W9-BVG-112

PROPERTY

ASPEN CASEBOOK SERIES

PROPERTY
Eighth Edition

Jesse Dukeminier

Late Maxwell Professor of Law
University of California
Los Angeles

James E. Krier

Earl Warren DeLano Professor of Law
University of Michigan

Gregory S. Alexander

A. Robert Noll Professor of Law
Cornell University

Michael H. Schill

Dean and Harry N. Wyatt Professor of Law
University of Chicago

Lior Jacob Strahilevitz

Sidley Austin Professor of Law
University of Chicago

Wolters Kluwer
Law & Business

Published by Wolters Kluwer Law & Business in New York.

Wolters Kluwer Law & Business serves customers worldwide with CCH, Aspen Publishers, and Kluwer Law International products. (www.wolterskluwerlb.com)

To contact Customer Service, e-mail customer.service@wolterskluwer.com, call 1-800-234-1660, fax 1-800-901-9075, or mail correspondence to:

> Wolters Kluwer Law & Business
> Attn: Order Department
> PO Box 990
> Frederick, MD 21705

Printed in the United States of America.

1 2 3 4 5 6 7 8 9 0

ISBN 978-1-4548-3760-2

Library of Congress Cataloging-in-Publication Data

Property / Jesse Dukeminier, Late Maxwell Professor of Law, University of California Los Angeles, James E. Krier, Earl Warren DeLano Professor of Law, University of Michigan, Gregory S. Alexander, A. Robert Noll Professor of Law Cornell Law School, Michael H. Schill, Dean and Harry N. Wyatt Professor of Law, University of Chicago, Lior Jacob Strahilevitz, Sidley Austin Professor of Law, The University of Chicago Law School. — 8th ed.
    p. cm.
  Includes bibliographical references and index.
  ISBN 978-1-4548-3760-2 (alk. paper)
1. Property — United States — Cases. I. Dukeminier, Jesse, author.
  KF560.D8 2014
  346.7304 — dc23

                                                                    2013050699

SUSTAINABLE FORESTRY INITIATIVE Certified Sourcing www.sfiprogram.org SFI-01042

SFI label applies to the text stock

About Wolters Kluwer Law & Business

Wolters Kluwer Law & Business is a leading global provider of intelligent information and digital solutions for legal and business professionals in key specialty areas, and respected educational resources for professors and law students. Wolters Kluwer Law & Business connects legal and business professionals as well as those in the education market with timely, specialized authoritative content and information-enabled solutions to support success through productivity, accuracy and mobility.

Serving customers worldwide, Wolters Kluwer Law & Business products include those under the Aspen Publishers, CCH, Kluwer Law International, Loislaw, ftwilliam.com and MediRegs family of products.

CCH products have been a trusted resource since 1913, and are highly regarded resources for legal, securities, antitrust and trade regulation, government contracting, banking, pension, payroll, employment and labor, and healthcare reimbursement and compliance professionals.

Aspen Publishers products provide essential information to attorneys, business professionals and law students. Written by preeminent authorities, the product line offers analytical and practical information in a range of specialty practice areas from securities law and intellectual property to mergers and acquisitions and pension/benefits. Aspen's trusted legal education resources provide professors and students with high-quality, up-to-date and effective resources for successful instruction and study in all areas of the law.

Kluwer Law International products provide the global business community with reliable international legal information in English. Legal practitioners, corporate counsel and business executives around the world rely on Kluwer Law journals, looseleafs, books, and electronic products for comprehensive information in many areas of international legal practice.

Loislaw is a comprehensive online legal research product providing legal content to law firm practitioners of various specializations. Loislaw provides attorneys with the ability to quickly and efficiently find the necessary legal information they need, when and where they need it, by facilitating access to primary law as well as state-specific law, records, forms and treatises.

ftwilliam.com offers employee benefits professionals the highest quality plan documents (retirement, welfare and non-qualified) and government forms (5500/PBGC, 1099 and IRS) software at highly competitive prices.

MediRegs products provide integrated health care compliance content and software solutions for professionals in healthcare, higher education and life sciences, including professionals in accounting, law and consulting.

Wolters Kluwer Law & Business, a division of Wolters Kluwer, is headquartered in New York. Wolters Kluwer is a market-leading global information services company focused on professionals.

For Joanna

Summary of Contents

Contents

Part V.   Land Use Controls   777

Chapter 9.   Judicial Land Use Controls: The Law of Nuisance   779

List of Illustrations

Chapter 5

Chapter 6

Chapter 7

Chapter 8

Chapter 9

Chapter 10

Chapter 11

Chapter 12

Preface to the Eighth Edition

The first edition of this book appeared in 1981. It has changed considerably over the years since, thanks to periodic revisions occasioned by developments in the law and literature, but the original aims and methods of the book have held steady. They are set forth in the Preface to the First Edition, reprinted in part on the following page.

As always, our work on the book has benefitted from the contributions of students, colleagues, friends, and institutions. We are grateful to them for their help, and hope the following list does justice to everyone: John Echeverria and Lee Anne Fennell (colleagues in arms who helped us with our treatment of materials in the book); Phil Caruso, Kate Gilbert, Jack Grein, Frances Lewis, Andrew Robb, and Mark Rohan (for research assistance); Laura Watson (for research and editorial assistance); Troy Froebe and Darren Kelly (for design and editorial assistance); Lyndsey Clark, Katy Morris, and John Niederbuhl (for administrative assistance); and the law libraries of Cornell University, the University of Chicago, and the University of Michigan.

James E. Krier
Gregory S. Alexander
Michael H. Schill
Lior Jacob Strahilevitz

March 2014

From the Preface to the First Edition

Property is a thoroughly modern subject of thoroughly antiquated origins. Probably in no other area of law does one see more, or even as many, strains of the old in the new. As an institution for allocating resources and distributing wealth and power, property bears in fundamentally important ways on central issues in contemporary life; as a body of doctrine, it discharges these modern-day tasks with rules and concepts drawn from age-old ways of looking at social relations in an ordered society. Property law has, to be sure, undergone constant change, but—at least in Anglo-American experience—it has not been revolutionized. Its enduring mix of old and new, rife with uneasy tensions, reflects more than an institution that has evolved over centuries and across cultures; it reflects as well two often conflicting objectives—promoting stability and accommodating change—that property systems must serve. To study property is to study social history, social relations, and social reform.

It is also, of course, to study law. The primary objective of this coursebook is to help students learn the complicated structure and functions of property doctrine and something of legal method, legal reasoning, and legal analysis. We have, however, secondary objectives as well, suggested by our opening remarks. How, why, and with what implications does the property system order relations in present-day America? What sorts of incentives does it create in terms of constructive use of scarce, valuable resources? How fairly does it confer benefits and impose burdens? To what extent is today's system a valuable, or a useless, legacy of the past? What sorts of reforms are suggested, and what might they achieve?

To pursue such secondary questions as these, and especially to accomplish the primary end of learning law and legal method, we need large doses of doctrine, but also a sense of history and of methods of critiquing institutional performance. There is, then, lots of law in what follows—in cases, statutes, text, and problems. There is also a consistent effort to trace historical antecedents. Finally, there is a fairly systematic, but by no means dominating, attempt to critique—often through an economic lens. Economics, like property, is in large part about resources. The economics in the book can be managed easily, we think, even by the totally uninitiated; it can also be ignored or even scorned. So too for the history, if one likes.

Jesse Dukeminier
James E. Krier

February 1, 1981

Acknowledgments

The authors acknowledge the permissions kindly granted to reproduce excerpts from, or illustrations of, the materials indicated below.

Books and Articles

American Law Institute, Restatement (Third) of Property, Servitudes (2000). Copyright ©2000 by the American Law Institute.

Baird, Douglas G., Common Law Intellectual Property and the Legacy of International News Service v. Associated Press, 40 U. Chi. L. Rev. 411 (1983). Copyright ©1983 by University of Chicago Law Review. Reproduced with permission of the University of Chicago Law School via Copyright Clearance Center.

Barnett, Walter, Marketable Title Acts—Panacea or Pandemonium?, 53 Cornell L. Rev. 45, 52-54. Copyright ©1967 by Cornell Law Review. Reprinted by permission of the Cornell Law Review via Copyright Clearance Center.

Berger, Lawrence, The Public Use Requirement in Eminent Domain, 57 Or. L. Rev. 203 (1978).

Demsetz, Harold, Toward a Theory of Property Rights, 57 Am. Econ. Rev. 347 (Pap. & Proc. 1967). Reprinted by permission of the American Economic Association and the author.

Dukeminier, Jesse, and James E. Krier, The Rise of the Perpetual Trust, 50 UCLA L. Rev. 1303 (2003). Reprinted with permission.

Egan, Timothy, The Serene Fortress: Many Seek Security in Private Communities, N.Y. Times, Sept. 3, 1995. Copyright ©1995 by The New York Times Company. Reprinted by permission.

Krier, James E., and Christopher Serkin, Public Ruses, 2004 Mich. St. L. Rev. 859, 862-863. Reprinted by permission.

McDougal, Myres S., & John W. Brabner-Smith, Land Tide Transfer: A Regression, 48 Yale L.J. 1125 (1939). Reprinted by permission of The Yale Law Journal Company and Fred B. Rothman & Co.

Merrill, Thomas W. and Henry E. Smith, Optimal Standardization in the Law of Property: The Numerus Clausus Principle, 110 Yale L.J. 1, 22-23 (2000). Used by permission.

Miceli, Thomas J., and C.F. Sirmans, Torrens versus Title Insurance: An Economic Analysis of Land Title Systems, Illinois Real Estates Letter (Fall 1997). Reprinted with permission.

Michelman, Frank, Property, Utility, and Fairness: Comments on the Ethical Foundations of "Just Compensation Law," 80 Harv. L. Rev. 1168 (1967). Copyright ©1967 by the Harvard Law Review Association.

Multi-Board Residential Real Estate Contract, REALTOR Association of the Western Suburbs. Used by permission.

Perry, Sandra White, Letter to editors regarding Jessie Lide's house (1988).

Posner, Richard A., Economic Analysis of Law (7th ed. 2007). Copyright ©2007. Reprinted by permission of Aspen Publishers, Inc.

Powell, Richard R., The Law of Real Property (Michael A. Wolf gen. ed. 2000). Copyright ©2000 by Matthew Bender & Co., Inc.

Walch, Tad, Maeser School Crisis Over, Deseret Morning News, Sept. 25, 2007. Reprinted by permission.

Illustrations

Blackstone, Sir William, portrait by Sir Joshua Reynolds, from the National Portrait Gallery, London.

Brandeis, Louis Dembitz, photograph, collection of the Supreme Court of the United States.

Day, Robert, cartoon. ©1958, 1986, Robert Day/Conde Nast Publications/cartoonbank. com. All rights reserved.

Decoyman driving wild duck up the pipe, Vincent Brooks Day & Son, Lith., drawn by author. Used by permission of Providence Press.

Delfino v. Vealencis, Bristol, Connecticut, map of land, from Manuel Baucells & Steven A. Lippman, Justice Delayed Is Justice Denied: A Co-operative Game Theoretic Analysis of Hold Up in Co-Ownership, 22 Cardozo L. Rev. 1191, 1222 (2001).

Development Rights Transfer, from John J. Costonis, Space Adrift (1974). Copyright ©1974 by the University of Illinois Press.

DOONESBURY ©2001 G. B. Trudeau. Reprinted with permission of UNIVERSAL UCLICK. All rights reserved.

Emporia, Kansas, Berkley Hills Addition, house, 1991 photograph by Chad Johnson.

Giant Tire, Detroit, Michigan, photograph by Wendy L. Wilkes.

Gray, J.C., portrait, Harvard Law Library. Used by permission.

Gray's Mansion, Chanute, Kansas, photograph by Vernon R. Parham, M.D.

Green Lawn Subdivision, Detroit, Michigan, photograph by Wendy L. Wilkes.

Gulf Terrace Condominium, Destin, Florida, photograph by Lucy Howell.

Gwernhaylod House, Overton-on-Dee, Wales, photograph, 1956. © Crown copyright: Royal Commission of the Ancient and Historical Monuments of Wales, reproduced with permission of the National Monuments Record of Wales.

Haunted House, Nyack, New York, photograph. Reproduced by permission of AP/Wide World Photos.

Henry VIII, painting by Hans Holbein the Younger. Copyright ©Fundacion Coleccion Thyssen-Bornemisza, Madrid.

Holmes, Oliver Wendell, photograph, collection of the Supreme Court of the United States.

Howard v. Kunto, Washington, map ©1995 by Barry C. Nelson.

Kelo house, New London, Connecticut, photograph. Used with permission of the Institute for Justice (www.ij.org).

Klimt, Gustav, painting entitled "Schloss Kammer am Attersee II." Private collection. Reproduced by permission of Galerie St. Etienne, New York.

Lachaise, Gaston, sculpture, Standing Woman, 1932. Bronze, 88 1/2'' high (225 cm.). University of California, Los Angeles, Franklin D. Murphy Sculpture Garden. Photographer: Donald Blumberg.

Ladue, Missouri, residences, 1999, photographs by Stuart Banner.

Lakeside Village Condominiums, Culver City, California, photograph by Jesse Dukeminier.

Lake Naomi, Pennsylvania, photograph, from Emma Miller Waygood, Changing Times in the Poconos (1972). Reprinted by permission of Mary Brower.

Lake Naomi, Pennsylvania, map, from the appellant's brief in Miller v. Lutheran Conference & Camp Assn., courtesy of Barlow Burke.

Leicester Square, London, etching, from the British Museum, London.

Leicester Square, London, 2012 photograph by Kim K. Alexander.

Lide, Jessie, Knoxville, Tennessee, house, 1956 photograph, courtesy of Sandra White Perry.

Livery of seisin, etching, from Daniel Coquillette, The Anglo-American Legal Heritage: Introductory Materials (1999), with copyright permission from Akademie Verlag, GmbH, Berlin.

Loretto's Apartment House, New York City, photograph by Michael S. Gruen.

Lucas v. South Carolina Coastal Council, lots, 2000, photograph by David S. Sanders.

Maslin, Michael, cartoon. ©2009 Michael Maslin/Conde Nast Publications/ www.cartoonbank.com. All rights reserved.

Marshall, John, portrait by Chester Harding. Reproduced by permission of the Boston Athenæum.

Messersmith, Caroline, Dickinson, North Dakota, house, 1999 photograph by Richard Volesky.

Metropolitan Opera Bill (von Stade), 2000, photograph by Charles Cronin.

Nahrstedt, Natore, photograph by Alan J. Duignan from Los Angeles Times, Dec. 24, 1992. Reproduced by permission.

Neponsit, New York houses, 1980, photograph by David S. Sanders.

Nollan v. California Coastal Commission, house and beach, 2001, photographs by David S. Sanders.

Odd Fellows Building and tract of land used for parking lot, Los Banos, California, photographs by Todd Benjamin.

O'Keeffe, Georgia, painting entitled "Seaweed," 1926. Copyright ©2009 Georgia O'Keeffe Museum/Artist Rights Society (ARS) New York. Reprinted by permission.

O'Keeffe, Georgia, 1968 photograph by Arnold Newman. Copyright ©Arnold Newman/ Getty Images (1968).

Oxford House, Edmonds, Washington, photograph, courtesy of Oxford House.

Pierre Apartments, Hackensack, New Jersey, photograph by David S. Sanders.

Residences on lots 19, 20, and 4, Chanute, Kansas, photograph by Vernon R. Parham, M.D.

River View Towers, Fort Lee, New Jersey, photograph by David S. Sanders.

Sea wall, Bay Head, New Jersey, photograph by The Star-Ledger, Newark, New Jersey.

Snout houses, photographs, from N.Y. Times, April 20, 2000. Photographer: Shane Young. Reproduced by permission of NYT Permissions.

Starke, Leslie, cartoon. ©1947 Leslie Stark/Conde Nast Publications/ www.cartoonbank. com. All rights reserved.

Steiner, Peter, cartoon. ©1996 Peter Steiner/Conde Nast Publications/ www.cartoonbank.com. All rights reserved.

Stoyanoff house, Ladue, Missouri, 2001 drawing by Stephen Harby.

Symphony Space, New York City, photograph by Charles Langelia, 2001 advertising poster.

Trever, John, cartoon. ©2005 John Trever and the Albuquerque Journal. Reprinted by permission.

Van Pelt, J. F., photograph, from The Steve Hill Collection, Mitchell Community College, North Carolina. Reproduced by permission of Bill Moose.

Van Pelt Residence, Statesville, North Carolina, etching, courtesy of Bill Moose.

Van Sandt v. Royster, Lots 19, 20, and 4, map by Greg R. Vetter and Marcilynn A. Burke.

Vealencis, Helen, photograph from Manel Baucells & Steven A. Lippman, Justice Delayed Is Justice Denied: A Cooperative Game Theoretic Analysis of Hold-Up in Co-Ownership, 22 Cardozo L. Rev. 1191, 1249 (2001).

Weber, Robert, cartoon. ©1977 Robert Weber/Conde Nast Publications/www.cartoon-bank.com. All Rights Reserved.

Wells Fargo Legacy Trust advertisement. Reprinted with permission of Wells Fargo Bank South Dakota, N. A.

World's Columbian Exposition, Chicago, 1893, photograph, ICHi-02530, View looking east at the Court of Honor, photographer—C. D. Arnold. Reproduced by permission of the Chicago History Museum.

This book has a supplementary website:
www.dukeminier-property.com

▲ *Home page*

The website is **geared to the book chapter by chapter**, and **within each chapter by topic.**

Your professor can provide the username and password for accessing the website.

 At various points in this book, you will see a **computer icon**, pictured left, indicating that the website contains **information of interest** to the particular material—including **background**, **illustrations**, and **explanations**.

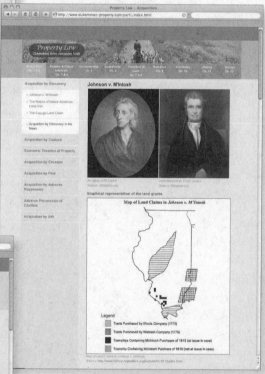

Acquisition, Chapters 1 & 2 ▲

▲ *Co-ownership, Chapter 5*

We welcome any comments or suggestions you might have about improving the site and making it more useful and interesting to you.

Please email your feedback to Greg Alexander at **gsa9@cornell.edu.**

PROPERTY

I
An Introduction to Some Fundamentals

The first two chapters of this book pursue a common theme—how some-one might acquire property other than by purchase—across a wide range of legal terrain. One purpose of the exercise is to lay down the chief doctrinal foundations of property law. Another is to introduce some basic concepts, issues, and analytic methods of ongoing importance.

1

First in Time: Acquisition of Property by Discovery, Capture, and Creation

Qui prior est tempore potior est jure.
(Who is prior in time is stronger in right.) —

Maxim of Roman Law

First come, first served. —

Henry Brinklow,
Complaynt of Roderick Mors, Ch. 17 (c. 1545)

How does property come to be, and why, and so what? Most of us most of the time take these questions for granted, which is to say that we take property for granted. But taking something for granted is not exactly the best path to understanding it. So we begin with the origins of property.

A. *Acquisition by Discovery*

Thus in the beginning all the world was *America*—

John Locke,
Two Treatises of Government,
Book II, Ch. V ("Of Property") (c. 1690)

Johnson v. M'Intosh
Supreme Court of the United States, 1823
21 U.S. (8 Wheat.) 543

Error to the District Court of Illinois. This was an action of ejectment for lands in the State and District of Illinois, claimed by the plaintiffs under a purchase and conveyance from the Piankeshaw Indians, and by the defendant, under a [later] grant from the United States. It came up on a case stated, upon which there was a judgment below for the defendant. . . .

CHIEF JUSTICE MARSHALL delivered the opinion of the Court.

The plaintiffs in this cause claim the land, in their declaration mentioned, under two grants, purporting to be made, the first in 1773, and the last in 1775, by the chiefs of certain Indian tribes, constituting the Illinois and the Piankeshaw nations; and the question is, whether this title can be recognised in the Courts of the United States?

The facts, as stated in the case agreed, show the authority of the chiefs who executed this conveyance, so far as it could be given by their own people; and likewise show, that the particular tribes for whom these chiefs acted were in rightful possession of the land they sold. The inquiry, therefore, is, in a great measure, confined to the power of Indians to give, and of private individuals to receive, a title which can be sustained in the Courts of this country.

As the right of society, to prescribe those rules by which property may be acquired and preserved is not, and cannot be drawn into question; as the title to lands, especially, is and must be admitted to depend entirely on the law of the nation in which they lie; it will be necessary, in pursuing this inquiry, to examine, not singly those principles of abstract justice, which the Creator of all things has impressed on the mind of his creature man, and which are admitted to regulate, in a great degree, the rights of civilized nations, whose perfect independence is acknowledged; but those principles also which our own government has adopted in the particular case, and given us as the rule for our decision.

On the discovery of this immense continent, the great nations of Europe were eager to appropriate to themselves so much of it as they could respectively acquire. Its vast extent offered an ample field to the ambition and enterprise of all; and the character and religion of its inhabitants afforded an apology for considering them as a people over whom the superior genius of Europe might claim an ascendency. The potentates of the old world found no difficulty in convincing themselves that they made ample compensation to the inhabitants of the new, by bestowing on them civilization and Christianity, in exchange for unlimited independence. But, as they were all in pursuit of nearly the same object, it was necessary, in order to avoid conflicting settlements, and consequent war with each other, to establish a principle, which all should acknowledge as the law by which the right of acquisition, which they all asserted, should be regulated as between themselves. This principle was, that discovery gave title to the government by whose subjects, or by whose authority, it was made, against all other European governments, which title might be consummated by possession.

The exclusion of all other Europeans, necessarily gave to the nation making the discovery the sole right of acquiring the soil from the natives, and establishing settlements upon it. It was a right with which no Europeans could interfere. It was a right which all asserted for themselves, and to the assertion of which, by others, all assented.

Those relations which were to exist between the discoverer and the natives, were to be regulated by themselves. The rights thus acquired being exclusive, no other power could interpose between them.

In the establishment of these relations, the rights of the original inhabitants were, in no instance, entirely disregarded; but were necessarily, to a considerable extent, impaired. They were admitted to be the rightful occupants of the soil, with a legal as well as just claim to retain possession of it, and to use it according to their own discretion, but their rights to complete sovereignty, as independent nations, were necessarily diminished, and their power to dispose of the soil at their own will, to whomsoever they pleased, was denied by the original fundamental principle, that discovery gave exclusive title to those who made it.

While the different nations of Europe respected the right of the natives, as occupants, they asserted the ultimate dominion to be in themselves; and claimed and exercised, as a consequence of this ultimate dominion, a power to grant the soil, while yet in possession of the natives. These grants have been understood by all, to convey a title to the grantees, subject only to the Indian right of occupancy.

The history of America, from its discovery to the present day, proves, we think, the universal recognition of these principles.

Spain did not rest her title solely on the grant of the Pope. Her discussions respecting boundary, with France, with Great Britain, and with the United States, all show that she placed it on the rights given by discovery. Portugal sustained her claim to the Brazils by the same title.

France, also, founded her title to the vast territories she claimed in America on discovery. However conciliatory her conduct to the natives may have been, she still asserted her right of dominion over a great extent of country not actually settled by Frenchmen, and her exclusive right to acquire and dispose of the soil which remained in the occupation of Indians. . . .

The claim of the Dutch was always contested by the English; not because they questioned the title given by discovery, but because they insisted on being themselves the rightful claimants under that title. Their pretensions were finally decided by the sword.

No one of the powers of Europe gave its full assent to this principle, more unequivocally than England. The documents upon this subject are ample and complete. So early as the year 1496, her monarch granted a commission to the Cabots, to discover countries then unknown to *Christian people*, and to take possession of them in the name of the king of England. Two years afterwards, Cabot proceeded on this voyage, and discovered the continent of North America, along which he sailed as far south as Virginia. To this discovery the English trace their title.

In this first effort made by the English government to acquire territory on this continent, we perceive a complete recognition of the principle which has been mentioned. The right of discovery given by this commission, is confined to countries "then unknown to all Christian people"; and of these countries Cabot was empowered to take possession in the name of the king of England. Thus asserting a right to take possession, notwithstanding the occupancy of the natives, who were heathens, and, at the same time, admitting the prior title of any Christian people who may have made a previous discovery.

The same principle continued to be recognised. [Omitted here is a discussion of various charters from the English crown, granting lands in America.]

Thus has our whole country been granted by the crown while in the occupation of the Indians. These grants purport to convey the soil as well as the right of dominion to the grantees. In those governments which were denominated royal, where the right to the soil was not vested in individuals, but remained in the crown, or was vested in the colonial government, the king claimed and exercised the right of granting lands, and of dismembering the government at his will. The grants made out of the two original colonies, after the resumption of their charters by the crown, are examples of this. The governments of New-England, New-York, New-Jersey, Pennsylvania, Maryland, and a part of Carolina, were thus created. In all of them, the soil, at the time the grants were made, was occupied by the Indians. Yet almost every title within those governments is dependent on these grants. In some instances, the soil was conveyed by the crown unaccompanied by the powers of government, as in the case of the northern neck of Virginia. It has never been objected to this, or to any other similar grant, that the title as well as possession was in the Indians when it was made, and that it passed nothing on that account.

These various patents cannot be considered as nullities; nor can they be limited to a mere grant of the powers of government. A charter intended to convey political power only, would never contain words expressly granting the land, the soil, and the waters. Some of them purport to convey the soil alone; and in those cases in which the powers of government, as well as the soil, are conveyed to individuals, the crown has always acknowledged itself to be bound by the grant. Though the power to dismember regal governments was asserted and exercised, the power to dismember proprietary governments was not claimed; and, in some instances, even after the powers of government were revested in the crown, the title of the proprietors to the soil was respected. . . .

Further proofs of the extent to which this principle has been recognised, will be found in the history of the wars, negotiations, and treaties, which the different nations, claiming territory in America, have carried on, and held with each other. . . .

Thus, all the nations of Europe, who have acquired territory on this continent, have asserted in themselves, and have recognised in others, the exclusive right of the discoverer to appropriate the lands occupied by the Indians. Have the American States rejected or adopted this principle?

By the treaty which concluded the war of our revolution, Great Britain relinquished all claim, not only to the government, but to the "propriety and territorial rights of the United States," whose boundaries were fixed in the second article. By this treaty, the powers of government, and the right to soil, which had previously been in Great Britain, passed definitively to these States. We had before taken possession of them, by declaring independence; but neither the declaration of independence, nor the treaty confirming it, could give us more than that which we before possessed, or to which Great Britain was before entitled. It has never been doubted, that either the United States, or the several States, had a clear title to all the lands within the boundary lines described in the treaty, subject only to the Indian right of occupancy, and that the exclusive power to extinguish that right, was vested in that government which might constitutionally exercise it.

Virginia, particularly, within whose chartered limits the land in controversy lay, passed an act, in the year 1779, declaring her

> exclusive right of pre-emption from the Indians, of all the lands within the limits of her own chartered territory, and that no person or persons whatsoever, have, or ever had, a right to purchase any lands within the same, from any Indian nation, except only persons duly authorized to make such purchase; formerly for the use and benefit of the colony, and lately for the Commonwealth.

[handwritten margin note: further proving this principle]

The act then proceeds to annul all deeds made by Indians to individuals, for the private use of the purchasers.

Without ascribing to this act the power of annulling vested rights, or admitting it to countervail the testimony furnished by the marginal note opposite to the title of the law, forbidding purchases from the Indians, in the revisals of the Virginia statutes, stating that law to be repealed, it may safely be considered as an unequivocal affirmance, on the part of Virginia, of the broad principle which had always been maintained, that the exclusive right to purchase from the Indians resided in the government.

In pursuance of the same idea, Virginia proceeded, at the same session, to open her land office, for the sale of that country which now constitutes Kentucky, a country, every acre of which was then claimed and possessed by Indians, who maintained their title with as much persevering courage as was ever manifested by any people.

[handwritten margin note: sold land even though Indians possessed land]

The States, having within their chartered limits different portions of territory covered by Indians, ceded that territory, generally, to the United States, on conditions expressed in their deeds of cession, which demonstrate the opinion, that they ceded the soil as well as jurisdiction, and that in doing so, they granted a productive fund to the government of the Union. The lands in controversy lay within the chartered limits of Virginia, and were ceded with the whole country northwest of the river Ohio. . . . The ceded territory was occupied by numerous and warlike tribes of Indians; but the exclusive right of the United States to extinguish their title, and to grant the soil, has never, we believe, been doubted. . . .

Our late acquisitions from Spain are of the same character; and the negotiations which preceded those acquisitions, recognise and elucidate the principle which has been received as the foundation of all European title in America.

The United States, then, have unequivocally acceded to that great and broad rule by which its civilized inhabitants now hold this country. They hold, and assert in themselves, the title by which it was acquired. They maintain, as all others have maintained, that discovery gave an exclusive right to extinguish the Indian title of occupancy, either by purchase or by conquest; and gave also a right to such a degree of sovereignty, as the circumstances of the people would allow them to exercise.

The power now possessed by the government of the United States to grant lands, resided, while we were colonies, in the crown, or its grantees. The validity of the titles given by either has never been questioned in our Courts. It has been exercised uniformly over territory in possession of the Indians. The existence of this power must negative the existence of any right which may conflict with, and control it. An absolute title to lands cannot exist, at the same time, in different persons, or in different governments. An absolute must be an exclusive title, or at least a title which excludes all others not compatible with it. All our institutions recognise the absolute title of the crown, subject only to the Indian right of occupancy, and recognise the absolute title of the crown to extinguish that right. This is incompatible with an absolute and complete title in the Indians.

We will not enter into the controversy, whether agriculturists, merchants, and manufacturers, have a right, on abstract principles, to expel hunters from the territory they possess, or to contract their limits. Conquest gives a title which the Courts of the conqueror cannot deny, whatever the private and speculative opinions of individuals may be, respecting the original justice of the claim which has been successfully asserted. The British government, which was then our government, and whose rights have passed to the United States, asserted a title to all the lands occupied by Indians, within the chartered limits of the British colonies. It asserted also a limited sovereignty over them, and the exclusive right of extinguishing the title which occupancy gave to them. These claims have been maintained and established as far west as the river Mississippi, by the sword. The title to a vast portion of the lands we now hold, originates in them. It is not for the Courts of this country to question the validity of this title, or to sustain one which is incompatible with it.

Although we do not mean to engage in the defence of those principles which Europeans have applied to Indian title, they may, we think, find some excuse, if not justification, in the character and habits of the people whose rights have been wrested from them.

The title by conquest is acquired and maintained by force. The conqueror prescribes its limits. Humanity, however, acting on public opinion, has established, as a general rule, that the conquered shall not be wantonly oppressed, and that their condition shall remain as eligible as is compatible with the objects of the conquest. Most usually, they are incorporated with the victorious nation, and become subjects or citizens of the government with which they are connected. The new and old members of the society mingle with each other; the distinction between them is gradually lost, and they make one people. Where this incorporation is practicable, humanity demands, and a wise policy requires, that the rights of the conquered to property should remain unimpaired; that the new subjects should be governed as equitably as the old, and that confidence in their security should gradually banish the painful sense of being separated from their ancient connexions, and united by force to strangers.

When the conquest is complete, and the conquered inhabitants can be blended with the conquerors, or safely governed as a distinct people, public opinion, which not even the conqueror can disregard, imposes these restraints upon him; and he cannot neglect them without injury to his fame, and hazard to his power.

But the tribes of Indians inhabiting this country were fierce savages, whose occupation was war, and whose subsistence was drawn chiefly from the forest. To leave them in possession of their country, was to leave the country a wilderness; to govern them as a distinct people, was impossible, because they were as brave and as high spirited as they were fierce, and were ready to repel by arms every attempt on their independence.

What was the inevitable consequence of this state of things? The Europeans were under the necessity either of abandoning the country, and relinquishing their pompous claims to it, or of enforcing those claims by the sword, and by the adoption of principles adapted to the condition of a people with whom it was impossible to mix, and who could not be governed as a distinct society, or of remaining in their neighbourhood, and exposing themselves and their families to the perpetual hazard of being massacred.

Frequent and bloody wars, in which the whites were not always the aggressors, unavoidably ensued. European policy, numbers, and skill prevailed. As the white population advanced, that of the Indians necessarily receded. The country in the immediate neighbourhood of agriculturists became unfit for them. The game fled into thicker and more unbroken forests, and the Indians followed. The soil, to which the crown originally claimed title, being no longer occupied by its ancient inhabitants, was parcelled out according to the will of the sovereign power, and taken possession of by persons who claimed immediately from the crown, or mediately, through its grantees or deputies.

That law which regulates, and ought to regulate in general, the relations between the conqueror and conquered, was incapable of application to a people under such circumstances. The resort to some new and different rule, better adapted to the actual state of things, was unavoidable. Every rule which can be suggested will be found to be attended with great difficulty.

However extravagant the pretension of converting the discovery of an inhabited country into conquest may appear; if the principle has been asserted in the first instance, and afterwards sustained; if a country has been acquired and held under it; if the property of the great mass of the community originates in it, it becomes the law of the land, and cannot be questioned. So, too, with respect to the concomitant principle, that the Indian inhabitants are to be considered merely as occupants, to be protected, indeed, while in peace, in the possession of their lands, but to be deemed incapable of transferring the absolute title to others. However this restriction may be opposed to natural right, and to the usages of civilized nations, yet, if it be indispensable to that system under which the country has been settled, and be adapted to the actual condition of the two people, it may, perhaps, be supported by reason, and certainly cannot be rejected by Courts of justice. . . .

It has never been contended, that the Indian title amounted to nothing. Their right of possession has never been questioned. The claim of government extends to the complete ultimate title, charged with this right of possession, and to the exclusive power of acquiring that right. . . .

After bestowing on this subject a degree of attention which was more required by the magnitude of the interest in litigation, and the able and elaborate arguments of the bar, than by its intrinsic difficulty, the Court is decidedly of opinion, that the plaintiffs do not exhibit a title which can be sustained in the Courts of the United States; and that there is no error in the judgment which was rendered against them in the District Court of Illinois.

Judgment affirmed, with costs.

NOTES AND QUESTIONS

1. *A logical place to begin.* Our concern here is not the complexities of title to land once occupied exclusively by Native Americans.[1] We are interested, instead, in getting a study of property under way, and Johnson v. M'Intosh provides an apt point of departure for several reasons.

First, how better to start a course in the American law of property than with the foundations of landownership in the United States? Land, you will learn, plays an important part in property law, and not just because so much of that law aims to resolve—better yet, avoid—conflicts over real property (as land is called). Landownership also commonly determines the ownership and control of a host of other natural resources, such as wild animals, water and minerals, peace and quiet, clean air, and open space. Moreover, many of the general legal principles pertaining to real property also apply to personal property (that is, property other than land). So landownership is important, and, as Johnson v. M'Intosh suggests, most landowners in the United States trace their ownership—their title—back to grants (or patents, as they are called in the case of conveyances of public land out of the government) from the United States. The United States, in turn, traces its title, by grant and otherwise, all the way back to the discovery of America by the white man.[2]

2. *Discovery . . . or conquest?* Discovery and conquest, both of which are mentioned in Chief Justice Marshall's[3] opinion in the *Johnson* case, are terms of art referring to methods of acquiring territory in international law. Acquisition by

---

1. Students wishing to pursue these and other issues regarding the legal situation of Native Americans might well begin their inquiries with Felix Cohen's Handbook of Federal Indian Law (rev. ed. 1982). Cohen (1907-1953), a man of great heart and energy, made important contributions to a number of fields, including legal philosophy. He was the son of another leading philosopher, Morris Cohen (1880-1947), whose views on "Property and Sovereignty" will be considered shortly.

2. Mention of tracing introduces the idea of a *chain of title*: The links in the chain are the transactions (conveyances) by which a parcel of land moves from owner to owner over time. The significance and operation of chain of title are examined in Chapters 7 and 8 of this book.

3. John Marshall (1755-1835), the fourth Chief Justice of the United States (from 1801 to 1835), is one of the great figures in the constitutional history of the United States. Marshall had little formal education (and only six weeks of formal legal training!) but had a remarkable mind and character. He was prominent as a diplomat, as a legislator, and as Secretary of State before being nominated as Chief Justice by President John Adams. A strong defender of the Constitution, the architect of the doctrine of judicial review, "Marshall raised the office [of Chief Justice] and the Supreme Court to stature and power previously lacking." Under his leadership, the practice of individual opinions by individual justices largely ceased, dissents were discouraged, and the "Court came to speak with one voice. Usually the voice was Marshall's." The quotations are from Robert Faulkner's essay on Marshall in 4 Encyclopedia of the American Constitution 1672-1676 (2000). See also Biographical Dictionary of the Common Law 354-355 (A.W.B. Simpson ed. 1984).

discovery entails "the sighting or 'finding' of hitherto unknown or uncharted territory; it is frequently accompanied by a landing and the symbolic taking of possession," acts that give rise to an inchoate title that must (on one view) subsequently be perfected, within a reasonable time, by settling in and making an effective occupation. 4 Encyclopedia of Public International Law 839-840 (1992). *Conquest* is the taking of possession of enemy territory through force, followed by formal annexation of the defeated territory by the conqueror. See Parry & Grant Encyclopaedic Dictionary of International Law 96 (2000).

Neither of these two modes of territorial acquisition has much immediate relevance today. As to discovery, there are virtually no unknown territories on earth (what about a new volcanic island emerging in the high seas?), and territories beyond the earth are governed by special treaties and agreements placing the moon and other celestial bodies outside the reach of national appropriation. As to conquest, it has come to be proscribed by contemporary international law as a method of territorial acquisition. 4 Encyclopedia of Public International Law, supra.

In earlier times, though, discovery and conquest were of great importance, as Johnson v. M'Intosh suggests. In that case the two doctrines worked in concert. Discovery, Marshall wrote, "gave an exclusive right to extinguish the Indian title of occupancy, either by purchase or by conquest."[4] See page 7. The first "discoverer" had a preemptive right to deal with the Indians, as against subsequent "discoverers." But why did discovery play any role at all? In principle, only a *res nullius* or *terra nullius* (a thing or territory belonging to no one), a "hitherto unknown territory," can be discovered. See 4 Encyclopedia of Public International Law, supra. North America in the fifteenth century was not unknown to its indigenous occupants. Why didn't it *belong* to them?

The answer is discomfiting. During the so-called classical era of discovery (1450-1600), prior possession by aboriginal populations (which were sometimes called savage populations, or semi-civilized ones) was commonly thought not to matter. "In previous centuries European international lawyers were sometimes reluctant to admit that non-European societies could constitute states for the purposes of international law, and territory inhabited by non-European peoples was sometimes regarded as *terra nullius*." Peter Malanczuk, Akehurst's Modern Introduction to International Law 148 (7th ed. 1997). Marshall was alluding to this attitude when he said of North America that "the character and religion of its inhabitants afforded an apology for considering them as a people over whom the superior genius of Europe might claim an ascendency."[5] See page 4.

---

4. Note that the modern indictment of acquisition by conquest is not "regarded as being retroactive to titles made by conquest in an earlier period." Robert Y. Jennings, The Acquisition of Territory in International Law 56 (1963).

5. The sarcasm and irony seen here and elsewhere in Marshall's opinion suggest his embarrassment with what he had to write, and there is independent evidence that he was sympathetic to the plight of Native Americans. In an 1828 letter to Justice Joseph Story, for example, Marshall mentioned some reasons to be forgiving of the "conduct of our forefathers in expelling the original occupants of the soil," but went on to state his view that "every oppression now exercised on a helpless people depending on our magnanimity and justice for the preservation of their existence impresses a deep stain on the American character." Quoted in The Political and Economic Doctrines of John Marshall 124-125 (John E. Oster ed. 1914).

For more on the historical context of Johnson v. M'Intosh, see Blake Watson, Buying America from the Indians: *Johnson v. McIntosh* and the History of Native Land Rights (2012); Robert J. Miller, Native America, Discovered and Conquered: Thomas Jefferson, Lewis & Clark, and Manifest Destiny (2006). We shall return to the subject shortly, after considering some additional reasons to begin a study of property with Johnson v. M'Intosh.

3. *Occupancy theory and the principle of first in time.* The doctrine of discovery at work in *Johnson* may be of little importance today, but exactly the opposite is true of the doctrine's foundation—the principle of first in time.

"The notion that being there first somehow justifies ownership rights is a venerable and persistent one." Lawrence C. Becker, Property Rights: Philosophical Foundations 24 (1977). The theory of first occupancy, or first possession, dates back to Roman law and played a considerable part in the writings of Hugo Grotius and Samuel Pufendorf in the seventeenth century (you will soon bump into these figures again; see pages 20, 24). As Grotius saw it, the riches of the earth were initially held in common (nothing belonged to any one individual). But because avarice eventually led to scarcity, the institution of private property became necessary to preserve peace. Private ownership was imagined to have developed according to agreements, explicit ones or those implied by occupation; it was to be "supposed" that whatever each person had taken possession of should be that person's property. Eventually, systems of government were introduced (how?), and the original rules of acquisition were modified. Still, though, the government had to recognize the pre-established property rights of its citizens.

> [T]he institution of private property really protected men's natural equality of rights. "Now property ownership was introduced for the purpose of preserving equality to this end, in fact, that each should enjoy his own." But what is this "own" to which each man has an equal right? . . . In fact, the "own" which the laws of property protect is whatever an individual has managed to get hold of, and equality of right, applied to property, means only that every man has an equal right to grab. The institution of property was an agreement among men legalizing what each had already grabbed, without any right to do so, and granting, for the future, a formal right of ownership to the first grabber. As a result of this agreement, which, by a remarkable oversight, puts no limit on the amount of property any one person may occupy, everything would soon pass into private ownership, and the equal right to grab would cease to have any practical value. [Richard Schlatter, Private Property: The History of an Idea 130-131 (1951).][6]

---

6. For implicit disagreement with Schlatter's account, see Adam Mossoff, What Is Property? Putting the Pieces Back Together, 45 Ariz. L. Rev. 371, 379-386 (2003), arguing that the words "one's own" in the arguments of Grotius and Pufendorf refer not just to what one can get hold of, but to the idea that one has a right to life and liberty, and that actions based on this right are necessary and sufficient to create a right of property. John Locke's labor theory, to which we will turn momentarily, begins with the same theoretical starting point.

We will be making brief reference to various philosophical perspectives on property from time to time. The literature on the general subject is vast, but the following short list might prove useful to interested students: Becker, supra; C.B. Macpherson, Property: Mainstream and Critical Positions (1978); Stephen R. Munzer, A Theory of Property (1990); J.E. Penner, The Idea of Property in Law (1997); Alan Ryan, Property (1987); Alan Ryan, Property and Political Theory (1984); Schlatter, supra; Jeremy Waldron, The Right to Private Property (1988); Theories of Property (Anthony Parel & Thomas Flanagan eds. 1979); and the essays collected in Property, 22 Nomos (1980).

John Marshall
Chief Justice of the United States, 1801-1835
by Chester Harding (1828)
Collection of the Boston Athenaeum

Occupancy fares rather well as a positive (descriptive or explanatory) theory of the origins of property. Sir William Blackstone put it to that use in his famous Commentaries on the Laws of England, completed a few years before the American Revolution (see page 24). See also Richard A. Epstein, Possession as the Root of Title, 13 Ga. L. Rev. 1221, 1222 (1979) (the common and civil law alike adopted the proposition that "taking possession of unowned things is the only possible way to acquire ownership of them"; the universal principle is "original possession"). And, as Becker observed above, the idea that being prior in time matters is not only "venerable" but "persistent." You will see it running throughout the materials in this book, particularly in the next section on Acquisition by Capture. For an overview of its active role in contemporary property law, see Lawrence Berger, An Analysis of the Doctrine that "First in Time Is First in Right," 64 Neb. L. Rev. 349 (1985).

Despite its persistence, however, the normative case for first possession—its force as a justification—is commonly thought to be rather weak. See Morris Cohen, Property and Sovereignty, 13 Cornell L.Q. 8, 15-16 (1927). But Cohen was not single-minded; he did find "a kernel of value" in the principle. Epstein provides a more spirited defense in his essay on Possession as the Root of Title, supra. See also Richard A. Epstein, Past and Future: The Temporal Dimension in the Law of Property, 64 Wash. U. L.Q. 667 (1986). Can you anticipate the arguments in these articles, constructing for yourself a list of the pros and cons of first in time?

4. *Labor theory and John Locke.* The famous philosopher John Locke (1632-1704) drew first occupancy into his labor theory of property, but in a way that was thought to give it greater moral weight. The problem is this: So what if someone possesses something first; why should anyone else be obliged to respect the claim of the first possessor? Locke reasoned that the obligation "was imposed by the law of nature, and bound all men fast long before mere human conventions had been thought of." Schlatter, supra, at 154. Here is a slightly modernized statement of the core of Locke's argument:

> Though the earth and all inferior creatures be common to all men, yet every man has a property in his own person. This nobody has any right to but himself. The labor of his body, and the work of his hands, we may say, are properly his. Whatsoever then he removes out of the state that nature has provided, and left it in, he has mixed his labor with, and joined to it something that is his own, and thereby makes it his property. It being by him removed from the common state nature placed it in, has by this labor something annexed to it, that excludes the common right of other men. For this labor being the unquestionable property of the laborer, no man but he can have a right to what that is once joined to, at least where there is enough, and as good left in common for others. [John Locke, Two Treatises of Government, Book II, Ch. V (1690).]

Locke's labor theory appears in several versions, most of them deficient in one respect or another. Like what? See Carol M. Rose, Property and Persuasion 11 (1994) (why does one own one's labor? In any event, how broad is the right that one establishes by mixing one's labor with something else?). Still, though, labor theory has its appeal, and the law of property continues to feel its influence (just as with its forerunner, occupancy theory). We mention a few examples here as an aside and ask you to watch for others as your studies progress.

Consider, then, the law of *accession*, which comes into play when one person adds to the property of another: by labor alone, *A* chopping *B*'s trees and making flower boxes from them; by labor and the addition of new material, *C* using her own oils and *D*'s canvas to produce a valuable painting. As between *A* and *B*, or *C* and *D*, which party is entitled to the final product? Is the other party entitled to damages equal to the value of his or her contribution? These issues look to be simple ones, but they are not. What factors do you suppose the courts would consider in resolving them? See Ray A. Brown, The Law of Personal Property 49-62 (Walter V. Raushenbush ed., 3d ed. 1975).

For an interesting theoretical analysis of the law of accession, see Thomas W. Merrill, Accession and Original Ownership, 1 J. Legal Analysis 459 (2009). A particular virtue of Merrill's treatment is that it shows a number of connections between accession and several other topics considered in the first two chapters of this book.

Another illustration of labor theory at work is found in Haslem v. Lockwood, 37 Conn. 500 (1871), where the plaintiff had raked into heaps manure that had accumulated in a public street, intending to carry it away the next day. Before he could do so, the defendant found the heaps of manure and hauled them off in his cart. In an action in trover for the value of the manure, the court held for the plaintiff. The manure belonged originally to the owners of the animals that dropped it, but had been abandoned. As abandoned property, it belonged to the first occupant, the plaintiff, who "had changed its original condition and greatly enhanced its value by his labor . . . ." 37 Conn. at 506. The defendant argued that the plaintiff had lost his rights when he left the heaps unattended overnight. The court asked, "if a party finds property comparatively worthless . . . and greatly increases its value by his labor and expense, does he lose his right if he leaves it a reasonable time to procure the means to take it away, when such means are necessary for its removal?" 37 Conn. at 507. Answer: No.

5. *John Locke and Johnson v. M'Intosh.* Return now to the *Johnson* case where we left it at the end of Note 2 above. Locke appears to have shared the common European view that the Native Americans had no substantial claim to the New World they had so long occupied.

> [He] reasoned that the Indians' occupancy of their aboriginal lands did not involve an adequate amount of "labor" to perfect a "property" interest in the soil. His argument helped frame and direct later liberal debates in colonial America on the natural rights of European agriculturists to dispossess tribal societies of their land base. [Robert A. Williams, Jr., The Medieval and Renaissance Origins of the Status of the American Indian in Western Legal Thought, 57 S. Cal. L. Rev. 1, 3 n.4 (1983).]

See generally Robert A. Williams, Jr., The American Indian in Western Legal Thought (1990).

Notwithstanding the foregoing, there is considerable evidence that American lawyers and government officials actually did, for a time, regard the Indians as owners of their lands. See Stuart Banner, How the Indians Lost Their Land: Law and Power on the Frontier (2005). In a detailed and very convincing account,

Professor Banner shows that acknowledgment of Indian ownership was common in the early 1790s. But by the time of the decision in *Johnson* some 30 years later, conventional wisdom was to the opposite effect: The Indians were not owners but merely had a right of occupancy. "A major change in American legal thought had taken place during the intervening three decades. . . . Like many transformations in legal thought, this one was so complete that contemporaries often failed to notice that it had occurred. They came to believe instead that they were simply following the rule laid down by their English colonial predecessors, and that the Indians had *never* been accorded full ownership of their land. And that view, expressed most prominently by the Supreme Court in *Johnson v. M'Intosh*, has persisted right up until today." Id. at 150.

Notice finally that in the penultimate paragraph of the *Johnson* opinion (page 9) the Court recognized an Indian title of occupancy, which only the government could purchase. Given that the European settlers had such superior might, why did they not instead simply conquer the Indians altogether, and grant them nothing? A persuasive answer is suggested in Eric Kades, The Dark Side of Efficiency: *Johnson v. M'Intosh* and the Expropriation of American Indian Lands, 148 U. Pa. L. Rev. 1065 (2000). Professor Kades argues that the settlers' objective was efficient expropriation; they wanted to get land at the least cost to themselves, with cost defined broadly to include lives lost in battle, diversion of capital to military production, and so on. In this light, purchase was often the cheapest course. To see why, consider that the decision in *Johnson*, echoing a long line of colonial statutes, royal proclamations, and administrative rulings, decreed that the sovereign (first Britain, then the United States) was the only buyer empowered to purchase Indian lands. The government was a so-called monopsonist—a sole buyer—and this fact helped reduce the price paid for the Indian title of occupancy. Moreover, major portions of early American land law (favorable financing, squatters' rights, and Homestead Acts) had the purpose and effect of weakening Indian resistance by luring settlers to the frontier. They brought with them European diseases against which tribes had no immunity; they cleared land and hunted prodigiously to get hides and fur. A native population decimated by sickness and deprived of sources of food and other necessities had little bargaining power. The title of occupancy went for a pittance. See also Eric Kades, History and Interpretation of the Great Case of *Johnson v. M'Intosh*, 19 Law & Hist. Rev. 67 (2001).

Despite the ongoing force of Johnson v. M'Intosh, scholars continue to contest its rationale and contemporary relevance. A summary of the critical commentary is provided in the final chapter of Blake Watson's book, supra. See also Blake Watson, The Doctrine of Discovery and the Elusive Definition of Indian Title, 15 Lewis & Clark L. Rev. 995 (2011). Watson argues that the nature of Indian title is unique, with no analogies in American law. A contrary view is offered in Michael C. Blumm, Why Aboriginal Title Is a Fee Simple Absolute, 15 Lewis & Clark L. Rev. 975 (2011). Professor Blumm argues that the problem with *Johnson* is more in its interpretation by other courts than in what the case actually held. Justice Marshall, he believes, aimed to protect native land rights as much as he thought possible.

6. *Property and power.* Property confers and rests upon power. It bestows on owners a form of sovereignty over others, because property means that the sovereign state stands behind the owners' assertions of right.[7] But as Morris Cohen observed:

> [T]he recognition of private property as a form of sovereignty is not itself an argument against it [for] some form of government we must always have. . . . While, however, government is a necessity, not all forms of it are of equal value. At any rate it is necessary to apply to the law of property all those considerations of social ethics and enlightened public policy which ought to be brought to the discussion of any just form of government. [Cohen, supra, at 14.]

In this respect, the ongoing history of relations between Native Americans and the U.S. government has not been a very happy one. "That there was tragedy, deception, barbarity, and virtually every other vice known to man in the 300-year history of the expansion of the original 13 Colonies into a Nation which now embraces more than three million square miles and 50 States cannot be denied." This is the view of then-Justice (now late Chief Justice) William Rehnquist, stated in a dissenting opinion written some 150 years after Johnson v. M'Intosh. See United States v. Sioux Nation of Indians, 448 U.S. 371, 437 (1980).

7. *Progressive property theory.* Recently, progressive property theorists have emphasized the social character of property. They reject the notion that the right to exclude is essential to ownership, and consider property's social nature as key to understanding property relations. They argue that ownership is a matter of obligations as well as rights. They also reject the idea that any one value or good is the foundation of property, arguing in favor of a pluralist conception of property that includes multiple goods such as individual autonomy, personhood, security, equal dignity, and community. See Gregory S. Alexander et al., A Statement of Progressive Property, 94 Cornell L. Rev. 743 (2009); Gregory S. Alexander, The Social-Obligation Norm in American Property Law, 94 Cornell L. Rev. 745 (2009) (developing a human-flourishing theory of property that views property owners as owing obligations to contribute to community members' development of basic capabilities); Eduardo M. Peñalver, Land Virtues, 94 Cornell L. Rev. 821 (2009) (proposing a virtue-based vision of property, especially land, according to which

---

7. See Gregory S. Alexander, Time and Property in the American Republican Legal Culture, 66 N.Y.U. L. Rev. 273, 277 (1991):

> [W]hile the liberal vision underlying individual property rights depicts the self as separated from politics, it is politics that defines the personal sphere—individual property rights depend on state power. Moreover, property is inescapably relational. When the state recognizes and enforces one person's property right, it simultaneously denies property rights in others. Thus the owner's security as to particular assets comes at the expense of others being vulnerable to the owner's control over those assets. Ownership is power over persons, not merely things.

These remarks suggest a perspective on property that was probably first associated with Critical Legal Studies (CLS), though some of the core Critical ideas date back 50 years and more to the Legal Realists (of whom Morris Cohen was one). Commonly called a movement, CLS has nevertheless been extraordinarily heterogeneous in terms of the points of view represented by its affiliates. If there is a common denominator, it is leftist disenchantment with existing social and legal institutions, with "liberal legalism," and with the idea that law transcends politics and is or can be objective or politically neutral. See generally Mark Kelman, A Guide to Critical Legal Studies (1987).

property law can and should inculcate virtues that promote decision making to strike a proper balance between self-interest and obligations to others); Joseph William Singer, Democratic Estates: Property Law in a Free and Democratic Society, 94 Cornell L. Rev. 1009 (2009) (property law should reflect democratic aspirations, with owners' obligations based on the characteristics of a robustly democratic society).

Progressive property theory (PPT) has not gone unchallenged. See the Responses in the Special Issue: Property and Obligation, in 94 Cornell L. Rev. 889-1007 (2009) (Responses by Eric R. Claeys, Jedediah Purdy, Henry E. Smith, and Katrina M. Wyman). PPT also has friendly critics. See Ezra Rosser, The Ambition and Transformative Potential of Progressive Property, 101 Cal. L. Rev. 107 (2013) (criticizing PPT for neglecting issues of race-related acquisition and distribution); Jane B. Baron, The Contested Commitments of Property, 61 Hastings L. Rev. 917 (2010) (criticizing PPT's focus on exclusion, arguing that the real contest between progressive and exclusion theorists is metaphorical—a "machine" metaphor of property versus a "conversation" metaphor).

8. *Epilogue and prologue.* See Rose, supra, at 19-20:

> [P]erhaps the deepest aspect of the common law text of possession lies in the attitude that this text strikes with respect to the relationship between human beings and nature. At least some Indians professed bewilderment at the concept of owning the land. Indeed they prided themselves on not marking the land but rather on moving lightly through it, living with the land and with its creatures as members of the same family rather than as strangers who visited only to conquer the objects of nature. The doctrine of first possession, quite to the contrary, reflects the attitude that human beings are outsiders to nature. It gives the earth and its creatures over to those who mark them so clearly as to transform them, so that no one else will mistake them for unsubdued nature.
>
> To be sure, we may admire nature and enjoy wildness. But those sentiments find little resonance in the doctrine of first possession. Its texts are those of cultivation, manufacture, and development. We cannot have our fish both loose and fast, as Herman Melville might put it. The common law of first possession makes a choice. The common law gives preference to those who convince the world that they can catch the fish and hold it fast. This may be a reward to useful labor, but it is more precisely the articulation of a specific vocabulary within a structure of symbols understood by a commercial people. It is this commonly understood and shared set of symbols that gives significance and form to what might seem the quintessentially individualistic act: the claim that one has, by "possession," separated for one's self property from the great commons of unowned things.

B.   Acquisition by Capture

Pierson v. Post

Supreme Court of New York, 1805
3 Cai. R. 175, 2 Am. Dec. 264

This was an action of trespass on the case commenced in a justice's court, by the present defendant against the now plaintiff.

The declaration stated that Post, being in possession of certain dogs and hounds under his command, did, "upon a certain wild and uninhabited, unpossessed and waste land, called the beach, find and start one of those noxious beasts called a fox," and whilst there hunting, chasing and pursuing the same with his dogs and hounds, and when in view thereof, Pierson, well knowing the fox was so hunted and pursued, did, in the sight of Post, to prevent his catching the same, kill and carry it off. A verdict having been rendered for the plaintiff below, the defendant there sued out a *certiorari*, and now assigned for error, that the declaration and the matters therein contained were not sufficient in law to maintain an action. . . .

TOMPKINS, J., delivered the opinion of the court.[8] This cause comes before us on a return to a *certiorari* directed to one of the justices of Queens county.

The question submitted by the counsel in this cause for our determination is, whether Lodowick Post, by the pursuit with his hounds in the manner alleged in his declaration, acquired such a right to, or property in, the fox, as will sustain an action against Pierson for killing and taking him away?

The cause was argued with much ability by the counsel on both sides, and presents for our decision a novel and nice question. It is admitted that a fox is an animal *ferae naturae*, and that property in such animals is acquired by occupancy only. These admissions narrow the discussion to the simple question of what acts amount to occupancy, applied to acquiring right to wild animals?

If we have recourse to the ancient writers upon general principles of law, the judgment below is obviously erroneous. Justinian's Institutes, lib. 2, tit. 1, s.13, and Fleta, lib. 3, c.2, p. 175, adopt the principle, that pursuit alone vests no property or right in the huntsman; and that even pursuit, accompanied with wounding, is equally ineffectual for that purpose, unless the animal be actually taken. The same principle is recognised by Bracton, lib. 2, c.1, p. 8.

Puffendorf, lib. 4, c.6, s.2, and 10, defines occupancy of beasts *ferae naturae*, to be the actual corporal possession of them, and Bynkershoek is cited as coinciding in this definition. It is indeed with hesitation that Puffendorf affirms that a wild beast mortally wounded, or greatly maimed, cannot be fairly intercepted by another, whilst the pursuit of the person inflicting the wound continues. The foregoing authorities are decisive to show that mere pursuit gave Post no legal right to the fox, but that he became the property of Pierson, who intercepted and killed him.

It therefore only remains to inquire whether there are any contrary principles, or authorities, to be found in other books, which ought to induce a different

8. Daniel Tompkins (1774-1825) was an important figure in the early Republic, especially in New York politics. A self-made man of humble origins, he graduated first in his class from Columbia College. He was an enormously popular figure with the electorate, served twice as Governor of New York State (1807-1817), and was the sixth Vice-President of the United States (1817-1825) during James Monroe's administration. Throughout his public service Tompkins had serious financial problems and was a heavy drinker. During his tenure as Vice-President he occasionally presided over the Senate while inebriated. He died in 1825, disgraced, deeply in debt, and probably alcoholic. See Ray W. Irwin, Daniel D. Tompkins: Governor of New York and Vice President of the United States (1968).—EDS.

decision. Most of the cases which have occurred in England, relating to property in wild animals, have either been discussed and decided upon the principles of their positive statute regulations, or have arisen between the huntsman and the owner of the land upon which beasts *ferae naturae* have been apprehended; the former claiming them by title of occupancy, and the latter *ratione soli*. Little satisfactory aid can, therefore, be derived from the English reporters.

Barbeyrac, in his notes on Puffendorf, does not accede to the definition of occupancy by the latter, but, on the contrary, affirms, that actual bodily seizure is not, in all cases, necessary to constitute possession of wild animals. He does not, however, *describe* the acts which, according to his ideas, will amount to an appropriation of such animals to private use, so as to exclude the claims of all other persons, by title of occupancy, to the same animals; and he is far from averring that pursuit alone is sufficient for that purpose. To a certain extent, and as far as Barbeyrac appears to me to go, his objections to Puffendorf's definition of occupancy are reasonable and correct. That is to say, that actual bodily seizure is not indispensable to acquire right to, or possession of, wild beasts; but that, on the contrary, the mortal wounding of such beasts, by one not abandoning his pursuit, may, with the utmost propriety, be deemed possession of him; since, thereby, the pursuer manifests an unequivocal intention of appropriating the animal to his individual use, has deprived him of his natural liberty, and brought him within his certain control. So also, encompassing and securing such animals with nets and toils, or otherwise intercepting them in such a manner as to deprive them of their natural liberty, and render escape impossible, may justly be deemed to give possession of them to those persons who, by their industry and labour, have used such means of apprehending them. Barbeyrac seems to have adopted, and had in view of his notes, the more accurate opinion of Grotius, with respect to occupancy. . . . The case now under consideration is one of mere pursuit, and presents no circumstances or acts which can bring it within the definition of occupancy by Puffendorf, or Grotius, or the ideas of Barbeyrac upon that subject.

The case cited from 11 Mod. 74-130, I think clearly distinguishable from the present; inasmuch as there the action was for maliciously hindering and disturbing the plaintiff in the exercise and enjoyment of a private franchise; and in the report of the same case, (3 Salk. 9) Holt, Ch. J., states, that the ducks were in the plaintiff's decoy pond, and so in his possession, from which it is obvious the court laid much stress in their opinion upon the plaintiff's possession of the ducks, *ratione soli*.

We are the more readily inclined to confine possession or occupancy of beasts *ferae naturae*, within the limits prescribed by the learned authors above cited, for the sake of certainty, and preserving peace and order in society. If the first seeing, starting, or pursuing such animals, without having so wounded, circumvented or ensnared them, so as to deprive them of their natural liberty, and subject them to the control of their pursuer, should afford the basis of actions against others for intercepting and killing them, it would prove a fertile source of quarrels and litigation.

rude

However uncourteous or unkind the conduct of Pierson towards Post, in this instance, may have been, yet his act was productive of no injury or damage for which a legal remedy can be applied. We are of opinion the judgment below was erroneous, and ought to be reversed.

LIVINGSTON, J.[9] My opinion differs from that of the court. Of six exceptions, taken to the proceedings below, all are abandoned except the third, which reduces the controversy to a single question.

Whether a person who, with his own hounds, starts and hunts a fox on waste and uninhabited ground, and is on the point of seizing his prey, acquires such an interest in the animal, as to have a right of action against another, who in view of the huntsman and his dogs in full pursuit, and with knowledge of the chase, shall kill and carry him away?

This is a knotty point, and should have been submitted to the arbitration of sportsmen, without poring over Justinian, Fleta, Bracton, Puffendorf, Locke, Barbeyrac, or Blackstone, all of whom have been cited; they would have had no difficulty in coming to a prompt and correct conclusion. In a court thus constituted, the skin and carcass of poor *reynard* would have been properly disposed of, and a precedent set, interfering with no usage or custom which the experience of ages has sanctioned, and which must be so well known to every votary of Diana. But the parties have referred the question to our judgment, and we must dispose of it as well as we can, from the partial lights we possess, leaving to a higher tribunal, the correction of any mistake which we may be so unfortunate as to make. By the pleadings it is admitted that a fox is a "wild and noxious beast." Both parties have regarded him, as the law of nations does a pirate, "*hostem humani generis*," and although "*de mortuis nil nisi bonum*," be a maxim of our profession, the memory of the deceased has not been spared. His depredations on farmers and on barn yards have not been forgotten; and to put him to death wherever found, is allowed to be meritorious, and of public benefit. Hence it follows, that our decision should have in view the greatest possible encouragement to the destruction of an animal, so cunning and ruthless in his career. But who would keep a pack of hounds; or what gentleman, at the sound of the horn, and at peep of day, would mount his steed, and for hours together, "*sub jove frigido*," or a vertical sun, pursue the windings of this wily quadruped, if, just as night came on, and his stratagems and strength were nearly exhausted, a saucy intruder, who had not shared in the honours or labours of the chase, were permitted to come in at the death, and bear away in triumph the object of pursuit? Whatever Justinian may have thought of the matter, it must be recollected that his code was compiled many hundred years ago, and it would be very hard indeed, at the distance of so many centuries,

---

9. Professor Craig Oren has informed us that Livingston, J., was probably Henry Brockholst Livingston (1757-1823). Born into a socially prominent family in New York City, he served in the American Revolution and later as assistant to John Jay when Jay was minister to Spain. Coming back from Spain, Livingston was captured by the British but subsequently released. During his career as a lawyer he became an ardent Jeffersonian and wrote a number of newspaper articles opposing Jay's Treaty. In 1806, President Jefferson appointed him to the U.S. Supreme Court, where he served until his death.

not to have a right to establish a rule for ourselves. In his day, we read of no order of men who made it a business, in the language of the declaration in this cause, "with hounds and dogs to find, start, pursue, hunt, and chase," these animals, and that, too, without any other motive than the preservation of Roman poultry; if this diversion had been then in fashion, the lawyers who composed his institutes would have taken care not to pass it by, without suitable encouragement. If any thing, therefore, in the digests or pandects shall appear to militate against the defendant in error, who, on this occasion, was the foxhunter, we have only to say *tempora mutantur*; and if men themselves change with the times, why should not laws also undergo an alteration?

It may be expected, however, by the learned counsel, that more particular notice be taken of their authorities. I have examined them all, and feel great difficulty in determining, whether to acquire dominion over a thing, before in common, it be sufficient that we barely see it, or know where it is, or wish for it, or make a declaration of our will respecting it; or whether, in the case of wild beasts, setting a trap, or lying in wait, or starting, or pursuing, be enough; or if an actual wounding, or killing, or bodily tact and occupation be necessary. Writers on general law, who have favoured us with their speculations on these points, differ on them all; but, great as is the diversity of sentiment among them, some conclusion must be adopted on the question immediately before us. After mature deliberation, I embrace that of Barbeyrac, as the most rational, and least liable to objection. If at liberty, we might imitate the courtesy of a certain emperor, who, to avoid giving offence to the advocates of any of these different doctrines, adopted a middle course, and by ingenious distinctions, rendered it difficult to say (as often happens after a fierce and angry contest) to whom the palm of victory belonged. He ordained, that if a beast be followed with *large dogs and hounds,* he shall belong to the hunter, not to the chance occupant; and in like manner, if he be killed or wounded with a lance or sword; but if chased with *beagles only,* then he passed to the captor, not to the first pursuer. If slain with a dart, a sling, or a bow, he fell to the hunter, if still in chase, and not to him who might afterwards find and seize him.

Now, as we are without any municipal regulations of our own, and the pursuit here, for aught that appears on the case, being with dogs and hounds of *imperial stature,* we are at liberty to adopt one of the provisions just cited, which comports also with the learned conclusion of Barbeyrac, that property in animals *ferae naturae* may be acquired without bodily touch or manucaption, provided the pursuer be within reach, or have a *reasonable* prospect (which certainly existed here) of taking, what he has *thus* discovered with an intention of converting to his own use.[10]

10. The tone of Livingston's dissent probably reflects an intention on his part to mock the majority's pedantry. But he would have done well to pay attention to the views of at least one classic figure, John Locke (recall Note 4 on page 14), who argued from his labor theory of property that on facts like those in *Pierson*, a wild animal should rightly go to the person who first invested labor in pursuit, notwithstanding capture had not yet been achieved. See John Locke, Two Treatises of Government, Book II, §30 (1690): "[T]he hare that anyone is hunting, is thought his who pursues her during the chase. For being a beast that is still looked upon as common, . . . whoever has employed so much labor about any of that kind, as to find and pursue her, has thereby removed her from the state of nature, wherein she was common, and hath begun a property." This was exactly the view advocated by Livingston.

When we reflect also that the interest of our husbandmen, the most useful of men in any community, will be advanced by the destruction of a beast so pernicious and incorrigible, we cannot greatly err, in saying, that a pursuit like the present, through waste and unoccupied lands, and which must inevitably and speedily have terminated in corporal possession, or bodily *seisin*, confers such a right to the object of it, as to make any one a wrongdoer, who shall interfere and shoulder the spoil. The justice's judgment ought, therefore, in my opinion, to be affirmed.

Judgment of reversal.

NOTES AND QUESTIONS

1. Pierson v. Post, one of the old chestnuts of property law, has in recent years figured in a flurry of law review articles:

Bethany R. Berger, It's Not about the Fox: The Untold History of *Pierson v. Post*, 55 Duke L.J. 1089 (2006), speculates that the real dispute in the case had little to do with rights to a fox; the issue, rather, was whether the use of local common areas should be determined by the tastes of the newly wealthy (Post) or the old agricultural traditionalists (Pierson).

Andrea McDowell, Legal Fictions in *Pierson v. Post*, 105 Mich. L. Rev. 735 (2007), argues that the dispute was a torts case in disguise. Neither party actually wanted the fox. Post simply wanted to run a hunt free of interference from others, whereas Pierson's aim was to get rid of varmints, not gain possession of them.

Angela Fernandez, The Lost Record of *Pierson v. Post*, the Famous Fox Case, 27 Law & Hist. Rev. 149 (2009), relates the author's discovery in 2008 of the long-lost judgment roll in the case and describes various previously unknown points of interest disclosed by the record—for example, the date of the incident (December 10, 1802); a description of the jury trial before a justice of the peace where the parties appeared without lawyers on December 30, 1802; the amount of damages Post claimed (up to $25) and was awarded (75¢ by the jury and $5 in costs); the amount Pierson won on appeal ($121.37); confirmation of the names of the lawyers; and all six grounds of appeal claimed by Pierson's lawyer, Nathan Sanford, which included allegations of some serious procedural error by the justice of the peace.

In another article, *Pierson v. Post*: A Great Debate, James Kent, and the Project of Building a Learned Law for New York State, 34 Law & Soc. Inq. 301 (2009), Professor Fernandez argues that the length of time the case took to be heard on appeal, plus the procedural error involved in the original finding for Post, which could easily have led to a quick and simple reversal for Pierson, suggest that something besides just the legal merits was at work in the case, specifically, that the judges and lawyers involved with it at the appellate level saw an opportunity for a learned debate. The chief justice of the court at the time of the appeal, James Kent, demonstrated considerable interest in the case, as evidenced by annotations he made on a later copy of the case and his treatment of it in his famous Commentaries on American Law (four volumes, 1826-1830). Professor Fernandez wonders whether Kent might have been the mastermind behind the case in 1805. She can't be sure, of course, but thinks, at least, that the published report of the case (the one we have reproduced) is best understood as a product of the intellectual interests and schooling of the lawyers and judges involved in the appeal, who were engaged in the project of building elaborate "high law" for the new nation.

2. *"Fox shoots man."* That was the headline of a January 2011 report by Reuters. "A wounded fox shot its would-be killer in Belarus by pulling the trigger on the hunter's gun as the pair scuffled after the man tried to finish the animal off with the butt of the rifle." Both fox and hunter survived.

3. The majority and dissenting opinions in Pierson v. Post are peppered with references to a number of obscure legal works and legal scholars. Justinian's Institutes is a Roman law treatise of the sixth century; Bracton was the author of a thirteenth-century tome on English law; Fleta refers to a Latin textbook on English law written in 1290 or thereabouts, supposedly in Fleet prison and possibly by one of the corrupt judges Edward I put there. Barbeyrac, Bynkershoek, Grotius, and Pufendorf (sometimes spelled Puffendorf) were legal scholars who wrote in the seventeenth and eighteenth centuries; the last two of them figured in our discussion of Johnson v. M'Intosh, as did John Locke, the English philosopher (1632-1704) and William Blackstone (1723-1780). See pages 12-15. Blackstone was the first professor of English law at an English university. His famous Commentaries on the Laws of England (1765-1769), the first accessible general statement of English law, was popular and influential in both England and the United States, despite being scorned by the likes of Jeremy Bentham (on whom see page 51) for uncritical acceptance of previous writers and blind admiration of the past. After resigning a professorship at Oxford, Blackstone was appointed to the bench, where in a famous opinion in Perrin v. Blake he concisely formulated the conservative creed of property lawyers of his time: "The law of real property in this country, wherever its materials were gathered, is now formed into a fine artificial system, full of unseen connexions and nice dependencies; and he that breaks one link of the chain, endangers the dissolution of the whole."1 Francis Hargrave, Tracts Relative to the Law of England 489, 498 (1787).

4. The discussion in Note 3 on page 12 introduced the principle of first in time and suggested the dominant role it plays in the law of property. Did the majority and dissenting justices in Pierson v. Post agree that first in time was the governing principle? Note that the majority held as it did "for the sake of certainty, and preserving peace and order in society." See page 20. How did its opinion (that mere chase is insufficient to confer the rights of first possession) advance those goals? The benefits of peace and order seem obvious enough. What are the advantages of certainty in a property system? Are there any disadvantages in promoting certainty? Consider in this regard the dissenting opinion of Justice Livingston, who wanted to promote the destruction of "pernicious beasts." He believed that his rule would do that more effectively than the rule of the majority opinion. Was he correct?

Sir William Blackstone
Attributed to Sir Joshua Reynolds
National Portrait Gallery, London

On the methods of reasoning reflected in the majority and dissenting opinions in Pierson v. Post, see Linda Holdeman Edwards, The Convergence of Analogical and Dialectic Imaginations in Legal Discourse, 20 Legal Stud. F. 7 (1996).

5. Livingston was also of the view that the question in Pierson v. Post "should have been submitted to the arbitration of sportsmen."[11] See page 21. In that event, Post probably would have won, because "it appeared from the record that all hunters in the region regarded hot pursuit as giving rights to take an unimpeded first possession." Richard A. Epstein, Possession as the Root of Title, 13 Ga. L. Rev. 1221, 1231 (1979). The local custom, in short, was contrary to the rule adopted by the majority. Should the majority have abided by the custom? Consider the following case.

Ghen v. Rich

United States District Court
District of Massachusetts, 1881
8 F. 159

NELSON, J. This is a libel to recover the value of a fin-back whale. The libellant lives in Provincetown and the respondent in Wellfleet. The facts, as they appeared at the hearing, are as follows:

> In the early spring months the easterly part of Massachusetts bay is frequented by the species of whale known as the fin-back whale. Fishermen from Provincetown pursue them in open boats from the shore, and shoot them with bomb-lances fired from guns made expressly for the purpose. When killed they sink at once to the bottom, but in the course of from one to three days they rise and float on the surface. Some of them are picked up by vessels and towed into Provincetown. Some float ashore at high water and are left stranded on the beach as the tide recedes. Others float out to sea and are never recovered. The person who happens to find them on the beach usually sends word to Provincetown, and the owner comes to the spot and removes the blubber. The finder usually receives a small salvage for his services. Try-works are established in Provincetown for trying out the oil. The business is of considerable extent, but, since it requires skill and experience, as well as some outlay of capital, and is attended with great exposure and hardship, few persons engage in it. The average yield of oil is about 20 barrels to a whale. It swims with great swiftness, and for that reason cannot be taken by the

---

11. Arbitration would no doubt have been cheaper but maybe not so satisfying to the real contestants (who seem to have been the fathers of the plaintiff and defendant). The following recollection of Pierson v. Post is quoted in James T. Adams, Memorials of Old Bridgehampton 166 (1916, 1962):

Jesse Pierson, son of Capt. David, . . . saw a fox run down an unused well near Peter's Pond, and killed and took the fox. Lodowick Post and a company with him were in pursuit and chasing the fox, and saw Jesse with it and claimed it as theirs, while Jesse persisted in his claim. Capt. Pierson said his son Jesse should have the fox and Capt. Post said the same of his son Lodowick and hence the law suit contested and appealed to the highest court in the State. . . . This became the leading case often cited. . . . To the public the decision was worth its cost. To the parties, who each expended over a thousand pounds, the fox cost very dear.

But this only went to show that "the love of law suits had not entirely disappeared, although, as by this time lawyers were employed, they were much more in the nature of luxuries." Id. at 165.

harpoon and line. Each boat's crew engaged in the business has its peculiar mark or device on its lances, and in this way it is known by whom a whale is killed.

The usage on Cape Cod, for many years, has been that the person who kills a whale in the manner and under the circumstances described, owns it, and this right has never been disputed until this case. The libellant has been engaged in this business for ten years past. On the morning of April 9, 1880, in Massachusetts bay, near the end of Cape Cod, he shot and instantly killed with a bomb-lance the whale in question. It sunk immediately, and on the morning of the 12th was found stranded on the beach in Brewster, within the ebb and flow of the tide, by one Ellis, 17 miles from the spot where it was killed. Instead of sending word to Provincetown, as is customary, Ellis advertised the whale for sale at auction, and sold it to the respondent, who shipped off the blubber and tried out the oil. The libellant heard of the finding of the whale on the morning of the 15th, and immediately sent one of his boat's crew to the place and claimed it. Neither the respondent nor Ellis knew the whale had been killed by the libellant, but they knew or might have known, if they had wished, that it had been shot and killed with a bomb-lance, by some person engaged in this species of business.

The libellant claims title to the whale under this usage. The respondent insists that this usage is invalid. It was decided by Judge Sprague, in Taber v. Jenny, 8 F. Cas. 159, that when a whale has been killed, and is anchored and left with marks of appropriation, it is the property of the captors; and if it is afterwards found, still anchored, by another ship, there is no usage or principle of law by which the property of the original captors is diverted, even though the whale may have dragged from its anchorage. The learned judge says:

> When the whale had been killed and taken possession of by the boat of the Hillman, (the first taker,) it became the property of the owners of that ship, and all was done which was then practicable in order to secure it. They left it anchored, with unequivocal marks of appropriation.

In Bartlett v. Budd, 2 F. Cas. 966, the facts were these: The first officer of the libellant's ship killed a whale in the Okhotsk sea, anchored it, attached a waif[12] to the body, and then left it and went ashore at some distance for the night. The next morning the boats of the respondent's ship found the whale adrift, the anchor not holding, the cable coiled round the body, and no waif or irons attached to it. Judge Lowell held that, as the libellants had killed and taken actual possession of the whale, the ownership vested in them. In his opinion the learned judge says:

> A whale, being *ferae naturae*, does not become property until a firm possession has been established by the taker. But when such possession has become firm and complete, the right of property is clear, and has all the characteristics of property.

He doubted whether a usage set up but not proved by the respondents, that a whale found adrift in the ocean is the property of the finder, unless the first taker should appear and claim it before it is cut in, would be valid, and remarked that "there would be great difficulty in upholding a custom that

---

12. Worry not! To a whaler a "waif" is not a homeless child but a pole with a little flag on top. — EDS.

should take the property of A. and give it to B., under so very short and uncertain a substitute for the statute of limitations, and one so open to fraud and deceit." Both the cases cited were decided without reference to usage, upon the ground that the property had been acquired by the first taker by actual possession and appropriation.

In Swift v. Gifford, 23 F. Cas. 558, Judge Lowell decided that a custom among whalemen in the Arctic seas, that the iron holds the whale, was reasonable and valid. In that case a boat's crew from the respondent's ship pursued and struck a whale in the Arctic ocean, and the harpoon and the line attached to it remained in the whale, but did not remain fast to the boat. A boat's crew from the libellant's ship continued the pursuit and captured the whale, and the master of the respondent's ship claimed it on the spot. It was held by the learned judge that the whale belonged to the respondents. It was said by Judge Sprague, in Bourne v. Ashley, an unprinted case referred to by Judge Lowell in Swift v. Gifford, that the usage for the first iron, whether attached to the boat or not, to hold the whale was fully established; and he added that, although local usages of a particular port ought not to be allowed to set aside the general maritime law, this objection did not apply to a custom which embraced an entire business, and had been concurred in for a long time by every one engaged in the trade.

In Swift v. Gifford, Judge Lowell also said:

> The rule of law invoked in this case is one of very limited application. The whale fishery is the only branch of industry of any importance in which it is likely to be much used, and if a usage is found to prevail generally in that business, it will not be open to the objection that it is likely to disturb the general understanding of mankind by the interposition of an arbitrary exception.

I see no reason why the usage proved in this case is not as reasonable as that sustained in the cases cited. Its application must necessarily be extremely limited, and can affect but a few persons. It has been recognized and acquiesced in for many years. It requires in the first taker the only act of appropriation that is possible in the nature of the case. Unless it is sustained, this branch of industry must necessarily cease, for no person would engage in it if the fruits of his labor could be appropriated by any chance finder. It gives reasonable salvage for securing or reporting the property. That the rule works well in practice is shown by the extent of the industry which has grown up under it, and the general acquiescence of a whole community interested to dispute it. It is by no means clear that without regard to usage the common law would not reach the same result. That seems to be the effect of the decisions in Taber v. Jenny and Bartlett v. Budd. If the fisherman does all that it is possible to do to make the animal his own, that would seem to be sufficient. Such a rule might well be applied in the interest of trade, there being no usage or custom to the contrary. Holmes, The Common Law, 217. But be that as it may, I hold the usage to be valid, and that the property in the whale was in the libellant.

The rule of damages is the market value of the oil obtained from the whale, less the cost of trying it out and preparing it for the market, with interest on the amount so ascertained from the date of conversion. As the question is new and important, and the suit is contested on both sides, more for the purpose of having it settled than for the amount involved, I shall give no costs.

Decree for libellant for $71.05, without costs.

NOTES AND QUESTIONS

1. A libel is the admiralty law equivalent of a lawsuit, and the libellant (or libelant) is the equivalent of the plaintiff in an action at law. Was the custom or usage relied upon in Ghen v. Rich essential to the libellant's case, or would the rule in Pierson v. Post, page 18, have served as well?

2. Ghen v. Rich describes several whaling customs, and evidence of others can be found in a surprising array of sources, including Herman Melville's Moby-Dick Ch. 89 (1851),[13] Oliver Wendell Holmes's famous lectures on The Common Law 212 (1881), a number of court reports, and various journals and historical accounts. Much of the literature is considered in Robert C. Ellickson, A Hypothesis of Wealth-Maximizing Norms: Evidence from the Whaling Industry, 5 J. Law, Econ. & Org. 83 (1989), part of a larger study on relationships between formal law and informal norms. See Robert C. Ellickson, Order Without Law: How Neighbors Settle Disputes (1991).

Ellickson concludes that all the supposed and actual whaling norms boiled down to essentially three. One usage entailed the fast-fish/loose-fish understanding "that a claimant owned a whale, dead or alive, so long as the whale was fastened by line or otherwise to the claimant's boat or ship." Another usage, iron-holds-the-whale, "conferred an exclusive right to capture upon the whaler who had first affixed a harpoon or other whaling craft to the body of the whale. . . . [T]he iron did not have to be connected by a line or otherwise to the claimant," so long as the claimant remained in fresh pursuit. The third usage "called for the value of the carcass to be split between the first harpooner and the ultimate seizer by way of a reasonable salvage award to the latter." Ellickson, Wealth-Maximizing Norms, supra, at 89-93. Each usage, Ellickson argues, "was adapted to its particular context"—to the disparate circumstances of various whales and waters—and all of them were developed and observed by whalers (and observed by courts, too) as informal or extralegal property rights regimes that maximized the whalers' aggregate wealth.

---

13. Chapter 89 of Moby-Dick bears the title "Fast-Fish and Loose-Fish." "A Fast-Fish belongs to the party fast to it," Melville wrote. "A Loose-Fish is fair game for anybody who can soonest catch it." The issue in Ghen v. Rich was when a fish was to be considered fast and when loose.

Recall that Professor Rose alluded to all of this in the excerpt that concluded our discussion of Johnson v. M'Intosh and the "discovery" of America (see page 18). In Moby-Dick one can find, in turn, Melville's own ironic allusion to the question of that discovery, again in Chapter 89: "What was America in 1492 but a Loose-Fish, in which Columbus struck the Spanish standard by way of waifing it for his royal master and mistress?" And "What is the great globe itself but a Loose-Fish? And what are you, reader, but a Loose-Fish and a Fast-Fish, too?"

So should a usage of whalers have determined the outcome of Ghen v. Rich?[14] And to get back to where we began all of this (in Note 5 on page 26), should the norms of hunters have decided Pierson v. Post? More generally, when and why should custom matter, and when and why not? See Ellickson, supra, at 95-96 (risk of overwhaling); Richard A. Epstein, Possession as the Root of Title, 13 Ga. L. Rev. 1221, 1231-1236 (1979); Benjamin van Drimmelen, The International Mismanagement of Whaling, 10 UCLA Pac. Basin L.J. 240 (1991).

3. The conservation organization Greenpeace tries to frustrate the capture of whales by interposing its own boats between whalers and their prey. Suppose conservationists as a group can demonstrate that this is their shared custom, and they have adopted it because they think it maximizes the aggregate wealth of the world by preventing overwhaling. Should the custom count? The case that follows, though decided almost three centuries ago, bears directly on the question.

Keeble v. Hickeringill

Queen's Bench, 1707
11 East 574, 103 Eng. Rep. 1127
11 Mod. 74, 130 (as Keble v. Hickringill)
3 Salk. 9 (as Keeble v. Hickeringhall)

Action upon the case. Plaintiff declares that he was, 8th November in the second year of the Queen, lawfully possessed of a close of land called Minott's Meadow, [containing] a decoy pond, to which divers wildfowl used to resort and come: and the plaintiff had at his own costs and charges prepared and procured divers decoy ducks, nets, machines and other engines for the decoying and taking of the wildfowl, and enjoyed the benefit in taking them: the defendant, knowing which, and intending to damnify the plaintiff in his vivary, and to fright and drive away the wildfowl used to resort thither, and deprive him of his profit, did, on the 8th of November, resort to the head of the said pond and vivary, and did discharge six guns laden with gunpowder, and with the noise and stink of the gunpowder did drive away the wildfowl then being in the pond: and on the 11th and 12th days of November the defendant, with design to damnify the plaintiff, and fright away the wildfowl, did place himself with a gun near the vivary, and there did discharge the said gun several times that was then charged with the gunpowder against the said decoy pond, whereby the wildfowl were frighted away, and did forsake the

14. In Ghen v. Rich, Judge Nelson worried that unless he sustained the usage in question, "this branch of industry must necessarily cease, for no person would engage in it if the fruits of his labor could be appropriated by any chance finder." See page 28. Recall that when Justice Livingston expressed the same concern (but with respect to foxes) in his dissenting opinion in Pierson v. Post, we questioned his reasoning. See page 24. Should we question Judge Nelson's? And by the way, do you agree with Nelson's statement (on page 28) that whaling customs "can affect but a few persons"? According to an interview with environmentalist Amory Lovins, in 1850 whaling was the fifth biggest industry in the United States, and most houses were lit by whale-oil lamps. Within a decade, however, competition from coal-based oil and gas had grabbed five-sixths of the market—this because whales were growing scarce and whale oil expensive. See Elizabeth Kolbert, Mr. Green, The New Yorker, Jan. 22, 2007, at 34, 39.

said pond. Upon not guilty pleaded, a verdict was found for the plaintiff and 20*l.* damages.

HOLT, C.J.[15] I am of opinion that this action doth lie. It seems to be new in its instance, but is not new in the reason or principle of it. For, 1st, this using or making a decoy is lawful. 2dly, this employment of his ground to that use is profitable to the plaintiff, as is the skill and management of that employment. As to the first, every man that hath a property may employ it for his pleasure and profit, as for alluring and procuring decoy ducks to come to his pond. To learn the trade of seducing other ducks to come there in order to be taken is not prohibited either by the law of the land or the moral law; but it is as lawful to use art to seduce them, to catch them, and destroy them for the use of mankind, as to kill and destroy wildfowl or tame cattle. Then when a man useth his art or his skill to take them, to sell and dispose of for his profit; this is his trade; and he that hinders another in his trade or livelihood is liable to an action for so hindering him. . . .

[W]here a violent or malicious act is done to a man's occupation, profession, or way of getting a livelihood, there an action lies in all cases. But if a man doth him damage by using the same employment; as if Mr. Hickeringill had set up another decoy on his own ground near the plaintiff's, and that had spoiled the custom of the plaintiff, no action would lie, because he had as much liberty to make and use a decoy as the plaintiff. This is like the case of 11 H. 4, 47.[16] One schoolmaster sets up a new school to the damage of an antient school, and thereby the scholars are allured from the old school to come to his new. (The action was held there not to lie.) But suppose Mr. Hickeringill should lie in the way with his guns, and fright the boys from going to school, and their parents would not let them go thither; sure that schoolmaster might have an action for the loss of his scholars. 29 E. 3, 18. A man hath a market, to which he hath toll for horses sold: a man is bringing his horse to market to sell: a stranger hinders and obstructs him from going thither to the market: an action lies, because it imports damage. . . .

And when we do know that of long time in the kingdom these artificial contrivances of decoy ponds and decoy ducks have been used for enticing into those ponds wildfowl, in order to be taken for the profit of the owner of the pond, who is at the expence of servants, engines, and other management, whereby the markets of the nation may be furnished; there is great reason to give encouragement thereunto; that the people who are so instrumental by their skill and industry so to furnish the markets should reap the benefit and have their action. But, in

---

15. Chief Justice Holt was one of the greatest English judges. After the flight of James II to France, abandoning the throne, Holt, as a member of the House of Commons, played a leading role in establishing a constitutional monarchy under William and Mary, a system that survives today. Subsequently he was appointed Chief Justice, which office he held from 1689 to 1710. He was noted for his integrity and independence and for his common sense as well as his deep learning in the law. Holt laid down the rule that the status of slavery could not exist in England; as soon as a slave breathed the air of England he was free. Smith v. Brown & Cooper, 2 Salk. 666, 90 Eng. Rep. 1172 (1703). Chief Justice Holt was the first of a line of enlightened judges who, in the eighteenth century, shaped English law to accommodate the needs of a mercantile society that would dominate world trading. Lord Mansfield, who served as Chief Justice from 1756 to 1788, was perhaps the most notable of these.—EDS.

16. The citation indicates a case decided in the eleventh year of the reign of Henry IV (1410). A variant is Y.B. 11 H.IV, 47. *Y.B.* refers to one of the Year Books, a collection (running from 1283 to 1535) of anonymous notes reporting cases.—EDS.

short, that which is the true reason is that this action is not brought to recover damage for the loss of the fowl, but for the disturbance; as 2 Cro. 604, Dawney v. Dee. So is the usual and common way of declaring.

NOTES AND QUESTIONS

1. *Early English reports.* There were no official reports of judicial decisions in England prior to the nineteenth century; entrepreneurs gathered up information about cases in one way or another and published them on their own. Students of the matter consider some of these unofficial sources to be more reliable than others. We have not indicated all the reports of *Keeble.* That from East (reprinted in Volume 103 of the English Reports), which we have used, is thought to be particularly trustworthy, the reporter claiming that his account came directly from a copy of Chief Justice Holt's manuscript. Modern (Mod.) is not esteemed, nor is the third volume of Salkeld (Salk.). See generally John W. Wallace, The Reporters (4th ed. 1882).

2. Keeble *and* Pierson. Go back to page 20, and you will see that the court in Pierson v. Post reckoned with *Keeble,* though it referred to it not by name but only by citation—the "case cited from 11 Mod. 74-130" and "the report of the same case, (3 Salk. 9)." The report in 3 Salk. 9 suggested to the court that the result in *Keeble* was influenced by the fact that the ducks were in the plaintiff's decoy pond, such that the plaintiff had possession of the ducks "*ratione soli.*" *Ratione soli* refers to the conventional view that an owner of land has possession—*constructive* possession, that is—of wild animals on the owner's land; in other words, land-owners are regarded as the prior possessors of any animals *ferae naturae* on their land, until the animals take off.[17]

We shall return to *ratione soli* shortly. The point for now is that it appears to have had little, if any, bearing on the final decision in *Keeble,* the statement of the court in Pierson v. Post to the contrary notwithstanding. The *Keeble* case was argued several times, and there was indeed a stage at which Chief Justice Holt seemed to be of the view that the plaintiff had (constructive) possession of the ducks in question. The arguments of counsel led him to change his mind, however, and to rest the judgment on the theory spelled out in the opinion from East that you have read—the theory of malicious interference with trade.

But the East report was unavailable at the time of Pierson v. Post; it was not published until 1815, a decade after the decision in *Pierson* was handed down. Hence the court had to rely on the accounts in Modern and Salkeld, which, as we saw, are probably untrustworthy.

---

17. The word *constructive,* a modifier familiar to all lawyers, will appear recurrently in this and other courses. One could say that the word is a way of pretending that whatever word it modifies depicts a state of affairs that actually exists when actually it does not. The pretense is made whenever judges wish, usually for good but often undisclosed reasons, a slightly different reality than the one confronting them. One might call this reasoning by strict analogy: Situation *A* is magically transformed into Situation *B* by incantation of the word *constructive.* Then the rule governing Situation *B* is applied to Situation *A* because the two situations are, after all, identical! Why might judges wish to pretend that a landowner possesses the wild animals on his land when actually he does not? See Problem 1 on pages 33-34.

3. *An abuse of right doctrine?* The *Keeble* case gives rise to a general question: Should an otherwise privileged act that causes harm to another person be legally actionable if the actor's reason for action was to cause harm? The question involves the doctrine of abuse of right, which provides that an owner abuses her property right when she exercises that right with the subjective intent of harming someone. The doctrine is widely recognized in the civil law, but since the decision in Bradford v. Pickles [1895], A.C. 587, the law in the U.K. and Commonwealth jurisdictions has generally been thought to be that motive is irrelevant. For a penetrating argument to the contrary, see Larissa Katz, Spite and Extortion: A Jurisdictional Principle of Abuse of Property Right, 122 Yale L.J. 1444 (2013). See also the fine book by Michael Taggart, Private Property and the Abuse of Rights in Victorian England: The Story of Edward Pickles and the Bradford Water Supply (2002).

4. *Interference with capture.* Suppose East had been available. Would the outcome of *Pierson* have been different? Should it have been? Was it essential to the outcome in *Keeble* that the plaintiff was engaged in something like a trade, as opposed to mere sport? Suppose *X* is an avid hunter who tracks down a deer on a piece of open hunting land during the hunting season. The deer is at very close range and just as *X* is about to shoot it another hunter, *Y*, appears and does so. Who gets the deer? Was it essential to the outcome in *Keeble* that the ducks were frightened off, rather than captured by a competitor of the plaintiff? Suppose that *Y* is not a hunter but a zealous animal lover who at the last instant frightens the deer away. Does *X* have any recourse?[18]

The second of the two situations described above gets us back to the activities of Greenpeace and other conservation groups mentioned in Note 3 on page 30. An article in the N.Y. Times, Nov. 23, 1990, at A22, reports that interference with the capture or killing of wild animals has become such a problem that most states and the federal government have enacted legislation outlawing hunter harassment on public land. Some challenges to the anti-harassment laws have succeeded on grounds of unconstitutional vagueness and violation of the First Amendment's protection of free speech. See also James E. Krier, Capture and Counteraction: Self-Help by Environmental Zealots, 30 U. Rich. L. Rev. 103 (1997).

PROBLEMS: MORE ON THE RULE OF CAPTURE AND WILD ANIMALS (AND A NOTE ON DUCK DECOYS)

1. A trespasser who captures a wild animal on the land of another might still have no rights to the animal as against the landowner, even though the landowner never had actual physical possession or control and even though the trespasser

---

18. An illuminating way to begin thinking about both of these questions is this: Try to imagine what instrumental ends—or objectives or policies—the decisions in *Pierson* and *Keeble* might have aimed to serve. Consider the schoolmaster of the "antient school" discussed in *Keeble*. A subsequent schoolmaster *scares* away the first school's students. Cause of action. *Lures* away the first school's students. No cause of action. Why the difference in results, especially given that the "antient school" was in each instance first in time? See Harold Demsetz, Wealth Distribution and the Ownership of Rights, 1 J. Legal Stud. 223, 231-232 (1972).

does. The court might say that the landowner had "constructive" possession of the animal. See footnote 17 on page 32. Why? See Ray A. Brown, The Law of Personal Property 17 (Walter B. Raushenbush 3d ed. 1975), suggesting that the courts reason as they do because a trespasser should not "be allowed to profit from his wrong." Notice the explanation gives rise to yet another question: Why is trespass considered to be "wrong"? More on that later. Suppose that T, a trespasser, captures a wild animal on the land of O, a landowner, and carries it off to her own land where she confines it in a cage. Subsequently, $T1$ trespasses on T's land and takes away the animal. In a suit by T against $T1$ for return of the animal, $T1$ defends on the ground that T had no rights of ownership in the animal. How would you respond, and why? Would your response be different if O had gone on to the land of T and taken the animal back, and T is now suing O for its return?

2. F has established a herd of deer that she keeps for pleasure and an occasional roast of venison. The deer roam about on open government grazing land during the day, but are sufficiently tame and domesticated that they return to a large shelter on F's land in the evening. (This is referred to as *animus revertendi*, or intention to return.) H, a hunter, licensed to hunt deer on the land, shoots one of F's deer one day during the hunting season. F sues H for return of the carcass. Who prevails? See Brown, supra, at 18. What policies might be served by holding for F? For H?[19]

On *animus revertendi* and the origins of domestic animals, see Robert C. Ellickson, Stone-Age Property in Domestic Animals, available at http://ssrn.com/abstract=2241675 (2013).

3. P imports two silver gray foxes, a male and a female, from Canada for breeding purposes on her Mississippi ranch. The natural habitat of the animals is the north central United States and Canada. The foxes are wild and once having escaped any captivity have no inclination to return. For this reason, P keeps her pair securely confined in a floored pen with plank walls five feet high. Despite these measures, the male gnaws his way out. P sets traps to recapture him, but to no avail. Some time later the fox is killed by D in a pine thicket 15 miles from P's ranch. D skins the fox and preserves the hide. P, learning of this, sues for return of the hide. Who should prevail, and why? See Brown, supra, at 18.

4. F, a farmer, is bothered by wild migrating geese on her land and shoots them in violation of the fish and game laws. The government confiscates the carcasses, and F sues for their return. The government wins, the court explaining that the government owns wild animals, may regulate their taking, and may confiscate animals taken in violation of regulations. See State ex rel. Visser v. State Fish & Game Commn., 437 P.2d 373 (Mont. 1968). So when the geese return the next year, F sues the government for damage to her cornfield caused by the geese

---

19. As an aside—but a revealing one—suppose that F has a neighbor who also keeps a herd of deer. A doe belonging to F roams onto the neighbor's land, takes up with a buck in the neighbor's herd, is fed by the neighbor, and eventually bears a fawn sired, presumably, by the neighbor's buck. Who owns the fawn, and why? See Carruth v. Easterling, 150 So. 2d 852 (Miss. 1963), and the marvelous essay by Felix Cohen, Dialogue on Private Property, 9 Rutgers L. Rev. 357, 365-369 (1954).

In his article, Cohen claimed that this so-called rule of increase is universal, observed in all legal cultures. It appears, however, that the English common law made an exception in the case of cygnets (baby swans), "which were divided equally between the owner of the cock and the owner of the hen . . . because of the strict monogamy of swan cocks." Thomas W. Merrill, Accession and Original Ownership, 1 J. Legal Analysis 459, 465 n.6 (2009).

Drawn by Author.   Vincent Brooks Day & Son lith.

DECOYMAN DRIVING WILD DUCK UP THE PIPE.

the government has been said to own. The government wins again, the court holding that the government does not own wild fowl and is not liable for damage caused by them. See Sickman v. United States, 184 F.2d 616 (7th Cir. 1950), cert. denied, 341 U.S. 939, reh'g denied, 342 U.S. 874 (1951). Can you square these two holdings? See Douglas v. Seacoast Prods., Inc., 431 U.S. 265, 284 (1977).[20]

5. *A note on duck decoys.* Duck decoys, invented in Holland in the sixteenth century and introduced into England in the seventeenth, provided an efficient system for capturing wild ducks on a commercial scale. A typical decoy consisted of a large pool of water from which radiated creeks, called pipes, which were roofed with netting. Ducks were attracted to the pool by the use of decoys; next, a specially trained dog, a piper, would appear at the front of a pipe and lure them closer (ducks, like humans, are curious and aggressive animals). When the ducks were well into a pipe a decoy man, previously hidden by a screen, would appear behind them (but out of sight of the pool) and frighten them farther into the pipe, where they were trapped. This technique enabled the capture of very large numbers of ducks, but didn't work well if there were disturbances—such as guns going off.

The use of duck decoys in the English fens died out in the mid-1900s (although a few are operated in Britain, and also in Holland, to capture birds for banding). The decoy at Minott's Meadow silted up long ago, but our late colleague Brian Simpson visited the area and he reported that the site of the decoy can still be identified, though not with absolute precision. Another site, at Pond Hall, can also be made out. The Pond Hall Decoy was owned by Hickeringill. Professor Simpson gathers from his research that the Minott's Meadow Decoy was constructed after Hickeringill's decoy at Pond Hall, and unusually close to it. This might have provoked Hickeringill, "a very eccentric parson," to retaliate as he did. Hickeringill, after all, had been first in time.

For more on duck decoys in general, and Keeble v. Hickeringill in particular, see A.W. Brian Simpson, Leading Cases in the Common Law (1995), Chapter 3 of which is entitled "The Timeless Principles of the Common Law: Keeble v. Hickeringill (1700)." The chapter begins: "The contribution of ducks to the common law system has been limited, but significant; they have concentrated the minds of lawyers upon fundamental issues of timeless principle." Id. at 45.

NOTES, QUESTIONS, AND PROBLEMS: THE RULE OF CAPTURE AND OTHER "FUGITIVE" RESOURCES

[I]nquiries into the acquisition of title to wild animals . . . may seem purely academic; how often, after all, do we expect to get into disputes about the ownership of wild pigs . . . ? These cases are not entirely silly, though. . . . [A]nalogies to the capture of wild animals show up time and again when courts have to deal on a nonstatutory basis with some "fugitive" resource that

---

20. But what if damage were caused by wildlife that the government had *reintroduced* to the local environment? See Christy v. Hodel, 857 F.2d 1324, 1335 n.9 (9th Cir. 1988), cert. denied, 490 U.S. 1114 (1989).

is being reduced to property for the first time. . . . [Carol M. Rose, Possession as the Origin of Property, 52 U. Chi. L. Rev. 73, 75 (1985).]

1. *Oil and gas.* Oil and natural gas commonly collect in reservoirs that underlie many acres of land owned by many different people.[21] The resources have a fugitive character in that they wander from place to place. Oil or gas once under the land of *A* might migrate to space under the land of *B* as the result of natural circumstances or because *B* drops a well and mines a common pool beneath *A*'s and *B*'s land. The oil or gas mined by *B* may even have been placed in the pool by *A* (gas and oil extracted elsewhere are often reinjected for storage or secondary recovery).

When these obviously problematic situations first led to litigation—usually (but not always) a suit by someone like *A* to recover the value of gas or oil drawn away by someone like *B*—the courts were induced by the fugitive nature of the resources in question to liken them to wild animals. And because ownership of wild animals had long been settled in terms of the rule of capture, the courts reasoned that ownership of oil and gas should be determined in the same manner. The resources, one early case said,

> may be classed by themselves, if the analogy be not too fanciful, as minerals *fera natura*. In common with animals, and unlike other minerals, they have the power and the tendency to escape without the volition of the owner. . . . They belong to the owner of the land, and are part of it, so long as they are on or in it, and are subject to his control; but when they escape, and go into other land, or come under another's control, the title of the former owner is gone. Possession of the land, therefore, is not necessarily possession of the gas. If an adjoining, or even a distant, owner, drills his own land, and taps your gas, so that it comes into his well and under his control, it is no longer yours, but his. [Westmoreland & Cambria Natl. Gas Co. v. DeWitt, 18 A. 724, 725 (Pa. 1889).]

Go back to the examples involving *A* and *B* above and consider the following:

(a) Does *A* have any remedy at all if *B* starts draining the pool? See Barnard v. Monongahela Natural Gas Co., 65 A. 801 (Pa. 1907) (*A* can go and do likewise). Compare Union Gas & Oil Co. v. Fyffe, 294 S.W. 176 (Ky. 1927) (suggesting that *A* might be able to get an injunction against excessive drilling or nonratable extraction). Which of these approaches is better, and why?

(b) Suppose *B*'s well starts on her land but angles down such that it "bottoms" underneath land owned by *A*. Does the rule of capture still apply? See 1

---

21. Or located in several countries, a point you should bear in mind when we come eventually to consider the implications of the rule of capture. See, e.g., Thomas C. Hayes, Confrontation in the Gulf: The Oilfield Lying Below the Iraq-Kuwait Dispute, N.Y. Times, Sept. 3, 1990, §1 at 7:

> At the heart of Iraq's dispute with Kuwait over oil, money and boundaries lies a huge banana-shaped oil formation some 10,200 feet below the desert sands.
> One of the world's largest oil reservoirs, the Rumaila field runs beneath the Iraq-Kuwait border, and the bulk of the 50-mile-long formation lies under Iraq. Yet much of the oil pumped from Rumaila in the last decade was taken by the Kuwaitis. Just as the pump at the edge of a lake can pull water from the entire lake, Kuwait's wells could eventually, in theory, bring up oil from the entire Rumaila pool.

> As Iraq sees it, Kuwait had been stealing its oil. Today BP and China's CNPC have a contract to drill in the border-straddling oil pool.

Howard R. Williams & Charles J. Meyers, Oil and Gas Law 55, 59 (1986); John D. McKinnis, Directional Drilling, Subsurface Trespass, and Conversion, 4 J. Min. L. & Policy 235 (1988-1989).

(c) Suppose that *A* has reinjected gas (it could as well be oil) that moves under *B*'s land. *B* sues to recover damages for the use and occupation of her land by *A*'s gas. What result? See Hammonds v. Central Kentucky Natural Gas Co., 75 S.W.2d 204 (Ky. 1934).

The court in the *Hammonds* case just cited held that *A* was not liable because, under the rule of capture, the gas was no longer hers. Because fugitive resources are to be treated like "wild animals," when they "escape" or are "restored to their natural wild and free state, the dominion and individual proprietorship of any person over them is at an end and they resume their status as common property." 75 S.W.2d at 206.

Hammonds has been criticized and rejected by a number of jurisdictions on the grounds that the analogy to wild animals is silly, that reinjected gas or oil hasn't really "escaped," and that in any event it is not "returned to its natural habitat" by reinjection. The Supreme Court of Kentucky eventually overruled *Hammonds*. See Texas American Energy Corp. v. Citizens Fidelity Bank & Trust Co., 736 S.W.2d 25 (Ky. 1987). We presume it is also the case today that reinjection does not ordinarily give rise to liability for the use and occupation of parts of a reservoir underlying the land of neighbors, even though ownership of the reinjected minerals remains intact. See, e.g., Railroad Commn. of Texas v. Manziel, 361 S.W.2d 560 (Tex. 1962).

There is a reason independent of strained analogies to discard the rule in *Hammonds*: It denied society at large the benefits of economical underground storage. (Do you see why?) There are also reasons—again independent of strained analogies—to discard the rule of capture altogether, yet it still applies to so-called native, or pre-severed, gas and oil. Should it? For that matter, should the rule of capture even be applied to wild animals themselves? We shall consider all of this a little later, in the course of examining some consequences of the rule and some means of mitigating them. See pages 52-53.

2. *Water.* The rule of capture has played a formative role in the case of another migratory resource—water. *Groundwater* (water found in underground aquifers), for example, was governed early on by the English rule of absolute ownership, which allowed each landowner over an aquifer to withdraw freely without regard to effects on neighbors.[22] "[F]ramed in property language, the rule was in reality a rule of capture, for a landowner's pump could induce water under the land of his neighbor to flow to his well—water that was in theory the neighbor's property while it remained in place." Restatement (Second) of Torts ch. 41, commentary at 256 (1977). Whoever first captured the water, then, was really its owner. The so-called English rule survives in just three states, as during the twentieth century many jurisdictions abandoned the English rule in favor of the American rule. The American rule of reasonable use is itself a rule of capture but with the slight

---

22. What sorts of effects? See generally the Note on Lateral and Subjacent Support on page 786.

addition that wasteful uses of water, if they actually harmed neighbors, were considered unreasonable and hence unlawful. As with the English rule, there was no principle of apportionment among overlying users. Today groundwater extraction is commonly governed by legislative and administrative programs. See Joseph W. Dellapenna, A Primer on Groundwater Law, 49 Idaho L. Rev. 265 (2013).

In the Western states, *surface waters* and some groundwater are allocated according to an explicit rule of first in time, called prior appropriation. The basic principle is that the person who first appropriates (captures) water and puts it to reasonable and beneficial use has a right superior to later appropriators. (Obviously, complications can arise. Suppose that *A* begins efforts to appropriate water from a stream—starts building diversion works—before *B*, but that *B* finishes her works and puts the water to beneficial use before *A*. Who is prior to whom? What would Pierson v. Post say?) Prior appropriation doctrine developed as a direct consequence of the scarcity of water in the arid West. Eastern states, where water is abundant, use one or another variant of riparian rights, the thrust of which is that each owner of land along a water source (riparian land) has a right to use the water, subject to the rights of other riparians. At first glance, riparian rights have no relation to a rule of capture, or first in time, but on a closer look they do—because the claims of riparians rest on their underlying holdings of riparian land, and the land itself was originally acquired by first possession. See Richard A. Epstein, Possession as the Root of Title, 13 Ga. L. Rev. 1221, 1234 (1979).

The extraordinarily low ratio of streams to land in the West made riparian law a poor means by which to allocate water there; hence prior appropriation. Neither system is perfect. Riparian rights, for example, take little or no account of the relative productivity of the land the water services, encourage the development of uneconomical "bowling-alley" parcels of land perpendicular to the banks of a stream, and ration poorly when stream levels are low. Prior appropriation encourages premature development and excessive diversion. It also rations poorly when supplies dwindle periodically.

3. *Water law and Johnson v. M'Intosh.* How should the traditional rights of indigenous populations to use water resources be vindicated? Does the role that clean water often plays in religious life matter? For an interesting exploration, see Rhett B. Larson, Water, Worship, and Wisdom: Indigenous Traditional Ecological Knowledge and the Human Right to Water, 19 ISLA J. of Intl. & Comp. L. 43 (2012).

4. *Analogies and their consequences.* The rule of capture follows directly from the powerful principle of first in time. The rule was applied early on to wild animals and then later, by analogy, to other fugitive resources of the sorts we have considered.[23] Reasoning by analogy from the familiar to the new is a common human tendency and a handy problem-solving technique; it is also standard practice among lawyers and judges faced with cases of first impression. See generally

---

23. The rule of capture even came into play in the lawsuit that arose when two baseball fans asserted conflicting claims to Barry Bonds' record-breaking home-run baseball. Popov v. Hayashi, Superior Court of California, Dec. 18, 2002. But the case was resolved with reference to other doctrines as well, and is best considered in connection with the law of finders, which we take up in the next chapter. See page 142.

Edward H. Levi, An Introduction to Legal Reasoning (1948). Rather than undertaking a general inquiry into the matter, we want to focus on the particular analogy drawn in the materials we have been discussing. What might be the consequences of applying the rule of capture to wild animals—and then to oil, gas, water, and other natural resources? What might those consequences have to do with the concept of "common property" mentioned in the quotation from *Hammonds* on page 38? The following reading addresses these fundamentally important questions.

Harold Demsetz, Toward a Theory of Property Rights

57 Am. Econ. Rev. 347-357 (Pap. & Proc. 1967)

The Concept and Role of Property Rights

In the world of Robinson Crusoe property rights play no role. Property rights are an instrument of society and derive their significance from the fact that they help a man form those expectations which he can reasonably hold in his dealings with others. These expectations find expression in the laws, customs, and mores of a society. An owner of property rights possesses the consent of fellowmen to allow him to act in particular ways. An owner expects the community to prevent others from interfering with his actions, provided that these actions are not prohibited in the specifications of his rights.

It is important to note that property rights convey the right to benefit or harm oneself or others. Harming a competitor by producing superior products may be permitted, while shooting him may not. A man may be permitted to benefit himself by shooting an intruder but be prohibited from selling below a price floor. It is clear, then, that property rights specify how persons may be benefited and harmed, and, therefore, who must pay whom to modify the actions taken by persons. The recognition of this leads easily to the close relationship between property rights and externalities.

Externality is an ambiguous concept.[24] For the purposes of this paper, the concept includes external costs, external benefits, and pecuniary as well as nonpecuniary externalities. No harmful or beneficial effect is external to the world. Some person or persons always suffer or enjoy these effects. What converts a harmful or beneficial effect into an externality is that the cost of bringing the effect to bear on the decisions of one or more of the interacting persons is too high to make it worthwhile, and this is what the term shall mean here. "Internalizing" such effects refers to a process, usually a change in property rights, that enables these effects to bear (in greater degree) on all interacting persons.

A primary function of property rights is that of guiding incentives to achieve a greater internalization of externalities. Every cost and benefit associated with social interdependencies is a potential externality. One condition is necessary to make costs and benefits externalities. The cost of a transaction in the rights

---

24. If you find this paragraph and the three that follow it difficult, skip ahead to the Note on "Externalities" on page 46, then return to the Demsetz essay.—EDS.

between the parties (internalization) must exceed the gains from internalization. In general, transacting costs can be large relative to gains because of "natural" difficulties in trading or they can be large because of legal reasons. In a lawful society the prohibition of voluntary negotiations makes the cost of transacting infinite. Some costs and benefits are not taken into account by users of resources whenever externalities exist, but allowing transactions increases the degree to which internalization takes place. . . .

The Emergence of Property Rights

If the main allocative function of property rights is the internalization of beneficial and harmful effects, then the emergence of property rights can be understood best by their association with the emergence of new or different beneficial and harmful effects.

Changes in knowledge result in changes in production functions, market values, and aspirations. New techniques, new ways of doing the same things, and doing new things—all invoke harmful and beneficial effects to which society has not been accustomed. It is my thesis in this part of the paper that the emergence of new property rights takes place in response to the desires of the interacting persons for adjustment to new benefit-cost possibilities.

The thesis can be restated in a slightly different fashion: property rights develop to internalize externalities when the gains of internalization become larger than the cost of internalization. Increased internalization, in the main, results from changes in economic values, changes which stem from the development of new technology and the opening of new markets, changes to which old property rights are poorly attuned. A proper interpretation of this assertion requires that account be taken of a community's preferences for private ownership. Some communities will have less-developed private ownership systems and more highly developed state ownership systems. But, given a community's tastes in this regard, the emergence of new private or state-owned property rights will be in response to changes in technology and relative prices.

I do not mean to assert or to deny that the adjustments in property rights which take place need be the result of a conscious endeavor to cope with new externality problems. These adjustments have arisen in Western societies largely as a result of gradual changes in social mores and in common law precedents. At each step of this adjustment process, it is unlikely that externalities per se were consciously related to the issue being resolved. These legal and moral experiments may be hit-and-miss procedures to some extent but in a society that weights the achievement of efficiency heavily, their viability in the long run will depend on how well they modify behavior to accommodate to the externalities associated with important changes in technology or market values.

A rigorous test of this assertion will require extensive and detailed empirical work. . . . In this part of the discussion, I shall present one group of such examples in some detail. They deal with the development of private property rights in land among American Indians. . . .

The question of private ownership of land among aboriginals has held a fascination for anthropologists. It has been one of the intellectual battlegrounds in the attempt to assess the "true nature" of man unconstrained by the "artificialities" of civilization. In the process of carrying on this debate, information has been uncovered that bears directly on the thesis with which we are now concerned. What appears to be accepted as a classic treatment and a high point of this debate is Eleanor Leacock's memoir on The Montagnes "Hunting Territory" and the Fur Trade. Leacock's research followed that of Frank G. Speck who had discovered that the Indians of the Labrador Peninsula had a long-established tradition of property in land. This finding was at odds with what was known about the Indians of the American Southwest and it prompted Leacock's study of the Montagnes who inhabited large regions around Quebec.

Leacock clearly established the fact that a close relationship existed, both historically and geographically, between the development of private rights in land and the development of the commercial fur trade. . . . The factual material uncovered by Speck and Leacock fits the thesis of this paper well, and in doing so, it reveals clearly the role played by property right adjustments in taking account of what economists have often cited as an example of an externality — the overhunting of game.

Because of the lack of control over hunting by others, it is in no person's interest to invest in increasing or maintaining the stock of game. Overly intensive hunting takes place. Thus a successful hunt is viewed as imposing external costs on subsequent hunters — costs that are not taken into account fully in the determination of the extent of hunting and of animal husbandry.

Before the fur trade became established, hunting was carried on primarily for purposes of food and the relatively few furs that were required for the hunter's family. The externality was clearly present. Hunting could be practiced freely and was carried on without assessing its impact on other hunters. But these external effects were of such small significance that it did not pay for anyone to take them into account. There did not exist anything resembling private ownership in land. . . . We may safely surmise that the advent of the fur trade had two immediate consequences. First, the value of furs to the Indians was increased considerably. Second, and as a result, the scale of hunting activity rose sharply. Both consequences must have increased considerably the importance of the externalities associated with free hunting. The property right system began to change, and it changed specifically in the direction required to take account of the economic effects made important by the fur trade. The geographical or distributional evidence collected by Leacock indicates an unmistakable correlation between early centers of fur trade and the oldest and most complete development of the private hunting territory. . . . An anonymous account written in 1723 states that the "principle of the Indians is to mark off the hunting ground selected by them by blazing the trees with their crest so that they may never encroach on each other. . . . By the middle of the century these allotted territories were relatively stabilized."

The principle that associates property right changes with the emergence of new and reevaluation of old harmful and beneficial effects suggests in this instance that the fur trade made it economic to encourage the husbanding of fur-bearing animals. Husbanding requires the ability to prevent poaching and this, in turn, suggests that socioeconomic changes in property in hunting land will take place. The chain of reasoning is consistent with the evidence cited above. Is it inconsistent with the absence of similar rights in property among the southwestern Indians?

Two factors suggest that the thesis is consistent with the absence of similar rights among the Indians of the southwestern plains. The first of these is that there were no plains animals of commercial importance comparable to the fur-bearing animals of the forest, at least not until cattle arrived with Europeans. The second factor is that animals of the plains are primarily grazing species whose habit is to wander over wide tracts of land. The value of establishing boundaries to private hunting territories is thus reduced by the relatively high cost of preventing the animals from moving to adjacent parcels. Hence both the value and cost of establishing private hunting lands in the Southwest are such that we would expect little development along these lines. The externality was just not worth taking into account.

The lands of the Labrador Peninsula shelter forest animals whose habits are considerably different from those of the plains. Forest animals confine their territories to relatively small areas, so that the cost of internalizing the effects of husbanding these animals is considerably reduced. This reduced cost, together with the higher commercial value of fur-bearing forest animals, made it productive to establish private hunting lands. . . .

The Coalescence and Ownership of Property Rights

I have argued that property rights arise when it becomes economic for those affected by externalities to internalize benefits and costs. But I have not yet examined the forces which will govern the particular form of right ownership. Several idealized forms of ownership must be distinguished at the outset. These are communal ownership, private ownership, and state ownership.

By communal ownership, I shall mean a right which can be exercised by all members of the community. Frequently the rights to till and to hunt the land have been communally owned. The right to walk a city sidewalk is communally owned. Communal ownership means that the community denies to the state or to individual citizens the right to interfere with any person's exercise of communally owned rights. Private ownership implies that the community recognizes the right of the owner to exclude others from exercising the owner's private rights. State ownership implies that the state may exclude anyone from the use of a right as long as the state follows accepted political procedures for determining who may not use state-owned property.[25] I shall not examine in detail the alternative

25. What Demsetz refers to as communally owned property is usually called an open-access commons (or, in lay terms, public property), meaning property open to everyone, or at least everyone in a given community, as with a public park. As to private ownership, Demsetz usually uses it to mean ownership by a single individual or entity (other than the government). On other occasions, however, he has in mind ownership by a

of state ownership. The object of the analysis which follows is to discern some broad principles governing the development of property rights in communities oriented to private property.

It will be best to begin by considering a particularly useful example that focuses our attention on the problem of land ownership. Suppose that land is communally owned. Every person has the right to hunt, till, or mine the land. This form of ownership fails to concentrate the cost associated with any person's exercise of his communal right on that person. If a person seeks to maximize the value of his communal rights, he will tend to overhunt and overwork the land because some of the costs of his doing so are borne by others. The stock of game and the richness of the soil will be diminished too quickly. It is conceivable that those who own these rights, i.e., every member of the community, can agree to curtail the rate at which they work the lands if negotiating and policing costs are zero. Each can agree to abridge his rights. It is obvious that the costs of reaching such an agreement will not be zero. What is not obvious is just how large these costs may be.

Negotiating costs will be large because it is difficult for many persons to reach a mutually satisfactory agreement, especially when each hold-out has the right to work the land as fast as he pleases. But, even if an agreement among all can be reached, we must yet take account of the costs of policing the agreement, and these may be large, also. . . . If a single person owns land, he will attempt to maximize its present value by taking into account alternative future time streams of benefits and costs and selecting that one which he believes will maximize the present value of his privately-owned land rights. We all know that this means that he will attempt to take into account the supply and demand conditions that he thinks will exist after his death. It is very difficult to see how the existing communal owners can reach an agreement that takes account of these costs.

In effect, an owner of a private right to use land acts as a broker whose wealth depends on how well he takes into account the competing claims of the present and the future. But with communal rights there is no broker, and the claims of the present generation will be given an uneconomically large weight in determining the intensity with which the land is worked. Future generations might desire to pay present generations enough to change the present intensity of land usage. But they have no living agent to place their claims on the market. Under a communal property system, should a living person pay others to reduce the rate at which they work the land, he would not gain anything of value for his efforts. Communal property means that future generations must speak for themselves. No one has yet estimated the costs of carrying on such a conversation.

---

group of individuals (a family, for example) short of the public at large — now sometimes called a limited-access commons. (A limited-access commons might take a legal form called concurrent ownership, the varieties of which will be considered in Chapter 5.) The key to understanding Demsetz's argument is to see the distinction between (1) situations like the open-access commons, where no one is entitled to exclude anybody from using a particular asset or resource, and (2) situations where someone (an owner) is entitled to exclude others (except concurrent owners, if any) from using a particular asset or resource. — EDS.

The land ownership example confronts us immediately with a great disadvantage of communal property. The effects of a person's activities on his neighbors and on subsequent generations will not be taken into account fully. Communal property results in great externalities. The full costs of the activities of an owner of a communal property right are not borne directly by him, nor can they be called to his attention easily by the willingness of others to pay him an appropriate sum. . . .

The state, the courts, or the leaders of the community could attempt to internalize the external costs resulting from communal property by allowing private parcels owned by small groups with similar interests. The logical groups in terms of similar interests, are, of course, the family and the individual. Continuing with our use of the land ownership example, let us initially distribute private titles to land randomly among existing individuals and, further, let the extent of land included in each title be randomly determined.

The resulting private ownership of land will internalize many of the external costs associated with communal ownership, for now an owner, by virtue of his power to exclude others, can generally count on realizing the rewards associated with husbanding the game and increasing the fertility of his land. This concentration of benefits and costs on owners creates incentives to utilize resources more efficiently.

But we have yet to contend with externalities. Under the communal property system the maximization of the value of communal property rights will take place without regard to many costs, because the owner of a communal right cannot exclude others from enjoying the fruits of his efforts and because negotiation costs are too high for all to agree jointly on optimal behavior. The development of private rights permits the owner to economize on the use of those resources from which he has the right to exclude others. Much internalization is accomplished in this way. But the owner of private rights to one parcel does not himself own the rights to the parcel of another private sector. Since he cannot exclude others from their private rights to land, he has no direct incentive (in the absence of negotiations) to economize in the use of his land in a way that takes into account the effects he produces on the land rights of others. If he constructs a dam on his land, he has no direct incentive to take into account the lower water levels produced on his neighbor's land.

This is exactly the same kind of externality that we encountered with communal property rights, but it is present to a lesser degree. Whereas no one had an incentive to store water on any land under the communal system, private owners now can take into account directly those benefits and costs to their land that accompany water storage. But the effects on the land of others will not be taken into account directly.

The partial concentration of benefits and costs that accompany private ownership is only part of the advantage this system offers. The other part, and perhaps the most important, has escaped our notice. The cost of negotiating over the remaining externalities will be reduced greatly. Communal property rights allow anyone to use the land. Under this system it becomes necessary for all to reach an agreement on land use. But the externalities that accompany private ownership of property do not affect all owners, and, generally speaking, it will be necessary for only a few to reach an agreement that takes these effects into account. The cost of negotiating an internalization of these effects is thereby reduced considerably. The point is important enough to elucidate.

Suppose an owner of a communal land right, in the process of plowing a parcel of land, observes a second communal owner constructing a dam on adjacent land. The farmer prefers to have the stream as it is, and so he asks the engineer to stop his construction. The engineer says, "Pay me to stop." The farmer replies, "I will be happy to pay you, but what can you guarantee in return?" The engineer answers, "I can guarantee you that I will not continue constructing the dam, but I cannot guarantee that another engineer will not take up the task because this is communal property; I have no right to exclude him." What would be a simple negotiation between two persons under a private property arrangement turns out to be a rather complex negotiation between the farmer and everyone else. This is the basic explanation, I believe, for the preponderance of single rather than multiple owners of property. Indeed, an increase in the number of owners is an increase in the communality of property and leads, generally, to an increase in the cost of internalizing.

The reduction in negotiating cost that accompanies the private right to exclude others allows most externalities to be internalized at rather low cost. Those that are not are associated with activities that generate external effects impinging upon many people. The soot from smoke affects many homeowners, none of whom is willing to pay enough to the factory to get its owner to reduce smoke output. All homeowners together might be willing to pay enough, but the cost of their getting together may be enough to discourage effective market bargaining. The negotiating problem is compounded even more if the smoke comes not from a single smoke stack but from an industrial district. In such cases, it may be too costly to internalize effects through the marketplace.

NOTE: "EXTERNALITIES"

"Externality," Demsetz says, "is an ambiguous concept." It is also an important one that you will be confronting more than occasionally in this book and elsewhere.[26] Let us try to explain.

Externalities exist whenever some person, say X, makes a decision about how to use resources without taking full account of the effects of the decision. X ignores some of the effects—some of the costs or benefits that would result from a particular activity, for example—because they fall on others. They are "external" to

---

26. The concept of externalities is a core concern in a large and growing body of work on the relationships between law and economics, as can be gathered from any of a number of instructive textbooks on the general subject. See, e.g., Robert Cooter & Thomas Ulen, Law and Economics (6th ed. 2012); A. Mitchell Polinsky, An Introduction to Law and Economics (3d ed. 2003); Richard A. Posner, Economic Analysis of Law (8th ed. 2011).

X, hence the label *externalities*. As a consequence of externalities, resources tend to be misused or "misallocated," which is to say used in one way when another would make society as a whole better off. It is not difficult to see why this is so. We will suggest the reasons in the abstract, leaving you to find concrete examples in Demsetz's discussion and your own experience. As the course develops, many instances of externalities and their consequences will become apparent.

Suppose that X is currently using his land in a way that imposes a total annual cost of $1,000 on people living in the surrounding area (the "neighbors"). Suppose too that X could change his use to one that would impose no costs on the neighbors, but the change would cost X $500 a year (in time and trouble or lost profits, for instance; construct a concrete example of our abstract hypothetical in your mind). The likelihood is that X will continue his current use, even though the alternative would make the *aggregate* of the people in question $500 better off annually (a $1,000 gain to the neighbors minus the $500 cost to X).[27] We could expect X to continue his current use because the alternative would make *him* worse off, notwithstanding the net gain it would yield in the aggregate.

The example is one of external costs—costly effects of X's current land use that, because they fall on others, X does not consider in making the decision to use his land in that way. However, the example also illustrates the problem of external benefits. Once X's current use is the prevailing situation, a change by X to a use imposing no costs on the neighbors would confer a benefit on them—the removal of the costs. Because these benefits fall on others, X ignores them in considering whether to change to the alternative. A more typical example of external benefits would be a situation in which X is using his land in a way that imposes no costs and confers no benefits on the neighbors. X could change to an alternative use that would increase his costs by $500 but confer benefits of $1,000 on the neighbors. The likelihood, again, is that he would not make the change because he would not take account of the external effects—here the benefits—of his decision. All the examples illustrate how external costs and benefits encourage the misuse of resources.

No doubt the discussion thus far leads you to suggest that if the alternative use of X's land would cost him $500 but make the neighbors $1,000 better off, then obviously it is in the neighbors' self-interest to offer, and X's self-interest to accept, some payment between $500 and $1,000 in exchange for X's agreement to pursue the alternative land use. Since any payment in that range would appear to make all parties concerned better off in their own terms, offer and acceptance—and thus a correction in the misuse or misallocation of X's land—seem

27. The technical terminology is to say the current use is "inefficient" because another use would increase the value of the resources involved and make all the parties better off, measured in their own terms (and given their own wealth). The use that would make them best off in those terms is the "efficient" or value-maximizing one—X's alternative use in all of our examples. For reasons that will perhaps become clear as you read this Note, the foregoing definitions should not be taken to suggest that efficient outcomes are necessarily to be preferred to inefficient alternatives. Or, to put the point more broadly, the economic perspective is useful but should hardly be an exclusive or conclusive way of looking at the world.

likely to take place. The suggestion is a good one, and it gets us to the core of the externalities problem. Notice what the offer of payment from the neighbors to X would accomplish. It would force X, in deciding how to use his land, to take account of the effect of his decision on others. It would do so because X, confronted with the offer, must now consider that if he continues his present use he forgoes payment from the neighbors, and the forgone payment is a cost to X of his decision—a cost X previously ignored because it was not brought to bear on him (it was external).[28]

An offer from the neighbors, then, would appear to resolve the problem, but it is hardly clear that an offer will be forthcoming. Suppose there are 100 neighbors affected to some degree by X's land use decisions, but none by more than $150. Notice that it is not in the self-interest of any one neighbor to offer X even the minimum amount (say $501) necessary to encourage X to begin thinking about changing his ways. Some sort of group offer is needed, but it may not come about. In particular, it is very unlikely to take place if the costs of *arranging* an offer to X ("transaction costs") are sufficiently high that they, combined with the amount required to induce X to alter his land use, add up to more than $1,000. Payment under these circumstances would be highly unlikely simply because the neighbors would be worse off if they paid than if they did not.

There are a number of reasons why transaction costs might be high. We have been assuming that X's identity is known. But what if instead, and not unrealistically, the neighbors are simply aware of effects but not their cause? Investigation will be necessary for the neighbors to find the person (X) with whom they must bargain, and this could be expensive. Efforts must also be made to raise money in the neighborhood, and these too might be costly. There are, after all, 100 neighbors involved. Dealing with so many people can be expensive, especially if they are spread over a large area, have infrequent contacts with one another, or are difficult to identify and approach because they are indistinguishable from other, unaffected people in the area.

One other factor can make matters even worse. If the effects of X's alternative land use are such that a change to that use necessarily confers a benefit (to some degree) on all 100 neighbors, then each has an incentive to take a "free ride."[29] The freerider reasons that no contribution to a group payment is necessary, because the contributions of others will amount to enough to induce X to change, so that the freerider benefits at no cost. Since each neighbor tends to reason this way, none is inclined to contribute much, if anything. The reasoning is not made explicit, of course. The freerider claims to be one of the unaffected or one only slightly affected (contributing a token dollar to get rid of the nagging

---

28. Conversely, of course, if X changes his present use, he gets the payment, and this is a benefit to X of his decision, one he had ignored before the offer because—again—it was external to him. For obvious reasons, economists say that the process of offers just discussed "internalizes" externalities. But offers or bargains are not the only means of internalization, as the excerpt from Demsetz shows.

29. Under what sorts of circumstances would a change in land use by X "necessarily" confer benefits on others?

fund raiser). The costs of overcoming freeriding can be high; if many people are involved, they can be prohibitive.[30]

There are other reasons why transaction costs might be high (for example, lawyers' fees if legal advice is necessary in the course of transacting), but those discussed above are probably the typically most important ones. The general point is this: When transaction costs become sufficiently high, the external effects of using resources are unlikely to be taken into account through any sort of bargaining process, and the resources are likely to be misused.

This is virtually all we have to understand for now: Externalities are, in essence, a function of transaction costs, and they encourage the misuse (the inefficient use) of resources. Very shortly, we will begin considering the range of ways a legal system (a property system in particular) might respond to the presence of high transaction costs. Before doing so, however, it might be useful to note a few points by way of summary:

(a) An externality is not simply an effect of one person's activity on another person; rather, it is an effect that the first person is not forced to take into account. X's activity benefits X \$100 and costs A \$50. A offers X \$50 to change his activity, and X refuses. The harmful or costly effect on A will thus continue, but it is not an "externality" because X has taken account of it in deciding to forgo the payment offered by A. This hardly means you should rest easy (especially if you are A!); notice that X is benefitting at A's expense. It simply means you should not call the effect on A an externality. You might want to call it "unfair," but you should have a reason for doing so. Suppose A has the legal right to stop X's activity and will only permit the activity to continue if X pays A \$75. X will probably do so because to stop would cost him \$100. Now A is benefitting at X's expense. The two situations have affected the distribution of wealth or income between X and A, but not the efficiency of the resource use. In considering which situation is "fair," do you agree that you might want to know something about the wealth of each party, the nature of the conduct of each, and so forth, as well as just what "fair" means in your system of values?

(b) Externalities do not necessarily lead to inefficient resource use. X, in the example above, will continue his conduct whether or not he takes account of its effects on A, and the conduct in the example happens to be efficient. Externalities

30. The freeriding problem arises when efforts are made to extract contributions *from* members of a group in order to carry out transactions that will confer collective or nonexclusive benefits on the group—on contributors and noncontributors alike. Collective or nonexclusive effects are typical of many (but not all) externalities.

A problem similar to freeriding—and one that, like freeriding, occasions high transaction costs—arises when payments must be made *to* a group in order to carry out a transaction, and where, unless each member of the group accepts payment, the transaction fails entirely. Suppose X wishes to change to a land use that will increase his profits by \$1,000 but impose \$50 in costly effects on each of 10 neighbors. Suppose, too, that X is prohibited by law from engaging in the use unless he first obtains the permission of each person affected. X will be inclined to offer payments (between \$50 and \$100) to each neighbor, but each has an incentive to "hold out" for an exorbitantly higher amount, knowing that without his permission X cannot pursue a venture worth far more to X than \$100. Holding out can frustrate transactions the completion of which would, as in the example posed, be beneficial to all concerned.

None of the foregoing discussion should be taken to imply that transaction costs are necessarily low when only a few parties are involved in a conflict over the use of a resource. We save this complication for later. See, e.g., Note 3 on pages 795-797.

do *encourage* inefficient use of resources, however, for the reasons we discussed. This is why we have said throughout this Note that they "tend" or are "likely" to lead to misuse of resources.

(c) It would be unwise for a society simply to ban all activities with (costly) external effects or to make all those engaging in them pay for the effects.[31] First of all, whose activity is to be banned? But for the presence of *both X* and *A* in the example above, there would be no external effect. Externalities are reciprocal; they arise from interactions or conflicts among people in the use of resources.[32] Secondly, if your intuition insists that *X* is responsible, notice that banning *X*'s conduct would foreclose the efficient use of the resource. So too would a requirement that *X* pay *A* a negotiated sum as a condition to continuing his activity, if the transaction costs involved in *X* paying *A* were sufficiently high. We can note from this (contrary to the technical terminology introduced in footnote 27) that what appears to be an "inefficient" use of resources might in fact be "efficient" because any effort to alter the situation could entail costs larger than the benefits realized from the move! See Harold Demsetz, From Economic Man to Economic System 109-110 (2008). In figuring the costs and benefits of moving from one regime to the other, however, it is important to consider more than just transaction costs, narrowly understood. There are all sorts of ways the law can intervene to improve the use of resources, including ways that make transactions unnecessary. For extensive and illuminating discussion of this theme, see Lee Anne Fennell, The Problem of Resource Access, 126 Harv. L. Rev. 1471 (2013).

NOTES AND QUESTIONS

1. *Demsetz*. According to Demsetz, a system of communal ownership (common property) tends to increase externalities, and a system of private ownership (private property) tends to reduce them. How?

Notice Demsetz's observation on page 40: "Harming a competitor by producing superior products may be permitted, while shooting him may not." Why? (Recall in this connection the discussion of "interference with capture" in Note 4 on page 33.)

---

31. Failure to see this leads to much of the confusion on the subject of externalities; yet, unhappily, the *externality* label contributes to the problem. The term can quite understandably, but also quite misleadingly, be taken to suggest that the best response to external costs is always to ban or otherwise control the activities seen to give rise to them.

32. See in this regard the classic essay by Ronald Coase, The Problem of Social Cost, 3 J.L. & Econ. 1 (1960). The essay develops the Coase Theorem (though nowhere in his essay does Coase call it such), which holds that in the absence of transaction costs it is irrelevant from the standpoint of efficiency whether *X* is liable to *A* for costly effects or not. Resources will be put to efficient use in either event. Do you see why? And does "efficient use in either event" necessarily mean "the *same* use in either event"? You should be able to work out the answer to the first question. On the second, see, e.g., Richard Craswell, Passing on the Costs of Legal Rules: Efficiency and Distribution in Buyer-Seller Relationships, 43 Stan. L. Rev. 361, 385-391 (1991) (discussing wealth effects and endowment effects).

The Problem of Social Cost is reprinted in Ronald Coase, The Firm, the Market, and the Law (1988), which collects (together with some fresh commentary) most of Coase's chief articles over the years. The book is a slim volume at 213 pages—but only in that one respect. In 1991, Ronald Coase was awarded the Nobel Memorial Prize in Economic Science. He died in September 2013, just a few months short of his 103rd birthday.

The law aims to discourage trespass (see Problem 1 on pages 33-34). A trespasser, it is typically said, should not be allowed to profit from his wrong. But why is trespass considered "wrong"? Can you see that Demsetz gives some hints?

2. *The utilitarian theory of property.* Demsetz's essay provides a utilitarian account of property, the theoretical foundations of which trace back to the work of David Hume in the eighteenth century, and then, later, to Jeremy Bentham. Utilitarian theory marked the break of philosophies of property from their earlier natural rights foundations. Suddenly the concept of property was, just as any man-made object is, merely an artifact—a human invention, a social institution, a means of organization. Utilitarian theory is, without doubt, the dominant view of property today, at least among lawyers and especially among those working in law and economics, who suggest that a primary function of property rights is to promote the efficient use of resources.

But surely there is more to property than that. Property systems are a means of distributing and redistributing the wealth of a society, a point pursued through two volumes in Richard T. Ely, Property and Contract in Their Relations to the Distribution of Wealth (1914) (see id. at 79-93 for "Illustrations Showing the Importance of Property in Wealth Distribution"). And property—private property at any rate—is said to nourish individuality and healthy diversity: It "performs the function of maintaining independence, dignity and pluralism in society by creating zones within which the majority has to yield to the owner. Whim, caprice, irrationality and 'antisocial' activities are given the protection of law; the owner may do what all or most of his neighbors decry." Charles A. Reich, The New Property, 73 Yale L.J. 733, 771 (1964).

A related point is the view that private property is essential to political freedom. See, e.g., Milton Friedman, Capitalism and Freedom (1962). Friedman, like many classical (and modern) liberal theorists, stresses the importance of free transferability in his account. Modern civic republicans, pursuing the Jeffersonian tradition, argue in contrast that a tension arises from unfettered alienability. Alienability promotes political freedom because it "liberates individuals from one form of dependency, feudal hierarchy, but exposes them to another dependency, markets and manufacturing. By debasing the moral personality of individuals and the polity, the free transferability policy would create a new form of dependency. Individuals would be subjects of the market, and the common welfare would be subordinated to the limitless pursuit of self-interest." So property should be transferable in order to avoid privilege and inequality, but should also be stable and nontransferable, "to avoid being reduced to a mere commodity, the object of acquisitive pursuit that would destroy republican virtue." Gregory S. Alexander, Time and Property in the American Republican Legal Culture, 66 N.Y.U. L. Rev. 273, 293-294, 300 (1991). See also Gregory S. Alexander, Commodity and Propriety 337-340 (1997).[33]

_____

33. Given the discussion to this point, it should be easy enough to see why lawyers avoid talking about property as a relationship between a person (the owner) and a thing (that is owned). Property, rather, concerns relationships among people with respect to things, "such that the so-called owner can exclude others from

Go back to the suggestion that an important function of property rights is to promote economic efficiency. Free transferability contributes to efficiency by facilitating the movement of resources from lower to higher valued uses, letting property owner *A* sell to buyer *B* at a price that makes both parties better off (if it didn't, there would be no sale). So, as we'll see, concerns with undue restraints on transfer run throughout the law of property. On the other hand, might there not be reasons, whether of justice or efficiency or both, to depart from this pattern and self-consciously forbid or at least limit transfer in certain instances? A case in point is the sale of human organs and tissues, considered later in this chapter (see pages 91-104), but there are many other (and usually less provocative) instances in which restrictions on transfer might provide a good remedy for perceived ills — say the practices of ticket-scalpers, zealous land-use regulators, or abusive patent-trolls (profiteers that secure patents not for their own use but only to hold up producers who later need the patented items or processes for their own productive activities). See Lee Anne Fennell, Adjusting Alienability, 122 Harv. L. Rev. 1403 (2009).

For more on the functions of property, including a discussion of its role as an "educative institution," see Carol M. Rose, Property as the Keystone Right?, 71 Notre Dame L. Rev. 329 (1996).

3. *Common property and the rule of capture: some problems and some solutions.* Common property and the rule of capture tend to go hand in hand. In an open-access commons, individuals don't really own things for themselves until they reduce them to possession, to the exclusion of other commoners. One consequence, as you should by now have gathered, is that "fugitive resources" like wild animals, oil and gas, groundwater, and the like, tend to be overconsumed; another consequence is overinvestment in capture technology. See, e.g., Dean Lueck, The Rule of First Possession and the Design of the Law, 38 J.L. & Econ. 393 (1995); Alan E. Friedman, The Economics of the Common Pool: Property Rights in Exhaustible Resources, 18 UCLA L. Rev. 855 (1971).

How might these problems be mitigated? Demsetz would suggest individual property rights in many cases. (Would he suggest them in all?) Another alternative is judicial controls, as through the law of nuisance (considered in Chapter 9), or legislative and administrative regulation of one sort or another.[34] *Groundwater*

---

certain activities or permit others to engage in those activities and in either case secure the assistance of the law in carrying out his decision." Felix Cohen, Dialogue on Private Property, 9 Rutgers L. Rev. 357, 373 (1954). This is why Demsetz says, on page 40, that in the world of Robinson Crusoe property would play no role (at least until Friday appeared!).

See generally Stephen R. Munzer, Property as Social Relations, in New Essays in the Legal and Political Theory of Property 36 (Stephen R. Munzer ed. 2001).

34. Don't assume that government regulation is a magic solution to resource mismanagement. The government can fail just as the market can, particularly when the costs of regulation would fall on small, intensely interested groups, and the benefits would flow to the public at large and to future generations. (Do you see the problem?) The U.S. Forest Service, Bureau of Reclamation, and Bureau of Land Management, for example, are routinely said to waste the resources over which they have jurisdiction, sometimes by regulating too much but more commonly by regulating too little in favor of special interest groups representing agriculture and the timber and cattle industries. See, e.g., Terry L. Anderson & Donald R. Leal, Free Market Environmentalism (rev. ed. 2001). We shall examine the problem of government failure most closely in Chapter 11 when we consider

extraction, for example, is commonly regulated through well-spacing requirements, limitations on the drilling of new wells, controls on quantities withdrawn,
and so on. Some jurisdictions establish groundwater management districts under
the direction of an administrative agency. Regarding *oil and gas*, most if not all
producing states control well spacing and rates of extraction. One interesting
technique is compulsory unitization: Upon vote of some proportion (usually two-
thirds) of the owners of land or drilling leases overlying an oil or gas field, a unit
of *all* owners is formed. All members of the unit share in production no matter whose well extracts the resource, with the result that the field is managed as
though it had only a single owner trying to maximize its value. See Jacqueline
Lang Weaver & David F. Asmus, Unitizing Oil and Gas Fields Around the World:
A Comparative Analysis of National Laws and Private Contracts, 28 Hous. J. Intl.
L. 3 (2006). As to *wildlife*, fish and game laws are familiar to everyone, and their
justification should now be apparent. And it bears mention that there is much current interest in a property rights approach to wildlife management—especially
with regard to commercial fishing. An example is individual transferable quotas,
or ITQs. Each ITQ, which can be sold by one fisherman to another, allows its
holder to capture a given percentage of the total catch allowed by the government. For discussion, see Katrina M. Wyman, The Property Rights Challenge in
Marine Fisheries, 50 Ariz. L. Rev. 511 (2008).

   4. *Pollution and the "tragedy of the commons."* Pollution and other environmental problems have important relationships to property, and we shall be discussing
them from time to time throughout this book. For now, consider what the foregoing materials have to say about some core causes of environmental problems. By
and large, the materials are concerned with taking things (like animals, oil and
gas, water) *out of* the environment; they also suggest, however, why people put
things *into* the environment—why they litter the countryside, operate factories
in ways that pollute the air and water, and so on. The problem, again, is common
property. On one view, resources owned in common (including environmental
resources like clean air and water) will always be abused, absent coercive intervention by the government. See Garrett Hardin, The Tragedy of the Commons,
162 Science 1243 (1968). Another view, developed later, suggests that Hardin
overstates the problem. Theory and evidence alike indicate circumstances under
which the owners of common property resources can cooperate to manage them
effectively. See the discussion in Note 6 on page 55.

   On property rights solutions to pollution problems, see the discussion at
pages 806-808 of this book. See generally Bruce Yandle & Andrew P. Morriss,
The Technologies of Property Rights: Choice Among Alternative Solutions to
Tragedies of the Commons, 28 Ecology L.Q. 123 (2001).

   5. *The "tragedy of the anticommons."* On page 43 Demsetz refers to common
property, private property, and state property as though these were the only

---

some alleged abuses of the zoning power. For an assessment of the role that scientists play in altering the interest group dynamic regarding federal lands, see Eric Biber, Which Science? Whose Science? How Scientific
Disciplines Can Shape Environmental Law, 79 U. Chi. L. Rev. 471 (2012).

possible forms of ownership, but they are not. An interesting addition to the list is the "anticommons," first suggested, mostly as a thought experiment, by Frank I. Michelman, Ethics, Economics and the Law of Property, in 24 Nomos 3 (1982). More recently, though, it has come to be seen as an important real-world category, thanks to Michael A. Heller, The Tragedy of the Anticommons: Property in the Transition from Marx to Markets, 111 Harv. L. Rev. 621 (1998). Just as a resource held in common entails few (if any) rights to exclude others, an anticommons entails *multiple* people with rights to veto the exploitation of a resource. And just as common property can lead to overconsumption of the resource in question (with the problem of overconsumption increasing as the number of commoners does), so an anticommons leads to *under*consumption (with the problem of underconsumption increasing as the number of anticommoners does). The anticommons is a fine thing when the whole idea is to keep people from using a resource (imagine a wilderness preserve, or a nuclear waste site), but counterproductive otherwise.

Heller illustrates that point by discussing Moscow's empty storefronts:

> Socialist rule stifled markets and often left store shelves bare. One promise of the transition "from Marx to markets" was that new entrepreneurs would acquire the stores, create businesses, and fill the shelves. However, after several years of reform, storefronts often remained empty, while flimsy metal kiosks, stocked full of goods, mushroomed up on Moscow streets. Why did new merchants not come in from the cold? [Id. at 622-623.]

The answer, according to Heller, owes to the way the government is creating new property rights. Usually, for example, no one person or entity is given ownership of a storefront. Instead, the incidents of ownership are broken up and distributed among a number of competing owners: one person has the right to sign a lease, another to receive some of the lease revenue, another to sell the property altogether, another to occupy the premises, and so on. "Each owner," says Heller, "can block the others from using the space as a storefront. No one can set up shop without collecting the consent of all of the other owners." Id. at 623.[35]

---

35. Professor Heller presents an expanded version of his analysis, written for a lay audience, in The Gridlock Economy: How Too Much Ownership Wrecks Markets, Stops Innovation, and Costs Lives (2008). For more on the commons and the anticommons, see Stephen R. Munzer, The Commons and the Anticommons in the Law and Theory of Property, in The Blackwell Guide to the Philosophy of Law and Legal Theory 148 (Martin P. Golding & William A. Edmundson eds. 2005); Lee Anne Fennell, Common Interest Tragedies, 98 Nw. U. L. Rev. 907 (2004); James M. Buchanan & Yong J. Yoon, Symmetric Tragedies: Commons and Anticommons, 43 J.L. & Econ. 1 (2000).

Yet another variant on common ownership is the "semicommons," so named because it combines private and common ownership. For an example, recall the hunting territories that figure in Demsetz's discussion (see pages 42-43). Demsetz overlooks a particular feature of the territories noted in the Leacock memoir: Owners of the territories *could* exclude other members of the tribe from hunting beaver for sale, but *could not* exclude them from hunting beaver for personal consumption. In other words, the territories remained common for some purposes, but not others—they were semicommon. Perhaps for this reason, beaver ended up being overharvested even after the territories were established. See John C. McManus, An Economic Analysis of Indian Behavior in the North American Fur Trade, 32 J. Econ. Hist. 36, 39, 46, 51 (1972).

On the semicommons, see Henry E. Smith, Semicommon Property Rights and Scattering in the Open Fields, 29 J. Legal Stud. 131 (2000). For an overview of all the variations on common property, see Lee Anne Fennell, Commons, Anticommons, Semicommons, in Research Handbook on the Economics of Property Law (Kenneth Ayotte & Henry E. Smith eds. 2009); Commons and Anticommons (Michael A. Heller ed. 2009).

Setting up a kiosk, by contrast, was relatively straightforward. An entrepreneur just needed to bribe a small number of government officials and the local Russian mafia, of whom it was said, "they don't charge too much, they tell you exactly how much they want up front, and when an agreement is made, they live up to it." Id. at 643 (quoting James P. Gallagher, Russia's Kiosk Capitalists Keep Wary Eye on Hard-Line Premier, Chi. Trib., Jan. 5, 1993, at 1).

6. *Some virtues of common property.* Demsetz concentrates on the problematic aspects of common property, to the neglect of its virtues. Which are what? Well, it all depends on the case, but a general list would include the economies of scale that can be realized through shared ownership; relatedly, the amassing of capital that makes it possible to "buy large" and thus realize scale economies; the risk-spreading benefits of shared ownership; the pleasures and rewards of mixing with others, whether at work or play. And some resources—such as roadways, recreational areas, open spaces for gatherings, beaches—are "inherently public," affording the greatest utility when widely accessible.[36] Consider also that in instances where resources are so abundant that depletion is not an issue, a commons can make considerable sense. The resource is freely there for all; there is little if any occasion for transactions between users; and the costs of setting up a private property regime (who owns what share? what are the rules and how are they enforced?) are avoided entirely. Even if conservation is an issue, it is not necessarily foreclosed by common ownership. Sometimes, for instance, local customs develop to limit undue exploitation. At other times, a resource is held in common, but by a close-knit group—a relatively limited number of people who share values and interests (this is the limited-access commons introduced in footnote 25 on page 43). Limited numbers and shared outlooks tend to reduce strategic behavior among the group members, thus facilitating constructive collective action. No guarantees, though. Just as open-access does not always result in a tragedy of the commons, limited-access does not always avoid it. See generally Elinor Ostrom, Governing the Commons: The Evolution of Institutions for Collective Action (1990). For an overview of her work, see Lee Anne Fennell, Ostrom's Law: Property Rights in the Commons, 5 Intl. J. of the Commons 9 (2011). In 2009, Ostrom, a political scientist, was awarded the Nobel Memorial Prize in Economic Science; she died in 2012.

7. *The evolution of property rights.* Demsetz's article has long been read as a study in the evolution of property rights,[37] and criticized in that light for only suggesting why, but not explaining how, property rights—more specifically, private property rights—formed in the first instance. The genesis cannot be attributed

---

36. See Carol M. Rose, The Comedy of the Commons: Custom, Commerce, and Inherently Public Property, 53 U. Chi. L. Rev. 711 (1986). Among other things, Rose discusses legal doctrines that facilitate the provision of inherently public property; we take them up in Chapter 10. See pages 845-846 (creations of roadways through public prescriptive easements), 847-856 (provision of beach access through public trust doctrine).

37. Witness, for example, a 2001 conference on the evolution of property rights, the chief purpose of which was to re-examine Demsetz's work. The conference papers are collected in Symposium, The Evolution of Property Rights, 31 J. Legal Stud. No. 2, Pt. 2 (2002). Some 40 years after publication of his original article, Demsetz revealed that an evolutionary account had never been his aim. See Harold Demsetz, Frischmann's View of "Toward a Theory of Property Rights," 4 Rev. L. & Econ. 127, 128 (2008).

to the government, because de facto rights emerged long before governments appeared on the scene. Nor can the first rights be easily explained as the product of collective action by commoners residing together in a state of nature. After all, Demsetz shows that high transaction costs meant commoners could not organize themselves to manage resources in their own group interest. How, then, could they be expected to collaborate in setting up a property rights regime? The answer, we now believe, entails some variation on the discussion, in Note 6 above, of the coordination advantages enjoyed by close-knit groups. On this view, early property regimes (and other organizational features of primitive societies) owed to the activities of tribes and the like whose members cooperated in the formation of property norms and, later, centralized authorities (a chief, a tribal council) to settle disputes and enforce rights.

A difficulty with this explanation is that primitive possessory rights probably developed well before humans had the intellectual equipment to cooperate in the design of property systems. So consider another explanation of the genesis of property rights, one that turns on individual as opposed to group behavior. The argument, based on evolutionary game theory, is that individual self-interest led early human ancestors (and many nonhuman animal species before them) to respect the possessions of each other, such that a convention of deference to possession developed "naturally" (as in natural selection) even though no individual or group ever intended such a uniform practice in the first place. The key consideration is the costs of fighting over a resource as compared to the costs of avoiding conflict. When the former exceed the latter, selection favors the development of deferential behavior. Perhaps property rights began in this fashion.[38] Then, much later, more complex and robust property regimes could be designed by modern humans endowed with the brain power to engage in constructive collaboration. See James E. Krier, Evolutionary Theory and the Origin of Property Rights, 95 Cornell L. Rev. 139 (2009); Jeffrey Evans Stake, The Property "Instinct," 359 Philosophical Transactions of the Royal Society London B 1763 (2004).

C. Acquisition by Creation

An observer from abroad has argued that the following principle "is part of the common law":

> Any expenditure of mental or physical effort, as a result of which there is created an entity, whether tangible or intangible, vests in the person who brought the entity into being, a proprietary right to the commercial exploitation of that entity, which right is separate and independent from the ownership of that entity. [D.F. Libling, The Concept of Property: Property in Intangibles, 94 L.Q. Rev. 103, 104 (1978).]

---

38. Even in modern times, possession plays a central role in property doctrine. See, e.g., the epigraphs at the beginning of Chapter 2, page 125.

The assertion is that if you create something—if in that sense you are first in time—then that something is most certainly yours to exploit, because, Libling argues, "the foundation of proprietary rights is the expenditure of labour and money (which merely represents past effort)." Id. at 119. So the underlying idea seems to derive from John Locke, who reasoned that you own the fruits of your labor in consequence of having "a property in your own person." See Note 4 on page 14.

The trouble is that the fruits of your labor are *not* always yours alone to exploit, and you do *not* always have full rights of property in your own person. Why? The materials in this section address that question.

1.   Property in One's Ideas and Expressions: General Principles of Intellectual Property

The law of property in ideas—or intellectual property, as it is called—is a large and lively subject treated in depth in advanced courses. Our aim here is most certainly *not* to study all the doctrines and details. Instead, our objectives are to introduce the key features of property rights in ideas and to examine the extent to which they resemble property rights in things.

International News Service v. Associated Press

Supreme Court of the United States, 1918
248 U.S. 215

JUSTICE PITNEY delivered the opinion of the Court.

The parties are competitors in the gathering and distribution of news and its publication for profit in newspapers throughout the United States. The Associated Press [or AP, complainant] . . . gathers in all parts of the world, by means of various instrumentalities of its own, by exchange with its members, and by other appropriate means, news and intelligence of current and recent events of interest to newspaper readers and distributes it daily to its members for publication in their newspapers. . . .

Defendant [INS] is a corporation organized under the laws of the State of New Jersey, whose business is the gathering and selling of news to its customers and clients, consisting of newspapers published throughout the United States, under contracts by which they pay certain amounts at stated times for defendant's service. . . .

The parties are in the keenest competition between themselves in the distribution of news throughout the United States; and so, as a rule, are the newspapers that they serve, in their several districts. . . .

The bill was filed to restrain the pirating of complainant's news by defendant in three ways: First, by bribing employees of newspapers published by complainant's members to furnish AP news to INS before publication, for transmission by telegraph and telephone to defendant's clients for publication by them; Second, by inducing AP members to violate its by-laws and permit defendant to obtain news before publication; and Third, by copying news from bulletin boards and from early editions of complainant's newspapers and selling this, either bodily or after rewriting it, to defendant's customers.[39]

The District Court, upon consideration of the bill and answer, with voluminous affidavits on both sides, granted a preliminary injunction under the first and second heads; but refused at that stage to restrain the systematic practice admittedly pursued by INS, of taking news bodily from the bulletin boards and early editions of AP's newspapers and selling it as its own. . . . The only matter that has been argued before us is whether INS may lawfully be restrained from appropriating news taken from bulletins issued by AP or any of its members, or from newspapers published by them, for the purpose of selling it to INS clients. AP asserts that INS's admitted course of conduct in this regard both violates AP's property right in the news and constitutes unfair competition in business. And notwithstanding the case has proceeded only to the stage of a preliminary injunction, we have deemed it proper to consider the underlying questions, since they go to the very merits of the action and are presented upon facts that are not in dispute. As presented in argument, these questions are: 1. Whether there is any property in news; 2. Whether, if there be property in news collected for the purpose of being published, it survives the instant of its publication in the first newspaper to which it is communicated by the news-gatherer; and 3. Whether defendant's admitted course of conduct in appropriating for commercial use matter taken from bulletins or early editions of AP publications constituted unfair competition in trade. . . .

AP's news matter is not copyrighted. It is said that it could not, in practice, be copyrighted, because of the large number of dispatches that are sent daily; and . . . news is not within the operation of the copyright act. Defendant, while apparently conceding this, nevertheless invokes the analogies of the law of literary property and copyright, insisting as its principal contention that, assuming AP has a right of property in its news, it can be maintained (unless the copyright act be complied with) only by being kept secret and confidential, and that upon the publication with AP's consent of uncopyrighted news by any of AP's members in a newspaper or upon a bulletin board, the right of property is lost, and the subsequent use of the news by the public or by INS for any purpose whatever becomes lawful. . . .

In considering the general question of property in news matter, it is necessary to recognize its dual character, distinguishing between the substance of the

---

39. According to one account, the actions of INS (which was owned by William Randolph Hearst) owed to the fact that its correspondents were barred "during much of World War I by British and French censors from sending war dispatches to the United States, because Hearst had offended the British and French by siding with Germany at the outset of the war." Richard A. Posner, Misappropriation: A Dirge, 40 Hous. L. Rev. 621, 627 (2003). Another account says simply that INS was barred because it violated censorship regulations. L. Ray Patterson & Stanley W. Lindberg, The Nature of Copyright: A Law of Users' Rights 180 (1991). —EDS.

information and the particular form or collocation of words in which the writer has communicated it.

No doubt news articles often possess a literary quality, and are the subject of literary property at the common law; nor do we question that such an article, as a literary production, is the subject of copyright by the terms of the act as it now stands.

But the news element—the information respecting current events contained in the literary production—is not the creation of the writer, but is a report of matters that ordinarily are *publici juris*; it is the history of the day. It is not to be supposed that the framers of the constitution, when they empowered Congress "to promote the progress of science and useful arts, by securing for limited times to authors and inventors the exclusive right to their respective writings and discoveries" (Const., Art. I, §8, par. 8), intended to confer upon one who might happen to be the first to report a historic event the exclusive right for any period to spread the knowledge of it.

We need spend no time, however, upon the general question of property in news matter at common law, or the application of the copyright act, since it seems to us the case must turn upon the question of unfair competition in business. . . . The peculiar value of news is in the spreading of it while it is fresh; and it is evident that a valuable property interest in the news, as news, cannot be maintained by keeping it secret. Besides, except for matter improperly disclosed, or published in breach of trust or confidence, or in violation of law, none of which is involved in this branch of the case, the news of current events may be regarded as common property. What we are concerned with is the business of making it known to the world, in which both parties to the present suit are engaged. . . . The parties are competitors in this field; and, on fundamental principles, applicable here as elsewhere, when rights or privileges of the one are liable to conflict with those of the other, each party is under a duty so to conduct its own business as not unnecessarily or unfairly to injure that of the other.

. . . The question here is not so much the rights of either party as against the public but their rights as between themselves. And although we may and do assume that neither party has any remaining property interest as against the public in uncopyrighted news matter after the moment of its first publication, it by no means follows that there is no remaining property interest in it as between themselves. For, to both of them alike, news matter, however little susceptible of ownership or dominion in the absolute sense, is stock in trade, to be gathered at the cost of enterprise, organization, skill, labor, and money, and to be distributed and sold to those who will pay money for it, as for any other merchandise. Regarding the news, therefore, as but the material out of which both parties are seeking to make profits at the same time and in the same field, we hardly can fail to recognize that for this purpose, and as between them, it must be regarded as *quasi* property, irrespective of the rights of either as against the public. . . .

The peculiar features of the case arise from the fact that, while novelty and freshness form so important an element in the success of the business, the very processes of distribution and publication necessarily occupy a good deal of time.

AP's service, as well as defendant's, is a daily service to daily newspapers; most of the foreign news reaches this country at the Atlantic seaboard, principally at the city of New York, and because of this, and of time differentials due to the earth's rotation, the distribution of news matter throughout the country is principally from east to west; and, since in speed the telegraph and telephone easily outstrip the rotation of the earth, it is a simple matter for defendant to take complainant's news from bulletins or early editions of complainant's members in the eastern cities and at the mere cost of telegraphic transmission cause it to be published in western papers issued at least as early as those served by complainant. Besides this, and irrespective of time differentials, irregularities in telegraphic transmission on different lines, and the normal consumption of time in printing and distributing the newspaper, result in permitting pirated news to be placed in the hands of defendant's readers sometimes simultaneously with the service of competing AP papers, occasionally even earlier.

INS insists that when, with the sanction and approval of complainant, and as the result of the use of its news for the very purpose for which it is distributed, a portion of AP's members communicate to the general public by posting it upon bulletin boards so that all may read, or by issuing it to newspapers and distributing it indiscriminately, complainant no longer has the right to control the use to be made of it; that when it thus reaches the light of day it becomes the common possession of all to whom it is accessible; and that any purchaser of a newspaper has the right to communicate the intelligence which it contains to anybody and for any purpose, even for the purpose of selling it for profit to newspapers published for profit in competition with complainant's members.

The fault in the reasoning lies in applying as a test the right of the complainant as against the public, instead of considering the rights of complainant and defendant, competitors in business, as between themselves. The right of the purchaser of a single newspaper to spread knowledge of its contents gratuitously, for any legitimate purpose not unreasonably interfering with complainant's right to make merchandise of it, may be admitted; but to transmit that news for commercial use, in competition with complainant—which is what defendant has done and seeks to justify—is a very different matter. In doing this defendant, by its very act, admits that it is taking material that has been acquired by complainant as the result of organization and the expenditure of labor, skill, and money, and which is salable by complainant for money, and that defendant in appropriating it and selling it as its own is endeavoring to reap where it has not sown, and by disposing of it to newspapers that are competitors of complainant's members is appropriating to itself the harvest of those who have sown. Stripped of all disguises, the process amounts to an unauthorized interference with the normal operation of complainant's legitimate business precisely at the point where the profit is to be reaped, in order to divert a material portion of the profit from those who have earned it to those who have not; with special advantage to defendant in the competition because of the fact that it is not burdened with any part of the expense of gathering the news. The transaction speaks for itself, and a court of equity ought not to hesitate long in characterizing it as unfair competition in business. . . .

The contention that the news is abandoned to the public for all purposes when published in the first newspaper is untenable. Abandonment is question of intent, and the entire organization of the AP negatives such a purpose. The cost of the service would be prohibitive if the reward were to be so limited. No single newspaper, no small group of newspapers, could sustain the expenditure. Indeed, it is one of the most obvious results to defendant's theory that, by permitting indiscriminate publication by anybody and everybody for purposes of profit in competition with the news-gatherer, it would render publication profitless, or so little profitable as in effect to cut off the service by rendering the cost prohibitive in comparison with the return. . . .

It is said that the elements of unfair competition are lacking because there is no attempt by defendant to palm off its goods as those of the complainant, characteristic of the most familiar, if not the most typical cases of unfair competition. But we cannot concede that the right to equitable relief is confined to that class of cases. In the present case the fraud upon complainant's rights is more direct and obvious. Regarding news matter as the mere material from which these two competing parties are endeavoring to make money, and treating it, therefore, as *quasi* property for the purposes of their business because they are both selling it as such, defendant's conduct differs from the ordinary case of unfair competition in trade principally in this that, instead of selling its own goods as those of complainant, it substitutes misappropriation in the place of misrepresentation, and sells complainant's goods as its own. . . .

The decree of the Circuit Court of Appeals will be Affirmed.

[The concurring opinion of Justice Holmes, joined by Justice McKenna, and the dissenting opinion of Justice Brandeis are omitted.]

NOTES AND QUESTIONS

1. *The rest of the story.* Contrary to conventional accounts, there was no evidence that INS was copying bulletins on the East Coast and transmitting them to newspapers on the West Coast. INS was just a convenient defendant that AP needed to establish a broad legal precedent that would protect its position as a natural monopoly. In the early twentieth century, the wire service was primarily a large network of leased telegraph lines. The cost of creating the network dwarfed the cost of gathering the news, an activity that AP spent little time or effort actually doing. Enhancing its market power even further, AP was a member of an international cartel that gave it exclusive rights to bulletins of foreign news services and access to foreign government communiqués. Technological and economic changes (e.g., substituting teletype machines for telegraph operators) threatened AP's monopoly position, opening it up to previously unknown competition. To block its potential competitors, AP sought a broad legal principle that recognized a property right in news. What it needed was a ready defendant whom it could charge with copying "its" news. It found one in INS. The chief of INS's bureau in Cleveland had bribed an AP reporter to provide him

with the news there. As for copying, INS had copied some of AP's material, but not very much or very often. The claim of copying was just a convenient excuse for bringing a lawsuit.

After the Supreme Court's decision, AP and INS settled. It was in their self-interest to do so because their relationship was mutually advantageous. INS, which was owned by William Randolph Hearst, wanted to continue to obtain the benefits of AP's service. On the other side, the members of AP, a cooperative of subscribers, did not wish to offend the powerful Mr. Hearst. At the end of the day, the case had very little effect on the way INS did business. For a full account of the story, see Douglas G. Baird, The Story of INS v. AP: Property, Natural Monopoly, and the Uneasy Legacy of a Concocted Controversy, in Intellectual Property Stories 9 (Jane C. Ginsburg & Rochelle Cooper Dreyfuss eds. 2006).

2. *Copying and the common law.* In Cheney Brothers v. Doris Silk Corp., 35 F.2d 279 (2d Cir. 1929), cert. denied, 281 U.S. 738 (1930), the plaintiff sought protection of designs of silks that it manufactured. Some of the silks succeeded commercially and some of them did not, and even commercially successful patterns did not last more than eight or nine months on the market. The defendant, Doris Silk, made copies of successful Cheney Brothers prints and sold them at a cheaper price. Cheney Brothers asked for an injunction, although only for the duration of one season. Neither patent nor copyright law provided protection, for practical and legal reasons, so Cheney Brothers relied on *INS*.

The Second Circuit, in an opinion by Learned Hand, denied relief, stating a basic rule: "In the absence of some recognized right at common law, or under the statutes . . . a man's property is limited to the chattels which embody his invention. Others may imitate these at their pleasure." The court distinguished *INS* by limiting it to its facts.

Today, in general, fashion designs are not protected under intellectual property law in the United States, but legislation is pending in both houses of Congress to provide such protection under the federal Copyright Act. Scholars continue to debate the desirability of expanding intellectual property protection in the fashion industry. Compare Kal Raustiala & Christopher Sprigman, The Knockoff Economy: How Imitation Sparks Innovation (2012) (copyright protection not necessary to spur innovation in the fashion industry), with C. Scott Hemphill & Jeannie Suk, The Law, Culture, and Economics of Fashion, 61 Stan. L. Rev. 1147 (2009) (stronger copyright protections are appropriate).

3. *The "hot news" doctrine.* If the general principle today is that of *Cheney Brothers*—in the absence of some recognized right, people are free to imitate or copy the original—then what is the current status of *INS*? The misappropriation doctrine developed in the case eventually fell into disuse, but recent years have seen a revival of sorts. Led by the Second Circuit, a few courts have developed a "hot news" doctrine, largely on the basis of *INS*. Under the Second Circuit's hot news doctrine, a newsgatherer may recover from a defendant when (1) the news-gathering or collection process involves significant expenditures; (2) the collected news or information is time-sensitive; (3) the defendant free rides on the collected material; (4) the freeriding directly competes with the newsgatherer's market; and

(5) the freeriding is likely to diminish incentives to collect news/information in a timely fashion. National Basketball Assn. v. Motorola, Inc., 105 F.3d 841, 852-853 (2d Cir. 1997). See also Barclays Capital, Inc. v. Theflyonthewall.com, Inc., 650 F.3d 876 (2d Cir. 2011) (no misappropriation found when tfotw.com leaked stock tips; claim was preempted by the Copyright Act). See generally Shyamkrishna Balganesh, "Hot News": The Enduring Myth of Property in the News, 111 Colum. L. Rev. 419 (2011).

4. *Intellectual property and labor theory.* As noted at the outset of this section, intellectual property is often defended on the basis of John Locke's labor theory of property. Indeed, from one perspective intellectual creation seems more like creation out of nothing than creation of tangible products from resources removed from an original commons. On this reasoning, intellectual property does not seem to involve the same complications of trying to separate out the relative contributions of individual laborers and the materials on which they have labored. See Gregory S. Alexander & Eduardo M. Peñalver, An Introduction to Property Theory 192 (2010). But is it actually the case that intellectual creations spring from nothing beyond the mind of the creator? See id. at 193-194.

In this connection, recall the Court's observation in *INS* (at page 60) that the defendant was "endeavoring to reap where it has not sown. . . ." So what? Consider the following from Douglas G. Baird, Common Law Intellectual Property and the Legacy of *International News Service v. Associated Press,* 50 U. Chi. L. Rev. 411, 413-414 (1983):

> That an individual has the right to reap what he has sown . . . is far from self-evident even as applied to tangible property. . . . We typically can reap only the wheat we sow on our own land, and how land becomes private property in the first place remains a mystery. In any event, wheat and information are fundamentally different from one another. It is the nature of wheat or land or any other tangible property that possession by one person precludes possession by anyone else. . . . Many people, however, can use the same piece of information. . . .
>
> The value of the information to AP derived in part from its ability to keep its rivals from copying the information it gathered. But deciding that it could not enjoy its news exclusively is not the same as telling a farmer he must hand over wheat he has grown to someone who merely watched him grow it. Deciding against AP would not mean that it would lose all revenue from its news-gathering efforts. People would still pay for the AP's news. . . .
>
> That the analogy between wheat and information does not apply with full force, however, does not mean that it should not apply at all. One can still argue that individuals have the right to enjoy the fruits of their labors, even when the labors are intellectual. But granting individuals exclusive rights to the information they gather conflicts with other rights in a way that granting exclusive rights to tangible property does not. In a market economy, granting individuals exclusive rights to property is an effective way of allocating scarce resources. Saying that someone should be able to own a particular good or piece of land and should be able to keep others from getting it unless they pay him is unobjectionable once one accepts the desirability of a market economy. Granting exclusive rights to information does not, however, necessarily promote a market economy. Competition depends upon imitation. One person invests labor and money to create a product, such as a food processor, that people will buy. Others may imitate him and take advantage of the new market by selling their own food processors. Their machines may incorporate their own ideas about how such machines should be made. As a result, the quality of the machines may rise and their price may fall. The first person is made worse off than he would be if he had had an exclusive right to his idea, because his competitors are enjoying the fruits of his

labor and are not paying for it. Nevertheless, the public as a whole may be better off, as long as this freedom to imitate does not destroy the incentive for people to come up with new devices.

For further elaboration on some of these ideas and an exploration of the quasi-property concept that loomed large in *INS*, see Shyamkrishna Balganesh, Quasi-Property: Like, But Not Quite Property, 160 U. Pa. L. Rev. 1889 (2012).

5. *Intellectual property law.* The law of intellectual property—primarily copyright, patent, and trademark—grants limited monopolies over protected material. The point of the monopolies is to promote creative activity; the point of the limits is to advance competition (which in turn facilitates consumption by holding prices down). The design of the systems entails difficult trade-offs, which in this country are made in the main by Congress (though there are common law copyrights in addition to statutory ones, and trademarks are regulated through a mixed system of state common law rules and optional federal registration).

a. Copyright

Copyright owners have the right to prevent others from reproducing the work, creating derivative works, distributing copies of the work to the public, performing the work publicly, displaying the work publicly, and performing the work by digital audio transmission. Of course, copyright holders may and frequently do sell others licenses to use their works in particular ways; they may also assign (transfer) their copyrights to others. Copyright protection has gradually been extended in duration over the years. Hence it is necessary to know when a particular work was created and, for works created before 1978, whether the copyright was renewed. Generally, for works created on or after January 1, 1978, the rule is that protection extends for the life of the author plus 70 years, and this term cannot be renewed.

Federal law imposes three requirements for copyright protection: originality, work of authorship, and fixation. *Originality* means that the work must be an independent creation of the author and must demonstrate at least some minimal degree of creativity.

Work of authorship is a fairly broad term. The federal statute identifies eight types of such works: literary works; musical works; dramatic works; pantomimes and choreographic works; pictorial, graphic, and sculptural works; motion pictures and other audiovisual works; sound recordings; and architectural works. The term "literary works" is interpreted to include computer programs. What is not covered is important: First, not covered is any "idea, procedure, process, system, method of operation, concept, principle, or discovery." 17 U.S.C. §102(b). Running throughout copyright law is the idea-expression distinction. Copyright law protects expressions, not ideas. It protects the form or mode by which ideas are expressed rather than the ideas themselves. Second, not covered are strictly functional works, such as systems or procedures, which are protected by patent law, not copyright.

Fixation means that the work be fixed in some kind of tangible medium, such as on a printed page, a CD, a canvas, or a computer hard drive. Even human skin may constitute a tangible medium of expression, enabling tattoo artists to qualify for copyright protection. See Matthew Beasley, Note, Who Owns Your Skin: Intellectual Property Law and Norms Among Tattoo Artists, 85 S. Cal. L. Rev. 1137, 1145 (2012).

In recent years, the Supreme Court has expressed concerns about the importance of not unduly restricting public access to information. The following case concerns the question of whether copyright protection is available for collections of basic information, in this case telephone numbers. Consider the implications of the decision for intellectual property protection of other types of databases.

Feist Publications, Inc. v. Rural Telephone Service Co.

Supreme Court of the United States, 1991
499 U.S. 340

Justice O'Connor delivered the opinion of the Court.

This case requires us to clarify the extent of copyright protection available to telephone directory white pages.

Rural Telephone Service Company is a certified public utility that provides telephone service to several communities in northwest Kansas. It is subject to a state regulation that requires all telephone companies operating in Kansas to issue annually an updated telephone directory. Accordingly, as a condition of its monopoly franchise, Rural publishes a typical telephone directory, consisting of white pages and yellow pages. The white pages list in alphabetical order the names of Rural's subscribers, together with their towns and telephone numbers. The yellow pages list Rural's business subscribers alphabetically by category and feature classified advertisement of various sizes. Rural distributes its directory free of charge to its subscribers, but earns revenue by selling yellow pages advertisements.

Feist Publications, Inc., is a publishing company that specializes in area-wide telephone directories. Unlike a typical directory, which covers only a particular calling area, Feist's area-wide directories cover a much larger geographical range, reducing the need to call directory assistance or consult multiple directories. The Feist directory that is the subject of this litigation covers 11 different telephone service areas in 15 counties and contains 46,878 white pages listings—compared to Rural's approximately 7,700 listings. Like Rural's directory, Feist's is distributed free of charge and includes both white pages and yellow pages. Feist and Rural compete vigorously for yellow pages advertising.

As the sole provider of telephone service in its service area, Rural obtains subscriber information quite easily. Persons desiring telephone service must apply to Rural and provide their names and addresses; Rural then assigns them a telephone number. Feist is not a telephone company, let alone one with monopoly status, and therefore lacks independent access to any subscriber information. To obtain white pages listings for its area-wide directory, Feist approached each of the 11 telephone companies operating in northwest Kansas and offered to pay for the right to use its white pages listings.

Of the 11 telephone companies, only Rural refused to license its listings to Feist. Rural's refusal created a problem for Feist, as omitting these listings would have left a gaping hole in its area-wide directory, rendering it less attractive to potential yellow pages advertisers. In a decision subsequent to that which we review here, the District Court determined that this was precisely the reason Rural refused to license its listings. The refusal was motivated by an unlawful purpose "to extend its monopoly in telephone service to a monopoly in yellow pages advertising." Rural Telephone Service Co. v. Feist Publications, Inc., 737 F. Supp. 610, 622 (Kan. 1990).

Unable to license Rural's white pages listings, Feist used them without Rural's consent. Feist began by removing several thousand listings that fell outside the geographic range of its area-wide directory, then hired personnel to investigate the 4,935 that remained. These employees verified the data reported by Rural and sought to obtain additional information. As a result, a typical Feist listing includes the individual's street address; most of Rural's listings do not. Notwithstanding these additions, however, 1,309 of the 46,878 listings in Feist's 1983 directory were identical to listings in Rural's 1982-1983 white pages. Four of these were fictitious listings that Rural had inserted into its directory to detect copying.

Rural sued for copyright infringement in the District Court for the District of Kansas, taking the position that Feist, in compiling its own directory, could not use the information contained in Rural's white pages. . . . The District Court granted summary judgment to Rural. . . . [T]he Court of Appeals for the Tenth Circuit affirmed "for substantially the reasons given by the district court." We granted certiorari to determine whether the copyright in Rural's directory protects the names, towns, and telephone numbers copied by Feist.

This case concerns the interaction of two well-established propositions. The first is that facts are not copyrightable; the other, that compilations of facts generally are. Each of these propositions possesses an impeccable pedigree. . . .

There is an undeniable tension between these two propositions. Many compilations consist of nothing but raw data—i.e., wholly factual information not accompanied by any original written expression. On what basis may one claim a copyright in such a work? Common sense tells us that 100 uncopyrightable facts do not magically change their status when gathered together in one place. Yet copyright law seems to contemplate that compilations that consist exclusively of facts are potentially within its scope.

The key to resolving the tension lies in understanding why facts are not copyrightable. The *sine qua non* of copyright is originality. To qualify for copyright protection, a work must be original to the author. . . . To be sure, the requisite level of creativity is extremely low; even a slight amount will suffice. The vast majority of works make the grade quite easily, as they possess some creative spark, "no matter how crude, humble or obvious" it might be. Originality does not signify novelty; a work may be original even though it closely resembles other works, so long as the similarity is fortuitous, not the result of copying. To illustrate, assume that two poets, each ignorant of the other, compose identical poems. Neither work is novel, yet both are original and, hence, copyrightable. . . .

It is this bedrock principle of copyright that mandates the law's seemingly disparate treatment of facts and factual compilations. . . . The distinction is one between creation and discovery: the first person to find and report a particular fact has not created the fact; he or she has merely discovered its existence. . . . Census-takers, for example, do not "create" the population figures that emerge from their efforts; in a sense, they copy these figures from the world around them. . . . Census data therefore do not trigger copyright, because these data are not "original" in the constitutional sense. . . .

Factual compilations, on the other hand, may possess the requisite originality. The compilation author typically chooses which facts to include, in what order to place them, and how to arrange the collected data so that they may be used effectively by readers. These choices as to selection and arrangement, so long as they are made independently by the compiler and entail a minimal degree of creativity, are sufficiently original that Congress may protect such compilations through the copyright laws. . . . Thus, even a directory that contains absolutely no protectible written expression, only facts, meets the constitutional minimum for copyright protection if it features an original selection or arrangement. . . .

This protection is subject to an important limitation. The mere fact that a work is copyrighted does not mean that every element of the work may be protected. Originality remains the sine qua non of copyright; accordingly, copyright protection may extend only to those components of a work that are original to the author. . . .

This inevitably means that the copyright in a factual compilation is thin. Notwithstanding a valid copyright, a subsequent compiler remains free to use the facts contained in another's publication to aid in preparing a competing work, so long as the competing work does not feature the same selection and arrangement. . . .

It may seem unfair that much of the fruit of the compiler's labor may be used by others without compensation. . . . The primary objective of copyright is not to reward the labor of authors, but "[t]o promote the Progress of Science and useful Arts." Art. I, 8, cl. 8. To this end, copyright assures authors the right to their original expression, but encourages others to build freely upon the ideas and information conveyed by a work. This principle, known as the idea/expression or fact/expression dichotomy, applies to all works of authorship. As applied to a factual compilation, assuming the absence of original written expression, only the compiler's selection and arrangement may be protected; the raw facts may be copied at will. This result is neither unfair nor unfortunate. It is the means by which copyright advances the progress of science and art. . . .

Most courts . . . understood from this Court's decisions that there could be no copyright without originality. . . .

But some courts misunderstood the [copyright] statute. . . . [They inferred] erroneously that directories and the like were copyrightable *per se*, "without any further or precise showing of original-personal-authorship." . . . [They] developed a new theory to justify the protection of factual compilations. Known alternatively as "sweat of the brow" or "industrious collection," the underlying notion was that copyright was a reward for the hard work that went into compiling facts. . . .

[This] "sweat of the brow" doctrine had numerous flaws, the most glaring being that it extended copyright protection in a compilation beyond selection and arrangement—the compiler's original contributions—to the facts them-selves. Under the doctrine, the only defense to infringement was independent creation. A subsequent compiler was "not entitled to take one word of information previously published," but rather had to "independently wor[k] out the matter for himself, so as to arrive at the same result from the same common sources of information." [Jeweler's Circular Publishing Co. v. Keystone Publishing Co., 281 F. 83, 88-89 (2d Cir. 1922).] "Sweat of the brow" courts thereby eschewed the most fundamental axiom of copyright law—that no one may copyright facts or ideas. . . .

Decisions of this Court applying the 1909 Act make clear that the statute did not permit the "sweat of the brow" approach. The best example is International News Service v. Associated Press, 248 U.S. 215 (1918). In that decision, the Court stated unambiguously that the 1909 Act conferred copyright protection only on those elements of a work that were original to the author. . . .

There is no doubt that Feist took from the white pages of Rural's directory a substantial amount of factual information. At a minimum, Feist copied the names, towns, and telephone numbers of 1,309 of Rural's subscribers. Not all copying, however, is copyright infringement. To establish infringement, two elements must be proven: (1) ownership of a valid copyright, and (2) copying of constituent elements of the work that are original. The first element is not at issue here; Feist appears to concede that Rural's directory, considered as a whole, is subject to a valid copyright because it contains some foreword text, as well as original material in its yellow pages advertisements.

The question is whether Rural has proved the second element. In other words, did Feist, by taking 1,309 names, towns, and telephone numbers from Rural's white pages, copy anything that was "original" to Rural? Certainly, the raw data does not satisfy the originality requirement. Rural may have been the first to discover and report the names, towns, and telephone numbers of its subscribers, but this data does not "'ow[e] its origin'" to Rural. . . . Rather, these bits of information are uncopyrightable facts; they existed before Rural reported them, and would have continued to exist if Rural had never published a telephone directory. . . .

The question that remains is whether Rural selected, coordinated, or arranged these uncopyrightable facts in an original way. As mentioned, original-ity is not a stringent standard; it does not require that facts be presented in an innovative or surprising way. It is equally true, however, that the selection and arrangement of facts cannot be so mechanical or routine as to require no creativity whatsoever. The standard of originality is low, but it does exist. . . .

The selection, coordination, and arrangement of Rural's white pages do not satisfy the minimum constitutional standards for copyright protection. As mentioned at the outset, Rural's white pages are entirely typical. . . . In preparing its white pages, Rural simply takes the data provided by its subscribers and lists it alphabetically by surname. The end product is a garden-variety white pages directory, devoid of even the slightest trace of creativity.

Rural's selection of listings could not be more obvious: It publishes the most basic information—name, town, and telephone number—about each person who applies to it for telephone service. This is "selection" of a sort, but it lacks the modicum of creativity necessary to transform mere selection into copyrightable expression. Rural expended sufficient effort to make the white pages directory useful, but insufficient creativity to make it original. . . .

Nor can Rural claim originality in its coordination and arrangement of facts. The white pages do nothing more than list Rural's subscribers in alphabetical order. This arrangement may, technically speaking, owe its origin to Rural; no one disputes that Rural undertook the task of alphabetizing the names itself. But there is nothing remotely creative about arranging names alphabetically in a white pages directory. . . .

We conclude that the names, towns, and telephone numbers copied by Feist were not original to Rural and therefore were not protected by the copyright in Rural's combined white and yellow pages directory. As a constitutional matter, copyright protects only those constituent elements of a work that possess more than a *de minimis* quantum of creativity. Rural's white pages, limited to basic subscriber information and arranged alphabetically, fall short of the mark. As a statutory matter, 17 U.S.C. §101 does not afford protection from copying to a collection of facts that are selected, coordinated, and arranged in a way that utterly lacks originality. Given that some works must fail, we cannot imagine a more likely candidate. Indeed, were we to hold that Rural's white pages pass muster, it is hard to believe that any collection of facts could fail. . . .

The judgment of the Court of Appeals is *Reversed*.

NOTES AND QUESTIONS

1. *The originality requirement, the "sweat-of-the-brow" doctrine, and labor theory.* *Feist* is perhaps the most important recent copyright decision dealing with the requirement that the work be original. Until *Feist*, several decisions had applied the "sweat-of-the-brow" doctrine. Under that doctrine, an author gains copyright protection simply on the basis of effort and expense; no originality is required. *Feist* is important, among other reasons, because it rejects that doctrine: "[O]riginality, not 'sweat of the brow,' is the touchstone of copyright protection in directories and other fact-based works. . . ." *Feist* is also important because of the Court's interpretation of originality. The test for originality, the Court indicates, is a modicum of creativity. Compilations of preexisting data may be copyrighted if they displayed sufficient creativity.

This is not the first time that we have seen the idea behind the sweat-of-the-brow doctrine. As the Court in *Feist* indicated, it is evident in the *INS* case. But even prior to that, we saw it in Pierson v. Post. Sweat-of-the-brow reasoning is the thrust of Justice Livingston's dissenting opinion in that case. There is some appeal to the idea that a person should be rewarded for her efforts, but recall Douglas Baird's observation, made in connection with *INS* (see pages 63-64), that we do not always reap where we sow. Why did the Court in *Feist* reject the sweat-of-the brow doctrine? And what about creativity—is that a better approach? (If so, better in what respect?)

2. *Databases. Feist* throws into question the status, vis-à-vis copyright protection, of various sorts of factual compilations. For example, what is the status of automated databases after *Feist*? Are they entitled to protection, or do they lack sufficient creativity? The status of such factual compilations is unclear after *Feist,* and lower federal courts have interpreted *Feist* in quite different ways. Compare, e.g., BellSouth Advertising & Publishing Corp. v. Donnelley Information Publishing, 999 F.2d 1436 (11th Cir. 1993) (yellow pages directory unprotectable because act of separating categories of businesses would "merge with the idea of listing such entities as a class of businesses in a business directory"), with Key Publications, Inc. v. Chinatown Today Publishing Enterprises, 945 F.2d 508 (2d Cir. 1991) (court protected copied directory that differed from BellSouth directory only by solely including businesses thought to be of interest to Chinese-Americans). Recent district court cases involving web site content indicate that the originality threshold for content and compilations remains rather low. See, e.g., Salestraq America, LLC v. Zyskowski, 635 F. Supp. 2d 1178 (D. Nev. 2009) (collection and compilation of information regarding residential properties' floor-plan measurements, architectural features, location information and other key attributes could satisfy the *Feist* test); Craigslist Inc. v. 3Taps Inc., 942 F. Supp. 2d 962, 2013 WL 1819999 (N.D. Cal. 2013) (Craigslist's user-generated classified advertisements and Craigslist's organization of those advertisements, categorized first by geographic area and then by product or service, demonstrate sufficient originality to defeat a motion to dismiss filed by web sites that copied Craigslist content).

Owners of databases and other factual compilations sometimes rely on alternative legal means of protecting their "sweat-of-the-brow" investments. Contract law has been especially popular in the wake of *Feist.* See, e.g., ProCD, Inc. v. Zeidenberg, 86 F.3d 1447 (7th Cir. 1996). Some cases hold that a person who copies a database may be liable for breach of contract even though the database is composed entirely of unprotectable facts.

3. *Infringement.* The copyright holder must satisfy three requirements to prevail in an infringement action: (1) he holds a valid copyright in the work; (2) defendant copied the work; and (3) the copying was an "improper appropriation." The final element—"improper appropriation"—requires the copyright holder show that the defendant copied so much of the original material that the two works are substantially similar.

The most important defense in an infringement action is *fair use.* It is also perhaps the most confusing (and confused) area of copyright law. The next case illustrates the operation of the fair use doctrine in the context of the aftermath of the infamous Watergate controversy, which resulted in the resignation of President Richard Nixon.

Harper & Row Publishers, Inc. v. Nation Enterprises

Supreme Court of the United States, 1985
471 U.S. 539

JUSTICE O'CONNOR delivered the opinion of the Court.

This case requires us to consider to what extent the "fair use" provision of the Copyright Revision Act of 1976 sanctions the unauthorized use of quotations from a public figure's unpublished manuscript.

[In February 1977, shortly after leaving the White House, President Ford contracted with Harper & Row and Reader's Digest to publish his as yet unwritten memoirs. The memoirs would contain fresh material concerning the Watergate crisis and Ford's pardon of former President Nixon. Ford's agreement with the publishers gave them exclusive rights to license prepublication excerpts. Two years later, when the memoirs were almost completed, prepublication rights were licensed to Time magazine for $25,000 (half in advance and the other at publication). Several weeks before the Time article was to be released, an article based on Ford's memoirs appeared in The Nation. It had been written by Victor Navasky, editor of The Nation, and based on a "purloined manuscript" of Ford's memoirs that had been given to Navasky by an unidentified person. Navasky knew that his possession of the manuscript was unauthorized and that it had to be returned quickly to his "source" to avoid discovery. He put together "a real hot news story" composed of quotes, paraphrases, and facts drawn exclusively from the manuscript; he attempted no independent commentary, research, or criticism because of the need for speed in order to "make news." His 2,250-word article appeared in April 1979, and led Time to cancel its piece and refuse to pay the second half of the contracted $25,000. The publishers brought suit for copyright infringement and won at trial, but the Court of Appeals reversed, finding that The Nation's story constituted a fair use of the Ford manuscript. The Supreme Court granted certiorari and, in the opinion below, reverses the judgment of the Court of Appeals.]

. . . The Nation has admitted to lifting verbatim quotes of the author's original language totaling between 300 and 400 words and constituting some 13% of The Nation article. In using generous verbatim excerpts of Mr. Ford's unpublished manuscript to lend authenticity to its account of the forthcoming memoirs, The Nation effectively arrogated to itself the right of first publication, an important marketable subsidiary right. For the reasons set forth below, we find that this use of the copyrighted manuscript, even stripped to the verbatim quotes conceded by The Nation to be copyrightable expression, was not a fair use within the meaning of the Copyright Act.

Fair use was traditionally defined as "a privilege in others than the owner of the copyright to use the copyrighted material in a reasonable manner without his consent." H. Ball, Law of Copyright and Literary Property 260 (1944) (hereinafter Ball). The statutory formulation of the defense of fair use in the Copyright Act reflects the intent of Congress to codify the common-law doctrine. Section 107 requires a case-by-case determination whether a particular use is fair, and the statute notes four nonexclusive factors to be considered. This approach was "intended to restate the [pre-existing] judicial doctrine of fair use, not to change, narrow, or enlarge it in any way." H.R. Rep. No. 94-1476, p. 66 (1976) (hereinafter House Report), U.S. Code Cong. & Admin. News 1976, pp. 5659, 5680.

The Copyright Act . . . recognized for the first time a distinct statutory right of first publication, which had previously been an element of the common-law protections afforded unpublished works. The Report of the House Committee on the Judiciary confirms that "Clause (3) of section 106, establishes the exclusive right of publications . . . . Under this provision the copyright owner would have the right to control the first public distribution of an authorized copy . . . of his work." Id. at 62 U.S. Code Cong. & Admin. News 1976, p. 5675.

Though the right of first publication, like the other rights enumerated in §106, is expressly made subject to the fair use provision of §107, fair use analysis must always be tailored to the individual case. The nature of the interest at stake is highly relevant to whether a given use is fair. From the beginning, those entrusted with the task of revision recognized the "overbalancing reasons to preserve the common law protection of undisseminated works until the author or his successor chooses to disclose them." Copyright Law Revision, Report of the Register of Copyrights on the General Revision of the U.S. Copyright Law, 87th Cong., 1st Sess., 41 (Comm. Print 1961). The right of first publication implicates a threshold decision by the author whether and in what form to release his work. First publication is inherently different from other §106 rights in that only one person can be the first publisher; as the contract with Time illustrates, the commercial value of the right lies primarily in exclusivity. Because the potential damage to the author from judicially enforced "sharing" of the first publication right with unauthorized users of his manuscript is substantial, the balance of equities in evaluating such a claim of fair use inevitably shifts. . . .

. . . We conclude that the unpublished nature of a work is "[a] key, though not necessarily determinative, factor" tending to negate a defense of fair use. Senate Report, at 64.

We also find unpersuasive respondents' argument that fair use may be made of a soon-to-be-published manuscript on the ground that the author has demonstrated he has no interest in nonpublication. This argument assumes that the unpublished nature of copyrighted material is only relevant to letters or other confidential writings not intended for dissemination. It is true that common-law copyright was often enlisted in the service of personal privacy. In its commercial guise, however, an author's right to choose when he will publish is no less deserving of protection. The period encompassing the work's initiation, its preparation, and its grooming for public dissemination is a crucial one for any literary endeavor. . . . The obvious benefit to author and public alike of assuring authors the leisure to develop their ideas free from fear of expropriation outweighs any short-term "news value" to be gained from premature publication of the author's expression. The author's control of first public distribution implicates not only his personal interest in creative control but his property interest in exploitation of prepublication rights, which are valuable in themselves and serve as a valuable adjunct to publicity and marketing. Under ordinary circumstances, the author's right to control the first public appearance of his undisseminated expression will outweigh a claim of fair use.

Respondents, however, contend that First Amendment values require a different rule under the circumstances of this case. The thrust of the decision below is that "[t]he scope of [fair use] is undoubtedly wider when the information conveyed relates to matters of high public concern." Consumers Union of the United States, Inc. v. General Signal Corp., 724 F.2d 1044, 1050 (2d Cir. 1983). . . .

Respondents' theory . . . would expand fair use to effectively destroy any expectation of copyright protection in the work of a public figure. Absent such protection, there would be little incentive to create or profit in financing such memoirs, and the public would be denied an important source of significant historical information. The promise of copyright would be an empty one if it could be avoided merely by dubbing the infringement a fair use "news report" of the book. . . .

In view of the First Amendment protections already embodied in the Copyright Act's distinction between copyrightable expression and uncopyrightable facts and ideas, and the latitude for scholarship and comment traditionally afforded by fair use, we see no warrant for expanding the doctrine of fair use to create what amounts to a public figure exception to copyright. Whether verbatim copying from a public figure's manuscript in a given case is or is not fair must be judged according to the traditional equities of fair use.

. . . The four factors identified by Congress as especially relevant in determining whether the use was fair are: (1) the purpose and character of the use; (2) the nature of the copyrighted work; (3) the substantiality of the portion used in relation to the copyrighted work as a whole; (4) the effect on the potential market for or value of the copyrighted work. We address each one separately.

Purpose of the Use. The Second Circuit correctly identified news reporting as the general purpose of The Nation's use. News reporting is one of the examples enumerated in §107 to "give some idea of the sort of activities the courts might regard as fair use under the circumstances." Senate Report, at 61. This listing was not intended to be exhaustive . . . or to single out any particular use as presumptively a "fair" use. . . . The fact that an article arguably is "news" and therefore a productive use is simply one factor in a fair use analysis. . . .

The fact that a publication was commercial as opposed to nonprofit is a separate factor that tends to weigh against a finding of fair use. In arguing that the purpose of news reporting is not purely commercial, The Nation misses the point entirely. The crux of the profit/nonprofit distinction is not whether the sole motive of the use is monetary gain but whether the user stands to profit from exploitation of the copyrighted material without paying the customary price.

In evaluating character and purpose we cannot ignore The Nation's stated purpose of scooping the forthcoming hardcover and Time abstracts. The Nation's use had not merely the incidental effect but the intended purpose of supplanting the copyright holder's commercially valuable right of first publication. Also relevant to the "character" of the use is "the propriety of the defendant's conduct." "Fair use presupposes 'good faith' and 'fair dealing.'" Time Inc. v. Bernard Geis Associates, 293 F. Supp. 130, 146 (S.D.N.Y. 1968). . . . Fair use distinguishes between a true scholar and a chiseler who infringes a work for personal profit.

Nature of the Copyrighted Work. Second, the Act directs attention to the nature of the copyrighted work. "A Time to Heal" may be characterized as an unpublished historical narrative or autobiography. The law generally recognizes a greater need to disseminate factual works than works of fiction or fantasy. . . . Some of the briefer quotes from the memoirs are arguably necessary adequately to convey the facts; for example, Mr. Ford's characterization of the White House tapes as the "smoking gun" is perhaps so integral to the idea expressed as to be inseparable from it. But The Nation did not stop at isolated phrases and instead excerpted subjective descriptions and portraits of public figures whose power lies in the author's individualized expression. Such use, focusing on the most expressive elements of the work, exceeds that necessary to disseminate the facts. . . .

Amount and Substantiality of the Portion Used. Next, the Act directs us to examine the amount and substantiality of the portion used in relation to the copyrighted work as a whole. In absolute terms, the words actually quoted were an insubstantial portion of "A Time to Heal." The District Court, however, found that "[T]he Nation took what was essentially the heart of the book." 557 F. Supp., at 1072. . . . The portions actually quoted were selected by Mr. Navasky as among the most powerful passages in those chapters. He testified that he used verbatim excerpts because simply reciting the information could not adequately convey the "absolute certainty with which [Ford] expressed himself," or show that "this comes from President Ford," or carry the "definitive quality" of the original. In short, he quoted these passages precisely because they qualitatively embodied Ford's distinctive expression. . . .

Stripped to the verbatim quotes, the direct takings from the unpublished manuscript constitute at least 13% of the infringing article. The Nation article is structured around the quoted excerpts which serve as its dramatic focal points. In view of the expressive value of the excerpts and their key role in the infringing work, we cannot agree with the Second Circuit that the "magazine took a meager, indeed an infinitesimal amount of Ford's original language." 723 F.2d, at 209.

Effect on the Market. Finally, the Act focuses on "the effect of the use upon the potential market for or value of the copyrighted work." This last factor is undoubtedly the single most important element of fair use. . . . The trial court found not merely a potential but an actual effect on the market. Time's cancellation of its projected serialization and its refusal to pay the $12,500 were the direct effect of the infringement. . . . Rarely will a case of copyright infringement present such clear-cut evidence of actual damage. Petitioners assured Time that there would be no other authorized publication of any portion of the unpublished manuscript prior to April 23, 1979. . . . Time cited The Nation's article, which contained verbatim quotes from the unpublished manuscript, as a reason for its nonperformance. . . .

Placed in a broader perspective, a fair use doctrine that permits extensive prepublication quotations from an unreleased manuscript without the copyright owner's consent poses substantial potential for damage to the marketability of first serialization rights in general. . . .

. . . The Nation conceded that its verbatim copying of some 300 words of direct quotation from the Ford manuscript would constitute an infringement unless excused as a fair use. Because we find that The Nation's use of these verbatim excerpts from the unpublished manuscript was not a fair use, the judgment of the Court of Appeals is reversed, and the case is remanded for further proceedings consistent with this opinion.

[The dissenting opinion of Justice Brennan is omitted.]

NOTES AND QUESTIONS

1. *Newsworthiness.* Should the public's interest in learning the information from Ford's memoirs sooner matter? After all, the Court in *Harper & Row* acknowledged that there is "a greater need to disseminate factual works than works of fiction or fantasy." (Page 74.) Is there not an even greater need to disseminate news than other types of factual work? If so, should there be a presumption that news falls within the ambit of fair use?

2. *Facts or form?* What did The Nation appropriate, Harper & Row's unprotected facts or its protected literary form? In dissent, Justice Brennan criticized the majority for conflating the two. Can the underlying facts of what President Ford said be separated from the way he said it?

3. *Amount and substantiality of portion used.* Recall that §107's third factor is "the amount and substantiality of the portion used in relation to the copyrighted work as a whole." In applying this factor, does quantity or quality matter? The answer is both. Courts have used a quantitative approach at times. See, e.g., Iowa State Univ. Research Found., Inc. v. American Broadcasting Co., 621 F.2d 57 (2d Cir. 1980) (no fair use where defendant broadcast 8 percent of plaintiff's film). At other times, they have focused on qualitative considerations. See, e.g., Meredith Corp. v. Harper & Row Publishers, Inc., 378 F. Supp. 686 (S.D.N.Y. 1974), aff'd, 500 F.2d 1221 (2d Cir. 1974) (no fair use where material used was particularly important to copyrighted work as a whole).

4. *What's the denominator?* The majority emphasized that 13 percent of The Nation's article consisted of direct quotes from Harper & Row's manuscript. Justice Brennan's dissent countered that direct quotes constituted some 300 words from a 200,000-word book, comprising roughly one-seventh of 1 percent of the manuscript. Is either of these percentages more relevant than the other for resolving the fair use controversy in *Harper & Row?*

5. *Unclean hands/bad faith.* As the Court in *Harper & Row* noted, the fair use defense is an equitable doctrine, hence the "propriety of [the] defendant's conduct" is taken into account. In the case itself, The Nation, the Court pointed out, "knowingly exploited a purloined manuscript." How much weight should be given to the fact that the defendant did or did not act in bad faith? The lower federal courts are divided on this question. Compare Atari Games Corp. v. Nintendo of Am. Inc., 975 F.2d 832 (Fed. Cir. 1992) (holding that "an individual must possess an authorized copy of a literary work" in order to assert the fair use defense), with Religious Tech Ctr. v. Netcom On-line Communication Serv., Inc., 923 F. Supp. 1231, 1244 n.14 (N.D. Cal. 1995) (stating that nothing in *Harper & Row* indicates that bad faith is conclusive of the fair use issue).

6. *Parodies and other "transformations."* In an important case decided after *Harper & Row*, the Supreme Court in Campbell v. Acuff-Rose Music, Inc., 510 U.S. 569 (1994), extended considerable copyright protection to parodies by holding that the commercial nature of the defendant's use could not preclude a defendant from prevailing under the fair use test. The case involved a copyright infringement claim by the owner of the song, made famous by Roy Orbison, "Oh, Pretty Woman" against 2 Live Crew, a popular rap group, which recorded a parody of the original song. The Court remanded the case for further proceedings, and indicated that many parodies will qualify for fair use protection. The Court held that the extent to which a defendant's work is "transformative" would be important for parodic works. Although acknowledging that transformative use is not absolutely necessary for fair use protection, the Court stated that "the more transformative the new work, the less will be the significance of other factors, like commercialism, that may weigh against a finding of fair use." 510 U.S. at 579.

See also Cariou v. Prince, 714 F.3d 694 (2d Cir. 2013), arising from artist Richard Prince's use of photographs from Patrick Cariou's book Yes Rasta. The photographs in question were portraits Cariou took in Jamaica; Prince claimed he had made fair use of the pictures by altering them in various "dystopian" ways (for example, substituting white circles and ovals of eyes, noses, and mouths). The court held that fair use does not require that secondary uses somehow comment on the original work. The test, rather, is whether a reasonable observer would find the secondary uses to be "transformative." Prince's work, the court said, manifested "an entirely different aesthetic" from Cariou's photographs.

b.   Patent

The patent system is usually thought to be rooted in utilitarian reasons. The U.S. Constitution supports this view: "[t]o promote the Progress of Science and the useful Arts. . . ." U.S. Const. art. I, §8. As we indicated earlier (see page 64), patent law involves a trade-off: It grants a limited monopoly to patentees, thus encouraging creative and socially useful enterprise. The specific protection that the federal patent statute grants to the patent holder is the right to prevent others from making, using, selling (and so on) the patented invention during the term of the patent. (Note, however, that the patentee's use of the item or product may be regulated or even prohibited by law.) Currently, the term of patents is 20 years from the date the application is filed with the U.S. Patent and Trademark Office (PTO).

Under the federal patent statute, patent applications must meet five requirements in order for the patent to be granted: patentability, novelty, utility, non-obviousness, and enablement.

Patentability means that the invention fits in one of the general categories of patentable subject matter, namely "process, machine, manufacture, or any composition of matter." 35 U.S.C. §101. *Novelty* means that the invention has not been preceded in identical form in public prior art. *Utility* is a minimal requirement that is easily met so long as the invention offers some actual benefit to humans. *Non-obviousness* is the most important requirement; it asks whether the invention is a sufficiently big technical advance over the prior art. Finally, *enablement* requires that the patent application describe the invention in sufficient detail that "one of ordinary skill in the art" would be able to use the invention.

In recent years, one of the major controversies in patent law has concerned the scope of patentable subject matter. Courts have taken an expansive view of the statutory subject matter requirement so that today eligible subject matter includes genetic materials such as DNA sequences, proteins, and business methods. Biotechnology-related inventions have been among the most interesting—and controversial—topics in recent decades.

Diamond v. Chakrabarty

Supreme Court of the United States, 1980
447 U.S. 303

CHIEF JUSTICE BURGER delivered the opinion of the Court.
[In 1972, respondent Chakrabarty, a microbiologist, filed a patent application related to Chakrabarty's invention of a human-made, genetically engineered bacterium capable of breaking down multiple components of crude oil, thus making it valuable for the treatment of oil spills. Chakrabarty's claims were of three types: first, process claims for the method of producing the bacteria; second, claims for an inoculum comprised of a carrier material floating on water, such as straw, and the new bacteria; and third, claims to the bacteria themselves. The patent examiner allowed the claims falling into the first two categories, but rejected claims for the bacteria on the grounds that micro-organisms are products of nature, and that as living things they are not patentable subject matter under 35 U.S.C. §101. The Court of Customs and Patent Appeals eventually reversed that decision, and the case went to the Supreme Court, which affirmed the appellate decision.]

The question before us in this case is a narrow one of statutory interpretation requiring us to construe 35 U.S.C. §101, which provides: "Whoever invents or discovers any new and useful process, machine, manufacture, or composition of matter, or any new and useful improvement thereof, may obtain a patent therefor, subject to the conditions and requirements of this title." Specifically, we must determine whether respondent's micro-organism constitutes a "manufacture" or "composition of matter" within the meaning of the statute. . . .

[T]his Court has read the term "manufacture" in §101 in accordance with its dictionary definition to mean "the production of articles for use from raw or prepared materials by giving to these materials new forms, qualities, properties, or combinations, whether by hand-labor or by machinery." Similarly, "composition of matter" has been construed consistent with its common usage to include "all compositions of two or more substances and . . . all composite articles, whether they be the results of chemical union, or of mechanical mixture, or whether they be gases, fluids, powders or solids." In choosing such expansive terms as "manufacture" and "composition of matter," modified by the comprehensive "any," Congress plainly contemplated that the patent laws would be given wide scope.

The relevant legislative history also supports a broad construction. The Patent Act of 1793, authored by Thomas Jefferson, defined statutory subject matter as "any new and useful art, machine, manufacture, or composition of matter, or any new or useful improvement [thereof]." The Act embodied Jefferson's philosophy that "ingenuity should receive a liberal encouragement." Subsequent patent statutes in 1836, 1870 and 1874 employed this same broad language. In 1952, when the patent laws were recodified, Congress replaced the word "art" with "process," but otherwise left Jefferson's language intact. The Committee Reports accompanying the 1952 Act inform us that Congress intended statutory subject matter to "include anything under the sun that is made by man."

This is not to suggest that §101 has no limits or that it embraces every discovery. The laws of nature, physical phenomena, and abstract ideas have been held not patentable. Thus, a new mineral discovered in the earth or a new plant found in the wild is not patentable subject matter. Likewise, Einstein could not patent his celebrated law that $E=mc^2$; nor could Newton have patented the law of gravity. . . .

Judged in this light, respondent's micro-organism plainly qualifies as patentable subject matter. His claim is not to a hitherto unknown natural phenomenon, but to a nonnaturally occurring manufacture or composition of matter—a product of human ingenuity. . . . [T]he patentee has produced a new bacterium with markedly different characteristics from any found in nature and one having the potential for significant utility. His discovery is not nature's handiwork, but his own; accordingly it is patentable subject matter under §101. . . .

Two contrary arguments are advanced, neither of which we find persuasive. . . . The petitioner's first argument rests on the enactment of the 1930 Plant Patent Act, which afforded patent protection to certain asexually reproduced plants, and the 1970 Plant Variety Protection Act, which authorized protection for certain sexually reproduced plants but excluded bacteria from its protection. In the petitioner's view, the passage of these Acts evidences congressional understanding that the terms "manufacture" or "composition of matter" do not include living things; if they did, the petitioner argues, neither Act would have been necessary.

We reject this argument. Prior to 1930, two factors were thought to remove plants from patent protection. The first was the belief that plants, even those artificially bred, were products of nature for purposes of the patent law. . . . The second obstacle to patent protection for plants was the fact that plants were thought not amenable to the "written description" requirement of the patent law. See 35 U.S.C. §112. Because new plants may differ from old only in color or perfume, differentiation by written description was often impossible. . . .

In enacting the Plant Patent Act, Congress addressed both of these concerns. It explained at length its belief that the work of the plant breeder "in aid of nature" was patentable invention. S. Rep. No. 315, 71st Cong., 2d Sess., 6-8 (1930); H.R. Rep. No. 1129, 71st Cong., 2d Sess., 7-9 (1930). And it relaxed the written description requirement in favor of "a description . . . as complete as is reasonably possible." 35 U.S.C. §162. No Committee or Member of Congress, however, expressed the broader view, now urged by the petitioner, that the terms "manufacture" or "composition of matter" exclude living things. . . .

Congress thus recognized that the relevant distinction was not between living and inanimate things, but between products of nature, whether living or not, and human-made inventions. Here, respondent's micro-organism is the result of human ingenuity and research. Hence, the passage of the Plant Patent Act affords the Government no support. . . .

The petitioner's second argument is that micro-organisms cannot qualify as patentable subject matter until Congress expressly authorizes such protection. His position rests on the fact that genetic technology was unforeseen when Congress enacted §101. From this it is argued that resolution of the patentability of inventions such as respondent's should be left to Congress. The legislative process, the petitioner argues, is best equipped to weigh the competing economic, social, and scientific considerations involved, and to determine whether living organisms produced by genetic engineering should receive patent protection. In support of this position, the petitioner relies on our recent holding in Parker v. Flook, 437 U.S. 584 (1978), and the statement that the judiciary "must proceed cautiously when . . . asked to extend patent rights into areas wholly unforeseen by Congress." Id. at 596.

It is, of course, correct that Congress, not the courts, must define the limits of patentability; but it is equally true that once Congress has spoken it is "the province and duty of the judicial department to say what the law is." Marbury v. Madison, 1 Cranch 137 (1803). Congress has performed its constitutional role in defining patentable subject matter in §101; we perform ours in construing the language Congress has employed. In so doing, our obligation is to take statutes as we find them, guided, if ambiguity appears, by the legislative history and statutory purpose. Here, we perceive no ambiguity. The subject-matter provisions of the patent law have been cast in broad terms to fulfill the constitutional and statutory goal of promoting "the Progress of Science and the useful Arts" with all that means for the social and economic benefits envisioned by Jefferson. Broad general language is not necessarily ambiguous when congressional objectives require broad terms.

Nothing in *Flook* is to the contrary. That case applied our prior precedents to determine that a "claim for an improved method of calculation, even when tied to a specific end use, is unpatentable subject matter under §101." 437 U.S., at 595 n.18. The Court carefully scrutinized the claim at issue to determine whether it was precluded from patent protection under "the principles underlying the prohibition against patents for 'ideas' or phenomena of nature." Id. at 593. We have done that here. *Flook* did not announce a new principle that inventions in areas not contemplated by Congress when the patent laws were enacted are unpatentable per se.

To read that concept into *Flook* would frustrate the purposes of the patent law. This Court frequently has observed that a statute is not to be confined to the "particular application[s] . . . contemplated by the legislators." Barr v. United States, 324 U.S. 83, 90 (1945). . . . This is especially true in the field of patent law. A rule that unanticipated inventions are without protection would conflict with the core concept of the patent law that anticipation undermines patentability. . . . Congress employed broad general language in drafting §101 precisely because such inventions are often unforeseeable.

To buttress his argument that petitioner, with support of *amicus*, points to grave risks that may be generated by research endeavors such as respondent's. The briefs present a gruesome parade of horribles. Scientists, among them Nobel laureates, are quoted suggesting that genetic research may pose a serious threat to the human race, or, at the very least, that the dangers are far too substantial to permit such research to proceed apace at this time. We are told that genetic research and related technological developments may spread pollution and disease, that it may result in a loss of genetic diversity, and that its practice may tend to depreciate the value of human life. These arguments are forcefully, even passionately, presented; they remind us that, at times, human ingenuity seems unable to control fully the forces it creates—that, with Hamlet, it is sometimes better "to bear those ills we have than fly to others that we know not of."

It is argued that this Court should weigh these potential hazards in considering whether respondent's invention is patentable subject matter under §101. We disagree. The grant or denial of patents on micro-organisms is not likely to put an end to genetic research or to its attendant risks. The large amount of research that has already occurred when no researcher had sure knowledge that patent protection would be available suggests that legislative or judicial fiat as to patentability will not deter the scientific mind from probing into the unknown any more than Canute could command the tides. Whether respondent's claims are patentable may determine whether research efforts are accelerated by the hope of reward or slowed by want of incentives, but that is all.

What is more important is that we are without competence to entertain these arguments—either to brush them aside as fantasies generated by fear of the unknown, or to act on them. The choice we are urged to make is a matter of high policy for resolution within the legislative process after the kind of investigation, examination, and study that legislative bodies can provide and courts cannot.

JUSTICE BRENNAN, with whom JUSTICE WHITE, JUSTICE MARSHALL, and JUSTICE POWELL join, dissenting.

. . . The patent laws attempt to reconcile this Nation's deep seated antipathy to monopolies with the need to encourage progress. . . . Given the complexity and legislative nature of this delicate task, we must be careful to extend patent protection no further than Congress has provided. In particular, were there an absence of legislative direction, the courts should leave to Congress the decisions whether and how far to extend the patent privilege into areas where the common understanding has been that patents are not available.

In this case, however, we do not confront a complete legislative vacuum. The sweeping language of the Patent Act of 1793, as re-enacted in 1952, is not the last pronouncement Congress has made in this area. In 1930 Congress enacted the Plant Patent Act affording patent protection to developers of certain asexually reproduced plants. In 1970 Congress enacted the Plant Variety Protection Act to extend protection to certain new plant varieties capable of sexual reproduction. Thus, we are not dealing—as the Court would have it—with the routine problem of "unanticipated inventions." . . . In these two Acts Congress has addressed the general problem of patenting animate inventions and has chosen carefully limited language granting protection to some kinds of discoveries, but specifically excluding others. These Acts strongly evidence a congressional limitation that excludes bacteria from patentability.

The Acts evidence Congress' understanding, at least since 1930, that §101 does not include living organisms. If newly developed living organisms not naturally occurring had been patentable under §101, the plants included in the scope of the 1930 and 1970 Acts could have been patented without new legislation. Those plants, like the bacteria involved in this case, were new varieties not naturally occurring. . . . I cannot share the Court's implicit assumption that Congress was engaged in either idle exercises or mere correction of the public record when it enacted the 1930 and 1970 Acts. . . . Because Congress thought it had to legislate in order to make agricultural "human-made inventions" patentable and because the legislation Congress enacted is limited, it follows that Congress never meant to make items outside the scope of the legislation patentable. . . .

Congress plainly has legislated in the belief that §101 does not encompass living organisms. It is the role of Congress, not this Court, to broaden or narrow the reach of the patent laws. This is especially true where, as here, the composition sought to be patented uniquely implicates matters of public concern.

NOTES AND QUESTIONS

1. *Aftermath.* The patent on Dr. Chakrabarty's invention was finally issued in March 1981. In the meantime, General Electric, which owned the patent, had announced that new techniques had made Chakrabarty's invention obsolete and that the company had no plans to develop his method.

2. Chakrabarty *and the then-nascent biotechnology industry. Chakrabarty* is important, among other reasons, because it provided a significant boost to the biotechnology industry, which was then in its nascent stage. In holding that a living, genetically altered microorganism constituted a patentable subject matter, the Supreme Court opened the door to subsequent waves of patent applications involving rapid advances in biotechnology. Prior to *Chakrabarty*, the patentability of genetically engineered organisms had seemed doubtful because of the long-established exclusion for "products of nature." See Funk Bros. Seed Co. v. Kalo Inoculant Co., 333 U.S. 127 (1948). *Chakrabarty* put those doubts to rest.

3. After *Chakrabarty*, what counts as a "product of nature"? The Supreme Court addressed that issue in Association for Molecular Pathology v. Myriad Genetics, Inc., 133 S. Ct. 2107 (2013). Myriad discovered genetic mutations that were associated with substantially elevated risks of breast and ovarian cancers. Myriad then obtained patents on the DNA sequences whose presence indicated a heightened cancer risk. The Court held that isolating a sequence that already existed in human DNA did not satisfy *Chakrabarty*'s requirements. "In *Chakrabarty*, scientists added four plasmids to a bacterium, which enabled it to break down various components of crude oil. . . . In this case, by contrast, Myriad did not create anything. To be sure, it found an important and useful gene, but separating that gene from its surrounding genetic material is not an act of invention." 133 S. Ct. at 2117. *Myriad* was not a total defeat for its namesake, though. Coding exons and adjacent non-coding introns combine to form human DNA, and Myriad also had removed the introns from naturally occurring DNA sequences, resulting in cDNA sequences that do not appear naturally in the human body. The Court held that such cDNA could be patented: "[T]he lab technician unquestionably creates something new when cDNA is made. cDNA retains the naturally occurring exons of DNA, but it is distinct from the DNA from which it was derived." 133 S. Ct. at 2119. In a footnote, the Court mentioned that inventors seeking to patent cDNA would still need to establish other elements of patentability such as novelty, non-obviousness, and specification. 133 S. Ct. at 2119 n.9. Creators of novel cDNA sequences may encounter particular difficulties satisfying patent law's non-obviousness requirement.

4. *Institutional competence.* The majority and dissent agree that whether living things can be patented is the sort of difficult philosophical and economic question that should be decided by Congress, not the courts. But the justices have differing assessments of what follows from that assumption. If the courts wish to maximize the likelihood of serious congressional investigation into a novel and important issue in property law or intellectual property law, what should they do? Should they recognize the ambiguous property right, as the majority did, or refuse to recognize such a right, as the dissent urged? Is the legislature more likely to create a property right that a court said was nonexistent under an existing statute or to abrogate a property right that the court said already exists? Constitutional provisions discussed in Chapter 12 also may affect the calculus.

A BRIEF NOTE ON TRADEMARKS

Volkswagen's VW, Nike's swoosh, Pepsi-Cola's script-written name, and M&M's slogan, "melts in your mouth, not in your hand"—all are examples of trademarks. Trademarks have been around almost as long as trade itself. (Potters' marks, for example, have been found on artifacts from ancient civilizations in China, India, Greece, Egypt, and elsewhere, dating back as far as 4,000 years.)

Originally, trademark protection in the United States was a matter of the state common law of unfair competition. This common law foundation is now supplemented by the federal Lanham Act, amended several times over the years. The act allows a trademark owner to register the mark, but registration is not required for the mark's validity. Under the act, a trademark refers to any "word, name, symbol, or device" used to identify particular goods and their source. Trademark law protects the first person or entity to use a distinctive mark in commerce (the first-in-time principle again). In contrast to copyright and patent law, trademark law depends not at all "upon . . . invention, discovery, or any work of the brain." Trade-Mark Cases, 100 U.S. 82, 94 (1879). The chief purposes of trademark protection are to prevent consumer confusion about the origin of the goods or service, to encourage trademark owners to invest in and maintain a consistent level of quality in the goods they produce, and to prevent competitors from freeriding on the goodwill achieved by others.

Generally speaking, three requirements must be met for trademark protection: distinctiveness, non-functionality, and first use in trade. *Distinctiveness* requires that the mark distinguish the goods or services of one person from those of another. The Lanham Act categorizes marks according to varying degrees of distinctiveness. *Non-functionality* reflects the fact that patent law protects goods on the basis of functionality. Hence, if an aspect of a good is exclusively functional, it cannot be protected by trademark law. A product feature is considered functional "if it is essential to the use or purpose of the article or if it affects the cost or quality of the article, that is, if exclusive use of the feature would put competitors at a significant non-reputation-related disadvantage." Qualitex Co. v. Jacobson Prods. Co., Inc., 514 U.S. 159, 165 (1995). Finally, the *first use in trade* requirement means that the exclusive right to a mark depends on first actual use in commerce, as opposed to first adoption. There are important analytical similarities between trademark rights and rights of publicity. Both regimes are considered below.

2. Property in One's Persona (the Right of Publicity)

According to George M. Armstrong, Jr., The Reification of Celebrity: Persona as Property, 51 La. L. Rev. 443 (1991):

> Only two decades ago a celebrity had no cause of action against an advertiser who imitated her voice. Until the 1970's any commercial value associated with celebrity was personal to the star and entered the public domain at death. As recently as the early 1950's celebrities could not

assign the right to use their name and likeness. At the beginning of this century the law denied relief even to the living person whose name or likeness was the object of illicit appropriation.

Things are different now. About half the states now recognize (by legislation or judicial decision) a right of publicity as a kind of property interest, assignable during life, descendible at death. The right of publicity forbids unauthorized commercial use of one's name, likeness, and other aspects of one's "identity." The right of publicity seems to be rooted in the right of privacy. Judge Richard Posner observes that the courts first recognized an explicit right of privacy in a case where the defendant, without consent, used the plaintiff's name and picture in an advertisement. "Paradoxically, this branch of the right of privacy is most often invoked by celebrities avid for publicity . . . ; they just want to make sure they get the highest possible price for the use of their name and picture." Richard A. Posner, Economic Analysis of Law 57 (8th ed. 2011).

An ongoing concern with intellectual property rights—whether patents, copyrights, trademarks, or rights of publicity—is the risk of going too far, protecting too much, at unnecessary cost to the public. Consider the following.

White v. Samsung Electronics America, Inc.

United States Court of Appeals
Ninth Circuit, 1992
971 F.2d 1395

GOODWIN, J. This case involves a promotional "fame and fortune" dispute. . . . Plaintiff Vanna White is the hostess of "Wheel of Fortune," one of the most popular game shows in television history. An estimated forty million people watch the program daily. Capitalizing on the fame which her participation in the show has bestowed on her, White markets her identity to various advertisers.

The dispute in this case arose out of a series of advertisements prepared for Samsung by Deutsch. The series ran in at least half a dozen publications with widespread, and in some cases national, circulation. Each of the advertisements in the series followed the same theme. Each depicted a current item from popular culture and a Samsung electronic product. Each was set in the twenty-first century and conveyed the message that the Samsung product would still be in use by that time. By hypothesizing outrageous future outcomes for the cultural items, the ads created humorous effects. For example, one lampooned current popular notions of an unhealthy diet by depicting a raw steak with the caption: "Revealed to be health food. 2010 A.D."

The advertisement which prompted the current dispute was for Samsung video-cassette recorders (VCRs). The ad depicted a robot, dressed in a wig, gown, and jewelry which Deutsch consciously selected to resemble White's hair and dress. The robot was posed next to a game board which is instantly recognizable as the Wheel of Fortune game show set, in a stance for which White is famous. The caption of the ad read: "Longest-running game show. 2012 A.D." Defendants referred to the ad as the "Vanna White" ad. Unlike the other celebrities used in the campaign, White neither consented to the ads nor was she paid.

Following the circulation of the robot ad, White sued Samsung and Deutsch in federal district court under: (1) California Civil Code §3344; (2) the California common law right of publicity; and (3) §43(a) of the Lanham Act, 15 U.S.C. §1125(a). The district court granted summary judgment against White on each of her claims. White now appeals.

I. Section 3344

White first argues that the district court erred in rejecting her claim under section 3344. Section 3344(a) provides, in pertinent part, that "any person who knowingly uses another's name, voice, signature, photograph, or likeness, in any manner, . . . for purposes of advertising or selling, . . . without such person's prior consent . . . shall be liable for any damages sustained by the person or persons injured as a result thereof."

White argues that the Samsung advertisement used her "likeness" in contravention of section 3344. . . . Samsung and Deutsch used a robot with mechanical features, and not, for example, a manikin molded to White's precise features. Without deciding for all purposes when a caricature or impressionistic resemblance might become a "likeness," we agree with the district court that the robot at issue here was not White's "likeness" within the meaning of section 3344. Accordingly, we affirm the court's dismissal of White's section 3344 claim.

II. Right of Publicity

White next argues that the district court erred in granting summary judgment to defendants on White's common law right of publicity claim. In Eastwood v. Superior Court, 198 Cal. Rptr. 342 (Cal. App. 1983), the California court of appeal stated that the common law right of publicity cause of action "may be pleaded by alleging (1) the defendant's use of the plaintiff's identity; (2) the appropriation of plaintiff's name or likeness to defendant's advantage, commercially or otherwise; (3) lack of consent; and (4) resulting injury." Id. at 417 (citing Prosser, Law of Torts (4th ed. 1971) §117, pp. 804-807). The district court dismissed White's claim for failure to satisfy Eastwood's second prong, reasoning that defendants had not appropriated White's "name or likeness" with their robot ad. We agree that the robot ad did not make use of White's name or likeness. However, the common law right of publicity is not so confined. . . .

The "name or likeness" formulation referred to in Eastwood originated not as an element of the right of publicity cause of action, but as a description of the types of cases in which the cause of action had been recognized. The source of this formulation is Prosser, Privacy, 48 Cal. L. Rev. 383, 401-07 (1960), one of the earliest and most enduring articulations of the common law right of publicity cause of action. In looking at the case law to that point, Prosser recognized that right of publicity cases involved one of two basic factual scenarios: name appropriation, and picture or other likeness appropriation. . . .

Even though Prosser focused on appropriations of name or likeness in discussing the right of publicity, he noted that "it is not impossible that there might be appropriation of the plaintiff's identity, as by impersonation, without the use of either his name or his likeness, and that this would be an invasion of his right of privacy." Id. at 401, n.155. At the time Prosser wrote, he noted however, that "no such case appears to have arisen." Id.

Since Prosser's early formulation, the case law has borne out his insight that the right of publicity is not limited to the appropriation of name or likeness. . . .

In Carson v. Here's Johnny Portable Toilets, Inc., 698 F.2d 831 (6th Cir. 1983), the defendant had marketed portable toilets under the brand name "Here's Johnny"—Johnny Carson's signature "Tonight Show" introduction—without Carson's permission. The district court had dismissed Carson's Michigan common law right of publicity claim because the defendants had not used Carson's "name or likeness." Id. at 835. In reversing the district court, the sixth circuit found "the district court's conception of the right of publicity . . . too narrow" and held that the right was implicated because the defendant had appropriated Carson's identity by using, inter alia, the phrase "Here's Johnny." Id. at 835-37.

The cases teach not only that the common law right of publicity reaches means of appropriation other than name or likeness, but that the specific means of appropriation are relevant only for determining whether the defendant has in fact appropriated the plaintiff's identity. The right of publicity does not require that appropriations of identity be accomplished through particular means to be actionable. . . .

. . . As the *Carson* court explained: "the right of publicity has developed to protect the commercial interest of celebrities in their identities. The theory of the right is that a celebrity's identity can be valuable in the promotion of products, and the celebrity has an interest that may be protected from the unauthorized commercial exploitation of that identity. . . . If the celebrity's identity is commercially exploited, there has been an invasion of his right whether or not his "name or likeness" is used. *Carson*, 698 F.2d at 835.

It is not important how the defendant has appropriated the plaintiff's identity, but whether the defendant has done so. . . . A rule which says that the right of publicity can be infringed only through the use of nine different methods of appropriating identity merely challenges the clever advertising strategist to come up with the tenth.

Indeed, if we treated the means of appropriation as dispositive in our analysis of the right of publicity, we would not only weaken the right but effectively eviscerate it. The right would fail to protect those plaintiffs most in need of its protection. Advertisers use celebrities to promote their products. The more popular the celebrity, the greater the number of people who recognize her, and the greater the visibility for the product. The identities of the most popular celebrities are not only the most attractive for advertisers, but also the easiest to evoke without resorting to obvious means such as name, likeness, or voice. . . .

Viewed separately, the individual aspects of the advertisement in the present case say little. Viewed together, they leave little doubt about the celebrity the ad is meant to depict. The female-shaped robot is wearing a long gown, blond wig, and large jewelry. Vanna White dresses exactly like this at times, but so do many other women. The robot is in the process of turning a block letter on a game-board. Vanna White dresses like this while turning letters on a game-board but perhaps similarly attired Scrabble-playing women do this as well. The robot is standing on what looks to be the Wheel of Fortune game show set. Vanna White dresses like this, turns letters, and does this on the Wheel of Fortune game show. She is the only one. Indeed, defendants themselves referred to their ad as the "Vanna White" ad. We are not surprised.

Television and other media create marketable celebrity identity value. Considerable energy and ingenuity are expended by those who have achieved celebrity value to exploit it for profit. The law protects the celebrity's sole right to exploit this value whether the celebrity has achieved her fame out of rare ability, dumb luck, or a combination thereof. . . . Because White has alleged facts showing that Samsung and Deutsch had appropriated her identity, the district court erred by rejecting, on summary judgment, White's common law right of publicity claim. . . .

III.   The Lanham Act

[Under the Lanham Act, White had to show that the robot ad created a likelihood of confusion. The court concluded that the trial court erred in rejecting White's claim at the summary judgment stage, because there was a genuine issue of fact regarding a likelihood of confusion as to her endorsement; the question was one for the jury.

Judge Alarcon concurred in part and dissented in part. He would have affirmed the trial court's judgment in all respects. In his views, the protection of intellectual property issues require a balancing of competing interests (1) rewarding the investment of creators; (2) avoiding monopolies that inhibit creation by others. Hence the law usually allows the copying of an idea but protecting unique expressions of it. Samsung, he thought, clearly used the idea, but just as clearly did not appropriate White's expression of it.

The defendants in the *White* case subsequently petitioned for a rehearing, which was denied. White v. Samsung Electronic America, Inc., 989 F.2d 1512 (9th Cir. 1992), cert. denied, 508 U.S. 951 (1993). The denial of rehearing prompted the following dissent by Judge Kozinski.]

Something very dangerous is going on here. Private property, including intellectual property, is essential to our way of life. It provides an incentive for investment and innovation; it stimulates the flourishing of our culture; it protects the moral entitlements of people to the fruits of their labors. But reducing too much to private property can be bad medicine. Private land, for instance, is far more useful if separated from other private land by public streets, roads and highways. Public parks, utility rights-of-way and sewers reduce the amount of land in private hands, but vastly enhance the value of the property that remains.

So too it is with intellectual property. Overprotecting intellectual property is as harmful as underprotecting it. Creativity is impossible without a rich public domain. Nothing today, likely nothing since we tamed fire, is genuinely new: Culture, like science and technology, grows by accretion, each new creator building on the works of those who came before. Overprotection stifles the very creative forces it's supposed to nurture.

The panel's opinion is a classic case of overprotection. Concerned about what it sees as a wrong done to Vanna White, the panel majority erects a property right of remarkable and dangerous breadth: Under the majority's opinion, it's now a tort for advertisers to remind the public of a celebrity. Not to use a celebrity's name, voice, signature or likeness; not to imply the celebrity endorses a product; but simply to evoke the celebrity's image in the public's mind. This Orwellian notion withdraws far more from the public domain than prudence and common sense allow. It conflicts with the Copyright Act and the Copyright Clause. It raises serious First Amendment problems. It's bad law, and it deserves a long, hard second look. . . .

The ad that spawned this litigation starred a robot dressed in a wig, gown and jewelry reminiscent of Vanna White's hair and dress; the robot was posed next to a Wheel-of-Fortune-like game board. The caption read "Longest-running game show. 2012 A.D." The gag here, I take it, was that Samsung would still be around when White had been replaced by a robot.

Perhaps failing to see the humor, White sued, alleging Samsung infringed her right of publicity by "appropriating" her "identity." Under California law, White has the exclusive right to use her name, likeness, signature and voice for commercial purposes. But Samsung didn't use her name, voice or signature, and it certainly didn't use her likeness. The ad just wouldn't have been funny had it depicted White or someone who resembled her—the whole joke was that the game show host(ess) was a robot, not a real person. No one seeing the ad could have thought this was supposed to be White in 2012.

The district judge quite reasonably held that, because Samsung didn't use White's name, likeness, voice or signature, it didn't violate her right of publicity. Not so, says the panel majority: The California right of publicity can't possibly be limited to name and likeness. If it were, the majority reasons, a "clever advertising strategist" could avoid using White's name or likeness but nevertheless remind people of her with impunity, "effectively eviscerat[ing]" her rights. To prevent this "evisceration," the panel majority holds that the right of publicity must extend beyond name and likeness, to any "appropriation" of White's "identity"— anything that "evoke[s]" her personality.

But what does "evisceration" mean in intellectual property law? Intellectual property rights aren't like some constitutional rights, absolute guarantees protected against all kinds of interference, subtle as well as blatant. They cast no penumbras, emit no emanations: The very point of intellectual property laws is that they protect only against certain specific kinds of appropriation. I can't publish unauthorized copies of, say, Presumed Innocent; I can't make a movie out of it. But I'm perfectly free to write a book about an idealistic young prosecutor on trial for a crime he didn't commit. . . . All creators draw in part on the work of those who came before, referring to it, building on it, poking fun at it; we call this creativity, not piracy.

The majority isn't, in fact, preventing the "evisceration" of Vanna White's existing rights; it's creating a new and much broader property right, a right unknown in California law. It's replacing the existing balance between the interests of the celebrity and those of the public by a different balance, one substantially more favorable to the celebrity. Instead of having an exclusive right in her name, likeness, signature or voice, every famous person now has an exclusive right to anything that reminds the viewer of her. After all, that's all Samsung did: It used an inanimate object to remind people of White, to "evoke" [her identity].

Consider how sweeping this new right is. What is it about the ad that makes people think of White? It's not the robot's wig, clothes or jewelry; there must be ten million blond women (many of them quasi-famous) who wear dresses and jewelry like White's. It's that the robot is posed near the "Wheel of Fortune" game board. Remove the game board from the ad, and no one would think of Vanna White. But once you include the game board, anybody standing beside it—a brunette woman, a man wearing women's clothes, a monkey in a wig and gown—would evoke White's image, precisely the way the robot did. It's the "Wheel of Fortune" set, not the robot's face or dress or jewelry that evokes White's image. The panel is giving White an exclusive right not in what she looks like or who she is, but in what she does for a living.

This is entirely the wrong place to strike the balance. Intellectual property rights aren't free: They're imposed at the expense of future creators and of the public at large. . . . This is why intellectual property law is full of careful balances between what's set aside for the owner and what's left in the public domain for the rest of us: The relatively short life of patents; the longer, but finite, life of copyrights; copyright's idea-expression dichotomy; the fair use doctrine; the prohibition on copyrighting facts; the compulsory license of television broadcasts and musical compositions; federal preemption of overbroad state intellectual property laws; the nominative use doctrine in trademark law; the right to make soundalike recordings. All of these diminish an intellectual property owner's rights. All let the public use something created by someone else. But all are necessary to maintain a free environment in which creative genius can flourish.

The intellectual property right created by the panel here has none of these essential limitations: No fair use exception; no right to parody; no idea-expression dichotomy. It impoverishes the public domain, to the detriment of future creators and the public at large. Instead of well-defined, limited characteristics such as name, likeness or voice, advertisers will now have to cope with vague claims of "appropriation of identity," claims often made by people with a wholly exaggerated sense of their own fame and significance. Future Vanna Whites might not get the chance to create their personae, because their employers may fear some celebrity will claim the persona is too similar to her own. The public will be robbed of parodies of celebrities, and our culture will be deprived of the valuable safety valve that parody and mockery create.'

Moreover, consider the moral dimension, about which the panel majority seems to have gotten so exercised. Saying Samsung "appropriated" something of White's begs the question: Should White have the exclusive right to something as broad and amorphous as her "identity"? Samsung's ad didn't simply copy White's schtick—like all parody, it created something new. True, Samsung did it to make money, but White does whatever she does to make money, too; the majority talks of "the difference between fun and profit," but in the entertainment industry fun is profit. Why is Vanna White's right to exclusive for-profit use of her persona—a persona that might not even be her own creation, but that of a writer, director or producer—superior to Samsung's right to profit by creating its own inventions? Why should she have such absolute rights to control the conduct of others, unlimited by the idea-expression dichotomy or by the fair use doctrine?

Finally, I can't see how giving White the power to keep others from evoking her image in the public's mind can be squared with the First Amendment. Where does White get this right to control our thoughts? The majority's creation goes way beyond the protection given a trademark or a copyrighted work, or a person's name or likeness. All those things control one particular way of expressing an idea, one way of referring to an object or a person. But not allowing any means of reminding people of someone? That's a speech restriction unparalleled in First Amendment law. . . .

For better or worse, we are the Court of Appeals for the Hollywood Circuit. Millions of people toil in the shadow of the law we make, and much of their livelihood is made possible by the existence of intellectual property rights. But much of their livelihood—and much of the vibrancy of our culture—also depends on the existence of other intangible rights: The right to draw ideas from a rich and varied public domain, and the right to mock, for profit as well as fun, the cultural icons of our time.

NOTES AND QUESTIONS

1. *The posthumous right of publicity.* In many jurisdictions, the right of publicity persists after death (for 20 to 100 years, depending on the state), and can descend by will or intestacy. Most states extend the right of publicity to everyone, although usually it has substantial value only to celebrities—even (or especially!) dead ones. For some time, Forbes has issued annual reports on the top-earning dead celebrities. For example, "13 famous names . . . earned a combined $194 million over the last 12 months," according to the report released in October 2008. The king of the hill most years has been Elvis Presley; "without so much as lifting a finger, the Memphis Flash earned a whopping $52 million in the last year." (But bear in mind that much postmortem celebrity income will owe to royalties, not to publicity rights.)

2. *The right of publicity and the First Amendment.* The interplay between the right of publicity and the First Amendment has led to mixed messages from the courts. In one case, Tiger Woods sued a company that marketed copies of a painting that commemorated Woods's win in the 1997 Masters golf tournament. The painting

showed three views of Woods in different poses in the foreground, with images of the clubhouse and past Masters winners in the background. The Sixth Circuit rejected Woods's right of publicity claim, holding that the artistic aspect of the painting gave it First Amendment protection. ETW Corp. v. Jireh Publishing, Inc., 332 F.3d 915 (6th Cir. 2003). Previously, the Supreme Court held that the First Amendment did not bar a right of publicity lawsuit brought by "the human cannonball," Hugo Zacchini, against a television station that broadcast his act of being fired 200 feet through the air. Zacchini v. Scripps-Howard Broadcasting Co., 433 U.S. 562 (1977).

3.   Property in One's Person (Body Parts)

Remember the foundation of Locke's labor theory of property, stated on page 14: "every man has a property in his own person." Slavery, obviously, was in opposition to that proposition (and so, it appears, were some of Locke's activities), but slavery has been abolished. So, can we now say, without qualification, that you have property in yourself? Consider the following case.

Moore v. Regents of the University of California
Supreme Court of California, 1990
793 P.2d 479, cert. denied, 499 U.S. 936 (1991)

[*Background*: In 1976 John Moore sought treatment for hairy-cell leukemia at the Medical Center of the University of California, Los Angeles. (We shall at times refer to the doctors at the Center and to the Regents of the University who own the Center collectively as "defendants.") The defendants conducted tests, took blood and tissue samples, confirmed the diagnosis, and told Moore that his condition was life-threatening and that his spleen should be removed. What they did not tell Moore was that his cells were unique and that access to them was of great scientific and commercial value.

Moore consented to the splenectomy and to some seven years of follow-up tests and procedures that he was led to believe were important to his treatment. His spleen was retained for research purposes without his knowledge or consent, and during the post-operative period samples of tissue and blood and other fluids were taken on each of Moore's visits. At some point Moore was informed that his bodily substances were being used for research, but he was never informed of the commercial value of the research or of the defendants' financial interest in it. The defendants subsequently established a cell line from Moore's cells (named the Mo cell line, after Moore), received a patent for it, and entered into various commercial agreements. Hundreds of thousands of dollars had been paid to the defendants under these agreements by the mid-1980s, and the potential market for products from Moore's cell line is estimated to run into the billions of dollars.

Moore sued for damages in 1984, his complaint stating a number of causes of action, including conversion (wrongful exercise of ownership rights over the personal property of another; Moore alleged that his blood and bodily substances, and the cell line derived from them, were "his tangible personal property"), lack of informed consent, breach of fiduciary duty, fraud and deceit, unjust enrichment, intentional infliction of emotional distress, negligent misrepresentation, and others. The trial court sustained the defendants' demurrers to the conversion cause of action and held that because the conversion cause of action was incorporated into all the other causes of action, those too were defective.

The court of appeal reversed, finding that Moore had adequately stated a cause of action for conversion. Moore v. Regents of the University of California, 249 Cal. Rptr. 494 (Cal. App. 1988). The court could find "no legal authority, public policy, nor universally known facts of biological science . . . which compel a conclusion that this plaintiff cannot have a sufficient legal interest in his own bodily tissues amounting to personal property. Absent plaintiff's consent to defendants' disposition of the tissues, or lawful justification, such as abandonment, the complaint adequately pleads all the elements of a cause of action for conversion."

"We have approached this issue with caution," the court said. "The evolution of civilization from slavery to freedom, from regarding people as chattels to recognition of the individual dignity of each person, necessitates prudence in attributing the qualities of property to human tissue. There is, however, a dramatic difference between having property rights in one's own body and being the property of another. . . . We are not called on to determine whether use of human tissue or body parts ought to be 'gift based' or subject to a 'free market.' That question of policy must be determined by the Legislature. In the instant case, the cell line has already been commercialized by defendants. We are presented a *fait accompli*, leaving only the question of who shares in the proceeds. . . ."

The court then considered the meaning of property and concluded that the essential element is dominion, or rights of use, control, and disposition. It went on to discuss the "many cases" (involving search and seizure, consent to medical procedures, rights to dead bodies, and other instances) that recognize "rights of dominion over one's own body, and the interests one has therein. . . . These rights and interests are so akin to property interests that it would be a subterfuge to call them something else."

The court concluded by dealing with a series of contentions by defendants. There were no grounds to infer that Moore had abandoned his tissue or consented to its use in research unrelated to his treatment. And the fact that the defendants' skill and effort had enhanced the value of Moore's tissue went not to the issue of conversion but to the measure of damages for the conversion. "Plaintiff's cells and genes are a part of his person," the court said, citing the right of publicity cases that "'afford legal protection to an individual's proprietary interest in his own identity.'" To hold that patients do not have the ultimate power to control the destiny of their tissues "would open the door to a massive invasion of human privacy and dignity in the name of medical progress." The court saw no

Pages from the Mo Cell Line Patent

reason to believe that medical research would suffer by requiring the consent of the donor of tissue before it can be appropriated. True, a potential donor, once informed, might refuse consent, but the court "would give the patient that right. As to defendants' concern that a patient might seek the greatest economic gain for his participation, this argument is unpersuasive because it fails to explain why defendants . . . are any more to be trusted with these momentous decisions than the person whose cells are being used." If giving patients a financial interest in their tissues inhibited donations and increased the costs of medical care, that problem could be addressed by the legislature.

Upon petition by the defendants, the court of appeal's judgment was reviewed by the California Supreme Court. The case takes up 65 pages of the official reporter; what follows is the essence of the views stated, particularly regarding the cause of action for conversion.]

PANELLI, J. We granted review in this case to determine whether plaintiff has stated a cause of action against his physician and other defendants for using his cells in potentially lucrative medical research without his permission. . . . We hold that the complaint states a cause of action for breach of the physician's disclosure obligations, but not for conversion. . . .

A.   Breach of Fiduciary Duty and Lack of Informed Consent

Moore repeatedly alleges that Golde [the attending physician] failed to disclose the extent of his research and economic interests in Moore's cells before obtaining consent to the medical procedures by which the cells were extracted. These allegations, in our view, state a cause of action against Golde for invading a legally protected interest of his patient. This cause of action can properly be characterized either as the breach of a fiduciary duty to disclose facts material to the patient's consent or, alternatively, as the performance of medical procedures without first having obtained the patient's informed consent. . . .

B.   Conversion

Moore also attempts to characterize the invasion of his rights as a conversion—a tort that protects against interference with possessory and ownership interests in personal property. He theorizes that he continued to own his cells following their removal from his body, at least for the purpose of directing their use, and that he never consented to their use in potentially lucrative medical research. . . . As a result of the alleged conversion, Moore claims a proprietary interest in each of the products that any of the defendants might ever create from his cells or the patented cell line.

No court, however, has ever in a reported decision imposed conversion liability for the use of human cells in medical research. While that fact does not end our inquiry, it raises a flag of caution. In effect, what Moore is asking us to do is to impose a tort duty on scientists to investigate the consensual pedigree of each human cell sample used in research. To impose such a duty, which would affect medical research of importance to all of society, implicates policy concerns far removed from the traditional, two-party ownership disputes in which the law of conversion arose. . . .

[W]e first consider whether the tort of conversion clearly gives Moore a cause of action under existing law. We do not believe it does. . . .

Since Moore clearly did not expect to retain possession of his cells following their removal, to sue for their conversion he must have retained an ownership interest in them. But there are several reasons to doubt that he did retain any such interest. First, no reported judicial decision supports Moore's claim, either directly or by close analogy. Second, California statutory law drastically limits any continuing interest of a patient in excised cells. Third, the subject matters of the Regents' patent—the patented cell line and the products derived from it—cannot be Moore's property.

Neither the Court of Appeal's opinion, the parties' briefs, nor our research discloses a case holding that a person retains a sufficient interest in excised cells to support a cause of action for conversion. We do not find this surprising, since the laws governing such things as human tissues, transplantable organs, blood, fetuses, pituitary glands, corneal tissue, and dead bodies deal with human biological materials as objects sui generis, regulating their disposition to achieve policy goals rather than abandoning them to the general law of personal property. . . . Lacking direct authority for importing the law of conversion into this context, Moore relies, as did the Court of Appeal, primarily on decisions addressing privacy rights. One line of cases involves unwanted publicity. These [cases] hold that every person has a proprietary interest in his own likeness and that unauthorized, business use of a likeness is redressible as a tort. . . .

Not only are the wrongful-publicity cases irrelevant to the issue of conversion, but the analogy to them seriously misconceives the nature of the genetic materials and research involved in this case. Moore . . . argues that "[i]f the courts have found a sufficient proprietary interest in one's persona, how could one not have a right in one's own genetic material, something far more profoundly the essence of one's human uniqueness than a name or a face?" However, as the defendants' patent makes clear—and the complaint, too, if read with an understanding of the scientific terms which it has borrowed from the patent—the goal and result of defendants' efforts has been to manufacture lymphokines. Lymphokines, unlike a name or a face, have the same molecular structure in every human being and the same important functions in every human being's immune system. Moreover, the particular genetic material which is responsible for the natural production of lymphokines, and which defendants use to manufacture lymphokines in the laboratory, is also the same in every person; it is no more unique to Moore than the number of vertebrae in the spine or the chemical formula of hemoglobin.

. . . [T]he Court of Appeal in this case concluded that "[a] patient must have the ultimate power to control what becomes of his or her tissues. To hold otherwise would open the door to a massive invasion of human privacy and dignity in the name of medical progress." Yet one may earnestly wish to protect privacy and dignity without accepting the extremely problematic conclusion that interference with those interests amounts to a conversion of personal property. Nor is it necessary to force the round pegs of "privacy" and "dignity" into the square hole of "property" in order to protect the patient, since the fiduciary-duty and informed-consent theories protect these interests directly by requiring full disclosure.

The next consideration that makes Moore's claim of ownership problematic is California statutory law, which drastically limits a patient's control over excised cells. Pursuant to Health and Safety Code section 7054.4, "[n]otwithstanding any other provision of law, recognizable anatomical parts, human tissues, anatomical human remains, or infectious waste following conclusion of scientific use shall be disposed of by interment, incineration, or any other method determined by the state department [of health services] to protect the public health and safety." Clearly the Legislature did not specifically intend this statute to resolve the question of whether a patient is entitled to compensation for the nonconsensual use of excised cells. A primary object of the statute is to ensure the safe handling of potentially hazardous biological waste materials. Yet one cannot escape the conclusion that the statute's practical effect is to limit, drastically, a patient's control over excised cells. By restricting how excised cells may be used and requiring their eventual destruction, the statute eliminates so many of the rights ordinarily attached to property that one cannot simply assume that what is left amounts to "property" or "ownership" for purposes of conversion law. . . .

Finally, the subject matter of the Regents' patent—the patented cell line and the products derived from it—cannot be Moore's property. This is because the patented cell line is both factually and legally distinct from the cells taken from Moore's body. Federal law permits the patenting of organisms that represent the product of "human ingenuity," but not naturally occurring organisms. . . . It is this *inventive effort* that patent law rewards, not the discovery of naturally occurring raw materials. Thus, Moore's allegations that he owns the cell line and the products derived from it are inconsistent with the patent, which constitutes an authoritative determination that the cell line is the product of invention. . . .

[Having concluded that Moore's claim found no support under the existing law of conversion, the majority considered whether the law of conversion should be extended to allow the claim.]

. . . There are three reasons why it is inappropriate to impose liability for conversion based upon the allegations of Moore's complaint. First, a fair balancing of the relevant policy considerations counsels against extending the tort. Second, problems in this area are better suited to legislative resolution. Third, the tort of conversion is not necessary to protect patients' rights. For these reasons, we conclude that the use of excised human cells in medical research does not amount to a conversion.

Of the relevant policy considerations, two are of overriding importance. The first is protection of a competent patient's right to make autonomous medical decisions. . . . The second important policy consideration is that we not threaten with disabling civil liability innocent parties who are engaged in socially useful activities, such as researchers who have no reason to believe that their use of a particular cell sample is, or may be, against a donor's wishes. . . .

Indeed, so significant is the potential obstacle to research stemming from uncertainty about legal title to biological materials that the Office of Technology Assessment reached this striking conclusion: "[R]egardless of the merit of claims by the different interested parties, resolving the current uncertainty may be more important to the future of biotechnology than resolving it in any particular way." . . .

We need not, however, make an arbitrary choice between liability and nonliability. Instead, an examination of the relevant policy considerations suggests an appropriate balance: Liability based upon existing disclosure obligations, rather than an unprecedented extension of the conversion theory, protects patients' rights of privacy and autonomy without unnecessarily hindering research.

To be sure, the threat of liability for conversion might help to enforce patients' rights indirectly. This is because physicians might be able to avoid liability by obtaining patients' consent, in the broadest possible terms, to any conceivable subsequent research use of excised cells. Unfortunately, to extend the conversion theory would utterly sacrifice the other goal of protecting innocent parties. Since conversion is a strict liability tort, it would impose liability on all those into whose hands the cells come, whether or not the particular defendant participated in, or knew of, the inadequate disclosures that violated the patient's right to make an informed decision. In contrast to the conversion theory, the fiduciary-duty and informed-consent theories protect the patient directly, without punishing innocent parties or creating disincentives to the conduct of socially beneficial research.

Research on human cells plays a critical role in medical research. This is so because researchers are increasingly able to isolate naturally occurring, medically useful biological substances and to produce useful quantities of such substances through genetic engineering. . . . The extension of conversion law into this area will hinder research by restricting access to the necessary raw materials. Thousands of human cell lines already exist in tissue repositories. . . . At present, human cell lines are routinely copied and distributed to other researchers for experimental purposes, usually free of charge. This exchange of scientific materials, which still is relatively free and efficient, will surely be compromised if each cell sample becomes the potential subject matter of a lawsuit.

To expand liability by extending conversion law into this area would have a broad impact. The House Committee on Science and Technology of the United States Congress found that "49 percent of the researchers at medical institutions surveyed used human tissues or cells in their research." . . . In addition, "there are nearly 350 commercial biotechnology firms in the United States actively engaged in biotechnology research and commercial product development and approximately 25 to 30 percent appear to be engaged in research to develop a human therapeutic or diagnostic reagent. . . . Most, but not all, of the human therapeutic products are derived from human tissues and cells, or human cell lines or cloned genes." . . .

In deciding whether to create new tort duties we have in the past considered the impact that expanded liability would have on activities that are important to society, such as research. . . .

[T]he theory of liability that Moore urges us to endorse threatens to destroy the economic incentive to conduct important medical research. If the use of cells in research is a conversion, then with every cell sample a researcher purchases a ticket in a litigation lottery. Because liability for conversion is predicated on a continuing ownership interest, "companies are unlikely to invest heavily in developing, manufacturing, or marketing a product when uncertainty about clear title exists." . . .

If the scientific users of human cells are to be held liable for failing to investigate the consensual pedigree of their raw materials, we believe the Legislature should make that decision. Complex policy choices affecting all society are involved, and [l]egislatures, in making such policy decisions, have the ability to gather empirical evidence, solicit the advice of experts, and hold hearings at which all interested parties present evidence and express their views. . . .

[T]here is no pressing need to impose a judicially created rule of strict liability, since enforcement of physicians' disclosure obligations will protect patients against the very type of harm with which Moore was threatened. So long as a physician discloses research and economic interests that may affect his judgment, the patient is protected from conflicts of interest. Aware of any conflicts, the patient can make an informed decision to consent to treatment, or to withhold consent and look elsewhere for medical assistance. As already discussed, enforcement of physicians' disclosure obligations protects patients directly, without hindering the socially useful activities of innocent researchers.

For these reasons, we hold that the allegations of Moore's third amended complaint state a cause of action for breach of fiduciary duty or lack of informed consent, but not conversion. . . .

Lucas, C.J., Eagleson, J., and Kennard, J., concurred.

ARABIAN, J., concurring. I join in the views cogently expounded by the majority. I write separately to give voice to a concern that I believe informs much of that opinion but finds little or no expression therein. I speak of the moral issue.

Plaintiff has asked us to recognize and enforce a right to sell one's own body tissue *for profit*. He entreats us to regard the human vessel—the single most venerated and protected subject in any civilized society—as equal with the basest commercial commodity. He urges us to commingle the sacred with the profane. He asks much. . . .

It is true, that this court has not often been deterred from deciding difficult legal issues simply because they require a choice between competing social or economic policies. . . . The difference here, however, lies in the nature of the conflicting moral, philosophical and even religious values at stake, and in the profound implications of the position urged. The ramifications of recognizing and enforcing a property interest in body tissues are not known, but are greatly feared—the effect on human dignity of a marketplace in human body parts, the impact on research and development of competitive bidding for such materials, and the exposure of researchers to potentially limitless and uncharted tort liability. . . .

Whether, as plaintiff urges, his cells should be treated as property susceptible to conversion is not, in my view, ours to decide. . . .

Where then shall a complete resolution be found? Clearly the Legislature, as the majority opinion suggests, is the proper deliberative forum. . . . Indeed, a legislative response creating a licensing scheme, which establishes a fixed rate of profit sharing between researcher and subject, has already been suggested. Such an arrangement would not only avoid the moral and philosophical objections to a free market operation in body tissue, but would also address stated concerns by eliminating the inherently coercive effect of a waiver system and by compensating donors regardless of temporal circumstances. . . .

[The concurring and dissenting opinion of Justice Broussard is omitted.]

MOSK, J. I dissent. Contrary to the principal holding of the Court of Appeal, the majority conclude that the complaint does not—in fact cannot—state a cause of action for conversion. I disagree with this conclusion for all the reasons stated by the Court of Appeal, and for additional reasons. . . .

The concepts of property and ownership in our law are extremely broad. . . .

Being broad, the concept of property is also abstract: rather than referring directly to a material object such as a parcel of land or the tractor that cultivates it, the concept of property is often said to refer to a "bundle of rights" that may be exercised with respect to that object—principally the rights to possess the property, to use the property, to exclude others from the property, and to dispose of the property by sale or by gift. . . . But the same bundle of rights does not attach to all forms of property. For a variety of policy reasons, the law limits or even forbids the exercise of certain rights over certain forms of property. For example, both law and contract may limit the right of an owner of real property to use his parcel as he sees fit. Owners of various forms of personal property may likewise be subject to restrictions on the time, place, and manner of their use. Limitations on the disposition of real property, while less common, may also be imposed. Finally, some types of personal property may be sold but not given away,[40] while others may be given away but not sold,[41] and still others may neither be given away nor sold.[42]

In each of the foregoing instances, the limitation or prohibition diminishes the bundle of rights that would otherwise attach to the property, yet what remains ·

---

40. A person contemplating bankruptcy may sell his property at its "reasonably equivalent value," but he may not make a gift of the same property.

· 41. A sportsman may give away wild fish or game that he has caught or killed pursuant to his license, but he may not sell it.

The transfer of human organs and blood is a special case discussed below.

42. E.g., a license to practice a profession, or a prescription drug in the hands of the person for whom it is prescribed.

is still deemed in law to be a protectible property interest. . . . The same rule applies to Moore's interest in his own body tissue. . . . Above all, at the time of its excision he at least had *the right to do with his own tissue whatever the defendants did with it*: i.e., he could have contracted with researchers and pharmaceutical companies to develop and exploit the vast commercial potential of his tissue and its products. . . .

Having concluded—mistakenly, in my view—that Moore has no cause of action for conversion under existing law, the majority next consider whether to "extend" the conversion cause of action to this context. Again . . . I respectfully disagree with [their reasoning].

. . . [O]ur society acknowledges a profound ethical imperative to respect the human body as the physical and temporal expression of the unique human persona. One manifestation of that respect is our prohibition against direct abuse of the body by torture or other forms of cruel or unusual punishment. Another is our prohibition against indirect abuse of the body by its economic exploitation for the sole benefit of another person. The most abhorrent form of such exploitation, of course, was the institution of slavery. Lesser forms, such as indentured servitude or even debtor's prison, have also disappeared. Yet their specter haunts the laboratories and boardrooms of today's biotechnological research-industrial complex. It arises wherever scientists or industrialists claim, as defendants claim here, the right to appropriate and exploit a patient's tissue for their sole economic benefit—the right, in other words, to freely mine or harvest valuable physical properties of the patient's body. . . .

A second policy consideration adds notions of equity to those of ethics. Our society values fundamental fairness in dealings between its members, and condemns the unjust enrichment of any member at the expense of another. This is particularly true when, as here, the parties are not in equal bargaining positions. . . . Yet defendants deny that Moore is entitled to any share whatever in the proceeds of this cell line. This is both inequitable and immoral. . . .

There will be . . . equitable sharing if the courts recognize that the patient has a legally protected property interest in his own body and its products: "property rights in one's own tissue would provide a morally acceptable result by giving effect to notions of fairness and preventing unjust enrichment. . . ."

I do not doubt that the Legislature is competent to act on this topic. The fact that the Legislature may intervene if and when it chooses, however, does not in the meanwhile relieve the courts of their duty of enforcing—or if need be, fashioning—an effective judicial remedy for the wrong here alleged. . . .

The inference I draw from the current statutory regulation of human biological materials, moreover, is the opposite of that drawn by the majority. By selective quotation of the statutes the majority seem to suggest that human organs and blood cannot legally be sold on the open market—thereby implying that if the Legislature were to act here it would impose a similar ban on monetary compensation for the use of human tissue in biotechnological research and development. But if that is the argument, the premise is unsound: contrary to popular misconception, it is not true that human organs and blood cannot legally be sold.

As to organs, the majority rely on the Uniform Anatomical Gift Act (Health & Saf. Code, §7150 et seq., hereafter the UAGA) for the proposition that a competent adult may make a post mortem gift of any part of his body but may not receive "valuable consideration" for the transfer. But the prohibition of the UAGA against the sale of a body part is much more limited than the majority recognize: by its terms the prohibition applies only to sales for "transplantation" or "therapy." Yet a different section of the UAGA authorizes the transfer and receipt of body parts for such additional purposes as "medical or dental education, research, or advancement of medical or dental science. No section of the UAGA prohibits anyone from selling body parts for any of those additional purposes; by clear implication, therefore, such sales are legal. Indeed, the fact that the UAGA prohibits *no* sales of organs other than sales for "transplantation" or "therapy" raises a further implication that it is also legal for anyone to sell human tissue to a biotechnology company for research and development purposes. . . .

The majority's final reason for refusing to recognize a conversion cause of action on these facts is that "there is no pressing need" to do so because the complaint also states another cause of action that is assertedly adequate to the task. . . .

I disagree, however, with the majority's further conclusion that in the present context a nondisclosure cause of action is an adequate—in fact, a superior—substitute for a conversion cause of action. . . .

The majority do not spell out how those obligations will be "enforced"; but because they arise from judicial decision (the majority opinion herein) rather than from legislative or administrative enactment, we may infer that the obligations will primarily be enforced by the traditional judicial remedy of an action for damages for their breach. . . .

The remedy is largely illusory. "[A]n action based on the physician's failure to disclose material information sounds in negligence. As a practical matter, however, it may be difficult to recover on this kind of negligence theory because the patient must prove a *causal connection* between his or her injury and the physician's failure to inform." (Martin & Lagod, Biotechnology and the Commercial Use of Human Cells: Toward an Organic View of Life and Technology (1989), 5 Santa Clara Computer & High Tech L.J. 211, 222, fn. omitted, italics added.) There are two barriers to recovery. First, "the patient must show that if he or she had been informed of all pertinent information, he or she would have declined to consent to the procedure in question." (Id.) . . .

The second barrier to recovery is still higher, and is erected on the first: it is not even enough for the plaintiff to prove that he personally would have refused consent to the proposed treatment if he had been fully informed; he must also prove that in the same circumstances *no reasonably prudent person* would have given such consent. . . .

The second reason why the nondisclosure cause of action is inadequate for the task that the majority assign to it is that it fails to solve half the problem before us: it gives the patient only the right to *refuse* consent, i.e., the right to prohibit the commercialization of his tissue; it does not give him the right to *grant* consent to that commercialization on the condition that he share in its proceeds. . . .

Third, the nondisclosure cause of action fails to reach a major class of potential defendants: all those who are outside the strict physician-patient relationship with the plaintiff. Thus the majority concede that here only defendant Golde, the treating physician, can be directly liable to Moore on a nondisclosure cause of action. . . .

NOTES AND QUESTIONS

1. *The rest of the story.* After losing on his conversion claim, Moore eventually resolved his remaining claims in a confidential settlement. Whatever amount he received, much of it probably went to pay attorneys' fees. Moore became an advocate for patients' rights. In 2001, his battle with cancer ended when he died at the age of 56.

2. *Another story.* "Doctors took her cells without asking. Those cells never died. They launched a medical revolution and a multimillion-dollar industry. More than twenty years later her children found out." So says the dust jacket of Rebecca Skloot's best-selling book, The Immortal Life of Henrietta Lacks (2010). Ms. Lacks, a poor black woman, died of cervical cancer in 1951; she was 31 years old. Shortly before her death, and without her knowledge or consent, doctors took some of her tumor cells. The cells (named HeLa cells) were able to live on in a laboratory, something that had never happened before; they have since been used in thousands of studies around the world. The research "yielded profound insights into cell biology, vaccines, in vitro fertilization and cancer." The Lacks family knew nothing of this until 1973, after which some of them began a long search for more information, the culmination of which is an August 2013 agreement with the National Institutes of Health that responds to the family's central concerns—privacy, and some sense of control over the use of data. Under the agreement, researchers will have to apply for access to the data and must submit annual reports about their studies. Two members of the Lacks family will be part of the N.I.H. working group that reviews applications. The agreement does not provide the family with proceeds from any commercial products developed from research on the HeLa cells. Carl Zimmer, Family Gets Role in Use of "Immortal Life" Cells, N.Y. Times, Aug. 8, 2013, at A1.

3. *A bundle of rights.* In his concurring opinion, Justice Arabian states that recognition of property rights in one's cells would necessarily entail "a right to sell one's own body tissue *for profit*." (Page 98.) But this hardly follows, as can be seen in the first few paragraphs of Justice Mosk's dissent, discussing property as "a bundle of rights." (Page 99.) According to this conception, conventional among lawyers, property entails a number of disparate rights—the right to possess, the right to use, the right to exclude, the right to transfer, etc. But in particular cases you might own property yet not have all of these rights. Consider the right to transfer. On most occasions you may sell or give away what you own, but not always. As the examples in footnotes 40-42 show, there are instances where

you may sell but not give, instances where you may give but not sell, and instances where you may do neither. Notwithstanding, we still talk about what you own as your "property."[43]

Could not the majority in *Moore* have used these observations to craft a more satisfactory opinion? If the majority had used Justice Mosk's bundle-of-rights approach, it could first have held the cells still to be Moore's property and then gone on to consider the question of alienability. Framing the matter in this way would readily allow the conclusion that because the cells were Moore's, they were not some doctor's to take, but neither were they Moore's *to sell in a market trans-action*. In other words, the majority could have limited Moore's property rights but nevertheless acknowledged and protected them through the cause of action for conversion. Concerns about the impact of conversion liability on medical research and development could in turn have been eased by an appropriately tailored measure of damages. The literature mentions any number of alternatives, such as royalties, a percentage of profits, or a lump sum.

4. *Compare* Moore *to* Chakrabarty. Recall our discussion of institutional competence in connection with Diamond v. Chakrabarty. See page 82. In *Moore*, the majority also emphasizes the importance of letting legislatures decide controversial questions about what is and isn't property, as does Justice Arabian's concurrence. But their resolution of the case—a refusal to recognize Moore's property rights—resembles the dissent in *Chakrabarty* rather than the majority. As it happens, there was no legislative override of the decision in *Moore* and rather little sustained legislative attention paid to the issue after the case was decided. The topic has received little attention in other states' legislatures as well, perhaps because the decision favored well-represented interests in biotechnology at the expense of individuals who are not part of any organized interest group and may not even realize that they have an economic stake in the issue.

5. *The problem of commodification.* There has been some legislative deliberation regarding some of the issues and concerns underlying *Moore*, as the decision shows in citing the Uniform Anatomical Gift Act, adopted in one version or another by every state in the country. The Uniform Act prohibits *sales* (that is, transfers for "valuable consideration") of body parts for purposes of transplantation or therapy (but not for purposes of research). Federal legislation takes the same tack. The National Organ Transplantation Act (NOTA), makes it "unlawful for any person to knowingly acquire, receive, or otherwise transfer any human organ for valuable consideration for use in human transplantation if the transfer affects interstate commerce." 42 U.S.C.A. §274e. Notice that the state and federal statutes implicitly recognize property rights in body parts, permitting gifts from living or cadaveric donors and even permitting sales, unless the sales are for

---

43. When sales are prohibited but gifts allowed, property is sometimes said to be market-inalienable. When the situation is reversed, one might say property is only market-alienable. When neither mode of transfer is permitted, the property is said to be inalienable. See Margaret Jane Radin, Market-Inalienability, 100 Harv. L. Rev. 1849 (1987); Susan Rose Ackerman, Inalienability and the Theory of Property Rights, 85 Colum. L. Rev. 931 (1985).

transplantation. (To use the terminology introduced in footnote 43, the regime is one of partial market-inalienability.)

The ban on sales of organs for transplantation is driven, in part at least, by a concern with commodification (recall Justice Arabian's concurring opinion). Some things, the argument runs, are not mere commodities to be trafficked in markets, for reasons (in part or entirely) of morality. So we have prohibitions of slavery, child labor, and prostitution—and sale of body parts for transplantation. But body parts for transplantation are unfortunately in short supply, and allowing market incentives could help solve the problem. But if people could sell their kidneys (each of us carries a spare), wouldn't poor people be the sellers and wealthy people the buyers? If so, are the poor being exploited, or just allowed to exercise free choice? Should there be a "means test" applied to sales of body parts, such that low-income people are excluded from the market? And so on. The problem of commodification, generally and in the particular case of body parts, is deeply difficult and divisive. See, e.g., Margaret Jane Radin, Contested Commodities (1996); Meredith M. Render, The Law of the Body, 62 Emory L.J. 549 (2013).

4. The Bundle of Rights' Frontiers: Exclusion, Abandonment, and Destruction

Earlier in this chapter (see footnote 33 on pages 51-52) we introduced Felix Cohen's notion of property as a relationship among people that entitles so-called owners to *include* (that is, permit) or *exclude* (that is, deny) use or possession of the owned property by other people; we then went on to discuss in the text the importance of free *transferability* of property rights. The materials following the *Moore* case focused on the right to include—to sell, for example, to another—but that right alone does not of itself result in a fully effective power to transfer. The right to exclude is needed as well. The two rights together are the necessary and sufficient conditions of transferability. Do you see why?

The law of trespass, introduced in Problem 1 on pages 33-34, protects the right to exclude, but then so too does the law of conversion at issue in *Moore*. Indeed, conversion developed in part as a substitute for the old action of trespass to chattels (chattels are personal property). So *Moore* can be seen to involve not just the right to include, but also the right to exclude. On that latter right, consider briefly the two cases that follow.

Jacque v. Steenberg Homes, Inc., 563 N.W.2d 154 (Wis. 1997). "Steenberg Homes had a mobile home to deliver. Unfortunately for Harvey and Lois Jacque (the Jacques), the easiest route of delivery was across their land. Despite adamant protests by the Jacques, Steenberg plowed a path through the Jacques' snow-covered field and via that path, delivered the mobile home. Consequently, the Jacques sued Steenberg Homes for intentional trespass. Although the jury awarded the Jacques $1 in nominal damages and $100,000 in punitive damages, the circuit court set aside the jury's award of $100,000. The court of appeals affirmed, reluctantly concluding that it could not reinstate the punitive damages because . . . an award of nominal damages will not sustain a punitive damage award. We conclude that when nominal damages are awarded for an intentional trespass to land, punitive damages may, in the discretion of the jury, be awarded. . . .

"Steenberg determined that the easiest route to deliver the mobile home was across the Jacques' land. . . . [T]he only alternative was a private road which was covered in up to seven feet of snow and contained a sharp curve which would require sets of 'rollers' to be used when maneuvering the home around the curve. Steenberg asked the Jacques on several occasions whether it could move the home across the Jacques' farm field. The Jacques refused. The Jacques were sensitive about allowing others on their land because they had lost property valued at over $10,000 to other neighbors in an adverse possession action in the mid-1980's.[44] Despite repeated refusals from the Jacques, Steenberg decided to sell the mobile home, which was to be used as a summer cottage, and delivered it on February 15, 1994. . . . "[Steenberg's] assistant manager asked Mr. Jacque how much money it would take to get permission. Mr. Jacque responded that it was not a question of money; the Jacques did not want Steenberg to cross their land. Mr. Jacque testified that he told Steenberg to '[F]ollow the road, that is what the road is for.' . . .

"At trial, one of Steenberg's employees testified that, upon coming out of the Jacques' home, the assistant manager stated: 'I don't give a _____ what [Mr. Jacque] said, just get the home in there any way you can.' The other Steenberg employee confirmed this testimony and further testified that the assistant manager told him to park the company truck in such a way that no one could get down the town road to see the route the employees were taking with the home. The assistant manager denied giving these instructions, and Steenberg argued that the road was blocked for safety reasons.

"The employees, after beginning down the private road, ultimately used a 'bobcat' to cut a path through the Jacques' snow-covered field and hauled the home across the Jacques' land to the neighbor's lot. One employee testified that upon returning to the office and informing the assistant manager that they had gone across the field, the assistant manager reacted by giggling and laughing. . . . When a neighbor informed the Jacques that Steenberg had, in fact, moved the mobile home across the Jacques' land, Mr. Jacque called the Manitowoc County Sheriff's Department. After interviewing the parties and observing the scene, an officer from the sheriff's department issued a $30 citation to Steenberg's assistant manager. . . .

"We turn first to the individual landowner's interest in protecting his or her land from trespass. The United States Supreme Court has recognized that the private landowner's right to exclude others from his or her land is 'one of the most essential sticks in the bundle of rights that are commonly characterized

---

44. Adverse possession is a property doctrine that permits a persistent trespasser on a parcel of land to become its owner. We discuss adverse possession at great length in Chapter 2. — EDS.

as property.' Kaiser Aetna v. United States, 444 U.S. 164, 176 (1979). . . . This court has long recognized '[e]very person['s] right to the exclusive enjoyment of his own property for any purpose which does not invade the rights of another person.' Diana Shooting Club v. Lamoreux, 114 Wis. 44, 59, 89 N.W. 880 (1902).

"Yet a right is hollow if the legal system provides insufficient means to protect it. . . . Harvey and Lois Jacque have the right to tell Steenberg Homes and any other trespasser, 'No, you cannot cross our land.' But that right has no practical meaning unless protected by the State, [and a nominal dollar] does not constitute state protection.

". . . A series of intentional trespasses, as the Jacques had the misfortune to discover in an unrelated action, can threaten the individual's very ownership of land.

"In sum, the individual has a strong interest in excluding trespassers from his or her land. . . .

"Society has an interest in punishing and deterring intentional trespassers beyond that of protecting the interests of the individual landowner. Society has an interest in preserving the integrity of the legal system. Private landowners should feel confident that wrongdoers who trespass upon their land will be appropriately punished. When landowners have confidence in the legal system, they are less likely to resort to 'self-help' remedies. . . ."

State v. Shack, 277 A.2d 369 (N.J. 1971). "Defendants entered upon private property to aid migrant farmworkers employed and housed there. Having refused to depart upon the demand of the owner, defendants [were convicted of trespassing].

"Before us, no one seeks to sustain these convictions. The complaints were prosecuted in the Municipal Court and in the County Court by counsel engaged by the complaining landowner, Tedesco. However Tedesco did not respond to this appeal, and the county prosecutor, while defending abstractly the constitutionality of the trespass statute, expressly disclaimed any position as to whether the statute reached the activity of these defendants.

"Complainant, Tedesco, a farmer, employs migrant workers for his seasonal needs. As part of their compensation, these workers are housed at a camp on his property.

"Defendant Tejeras is a field worker for the Farm Workers Division of the Southwest Citizens Organization for Poverty Elimination, known by the acronym SCOPE, a nonprofit corporation funded by the Office of Economic Opportunity pursuant to an act of Congress, 42 U.S.C.A. §§2861-2864. The role of SCOPE includes providing for the 'health services of the migrant farm worker.'

"Defendant Shack is a staff attorney with the Farm Workers Division of Camden Regional Legal Services, Inc., known as 'CRLS,' also a nonprofit corporation funded by the Office of Economic Opportunity pursuant to an act of Congress, 42 U.S.C.A. §2809(a)(3). The mission of CRLS includes legal advice and representation for these workers.

"Differences had developed between Tedesco and these defendants prior to the events which led to the trespass charges now before us. Hence when defendant Tejeras wanted to go upon Tedesco's farm to find a migrant worker who needed medical aid for the removal of 28 sutures, he called upon defendant Shack for his help with respect to the legalities involved. Shack, too, had a mission to perform on Tedesco's farm; he wanted to discuss a legal problem with another migrant worker there employed and housed. Defendants arranged to go to the farm together. Shack carried literature to inform the migrant farmworkers of the assistance available to them under federal statutes, but no mention seems to have been made of that literature when Shack was later confronted by Tedesco.

"Defendants entered upon Tedesco's property and as they neared the camp site where the farmworkers were housed, they were confronted by Tedesco who inquired of their purpose. Tejeras and Shack stated their missions. In response, Tedesco offered to find the injured worker, and as to the worker who needed legal advice, Tedesco also offered to locate the man but insisted that the consultation would have to take place in Tedesco's office and in his presence. Defendants declined, saying they had the right to see the men in the privacy of their living quarters and without Tedesco's supervision. Tedesco thereupon summoned a State Trooper who, however, refused to remove defendants except upon Tedesco's written complaint. Tedesco then executed the formal complaints charging violations of the trespass statute.

"The constitutionality of the trespass statute, as applied here, is challenged on several scores. . . .

"These constitutional claims are not established by any definitive holding. We think it unnecessary to explore their validity. The reason is that we are satisfied that under our State law the ownership of real property does not include the right to bar access to governmental services available to migrant workers and hence there was no trespass within the meaning of the penal statute. The policy considerations which underlie that conclusion may be much the same as those which would be weighed with respect to one or more of the constitutional challenges, but a decision in nonconstitutional terms is more satisfactory, because the interests of migrant workers are more expansively served in that way than they would be if they had no more freedom than these constitutional concepts could be found to mandate if indeed they apply at all.

"Property rights serve human values. They are recognized to that end, and are limited by it. Title to real property cannot include dominion over the destiny of persons the owner permits to come upon the premises. Their well-being must remain the paramount concern of a system of law. Indeed, the needs of the occupants may be so imperative and their strength so weak, that the law will deny the occupants the power to contract away what is deemed essential to their health, welfare, or dignity.

"Here we are concerned with a highly disadvantaged segment of our society. We are told that every year farmworkers and their families numbering more than one million leave their home areas to fill the seasonal demand for farm labor in the United States. The migrant farmworkers come to New Jersey in substantial numbers. . . .

"The migrant farmworkers are a community within but apart from the local scene. They are rootless and isolated. Although the need for their labors is evident, they are unorganized and without economic or political power. It is their plight alone that summoned government to their aid. In response, Congress provided under Title III-B of the Economic Opportunity Act of 1964 (42 U.S.C.A. §2701 et seq.) for 'assistance for migrant and other seasonally employed farmworkers and their families.' . . .

"These ends would not be gained if the intended beneficiaries could be insulated from efforts to reach them. It is in this framework that we must decide whether the camp operator's rights in his lands may stand between the migrant workers and those who would aid them. The key to that aid is communication. Since the migrant workers are outside the mainstream of the communities in which they are housed and are unaware of their rights and opportunities and of the services available to them, they can be reached only by positive efforts tailored to that end. . . .

"A man's right in his real property of course is not absolute. It was a maxim of the common law that one should so use his property as not to injure the rights of others. Although hardly a precise solvent of actual controversies, the maxim does express the inevitable proposition that rights are relative and there must be an accommodation when they meet. Hence it has long been true that necessity, private or public, may justify entry upon the lands of another. . . .

"Thus approaching the case, we find it unthinkable that the farmer-employer can assert a right to isolate the migrant worker in any respect significant for the worker's well-being. The farmer, of course, is entitled to pursue his farming activities without interference, and this defendants readily concede. But we see no legitimate need for a right in the farmer to deny the worker the opportunity for aid available from federal, State, or local services, or from recognized charitable groups seeking to assist him. Hence representatives of these agencies and organizations may enter upon the premises to seek out the worker at his living quarters. So, too, the migrant worker must be allowed to receive visitors there of his own choice, so long as there is no behavior hurtful to others, and members of the press may not be denied reasonable access to workers who do not object to seeing them. . . .

"It follows that defendants here invaded no possessory right of the farmer-employer. Their conduct was therefore beyond the reach of the trespass statute. The judgments are accordingly reversed and the matters remanded to the County Court with directions to enter judgments of acquittal."

NOTES AND QUESTIONS

1. William Blackstone (see page 24) grandly defined the right of property as "that sole and despotic dominion which one man claims and exercises over the external things of the world, in total exclusion of the right of any other

individual in the universe." 2 Commentaries *2. Two centuries later, the U.S. Supreme Court, in the *Kaiser Aetna* case cited and quoted in *Jacque* (see pages 105-106), described the right to exclude as an essential feature of property. See also Thomas W. Merrill, The Property Strategy, 160 U. Pa. L. Rev. 2061 (2012); Thomas W. Merrill, Property and the Right to Exclude, 77 Neb. L. Rev. 730 (1998). Why could the farmers in *Jacque* be despotic, but the farmer in *Shack* not?

2. Even in Blackstone's time, there were limitations on the right to exclude; nowadays there are many more. Here is a list of just some of the examples you will encounter as you work your way through this book (watch for others): civil rights legislation forbidding various forms of discrimination; rent controls and other limitations on a landlord's right to evict tenants; the law of adverse possession; bodies of doctrine granting public rights of access to private beaches; legislation protecting homeowners who have defaulted on mortgage payments. Laws in many American states and European nations have even protected the public's right to roam on unimproved, privately owned land. See John A. Lovett, Progressive Property in Action: The Land Reform (Scotland) Act 2003, 89 Neb. L. Rev. 739 (2011); Brian Sawers, The Right to Exclude from Unimproved Land, 83 Temple L. Rev. 665 (2011).

As *Shack* and the foregoing examples suggest, limitations on the right to exclude might find their source in federal or state constitutional provisions, in federal, state, or local legislation, or in the common law. The same is generally true of limitations on the right to include, or transfer, studied in connection with the *Moore* case. These limitations on the right to transfer seem to reflect a range of considerations rather than one overarching principle, and this is no doubt true of the right to exclude as well. See Gregory S. Alexander & Eduardo M. Peñalver, An Introduction to Property Theory 135-149 (2012). Recall, for example, Morris Cohen, who addressed the relationships between property and power in his essay on Property and Sovereignty, published on the eve of the Great Depression (see Note 6 on page 17). Acknowledging that "the essence of private property is always the right to exclude others," Cohen nevertheless maintained that it should not be regarded as inviolable. To the contrary, Cohen argued, "the right of property must be supported by restrictions or positive duties on the part of the owners, enforced by the state as much as the right to exclude others which is the essence of property." Some 50 years later, C.B. Macpherson argued in a similar vein that the right to exclude is no more the essence of property—as a matter of logic or as a matter of propriety—than *the right not to be excluded* (as in the case of common property, which figured throughout the preceding section of this chapter). And when property is so understood, he said, the problem is no longer one "of putting limits on the property right, but of supplementing the individual right to exclude others by the individual right not to be excluded by others." This latter right "may provisionally be stated as the individual right to equal access to the means of labour and/or the means of life." C.B. Macpherson, Property: Mainstream and Critical Positions 201 (1978). A related but more general argument is set out in Gregory S. Alexander, The Social-Obligation Norm in American Property Law, 94 Cornell L. Rev. 745 (2009). Alexander sees in

American property law, on both the private and public sides, a social-obligation norm imposing on all individuals a duty to promote the capabilities essential to human flourishing—meaning, as to property owners, a duty sometimes to share their surplus resources with the needy.

3. There is, of course, an opposing point of view about the right to exclude. Richard A. Epstein, for example, speaks in defense of a firm right to exclude in two essays: Rights and "Rights Talk" (Book Review), 105 Harv. L. Rev. 1106 (1992), and Property and Necessity, 13 Harv. J.L. & Pub. Poly. 2 (1990). "What is wrong," Professor Epstein asks, "with a system of absolute rights that allows individuals to exclude some persons on a whim and admit others only by mutual consent?" His answer: "By and large, nothing," because by and large absolute rights simply establish the conditions for subsequent market transactions. Buyers and sellers may deal as they see fit, but so long as there are many buyers and sellers market forces will check abuse. "Those who exercise absolute rights in a capricious fashion pay for their folly by losing their markets." Epstein, Rights and "Rights Talk," supra, at 1109. Epstein argues that narrow limitations on the right to exclude are appropriate only when conditions (such as monopoly) create obstacles to market transactions. Epstein, Property and Necessity, supra, at 7. This approach might leave some people out in the cold, but avoiding that problem comes at the cost "of forcing individuals to open their property to persons whom they would prefer, for whatever reason, to exclude." Epstein, Property and Necessity, supra, at 7.

4. Owners of property can exclude in ways other than putting up fences or posting No Trespassing! signs. Such as what? And why might an owner choose one means rather than another? These interesting questions are addressed in Lior Jacob Strahilevitz, Information and Exclusion 42-53, 75-92 (2011).

The court in *Shack* was concerned that an owner of land might use his monopoly over a resource to exercise dominion over people. *Shack* is hardly the only property case in which courts worry about one person unilaterally exercising control over a resource in a way that might harm neighbors and other third parties. Perhaps the two most controversial rights in the bundle of ownership are the rights to abandon property and to destroy property. Both rights entail the unilateral relinquishment of property. As we shall see, courts treat the abandonment and destruction of different kinds of resources very differently.

Pocono Springs Civic Association, Inc. v. MacKenzie

Superior Court of Pennsylvania, 1995
667 A.2d 233

ROWLEY, J. The issue in this appeal is whether real property owned by appellants Joseph W. MacKenzie and Doris C. MacKenzie has been abandoned, as they claim. In an order entered January 5, 1995, the trial court granted summary judgment, in the amount of $1,739.82, in favor of appellee Pocono Springs Civic

Association, Inc., which argued successfully to the trial court that appellants had not abandoned their property located in appellee's development, and, therefore appellants were still obligated to pay association fees.[45]

. . . [T]he facts are in no manner disputed. Our determination, therefore, is simply whether the trial court erred as a matter of law in finding that appellee's right to summary judgment is clear and free from doubt.

We briefly outline the facts and procedural background of the case as follows: Appellants purchased a vacant lot at Pocono Springs Development, located in Wayne County, on October 14, 1969. In 1987, appellants decided to sell their still-vacant lot. A subsequent offer for the purchase of appellants' lot was conditioned upon the property being suitable for an on-lot sewage system. Upon inspection, the lot was determined to have inadequate soil for proper percolation, and appellants' sale was lost. Believing their investment to be worthless, appellants attempted to abandon their lot at Pocono Springs Development. Appellants claimed that because they successfully abandoned their lot, they are relieved from any duty to pay the association fees sought by appellee. The trial court held, however, that the appellant's abandonment defense is "not a valid defense." We agree with the trial court, and affirm. . . .

Appellants' argument, that they successfully abandoned their lot at Pocono Springs Development, is based upon several actions that they believe disassociate them from the land. First, appellants, after learning that the lot would not meet township sewage requirements, attempted to turn the lot over to appellee. Appellee declined to accept the property. Second, appellants tried to persuade appellee to accept the lot as a gift, to be used as a park-like area for the community. Appellee again declined. Third, in 1986 appellants ceased paying real estate taxes on their lot, and in 1988 the Wayne County Tax Claim Bureau offered the property for sale, due to delinquent tax payments. There were no purchasers. Fourth, in 1990, the lot was again offered for sale by the Tax Claim Bureau. The property again was not sold. The Bureau then placed the lot on its "repository" list. Fifth, appellants signed a notarized statement, mailed to "all interested parties," which expressed their desire to abandon the lot. Sixth, appellants do not accept mail regarding the property. These occurrences, together with appellants having neither visited the lot nor utilized the development's services since 1986, cause appellants to "assert that they do not have 'perfect' title to Lot #20, in Pocono Springs [Development,] [thus] they can and have abandoned said property back to the sovereign." On the basis of the above, appellants argue that their conduct manifests an intent to abandon, and that their intent to abandon should be a question of fact which precludes summary judgment.

---

45. The covenant upon which appellee relies reads as follows:

   An association of all property owners is to be formed by the Grantor and designated by such name as may be deemed appropriate, and when formed, the buyer covenants and agrees that he, his executors, heirs and assigns, shall be bound by the by-laws, rules and regulations as may be duly formulated and adopted by such association and that they shall be subject to the payment of annual dues and assessments of the same.

Deed, Covenant Number 11.

The law of abandonment in Pennsylvania does not support appellants' argument. This Court has held that abandoned property is that:

> to which an owner has voluntarily relinquished all right, title, claim and possession with the intention of terminating his ownership, but without vesting it in any other person and with the intention of not reclaiming further possession or resuming ownership, possession or enjoyment.

Commonwealth v. Wetmore, 447 A.2d 1012, 1014 (Pa. Super. 1982). However, in the instant case, appellants have not relinquished their rights, title, claim and possession of their lot. They remain owners of real property in fee simple, with a recorded deed and "perfect" title. Absent proof to the contrary, possession is presumed to be in the party who has record title. Overly v. Hixson, 82 A.2d 573 (Pa. Super. 1951). As appellants themselves concede, with commendable candor, no authority exists in Pennsylvania that allows for the abandonment of real property when owned in fee simple with perfect title.[46] . . . Yet, appellants nonetheless maintain that their non-use, refusal to pay taxes, and offers to sell create an abandonment, because of a displayed intent to abandon.

. . . [T]he record shows that they have retained "perfect" title to their lot. Neither title nor deed has been sold or transferred. . . . Perfect title, under Pennsylvania law, cannot be abandoned. O'Dwyer v. Ream, 136 A.2d 90 (Pa. 1957). In *O'Dwyer*, our Supreme Court held that once it is determined that good title exists, then the abandonment theory cannot succeed. See also A. D. Graham & Company, Inc. v. Pennsylvania Turnpike Commission, 33 A.2d 22, 29 (Pa. 1943) (which held that the doctrine of abandonment does not apply to perfect titles, only to imperfect titles). Appellants do not cite, and our own research has not discovered, any more recent cases that would cause us to question the authority of the cited decisions. Absent authority to support their argument, therefore, the appeal cannot be successful for appellants.

Appellants further claim that the trial court erred in granting summary judgment because whether they abandoned their lots should be a question of intent, for a jury to determine. . . . In the instant case, appellants' intent is irrelevant. What is controlling is our law, which states that real property cannot be abandoned. The law, therefore, leaves nothing for a jury to decide on this claim, which amounts to a legal impossibility.

. . . Therefore, we are constrained to find that appellee is entitled to judgment as a matter of law.

NOTES AND QUESTIONS

1. In feudal times, all land tenants owed a service to the lord, which was contracted for when the lord granted the land to the original tenant and bound heirs and assignees (see pages 210-215). Land could not be abandoned because such

---

46. Most commonly, abandonment involves personal property or railway lines not owned in fee simple.

abandonment would mean no one was obligated to perform service to the lord while the land was unowned. The modern equivalent of these feudal incidents are property taxes (and in case of land in a homeowners' association like Pocono Springs, assessments). In the modern era, should we expect that valuable real estate that has been abandoned will remain unclaimed, such that no one will be responsible for paying property taxes on it, for long?

2. What would you advise the MacKenzies to do to stop the hemorrhaging of cash?

3. *Further background on* Pocono Springs. We corresponded with the MacKenzie daughters, Sandra M. Lloyd and Holly Carlson. According to Lloyd and Carlson, their grandmother gave the MacKenzies a gift of money so that they could purchase the property in Pocono Springs. They bought it under the mistaken impression that the land could be developed for residential purposes. The MacKenzies felt compelled to litigate because they were advised by counsel that without a favorable ruling from the court the property would "become the ultimate family white elephant," one that would eventually burden their daughters. Following a telephone conversation with the attorney for the MacKenzies, Professor Eduardo Peñalver reported to us that of 3,000 lots in the Pocono Springs development, only about 400 proved capable of development. The other lots remained vacant as of 2010. The attorney stated that the association's board was dominated by a few individuals who had been able to build on their lots. They would not accept land from the owners who were unable to build. After extensive litigation, the MacKenzies and other owners refused to pay their judgments. Most of them were of retirement age and not concerned about their credit ratings. The attorney reported that only about 10 percent of the owners paid the assessments; the rest just walked away.

Hawkins v. Mahoney

Supreme Court of Montana, 1999
990 P.2d 776

TRIEWEILER, J. The Plaintiff, Sherman Hawkins . . . is an inmate at Montana State Prison in Deer Lodge, Montana. On July 12, 1997, Hawkins escaped from the prison. Immediately following his escape, Montana State Prison officials packed up Hawkins' personal property, sealed it with security tape, placed Hawkins' name on each box and removed the boxes from his cell. Hawkins' personal property was placed in the Montana State Prison storage room on July 12, 1997.

On July 14, 1997, two days after Hawkins escaped, Hawkins was apprehended and returned to the prison. Upon his return, prison officials placed Hawkins in administrative segregation in the maximum security unit. On July 20, 1997, Hawkins was found guilty of escape following a Department of Corrections disciplinary hearing. He received the following sanctions: ten days in disciplinary segregation, loss of good-time, and a recommendation for reclassification to the maximum security unit. The disciplinary hearings officer did not order Hawkins' personal property destroyed. During the next 30 days Hawkins requested the return of his personal property several times.

In September 1997 prison officials escorted Hawkins to the storage room and allowed Hawkins to remove all of his legal papers and legal materials from the boxes of his personal property. Prison officials informed Hawkins that, by policy, when an inmate escapes, all of his property is considered abandoned and is subsequently destroyed. Prison officials then informed Hawkins that his remaining personal property would either be destroyed or sold. Hawkins' remaining property included: a television, stereo, word processor, eyeglasses and books. Hawkins estimated that the approximate value of his personal property was $2290. Sometime after September 1997, prison officials destroyed or sold Hawkins' remaining personal property.

Hawkins subsequently filed this action against five Montana State Prison officials and the State of Montana and alleged that the individual Defendants destroyed his property without affording him due process of law . . . . The District Court concluded that Hawkins had abandoned his property by his escape and that the abandonment constituted a complete defense to any action brought by Hawkins which depended on his ownership of the property. . . .

Hawkins contends that the District Court erred in finding that, when he escaped from the Montana State Prison, he abandoned his personal property which he kept in his cell. Hawkins asserts that because he was returned to the prison within two days, and the Defendants had his personal property in the prison storage room, the Defendants should have returned the property to him when he requested it.

The Defendants respond that Hawkins abandoned his property when he escaped from prison and as a result of his abandonment, the Montana State Prison became the owner of the property "to do with it as it pleased." Defendants contend that Hawkins' escape evidenced his intent to terminate his ownership of the property, stating: "Hawkins, therefore, had a choice. He could keep his rights to his property or he could escape. The choices are mutually exclusive; he could not accomplish both."

The District Court . . . relied on a 1989 Missouri Court of Appeals decision, Herron v. Whiteside, 782 S.W.2d 414 (Mo. App. 1989), to conclude that Hawkins had abandoned his property. [The *Herron* court] held that a prisoner's escape from confinement constitutes, as a matter of law, abandonment of the personal property the prisoner left at the prison. Id. at 416. In that case, during Herron's one day escape, prison officials allowed prison employees to give away his property and allowed other inmates to take Herron's property from his cell. Id. at 415.

We . . . conclude that . . . *Herron* is factually distinguishable from this case. In *Herron*, the prison employees and inmates ransacked Herron's cell after he escaped and appropriated Herron's property for themselves. The state did not take Herron's personal property into protective custody after his escape. Whereas, in this case, after Hawkins escaped from the prison, the Defendants removed Hawkins' personal property from his cell, placed his possessions in boxes with

Hawkins' name on them and then placed the boxes in the prison storage room. After Hawkins returned to the prison, he asked about his personal property and asked that it be returned to him.

With regard to a former owner's rights to abandoned property, it has been stated that:

> Personal property, upon being abandoned, ceases to be the property of any person, unless and until it is reduced to possession with the intent to acquire title to, or ownership of, it. Such property may, accordingly, be appropriated by anyone, *if it has not been reclaimed by the former owner*, and ownership of it vests by operation of law, in the person first lawfully appropriating it and reducing it to possession with the intention to become its owner, provided such taking is fair.

1 C.J.S. *Abandonment* §12 (1985) (emphasis added). In Gregg v. Caldwell-Guadalupe Pick-Up Stations, 286 S.W. 1083, 1084 (Tex. Civ. App. 1926), the Texas court stated: "[a]bandoned property is no man's property until reduced to possession with intent to acquire title." . . . The intention must be discovered from all the circumstances of the case. . . .

In this case there is no contention that Hawkins expressed an intention to abandon his property. The intent was presumed or inferred when he left the prison without taking the property with him. . . .

The intent to abandon property is a requisite element of abandonment. If there is no expressed intent, then the intent may be inferred by the acts of the owner. In *Herron*, the Missouri court held that a prisoner's escape convincingly infers the intent to abandon property. *Herron*, 782 S.W.2d at 417. That court essentially held that intent to abandon property is a conclusive presumption, or an irrebuttable presumption. However, we know of no persuasive reason why such a presumption should be conclusive prior to the time when possession of the property is acquired by someone else with the intent to acquire ownership.

It does not appear, based on the facts we assume to be true, that at any point after Hawkins' escape and before Hawkins' request for the return of his property, that the Montana State Prison reduced Hawkins' property to possession with the intent to acquire title to, or ownership of it.

We conclude that the presumption or inference of intent to abandon one's property, based solely upon the acts of the owner, is a rebuttable presumption. . . . Therefore, upon Hawkins' return to the prison and request for his property prior to it being claimed by anyone else, he effectively rebutted the presumption that he ever intended to abandon his property. Accordingly, when Hawkins reclaimed his property by requesting it be returned to him, Hawkins regained his status as the owner of his personal property against all others. . . .

We conclude that the District Court erred when it held that Hawkins had abandoned his personal property and had no right to request the return of his personal property. . . . The judgment of the District Court is reversed and this case is remanded to the District Court for further proceedings consistent with this opinion.

[The dissenting opinions of Justice Gray and Chief Justice Turnage are omitted.]

NOTES AND QUESTIONS

1. Note the contrast between *Pocono Springs* and *Hawkins*. Pennsylvania, like every other American state, holds that a fee simple interest in land cannot be abandoned. Montana, like every other American state, holds that chattel property may be abandoned. What explains American law's permissive attitude with respect to the abandonment of chattels and simultaneous prohibition on the abandonment of real property? The question is explored in two law review articles that appeared a few months apart, Lior Jacob Strahilevitz, The Right to Abandon, 158 U. Pa. L. Rev. 355 (2010), and Eduardo Peñalver, The Illusory Right to Abandon, 109 Mich. L. Rev. 191 (2010).

Strahilevitz argues that the per se prohibition on the abandonment of real estate arose for historical reasons but cannot be justified presently any more than a ban on the abandonment of chattel property could be justified. To Strahilevitz, the relevant question is whether the property in question has positive economic value (in which case abandonment usually ought to be permitted) or negative economic value (in which case abandonment usually ought to be prohibited). Strahilevitz argues that the costs of permitting abandonment (which include confusion about whether it may be claimed by third parties, deterioration of a resource's value while it is unowned, violent squabbles as people race to acquire an abandoned resource, and concerns that neighbors or the state may be responsible for disposing of or cleaning up a resource) are equally applicable to real property and chattel property alike. So too are the benefits associated with abandonment (primarily that it facilitates the transfer of a resource from someone who does not value it very highly to someone who does, that it allows an owner to transfer a resource without having to devote effort to discovering who might want or deserve it, and that the availability of a right to abandon a resource may prevent an owner from exercising his right to destroy or deplete a resource). Indeed, concludes Strahilevitz, because land is immobile and comes along with a comprehensive system for recording who owns what (see pages 693-699), the case for permitting the abandonment of positive-value real estate is *stronger* than the case for permitting the abandonment of positive-value chattel property. Do you see why?

Peñalver, by contrast, approaches the puzzle by arguing that while the abandonment of chattels is theoretically permitted by the common law, as a practical matter chattel abandonment rarely, if ever, occurs. He posits that the prohibition on the abandonment of land precludes the lawful abandonment of chattels by depriving would-be abandoners of a location where they can leave abandoned property. Strahilevitz responds to this point by suggesting that governments often permit chattel abandonment to occur on public land (for example, the National Park Service promotes geocaching on some of its land), that private owners may do the same (such as book swap rooms in dormitories), and that private landowners frequently abandon chattel property on their own land (for example, a landowner who leaves firewood on her front lawn with a sign that says, "take as much wood as you can carry"). Peñalver retorts that the consensual, not unilateral, nature of some of these transfers makes it inappropriate to characterize them as true abandonment. More broadly, Peñalver suggests that the common law's hostility to abandonment is grounded in deeply embedded norms of social obligation that permeate American property law. Walking away from land entails walking away from duties owed to others without their permission, with no guarantee that a new steward for the land will show up to assume an owner's obligations.

2. *More on* Hawkins. The common law elements of abandonment are (1) the owner must intend to relinquish all interests in the property, with no intention that it be acquired by any particular person, and (2) there must be a voluntary act by the owner effectuating that intent. Abandoned property belongs to the first person who subsequently takes control of it. The court holds that Hawkins did not abandon his property upon escaping prison because he was able to rebut an inference that he intended to abandon the chattels. Is there a better way to make sense of the sequence of events described in the case, whereby Hawkins escapes without his property, the prison places the property in boxes with Hawkins's name on them, and Hawkins asks for the property's return after being apprehended? See Strahilevitz, supra, 158 U. Pa. L. Rev. at 376. Should the majority have taken into consideration the state's policy interest in deterring prison escape attempts? Are such considerations something that an inmate pondering an escape would contemplate?

3. *Is taking out the trash abandonment?* Suppose a business throws away various documents, including a list of all its employees and their home addresses. A union organizer removes the documents from the dumpster and then contacts the employees at their home addresses as part of a unionization campaign at the business. What result? Compare Long v. Dilling Mechanical Contractors, 705 N.E.2d 1022 (Ind. App. 1999) (no criminal liability because Dilling abandoned items placed in its dumpster), with Sharpe v. Turley, 191 S.W.3d 362 (Tex. App. 2006) (an owner who deposits trash in a dumpster does not abandon it, but is instead transferring it to the waste hauling firm with whom the owner has contracted). For an exploration of the burdens imposed on people who have to decide whether property is abandoned, lost, or something else, see Matt Corriel, Comment, Up for Grabs: A Workable System for the Unilateral Acquisition of Chattels, 161 U. Pa. L. Rev. 807 (2013).

4. *Can one's name be abandoned?* Basketball legend Lew Alcindor led the UCLA men's basketball team to national championships in 1967, 1968, and 1969. In 1971, while starring in the NBA, Alcindor permanently changed his name to Kareem Abdul-Jabbar as an affirmation of his Muslim faith. During the 1993 Men's College Basketball Tournament, General Motors ran advertisements for its Oldsmobile Eighty-Eight that compared the car's record of excellence (being named a Consumer Digest Best Buy three years in a row) to Lew Alcindor's excellence (being named NCAA Tournament Most Valuable Player three years in a row). Abdul-Jabbar sued General Motors for violating his right of publicity and trademark rights in his name. Abdul-Jabbar conceded that he had stopped using the name Lew Alcindor for commercial purposes more than a decade ago. General Motors argued that this non-use amounted to abandonment. The Ninth

Circuit ruled in Abdul-Jabbar's favor. *Abdul-Jabbar v. General Motors Corp.*, 85 F.3d 407 (9th Cir. 1996).

Although trademark law considers a mark abandoned when "its use has been discontinued with intent not to resume such use," 15 U.S.C. §1127, the court deemed this clear language inapplicable to people's birth names. "One's birth name is an integral part of one's identity; it is not bestowed for commercial purposes, nor is it 'kept alive' through commercial use. A proper name thus cannot be deemed 'abandoned' throughout its possessor's life, despite his failure to use it, or continue to use it, commercially." 85 F.3d at 411. With respect to the right of publicity, the court held that celebrities could continue to exploit their current or former names despite non-use. 85 F.3d at 415. Is there a coherent reason why trademark rights to one's name ought to be treated like fee simple interests in land, such that neither can be abandoned as a matter of law? Do any of the reasons for prohibiting the abandonment of real estate apply to identities? Are there other reasons why the law might prohibit the abandonment of one's identity for commercial purposes? After *Abdul-Jabbar*, does an individual who prefers to let anyone use his name and identity without permission have any credible way to signal this willingness to interested members of the public?

Speaking of abandonment, General Motors ceased production of the Oldsmobile Eighty-Eight in 1999.

Eyerman v. Mercantile Trust Co.

Missouri Court of Appeals, 1975
524 S.W.2d 210

RENDLEN, J. Plaintiffs appeal from denial of their petition seeking injunction to prevent demolition of a house at #4 Kingsbury Place in the City of St. Louis. The action is brought by individual neighboring property owners and certain trustees for the Kingsbury Place Subdivision. We reverse.

Louise Woodruff Johnston, owner of the property in question, died January 14, 1973, and by her will directed the executor "to cause our home at 4 Kingsbury Place . . . to be razed and to sell the land upon which it is located . . . and to transfer the proceeds of the sale . . . to the residue of my estate." Plaintiffs assert that razing the home will adversely affect their property rights, violate the terms of the subdivision trust indenture for Kingsbury Place, produce an actionable private nuisance and is contrary to public policy.

The area involved is a "private place" established in 1902 by trust indenture which provides that Kingsbury Place and Kingsbury Terrace will be so maintained, improved, protected and managed as to be desirable for private residences. The trustees are empowered to protect and preserve "Kingsbury Place" from encroachment, trespass, nuisance or injury, and it is "the intention of these presents, forming a general scheme of improving and maintaining said property as desirable residence property of the highest class." The covenants run with the land and the indenture empowers lot owners or the trustees to bring suit to enforce them.

Except for one vacant lot, the subdivision is occupied by handsome, spacious two and three-story homes, and all must be used exclusively as private residences. The indenture generally regulates location, costs and similar features for any structures in the subdivision, and limits construction of subsidiary structures except those that may beautify the property, for example, private stables, flower houses, conservatories, play houses or buildings of similar character.

On trial the temporary restraining order was dissolved and all issues found against the plaintiffs. . . .

Whether #4 Kingsbury Place should be razed is an issue of public policy involving individual property rights and the community at large. The plaintiffs have pleaded and proved facts sufficient to show a personal, legally protectible interest.

Demolition of the dwelling will result in an unwarranted loss to this estate, the plaintiffs and the public. The uncontradicted testimony was that the current value of the house and land is $40,000.00; yet the estate could expect no more than $5,000.00 for the empty lot, less the cost of demolition at $4,350.00, making a grand loss of $39,350.33 if the unexplained and capricious direction to the executor is effected. Only $650.00 of the $40,000.00 asset would remain.

Kingsbury Place is an area of high architectural significance, representing excellence in urban space utilization. Razing the home will depreciate adjoining property values by an estimated $10,000.00 and effect corresponding losses for other neighborhood homes. The cost of constructing a house of comparable size and architectural exquisiteness would approach $200,000.00.

The importance of this house to its neighborhood and the community is reflected in the action of the St. Louis Commission on Landmarks and Urban Design designating Kingsbury Place as a landmark of the City of St. Louis. This designation, under consideration prior to the institution of this suit, points up the aesthetic and historical qualities of the area and assists in stabilizing Central West End St. Louis. It was testified by the Landmarks Commission chairman that the private place concept, once unique to St. Louis, fosters higher home maintenance standards and is among the most effective methods for stabilizing otherwise deteriorating neighborhoods. The executive director of Heritage St. Louis, an organization operating to preserve the architecture of the city, testified to the importance of preserving Kingsbury Place intact:

> The reasons (sic) for making Kingsbury Place a landmark is that it is a definite piece of urban design and architecture. It starts out with monumental gates on Union. There is a long corridor of space, furnished with a parkway in the center, with houses on either side of the street, . . . The existence of this piece of architecture depends on the continuity of the (sic) both sides. Breaks in this continuity would be as holes in this wall, and would detract from the urban design qualities of the streets. . . . Many of these houses are landmarks in themselves, but they add up to much more. . . . I would say Kingsbury Place, as a whole, with its design, with its important houses . . . is a most significant piece of urban design by any standard.

To remove #4 Kingsbury from the street was described as having the effect of a missing front tooth. The space created would permit direct access to Kingsbury

Place from the adjacent alley, increasing the likelihood the lot will be subject to uses detrimental to the health, safety and beauty of the neighborhood. The mere possibility that a future owner might build a new home with the inherent architectural significance of the present dwelling offers little support to sustain the condition for destruction.

[N]o individual, group of individuals nor the community generally benefits from the senseless destruction of the house; instead, all are harmed and only the caprice of the dead testatrix is served. Destruction of the house harms the neighbors, detrimentally affects the community, causes monetary loss in excess of $39,000.00 to the estate and is without benefit to the dead woman. No reason, good or bad, is suggested by the will or record for the eccentric condition. This is not a living person who seeks to exercise a right to reshape or dispose of her property; instead, it is an attempt by will to confer the power to destroy upon an executor who is given no other interest in the property. To allow an executor to exercise such power stemming from apparent whim and caprice of the testatrix contravenes public policy.

The Missouri Supreme Court held in State ex rel. McClintock v. Guinotte, 204 S.W. 806, 808 (Mo. en banc 1918), that the taking of property by inheritance or will is not an absolute or natural right but one created by the laws of the sovereign power. The court points out the state "may foreclose the right absolutely, or it may grant the right upon conditions precedent, which conditions, if not otherwise violative of our Constitution, will have to be complied with before the right of descent and distribution (whether under the law or by will) can exist." Further, this power of the state is one of inherent sovereignty which allows the state to "say what becomes of the property of a person, when death forecloses his right to control it." Id. at 808, 809. While living, a person may manage, use or dispose of his money or property with fewer restraints than a decedent by will. One is generally restrained from wasteful expenditure or destructive inclinations by the natural desire to enjoy his property or to accumulate it during his lifetime. Such considerations however have not tempered the extravagance or eccentricity of the testamentary disposition here on which there is no check except the courts.

In the early English case of Egerton v. Brownlow, 10 Eng. Rep. 359, 417 (Queen's Bench 1853), it is stated: "The owner of an estate may himself do many things which he could not (by a condition) compel his successor to do. One example is sufficient. He may leave his land uncultivated, but he cannot by a condition compel his successor to do so. The law does not interfere with the owner and compel him to cultivate his land, (though it may be for the public good that land should be cultivated) so far the law respects ownership; but when, by a condition, he attempts to compel his successor to do what is against the public good, the law steps in and pronounces the condition void and allows the devisee to enjoy the estate free from the condition." . . .

In the case of In re Scott's Will, Board of Commissioners of Rice County v. Scott et al., 93 N.W. 109 (Minn. 1903), the Supreme Court of Minnesota stated, when considering the provision of a will directing the executor to destroy money belonging to the estate: "We assume, for purpose of this decision, that the direction in the codicil to the executor to destroy all of the residue of the money or cash or evidences of credit belonging to the estate was void." Id. at 109. See also Restatement, Second, Trusts §124, at 267: "Although a person may deal capriciously with his own property, his self interest ordinarily will restrain him from doing so. Where an attempt is made to confer such a power upon a person who is given no other interest in the property, there is no such restraint and it is against public policy to allow him to exercise the power if the purpose is merely capricious." . . .

The term "public policy" cannot be comprehensively defined in specific terms but the phrase "against public policy" has been characterized as that which conflicts with the morals of the time and contravenes any established interest of society. Acts are said to be against public policy "when the law refuses to enforce or recognize them, on the ground that they have a mischievous tendency, so as to be injurious to the interests of the state, apart from illegality or immorality." . . .

Public policy may be found in the Constitution, statutes and judicial decisions of this state or the nation. In re Rahn's Estate, 291 S.W. 120 (Mo. 1927). But in a case of first impression where there are no guiding statutes, judicial decisions or constitutional provisions, "a judicial determination of the question becomes an expression of public policy provided it is so plainly right as to be supported by the general will." In re Mohler's Estate, 22 A.2d 680, 683 (Pa. 1941). In the absence of guidance from authorities in its own jurisdiction, courts may look to the judicial decisions of sister states for assistance in discovering expressions of public policy. . . .

Although public policy may evade precise, objective definition, it is evident from the authorities cited that this senseless destruction serving no apparent good purpose is to be held in disfavor. A well-ordered society cannot tolerate the waste and destruction of resources when such acts directly affect important interests of other members of that society. It is clear that property owners in the neighborhood of #4 Kingsbury, the St. Louis Community as a whole and the beneficiaries of testatrix's estate will be severely injured should the provisions of the will be followed. No benefits are present to balance against this injury and we hold that to allow the condition in the will would be in violation of the public policy of this state.

Having thus decided, we do not reach the plaintiffs' contentions regarding enforcement of the restrictions in the Kingsbury Place trust indenture and actionable private nuisance, though these contentions may have merit.

The judgment is reversed and the cause remanded to the Circuit Court to enter judgment as prayed.

Dowd, P.J., concurs.

CLEMENS, J., dissenting. . . . The simple issue in this case is whether the trial court erred by refusing to enjoin a trustee from carrying out an explicit testamentary directive. In an emotional opinion, the majority assumes a psychic knowledge of the testatrix' reasons for directing her home be razed; her testamentary disposition is characterized as "capricious," "unwarranted," "senseless," and "eccentric." But the record is utterly silent as to her motives.

The majority's reversal of the trial court here spawns bizarre and legally untenable results. By its decision, the court officiously confers a "benefit" upon testamentary beneficiaries who have never litigated or protested against the razing. The majority opinion further proclaims that public policy demands we enjoin the razing of this private residence in order to prevent land misuse in the City of St. Louis. But the City, like the beneficiaries, is not a party to this lawsuit. The fact is the majority's holding is based upon wispy, self-proclaimed public policy grounds that were only vaguely pleaded, were not in evidence, and were only sketchily briefed by the plaintiffs.

The only plaintiffs in this case are residents of Kingsbury Place and trustees under its indenture. In seeking to enjoin the removal of testatrix' home at #4 Kingsbury Place, these plaintiffs claim they are entitled to an injunction first, by virtue of language in the trust indenture; secondly, because the razing would constitute a nuisance; and thirdly on the ground of public policy. But plaintiffs have not shown the indenture bars razing testatrix' home or that the razing would create a nuisance. And no grounds exist for ruling that the razing is contrary to public policy.

The Trust Indenture. Kingsbury Place is a "private place" established in 1902 by trust indenture. Except for one well-tended vacant lot (whose existence the majority ignores in saying the street minus #4 Kingsbury Place would be like "a missing front tooth") the trust indenture generally regulates size, constructions and cost of structures to be built on Kingsbury Place. It empowers the trustees to maintain vacant lots and to protect the street from "encroachment, trespass, nuisance and injury." The indenture's acknowledgment that vacant lots did and would exist shows that such lots were not to be considered an "injury." The fact the indenture empowers the trustees to maintain vacant lots is neither an express nor an implied ban against razing residences. The indenture simply recognizes that Kingsbury Place may have vacant lots from time to time—as it now has—and that the trustees may maintain them—as they now do. The indenture itself affords plaintiffs no basis for injunctive relief.

Nuisance. Plaintiffs contend the non-existence of the Johnston dwelling would create a nuisance. Plaintiffs opined the home's removal would be detrimental to neighbors' health and safety, would lower property values in the area and would be undesirable aesthetically, architecturally, socially and historically. These opinions were based upon conjecture rather than upon a reasonable degree of certainty; hence, they were not binding on the trial court. . . . The record reveals the one existing vacant lot on Kingsbury Place is well-maintained by the trustees; it does not constitute a nuisance. There is no reason to presume a second vacant lot would be left untended or that private police would cease patrolling. The facts do not support an inference that plaintiffs' rights in the use of their own lands would be invaded by removing the Johnston home. They are not entitled to injunctive relief on the basis of imagined possibilities.

Public Policy. The majority opinion bases its reversal on public policy. But plaintiffs themselves did not substantially rely upon this nebulous concept. Plaintiffs' brief contends merely that an "agency of the City of St. Louis has recently (?) designated Kingsbury Place as a landmark," citing §24.070, Revised Code of the City of St. Louis. Plaintiffs argue removal of the Johnston home would be "intentional . . . destruction of a landmark of historical interest." Neither the ordinance cited in the brief nor any action taken under it were in evidence. Indeed, the Chairman of the Landmarks and Urban Design Commission testified the Commission did not declare the street a landmark until after Mrs. Johnston died. A month after Mrs. Johnston's death, several residents of the street apparently sensed the impending razing of the Johnston home and applied to have the street declared a landmark. The Commissioner testified it was the Commission's "civic duty to help those people."

The majority opinion . . . suggests the court may declare certain land uses, which are not illegal, to be in violation of the City's public policy. And the majority so finds although the City itself is not a litigant claiming injury to its interests. The majority's public-policy conclusions are based not upon evidence in the lower court, but upon incidents which may have happened thereafter.

The court has resorted to public policy in order to vitiate Mrs. Johnston's valid testamentary direction. But this is not a proper case for court-defined public policy. . . .

The leading Missouri case on public policy as that doctrine applies to a testator's right to dispose of property is In re Rahn's Estate. . . . There, an executor refused to pay a bequest on the ground the beneficiary was an enemy alien, and the bequest was therefore against public policy. The court denied that contention: "We may say, at the outset, that the policy of the law favors freedom in the testamentary disposition of property and that it is the duty of the courts to give effect to the intention of the testator, as expressed in his will, provided such intention does not contravene an established rule of law." And the court wisely added, "it is not the function of the judiciary to create or announce a public policy of its own, but solely to determine and declare what is the public policy of the state or nation as such policy is found to be expressed in the Constitution, statutes, and judicial decisions of the state or nation, . . . not by the varying opinions of laymen, lawyers, or judges as to the demands or the interests of the public." And, in cautioning against judges declaring public policy the court stated: "Judicial tribunals hold themselves bound to the observance of rules of extreme caution when invoked to declare a transaction void on grounds of public policy, and prejudice to the public interest must clearly appear before the court would be warranted in pronouncing a transaction void on this account." In resting its decision on public-policy grounds, the majority opinion has transgressed the limitations declared by our Supreme Court in *Rahn's Estate.*

. . . It requires judicial imagination to hold, as the majority does, that the mere presence of a second vacant lot on Kingsbury Place violates public policy.

As much as our aesthetic sympathies might lie with neighbors near a house to be razed, those sympathies should not so interfere with our considered legal judgment as to create a questionable legal precedent. Mrs. Johnston had the right during her lifetime to have her house razed, and I find nothing which precludes her right to order her executor to raze the house upon her death. . . .

NOTES AND QUESTIONS

1. *Aftermath.* The house at #4 Kingsbury Place still stands. It last sold in 1992 for $370,000, and its estimated value in 2014 was more than $900,000, according to Zillow.com.

2. *Do justifications matter?* Recall the discussion on page 99 of property as a bundle of rights, including rights to possess, to use, to transfer, to exclude. Is there (should there be) a right to destroy? If you were representing a client in Missouri who earnestly wished to live in his home until his death and then to have it destroyed, would there be any way to help him accomplish this goal under *Eyerman?* Would articulating a rationale in the will for the destruction of the house convince the courts to permit enforcement? See National City Bank v. Case Western Reserve University, 369 N.E.2d 814, 818-819 (Ohio Com. Pl. 1976).

3. *What about pro-destruction social norms?* How should the law respond if someone wants to be buried wearing her diamond wedding ring and other jewelry, as is commonly the case? See Meksras Estate, 63 Pa. D. & C.2d 371 (C.P. Phila. County 1974). For that matter, if someone elects *not* to be an organ donor, should *Eyerman*'s rule apply? These questions and related ones are considered in Lior Jacob Strahilevitz, The Right to Destroy, 114 Yale L.J. 781 (2005). The same source considers the right to destroy artistic works of the owner's creation, as does Joseph L. Sax, Playing Darts with a Rembrandt: Public and Private Rights in Cultural Treasures (1999).

4. *Does the right to destroy facilitate extortion?* Might protecting the right to destroy property cause owners to issue bluffs and threats as a way of extracting money from each other? See Stephen E. Sachs, Comment, Saving Toby: Extortion, Blackmail, and the Right to Destroy, 24 Yale L. & Poly. Rev. 251 (2006).

2

Subsequent in Time: Acquisition of Property by Find, Adverse Possession, and Gift

Possession, as we saw in the preceding chapter, is a powerful concept in the law of property. By virtue of *first* possession one can make an unowned thing, or a thing before enjoyed only by all in common, one's own. But suppose the principle of first in time, so dominant in Chapter 1, no longer holds. Suppose that something *already* owned by someone else, say *A*, *subsequently* comes into the possession of *B*, and without *A*'s consent. Surprisingly enough, *B* might still become the thing's "owner," as the first two sections of this chapter make clear. Even without being declared owner, *B* might nevertheless be granted considerable protection by the legal system. But when does *B* have "possession," so as to enjoy this favored position, and why are possessors favored anyway? These important questions figured in the last chapter and they do so again in this one.

Another common theme persists. Chapter 1 was concerned, among other things, with acquisition of property other than by purchase, and this chapter is as well—right through to its final section, where we examine the law of gifts. Possession plays a role there, too.

A. Acquisition by Find

Possession is eleven points in the law.—

> *Colley Cibber,*
> Woman's Wit, Act I (1697)

Possession is very strong; rather more than nine points of the law.—

> *Lord Mansfield,*
> Corporation of Kingston-upon-Hull v. Horner,
> 98 Eng. Rep. 807, 815 (1774)

Finders keepers, losers weepers.—

> *Old Scottish Proverb*

Armory v. Delamirie

King's Bench, 1722
1 Strange 505

The plaintiff being a chimney sweeper's boy found a jewel and carried it to the defendant's shop (who was a goldsmith)[1] to know what it was, and delivered it into the hands of the apprentice, who under pretence of weighing it, took out the stones, and calling to the master to let him know it came to three halfpence, the master offered the boy the money, who refused to take it, and insisted to have the thing again; whereupon the apprentice delivered him back the socket without the stones. And now in trover against the master these points were ruled:

1. That the finder of a jewel, though he does not by such finding acquire an absolute property or ownership, yet he has such a property as will enable him to keep it against all but the rightful owner, and consequently may maintain trover.

2. That the action well lay against the master, who gives a credit to his apprentice, and is answerable for his neglect.

3. As to the value of the jewel several of the trade were examined to prove what a jewel of the finest water that would fit the socket would be worth; and the Chief Justice (Pratt) directed the jury, that unless the defendant did produce the jewel, and shew it not to be of the finest water, they should presume the strongest against him, and make the value of the best jewels the measure of their damages: which they accordingly did.

NOTES AND QUESTIONS

1. Based on judicial statements like that in the *Armory* case, it is often said "that the title of the finder is good as against the whole world but the true owner. . . ." Ray A. Brown, The Law of Personal Property 26 (Walter B. Raushenbush 3d ed. 1975). To test the generalization, suppose that *F1* loses a watch he had earlier found and that it is subsequently found by *F2*. *F1* sues *F2* for return of the watch. Who wins? The answer, as it happens, is that *F1* wins. Knowing this, can you revise the statement from Brown quoted above so that it accurately states the law?

We saw in the last chapter that lawyers conceive of property as referring to relationships among people with respect to things, not to a relationship between

---

1. Some information about the parties in this famous case: The plaintiff was, as indicated, a chimney sweeper's boy named Armory. Chimney sweepers—or sweeps, as we would say today—came into demand in the seventeenth century, when middle-class people started living in houses with fireplaces in every room. Flues were made to be small (about 9 by 14 inches), so that several could fit into one chimney. Hence sweeps employed little boys, sometimes as young as age four, to clean the flues, removing soot with brooms and scrapers as they worked their way up the tight spaces. The boys wore stovepipe hats to dislodge soot and keep it out of their eyes. See Neal Singer, Chimney Sweeps Are Plunging into Their Work Again, Smithsonian Magazine, Sept. 1995, at 97.

As for the defendant, his surname (de Lamerie, given name Paul) was misspelled by the court reporter. He was a goldsmith, but made his reputation working in silver. He was the most celebrated and prolific silversmith of the finest period of English silver work, the first half of the eighteenth century. His work can be seen in many American museums, and his finest pieces have sold at auction for more than $1 million.—EDS.

a person and a thing. See footnote 33 on page 51. The *F1-F2* problem provides an illustration of that proposition. The meaning of the phrase *true owner* depends upon who the other claimants are. Title, or ownership, is *relative*. B can have title as against C but not as against A.

The rule that a prior possessor prevails over a subsequent possessor applies in cases involving land as well as in cases involving personal property. See Percy Bordwell, Ejectment Takes Over, 55 Iowa L. Rev. 1089 (1970).

2. In Armory v. Delamirie the plaintiff sued defendant in trover. *Trover* is a common law action for money damages resulting from the defendant's conversion to his own use of a chattel owned or possessed by the plaintiff. The plaintiff waives his right to obtain the return of the chattel and insists that the defendant be subjected to a forced purchase of the chattel from him. If the defendant loses, he must pay money damages to the plaintiff. What is the measure of damages: the value of the chattel at the time the conversion occurs or the value of the plaintiff's interest (i.e., the value of the chattel discounted by the probability that the true owner will appear and reclaim it)? Which measure did the court adopt? Is it sound?

3. Suppose that in 1723 the true owner of the jewel involved in the *Armory* case appeared at the goldsmith's shop and demanded return of the jewel. What are the rights of the goldsmith and the true owner as against each other and as against the chimney sweeper's boy? See the case of The Winkfield, [1902] P. 42 (1901), involving a voluntary bailment,[2] where the court said: "The wrongdoer, having once paid full damages to the bailee, has an answer to any action by the bailor."

In voluntary bailment situations, as in The Winkfield, the courts usually bar an action by the true owner against the present possessor if the bailee has recovered from the present possessor. See Note, Bailment: The Winkfield Doctrine, 34 Cornell L.Q. 615 (1949). Should they bar an action by the true owner against the present possessor when a *finder* or *prior wrongful possessor* has recovered from the present possessor? Why might this case be treated differently? See Brown, supra, at §11.11.

4. Would it have made any difference in Armory v. Delamirie if the chimney sweeper's boy had taken the jewel off a dressing table in the house where he was cleaning the chimney? In Anderson v. Gouldberg, 53 N.W. 636 (Minn. 1892), the plaintiffs trespassed upon the timberland of a third party, cut logs, and hauled

---

2. A bailment is the rightful possession of goods by a person (the bailee) who is not the owner. A voluntary bailment occurs when the owner of the goods (the bailor) gives possession to the bailee, as when you leave your clothes with a laundry or check your coat at a restaurant or turn over your car keys to a parking lot attendant or deposit mail in the post office. In the case of found goods, the bailment is involuntary from the standpoint of the owner but not from that of the finder, who has, after all, chosen to take possession; by doing so, the finder assumes the obligations of a bailee. What are those obligations? Traditionally, the answer to that question has turned on an elaborate scheme of classification according to which some bailees were held to a standard of great care, some (such as finders) to a standard of minimal care, and the balance to an ordinary negligence standard of reasonable care under the circumstances. The modern view is that the latter standard should apply across the board. See Richard H. Helmholz, Bailment Theories and the Liability of Bailees: The Elusive Uniform Standard of Reasonable Care, 41 U. Kan. L. Rev. 97 (1992).

them to a mill, where the defendants took them. In an action of *replevin* (a lawsuit to obtain return of the goods, not damages), the court ruled for the plaintiffs and said:

> Therefore the only question is whether bare possession of property, though wrongfully obtained, is sufficient title to enable the party enjoying it to maintain replevin against a mere stranger, who takes it from him. We had supposed that this was settled in the affirmative as long ago, at least, as the early case of Armory v. Delamirie, 1 Strange 505, so often cited on that point.
>
> When it is said that to maintain replevin the plaintiff's possession must have been lawful, it means merely that it must have been lawful as against the person who deprived him of it; and possession is good title against all the world except those having a better title.
>
> Counsel says that possession only raises a presumption of title, which, however, may be rebutted. Rightly understood, this is correct; but counsel misapplies it. One who takes property from the possession of another can only rebut this presumption by showing a superior title in himself, or in some way connecting himself with one who has. One who has acquired the possession of property, whether by finding, bailment, or by mere tort, has a right to retain that possession as against a mere wrongdoer who is a stranger to the property. Any other rule would lead to an endless series of unlawful seizures and reprisals in every case where property had once passed out of the possession of the rightful owner. [53 N.W. at 637.]

Richard H. Helmholz, Wrongful Possession of Chattels: Hornbook Law and Case Law, 80 Nw. U. L. Rev. 1221 (1986), notes that cases like *Anderson*, involving two wrongdoers, seldom arise. After surveying a number of substantive areas (including the law of finders), Helmholz concludes that in the more common case of disputes between a prior wrongful possessor and an honest subsequent one, courts regularly prefer the latter—in quiet defiance of the hornbook rule. The rule of prior possession is said to be explicitly invoked only in support of honest claimants. See also John V. Orth, *Russell v. Hill* (N.C. 1899): Misunderstood Lessons, 73 N.C. L. Rev. 2031 (1995). Quite to the contrary, however, is a more recent case, Payne v. TK Auto Wholesalers, 911 A.2d 747 (Conn. App. 2006), citing *Anderson* favorably and recognizing the possessory interest of a wrongdoer as against all but the true owner of the property in question.

5. Should the courts be more willing to grant replevin to the prior possessor than to grant money damages? See Annot., 150 A.L.R. 163 (1944). Should it matter whether the true owner is known?

Replevin and trover are actions involving personal property. The action similar to replevin in real property cases[3] is an action for possession (ejectment), and the action similar to trover is an action for damages (trespass).[4] The courts

---

3. Real property is that sort of property for which a "real action," as distinct from a "personal action," could be brought in the king's courts in feudal times. The word *real* is derived from the Latin *res* meaning "thing" and was applied to actions concerning land because, if an owner had been wrongfully deprived of land, the remedy was restoration of the land (i.e., the thing) itself, whereas in a "personal action" (which was, in early times, all that could be brought in respect of movable goods), the court would allow payment of the value of the goods instead of compelling their return. After considerable hesitancy, the law finally developed the action of replevin for the specific return of movable goods, but by this time the name personal property had become stuck to them.

4. The common law actions of trover, replevin, ejectment, and trespass, which were complicated by numerous procedural niceties, have in most states been simplified and in many renamed. We leave these details for your course in Civil Procedure, but note that the essential difference in remedies afforded by these actions—the return of the thing as opposed to damages—is preserved in modern codes of civil procedure.

appear to be more reluctant to give the prior possessor of land, who has no title, permanent damages than to put the prior possessor back into possession.

Hannah v. Peel

King's Bench Division, 1945
[1945] K.B. 509

Action tried by BIRKETT, J. On December 13, 1938, the freehold of Gwernhaylod House, Overton-on-Dee, Shropshire, was conveyed to the defendant, Major Hugh Edward Ethelston Peel, who from that time to the end of 1940 never himself occupied the house and it remained unoccupied until October 5, 1939, when it was requisitioned [for quartering soldiers], but after some months was released from requisition. Thereafter it remained unoccupied until July 18, 1940, when it was again requisitioned, the defendant being compensated by a payment at the rate of 250 *l.* a year. In August, 1940, the plaintiff, Duncan Hannah, a lance-corporal, serving in a battery of the Royal Artillery, was stationed at the house and on the 21st of that month, when in a bedroom, used as a sick-bay, he was adjusting the black-out curtains when his hand touched something on the top of a window-frame, loose in a crevice, which he thought was a piece of dirt or plaster. The plaintiff grasped it and dropped it on the outside window ledge. On the following morning he saw that it was a brooch covered with cobwebs and dirt. Later, he took it with him when he went home on leave and his wife having told him it might be of value, at the end of October, 1940, he informed his commanding officer of his find and, on his advice, handed it over to the police, receiving a receipt for it. In August, 1942, the owner not having been found the police handed the brooch to the defendant, who sold it in October, 1942, for 66*l.*, to Messrs. Spink & Son, Ltd., of London, who resold it in the following month for 88*l.* There was no evidence that the defendant had any knowledge of the existence of the brooch before it was found by the plaintiff. The defendant had offered the plaintiff a reward for the brooch, but the plaintiff refused to accept this and maintained throughout his right to the possession of the brooch as against all persons other than the owner, who was unknown. By a letter, dated October 5, 1942, the plaintiff's solicitors demanded the return of the brooch from the defendant, but it was not returned and on October 21, 1943, the plaintiff issued his writ claiming the return of the brooch, or its value, and damages for its detention. By his defence, the defendant claimed the brooch on the ground that he was the owner of Gwernhaylod House and in possession thereof. . . .

BIRKETT, J. There is no issue of fact in this case between the parties. As to the issue in law, the rival claims of the parties can be stated in this way: The plaintiff says: "I claim the brooch as its finder and I have a good title against all the world, save only the true owner." The defendant says: "My claim is superior to yours in as much as I am the freeholder. The brooch was found on my property, although I was never in occupation, and my title, therefore, ousts yours and in the absence

Gwernhaylod House, Overton-on-Dee
Gwernhaylod, a Welsh word, means sunny marsh. Gwernhaylod House
was originally built ein 1460, rebuilt in 1740, and torn down in 1950.

of the true owner I am entitled to the brooch or its value." Unhappily the law on this issue is in a very uncertain state and there is need of an authoritative decision of a higher court. Obviously if it could be said with certainty that this is the law, that the finder of a lost article, wherever found, has a good title against all the world save the true owner, then, of course, all my difficulties would be resolved; or again, if it could be said with equal certainty that this is the law, that the possessor of land is entitled as against the finder to all chattels found on the land, again my difficulties would be resolved. But, unfortunately, the authorities give some support to each of these conflicting propositions. . . .

The case of Bridges v. Hawkesworth, 21 L.J. (Q.B.) 75, 15 Jur. 1079, was . . . an appeal against a decision of the county court judge at Westminster. The facts appear to have been that in the year 1847 the plaintiff, who was a commercial traveller, called on a firm named Byfield & Hawkesworth on business, as he was in the habit of doing, and as he was leaving the shop he picked up a small parcel which was lying on the floor. He immediately showed it to the shopman, and opened it in his presence, when it was found to consist of a quantity of Bank of England notes, to the amount of 65*l*. The defendant, who was a partner in the firm of Byfield & Hawkesworth, was then called, and the plaintiff told him he had found the notes, and asked the defendant to keep them until the owner appeared to claim them. Then various advertisements were put in the papers asking for the owner, but the true owner was never found. No person having appeared to claim them, and three years having elapsed since they were found, the plaintiff applied to the defendant to have the notes returned to him, and offered to pay the expenses of the advertisements, and to give an indemnity. The defendant refused to deliver them up to the plaintiff, and an action was brought in the county court of Westminster in consequence of that refusal. The county court judge decided that the defendant, the shopkeeper, was entitled to the custody of the notes as against the plaintiff, and gave judgment for the defendant. Thereupon the appeal was brought which came before the court composed by Patteson, J., and Wightman, J. Patteson, J., said: "The notes which are the subject of this action were incidentally dropped, by mere accident, in the shop of the defendant, by the owner of them. The facts do not warrant the supposition that they had been deposited there intentionally, nor has the case been put at all upon that ground. The plaintiff found them on the floor, they being manifestly lost by someone. The general right of the finder to any article which has been lost, as against all the world, except the true owner, was established in the case of Armory v. Delamirie, 1 Str. 505, which has never been disputed. This right would clearly have accrued to the plaintiff had the notes been picked up by him outside the shop of the defendant and if he once had the right, the case finds that he did not intend, by delivering the notes to the defendant, to waive the title (if any) which he had to them, but they were handed to the defendant merely for the purpose of delivering them to the owner should he appear." Then a little later: "The case, therefore, resolves itself into the single point on which it appears that the learned judge decided it, namely, whether the circumstance of the notes being found inside the defendant's shop gives him, the defendant, the right to have them as against the plaintiff, who found them." After discussing the cases, and the argument, the learned judge said: "If the discovery had never been communicated to the defendant, could the real owner have had any cause of action against him because they were found in his house? Certainly not. The notes never were in the custody of the defendant, nor within the protection of his house, before they were found, as they would have been had they been intentionally deposited there; and the defendant has come under no responsibility, except from the communication made to him by the plaintiff, the finder, and the steps taken by way of advertisement. . . . We find, therefore, no circumstances in this case to take it out of the general rule of law, that the finder of a lost article is entitled to it as against all persons except the real owner, and we think that that rule must prevail, and that the learned judge was mistaken in holding that the place in which they were found makes any legal difference. Our judgment, therefore, is that the plaintiff is entitled to these notes as against the defendant."

It is to be observed that in Bridges v. Hawkesworth, which has been the subject of immense disputation, neither counsel put forward any argument on the fact that the notes were found in a shop. Counsel for the appellant assumed throughout that the position was the same as if the parcel had been found in a private house, and the learned judge spoke of "the protection of his" (the shopkeeper's) "house." The case for the appellant was that the shopkeeper never knew of the notes. Again, what is curious is that there was no suggestion that the place where the notes were found was in any way material; indeed, the judge in giving the judgment of the court expressly repudiates this and said in terms "The learned judge was mistaken in holding that the place in which they were found makes any legal difference." It is, therefore, a little remarkable that in South Staffordshire Water

Co. v. Sharman, [1896] 2 Q.B. 44, Lord Russell of Killowen, C.J., said: "The case of Bridges v. Hawkesworth stands by itself, and on special grounds; and on those grounds it seems to me that the decision in that case was right. Someone had accidentally dropped a bundle of banknotes in a public shop. The shopkeeper did not know they had been dropped, and did not in any sense exercise control over them. The shop was open to the public, and they were invited to come there." That might be a matter of some doubt. Customers were invited there, but whether the public at large was, might be open to some question. Lord Russell continued: "A customer picked up the notes and gave them to the shopkeeper in order that he might advertise them. The owner of the notes was not found, and the finder then sought to recover them from the shopkeeper. It was held that he was entitled to do so, the ground of the decision being, as was pointed out by Patteson, J., that the notes, being dropped in the public part of the shop, were never in the custody of the shopkeeper, or 'within the protection of his house.'" Patteson, J., never made any reference to the public part of the shop and, indeed, went out of his way to say that the learned county court judge was wrong in holding that the place where they were found made any legal difference. . . .

With regard to South Staffordshire Water Co. v. Sharman, [1896] 2 Q.B. 44, the first two lines of the headnote are: "The possessor of land is generally entitled, as against the finder, to chattels found on the land." I am not sure that this is accurate. The facts were that the defendant Sharman, while cleaning out, under the orders of the plaintiffs, the South Staffordshire Water Company, a pool of water on their land, found two rings embedded in the mud at the bottom of the pool. He declined to deliver them to the plaintiffs, but failed to discover the real owner. In an action brought by the company against Sharman in detinue it was held that the company was entitled to the rings. Lord Russell of Killowen, C.J., said: "The plaintiffs are the freeholders of the locus in quo, and as such they have the right to forbid anybody coming on their land or in any way interfering with it. They had the right to say that their pool should be cleaned out in any way that they thought fit, and to direct what should be done with anything found in the pool in the course of such cleaning out. It is no doubt right, as the counsel for the defendant contended, to say that the plaintiffs must show that they had actual control over the locus in quo and the things in it; but under the circumstances, can it be said that the Minster Pool and whatever might be in that pool were not under the control of the plaintiffs? In my opinion they were. . . . The principle on which this case must be decided, and the distinction which must be drawn between this case and that of Bridges v. Hawkesworth, is to be found in a passage in Pollock and Wright's essay on Possession in the Common Law, p. 41: 'The possession of land carries with it in general, by our law, possession of everything which is attached to or under that land, and, in the absence of a better title elsewhere, the right to possess it also. . . .'" And it makes no difference that the possessor is not aware of the thing's existence. . . .

Then Lord Russell cited the passage which I read earlier in this judgment and continued: "It is somewhat strange"—I venture to echo those words—"that there is no more direct authority on the question; but the general principle seems to me to be that where a person has possession of house or land, with a manifest intention to exercise control over it and the things which may be upon or in it, then, if something is found on that land, whether by an employee of the owner or by a stranger, the presumption is that the possession of that thing is in the owner of the locus in quo." It is to be observed that Lord Russell there is extending the meaning of the passage he had cited from Pollock and Wright's essay on Possession in the Common Law, where the learned authors say that the possession of "land carries with it possession of everything which is attached to or under that land." Then Lord Russell adds possession of everything which may be on or in that land. South Staffordshire Water Co. v. Sharman, which was relied on by counsel for the defendant, has also been the subject of some discussion. It has been said that it establishes that if a man finds a thing as the servant or agent of another, he finds it not for himself, but for that other, and indeed that seems to afford a sufficient explanation of the case. The rings found at the bottom of the pool were not in the possession of the company, but it seems that though Sharman was the first to obtain possession of them, he obtained them for his employers and could claim no title for himself.

The only other case to which I need refer is Elwes v. Brigg Gas Co., 33 Ch. D. 562, in which land had been demised to a gas company for ninety-nine years with a reservation to the lessor of all mines and minerals. A pre-historic boat embedded in the soil was discovered by the lessees when they were digging to make a gasholder. It was held that the boat, whether regarded as a mineral or as part of the soil in which it was embedded when discovered, or as a chattel, did not pass to the lessees by the demise, but was the property of the lessor though he was ignorant of its existence at the time of granting the lease. Chitty, J., said: "The first question which does actually arise in this case is whether the boat belonged to the plaintiff at the time of the granting of the lease. I hold that it did, whether it ought to be regarded as a mineral, or as part of the soil within the maxim above cited, or as a chattel. If it was a mineral or part of the soil in the sense above indicated, then it clearly belonged to the owners of the inheritance as part of the inheritance itself. But if it ought to be regarded as a chattel, I hold the property in the chattel was vested in the plaintiff, for the following reasons." Then he gave the reasons, and continued: "The plaintiff then being thus in possession of the chattel, it follows that the property in the chattel was vested in him. Obviously the right of the original owner could not be established; it had for centuries been lost or barred, even supposing that the property had not been abandoned when the boat was first left on the spot where it was found. The plaintiff, then, had a lawful possession, good against all the world, and therefore the property in the boat. In my opinion it makes no difference, in these circumstances, that the plaintiff was not aware of the existence of the boat."[5]

[handwritten margin note: FOUND PRE-HISTORIC BOAT]

5. "Thus the case ended," says a comment on *Elwes* written a century later. "Mr. Elwes, having gained possession of the boat, exhibited it in a specially constructed brick building in the estate yard, near Brigg Station. There for twenty-three years many thousands of visitors paid for admission to see it." Subsequently Elwes gave the boat to a public museum at Hull. "[I]t was carefully removed to Hull, via the River Ancholme (appropriately

A review of these judgments shows that the authorities are in an unsatisfactory state. . . .

It is fairly clear from the authorities that a man possesses everything which is attached to or under his land. Secondly, it would appear to be the law from the authorities I have cited, and particularly from Bridges v. Hawkesworth, that a man does not necessarily possess a thing which is lying unattached on the surface of his land even though the thing is not possessed by someone else. A difficulty, however, arises . . . because the rule which governs things an occupier possesses as against those which he does not, has never been very clearly formulated in our law. . . .

There is no doubt that in this case the brooch was lost in the ordinary meaning of that term, and I should imagine it had been lost for a very considerable time. Indeed, from this correspondence it appears that at one time the predecessors in title of the defendant were considering making some claim. But the moment the plaintiff discovered that the brooch might be of some value, he took the advice of his commanding officer and handed it to the police. His conduct was commendable and meritorious. The defendant was never physically in possession of these premises at any time. It is clear that the brooch was never his, in the ordinary acceptation of the term, in that he had the prior possession. He had no knowledge of it, until it was brought to his notice by the finder. A discussion of the merits does not seem to help, but it is clear on the facts that the brooch was "lost" in the ordinary meaning of that word, that it was "found" by the plaintiff in the ordinary meaning of that word, that its true owner has never been found, that the defendant was the owner of the premises and had his notice drawn to this matter by the plaintiff, who found the brooch. In those circumstances I propose to follow the decision in Bridges v. Hawkesworth, and to give judgment in this case for the plaintiff for 66l.

Judgment for plaintiff.

NOTES AND QUESTIONS

1. Did Major Peel lose because he did not have prior possession, or did he not have prior possession because he lost?

2. How effective was the court's marshalling of precedent to support its decision? Was its reasoning persuasive? Was the court relying upon horse sense? Do the words of the court act as a guide for the prediction of the outcome of similar, but not too similar, cases?

3. Suppose Major Peel had resided in Gwernhaylod House from December 1938 until the first requisition in October 1939. Would the result in Hannah v. Peel be the same? See Parker v. British Airways Bd., [1982] 2 W.L.R. 503, 516-517:

---

enough), though in a rather different method from the trip it made on the same river some two thousand or more years ago. Would that it had remained in Brigg! In 1943 the boat was destroyed in an air raid on the museum premises." Michael L. Nash, Are Finders Keepers? One Hundred Years Since *Elwes v. Brigg Gas Co.*, 137 New L.J. 118, 119 (1987).—Eds.

"I would be inclined to say that the occupier of a house will almost invariably possess any lost article on the premises. He may not have taken any positive steps to demonstrate his *animus possidendi*, but so firm is his control that the *animus* can be seen to attach to it" (per Eveleigh, L.J.). Cf. Margaret J. Radin, Property and Personhood, 34 Stan. L. Rev. 957, 987, 991-996 (1982) (sanctity of the home); Stephanie M. Stern, Residential Protectionism and the Legal Mythology of Home, 107 Mich. L. Rev. 1093 (2009) (drawing on studies in psychology, sociology, and demography to argue that very little evidence supports the notion that people regard their homes as special objects).

Or suppose (as was the fact) that the house had never been occupied by Peel but also never requisitioned by the government. Hannah, while stationed at a nearby military base, went for a walk in the woods around Gwernhaylod House, was intrigued by the imposing mansion, entered by the unlocked front door, and found the brooch. Would the result in Hannah v. Peel be the same? Recall Problem 1 on page 33, and see Favorite v. Miller, 407 A.2d 974, 977 (Conn. 1978) (owner of locus prevails as against trespassing finder unless trespass "trivial or merely technical"); Bishop v. Ellsworth, 234 N.E.2d 49, 52 (Ill. App. 1968) ("if the discoverer is a trespasser such trespasser can have no claim to possession of such property even if it might otherwise be considered lost"). But see Hendle v. Stevens, 586 N.E.2d 826, 832 (Ill. App. 1992) ("we think the *Bishop* court's statement that a trespasser has no claim to possession of lost property is erroneous").

McAvoy v. Medina

Supreme Judicial Court of Massachusetts, 1866
93 Mass. (11 Allen) 548

Tort to recover a sum of money found by the plaintiff in the shop of the defendant.

At the trial in the superior court, before Morton, J., it appeared that the defendant was a barber, and the plaintiff, being a customer in the defendant's shop, saw and took up a pocket-book which was lying upon a table there, and said, "See what I have found." The defendant came to the table and asked where he found it. The plaintiff laid it back in the same place and said, "I found it right there." The defendant then took it and counted the money, and the plaintiff told him to keep it, and if the owner should come to give it to him; and otherwise to advertise it; which the defendant promised to do. Subsequently the plaintiff made three demands for the money, and the defendant never claimed to hold the same till the last demand. It was agreed that the pocket-book was placed upon the table by a transient customer of the defendant and accidentally left there, and was first seen and taken up by the plaintiff, and that the owner had not been found.

The judge ruled that the plaintiff could not maintain his action, and a verdict was accordingly returned for the defendant; and the plaintiff alleged exceptions. . . .

DEWEY, J. It seems to be the settled law that the finder of lost property has a valid claim to the same against all the world except the true owner, and generally that the place in which it is found creates no exception to this rule. 2 Parsons on Con. 97. Bridges v. Hawkesworth, 7 Eng. Law & Eq. R. 424.

But this property is not, under the circumstances, to be treated as lost property in that sense in which a finder has a valid claim to hold the same until called for by the true owner. This property was voluntarily placed upon a table in the defendant's shop by a customer of his who accidentally left the same there and has never called for it. The plaintiff also came there as a customer, and first saw the same and took it up from the table. The plaintiff did not by this acquire the right to take the property from the shop, but it was rather the duty of the defendant, when the fact became thus known to him, to use reasonable care for the safe keeping of the same until the owner should call for it. In the case of Bridges v. Hawkesworth the property, although found in a shop, was found on the floor of the same, and had not been placed there voluntarily by the owner, and the court held that the finder was entitled to the possession of the same, except as to the owner. But the present case more resembles that of Lawrence v. The State, 1 Humph. (Tenn.) 228, and is indeed very similar in its facts. The court there take a distinction between the case of property thus placed by the owner and neglected to be removed, and property lost. It was there held that "to place a pocket-book upon a table and to forget to take it away is not to lose it, in the sense in which the authorities referred to speak of lost property."

We accept this as the better rule, and especially as one better adapted to secure the rights of the true owner.

In view of the facts of this case, the plaintiff acquired no original right to the property, and the defendant's subsequent acts in receiving and holding the property in the manner he did does not create any.

Exceptions overruled.

NOTES AND QUESTIONS

1. *The rule in* McAvoy. An essay by Walter Wheeler Cook, Ownership and Possession, in 11 Encyclopedia of the Social Sciences 521, 524 (1935), says this: "It is obvious . . . that from the point of view of social policy the shopkeeper ought to be preferred to the customer, as in that event the article would be more likely to get back into the possession of the real owner." Do you agree? Are you sure?

2. *Mislaid, lost, and abandoned property.* A typical summary of the common law rules on finders runs like this: "A finder of property acquires no rights in mislaid property, is entitled to possession of lost property against everyone except the true owner, and is entitled to keep abandoned property." Michael v. First Chicago Corp., 487 N.E.2d 403, 409 (Ill. App. 1985).

Like many typical summaries, this one is a bit misleading. The statement regarding mislaid property is correct, but the statement regarding lost property is not—at least in some jurisdictions. Notice, for example, that the statement

"There's my wallet—right where I left it."

Was the wallet lost, or mislaid?

neglects the distinctions, suggested in Hannah v. Peel, having to do with the circumstances under which lost goods are found: Embedded in the soil, or not? Found in a public place, or a private one? Such considerations can matter. Should they?

The statement is also probably inaccurate as to abandoned property, meaning items intentionally and voluntarily relinquished, with no intent to reclaim. The dominant concern of the law of finders—to protect true owners—drops out in the case of abandoned property, because the true owner has renounced any claim, but the interests of the owner of the place of the find remain. Should they count?

3. *Employees and other agents.* A janitor cleaning up in a hotel finds a sum of money and turns it in to the manager. After a year the money is unclaimed, and the janitor sues for its return. Who wins? The law here sprawls all over the lot, with decisions commonly turning on the lost-mislaid-abandoned distinction, or on the place of the find, or on the law of principal and agent. See, e.g., Jackson v. Steinberg, 200 P.2d 376 (Or. 1948) ($800 found by chambermaid under paper lining in dresser drawer awarded to hotel owner on theory that it was mislaid property that the maid had a duty to deliver to her employer); Erickson v. Sinykin, 26 N.W.2d 172 (Minn. 1947) (money found by interior decorator held

abandoned, and decorator, unlike a maid or janitor, had no duty to report find to employer); Kalyvakis v. The T.S.S. Olympia, 181 F. Supp. 32 (S.D.N.Y. 1960) ($3,000 found by ship steward on floor of ship's public men's room awarded to finder on ground that it was lost or abandoned; court rejected English master-servant (principal-agent) exception as not in accord with the weight of American authority).

What about finds by police officers? They commonly come across money in the course of their duties, and sometimes they (or their supervisors) want to keep it. A 1995 Oklahoma case arose when the Hoel family saw money scattered along a road as they drove home from dinner. Mrs. Hoel contacted authorities, while Mr. Hoel and one of his sons secured the scene. A little while later a deputy sheriff arrived and took possession of the money, $4,600 in hundred dollar bills. The Hoels told him they wanted the money if its rightful owner were not located. A half year later, the sheriff's office started an action seeking permission to deposit the money in the Sheriff's Training Fund, arguing that the Hoels had never taken possession of it. The court held for the Hoels. They hadn't taken literal possession of the money, but only because the deputy had ordered them not to touch it. They had taken charge of the scene before the deputy arrived, and that was enough to give them the rights of a finder—rights superior to anyone (even a sheriff!) but the true owner of the funds. See Hoel v. Powell, 904 P.2d 153 (Okla. App. 1995). See also Pennsylvania v. $7,000 in U.S. Currency, 742 A.2d 711 (Pa. Commw. Ct. 1999), and In re Funds in the Possession of Conemaugh Township, 724 A.2d 990 (Pa. Commw. Ct. 1999).

4. *Treasure trove.* At English common law treasure trove (derived from the Old French *tresor trové*, found treasure) belonged to the king. Treasure trove was any money or coin, gold, silver plate, or bullion hidden in the earth. When the Romans were driven out of England and northern Europe, they concealed their money and treasures underground, and the kings or conquering generals, knowing this, seized the goods for themselves and punished severely any person who did not deliver up found treasures. The law drew a distinction between treasures hidden with the intention of returning to reclaim them, which went to the king, and abandoned property, which went to the finder. Nowadays, it appears, the practice of the British Crown is to give treasure trove to British museums, provided they agree to make a payment of half the value to the finder. According to a 2010 report on the BBC News, an amateur treasure hunter in Scotland found gold ornaments after exploring with his new metal detector and digging a hole when alerted by it. The trove, four neck ornaments over two thousand years old, had a value of about £1 million, half of which had to be paid to the finder (who said he would give a share to the landowner). Under American law, treasure trove has been treated in various ways over the years. Nowadays it is usually taken to include any hidden money, gold, and silver, whether or not buried underground, and the tendency is to treat it like any other found property (meaning it might be classified as lost or mislaid or abandoned). See, e.g., Corliss v. Wenner, 34 P.3d 1100 (Idaho App. 2001), refusing to recognize the doctrine of treasure trove and noting that this is the trend among state and federal courts. *Corliss* is discussed in

Richard B. Cunningham, The Twilight of Treasure Trove, in Legal Perspectives on Cultural Resources 37 (Jennifer R. Richman & Marion P. Forsyth eds. 2004). In any event, the finders might end up weepers rather than keepers. Consider the story of two laborers building a driveway on Sun Valley, Idaho property belonging to Jann Wenner, the owner of *Rolling Stone.* In the course of their work, the two men found four pounds of gold coins that had been buried in a jar. Much like the finders of money in a crashed plane in the 1998 movie, A Simple Plan, the two men schemed to keep the coins secret for a time and then share them, but the plan fell apart and the men fell out. After several years of litigation, a judge decided that Wenner had the right to the coins, estimated to be worth about $25,000. The judge rejected the law of treasure trove, considering it unsuited for modern times. He thought that because the two finders were working for Wenner, they were acting on his behalf. The coins, like the dirt the men were excavating to build the driveway, belonged to Wenner as the owner of the land. See Tad Friend, The Gold Diggers, The New Yorker, May 3, 1999, at 80.

For three more recent cases involving the categorical finders' rules considered in all the foregoing discussion, see Benjamin v. Lindner Aviation, Inc., 534 N.W.2d 400 (Iowa 1995), In re Seizure of $82,000 More or Less, 119 F. Supp. 2d 1013 (W.D. Mo. 2000), and Terry v. Lock Hospitality, 37 S.W.2d 202 (Ark. 2001). In *Benjamin*, $18,000 was found in the wing of an old airplane by an inspector removing rusty screws. Obviously, the money had not been "lost." The court deemed it to be mislaid property, possessed by the owner of the airplane. It had not been concealed long enough to be a treasure trove, and was not abandoned because no one would abandon so much money (not even a thief or a drug dealer?). *Benjamin* was distinguished by the court in the *In re Seizure* case, notwithstanding similar facts—money found in the gas tank of a car. The important difference was that the car had been seized by the government because it had been used to transport drug proceeds, and then sold (without discovery of the stash) to a buyer who subsequently noticed a fuel problem. A mechanic hired to fix the problem found the cash and informed the Drug Enforcement Agency, which claimed the money as against the buyer of the car. The court held for the buyer on the ground that the money had been abandoned, not mislaid; the culprits who hid it in the gas tank couldn't claim it without risking arrest for drug dealing, so they chose to leave it behind. Thus abandoned, it belonged to the buyer as the first person to find it (the mechanic was merely the buyer's agent). *Terry* involved a box of money, $38,000 in old currency hidden above the ceiling, which was discovered by contractors working on a motel. Possession of the find was awarded to the motel owner—for exactly the reasons set out in *Benjamin*, on which the court relied.

5. *Shipwrecks.* Under English common law, "wreck"—which referred very narrowly to cargo washed ashore from a ship lost at sea with no survivors—went to the crown. Blackstone claimed that this right in the king was "grounded on the consideration of his guarding and protecting the seas from pirates and robbers." 1 William Blackstone, Commentaries *290. Under traditional maritime law, a ship lost at sea and settled on the ocean floor remained the owner's property—unless

"The way I see it, we divvy up — a third for you, a third for me, and a third
for Sam — and what the George A. Fuller Company don't know won't hurt them."

title to the vessel had been abandoned—but anyone subsequently reducing the ship or its cargo to possession was entitled to a salvage award. See Columbus-America Discovery Group v. Atlantic Mutual Ins. Co., 974 F.2d 450 (4th Cir. 1992) (holding that the insurers of the *Central America*, which had sunk in 1857, had not abandoned their title and were still owners of $1 billion in gold on board; the salvors who had found the ship were entitled to a salvage award).

In this country, the law of finders has usually been applied to ships lost in territorial waters, and the finder held entitled to an abandoned shipwreck unless the wreck was embedded in land owned or possessed by another. Given this, the United States and individual states have successfully asserted claims to shipwrecks embedded in their territorial waters and thus constructively possessed. In the Abandoned Shipwreck Act of 1987, 43 U.S.C.A. §§2101-2106, the United States asserts title to any abandoned shipwreck embedded in submerged lands of a state and simultaneously transfers its title to the state in which the wreck is located. The purpose is to turn over management of embedded shipwrecks in state waters to the states and permit them to develop their own rules for salvage or preservation unimpeded by the general law. (The act provides that the law of finds and the law of salvage shall not apply to abandoned shipwrecks covered by its provisions.) For criticism of the act, see Forrest Booth, Who Owns Sunken Treasure? The Supreme Court, the Abandoned Shipwreck Act, and the Brother Jonathan, 11 U.S.F. Mar. L.J. 77 (1998-1999).

Maritime law and its principle of salvage awards, mentioned above, contrasts sharply with property law, which awards a finder all or nothing, subject to the rights of the true owner. Should the law of finders be changed so that the finder is entitled to an award (a reward) if the property in question is returned to its owner or held to be in possession of the owner of the locus?[6] Or should the law be changed so that in hard cases, when no clear policy objective seems to dominate, the value of the find should be split between the finder and the owner of the locus?[7]

---

6. There is no common law right to a reward, though statutes in some states may confer such a right. Moreover, finders and custodians may claim any reward that the owner of the goods has offered, as well as reimbursement for reasonable expenses incurred in securing and caring for the property in question—this as a consequence of the law of bailments. See footnote 2 on page 127.

The right to a reward seems to be more common among civil law jurisdictions in Europe (civil law here meaning codified law that derives from the Roman law tradition). An example is Article 971 of the German Civil Code:

(1) The finder may demand a finder's fee from the person entitled to receive the thing. The finder's fee amounts to five per cent of the value of the thing up to one thousand Deutsch marks, three per cent of the value above this figure, and in the case of animals three per cent. If the thing represents value only to the person entitled to receive it, the finder's fee shall be fixed in an equitable manner.

(2) The claim is not allowed if the finder violates the duty of reporting or hides the found property when inquiry is made.

7. Another kind of division—between custody and eventual ownership—is also possible: "[W]here the article is found in a quasi-public place, the occupier will be allowed to hold it, but he must relinquish it to the finder if the owner remains unascertained after a reasonable time." David Riesman, Jr., Possession and the Law of Finders, 52 Harv. L. Rev. 1105, 1125 (1939) (a classic essay well worth reading in its entirety). What do you think of Riesman's suggestion? What is it supposed to accomplish? Could it at times be fruitfully

6. *Barry Bonds' record-setting home-run baseball.* Recall mention in the last chapter (see footnote 23 on page 39) of Popov v. Hayashi, Superior Court of California, 2002, the case resulting from competing claims to the ball that Barry Bonds hit out of the park for his record-breaking seventy-third home run of the 2001 season. The facts, essentially, were these: Popov came to the game prepared, wearing a glove and positioning himself in the area where Bonds hit most of his home runs. Popov caught the home-run ball, although maybe not securely; he was engulfed by a crowd as the ball entered his glove, tackled, grabbed, hit, and kicked. The ball ended up on the ground. Hayashi picked it up and put it in his pocket. After a while he disclosed it. Popov grabbed for it, unsuccessfully. Security guards took Hayashi away.

Popov sued on various grounds. The judge found that it was never clear whether Popov would have retained control of the ball if the crowd had not interfered with his efforts. "Prior to the time the ball was hit," the judge wrote, "it was possessed and owned by Major League Baseball. At the time it was hit it became intentionally abandoned property. The first person who came in possession of the ball became its new owner." But the parties disagreed about the definition of possession. The judge appointed a panel of four law professors to help him resolve the disagreement, and held an open forum at the University of California, Hastings College of Law in San Francisco. The professors also disagreed on the issue of possession. Various precedents, including Pierson v. Post (see page 18), were considered. The judge concluded that the meaning of possession was contextual: a hunter acquires possession of an animal by mortally wounding it, not by the actual eventual capture; in the case of maritime salvage, possession of a wreck requires as much control as the situation permits; in the case of a baseball, possession requires full control. But, though Popov had not established that he had full control, he might have done so if the mob had not intervened, and the judge held that where an actor takes significant but incomplete steps toward full control and is interrupted by wrongful acts, he has a pre-possessory interest, a qualified right of possession. Hayashi picked up the ball subject to that right. He was not a wrongdoer, but to give him the ball would be unfair to Popov. By the same token, to give it to Popov would be unfair to Hayashi. The judge concluded: "Both men have a superior claim to the ball as against all the world. Each man has a claim of equal dignity as to the other." This being the case, the judge applied the concept of equitable division, citing Richard H. Helmholz, Equitable Division and the Law of Finders, 52 Fordham L. Rev. 313 (1983), who considered that the concept provided a good way to resolve competing claims, each as strong as the other.

---

combined with Helmholz's idea of equitable division? Can you imagine how the concept of possession underlying the common law of finders probably led the courts to neglect various sorts of division (in time or value or both) in favor of the all-or-nothing approach that characterizes the law of finders?

For an example of a decision recognizing the important but regularly overlooked distinction between custody of the found item for now and ownership of the found item eventually, see Paset v. Old Orchard Bank & Trust Co., 378 N.E.2d 1264 (Ill. App. 1978) (making locus owner temporary custodian and then vesting ownership in finder).

According to a July 19, 2005 report on CourtTV.com, the judge ordered that the ball be sold and the proceeds divided equally between the two men. The ball was estimated to be worth as much as $1.5 million, but ended up selling at auction for $450,000. The shortfall, according to the CourtTV account, gave rise to another legal battle. Popov's attorney obtained a freeze on his client's half of the money to help pay a legal bill of $473,530.32.

For law review commentary, see, e.g., Steven Semeraro, An Essay on Property Rights in Milestone Home Run Baseballs, 56 SMU L. Rev. 2281 (2003); Patrick Stoklas, Popov v. Hayashi, A Modern Day Pierson v. Post: A Comment on What the Court Should Have Done with the Seventy-Third Home Run Baseball Hit by Barry Bonds, 34 Loy. U. Chi. L.J. 901 (2003); Paul Finkelman, Fugitive Baseballs and Abandoned Property: Who Owns the Home Run Ball, 23 Cardozo L. Rev. 1609 (2002).

7. *Legislation.* Many states have legislation covering lost, mislaid, and abandoned property—sometimes very lengthy and complicated legislation. A typical statute might require finders to deposit the property at a designated place, provide for notice to possible owners, and provide for an award of title—say to the finder—if the property owner does not appear within a specified period. Some statutes apply only to "lost property." These statutes have often been construed narrowly to apply only to "lost" property as defined by common law and not to abolish the common law distinctions between types of found property.

8. *Items from the news.* An article by Norimitsu Onishi, Never Lost, But Found Daily: Japanese Honesty, N.Y. Times, Jan. 8, 2004, at A1, reports on the extraordinary tendency of Japanese citizens to take found items into one of many lost-and-found centers spread throughout Japan. Even cash is commonly turned in—$23 million in 2002, for example. For a comparative study of the Japanese system, see Mark D. West, Losers: Recovering Lost Property in Japan and the United States, 37 Law & Socy. Rev. 369 (2003), who attributes much of the system's success to four factors: the uniformity and simplicity of Japanese finders' law, as compared to that in the United States; the fact that the system has been in place for a long time and thus is familiar to citizens; the many conveniently located lost-and-found centers; and the sticks and carrots of Japanese law (finders who take possession of lost goods but do not turn them in are subject to criminal penalties, owners who claim objects are required to pay a finder's fee ranging from 5 to 20 percent of the objects' value, and if no one claims an object within a specified period, the finder gets it).

Some of the features of the Japanese system can be found in some parts of the United States, and U.S. finders might be pretty honest in any event. See, e.g., Marc Santora, Teeth Missing? Try Lost and Found, N.Y. Times, Aug. 2, 2002, at B1, reporting on the lost and found operation at Grand Central Terminal in Manhattan, and expressing some surprise that so many lost items get turned in, even though the finders can claim no reward, nor do they get unclaimed goods, which go to charity. Or consider a letter to the editor by Greg Smithsimon, published in the N.Y. Times, Mar. 25, 2007. Students in Smithsimon's urban studies course at Barnard College conducted an experiment; they dropped wallets all over New York City to see if finders returned them; "in 132 drops from the Bronx to Brooklyn, the wallet was stolen only two times." And the two that weren't returned? They had been "taken during drops made on the tony Upper East Side, from blocks where median family income is $126,000 per year. Perhaps what goes around doesn't come around."

B.   Acquisition by Adverse Possession

This section continues the inquiry begun in the last, on finders. Something is owned by *A*; subsequently, and without *A*'s consent, it comes into the possession of *B*. *B* might become the thing's owner; short of that, *B* still has some rights. But, again, when is *B* in "possession," and why is *B*'s possession—which might be openly adverse to the claims of *A*—even recognized by the legal system? These are exactly the questions considered in the last section, examined now in a new setting.

1.   The Theory and Elements of Adverse Possession

Powell on Real Property §91.01
(Michael A. Wolf gen. ed. 2009)

Every American jurisdiction has one or more statutes of limitations that fix the period of time beyond which the owner of land can no longer bring an action, or undertake self-help, for the recovery of land from another person in possession. These statutes of limitations differ substantially in the duration of the established periods, in provisions for extending the normally operative period, and in other particulars. These statutes are complemented and amplified by a large body of case law that elaborates on the kind of possession by another that is sufficient to cause the statutory period to begin to run, and to continue running, against the true owner. Thus, the law of adverse possession is a synthesis of statutory and decisional law.

Statutes of limitations have a long history in Anglo-American law, extending back beyond the thirteenth century. In a 1275 statute, the practice began of naming past events, beyond which no suitor in an action affecting land could search and retrieve evidence supporting title. This permitted recent seisin, even if tortiously acquired, to become protected ownership. As time passed, and as the historical events named in the statute receded into antiquity, this kind of statute lost its usefulness. A statute of 1540 adopted the more modern procedure of stipulating a period of years within which various actions had to be commenced by the real property owner. This type of statute reached its culmination in a 1623 version, which furnished the pattern for many American enactments.[8] . . .

---

8. 21 Jac. I, Ch. 16, §§1, 2 (1623): "For quieting of men's estates and avoiding of suits [described types of action] shall be sued and taken within twenty years next after the title and cause of action first descended or

Adverse possession functions as a method of transferring interests in land without the consent of the prior owner, and even in spite of the dissent of such owners. It rests upon social judgments that there should be a restricted duration for the assertion of "aging claims," and that the passage of a reasonable time period should assure security to a person claiming to be an owner. The theory upon which adverse possession rests is that the adverse possessor may acquire title at such time as an action in ejectment (or other action for possession of real property) by the record owner would be barred by the statute of limitations.

Henry W. Ballantine, Title by Adverse Possession

32 Harv. L. Rev. 135 (1918)

Title by adverse possession sounds, at first blush, like title by theft or robbery, a primitive method of acquiring land without paying for it. When the novice is told that by the weight of authority not even good faith is a requisite, the doctrine apparently affords an anomalous instance of maturing a wrong into a right contrary to one of the most fundamental axioms of the law.

> For true it is, that neither fraud nor might
> Can make a title where there wanteth right.[9]

The policy of statutes of limitation is something not always clearly appreciated. Dean Ames, in contrasting prescription in the civil law with adverse possession in our law, remarks: "English lawyers regard not the merit of the possessor, but the demerit of the one out of possession." It has been suggested, on the other hand, that the policy is to reward those using the land in a way beneficial to the community. This takes too much account of the individual case. The statute has not for its object to reward the diligent trespasser for his wrong nor yet to penalize the negligent and dormant owner for sleeping upon his rights; the great purpose is automatically to quiet all titles which are openly and consistently asserted, to provide proof of meritorious titles, and correct errors in conveyancing.

Oliver Wendell Holmes, The Path of the Law

10 Harv. L. Rev. 457, 476-477 (1897)

Let me now give an example to show the practical importance, for the decision of actual cases, of understanding the reasons of the law, by taking an example from

---

fallen, and at no time after the said twenty years; . . . and that no person or persons shall at any time hereafter make any entry into any lands, tenements or hereditaments, but within twenty years next after his or their right of title which shall hereafter first descend or accrue to the same, and in default thereof, such persons, so not entering and their heirs, shall be utterly excluded and disabled from such entry after to be made. . . ."

9. Quoted in Altham's Case, 8 Coke Rep. 153, 77 Engl. reprint, 707.

rules which, so far as I know, never have been explained or theorized about in any adequate way. I refer to statutes of limitation and the law of prescription. The end of such rules is obvious, but what is the justification for depriving a man of his rights, a pure evil as far as it goes, in consequence of the lapse of time? Sometimes the loss of evidence is referred to, but that is a secondary matter. Sometimes the desirability of peace, but why is peace more desirable after twenty years than before? It is increasingly likely to come without the aid of legislation. Sometimes it is said that, if a man neglects to enforce his rights, he cannot complain if, after a while, the law follows his example. . . .

I should suggest that the foundation of the acquisition of rights by lapse of time is to be looked for in the position of the person who gains them, not in that of the loser. Sir Henry Maine has made it fashionable to connect the archaic notion of property with prescription. But the connection is further back than the first recorded history. It is in the nature of man's mind. A thing which you have enjoyed and used as your own for a long time, whether property or an opinion, takes root in your being and cannot be torn away without your resenting the act and trying to defend yourself, however you came by it. The law can ask no better justification than the deepest instincts of man. It is only by way of reply to the suggestion that you are disappointing the former owner, that you refer to his neglect having allowed the gradual dissociation between himself and what he claims, and the gradual association of it with another. If he knows that another is doing acts which on their face show that he is on the way toward establishing such an association, I should argue that in justice to that other he was bound at his peril to find out whether the other was acting under his permission, to see that he was warned, and, if necessary, stopped.

NOTES AND QUESTIONS

1. What do you make of the passage from Oliver Wendell Holmes (written a few years before he joined the U.S. Supreme Court)? Does it suggest that adverse possession is motivated by economic concerns, or psychological ones, or moral ones? As it happens, each view finds some support. See, e.g., Richard A. Posner, Economic Analysis of Law 97-98 (8th ed. 2011) (Holmes was suggesting an economic explanation, based on diminishing marginal utility of income); Robert C. Ellickson, Bringing Culture and Human Frailty to Rational Actors: A Critique of Classical Law and Economics, 65 Chi.-Kent L. Rev. 23, 39 (1989) (Holmes "is more faithfully interpreted as anticipating (in a primitive way)" much later developments in cognitive psychology—in particular, prospect theory, which holds in part that people regard loss of an asset in hand as more significant than forgoing the opportunity to realize an apparently equivalent gain); Jeffrey E. Stake, The Uneasy Case for Adverse Possession, 89 Geo. L.J. 2419 (2001) (expanding on Ellickson); Joseph W. Singer, The Reliance Interest in Property, 40 Stan. L. Rev. 611, 667 (1988) ("The possessor has come to expect continued access to the property and the true owner has fed those expectations by her actions (or her failure to act). It is morally wrong for the true owner to allow a relationship of

dependence to be established and then to cut off the dependent party," citing the passage from Holmes.).

2. The excerpt from Powell that began this section says that adverse possession functions as a means of "transferring" ownership, and so it does, but not so straightforwardly as you might think. The running of the statute of limitations not only bars an action by the erstwhile owner but also vests a *new* title, created by operation of law, in the adverse possessor. Once acquired, this new title "relates back" to the date of the event that started the statute of limitations running, and the law acts as though the adverse possessor were the owner from that date. With what implications? Consider the rule of increase, introduced in footnote 19 on page 34. By the rule of increase, the offspring of animals belong to the owner of the mother. Suppose that at point 1 in time *A* takes possession of *B*'s cow without *B*'s consent; that at point 2 in time a calf is born to the cow; and that at point 3 in time *A* gets title to the cow by adverse possession. *A*'s title relates back to point 1 in time. Given that it is now *as though A* owned the cow since that time, *A* owns the calf too, even though *A* might not have possessed *the calf* for the statutory period. (Notice that adverse possession applies to personal property as well as land—sometimes, however, with special twists that we will take up later.)

3. How (if at all) might one reconcile adverse possession with the principle of first in time that figured so prominently in Chapter 1? See Richard A. Epstein, Past and Future: The Temporal Dimension in the Law of Property, in Symposium, Time, Property Rights, and the Common Law, 64 Wash. U. L.Q. 667, 673, 676 (1986).

Lay people in particular tend to take a dim view of adverse possession doctrine, regarding it as a variety of rip-off. In this connection, consider the views expressed in a recent book by Eduardo M. Peñalver & Sonia K. Katyal, Property Outlaws 150-156 (2010). The authors aim to rehabilitate the reviled character of the intentional property lawbreaker by showing how such outlaws have enabled the reevaluation of (and sometimes changes in) the distribution and content of property rights. They figure that their views with respect to adverse possession, understood as a mechanism for redistribution, probably have the most bearing on less developed areas of the globe, as opposed to countries like the United States. But, they wonder, is this so even after the great economic downturn?

Even in rich countries and in good times, doesn't adverse possession make sense? Suppose (you think) you own a house, but in fact way back in your chain of title lurks a person who got the property by adversely possessing it—maybe by inadvertence, maybe knowingly. Without the doctrine, where would you stand? And on the knowing adverse possessor, see the discussion in footnote 19 on page 162.

4. Regarding the length of the statute of limitations for adverse possession, 20 years used to be common, but the modern trend is to shorten this to something on the order of 6 to 10 years (although one can find periods as short as 3 years and as long as 30 years). See William G. Ackerman & Shane T. Johnson, Outlaws of the Past: A Western Perspective on Prescription and Adverse Possession, 31 Land & Water L. Rev. 79, 111-112 (1996). What considerations should influence

the matter of selecting a statutory period? See Robert C. Ellickson, Adverse Possession and Perpetuities Law: Two Dents in the Libertarian Model of Property Rights, in Symposium, supra, at 723, 725-734 (discussing the interests of landowners, adverse possessors, buyers of land, and society at large).

——————————————

As noted in the Powell excerpt, "the law of adverse possession is a synthesis of statutory and decisional law," with judicial rules supplementing the statutes of limitation that make up the core of adverse possession. The essence of these supplemental rules is this: Adverse possession requires that there be (1) an entry that is actual and exclusive, (2) open and notorious, (3) continuous for the statutory period, and (4) adverse and under a claim of right. What might be the substance and purpose of each of these requirements? The answer to the question is pretty straightforward, at least for our present introductory purposes, and at least as to all but the fourth item. Consider:

(1) One obvious reason that an *entry* is required is that adverse possession depends on a statute of limitations running against a cause of action, and the entry (without permission, adverse to the rights of the property owner, but more on this when we get to the fourth item) creates that cause of action—for trespass—and thereby triggers the statute. Entry also helps stake out what it is the adverse possessor might end up claiming. Some case law and academic commentary suggests that an actual entry is required because it shows an interloper who at least is working the property, making it productive, and by these means earning some rights. (This *earning* principle is mentioned, with skepticism, in the excerpt by Ballantine on page 145, and it will come up from time to time later.)

Notice that an adverse possessor's entry must be *exclusive*. The idea here is that if the owner or members of the public generally are using the land along with the adverse possessor, that tends to indicate that the possession is not adverse at all, because the adverse possessor is taking no steps to exclude others. That inference is weaker, however, if the owner or members of the public make only very occasional or incidental use of the land in question.

(2) Entry must be by acts sufficiently *open and notorious* that they would put reasonably attentive property owners on notice that someone is on their property.[10] This requirement reflects the *sleeping* principle underlying adverse possession;

———

10. Notoriety is usually straightforward, but not always. Consider an instance where adverse possession goes underground. Suppose that *A* and *B* are neighbors whose parcels of land lie over a cave, the entrance to which is on *A*'s land. *A* discovers the entrance, explores the full domain of the cave, and then opens it up to the public for a fee. *A*'s business, well-known to *B*, runs for many years. After the statute of limitations has expired, *B* learns that part of the cave is under his land and brings suit to quiet his title to that part; *A* in turn claims title to all the cave by adverse possession. Was *A*'s possession open and notorious? No, according to Marengo Cave Co. v. Ross, 10 N.E.2d 917 (Ind. 1937).

It is implicit in *Marengo* that the owner of a surface parcel also owns the part of a common cave underlying the parcel. This follows from the so-called *ad coelum* doctrine: *Cujus est solum, ejus est usque ad coelum et ad infernos* (to whomsoever the soil belongs, he owns also to the sky and to the depths). Would it make more sense to say that the owner of the land on which sits the entrance to a cave owns the cave? To say that whoever discovers a cave and opens it to access owns the cave? To say that all the overlying landowners own the cave together, in

see Ballantine again, mentioning a purpose "to penalize the negligent and dormant owner for sleeping upon his rights." If the adverse possessor's entry were not reasonably observable, we couldn't rightly blame an owner for being "dormant." (Understand that the notoriety requirement is aimed at constructive not actual notice; the test of notoriety is objective. If the adverse possessor's acts would be noticed by an ordinary person, then the owner is regarded as knowing what should have been known. But suppose the adverse possessor is a sneak whose acts are not apparent at all, but happen to be known by the property owner. Does the owner's actual notice matter? Does the principle of earning have a bearing on this question?)

(3) Entry must be *continuous* for the statutory period, but not literally constant. An adverse possessor is permitted to come and go in the ordinary course, given the nature of the property in question (being on the farm most of the time; using the summer fishing camp for regular summer fishing trips; etc.). Note that the continuity requirement reflects, harmoniously, both the earning and sleeping principles.[11]

In the leading case of Ewing v. Burnet, 36 U.S. (11 Pet.) 41 (1837), adverse possession of an unimproved lot in Cincinnati, used principally for digging sand and gravel, was established when the claimant paid taxes on the lot,[12] from time to time dug sand and gravel from it, permitted others to do so, and brought actions of trespass against others for doing so without his permission. Notice then that adverse possession may exist even if the occupant does not reside on the property and for long periods does not use it at all. A commonly stated generalization that follows from cases like *Ewing* is this: The sort of entry and possession that will ripen into title by adverse possession is use of the property in the manner that an average true owner would use it under the circumstances, such that neighbors and other observers would regard the occupant as a person exercising exclusive dominion. But generalizations are dangerous. In Pettis v. Lozier, 349 N.W.2d 372 (Neb. 1984), adverse possession of an eight-acre suburban wooded tract was not established notwithstanding that the claimant occasionally used the land for a

---

common? Given *ad coelum* and the three alternatives, which is best? For contending views on that question, see the majority, concurring, and dissenting opinions in Edwards v. Sims, 24 S.W.2d 619 (Ky. 1929), and Edwards v. Lee's Admr., 96 S.W.2d 1028 (Ky. 1936).

Although *ad coelum* is sometimes taken seriously in the case of caves, the doctrine has little place in modern times. Think of airplanes; think of carbon sequestration. For a thorough overview, see John G. Sprankling, Owning the Center of the Earth, 55 UCLA L. Rev. 979 (2008).

11. Distinguish the adverse possessor's occasional absence from the property, on the one hand, and *abandonment* on the other. If the adverse possessor abandons the property—leaves with no intention to return—before the statute has run, the statute stops, a new entry is required, and the whole process must begin anew. Distinguish also *interruption* by the true owner before the statute has run—say by bringing a successful ejectment action against the adverse possessor, or by re-entering the property. In the case of a successful ejectment action, the lawsuit interrupts the period of possession even if the owner does not thereafter actually oust the adverse possessor, who must start all over. See, e.g., Irving Pulp & Paper Ltd. v. Kelly, 654 A.2d 416 (Me. 1995). As to re-entry by the true owner, it must be open and hostile and effective. See 3 American Law of Property §15.9 (1952).

12. A number of states require that adverse possessors pay property taxes in order to have the statute of limitations running in their behalf. The requirement can help owners of large or remote parcels to monitor whether there might be interlopers occupying their land. Tax payments are a matter of public record, easy enough to check periodically.

variety of purposes throughout the statutory period—kept geese and livestock there, put up three large packing crates to serve as sheds for his animals, planted native grass and 25 pine trees (all the trees died), did some vegetable gardening, built a watering tank, set out a beehive, dumped trash and junk and old cars, did some fencing, used the property for recreation, posted "No Hunting" and "No Trespassing" signs, twice removed "For Sale" signs, and once told a prospective purchaser of the tract that it belonged to him.

(4) Turn finally to the requirement that entry must be *adverse and under a claim of right*—or, as it is sometimes expressed, hostile and under a claim of title.[13] Here the law reflects much contention and confusion, the latter probably caused in part by the fact that "adversity" and "hostility" imply possessors wrongfully seeking something not theirs, whereas "claim of right" and "claim of title" imply possessors thinking something *is* theirs. In any event, there are different points of view on what the requirement should entail.

Begin with a rather notorious case on the subject. If you read it carefully, you will see that the majority decision cannot possibly mean what it says.

Van Valkenburgh v. Lutz

Court of Appeals of New York, 1952
106 N.E.2d 28

[*Prologue: Background information taken by the editors from the record and briefs submitted to the New York Court of Appeals.* Shortly after their marriage in 1912, Mary and William Lutz bought at auction two wooded lots in Yonkers, a suburb of New York, taking title in the husband's name. The lots, numbered 14 and 15, were situated high on a hill above Leroy Avenue, at the time an unimproved "paper" street. To the west was a wooded triangular tract—consisting of lots 19, 20, 21, and 22—the ownership of which is at issue in this case. (Lots 19-22 appear as one lot—lot 19—on the current Yonkers tax map reproduced as Figure 2-1.) Instead of climbing the steep grade from Leroy Avenue to reach lots 14 and 15, the Lutzes found it easier to cross the triangular tract which they did not own; Lutz cleared a "traveled way" near the northern boundary of the tract to reach Gibson Place on the west.

With the help of his brother Charlie and his wife Mary, William Lutz cleared lots 14 and 15 and built a house for his family on them. The Lutzes also partially cleared the triangular tract and built for Charlie a one-room structure on lot 19. By 1920 the buildings were occupied. In 1921 Mary's fifth and last child was born to her in the main house.

In 1928 the city graded Leroy Avenue and broke the private water line leading to the main Lutz house. Lutz, who was working in New York City at the time, went home to repair it. As a result, he lost his job; thereafter Lutz stayed home

---

13. "Claim of title" must not be confused with the concept of "color of title," considered in the Note on page 162 and the Problems that follow it.

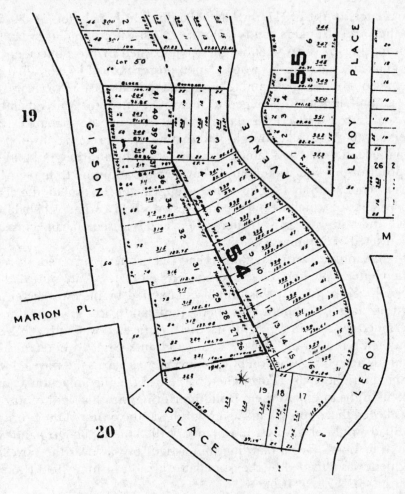

Figure 2-1
Yonkers Tax Map, 1984

(For more images, consult Google Maps, Leroy Ave., Yonkers.)

tending a garden on the triangular property, selling vegetables, and doing odd jobs for neighbors. The Lutz children grew up, and all except the youngest son, Eugene, moved away.

In 1937 Joseph and Marion Van Valkenburgh bought lots west of Gibson Place and built a new home there. Some nine years later, in 1946, bad blood developed between the Lutzes and the Van Valkenburghs. In April of that year Mary Lutz was annoyed by the presence of the Van Valkenburgh children in her garden, and she called her husband over. The Van Valkenburgh children ran home, Lutz behind them brandishing an iron pipe and crying, "I'll kill you." Van Valkenburgh then appeared and began a heated argument with Lutz. He subsequently swore out a complaint of criminal assault, and Lutz was arrested, jailed, then released on bail.

A year later, in April 1947, the Van Valkenburghs bought lots 19, 20, 21, and 22 from the City of Yonkers at a foreclosure sale for nonpayment of taxes.[14] On the following July 6, Van Valkenburgh, accompanied by two policemen, visited the triangular tract and, in his words, "took possession" of it. He called to Mrs. Lutz to come out of her house and told her that the Lutzes were to clear from the property all buildings that belonged to them. On July 8 the Van Valkenburghs' attorney sent Lutz a registered letter informing him that the triangular tract was now owned by the Van Valkenburghs and that he should remove any of his property from the land. A few days later Lutz went to see the attorney and told him he wanted proof of the Van Valkenburghs' ownership and time to harvest his vegetable crop. Then, on July 13, Lutz failed to appear for the trial on the charge of criminal assault, for which he had been arrested a year earlier. A bench warrant was issued, and Lutz was again arrested, jailed, and released on bail. Subsequently he was convicted of criminal assault.

In the meantime Van Valkenburgh had the property surveyed. In response to another letter from the Van Valkenburghs' attorney, Lutz returned to the attorney's office on July 21, this time accompanied by his own lawyer. At this meeting Lutz agreed to remove his sheds, junk, and garden within thirty days, but he claimed a prescriptive right[15] to use the traveled way to reach his property. Lutz then removed the chicken coops and junk. Shortly thereafter the Van Valkenburghs invited legal action by erecting a fence across the traveled way that Lutz claimed a right to use. Lutz joined battle by bringing an action against the Van Valkenburghs to enjoin them from interfering with his right of way. In the suit Lutz alleged that Marion Van Valkenburgh was the owner of the property, but that Lutz had a right of way over it. In January 1948 the trial court handed down a judgment in Lutz's favor, awarding him a right of way over the traveled way; this judgment was affirmed by the Appellate Division in June 1948 (Lutz v. Van Valkenburgh, 81 N.Y.S.2d 161).

The action in this case was commenced against the Lutzes on April 8, 1948. Perhaps realizing the blunder made in the prior lawsuit (the admission that Marion Van Valkenburgh owned lots 19-22), Lutz fired his Yonkers lawyer and hired one from Wall Street. Not to be outdone, the Van Valkenburghs also sought out and employed a Wall Street firm. In August 1948 William Lutz died, devising all his property to his wife Mary. The Van Valkenburghs' suit was tried in June 1950. The testimony in the case totaled some 250 pages, and in addition there were 56 exhibits consisting of deeds, surveys, and photographs. Several neighbors

---

14. Although the laws regarding tax foreclosure sales vary from state to state, usually the purchaser at the sale (such as the Van Valkenburghs) receives title to the property free and clear of any claims by other parties (including possessors like the Lutzes), provided appropriate notice was given. Yet, oddly, the Van Valkenburghs never raised this point in their lawsuit, perhaps because notice had not been given to the Lutzes.

15. Prescription differs from adverse possession in terms of the sorts of interests acquired. By adverse possession one may acquire the title or ownership, and the exclusive possession, of land formerly belonging to someone else, say X, whereas prescription gives rise to rights of use, such as rights of way and other easements, but title to the land remains in X. In some jurisdictions the elements of the two doctrines are essentially identical, in others not, as we shall see in Chapter 10.

who had lived in the area a long time testified for the Lutzes. Not one testified for the Van Valkenburghs, who lost in the trial court and appealed.]

DYE, J. These consolidated actions were brought to compel the removal of certain encroachments upon plaintiffs' lands, for delivery of possession and incidental relief. The subject property consists of four unimproved building lots designated as 19, 20, 21 and 22 in block 54 on the official tax map of the city of Yonkers, N.Y. These lots together form a parcel somewhat triangular in shape with dimensions of approximately 150 by 126 by 170 feet fronting on Gibson Place, a street to be laid out within the subdivision running in a northwesterly direction from Leroy Avenue and now surfaced for automobile travel as far as lots 26, 27 and 28. The subject premises were purchased by the plaintiffs from the city of Yonkers by deed dated April 14, 1947. At that time the defendants were, and had been since 1912, owners of premises designated as lots 14 and 15 in block 54, as shown on the same map. The defendants' lots front on Leroy Avenue and adjoin lot 19 owned by the plaintiffs at the rear boundary line. All of these lots, though differently numbered, appear on a map of the subdivision of the Murray Estate opened prior to 1912 and numbering 479 lots. At that time that part of the Murray subdivision was covered with a natural wild growth of brush and small trees.

The defendants interposed an answer denying generally the allegations of the complaint and alleging as an affirmative defense, and as a counterclaim, that William Lutz had acquired title to the subject premises by virtue of having held and possessed the same adversely to plaintiffs and predecessors for upwards of thirty years.

The issue thus joined was tried before Hon. Frederick P. Close, Official Referee, who found that title to said lots "was perfected in William Lutz by virtue of adverse possession by the year 1935" and not thereafter disseized. The judgment entered thereon in favor of the defendants was affirmed in the Appellate Division, Second Department, without opinion, one Justice dissenting on the ground that the evidence was insufficient to establish title by adverse possession.

To acquire title to real property by adverse possession not founded upon a written instrument, it must be shown by clear and convincing proof that for at least fifteen years (formerly twenty years) there was an "actual" occupation under a claim of title, for it is only the premises so actually occupied "and no others" that are deemed to have been held adversely (Civ. Prac. Act, §§34, 38, 39). The essential elements of proof being either that the premises (1) are protected by a substantial inclosure, or are (2) usually cultivated or improved (Civ. Prac. Act, §40).[16]

---

16. At the time of the *Lutz* case, N.Y. Civil Practice Act §§34, 38, 39, and 40 provided:

§34. An action to recover real property or the possession thereof cannot be maintained by a party other than the people, unless the plaintiff, his ancestor, predecessor or grantor, was seized or possessed of the premises in question within fifteen years before the commencement of the action. . . .

§38. For the purpose of constituting an adverse possession, by a person claiming a title founded upon a written instrument or a judgment or decree, land is deemed to have been possessed and occupied in either of the following cases:

Concededly, there is no proof here that the subject premises were "protected by a substantial inclosure" which leaves for consideration only whether there is evidence showing that the premises were cultivated or improved sufficiently to satisfy the statute.

We think not. The proof concededly fails to show that the cultivation incident to the garden utilized the whole of the premises claimed. Such lack may not be supplied by inference on the showing that the cultivation of a smaller area, whose boundaries are neither defined nor its location fixed with certainty, "must have been . . . substantial" as several neighbors were "supplied . . . with vegetables." This introduces an element of speculation and surmise which may not be considered since the statute clearly limits the premises adversely held to those "actually" occupied "and no others" (Civ. Prac. Act, §39) which we have recently interpreted as requiring definition by clear and positive proof (St. William's Church v. People, 296 N.Y. 861, revg. 269 App. Div. 874, motion for reargument denied 296 N.Y. 1000).

Furthermore, on this record, the proof fails to show that the premises were improved (Civ. Prac. Act, §40). According to the proof the small shed or shack (about 5 by 10½ feet) which, as shown by survey map, was located on the subject premises about 14 feet from the Lutz boundary line, . . . was built in about the year 1923 and, as Lutz himself testified, he knew at the time it was not on his land, and his wife, a defendant here, also testified to the same effect.

The statute requires as an essential element of proof, recognized as fundamental on the concept of adversity since ancient times, that the occupation of premises be "under a claim of title" (Civ. Prac. Act, §39), in other words, hostile (Belotti v. Bickhardt, 228 N.Y. 296), and when lacking will not operate to bar the legal title (Doherty v. Matsell, 119 N.Y. 646), no matter how long the occupation may have continued (La Frombois v. Jackson, 8 Cow. 589; Colvin v. Burnet, 17 Wend. 564).

Similarly, the garage encroachment, extending a few inches over the boundary line, fails to supply proof of occupation by improvement. Lutz himself testified that when he built the garage he had no survey and thought he was getting

---

1. Where it has been usually cultivated or improved.

2. Where it has been protected by a substantial inclosure.

3. Where, although not inclosed, it has been used for the supply of fuel or of fencing timber, either for the purposes of husbandry or for the ordinary use of the occupant.

Where a known farm or single lot has been partly improved, the portion of the farm or lot that has been left not cleared or not inclosed, according to the usual course and custom of the adjoining country, is deemed to have been occupied for the same length of time as the part improved and cultivated.

§39. Where there has been an actual continued occupation of premises under a claim of title, exclusive of any other right, but not founded upon a written instrument or a judgment or decree, the premises so actually occupied, and no others, are deemed to have been held adversely.

§40. For the purpose of constituting an adverse possession by a person claiming title not founded upon a written instrument or a judgment or decree, land is deemed to have been possessed and occupied in either of the following cases, and no others:

1. Where it has been protected by a substantial inclosure.

2. Where it has been usually cultivated or improved.

These provisions were subsequently revised, among other ways, by reducing the statutory period from 15 to 10 years. —EDS.

it on his own property, which certainly falls short of establishing that he did it under a claim of title hostile to the true owner. The other acts committed by Lutz over the years, such as placing a portable chicken coop on the premises which he moved about, the cutting of brush and some of the trees, and the littering of the property with odds and ends of salvaged building materials, cast-off items of house furnishings and parts of automobiles which the defendants and their witnesses described as "personal belongings," "junk," "rubbish" and "debris," were acts which under no stretch of the imagination could be deemed an occupation by improvement within the meaning of the statute, and which, of course, are of no avail in establishing adverse possession.

We are also persuaded that the defendant's subsequent words and conduct confirm the view that his occupation was not "under a claim of title." When the defendant had the opportunity to declare his hostility and assert his rights against the true owner, he voluntarily chose to concede that the plaintiffs' legal title conferred actual ownership entitling them to the possession of these and other premises in order to provide a basis for establishing defendant's right to an easement by adverse possession—the use of a well-defined "traveled way" that crossed the said premises. In that action (Lutz v. Van Valkenburgh, 274 App. Div. 813), William Lutz, a defendant here (now deceased), chose to litigate the issue of title and possession and, having succeeded in establishing his claim of easement by adverse possession, he may not now disavow the effect of his favorable judgment (Goebel v. Iffla, 111 N.Y. 170), or prevent its use as evidence to show his prior intent. Declarations against interest made by a prescriptive tenant are always available on the issue of his intent (6 Wigmore on Evidence, §1778).

On this record we do not reach the question of disseisin by oral disclaimer, since the proof fails to establish actual occupation for such time or in such manner as to establish title. What we are saying is that the proof fails to establish actual occupation for such a time or in such a manner as to establish title by adverse possession (Civ. Prac. Act, §§39, 40; St. William's Church v. People, supra).

The judgments should be reversed, the counterclaim dismissed and judgment directed to be entered in favor of plaintiff Joseph D. Van Valkenburgh for the relief prayed for in the complaint subject to the existing easement (Lutz v. Van Valkenburgh, 274 App. Div. 813), with costs in all courts.

FULD, J. (dissenting). In my judgment, the weight of evidence lies with the determination made by the court at Special Term and affirmed by the Appellate Division. But whether that is so or not, there can be no doubt whatsoever that the record contains some evidence that the premises here involved were occupied by William Lutz, defendant's late husband, for fifteen years under a claim of title—and that, of course, should compel an affirmance.

The four lots in suit, located in the city of Yonkers, comprise a fairly level parcel of land, triangular in shape, with approximate dimensions of 150 by 126 by 170 feet. It is bounded on the north by a "traveled way," on the west and south by Gibson Place, an unopened street, and on the southeast by a vacant lot. Immediately to the east of the parcel, the land descends sharply to Leroy Avenue, forming a steep hill; on the hill are situated two lots, purchased by Lutz in 1912, upon which his family's home has stood for over thirty years.

Wild and overgrown when the Lutzes first moved into the neighborhood, the property was cleared by defendant's husband and had been, by 1916, the referee found, developed into a truck farm "of substantial size." Lutz, together with his children, worked the farm continuously until his death in 1948; indeed, after 1928, he had no other employment. Each year, a new crop was planted and the harvest of vegetables was sold to neighbors. Lutz also raised chickens on the premises, and constructed coops or sheds for them. Fruit trees were planted, and timber was cut from that portion of the property not used for the farm. On one of the lots, Lutz in 1920 built a one-room dwelling, in which his brother Charles has lived ever since.

Although disputing the referee's finding that the dimensions of Lutz's farm were substantial, the court's opinion fails to remark the plentiful evidence in support thereof. For instance, there is credible testimony in the record that "nearly all" of the property comprised by the four lots was cultivated during the period to which the referee's finding relates. A survey introduced in evidence indicates the very considerable extent to which the property was cultivated in 1950, and many witnesses testified that the farm was no larger at that time than it had ever been. There is evidence, moreover, that the cultivated area extended from the "traveled way" on *one side* of the property to a row of logs and brush—placed by Lutz for the express purpose of marking the farm's boundary—at the *opposite end* of the premises.

According to defendant's testimony, she and her husband, knowing that they did not have record title to the premises, intended from the first nevertheless to occupy the property as their own. Bearing this out is the fact that Lutz put down the row of logs and brush, which was over 100 feet in length, to mark the southwestern boundary of his farm; this marker, only roughly approximating the lot lines, extended beyond them into the bed of Gibson Place. The property was, moreover, known in the neighborhood as "Mr. Lutz's gardens," and the one-room dwelling on it as "Charlie's house"; the evidence clearly indicates that people living in the vicinity believed the property to be owned by Lutz. And it is undisputed that for upwards of thirty-five years—until 1947, when plaintiffs became the record owners—no other person ever asserted title to the parcel.

With evidence such as that in the record, I am at a loss to understand how this court can say that support is lacking for the finding that the premises had been occupied by Lutz under a claim of title. The referee was fully justified in concluding that the character of Lutz's possession was akin to that of a true owner and indicated, more dramatically and effectively than could words, an intent to claim the property as his own. Recognizing that "A claim of title may be made by acts alone, quite as effectively as by the most emphatic assertions" (Barnes v. Light, 116 N.Y. 34, 39), we have often sustained findings based on evidence of actual occupation and improvement of the property in the manner that "owners are accustomed to possess and improve their estates." (La Frombois v. Jackson, 8 Cow. 589, 603. . . .)

That Lutz knew that he did not have the record title to the property—a circumstance relied upon by the court—is of no consequence, so long as he intended, notwithstanding that fact, to acquire and use the property as his own. As we stated in Ramapo Mfg. Co. v. Mapes (216 N.Y. 362, 370-371), "the bona fides of the claim of the occupant is not essential and it will not excuse the negligence of the owner in forbearing to bring his action until after the time in the Statute of Limitations shall have run against him to show that the defendant knew all along that he was in the wrong. (Humbert v. Rector, etc., of Trinity Church, 24 Wend. 587.)"

Quite obviously, the fact that Lutz alleged in the 1947 easement action—twelve years after the title had, according to the referee, vested in him through adverse possession—that one of the plaintiffs was the owner of three of the lots, simply constituted evidence pointing the other way, to be weighed with the other proof by the courts below. While it is true that a disclaimer of title by the occupant of property, made before the statutory period has run, indelibly stamps his possession as nonadverse and prevents title from vesting in him . . . , a disclaimer made after the statute has run carries with it totally different legal consequences. Once title has vested by virtue of adverse possession, it is elementary that it may be divested, not by an oral disclaimer, but only by a transfer complying with the formalities prescribed by law. . . .

Hence, an oral acknowledgment of title in another, made after the statutory period is alleged to have run, "is only evidence tending to show the character of the previous possession." (Smith v. Vermont Marble Co., 99 Vt. 384, 394. . . .)

Here, Official Referee Close, of the opinion that the 1947 admission was made by Lutz under the erroneous advice of his attorney (cf. Shirey v. Whitlow, 80 Ark. 444, 446-447), chose to rest his decision rather on evidence of Lutz's numerous and continual acts of dominion over the property—proof of a most persuasive character. Even if we were to feel that the referee was mistaken in so weighing the evidence, we would be powerless to change the determination, where, as we have seen, there is some evidence in the record to support his conclusion.

In view of the extensive cultivation of the parcel in suit, there is no substance to the argument that the requirements of sections 39 and 40 of the Civil Practice Act were not met. Under those provisions, only the premises "actually occupied" in the manner prescribed—that is, "protected by a substantial inclosure" or "usually cultivated or improved"—are deemed to have been held adversely. The object of the statute, we have recognized, "is that the real owner may, by unequivocal acts of the usurper, have notice of the hostile claim and be thereby called upon to assert his legal title." (Monnot v. Murphy, 207 N.Y. 240, 245; see, also, Trustees of Town of East Hampton v. Kirk, 84 N.Y. 215, 220.) Since the character of the acts sufficient to afford such notice "depends upon the nature and situation of the property and the uses to which it can be applied," it is settled that the provisions of sections 39 and 40 are to be construed, not in a narrow or technical sense, but with reference to the nature, character, condition, and location of the property under consideration. . . .

Judge Dye considers it significant that the proof "fails to show that the cultivation incident to the garden utilized the whole of the premises claimed" [see page 154]. There surely is no requirement in either statute or decision that proof of adverse possession depends upon cultivation of "*the whole*" plot or of *every foot* of the property in question. And, indeed, the statute—which, as noted, reads "*usually* cultivated or improved"—has been construed to mean only that the claimant's occupation must "consist of acts such as are usual in the ordinary cultivation and improvement of similar lands by thrifty owners." (Ramapo Mfg. Co. v. Mapes, supra, 216 N.Y. 362, 373.) The evidence demonstrates that by far the greater part of the four lots was regularly and continuously used for farming, and, that being so, the fact that a portion of the property was not cleared should not affect the claimant's ability to acquire title by adverse possession: any frugal person, owning and occupying lands similar to those here involved, would have permitted, as Lutz did, some of the trees to stand—while clearing the bulk of the property—in order to provide a source of lumber and other tree products for his usual needs. The portion of the property held subservient to the part actively cultivated is as much "occupied" as the portion actually tilled. The nature of the cultivation engaged in by Lutz was more than adequate, as his neighbors' testimony establishes, to give the owner notice of an adverse claim and to delimit the property to which the claim related. The limits of the parcel in suit were indicated in a general way by boundaries natural as well as man-made: the declivity to Leroy Avenue, the "traveled way," and Gibson Place. Apart from that, however, the evidence discloses that the bulk of each of the four lots was cultivated, and—even putting to one side the fact that the cottage, called "Charlie's house," had been actually occupied and lived in for upwards of thirty years—such substantial use was enough to put the owner on notice that his whole lot was claimed.

In short, there is ample evidence to sustain the finding that William Lutz actually occupied the property in suit for over fifteen years under a claim of title. Since, then, title vested in Lutz by 1935, the judgment must be affirmed. To rule otherwise, on the ground that the weight of evidence is against that finding—a view which I do not, in any event, hold—is to ignore the constitutional provision that limits our jurisdiction to the review of questions of law (N.Y. Const., art. VI, §7; see also, Civ. Prac. Act, §605).

I would affirm the judgment reached by both of the courts below.

Lewis, Conway and Froessel, JJ., concur with Dye, J.; Fuld, J., dissents in opinion in which Loughran, Ch. J., and Desmond, J., concur.

[*Epilogue:* Litigation between the Van Valkenburghs and the Lutzes did not end with the principal case. The Van Valkenburghs' judgment included costs and disbursements, and an execution was issued directing the sale of lots 14 and 15 (the Lutz home) to pay the judgment. In the meantime Mary Lutz had transferred all her interest in her home to her son Eugene, who resided there with his mother, his wife, and his child. Eugene moved to set aside the execution, and the motion was granted; the Van Valkenburghs moved for a rehearing, and this was denied. The Van Valkenburghs then appealed the order denying the rehearing instead of appealing, as they should have, the order granting Eugene's motion.

They lost. Van Valkenburgh v. Lutz, 175 N.Y.S.2d 203 (App. Div. 1958). By a lawyer's procedural error, the Lutz home was saved for Mary and Eugene. (*Query:* Was the lawyer liable to the Van Valkenburghs for malpractice?)

William Lutz's brother Charlie was mentally incompetent; after the principal case, Eugene was appointed as his guardian. Charlie had not been a party to the prior proceedings, so he was in position to contest them. Through his guardian he brought an action against the Van Valkenburghs to enjoin removal of "his" house from lot 19. Charlie claimed that he and his brother William had constructed the house over 20 years earlier and that when this house was being constructed he believed he was building it on William's land. He further claimed that, since 1917, he had been in possession of the house as the tenant of William, the owner, and that he paid rent to William for the house. This lawsuit wound its way up and down the courts until 1968, when the Court of Appeals unanimously ruled for the Van Valkenburghs on the ground that Charlie's occupation was not under a claim of title. Lutz v. Van Valkenburgh, 237 N.E.2d 844 (N.Y. 1968). By this time Charlie was well into his eighties.

Eugene Lutz and his wife continued to live in the Lutz house. The traveled way, bounded by a tall chain link fence, and the house were guarded by two ferocious dogs, whose menacing bark warned strangers away. The Van Valkenburghs are dead. The triangular tract—the subject of this bitter dispute between neighbors—is now owned by a church. For more about the *Lutz* case and the contestants, see R.H. Helmholz, The Saga of *Van Valkenburgh v. Lutz*: Animosity and Adverse Possession in Yonkers, in Property Stories 59 (Gerald Korngold & Andrew P. Morriss eds. 2d ed. 2009); Note, New York Adverse Possession Law as a Conspiracy of Forgetting: *Van Valkenburgh v. Lutz* and the Examination of Intent, 14 Cardozo L. Rev. 1089 (1993).]

NOTES AND QUESTIONS

1. *Huh?* We noted earlier that the majority decision in *Lutz* can't really mean what it says. According to the decision, the Lutzes lost, among other reasons, because they did not meet the requirement, set out in §39 of the New York statute (see footnote 16), of occupation "under a claim of title" (which the court took to include a "hostile" claim; see pages 154-155). The court then concluded that the structure built for Charlie didn't count because "Lutz knew at the time it was not on his land," and that the garage encroachment didn't count because "Lutz thought he was getting it on his own property, which certainly falls short of establishing that he did it under a claim of title hostile to the true owner." Putting these bits together, the decision amounts to saying, nonsensically, that in New York you can only adversely possess land that is already yours! Do you see that?

2. *States of mind.* The requirement that adverse possession be accompanied by a "claim of title" is embodied in the statutes of various states, and even when it is not, a considerable number of courts have read it in, whether in terms of claim of title, claim of right, or hostility.

But what does this requirement mean? A good way to approach the inquiry is in terms of the state of mind required of the adverse possessor, and in this respect existing doctrine reflects three different views: (1) State of mind is irrelevant. (2) The required state of mind is, "I thought I owned it." (3) The required state of mind is, "I thought I didn't own it, but I intended to make it mine." These have been called, respectively, "the objective standard, the good-faith standard, and the aggressive trespass standard." Margaret Jane Radin, Time, Possession, and Alienation, 64 Wash. U. L.Q. 739, 746-747 (1986).

The first view is firmly held in England, where the statute of limitations begins to run as soon as the true owner is dispossessed by someone taking possession inconsistent with—not subordinate to—his title. See Robert Megarry & H.W.R. Wade, The Law of Real Property 1307 (Charles Harpum 6th ed. 2000). The point behind this view is simple: Once there is an entry against the true owner, she has a cause of action. Given that, shouldn't the statute of limitations be running, *whatever* the entrant's state of mind? See 3 American Law of Property §15.4 (1952), endorsing the view and suggesting it is the majority position in the United States; Totman v. Malloy, 725 N.E.2d 1045, 1048 (Mass. 2000) ("We have long held that the state of mind of the claimant is not relevant to a determination whether the possession of land is nonpermissive."); Tioga Coal Co. v. Supermarkets Gen. Corp., 546 A.2d 1 (Pa. 1988) (if all other requirements of adverse possession have been met, hostility will be implied, regardless of the subjective state of mind of the adverse possessor); Chaplin v. Sanders, 676 P.2d 431, 436 (Wash. 1984) (adverse possessor's "subjective belief regarding his true interest in the land and his intent to dispossess or not dispossess another is irrelevant").

The second view, requiring a good-faith claim, is voiced from time to time in American decisions. An example is Halpern v. Lacy Inv. Corp., 379 S.E.2d 519 (Ga. 1989), where the court said:

> We hold that the correct rule is that one must enter upon the land claiming in good faith the right to do so. To enter upon the land without any honest claim of right to do so is but a trespass and can never ripen into prescriptive title. In the language used in Hannah v. Kenny, 210 Ga. 824, 83 S.E.2d 1 (1954), such a person is called a "squatter." . . . Here there was evidence that the Halperns knew the parcel of land was owned by another yet they simply took possession when their offer to purchase was declined. There was evidence to support a finding that this possession never changed its character.
>
> One may maintain hostile possession of land in good faith. . . . [H]ostile possession and claim of right are legal equivalents for all practical purposes. The holding is that most who have hostile possession of land do so with a good faith claim of right and therefore a jury or other factfinder may, in the absence of a contrary showing, infer from hostile possession that it is done in good faith that a claim of right exists. [379 S.E.2d at 521.][17]

17. Notice the reference to "squatters," who, the court suggests, cannot become adverse possessors. Why should that be? In any event, and especially given the increasingly apparent problem of homelessness in the United States (to which we shall return), should squatters have rights—say to occupy vacant and abandoned buildings?

Professor Helmholz claims that the good-faith requirement plays a larger role than might at first appear. Based on an extensive survey of cases, he concludes that many courts do take account of state of mind—though they might not say as much—in cases where the evidence strongly suggests that the adverse possessor was well aware he was trespassing. Manipulating the hostility and claim-of-right requirements, the courts "regularly award title to the good faith trespasser, where they will not award it to the trespasser who knows what he is doing at the time he enters the land in dispute." Richard H. Helmholz, Adverse Possession and Subjective Intent, 61 Wash. U. L.Q. 331, 356-358 (1983). A reply to Helmholz's article argues that the cases surveyed provide no basis for his conclusions. Roger A. Cunningham, Adverse Possession and Subjective Intent: A Reply to Professor Helmholz, 64 Wash. U. L.Q. 1 (1986). The third view, that of the aggressive trespasser, is reflected in Preble v. Maine Cent. R. Co., quoted and discussed on pages 165-166. That case stands for the proposition that (at least in the case of boundary disputes) to qualify as adverse possessors, occupants must intend to take the property even if they know it doesn't belong to them. One way of dealing with aggressive (sometimes called bad-faith) adverse possession is to award title, but only if the adverse possessor agrees to pay fair market value to the dispossessed former owner. Title would go to the adverse possessor for some of the reasons we have adverse possession to begin with—for example, to protect the interests of third parties who relied upon the appearance of ownership. But the obligation to compensate would be imposed to punish and deter the consciously wrongful activity. For a discussion, see Thomas W. Merrill, Property Rules, Liability Rules, and Adverse Possession, 79 Nw. U. L. Rev. 1122 (1984). See also Comment, Compensation for the Involuntary Transfer of Property Between Private Parties: Application of a Liability Rule to the Law of Adverse Possession, 79 Nw. U. L. Rev. 759 (1984), advancing the same idea for *all* adverse possession cases.[18] Both articles were provoked by Warsaw v. Chicago Metallic Ceilings, Inc., 676 P.2d 584 (Cal. 1984), concerning a prescriptive easement, when the court considered, but ultimately rejected, a compensation requirement (we take up prescriptive easements in Chapter 10). The compensation requirement is analyzed in Richard A. Epstein, Past and Future: The Temporal Dimension in the Law of Property, 64 Wash. U. L.Q. 667, 688-689 (1986) (favoring instead a two-tier statute of limitations with a longer period for bad-faith possessors); Thomas

---

18. In the title of these two articles you see mention of *property rules* and *liability rules*. The labels have become terms of art after an influential article by Guido Calabresi & A. Douglas Melamed, Property Rules, Liability Rules and Inalienability: One View of the Cathedral, 85 Harv. L. Rev. 1089 (1972). When a property interest is protected by a property rule, the interest cannot be taken from its owner without the owner's consent; all transfers are *voluntary*. When a property interest is protected by a liability rule, the interest can be taken without the owner's consent but only upon payment of judicially determined damages; transfers are *forced*. Ordinary adverse possession doctrine protects (1) the owner's interest with a property rule before the statute of limitations has run, then (2) the adverse possessor's interest with a property rule after the statute has run. The compensation approach discussed above would observe (1) but as to (2) would leave in the owner—after the statute has run—an interest protected by a liability rule. Transfer of the owner's interest to the adverse possessor could be forced but only upon payment of compensatory damages by the latter.

We shall explore the property rule-liability rule dichotomy in various places throughout this book. See in particular Note 3 on page 805.

J. Miceli & C.F. Sirmans, An Economic Theory of Adverse Possession, 15 Intl. Rev. L. & Econ. 161 (1995).[19]

3. *The demise and rebirth of* Lutz. The majority decision in *Lutz* was overruled (although not in so many words) by Walling v. Przybylo, 851 N.E.2d 1167, 1169-1170 (N.Y. 2006), the court holding that there can be a claim of right even if the adverse possessor knows that the land in question belongs to someone else. The court found the facts in *Lutz* to be "distinguishable," and described as "mistaken dictum" any language in *Lutz* "that may seem inconsistent with our holding here." But that was not the end of the story. New York legislators were unhappy with *Walling*; they wanted a rule that would "discourage persons from attempting to possess land they knew did not belong to them." The governor vetoed their first effort to change the law, but the second succeeded, in 2008. See, e.g., N.Y. Real Prop. Actions & Proc. §501(3) (McKinney 2009), defining the "claim of right" requirement: "A claim of right means a reasonable basis for the belief that the property belongs to the adverse possessor or property owner, as the case may be." The new provision is said to be "'all about good faith.'"

The quotations in the foregoing are drawn from Practice Commentaries written by Rudolph de Winter and Larry M. Loeb, appended to §501. The Commentaries end as follows: "It remains for the courts to determine if the new legislation accomplishes the Legislature's goals. It is possible that §501 may be read to be circular. A party possessing property may be found to not initially have had a claim of right but having possessed the property for the statutory period may acquire a claim of right and mature into an adverse possessor."

NOTE: COLOR OF TITLE AND CONSTRUCTIVE ADVERSE POSSESSION

The "claim of title" required by the New York statutes, and at issue in Van Valkenburgh v. Lutz, is quite different from "color of title." *Claim of title* is simply one way of expressing the requirement of hostility or claim of right on the part of an adverse possessor. *Color of title*, on the other hand, refers to a claim founded on a written instrument (a deed, a will) or a judgment or decree that is for some reason defective and invalid (as when the grantor does not own the land conveyed by deed or is incompetent to convey, or the deed is improperly executed). Claim under color of title was not required by English law and is not required in most American jurisdictions. In a few states, color of title is essential to acquiring title

---

19. For a dramatically different approach to bad-faith adverse possessors, see Lee Anne Fennell, Efficient Trespass: The Case for "Bad Faith" Adverse Possession, 100 Nw. U. L. Rev. 1037 (2006), suggesting that better terms for "good-faith" and "aggressive" (or "bad-faith") would be "inadvertent" and "knowing," so as not to color the behavior in question. Id. at 1037-1038 n.1. Professor Fennell develops the argument for an efficient adverse possession doctrine, one in which the contested land would move from a lower-valuing owner to a higher-valuing trespasser. One element of her argument runs directly counter to the conventional wisdom: Her suggested approach would operate *only* on behalf of knowing trespassers—that is, on behalf of what are usually regarded today as undeserving claimants.

by adverse possession. What might be the rationale for the concept of color of title? Should it be required in all cases? Dispensed with in all?

Even though color of title is not a prerequisite for adverse possession in most states, it has important advantages for the adverse possessor. Notice, for example, that the statutes involved in Van Valkenburgh v. Lutz set out different requirements for claims of title "founded upon a written instrument or a judgment or decree" and those not so founded. (See footnote 16 on pages 153-154.) The requirements in the first case are slightly more lenient than those in the second. In some states a shorter statute of limitations is applicable to adverse possessors with color of title than to those without. In all states entry with color of title may have an advantage where the adverse possessor enters into possession of only a part of the property. Actual possession under color of title of only a part of the land covered by the defective writing is *constructive* possession of all that the writing describes. The advantage that a person may gain from constructive possession is that the activities relied upon to establish adverse possession reach not only the part of the premises actually occupied, but the entire premises described in a deed to the claimant. This doctrine of constructive adverse possession under color of title, established by judicial rule in some states and by statute in others, is, however, subject to some limitations. Several of them are explored in the Problems that follow.

PROBLEMS

1. *O* owns and has been in possession of a 100-acre farm since 1975. In 1994 *A* entered the back 40 acres under color of an invalid deed from *Z* (who had no claim to the land) for the entire 100 acres. Since her entry, *A* has occupied and improved the back 40 in the usual manner for the period required by the statute of limitations. *A* brings suit to evict *O* from the farm, claiming title by constructive adverse possession. What result? See Patrick v. Goolsby, 11 S.W.2d 677 (Tenn. 1928). Suppose that in 1975 *O* took title to the farm under an invalid deed and has been in possession for a period sufficient to satisfy the statute of limitations. Would the result in the suit by *A* be different? What if the statute has not yet run in *O*'s favor?

2. Two contiguous lots, 1 and 2, are owned by *X* and *Y* respectively. (*X* and *Y* are not in possession.) The lots are conveyed by an invalid deed from *Z* to *A*, who enters lot 1 and occupies it in the usual manner for the period required by the statute of limitations. Subsequently *A* sues *X* and *Y* to quiet title to lots 1 and 2. What result? Would it matter if *X* had signed the deed? If *X* had signed the deed and *A* had entered lot 2? See Wheatley v. San Pedro, Los Angeles & Salt Lake Railroad, 147 P. 135 (Cal. 1915); Brock v. Howard, 200 S.W.2d 734 (Ky. 1947).

The case that follows concerns a boundary dispute, now the most frequently litigated of adverse possession claims. You will notice that the question of the claimant's state of mind, a matter considered at length after the *Lutz* case (see Note 2 beginning on page 159), comes up once again, in the special context of mistake. The notoriety requirement can take on a special twist here as well.

Mannillo v. Gorski

Supreme Court of New Jersey, 1969
255 A.2d 258

HANEMAN, J. Plaintiffs filed a complaint in the Chancery Division seeking a mandatory and prohibitory injunction against an alleged trespass upon their lands. Defendant counterclaimed for a declaratory judgment which would adjudicate that she had gained title to the disputed premises by adverse possession under N.J.S. 2A:14-6, N.J.S.A., which provides:

Every person having any right or title of entry into real estate shall make such entry within 20 years next after the accrual of such right or title of entry, or be barred therefrom thereafter.

After plenary trial, judgment was entered for plaintiffs. Mannillo v. Gorski, 100 N.J. Super. 140, 241 A.2d 276 (Ch. Div. 1968). Defendant appealed to the Appellate Division. Before argument there, this Court granted defendant's motion for certification.

The facts are as follows: In 1946, defendant and her husband entered into possession of premises in Keansburg known as Lot No. 1007 in Block 42, under an agreement to purchase. Upon compliance with the terms of said agreement, the seller conveyed said lands to them on April 16, 1952. Defendant's husband thereafter died. The property consisted of a rectangular lot with a frontage of 25 feet and a depth of 100 feet. Plaintiffs are the owners of the adjacent Lot 1008 in Block 42 of like dimensions, to which they acquired title in 1953.

In the summer of 1946 Chester Gorski,[20] one of the defendant's sons, made certain additions and changes to the defendant's house. He extended two rooms at the rear of the structure, enclosed a screened porch on the front, and put a concrete platform with steps on the west side thereof for use in connection with a side door. These steps were built to replace existing wooden steps. In addition, a concrete walk was installed from the steps to the end of the house. In 1953, defendant raised the house. In order to compensate for the resulting added height from the ground, she modified the design of the steps by extending them toward both the front and the rear of the property. She did not change their width.

Defendant admits that the steps and concrete walk encroach upon plaintiffs' lands to the extent of 15 inches. She contends, however, that she has title to said land by adverse possession. N.J.S.A. 2A:14-6, quoted above. Plaintiffs assert contrawise that defendant did not obtain title by adverse possession as her possession was not of the requisite hostile nature. They argue that to establish title by adverse possession, the entry into and continuance of possession must be accompanied by an intention to invade the rights of another in the lands, i.e., a knowing wrongful taking. They assert that, as defendant's encroachment was not accompanied by an intention to invade plaintiffs' rights in the land, but rather by the mistaken

---

20. Chester Gorski was 14 years old at the time and, in adulthood, became a general contractor, building houses. —EDS.

belief that she owned the land, and that therefore an essential requisite to establish title by adverse possession, i.e., an intentional tortious taking, is lacking.

The trial court concluded that defendant had clearly and convincingly proved that her possession of the 15-inch encroachment had existed for more than 20 years before the institution of this suit and that such possession was "exclusive, continuous, uninterrupted, visible, notorious and against the right and interest of the true owner." There is ample evidence to sustain this finding except as to its visible and notorious nature, of which more hereafter. However, the judge felt impelled by existing New Jersey case law, holding as argued by plaintiffs above, to deny defendant's claim and entered judgment for plaintiffs. 100 N.J. Super., at 150, 241 A.2d 276. The first issue before this Court is, therefore, whether an entry and continuance of possession under the mistaken belief that the possessor has title to the lands involved, exhibits the requisite hostile possession to sustain the obtaining of title by adverse possession.

The first detailed statement and acceptance by our then highest court, of the principle that possession as an element of title by adverse possession cannot be bottomed on mistake, is found in Folkman v. Myers, 93 N.J. Eq. 208, 115 A. 615 (E. & A. 1921). . . . In so doing, the former Court of Errors and Appeals aligned this State with that branch of a dichotomy which traces its genesis to Preble v. Maine Cent. R. Co., 85 Me. 260, 27 A. 149, 21 L.R.A. 829 (Sup. Jud. Ct. Me. 1893) and has become known as the Maine doctrine. In *Preble*, the court said at 27 A. at p. 150:

> Indeed, the authorities all agree that this intention of the occupant to claim the ownership of land not embraced in his title is a necessary element of adverse possession; and in case of occupancy by mistake beyond a line capable of being ascertained this intention to claim title to the extent of the occupancy must appear to be absolute, and not conditional; otherwise the possession will not be deemed adverse to the true owner. It must be an intention to claim title to all land within a certain boundary on the face of the earth, whether it shall eventually be found to be the correct one or not. If, for instance, one in ignorance of his actual boundaries takes and holds possession by mistake up to a certain fence beyond his limits, upon the claim and in the belief that it is the true line, with the intention to claim title, and thus, if necessary, to acquire "title by possession" up to that fence, such possession, having the requisite duration and continuity, will ripen into title.
>
> If, on the other hand, a party through ignorance, inadvertence, or mistake occupies up to a given fence beyond his actual boundary, because he believes it to be the true line, but has no intention to claim title to that extent if it should be ascertained that the fence was on his neighbor's land, an indispensable element of adverse possession is wanting. In such a case the intent to claim title exists only upon the condition that the fence is on the true line. The intention is not absolute, but provisional, and the possession is not adverse.

This thesis, it is evident, rewards the possessor who entered with a premeditated and predesigned "hostility"—the intentional wrongdoer—and disfavors an honest, mistaken entrant. 3 American Law of Property (Casner ed. 1952), §104, pp. 773, 785. . . .

The other branch of the dichotomy relies upon French v. Pearce, 8 Conn. 439 (Sup. Ct. Conn. 1831). The court said in Pearce on the question of the subjective hostility of a possessor, at pp. 442, 445-446:

Into the recesses of his (the adverse claimant's) mind, his motives or purposes, his guilt or innocence, no enquiry is made.

. . . The very nature of the act (entry and possession) is an assertion of his own title, and the denial of the title of all others. It matters not that the possessor was mistaken, and had he been better informed, would not have entered on the land.

The Maine doctrine has been the subject of much criticism in requiring a knowing wrongful taking. The criticism of the Maine and the justification of the Connecticut branch of the dichotomy is well stated in 6 Powell, Real Property (1969), §1015, pp. 725-728:

Do the facts of his possession, and of his conduct as if he were the owner, make immaterial his mistake, or does such a mistake prevent the existence of the prerequisite claim of right? The leading case holding the mistake to be of no importance was French v. Pearce, decided in Connecticut in 1831. . . . This viewpoint has gained increasingly widespread acceptance. The more subjectively oriented view regards the "mistake" as necessarily preventing the existence of the required claim of right. The leading case on this position is Preble v. Maine Central R.R., decided in 1893. This position is still followed in a few states. It has been strongly criticized as unsound historically, inexpedient practically, and as resulting in better treatment for a ruthless wrongdoer than for the honest landowner. . . . On the whole the law is simplified, in the direction of real justice, by a following of the Connecticut leadership on this point.

Again, 4 Tiffany, Real Property (3d ed. 1939), 1159, pp. 474-475, criticizes the employment of mistake as negating hostility as follows:

In no case except in that of a mistake as to boundary has the element of mistake been regarded as having any significance, and there is no reason for attributing greater weight thereto when the mistake is as to the proper location of a boundary than when it is a mistake as to the title to all the land wrongfully possessed. And to introduce the element of mistake, and then limit its significance by an inquiry as to the intention which the possessor may have as to his course of action in case there should be a mistake, an intention which has ordinarily no existence whatsoever, is calculated only to cause confusion without, it is conceived, any compensating advantage.

We are in accord with the criticism of the Maine doctrine and favor the Connecticut doctrine for the above quoted reasons.[21] As far as can be seen, overruling the former rule will not result in undermining any of the values which stare decisis is intended to foster. The theory of reliance, a cornerstone of stare decisis, is not here apt, as the problem is which of two mistaken parties is entitled to land. Realistically, the true owner does not rely upon entry of the possessor by mistake as a reason for not seeking to recover possession. Whether or not the entry is caused by mistake or intent, the same result eventuates — the true owner is ousted from possession. In either event his neglect to seek recovery of possession, within the requisite time, is in all probability the result of a lack of knowledge that he is being deprived of possession of lands to which he has title.

21. Maine itself has abandoned the Maine doctrine. See Dombkowski v. Ferland, 893 A.2d 599 (Me. 2006). —EDS.

Accordingly, we discard the requirement that the entry and continued possession must be accompanied by a knowing intentional hostility and hold that any entry and possession for the required time which is exclusive, continuous, uninterrupted, visible and notorious, even though under mistaken claim of title, is sufficient to support a claim of title by adverse possession.

However, this conclusion is not dispositive of the matter sub judice. Of equal importance under the present factual complex, is the question of whether defendant's acts meet the necessary standard of "open and notorious" possession. . . .

Generally, where possession of the land is clear and unequivocal and to such an extent as to be immediately visible, the owner may be presumed to have knowledge of the adverse occupancy. . . . However, when the encroachment of an adjoining owner is of a small area and the fact of an intrusion is not clearly and self-evidently apparent to the naked eye but requires an on-site survey for certain disclosure as in urban sections where the division line is only infrequently delineated by any monuments, natural or artificial, such a presumption is fallacious and unjustified. The precise location of the dividing line is then ordinarily unknown to either adjacent owner and there is nothing on the land itself to show by visual observation that a hedge, fence, wall or other structure encroaches on the neighboring land to a minor extent. Therefore, to permit a presumption of notice to arise in the case of minor border encroachments not exceeding several feet would fly in the face of reality and require the true owner to be on constant alert for possible small encroachments. The only method of certain determination would be by obtaining a survey each time the adjacent owner undertook any improvement at or near the boundary, and this would place an undue and inequitable burden upon the true owner. Accordingly we hereby hold that no presumption of knowledge arises from a minor encroachment along a common boundary. In such a case, only where the true owner has actual knowledge thereof may it be said that the possession is open and notorious.

It is conceivable that the application of the foregoing rule may in some cases result in undue hardship to the adverse possessor who under an innocent and mistaken belief of title has undertaken an extensive improvement which to some extent encroaches on an adjoining property. In that event the situation falls within the category of those cases of which Riggle v. Skill, 9 N.J. Super. 372, 74 A.2d 424 (Ch. Div. 1950), affirmed 7 N.J. 268, 81 A.2d 364 (1951) is typical and equity may furnish relief. Then, if the innocent trespasser of a small portion of land adjoining a boundary line cannot without great expense remove or eliminate the encroachment, or such removal or elimination is impractical or could be accomplished only with great hardship, the true owner may be forced to convey the land so occupied upon payment of the fair value thereof without regard to whether the true owner had notice of the encroachment at its inception. Of course, such a result should eventuate only under appropriate circumstances and where no serious damage would be done to the remaining land as, for instance, by rendering the balance of the parcel unusable or no longer capable of being built upon by reason of zoning or other restrictions.

We remand the case for trial of the issues (1) whether the true owner had actual knowledge of the encroachment, (2) if not, whether plaintiffs should be obliged to convey the disputed tract to defendant, and (3) if the answer to the latter question is in the affirmative, what consideration should be paid for the conveyance. The remand, of course, contemplates further discovery and a new pretrial.

Remanded for trial in accordance with the foregoing.

[After the case was remanded for trial, the parties settled. Mrs. Gorski paid Mannillo $250, and in exchange Mannillo gave her the land covered by the encroachment.]

NOTES, QUESTIONS, AND PROBLEMS

1. *Mistake.* Most jurisdictions have abandoned the Maine doctrine. Is that a good thing? Recall the discussion in Note 2 on page 159.

2. *Notoriety.* The court in *Mannillo* says that in the case of minor encroachments, the owner of the land must have "actual knowledge thereof" in order for the adverse claimant to satisfy the notoriety requirement. Suppose that a friend of the plaintiffs' had told them one day more than 20 years prior to the lawsuit, "I hear there's a problem with your neighbor's house, that the new part they built might go too far." Plaintiffs thereafter do nothing. Are they on any sort of notice? In any event, if "actual notice" is truly required in the case of minor encroachments, still a question remains: "Actual notice" of what? Suppose the plaintiffs knew of an encroachment but thought that it was only 3 inches. Is there notorious possession as to 3 inches, or 15 inches, or no inches?

3. *Mistaken boundaries.* A and B own adjacent lots. A erects a fence on what she mistakenly assumes to be the true boundary line dividing the lots; in fact the fence is erected on B's lot three feet beyond the boundary. A thereafter acts as the owner of all the land on her side of the fence for the statutory period. Suppose that as a consequence of these actions A acquires title by adverse possession. Later, after the statute has run, a survey by B reveals the mistake. B tells this to A, and A, "to avoid a hassle," tears down her fence and erects a new fence on the original true boundary. Three years later A talks to a lawyer, changes her mind, and sues to eject B from the three feet. What result? See Kline v. Kramer, 386 N.E.2d 982 (Ind. App. 1979); Mugaas v. Smith, 206 P.2d 332 (Wash. 1949).

Boundary disputes may also be resolved by the doctrines of agreed boundaries, acquiescence, and estoppel. The doctrine of agreed boundaries provides that if there is uncertainty between neighbors as to the true boundary line, an oral agreement to settle the matter is enforceable if the neighbors subsequently accept the line for a long period of time. The doctrine of acquiescence provides that long acquiescence—though perhaps for a period of time shorter than the statute of limitations—is evidence of an agreement between the parties fixing the boundary line. The doctrine of estoppel comes into play when one neighbor makes representations about (or engages in conduct that tends to indicate) the location of a common boundary, and the other neighbor then changes her position in reliance on the representations or conduct. The first neighbor is then estopped to deny the validity of his statements or acts. Estoppel has also been applied when one neighbor remains silent in the face of expenditures by another that suggest the latter's notion of the boundary's location. The three doctrines are commonly interwoven by the courts, leaving the law vague and tricky to apply. See Mehdizadeh v. Mincer, 54 Cal. Rptr. 2d 284 (Ct. App. 1996); Olin L. Browder, Jr., The Practical Location of Boundaries, 56 Mich. L. Rev. 487 (1958); Stewart E. Sterk, Estoppel in Property Law, 77 Neb. L. Rev. 756, 788-794 (1998).

4. *Mistaken improvers.* At the end of the opinion in *Mannillo* (see pages 167-168), the court discusses the problem of the innocent improver, someone who mistakenly builds on land belonging to another but is subsequently ousted from the land before the statutory period for adverse possession has run. The early common law on this matter was rather harsh: anything built on the wrong land, whether in good faith or not, became the property of the landowner (subject to the usual exceptions for delay, acquiescence, and estoppel). The modern tendency, as *Mannillo* indicates, is to ease the plight of innocent improvers — in that case, by forcing a conveyance (at market value) of land from the owner to the improver. A variation is to give the landowner the option to buy the improvement (again, at market value) instead. Some states have legislation (often called "occupying claimant" or "betterment" acts) that set out these and other remedies.

If the inconvenience caused by an innocent encroachment is so minor as to be trivial, relief might be denied altogether. If, on the other hand, the encroachment takes up a substantial part of the land in question, removal might be ordered notwithstanding the good faith of the encroaching party, depending upon how the court in a particular case strikes a balance between competing considerations. See, e.g., Amkco Ltd., Co. v. Wellborn, 21 P.3d 24 (N.M. 2001), involving an unintentional encroachment that took up almost 10 percent of the plaintiff's land. The court applied a two-part test. First, the plaintiff has to show that it would suffer irreparable harm if removal were denied. But even if irreparable harm is proved, still the relief might be denied under a balancing test that compares the hardship to the plaintiff if removal is denied to the hardship to the defendant if it is granted. If this relative hardship test precludes removal of the encroachment, the encroaching party acquires either title or an easement in the land and pays damages accordingly.

Compare intentional encroachments, as to which most courts require removal of the offending structure, no matter how costly that might be. Why treat intentional encroachers so harshly? See Stewart E. Sterk, Property Rules, Liability Rules, and Uncertainty About Property Rights, 106 Mich. L. Rev. 1285, 1296-1297, 1319-1323 (2008).

2.   The Mechanics of Adverse Possession

Howard v. Kunto
Court of Appeals of Washington, 1970
477 P.2d 210

PEARSON, J. Land surveying is an ancient art but not one free of the errors that often creep into the affairs of men. In this case, we are presented with the question of what happens when the descriptions in deeds do not fit the land the deed holders are occupying. Defendants appeal from a decree quieting title in the plaintiffs of a tract of land on the shore of Hood Canal in Mason County.

At least as long ago as 1932 the record tells us that one McCall resided in the house now occupied by the appellant-defendants, Kunto. McCall had a deed that described a 50-foot wide parcel on the shore of Hood Canal. The error that brings this case before us is that the 50 feet described in the deed is not the same 50 feet upon which McCall's house stood. Rather, the described land is an adjacent 50-foot lot directly west of that upon which the house stood. In other words, McCall's house stood on one lot and his deed described the adjacent lot. Several property owners to the west of defendants, not parties to this action, are similarly situated.

Over the years since 1946, several conveyances occurred, using the same legal description and accompanied by a transfer of possession to the succeeding occupants. The Kuntos' immediate predecessors in interest, the Millers, desired to build a dock. To this end, they had a survey performed which indicated that the deed description and the physical occupation were in conformity. Several boundary stakes were placed as a result of this survey and the dock was constructed, as well as other improvements. The house as well as the others in the area continued to be used as summer recreational retreats.

The Kuntos then took possession of the disputed property under a deed from the Millers in 1959. In 1960 the respondent-plaintiffs, Howard, who held land east of that of the Kuntos, determined to convey an undivided one-half interest in their land to the Yearlys. To this end, they undertook to have a survey of the entire area made. After expending considerable effort, the surveyor retained by the Howards discovered that according to the government survey, the deed descriptions and the land occupancy of the parties did not coincide. Between the Howards and the Kuntos lay the Moyers' property. When the Howards' survey was completed, they discovered that they were the record owners of the land occupied by the Moyers and that the Moyers held record title to the land occupied by the Kuntos. Howard approached Moyer and in return for a conveyance of the land upon which the Moyers' house stood, Moyer conveyed to the Howards record title to the land upon which the Kunto house stood. Until plaintiffs Howard obtained the conveyance from Moyer in April, 1960, neither Moyer nor any of his predecessors ever asserted any right to ownership of the property actually being

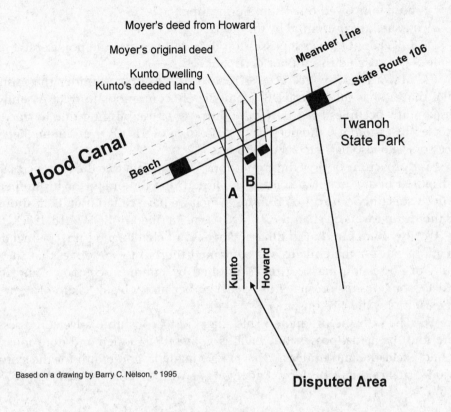

Figure 2-2

possessed by Kunto and his predecessors. This action was then instituted to quiet title in the Howards and Yearlys. The Kuntos appeal from a trial court decision granting this remedy.

At the time this action was commenced on August 19, 1960,[22] the defendants had been in occupance of the disputed property less than a year. The trial court's reason for denying their claim of adverse possession is succinctly stated in its memorandum opinion: "In this instance, defendants have failed to prove, by a preponderance of the evidence, a continuity of possession or estate to permit tacking of the adverse possession of defendants to the possession of their predecessors."

22. The inordinate delay in bringing this matter to trial appears from the record to be largely inexcusable. However, neither counsel who tried the case was at fault in any way. . . .

Finding of fact 6,[23] which is challenged by defendants, incorporates the above concept and additionally finds defendant's possession not to have been "continuous" because it involved only "summer occupancy."

Two issues are presented by this appeal:

(1) Is a claim of adverse possession defeated because the physical use of the premises is restricted to summer occupancy?

(2) May a person who receives record title to tract A under the mistaken belief that he has title to tract B (immediately contiguous to tract A) and who subsequently occupies tract B, for the purpose of establishing title to tract B by adverse possession, use the periods of possession of tract B by his immediate predecessors who also had record title to tract A?

In approaching both of these questions, we point out that the evidence, largely undisputed in any material sense, established that defendant or his immediate predecessors did occupy the premises, which we have called tract B, as though it was their own for more than the 10 years as prescribed in RCW 4.16.020.[24]

We also point out that finding of fact 6 is not challenged for its factual determinations but for the conclusions contained therein to the effect that the continuity of possession may not be established by summer occupancy, and that a predecessor's possession may not be tacked because a legal "claim of right" did not exist under the circumstances.

We start with the oft-quoted rule that: "[T]o constitute adverse possession, there must be actual possession which is *uninterrupted*, open and notorious, hostile and exclusive, and under a *claim of right* made in good faith for the statutory period." (Italics ours.) Butler v. Anderson, 71 Wash. 2d 60, 64, 426 P.2d 467, 470 (1967).[25]

---

23. "In the instant case the defendants' building was not simply over the line, but instead was built wholly upon the wrong piece of property, not the property of defendants, described in Paragraph Four of the complaint herein, but on the property of the plaintiffs, described in Paragraph Three of the complaint and herein. That the last three deeds in the chain of title, covering and embracing defendants' property, including defendants' deed, were executed in other states, specifically, California and Oregon. And there is no evidence of pointing out to the grantees in said three deeds, aforesaid, including defendants' deed, of any specific property, other than the property of defendants, described in their deed, and in Paragraph Four (4) of the complaint, and herein; nor of any immediate act of the grantees, including defendants, in said three (3) deeds, aforesaid, of taking possession of any property, other than described in said three (3) deeds, aforesaid; and the testimony of husband defendant, was unequivocally that he had no intention of possessing or holding anything other than what the deed called for; and, that there is no showing of any continuous possession by defendants or their immediate predecessors in interest, since the evidence indicates the property was in the nature, for use, as a summer occupancy, and such occupancy and use was for rather limited periods of time during comparatively short portions of the year, and was far from continuous."

24. This statute provides:

4.16.020 Actions to be commenced within ten years. The period prescribed in RCW 4.16.010 for the commencement of actions shall be as follows:
Within ten years;
Actions for the recovery of real property, or for the recovery of the possession thereof; and no action shall be maintained for such recovery unless it appears that the plaintiff, his ancestor, predecessor or grantor was seized or possessed of the premises in question within ten years before the commencement of the action.

25. In 1984 the Washington Supreme Court overruled Howard v. Kunto to the extent that the case suggests a *good-faith* requirement for adverse possession. See Chaplin v. Sanders, cited and quoted in this book at page 160. — Eds.

We reject the conclusion that summer occupancy only of a summer beach home destroys the continuity of possession required by the statute. It has become firmly established that the requisite possession requires such possession and dominion "as ordinarily marks the conduct of owners in general in holding, managing, and caring for property of like nature and condition." Whalen v. Smith, 183 Iowa 949, 953, 167 N.W. 646, 647 (1918). . . .

We hold that occupancy of tract B during the summer months for more than the 10-year period by defendant and his predecessors, together with the continued existence of the improvements on the land and beach area, constituted "uninterrupted" possession within this rule. To hold otherwise is to completely ignore the nature and condition of the property. . . .

We find such rule fully consonant with the legal writers on the subject. In F. Clark, Law of Surveying and Boundaries, §561 (3d ed. 1959) at 565: "Continuity of possession may be established although the land is used regularly for only a certain period each year." Further, at 566:

> This rule . . . is one of substance and not of absolute mathematical continuity, provided there is no break so as to sever two possessions. It is not necessary that the occupant should be actually upon the premises continually. If the land is occupied during the period of time during the year it is capable of use, there is sufficient continuity.

We now reach the question of tacking. The precise issue before us is novel in that none of the property occupied by defendant or his predecessors coincided with the property described in their deeds, but was contiguous.

In the typical case, which has been subject to much litigation, the party seeking to establish title by adverse possession claims *more* land than that described in the deed. In such cases it is clear that tacking is permitted.

In Buchanan v. Cassell, 53 Wash. 2d 611, 614, 335 P.2d 600, 602 (1959), the Supreme Court stated: "This state follows the rule that a purchaser may tack the adverse use of its predecessor in interest to that of his own where the land was intended to be included in the deed between them, but was mistakenly omitted from the description." El Cerito, Inc. v. Ryndak, 60 Wash. 2d 847, 376 P.2d 528 (1962).[26]

The general statement which appears in many of the cases is that tacking of adverse possession is permitted if the successive occupants are in "privity." See Faubion v. Elder, 49 Wash. 2d 300, 301 P.2d 153 (1956). The deed running between the parties purporting to transfer the land possessed traditionally furnishes the privity of estate which connects the possession of the successive occupants. Plaintiff contends, and the trial court ruled, that where the deed does not describe *any* of the land which was occupied, the actual transfer of possession is insufficient to establish privity.

---

26. In Baylor v. Soska, 658 A.2d 743 (Pa. 1995), the court held that tacking is not permitted unless the disputed parcel is actually described by the deed as the land conveyed. This view would prevent tacking in Howard v. Kunto. Which view is better? — EDS.

To assess the cogency of this argument and ruling, we must turn to the historical reasons for requiring privity as a necessary prerequisite to tacking the possession of several occupants. Very few, if any, of the reasons appear in the cases, nor do the cases analyze the relationships that must exist between successive possessors for tacking to be allowed. See W. Stoebuck, The Law of Adverse Possession in Washington in 35 Wash. L. Rev. 53 (1960).

The requirement of privity had its roots in the notion that a succession of trespasses, even though there was no appreciable interval between them, should not, in equity, be allowed to defeat the record title. The "claim of right," "color of title" requirement of the statutes and cases was probably derived from the early American belief that the squatter should not be able to profit by his trespass.[27]

However, it appears to this court that there is a substantial difference between the squatter or trespasser and the property purchaser, who along with several of his neighbors, as a result of an inaccurate survey or subdivision, occupies and improves property exactly 50 feet to the east of that which a survey some 30 years later demonstrates that they in fact own. It seems to us that there is also a strong public policy favoring early certainty as to the location of land ownership which enters into a proper interpretation of privity.

On the irregular perimeters of Puget Sound exact determination of land locations and boundaries is difficult and expensive. This difficulty is convincingly demonstrated in this case by the problems plaintiff's engineer encountered in attempting to locate the corners. It cannot be expected that every purchaser will or should engage a surveyor to ascertain that the beach home he is purchasing lies within the boundaries described in his deed. Such a practice is neither reasonable nor customary. Of course, 50-foot errors in descriptions are devastating where a group of adjacent owners each hold 50 feet of waterfront property.

The technical requirement of "privity" should not, we think, be used to upset the long periods of occupancy of those who in good faith received an erroneous deed description. Their "claim of right" is no less persuasive than the purchaser who believes he is purchasing *more* land than his deed described.

In the final analysis, however, we believe the requirement of "privity" is no more than judicial recognition of the need for some reasonable connection between successive occupants of real property so as to raise their claim of right above the status of the wrongdoer or the trespasser. We think such reasonable connection exists in this case.

Where, as here, several successive purchasers received record title to tract A under the mistaken belief that they were acquiring tract B, immediately contiguous thereto, and where possession of tract B is transferred and occupied in a continuous manner for more than 10 years by successive occupants, we hold there is sufficient privity of estate to permit tacking and thus establish adverse possession as a matter of law.

---

27. The English common law does not require privity as a prerequisite for tacking. See F. Clark, Law of Surveying and Boundaries, §561 (3d ed. 1959) at 568.

We see no reason in law or in equity for differentiating this case from Faubion v. Elder, 49 Wash. 2d 300, 301 P.2d 153 (1956), where the appellants were claiming *more* land than their deed described and where successive periods of occupation were allowed to be united to each other to make up the time of adverse holding. . . .

This application of the privity requirement should particularly pertain where the holder of record title to tract B acquired the same with knowledge of the discrepancy.

Judgment is reversed with directions to dismiss plaintiffs' action and to enter a decree quieting defendants' title to the disputed tract of land in accordance with the prayer of their cross-complaint.

QUESTIONS

1. In *Mannillo* (page 164), the court held that an adverse occupation might be so small as to not be open and notorious. Was there not a related but unaddressed problem in Howard v. Kunto? Consider the observation of Robert M. Pirsig in his book Zen and the Art of Motorcycle Maintenance 48 (1974): "Some things you miss because they're so tiny you overlook them. But some things you don't see because they're so huge."

2. Suppose that instead of building a summer house on "their" lot, the Kuntos and their predecessors had camped every summer on the lot and, being good environmentalists, had left no traces when they removed their camp in the fall. Would this satisfy the requirement of continuity? Compare Ray v. Beacon Hudson Mountain Corp., 666 N.E.2d 532 (N.Y. 1996).

For an argument that adverse possession rules favor economic exploitation of wild lands by permitting successful claims of adverse possession of wild lands to rest on limited, sporadic activities that would not be sufficient for developed lands, see John G. Sprankling, An Environmental Critique of Adverse Possession, 79 Cornell L. Rev. 816 (1994). Inasmuch as strengthening the standard for adverse possession of wild lands might result in claimants inflicting more environmental injury, Professor Sprankling suggests exempting wild lands altogether from adverse possession. See also Alexandra B. Klass, Adverse Possession and Conservation: Expanding Traditional Notions of Use and Possession, 77 U. Colo. L. Rev. 283 (2006).

PROBLEMS: TACKING

An important issue in Howard v. Kunto concerns so-called tacking and the requirement of privity among a series of adverse possessors. But tacking comes into play in different guises. Suppose, for example, that X buys certain property described in a deed from the seller, who as it happens had also (but unknowingly) adversely possessed a strip adjacent to the described land. If the evidence shows that the deed to X was intended by the parties to convey not only the described land but also the adversely possessed strip, is X allowed to "tack" that strip onto the land described in the deed? In Buchanan v. Cassell, cited in Howard v. Kunto at page 173, the court held that X could do exactly that. Howard v. Kunto, relying on the clear intentions of the parties in privity with one another, extends *Buchanan* to a situation where the deed describes none of the land in question, such that there is nothing onto which the adversely possessed land can be tacked.

Another kind of tacking issue arises when land is adversely possessed by a series of people, no one of whom occupies the land for the statutory period, though all of them taken together do. May the bits of time of each possessor be tacked together? Is privity required? The following problems explore these matters, as well as the related situation when adverse possession is asserted against a series of owners. Assume in each problem that the jurisdiction has a 10-year statute of limitations.

1. In 2000 A enters adversely upon Blackacre,[28] owned by O. In 2007 B tells A, "Get out of here, I'm taking over." A, feeling threatened, leaves, and B enters into possession. In 2010 who owns Blackacre? Can O or A eject B? See 3 American Law of Property §15.10 (1952). For the contrary English law, see footnote 27 and Robert Megarry & H.W.R. Wade, Real Property 1422-1423 (Charles Harpum 7th ed. 2008) ("time runs against the true owner from the time when adverse possession began, and so long as adverse possession continues unbroken it makes no difference who continues it"). Which view is better? To what extent does your answer turn on what you see as the purposes of adverse possession?

Suppose that in 2007 A leaves under threat of force, but six months later A recovers possession from B. If O does nothing, will A own Blackacre 10 years from the date of his entry in 2000, or 10 years and six months from the date of his entry in 2000, or in 2017? See 3 American Law of Property, supra, §15.10.

Suppose that in 2007 A abandons Blackacre, and B immediately goes into possession. If O does nothing, will B own Blackacre in 2010?

2. In 1994 A enters adversely upon Blackacre, owned by O. In 1995 O dies, leaving a will that devises Blackacre to B for life, remainder to C. In 2010 B dies without ever having entered upon Blackacre. Who owns Blackacre?

3. O, owner of Blackacre, dies in 1995 leaving a will that devises Blackacre to B for life, remainder to C. In 1996 A enters adversely upon the land. In 2010 B dies. Who owns Blackacre? See 3 American Law of Property, supra, §15.8; Harper v. Paradise, 210 S.E.2d 710 (Ga. 1974), reproduced at page 741; Piel v. Dewitt, 351 N.E.2d 48 (Ind. App. 1976). But cf. Wallace v. Magie, 522 P.2d 989 (Kan. 1974).

---

28. Hypothetical tracts of land traditionally have been referred to as Blackacre, Whiteacre, and Greenacre—just why no one knows for sure. One of the earliest law treatises written in English, Coke on Littleton 148b (1628), refers to Blackacre and Whiteacre. The Oxford English Dictionary suggests the terms indicate lands growing different crops (peas and beans are black, corn and potatoes are white, hay is green). Or the terms might originally have referred to lands receiving different rents (black rents are payable in produce, white rents in silver). Students have sometimes suggested that Wiseacre be added to the list.

PROBLEMS: DISABILITIES

In every state the statute of limitations is extended if specified disabilities are present. Disability provisions differ, but the following example is typical:

> An action to recover the title to or possession of real property shall be brought within ten years after the cause thereof accrued, but if a person entitled to bring such action, at the time the cause thereof accrues, is within the age of minority, of unsound mind, or imprisoned, such person, after the expiration of ten years from the time the cause of action accrues, may bring such action within five years after such disability is removed.

Particularly note two matters: A disability is immaterial unless it existed at the time when the cause of action accrued. And after the words "such person" you should insert, as a result of judicial construction, the words "or anyone claiming from, by, or under such person." (Do you see why a court would read those words into the statute?)

When in the following examples would the adverse possessor acquire title under the statute set out above? In each case, *O* is the owner in 1995, and *A* enters adversely on May 1, 1995. The age of majority is 18. (In reading the examples, understand that to die "intestate" means to die without a will. In such cases, the decedent's estate goes to heirs, if the decedent has any.)

1. *O* is insane in 1995. *O* dies insane and intestate in 2008.

(a) *O*'s heir, *H*, is under no disability in 2008.

(b) *O*'s heir, *H*, is six years old in 2008.

2. *O* has no disability in 1995. *O* dies intestate in 2004. *O*'s heir, *H*, is two years old in 2004.

3. *O* is eight years old in 1995. In 2002 *O* becomes mentally ill, and *O* dies intestate in 2011. *O*'s heir, *H*, is under no disability. Does the adverse possessor here acquire title in 2005, 2010, or at some later date? If the answer is 2005 or 2010, how are *O*'s interests to be protected?

Consider again the purposes of adverse possession and note how some of them conflict in the case of disabilities. Does reflection on Problem 3 suggest that disability doctrine is unnecessary?

4. *O* disappears in 1998 and is not heard from again. You represent *B*, who wishes to buy from *A*. What advice do you give *B*?

NOTE: ADVERSE POSSESSION AGAINST
THE GOVERNMENT

Under the common law rules, adverse possession does not run against the government—local, state, or federal. In England the maxim *nullum tempus occurrit regi* (no time runs against the king) barred the running of the statute of limitations against the sovereign. In barring adverse possession against the government, American courts have relied on this rule as well as state constitutional provisions restricting the alienation of state lands. Courts often say, in justification, that the state owns its land in trust for all the people, who should not lose the land because of the negligence of a few state officers or employees.

A number of states, however, have changed the common law rules, whether by legislation or judge-made law.[29] A few permit adverse possession against government land on the same terms as against private land. Others permit it only if possession continues for a period much longer than that applied in the case of private lands. Still others permit it only against government lands held in a proprietary (as opposed to a public or governmental) capacity. See, e.g., American Trading Real Estate Properties, Inc. v. Town of Trumbull, 574 A.2d 796 (Conn. 1990); Devins v. Borough of Bogota, 592 A.2d 199 (N.J. 1991).

Are there good reasons to treat government lands differently from those privately owned? What types of land might justifiably be subjected to adverse possession and what types not?

 3.   Adverse Possession of Chattels

O'Keeffe v. Snyder

Supreme Court of New Jersey, 1980
416 A.2d 862

POLLOCK, J. This is an appeal from an order of the Appellate Division granting summary judgment to plaintiff, Georgia O'Keeffe, against defendant, Barry Snyder, d/b/a Princeton Gallery of Fine Arts, for replevin of three small pictures painted by O'Keeffe. In her complaint, filed in March, 1976, O'Keeffe alleged she was the owner of the paintings and that they were stolen from a New York art gallery in 1946. Snyder asserted he was a purchaser for value of the paintings, he had title by adverse possession, and O'Keeffe's action was barred by the expiration of the six-year period of limitations . . . pertaining to an action in replevin. Snyder impleaded third party defendant, Ulrich A. Frank, from whom Snyder purchased the paintings in 1975 for $35,000.

The trial court granted summary judgment for Snyder on the ground that O'Keeffe's action was barred because it was not commenced within six years of the alleged theft. The Appellate Division reversed and entered judgment for O'Keeffe. A majority of that court concluded that the paintings were stolen, the defenses of expiration of the statute of limitations and title by adverse possession were identical, and Snyder had not proved the elements of adverse possession. Consequently, the majority ruled that O'Keeffe could still enforce her right to possession of the paintings.

. . . We reverse and remand the matter for a plenary hearing in accordance with this opinion.

---

29. Even absent such changes, the government may be estopped from asserting any right to land where a person improves the land with the knowledge and acquiescence of government officials. See, e.g., Clinton Natl. Bank v. City of Camanche, 251 N.W.2d 248 (Iowa 1977).

The record, limited to pleadings, affidavits, answers to interrogatories, and depositions, is fraught with factual conflict. Apart from the creation of the paintings by O'Keeffe and their discovery in Snyder's gallery in 1976, the parties agree on little else.

O'Keeffe contended the paintings were stolen in 1946 from a gallery, An American Place. The gallery was operated by her late husband, the famous photographer Alfred Stieglitz.

An American Place was a cooperative undertaking of O'Keeffe and some other American artists identified by her as Marin, Hardin, Dove, Andema, and Stevens. In 1946, Stieglitz arranged an exhibit which included an O'Keeffe painting, identified as Cliffs. According to O'Keeffe, one day in March, 1946, she and Stieglitz discovered Cliffs was missing from the wall of the exhibit. O'Keeffe estimates the value of the painting at the time of the alleged theft to have been about $150.

About two weeks later, O'Keeffe noticed that two other paintings, Seaweed and Fragments, were missing from a storage room at An American Place. She did not tell anyone, even Stieglitz, about the missing paintings, since she did not want to upset him.

Before the date when O'Keeffe discovered the disappearance of Seaweed, she had already sold it (apparently for a string of amber beads) to a Mrs. Weiner, now deceased. Following the grant of the motion for summary judgment by the trial court in favor of Snyder, O'Keeffe submitted a release from the legatees of Mrs. Weiner purportedly assigning to O'Keeffe their interest in the sale.

O'Keeffe testified on depositions that at about the same time as the disappearance of her paintings, 12 or 13 miniature paintings by Marin also were stolen from An American Place. According to O'Keeffe, a man named Estrick took the Marin paintings and "maybe a few other things." Estrick distributed the Marin paintings to members of the theater world who, when confronted by Stieglitz, returned them. However, neither Stieglitz nor O'Keeffe confronted Estrick with the loss of any of the O'Keeffe paintings.

There was no evidence of a break and entry at An American Place on the dates when O'Keeffe discovered the disappearance of her paintings. Neither Stieglitz nor O'Keeffe reported them missing to the New York Police Department or any other law enforcement agency. Apparently the paintings were uninsured, and O'Keeffe did not seek reimbursement from an insurance company. Similarly, neither O'Keeffe nor Stieglitz advertised the loss of the paintings in Art News or any other publication. Nonetheless, they discussed it with associates in the art world and later O'Keeffe mentioned the loss to the director of the Art Institute of Chicago, but she did not ask him to do anything because "it wouldn't have been my way." O'Keeffe does not contend that Frank or Snyder had actual knowledge of the alleged theft.

Stieglitz died in the summer of 1946, and O'Keeffe explains she did not pursue her efforts to locate the paintings because she was settling his estate. In 1947, she retained the services of Doris Bry to help settle the estate. Bry urged O'Keeffe to report the loss of the paintings, but O'Keeffe declined because "they never got anything back by reporting it." Finally, in 1972, O'Keeffe authorized Bry to report the theft to the Art Dealers Association of America, Inc., which maintains for its members a registry of stolen paintings. The record does not indicate whether such a registry existed at the time the paintings disappeared.

In September, 1975, O'Keeffe learned that the paintings were in the Andrew Crispo Gallery in New York on consignment from Bernard Danenberg Galleries. On February 11, 1976, O'Keeffe discovered that Ulrich A. Frank had sold the paintings to Barry Snyder, d/b/a Princeton Gallery of Fine Art. She demanded their return and, following Snyder's refusal, instituted this action for replevin.

Frank traces his possession of the paintings to his father, Dr. Frank, who died in 1968. He claims there is a family relationship by marriage between his family and the Stieglitz family, a contention that O'Keeffe disputes. Frank does not know how his father acquired the paintings, but he recalls seeing them in his father's apartment in New Hampshire as early as 1941-1943, a period that precedes the alleged theft. Consequently, Frank's factual contentions are inconsistent with O'Keeffe's allegation of theft. Until 1965, Dr. Frank occasionally lent the paintings to Ulrich Frank. In 1965, Dr. and Mrs. Frank formally gave the paintings to Ulrich Frank, who kept them in his residences in Yardley, Pennsylvania and Princeton, New Jersey. In 1968, he exhibited anonymously Cliffs and Fragments in a one day art show in the Jewish Community Center in Trenton. All of these events precede O'Keeffe's listing of the paintings as stolen with the Art Dealers Association of America, Inc. in 1972.

Frank claims continuous possession of the paintings through his father for over thirty years and admits selling the paintings to Snyder. Snyder and Frank do not trace their provenance, or history of possession of the paintings, back to O'Keeffe.

As indicated, Snyder moved for summary judgment on the theory that O'Keeffe's action was barred by the statute of limitations and title had vested in Frank by adverse possession. For purposes of his motion, Snyder conceded that the paintings had been stolen. On her cross motion, O'Keeffe urged that the paintings were stolen, the statute of limitations had not run, and title to the paintings remained in her. . . .

The Appellate Division accepted O'Keeffe's contention that the paintings had been stolen. However, in his deposition, Ulrich Frank traces possession of the paintings to his father in the early 1940s, a date that precedes the alleged theft by several years. The factual dispute about the loss of the paintings by O'Keeffe and their acquisition by Frank, as well as the other subsequently described factual issues, warrant a remand for a plenary hearing. . . .

Without purporting to limit the scope of the trial, other factual issues include whether . . . the paintings were not stolen but sold, lent, consigned, or given by Stieglitz to Dr. Frank or someone else without O'Keeffe's knowledge before he died; and [whether] there was any business or family relationship between Stieglitz and Dr. Frank so that the original possession of the paintings by the Frank family may have been under claim of right.

Seaweed
by Georgia O'Keeffe (1926)
Collection of Juan Hamilton

On the limited record before us, we cannot determine now who has title to the paintings. The determination will depend on the evidence adduced at trial. Nonetheless, we believe it may aid the trial court and the parties to resolve questions of law that may become relevant at trial.

Our discussion begins with the principle that, generally speaking, if the paintings were stolen, the thief acquired no title and could not transfer good title to others regardless of their good faith and ignorance of the theft. Proof of theft would advance O'Keeffe's right to possession of the paintings absent other considerations such as expiration of the statute of limitations.

Another issue that may become relevant at trial is whether Frank or his father acquired a "voidable title" to the paintings under N.J.S.A. 12A:2-403(1). That section, part of the Uniform Commercial Code (U.C.C.),[30] does not change the basic principle that a mere possessor cannot transfer good title. Nonetheless, the U.C.C. permits a person with voidable title to transfer good title to a good faith purchaser for value in certain circumstances. If the facts developed at trial merit application of that section, then Frank may have transferred good title to Snyder, thereby providing a defense to O'Keeffe's action. . . .

On this appeal, the critical legal question is when O'Keeffe's cause of action accrued. The fulcrum on which the outcome turns is the statute of limitations . . . , which provides that an action for replevin of goods or chattels must be commenced within six years after the accrual of the cause of action.

The trial court found that O'Keeffe's cause of action accrued on the date of the alleged theft, March, 1946, and concluded that her action was barred. The Appellate Division found that an action might have accrued more than six years before the date of suit if possession by the defendant or his predecessors satisfied the elements of adverse possession. As indicated, the Appellate Division concluded that Snyder had not established those elements and that the O'Keeffe action was not barred by the statute of limitations. . . .

The purpose of a statute of limitations is to "stimulate to activity and punish negligence" and "promote repose by giving security and stability to human affairs." Wood v. Carpenter, 101 U.S. 135, 139, 25 L. Ed. 807, 808 (1879). A statute

---

30. Uniform Commercial Code §2-403 provides:

§2-403. *Power to Transfer; Good Faith Purchase of Goods; "Entrusting."*

(1) A purchaser of goods acquires all title which his transferor had or had power to transfer except that a purchaser of a limited interest acquires rights only to the extent of the interest purchased. A person with voidable title has power to transfer a good title to a good faith purchaser for value. When goods have been delivered under a transaction of purchase the purchaser has such power even though

(a) the transferor was deceived as to the identity of the purchaser, or

(b) the delivery was in exchange for a check which was later dishonored, or

(c) it was agreed that the transaction was to be a "cash sale," or

(d) the delivery was procured through fraud punishable as larcenous under the criminal law.

(2) Any entrusting of possession of goods to a merchant who deals in goods of that kind gives him power to transfer all rights of the entruster to a buyer in the ordinary course of business.

(3) "Entrusting" includes any delivery and any acquiescence in retention of possession regardless of any condition expressed between the parties to the delivery or acquiescence and regardless of whether the procurement of the entrusting or the possessor's disposition of the goods have been such as to be larcenous under the criminal law. — EDS.

of limitations achieves those purposes by barring a cause of action after the statutory period. In certain instances, this Court has ruled that the literal language of a statute of limitations should yield to other considerations.

To avoid harsh results from the mechanical application of the statute, the courts have developed a concept known as the discovery rule. The discovery rule provides that, in an appropriate case, a cause of action will not accrue until the injured party discovers, or by exercise of reasonable diligence and intelligence should have discovered, facts which form the basis of a cause of action. The rule is essentially a principle of equity, the purpose of which is to mitigate unjust results that otherwise might flow from strict adherence to a rule of law. . . .

[W]e conclude that the discovery rule applies to an action for replevin of a painting. . . . O'Keeffe's cause of action accrued when she first knew, or reasonably should have known through the exercise of due diligence, of the cause of action, including the identity of the possessor of the paintings. . . .

In determining whether O'Keeffe is entitled to the benefit of the discovery rule, the trial court should consider, among others, the following issues: (1) whether O'Keeffe used due diligence to recover the paintings at the time of the alleged theft and thereafter; (2) whether at the time of the alleged theft there was an effective method, other than talking to her colleagues, for O'Keeffe to alert the art world; and (3) whether registering paintings with the Art Dealers Association of America, Inc. or any other organization would put a reasonably prudent purchaser of art on constructive notice that someone other than the possessor was the true owner.

The acquisition of title to real and personal property by adverse possession is based on the expiration of a statute of limitations. . . .

To establish title by adverse possession to chattels, the rule of law has been that the possession must be hostile, actual, visible, exclusive, and continuous. . . . There is an inherent problem with many kinds of personal property that will raise questions whether their possession has been open, visible, and notorious. . . . For example, if jewelry is stolen from a municipality in one county in New Jersey, it is unlikely that the owner would learn that someone is openly wearing that jewelry in another county or even in the same municipality. Open and visible possession of personal property, such as jewelry, may not be sufficient to put the original owner on actual or constructive notice of the identity of the possessor.

The problem is even more acute with works of art. Like many kinds of personal property, works of art are readily moved and easily concealed. O'Keeffe argues that nothing short of public display should be sufficient to alert the true owner and start the statute running. Although there is merit in that contention from the perspective of the original owner, the effect is to impose a heavy burden on the purchasers of paintings who wish to enjoy the paintings in the privacy of their homes. . . .

The problem is serious. According to an affidavit submitted in this matter by the president of the International Foundation for Art Research, there has been an "explosion in art thefts" and there is a "worldwide phenomenon of art theft which has reached epidemic proportions."

The limited record before us provides a brief glimpse into the arcane world of sales of art, where paintings worth vast sums of money sometimes are bought without inquiry about their provenance. There does not appear to be a reasonably available method for an owner of art to record the ownership or theft of paintings. Similarly, there are no reasonable means readily available to a purchaser to ascertain the provenance of a painting. It may be time for the art world to establish a means by which a good faith purchaser may reasonably obtain the provenance of a painting. An efficient registry of original works of art might better serve the interests of artists, owners of art, and bona fide purchasers than the law of adverse possession with all of its uncertainties. Although we cannot mandate the initiation of a registration system, we can develop a rule for the commencement and running of the statute of limitations that is more responsive to the needs of the art world than the doctrine of adverse possession.

We are persuaded that the introduction of equitable considerations through the discovery rule provides a more satisfactory response than the doctrine of adverse possession. The discovery rule shifts the emphasis from the conduct of the possessor to the conduct of the owner. The focus of the inquiry will no longer be whether the possessor has met the tests of adverse possession, but whether the owner has acted with due diligence in pursuing his or her personal property.

For example, under the discovery rule, if an artist diligently seeks the recovery of a lost or stolen painting, but cannot find it or discover the identity of the possessor, the statute of limitations will not begin to run. The rule permits an artist who uses reasonable efforts to report, investigate, and recover a painting to preserve the rights of title and possession.

Properly interpreted, the discovery rule becomes a vehicle for transporting equitable considerations into the statute of limitations for replevin. . . .

It is consistent also with the law of replevin as it has developed apart from the discovery rule. In an action for replevin, the period of limitations ordinarily will run against the owner of lost or stolen property from the time of the wrongful taking, absent fraud or concealment. Where the chattel is fraudulently concealed, the general rule is that the statute is tolled. . . .

A purchaser from a private party would be well-advised to inquire whether a work of art has been reported as lost or stolen. However, a bona fide purchaser who purchases in the ordinary course of business a painting entrusted to an art dealer should be able to acquire good title against the true owner. Under the U.C.C. entrusting possession of goods to a merchant who deals in that kind of goods gives the merchant the power to transfer all the rights of the entruster to a buyer in the ordinary course of business. In a transaction under that statute, a merchant may vest good title in the buyer as against the original owner. The interplay between the statute of limitations as modified by the discovery rule and the U.C.C. should encourage good faith purchases from legitimate art dealers and discourage trafficking in stolen art without frustrating an artist's ability to recover stolen art works.

The discovery rule will fulfill the purposes of a statute of limitations and accord greater protection to the innocent owner of personal property whose goods are lost or stolen. . . .

By diligently pursuing their goods, owners may prevent the statute of limitations from running. The meaning of due diligence will vary with the facts of each case, including the nature and value of the personal property. For example, with respect to jewelry of moderate value, it may be sufficient if the owner reports the theft to the police. With respect to art work of greater value, it may be reasonable to expect an owner to do more. In practice, our ruling should contribute to more careful practices concerning the purchase of art.

The considerations are different with real estate, and there is no reason to disturb the application of the doctrine of adverse possession to real estate. Real estate is fixed and cannot be moved or concealed. The owner of real property knows or should know where his property is located and reasonably can be expected to be aware of open, notorious, visible, hostile, continuous acts of possession on it.

Our ruling not only changes the requirements for acquiring title to personal property after an alleged unlawful taking, but also shifts the burden of proof at trial. Under the doctrine of adverse possession, the burden is on the possessor to prove the elements of adverse possession. Under the discovery rule, the burden is on the owner as the one seeking the benefit of the rule to establish facts that would justify deferring the beginning of the period of limitations. . . .

Read literally, the effect of the expiration of the statute of limitations . . . is to bar an action such as replevin. The statute does not speak of divesting the original owner of title. By its terms the statute cuts off the remedy, but not the right of title. Nonetheless, the effect of the expiration of the statute of limitations, albeit on the theory of adverse possession, has been not only to bar an action for possession, but also to vest title in the possessor. There is no reason to change that result although the discovery rule has replaced adverse possession. History, reason, and common sense support the conclusion that the expiration of the statute of limitations bars the remedy to recover possession and also vests title in the possessor. . . . Before the expiration of the statute, the possessor has both the chattel and the right to keep it except as against the true owner. The only imperfection in the possessor's right to retain the chattel is the original owner's right to repossess it. Once that imperfection is removed, the possessor should have good title for all purposes. . . .

We next consider the effect of transfers of a chattel from one possessor to another during the period of limitation under the discovery rule. Under the discovery rule, the statute of limitations on an action for replevin begins to run when the owner knows or reasonably should know of his cause of action and the identity of the possessor of the chattel. Subsequent transfers of the chattel are part of the continuous dispossession of the chattel from the original owner. The important point is not that there has been a substitution of possessors, but that there has been a continuous dispossession of the former owner. . . .

For the purpose of evaluating the due diligence of an owner, the dispossession of his chattel is a continuum not susceptible to separation into distinct acts. Nonetheless, subsequent transfers of the chattel may affect the degree of difficulty encountered by a diligent owner seeking to recover his goods. To that extent, subsequent transfers and their potential for frustrating diligence are relevant in applying the discovery rule. An owner who diligently seeks his chattel should be entitled to the benefit of the discovery rule although it may have passed through many hands. Conversely an owner who sleeps on his rights may be denied the benefit of the discovery rule although the chattel may have been possessed by only one person.

We reject the alternative of treating subsequent transfers of a chattel as separate acts of conversion that would start the statute of limitations running anew. At common law, apart from the statute of limitations, a subsequent transfer of a converted chattel was considered to be a separate act of conversion. . . . Adoption of that alternative would tend to undermine the purpose of the statute in quieting titles and protecting against stale claims.

The majority and better view is to permit tacking, the accumulation of consecutive periods of possession by parties in privity with each other. . . .

We reverse the judgment of the Appellate Division in favor of O'Keeffe and remand the matter for trial in accordance with this opinion.

[Dissenting opinions by Justice Sullivan and Justice Handler are omitted.]

A NOTE ON GEORGIA O'KEEFFE

Georgia O'Keeffe, born on a dairy farm in 1887 in Sun Prairie, Wisconsin, grew up in the rural Midwest. After studying art under various teachers in Chicago and New York, she decided to paint shapes that, she claimed, were "in [her] head." In 1915, she sent some of her drawings—of budding and organic shapes, reflecting an intense feminine sensibility—to a friend in New York, admonishing her to show them to no one. The friend, disregarding O'Keeffe's wishes, showed them to Alfred Stieglitz, the noted New York photographer and gallery owner. Upon seeing the drawings, Stieglitz remarked, "At last, a woman on paper," and promptly displayed them in his gallery. When, shortly thereafter, O'Keeffe came to New York and learned of this, she was furious. She rushed to the gallery and demanded that her private work, shown without her permission, be taken down. Stieglitz refused. To keep her work from being seen, he told her, would be like depriving the world of a child about to be born (with Stieglitz as midwife). The drawings remained on the wall, provoking much controversy about O'Keeffe's sexual symbolism, which she denied was there.

Stieglitz, obsessed with this woman 20 years his junior, soon left his wife and daughter and moved in with her. "He photographed me until I was crazy," O'Keeffe—with a mischievous chuckle—recalled in her nineties. He photographed every square inch of O'Keeffe nude, then exhibited the pictures in a show, creating a scandal and bringing O'Keeffe instant fame.

Soon thereafter, O'Keeffe began to produce many of her spectacular flower paintings, which critics once again found full of Freudian symbolism. O'Keeffe replied to them:

> Well—I made you take time to look at what I saw and when you took time to really notice my flower you hung all your own associations with flowers on my flower and you write about my flower as if I think and see what you think and see of the flower—and I don't.[31]

O'Keeffe, now established in the New York art world, became the embodiment of Stieglitz's belief that women could turn out art as powerful as any man's.

O'Keeffe and Stieglitz married in 1924. When, a few years later, Stieglitz entered into a liaison with a woman half O'Keeffe's age, and put her in charge of his gallery, O'Keeffe—needing space—began spending long summers in New Mexico. She found that New Mexico was where she belonged, but she could not leave Stieglitz, to whom she remained intensely devoted. She returned to New York every fall to renew her bond with him, though she never answered amiably when addressed as "Mrs. Stieglitz."

When Stieglitz died in 1946, at age 82, O'Keeffe first booted his lover out of his gallery, and then she moved to New Mexico for good. In the isolated Penitente village of Abiquiu (pop. 150), on a rise overlooking the green Chama River valley and barren pink and white and ochre hills beyond, she had many years before found a roofless adobe building with a door she "just had to paint" and had to own. Now, after lengthy negotiations, including long afternoon visits by the priests, O'Keeffe was able to wrest title away from the local Catholic church. O'Keeffe fixed up the adobe, fitted it with Zenlike simplicity, walled it in with a garden and orchard, and lived there, mostly alone, with some chow dogs she described as "good biters," until her death in 1986 at age 99. She left most of her estate of $70 million (comprised largely of 400 works of art she had created) to a handsome young man by the name of Juan Hamilton, who, when O'Keeffe was 86, knocked on her door at Abiquiu looking for work. Hamilton bore an uncanny resemblance to the youthful Stieglitz. He moved in with O'Keeffe soon after being admitted at her door, becoming her indispensable companion and, some say, lover. When her old friend of many years, the mother of Harvard's former president Derek Bok, called Hamilton a fortune hunter, O'Keeffe icily rebuffed her and cut Harvard out of her will.

NOTES AND QUESTIONS

1. Back to the case of O'Keeffe v. Snyder. The parties subsequently settled before a retrial. The paintings were divided. O'Keeffe took "Seaweed," Snyder took another painting, and the third was sold at auction at Sotheby's to pay lawyers' bills.

---

31. Or O'Keeffe might have replied—as Freud, who loved cigars, is reputed to have said—"Sometimes a cigar is just a cigar."

Georgia O'Keeffe, 1968

© Arnold Newman/Getty Images

2. Note that the opinion in *O'Keeffe* permits tacking of periods of possession, but—it appears—only so long as the possessors are in privity with each other. See page 186. Given the focus in *O'Keeffe* on the conduct of the owner, and given that the "important point is not that there has been a substitution of possessors, but that there has been a continuous dispossession of the former owner," why is privity required?

For an analysis of O'Keeffe v. Snyder, see Paula A. Franzese, "Georgia on My Mind"—Reflections on *O'Keeffe v. Snyder*, 9 Seton Hall L. Rev. 1, 14-15 (1989).

3. At least one state, California, has adopted the discovery rule by statute. See Cal. Civ. Proc. Code §338(c) (West 2013) But New York, probably the site of most purchases of major works of art in the United States, has rejected it on the ground that it provides insufficient protection for owners of stolen artwork. See Solomon R. Guggenheim Found. v. Lubell, 569 N.E.2d 426 (N.Y. 1991). The *Guggenheim* case held that the statute of limitations for replevin does not begin to run in favor of a good-faith purchaser until the true owner makes a demand for return and the good-faith purchaser refuses. Until demand is made, possession of the stolen property by a good-faith purchaser for value is not considered wrongful. The court thought it inappropriate to put a duty of reasonable diligence on the true owner, reasoning that such an approach would encourage illicit trafficking in stolen art by putting the burden on the true owner to demonstrate that it had undertaken a reasonable search. Moreover, the court believed that it would be difficult, if not impossible, to craft a reasonable diligence requirement that could take into account all the variables in a particular situation and not unduly

burden the true owner. The better rule, the court said, is to protect true own-ers by requiring potential purchasers to investigate the provenance of works of art. The true owner's diligence remains relevant, however, in that unreasonable delay, if it works to the prejudice of the good-faith purchaser, might permit the latter to assert the equitable defense of laches.

4. *Purchasing from a thief: conflicting views.* In the United States (and adverse possession aside), a purchaser cannot obtain good title from a thief—a point implicit in the first sentence of subsection (1) of Uniform Commercial Code §2-403, set out in footnote 30 on page 182. Notice, however, that a purchaser might be able to obtain good title from other sorts of scoundrels, as the court in *O'Keeffe* suggests on pages 180-182. If Frank had a "voidable title" for one of the reasons suggested in subsections (a) through (d) of the Code provision (for example, paying for the paintings by a check that bounced), then Frank could convey good title to Snyder if Snyder was "a good faith purchaser for value," meaning, essentially, a buyer not on notice that matters are amiss. If O'Keeffe had entrusted the paintings to Stieglitz's gallery for appraisal but not for sale, Stieglitz—being "a merchant who deals in goods of that kind"—could transfer a good title to a good-faith buyer in the ordinary course of business. See U.C.C. §2-403(2).

Some countries in Europe and elsewhere follow similar rules, but not all of them do. Several recognize the doctrine of market overt, according to which a bona fide purchaser may acquire good title from a thief if the sale in question takes place in an open market. Opportunities for the laundering of stolen objects arise as a result. The problem has not gone unnoticed in the art world (nor, we presume, the underworld). See, e.g., Note, International Transfers of Stolen Cultural Property: Should Thieves Continue to Benefit from Domestic Laws Favoring Bona Fide Purchasers?, 13 Loy. L.A. Intl. & Comp. L.J. 427 (1990).

Whom should the law protect in instances like those discussed, the innocent owner or the innocent bona fide purchaser? What interests are in conflict? Does reflection on the voidable-title and entrusting exceptions contained in Uniform Commercial Code §2-403 suggest a way to resolve the conflict? See Robert Cooter & Thomas Ulen, Law and Economics 159-161 (5th ed. 2008).

C. Acquisition by Gift

To complete our study of possession, we turn to gifts of personal property, where, as we shall see, possession plays a very important role. There are three require-ments to make a gift of personal property. First, the donor must *intend* to make a present transfer of an existing interest in the property. Intent is commonly a prob-lem in litigated gift cases. Second, the donor must *deliver* possession ("hand over the property") to the donee with the manifested intention to make a gift. Delivery and intent interact and overlap with each other to a considerable degree, but they are discrete requirements nonetheless, and both must be present. Finally, *acceptance* by the donee is also required but seldom an issue. Courts presume acceptance upon delivery, unless a donee expressly refuses a gift. Intention to make a gift may be shown by oral evidence; delivery requires objective acts.

More on delivery. The requirement of transfer of possession is feudal in origin. In feudal times, when few could read or write, a symbolic ceremony transferring possession was an important ritual signifying the transfer. Land could be transferred only by delivering a clod of dirt or a branch to the grantee on the land itself. The ceremony was called "livery of seisin" (see page 243); chattels had to be handed over. In 1677 the Statute of Frauds abolished livery of seisin and initiated the requirement of a deed to pass title to land. However, the visual ceremony of transferring possession still survives if the object transferred is on top of the land. In a famous article, Professor Mechem suggested the following reasons for the survival of the delivery requirement in gifts of personal property:

> 1. Handing over the object makes vivid and concrete to the donor the significance of the act performed. By feeling the "wrench of delivery," the donor realizes an irrevocable gift has been made.
> 2. The act is unequivocal evidence of a gift to the actual witnesses of the transaction.
> 3. Delivery of the object to the donee gives the donee, after the act, prima facie evidence in favor of the alleged gift. [Philip Mechem, Gifts of Chattels and of Choses in Action Evidenced by Commercial Instruments, 21 Ill. L. Rev. 341, 348-349 (1926).]

If manual delivery is not practicable because of the size or weight of the object, or its inaccessibility, constructive or symbolic delivery may be permitted. *Constructive* delivery is handing over a key or some object that will open up access to the subject matter of the gift. *Symbolic* delivery is handing over something symbolic of the property given. The usual case of symbolic delivery involves handing over a written instrument declaring a gift of the subject matter; for example, Joe hands to Marilyn a paper reading, "I give my grand piano to Marilyn. s/ Joe." The traditional rule of gifts is: If an object can be handed over, it must be. But there are indications that the rule is eroding. For example, one court found valid *constructive* delivery where a donor who had received a check from another endorsed the check in blank and put it on a table in her apartment, which she shared with the donee, along with a note giving the check to the donee, and then left with the intention of committing suicide (which she did). Scherer v. Hyland, 380 A.2d 698 (N.J. 1977). Under the traditional rule, constructive delivery would not be recognized here. (Do you see why?) However, the court stated that it would find a constructive delivery adequate "when the evidence of donative intent is concrete and undisputed, when there is every indication that the donor intended to make a present transfer of the subject-matter of the gift, and when the steps taken by the donor to effect such a transfer must have been deemed by the donor as sufficient to pass the donor's interest to the donee."

The restriction on *symbolic* delivery has also been relaxed somewhat. Some states have statutes providing that symbolic delivery by a writing is always permitted. E.g., Cal. Civ. Code §1147 (West 2013).

With only three requirements, gift law is beguilingly simple, and we shall see that the requirements of donative intent and delivery are far more complex than meets the eye. In studying the materials that follow, it will be helpful to keep in mind this observation from a commentator: "[A] close examination of the cases leaves a reader with a sense that ad hoc considerations of fairness and justice or propriety do much of the work in leading judges to decisions." Roy Kreitner, The Gift Beyond the Grave: Revising the Question of Consideration, 101 Colum. L. Rev. 1876, 1906 (2001).

PROBLEMS

1. *O* owns a pearl ring. While visiting her daughter *A*, *O* leaves the ring on the bathroom sink. After *O* leaves, *A* discovers the ring. When *A* telephones *O* to tell her of the discovery, *O* tells *A* to keep the ring as a gift. Has *O* made a gift to *A*? If so, can *O* change her mind the next day and require *A* to return the ring?

Suppose that *A* does not telephone *O* to tell her the ring has been found. A week later, at a dinner with friends, *A* surprises *O* by producing the ring. *O* takes the ring, looks at it, then gives it back to *A*, saying, "I want you to have it. It's yours." *A* tries the ring on, but it is too large for *A*'s finger. *O* then says, "Let me wear it until you can get it cut down to fit you." *O* leaves the dinner wearing the ring, is struck by a car, and is killed. *A* sues *O*'s executor for the ring. What result? Garrison v. Union Trust Co., 129 N.W. 691 (Mich. 1910).

Suppose that at the dinner above, *O* had not said the words quoted, but instead had said, "I promise to leave you this ring when I die." What result? For criticism of the distinction between gifts and gift promises, see Jane B. Baron, Gifts, Bargains, and Form, 64 Ind. L.J. 155 (1989). The traditional rule that gift promises are legally unenforceable for lack of consideration is defended in Melvin Eisenberg, The World of Contract and the World of Gift, 85 Cal. L. Rev. 821 (1997).

Suppose *A* gives *B* a $21,000 engagement ring. Later the engagement is broken. Does it matter who broke the engagement in determining who now owns the ring? See Lindh v. Surman, 742 A.2d 643 (Pa. 1999) (4 to 3, adopting a no-fault approach, holding that the ring must be returned to the donor regardless of who broke the engagement, in an opinion by "Madame Justice Newman," dissent by "Mr. Justice Cappy in which Messrs. Justice Castillo and Saylor join" [Law French resurrected?]). The traditional rule is that the donor cannot recover the ring if the donor is at fault. See Annot., 44 A.L.R.5th 1 (1996).

2. *O* writes a check to *B* on her checking account and hands it to *B*. Before *B* can cash the check, *O* dies. What result? See Woo v. Smart, 442 S.E.2d 690 (Va. 1994) (holding no gift until check paid, because donor retains dominion and control of funds; donor could stop payment or die, revoking command to bank to pay the money). But see In re Estate of Smith, 694 A.2d 1099 (Pa. Super. Ct. 1997) (holding valid gifts of checks on facts similar to those in *Woo*).

3. Suppose that *O*, while wearing a wristwatch, hands *A* a signed writing saying: "I hereby give *A* the wristwatch I am wearing." Is this a valid gift? The traditional rule is that the watch must be handed over, if practicable. Restatement (Third) of Property, Wills and Other Donative Transfers §6.2 illustration 22 (2003), says that

a gift of a watch by a document is valid, even though it would be easy to take it off and hand it over. Although without case support at present, the Restatement rule may be the rule of the future. Which is the better rule? Should the donor be made to feel the "wrench of manual delivery"? Would the average person know the difference between a paper reading, "I give you my watch," which the Restatement says should be a good gift, and a paper reading, "I will give you my watch," which is an unenforceable gratuitous promise?

4. Robert Hocks rented a safe deposit box jointly with his sister Joan. He planned to give her everything he put in the box. At a restaurant, Robert handed Joan four $5,000 bearer bonds, saying, "I want to give these to you." Joan put the bonds in the safe deposit box. Subsequently, Robert clipped the coupons and collected the interest on the bonds.

During the next several years, Robert added 22 more bonds to the box, as well as a diamond ring. Only Robert, not Joan, went into the box, though Joan had a right to do so. To avoid "a lot of hassle" from Robert's wife, Joan suggested to Robert that he should leave a note in the box indicating her interest. Robert placed a handwritten note in the box: "Upon my death, the contents of this safety deposit box #7069 will belong to and are to be removed only by my sister Joan Jeremiah." Upon Robert's death, is Joan entitled to the contents of the box? See Hocks v. Jeremiah, 759 P.2d 312 (Or. App. 1988) (holding Joan entitled only to the first four bonds that were hand delivered to her; the remaining contents were not delivered even though Joan was a joint tenant of the box).

5. Here is an item from the New York Post web site, dated June 18, 2013, and titled "Kraft: Putin stole Super Bowl ring." While on a business trip to Russia in 2005, Robert Kraft, owner of the New England Patriots, took off his Super Bowl ring, worth $25,000, and showed it to Russian President Vladimir Putin. According to Kraft, Putin put on the ring and said, "I can kill someone with this ring." Kraft claims that he "put [his] hand out and [Putin] put [the ring] in his pocket, and three KGB guys got around him and walked out." Kraft later released a statement, saying, "I decided to give [President Putin] the ring as a symbol of the respect and admiration that I have for the Russian people and [his] leadership."

Did Robert Kraft make a gift of his Super Bowl ring to Vladimir Putin at any time?

Newman v. Bost

Supreme Court of North Carolina, 1898
29 S.E. 848

Action tried before COBLE, J., and a jury. . . . The plaintiff alleged in her complaint that the intestate of the defendant, while in his last sickness, gave her all the furniture and other property in his dwelling-house as a gift causa mortis. Among other things claimed, there was a policy of insurance of $3,000 on the life of intestate and other valuable papers, which she alleged were in a certain bureau drawer in intestate's bedroom. She alleged that defendant administrator has collected the policy of life insurance and sold the household and kitchen furniture, and this suit is against *defendant as administrator* to recover the value of the property alleged to have been converted by him. There are other matters involved, claims for services, claim for fire insurance collected by intestate in his lifetime, etc.

On the trial it appeared that the intestate's wife died about ten years before he died, and without issue; that the intestate lived in his dwelling, after his wife's death, in Statesville until his death, and died without issue; that about the last day of March, 1896, he was stricken with paralysis and was confined to his bed in his house and was never able to be out again till he died on 12 April, 1896; that shortly after he was stricken he sent for Enos Houston to nurse him in his last illness; that while helpless in his bed soon after his confinement and *in extremis* he told Houston he had to go—could not stay here—and asked Houston to call plaintiff into his room; he then asked the plaintiff to hand him his private keys, which plaintiff did, she having gotten them from a place over the mantel in intestate's bedroom in his presence and by his direction; he then handed plaintiff the bunch of keys and told her to take them and keep them, that he desired her to have them and everything in the house; he then pointed out the bureau, the clock and other articles of furniture in the house and asked his chamber door to be opened and pointed in the direction of the hall and other rooms and repeated that everything in the house was hers—he wanted her to have everything in the house; his voice failed him soon after the delivery of the keys and these declarations, so that he could never talk again to be understood, except to indicate yes and no, and this generally by a motion of the head; the bunch of keys delivered to the plaintiff, amongst others, included one which unlocked the bureau pointed out to plaintiff as hers (and other furniture in the room), and the bureau drawer which this key unlocked, contained in it a life insurance policy, payable to intestate's estate, and a few small notes, a large number of papers, receipts, etc., etc., and there was no other key that unlocked this bureau drawer; this bureau drawer was the place where intestate kept all his valuable papers; plaintiff kept the keys as directed from time given her and still has them; at the death of intestate's wife he employed plaintiff, then an orphan about eighteen years old, to become his housekeeper, and she remained in his service for ten years and till his death, and occupied rooms assigned her in intestate's residence; in 1895 the intestate declared his purpose to marry plaintiff within twelve months; nobody resided in the house with them; immediately after the death of intestate, Houston told of the donation to Mr. Burke, and the plaintiff informed her attorney, Mr. Burke, of it, and she made known her claim to the property in the house and kept the keys and forbade the defendant from interfering with it in any way, both before and after he qualified as administrator.

Other facts in relation to the plaintiff's claim appear in the opinion. There was a verdict, followed by judgment for the plaintiff, and defendant appealed.

FURCHES, J. The plaintiff in her complaint demands $3,000 collected by defendant, as the administrator of J.F. Van Pelt,[32] on a life insurance policy, and now in his hands; $300, the value of a piano upon which said Van Pelt collected that amount of insurance money; $200.94, the value of household property sold by defendant as belonging to the estate of his intestate, and $45, the value of property in the plaintiff's bedroom and sold by the defendant as a part of the property belonging to the intestate's estate.

The $3,000, money collected on the life insurance policy, and the $200.94, the price for which the household property sold, plaintiff claims belonged to her by reason of a donatio causa mortis from said Van Pelt. The $45, the price for which her bedroom property sold, and the $300 insurance money on the piano, belonged to her also by reason of gifts inter vivos.

The rules of law governing all of these claims of the plaintiff are in many respects the same, and the discussion of one will be to a considerable extent a discussion of all.

To constitute a donatio causa mortis, two things are indispensably necessary: an intention to make the gift, and a delivery of the thing given. Without both of these requisites, there can be no gift causa mortis. And both these are matters of fact to be determined by the jury, where there is evidence tending to prove them.

The intention to make the gift need not be announced by the donor in express terms, but may be inferred from the facts attending the delivery—that is, what the donor said and did. But it must always clearly appear that he knew *what he was doing*, and that he intended a gift. So far, there was but little diversity of authority, if any.

32. J.F. Van Pelt was a man of some standing in Statesville, North Carolina. He moved there in 1859 and entered the grocery business. When the Civil War broke out, his partner joined the Confederate army, and Van Pelt stayed at home to run their business. He was mayor of the town from 1873 to 1877 and from 1883 to 1885. He was also manager of Statesville's Opera Hall. His obituary in the Statesville Semi-Weekly Landmark, April 14, 1896, printed under the heading "Called to Account," noted: "With limited education, he was possessed of splendid business judgment and had, by judicious management, accumulated a good property. He had been retired from active business for several years."

Van Pelt was 62 years old when he died in his home on Front Street, having moved there when his Walnut Street residence burned. (In the Walnut Street house was a piano, which the plaintiff, Julia Newman, claimed had been given her and on which Van Pelt had collected the fire insurance proceeds.) Van Pelt died intestate. His heirs were a sister living in China Grove, North Carolina, and a brother living in Alabama.

The trial in Newman v. Bost occupied four days. The attorneys for the parties took over one day making their closing arguments to the jury. Julia Newman's lawyer, in closing, "spoke for about two and a half hours, finishing at 2 o'clock, when court adjourned for dinner." Id., January 18, 1898. (O, for the days when eloquent lawyering could produce a hungry jury!) After dinner and lengthy deliberation, the jury unanimously found for Julia.

Sometime after the trial Julia Newman left Statesville. About a month before Van Pelt's death, Julia had bought 36 acres of land from him. She sold the land in 1907, at a nice profit. The deed listed Julia, still unmarried, as living in Maryland. The information in this footnote was furnished the editors by Bill Moose of Mitchell Community College, Statesville, N.C. The photograph of Van Pelt is from the collection of Steve Hill in Statesville.—EDS.

As to what constitutes or may constitute delivery, has been the subject of discussion and adjudication in most or all the courts of the Union and of England, and they have by no means been uniform—some of them holding that a symbolical delivery—that is, some other article delivered in the name and stead of the thing intended to be given, is sufficient; others holding that a symbolical delivery is not sufficient, but that a constructive delivery—that is, the delivery of a key to a locked house, trunk or other receptacle is sufficient. They distinguish this from a symbolical delivery, and say that this is in *substance* a delivery of the thing, as it is the means of using and enjoying the thing given; while others hold that there must be an actual manual delivery to perfect a gift causa mortis.

This doctrine of donatio causa mortis was borrowed from the Roman Civil Law by our English ancestors. There was much greater need for such a law at the time it was incorporated into the civil law and into the English law than there is now. Learning was not so general, nor the facilities for making wills so great then as now. . . .

It seems to us that, . . . after the statute of fraud and of wills, this doctrine of causa mortis is in direct conflict with the spirit and purpose of those statutes—the prevention of fraud. It is a doctrine, in our opinion, not to be extended but to be strictly construed and confined within the bounds of our adjudged cases. We were at first disposed to confine it to cases of actual *manual* delivery, and are only prevented from doing so by our loyalty to our own adjudications. . . .

Many of the cases cited by the plaintiff are distinguishable from ours, if not all of them. Thomas v. Lewis (a Virginia case), 37 Am. St., 878, was probably more relied on by the plaintiff than any other case cited, and for that reason we mention it by name. This case, in its essential facts, is distinguishable from the case under consideration. There, the articles present were taken out of the bureau drawer, handed to the donor, and then delivered by him to the donee. According to all the authorities, this was a good gift causa mortis. The box and safe, the key to which the donor delivered to the donee, were not present but were deposited in the vault of the bank; and so far as shown by the case it will be presumed, from the place where they were and the purpose for which things are usually deposited in a bank vault, that they were only valuable as a depository for such purposes, as holding and preserving money and valuable papers, bonds, stocks and the like. This box and safe would have been of little value to the donee for any other purpose. But more than this, the donor expressly stated that all you find *in this box and this safe is yours*. There is no mistake that it was the intention of the donor to give what was contained in the box and in the safe.

As my Lord Coke would say: "Note the diversity" between that case and the case at bar. There, the evidence of debt contained in the bureau, which was present, was taken out, given to the donor, and by him delivered to the donee. This was an actual manual delivery, good under all the authorities. But no such thing was done in this case as to the life insurance policy. It was neither taken out of the drawer nor mentioned by the donor, unless it is included in the testimony of Enos Houston who, at one time, in giving his testimony says that Van Pelt gave her the keys, saying "what is in this house is yours," and at another time on cross-examination, he said to Julia, "I intend to give you this furniture in this house," and at another time, "What property is in this house is yours." The bureau in which was found the life insurance policy, after the death of Van Pelt, was present in the room where the keys were handed to Julia, and the life insurance policy could easily have been taken out and handed to Van Pelt, and by him delivered to Julia, as was done in the case of Thomas v. Lewis, supra. But this was not done. The safe and box, in Thomas v. Lewis, were not present, so that the contents could not have been taken out and delivered to the donee by the donor. The ordinary use of a stand of bureaus is not for the purpose of holding and securing such things as a life insurance policy, though they may be often used for that purpose, while a safe and a box deposited in the vault of a bank are. A bureau is an article of household furniture, used for domestic purposes, and generally belongs to the ladies' department of the household government, while the safe and box, in Thomas v. Lewis, are not. The bureau itself, mentioned in this case, was such property as would be valuable to the plaintiff. . . .

It is held that the law of delivery in this State is the same in gifts inter vivos and causa mortis. Adams v. Hayes, 24 N.C. 361. . . . [T]here can be no gift of either kind without both the intention to give and the delivery. . . .

The leading case in this State is Adams v. Hayes. . . .

Following this case, . . . we feel bound to give effect to *constructive delivery*, where it plainly appears that it was the intention of the donor to make the gift, and where the things intended to be given are *not* present, or, where present, are incapable of *manual* delivery from their size or weight. But where the articles are present and are capable of manual delivery, *this must be had*. This is as far as we can go. It may be thought by some that this is a hard rule—that a dying man cannot dispose of his own. But we are satisfied that when properly considered, it will be found to be a just rule. But it is not a hard rule. The law provides how a man can dispose of all his property, both real and personal. To do this, it is only necessary for him to observe and conform to the requirements of these laws. . . . The law provides that every man may dispose of all of his property by will, when made in writing. And it is most singular how guarded the law is to protect the testator against fraud and impositions by requiring that every word of the will must be written and signed by the testator, or, if written by someone else, it must be attested by at least *two* subscribing witnesses who shall sign the same in his presence and at his request, or the will is void. . . .

In gifts causa mortis it requires but one witness, probably one servant as a witness to a gift of all the estate a man has; no publicity is to be given that the gift has been made, and no probate or registration is required.

The statute of wills is a statute against fraud, considered in England and in this State to be demanded by public policy. And yet, if symbolical deliveries of gifts causa mortis are to be allowed, or if constructive deliveries be allowed to the extent claimed by the plaintiff, the statute of wills may prove to be of little value. For such considerations, we see every reason for restricting and none for extending the rules heretofore established as applicable to gifts causa mortis.

Residence of Mr. J.F. Van Pelt, Walnut Street

from The (Statesville, N.C.) Landmark Trade Edition, May 22, 1890

This house, and with it "Miss Julia's piano," burned between 1890 and 1896.

It being claimed and admitted that the life insurance policy was present in the bureau drawer in the room where it is claimed the gift was made, and being capable of actual manual delivery, we are of the opinion that the title of the insurance policy did not pass to the plaintiff, but remained the property of the intestate of the defendant.

But we are of the opinion that the bureau and any other article of furniture, locked and unlocked by any of the keys given to the plaintiff, did pass and she became the owner thereof. This is upon the ground that while these articles were present, from their size and weight they were incapable of actual manual delivery; and that the delivery of the keys was a constructive delivery of these articles, equivalent to an actual delivery if the articles had been capable of manual delivery.

[W]e are of the opinion that the other articles of household furniture (except those in the plaintiff's private bed chamber) did not pass to the plaintiff, but remained the property of the defendant's intestate.

We do not think the articles in the plaintiff's bed chamber passed by the donatio causa mortis for the same reason that the other articles of household furniture did not pass—want of delivery—either constructive or manual. But as to the furniture in the plaintiff's bedroom ($45) it seems to us that there was sufficient evidence of both gift and delivery to support the finding of the jury, as a gift inter vivos. The intention to give this property is shown by a number of witnesses and contradicted by none.

The only debatable ground is as to the sufficiency of the delivery. But when we recall the express terms in which he repeatedly declared that it was hers; that he had bought it for her and had given it to her; that it was placed in her private chamber, her bedroom, where we must suppose that she had the entire use and control of the same, it would seem that this was sufficient to constitute a delivery. There was no evidence, that we remember, disputing these facts. But, if there was, the jury have found for the plaintiff, upon sufficient evidence at least to go to the jury, as to this gift and its delivery. As to the piano there was much evidence tending to show the intention of Van Pelt to give it to the plaintiff, and that he had given it to her, and we remember no evidence to the contrary. And as to this, like the bedroom furniture, the debatable ground, if there is any debatable ground, is the question of delivery. It was placed in the intestate's parlor where it remained until it was burned. The intestate insured it as his property, collected and used the insurance money as his own, often saying that he intended to buy the plaintiff another piano, which he never did. It must be presumed that the parlor was under the dominion of the intestate, and not of his cook, housekeeper, and hired servant. And unless there is something more shown than the fact that the piano was bought by the intestate, placed in his parlor, and called by him "Miss Julia's piano," we cannot think this constituted a delivery. But, as the case goes back for a new trial, if the plaintiff thinks she can show a delivery she will have an opportunity of doing so. But she will understand that she must do so according to the rules laid down in this opinion — that she must show actual or constructive delivery equivalent to actual manual delivery. We see no ground upon which the plaintiff can recover the insurance money, if the piano was not hers.

We do not understand that there was any controversy as to the plaintiff's right to recover her services, which the jury have estimated to be $125. The view of the case we have taken has relieved us from a discussion of the exceptions to evidence, and as to the charge of the Court. There is no such thing in this State as *symbolical delivery* in gifts either inter vivos or causa mortis. . . .

New trial.

NOTES AND PROBLEMS

1. A gift *causa mortis*, that is, a gift made in contemplation of and in expectation of immediate approaching death,[33] is a substitute for a will. If the donor lives, the gift is revoked, although some courts may hold that revocation occurs only if the donor elects to revoke upon recovering. Because the courts see upholding gifts causa mortis as undercutting the safeguards of the Statute of Wills, traditionally they have more strictly applied the requirements for a valid gift causa mortis than for a gift inter vivos. They also have placed restrictions on gifts causa mortis not applicable to inter vivos gifts. For example, if the donee already is in possession of the property, there must be a redelivery to effect a valid gift causa mortis but not if the gift is inter vivos. If Van Pelt had put a small cinnabar box in Julia's bedroom, he could during his lifetime, before death drew near, declare that he

---

33. Although older cases have been to the contrary, more recent ones tend to find that the "contemplation of imminent death" requirement is met where a person made gifts in anticipation of suicide that subsequently occurred. See, e.g., In re Estate of Smith, 694 A.2d 1099 (Pa. Super. Ct. 1997); Scherer v. Hyland, 380 A.2d 698 (N.J. 1977).

was giving the box to Julia. But if he waited until he was on his deathbed, he would have to deliver the box to her again.

Given changes in the law of wills, the strict approach to gifts *causa mortis* may no longer be justified. The modern trend is to enforce the decedent's intent even if there is evidence of some failure to comply with the wills act formalities, so long as there is clear and convincing evidence of donative intent. See, e.g., Uniform Probate Code §2-503 (2008).

2. Suppose that Van Pelt had said to Julia, "I want to give you my insurance policy in that bureau over there, so Enos please get it and give it to her." Enos, however, leaves the policy where it was. Is there a valid gift? See Wilcox v. Matteson, 9 N.W. 814 (Wis. 1881). What if Van Pelt instead had said, "I want to give you my bureau there. Enos, move it into her room." Enos does so. The bureau contains the life insurance policy. On the reasoning of Newman v. Bost, is there a valid gift?

3. Suppose that Van Pelt had called Julia in and said, "I want to give you my bureau and the insurance policy locked in it. Here is the key." Julia takes the key but the bureau stays where it is. On the reasoning of Newman v. Bost, has a valid gift been made?

4. Suppose that Van Pelt had called Julia in and said, "I want to give you my little strong box here and the insurance policy locked in it. Here is the key." Julia takes the key but the box stays where it is. On the reasoning of Newman v. Bost, has a valid gift been made? See Bynum v. Fidelity Bank of Durham, 19 S.E.2d 121 (N.C. 1942).

5. If Van Pelt had said to his wife before she died, "Dear, I give you the piano," would there be a gift? See Restatement (Third) of Property, Wills and Other Donative Transfers §6.2 illustration 7 (2003). Would this be sufficient for a gift to Julia? If not, how could Van Pelt give the piano to Julia?

Gruen v. Gruen

Court of Appeals of New York, 1986
496 N.E.2d 869

SIMONS, J. Plaintiff commenced this action seeking a declaration that he is the rightful owner of a painting which he alleges his father, now deceased, gave to him. He concedes that he has never had possession of the painting but asserts that his father made a valid gift of the title in 1963 reserving a life estate for himself. His father retained possession of the painting until he died in 1980. Defendant, plaintiff's stepmother, has the painting now and has refused plaintiff's requests that she turn it over to him. She contends that the purported gift was testamentary in nature and invalid insofar as the formalities of a will were not met or, alternatively, that a donor may not make a valid inter vivos gift of a chattel and retain a life estate with a complete right of possession. Following a seven-day nonjury trial, Special Term found that plaintiff had failed to establish any of the elements of an inter vivos gift and that in any event an attempt by a donor to retain a present possessory life estate in a chattel invalidated a purported gift of it. The Appellate Division held that a valid gift may be made reserving a life estate and, finding the elements of a gift established in this case, it reversed and remitted the matter for a determination of value (104 A.D.2d 171, 488 N.Y.S.2d 401). That determination has now been made and defendant appeals directly to this court, pursuant to CPLR 5601(d), from the subsequent final judgment entered in Supreme Court awarding plaintiff $2,500,000 in damages representing the value of the painting, plus interest. We now affirm.

The subject of the dispute is a work entitled "Schloss Kammer am Attersee II" painted by a noted Austrian modernist, Gustav Klimt.[34] It was purchased by plaintiff's father, Victor Gruen, in 1959 for $8,000. On April 1, 1963 the elder Gruen, a successful architect with offices and residences in both New York City and Los Angeles during most of the time involved in this action,[35] wrote a letter to plaintiff, then an undergraduate student at Harvard, stating that he was giving him the Klimt painting for his birthday but that he wished to retain the possession of it for his lifetime. This letter is not in evidence, apparently because plaintiff destroyed it on instructions from his father. Two other letters were received, however, one dated May 22, 1963 and the other April 1, 1963. Both had been dictated by Victor Gruen and sent together to plaintiff on or about May 22, 1963. The letter dated May 22, 1963 reads as follows:

Dear Michael:

I wrote you at the time of your birthday about the gift of the painting by Klimt. Now my lawyer tells me that because of the existing tax laws, it was wrong to mention in that letter that I want to use the painting as long as I live. Though I still want to use it, this should not appear in the

34.   Gustav Klimt (1862-1918) was one of the founders of the Vienna Secession, a group of young fin-de-siècle Viennese artists who sought to liberate Viennese art from the dominance of naturalist style, opening it to such contemporary European influences as art nouveau. He created many murals for public buildings, both in Vienna and elsewhere, but perhaps his greatest fame was as a painter of portraits and landscapes that exhibited an exotic and often erotic style. See Gerbert Frodl, Klimt (trans. Alexandra Campbell 1990). In 2006, a Klimt painting, "Adele Block-Bauer I," was purchased by cosmetics magnate Ronald S. Lauder for $135 million. It was at the time the highest sum ever paid for a painting. The work purchased by Lauder had been the subject of an extensive restitution battle between the Austrian government and a niece of Ms. Block-Bauer, who contended, successfully, that the Nazis had stolen the painting and four other Klimt works during World War II.

Schloss Kammer, the subject of the painting in dispute, was Klimt's favorite vacation spot. It is located in the Salzkammergut, a beautiful lake district outside of Salzburg, Austria. We owe this information to Professor Susan French, who has told the whole (and fascinating) story of the case in her essay, Susan F. French, Gruen v. Gruen: A Tale of Two Stories, in Property Stories 75 (Gerald Korngold & Andrew P. Morriss eds. 2d ed. 2009).—EDS.

35.   Victor Gruen, born in Vienna, was an urban designer and architect who came to this country in 1933. His firm, Victor Gruen Associates, has been one of the most influential in shaping the urban environment since World War II. It designed the first regional shopping center, Northland near Detroit, which inspired similar plans for enormous enclosed shopping malls in other cities. Gruen was the author of several books on urban planning, in which he said his main aim was to design cities that were worthwhile to live in as well as functional. "Some say there is no need for a city, a center," Gruen once said. "They say you can communicate in the future with television phones. You may be able eventually to talk to your girl friend by television, but you can't kiss her that way." His best book is The Heart of Our Cities (1964).

Gruen viewed Vienna as the most livable of cities, largely because the automobile—which he disliked—had been banned from downtown. In the last years of his life he returned to live in Vienna, where he died in 1980. See generally M. Jeffrey Hardwick, Mall Maker: Victor Gruen, Architect of an American Dream (2003).—EDS.

letter. I am enclosing, therefore, a new letter and I ask you to send the old one back to me so that it can be destroyed.

I know this is all very silly, but the lawyer and our accountant insist that they must have in their possession copies of a letter which will serve the purpose of making it possible for you, once I die, to get this picture without having to pay inheritance taxes on it.

Love,

s/ *Victor*

Enclosed with this letter was a substitute gift letter, dated April 1, 1963, which stated:

Dear Michael:

The 21st birthday, being an important event in life, should be celebrated accordingly. I therefore wish to give you as a present the oil painting by Gustav Klimt of Schloss Kammer which now hangs in the New York living room. You know that Lazette and I bought it some 5 or 6 years ago, and you always told us how much you liked it.

Happy birthday again.

Love

s/ *Victor*

Plaintiff never took possession of the painting nor did he seek to do so. Except for a brief period between 1964 and 1965 when it was on loan to art exhibits and when restoration work was performed on it, the painting remained in his father's possession, moving with him from New York City to Beverly Hills and finally to Vienna, Austria, where Victor Gruen died on February 14, 1980. Following Victor's death plaintiff requested possession of the Klimt painting and when defendant refused, he commenced this action.

The issues framed for appeal are whether a valid inter vivos gift of a chattel may be made where the donor has reserved a life estate in the chattel and the donee never has had physical possession of it before the donor's death and, if it may, which factual findings on the elements of a valid inter vivos gift more nearly comport with the weight of the evidence in this case, those of Special Term or those of the Appellate Division. The latter issue requires application of two general rules. First, to make a valid inter vivos gift there must exist the intent on the part of the donor to make a present transfer; delivery of the gift, either actual or constructive to the donee; and acceptance by the donee (Matter of Szabo, 10 N.Y.2d 94, 98, 217 N.Y.S.2d 593, 176 N.E.2d 395; Matter of Kelly, 285 N.Y. 139, 150, 33 N.E.2d 62 [dissenting in part opn.]). Second, the proponent of a gift has the burden of proving each of these elements by clear and convincing evidence.

Donative Intent

There is an important distinction between the intent with which an inter vivos gift is made and the intent to make a gift by will. An inter vivos gift requires that

Schloss Kammer am Attersee II
by Gustav Klimt
Courtesy of the Galerie St. Etienne, New York

the donor intend to make an irrevocable present transfer of ownership; if the intention is to make a testamentary disposition effective only after death, the gift is invalid unless made by will.

Defendant contends that the trial court was correct in finding that Victor did not intend to transfer any present interest in the painting to plaintiff in 1963 but only expressed an intention that plaintiff was to get the painting upon his death. The evidence is all but conclusive, however, that Victor intended to transfer ownership of the painting to plaintiff in 1963 but to retain a life estate in it and that he did, therefore, effectively transfer a remainder interest in the painting to plaintiff at that time. Although the original letter was not in evidence, testimony of its contents was received along with the substitute gift letter and its covering letter dated May 22, 1963. The three letters should be considered together as a single instrument (see Matter of Brandreth, 169 N.Y. 437, 440, 62 N.E. 563) and when they are they unambiguously establish that Victor Gruen intended to make a present gift of title to the painting at that time. But there was other evidence for after 1963 Victor made several statements orally and in writing indicating that he had previously given plaintiff the painting and that plaintiff owned it. Victor Gruen retained possession of the property, insured it, allowed others to exhibit it and made necessary repairs to it but those acts are not inconsistent with his retention of a life estate. . . . Victor's failure to file a gift tax return on the transaction was partially explained by allegedly erroneous legal advice he received, and while that omission sometimes may indicate that the donor had no intention of making a present gift, it does not necessarily do so and it is not dispositive in this case.

Defendant contends that even if a present gift was intended, Victor's reservation of a lifetime interest in the painting defeated it. . . .

Defendant recognizes that a valid inter vivos gift of a remainder interest can be made not only of real property but also of such intangibles as stocks and bonds. Indeed, several of the cases she cites so hold. That being so, it is difficult to perceive any legal basis for the distinction she urges which would permit gifts of remainder interests in those properties but not of remainder interests in chattels such as the Klimt painting here. The only reason suggested is that the gift of a chattel must include a present right to possession. The application of *Brandreth* to permit a gift of the remainder in this case, however, is consistent with the distinction, well recognized in the law of gifts as well as in real property law, between ownership and possession or enjoyment. Insofar as some of our cases purport to require that the donor intend to transfer both title and possession immediately to have a valid inter vivos gift (see Gannon v. McGuire, 160 N.Y. 476, 481, 55 N.E. 7; Young v. Young, 80 N.Y. 422, 430), they state the rule too broadly and confuse the effectiveness of a gift with the transfer of the possession of the subject of that gift. The correct test is "'whether the maker intended the [gift] to have *no effect* until after the maker's death, or whether he intended it to transfer *some present interest*'" (McCarthy v. Pieret, 281 N.Y. 407, 409, 24 N.E.2d 102 [emphasis added]; see also 25 N.Y. Jur., Gifts, §14, at 156-157). As long as the evidence establishes an intent to make a present and irrevocable transfer of title or the right of ownership, there is a present transfer of some interest and the gift is effective immediately.

Thus, in Speelman v. Pascal, [10 N.Y.2d 313, 222 N.Y.S.2d 324, 178 N.E.2d 723], we held valid a gift of a percentage of the future royalties to the play "My Fair Lady" before the play even existed. There, as in this case, the donee received title or the right of ownership to some property immediately upon the making of the gift but possession or enjoyment of the subject of the gift was postponed to some future time.

Defendant suggests that allowing a donor to make a present gift of a remainder with the reservation of a life estate will lead courts to effectuate otherwise invalid testamentary dispositions of property. The two have entirely different characteristics, however, which make them distinguishable. Once the gift is made it is irrevocable and the donor is limited to the rights of a life tenant not an owner. Moreover, with the gift of a remainder title vests immediately in the donee and any possession is postponed until the donor's death whereas under a will neither title nor possession vests immediately. Finally, the postponement of enjoyment of the gift is produced by the express terms of the gift not by the nature of the instrument as it is with a will (see Robb v. Washington & Jefferson Coll., 185 N.Y. 485, 493, 78 N.E. 359).

Delivery

In order to have a valid inter vivos gift, there must be a delivery of the gift, either by a physical delivery of the subject of the gift or a constructive or symbolic delivery such as by an instrument of gift, sufficient to divest the donor of dominion and control over the property. As the statement of the rule suggests, the requirement of delivery is not rigid or inflexible, but is to be applied in light of its purpose to avoid mistakes by donors and fraudulent claims by donees. Accordingly, what is sufficient to constitute delivery "must be tailored to suit the circumstances of the case" (Matter of Szabo, supra, 10 N.Y.2d at p.98, 217 N.Y.S.2d 593, 176 N.E.2d 395). The rule requires that "'[t]he delivery necessary to consummate a gift must be as perfect as the nature of the property and the circumstances and surroundings of the parties will reasonably permit'" (id.).

Defendant contends that when a tangible piece of personal property such as a painting is the subject of a gift, physical delivery of the painting itself is the best form of delivery and should be required. Here, of course, we have only delivery of Victor Gruen's letters which serve as instruments of gift. Defendant's statement of the rule as applied may be generally true, but it ignores the fact that what Victor Gruen gave plaintiff was not all rights to the Klimt painting, but only title to it with no right of possession until his death. Under these circumstances, it would be illogical for the law to require the donor to part with possession of the painting when that is exactly what he intends to retain.

Nor is there any reason to require a donor making a gift of a remainder interest in a chattel to physically deliver the chattel into the donee's hands only to have the donee redeliver it to the donor. As the facts of this case demonstrate, such a requirement could impose practical burdens on the parties to the gift while serving the delivery requirement poorly. Thus, in order to accomplish this type of delivery the parties would have been required to travel to New York for the symbolic transfer and redelivery of the Klimt painting which was hanging on the wall of Victor Gruen's Manhattan apartment. Defendant suggests that such a requirement would be stronger evidence of a completed gift, but in the absence of witnesses to the event or any written confirmation of the gift it would provide less protection against fraudulent claims than have the written instruments of gift delivered in this case.

Acceptance

Acceptance by the donee is essential to the validity of an inter vivos gift, but when a gift is of value to the donee, as it is here, the law will presume an acceptance on his part. Plaintiff did not rely on this presumption alone but also presented clear and convincing proof of his acceptance of a remainder interest in the Klimt painting by evidence that he had made several contemporaneous statements acknowledging the gift to his friends and associates, even showing some of them his father's gift letter, and that he had retained both letters for over 17 years to verify the gift after his father died. Defendant relied exclusively on affidavits filed by plaintiff in a matrimonial action with his former wife, in which plaintiff failed to list his interest in the painting as an asset. These affidavits were made over 10 years after acceptance was complete and they do not even approach the evidence in Matter of Kelly (285 N.Y. 139, 148-149, 33 N.E.2d 62 [dissenting in part opn.], supra) where the donee, immediately upon delivery of a diamond ring, rejected it as "too flashy." We agree with the Appellate Division that interpretation of the affidavit was too speculative to support a finding of rejection and overcome the substantial showing of acceptance by plaintiff.

Accordingly, the judgment appealed from and the order of the Appellate Division brought up for review should be affirmed, with costs.

NOTES AND QUESTIONS

1. If Victor Gruen had wanted to give Michael the complete ownership of the painting and not reserve a life estate, could he have done so by a letter sent to Michael at Harvard?

2. Suppose that Victor Gruen had typed and signed a letter to Michael: "I give you the Klimt painting when I die." Would this be a valid lifetime gift? It would not. The letter is a will. It shows no intention to give Michael any rights *now*, but only when Victor dies. As a will, the instrument is not valid unless properly executed as a will, with witnesses.

Carefully distinguish a will from what Victor actually did. He wrote: "I give you the Klimt painting, reserving possession for my life." This gives Michael a *present* ownership interest in the painting, with possession postponed until Victor's death.

Gruen v. Gruen introduces you to the concept of a life estate (in Victor) and a remainder (in Michael). Each of these estates is a separate interest in the same property, entitling first the life tenant to possession, and then, after his death, the remainderman. We will examine these estates in Chapters 3 and 4.

3. Should Victor's widow, Kamija, have had any rights with respect to the painting? If Victor had retained it until death and devised it to Michael, Kamija might have been able to claim a portion of the value of the painting as part of her statutory elective share, a subject that we will study in Chapter 5. See pages 409-410. Should the result be different if Victor had transferred a remainder interest during his life, retaining a life interest in the painting? See Uniform Probate Code §2-205(2)(A) (2008) (value of assets transferred during decedent's life with retained lifetime possessory interest is subject to surviving spouse's elective share).

4. When Michael finally received the painting from Kamija, he immediately arranged for Sotheby's to auction it in London. Sotheby's sold the painting on June 30, 1987, for $5.3 million, then a record price for Klimt's work. Ten years later, the buyer sold the painting at auction for $23.5 million. The painting ended up in Galleria Nazionale d'Arte Moderna, in Rome, Italy. See French, A Tale of Two Stories, supra, at 95.

5. For an exhaustive treatment of the law of gifts, comparing U.S. law with its counterparts in other countries, see Richard Hyland, Gifts: A Study in Comparative Law (2009).

II

The System of Estates
(Leaseholds Aside)

For property law, the system of estates represents the most obvious of many links between past and present. The very word *estate*, drawn from and implying *status*, signifies the feudal origins of the system—origins that we will consider on brief occasions in the following chapters. So does the distinction, still current, between *freehold* and *nonfreehold* estates—the first referring to normal tenures of feudal times, the second to mere leases.

From its feudal origins the system of estates evolved into an elaborate hierarchy of interests in land, accompanied by an equally elaborate taxonomy by which to classify them. Those who held estates in land, free or otherwise, found it to their advantage to create new estates and new interests, or they managed to do as much without knowing they had.[1] It became commonplace for two or more persons to have interests in the same land—for example, one person with a right to possession now (present interest) and another person with a right to possession later (future interest), or two or more persons with rights to concurrent possession, now or in the future (co-ownership or cotenancy). The various estates developed as a consequence of the language or other facts giving rise to their creation, and each estate carried with it characteristics different from the others. It was necessary, it must have been thought, to have some grand scheme to keep everything straight. Hence the taxonomy that you will be studying.

Regarding that taxonomy, you should come to see that much of it is obsolete today, dealing with distinctions that have, or should have, lost their relevance. Nevertheless, the unduly elaborate classification of the estate system persists. (Why do you suppose that is so?) Justice Holmes once said, "It is revolting to have no better reason for a rule than that it was laid down in the time of Henry IV. It is still more revolting if the grounds upon which it was laid down have vanished long since, and the rule simply persists from imitation of the past." Oliver Wendell Holmes, The Path of the Law, 10 Harv. L. Rev. 457, 469 (1897). Holmes was speaking in another context, but he might as well have been talking about the system of estates. As we shall see,

---

1. Actually, this process still goes on, in a way. We might, for example, regard the condominium as a new sort of estate, though one with a line going back to classical times, and we acknowledge today nonfreehold estates that were unknown at common law. But generally speaking, the common law prohibits creation of novel estates or other property interests. See Note 4 on pages 221-222.

the estates system is riddled with rules that have lost their purpose (though the situation is much better now than it was in Holmes's time and likely to improve still more). Labels have been even more enduring, a good example of the triumph of form over substance.

Leaseholds—the landlord-tenant estates—are an element of the estate system, but the rules governing landlord-tenant relations are sufficiently distinct to merit separate treatment. Accordingly, we save the topic for close study in Part III.

Benjamin N. Cardozo, The Nature of the Judicial Process
54-55 (1921)

Let me speak first of those fields where there can be no progress without history. I think the law of real property supplies the readiest example. No lawgiver meditating a code of laws conceived the system of feudal tenures. History built up the system and the law that went with it. Never by a process of logical deduction from the idea of abstract ownership could we distinguish the incidents of an estate in fee simple from those of an estate for life, or those of an estate for life from those of an estate for years. Upon these points, "a page of history is worth a volume of logic."[2] So it is wherever we turn in the forest of the law of land. Restraints upon alienation, the suspension of absolute ownership, contingent remainders, executory devises, private trusts and trusts for charities, all these heads of the law are intelligible only in the light of history, and get from history the impetus which must shape their subsequent development. I do not mean that even in this field, the method of philosophy plays no part at all. Some of the conceptions of the land law, once fixed, are pushed to their logical conclusions with inexorable severity. The point is rather that the conceptions themselves have come to us from without and not from within, that they embody the thought, not so much of the present as of the past, that separated from the past their form and meaning are unintelligible and arbitrary, and hence that their development, in order to be truly logical, must be mindful of their origins.

2. Holmes, J., in N.Y. Trust Co. v. Eisner, 256 U.S. 345, 349 [(1921)].

Possessory Estates

A. *Up from Feudalism*

The Norman Conquest in 1066 determined to considerable degree the central features of English law. Beginning with William the Conqueror's reign, the English, influenced by Norman, French, and Roman ideas, developed a legal system that spread throughout the English-speaking world, America included. Here we trace in broad outline the development of English property law in particular, emphasizing those parts of the history still important in understanding modern concepts.

1. Tenure

Begin with the social system imposed by William. It was a strictly organized hierarchy in which fighters and priests held a dominant place. A central feature of the system was land tenure, according to which one's position was defined in terms of one's relationship to land. Everyone, save the king, was made subservient to someone else, literally his land lord. And all were subservient to the crown, from whom all land titles derived.

The Anglo-Saxons who resisted William forfeited their lands, which were parceled out to William's supporters. They became his tenants in chief, each of them holding land under an agreement to render the king specific services, usually military in nature, such as furnishing knights to fight for the king. A tenant in chief could provide knights by paying them and keeping them in his household ready to fight, but more frequently he provided his quota by *subinfeudation*. This took the form of the tenant in chief granting a parcel of his land to a subtenant in exchange for the service of one or more knights or for some other service necessary to support the land lord. A tenant in chief and a lesser tenant could not shift a service from the land, which was forfeited if the service was not performed, but they could, as between themselves, determine who would perform it. The lesser tenants might also subinfeudate, so that a feudal pyramid was built up, with services flowing to the king at the top and protection extending downward to the actual occupants of the land at the bottom. The title to one tract of land might look like this:

King

|

Tenant in chief

|

Mesne lord[1]

|

Tenant in demesne

|

The tenant in demesne had possessory use of the land (so-called *seisin*, of which more later); the lords above him had the rights to services. To assist in the collection of feudal services, William ordered the royal clerks to prepare Domesday Book (pronounced doomsday, because from it there was no appeal), a record of the holder of each tract of land in England and the services by which the land was held. This remarkable survey, which attempted to enumerate every town, mill, church, woodland, and tenement in the kingdom, was completed in 1086 and still exists in the Public Records Office in London.

2.   Feudal Tenures and Services

William's principal aims in establishing his rule were military security, revenues, and support of the church. There were, accordingly, three major tenures — military, economic, and religious — each with accompanying services. The principal military tenure was *knight service*, which required the tenant to provide a specified number of men to fight for the king for 40 days each year. Almost all land granted by William was in knight service, but within a hundred years after the Conquest, the king had begun to take money payment (scutage or shield money) instead of knights, and use it to hire mercenaries. At this point tenants by knight service lost their military function and were slowly transformed into country gentlemen. Another military tenure was *grand sergeanty*, created to provide among other things a splendid court life and pageantry for the knights, such as by carrying the royal banner. (Several grand sergeanties survive today in connection with coronation services.) Petty sergeanty existed too, for nonpersonal services, but in time it came to be regarded as *socage*.

Socage was an economic tenure, its services intended to provide subsistence and maintenance for overlords. Any kind of service might be required, such as money rent or 10 days of plowing or keeping a bridge in repair or delivering a dish of mushrooms fresh for the king's breakfast in London. So strong was the

---

1. *Mesne* (law French, pronounced mean) means intermediate; a mesne lord was lord to those who stood below him in the feudal ladder and tenant to those above. A tenant in chief could be a mesne lord, but the king, standing at the top, could not be.

notion of tenure that, upon a grant of land, some service—even if merely symbolic—was thought to be due. A father granting land to a younger son might require annual delivery of an arrow with eagle's feathers, or a rose every midsummer. One Roland is recorded as having held 110 acres for which on Christmas Day, every year, he was to perform before the king "altogether, and once, a leap, a puff, and a fart."[2] These nominal services were not as silly as they seem. They provided evidence of the tenurial relationship and thus were important for establishing the lord's right to incidents, which we shall discuss momentarily.

Finally, for a society ruled as much by the cross as the sword, it was important to bestow land on the church. Here again, however, the notion that land must be held to enhance the power of a temporal lord required some service from the ecclesiastics, and so there were religious tenures with such services as singing mass every Friday or, if no specific services were retained, praying for the repose of the grantor's soul. This last service was called *frankalmoign.*

The military tenures, socage, and the religious tenures were free tenures held by free men, vassals but not peasants. But there were unfree tenures as well. The king and the greater lords almost always kept possession of some choice portions of their lands for a castle or a manor house, with surrounding farm and pasturage, and these were worked by peasants, known at the time as villeins. (The word is from *vill*, a settlement often but not always coinciding with a manorial unit. From the medieval mind with its strong class bias comes the modern meaning of a villain as a scoundrel.) In the early years after the Conquest, villeins comprised the vast majority of the tenant population. They held their land at the will of the lord of the manor and were denied protection by the king's courts. In this sense villeins were not part of the feudal system based upon personal loyalty and service contracts, but held their land by a much more precarious relationship. Nonetheless, in time villein tenants came to hold "by the custom of the manor"; their rights were set forth on manorial records and a copy given to the tenants. With this change their holdings came to be called copyhold. By the fifteenth century, copyholders had gained entry into the royal courts, which assisted any tenant ejected by the lord in a manner not in accordance with the custom of the manor. By the civil wars of the seventeenth century, their holdings had become as secure as freeholds; copyhold had lost its taint of servility and had become merely another form of landholding.[3]

---

2. Thomas Blount, Ancient Tenures 60 (2d ed. 1784). See also John Southworth, The English Medieval Minstrel 47 (1989), reporting that Roland's service was performed by Roland's descendants for about 200 years. This rather rude entertainment goes back at least as far as the Romans. A bronze Roman statue (first century A.D.) of a comedian preparing to perform this feat is in the collection of Roman sculpture at the Getty Museum in Los Angeles.

3. Copyhold land was finally made freehold by the Law of Property Act of 1922. Copyhold tenure has never been of any importance in the United States, where all land either is held as freehold from the state or is held allodially, i.e., with no notion of holding from anyone.

3. Feudal Incidents

Besides the services, a tenant owed other duties and was subject to several liabilities benefiting his lord. These were called *incidents*. Feudal services were fixed obligations. In the course of the Middle Ages, the economic importance of services declined because they could not be changed when social conditions or money values made them outmoded. Many of the services were commuted into money rents, which lost value with inflation, particularly during the thirteenth and fourteenth centuries. On the other hand, feudal incidents, which gave the lord possession of the land or its equivalent, kept pace with inflation and maintained their value. Thus the feudal incidents, jealously guarded by the crown, lasted long after the feudal services disappeared.

The feudal incidents included homage and fealty, aids, forfeiture, and certain liabilities at the death of tenants. *Homage and fealty* was one of the most significant features of feudal society. Each military tenant pledged utter support to his lord in a solemn ceremony. He knelt, put his hands between the lord's hands, swore a binding oath of loyalty, and thereby became the lord's man. William and his successors shrewdly required a separate oath of loyalty to the crown. Therefore the tenant might say: "I become your man from this day forward for the tenement which I hold of you, and I will bear you faith in life and limb and earthly worship against all men, saving only the faith I owe to our sovereign lord the king." Since a man gave his allegiance to the king, he deserved the king's protection in disputes with his lord.[4]

Aids entitled a lord to demand help from his tenants in case of financial emergencies. At first, the occasions for aids were many, but in 1215 the Magna Carta limited them to three: the ransoming of the lord from his captors, the knighting of his eldest son, and the marriage of his eldest daughter.

As to *forfeiture*, although the lords had accepted by the thirteenth century the principle of hereditary succession (for example, a tenant's son inherited his father's position), they insisted on the incident of revocability or forfeiture. If a tenant breached his oath of loyalty or refused to perform feudal services, his land was forfeited to the lord. If a tenant committed high treason, the king was entitled to seize and keep the tenant's land, whether held from the king or a mesne lord.

Finally, regarding liabilities at the death of a tenant, there was a cluster of incidents. *Wardship and marriage* meant that when a tenant died leaving an heir under 21, the tenant's lord was the heir's guardian, entitled to possession of the

---

4. The rise of the royal courts was largely due to the king's acts to protect free tenants from their lords, who used self-help to dispossess their tenants unjustly. In 1166 Henry II issued an ordinance giving the dispossessed free tenant a speedy remedy to recover possession; this was called the *assize of novel disseisin*. A jury was summoned to determine whether the tenant had been in prior possession and had been ousted without a judgment; if so, the tenant was entitled to be put back in possession. Some 10 years later the *assize of mort d'ancestor* was instituted to permit an heir to claim, on the death of his ancestor, possession of land from which he was unjustly excluded by the lord. Thus the lords could not vindicate their claims by self-help, but were required to get a judgment to dispossess free tenants. Compare the treatment of leasehold tenants at pages 482-492.

tenant's land, together with its rents and profits, but with the obligation to provide the heir subsistence and not commit waste. The lord also had the right to sell the heir in marriage, and if the heir refused a suitable arrangement he had to pay a fine. Wardship and marriage ended when the tenant came of age. It applied only to the military tenures, the idea being that the lord had to be compensated for his loss of military services while the heir was a minor. Control over marriage of a female heir may have been necessary to keep her from marrying the son of an enemy who, as husband, gained control of the wife's lands,[5] but it was extended to control over marriage of male heirs as well. After land became alienable, and knight's service was transformed into a money payment, wardship and marriage were simply windfalls to the lord. Since the lord was not accountable for the profits, he could—and often did—sell the wardship or the marriage.

A second liability at the death of a tenant was *relief.* When a tenant died, the heir had to pay the lord an appropriate sum, perhaps a year's rent, to come into his inheritance. The sum served to "relieve" the land from the lord's grasp. Given that the life expectancy of males in the centuries after the Conquest was hardly more than 35 years—such was the effect of disease and violence—the overlord might reasonably expect to have wardship and marriage one out of every four years over any substantial period of time. A relief might become payable once a decade. So these incidents were very lucrative.

Third, there was *escheat.* If a tenant died without heirs, the land returned to the lord from whom it was held. Similarly, if a tenant were convicted of a felony, the land escheated to the lord after the king had exercised his right to waste the criminal's land for a year and a day. A modified form of escheat is in force today: When a person dies intestate (that is, without a will) without heirs, the person's property escheats to the state.[6]

4. Avoidance of Feudal Incidents

One of the persistent themes of English and American legal history is the continuing efforts of the rich to avoid taxes. In feudal times, this meant avoidance of feudal incidents. For example, in early feudal times there were two ways to transfer possession of land. A tenant in demesne could *substitute* for himself some new tenant who would hold the land from his lord. Substitution required the lord's consent and homage to the lord from the new tenant. Or the tenant could, without the lord's consent, add a new rung to the bottom of the feudal ladder,

---

5. Control of marriage of a female heir led, in some cases, to the practice of ravishment. If the lord turned down the man preferred by the female heir, she might be abducted kicking and screaming (but not too much) and ravished by the man. The law then gave the pair a choice: marry or the ravisher must die. Thus did the female heir get her chosen mate, but the lord extracted a fine for their playing fast and loose with his rights.

6. If you think that escheat is a thing of the past, or that it occurs only in small estates, think again. Roman Blum, a Holocaust survivor who died in 2013 at age 97 with no known heirs and without a will, left an estate valued at nearly $40 million. Julie Satow, He Left a Fortune, to No One, N.Y. Times, Apr. 28, 2013, at 1 (Metropolitan section). We have seen estimates that $5 billion escheats annually to American state governments.

becoming a mesne lord himself and having a tenant who rendered him services. As we saw at page 209, this was called *subinfeudation*. (The distinction between substitution and subinfeudation is very similar to the distinction between assignment and subleasing in landlord-tenant law, a matter to be considered in Chapter 6 at pages 465-482.) Subinfeudation could not diminish the feudal services because a lord could proceed directly against the tenant in possession, using the remedies of distraint and distress and, ultimately, expulsion. But subinfeudation could be used to avoid the feudal incidents. Suppose that *T*, holding of *L* by knight service, subinfeudated to the church in frankalmoign or to *T1*, reserving as service one rose at midsummer. Knight service must still be rendered *L*, but this subinfeudation seriously devalued *L*'s incidents of wardship, marriage, relief, and escheat. Instead of *L* getting possession of the land when *T* died with a minor heir or without heirs, *L* was entitled to whatever service *T* could claim from the church or *T1*—prayers, one rose, whatever. The king and the barons, with much to lose by subinfeudation, took steps to curb the practice, finally succeeding with the enactment of the Statute Quia Emptores in 1290. The statute prohibited subinfeudation altogether, and thus the mischief of devaluing feudal incidents by this route was stopped.

5. The Decline of Feudalism

Quia Emptores (taking its name from the first two words of the statute, written in Latin) was intended to shore up the feudal system, but actually it marked the beginning of the end. It prohibited subinfeudation in fee simple.[7] But as a price for putting an end to subinfeudation, the great lords had to concede to all free tenants the right to substitute a new tenant for all or part of their land without the lord's consent. The new tenant would hold of the lord by the same services as the old, and if only part of the land were conveyed to a new tenant the feudal services were to be apportioned. The major historic consequences of Quia Emptores were two. The statute established a principle of free alienation of land, which turned out to be a major force in the development of property law. Alienability—the power to transfer resources to another person—is essential to a market economy. Second, in time, with the working of escheat and forfeiture, existing mesne lordships tended to disappear, and most land came to be held directly from the crown. As it turned out, the one person who had nothing to lose and all to gain by the statute was the king. By the time of the Tudors, mesne lords had become uncommon, and Henry VIII, perceiving that feudal incidents could be sources of substantial revenue, doggedly pursued their collection. He forced through the Statute of Uses (1536), designed primarily to prevent evasions of these incidents,

---

7. The fee simple—the greatest modern estate known to law—is discussed beginning at page 215. Subinfeudation of lesser estates was not prohibited, and Quia Emptores proved no block to the development of modern landlord-tenant law.

and set up the Court of Wards and Liveries to collect them. We shall return to this thread of the story later at page 289.

After Quia Emptores, with free substitution permitted, the relationship between tenant and lord was basically an economic one. The tenant was now the "owner"; services and incidents were a form of taxes or wages. The personal relationship—a key feature of feudalism—began to atrophy. A market economy started to develop. The Black Death in 1349 wiped out a huge number of villein tenants. The survivors could obtain well-paid work outside the manor, and many of them became wage earners who rented their dwellings. The manors had to turn to hired labor. When wages rose swiftly, the landlords and employers of labor attempted to freeze wages by a parliamentary act, the Statute of Labourers, but the laws of supply and demand proved stronger than those of Parliament. Wages continued to rise, and peasants, welcoming independence, continued to escape from the communal obligations of manorial life. Yet so important a social system as feudalism, which governed people's lives for several centuries, did not perish outright. Feudalism has its continuations in the law, as we shall see.

NOTE

Occasionally in this country one runs across feudal services reserved by a grantor before the American Revolution. Here's one instance: In 1772 Henry William Stiegel and his wife conveyed to their fellow Lutherans in Manheim, Pennsylvania, a plot of ground on which to build a church. The consideration was five shillings and "in the month of June yearly forever hereafter the rent of one red rose if the same shall be lawfully demanded." On the second Sunday in June, each year, the Zion Evangelical Lutheran Church of Manheim continues to pay the feudal obligation of one red rose to a Stiegel descendant.[8] See also the quit rents reserved by the Dutch patroons and other great landowners in New York, Pennsylvania, and Maryland, discussed in Eric Kades, The End of the Hudson Valley's Peculiar Institution: The Anti-Rent Movement's Politics, Social Relations, and Economics, 27 Law & Soc. Inquiry 941 (2002).

B. The Fee Simple

Out of feudalism developed a system of estates in land. A tenant had a *status* as a tenant of the fee or a tenant for life. In the course of time status became *estate*. Each estate is defined by the length of time it may endure. A fee simple may endure forever; a life estate, for the life of a person; a term of years, for some period of time measured by the calendar.

The modern relevance of estates. The estate system is central to our laws, both in theory and in practice. It is an essential part of the processes by which property interests are transferred from one party to another during life (*inter vivos*) or at

---

8. Professor Craig Oren informs us that this practice still continues. Indeed, according to one of his students, who is from Manheim, it is a big event in the town.

death. Lawyers explicitly refer to the type of estate that is being transferred when they draft deeds, wills, and other legal instruments involved in property transactions. So too for lay people who undertake a transfer (one hopes correctly) without any legal assistance beyond a form book. The estate system is designed to make clear who is transferring what to whom — not just what physical parcel of land or item of personal property, but also what sort of ownership, measured in terms of the duration of the transferee's interest.

The estates system developed gradually over the course of several centuries, and the process has rendered it unduly complex. Happily, various simplifying measures have been adopted, and still others proposed. Among the latter, perhaps the most significant is the new Restatement (Third) of Property, Wills and Other Donative Transfers. We will discuss relevant provisions of the Third Restatement as we go along.

The first estate we take up is the fee simple absolute, usually just called the "fee simple." (There are other types of fees simple as well — the defeasible fees simple soon to be considered.) To help explain possessory estates (and, in Chapter 4, future interests), we will use graphical depictions. All of the depictions are based on a metaphor developed by the great English legal historians Pollock and Maitland, who conceived of estates in terms of a "plane of time."[9] In these terms, and taking ∞ to signify infinity, the fee simple absolute looks like this:

Time line 3-1

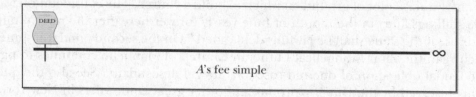

A's fee simple

1.   How the Fee Simple Developed

a.   Rise of Heritability

One of the key features of feudalism was that land was not owned by the possessor but was held by the possessor as tenant of someone else. Because of the highly personal nature of the lord-tenant relationship, in the period immediately following the Norman Conquest the tenant's holding (called his fee or fief) could not be inherited by his heir; in effect the tenant had only lifetime tenure. Upon the tenant's death his time on the land ceased, and the lord was under no obligation to recognize the tenant's heir as his successor. Customarily, though, for an

---

9. 1 Frederick Pollock & Frederic W. Maitland, The History of English Law Before the Time of Edward I 10 (2d ed. reissue 1968). The plane-of-time metaphor is, of course, strange. Given that a plane is two-dimensional, whereas time is a single dimension, a "plane of time" is hard (read impossible) to picture. But picture it anyway, because for our purposes the metaphor works nicely.

appropriate sum (a relief) the lord would regrant the land to the heir, securing from him homage and an oath of fealty. In time the lord recognized an obligation to admit the dead tenant's son, and so, in advance, would consent to descent. This advance consent was denoted by a conveyance from the lord "to A and his heirs." Still later, by the beginning of the thirteenth century, inheritance of a fee became a matter of right, but the payment of a relief to the lord continued.[10]

b. Rise of Alienability

In the first 200 years after the Conquest the fee was not freely alienable inter vivos by a deed during the life of the owner nor devisable by will at the death of the owner; hence the practical effect of a conveyance "to A and his heirs" was to give A a fee that would pass to A's heir, to the heir's heir, and so on down the centuries. But as the demand for land increased, the idea that a tenant should be able to convey the fee to another during his life openly and without the lord's consent gained currency. By the end of the thirteenth century, Quia Emptores settled that the fee was freely alienable.

c. Rise of the Fee Simple Estate

Once the fee became alienable, the feudal realities behind a conveyance to A "and his heirs" became meaningless. This transformation is vividly illustrated in connection with escheat. Suppose that L conveys land "to A and his heirs" and subsequently A conveys the land "to B and his heirs." Then A dies without heirs. Will the land escheat to L? Soon after Quia Emptores the judges answered no; the land will escheat only if the current tenant of the fee dies without heirs. Thus the fee, which started out as simply a *holding*, became an alienable fee simple, a *freehold estate* not terminable at the will of the lord, with an existence all its own.

The development of the fee simple estate is an example of that most striking phenomenon of English land law, the reification of abstractions, a process of thinking that still pervades our law. Instead of thinking of the land itself, the lawyer thinks of an *estate in land*, which is imagined as almost having a real existence apart from the land. *O*, owner of Blackacre, has an estate known as a *fee simple*, which is given the qualities and characteristics of a thing. During life, *O* can convey his fee simple to another; if he owns the fee simple at death, it passes under his will or descends

---

10. For an interesting argument that, contrary to the conventional historical account, the alienability of land, especially with respect to the use of land for credit, did not develop in a constantly progressive fashion, see Claire Priest, Creating an American Property Law: Alienability and Its Limits in American History, 120 Harv. L. Rev. 385 (2006). Professor Priest argues that well into the eighteenth century English land law imposed restrictions on creditors' ability to seize land in payment of debts, indicating that stability of land ownership was valued more than advancing credit. However, the enactment of the Debt Recovery Act in 1732, which applied to the American colonies but not to England itself, removed the traditional English protections of land from creditors, thereby expanding the creditworthiness of land and land's alienability generally.

to his heirs. Creditors may reach the fee simple and sell it to pay debts in default. Note how, in the preceding two sentences, we have spoken of a fee simple as a thing. In the next chapter we shall talk of future estates in land as things: They vest, divest, merge, are destroyed, shift, spring. These estates are almost visible entities. Imagining estates was a wonderful flight of the judicial mind in the thirteenth century, and now, after hundreds of years, it seems a quite natural way of regarding that which we cannot see. (Bear in mind, however, that modern analysis insists that an estate is "a bundle of rights," that is, estate is a word denoting legal relations between persons with respect to a thing.[11] What rights are in the bundle involves issues of public policy, not merely an analysis of qualities of imagined objects, and rights in the bundle have varied from century to century and from place to place.)

The fee simple absolute is as close to unlimited ownership as our law recognizes. It is the largest estate in terms of duration. It may endure forever.

Interests in personal property. Although the law of estates grew out of dispositions of land, courts permitted the same kinds of interests to be created in personal property. For historical reasons there is a fee simple only in land, not in personal property. But occasionally people speak of a fee simple in personal property, and no great harm is done.

2.   Creation of a Fee Simple

At early common law a fee simple was created by the grantor conveying land to *A and his* [or her] *heirs.* As noted above, the words "and his heirs," inserted in a conveyance, indicated that *A*'s interest in the land was inheritable by his heirs, but such words did not give *A*'s prospective heirs any interest in the land. *A*'s son would inherit the land from *A* if *A* still owned the land at his death, but *A*'s son had no interest during *A*'s lifetime.

The judges reached this result by construing the words "and his heirs" as *words of limitation,* which define the estate granted to *A,* to wit, a fee simple. The heirs do not take as "purchasers," an old common law word referring to persons who are given an interest in land by an instrument (as opposed to persons who inherit land by intestate succession). In a conveyance "to *A* and his heirs," then, the words "to *A*" are *words of purchase,* identifying *A* as the grantee, and the words "and his heirs" are words of limitation indicating that *A* takes a fee simple.

At common law, words indicating that the land was inheritable, such as to *A* "and his heirs," were necessary to create a fee simple.[12] This remained true long

---

11. Analyzing rights in land to be legal relations between persons with respect to land, and not—as older analysis had it—legal relations of a person to the land, was given systematic exposition by Wesley N. Hohfeld in the first quarter of the twentieth century and was adopted by the first Restatement of Property §§1-10 (1936).

12. An *inter vivos* conveyance (that is, a conveyance made by the grantor during his life) "to *A,* his successors and assigns forever" or "to *A* in fee simple" gave *A* a life estate only. In a *testamentary* conveyance (one made by a testator in his or her will), the words "and his heirs" were never necessary. Even in earlier times any words indicating that the testator intended a fee simple would suffice, e.g., "to *A* absolutely." Today it is assumed that the testator intends to dispose of as large an estate as the testator had.

after the original reason for inserting "and his heirs" in feudal conveyances disappeared. But it is no longer necessary to put words of inheritance in a deed in any state. Statutes and judicial decisions now provide that a grantor is presumed, in the absence of words indicating otherwise, to transfer the grantor's entire estate. A grant by O "to A," without more, conveys a fee simple to A. Although the phrase "and his heirs" is no longer required, lawyers, being creatures of habit, continue to insert it.

PROBLEMS

1. In 1600 O conveys Blackacre "to A for life, then to B forever." What estates do A and B have? If A dies and then B dies, who owns Blackacre? Suppose the conveyance takes place in 2014?

2. In 1600 O conveys Whiteacre "to A for life, remainder to the heirs of B." B is alive in 1600 but dies (without a will) soon thereafter. B's heir is C. Subsequently A dies. What estate does C have?

3. O conveys Greenacre "to A and her heirs." A's only child, B, is a spendthrift and runs up large, unpaid bills. B's creditors can attach B's property to satisfy their claims. Does B have an interest in Greenacre, reachable by B's creditors? Suppose A wishes to sell Greenacre and use the proceeds to take a trip around the world. Can B prevent A from doing this?

3. Inheritance of a Fee Simple

Now you are going to have to gain command of some technical terms often used imprecisely by nonlawyers, but if you pay close attention you will not find them difficult. They are the common coinage of hundreds of problems relating to inheritance.

Heirs.   If a person dies *intestate* (that is, without a will), the decedent's real property descends to his or her heirs.[13] Heirs are persons who survive the decedent and are designated as intestate successors under the state's statute of descent. No one is heir of the living; a living person has no heirs (yet!). Hence, if there is a conveyance "to the heirs of A" (a living person), we do not know who will take until A dies and A's heirs are ascertained.

A spouse was not an heir at common law; a spouse was given only dower or curtesy in land (see pages 407-408). Today in all states the surviving spouse is

---

13. The persons who succeed to an intestate's personal property are called next of kin. At common law, where primogeniture applied to land but not to personal property, heir and next of kin were not necessarily the same. Today in almost all states the same persons succeed to land and to personal property. In these states, "heirs" and "next of kin" are equivalent terms.

Persons who take property under a decedent's *will* are called devisees or sometimes, if taking personal property, legatees.

designated as an intestate successor of some share in the decedent's land; the size of the share often depends on who else survives. For example, the surviving spouse might take one-half if the decedent leaves one child, one-third if the decedent leaves two or more children, and all if the decedent leaves no children, no more remote issue, and no parents.

Under modern statutes of descent, classes of kindred are usually preferred as heirs in the following manner: first issue; and if no issue, then parents; and if none, then collaterals.

Issue. If the decedent leaves issue, they take to the exclusion of all other kindred. The word issue is synonymous with descendants. Despite its physiological specificity, issue does not refer to children only but includes further descendants. The distribution is made among the decedent's issue per stirpes ("by the stocks"), which generally means that if any child of the decedent dies before the decedent leaving children who survive the decedent, such child's share goes to his or her children by right of representation.

Until 1925, the rule of primogeniture applied to most of the land in England. The eldest son inherited the land. If the eldest son predeceased the decedent, leaving issue, his eldest son or other issue represented him under some rather complex rules always preferring males over females of equal degree of kinship. Only if there were no sons would the decedent's daughters inherit. Once appropriate for the military tenures, primogeniture became the common law for almost all. Primogeniture was followed in some American states before the Revolution, but was completely abolished by the end of the eighteenth century. Children now share equally.

A child born out of wedlock was *filius nullius*, the child of no one, and could inherit from neither mother nor father at common law. Today a child born out of wedlock inherits from the mother and, if paternity is acknowledged or proved, from the father. Adoption was unknown in England until 1926. Today, in American states, adopted children inherit from their adoptive parents and sometimes from their natural parents as well.

Ancestors. By statute parents usually take as heirs if the decedent leaves no issue.

Collaterals. All persons related by blood to the decedent who are neither descendants nor ancestors are collateral kin. This includes brothers, sisters, nephews, nieces, uncles, aunts, and cousins. If a decedent leaves no spouse, no issue, and no parents, the decedent's brothers and sisters (and their descendants by representation) take in all jurisdictions. The rules for determining which of the more remote collateral kindred take were rather complicated at common law and remain so today.

Escheat. If a person died intestate without any heirs, the person's real property escheated to the overlord in feudal times. Now such property escheats to the state where the property is located. If no next of kin could be found, the personal property of an intestate went to the crown under the principle of *bona vacantia* (goods without an owner). Today such property goes to the state. See generally John V. Orth, Escheat: Is the State the Last Heir?, 13 Green Bag 2d 73 (2009).

NOTES AND PROBLEMS

1. *O*, owner of Blackacre, has two children, *A* (daughter) and *B* (son). Subsequently *B* dies testate, devising all his property to *W*, his wife. *B* is survived by three children, *B1* (daughter), *B2* (son), and *B3* (daughter). *A1* (son) is born to *A*. Then *O* dies intestate. Who owns Blackacre in England in 1800? Under modern American law?

2. *O* conveys Blackacre "to *A* and her heirs." If *A* dies intestate without issue, will Blackacre escheat to the state?

3. *O* conveys Blackacre "to *A* for life, remainder to *B* and her heirs." *B* then dies intestate without heirs. *A* then dies. Who owns Blackacre?

4. *Standardization of estates.* Once the estates system developed, judges decided that standardization of estates furthered alienability by facilitating standardized transfers of the same resources, either by the owner or by the owner's heirs or devisees. Hence a fee simple, which is defined as an estate capable of being inherited by whoever turns out to be the heirs of the fee simple owner, can have no limitations put upon its inheritability. This distinguishes the fee simple from the fee tail (below). Except for a limitation that creates a fee tail, a limitation that purports to limit inheritance to a particular class of heirs creates a fee simple, inheritable by heirs generally. Example: Royal Whiton, not overly fond of his daughter-in-law and her family, devises land "to my granddaughter Sarah and her heirs on her father's side." Sarah takes a fee simple. It can be inherited by her heirs on her mother's side. Johnson v. Whiton, 34 N.E. 542 (Mass. 1893). "A man cannot create a new kind of inheritance [i.e., estate]," said Holmes, J., in deciding this case. If Whiton's will were given effect, Holmes continued, this would "put it out of the power of the owners to give a clear title for generations."[14]

The prohibition of new or customized property interests, known in the civil law as the *numerus clausus* principle, applies not only to estates but to all types of property interests. By requiring that owners create only legally recognized property interests, which have a standardized form, the principle directly restricts freedom of ownership. What is the reason for this restriction? Professor Heller suggests that the purpose of the *numerus clausus* principle is to limit fragmentation of ownership and thus promote the easy transferability of property rights. See Michael A. Heller, The Boundaries of Private Property, 108 Yale L.J. 1163, 1176-1178 (1999). (On the importance of transferability, recall the discussion in this book at page 52.) Professors Merrill and Smith have a different explanation.

---

14. If your client does not want his granddaughter's heirs on her mother's side to inherit the land, how should his will be drafted?

See Thomas W. Merrill & Henry E. Smith, Optimal Standardization in the Law of Property: The *Numerus Clausus* Principle, 110 Yale L.J. 1, 8 (2000), where they argue that the principle

> stems from the in rem nature of property rights: When property rights are created, third parties must expend time and resources to determine the attributes of these rights, both to avoid violating them and to acquire them from present holders. The existence of unusual property rights increases the cost of processing information about property rights. Those creating or transferring idiosyncratic property rights cannot always be expected to take these increases in measurement costs fully into account, making them a true externality. Standardization of property rights reduces these measurement costs.

For criticisms of the Merrill and Smith view, see Henry Hansmann & Reiner Kraakman, Property, Contract, and Verification: The *Numerus Clausus* Problem and the Divisibility of Rights, 31 J. Legal Studies 373 (2002) (arguing that the *numerus clausus* principle is not cost-minimizing because parties are free to tinker with the content of the property forms); Hanoch Dagan, The Craft of Property, 91 Cal. L. Rev. 1517, 1565-1570 (2003) (arguing that the principle consolidates expectations and expresses normative ideals for core types of interpersonal relationships); Nestor M. Davidson, Standardization and Pluralism in Property Law, 61 Vand. L. Rev. 1597 (2008) (*numerus clausus* principle is based neither on efficiency nor on coherent categories of meaning, but on the need for a stable framework of forms by which to express the ongoing development of property rules in response to competing social and political goals); Avihay Dorfman, Property and Collective Undertaking: The Principle of Numerus Clausus, 61 U. Toronto L.J. 467 (2011) (arguing that at the core of the numerus clausus principle is the legitimation question of how political authority is possible in the context of legislating new forms of property rights). See also Bernard Rudden, Economic Theory v. Property Law: The *Numerus Clausus* Problem, in Oxford Essays in Jurisprudence 239 (3d series, John Eekelaar & John Bell eds. 1987).

C. The Fee Tail

One of the great and continuing conflicts in the development of English property law arose out of the desire of the heads of rich families to make land inalienable. In a real sense, land was family power, status, and wealth, and those who controlled it wanted to make it impossible—or, if not impossible, at least very difficult—for their descendants to alienate it. The family bond was strong; the family was thought of as a chain of ancestors and descendants extending through time, with the primogenitary heir as current head.

The medieval dynasts sought an estate where the current owner could not cut off the inheritance rights of his issue. In the earliest period after the Conquest, they attempted to create such an estate by a conveyance "to *A* and the heirs of his body." The purpose was to give the land to *A* and his descendants, generation after generation. The courts, however, held that if issue were born to *A*, *A* could transfer a fee simple, cutting off the inheritance rights of his issue. Hence *A*'s estate was known as a *fee simple conditional*, a fee simple conditional upon having issue.

The judicial construction of this kind of grant was much resented by the barons, who petitioned Parliament to redress their grievances. In 1285 Parliament responded by enacting the Statute de Donis Conditionalibus, which replaced the fee simple conditional with the *fee tail*.[15] A fee tail, like the superseded fee simple conditional, is an estate in land created by a conveyance "to *A* and the heirs of his body."[16] It is an estate precisely tailored to the desires of the medieval dynasts. The fee tail descends to *A*'s lineal descendants ("heirs of the body," meaning children, grandchildren, etc.) generation after generation,[17] and it expires when the original tenant in fee tail, *A*, and all of *A*'s lineal descendants are dead. When *A*'s bloodline runs out and the fee tail ends, the land will revert to the grantor or the grantor's heirs by way of reversion or, if specified in the instrument, will go to some other branch of the family. For example, *O* might convey land "to my son *A* and the heirs of his body, and if *A* dies without issue, to my daughter *B* and her heirs." By this conveyance *A* is given a fee tail, and *B* is given a remainder in fee simple to become possessory when and if the fee tail expires. Every fee tail has a reversion or a remainder after it.

Time line 3-2

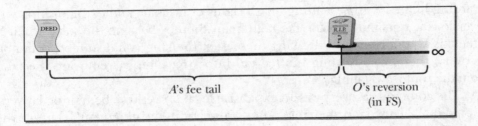

As originally authorized by the Statute de Donis, the tenant in fee tail could alienate his possessory interest, which ended upon his death, but he could not affect the rights of his issue to succeed to the land upon his death. In the 200 years after de Donis, the king and the judges began to perceive many mischiefs in

15. In Iowa and South Carolina, courts have held that the Statute de Donis is not in force because its purpose of maintaining a landed aristocracy is contrary to American institutions. Hence a fee simple conditional, obsolete in England since 1285, can be created in these two states. See Powell on Real Property §14.04 (Michael A. Wolf gen. ed. 2009).

16. A conveyance "to *A* and his issue" or "to *A* and his children" might create a fee tail, but the law was complicated by the necessity for the word *heirs* in a deed and by rules laid down in Wild's Case. See 5 American Law of Property §§22.15-22.28 (1952).

17. A *fee tail male* could also be created, limiting descent to male descendants. A *fee tail female* (or as punsters might have it, a *femme fee tail*) could be created in favor of female descendants, although in fact this was rarely done. Or a *fee tail special* might be created in a marriage settlement, limiting descent to issue of the husband by a named (special) wife.

the inability of the fee tail tenant to cut out succession by his issue. As Blackstone noted:

> Children grew disobedient when they knew they could not be set aside: farmers were ousted of their leases made by tenants in tail; for, if such leases had been valid, then under colour of long leases the issue might have been virtually disinherited: creditors were defrauded of their debts; for, if a tenant in tail could have charged his estate with their payment, he might also have defeated his issue, by mortgaging it for as much as it was worth: innumerable latent entails were produced to deprive purchasers of the lands they had fairly bought; of suits in consequence of which our ancient books are full: and treasons are encouraged; as estates-tail were not liable to forfeiture longer than for the tenant's life. [2 William Blackstone, Commentaries *116.]

The king was interested primarily in the last item on Blackstone's list. Soon after the enactment of de Donis, the great barons overwhelmed the monarchy and became the ruling class contending for the crown. There followed the anarchic period in English history culminating in the Wars of the Roses. When Edward IV took the throne in 1461, he observed how the great families had developed in the fee tail a secure land base from which they could challenge the king, and he sought a means to undermine it.

In Taltarum's Case, Y.B. 12 Edw. IV, 19 (1472), the court developed such a means. With Edward's countenance, the judges approved a method by which a tenant in tail could "bar the entail." By bringing a collusive lawsuit known as a common recovery, the fee tail tenant in possession could obtain a court decree awarding him a *fee simple*, cutting off all rights of his issue and extinguishing any reversion or remainder.[18] The fee tail tenant thereby became the sole owner. If a fee tail were forfeited to the king thereafter, the king could suffer a common recovery, thereby converting the fee tail into a fee simple, removing the land from the traitorous family forever.

The common recovery was an expensive legal procedure, benefiting lawyers, but it did make the land alienable. After 400 years, in the nineteenth century, the common recovery was finally abolished, and a fee tail tenant was given power to disentail simply by conveying a fee simple by deed to another.[19]

Thwarted in Taltarum's Case, which approved a means of barring entails, lawyers for the dynastic landed gentry, who continued to desire to control inheritance, began to create life estates in one generation followed by remainders in the next generation, whence developed the modern law of future interests, discussed in the next chapter.

---

18. If you really want to get into the details of the common recovery, with all its legal hocus pocus, see A.W. Brian Simpson, A History of the Land Law 125-138 (2d ed. 1986).

19. The power to disentail did not end the usefulness of the fee tail in England. Only a fee tail tenant *in possession* could disentail. Some 200 years after Taltarum's Case, lawyers for landowners seized upon this requirement to create what became known as a "strict settlement." In brief, land was limited to *A* for life, then to *A*'s eldest son in tail, then to *A*'s second son in tail, and so forth. When *A*'s eldest son, *B*, became of age or married, *A* surrendered possession to *B*, who suffered a common recovery, giving *B* a fee simple. *B* then turned around and made a new limitation to *A* for life, then to *B* for life, then to *B*'s eldest son in tail, and so forth. Thus inalienability was pushed forward generation by generation.

Abolition of the Fee Tail

For Thomas Jefferson, the fee tail and primogeniture were odious means of perpetuating a hereditary aristocracy. Jefferson persuaded the Virginia legislature to abolish both around the time of the American Revolution, and other legislatures soon followed suit.[20] Today the fee tail can be created only in Delaware, Maine, Massachusetts, and Rhode Island. In these states, a fee tail tenant can convert a fee tail into a fee simple by a deed executed during life, but cannot bar the entail by will.[21] Even in these states, a fee tail is rarely encountered, however. The fee tail has been replaced by the life estate as a device for controlling inheritance.

About the only problem related to the fee tail that arises in modern times is this: When an instrument uses language that would have created a fee tail at common law, what estate is thereby created today? Suppose that *O* conveys "to my son *A* and the heirs of his body, and if *A* dies without issue to my daughter *B* and her heirs." What interests are created under modern law? In each state in which the fee tail is abolished, a statute specifies what estate is created in *A* by the language of *O*'s conveyance and what interest, if any, is created in *B*. Although a few states provide that *A* takes a life estate, and *A*'s issue take a remainder in fee simple, the large majority of states fall into one of two categories:

(1) In states falling into the first category, statutes provide that a limitation "to *A* and the heirs of his body" creates a fee simple in *A*, and any further words having to do with *A*'s death without issue are void. Hence neither *A*'s issue nor *B* take anything under the above conveyance. The justification for this type of statute is that inasmuch as *A* could disentail and destroy the interests of *A*'s issue and *B*, the statute does it automatically.

(2) In states in the second category, statutes provide that a limitation "to *A* and the heirs of his body" creates a fee simple in *A*, but they further provide that to the interest created in *B* if *A* dies without issue will be given effect in one circumstance. *B* will take the fee simple if, and only if, *at A's death*, *A* leaves no surviving issue (and not, as at common law, when *A*'s whole line of issue runs out).[21] If *A* leaves surviving issue at his death, *B*'s interest fails, and *A*'s fee simple cannot be divested thereafter. In such case, *A* can devise his fee simple to whomever he chooses.

The new Restatement of Property provides that "[t]he fee tail estate is not recognized in American law." Restatement (Third) of Property, Wills and Other

---

20. See Stanley N. Katz, Thomas Jefferson and the Right to Property in Revolutionary America, 19 J.L. & Econ. 467 (1976). Professor Claire Priest has argued that the use of the entail in colonial America is best understood not as an instrument for perpetuating aristocracy but as a means of reducing risk in a family-based agricultural economy. During the Founding Era, she points out, the fee tail was reformed, not abolished, in many states; the reform measures were motivated less by political symbolism than by an effort to make land title registries simpler and more reliable, thereby broadening land markets. Where the fee tail was abolished — primarily in the slave South — the motive, she contends, was to strengthen the system of slavery. See Claire Priest, Understanding the End of Entail: Information, Institutions, and Slavery in the American Revolution Period (unpubl. ms. 2009, on file with the editors).

21. *B*'s future interest is known as a divesting executory interest, which will shift the fee simple to *B* if *A* leaves no issue at his death. Executory interests are explained beginning at page 286.

Donative Transfers §24.4 (2011). It goes on to state that language that would have created a fee tail at common law creates a fee simple absolute. This means that any gift over following what would, at common law, have been a fee tail is void. A comment to the Restatement observes that even under its new rule it is possible to create a substantially equivalent estate by a disposition such as "to A for life, then to A's issue from time to time living forever." Id. §24.4 comment c. Such a disposition is valid except to the extent restricted by the Rule Against Perpetuities, which we take up in Chapter 4. In recent years, several states have abolished the Rule Against Perpetuities, making it possible in these states to create the substantial equivalent of the old fee tail.

D. The Life Estate

Because the early feudal relation between lord and tenant involved only lifetime tenure, the law had little problem recognizing an *estate for life.* Judicial recognition of a life estate had two important consequences. First, it meant that the grantor of a life estate could control who takes the property at the life tenant's death. The life estate ultimately supplanted the fee tail as a device to control inheritance. Second, as land and stocks and bonds came to be viewed as income-producing capital, trust management for the life tenant developed. Under modern trust management, one person (often a corporate person such as a bank) manages property for the benefit of the life tenant, paying the life tenant the income therefrom. Today most life estates are created in trust. The amount of property in private trusts benefiting life tenants exceeds several hundred billion dollars in this country.

A conveyance "to A for life" gives A a life estate that lasts for the duration of A's life. A can transfer his life estate to B, in which case B has a life estate *pur autre vie*—that is, an estate that is measured by A's life-span, not B's. If B dies during A's lifetime, the life estate passes to B's heirs or devisees until A dies. See Collins v. Held, 369 N.E.2d 641 (Ind. App. 1977). Every life estate is followed by a future interest—either a reversion in the transferor or a remainder in a transferee, or both. Hence, suppose that O conveys Blackacre "to A for life." A has a life estate, and O has a reversion.

Time line 3-3

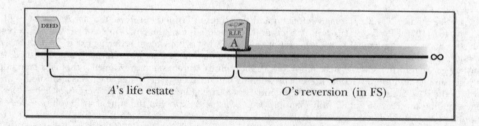

A's life estate   O's reversion (in FS)

White v. Brown

Supreme Court of Tennessee, 1977
559 S.W.2d 938

BROCK, J. This is a suit for the construction of a will. The Chancellor held that the will passed a life estate, but not the remainder,[22] in certain realty, leaving the remainder to pass by inheritance to the testatrix's heirs at law. The Court of Appeals affirmed.

Mrs. Jessie Lide died on February 15, 1973, leaving a holographic [handwritten] will which, in its entirety, reads as follows:

> April 19, 1972
>
> I, Jessie Lide, being in sound mind declare this to be my last will and testament. I appoint my niece Sandra White Perry to be the executrix of my estate.
> I wish Evelyn White to have my home to live in and not to be sold.
> I also leave my personal property to Sandra White Perry. My house is not to be sold.
>
> Jessie Lide
> (Underscoring by testatrix)

Mrs. Lide was a widow and had no children. Although she had nine brothers and sisters, only two sisters residing in Ohio survived her. These two sisters quitclaimed any interest they might have in the residence to Mrs. White. The [twelve] nieces and nephews of the testatrix, her heirs at law [other than her two sisters and Sandra White Perry], are defendants in this action.

Mrs. White, her husband, who was the testatrix's brother, and her daughter, Sandra White Perry, lived with Mrs. Lide as a family for some twenty-five years. After Sandra married in 1969 and Mrs. White's husband died in 1971, Evelyn White continued to live with Mrs. Lide until Mrs. Lide's death in 1973 at age 88.

Mrs. White, joined by her daughter as executrix, filed this action to obtain construction of the will, alleging that she is vested with a fee simple title to the home. The defendants contend that the will conveyed only a life estate to Mrs. White, leaving the remainder to go to them under our laws of intestate succession. The Chancellor held that the will unambiguously conveyed only a life interest in the home to Mrs. White and refused to consider extrinsic evidence concerning Mrs. Lide's relationship with her surviving relatives. Due to the debilitated condition of the property and in accordance with the desire of all parties, the Chancellor ordered the property sold with the proceeds distributed in designated shares among the beneficiaries.[23]

---

22. The court apparently misspoke. The interest created in heirs when the owner of a fee simple estate in land devises only a life estate in the land is a reversion, not a remainder, as we shall see in Chapter 4. We are grateful to Professor Louise Halper for bringing the court's mistake to our attention. —EDS.

23. The brief for the appellee states that the chancellor ordered the proceeds divided between the life tenant, Evelyn White, and the testatrix's heirs, as remaindermen, according to the value of their respective interests ascertained from life expectancy tables, on which see page 234. —EDS.

I.

Our cases have repeatedly acknowledged that the intention of the testator is to be ascertained from the language of the entire instrument when read in the light of surrounding circumstances. But, the practical difficulty in this case, as in so many other cases involving wills drafted by lay persons, is that the words chosen by the testatrix are not specific enough to clearly state her intent. Thus, in our opinion, it is not clear whether Mrs. Lide intended to convey a life estate in the home to Mrs. White, leaving the remainder interest to descend by operation of law, or a fee interest with a restraint on alienation. Moreover, the will might even be read as conveying a fee interest subject to a condition subsequent (Mrs. White's failure to live in the home).

In such ambiguous cases it is obvious that rules of construction, always yielding to the cardinal rule of the testator's intent, must be employed as auxiliary aids in the courts' endeavor to ascertain the testator's intent.

In 1851 our General Assembly enacted two such statutes of construction, thereby creating a statutory presumption against partial intestacy.

Chapter 33 of the Public Acts of 1851 (now codified as T.C.A. §§64-101 and 64-501) reversed the common law presumption[24] that a life estate was intended unless the intent to pass a fee simple was clearly expressed in the instrument. T.C.A. §64-501 provides:

> Every grant or devise of real estate, or any interest therein, shall pass all the estate or interest of the grantor or devisor, unless the intent to pass a less estate or interest shall appear by express terms, or be necessarily implied in the terms of the instrument.

Chapter 180, Section 2 of the Public Acts of 1851 (now codified as T.C.A. §32-301) was specifically directed to the operation of a devise. In relevant part, T.C.A. §32-301 provides:

> A will . . . shall convey all the real estate belonging to [the testator] or in which he had any interest at his decease, unless a contrary intention appear by its words and context.

Thus, under our law, unless the "words and context" of Mrs. Lide's will clearly evidence her intention to convey only a life estate to Mrs. White, the will should be construed as passing the home to Mrs. White in fee. "'If the expression in the will is doubtful, the doubt is resolved against the limitation and in favor of the absolute estate.'" Meacham v. Graham, 98 Tenn. 190, 206, 39 S.W. 12, 15 (1897) (quoting Washbon v. Cope, 144 N.Y. 287, 39 N.E. 388).

---

24. Because the feudal lord granted land solely as compensation for personal services, the grant was for no longer than the life of the grantee. Later the grant was extended to the sons and other issue of the grantee under the designation of "heirs." Heirs were thus entitled to stand in the place of their ancestor after his death if mentioned in the grant—but only if specifically mentioned. Thereafter, the word "heirs," when used in a conveyance to a man "and his heirs," came to include collateral as well as lineal heirs, ultimately indicating that such grantee took an estate that would pass to his heirs or the heirs of anyone to whom he aliened it. That is, "heirs" ceased to be a word of purchase and became a word of limitation. 1 Tiffany, Real Property §28 (3d ed. 1939).

Jessie Lide's House, 1956
Jessie Lide on right, Sandra White in middle

Several of our cases demonstrate the effect of these statutory presumptions against intestacy by construing language which might seem to convey an estate for life, without provision for a gift over after the termination of such life estate, as passing a fee simple instead. In Green v. Young, 163 Tenn. 16, 40 S.W.2d 793 (1931), the testatrix's disposition of all of her property to her husband "to be used by him for his support and comfort during his life" was held to pass a fee estate. Similarly, in Williams v. Williams, 167 Tenn. 26, 65 S.W.2d 561 (1933), the testator's devise of real property to his children "for and during their natural lives" without provision for a gift over was held to convey a fee. And, in Webb v. Webb, 53 Tenn. App. 609, 385 S.W.2d 295 (1964), a devise of personal property to the testator's wife "for her maintenance, support and comfort, for the full period of her natural life" with complete powers of alienation but without provision for the remainder passed absolute title to the widow.

II.

Thus, if the sole question for our determination were whether the will's conveyance of the home to Mrs. White "to live in" gave her a life interest or a fee in the home, a conclusion favoring the absolute estate would be clearly required. The question, however, is complicated somewhat by the caveat contained in the will that the home is "not to be sold"—a restriction conflicting with the free alienation of property, one of the most significant incidents of fee ownership. We must determine, therefore, whether Mrs. Lide's will, when taken as a whole, clearly evidences her intent to convey only a life estate in her home to Mrs. White.

Under ordinary circumstances a person makes a will to dispose of his or her entire estate. If, therefore, a will is susceptible of two constructions, by one of which the testator disposes of the whole of his estate and by the other of which he disposes of only a part of his estate, dying intestate as to the remainder, this Court has always preferred that construction which disposes of the whole of the testator's estate if that construction is reasonable and consistent with the general scope and provisions of the will. A construction which results in partial intestacy will not be adopted unless such intention clearly appears. It has been said that the courts will prefer any reasonable construction or any construction which does not do violence to a testator's language, to a construction which results in partial intestacy.

The intent to create a fee simple or other absolute interest and, at the same time to impose a restraint upon its alienation can be clearly expressed. If the testator specifically declares that he devises land to A "in fee simple" or to A "and his heirs" but that A shall not have the power to alienate the land, there is but one tenable construction, viz., the testator's intent is to impose a restraint upon a fee simple. To construe such language to create a life estate would conflict with the express specification of a fee simple as well as with the presumption of intent to make a complete testamentary disposition of all of a testator's property. By extension, as noted by Professor Casner in his treatise on the law of real property:

> Since it is now generally presumed that a conveyor intends to transfer his whole interest in the property, it may be reasonable to adopt the same construction [conveyance of a fee simple], even in the absence of words of inheritance, if there is no language that can be construed to create a remainder. [6 American Law of Property §26.58 (A. J. Casner ed. 1952).]

In our opinion, testatrix's apparent testamentary restraint on the alienation of the home devised to Mrs. White does not evidence such a clear intent to pass only a life estate as is sufficient to overcome the law's strong presumption that a fee simple interest was conveyed.

Accordingly, we conclude that Mrs. Lide's will passed a fee simple absolute in the home to Mrs. White. Her attempted restraint on alienation must be declared void as inconsistent with the incidents and nature of the estate devised and contrary to public policy.

The decrees of the Court of Appeals and the trial court are reversed and the cause is remanded to the chancery court for such further proceedings as may be necessary, consistent with this opinion. Costs are taxed against appellees.

HARBISON, J., dissenting. With deference to the views of the majority, and recognizing the principles of law contained in the majority opinion, I am unable to agree that the language of the will of Mrs. Lide did or was intended to convey a fee simple interest in her residence to her sister-in-law, Mrs. Evelyn White.

The testatrix expressed the wish that Mrs. White was to have my home to live in and *not* to be *sold*. The emphasis is that of the testatrix, and her desire that Mrs. White was not to have an unlimited estate in the property was reiterated in the last sentence of the will, to wit: "My house is not to be sold."

The testatrix appointed her niece, Mrs. Perry, executrix and made an outright bequest to her of all personal property.

The will does not seem to me to be particularly ambiguous, and like the Chancellor and the Court of Appeals, I am of the opinion that the testatrix gave Mrs. White a life estate only, and that upon the death of Mrs. White the remainder will pass to the heirs at law of the testatrix.

The cases cited by petitioners in support of their contention that a fee simple was conveyed are not persuasive, in my opinion. Possibly the strongest case cited by the appellants is Green v. Young, 163 Tenn. 16, 40 S.W.2d 793 (1931), in which the testatrix bequeathed all of her real and personal property to her husband "to be used by him for his support and comfort during his life." The will expressly stated that it included all of the property, real and personal, which the testatrix owned at the time of her death. There was no limitation whatever upon the power of the husband to use, consume, or dispose of the property, and the Court concluded that a fee simple was intended.

In the case of Williams v. Williams, 167 Tenn. 26, 65 S.W.2d 561 (1933), a father devised property to his children "for and during their natural lives," but the will contained other provisions not mentioned in the majority opinion which seem to me to distinguish the case. Unlike the provisions of the present will, other clauses in the *Williams* will contained provisions that these same children were to have "all the residue of my estate personal or mixed of which I shall die possessed or seized, or to which I shall be entitled at the time of my decease, to have and to hold the same to them and their executors and administrators and assigns forever."

Further, following some specific gifts to grandchildren, there was another bequest of the remainder of the testator's money to these same three children. The language used by the testator in that case was held to convey the fee simple interest in real estate to the children, but its provisions hardly seem analogous to the language employed by the testatrix in the instant case.

In the case of Webb v. Webb, 53 Tenn. App. 609, 385 S.W.2d 295 (1964), the testator gave his wife all the residue of his property with a clear, unqualified and unrestricted power of use, sale or disposition. Thereafter he attempted to limit her interest to a life estate, with a gift over to his heirs of any unconsumed property. Again, under settled rules of construction and interpretation, the wife was found to have a fee simple estate, but, unlike the present case, there was no limitation whatever upon the power of use or disposition of the property by the beneficiary. . . .

In the present case the testatrix knew how to make an outright gift, if desired. She left all of her personal property to her niece without restraint or limitation. As to her sister-in-law, however, she merely wished the latter have her house "to live in," and expressly withheld from her any power of sale.

The majority opinion holds that the testatrix violated a rule of law by attempting to restrict the power of the donee to dispose of the real estate. Only by thus striking a portion of the will, and holding it inoperative, is the conclusion reached that an unlimited estate resulted.

In my opinion, this interpretation conflicts more greatly with the apparent intention of the testatrix than did the conclusion of the courts below, limiting the gift to Mrs. White to a life estate. I have serious doubt that the testatrix intended to create any illegal restraint on alienation or to violate any other rules of law. It seems to me that she rather emphatically intended to provide that her sister-in-law was not to be able to sell the house during the lifetime of the latter—a result which is both legal and consistent with the creation of a life estate.

In my opinion the judgment of the courts below was correct and I would affirm.

NOTES AND QUESTIONS

1. *Restraints on alienation: types and validity.* The rule against direct restraints on alienation is an old one, going back at least to the fifteenth century. It owes something to the Statute Quia Emptores (1290), which stripped the mesne lords, but not the king, of the power to block transfers of the land by their tenants without their consent.

The objections to restraints on alienation are mainly four. First, such restraints make property unmarketable. The particular land may be made unavailable for its highest and best use. Second, restraints tend to perpetuate the concentration of wealth by making it impossible for the owner to sell property and consume the proceeds of sale. The restrained owner cannot dissipate the capital and, perhaps, fall out of the ranks of the rich. Third, restraints discourage improvements on land. An owner is unlikely to sink his money into improvements on land that he cannot sell. If a mortgage cannot be placed on the land (giving the money-lender the right to sell the land if the borrower defaults on the loan), lenders will not make money available to finance improvements. Fourth, restraints prevent the owner's creditors from reaching the property, working hardship on creditors who rely on the owner's enjoyment of the property in extending credit. See 6 American Law of Property §26.3 (1952).

It is sometimes said that a restraint on alienation is "repugnant" to a fee simple and void for that reason. This argument begs the question. Do you see why? If not, see Percy Bordwell, Alienability and Perpetuities II, 23 Iowa L. Rev. 1, 14 (1937) (repugnancy argument makes alienability a characteristic of a fee simple, by definition, then rejects restraints as inconsistent with that definition).

Restraints on alienation have traditionally been classified as disabling restraints, forfeiture restraints, and promissory restraints. A *disabling restraint* withholds from the grantee the power of transferring his interest (e.g., *O* conveys Blackacre "to *A* and his heirs but any transfer hereafter in any manner of an interest in Blackacre shall be null and void"). A disabling restraint was involved in White v. Brown. A *forfeiture restraint* provides that if the grantee attempts to transfer his interest, it is forfeited to another person (e.g., *O* conveys Blackacre "to *A* and his heirs, but if *A* attempts to transfer the property by any means whatsoever, then to *B* and her heirs"). A *promissory restraint* provides that the grantee promises not to transfer his interest (e.g., *O* conveys Blackacre "to *A* and his heirs, and *A* promises for himself, his heirs and successors in interest that Blackacre will not be transferred by any means"). A promissory restraint, if valid, is enforceable by the contract remedies of damages or an injunction. Promissory restraints on alienation of land are rare except in the landlord-tenant context (see pages 473-482).

The Restatement (Second) of Property, Donative Transfers, ch. 4 (1983) generally treats all these restraints alike when they are imposed on a fee simple, and the new Restatement adheres to that view. See Restatement (Third) of Property, Wills and Other Donative Transfers, Scope Note Introducing Division VIII (2011). Following overwhelming authority, the Restatement provides that an absolute restraint on a fee simple is void. But with respect to partial restraints on a fee simple, the Restatement takes a more tolerant position than do most courts. The Restatement provides that a partial restraint (e.g., limiting conveyance to certain persons or putting a time limit on the restraint) is valid if, under all the circumstances of the case, the restraint is found to be reasonable in purpose, effect, and duration.

With respect to restraints on a life estate, the Restatement (Second) provides that an absolute disabling restraint is void (§4.1(1)), but a forfeiture restraint is valid (§4.2(1)). This different treatment of disabling and forfeiture restraints follows the majority of cases. What is the justification for this different treatment of disabling and forfeiture restraints? See 6 American Law of Property §§26.48-26.50 (1952) (forfeiture induces the life tenant to pay debts, whereas a disabling restraint, which allows the life tenant to not pay but keep the property, does not).

2. *Postscript to* White v. Brown. More about Jessie Lide's house from her niece Sandra White Perry:

I moved to that house when I was nine months old along with my parents (my father was Jessie Lide's brother). I lived in that house until I married at age 22. The house originally had 4 rooms—living room, dining room, kitchen, and one bedroom. Mama, Daddy, and I lived in one room of Jessie's four-room house. She also lived in one room—originally the kitchen. Jessie cleaned the living room every day. We never sat in it. The only time Jessie unlocked it was for a death in the family. In 1957, after renting the house for $3 a week for 38 years, Jessie purchased the house from her landlord for a price of $3,000 cash. At that time, the house had no hot water and no electrical plugs. After she purchased the house, three more rooms were added on—a bedroom for me, a kitchen for my mother, and a room to be used for storing things.

In 1964 the Chrysler Corporation offered her a price of $35,000 for the property. The company had purchased more than half the block and this house stood in the way. She refused to sell, stating this was her home.

[Jessie died in 1973.]

In 1976 my mother had a serious stroke, therefore making it impossible for her to live alone anymore. I had her move into my home and we rented out the Gratz Street house—after spending $8,000 on improvements.

In 1981 my mother died. My husband and I were unemployed at the time. We put the house up for sale. Being desperate along with threats from the bank (regarding the home improvement loan on the house), we were forced to sell to anyone that would have it. We sold it to a fellow named Brewster for $10,000. In 1986 he sold the house to the Chrysler Company next door for a price of $40,000. I had contacted the Chrysler Company in 1981, but they were not interested at that time in buying the property. [Letter from Sandra White Perry to the editors, dated Aug. 1, 1988.]

NOTE: VALUATION OF LIFE ESTATE
   AND REMAINDER

In White v. Brown the chancellor found that Evelyn White had a life estate in Jessie Lide's house. He ordered the house sold and the proceeds divided between the life tenant and the remaindermen. How can we determine the value of the life estate and of the remainder?

Assume that the house is worth $10,000. Since we do not know how long the life tenant will actually live, to value the life estate we assume the life tenant will die at the time predicted by a life expectancy (mortality) table. We also need an interest rate; we will assume the market interest rate is 6 percent. Now we can value the life estate and remainder.

To value the life estate, we need to ascertain the present value of the right to receive $600 annually (6 percent of $10,000) for the life tenant's life expectancy. We seek a sum that, invested for the life tenant's life expectancy at 6 percent, will pay $600 for the given number of years and exhaust itself on final payment—in short, the price of an annuity. To simplify the problem let us assume that the life tenant has a life expectancy of only three years. The right to $1 one year from now is not worth $1 now, but only the amount that, if increased by the interest it can earn in a year, will equal $1. Assuming a 6 percent rate of interest, 94 cents will grow to $1 a year from today. A dollar due in two years is worth 89 cents today (at 6 percent interest); by reinvesting interest, 89 cents today will grow into 94 cents one year from now, which will grow into $1 two years from now. The present value of the right to receive $1 per year for three years is the sum of 94 cents and 89 cents and 84 cents, or $2.67.

Now what is the present value of the right to receive $600 a year for the next three years? $600 × 2.67 = $1,600, which is the present value of the life estate.

In order to value a remainder we must know the number of years the right to receive the sum will be deferred. If we assume that the life tenant has a life expectancy of three years, 84 cents invested at 6 percent with interest compounded annually will be worth $1 at the end of three years. Therefore $8,400 will grow to $10,000 at the end of three years, when the remainder is due to fall in. Hence the remainder has a present value of $8,400.

For lack of a better method, courts, taxing authorities, and insurance companies value life estates and remainders by resort to life expectancy tables. Under Treasury regulations applicable at the time of Jessie Lide's death, if the life tenant is 10 years old, the life estate is worth 96 percent of the total asset value, and the remainder is worth 4 percent. If the life tenant is 70 years old, the life estate is worth 48 percent of the asset value, and the remainder is worth 52 percent. Treas. Reg. §25.2512-9(f), Table A2. If Evelyn White had been given a life estate in White v. Brown and were 70 years old, why might she and the remaindermen not be willing to sell the house voluntarily and divide the proceeds 48 percent to 52 percent?

Baker v. Weedon

Supreme Court of Mississippi, 1972
262 So. 2d 641

PATTERSON, J. This is an appeal from a decree of the Chancery Court of Alcorn County. It directs a sale of land affected by a life estate and future interests with provision for the investment of the proceeds. The interest therefrom is to be paid to the life tenant for her maintenance. We reverse and remand.

John Harrison Weedon was born in High Point, North Carolina. He lived throughout the South and was married twice prior to establishing his final residence in Alcorn County. His first marriage to Lula Edwards resulted in two siblings, Mrs. Florence Weedon Baker and Mrs. Delette Weedon Jones. Mrs. Baker was the mother of three children, Henry Baker, Sarah Baker Lyman and Louise Virginia Baker Heck, the appellants herein. Mrs. Delette Weedon Jones adopted a daughter Dorothy Jean Jones, who has not been heard from for a number of years and whose whereabouts are presently unknown.

John Weedon was next married to Ella Howell and to this union there was born one child, Rachel. Both Ella and Rachel are now deceased.

Subsequent to these marriages John Weedon bought Oakland Farm in 1905 and engaged himself in its operation. In 1915 John, who was then 55 years of age, married Anna Plaxico, 17 years of age. This marriage, though resulting in no children, was a compatible relationship. John and Anna worked side by side in farming this 152.95-acre tract of land in Alcorn County. There can be no doubt that Anna's contribution to the development and existence of Oakland Farm was significant. The record discloses that during the monetarily difficult years following World War I she hoed, picked cotton and milked an average of fifteen cows per day to protect the farm from financial ruin.

While the relationship of John and Anna was close and amiable, that between John and his daughters of his first marriage was distant and strained. He had no contact with Florence, who was reared by Mr. Weedon's sister in North Carolina, during the seventeen years preceding his death. An even more unfortunate relationship existed between John and his second daughter, Delette Weedon Jones. She is portrayed by the record as being a nomadic person who only contacted her father for money, threatening on several occasions to bring suit against him.

With an obvious intent to exclude his daughters and provide for his wife Anna, John executed his last will and testament in 1925. It provided in part:

> Second; I give and bequeath to my beloved wife, Anna Plaxico Weedon all of my property both real, personal and mixed during her natural life and upon her death to her children, if she has any, and in the event she dies without issue then at the death of my wife Anna Plaxico Weedon I give, bequeath and devise all of my property to my grandchildren, each grandchild sharing equally with the other.
>
> Third; In this will I have not provided for my daughters, Mrs. Florence Baker and Mrs. Delette Weedon Jones, the reason is, I have given them their share of my property and they have not looked after and cared for me in the latter part of my life.

Subsequent to John Weedon's death in 1932 and the probate of his will, Anna continued to live on Oakland Farm. In 1933 Anna, who had been urged by John to remarry in the event of his death, wed J.E. Myers. This union lasted some twenty years and produced no offspring which might terminate the contingent remainder vested in Weedon's grandchildren by the will.

There was no contact between Anna and John Weedon's children or grandchildren from 1932 until 1964. Anna ceased to operate the farm in 1955 due to her age and it has been rented since that time. Anna's only income is $1000 annually from the farm rental, $300 per year from sign rental and $50 per month by way of social security payments. Without contradiction Anna's income is presently insufficient and places a severe burden upon her ability to live comfortably in view of her age and the infirmities therefrom.

In 1964 the growth of the city of Corinth was approaching Oakland Farm. A right-of-way through the property was sought by the Mississippi State Highway Department for the construction of U.S. Highway 45 bypass. The highway department located Florence Baker's three children, the contingent remaindermen by the will of John Weedon, to negotiate with them for the purchase of the right-of-way. Dorothy Jean Jones, the adopted daughter of Delette Weedon Jones, was not located and due to the long passage of years, is presumably dead. A decree pro confesso was entered against her.

Until the notice afforded by the highway department the grandchildren were unaware of their possible inheritance. Henry Baker, a native of New Jersey, journeyed to Mississippi to supervise their interests. He appears, as was true of the other grandchildren, to have been totally sympathetic to the conditions surrounding Anna's existence as a life tenant. A settlement of $20,000 was completed for the right-of-way bypass of which Anna received $7500 with which to construct a new home. It is significant that all legal and administrative fees were deducted from the shares of the three grandchildren and not taxed to the life tenant. A contract was executed in 1970 for the sale of soil from the property for $2500. Anna received $1000 of this sum which went toward completion of payments for the home.

There was substantial evidence introduced to indicate the value of the property is appreciating significantly with the nearing completion of U.S. Highway 45 bypass plus the growth of the city of Corinth. While the commercial value of the property is appreciating, it is notable that the rental value for agricultural purposes is not. It is apparent that the land can bring no more for agricultural rental purposes than the $1000 per year now received.

The value of the property for commercial purposes at the time of trial was $168,500. Its estimated value within the ensuing four years is placed at $336,000, reflecting the great influence of the interstate construction upon the land. Mr. Baker, for himself and other remaindermen, appears to have made numerous honest and sincere efforts to sell the property at a favorable price. However, his endeavors have been hindered by the slowness of the construction of the bypass.

Anna, the life tenant and appellee here, is 73 years of age and although now living in a new home, has brought this suit due to her economic distress. She prays that the property, less the house site, be sold by a commissioner and that the proceeds be invested to provide her with an adequate income resulting from interest on the trust investment. She prays also that the sale and investment management be under the direction of the chancery court.

The chancellor granted the relief prayed by Anna under the theory of economic waste. His opinion reflects:

> . . . [T]he change of the economy in this area, the change in farming conditions, the equipment required for farming, and the age of this complainant leaves the real estate where it is to all intents and purposes unproductive when viewed in light of its capacity and that a continuing use under the present conditions would result in economic waste.[25]

The contingent remaindermen by the will, appellants here, were granted an interlocutory appeal to settle the issue of the propriety of the chancellor's decree in divesting the contingency title of the remaindermen by ordering a sale of the property.

The weight of authority reflects a tendency to afford a court of equity the power to order the sale of land in which there are future interests. Simes, Law of Future Interests, section 53 (2d ed. 1966), states:

> By the weight of authority, it is held that a court of equity has the power to order a judicial sale of land affected with a future interest and an investment of the proceeds, where this is necessary for the preservation of all interests in the land. When the power is exercised, the proceeds of the sale are held in a judicially created trust. The beneficiaries of the trust are the persons who held interests in the land, and the beneficial interests are of the same character as the legal interests which they formally held in the land.

See also Simes and Smith, The Law of Future Interests, §1941 (2d ed. 1956).

This Court has long recognized that chancery courts do have jurisdiction to order the sale of land for the prevention of waste. Kelly v. Neville, 136 Miss. 429, 101 So. 565 (1924). In Riley v. Norfleet, 167 Miss. 420, 436-437, 148 So. 777, 781 (1933), Justice Cook, speaking for the Court and citing *Kelly*, supra, stated: ". . . The power of a court of equity on a plenary bill, with adversary interest properly represented, to sell contingent remainders in land, under some circumstances, though the contingent remaindermen are not then ascertained or in being, as, for instance, to preserve the estate from complete or partial destruction, is well established."

While Mississippi and most jurisdictions recognize the inherent power of a court of equity to direct a judicial sale of land which is subject to a future interest, nevertheless the scope of this power has not been clearly defined. It is difficult to determine the facts and circumstances which will merit such a sale.

It is apparent that there must be "necessity" before the chancery court can order a judicial sale. It is also beyond cavil that the power should be exercised

---

25. What does the chancellor mean by "economic waste"? Is it the same as the legal concept of waste? See Note 4 on page 241. —EDS.

with caution and only when the need is evident. Lambdin v. Lambdin, 209 Miss. 672, 48 So. 2d 341 (1950). These cases, *Kelly, Riley* and *Lambdin,* supra, are all illustrative of situations where the freehold estate was deteriorating and the income therefrom was insufficient to pay taxes and maintain the property. In each of these this Court approved a judicial sale to preserve and maintain the estate. The appellants argue, therefore, that since Oakland Farm is not deteriorating and since there is sufficient income from rental to pay taxes, a judicial sale by direction of the court was not proper.

The unusual circumstances of this case persuade us to the contrary. We are of the opinion that deterioration and waste of the property is not the exclusive and ultimate test to be used in determining whether a sale of land affected by a future interest is proper, but also that consideration should be given to the question of whether a sale is necessary for the best interest of all the parties, that is, the life tenant and the contingent remaindermen. This "necessary for the best interest of all parties" rule is gleaned from Rogers, Removal of Future Interest Encumbrances—Sale of the Fee Simple Estate, 17 Vanderbilt L. Rev. 1437 (1964); Simes, Law of Future Interests, supra; Simes and Smith, The Law of Future Interests, §1941 (1956); and appears to have the necessary flexibility to meet the requirements of unusual and unique situations which demand in justice an equitable solution.

Our decision to reverse the chancellor and remand the case for his further consideration is couched in our belief that the best interest of all the parties would not be served by a judicial sale of the entirety of the property at this time. While true that such a sale would provide immediate relief to the life tenant who is worthy of this aid in equity, admitted by the remaindermen, it would nevertheless under the circumstances before us cause great financial loss to the remaindermen.

We therefore reverse and remand this cause to the chancery court, which shall have continuing jurisdiction thereof, for determination upon motion of the life tenant, if she so desires, for relief by way of sale of a part of the burdened land sufficient to provide for her reasonable needs from interest derived from the investment of the proceeds. The sale, however, is to be made only in the event the parties cannot unite to hypothecate the land for sufficient funds for the life tenant's reasonable needs. By affording the options above we do not mean to suggest that other remedies suitable to the parties which will provide economic relief to the aging life tenant are not open to them if approved by the chancellor. It is our opinion, shared by the chancellor and acknowledged by the appellants, that the facts suggest an equitable remedy. However, it is our further opinion that this equity does not warrant the remedy of sale of all of the property since this would unjustly impinge upon the vested rights of the remaindermen.

Reversed and remanded.

[*Postscript:* After the Mississippi Supreme Court handed down its opinion in Baker v. Weedon, John's grandchildren relented and agreed to sell all of the land except the five acres where Anna lived. Anna and her lawyer were appointed trustees, to invest the proceeds and pay the income to Anna for life. The land became the site of a printing plant printing National Geographic magazines. In her nineties Anna Weedon fell and broke her hip and was confined to a wheelchair, but she managed to live alone in her house until her death in 1996 at age 98. She survived two of her husband's three grandchildren.]

NOTES AND QUESTIONS

1. *Wisdom of creating a legal life estate.* Is it wise to create a legal life estate, as John Weedon did? What problems might arise during the life tenant's life that the life tenant cannot adequately solve? How would you handle the following problems in drafting John Weedon's will?

Sale. Circumstances might change so that a sale of the property is advantageous. The life tenant cannot sell a fee simple unless *all* other persons having an interest in the property consent or unless a court of equity orders sale and reinvestment of the proceeds.

Lease. It might be advantageous for the life tenant to lease the property for a period extending beyond the life tenant's death.

Mortgage. If the life tenant has no capital of her own, she may be unable to improve the property without borrowing from a bank and giving the bank a mortgage on the property. A bank ordinarily does not lend money if the security is a life estate rather than a fee simple.

Waste. The life tenant may want to take minerals out of the land or cut timber or take down a still usable building. The actions may constitute waste, entitling the remaindermen to an injunction or damages. See Note 4 below.

Insurance. The life tenant is under no duty to insure buildings on the land. If the life tenant does insure buildings and the buildings are destroyed by fire, the life tenant has been held entitled to the whole proceeds and the remaindermen nothing. Ellersbusch v. Myers, 683 N.E.2d 1352 (Ind. App. 1997).

The person creating a legal life estate can draft the instrument so as to give the life tenant a power to sell or mortgage a fee simple or to lease beyond the duration of the life estate. A life estate can be coupled with any number of powers to do specific acts not otherwise permitted the life tenant. However, if the life tenant is given the power to sell a fee simple, the drafter should consider what is to be done with the proceeds of sale and draft appropriate provisions. Should the proceeds be given outright to the life tenant or held by a trustee in trust for the life tenant's life?

2. *Legal life estates in personalty.* Legal life estates (that is, life estates not created in a trust) in personal property create special problems. Unlike land, personalty, especially tangibles, is movable and easily sold. The law of waste, which was developed to deal with problems resulting from the temporal division of ownership in land, does not adequately protect the holders of future interests in personalty against misappropriation or misuse of personalty by the present possessor. Some states have statutory solutions to this problem. Pennsylvania, for

example, statutorily provides that the holder of a legal life estate in personalty shall be treated as a trustee of the personalty. Pa. Cons. Stat. Ann. tit. 20, §6113 (2005). Other statutes require legal life tenants of personalty to account to a court periodically as though they were trustees. See N.Y. Surr. Ct. Proc. Act §2201 (McKinney 1997). Still other statutes permit courts to order legal life tenants to post a bond. See Conn. Gen. Stat. Ann. §45a-451 (2004). In the absence of statutes, courts generally have considerable discretion to determine whether the circumstances warrant ordering the life tenant to provide some form of security, especially where the life tenant expressly or implicitly has been given the power to sell the asset. William B. Stoebuck & Dale A. Whitman, The Law of Property §4.11 (3d ed. 2000).

3. *Protecting the life tenant by creating a trust.* A trust, which you have not yet studied, should always be considered by a lawyer when a client proposes to create a life estate. A trust is a more flexible and usually more desirable property arrangement than a legal life estate. *A trustee holds the legal fee simple* and as the "manager" of the property may be directed to pay all the income to the life tenant or to let the life tenant into possession. As manager, the trustee will have powers spelled out in the instrument creating the trust, or supplied by law, to administer the trust for the benefit of the life tenant and remaindermen. These powers usually give the trustee power to sell, lease, mortgage, remove minerals, or do whatever a prudent person would do with respect to the property. If the trustee sells the property, the trustee invests the proceeds of sale, paying the income therefrom to the life tenant.

The life tenant can be made trustee. For example, John Weedon could have devised his land to his wife Anna as trustee in trust for Anna for life, remainder to his grandchildren. As trustee, Anna would have a legal fee simple and would be the manager of the land, owing fiduciary duties to herself and to the remaindermen. She would also have an equitable life estate entitling her to possession of the land or to net rental income for her life. As trustee, Anna could sell the fee simple to the property if desirable, say for $168,500. She could then invest the $168,500 in stocks and bonds or other assets, and pay herself the income from them. On her death the remaindermen would be entitled to the assets owned by the trust, in whatever form those assets then took.

If John Weedon did not think Anna was capable of acting as a trustee, he could have named some other person trustee. Or he could have provided in his will that if Anna ever wanted to sell the land, a trust would come into existence at that time, and the court would appoint a suitable person as trustee.

The conceptual framework of the trust is detailed in the next chapter, at pages 295-303, but we want to introduce you to the trust early because, in our judgment, a legal life estate, as was created in Baker v. Weedon, should almost always be avoided. It was a property arrangement suited to the great landed families of England in an age when land was the chief form of wealth — the basis of the family dynasty and the stately homes that passed from generation to generation — and when urban development proceeded slowly and land values remained relatively stable.[26] A legal life estate is unsuited to a modern economy that regards land as just another form of income-producing wealth, which can swiftly appreciate in value under pressure for development and which must be managed effectively.

4. *Waste.* The law of waste can become relevant whenever two or more persons—suppose two here, called *A* and *B*—have rights to possess property at the same time (as in concurrent ownership, considered in Chapter 5) or consecutively (as in Baker v. Weedon or in the case of present and future interests generally). The central idea of the waste concept is that *A* should not be able to use the property in a manner that *unreasonably* interferes with the expectations of *B*. In this regard, the law of waste is aptly named, because it is designed to avoid just that—uses of property that fail to maximize the property's value. See Richard A. Posner, Economic Analysis of Law 92 (8th ed. 2011):

> [T]he common law doctrine of waste . . . mediates between the competing interests of life tenants and remaindermen. A life tenant will have an incentive to maximize not the value of the property—that is, the present value of the entire stream of future earnings obtainable from it—but only the present value of the earnings stream obtainable during his expected lifetime. He will therefore want to cut timber before it has attained its mature growth even though the present value of the timber would be greater if the cutting of some or all of it were postponed if the added value from waiting would enure to the remainderman. The law of waste forbids this.
>
> There might seem to be no need for such a law, because the life tenant and the remainderman could negotiate an optimal plan for exploiting the property. But since the tenant and remainderman . . . [are locked into dealing with each other—a so-called bilateral monopoly], transaction costs may be high. Also, the remaindermen may be children, who do not have the legal capacity to make binding contracts; they may even be unborn children.

The law of waste began developing in the twelfth century and evolved over time into a complex set of rules for reconciling the conflicting interests of people like *A* and *B*. The precise application of waste doctrine turns on a number of variables—the nature of the property interests of the competing parties, the conduct in question, the remedy sought—and easy generalizations are likely to prove inaccurate. Here we simply underscore some central points and interesting quirks and problems. For a fuller treatment, see Powell on Real Property §§56.01-56.12 (Michael A. Wolf gen. ed. 2009).

Suppose that *A* has a present possessory interest in property and that *B* has a future interest—a future right to possession. *A*'s interest might be of short or possibly long duration—a month-to-month tenancy at one extreme, or at the other a long term of years or (as in Baker v. Weedon) a life estate. Similarly, *B*'s interest might be certain to come into possession (as with the landlord's reversion following a tenancy) or tenuous. As to tenuous future interests, ones that

---

26. The legal life estate can no longer be created in England. It was abolished by the Law of Property Act of 1925. A life estate can exist only as an equitable interest, that is to say, someone must hold the legal fee simple in trust whenever a life estate is created. The purpose of this legislation was to ensure that a fee simple owner is always available with authority to sell, mortgage, or lease the land. See C. Dent Bostick, Loosening the Grip of the Dead Hand: Shall We Abolish Legal Future Interests in Land?, 32 Vand. L. Rev. 1061, 1090-1097 (1979), recommending that America follow the English lead.

may or may not become possessory, we will see a number of examples in Chapter 4. You should note, though, that Baker v. Weedon is a case in point. If Anna had children, John Weedon's grandchildren would not get the farm. With the foregoing in mind, we can simply say that typically the greater A's interest, the more freedom A has in using the property in question; correspondingly, the more tenuous B's interest, the less protection given B. (Keeping in mind Posner's discussion of the economic functions of waste, how would you justify these distinctions?)

What sort of conduct amounts to waste, then, turns in part on the nature of the interests involved. It also turns on the conduct in question. The courts have created three general categories of waste: affirmative waste, arising from voluntary acts; permissive waste, arising from a failure to act; and ameliorative waste, resulting from changes to the property, specifically changes that increase its value.

As to *affirmative waste*, liability results from injurious acts that have more than trivial effects. Generally, *injurious* has meant acts that substantially reduce the value of the property in question—but with some exceptions. Usually, for example, minerals can be extracted, even though doing so reduces the value of the property for holders of future interests, *if* the minerals were being extracted when the future interests were created.[27] Trees can be cut if clearing the land is regarded as good husbandry.

Permissive waste is essentially a question of negligence—failure to take reasonable care of the property. Kimbrough v. Reed, 943 P.2d 1232 (Idaho 1997), is illustrative. In this case, the life tenant let the water pump fall into disrepair with a resulting loss of lawn, shrubs, and trees. The life tenant was assessed damages for waste. See also McIntyre v. Scarbrough, 471 S.E.2d 199 (Ga. 1996), holding that a life tenant's failure to pay real estate taxes is waste, resulting in forfeiture of the life estate.

Ameliorative waste consists of uses by the tenant that increase rather than decrease the market value of the land. The traditional view was that such actions by the tenant gave rise to liability on the theory that the fee holder was entitled to take possession of the land in substantially the same condition as it was when first transferred to the tenant. Any material alterations were waste. (This notion underlies the court's opinion in Baker v. Weedon.) Today a significant number of courts reject this view. The leading case is Melms v. Pabst Brewing Co., 79 N.W. 738 (Wis. 1899), holding that life tenants may make substantial alterations or even demolish structures when conditions change, provided the market value of the remainder (or reversion, as the case may be) is not diminished by these actions. Such an outcome is virtually certain if the life tenant has a long life expectancy. See Thomas W. Merrill, Melms v. Pabst Brewing Co. and the Doctrine of Waste in American Property Law, 94 Marq. L. Rev. 1055 (2011).

---

27. This is known as the "open mines" doctrine. If the mines were opened by the grantor before he created the life estate, it is presumed that the grantor intended the life tenant to be able to continue mining. But if the mines were not open before the life estate was created, the life tenant cannot open them.

On the law of waste, see generally John A. Lovett, Doctrines of Waste in a Landscape of Waste, 72 Mo. L. Rev. 1209 (2007); Jedediah Purdy, The American Transformation of Waste Doctrine: A Pluralist Interpretation, 91 Cornell L. Rev. 653 (2006).

NOTE: SEISIN

The fee simple, the fee tail, and the life estate are *freehold estates*. The chief significance of this, at common law, was that a freeholder had *seisin*. Seisin was possession, of a particular kind and with peculiar consequences. Tenants seised of the land were responsible for feudal services, and feudal land law decreed that someone must always be seised. Dower and curtesy were given only to spouses of persons seised of the land (see page 408). Before 1536, a freehold estate could be created or transferred only by a ceremonial known as feoffment with *livery of seisin*. This usually included both the grantor and the grantee going on the land and the grantor, before witnesses, delivering seisin to the grantee by some symbolic act such as handing over a clod of dirt or some stalks or putting the grantee's hand on the ring of the door and uttering such words as "Know ye that I have given this land to (the grantee)." Even though livery was often accompanied by a written charter of feoffment, the act of turning over possession before witnesses attested a change of ownership in the clearest possible way.[28]

Seisin was endowed by the medieval mind with a real existence, illustrating again the philosophical tendency during that period to reify abstract ideas. Bracton, for example, writing between 1250 and 1268, regarded the lord of

---

28. If this ceremony strikes you as quaint, consider that manual delivery may still be required for gifts of tangible personal property. See pages 189-191. And with respect to modern transfers by will, just the right things must be said and done when the will is executed, or the will cannot be probated. See Thomas P. Gallanis, Family Property Law: Wills, Trusts, and Future Interests 112-134 (5th ed. 2011).

an English manor as seised of the estate until his corpse was carried from the manor house, when seisin passed to the heir. Henry de Bracton, De Legibus et Consuetudinibus Angliae, f. 41b.

E.   Leasehold Estates

Leasehold estates are nonfreehold possessory estates. Leasehold tenants do not have seisin. Leases originally were regarded as personal contracts between lessor and lessee outside the tenurial system. Leases were classed as personal property ("chattels real"). It was natural, then, that the law regarded the freeholder (land-lord) as still seised of the land even after he had granted a term of years and given up physical possession to the leasing tenant. When a lease is involved, the landlord holds seisin; the tenant merely has possession. Fortunately, this distinc-tion is of little importance today. It is usually not necessary to distinguish seisin from possession.

In the course of time, leaseholders were held to have an estate in land and were brought into the tenurial system. Modern leasehold estates include the term of years, the periodic tenancy, and the tenancy at will. Historically, the *term of years* was the most important of these. A term of years is an estate ending on a fixed cal-endar date, such as a term of five years or one year or six months. Terms of years are very common today in commercial and residential leasing. We shall consider leasehold estates at length in Chapter 6.

F.   Defeasible Estates

A fee simple may be absolute, meaning that it cannot be divested nor will it end upon the occurrence of any future event. Or a fee simple may be *defeasible*. Any estate may be made to be *defeasible*, meaning it will terminate, prior to its natural end point, upon the occurrence of some specified future event. For example, a life estate ends naturally at the death of the life tenant, whereas a defeasible life estate might end earlier than that (as in a conveyance that states, "*O* to *A* for life so long as the property is used only for residential purposes"). The most common defeasible freehold estates are the fees simple defeasible ("defeasible fees," as we will sometimes call them).

The modern functions of defeasible fees. Although, like estates generally, the ori-gins of defeasible fees are ancient, their functions remain relevant today. The primary purpose of defeasible fees is land use control; to a lesser extent they are used to control behavior not related to any particular use of land (for example, "to *A* and his heirs so long as *A* never drinks alcoholic beverages"). As instruments of land use control, defeasible fees are rather blunt, because their violation may result in forfeiture of ownership, and they have to a substantial extent been over-taken by restrictive covenants, which we will study in Chapter 10. But land owners still use them often enough to justify studying them.

There are three types of defeasible fees simple: the fee simple determinable, the fee simple subject to condition subsequent, and the fee simple subject to executory limitation (or, as some say it, subject to executory interest). A *fee simple determinable* is a fee simple so limited that it will end *automatically* when a stated event happens. Example: *O* conveys Blackacre "to the Hartford School Board, its successors and assigns, so long as the premises are used for school purposes." The fee simple may continue forever, but if the land ceases to be used for school purposes, the fee simple will come to an end or, using the old word, determine, and the fee simple will revert back to *O*, the grantor. A fee simple determinable is sometimes called a fee simple on a special limitation, indicating that the fee simple will expire by this limitation if it occurs.

A fee simple determinable is created by language connoting that the transferor is conveying a fee simple only until an event happens. In the example above, the words "so long as the premises are used for school purposes" connotes a determinable fee. Other language that would create a determinable fee includes "while used for school purposes," or "during the continuance of said school," or "until the Board no longer uses the land for a school," or any words with a *durational* aspect. Words that merely state the motive of the transferor in making a gift do not create a determinable fee; for example, a conveyance "to the Hartford School Board for school purposes" gives the Board a fee simple absolute and not a fee simple determinable.[29]

Every fee simple determinable is accompanied by a future interest. In the ordinary case the future interest is retained by the transferor, *O* in the above example, or his heirs, and called a *possibility of reverter*.[30] The possibility of reverter may be expressly retained or, as in the above example, arise by operation of law. It arises by operation of law because *O* has transferred less than his entire interest in Blackacre when he creates a determinable fee in the School Board.

(In the next two time lines and in several of the time lines both in this chapter and the next, ✳ represents the possessory estate's termination by operation of a limitation; ✕ represents the possessory estate's termination by operation of a condition.)

Time line 3-4

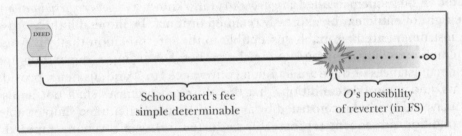

School Board's fee
simple determinable

O's possibility
of reverter (in FS)

29. This rule seems to be honored almost as often in the breach as in the observance. See Forsgren v. Sollie, 659 P.2d 1068 (Utah 1983), holding (3 to 2) that a deed providing, "This property is conveyed to be used as and for a church or residence purposes only," created a fee simple subject to condition subsequent.

30. When a future interest following a determinable fee is created in a transferee, it is called an executory interest. See pages 289-292.

A fee simple subject to condition subsequent is a fee simple that does not automatically terminate but *may be cut short* or divested at the transferor's election when a stated condition happens. Example: *O* conveys Whiteacre "to the Hartford School Board, its successors and assigns, but if the premises are not used for school purposes, the grantor has a right to re-enter and retake the premises." Observe that we have used a different verbal formula than that creating a determinable fee. The Board's fee simple may be cut short if *O* elects to exercise the right of entry, but it is not automatically terminated when the stated event happens. Unless and until entry is made, the fee simple continues. That is the essential difference between these two defeasible fees.

Time line 3-5

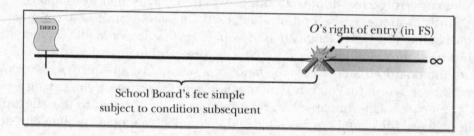

School Board's fee simple
subject to condition subsequent

A fee simple subject to condition subsequent is created by a conveyance of a fee simple, followed by language providing that the fee simple may be divested by the transferor if a specified event happens. In the above example, the clause beginning with "but if . . ." states a condition subsequent. Other language creating a condition subsequent, after conveying a fee simple, includes "provided, however, that when the premises . . . ," or "on condition that if the premises . . . ," or other words indicating that the estate may be cut short at the transferor's election. The difference between language creating a determinable fee and language creating a fee simple subject to condition subsequent is extremely subtle, but millions of dollars have turned on this difference in language.

The future interest retained by the transferor to divest a fee simple subject to condition subsequent is called a *right of entry* (also known as a *power of termination*).[31] The right of entry may be expressly retained or it may be implied if the words of the instrument are reasonably susceptible to the interpretation that this type of forfeiture estate was contemplated by the parties. For example, depending upon the circumstances of the transaction, a conveyance "to *A* and his heirs, provided always, and upon this condition, that the aforesaid premises shall not be used for a tavern," might be construed by a court to create either a fee simple subject to condition subsequent (enforceable by forfeiture) or a covenant imposed to benefit the grantor's retained land (enforceable by injunction or damages). It is

---

31. A right of entry, like a possibility of reverter, may be retained only by the transferor or his heirs. It may not be created in a transferee.

always wise, of course, to avoid litigation by expressly including a right of entry if that is intended.

A *fee simple subject to executory limitation* is the estate created when a grantor transfers a fee simple subject to condition subsequent, and in the same instrument creates a future interest in a third party rather than in himself. The future interest in the third party is called an executory interest. (We will study executory interests in Chapter 4.) Thus, if *O* conveys land "to the Hartford School Board, but if it ceases to use the land as a school, to the City Library," the School Board has a fee simple subject to executory limitation, and the City Library has an executory interest.[32] A fee simple subject to condition subsequent and a fee simple subject to executory limitation are created by the same language. The distinction between the two is based on the type of future interest following it. A fee simple subject to condition subsequent is followed by a right of entry, whereas a fee simple subject to executory limitation is followed by an executory interest.

Note well an important difference between the fee simple subject to condition subsequent and the fee simple subject to executory limitation: If the condition is breached the former is forfeited only if the right of entry is exercised, but the latter is forfeited immediately, regardless of any action on the part of the holder of the executory interest to take possession. The reason for this difference grows out of the English Statute of Uses (1536), which we will discuss in Chapter 4.

Time line 3-6

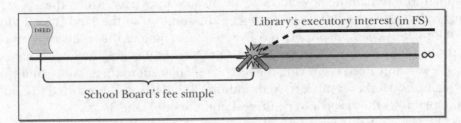

Lawyers, when using the term fee simple, ordinarily have in mind a fee simple absolute. We follow that practice. When we have a fee simple defeasible in mind, we say so.

---

32. Suppose instead that the conveyance was "to the Hartford School Board so long as it uses the land as a school, then to the City Library." Here *O* has created a fee simple determinable (thanks to the "so long as" language) in the School Board, followed by an executory interest in the Library. Hence the state of title is a fee simple determinable in the School Board followed by an executory interest.

Mahrenholz v. County Board of School Trustees

Appellate Court of Illinois, 1981
417 N.E.2d 138

JONES, J. This case involves an action to quiet title to real property located in Lawrence County, Illinois. Its resolution depends on the judicial construction of language in a conveyance of that property. The case is before us on the pleadings, plaintiffs' third amended complaint having been dismissed by a final order. The pertinent facts are taken from the pleadings.

On March 18, 1941, W.E. and Jennie Hutton executed a warranty deed in which they conveyed [1½ acres out of 40 acres they owned], to be known here as the Hutton School grounds, to the Trustees of School District No. 1, the predecessors of the defendants in this action. The deed provided that "this land to be used for school purpose only; otherwise to revert to Grantors herein." W.E. Hutton died intestate on July 18, 1951, and Jennie Hutton died intestate on February 18, 1969. The Huttons left as their only legal heir their son Harry E. Hutton.

The property conveyed by the Huttons became the site of the Hutton School. Community Unit School District No. 20 succeeded to the grantee of the deed and held classes in the building constructed upon the land until May 30, 1973. After that date, children were transported to classes held at other facilities operated by the District. The District has used the property since then for storage purposes only. . . .

[In July 1941, W.E. and Jennie Hutton conveyed to Earl and Madeline Jacqmain the remaining 38½ acres of the 40-acre tract from which the 1½ acres conveyed to the school board were taken. In addition to the land surrounding the school, this deed purported to convey to the Jacqmains the reversionary interest the Huttons held in the school land. On October 9, 1959, the Jacqmains executed a warranty deed conveying the 38½ acres adjacent to the school grounds to the plaintiffs, Herbert and Betty Mahrenholz. This deed also purported to convey to the plaintiffs the reversionary interest in the school land.]

On May 7, 1977, Harry E. Hutton, son and sole heir of W.E. and Jennie Hutton, conveyed to the plaintiffs all of his interest in the Hutton School land. This document was filed in the recorder's office of Lawrence County on September 7, 1977. On September 6, 1977, Harry Hutton disclaimed his interest in the property in favor of the defendants. The disclaimer was in the form of a written document entitled "Disclaimer and Release." It contained the legal description of the Hutton School grounds and recited that Harry E. Hutton disclaimed and released any possibility of reverter or right of entry for condition broken, or other similar interest, in favor of the County Board of School Trustees for Lawrence County, Illinois, successor to the Trustees of School District No. 1 of Lawrence County, Illinois. The document further recited that it was made for the purpose of releasing and extinguishing any right Harry E. Hutton may have had in the "interest retained by W.E. Hutton and Jennie Hutton . . . in that deed to the Trustees of School District No. 1, Lawrence County, Illinois dated March 18, 1941, and filed on the same date. . . ." The disclaimer was filed in the recorder's office of Lawrence County on October 4, 1977.

The plaintiffs filed a complaint in the circuit court of Lawrence County . . . in which they sought to quiet title to the school property in themselves. . . . On March 21, 1979, the trial court entered an order dismissing this complaint. In the order the court found that the

> [W]arranty deed dated March 18, 1941, from W.E. Hutton and Jennie Hutton to the Trustees of School District No. 1, conveying land here concerned, created a fee simple subject to a condition subsequent followed by the right of entry for condition broken, rather than a determinable fee followed by a possibility of reverter.

Plaintiffs have perfected an appeal to this court.

The basic issue presented by this appeal is whether the trial court correctly concluded that the plaintiffs could not have acquired any interest in the school property from the Jacqmains and Harry Hutton. Resolution of this issue must turn upon the legal interpretation of the language contained in the March 18, 1941, deed from W.E. and Jennie Hutton to the Trustees of School District No. 1: "this land to be used for school purpose only; otherwise to revert to Grantors herein." In addition to the legal effect of this language we must consider the alienability of the interest created and the effect of subsequent deeds.

The parties appear to be in agreement that the 1941 deed from the Huttons conveyed a defeasible fee simple estate to the grantee, and gave rise to a future interest in the grantors (see Restatement of the Law, Property, sec. 153), and that it did not convey a fee simple absolute, subject to a covenant. The fact that provision was made for forfeiture of the estate conveyed should the land cease to be used for school purposes suggests that this view is correct. Dunne v. Minsor (1924), 312 Ill. 333, 143 N.E. 842; Newton v. Village of Glen Ellyn (1940), 374 Ill. 50, 27 N.E.2d 821. Restatement of the Law, Property, secs. 44, 45.

The future interest remaining in this grantor or his estate can only be a possibility of reverter or a right of re-entry for condition broken. As neither interest may be transferred by will or by inter vivos conveyance (Ill. Rev. Stat., ch. 30, par. 37b), and as the land was being used for school purposes in 1959 when the Jacqmains transferred their interest in the school property to the plaintiffs, the trial court correctly ruled that the plaintiffs could not have acquired any interest in that property from the Jacqmains by the deed of October 9, 1959.

Consequently this court must determine whether the plaintiffs could have acquired an interest in the Hutton School grounds from Harry Hutton. The resolution of this issue depends on the construction of the language of the 1941 deed of the Huttons to the school district. As urged by the defendants and as the trial court found, the deed conveyed a fee simple subject to a condition subsequent followed by a right of reentry for condition broken. As argued by the plaintiffs, on the other hand, the deed conveyed a fee simple determinable followed by a possibility of reverter. In either case, the grantor and his heirs retain an interest in the property which may become possessory if the condition is broken. We emphasize here that although sec. 1 of An Act relating to Rights of Entry or Reentry for breach of condition subsequent and possibilities of reverter effective July 21, 1947 (Ill. Rev. Stat., ch. 30, par. 37b) provides that rights of re-entry for condition broken and possibilities of reverter are neither alienable or devisable, they are inheritable. (Deverick v. Bline (1950), 404 Ill. 302, 89 N.E.2d 43.) The type of interest held governs the mode of reinvestment with title if reinvestment is to occur. If the grantor had a possibility of reverter, he or his heirs become the owner of the property by operation of law as soon as the condition is broken. If he has a right of re-entry for condition broken, he or his heirs become the owner of the property only after they act to retake the property.

It is alleged, and we must accept, that classes were last held in the Hutton School in 1973. Harry Hutton, sole heir of the grantors, did not act to legally retake the premises but instead conveyed his interest in that land to the plaintiffs in 1977. If Harry Hutton had only a naked right of re-entry for condition broken, then he could not be the owner of that property until he had legally re-entered the land. Since he took no steps for a legal re-entry, he had only a right of re-entry in 1977, and that right cannot be conveyed inter vivos. On the other hand, if Harry Hutton had a possibility of reverter in the property, then he owned the school property as soon as it ceased to be used for school purposes. Therefore, assuming (1) that cessation of classes constitutes "abandonment of school purposes" on the land, (2) that the conveyance from Harry Hutton to the plaintiffs was legally correct, and (3) that the conveyance was not pre-empted by Hutton's disclaimer in favor of the school district, the plaintiffs could have acquired an interest in the Hutton School grounds if Harry Hutton had inherited a possibility of reverter from his parents.

The difference between a fee simple determinable (or, determinable fee) and a fee simple subject to a condition subsequent, is solely a matter of judicial interpretation of the words of a grant. . . . [T]he Huttons would have created a fee simple determinable if they had allowed the school district to retain the property *so long as* or *while* it was used for school purposes, or *until* it ceased to be so used. Similarly, a fee simple subject to a condition subsequent would have arisen had the Huttons given the land *upon condition that* or *provided that* it be used for school purposes. In the 1941 deed, though the Huttons gave the land "to be used for school purpose only, otherwise to revert to Grantors herein," no words of temporal limitation, or terms of express condition, were used in the grant.

The plaintiffs argue that the word "only" should be construed as a limitation rather than a condition. The defendants respond that where ambiguous language is used in a deed, the courts of Illinois have expressed a constructional preference for a fee simple subject to a condition subsequent. (Storke v. Penn Mutual Life Ins. Co. (1945), 390 Ill. 619, 61 N.E.2d 552.) Both sides refer us to cases involving deeds which contain language analogous to the 1941 grant in this case.

We believe that a close analysis of the wording of the original grant shows that the grantors intended to create a fee simple determinable followed by a possibility of reverter. Here, the use of the word "only" immediately following the grant "for school purpose" demonstrates that the Huttons wanted to give the land to the school district only as long as it was needed and no longer. The language "this land to be used for school purpose only" is an example of a grant which contains a limitation within the granting clause. It suggests a limited grant, rather than a full grant subject to a condition, and thus, both theoretically and linguistically, gives rise to a fee simple determinable.

The second relevant clause furnishes plaintiff's position with additional support. It cannot be argued that the phrase "otherwise to revert to grantors herein" is inconsistent with a fee simple subject to a condition subsequent. Nor does the word "revert" automatically create a possibility of reverter. But, in combination with the preceding phrase, the provisions by which possession is returned to the grantors seem to trigger a mandatory return rather than a permissive return because it is not stated that the grantor "may" re-enter the land. See City of Urbana v. Solo Cup Co. (4th Dist. 1979), 66 Ill. App. 3d 45, 22 Ill. Dec. 786, 383 N.E.2d 262.

The terms used in the 1941 deed, although imprecise, were designed to allow the property to be used for a single purpose, namely, for "school purpose." The Huttons intended to have the land back if it were ever used otherwise. Upon a grant of exclusive use followed by an express provision for reverter when that use ceases, courts and commentators have agreed that a fee simple determinable, rather than a fee simple subject to a condition subsequent, is created. (1 Simes and Smith, The Law of Future Interests (2nd ed. 1956) sec. 286 n.58.) Our own research has uncovered cases from other jurisdictions and sources in which language very similar to that in the Hutton deed has been held to create a fee simple determinable:

> A conveyance "for the use, intent and purpose of a site for a School House [and] whenever the said School District removes the School House from said tract of land or whenever said School House ceases to be used as the Public School House . . . then the said Trust shall cease and determine and the said land shall revert to the grantor and his heirs." [Consolidated School District v. Walter (1954), 243 Minn. 159, 66 N.W.2d 881, 882.]
>
> [I]t being absolutely understood that when said land ceases to be used for school purposes it is to revert to the above grantor, his heirs. [U.S. v. 1119.15 Acres of Land (E.D. Ill. 1942), 44 F. Supp. 449.]
>
> That I, S.S. Gray (Widower), for and in consideration of the sum of Donation to Wheeler School District to be used by said Wheeler Special School District for school and church purposes and to revert to me should school and church be discontinued or moved. [Williams v. Kirby School District (Ark. 1944), 181 S.W.2d 488, 490.]
>
> It is understood and agreed that if the above described land is abandoned by the said second parties and not used for school purposes then the above described land reverts to the party of the first part. [School District No. 6 v. Russell (1964), 156 Colo. 75, 396 P.2d 929, 930.]
>
> [T]o B and C [trustees of a school district] and their heirs and successors for school purposes and to revert to the grantor when it ceases to be so used. [Restatement of Property, sec. 44, comment 1, illustration V (1936).]

Thus, authority from this state and others indicates that the grant in the Hutton deed did in fact create a fee simple determinable. We are not persuaded by the cases cited by the defendants for the terms of conveyance in those cases distinguish them from the facts presented here. . . .

The estate created in Latham v. Illinois Central Railroad Co. (1912), 253 Ill. 93, 97 N.E. 254, was held to be a fee simple subject to a condition subsequent.

Land was conveyed to a railroad in return for the railroad's agreement to erect and maintain a passenger depot and a freight depot on the premises. The deed was made to the grantee, "their successors and assigns forever, for the uses and purposes hereinafter mentioned and for NONE other." Those purposes were limited to "railroad purposes only." The deed provided "that in case of non-user of said premises so conveyed for the uses and purposes aforesaid, that then and in that case the title to said premises shall revert back to [the grantors], their heirs, executors, administrators and assigns." The property was granted to the railroad to have and hold forever, "subject, nevertheless, to all the conditions, covenants, agreements and limitations in this deed expressed." The estate in *Latham* may be distinguished from that created here in that the former was a grant "forever" which was subjected to certain use restrictions while the Hutton deed gave the property to the school district only as long as it could use it. . . .

The defendants also direct our attention to the case of McElvain v. Dorris (1921), 298 Ill. 377, 131 N.E. 608. There, land was sold subject to the following condition: "This tract of land is to be used for mill purposes, and if not used for mill purposes the title reverts back to the former owner." When the mill was abandoned, the heirs of the grantor brought suit in ejectment and were successful. The Supreme Court of Illinois did not mention the possibility that the quoted words could have created a fee simple determinable but instead stated,

> Annexed to the grant there was a condition subsequent, by a breach of which there would be a right of re-entry by the grantor or her heirs at law. [Citations.] A breach of the condition in such a case does not, of itself, determine the estate, but an entry, or some act equivalent thereto, is necessary to revest the estate, and bringing a suit in ejectment is equivalent to such reentry. [298 Ill. at 379, 131 N.E. 608.]

It is urged by the defendants that McElvain v. Dorris stands for the proposition that the quoted language in the deed creates a fee simple subject to a condition subsequent. We must agree with the defendants that the grant in *McElvain* is strikingly similar to that in this case. However, the opinion in *McElvain* is ambiguous in several respects. First, that portion of the opinion which states that "Annexed to the grant there was a condition subsequent . . ." may refer to the provision quoted above, or it may refer to another provision not reproduced in the opinion. Second, even if the court's reference is to the quoted language, the holding may reflect only the court's acceptance of the parties' construction of the grant. (A similar procedure was followed in Trustees of Schools v. Batdorf (1955), 6 Ill. 2d 486, 130 N.E.2d Ill., as noted by defendants.) After all, as an action inejectment was brought in *McElvain,* the difference between a fee simple determinable and a fee simple subject to a condition subsequent would have no practical effect and the court did not discuss it.

To the extent that *McElvain* holds that the quoted language establishes a fee simple subject to a condition subsequent, it is contrary to the weight of Illinois and American authority. A more appropriate case with which to resolve the problem presented here is North v. Graham (1908), 235 Ill. 178, 85 N.E. 267. Land was conveyed to trustees of a church under a deed which stated that "said tract of land above described to revert to the party of the first part whenever it ceases to be used or occupied for a meeting house or church." Following an extended discussion of determinable fees, the court concluded that such an estate is legal in Illinois and that the language of the deed did in fact create that estate.

North v. Graham, like this case, falls somewhere between those cases in which appears the classic language used to create a fee simple determinable and that used to create a fee simple subject to a condition subsequent. . . .

Although the word "whenever" is used in the North v. Graham deed, it is not found in a granting clause, but in a reverter clause. The court found this slightly unorthodox construction sufficient to create a fee simple determinable, and we believe that the word "only" placed in the granting clause of the Hutton deed brings this case under the rule of North v. Graham.

We hold, therefore, that the 1941 deed from W.E. and Jennie Hutton to the Trustees of School District No. 1 created a fee simple determinable in the Trustees followed by a possibility of reverter in the Huttons and their heirs. Accordingly, the trial court erred in dismissing plaintiffs' . . . complaint which followed its holding that the plaintiffs could not have acquired any interest in the Hutton School property from Harry Hutton. We must therefore reverse and remand this cause to the trial court for further proceedings.

We refrain from deciding the following issues: (1) whether the 1977 conveyance from Harry Hutton was legally sufficient to pass his interest in the school property to the plaintiffs, (2) whether Harry Hutton effectively disclaimed his interest in the property in favor of the defendants by virtue of his 1977 disclaimer, and (3) whether the defendants have ceased to use the Hutton School grounds for "school purposes." . . .

Reversed and remanded.

NOTES, QUESTIONS, AND PROBLEM

1. *FSD or FSCD, and why does it matter?* Several possible situations exist where different legal consequences might result from classifying an estate as a fee simple determinable with a possibility of reverter rather than a fee simple subject to a right of entry. The most important situation relates to transferability of the future interest—the problem in the *Mahrenholz* case.

At common law a possibility of reverter and a right of entry descended to heirs upon the death of the owner of such interests. But, curiously enough, neither interest was transferable during life. A possibility of reverter was not transferable during life because it was not thought of as a property interest (a "thing") you could transfer but as a "mere possibility of becoming an estate" (as, before we understood the nature of matter, we would think of gas which might pass into a solid). A right of entry was not transferable because it too was not a "thing"; rather it was thought of as a special right in the grantor to forfeit the grantee's estate. It was like a chose in action (a right to sue), and choses in action were inalienable until modern times. You might assume that because we now think of these interests as things, and because these interests are inheritable by heirs and devisable by will, we would discard the rule that they cannot be transferred during life. But history has left curious traces in our law.

In most American states the possibility of reverter and the right of entry, like other property interests, are transferable inter vivos. This is the modern trend. But some states continue to follow the common law rule; the interests are not transferable inter vivos except to the owner of the possessory fee (called a release). A few states appear to draw a distinction between the two interests and hold that the possibility of reverter is transferable, but the right of entry is not. In a couple of states the right of entry has been given even harsher treatment: The mere attempt to transfer a right of entry during life destroys it. For discussion of these various positions, with citations to states, see Powell on Real Property §21.02 (Michael A. Wolf gen. ed. 2009).

In another situation where different legal consequences might flow from the fact that a possibility of reverter becomes possessory automatically whereas a right of entry requires a positive act by the grantor to terminate the fee simple, adverse possession is involved. The statute of limitations starts running on the possibility of reverter as soon as the determinable fee ends. With respect to the right of entry, theoretically the statute of limitations should not begin to run until the grantor attempts to exercise the right and is rebuffed, giving rise to a cause of action. However, this may be more theory than reality. In many states the statute begins to run on the right of entry when the condition occurs. Or, analogizing to the equitable doctrine of laches, which bars relief when delay works injury, prejudice, or disadvantage to the defendant, courts in other states may require the right of entry to be exercised within a reasonable time, which in turn may be defined as the period of the statute of limitations. See Mildram v. Town of Wells, 611 A.2d 84 (Me. 1992).

For discussion of these and other possible differences, see William B. Stoebuck & Dale A. Whitman, The Law of Property §2.7 (3d ed. 2000).

As *Mahrenholz* vividly illustrates, disputes and litigation can easily arise when lawyers are less careful than they should be in selecting precisely correct legal terminology as they draft deeds and other legal instruments used to transfer estates. Language matters—but perhaps sometimes too much. Given the trouble it invites, is it sensible to continue the distinction between the fee simple determinable and the fee simple subject to condition subsequent? Should dramatically different consequences turn on fine distinctions unwittingly overlooked? California and Kentucky have abolished the fee simple determinable with statutes providing that language creating a fee simple determinable at common law creates a fee simple subject to condition subsequent. Cal. Civ. Code §885.020 (West 2007); Ky. Rev. Stat. Ann. §381.218 (2006).

The new Restatement draft abolishes the distinctions among the three types of defeasible fees (the fee simple determinable, fee simple subject to a condition subsequent, and fee simple subject to an executory limitation). It replaces them with a single estate, the *fee simple defeasible*, defined as "a present interest that terminates upon the happening of a stated event that might or might not occur." Restatement (Third) of Property, Wills and Other Donative Transfers §24.3 (2011). Hence, if

O conveys land "to Grantee School District so long as the land is used for school purposes; upon the land being used for non-school purposes, the land is to revert to the Grantor," under the Restatement this would create a fee simple defeasible, rather than a fee simple determinable; the School District's interest would terminate upon the occurrence of an event that might or might not occur (the District using the land for non-school purposes). Id. §24.3 comment g.

2. *Problem. O* conveys Blackacre "to *A* and her heirs so long as the premises are not used for sale of beer, wine, or liquor, and if beer, wine, or liquor is sold on the premises *O* retains a right to re-enter the premises." Subsequently *A* opens a restaurant on Blackacre that serves several dishes cooked with wine or flamed with brandy and at Sunday brunch offers a complimentary glass of champagne. *A*'s restaurant is successful, and 11 years after its opening *B* wants to buy it and add a bar. Advise *B*.

3. *Sequel to* Mahrenholz. In *Mahrenholz* the land was given for "school purpose" only. What is a school purpose? In a sequel to *Mahrenholz,* the court held that use of the Hutton School property to store school equipment and supplies, primarily used desks, was for a school purpose, and therefore the Mahrenholzes were not entitled to the property. Mahrenholz v. County Bd. of School Trustees, 544 N.E.2d 128 (Ill. App. 1989).

Suppose that the school board permits the school auditorium to be used by various community groups, including a Christian Revival, or suppose it rents the auditorium to a promoter who stages various entertainments, including a touring ballet company and a rock band. Would the land revert? Or suppose that the school board executes an oil and gas lease and oil wells are drilled, striking oil. Would the land revert to the grantors' successors? Could the grantors' successors obtain an injunction to prevent taking oil from the land on the theory that such would constitute waste and a destruction of the value of the possibility of reverter? See Davis v. Skipper, 83 S.W.2d 318 (Tex. 1935) (holding that title did not revert because the church building was still being used for a church and because the present owner of a fee simple determinable has "all the incidents of a fee simple" and could therefore extract oil from the land).

4. *Substantial compliance?* Should courts adopt a substantial compliance approach in determining whether a use complies with a limitation or a condition? In Ator v. Unknown Heirs, 146 P.3d 821 (Okla. App. 2006), Thelma Ator and her husband deeded a parcel of vacant land to the School District of Owasso, Oklahoma, "for so long as said real property shall be used for such purposes as a part of a regularly organized and fully scheduled program of football practice and playing; . . . if at any time . . . [School District] shall fail to comply fully with the terms of this deed . . . or observe the spirit thereof, this grant shall become null and void and the full fee simple title to said property shall revert to and vest in [grantors], their heirs and assigns forever." Following the conveyance, the School District built on the conveyed property a football stadium and practice field known as Ator Field. Some 40 years later, however, the District built a new stadium elsewhere and no longer held any of its games at Ator Field, which became a practice and scrimmage facility for its eighth- and ninth-grade teams.

256   3. Possessory Estates

The District also permitted a private organization known as the Future Owasso Rams to use the property for its home games. Thelma Ator's sole heir claimed that the School District forfeited the property when it moved its regular football games from Ator Field to the new stadium and that she owned the land in fee simple as a consequence. The School District argued that substantial, not strict, compliance with the terms of the deed is all that the law requires and that the current use of Ator Field substantially complied with the limitation in Thelma Ator's deed. What is your reaction to this argument?

5. *Covenants distinguished.* Conditions imposed by the grantor in creating defeasible fees must be distinguished from covenants (promises) made by a grantee. A condition is much more onerous than a covenant. If a condition is breached, the land is or may be *forfeited* to the holder of the future interest. A covenant is a promise by the grantee that a specified act will or will not be performed. If a covenant is breached, the promisee may sue for an *injunction* or *damages.* Example: *O* conveys Blackacre "to *A,* who promises on behalf of himself, his heirs, and assigns that Blackacre will be used only for residential purposes." If *A* erects a slaughterhouse on Blackacre, *O* can sue *A* for an injunction to have the slaughterhouse removed or *O* can sue *A* for damages. We discuss covenants in Chapter 10.

6. *Duration of possibilities of reverter and rights of entry in Illinois.* At the time of the decision in *Mahrenholz,* Illinois had a statute that placed a 40-year limit on the duration of possibilities of reverter and rights of entry. The time limit applied to reverters and rights of entry existing at the time of enactment. The current version of the statute is Ill. Comp. Stat. Ann. c. 765, 3304 (2012). We discuss this type of statute in Chapter 4. See page 315.

Tad Walch, Maeser School Crisis Over

Deseret Morning News, Sept. 25, 2007, available at http://www.deseretnews.com/article/695212965/Maeser-School-crisis-over.html

Provo—The wacky, 109-year-old tale of the overlooked 1898 deed has a happy ending, with a settlement that averts a potential crisis for the award-winning renovation of central Provo's historic Maeser School.

The heirs of Ed Loose dropped their claim to about 1 acre of land given a century ago by Loose to the Provo School District. In exchange, the title companies that failed to uncover Loose's two forgotten, handwritten deeds, will pay for a memorial outside the school. Loose donated the land on one condition—it always remain a playground for the elementary school or be returned to his family.

The two title companies will pay $20,000—up to $10,000 for the memorial to Loose and $10,000 for a scholarship fund and attorney fees.

Loose donated the land in two parts, one in 1898 and the other in 1910, with deeds both apparently in his own hand.

The school district closed Maeser Elementary School five years ago and nearly demolished the historic building. The nonprofit Provo Housing Authority rescued it from the wrecking ball three years ago by buying it and launching a drive to renovate it as affordable senior housing.

The creative mix of 14 grants and loans worth $5.2 million that financed the project could have unraveled when the deeds surfaced.

The funding came with conditions, too—not only would the renovation have to be completed, but a dozen homes had to be built around the school and sold to first-time homebuyers through a self-help affordable housing program.

Construction was under way when Loose's great-grandson, Ed Peterson, learned of the deeds, which didn't turn up in four separate searches conducted by First American Title Insurance Co. and Fidelity Title Insurance Co. The news stunned housing authority executive director Doug Carlson.

"It was a surprise and shock," Carlson said. "This came totally out of the blue. For a brief moment, I was fearful three years of hard work and several million dollars were in jeopardy."

Peterson, named for his great-grandfather, said the heirs wanted to protect what he called a "classy" renovation that has won six major awards for beauty, historic rehabilitation and city planning.

"I'm tickled pink by what they've done there," he said. "It's a marvelous public project. My great-grandfather would be proud of it."

Peterson said the .95 acres may have been worth up to $250,000. The nonprofit housing authority didn't have the money to buy it and had been told by the title insurance companies the land was clear of any encumbrances.

"This is why you buy title insurance," Carlson said. "The money we spent in title insurance policies was money well spent."

The Maeser School Apartments opened in November and now has clear title. So do Jose and Meagan Sanchez, whose new home sits on a corner of the land Loose donated.

Construction on the final seven homes around the former school can now begin. They must be completed by next summer to meet a deadline for funding all of the projects.

The Charles Edwin Loose and Mary Jane Loose Memorial at Maeser School will be a plaza with a sandstone plaque bearing the images of the colorful Loose, present as a 12-year-old when the Golden Spike was driven in Utah, and his wife.

Peterson said $5,000 will go to a scholarship fund in his father's name, Edwin L. Peterson, at Utah State University. The scholarship is presented each year to a student who wants to teach geography, as Loose's grandson did at USU.

The final $5,000 goes to one of the heirs to cover attorney's fees.

First American Title and Fidelity Title will each contribute $10,000, according to a copy of the settlement obtained by the Deseret Morning News.

First American Title officials declined to talk about the Maeser/Loose deed specifically, but it isn't unusual for a title search to stop short of exploring back 100 years, company vice-president and regional counsel Blake Heiner said.

Loose's condition that if the playground was removed the property would be returned to his family called a right of reverter—is extremely rare.

"I would have to say, in my 30 years in this business, this is the first time I've seen a right of reverter anywhere but in a law school exam," Heiner said. "These type of things don't happen in today's world."

Many neighbors were angry to lose the school park, but efforts to build the required new homes elsewhere failed. Major Provo parks sit three and four blocks away from the former school.

Carlson said the public is invited to enjoy the Loose Plaza.

Mountain Brow Lodge No. 82, Independent Order of Odd Fellows v. Toscano

Court of Appeal of California, Fifth District, 1967
64 Cal. Rptr. 816

GARGANO, J. This action was instituted by appellant, a non-profit corporation,[33] to quiet its title to a parcel of real property which it acquired on April 6, 1950, by gift deed from James V. Toscano and Maria Toscano, both deceased. Respondents are the trustees and administrators of the estates of the deceased grantors and appellant sought to quiet its title as to their interest in the land arising from certain conditions contained in the gift deed.

The matter was submitted to the court on stipulated facts and the court rendered judgment in favor of respondents. However, it is not clear from the court's findings of fact and conclusions of law whether it determined that the conditions were not void and hence refused to quiet appellant's title for this reason, or whether it decided that appellant had not broken the conditions and then erroneously concluded that "neither party has a right to an anticipatory decree" until a violation occurs. Thus, to avoid prolonged litigation the parties have stipulated that when the trial court rendered judgment refusing to quiet appellant's title it simply decided that the conditions are not void and that its decision on this limited issue is the only question presented in this appeal. We shall limit our discussion accordingly.

The controversy between the parties centers on the language contained in the habendum clause of the deed of conveyance which reads as follows:

Said property is restricted for the use and benefit of the second party, only; and in the event the same fails to be used by the second party or in the event of sale or transfer by the second party of all or any part of said lot, the same is to revert to the first parties herein, their successors, heirs or assigns.

33. There is no authoritative explanation for the odd name "Odd Fellows." One explanation is that the original Odd Fellows were people who engaged in various, or odd, trades. Organizations already existed for larger trades, so tradespeople in other, smaller trades decided to form their own fellowship for fraternity and mutual support. Whatever the reason for the name, the Odd Fellowship was first created in England during the eighteenth century when the industrial revolution, which weakened the apprentice system, left young workers vulnerable if they became sick or injured. One of their principal emblems was a bundle of sticks, though it did not carry the same meaning as it does to modern property students. See Don R. Smith & Wayne Roberts, The Three Link Fraternity: Odd Fellowship in California (1993). — EDS.

Respondents maintain that the language creates a fee simple subject to a condition subsequent and is valid and enforceable. On the other hand, appellant contends that the restrictive language amounts to an absolute restraint on its power of alienation and is void. It apparently asserts that, since the purpose for which the land must be used is not precisely defined, it may be used by appellant for any purpose and hence the restriction is not on the land use but on who uses it. Thus, appellant concludes that it is clear that the reversionary clause was intended by grantors to take effect only if appellant sells or transfers the land.

Admittedly, the condition of the habendum clause which prohibits appellant from selling or transferring the land under penalty of forfeiture is an absolute restraint against alienation and is void. The common law rule prohibiting restraint against alienation is embodied in Civil Code section 711 which provides: "Conditions restraining alienation, when repugnant to the interest created, are void." However, this condition and the condition relating to the use of the land are in the disjunctive and are clearly severable. In other words, under the plain language of the deed the grantors, their successors or assigns may exercise their power of termination "if the land is not used by the second party" or "in the event of sale or transfer by the second party." Thus, the invalid restraint against alienation does not necessarily affect or nullify the condition on land use (Los Angeles Investment Company v. Gary, 181 Cal. 680, 186 P. 596, 9 A.L.R. 115).

The remaining question, therefore, is whether the use condition created a defeasible fee as respondents maintain or whether it is also a restraint against alienation and nothing more as appellant alleges. Significantly, appellant is a non-profit corporation organized for lodge, fraternal and similar purposes. Moreover, decedent, James V. Toscano, was an active member of the lodge at the time of his death. In addition, the term "use" as applied to real property can be construed to mean a "right which a person has to use or enjoy the property of another according to his necessities" (Mulford v. LeFranc (1864), 26 Cal. 88, 102). Under these circumstances it is reasonably clear that when the grantors stated that the land was conveyed in consideration of "love and affection" and added that it "is restricted for the *use* and benefit of the second party" they simply meant to say that the land was conveyed upon condition that it would be used for lodge, fraternal and other purposes for which the non-profit corporation was formed. Thus, we conclude that the portion of the habendum clause relating to the land use, when construed as a whole and in light of the surrounding circumstances, created a fee subject to a condition subsequent with title to revert to the grantors, their successors or assigns if the land ceases to be used for lodge, fraternal and similar purposes for which the appellant is formed.[34] No formal language is necessary to create a fee simple subject to a condition subsequent as long as the intent of the grantor is clear. It is the rule that the object in construing a deed is to ascertain the intention of the grantor from words which have been employed and

---

34. It is arguable that the gift deed created a fee simple determinable. However, in doubtful cases the preferred construction is in favor of an estate subject to a condition subsequent (2 Witkin, Summary Calif. Law., Real Prop. §97, pp. 949-950).

Odd Fellows Building, Los Banos
erected 1919, meeting rooms above, stores below

The tract of land given the lodge by the Toscanos,
adjacent to the rear of the building, is used as a parking lot.

from surrounding circumstances (Brannan v. Mesick, 10 Cal. 95; Aller v. Berkeley Hall School Foundation, 40 Cal. App. 2d 31, 103 P.2d 1052; Schofield v. Bany, 175 Cal. App. 2d 534, 346 P.2d 891).

It is of course arguable, as appellant suggests, that the condition in appellant's deed is not a restriction on land use but on who uses it. Be this as it may, the distinction between a covenant which restrains the alienation of a fee simple absolute and a condition which restricts land use and creates a defeasible estate was long recognized at common law and is recognized in this state.[35] Thus, conditions restricting land use have been upheld by the California courts on numerous occasions even though they hamper, and often completely impede, alienation. A few examples follow: Mitchell v. Cheney Slough Irrigation Co., 57 Cal. App. 2d 138, 134 P.2d 34 (irrigation ditch); Aller v. Berkeley Hall School Foundation, 40 Cal. App. 2d 31, 103 P.2d 1052 (exclusively private dwellings); Rosecrans v. Pacific Electric Railway Co., 21 Cal. 2d 602, 134 P.2d 245 (to maintain a train schedule); Schultz v. Beers, 111 Cal. App. 2d 820, 245 P.2d 334 (road purposes); Firth v. Marovich, 160 Cal. 257, 116 P. 729 (residence only).

Moreover, if appellant's suggestion is carried to its logical conclusion it would mean that real property could not be conveyed to a city to be used only for its own city purposes, or to a school district to be used only for its own school purposes, or to a church to be used only for its own church purposes. Such restrictions would also be restrictions upon who uses the land. And yet we do not understand this to be the rule of this state. For example, in Los Angeles Investment Company v. Gary, supra, 181 Cal. 680, 186 P. 596, land had been conveyed upon condition that it was not to be sold, leased, rented or occupied by persons other than those of Caucasian race. The court held that the condition against alienation of the land was void, but upheld the condition restricting the land use. Although a use restriction compelling racial discrimination is no longer consonant with constitutional principles under more recent decisions, the sharp distinction that the court drew between a restriction on land use and a restriction on alienation is still valid. For further example, in the leading and often cited case of Johnston v. City of Los Angeles, 176 Cal. 479, 168 P. 1047, the land was conveyed to the City of Los Angeles on the express condition that the city would use it for the erection and maintenance of a dam, the land to revert if the city ceased to use it for such purposes. The Supreme Court held that the condition created a defeasible estate, apparently even though it was by necessity a restriction on who could use the land.

Our independent research indicates that the rule is the same in other jurisdictions. In Regular Predestinarian Baptist Church of Pleasant Grove v. Parker, 373 Ill. 607, 27 N.E.2d 522, 137 A.L.R. 635, a condition "'To have and to hold

---

35. The distinction between defeasible estates and future interests which also curtail alienation was recognized at common law. In fact, the creation of future interests, through trusts and similar devises, whose vesting could be indefinitely postponed, resulted in the development of the rule against perpetuities. Significantly, the rule against perpetuities has no application to defeasible estates because reversions, possibilities of reverter and powers of termination are inherently vested in nature (Strong v. Shatto, 45 Cal. App. 29, 187 P. 150; Caffroy v. Fremlin, 198 Cal. App. 2d 176, 17 Cal. Rptr. 668).

. . . as long as the same is used by the Regular Predestinarian Baptist Church as a place of meeting . . .'" was deemed to have created a defeasible estate by the Supreme Court of Illinois.

In Frensley v. White, 208 Okl. 209, 254 P.2d 982, 983, the deed to the trustees of a religious organization contained the following language:

> To Have And To Hold said above described premises unto the said Trustees and their successors in office, as aforesaid, in trust, so long as said premises shall be held, kept and used by said church or any branch thereof, or any successor thereto for a place of divine worship, for the use of the ministry and membership of said church, subject to the usages, discipline and ministerial appointments of said church as from time to time authorized and declared by the General Council of the Assemblies of God Church and by the Annual Council within whose bounds said premises are, or may hereafter be situated.

The Supreme Court of Oklahoma treated the estate as a fee determinable, notwithstanding the extreme language of the deed which not only limited the land use but who could use it.

In Merchants Bank and Trust Company v. New Canaan Historical Society, 133 Conn. 706, 54 A.2d 696, 172 A.L.R. 1275, a parcel of real property was willed to the New Canaan Library Association "'upon the condition and provided, however, that if said property shall not be used by said Library Association for the purposes of its organization, this devise shall terminate and the property become a part of my residuary estate. . . .'" There, as here, the language of the condition did not precisely define the restricted use but expressly permitted any use for which the library association was formed. The Supreme Court of Errors of Connecticut clearly indicated that the will had created a fee determinable.

For the reasons herein stated, the first paragraph of the judgment below is amended and revised to read:

> 1. That at the time of the commencement of this action title to the parcel of real property situated in the City of Los Banos, County of Merced, State of California, being described as Lot 20 Block 72 according to the Map of the Town of Los Banos, was vested in the MOUNTAIN BROW LODGE NO. 82, INDEPENDENT ORDER OF ODD FELLOWS, subject to the condition that said property is restricted for the use and benefit of the second party only; and in the event the same fails to be used by the second party the same is to revert to the first parties herein, their successors, heirs or assigns.

As so modified the judgment is affirmed. Respondents to recover their costs on appeal.

STONE, J. I dissent. I believe the entire habendum clause which purports to restrict the fee simple conveyed is invalid as a restraint upon alienation. . . .

If the words "sale or transfer," which the majority find to be a restraint upon alienation, are expunged, still the property cannot be sold or transferred by the grantee because the property may be used by only the I.O.O.F. Lodge No. 82, upon pain of reverter. This use restriction prevents the grantee from conveying the property just as effectively as the condition against "sale or transfer . . . of all or any part of said lot."

Certainly, if we are to have realism in the law, the effect of language must be judged according to what it does. When two different terms generate the same ultimate legal result, they should be treated alike in relation to that result.

Section 711 of the Civil Code expresses an ancient policy of English common law. The wisdom of this proscription as applied to situations of this kind is manifest when we note that a number of fraternal, political and similar organizations of a century ago have disappeared, and others have ceased to function in individual communities. Should an organization holding property under a deed similar to the one before us be disbanded one hundred years or so after the conveyance is made, the result may well be a title fragmented into the interests of heirs of the grantors numbering in the hundreds and scattered to the four corners of the earth.

[I]t seems to me that . . . the entire habendum clause is repugnant to the grant in fee simple that precedes it. I would hold the property free from restrictions, and reverse the judgment.

NOTES AND QUESTION

1. *Use conditions that are indirect restraints on alienation.* Falls City, Nebraska, conveyed land to the Missouri Pacific Railway Company as long as the land was used as a site for the railroad company's divisional headquarters, and in case it should be abandoned for such use the land was to revert to the city. Subsequently, the railroad company moved its divisional headquarters from Falls City. In a quiet title action by the railroad against the city, the court held that the reverter provision was invalid as a restraint on alienation and that the railroad had a fee simple absolute:

> We find that the recent decision of the Nebraska Supreme Court in Cast v. National Bank of Commerce, Trust and Savings Association of Lincoln, 183 N.W.2d 485 (Neb. 1971), is controlling. In *Cast*, the court held, upon rehearing, that a condition attached to a defeasible fee simple is an [unenforceable] indirect restraint against alienation "if it materially affects marketability adversely." . . . If the condition subsequent in the conveyance expressly limits alienation of the property to an impermissibly small number of persons, it is void and unenforceable. Conversely, most use restrictions are valid and enforceable unless they also have the practical effect of "affecting marketability adversely" by unreasonably limiting the class of persons to whom it may be alienated. . . . In limiting the use of the property by the Railroad to use as its divisional headquarters only, the City, in practical effect, completely restricted alienation of the land to other grantees. Thus, even though the conditional restriction is couched in terms of the use of the property, like the conditional limitation in *Cast*, it unreasonably affects the marketability of the land adversely by completely restricting alienation. [Falls City v. Missouri Pacific Railway Co., 453 F.2d 771, 773-774 (8th Cir. 1971).]

2. *Form versus effect.* Suppose some particular limitation or condition contained in a defeasible fee — say a provision that limits the use of the property to a school for children with disabilities. If the provision is viewed merely as a restriction on

land use, then under the general rule it is valid. If it is viewed instead as a restraint on alienation (because, after all, the provision could significantly limit future transfers of the property), then under the general rule it is invalid unless reasonable under the circumstances (recall the discussion in Note 1 on page 232). But what of a limitation or condition that has the form of a land use restriction (as above) but the effect of a restraint on alienation? One approach to the issue is purely formal; an example is the majority opinion in *Toscano*. The other approach, illustrated by the dissenting opinion in *Toscano* and the decision in *Falls City*, looks at the effect, not the form, of the limitation, such that a nominal restriction on land use might fail as an unreasonable restraint on alienation.

The Restatement takes the wise position that substance, not form, should control, but recognizes that no precise rule as to validity can be formulated. Restatement (Second) of Property, Donative Transfers §3.4 comment b (1983). Form is relevant, but not conclusive. The grantor's purpose, where discernible, is also relevant, as is the practical effect of the restriction. If it has a significant impact on transferability, then it should be treated as a restraint on alienation, subject to the rules governing the validity of such restraints.

3. *Restrictions on family members.* Testators sometimes attempt to control, after their deaths, the use of their houses by family members. The results are mixed. In Cast v. National Bank of Commerce, Trust & Sav. Assn. of Lincoln, 183 N.W.2d 485 (Neb. 1971), the testator left a farm to Richard Cast in fee simple on condition that "Richard or one of his children shall occupy the farm as his or her residence for 25 years," with forfeiture for breach of condition. The court held the condition void as a restraint on alienation. See also Wills v. Pierce, 67 S.E.2d 239 (Ga. 1951), holding invalid a condition that a house "shall be used [by the grantee and his heirs] as a residence," with reverter to the grantor in case of breach.

Compare Casey v. Casey, 700 S.W.2d 46 (Ark. 1985), where the testator devised land to his son with a provision for forfeiture if the son's daughter were ever to own, possess, or be a guest on the land for more than one week a year. The court held the condition unreasonable and void because capricious and imposed for spite or malice.

Compare also Babb v. Rand, 345 A.2d 496 (Me. 1975), where the testator left a summer home "to John Freeman Rand in fee simple with the proviso that he shall never deny access or occupation to [the testator's other children] during their lifetime." The court held that this created a fee simple in John subject to a valid condition subsequent that continued until the death of the testator's last child.

Do these cases pose the same policy question as that involved in *Falls City*?

NOTE: CONDEMNATION OF DEFEASIBLE FEES AND THE VALUATION OF DEFEASIBLE FEES AND REVERSIONARY INTERESTS

Suppose a parcel of land is taken by a city government through its eminent domain power, and that the land taken was owned in fee simple defeasible, with a future interest retained in the grantor or the grantor's heirs. The city has to pay the fair market value of the land, but how should that award be divided among the holders of the present and future interests? The majority view is that where a defeasible fee is condemned, the holder of the fee takes the entire condemnation award; the holder of the reversionary interest takes nothing. The reason is that the reversionary interest is considered too remote and contingent to be capable of valuation. The Restatement of Property takes a slightly different view. If the defeasible fee would probably not end within a reasonably short period of time (not taking into account the condemnation), the fee owner should have the entire award. Restatement of Property §53 comment b (1936). In practice, the Restatement view reaches the same result as the majority view in most cases, as the end of the defeasible fee typically is not imminent. Consider the following two cases.

Ink v. City of Canton

Supreme Court of Ohio, 1965
212 N.E.2d 574

This cause originated in 1959 as an action in the Common Pleas Court of Stark County for a declaratory judgment with respect to the rights of the parties in a 33-acre tract of land known as Ink Park.

By two deeds, one in 1936 and the other in 1941, the lineal descendants of Harry H. Ink conveyed that tract to the city of Canton. The second deed was given to correct the description but otherwise the two deeds are substantially identical.

Plaintiffs are the grantors or the heirs of deceased grantors in those deeds.

In each deed, the granting clause reads:

. . . for the use and purpose of a public park, but for no other use or purpose whatsoever.

In each deed, the habendum clause reads:

To have and to hold said premises, with the appurtenances thereof, unto the said grantee and its successors, for so long a time as said grantee, and its successors, shall use and maintain said above described premises as and for a public park, and for no other use and purpose whatsoever; and in case said premises shall at any time hereafter cease to be occupied and used as a public park, or in case the restrictions, conditions, reservations and exceptions above mentioned shall be violated, then all the right, title and interest of said grantee and its successors in and to said premises shall be forfeited and shall cease and terminate, and said premises shall revert to and be vested in the above grantors, their heirs, successors and assigns, and said grantors, their heirs, successors and assigns, or any of them, may thereupon enter and take possession of all or any part of the aforesaid premises without notice. . . .

Each deed also provides:

The property hereby conveyed shall be known and designated as the "Harry H. Ink Park" in memory of the man who purchased it in 1914, with the idea of donating the same at some future date to the city of Canton . . . for park purposes.

The conveyance was accepted by the city, the tract was improved and developed as a public park, was named "Ink Park" and was used as a public park until 1961 when the state instituted proceedings to appropriate perpetual easements for highway and related purposes over all but 6½ of the 33½ acres. . . .

In the appropriation proceedings, the Director of Highways stated that the value of land taken was $96,247, that the value of structures was $2,875, and that the damages to the residue of the property not taken was $31,700, and deposited a total of $130,822 to be distributed to those having interests in the property. . . .

[The Common Pleas Court awarded the whole sum to the city. The Court of Appeals affirmed.]

TAFT, C.J. Plaintiffs . . . raise questions as to the effect of the state's appropriation of a substantial part of the Ink Park property on the respective rights of the city and of the plaintiffs to (1) the portion of that property still usable for park purposes and (2) the money paid by the state for the portions thereof appropriated and for damages to the residue.

Until the latter part of the Nineteenth Century, there were no reported cases which dealt with such questions. See Courter and Maskery, The Effect of Condemnation Proceedings upon Possibilities of Reverter and Powers of Termination, 38 University of Detroit Law Journal (1960) 46, 47.

Where property is conveyed in fee with a proviso that it is to be used only for a specified use and that the property shall revert to the grantor if such specified use ceases, it would appear reasonable to conclude that the property would so revert when its appropriation by eminent domain proceedings prevents that specified use. Such a conclusion would appear to be especially reasonable where, as in the instant case, the grantee paid nothing for what had been conveyed to him. A few cases have so held. Crow, Admr. v. Tidnam (1947), 198 Okla. 650, 181 P.2d 549; Lancaster School District v. Lancaster County (1929), 295 Pa. 112, 144 A. 901; Pedrotti v. Marin County (CCA 9-1946), 152 F.2d 829. However, the great weight of authority has held that there is no reverter in such an instance, and that the grantee takes the whole of the amount paid for the property appropriated. Courter and Maskery, supra; 46 Cornell Law Quarterly (1961) 631 et seq.; The Value of Possibilities of Reverter and Powers of Termination in Eminent Domain, Illinois Law Forum (1963) 693; Condemnation of Future Interests, 48 Virginia Law Review (1962) 461, 472 et seq.; Condemnation of Future Interests, 43 Iowa Law Review (1958) 241, 247.

This court's opinion in Board of County Commissioners v. Thormyer, Dir. (1959), 169 Ohio St. 291, 159 N.E.2d 612, 75 A.L.R.2d 1373, recognizes that such a holding may give a windfall to the grantee. He not only gets the value of what he had, i.e., the value of the property with the restriction as to its use, but he gets what may be a greater value than the property would have without any such restriction. At the same time, the grantor's right of reverter is destroyed and he gets nothing for it.

There may be some justification for such a conclusion where the grantee paid the grantor the full value of the property for the determinable fee. In such an instance, giving the grantor any part of the eminent domain award would represent a windfall to the grantor. Also, since the grantee would have paid the full value of the property, it is reasonably arguable that giving the whole of the award to the grantee would give him the value of no more than what the grantee had paid for when he acquired the determinable fee. See concurring opinion in McMechan v. Board of Edn. of Richland Twp. (1952), 157 Ohio St. 241, 253, 105 N.E.2d 270. However, where, as in the instant case, the grantee paid nothing to the grantor for the determinable fee, it seems apparent that, at the very least, the amount, if any, by which the value of an unrestricted fee exceeds the value of the restricted fee, is something that should go to the grantor. Before the appropriation, the grantee had no right to the greater value of the property, if it had a greater value without the restrictions imposed upon the grantee. The difference between that greater value and what the grantee lost as a result of the appropriation, i.e., the value of what the grantee had, would seem logically to belong to the grantor. That difference certainly represents the value of something which the grantor expressly refrained from conveying to the grantee. Where the amount of that difference can be determined, as it frequently can, and where the grantee had paid nothing for his determinable fee, there would appear to be no basis whatever for the reason usually advanced for giving the whole of the award in the appropriation proceedings to the grantee. That reason is that the right of reverter of the grantor is too remote and contingent to be capable of valuation.

The other reason sometimes advanced for giving the whole of the appropriation award to the grantee is that, since the law (i.e., the legal taking in eminent domain) has made it impossible to perform the condition under which the property is held, performance of that condition is excused. This is a statement of the conclusion reached rather than any reason for reaching that conclusion. The most that might be said for such a conclusion is that the provision for reverter on breach of the condition as to use is intended by the grantor to compel the grantees to make the specified use of the property. After the property is appropriated in eminent domain proceedings, such provision can no longer have any influence in compelling such use. Hence, the only justification for its existence has disappeared. However, this does not represent a reason for giving the grantee the value of something he has not lost (i.e., the amount, if any, by which the value of the property taken exceeds its lesser value for the restricted use that the grantee could have made of it) where the grantor expressly refrained from conveying that something to him.

As stated in Simes and Smith, Law of Future Interests, 2 Ed. (1956) Section 2013:

> . . . in the usual case the testator [grantor] neither thought of eminent domain nor provided therefor. Now, in fact it may be said that in most other cases of impossibility, the testator [grantor] did not foresee the situation which occurred, nor provide for it; and that is probably true. But it does not follow that this should be treated like the ordinary case of an impossible condition subsequent. It must be remembered that in the usual case the court must give the property either to the devisee [grantee] or to the devisor's [grantor's] heirs. There is no third alternative; whereas in the eminent domain case, the court may divide the award between them. . . .

In apparent recognition of the harshness of the majority rule giving the whole of the appropriation award to the owner of the determinable fee and nothing to the owner of the right of reverter, the American Law Institute Restatement of the Law of Property (1936) 188, Section 53, comment c, provides for a division of the eminent domain award between the owner of that determinable fee and the owner of the right of reverter where,

> viewed from the time of commencement of an eminent domain proceeding, and not taking into account any changes in the use of the land sought to be condemned which may result as a consequence of such proceeding, the event upon which a possessory estate in fee simple defeasible [determinable fee] is to end is an event the occurrence of which, within a reasonably short period of time, is probable.

Although not supported by any authority prior to its promulgation in 1936, this rule has received some support. See annotation, 81 A.L.R.2d 568, entitled Rights in Condemnation Award where Land Taken was Subject to Possible Rights of Reverter or Re-entry, which endeavors to explain the authorities with reference to this rule.

In the instant case, there was no event imminent, other than the impending appropriation proceedings, that could amount to a failure to use the Ink Park property for the purposes specified in the deeds conveying it to the city. Hence, this rule of the Restatement would not be applicable in the instant case. However, this limited departure by the Restatement and the authorities following it from the harsh majority rule, giving the whole of the appropriation award to the owner of the determinable fee, encourages us to consider whether some greater departure from that harsh rule should be made in the instant case.

We have already pointed out that the grantee paid nothing to the grantor for the determinable fee involved in the instant case; and that the reasons for giving any of the eminent domain award to the grantee are not the same in such a situation as where the grantee paid for what was conveyed to him.

There is another significant and, we believe, a decisive factor that should be considered in the instant case. The deeds conveying Ink Park to the city expressed an intention to impose upon the city a duty to use the property conveyed "as and for a public park . . ." to "be known and designated as" Ink Park. By accepting that conveyance, the city undertook a fiduciary obligation to use such property only for such purpose. Thus, until a court of equity in appropriate proceedings may give authority to do otherwise, the city must hold any interests in the Ink Park property not taken from it subject to the fiduciary obligations imposed upon it by the two deeds conveying that property to the city. . . .

Likewise, whatever money the city received in the eminent domain proceedings for the Ink Park land taken or on account of damages to the Ink Park land not taken can only be held by the city so long as it proposes to use, can reasonably use, and does use that money for Ink Park purposes; and any of that money which the city either does not propose to use, cannot reasonably use, or does not use for Ink Park purposes should revert to the plaintiffs. . . .

It follows that so long as the city proposes to, can reasonably and does use for Ink Park purposes the part of the Ink Park property not taken in eminent domain proceedings and the money it receives for the Ink Park land taken and on account of damages to such land not taken, neither such land nor money will revert to plaintiffs although plaintiffs will retain their rights of reverter both with respect to that land and that money.

However, for reasons hereinbefore stated, since the money paid for the land taken in the eminent domain proceedings represents its value for any use and the conveyance to the city was for a specific use only, the amount, if any, by which the value of that land for any use exceeds its value for the specific use only should be paid to the plaintiffs. The grantor never intended to convey for park or any other purposes the interests in the Ink Park property represented by such difference between its unrestricted value and its value for the uses specified in the two deeds. . . .

Part of the eminent domain award is for structures taken. To the extent that this part of the award represents payment for structures built by the city, this part should go to the city without being subject to any fiduciary obligation imposed by or right of reverter provided for in the deeds conveying Ink Park to the city.

For the foregoing reasons, the judgment of the Court of Appeals is reversed, and the cause is remanded to the Court of Appeals for further proceedings in accordance with this opinion.

Judgment reversed.

NOTES AND QUESTIONS

1. The City of Canton and the Ink heirs, acting together to sell their separate interests to a purchaser, can receive the full market value of the land from the purchaser. Thus, in that sense, the total value of their interests equals the full market value of the land.

Valuation of the interests separately, however, results in the paradox that the sum of the parts does not equal the whole. The value of the city's fee simple determinable is the value of the land as a public park discounted by the probability of cessation of park use. Since cessation of park use is solely within the control of the city (absent exercise of eminent domain by the state), the probability of cessation of park use — and the discount — is negligible. How is the value of land limited to public park use to be determined? There is no market in land parcels that can be used only for a public park from which we can ascertain what comparable properties sell for. How much would you give to own a public park?

The value of the possibility of reverter is the full market value of the land discounted by the probability that the reverter will never become possessory. Since cessation of park use lies in the discretion of the city, which is likely never to cease such use, the possibility of reverter is substantially worthless on the market.

The court appears to get out of the dilemma by saying that the city's determinable fee should be valued first and "the amount, if any, by which the value of that land for any use [i.e., full market value] exceeds its value for the specific use only [value for park use] should be paid to the plaintiffs." If the court really means this, who will end up with the lion's share of the condemnation proceeds?

Does a better solution appear to you than any solution considered by the court? See Victor P. Goldberg, Thomas W. Merrill & Daniel Unumb, Bargaining in the Shadow of Eminent Domain: Valuing and Apportioning Condemnation Awards Between Landlord and Tenant, 34 UCLA L. Rev. 1083, 1133-1135 (1987) (arguing that the ideal solution is to provide for a condemnation clause in the deed; alternatively, give proceeds to the grantee).

2. The valuation problem aside, were the plaintiffs in *Ink* paid for their future interest but also allowed to keep it?

3. *Postscript*. The decision in Ink v. City of Canton was handed down in December 1965 and remanded to the trial court. The city and the Ink heirs could not agree on how to divide the money according to the rule laid down in the *Ink* case, nor could they find the relevant evidence that would help the trial court fix the values of their respective interests. Perhaps responding to pressure from the city, which had agreed not to contest running the interstate highway through Ink Park, the state reconsidered its valuation of the Ink Park land and paid an additional $137,000 into the pot to be divided. In 1973 the city and the Ink heirs were finally able to come to a settlement. The pot had now grown, with interest, to $293,000. The settlement gave the city $130,000, the Ink heirs $160,000, and the lawyer for the Inks $3,000. In this settlement the Ink heirs released to the city their possibility of reverter in the remaining 6½ acres of Ink Park. The trial court approved the settlement. The city of Canton put its $130,000 in an Ink Park Land Fund, for the purpose of buying park land. In 1979, the city used this money to help pay for a replacement park of 24 acres, which cost $200,000. (This information was furnished to the editors by Professor William Roth, who investigated the aftermath of the *Ink* case.)

City of Palm Springs v. Living Desert Reserve, 82 Cal. Rptr. 2d 859 (Cal. App. 1999). In June 1986, the McCallum Desert Foundation conveyed 30 acres of land to the city of Palm Springs to be used as the site of the McCallum Desert Reserve and Equestrian Center. The deed gave the city a fee simple in the land subject to a condition subsequent: "In the event that the property is not used solely and perpetually as the site of the McCallum Desert Reserve and Equestrian Center, then the interest in the land and premises herein conveyed shall pass to the Living Desert Reserve, Palm Desert, California, and grantee shall forfeit all rights thereto."[36] In 1993 Palm Springs decided it would rather build a golf course on the land. It brought a condemnation action against Living Desert Reserve, claiming that the power of termination in Living Desert Reserve was not com-

---

36. The court characterized the interest as a fee simple subject to condition subsequent because California has statutorily abolished the distinctions between a fee simple subject to condition subsequent, fee simple determinable, and fee simple subject to executory limitation, providing that language that at common law would have created either a fee simple determinable or a fee simple subject to executory limitation creates a fee simple subject to condition subsequent. See Cal. Civ. Code §§885.010(a)(2) and 885.020 (West 2013).

pensable. The city argued that under Restatement of Property §53 (quoted in Ink v. City of Canton), not taking into account the condemnation proceeding, the possibility of breach of condition by the city was too remote and speculative, and the power of termination was valueless for purposes of condemnation.

The court agreed that the Restatement was followed in California, but it held that the violation of the condition was imminent. When the condemnor owns the present possessory interest in the land, the court held, the action of condemnation itself makes violation of the condition imminent. The Restatement applies only when a paramount authority condemns property and ousts the possessor. Otherwise the city could turn its fee simple subject to condition subsequent into an unrestricted fee simple by condemning the power of termination and paying nothing for it. The court chastised the city for making its argument: "the decision to assert that position did not display the high degree of fairness, justice, and virtue that should characterize public entities. Such inequitable behavior must not be rewarded." Since the condemnation proceeding made breach of the condition reasonably imminent, the Living Desert Reserve was entitled to be compensated for 100 percent of the value of the unrestricted fee in the land. Accord Leeco Gas & Oil Co. v. County of Nueces, 736 S.W.2d 629 (Tex. 1987).

NOTE: DEFEASIBLE LIFE ESTATES AND PERSONAL CONDUCT RESTRAINTS

In former years it was not uncommon to run across a life estate defeasible upon marriage. For example, a husband might devise property to his widow for life with a proviso that she loses it if she remarries. Such a provision is now rarely encountered, for several reasons. First, the provision rests upon a notion that a second husband is liable for support of his wife for her lifetime, even after divorce; therefore, the wife will not need support from her first husband. But the common law liability of husbands (second as well as first) to support their wives after divorce has almost passed from the American scene (see page 394). Second, at the death of one spouse, modern law has increased the protection of the surviving spouse, giving her an elective share of fee simple ownership in her deceased husband's estate and not, as at common law, merely support for her life. If dissatisfied with a life estate defeasible upon remarriage given her by her husband's will, the surviving wife can renounce the will and claim a share of outright ownership. Third, a proviso for forfeiture upon remarriage has lost favor since the 1940s, when the marital deduction was introduced into the Internal Revenue Code, because the proviso disqualifies the devise for the federal estate tax marital deduction. For a life estate to qualify for the marital deduction and pass free of estate taxation, the surviving spouse must be entitled to all the income for her entire life. Internal Revenue Code §2056(b)(5) & (7) (2011).

In addition, provisions calling for forfeiture of property upon marriage may violate the common law rule against restraints on marriage. The common law favors marriage and is jealous of provisions that hinder it. In determining whether a particular provision violates this policy favoring marriage, courts have said that the fundamental question is whether the provision has the *purpose* (1) of coercing abstention from marriage or (2) of providing support until marriage, without any desire to hinder marriage. If the transferor has the first purpose in mind, the provision is invalid. If the second purpose is his objective, the provision will be upheld. See Estate of Guidotti, 109 Cal. Rptr. 2d 674 (Cal. App. 2001) (language in husband's testamentary trust giving his wife a life interest only if she remains unmarried held void as a restraint on marriage).

A number of courts have taken the position that the purpose of the grantor can be discerned from the form of the limitation. A devise "to A for life so long as A remains unmarried, then to B," is thought to have the dominant motive of providing support until marriage, when presumably A's spouse will provide support, and not the purpose of discouraging marriage. A devise "to A for life, but if A marries, then to B," on the other hand, is thought to have the purpose of penalizing marriage. See Lewis v. Searles, 452 S.W.2d 153 (Mo. 1970). Is this reasoning sound? Restatement (Second) of Property, Donative Transfers §6.1 comment e (1983), says a determinable limitation has "some slight evidentiary value as indicative of a motive to provide support."

PROBLEM

H's will devises Blackacre "to my wife, *W*, for her use and benefit, so long as she remains unmarried." *H* devises the residue of his property to his daughter, *D*, a child by an earlier marriage. *W* does not remarry but moves into the apartment of her male friend, *A*. *W* subsequently dies, devising all her property to *A*. Who owns Blackacre? See Eller v. Wages, 136 S.E.2d 730 (Ga. 1964); Saunders v. Saunders, 490 P.2d 1260 (Or. 1971). See also Restatement (Second) of Property, supra, §6.1 comment f: "A restraint against marriage is construed as narrowly as possible, consistent with the language employed in describing the restraint and, hence, does not automatically include within it a restraint against cohabitation without marriage."

REVIEW PROBLEMS

(The answers to these Problems appear in Appendix A, beginning at page 1267.)

1. *O* conveys Blackacre "to *A* and her heirs, but if Blackacre is used for any purpose other than agricultural purposes, then *O* has the right to re-enter and take possession of the land." What is the state of title in Blackacre at common law?

2. Taking the facts of Problem 1, suppose that some years after the conveyance, *A* begins construction of several residences on Blackacre. *O* has died and devised her entire estate to *B*. What is the state of title in Blackacre at common law?

3. *O* conveys Blackacre "to *A* and her heirs so long as Blackacre is used for residential purposes only." What is the state of title in Blackacre at common law?

4. Taking the facts of Problem 3, suppose that some years after the conveyance, *A* begins construction of a factory on Blackacre. *O* has died and devised her entire estate to *B*. What is the state of title in Blackacre at common law?

5. *O* conveys Greenacre "to the Finger Lakes Land Trust [a charitable organization] on condition that Greenacre remains forever undeveloped and in its natural condition; in the event Greenacre is ever developed, residentially, commercially, or otherwise, then to the Land Conservancy [also a charitable organization] in fee simple absolute." What is the state of title in Greenacre at common law?

6. *O* conveys Wiseacre "to *A* and her heirs, and *A* promises, on behalf of her heirs and assigns forever, that Wiseacre shall be used solely for agricultural purposes." What is the state of title in Wiseacre at common law?

7. Taking the facts of Problem 6, suppose that some years after the conveyance, *A* begins construction of a factory on Wiseacre. What is the state of title in Wiseacre at common law when *A* begins construction? What remedies does *O* have against *A*?

8. *O* conveys Whiteacre "to *A* and his heirs; but if *A* ever drinks alcohol or alcoholic beverages, then to *B* and her heirs." Later, *B* executes and delivers a deed purporting to convey her interest in Whiteacre to *C*. Later still, *A* drinks whiskey and gets drunk. What is the state of title in Whiteacre at common law?

[Handwritten notes:]

8. FFSSEL
B = EI

1. Before: O = FSA
A = nothing

@ : O = right of reentry
A = FSSCS

2. B = right of re-entry

3. FSD

6.

4. B = reversion

5. FSSEL
LC = exec. interst

4

Future Interests

A. Introduction

The modern relevance of future interests. We turn now to future interests, which confer rights to the enjoyment of property at a future time. Although future interests have ancient origins, they are very relevant to modern law practice. Most future interests are created in the context of family wealth transfer transactions, particularly those implemented through a trust (to which you were briefly introduced in the last chapter, in Note 3 at page 240). Virtually every family property trust today involves one or more future interests. Such interests usually follow a life estate given to a designated beneficiary, commonly the grantor's spouse or a class of beneficiaries such as the grantor's children.

We will study the trust in more detail later (see pages 295-303), but to illustrate the relationship between a trust and future interests, consider this simple example. Suppose that *W*, a woman married to *H*, has two adult children and no grandchildren (yet). She wishes to plan her estate so that upon her death all of the income from her assets, currently valued at approximately $750,000, and so much of her assets as *H* needs for his support, health, and maintenance will be paid to *H* for his life. Upon *H*'s death, all of *W*'s remaining assets are to go to her children.

The best way to implement *W*'s plan is through a trust. Using the trust form, *W* can give the trustee, a person or institution in whom she has confidence, the power to invest the trust principal and the discretion to pay the appropriate amount of principal to *H*. *W*'s will might provide that she devises her estate to a named trustee, in trust, with directions to pay all income and so much of the trust principal as *H* needs for his support, health, and maintenance to *H* for his life, providing further that upon *H*'s death the trust shall terminate and the trustee shall distribute all of the trust assets outright to *W*'s children. During the term of the trust the trustee holds the legal title to the trust assets in fee simple, subject to the beneficial interests of *H* and *W*'s children. *H* has a life estate, and *W*'s children have a remainder (more precisely, a vested remainder).[1]

---

1. Future interests in trusts are sometimes referred to as "equitable" because, as we will discuss later (see page 297), trusts and trust interests are enforced by courts of equity.

After the courts held that the fee tail could be destroyed by a common recovery, cutting off the rights of issue and converting the fee tail into a fee simple (on which recall the discussion at page 225), lawyers began to create life estates followed by one or more future interests. Thus a testator might devise land "to my son *A* for life, and on *A*'s death to *A*'s daughter *B* and her heirs." By creating a future interest in his granddaughter, *B*, to become possessory upon his son *A*'s death, the testator is able to control inheritance of the land not only at his death but also at his son's death. Today, life estates followed by future interests are the foundation blocks of wills and estate planning.

Future interests are limited in number, but the ones permitted are quite enough. In fact, we are willing to bet that, before we are through, you will have a candidate or two for the discard file.

Future interests recognized in our legal system are:

(1) Interests retained by the transferor, known as:
    (a) Reversion
    (b) Possibility of reverter
    (c) Right of entry (also known as power of termination)
(2) Interests created in a transferee, known as:
    (a) Vested remainder
    (b) Contingent remainder
    (c) Executory interest

As you study the materials in this chapter, bear in mind that a future interest is always attached to some estate of the types considered in Chapter 3 (fee simple, life estate, etc.). For example, a person might have a remainder (the future interest) for life (the future interest is attached to, or is "in," a life estate) or in fee simple absolute or in some other estate. And this is true of all the future interests listed above, so be careful to label any future interest fully, identifying not just the interest but also the estate.

A future interest is not a mere expectancy, like the hope of a child to inherit from a parent. A future interest gives legal rights to its owner. It is a presently existing property interest, protected by the court as such. Take this case: *O* conveys Blackacre to *A* for life, then to *B* and her heirs. *B* has present legal rights and liabilities. *B* can sell or give away her remainder. She can enjoin *A* from committing waste. She can sue third parties who are injuring the land. If *B* dies during the life of *A*, *B*'s remainder will be transmitted to *B*'s heirs or devisees, and a federal estate tax or state inheritance tax may be levied upon its value. Although a future interest does not entitle its owner to present possession, it is a *presently existing interest* that may become possessory in the future.

B. Future Interests in the Transferor

1. Reversion

Historically, the earliest future interest to develop was a reversion. If O, a fee simple owner, granted the land "to A for life," the land would revert ("come back") to O at A's death. O's right to future possession is called a reversion. If O dies during A's life, O's reversion passes under his will or to his heirs, and at A's death whoever owns the reversion is entitled to possession of the land.

In a general sense, then, a reversion is the interest left in an owner when he carves out of his estate a lesser estate and does not provide who is to take the property when the lesser estate expires. But a more precise definition is necessary. "A reversion is," in the words of Professor Lewis Simes, "the interest remaining in the grantor, or in the successor in interest of a testator, who transfers a *vested estate of a lesser quantum* than that of the vested estate which he has." 1 American Law of Property §4.16 (1952) (emphasis added). The hierarchy of estates determines what is a lesser estate. The fee simple is a greater estate than a fee tail, which is a greater estate than a life estate, which is a greater estate than the leasehold estates. Hence if O, owning a fee simple, creates a fee tail, a life estate, or a term of years, and does not at the same time convey away a vested remainder in fee simple, O has a reversion. If A, owning only a life estate, creates a term of years, A has a reversion.

Because reversions result from the hierarchy of estates, they are thought of as the remnant of an estate that has not entirely passed away from the transferor. Hence all reversions are retained interests, which remain vested in the transferor.

When a reversion is retained, it may or may not be certain to become possessory in the future. Thus:

> *Example 1.* O conveys Blackacre "to A for life." O has a reversion in fee simple that is certain to become possessory. At A's death, either O or O's successors in interest will be entitled to possession.

Time line 4-1

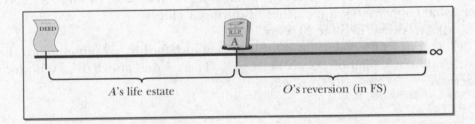

Example 2. O conveys Whiteacre "to *A* for life, then to *B* and her heirs if *B* survives *A*." *O* has a reversion in fee simple that is not certain to become possessory. If *B* dies before *A*, *O* will be entitled to possession at *A*'s death. On the other hand, if *A* dies before *B*, *O*'s reversion is divested on *A*'s death and will never become possessory.

Time line 4-2

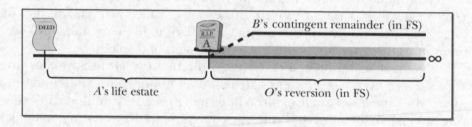

In the above examples, the *value* of the reversions may differ, because one is certain to become possessory and the other is not, but the *name* of *O*'s interest in both examples—a reversion—is the same. *Note well*: In *Example 2, O* has a reversion, not a possibility of a reversion. There is no such interest as a "possibility of reversion," and you should never use that phrase. Such talk is likely to produce confusion of a reversion with an entirely different interest, the possibility of reverter, which follows a determinable fee. Remember that the names of future interests are names arbitrarily given, like first names to children. Call the future interest by its correct name.

At common law a reversion was transferable during life and descendible and devisable at death. It remains so today.

PROBLEMS

1. *O* owns a fee simple and makes the following transfers. In which cases is there a reversion?

(a) *O* conveys "to *A* for life, then to *B* and her heirs."

(b) *O* conveys "to *A* for life, then to *B* and the heirs of her body."

(c) *O* conveys "to *A* for life, then to *B* and her heirs if *B* attains the age of 21 before *A* dies." At the time of the conveyance *B* is 15 years old. (If there is a reversion, what happens to it if *B* reaches 21 during *A*'s life?)

(d) *O* conveys "to *A* for 20 years."

2. *O* conveys Blackacre "to *A* for life, then to *B* for life." *O* subsequently dies with a will devising all of *O*'s property to *C*. Then *A* dies and *B* dies. Who owns Blackacre?

2.   Possibility of Reverter

A possibility of reverter arises when an owner carves out of his estate a *determinable* estate of the same quantum. Theoretically, a possibility of reverter can be retained when a life tenant conveys his life estate to another, determinable on the happening of an event, but the cases, almost without exception, deal with carving a fee simple determinable out of a fee simple absolute. Thus for all practical purposes a possibility of reverter is a future interest remaining in the transferor or his heirs when a fee simple determinable is created. Example: *O* conveys Blackacre "to Hartford School Board so long as used for school purposes." *O* has a possibility of reverter.

Time line 4-3

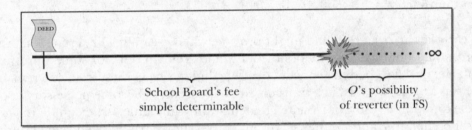

The possibility of reverter has been previously discussed in connection with its correlative possessory estate, the fee simple determinable. See pages 245, 253-254.

3. Right of Entry

When an owner transfers an estate subject to condition subsequent and retains the power to cut short or terminate the estate, the transferor has a right of entry. Example: *O* conveys Whiteacre "to Hartford School Board, but if it ceases to use the land for school purposes, *O* has the right to re-enter and retake the premises."

Time line 4-4

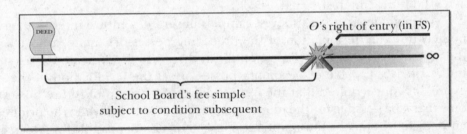

The right of entry has been previously discussed in connection with the fee simple subject to condition subsequent. See pages 246, 253-254.

C.   *Future Interests in Transferees*

There are three types of future interests in transferees: vested remainders, contingent remainders, and executory interests. A remainder or executory interest cannot be retained by the transferor; these interests are created only in transferees. Once created, a remainder or executory interest can be transferred back to the grantor, but the name originally given the interest does not change.

1.   Introduction

In early law an owner of land might provide, when creating a life estate, that the land would not revert to the donor but would "remain out" for some third person. Hence developed the concept of a remainder. The earliest form of a remainder was a future interest in a transferee that is certain to become possessory upon the expiration of the prior estate created at the same time. An example is "to *A* for life, then to *B* and her heirs." In this conveyance *B* has a vested remainder in fee simple. Upon *A*'s death, *B* or *B*'s successor in interest is entitled to possession in fee simple.

Although a vested remainder was recognized with little difficulty, it took several centuries for the law to approve a contingent remainder. In the case of the vested remainder above, the transferor has decided at the outset who is to take the property upon the life tenant's death. A contingent remainder permits the transferor to let future events determine this question. For example, upon *A*'s marriage, *O* (*A*'s father) might convey "to *A* for life, then to *A*'s eldest son and his heirs." If *A* has a son born thereafter, such son will take on *A*'s death; but if a son is not born, the land will revert to *O*. The contingent remainder gave difficulty to the judges because it left uncertain who would take the land upon *A*'s death, and the old law disliked uncertainty in succession to land titles (much as people disliked uncertainty in succession to the crown). Finally, after several hesitant starts, the contingent remainder, in the middle of the sixteenth century, was admitted as a valid future interest.

A remainder is, as the above examples illustrate, a future interest that waits politely until the termination of the preceding possessory estate, at which time the remainder moves into possession if it is then vested. A remainder is a future interest that is capable of becoming possessory at the termination of the prior estate. It is not required that the future interest be certain of future possession, only that it be possible for the interest to become possessory when the prior estate ends. If, at the time the future interest is created, it is not possible for it to become possessory upon the termination of the prior estate, the future interest is not a remainder.

Not long after the contingent remainder was recognized by the courts, the executory interest arose to complicate matters further. The executory interest, made possible by the Statute of Uses (1536), developed to do what a remainder cannot do: divest or cut short the preceding interest. An executory interest is a future interest in a transferee that can take effect only by divesting another interest. The difference between taking possession as soon as the prior estate ends and divesting the prior estate is the essential difference between a remainder and an executory interest. More on executory interests shortly.

PROBLEM

O conveys Blackacre "to *A* for life, then to *B* if *B* gives *A* a proper funeral." Does *B* have a remainder or an executory interest? If it is an executory interest, whose interest will be divested if *B* gives *A* a proper funeral?

2. Remainders

Now that you have a general idea of what a remainder is, we must explore the technical aspects of remainders further.

Remainders are classified into two general types: vested and contingent. A remainder is *vested* if (1) it is given to an ascertained person and (2) it is not subject to a condition precedent (other than the natural termination of the preceding estates). Or, to put it another way, a remainder is vested if it is created in an ascertained person and is ready to become possessory whenever and however all preceding estates expire. A remainder is *contingent* if (1) it is given to an unascertained person or (2) it is made contingent upon some event occurring other than the natural termination of the preceding estates. In the latter situation the remainder is said to be subject to a condition precedent. In either situation (owner unascertained or subject to condition precedent), the remainder is not now ready to become possessory upon the expiration of the preceding estate.

About vested remainders. A remainder may be *indefeasibly vested*, meaning that the remainder is certain of becoming possessory in the future and cannot be divested. Thus:

> *Example 3. O* conveys "to *A* for life, then to *B* and her heirs." *B* has an indefeasibly vested remainder certain to become possessory upon termination of the life estate. If *B* dies during *A*'s life, on *B*'s death *B*'s remainder passes to *B*'s devisees, or, if *B* dies without a will, passes to *B*'s heirs, or, if *B* dies without a will and without heirs, escheats to the state. *B* or *B*'s successor in interest is certain to take possession upon *A*'s death.

Time line 4-5

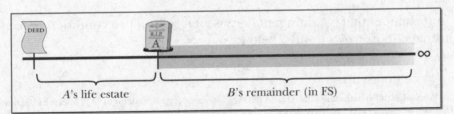

A's life estate   B's remainder (in FS)

Observe that the full state of B's title in *Example 3* is "B has a vested remainder in fee simple absolute." "Remainder" tells us the kind of future interest; "in fee simple absolute" tells us the kind of estate held as a remainder (and what kind of possessory estate the remainder will become when it becomes possessory).

A remainder may be vested but not certain of becoming possessory. It can be vested subject to being divested if an event happens. *Example 8*, on page 283, is an illustration.

A remainder created in a class of persons (such as in A's children) is vested if one member of the class is ascertained, and there is no condition precedent. The remainder is *vested subject to open* or *vested subject to partial divestment* if later-born children are entitled to share in the gift. Thus:

> *Example 4.* O conveys "to A for life, then to A's children and their heirs." A has one child, B. The remainder is vested in B subject to open to let in later-born children. B's exact share cannot be known until A dies. If A has no child at the time of the conveyance, the remainder is contingent because no taker is ascertained.

About contingent remainders. A remainder that is contingent because its takers are unascertained is illustrated by the following example:

> *Example 5.* O conveys "to A for life, then to the heirs of B." B is alive. The remainder is contingent because the heirs of B cannot be ascertained until B dies.[2] This paradox has a long history. Robert Megarry & H.W.R. Wade, The Law of Real Property 1177 (5th ed. 1984), report that after the validity of contingent remainders had become firmly established in the sixteenth century, the problem of the ownership of the inheritance remained unsolved. Some said that under the above remainder to the heirs of B, the fee simple was in abeyance, or *in nubibus* (in the clouds) or *in gremio legis* (in the bosom of the law). No living person has heirs, only heirs apparent. If B's heirs apparent do not survive B, they will not be B's heirs. The words "heirs of B" refer only to persons who survive B and are designated as B's intestate successors by the applicable statute of intestate succession.

Time line 4-6

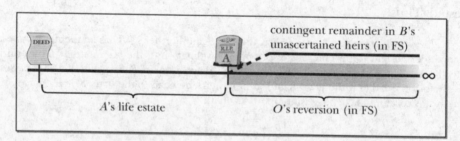

A remainder that is contingent because it is subject to a condition precedent is illustrated in *Examples 6* and *7* below:

---

2. Who owns this remainder? Can unborn persons own property? Restatement of Property §153 comment a (1936) says we cannot accurately say that an unborn person has a future interest. Yet it is quite clear that the law treats the limitation as if a future interest has been created.

Example 6. O conveys "to A for life, then to B and her heirs if B survives A." The language *if B survives A* subjects B's remainder to a condition precedent. B can take possession only if B survives A.

Example 7. O conveys "to A for life, then to B and her heirs if B survives A, and if B does not survive A to C and his heirs." The language *if B survives A* subjects B's remainder to the condition precedent of B surviving A, and the language *and if B does not survive A* subjects C's remainder to the opposite condition precedent. Here we have *alternative contingent remainders* in B and C. If the remainder in B vests, the remainder in C cannot, and vice versa.

PROBLEMS

1. O conveys "to A for life, and in the event of A's death to B and her heirs." Is B's remainder vested or contingent? If B, while A is still alive, later conveys her interest back to O, what does O have?

2. O conveys "to A for life, then to B for life, then to C and her heirs." What interests are created? Suppose the remainder to C had been "then to C and her heirs if C survives A and B." What interests are created?

3. O conveys "to A and B for their joint lives, then to the survivor in fee simple." Is the remainder vested or contingent?

4. O conveys "to A for life, then to A's children who shall reach 21." A's oldest child, B, is 17. Is the remainder vested or contingent?[3] B subsequently reaches 21. Is the remainder vested or contingent?

About vesting subject to divestment. Before divesting executory interests were recognized, it could generally be said that a vested remainder in fee simple was a remainder certain to become possessory, whereas a contingent remainder in fee simple was uncertain of possession. But the simple logic of turning classification on the certainty of possession was shattered by the Statute of Uses (1536) (see page 289), which permitted the creation of a shifting interest in a transferee that can divest a vested remainder before it becomes possessory. *Example 8* illustrates the fine distinction in modern law between a contingent remainder and a vested remainder subject to divestment.

Example 8. O conveys "to A for life, then to B and her heirs, but if B does not survive A to C and his heirs." Note carefully: B does *not* have a contingent remainder. B has a *vested remainder* in fee simple subject to divestment; C has a shifting executory interest which can become possessory only by divesting B's remainder.

The different classification of B's remainder in *Example 7* and in *Example 8* results solely from the way the conveyance is phrased. O's intent is exactly the

---

3. If A dies before B reaches 21, at common law the remainder was destroyed at A's death. Under modern law, the remainder is not destroyed, and A's children can take after A's death when they reach the age of 21. See pages 304-306.

same in both cases, but it is expressed differently. Expressing intent in different ways can produce stunning differences in result. *Examples 7* and *8* should make you keenly aware that, in the law of future interests, much turns on the exact language of the conveyance.

The key to understanding why *B*'s interest is contingent in *Example 7* and vested in *Example 8* is this: You must classify interests in sequence as they are written. You start reading to the right, classify the first interest, then move on to the second interest and classify it, and then move to the next interest. Gray put it this way: "Whether a remainder is vested or contingent depends upon the language employed. If the conditional element is incorporated into the description of, or into the gift to, the remainderman, then the remainder is contingent; but if, after words giving a vested interest, a clause is added divesting it, the remainder is vested." John C. Gray, The Rule Against Perpetuities §108 (4th ed. 1942). We have made it easy for you to see what language is "incorporated" into the gift by inserting commas in the conveyance indicating where you should stop and classify, before moving on to the next interest. In *Example 8*, stopping at the comma after the phrase "then to *B* and her heirs," you find that *B* has a vested remainder because there is no condition precedent within the commas setting off *B*'s gift. The phrase "but if *B* does not survive *A*," coming after the comma marking the end of *B*'s gift, is language incorporated into *C*'s gift, not *B*'s. The phrase thus states a condition subsequent (or divesting condition) with respect to *B*'s interest; it states a condition precedent with respect to *C*'s interest.

In classifying future interests after a life estate, you can bet on this rule: If the first future interest created is a contingent remainder in fee simple (as in *Example 7* above), the second future interest in a transferee will also be a contingent remainder. If the first future interest created is a vested remainder in fee simple (as in *Example 8* above), the second future interest in a transferee will be a divesting executory interest.

QUESTION

In *Example 7* above there is a reversion in *O*; in *Example 8* there is no reversion. In *Example 7* under what circumstances will the property revert to *O*? The key to answering this question is to realize that the life estate can terminate prior to the death of the life tenant. At early common law, a life estate was destroyed if the life tenant made a tortious conveyance (that is, breached his oath of homage to his lord by purporting to convey more than he had, for example, a fee simple). The life estate was not forfeited to the lord; the life estate simply ended, and seisin passed on to the holder of the next vested estate. Although life estates can no longer end for breach of feudal obligations, for purposes of classifying remainders *the law has continued to assume that a life estate can end prior to the death of the life tenant.*

The law has a preference for a vested remainder, and, where an instrument is ambiguous, the courts construe it in favor of a vested remainder. As Chief Justice Coke put it, "the law always delights in the vesting of estates, and contingencies are odious in the law, and are the causes of troubles, and vesting and settling of estates, the cause of repose and certainty." Roberts v. Roberts, 2 Bulst. 123, 131, 80 Eng. Rep. 1002, 1009 (K.B. 1613).

What difference does it make whether a remainder is vested or contingent? There are four great historic differences. First, a vested remainder *accelerates* into possession whenever and however the preceding estate ends—either at the life tenant's death or earlier if the life estate ends before the life tenant's death. A contingent remainder cannot become possessory so long as it remains contingent. Hence where there is a conveyance "to A for life, then to B, but if B dies under 21 to C," B, holding a vested remainder, is entitled to possession at A's death, even though B is under 21. If B is under 21, B's possessory estate remains subject to divestment until B reaches 21. If, on the other hand, the conveyance had read "to A for life, then to B if B reaches 21," B would not be entitled to possession at A's death prior to B's reaching 21.

Second, at early common law a contingent remainder, with a few exceptions, was *not assignable* during the remainderman's life and hence was unreachable by creditors. A contingent remainder was thought of as a mere possibility of becoming an interest and not as an interest ("thing") that could be transferred. (But oddly enough, when the question was whether the heirs of a dead remainderman inherited the remainder, the courts saw the remainder as an interest passing to them, if survivorship was not required by the instrument.) Inasmuch as today we regard contingent remainders as interests in property, in most states contingent remainders are now transferable during life and reachable by creditors. In a handful of states, the old common law is still followed. Vested remainders have always been transferable during life as well as at death.

The third difference between vested and contingent remainders is that at common law contingent remainders were *destroyed* if they did not vest upon termination of the preceding life estate, whereas vested remainders were not destructible in this manner. We shall consider the modern law on this later in this chapter.

The fourth difference is that contingent remainders are subject to the *Rule Against Perpetuities*, whereas vested remainders are not. In applying this rule, the distinction between vested and contingent remainders remains all-important. We consider the Rule Against Perpetuities at the end of this chapter.

In addition to the major common law differences, under some state statutes the owner of a contingent remainder may not have standing to sue for waste, or for partition, or for a trust accounting, whereas a vested remainderman has such standing. Legislatures have sometimes assumed that a vested interest is more worthy of protection than a contingent interest. (Does this make sense when the vested interest is held subject to divestment? Would it be better to distinguish between remainders certain to become possessory and remainders not certain of possession?)

3. Executory Interests

An executory interest is a future interest in a transferee that must, in order to become possessory,

(1) divest or cut short some interest in another *transferee* (this is known as a shifting executory interest), or

(2) divest the *transferor* in the future (this is known as a springing executory interest).[4]

Executory interests grew out of the more or less accidental circumstance that England had, in addition to courts of law, a separate Court of Equity (known also as the Court of Chancery). After the Conquest, every king had his chancellor, who had custody of the great seal and was head of all the king's clerks. The chancellor was almost always a cleric, often a high ecclesiastical official. He was also a member of the king's council—indeed, the specially learned member. When relief was not forthcoming from the common law courts, petitioners asked the king's council to interfere on behalf of the king for the love of God and in the way of charity. Because of the chancellor's learning and his position as "Keeper of the King's Conscience," the council more and more referred petitions to the chancellor, and by the end of the reign of Henry V (1413-1422) the Court of Chancery had become an established court of the realm.

The law courts adjudicated title, declaring who had rights in land. The chancellor did what conscience required by enforcing personal duties. The chancellor could not declare rights, but he could, if conscience demanded, punish those who insisted upon enforcing their rights. Thus he could bring powerful pressure on persons to obey him while not altering their legal rights. Quite naturally, lawyers appealed to the chancellor's conscience to impart a much needed element of elasticity into the rigidity of the land law and hence give to landowners wider powers over their property than they possessed at common law. The chancellor's rules also offered the possibility of avoiding taxation, and it was this that brought on the Statute of Uses.

a. Two Prohibitory Rules: No Shifting Interests; No Springing Interests

Prior to 1536 common law courts laid down two rules based upon their ideas of estates and of conveyancing. The first of these was that *no future interest could be created in favor of a transferee if the interest could operate to cut short a freehold estate.* Thus:

---

4. We differentiate here between a shifting executory interest and a springing executory interest because we think it helps the student better understand what an executory interest is, but there is no difference in legal consequences between the two.

Example 9. Prior to the Statute of Uses (1536), *O* conveys Whiteacre, a small tract of land, "to my eldest son *A* and his heirs, but if *A* inherits Blackacre (the family manor), then Whiteacre is to go to my second son *B* and his heirs." Under this conveyance, *A* takes a fee simple absolute and *B* takes nothing. *O* cannot shift title and thus is prevented from planning in this manner for contingent events.

The reason for the rule was that *O* could not create a right of entry in a · stranger,[5] which a shifting interest resembled.

The second rule was that *no freehold estate could be created to spring up in the future.* This was a rule against interests springing out of the grantor at some future date. Thus:

Example 10. Prior to the Statute of Uses, *O* conveys "to *A* and her heirs when *A* marries *B*." Under this conveyance, *A* takes nothing; *O* is left with the fee simple.

The reason for this rule? A freehold estate could not be created unless a feoffment with livery of seisin took place on the land. In *Example 10*, *A* could not take seisin at the time of the conveyance because *O* did not intend it to pass to *A* until *A* married. So *A* took nothing.

This rule did not prevent the creation of a remainder to commence in the future, provided there was a freehold estate in a transferee to support it. Thus in a grant "to *A* for life, then to *B* and her heirs," livery of seisin to *A* was sufficient to create *A*'s freehold life estate and also to sustain *B*'s remainder. *A* held seisin for his life, and on *A*'s death seisin immediately passed to *B* according to the terms of the original grant.

b. The Rise of the Use

The chancellor was concerned with conscience, not seisin, and paid no attention to the seisin rules of the law courts. When he thought persons should be required to perform their moral duties, the chancellor would step in and protect a transferee, regardless of what his legal rights might be. Hence there developed in equity a protected interest known as a "use" (meaning benefit).

Example 11. Before the Statute of Uses, *O* goes on the land and enfeoffs "*X* and his heirs to hold to the use of *A* and his heirs, but if *A* inherits the family manor, then to the use of *O*'s second son *B* and his heirs." (Compare *Example 9*.)

So far as the law courts were concerned, the feoffment with livery of seisin created a fee simple absolute in *X*; the law courts refused to compel the feoffee to uses, *X*, to hold the land for the benefit of *A*. The chancellor, however, thought that *X* had a good faith duty to hold seisin for the benefit of *A*, the *cestui que use*, a corruption of *cestui a que use le feoffment fuit fait* (the one for whose benefit the

5. See footnote 31 on page 246.

feoffment was made). If the shifting event happened, X had the duty to hold for the benefit of the other *cestui que use, B.* The chancellor enforced this duty. He would issue an order for the feoffee to uses to appear before him and, if satisfied that there was a just complaint, order the feoffee to perform some definite act, such as paying the rent to the *cestui que use* or letting the *cestui* into possession. The chancellor made no order concerning the title to the land in question, which was within the jurisdiction of the law courts, but he could coerce the legal owner by threatening him with imprisonment.

In *Example 11* we have a feoffment to uses. Another common method of creating a use was the bargain and sale deed.[6] Suppose that O and his grantee did not want to go out to the land (perhaps many miles removed from London) and perform livery of seisin; instead, in the London office of his solicitor, O sold Blackacre to A for £50 and gave a bargain and sale deed to "A and his heirs." Because there had been no feoffment with livery of seisin, legal title and seisin were still in O. But here again, to enforce the bargain the chancellor stepped in and required O to hold legal title to Blackacre for the benefit of A.

Springing uses as well as shifting uses might be created in equity. For example, O might wish to endow his daughter A with a suitable tract of land upon her marriage to B. A conveyance when A marries B—in the form of *Example 10*—violated the law courts' rule against springing interests. But O could avoid this rule by enfeoffing "X and his heirs to the use of O and his heirs and then to the use of A and her heirs when A marries B." Equity would enforce the springing use.

As time passed, it became evident that all sorts of benefits could be accomplished by "raising a use." For example, until 1540 land could not be devised by will—but O could obtain the practical equivalent of a will by enfeoffing "X and his heirs to the use of O during O's lifetime and then to the use of such persons as O shall appoint by will." By this device O could effectively circumvent the doctrine of primogeniture and leave land to a younger son or a daughter. Particularly because of its success in avoiding those medieval taxes known as feudal incidents, the use became universally popular.[7] By the time of the Wars of the Roses the greater part of the land in England was held in use.

---

6. When no consideration was given, a covenant to stand seised could raise a use in favor of family members. For example, O might covenant to stand seised in favor of his daughter A. Love and affection for relatives sufficed as good consideration to raise a use. The covenant to stand seised developed after the Statute of Uses as the normal method of making a family settlement. Unlike livery, it was secret, an advantage still sought by the rich today.

7. Feudal incidents were levied when seisin descended to the heir upon death (see pages 212-213). This catastrophe to family finances could be avoided by preventing the descent of seisin. How was this done? O simply enfeoffed a large group of persons as joint tenants who held seisin to O's own use. Under the theory of joint tenancy (page 344), upon the death of one joint tenant, seisin does not descend to his heir nor pass to the surviving tenants, who are viewed as seised of the whole property from the beginning of the tenancy. When the number of joint tenants holding seisin grew dangerously low, others could be enfeoffed jointly with them.

c.   Abolition of the Use: The Statute of Uses

Shortly after his break with Rome, Henry VIII ran short of money. He resolved to meet his needs by restoring feudal revenues, which had been depleted by the prevalence of uses. After various maneuvers, including threats, lawsuits, and cajolery, "the Statute of Uses was forced upon an unwilling Parliament by an extremely strong-willed king."[8] The statute was enacted in 1535, to become effective in 1536.

Henry VIII
by Hans Holbein the Younger, c. 1536

8. Frederic W. Maitland, Equity 34 (John Brunyate rev. ed. 1947).

It provided that if any person or persons were seised to the use of any other person or persons, the legal estate (seisin) would be taken away from the feoffee to uses and given to the *cestui que use*. In the language of the time, the statute "executed" the use, that is, converted it into a legal interest.

One effect of the statute was to expand legal future interests by converting what were "shifting uses" and "springing uses" in equity before 1536 into legal "shifting executory interests" and "springing executory interests." Thus:

> *Example 12.* After 1536 *O* bargains and sells "to *A* and his heirs, but if *B* returns from Rome, then to *B* and his heirs." Here the bargain and sale conveyance raised a use in *A* and a shifting use in *B*. These were immediately "executed" by the statute, leaving as the state of *legal* title: Fee simple in *A* subject to a shifting executory interest in *B* in fee simple.

> *Example 13.* After 1536 *O* covenants to stand seised "for the benefit of *A* and her heirs when *A* marries *B*." Here the covenant to stand seised raised a use—which was immediately "executed" by the statute, leaving as the state of *legal* title: Fee simple in *O* subject to a springing executory interest in *A* in fee simple.

That is the story of how executory interests came to be recognized. What are called executory interests today are interests that would have been void at law prior to the Statute of Uses because they violated the two rules stated above.

On the Statute of Uses, see A.W. Brian Simpson, A History of the Land Law 173-207 (2d ed. 1986).

d.   Modern Executory Interests

One effect of the Statute of Uses was to permit the creation of a new estate: *a fee simple subject to an executory limitation*. This is a fee simple that, upon the happening of a stated event, is automatically divested by an executory interest in a *transferee*. Such a fee simple can be created either in possession or in remainder. Thus:

> *Example 14.* *O* conveys "to *A* and his heirs, but if *A* dies without issue surviving him, to *B* and her heirs." *A* has a possessory fee simple subject to an executory limitation (or subject to divestment by *B*'s executory interest). *B*'s future interest can become possessory only by divesting *A*.

Time line 4-7

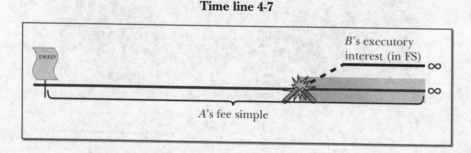

> *Example 15.* *O* conveys "to *A* for life, then to *B* and her heirs, but if *B* dies under the age of 21, to *C* and her heirs." *B* is age 15. *B* has a vested remainder in fee simple subject to an executory

limitation (or subject to divestment by *C*'s executory interest if *B* dies under age 21). Also see *Example 8* above.

Time line 4-8

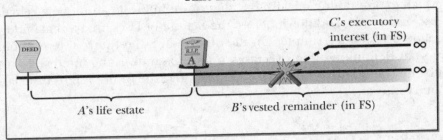

Executory interests are ordinarily treated as contingent interests, because they are subject to a condition precedent and do not vest until they become possessory.

Back to defeasible fees. In our discussion of defeasible fees at pages 244-247, we noted that executory interests might be created to follow those interests, rather than a possibility of reverter or a right of entry. A possibility of reverter or a right of entry can be created only in the transferor; an executory interest can be created only in a transferee. Thus, if the transferor wants to create a future interest in a transferee after a defeasible fee, it will necessarily be an executory interest.

> *Example 16. O* conveys "to Hartford School Board, but if the premises are not used for school purposes during the next 20 years, to Town Library." The School Board has a fee simple subject to an executory interest that will automatically divest the Board's fee simple if the condition happens. (In this respect the executory interest differs from a right of entry in *O*, which is optional, not automatic in divesting.)

Time line 4-9

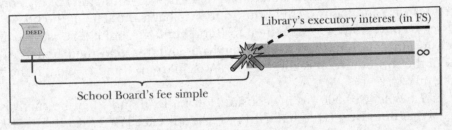

> *Example 17. O* conveys "to Hartford School Board so long as the premises are used for school purposes, then to Town Library." The School Board has a fee simple determinable followed by an executory interest. Town Library has an executory interest. (For an explanation of why the School Board has a determinable fee in Example 17 but a fee subject to executory limitation in Example 16, see page 247 in Chapter 3.)

Time line 4-10

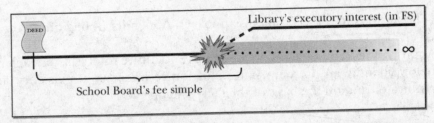

The interest given to Town Library in *Example 17* is not a divesting interest and should logically be classified as a remainder. It stands ready to *succeed* on the natural expiration of the preceding estate; it does *not divest* the determinable fee, which expires automatically. But the future interest cannot be a remainder because of the rule, laid down before the Statute of Uses, that a remainder cannot follow a vested fee simple. On the other hand, the future interest does not fit into our definition of an executory interest as a divesting interest. Forced to violate one rule or the other, courts chose to give the future interest the label of executory interest.

PROBLEMS AND NOTE

1. *O*, owner of Wiseacre, comes to you to draft an instrument of gift. *O* tells you he wants to convey Wiseacre to his son *A* for life, and upon *A*'s death *O* wants Wiseacre to go to *A*'s children if any are alive or, if none are then alive, to *O*'s daughter *B*. Consider the following conveyances, all carrying out *O*'s intent, but each creating different future interests. Identify the future interests.

(a) *O* conveys "to *A* for life, then to *A*'s children and their heirs, but if at *A*'s death he is not survived by any children, then to *B* and her heirs." At the time of the conveyance, *A* is alive and has no children. What is the state of the title?

Two years after the conveyance, twins, *C* and *D*, are born to *A*. What is the state of the title?

Suppose that *C* dies during *A*'s lifetime, and that *A* is survived by *B* and *D*. What is the state of the title?

(b) *O* conveys "to *A* for life, then to such of *A*'s children as survive him, but if none of *A*'s children survives him, to *B* and her heirs." At the time of the conveyance, *A* is alive and has two children, *C* and *D*. What is the state of the title?

(c) *O* conveys "to *A* for life, then to *B* and her heirs, but if *A* is survived at his death by any children, then to such surviving children and their heirs." At the time of the conveyance, *A* is alive and has two children, *C* and *D*. What is the state of the title?

2. *T* devises $10,000 "to my cousin, Don Little, if and when he survives his wife." What does Don Little have? In re Little's Estate, 170 A.2d 106 (Pa. 1961). Why do you suppose that the testator would make such a devise?

3. For a proposal to reform and simplify the system of estates through a Uniform Future Interests Act, see T.P. Gallanis, The Future of Future Interests, 60 Wash. & Lee L. Rev. 513 (2003).

REVIEW PROBLEMS

(The answers to these Problems appear in Appendix B, beginning on page 1269.)

Applying the traditional system of estates and future interests, for each problem below, identify all present estates and future interests in existence at the times indicated and on the basis of the facts stated.

1. *O* conveys "to *A* for life, then to *B* for life, then to *C*'s heirs." *A*, *B*, *C*, and *O* are all alive at the time of the conveyance. *C* is unmarried and has two living children, *X* and *Y*.

2. *O* conveys "to *A* upon her first wedding anniversary." *A* is alive and unmarried at the time of the conveyance. *O* is also then alive.

3. *O* conveys "to *A* for 10 years, then to such of *A*'s children as attain age 21." At the time of the conveyance, *A* and *O* were alive. *A* had two children, *X* and *Y*, ages 20 and 17, respectively.

4. Applying the same facts as in Problem 3, assume that *X* later attains age 21 and *Y* is still under age 21. *A* and *O* are both still alive.

5. Applying the same facts as in Problem 3, assume that *X* dies when *X* is age 22 and *Y* is age 19. *O* is still alive.

6. *O* conveys "to *A* for life, then to *A*'s children." *A* and *O* are alive at the time of the conveyance. *A* has one child, *X*.

7. Applying the same facts as in Problem 6, assume that *A* has another child, *Y*, and then *A* dies survived by *X*, *Y*, and *O*. Identify all of the estates and future interests existing as of *A*'s death.

8. *O* conveys "to *A* for life, then to *B* and her heirs; but if *B* marries *Z*, then to *C* and his heirs."

9. *O* conveys Blackacre "to *A* for life, then to *B* and her heirs so long as Blackacre is organically farmed."

10. *O* conveys a sum of money "to *A* if she graduates from college." *A* is not yet enrolled in college.

Remainder or executory interest: does it matter? As we have seen, historically the law of future interests divided those interests initially created in transferees into two distinct categories: remainders and executory interests. As we have also seen, the distinction is sometimes not obvious and is difficult to draw. (Consider, for example, the distinction between a contingent remainder and an executory interest.) So it is worth asking whether any legal consequences turn on a future interest being labeled a remainder or an executory interest. The answer is yes and no. At common law there certainly were important consequences. Executory interests were not subject to destruction by a gap in seisin, as were contingent remainders (see pages 304-306). And executory interests possibly were not caught within the web of Shelley's Case (see pages 306-307). These rules have been abolished in all but a handful of states, and, where abolished, there may be no significant differences in legal consequences between executory interests and remainders. See D. Benjamin Barros, Toward a Model Law of Estates and Future Interests, 66 Wash. & Lee L. Rev. 3 (2009); T.P. Gallanis, The Future of Future Interests, 60 Wash. & Lee L. Rev. 513 (2003); Lawrence W. Waggoner, Reformulating the Structure of Estates: A Proposal for Legislative Action, 85 Harv. L. Rev. 729 (1972); Jesse Dukeminier, Contingent Remainders and Executory Interests: A Requiem for the Distinction, 43 Minn. L. Rev. 13 (1958). See also Joseph William Singer,

Democratic Estates: Property Law in a Free and Democratic Society, 94 Cornell L. Rev. 1009 (2009). Modern statutes often include executory interests in an all-inclusive definition of a remainder. See, e.g., N.Y. Est., Powers & Trusts Law §6-3.2 (McKinney 2002).

Simplifying the law of future interests and the Restatement (Third). Reacting to the long overdue need to simplify the system of future interests and to eliminate ancient and obsolete distinctions, the Restatement (Third) of Property makes several major changes in the classification of future interests. First, it eliminates the historical division of future interests into five types (remainders, executory interests, reversions, possibilities of reverter, and rights of entry), and simply categorizes all future interests as "future interests." Restatement (Third) of Property, Wills and Other Donative Transfers §§25.1, 25.2 (2011). In addition, all future interests are alienable, devisable, and descendible if the owner's death does not cause the interest's termination (unless it is subject to a valid restraint on alienation). Id. §25.2 comment g.

> *Example 18.* O conveys Blackacre "to the School Board so long as the premises are used for educational purposes during O's lifetime; if the School Board allows the premises to be used for non-educational purposes, then the land reverts back to O." Under the Restatement (Third)'s new classification system, the School Board has a fee simple defeasible, and O's interest is classified simply as a future interest.

> *Example 19.* O conveys "to A for life, then to B if B survives to age 21." Historically, B's interest was classified as a contingent remainder. Under the Restatement (Third)'s new classification system, B's interest is classified simply as a future interest. Moreover, historically, O's interest during A's life and prior to B's reaching age 21 was classified as a reversion. Under the Restatement (Third)'s new classification system, O's interest is classified simply as a future interest.

The second change is that the Restatement (Third) eliminates the traditional categories of future interests as indefeasibly vested, vested subject to complete defeasance, vested subject to open, and contingent, and replaces them with only one distinction—vested or contingent. Id. §25.3. It provides that a future interest is contingent "if, for any reason, it might not take effect in possession or enjoyment." Id. §25.3 comment f. It further provides that either a vested or a contingent future interest can be subject to open.

> *Example 20.* O conveys Blackacre "to the School Board so long as the premises are used for educational purposes; if the School Board allows the premises to be used for non-educational purposes during O's lifetime, then the land reverts back to O." Under the Restatement (Third)'s new classification system, the School Board has a fee simple defeasible, and O has a future interest. O's future interest is classified as contingent because it is not certain to become possessory.

> *Example 21.* O conveys "to A for life, then to B, but if B predeceases A, then to return to O." Historically, B's interest was classified as a vested remainder subject to complete defeasance (divestment). Under the Restatement (Third)'s new classification system, B's future interest is classified as contingent because it will not take effect in possession or enjoyment in B if B fails to survive A. Moreover, historically, O's interest during A's and B's lifetimes was classified as vested subject to complete defeasance (divestment). Under the Restatement (Third)'s new

classification system, *O*'s future interest is classified as contingent because *B* might survive *A*, in which case *O* will not be entitled to possess or enjoy the property.

> *Example 22.* *O* conveys "to *A* for life, then to *B*, but if *B* predeceases *A*, then to *C*." Under the Restatement (Third)'s new classification system, *B*'s future interest is classified as contingent for the reason explained in *Example 21*. Historically, during *A*'s and *B*'s lifetimes *C*'s interest was classified as an executory interest. If *B* predeceased *A*, then *C*'s interest would have divested *B*'s vested remainder and become a vested remainder. Under the Restatement (Third)'s new classification system, *C*'s future interest is classified as contingent because *B* might survive *A*, in which case *C*'s interest will not take effect in possession or enjoyment either in *C* personally or in *C*'s successors in interest.

A third change concerns class gifts. The Restatement (Third) provides that in cases of future interests transferred to a class that is still open to new members, the interest of each class member existing from time to time is classified as subject to open. Moreover, the future interest may be classified either as vested or contingent. However, the interests of potential class members are always classified as contingent. Id. §25.4.

> *Example 23.* *O* conveys "to *A* for life, then to *A*'s children." At the time of the conveyance *A* had two children, *X* and *Y*, then alive. Historically, during *A*'s lifetime the remainder created in *X* and *Y* was classified as vested subject to open (executory interests were also recognized in *A*'s unborn or unadopted children). Under the Restatement (Third)'s new classification system, *X* and *Y* each have a vested future interest subject to open. Each of *A*'s unborn or unadopted children have a contingent future interest subject to open. Each one may or may not be born or adopted, so the interest is not certain to take effect in possession or enjoyment. Id. §25.4 illustration 1.

D. The Trust

The use, which the Statute of Uses never did completely abolish,[9] is the basis for the modern trust, a fundamental device in estate planning today. Trusts allow settlors to arrange their assets in ways that maximize flexibility in property management as well as transfer wealth to future generations.

The core of the trust is separation of "legal" and "equitable" title. The trustee holds legal title to the trust property and manages that property for the benefit of the beneficiaries, who have the right of beneficial enjoyment of the property. In the usual trust, the trustee has the power to sell trust assets and reinvest the proceeds in other assets. The net income of the trust is paid to the beneficiaries, and upon termination of the trust the trust assets as they then exist are handed over to the designated beneficiaries, free of the trust.

The dual ownership of the trust property was possible because of the existence of separate courts of law and equity. Although the trustee is the legal owner,

---

9. The common law courts held that the statute did not apply if the feoffee to uses (*trustee* in today's language) was given active duties, which is exactly the case in the modern trust.

THE SYSTEM OF ESTATES AND FUTURE INTERESTS

Suppose that a transferor who owns land in fee simple absolute conveys one of the possessory estates listed in the left column below. What future interests, if any, might then arise? The middle column shows the possible future interests in the transferor, and the right column shows the possible future interests in transferees.

| POSSESSORY ESTATES | POSSIBLE COMBINATIONS OF FUTURE INTERESTS | |
	In Transferor	In Transferee
Fee simple absolute	None	None
Defeasible fee simple:		
• Fee simple determinable	Possibility of reverter	None
• Fee simple subject ot a condition subsequent	Right of entry (power of termination)	None
• Fee simple subject to an executory limitation	None	Executory interest
Fee tail	Same as with Life estate	Same as with Life estate
Life estate	Reversion [indefeasibly vested] (when no remainder created)	
	Reversion [vested subject to defeasance] (when contingent remainder(s) created)	Contingent remainder(s)
	Possibility of reverter (if any)	Remainder vested subject to open
	Right of entry incident to reversion	Remainder vested subject to divestment
	Reversion [vested subject to defeasance or indefeasibly vested]	Executory interest (if any)
		Remainder vested subject to limitational defeasance
	None	Executory interests in unborn class members
	None	Indefeasibly vested remainder
Leaseholds	Same as with Life estates	Same as with Life estates

it is subject to orders of an equity court, which enforces the trustee's duties to the beneficiaries, who are said to hold equitable interests, that is, interests enforceable by courts of equity.

In the typical trust the beneficiaries hold equitable interests that correspond to the legal possessory estates and future interests you have studied. Thus:

> *Example 24. O* conveys Blackacre "to *X* in trust to pay the income to *A* for life, and then to pay the principal to *A*'s children who survive *A*." *X* is given the express power to sell Blackacre. *X* has the legal fee simple in Blackacre; *A* has an equitable life estate and is entitled to all the income generated by the property. *A*'s children have an equitable contingent remainder, and *O* has an equitable reversion. If *X* sells Blackacre for $200,000 and reinvests the $200,000 in Whiteacre and General Motors stock, the trust property then consists of these latter items. Upon *A*'s death *X* conveys the trust property to the persons entitled thereto, *A*'s children if any are alive or *O* if *A* has no surviving children.

The trustee is a fiduciary and thus subject to stringent duties in managing trust property. Most important is the duty of loyalty. The trustee must act for the exclusive benefit of the beneficiaries and is not permitted to benefit personally. For breach of this or any other fiduciary duty the trustee is subject to personal liability to the beneficiaries and may be removed by a court.

One of the many benefits of the trust is that settlors can protect the beneficiaries' interests by making them inalienable. Spendthrift trusts, as they are called, are possible because American courts in the late nineteenth century held that the common law rules against restraints on alienation, which you studied on pages 232-233, do not apply to beneficiaries' equitable interests. As a consequence, trusts can be drafted in such a way that trust beneficiaries have no power to transfer or borrow against their trust interests, and creditors have no power to reach those interests to satisfy beneficiaries' debts. Indeed, a few states in recent years have enacted statutes that permit settlors to create trusts in which the settlor's own equitable interest, usually a life estate, is immune from creditor claims. You will study these asset-protection trusts and other types of trusts in much more detail in courses on wills, trusts, and estate planning.

Spendthrift trusts first appeared in the late nineteenth century as the result of the famous case that follows.

Broadway National Bank v. Adams

Supreme Judicial Court of Massachusetts, 1882
133 Mass. 170

MORTON, C.J. The object of this bill in equity is to reach and apply in payment of the plaintiff's debt due from the defendant Adams the income of a trust fund created for his benefit by the will of his brother. The eleventh article of the will is as follows:

> I give the sum of seventy-five thousand dollars to my said executors and the survivors or survivor of them, in trust to invest the same in such manner as to them may seem prudent, and to pay

the net income thereof, semiannually, to my said brother Charles W. Adams, during his natural life, such payments to be made to him personally when convenient, otherwise, upon his order or receipt in writing; in either case free from the interference or control of his creditors, my intention being that the use of said income shall not be anticipated by assignment. At the decease of my said brother Charles, my will is that the net income of said seventy-five thousand dollars shall be paid to his present wife, in case she survives him, for the benefit of herself and all the children of said Charles, in equal proportions, in the manner and upon the conditions the same as herein directed to be paid him during his life, so long as she shall remain single. And my will is, that, after the decease of said Charles and the decease or second marriage of his said wife, the said seventy-five thousand dollars, together with any accrued interest or income thereon which may remain unpaid, as herein above directed, shall be divided equally among all the children of my said brother Charles, by any and all his wives, and the representatives of any deceased child or children by right of representation.

There is no room for doubt as to the intention of the testator. It is clear that, if the trustee was to pay the income to the plaintiff under an order of the court, it would be in direct violation of the intention of the testator and of the provisions of his will. The court will not compel the trustee thus to do what the will forbids him to do, unless the provisions and intention of the testator are unlawful.

The question whether the founder of a trust can secure the income of it to the object of his bounty, by providing that it shall not be alienable by him or be subject to be taken by his creditors, has not been directly adjudicated in this Commonwealth. The tendency of our decisions, however, has been in favor of such a power in the founder. . . . Sparhawk v. Cloon, 125 Mass. 263.

It is true that the rule of the common law is, that a man cannot attach to a grant or transfer of property, otherwise absolute, the condition that it shall not be alienated; such condition being repugnant to the nature of the estate granted. Co. Lit. 223 *a*. Blackstone Bank v. Davis, 21 Pick. 42.

Lord Coke gives as the reason of the rule, that "it is absurd and repugnant to reason that he, that hath no possibility to have the land revert to him, should restrain his feoffee in fee simple of all his power to alien," and that this is "against the height and puritie of a fee simple." By such a condition, the grantor undertakes to deprive the property in the hands of the grantee of one of its legal incidents and attributes, namely, its alienability, which is deemed to be against public policy. But the reasons of the rule do not apply in the case of a transfer of property in trust. By the creation of a trust like the one before us, the trust property passes to the trustee with all its incidents and attributes unimpaired. He takes the whole legal title to the property, with the power of alienation; the *cestui que trust* takes the whole legal title to the accrued income at the moment it is paid over to him. Neither the principal nor the income is at any time inalienable.

The question whether the rule of the common law should be applied to equitable life estates created by will or deed, has been the subject of conflicting adjudications by different courts, as is fully shown in the able and exhaustive arguments of the counsel in this case. As is stated in Sparhawk v. Cloon, above cited, from the time of Lord Eldon the rule has prevailed in the English Court of Chancery, to the extent of holding that when the income of a trust estate is given to any person (other than a married woman) for life, the equitable estate for life is alienable by, and liable in equity to the debts of, the *cestui que trust,* and that this quality is so inseparable from the estate that no provision, however express, which does not operate as a cesser or limitation of the estate itself, can protect it from his debts. . . .

The English rule has been adopted in several of the courts of this country.

Other courts have rejected it, and have held that the founder of a trust may secure the benefit of it to the object of his bounty, by providing that the income shall not be alienable by anticipation, nor subject to be taken for his debts.

The precise point involved in the case at bar has not been adjudicated in this Commonwealth; but the decisions of this court which we have before cited recognize the principle, that, if the intention of the founder of a trust, like the one before us, is to give to the equitable life tenant a qualified and limited, and not an absolute, estate in the income, such life tenant cannot alienate it by anticipation, and his creditors cannot reach it at law or in equity. It seems to us that this principle extends to and covers the case at bar. The founder of this trust was the absolute owner of his property. He had the entire right to dispose of it, either by an absolute gift to his brother, or by a gift with such restrictions or limitations, not repugnant to law, as he saw fit to impose. His clear intention, as shown in his will, was not to give his brother an absolute right to the income which might hereafter accrue upon the trust fund, with the power of alienating it in advance, but only the right to receive semiannually the income of the fund, which upon its payment to him, and not before, was to become his absolute property. His intentions ought to be carried out, unless they are against public policy. There is nothing in the nature or tenure of the estate given to the *cestui que trust* which should prevent this. The power of alienating in advance is not a necessary attribute or incident of such an estate or interest, so that the restraint of such alienation would introduce repugnant or inconsistent elements.

We are not able to see that it would violate any principles of sound public policy to permit a testator to give to the object of his bounty such a qualified interest in the income of a trust fund, and thus provide against the improvidence or misfortune of the beneficiary. The only ground upon which it can be held to be against public policy is, that it defrauds the creditors of the beneficiary.

It is argued that investing a man with apparent wealth tends to mislead creditors, and to induce them to give him credit. The answer is, that creditors have no right to rely upon property thus held, and to give him credit upon the basis of an estate which, by the instrument creating it, is declared to be inalienable by him, and not liable for his debts. By the exercise of proper diligence, they can ascertain the nature and extent of his estate, especially in this Commonwealth, where all wills and most deeds are spread upon the public records. There is the same danger of their being misled by false appearances, and induced to give credit to the equitable life tenant when the will or deed of trust provides for a cesser or limitation over, in case of an attempted alienation, or of bankruptcy or attachment, and the argument would lead to the conclusion that the English rule is equally in violation of public policy. We do not see why the founder of a trust may not directly provide that his property shall go to his beneficiary with the restriction that it shall not be alienable by anticipation, and that his creditors shall not have the right to attach it in advance, instead of indirectly reaching the same result by a provision for a cesser or a limitation over, or by giving his trustees a discretion as to paying it. He has the entire *jus disponendi*, which imports that he may give it absolutely, or may impose any restrictions or fetters not repugnant to the nature of the estate which he gives. Under our system, creditors may reach all the property of the debtor not exempted by law, but they cannot enlarge the gift of the founder of a trust, and take more than he has given.

The rule of public policy which subjects a debtor's property to the payment of his debts, does not subject the property of a donor to the debts of his beneficiary, and does not give the creditor a right to complain that, in the exercise of his absolute right of disposition, the donor has not seen fit to give the property to the creditor, but has left it out of his reach.

Whether a man can settle his own property in trust for his own benefit, so as to exempt the income from alienation by him or attachment in advance by his creditors, is a different question, which we are not called upon to consider in this case. But we are of opinion that any other person, having the entire right to dispose of his property, may settle it in trust in favor of a beneficiary, and may provide that it shall not be alienated by him by anticipation, and shall not be subject to be seized by his creditors in advance of its payment to him.

It follows that, under the provisions of the will which we are considering, the income of the trust fund created for the benefit of the defendant Adams cannot be reached by attachment, either at law or in equity, before it is paid to him. Bill dismissed.

John C. Gray, Restraints on the Alienation of Property
242-247 (2d ed. 1895)

[The fallacy of Broadway National Bank v. Adams] is, that the only objection to such inalienable life estates is that they defraud the creditors of the life tenant; and the courts labor, with more or less success, to show that these creditors are not defrauded.[10] . . . But, with submission, this is not the ground why equitable life estates cannot be made inalienable and free from debts. The true ground is that on which the whole law of property, legal and equitable, is based: — that inalienable rights of property are opposed to the fundamental principles of the common law; that it is against public policy that a man "should have an estate to live on, but not an estate to pay his debts with," Tillinghast v. Bradford, 5 R.I. 205, 212, . . . and should have the benefits of wealth without the responsibilities.

10. In Nichols v. Eaton, 91 U.S. 716, 726, and Broadway National Bank v. Adams, 133 Mass. 170, it is said that by means of the public records creditors can learn the existence of these trusts. But (1) Deeds settling personal property, e.g., marriage settlements, are not recorded. (2) In what registry is a creditor to look to see whether there is a will creating a spendthrift trust in favor of his debtor? That a debtor lives in a certain county is no reason why a trust may not be created for him by a will recorded in some other county or State.

John Chipman Gray

The common law has recognized certain classes of persons who may be kept in pupilage, viz. infants, lunatics, married women; but it has held that sane grown men must look out for themselves,—that it is not the function of the law to join the futile effort to save the foolish and the vicious from the consequences of their own vice and folly. It is wholesome doctrine, fit to produce a manly race, based on sound morality and wise philosophy. . . .

That grown men should be kept all their lives in pupilage, that men not paying their debts should live in luxury on inherited wealth, are doctrines as undemocratic as can well be conceived. They are suited to the times in which the Statute de Donis was enacted, and the law was administered in the interest of rich and powerful families. The general introduction of spendthrift trusts would be to form a privileged class, who could indulge in every speculation, could practise [sic] every fraud, and yet, provided they kept on the safe side of the criminal law, could roll in wealth. They would be an aristocracy, though certainly the most contemptible aristocracy with which a country was ever cursed.

NOTES AND QUESTIONS

1. *Gray's critique of spendthrift trusts.* John Chipman Gray was one of the towering figures of American property law. A teacher of property at Harvard from 1869 to 1913,[11] Gray assembled six volumes of cases on property, which law students painstakingly dissected. Famed for his erudition, rigorous logic, and oracular style, Gray was so outraged by judicial approval of the spendthrift trust that he wrote Restraints on the Alienation of Property (1st ed. 1883) denouncing the spendthrift trust on all scores: precedent, policy, and logic. Despite Gray's fulmination, the spendthrift trust is now accepted in a large majority of states. See generally 3 Austin W. Scott, William F. Fratcher & Mark L. Ascher, Scott and Ascher on Trusts §§14.9, 15.2-15.8 (5th ed. 2007). The historical development of the doctrine is explained in Gregory S. Alexander, The Dead Hand and the Law of Trusts in the Nineteenth Century, 37 Stan. L. Rev. 1189 (1985).

Although Gray's views on spendthrift trusts were rejected, his second book, the great Rule Against Perpetuities (1st ed. 1886), was enormously influential. It became *the* authority on perpetuities law, one of the few American law books to be accepted as authority on English law by English courts. We shall meet the Rule Against Perpetuities later in this chapter.

2. Why is a disabling restraint upon an equitable life estate valid when a disabling restraint upon a legal life estate (see page 232) is void? Why can wages be garnished by creditors of the wage earner, but income from a spendthrift trust cannot be reached by creditors?

11. Gray (1839-1915) was also one of the co-founders of the prestigious Boston law firm of Ropes & Gray where his trusts and estates clients included many of Boston's elite Back Bay families. Among his closest friends was Justice Oliver Wendell Holmes. Gray was the half-brother of U.S. Supreme Court Justice Horace Gray.

3. *Self-settled spendthrift trusts.* The spendthrift trust is only allowed for inherited wealth. A person can set up a spendthrift trust for another but not for himself. (Why not?) Thus persons who inherit wealth can be protected against creditors but persons who earn wealth cannot be. Does this make sense? Some states have recently abandoned this traditional trust doctrine. Under so-called asset protection trust statutes, a person may shield assets from his creditors by placing them in a spendthrift trust for his own benefit. E.g., Alaska Stat. §34.40.110 (2012); Del. Code Ann. tit. 12, §§3570-3576 (2012). There are a number of requirements for creating such trusts, which you may study in courses on Trusts and Estates. Are these statutes a good idea as a policy matter? The political dynamic behind them is much the same as that behind legislation permitting so-called perpetual trusts.

4. *Perpetual trusts.* A recent important development in trust law is state legislation permitting settlors to create what are called "perpetual" or "dynasty" trusts, meaning trusts that can continue to control the disposition of wealth forever into the future—literally in some jurisdictions and virtually in others. The legislation accomplishes this by changing the Rule Against Perpetuities, effectively abolishing the Rule as it applies to most family trusts. We will take up the Rule, and perpetual trusts with it, shortly. First, however, we should give a glance to three old rules that arguably shared one of the Rule's purposes, that of enhancing alienability by eliminating contingent future interests. A glance is sufficient because the rules have been abolished in most jurisdictions, but worthwhile nevertheless because they survive to some degree (even jurisdictions that have abolished them have not always done so retroactively), and because there isn't much point in knowing a rule has been abolished if you don't know what the rule was in the first place. Moreover, learning a little about these old rules will help you understand the Rule Against Perpetuities, still very much alive and kicking.

E.   Rules Furthering Marketability by Destroying Contingent Future Interests

A regular aim of people of means has long been to control their wealth over multiple future generations. Lawyers have found ways to help rich clients exercise such "dead hand" control at least since the late sixteenth and early seventeenth centuries, the period when members of the mercantile class in England began accumulating enormous fortunes. These parvenus were eager to purchase land, build stately homes, and become squires, entrenched against forfeiture, prodigal issue, and other catastrophes. Their lawyers implemented their dreams by using the newly valid shifting and springing executory interests and by exploring possible new uses of contingent remainders. (The latter had been little used before the sixteenth century, largely because, as we are about to see, they were destructible by the life tenant.) The most ambitious conveyancers began to draft extremely complicated documents creating elaborate series of future interests.[12] Judges, jealous of any maneuvers that made land inalienable, responded by developing new obstacles to these innovations, or by firming up existing ones.

The judges were especially wary of contingent interests, which, unlike vested interests, tended to make land unmarketable. The point is easy enough to see. When *O* conveyed Blackacre "to *A* for life, remainder to *B* and his heirs," a fee simple could be conveyed to a purchaser *A*, the life tenant, and *B*, with the vested remainder, simply by having *A* and *B* join in the deed. But with respect to contingent interests, obstacles to sale were much greater. If *O* conveyed land "to *A* for life, then to *A*'s heirs," the land could not be sold during *A*'s life because the heirs could not be ascertained until *A*'s death. If *T* devised land "to *A* for life, then to *B* if *B* survives *A*," *A* and *B* and *T*'s heir (who had a reversion) would have to agree to sell the land and how to divide the proceeds. Agreement was not likely, thanks mostly to high transaction costs (to use the parlance developed in Chapter 1). On top of these practical difficulties, the legal alienability of contingent interests was uncertain.

To destroy contingent interests and make land more marketable, judges developed four rules. We will quickly summarize the first three because they have been abolished, either by statute or judicial decision, in most states. The fourth rule, the Rule Against Perpetuities, is another matter.

1. Destructibility of Contingent Remainders

Here is a simple statement of the rule of destructibility of contingent remainders: *A legal remainder in land is destroyed if it does not vest at or before the termination of the preceding freehold estate.* If the remainder is still subject to a condition precedent when the preceding estate terminates, the remainder is wiped out, and the right of possession moves on to the next vested interest.

Although this rule apparently grew out of the feudal need for continuity of seisin, another policy came to support it: Destroying contingent remainders enhanced the alienability of land.

The destructibility doctrine is illustrated in the following example:

> *Example 25.* *O* conveys Blackacre "to *A* for life, then to *B* and her heirs if *B* reaches 21." If at *A*'s death *B* is under the age of 21, *B*'s remainder is destroyed. *O* now has the right of possession.

---

12. The most celebrated conveyancer of the seventeenth century was Sir Orlando Bridgeman (1606-1674). Even his enemies did not feel secure in their estates until they had consulted him. He invented, among other things, the strict settlement (see footnote 19 on page 224), and, to deal with an insane first son and heir of the Earl of Arundel, drew a daring series of instruments, the most important of which was upheld in the landmark Duke of Norfolk's Case, 22 Eng. Rep. 931 (Ch. 1681) (see page 308). Although Bridgeman's gamble in that case succeeded, his instrument raised the specter of a perpetuity, and from the case evolved the Rule Against Perpetuities.

Contingent remainders could also be destroyed another way. English courts held that the life estate could be terminated before the life tenant's death by forfeiture or merger. The life tenant therefore had the power to destroy contingent remainders whenever he wished. Thus:

> *Example 26.* O conveys Whiteacre "to *A* for life, then to *B* and her heirs if *B* survives *A.*" *A* conveys his life estate to *O*, the life estate merges into the reversion, destroying *B*'s contingent remainder.

The doctrine of merger (which is still in effect) requires a little explanation. It provides that if the life estate and the next vested estate in fee simple come into the hands of one person, the lesser estate is merged into the larger. Suppose there is a conveyance "to *A* for life, remainder to *B* and her heirs." If *A* conveys her life estate to *B*, the life estate and remainder merge, giving *B* a fee simple. This makes good sense, as there is no reason for keeping the estates separate. The courts extended the doctrine from situations like this to the very different situation where the life estate was followed by a contingent remainder and a reversion.[13] Applying the destructibility doctrine in *Example 26* makes land alienable now rather than at *A*'s death.

Because of the mysteries of the concept of seisin, the destructibility doctrine did not apply to executory interests. However, to give the destructibility doctrine as extensive a reach as possible, the courts held that you must construe a limitation as creating a contingent remainder rather than an executory interest if that construction is possible.

The destructibility doctrine proved ineffective in eliminating all future interests that might endure for an unreasonably long time. Clever lawyers could still tie up land for extended periods by creating contingent remainders in trusts (the doctrine only applied to legal contingent remainders) or by creating executory interests rather than contingent remainders. In fact, the exemption of executory interests from the destructibility rule was a main reason why judges developed the Rule Against Perpetuities.

After the Rule Against Perpetuities was fully developed in the nineteenth century, it appeared to be a good idea to subject all contingent future interests in transferees to one rule, the Rule Against Perpetuities, and abolish the destructibility doctrine. The new Restatement does not recognize the destructibility rule and states that it has been abolished by statute or case law in nearly all states. Restatement (Third) of Property, Wills and Other Donative Transfers §25.5 Reporter's Notes (2011).

To see the effect of abolition of the destructibility doctrine, suppose that *O* conveys Blackacre "to *A* for life, then to such of *A*'s children as attain the age of 21." Two years later *A* dies leaving two children: *C*, age 8, and *D*, age 4. Under the

---

13. *Exception:* If a life estate and the next vested estate are created simultaneously in the same person, they do not merge at that time so as to destroy intervening contingent remainders. This would violate the grantor's intent in creating separate estates. However, if the life estate and the next vested estate are thereafter conveyed to another person, they will then merge and destroy intervening contingent remainders.

destructibility doctrine, the contingent remainders would be destroyed because they had not vested by the time of A's death. If the doctrine has been abolished, however, the result is different. Upon A's death, C and D have executory interests that will divest O's possessory fee simple if either or both C and D reach age 21. (*Question*: If C reaches 21 and D is still alive, what interest in Blackacre does C have?)

2. The Rule in Shelley's Case

The Rule in Shelley's Case, which takes its name from a sixteenth-century case but is actually quite a bit older, can be simply stated.[14] It provides that if

(1) one instrument
(2) creates a life estate in land in A, and
(3) purports to create a remainder in persons described as A's heirs (or the heirs of A's body), and
(4) the life estate and remainder are both legal or both equitable,

the remainder becomes a remainder in fee simple (or fee tail) in A. (*Note well*: This is all that the Rule in Shelley's Case does.) The doctrine of merger may then come into play. According to this doctrine, a life estate in A merges into a vested remainder in fee (a larger estate) held by A. Thus:

> *Example 27.* O conveys Blackacre "to A for life, then to A's heirs." The Rule in Shelley's Case gives A a vested remainder in fee simple. A's life estate then merges into the remainder, leaving A with a fee simple in possession. The land is immediately alienable by A and not tied up for A's lifetime.

The life estate cannot merge into a vested remainder in fee simple if there is an intervening vested life estate, blocking merger. (Recall the discussion of merger on page 305.) The Rule in Shelley's Case is a rule of property, not a rule of construction; that is, it is intent-overriding.

The Rule in Shelley's Case has been abolished in an overwhelming majority of states. It is still effective only in a very small number of states. See Restatement (Third) of Property, Wills and Other Donative Transfers §16.2 Reporter's Note (2011).[15] See also Powell on Real Property §31.07(3) (Michael A. Wolf gen. ed. 2009); John V. Orth, Requiem for the Rule in Shelley's Case, 67 N.C. L. Rev. 681 (1989) (North Carolina abolished the rule in 1987). In a few states, however, abolition by statute is fairly recent and does not apply retroactively; litigation of

---

14. If you want an expanded analysis of the rule, see William A. Reppy, Jr., Judicial Overkill in Applying the Rule in Shelley's Case, 73 Notre Dame L. Rev. 83 (1997).

15. The Reporter's Note indicates that the Rule in Shelley's Case is still in effect in Arkansas, but the Rule has been statutorily abolished for instruments executed after July 16, 2003. See Ark. Code §18-12-303.

old instruments will continue for some time even in states that have abolished Shelley's Case.

3. The Doctrine of Worthier Title

The Doctrine of Worthier Title provides that where there is an inter vivos conveyance[16] of land by a grantor to a person, with a limitation over to the *grantor's own heirs* either by way of remainder or executory interest, no future interest in the heirs is created; rather, a reversion is retained by the grantor. Thus:

> *Example 28.* O conveys Blackacre "to A for life, then to O's heirs." In the absence of the Worthier Title Doctrine, there is a contingent remainder in favor of O's unascertained heirs. Under the Worthier Title Doctrine, however, no such remainder exists. Rather, O has a reversion.

The reasons for this doctrine are obscure, but probably it was motivated by the same policies as underlay the Rule in Shelley's Case. The doctrine furthers alienability; O could convey a reversion, whereas O's heirs, not being ascertained, could not convey the future interest. The doctrine also prevented feudal tax evasion; the feudal incidents were due only if O's heir acquired his interest by descent from O and not by purchase. Because these reasons were inapplicable to personal property, the doctrine was a rule of law that applied only to land. In Doctor v. Hughes, 122 N.E. 221 (N.Y. 1919), Judge Cardozo applied the doctrine as a rule of construction, with the effect that it applied to personal property as well as to real property. In that form, the doctrine generated an enormous amount of litigation. The New York legislature finally got involved and abolished the doctrine altogether. As a rule of construction, the doctrine may still survive in some states. It has been abolished in California, Illinois, Massachusetts, Minnesota, New York, North Carolina, Texas, and a number of other states. See Restatement (Third) of Property, Wills and Other Donative Transfers §16.3 Reporter's Note (2011). As with the Rule in Shelley's Case, however, even in states that have abolished the Worthier Title Doctrine, it is still a good idea to be familiar with it because of the possibility of litigation involving old instruments that are still subject to it.

4. The Rule Against Perpetuities

a. The Common Law Rule

The culmination of the long struggle between landowners who wanted to keep land within the family and the judges who for centuries had tried to stand

---

16. A similar rule used to apply to devises of land. Restatement (Third) of Property, Wills and Other Donative Transfers §16.3 comment c (2011), says no such rule now exists as to devises.

firm against these efforts is the Rule Against Perpetuities. The Rule originated in the Duke of Norfolk's Case, 22 Eng. Rep. 931 (Ch. 1681), and as fleshed out in the next 200 years it took the form of a compromise between the landed class and the judges.[17] At the time of the formulation of the Rule Against Perpetuities, heads of families were much concerned about securing family land from incompetent children. The judges accepted this and over time developed a period during which the father's wishes would prevail. He could realistically and perhaps wisely assess the capabilities of *living* members of his family. So, with respect to them, the father's informed judgment was given effect. But the head of family could know nothing of unborn persons. Hence, the father was permitted to control only so long as his judgment was informed with an understanding of the capabilities and needs of persons alive when the judgment was made. Later, judges permitted testators to extend their control beyond lives in being if any of the persons in the next generation was actually a minor. Finally, after about 150 years, the judges fixed the period as lives in being plus 21 years thereafter.

In the concise formulation made famous by John Chipman Gray, the Rule Against Perpetuities is: "No interest is good unless it must vest, if at all, not later than twenty-one years after some life in being at the creation of the interest." John C. Gray, The Rule Against Perpetuities §201 (4th ed. 1942).[18] The compromise it strikes is that property may be tied up with contingent interests for lives in being plus 21 years thereafter, but no longer. The effect was to permit a donor "[to] provide for all of those in his family whom he personally knew and the first generation after them upon attaining majority." 6 American Law of Property §24.16 (1952). When you think about it, permitting this extensive period of dead hand control represents a considerable victory for the rich desirous of controlling their fortunes after death.

(1)   *Mechanics of the Rule*

The first step in applying the common law version of the Rule Against Perpetuities is to determine whether the future interest in question is even subject to the Rule, which applies only to interests that are not vested at the time of the conveyance that creates them. This boils down to saying that only three interests are subject to the Rule: contingent remainders, executory interests, and class gifts. Contingent remainders and executory interests are subject to the Rule because they are not vested interests. Class gifts are a special case that we will consider later (see page 311).

---

17. For an account of the historical origins of the Rule, see George L. Haskins, Extending the Grasp of the Dead Hand: Reflections on the Origins of the Rule Against Perpetuities, 126 U. Pa. L. Rev. 19 (1977).

18. Gray was fabled because he reduced centuries of cases to this one sentence. But there are many complexities hidden in that sentence. His book became recognized as *the* authority on the Rule. See Stephen A. Siegel, John Chipman Gray, Legal Formalism, and the Transformation of Perpetuities Law, 36 U. Miami L. Rev. 439 (1982).

The next step is to determine whether the given interest might not vest within the perpetuity period of "lives in being plus 21 years." The Rule Against Perpetuities is a rule that strikes down contingent interests that *might* vest too remotely. The essential thing to grasp about the Rule is that *it is a rule of logical proof.* You must prove that a contingent interest is certain to *vest or terminate* no later than 21 years after the death of some person alive at the creation of the interest.[19] If you cannot prove that, then the contingent interest is void from the outset.

What you are looking for is a person (it only takes one) who will enable you to prove that the contingent interest will vest or fail within the life, or at the death, of that person, or within 21 years after that person's death. This person, if found, is called the *validating life.*[20] Anyone in the world can be a validating life, so long as that anyone was in being[21] at or before the time at which the interest in question was created. But inasmuch as a validating life will be found, if found at all, among persons whose lives are somehow causally connected with the vesting or termination of the interest, you look only at them in searching for a validating life. These include the preceding life tenant, the taker or takers of the contingent interest, anyone who can affect the identity of the takers (such as *A* in a gift to *A*'s children), and anyone else who can affect events relevant to the condition precedent. If you find that there is a person in this group who enables you to make the necessary proof, then you have found a validating life. If there is no person among this group of relevant lives by whom the requisite proof can be made, the interest is void unless it must vest or fail within 21 years.

Anyone who has read the foregoing will no doubt agree that the Rule Against Perpetuities really cannot be understood merely by parsing, however diligently, an explanatory text. Examples are crucial, so begin by considering the two that follow.

> *Example 29. O* transfers a sum "in trust for *A* for life, then to *A*'s first child to reach 21." *A* is the validating life. You can prove that any child of *A* who reaches 21 will necessarily reach 21 within 21 years of *A*'s death. The remainder must vest or fail within this period; it cannot possibly vest more than 21 years after *A* dies. The remainder is valid.

---

19. If the contingent interest is created by will, the life in being must be a person alive at the testator's death. If the contingent interest is created by an irrevocable inter vivos transfer, the life in being must be a person alive at the time of the transfer. In case of a revocable transfer, the Rule Against Perpetuities does not apply until the transfer becomes irrevocable, and hence the life in being must be a person alive when the power of revocation ceases.

20. The validating life is sometimes referred to as the "measuring life," but this is misleading because it may be read to imply that the law "measures" a "perpetuity period" for each case, which isn't so. A life is a "measuring life" only if it *validates* the interest. Hence, only valid interests have "measuring lives." Invalid interests are invalid because there exists no measuring life that makes them valid. Thus the search is for a validating life. See Lawrence W. Waggoner & Thomas P. Gallanis, Estates in Land and Future Interests in a Nutshell 93 (3d ed. 2005).

21. As elsewhere in property law, a child is considered as in being from the time of conception if later born alive.

Example 30. O transfers a sum "in trust for *A* for life, then to *A*'s first child to reach 25." *A* has no child age 25 or older. There is no validating life; the contingent remainder is void. You cannot prove that *A*'s first child to reach 25 will do so within 21 years after *A*'s death.

Example 30 illustrates a very important point about the search for a validating life. In looking at persons whose lives are in some way causally connected with the vesting or termination of the interest, we ask whether there is with respect to a given person an invalidating chain of possible events after the interest's creation. We ask what *might* happen, without regard to what, in the end, actually did happen. If what might happen is that the interest remains unvested following that person's life plus 21 years, then that person cannot be the validating life. All possible post-creation events, no matter how unlikely, must be taken into account. In *Example 30* there is an invalidating chain of possible events. Here is what might happen: *A*'s presently living children (all under 25) die; *A* has another child, *B*, a year later; *A* dies, leaving *B*, age 3, alive. *B* will not reach 25 within 21 years after *A*'s death. If the gift vests in *B*, it will vest 22 years after *A*'s death, and this is too remote. No other life enables you to make the proof required. Since the contingent remainder is void, it is struck from the instrument, leaving a life estate in *A*, with a reversion in *O*.

Sometimes a validating life will be a person who is not mentioned in the instrument. The key is that to be a validating life, a person must be someone who can affect vesting or termination of the interest. Thus:

Example 31. T devises[22] property "to my grandchildren who reach 21." *T* leaves two children and three grandchildren under 21. The validating life is the survivor of *T*'s two children.[23] All of *T*'s grandchildren must reach 21, if at all, within 21 years after the death of the survivor of *T*'s two children. Therefore, the gift is valid.

Under the what-might-happen test, an interest may be invalid on the basis of a seemingly absurd invalidating chain of events. Consider this example:

Example 32. T devises a sum "in trust for *A* for life, then to *A*'s children for the life of the survivor of them, then upon the death of the last surviving child of *A*, to *A*'s grandchildren." At the time of *T*'s death, *A* is an 80-year-old woman with two living children, *B* and *C*. The remainder to *A*'s grandchildren is void. The invalidating chain of possible events is the following: After *T*'s death, *A* might have a child, *X*, who in turn has a child, *Y*, conceived and born more than 21 years after the death of the survivor of *A*, *B*, and *C*. It matters not how unlikely it is that an 80-year-old woman would conceive a child. Under the common law Rule Against Perpetuities, it must be assumed that a person of any age can have a child, no matter what the person's physical condition. The presumption of lifetime fertility is conclusive,[24] notwithstanding contrary evidence.[25]

---

22. Would it make any difference if the transfer had been by deed rather than by will?

23. If the surviving child was one who was in gestation, or *en ventre sa mere*, at *T*'s death, that child is considered a life in being. See footnote 21 above.

24. The conclusive presumption of lifetime fertility owes its origin to an infamous English case, Jee v. Audley, 29 Eng. Rep. 1186 (Ch. 1787). We will spare you the details of this fascinating but difficult case. The story behind it is wonderfully told in A.W. Brian Simpson, Leading Cases in the Common Law 79-88 (1995).

25. The presumption of lifetime fertility works the other way around as well. A 2-year-old child is conclusively presumed to be capable of having children. In an influential article, the late Professor Barton Leach, an early critic of the common law Rule, dubbed the example of invalidity based on the presumption of an 80-year-old person's fertility the case of the "fertile octogenarian." A variation on this consequence of the lifetime fertility presumption is the possibility that a child might conceive a child. Professor Leach called this one the

If a transfer creates more than one interest subject to the Rule Against Perpetuities, you must test the validity of each interest separately. One interest may be valid and another one not. Moreover, the same person may or may not be the validating life for all interests. Different lives may validate different interests.

(2)   Class Gifts

Gifts to classes present a special case under the Rule Against Perpetuities. A corollary rule known as the "all-or-nothing rule"[26] holds that if a gift to one member of the class might vest too remotely, the whole class gift is void. Or, to put it another way, under the Rule Against Perpetuities a class gift is not vested *in any member* of the class until the interests of *all members* have vested. A gift that is vested subject to open (see page 282) is *not* vested under the Rule Against Perpetuities. For a class gift to be vested under the Rule, the class must be closed (that is, each and every member of the class must be in existence and identified), and all conditions precedent for each and every member of the class must be satisfied, within the perpetuities period. Thus suppose a gift "to *A* for life, then to *A*'s children," and *A* has living one child, *B*. *B*'s remainder is vested subject to open, but it is not vested under the Rule Against Perpetuities until *A* dies and all of *A*'s children are then in existence and identified. But because the remainder beneficiaries will all be ascertained at *A*'s death, the remainder is valid.

Class closing rule (a/k/a the rule of convenience). The possibility that more members may be added to a class at a remote point in the future creates a potential violation of the Rule Against Perpetuities for some class gifts.

> *Example 33.* *O* devises land "to *A*'s children who survive to age 25." Suppose that at *O*'s death *A* is alive and has three children, all of whom are younger than 25 and at least one of whom is younger than 4. Note first that no life estate precedes the interest given to *A*'s children.

---

case of the "precocious toddler." See W. Barton Leach, Perpetuities in a Nutshell, 51 Harv. L. Rev. 638, 643-644 (1938).

These presumptions are perhaps not entirely farfetched. According to wire service news reports, the oldest known mother is Rajo Devi, of India. In 2008, at the age of 70, she gave birth to a baby girl. The youngest mother on record is Lina Medina, of Lima, Peru. In 1939, at the age of 5, she delivered a premature baby boy by Cesarean section.

Yet another variation is the possibility that a person may conceive a child after her or his death through artificial insemination. Whether a person who deposits an egg or sperm in an artificial insemination bank is a parent of any child conceived after the depositor's death has not been decided. In perpetuities cases to date, courts have ignored the possibility of posthumous parentage of a child *en ventre sa frigidaire.* (Leach's term again! See W. Barton Leach, Perpetuities in the Atomic Age: The Sperm Bank and the Fertile Decedent, 48 ABA J. 942 (1962).) In many states statutes handle the problem by simply stating that the possibility of a child being born to a dead person is ignored. See Uniform Statutory Rule Against Perpetuities §1(d). For a different approach to the problem, see Sharona Hoffman & Andrew P. Morriss, Birth After Death: Perpetuities and the New Reproductive Technologies, 38 Ga. L. Rev. 575, 624-629 (2004) (proposing a rebuttable presumption that testator intended to exclude posthumously conceived children).

Some jurisdictions have changed the presumption of lifetime fertility in one respect or another. See the discussion on page 329.

26. The all-or-nothing rule was first announced in the English decision of Leake v. Robinson, 35 Eng. Rep. 979 (Ch. 1817).

The executory interest in *A*'s children is void. The invalidating chain of events is that *A* may have another child after *O*'s death, and that child may reach age 25 more than 21 years after the death of *A* and *A*'s three children who were alive at *O*'s death.

In some class gift situations a rule of construction known as the *rule of convenience* may save the interest. Under the rule of convenience, a class will close as soon as one member of the class is entitled to immediate possession or enjoyment, even if this means closing the class before it closes naturally, or physiologically—that is, when the possibility of births (or adoptions) ends (i.e., at the death of a class's ancestor). When the class closes prematurely under the rule of convenience no person born (conceived) thereafter can share in the gift. That is all the rule of convenience does. The rule does not terminate the interest of existing class members whose interests are not yet vested at the time of creation. They remain present members of the class. But neither are they guaranteed to share in the gift. They will do so only if they satisfy the relevant condition precedent.

As a rule of construction, the rule of convenience yields to evidence of a contrary intent. In practice, however, such evidence seldom exists, so the rule of convenience usually prevails. It is based on the notion that because of difficulties, or "inconveniences," in allowing persons born (or adopted) after distribution to participate in the gift, the donor would prefer to exclude such persons. The main inconvenience of keeping the class open beyond the distribution date is that the distributees would receive a defeasible interest, and such an interest is considerably less useful to them than one that is indefeasible.

The rule of convenience may save an otherwise invalid interest under the common law Rule Against Perpetuities in the following way.

> *Example 34.* Go back to *Example 33* ("to such of *A*'s children as survive to age 25"). Assume that at the time of *O*'s death *A* was alive and had three children, the eldest of whom had reached age 25 by the time of *O*'s death. Under the rule of convenience, because *A*'s eldest child had reached 25 by the time of *O*'s death—the time of distribution—the class closes prematurely at *O*'s death. The interest takes effect in possession at *O*'s death. Any child born to (or adopted by) *A* after *O*'s death is excluded from the class, saving the class gift. The children who were living at *O*'s death and are younger than 25 at that point constitute their own validating lives. They are all lives in being, each of whom will or will not reach age 25 within their own lives.

PROBLEMS AND NOTE

We said earlier that examples help when one is trying to understand the Rule Against Perpetuities. So do problems. Apply the Rule to determine the validity of each interest in the following dispositions. (Assume that all parties designated by a capital letter (e.g., *A*) have been born by the time of the transfer.)

✗ 1. *O* conveys "to *A* for life, then to *B* if *B* attains the age of 30." *B* is now 2 years old.

2. *O* conveys "to *A* for life, then to *A*'s children for their lives, then to *B* if *B* is then alive, and if *B* is not then alive, to *B*'s heirs."[27] Assume that *A* has no children at the time of conveyance.

3. *O*, a teacher of property law, declares that she holds in trust $1,000 "for all members of my present property class who are admitted to the bar." Is the gift good? Suppose that *O* had said "for the first child of *A* who is admitted to the bar." In analyzing the validity of the gift to *A*'s first child admitted to the bar, does it matter whether *A* was alive or dead at the time of the conveyance?

4. *O* conveys "to *A* for life, then to *A*'s children who reach 25." *A* is alive and has a child, *B*, age 26, living at the time of the conveyance. Is the remainder valid? (Contrast this Problem with *Example 33* on page 311. Do you see the relevant difference?)

5. *O* conveys "to *A* for life, then to *A*'s widow, if any, for life, then to *A*'s issue then living." Is the gift to *A*'s issue valid? See Dickerson v. Union Natl. Bank of Little Rock, 595 S.W.2d 677 (Ark. 1980).

6. *T* devises property "to *A* for life, and on *A*'s death to *A*'s children for their lives, and upon the death of *A* and *A*'s children, to [the person or persons indicated in the bracketed examples below]."

A and *B* survive *T*. *A* has one child, *X*, who also survives *T*. Is the devise of the remainder in fee simple valid or void under the Rule Against Perpetuities if the following words are inserted in the brackets?

(a)   ["*B* if *A* dies childless"]
(b)   ["*B* if *A* has no grandchildren then living"]
(c)   ["*B*'s children"]
(d)   ["*B*'s children then living"]
(e)   ["*A*'s grandchildren"]
(f)   ["*T*'s grandchildren"]

In solving the class gift problems above, focus first on when all the class members will be ascertained (within lives in being plus 21 years?) and second on when all conditions precedent, if any, will be met for all members of the class (within lives in being plus 21 years?).

7. *Saving clause in a trust.* In drafting a trust creating future interests, experienced lawyers almost always include a perpetuities saving clause. A saving clause is designed to terminate the trust, and distribute the assets, at the expiration of specified measuring lives plus 21 years, if the trust has not earlier terminated. Suppose that the testator wants to create a trust paying income to her only child *A* for life, then income to *A*'s children for their lives, then distributing the principal to *A*'s grandchildren. Here is a saving clause that might be inserted in the trust:

---

27. If by the distribution date *B* has died without surviving heirs, such that her intestate estate would escheat to the state, then the state is treated as an heir for purposes of construing the term "heirs" in the class gift. See Restatement (Third) of Property, Will and Other Donative Transfers §16.1 comment i (2004); Uniform Probate Code §2-711 (2011).

Notwithstanding any other provision in this instrument, this trust shall terminate, if it has not previously terminated, 21 years after the death of the survivor of *A* and *A*'s issue living at my death. In case of such termination, the then remaining principal and undistributed income of the trust shall be distributed to *A*'s issue then living per stirpes, or, if no issue of *A* is then living, to the American Red Cross.

If *A* actually has an afterborn child who lives more than 21 years after the death of *A* and all *A*'s issue living at the testator's death (the possibility that causes the gift of trust principal to violate the Rule), the trust will terminate under the saving clause and the principal will then be distributed.

You can use extraneous lives in a saving clause if you want to. If you want a trust to continue for a very long period of time, you might end the trust 21 years after the death of the survivor of the descendants of John D. Rockefeller[28] living at the creation of the trust. In either case all interests in the trust will necessarily vest, if at all, within the perpetuities period.[29]

(3) Future Interests in Transferors; Executory Interests Following Defeasible Fees; and Options

Future interests retained by the *transferor*—reversions, possibilities of reverter, and rights of entry—are not subject to the Rule Against Perpetuities. They are treated as vested as soon as they arise. This exemption leads to some startling differences in result when the transferor attempts to create an equivalent executory interest in a transferee. Compare these two cases involving future interests in the grantor:

Example 35. *O* conveys Blackacre "to the School Board so long as it is used for a school." The School Board has a fee simple determinable; *O* has a possibility of reverter exempt from the Rule Against Perpetuities.

Example 36. *O* conveys Blackacre "to the School Board, but if it ceases to use Blackacre for school purposes, *O* has a right to re-enter." The School Board has a fee simple subject to condition subsequent; *O* has a right of entry exempt from the Rule Against Perpetuities.

Now compare these two cases involving future interests in *transferees:*

28. Currently, there are approximately 140 living descendants of John D. Rockefeller. The descendants are worth billions, thanks to the seven trusts that the oil tycoon's son, John D. Rockefeller Jr., set up in 1934. The family now uses more than 100 trusts to manage its assets.

29. Be careful, though! The Restatement, reflecting what is probably the widely shared view, states that a perpetuity savings clause is ineffective if "the designated validating lives are unreasonable in number." It further explains, "The validating lives are unreasonable in number if it would be impractical to keep track of them all to determine when the last living member dies." Restatement (Third) of Property, Wills and Other Donative Transfers §27.1 comment d (2011). Accord Uniform Statutory Rule Against Perpetuities Act §1 comment part b. In fact, we have been told that practicing lawyers rarely use such devices. In their view the task of keeping track of the lives of a large group of individuals totally unrelated to the testator is impracticable. They are much more apt to designate the last survivor of the testator's descendants living at the testator's death, or even the last survivor of the descendants of the testator's grandparents.

Example 37. O conveys Blackacre "to the School Board so long as it is used for a school, then to *A* and her heirs." *A*'s executory interest violates the Rule Against Perpetuities.[30] It will not necessarily vest within *A*'s lifetime or within 21 years after *A*'s death. It may vest and become possessory centuries from now. When an interest violates the Rule Against Perpetuities, it is struck out and the remaining valid interests stand. Take a pencil and line out the void gift, "then to *A* and her heirs." This leaves a fee simple determinable in the School Board. Since *O* has not given away *O*'s entire interest, *O* has a possibility of reverter.

Example 38. O conveys Blackacre "to the School Board, but if it ceases to use Blackacre for school purposes to *A* and her heirs." The School Board has a fee simple subject to (an apparent) executory interest. *A*'s executory interest violates the Rule Against Perpetuities for the reason given in *Example 37*. Strike it out, beginning with "but if it ceases . . . ." This leaves standing a conveyance "to the School Board." The School Board has a fee simple absolute!

If you were counsel for *O* in *Examples 37* and *38*, how would you carry out *O*'s desires exactly, using two pieces of paper rather than one? Would a lawyer be liable for malpractice if the lawyer failed to use two pieces of paper?

Should the Rule Against Perpetuities apply to possibilities of reverter and rights of entry? In England these interests are subject to the Rule by statute. English Perpetuities and Accumulations Act, 1964, §12. In this country a number of states have limited these interests to a specified number of years, usually 30, after which the possessory fee becomes absolute. See, e.g., Cal. Civ. Code §885.030 (West 2007); Mass. Ann. Laws ch. 184A, §7 (2011); N.C. Gen. Stat. §41-32 (2011) (60 years). Some of these statutes permit a possibility of reverter or right of entry to be preserved for additional periods by recording in the courthouse, before the end of the allowable period, a notice of intent to preserve the future interest. See N.Y. Real Prop. Law §345 (2012). The Uniform Statutory Rule Against Perpetuities, enacted in about half the states (see page 331), validates executory interests in *Examples 37* and *38* for 90 years, but it does not change the common law exemption granted to interests in the transferor.

And what about options; should the Rule apply to them? Consider the following case.

The Symphony Space, Inc. v. Pergola Properties, Inc.[31]
Court of Appeals of New York, 1996
669 N.E.2d 799

KAYE, C.J. This case presents the novel question whether options to purchase commercial property are exempt from the prohibition against remote vesting embodied in New York's Rule against Perpetuities (EPTL 9-1.1[b]). Because

---

30. If *O* makes a gift to Charity *A* followed by a gift over to Charity *B* if a specified event happens, the executory interest in Charity *B* is exempt from the Rule Against Perpetuities. Thus in a deed of Blackacre to the School Board so long as it is used as a school, and then to City Library, the executory interest in City Library is valid. This exemption applies only if both the possessory estate and the future interest are in charitable organizations. It does not apply if either the possessory estate or the future interest is in a noncharity.

31. Fair warning: "No one can read the perpetuity cases . . . without some sense of nausea." W. Barton Leach & James K. Logan, Cases and Text on Future Interests and Estate Planning 672 (1961).—EDS.

an exception for commercial options finds no support in our law, we decline to exempt all commercial option agreements from the statutory Rule against Perpetuities.

Here, we agree with the trial court and Appellate Division that the option defendants seek to enforce violates the statutory prohibition against remote vesting and is therefore unenforceable.

I.   Facts

The subject of this proceeding is a two-story building situated on the Broadway block between 94th and 95th Streets on Manhattan's Upper West Side. In 1978, Broadwest Realty Corporation owned this building, which housed a theater and commercial space. Broadwest had been unable to secure a permanent tenant for the theater—approximately 58% of the total square footage of the building's floor space. . . . Broadwest also owned two adjacent properties, Pomander Walk (a residential complex) and the Healy Building (a commercial building). Broadwest had been operating its properties at a net loss.

Plaintiff Symphony Space, Inc., a not-for-profit entity devoted to the arts, had previously rented the theater for several one-night engagements.

In 1978, Symphony and Broadwest engaged in a transaction whereby Broadwest sold the entire building to Symphony for the below-market price of $10,010 and leased back the income-producing commercial property, excluding the theater, for $1 per year. Broadwest maintained liability for the existing $243,000 mortgage on the property as well as certain maintenance obligations. As a condition of the sale, Symphony, for consideration of $10, also granted Broadwest an option to repurchase the entire building. Notably, the transaction did not involve Pomander Walk or the Healy Building.

The purpose of this arrangement was to enable Symphony, as a not-for-profit corporation, to seek a property tax exemption for the entire building—which constituted a single tax parcel—predicated on its use of the theater. The sale-and-leaseback would thereby reduce Broadwest's real estate taxes by $30,000 per year, while permitting Broadwest to retain the rental income from the leased commercial space in the building, which the trial court found produced $140,000 annually. The arrangement also furthered Broadwest's goal of selling all the properties, by allowing Broadwest to postpone any sale until property values in the area increased and until the commercial leases expired. Symphony, in turn, would have use of the theater at minimal cost, once it received a tax exemption.

Thus, on December 1, 1978, Symphony and Broadwest—both sides represented by counsel—executed a contract for sale of the property from Broadwest to Symphony for the purchase price of $10,010. The contract specified that $10 was to be paid at the closing and $10,000 was to be paid by means of a purchase-money mortgage.

The parties also signed several separate documents, each dated December 31, 1978: (1) a deed for the property from Broadwest to Symphony; (2) a lease from Symphony to Broadwest of the entire building except the theater for rent of $1 per year and for the term January 1, 1979 to May 31, 2003, unless terminated earlier; (3) a 25-year, $10,000 mortgage and mortgage note from Symphony as mortgagor to Broadwest as mortgagee, with full payment due on December 31, 2003; and (4) an option agreement by which Broadwest obtained from Symphony the exclusive right to repurchase all of the property, including the theater.

It is the option agreement that is at the heart of the present dispute. Section 3 of that agreement provides that Broadwest may exercise its option to purchase the property during any of the following "Exercise Periods":

> (a) at any time after July 1, 1979, so long as the Notice of Election specifies that the Closing is to occur during any of the calendar years 1987, 1993, 1998 and 2003. . . .

Symphony ultimately obtained a tax exemption for the theater. In the summer of 1981, Broadwest sold and assigned its interest under the lease, option agreement, mortgage and mortgage note, as well as its ownership interest in the contiguous Pomander Walk and Healy Building, to defendants' nominee for $4.8 million. The nominee contemporaneously transferred its rights under these agreements to defendants Pergola Properties, Inc., Bradford N. Swett, Casandium Limited and Darenth Consultants as tenants in common.

Subsequently, defendants initiated a cooperative conversion of Pomander Walk, which was designated a landmark in 1982, and the value of the properties increased substantially. An August 1988 appraisal of the entire blockfront, including the Healy Building and the unused air and other development rights available from Pomander Walk, valued the property at $27 million assuming the enforceability of the option. By contrast, the value of the leasehold interest plus the Healy Building without the option were appraised at $5.5 million. . . .

[In 1985 Pergola Properties, on behalf of all the defendants, notified Symphony that it was exercising its option under section 3(a) of the option agreement, with the closing date scheduled for January 5, 1987. Symphony then initiated this declaratory judgment action against the defendants, arguing that the option agreement violated the New York statutory prohibition against remote vesting.]

Thereafter, the parties cross-moved for summary judgment in the instant declaratory judgment proceeding. The trial court granted Symphony's motion while denying that of defendants. In particular, the court concluded that the Rule against Perpetuities applied to the commercial option contained in the parties' agreement, that the option violated the Rule and that Symphony was entitled to exercise its equitable right to redeem the mortgage. . . .

In a comprehensive writing by Justice Ellerin, the Appellate Division likewise determined that the commercial option was unenforceable under the Rule against Perpetuities. . . . The Appellate Division certified the following question to us: "Was the order of the Supreme Court, as affirmed by this Court, properly made?" We conclude that it was and now affirm.

II. Statutory Background

The Rule against Perpetuities evolved from judicial efforts during the 17th century to limit control of title to real property by the dead hand of landowners reaching into future generations. Underlying both early and modern rules restricting future dispositions of property is the principle that it is socially undesirable for property to be inalienable for an unreasonable period of time. These rules thus seek "to ensure the productive use and development of property by its current beneficial owners by simplifying ownership, facilitating exchange and freeing property from unknown or embarrassing impediments to alienability" (Metropolitan Transp. Auth. v. Bruken Realty Corp., 67 N.Y.2d 156, 161, 501 N.Y.S.2d 306, 492 N.E.2d 379, citing De Peyster v. Michael, 6 N.Y. 467, 494).

The traditional statement of the common-law Rule against Perpetuities was set forth by Professor John Chipman Gray: "No interest is good unless it must vest, if at all, not later than twenty-one years after some life in being at the creation of the interest" (Gray, The Rule Against Perpetuities §201, at 191 (4th ed. 1942)).

In New York, the rules regarding suspension of the power of alienation and remoteness in vesting—the Rule against Perpetuities—have been statutory since 1830. . . .

New York's current statutory Rule against Perpetuities is found in EPTL 9-1.1. Subdivision (a) sets forth the suspension of alienation rule and deems void any estate in which the conveying instrument suspends the absolute power of alienation for longer than lives in being at the creation of the estate plus 21 years (see, EPTL 9-1.1[a][2]).[32] The prohibition against remote vesting is contained in subdivision (b), which states that "[n]o estate in property shall be valid unless it must vest, if at all, not later than twenty-one years after one or more lives in being at the creation of the estate and any period of gestation involved" (EPTL 9-1.1[b]). This Court has described subdivision (b) as "a rigid formula that invalidates any interest that may not vest within the prescribed time period" and has "capricious consequences" (Wildenstein & Co. v. Wallis, 79 N.Y.2d 641, 647-648, 584 N.Y.S.2d 753, 595 N.E.2d 828). Indeed, these rules are predicated upon the public policy of the State and constitute non-waivable, legal prohibitions (see, Metropolitan Transp. Auth. v. Bruken Realty Corp., 67 N.Y.2d at 161, 501 N.Y.S.2d 306, 492 N.E.2d 379).

In addition to these statutory formulas, New York also retains the more flexible common-law rule against unreasonable restraints on alienation. Unlike the

---

32. The New York rule against suspension of the power of alienation is a separate rule from the Rule Against Perpetuities. The power of alienation is suspended when there are no persons in being who can convey an absolute fee simple. If a transfer is made in trust, the power of alienation is suspended if *either* the trustee does not have the power to transfer a legal fee simple *or* the owners of all the equitable interests cannot convey an equitable fee simple, usually because interests are created in unborn or unascertained persons. Other states have similar rules against suspension of the power of alienation. See, e.g., N.J. Stat. §46:2F-10 (2013). See Thomas P. Gallanis, Family Property Law: Wills, Trusts, and Future Interests 846-847 (5th ed. 2011).

An option does not violate the rule against suspension of the power of alienation because the optionor and the optionee (here Symphony Space and Pergola Properties) can convey a legal fee simple if they act jointly. Hence the suspension rule is not involved in this case.—EDS.

statutory Rule against Perpetuities, which is measured exclusively by the passage of time, the common-law rule evaluates the reasonableness of the restraint based on its duration, purpose and designated method for fixing the purchase price. (See, Wildenstein & Co. v. Wallis, 79 N.Y.2d at 648, 584 N.Y.S.2d 753, 595 N.E.2d 828; Metropolitan Transp. Auth. v. Bruken Realty Corp., 67 N.Y.2d at 161-162, 501 N.Y.S.2d 306, 492 N.E.2d 379, supra.)

Against this background, we consider the option agreement at issue.

III. Validity of the Option Agreement

Defendants proffer three grounds for upholding the option: that the statutory prohibition against remote vesting does not apply to commercial options; that the option here cannot be exercised beyond the statutory period; and that this Court should adopt the "wait and see" approach to the Rule against Perpetuities. We consider each in turn.

A. Applicability of the Rule to Commercial Options

Under the common law, options to purchase land are subject to the rule against remote vesting (see, Simes, Future Interests §132 (2d ed. 1966); Simes and Smith, Future Interests §1244 (2d ed.); Leach, Perpetuities in a Nutshell, 51 Harv. L. Rev. 638, 660; see also, London & S.W. Ry. Co. v. Gomm, 20 Ch. D. 562). Such options are specifically enforceable and give the option holder a contingent, equitable interest in the land (Dukeminier, A Modern Guide to Perpetuities, 74 Cal. L. Rev. 1867, 1908; Leach, Perpetuities in Perspective: Ending the Rule's Reign of Terror, 65 Harv. L. Rev. 721, 736-737). This creates a disincentive for the landowner to develop the property and hinders its alienability, thereby defeating the policy objectives underlying the Rule against Perpetuities (see, Dukeminier, A Modern Guide to Perpetuities, 74 Cal. L. Rev. 1908; 5A Powell, Real Property ¶ 771[1]).

Typically, however, options to purchase are part of a commercial transaction. For this reason, subjecting them to the Rule against Perpetuities has been deemed "a step of doubtful wisdom" (Leach, Perpetuities in Perspective: Ending the Rule's Reign of Terror, 65 Harv. L. Rev. 737; see also, Dukeminier, A Modern Guide to Perpetuities, 74 Cal. L. Rev. 1908; Note, Options and the Rule Against Perpetuities, 13 U. Fla. L. Rev. 214, 214-215). As one vocal critic, Professor W. Barton Leach, has explained,

> [t]he Rule grew up as a limitation on family dispositions; and the period of lives in being plus twenty-one years is adapted to these gift transactions. The pressures which created the Rule do not exist with reference to arms-length contractual transactions, and neither lives in being nor twenty-one years are periods which are relevant to business men and their affairs. [Leach, Perpetuities: New Absurdity, Judicial and Statutory Correctives, 73 Harv. L. Rev. 1318, 1321-1322.]

Professor Leach, however, went on to acknowledge that, under common law, "due to an overemphasis on concepts derived from the nineteenth century, we are stuck with the application of the Rule to options to purchase," urging that "this should not be extended to other commercial transactions" (id., at 1322; see also, Simes and Smith, Future Interests §1244).

It is now settled in New York that, generally, EPTL 9-1.1(b) applies to options. In Buffalo Seminary v. McCarthy, 86 A.D.2d 435, 451 N.Y.S.2d 457, supra, the court held that an unlimited option in gross to purchase real property was void under the statutory rule against remote vesting, and we affirmed the Appellate Division on the opinion of then-Justice Hancock (58 N.Y.2d 867, 460 N.Y.S.2d 528, 447 N.E.2d 76). Since then, we have reiterated that options in real estate are subject to the statutory rule (see, e.g., Wildenstein & Co. v. Wallis, 79 N.Y.2d at 648, 584 N.Y.S.2d 753, 595 N.E.2d 828, supra).

Although the particular option at issue in *Buffalo Seminary* was part of a private transaction between neighboring landowners, the reasoning employed in that case establishes that EPTL 9-1.1(b) applies equally to commercial purchase options. In reaching its conclusion in *Buffalo Seminary*, the court explained that . . . the Legislature specifically intended to incorporate the American common-law rules governing perpetuities into the New York statute (id., at 441-442, 451 N.Y.S.2d 457).

Because the common-law rule against remote vesting encompasses purchase options that might vest beyond the permissible period, the court concluded that EPTL 9-1.1(b) necessarily encompasses such options (id., at 443, 451 N.Y.S.2d 451). Inasmuch as the common-law prohibition against remote vesting applies to both commercial and noncommercial options, it likewise follows that the Legislature intended EPTL 9-1.1(b) to apply to commercial purchase options as well.

Consequently, creation of a general exception to EPTL 9-1.1(b) for all purchase options that are commercial in nature, as advocated by defendants, would remove an entire class of contingent future interests that the Legislature intended the statute to cover. While defendants offer compelling policy reasons—echoing those voiced by Professor Leach—for refusing to apply the traditional rule against remote vesting to these commercial option contracts, such statutory reformation would require legislative action similar to that undertaken by numerous other State lawmakers (see, e.g., Cal. Prob. Code §21225; Fla. Stat. Annot. ch. 689.225; Ill. Stat. Annot. ch. 765, para. 305/4).

Our decision in Metropolitan Transp. Auth. v. Bruken Realty Corp., 67 N.Y.2d 156, 501 N.Y.S.2d 306, 492 N.E.2d 379, supra) is not to the contrary. In *Bruken*, we held that EPTL 9-1.1(b) did not apply to a preemptive right in a "commercial and governmental transaction" that lasted beyond the statutory perpetuities period. In doing so, we explained that, unlike options, preemptive rights (or rights of first refusal) only marginally affect transferability:

> An option grants to the holder the power to compel the owner of property to sell it whether the owner is willing to part with ownership or not. A preemptive right, or right of first refusal, does not give its holder the power to compel an unwilling owner to sell; it merely requires the owner, when and if he decides to sell, to offer the property first to the party holding the preemptive right so that he may meet a third-party offer or buy the property at some other price set by a previously stipulated method. [Id., at 163, 501 N.Y.S.2d 306, 492 N.E.2d 379.]

Enforcement of the preemptive right in the context of the governmental and commercial transaction, moreover, actually encouraged the use and development of the land, outweighing any minor impediment to alienability (id., at 165-166, 501 N.Y.S.2d 306, 492 N.E.2d 379).

Bruken merely recognized that the Legislature did not intend EPTL 9-1.1(b) to apply to those contingent future interests in real property that encourage the holder to develop the property by insuring an opportunity to benefit from the improvements and to recapture any investment (see, Metropolitan Transp. Auth. v. Bruken Realty Corp., 67 N.Y.2d at 165, 501 N.Y.S.2d 306, 492 N.E.2d 379; Morrison v. Piper, 77 N.Y.2d 165, 170, 565 N.Y.S.2d 444, 566 N.E.2d 643). In these limited circumstances, enforcement would promote the purposes underlying the rule.

Bruken, then, did not create a sweeping exception to EPTL 9-1.1(b) for commercial purchase options. Indeed, we have since emphasized that options to purchase are to be treated differently than preemptive rights, underscoring that preemptive rights impede alienability only minimally whereas purchase options vest substantial control over the transferability of property in the option holder (see, Wildenstein & Co. v. Wallis, 79 N.Y.2d at 648, 584 N.Y.S.2d 753, 595 N.E.2d 828, supra; Morrison v. Piper, 77 N.Y.2d at 169-170, 565 N.Y.S.2d 444, 566 N.E.2d 643, supra). We have also clarified that even preemptive rights are ordinarily subject to the statutory rule against remote vesting (see, Morrison v. Piper, 77 N.Y.2d 165, 565 N.Y.S.2d 444, 566 N.E.2d 643, supra). Only where the right arises in a governmental or commercial agreement is the minor restraint on transferability created by the preemptive right offset by the holder's incentive to improve the property.

Here, the option agreement creates precisely the sort of control over future disposition of the property that we have previously associated with purchase options and that the common-law rule against remote vesting—and thus EPTL 9-1.1(b)—seeks to prevent. As the Appellate Division explained, the option grants its holder absolute power to purchase the property at the holder's whim and at a token price set far below market value. This Sword of Damocles necessarily discourages the property owner from investing in improvements to the property. Furthermore, the option's existence significantly impedes the owner's ability to sell the property to a third party, as a practical matter rendering it inalienable.

That defendants, the holder of this option, are also the lessees of a portion of the premises does not lead to a different conclusion here.

Generally, an option to purchase land that originates in one of the lease provisions, is not exercisable after lease expiration, and is incapable of separation from the lease is valid even though the holder's interest may vest beyond the perpetuities period (see, Berg, Long-Term Options and the Rule Against Perpetuities, 37 Cal. L. Rev. 1, 21; Leach, Perpetuities: New Absurdity, Judicial and Statutory Correctives, 73 Harv. L. Rev. 1320; Simes and Smith, Future Interests §1244). Such options—known as options "appendant" or "appurtenant" to leases—encourage the possessory holder to invest in maintaining and developing the property by guaranteeing the option holder the ultimate benefit of any such investment. Options appurtenant thus further the policy objectives underlying the rule against remote vesting and are not contemplated by EPTL 9-1.1(b). . . .

To be sure, the option here arose within a larger transaction that included a lease. Nevertheless, not all of the property subject to the purchase option here is even occupied by defendants. The option encompasses the entire building — both the commercial space and the theater — yet defendants are leasing only the commercial space. With regard to the theater space, a disincentive exists for Symphony to improve the property, since it will eventually be claimed by the option holder at the predetermined purchase price. . . .

Put simply, the option here cannot qualify as an option appurtenant and significantly deters development of the property. If the option is exercisable beyond the statutory perpetuities period, refusing to enforce it would thus further the purpose and rationale underlying the statutory prohibition against remote vesting.

B.   Duration of the Option Agreement

1.   Duration Under Section 3(a) of the Agreement

Defendants alternatively claim that section 3(a) of the agreement does not permit exercise of the option after expiration of the statutory perpetuities period. According to defendants, only the possible closing dates fall outside the permissible time frame.

Where, as here, the parties to a transaction are corporations and no measuring lives are stated in the instruments, the perpetuities period is simply 21 years (see, Metropolitan Transp. Auth. v. Bruken Realty Corp., 67 N.Y.2d at 161, 501 N.Y.S.2d 306, 492 N.E.2d 379, supra). Section 1 of the parties' agreement allows the option holder to exercise the option "at any time during any Exercise Period" set forth in section three. Section 3(a), moreover, expressly provides that the option may be exercised "at any time after July 1, 1979," so long as the closing date is scheduled during 1987, 1993, 1998 or 2003.

Even factoring in the requisite notice, then, the option could potentially be exercised as late as July 2003 — more than 24 years after its creation in December 1978. Defendants' contention that section 3(a) does not permit exercise of the option beyond the 21-year period is thus contradicted by the plain language of the instrument.

Nor can EPTL 9-1.3 — the "saving statute" — be invoked to shorten the duration of the exercise period under section 3(a) of the agreement. That statute mandates that, "[u]nless a contrary intention appears," certain rules of construction govern with respect to any matter affecting the Rule against Perpetuities (EPTL 9-1.3[a]). The specified canons of construction include that "[i]t shall be presumed that the creator intended the estate to be valid" (EPTL 9-1.3[b]) and "[w]here the duration or vesting of an estate is contingent upon . . . the occurrence of any specified contingency, it shall be presumed that the creator of such estate intended such contingency to occur, if at all, within twenty-one years from the effective date of the instrument creating such estate" (EPTL 9-1.3[d]).

By presuming that the creator intended the estate to be valid, the statute seeks to avoid annulling dispositions due to inadvertent violations of the Rule against Perpetuities. The provisions of EPTL 9-1.3, however, are merely rules of construction. While the statute obligates reviewing courts, where possible, to avoid constructions that frustrate the parties' intended purposes . . . , it does not authorize courts to rewrite instruments that unequivocally allow interests to vest outside the perpetuities period (compare, EPTL 9-1.2 (reducing age contingency to 21 years, where interest is invalid because contingent on a person reaching an age in excess of 21 years)).

Indeed, by their terms, the rules of construction in EPTL 9-1.3 apply only if "a contrary intention" does not appear in the instrument. . . .

For example, where a deed contains contradictory phrases, one of which is valid under the Rule . . . , or where one of two possible interpretations of a term in an agreement would comply with the Rule . . . , the court will adopt the construction validating the disposition (see also, Restatement of Property §375 (1944)). By contrast, an option containing no limitation in duration demonstrates the parties' intent that it last indefinitely, and EPTL 9-1.3 does not permit "an extensive rewriting of the option agreement . . . so as to make it conform to the permissible period" (see, Buffalo Seminary v. McCarthy, 86 A.D.2d at 446, 451 N.Y.S.2d 457, supra).

The unambiguous language of the agreement here expresses the parties' intent that the option be exercisable "at any time" during a 24-year period pursuant to section 3(a). The section thus does not permit a construction that the parties intended the option to last only 21 years.

Given the contrary intention manifested in the instrument itself, the saving statute is simply inapplicable. . . .

C. "Wait and See" Approach

Defendants next urge that we adopt the "wait and see" approach to the Rule against Perpetuities: an interest is valid if it actually vests during the perpetuities period, irrespective of what might have happened (see, Dukeminier, A Modern Guide to Perpetuities, 74 Cal. L. Rev. 1867, 1880). The option here would survive under the "wait and see" approach since it was exercised by 1987, well within the 21-year limitation.

This Court, however, has long refused to "wait and see" whether a perpetuities violation in fact occurs. As explained in Matter of Fischer, 307 N.Y. 149, 157, 120 N.E.2d 688, "[i]t is settled beyond dispute that in determining whether a will has illegally suspended the power of alienation, the courts will look to what might have happened under the terms of the will rather than to what has actually happened since the death of the testator." . . .

The very language of EPTL 9-1.1, moreover, precludes us from determining the validity of an interest based upon what actually occurs during the perpetuities period. Under the statutory rule against remote vesting, an interest is invalid "unless it must vest, if at all, not later than twenty-one years after one or more lives in being" (EPTL 9-1.1[b]). That is, an interest is void from the outset if it may vest too remotely. . . . Because the option here could have vested after expiration of the 21-year perpetuities period, it offends the Rule.

We note that the desirability of the "wait and see" doctrine has been widely debated (see, 5A Powell, Real Property ¶ 827F[1], [3]; see also, Waggoner, Perpetuity Reform, 81 Mich. L. Rev. 1718 (describing "wait and see" as "(t)he most controversial of the reform methods")). Its incorporation into EPTL 9-1.1, in any event, must be accomplished by the Legislature, not the courts.

We therefore conclude that the option agreement is invalid under EPTL 9-1.1(b). . . .

IV. Remedy

As a final matter, defendants argue that, if the option fails, the contract of sale conveying the property from Broadwest to Symphony should be rescinded due to the mutual mistake of the parties. We conclude that rescission is inappropriate and therefore do not pass upon whether Broadwest's claim for rescission was properly assigned to defendant Pergola.

A contract entered into under mutual mistake of fact is generally subject to rescission (see, Matter of Gould v. Board of Educ., 81 N.Y.2d 446, 453, 599 N.Y.S.2d 787, 616 N.E.2d 142). CPLR 3005 provides that when relief against mistake is sought, it shall not be denied merely because the mistake is one of law rather than fact. Relying on this provision, defendants maintain that neither Symphony nor Broadwest realized that the option violated the Rule against Perpetuities at the time they entered into the agreement and that both parties intended the option to be enforceable.

CPLR 3005, however, does not equate all mistakes of law with mistakes of fact. . . . Indeed, this Court has held that the predecessor statute, Civil Practice Act §112-f, did not mandate the court to grant relief where taxes had been paid on the assumption that a taxing statute subsequently found to be unconstitutional was valid (id.). Likewise, CPLR 3005 "does not permit a mere misreading of the law by any party to cancel an agreement" (Siegel, Practice Commentaries, McKinney's Cons. Laws of N.Y., Book 7B, CPLR 3005, at 621).

Here, the parties' mistake amounts to nothing more than a misunderstanding as to the applicable law, and CPLR 3005 does not direct undoing of the transaction. . . .

The remedy of rescission, moreover, lies in equity and is a matter of discretion (Rudman v. Cowles Communications, 30 N.Y.2d 1, 13, 330 N.Y.S.2d 33, 280 N.E.2d 867). Defendants' plea that the unenforceability of the option is contrary to the intent of the original parties ignores that the effect of the Rule against Perpetuities—which is a statutory prohibition, not a rule of construction—is always to defeat the intent of parties who create a remotely vesting interest. As explained by the Appellate Division, there is "an irreconcilable conflict in applying a remedy which is designed to void a transaction because it fails to carry out

the parties' true intent to a transaction in which the mistake made by the parties was the application of the Rule against Perpetuities, the purpose of which is to defeat the intent of the parties" (214 A.D.2d 66, 80, 631 N.Y.S.2d 136).

The Rule against Perpetuities reflects the public policy of the State. Granting the relief requested by defendants would thus be contrary to public policy, since it would lead to the same result as enforcing the option and tend to compel performance of contracts violative of the Rule. Similarly, damages are not recoverable where options to acquire real property violate the Rule against Perpetuities, since that would amount to giving effect to the option (see, 5A Powell, Real Property ¶ 771[3]).

Accordingly, the order of the Appellate Division should be affirmed, with costs, and the certified question answered in the affirmative.

NOTES AND QUESTIONS

1. *Options to purchase and right of refusal under the Rule Against Perpetuities.* In recent years a large number of cases finding violations of the Rule Against Perpetuities involve options to purchase and rights of first refusal (preemptive options). An option to purchase, which is specifically enforceable in equity, creates an interest in the property involved. A purchase option is treated like a future interest, contingent upon exercise of the option. The general view, reflected in *Symphony Space*, is that purchase options are subject to the Rule Against Perpetuities and are void if exercisable beyond lives in being plus 21 years.

Unlike an option to purchase, a right of first refusal (sometimes called a preemptive right) does not give the holder the power to compel the owner to sell. It only requires the owner, if and when she decides to sell, to offer the property first to the holder of the right. Courts have generally held that rights of first refusal are not subject to the Rule Against Perpetuities. The reason commonly given is that because the holder of the right may choose to purchase the property, on the same terms as a bona fide offer, if and when the owner decides to sell, the holder of the right has no power to encumber an owner's ability to sell the property for an undue length of time. The right casts no uncertainty on the title, nor does it inhibit a sale of the property. See Bortolotti v. Hayden, 866 N.E.2d 882 (Mass. 2007). Some courts, though, hold that rights of first refusal are subject to the Rule and invalidate them if they are exercisable beyond the perpetuities period. See, e.g., Low v. Spellman, 629 A.2d 57 (Me. 1998); Arundel Corp. v. Marie, 860 A.2d 886 (Md. App. 2004). In New York, market-price rights of first refusal created in commercial or government (but not family) transactions, are not subject to the Rule, but are subject to the common law rule against unreasonable restraints on alienation (on which recall the discussion on pages 232-233). See Metropolitan Transp. Co. v. Bruken Realty Corp., 492 N.E.2d 379 (N.Y. 1986).

Does it make sense to subject commercial transactions to the Rule Against Perpetuities? Professor Stake argues that it does not. In his insightful account of *Symphony Space,* he states:

[T]here is little reason to apply the Rule to commercial options. There is also a reason that the Rule should *not* apply, as opposed to just an absence of reasons for applying it. The Rule invalidates some divisions of rights, divisions that are probably inefficient in the sense that the sum of the parts is less than the whole. The parts are very likely worth less than the whole because those kinds of divisions are rarely created by the market. With commercial options, however, it is less likely that the transfer has been designed to consume some of the value of the land by dividing it. Commercial actors usually want to increase the value of the land. [Jeffrey Evans Stake, Upper West Side Story: The Symphony Space, Inc. v. Pergola Properties, Inc., 669 N.E.2d 799 (1996), in Property Stories 265, 295 (Gerald Korngold & Andrew P. Morriss eds. 2d ed. 2009).]

The Uniform Statutory Rule Against Perpetuities (USRAP) abolishes the application of the Rule Against Perpetuities to options and other commercial transactions. See USRAP §4(1) (1990). Restatement (Third) of Property, Wills and Other Donative Transfers §27.3(1) (2011) follows suit. The Official Comment to USRAP states that while appropriate to gratuitous transactions, the Rule is "an inappropriate instrument of social policy to use as a control of [commercial] transactions." It observes, however, that contingent future interests created by commercial transactions should, as in New York, remain subject to scrutiny as unreasonable restraints on alienation. Another approach has been to limit the duration of certain commercial transactions to a flat period of years. See, e.g., Ill. Comp. Stat. Ann. ch. 765 305/4(a)(7) (2001) (40 years); Mass. Gen. Laws Ann. ch. 184A, §5 (2011) (30 years).

2. *Judicial reformation in* Symphony Space? In *Symphony Space* the court in Section IV of its opinion refused to reform the option so that it carried out the interest of the parties within the perpetuities period. It could have saved the option by providing that it could not be exercised more than 21 years after December 1978. Observe that the court noted that N.Y. Est., Powers & Tr. Law §9-1.2 would reduce an age contingency to 21 to save the gift. Why not reduce the option period similarly? Surely the parties, at the time they negotiated the option, would prefer that to invalidity of the option.

3. *Options to renew leases.* In Bleecker St. Tenants Corp. v. Bleecker Jones LLC, 945 N.E.2d (N.Y. 2011), the New York Court of Appeals held that options to renew leases fall outside the scope of New York's statutory Rule Against Perpetuities. The instant lease was a commercial lease providing for an initial term of 14 years with 9 consecutive options to renew for a 10-year period. After the initial 14-year lease term had expired, the tenant did not exercise any lease option but remained in possession as a month-to-month lessee until the landlord filed suit seeking to void the options under N.Y. Est., Powers & Tr. Law §9-1.1(b). The trial court held that the renewal options were appurtenant to the lease, exercisable during the lease term, and therefore were valid. The Appellate Division reversed, holding that the renewal option was void under the New York statutory Rule Against Perpetuities. The Court of Appeals reversed. It reasoned that because N.Y. Est., Powers & Tr. Law §9-1.1(b) codifies the common law Rule Against Perpetuities and the common law Rule did not apply to options to renew leases, such options fall outside the scope of the New York statute. Moreover, the court stated, options to renew leases are distinguishable from options to purchase in two respects: (1) an option

to renew a lease is exercisable pursuant to a lease agreement and is therefore inherently appurtenant to the lease; and (2) such an option lacks the power to divest title of the property to the option holder.

4. *What is it?* Return to the exemption of possibilities of reverter and rights of entry from the Rule Against Perpetuities (page 314). Take this case:

> *Example 39.* For $5,000 *O* conveys Blackacre "to the School Board for so long as the land is used for school purposes, and when the land ceases to be so used, *O*, his heirs or assigns, may repay the purchase price and demand a reconveyance of the property."

Is *O*'s interest an option? A preemptive right? Is it valid? See Schafer v. Deszcz, 698 N.E.2d 60 (Ohio App. 1997) (holding it to be a preemptive right violating the Rule Against Perpetuities).

If *O* had a possibility of reverter and could repossess the land free if the School Board ceases to use it for school use, why does it violate public policy if *O* may repossess the land only upon refunding the purchase price?

5. *Malpractice liability.* Is the lawyer for Broadwest who drew up the option agreement in *Symphony Space* liable in damages for negligence? See Millwright v. Romer, 322 N.W.2d 30 (Iowa 1982); John W. Weaver, Fear and Loathing in Perpetuities, 48 Wash. & Lee L. Rev. 1393 (1991).

6. *Postscript.* After prevailing in court, Symphony Space sold its air rights in 1998 for $10 million to a developer, Related Companies, which also bought the Healy Building next door. Related Companies built a 22-story residential tower over the theater and on the Healy Building site. Symphony Space used the money to rehabilitate its 830 seat theater, which is the venue for many off-beat and innovative presentations of the arts. The 22-story building, built on a steel platform spanning the theater, towers over the quaint Tudor cottages and gardens of the landmark Pomander Walk to the west.

For a discussion of *Symphony Space*, see Patricia Y. Rayhan, Perpetuities Perpetuated: Symphony Space v. Pergola Properties, Inc., 60 Alb. L. Rev. 1259 (1997).

b. The Perpetuity Reform Movement

(1) Early Reforms

The classic common law Rule Against Perpetuities fell into disfavor by the middle of the twentieth century, thanks largely to its remorseless nature. The Rule, as you now know, invalidates any interests not guaranteed to vest or terminate within a life in being plus 21 years, even in cases where vesting within the required time is in fact extraordinarily probable. Dissatisfaction with this feature in particular led to considerable agreement about the need for perpetuity reform, but no consensus how to proceed. Perhaps as a result, reform came in stages, with first one approach and then another. Eventually, four different methods were tried, and they are described below in chronological order. (Some of the approaches remain in effect in one jurisdiction or another.)

The first approach to reform departed from the common law Rule by focusing on actual rather than possible facts existing at the end of the estate preceding the future interest in question. For example, a Massachusetts statute (since repealed) provided that the validity of a future interest following a life estate was to be determined on the basis of actual facts existing at the end of the life estate. A problem remained, however, because the reform made no provision for instances of purely technical violations, such as cases where at the end of the preceding estate there was an utterly negligible probability that the future interest in question would remain unvested at the end of the perpetuity period.

The second stage of reform attended to this difficulty by the method of specific statutory repairs designed to avoid purely technical violations by altering the common law conventions in certain specific circumstances. An Illinois statute, for example, avoids the notorious "fertile octogenarian" problem (see footnotes 24 and 25 on page 310) by providing that anyone above the age of 65 and below 13 is deemed incapable of having a child. New York has a similar statute, as well as a statute designed to deal with the unborn widow (see Problem 5 on page 313) by presuming that a gift to the surviving "spouse" of a living person is a gift to a person in being. These sorts of statutes also authorize courts to reform instruments in limited instances. For example, age contingencies in excess of 21 that cause a gift to fail (see *Example 30* on page 310, and Problem 4 on page 313) are reduced to 21. For an argument that statutes reflecting this approach should expand the list of instances authorizing judicial reformation, see Ira M. Bloom, Perpetuities Refinement: There Is an Alternative, 62 Wash. L. Rev. 23 (1987) (advocating that New York extend judicial reformation to all cases).

The third stage of reform, sometimes called "immediate reformation," reflects this sentiment. Jurisdictions taking this approach have statutes authorizing (or sometimes directing) courts to reform a disposition in a way that avoids any perpetuity violation while effectuating the transferor's intent as nearly as possible (called *cy pres* in Law French); reformation may be made at any time. Missouri, Oklahoma, and Texas take this approach. For example, Tex. Prop. Code Ann. §5.043(a) (2003) provides:

> Within the limits of the rule against perpetuities, a court shall reform or construe an interest in real or personal property that violates the rule to effect the ascertainable general intent of the creator of the interest. A court shall liberally construe and apply this provision to validate an interest to the fullest extent consistent with the creator's intent.

The cy pres approach gained favor among a few academics during the second half of the twentieth century, but was rejected by many jurisdictions in favor of the fourth approach to reform, called wait-and-see, the basic idea of which is this: Rather than invalidating an interest at the time of its creation on the basis of the what-might-happen test, we wait and see whether a contingent interest actually vests within some permissible vesting period. There is a two-step analysis, the first step of which preserves what has been called the "validating side" of the common law Rule.[33] If the unvested future interest is valid under the common law Rule, that is the end of the matter, and there is no waiting. But if the interest is invalid under the common law Rule, the second step gives the interest a second chance. The interest is valid if in fact it vests or terminates within the permissible vesting period. If it is still in existence and not vested at the end of that period, then it is invalid.

An early version of wait-and-see was adopted in a 1947 Pennsylvania statute. Similar statutes are in effect in a small number of states, including Ohio and Vermont, but this version of wait-and-see did not gain wide favor, in large part because the statutes provide no means by which to demarcate the permissible vesting period. These statutes define the relevant period as, in the language of the now repealed Pennsylvania provision that first introduced such statutes, "the period allowed by the common law against perpetuities as measured by actual event," but this is misleading because such a period in fact does not exist. Because the common law Rule determines the validity or invalidity of an interest at the time of its creation and on the basis of possible future events, there is no need to mark off an actual "perpetuity period" by tracking the life span of so-called measuring lives (on which recall footnote 20 on page 309).[34] Professor Dukeminier proposed a "causal-relationship principle" to define the permissible vesting period for wait-and-see purposes. See Jesse Dukeminier, Wait-and-See: The Causal Relationship Principle, 102 L.Q. Rev. 250 (1986); Jesse Dukeminier, Perpetuities: The Measuring Lives, 85 Colum. L. Rev. 1648 (1985). His basic idea was that the "perpetuity period" for a given interest could be fixed by reference to the lives of persons who could affect the vesting (or termination) of the interest. No state currently has a causal-relationship type statute.[35] The drafters of the Uniform Statutory Rule Against Perpetuities tried to work with the causal-relationship principle but found it too speculative to be workable.

(2) The Uniform Statutory Rule Against Perpetuities

Most formerly wait-and-see states have since adopted the Uniform Statutory Rule Against Perpetuities (USRAP), first promulgated in 1986. The USRAP's most significant innovation over earlier versions of wait-and-see is the use of a flat 90-year permissible vesting period. If at the end of 90 years following the creation of the interest, the interest is still in existence and unvested, it is invalid.[36]

---

33. Lawrence W. Waggoner, The Uniform Statutory Rule Against Perpetuities: The Rationale for the 90-Year Waiting Period, 73 Cornell L. Rev. 157, 157 (1988).

34. The only case ever to apply a Pennsylvania-type statute, Estate of Pearson, 275 A.2d 336 (Pa. 1971), has been widely criticized for failing to explain who the measuring lives were and how they are to be identified under the statute. See Lawrence W. Waggoner, Perpetuity Reform, 81 Mich. L. Rev. 1718, 1764-1769 (1983).

35. Kentucky's causal-relationship type statute was repealed in 2010.

36. If the interest is invalid at the end of the 90-year period, the court reforms the disposition in a way designed most closely to approximate the transferor's manifested plan of disposition and still vest within 90 years.

The USRAP drafters thought a fixed period would avoid the need to trace a designated group of actual lives and to determine which of them is in fact the longest survivor and when he or she died. The USRAP's permissible vesting period is 90 years. Why 90 years? Professor Waggoner, the main drafter of the USRAP, gave this explanation:

> [T]he philosophy behind the 90-year period was to fix a period of time that approximates the period of time that would traditionally be allowed by the wait-and-see doctrine. . . . Using four hypothetical families deemed to be representative of actual families, the framers determined that, on average, the transferor's youngest descendant in being at the transferor's death—assuming the transferor's death to occur between ages 60 and 90, which is when 73 percent of the population die—is about 6 years old. The remaining life expectancy of a 6 year old is about 69 years. The 69 years, plus the 21-year tack-on period, gives [a permissible vesting] period of 90 years. Although this method may not be scientifically accurate to the nth degree, the Drafting Committee considered it reliable enough to support a waiting period of 90 years. [Lawrence W. Waggoner, The Uniform Statutory Rule Against Perpetuities Act: The Rationale of the 90-Year Waiting Period, 73 Cornell L. Rev. 157, 162, 166-168 (1988).][37]

The USRAP has had its detractors. One criticism is that the 90-year permissible vesting period is too long to wait. This objection illustrates why the term "wait-and-see" is misleading. Under the USRAP, it is not always necessary to wait 90 years. Indeed, in the vast majority of cases such a wait will be unnecessary because most unvested future interests will either vest or terminate long before then. This is why the term "permissible vesting period" is more accurate and helpful.

The USRAP has been enacted in more than 20 jurisdictions, including Arizona, Arkansas, California, Connecticut, Florida, Georgia, Massachusetts, Michigan, North Carolina, Oregon, and Utah. However, a number of enacting states have modified the USRAP in various ways that permit perpetual trusts, a topic that we take up next.

For various views on the USRAP, see Ira M. Bloom, Perpetuities Refinement: There Is an Alternative, 62 Wash. L. Rev. 23 (1987); Mary L. Fellows, Testing Perpetuities Reforms: A Study of Perpetuity Cases 1984-89, 25 Real Prop., Prob. & Tr. J. 597 (1990); Amy M. Hess, Freeing Property Owners From the RAP Trap: Tennessee Adopts the Uniform Statutory Rule Against Perpetuities, 62 Tenn. L. Rev. 267 (1995); Ronald C. Link & Kimberley A. Licata, Perpetuities Reform in

---

37. Professor Dukeminier strongly disagreed. He objected that there was no empirical evidence to support the USRAP's 90-year waiting period and that the statute unwisely extended dead hand control of property. See Jesse Dukeminier, The Uniform Statutory Rule Against Perpetuities: Ninety Years in Limbo, 34 UCLA L. Rev. 1023 (1987). The disagreement between Professors Waggoner and Dukeminier was played out in an extended debate in print. See, e.g., Lawrence W. Waggoner, Perpetuities Reform, 81 Mich. L. Rev. 1718 (1983); Jesse Dukeminier, Perpetuities: The Measuring Lives, 85 Colum. L. Rev. 1648 (1985); Lawrence W. Waggoner, Perpetuities: A Perspective on Wait-and-See, 85 Colum. L. Rev. 1714 (1985).

The English Law Commission Report on the Rules Against Perpetuities and Excessive Accumulations, Rep. No. 252 (1998), goes a step further than the USRAP, recommending that lives in being plus 21 years be discarded altogether and replaced by one fixed perpetuity period of 125 years. A minority thought the Rule should be abolished entirely. See Thomas P. Gallanis, The Rule Against Perpetuities and the Law Commission's Flawed Philosophy, 59 Cambridge L.J. 284 (2000).

North Carolina: The Uniform Statutory Rule Against Perpetuities, Nondonative Transfers, and Honorary Trusts, 74 N.C. L. Rev. 1783 (1996).

(3)   The Restatement (Third)'s Two-Generations Approach

The Restatement (Third) breaks new ground by adopting a different approach to implement the policy against excessive dead hand control. Although continuing the basic wait-and-see reform, it rejects both a lives-in-being and the USRAP's period-in-gross measures. Instead, it adopts a two-generations approach. It provides: "A trust or other donative disposition of property is subject to judicial modification . . . to the extent that [it] does not terminate on or before the expiration of the perpetuity period. . . . " Restatement (Third) of Property, Wills and Other Donative Transfers §27.1(a) (2011). It goes on to define the "perpetuity period" as "expir[ing] at the death of the last living measuring life." The "measuring lives" are comprised of a group consisting of the transferor, the beneficiaries who are related to the transferor and who are no more than two generations younger than the transferor, and the beneficiaries who are unrelated to the transferor and no more than the equivalent of two generations younger than the transferor. Id. §27.1(b).

Example 40, below, illustrates how the two-generations approach works:

> *Example 40.* O irrevocably conveys property in trust, directing the trustee to distribute the income at the trustee's discretion among O's descendants from time to time then living. The terms of the trust require the trust to terminate when O no longer has any living descendants. On termination, the trustee is directed to distribute the trust estate to a specified charity. At the creation of the trust, O had two adult children, C1 and C2, and two grandchildren, GC1 and GC2. After the trust was created, two more grandchildren, GC3 and GC4, were born. GC4 was born after O's death.

> Under the Restatement (Third)'s approach, the measuring lives would be O and O's children and grandchildren, C1, C2, GC1, GC2, GC3, and GC4. Suppose that GC4 was the last living measuring life and that GC4 has now died, say at age 88. GC4's death would mark the expiration of the perpetuity period. At GC4's death, O had 50 living descendants—8 great-grandchildren, 16 great-great-grandchildren, and 26 great-great-great-grandchildren. The trust would be subject to judicial modification, because the trust did not terminate on or before the expiration of the perpetuity period. The court should modify the trust by requiring it to terminate on the death of GC4 and order the trust principal to be distributed by representation to O's descendants living when the perpetuity period expired. If O's line of descendants had died out when or before the perpetuity period expired, no modification would be required, because the trust would have required distribution to the specified charity when O's last living descendant died.

The example is taken from Lawrence W. Waggoner, The American Law Institute Proposes a New Approach to Perpetuities: Limiting the Dead Hand to Two Younger Generations (University of Michigan Public Law Working Paper No. 200, 2010), available at http://ssrn.com/abstract=1614936.

An Introductory Note explains the rationale for the two-generations approach:

The objective of switching to a generation-based perpetuity period is not to produce a materially longer or shorter maximum period. Under the traditional lives-in-being approach, the longest living individual who serves as a measuring life will eventually die, but that individual can be someone who is more than two generations younger than the transferor and can outlive the transferor by many decades, maybe even a century,[38] but not much more and often less. Under the two-generations approach the longest-living individual who serves as a measuring life will eventually die, but that individual can be someone who is conceived and born after the transferor's death and can outlive the transferor by many decades, maybe even a century, but not much more and often less. Although the length of the two periods will be different in individual cases, the average length will probably work out to be about the same. [Restatement (Third) of Property, Wills and Other Donative Transfers ch. 27, Introductory Note (2011) (footnote added).]

Unlike the common law Rule, the two-generations approach focuses on the time of termination rather than the time of vesting. The rationale given for this shift is that the time of termination "coordinates more purposively with the Rule's objective of limiting dead-hand control, because the time of termination is when the property comes under the control of the ultimate beneficiaries." Id. An incidental benefit of the shift is that it makes the distinction between contingent and vested future interests irrelevant.

For a criticism of the Restatement (Third)'s approach, see Scott Andrew Shepard, Which the Deader Hand? A Counter to the American Law Institute's Proposed Revival of Dying Perpetuities Rules, 86 Tul. L. Rev. 559 (2012).

(4) Qualified Abolition of the Rule, and the Rise of the Perpetual Trust

Times have recently changed. The great melancholy speech of Henry IV in the Palace of Westminster aptly describes the current scene: "And changes fill the cup of alteration, With divers liquors." William Shakespeare, Henry IV, Part 2, Act III, Scene 1. Nearly one-quarter of the states have now enacted statutes either abolishing (actually or virtually) the Rule Against Perpetuities in the case of trusts containing a power of sale in the trustee, this at least being the characteristic pattern. (The Rule remains in force for legal interests—that is, other than the equitable interests created in a trust—but legal future interests are almost never found in practice today.) Where such statutes exist, perpetual (or virtually perpetual) trusts are now permitted.

This particular reform movement began in the early 1980s when Wisconsin, followed by South Dakota and Idaho, abolished the common law Rule Against

---

38. Final distribution of trust assets a century after the transferor's death is not entirely fanciful. In 2011, a $100 million trust established by Wellington Burt, of Saginaw, Michigan, finally terminated, and the assets were distributed to 12 great-, great-great-, and great-great-great-grandchildren ranging in age from 19 to 94 years old. Burt, described as a cantankerous lumber baron, died in 1919. His trust provided that the trust was to terminate and the assets were to be distributed 21 years after the death of his youngest grandchild in existence when Burt died. See Martha Neil, Perpetuities Rule Finally Ends $100M Waiting Game for Lumber Baron's Heirs, 92 Years After His Death, http://www.abajournal.com/news/perpetuities_rule_finally_ends_100m_waiting_game/ (last visited Dec. 4, 2013).

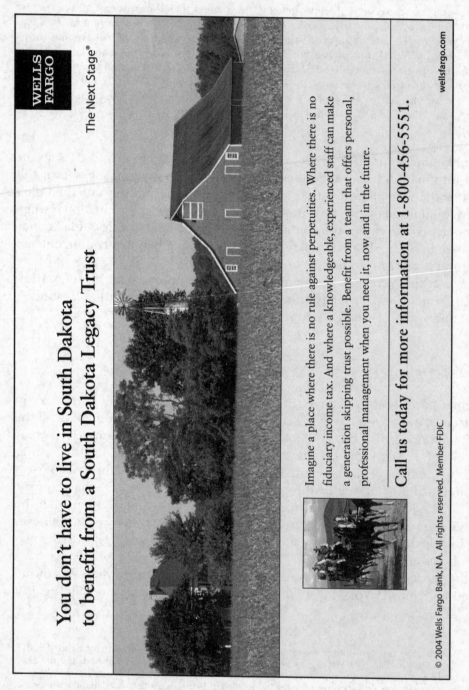

Wells Fargo advertisement for So. Dakota Dynasty Trusts

Perpetuities.[39] Thus, these states permitted trusts to last forever if the trustee has the power to sell the trust assets.

The movement subsequently spread, especially so since the mid-1980s (for reasons having to do with the federal estate tax, to be considered shortly). States were pushed to get on the bandwagon by lawyers for the rich seeking tax advantages, and trust companies seeking fees for managing perpetual trusts. If a state did not act, business would be lost to other states that did. See Robert H. Sitkoff & Max Schanzenbach, Jurisdictional Competition for Trust Funds: An Empirical Study of Perpetuities and Taxes, 115 Yale L.J. 356 (2005). For an indication of the states that permit perpetual trusts, and by what means, see Note 1 on page 339. You will note that some of these states do not directly abandon the Rule Against Perpetuities but accomplish as much by turning it into a default rule; settlors may opt out of the common law Rule by inserting in the trust instrument a simple statement to that effect.

Is this movement to abolish the Rule and to permit perpetual (sometimes called dynastic) trusts wise? What factors have led so many states to abandon the rule and permit perpetual trusts? What were the original policy reasons behind the Rule, and are those reasons relevant today? Are there other policies that the Rule might continue to serve today? The following excerpt addresses these questions.

Jesse Dukeminier & James E. Krier
The Rise of the Perpetual Trust
50 UCLA L. Rev. 1303, 1311-1316, 1317, 1319, 1321-1325, 1343 (2003)

The Rise of the Perpetual Trust

[T]wo reforms . . . — the wait-and-see doctrine, and then, especially, USRAP — might have weakened the Rule against Perpetuities, but they honored its purpose. Neither reform embodied any intention to free the dead hand of age-old restrictions; to the contrary, both shared that central policy of the Rule. But they, as much as the old Rule, are being undermined by the recent wave of state legislation permitting perpetual trusts. To account for that legislation, we have to begin with the federal estate tax.

The Generation-Skipping Transfer Tax

The federal estate tax, first enacted in 1916, levies a tax on any property interest transferred by will, intestacy, or survivorship to another person, except

---

39. These states replaced the common law Rule Against Perpetuities with the rule prohibiting suspension of the power of alienation, which we described earlier (see footnote 32 on page 318). Unlike the Rule Against Perpetuities, the anti-suspension rule is not aimed at remoteness of vesting but at maintaining the power of alienation. According to the anti-suspension rule, so long as living persons acting together can convey a fee, the disposition is valid, regardless of the time of possible vesting. The rule requires only that the power of alienation not be suspended beyond a life in being plus 21 years.

for transfers to spouses and charities. The tax can be avoided, however, by the use of life estates. At the death of a life tenant, the tenancy ends, leaving no transfer to be taxed. For seventy years, lawyers took advantage of this loophole by creating trusts with successive life estates, which could continue without any estate taxes being levied against succeeding generations until after the termination of the trust. And the trusts themselves could continue until the Rule against Perpetuities, in one or another variant, called a halt. Here is an example:

> *Case 4.* T devises property in trust to pay the income to his daughter A for life, then to pay the income to A's children for their lives, then to distribute the principal to A's grandchildren (with a saving clause or other wording to avoid a perpetuities violation). At T's death an estate tax is levied on the property, but no estate tax is levied at the death of A or at the death of A's children because these persons do not have interests transferable on death. An estate tax will not be levied again until the death of A's grandchildren, perhaps more than a hundred years after T's death.

In 1986 Congress closed this loophole in the tax laws, deciding that a transfer tax is due at the expiration of each generation. After 1986, if a transferor creates a life estate in a child that avoids ("skips") the federal estate tax at the child's death, as in *Case 4*, a generation-skipping transfer (GST) tax is due at the child's death if the property passes to the next generation. The GST tax is levied at the highest rate of the estate tax (50 percent in 2001). In *Case 4*, no federal estate tax is payable at A's death because A does not have a transmissible interest. However, at A's death, a generation-skipping transfer occurs, from T to his grandchildren. And so, at A's death, the GST tax is levied on the value of the nonexempt corpus of the trust. Upon the death of A's children, another generation-skipping transfer tax is levied.

At the same time it amended the federal transfer tax laws by adding the GST tax, Congress lightened the taxpayer burden by providing a $1 million exemption from the GST tax for each transferor (doubled in the case of married couples). An inflation adjustment in 2002 increased the amount to $1.1 million; it will increase again to $1.5 million in 2004 and ultimately, in gradual steps, to $3.5 million in 2009. The exemption can be allotted to direct gifts to grandchildren or to a trust producing one or more generation-skipping transfers. The estate tax law itself places no limitation on the duration of such trusts. A transferor can create a trust, with $1.1 million ($3.5 million after 2008) as principal, for his children for life, with successive life estates in succeeding generations, for as long as state perpetuities law allows. Thanks to the exemption, no estate tax or GST tax is due until the trust terminates. In states following the Rule against Perpetuities, these tax-exempt dynasty trusts can endure for lives-in-being at the creation of the trust, plus twenty-one years; in USRAP states they can last for that period or for ninety years.

State Legislation

When Congress enacted the GST tax, it probably assumed that most states would continue to adhere to the Rule against Perpetuities in one or another variation, but this has proved unfounded. Before 1986, only three states—Idaho, South Dakota, and Wisconsin—had abolished the Rule and adopted a prohibition against suspension of the power of alienation. Perpetual trusts have thus been permitted in these states for some time, provided there is some person, such as a trustee with a power of sale, who can transfer title to (alienate) the trust property. But since 1986, at least seventeen more states have enacted legislation permitting perpetual, or almost perpetual, trusts, with some significant variation in statutory terms. . . .

The . . . list will almost certainly grow. . . . The reason has little if anything to do with some wish on the part of wealthy people to control the lives of their unknown descendants; rather, it has to do with their interest in saving on federal transfer taxes imposed at the descendants' deaths, and on competition among the states to cater to that interest. . . . [P]erpetual trusts have long been permitted in Idaho, South Dakota, and Wisconsin, but they were seldom created before the appearance of the GST tax in 1986. Once the GST tax was enacted, however, perpetual trusts became much more attractive, and suddenly the three perpetual-trust states had a comparative advantage in attracting trust business and capital.

This did not go unnoticed. Delaware, the first state to permit perpetual trusts after 1986, did so explicitly to remain competitive in the trust market. One state after another followed suit, and, so far as one can tell, all for that same reason. New Jersey, for example, repealed its USRAP "to permit banks and trust companies to offer 'dynasty trusts' to their customers, such as those that are being offered by banks and trust companies located in other states," like Delaware and South Dakota. . . .

It is difficult to get hard data on the popularity of perpetual trusts among consumers, but there appears to be enough interest among the relatively wealthy to create a tidy market. [For an update on the situation, see the materials immediately following the excerpt.] South Dakota, for example, has enjoyed a substantial increase in trust business since 1986, most of it on behalf of nonresident clients ("S.D. is not a wealthy state, so there would be only a small proportion of its residents who would have call for such trusts"). . . .

Marketing is part of the picture; people involved in the trust business have not been shy in their efforts to attract customers. . . .

Problems and Palliatives

The wisdom of abolishing the Rule against Perpetuities in the case of perpetual trusts has to turn on the merits of the Rule's underlying policies. . . .

. . . There are essentially three concerns, each of which can be stated in terms of a problem arising from a persistent dead hand. The first, the problem of inalienability, is of little importance in our context because it can be avoided by any well-drafted trust. The second, which we shall call the problem of first-generation monopoly, is contentious; we shall satisfy ourselves simply with describing the competing outlooks. The third, the problem of duration, is a catch-all for a host of difficulties that can arise as an uncertain future unwinds, and it will require the bulk of our attention.

The Problem of Inalienability

Transferability (or "alienability") of property promotes efficiency; it allows the movement of resources from lower to higher valued uses through voluntary transactions between buyers and sellers that leave both sides of the bargain better off. So it is unsurprising that free alienability is one of the enduring principles of English, and subsequently American, property law. . . .

In the United States today, the assets of the wealthy consist largely of personal property, not land. Transfers of personal property, and of land as well, for the benefit of succeeding generations are almost always in trust, and trustees almost always have a power to sell the trust property and invest in other assets. In almost all states permitting perpetual trusts, trustees must be given this power by the instrument if it is not granted by statute. A well-drafted trust will grant the power in any event. Hence, perpetual trusts do not give rise to a problem of inalienability; the trust assets are freely marketable.

The Problem of First-Generation Monopoly

Another sort of inalienability problem . . . is what we call the problem of first-generation monopoly, meaning by "first generation" the generation of the settlor who sets up a perpetual trust. [Professor Lewis] Simes wrote:

> [I]t is good public policy to allow each person to dispose of his property as he pleases. The policy extends not only to the present generation but to future generations. If we are to permit the present generation to tie up all existing capital for an indefinitely long period of time, then future generations will have nothing to dispose of by will except what they have saved from their own income; and the property which each generation enjoys will already have been disposed of by ancestors long dead. The rule against perpetuities would appear to strike a balance between the unlimited disposition of property by the members of the present generation and its unlimited disposition by members of future generations.[40]

This is an old and appealing sentiment. . . . Simes . . . thought that the force of the argument against first-generation monopoly "can scarcely be denied." And yet it can. Professor Thomas Gallanis notes, for example, that sentiments about the dead hand rest on dubious assumptions about what people actually want.[40] . . . Consider, for example, the likely preferences of the mentally incompetent; of minor children; of bad money managers who lack the discipline to lash themselves to the mast; of people (maybe those same people!) hounded by creditors and vulnerable to bankruptcy; of people, supported by the state, who are beneficiaries of discretionary trusts, which the state cannot touch; of people contemplat-

40. Thomas P. Gallanis, The Rule Against Perpetuities and the Law Commission's Flawed Philosophy, 59 Cambridge L.J. 284, 287-290 (2000).

ing divorce and interested in having their property out of reach of the other half; of people who reap nice tax advantages from trusts, including spouses who benefit from the marital deduction, and beneficiaries of tax-exempt dynasty trusts, among others. And even as to the class of those who would prefer their property outright, it isn't clear that the aggregate satisfaction of all class members, present and future combined, is increased by the Rule against Perpetuities. . . .

. . . Beyond that, one should consider goals other than satisfaction of preferences. A goal of equality, for example, might support placing restraints on the ability of one generation to limit the opportunities of the next; a goal of donative freedom, on the other hand, would cut in the opposite direction. . . .

Equal opportunity aside, there is an argument that trusts concentrate economic power in the rich or, more accurately, in the trustees for the rich. In the case of trusts, the trustees, not the beneficiaries, have the power of investment. They decide where the trust capital is to be invested, and are required to act prudently—for example, by diversifying trust holdings. . . .

Consider finally the argument that the certainty of receiving trust income makes beneficiaries lazy and unproductive. . . . When the Republic was established, England had a "leisure class," composed of nobles and country gentlemen who lived off their land rents and inheritances and refrained from something as low as work. . . . But this country has never had a leisure class like England's. We have no sense of inherited hierarchy. Our work ethic, deeply imbedded from the times of the Puritans, has spared us a class of great drones. . . .

The Future of Perpetual Trusts

. . . The short of it is that Congress has come to be in charge of trust duration. The future of perpetual trusts is in its hands, to be dealt with through the tax system. The role of the states is to develop affordable means for modifying and terminating trusts when that is in the best interests of the beneficiaries. We have reached a great turning point in the law of trusts.

NOTES

1. *Current status of the Rule Against Perpetuities.* The Rule Against Perpetuities' status in the various jurisdictions presents a bewilderingly mixed picture, one that keeps changing as states continue to revise their statutes. The three major categories are: (1) the USRAP in effect unmodified (e.g., California, Connecticut, Georgia, Kansas, Massachusetts, Minnesota, Montana, Nebraska, New Mexico, Oregon, South Carolina, West Virginia); (2) non-USRAP versions of "wait-and-see" (e.g., Iowa, Maryland, Mississippi, Vermont); and (3) statutes permitting some version of dynastic trusts (e.g., Alaska, Colorado, Delaware, Florida, Idaho, Maine, Nevada, New Hampshire, New Jersey, Pennsylvania, South Dakota, and Utah). No state follows the Rule in its pure form. Still, it is necessary to study the

common law version because several statutory versions, notably the USRAP, provide that the "wait-and-see" part applies only if the court first determines that the interest in question is void under the common law version of the Rule.

2. *Effects of dynasty trust statutes.* In an important empirical study, Professors Robert Sitkoff and Max Schanzenbach found that through 2003, "roughly $100 billion in trust funds have poured into the states that have abolished the Rule." (That figure represents about 10 percent of the total trust assets for 2003.) Moreover, they found that after a state had validated perpetual trusts, "its reported trust assets through 2003 increased by as much as 20 percent relative to states that retained the Rule." Robert H. Sitkoff & Max Schanzenbach, Jurisdictional Competition for Trust Funds: An Empirical Analysis of Perpetuities and Taxes, 115 Yale L.J. 356, 410-111 (2005). One Georgia lawyer reports that 30 to 40 percent of his clients with taxable estates now have dynasty trusts, compared with about half that percentage four years ago. See Rachel Emma Silverman, Building Your Own Dynasty—States Toss Out Restrictions on Creating Perpetual Trusts; Downside: Fees Last Forever, Too, Wall St. J., Sept. 15, 2004, at D1.

3. *Criticisms of perpetual trusts.* Perpetual trusts are not without critics, and Professor Lawrence Waggoner is a leading example. Waggoner, the Reporter of the Restatement (Third) of Property, Wills and Other Donative Transfers (2011), has suggested several problems with perpetual trusts: (1) Genetic dilution—With each step down the generational ladder, the donor's relationship with descendant-beneficiaries weakens significantly. Waggoner points out that on average, a donor's genetic relationship with her descendants is cut in half at each succeeding generation. So, 300 years after the donor's death, her genetic relationship is reduced to about 0.0061 percent, about the same as a person has with any randomly selected member of the population. (2) Beneficiary proliferation—As the genetic relationship between donor and beneficiaries diminishes, Waggoner notes, the number of descendant-beneficiaries grows geometrically. For example, 150 years after creation of a perpetual trust, the trust could have as many as 450 such beneficiaries; 250 years after creation, more than 7,000 beneficiaries; and 350 years after creation, about 114,500 beneficiaries. Waggoner observes that if the beneficiaries were to hold a meeting, they would have to rent out Rungrado May Day Stadium, in Pyongyang, North Korea, or Salt Lake Stadium, in Kolkata, India. (3) Benefitting strangers—The older the trust, the less likely the donor is to know the descendant-beneficiaries and the less likely the beneficiaries are to know each other. Few people know their third or fourth cousins (descendants of great-great grandparent or of their great-great-great grandparents), yet they would be common beneficiaries in perpetual trusts a few hundred years old. See Lawrence W. Waggoner, The Folly of Perpetual Trusts (Univ. of Michigan Public Law and Legal Theory Working Paper No. 259, 2011, updated April 2013), available at http://ssrn.com/abstract=1975117. For other criticisms of perpetual trusts, see Ray D. Madoff, Immortality and the Law 78-85 (2010); Edward J. McCaffery, The Dirty Little Secret of (Estate) Tax Reform, 65 Stan. L. Rev. Online 21 (2012); Lucy A. Marsh, The Demise of Dynasty Trusts: Returning the Wealth to the Family, 5 Est. Plan. & Cmty. Prop. L.J. 23 (2012-13); Mark L.

Ascher, But I Thought the Earth Belonged to the Living, 89 Tex. L. Rev. 1149 (2011) (reviewing Lawrence M. Friedman, Dead Hands: A Social History of Wills, Trusts, and Inheritance (2009)). For a defense of dynastic trusts, see Bridget J. Crawford, Who Is Afraid of Perpetual Trusts?, 111 Mich. L. Rev. First Impressions 79 (2012).

4. *Restatement (Third) rejects perpetual trusts.* The American Law Institute has declared the perpetual trust movement "ill advised." Restatement (Third) of Property, Wills and Other Donative Transfers, Introductory Note to Chapter 27, at 564 (2011). The Restatement explains: "The movement to abrogate the Rule Against Perpetuities has not been based on the merits of removing the Rule's curb on excessive dead-hand control. The policy issues associated with allowing perpetual or near-perpetual trusts have not been seriously discussed in the state legislatures. The driving force has been the effort to compete for trust industry (financial services) business from other states." Id. (footnote omitted).

5. There is a rapidly growing literature on perpetual trusts and the race to repeal the Rule Against Perpetuities. For some examples, see Joel C. Dobris, Undoing Repeal of the Rule Against Perpetuities: Federal and State Tools for Breaking Dynasty Trusts, 27 Cardozo L. Rev. 2537 (2006); Max M. Schanzenbach & Robert H. Sitkoff, Perpetuities or Taxes? Explaining the Rise of the Perpetual Trust, 27 Cardozo L. Rev. 2465 (2006); Joshua C. Tate, Perpetual Trusts and the Settlor's Intent, 53 U. Kan. L. Rev. 595 (2005); Stewart E. Sterk, Jurisdictional Competition to Abolish the Rule Against Perpetuities: R.I.P. for the R.A.P., 24 Cardozo L. Rev. 2097 (2003); Stephen E. Greer, The Alaska Dynasty Trust, 18 Alaska L. Rev. 253 (2001); Verner F. Chaffin, Georgia's Proposed Dynasty Trust: Giving the Dead Too Much Control, 35 Ga. L. Rev. 1 (2000); Joel C. Dobris, The Death of the Rule Against Perpetuities, or the USRAP Has No Friends—An Essay, 35 Real Prop., Prob. & Tr. J. 601 (2000); Note, Dynasty Trusts and the Rule Against Perpetuities, 116 Harv. L. Rev. 2588 (2003). See also Eric Rakowski, The Future Reach of the Disembodied Will, 4 Pol. Phil. & Econ. 91 (2005).

6. For a defense of the common law Rule, see Jeffrey E. Stake, Darwin, Donations and the Illusions of Dead Hand Control, 64 Tul. L. Rev. 705 (1990). Professor Stake argues that the Rule frees current owners from dead hand behavioral constraints and enhances their enjoyment of ownership by reducing uncertainty.

5

Co-ownership and Marital Interests

As we have seen, ownership may be divided among two or more persons in the sense that they have *consecutive* rights of possession. The division results in possessory and future interests, not co-ownership. The latter term refers to situations when two or more persons have *concurrent* rights of present or future possession, and those situations are the central subject of this chapter.[1]

Actually, we shall not be looking here at all modes of co-ownership, nor shall we be looking only at concurrent interests. Partnerships, for example, involve co-ownership of partnership assets, but we ignore the subject because it is studied in detail in courses such as business associations. Similarly, some marital interests are not concurrent, but we nevertheless study them in Section B of this chapter. We do so because several important marital interests are concurrent or do involve forms of co-ownership and thus are conveniently studied here. Since we open the subject, we might as well give it unified treatment.

A. Common Law Concurrent Interests

1. Types, Characteristics, Creation

The common law has known at least five types of concurrent interests. We can ignore two of these, one because it is of no importance and the other because it is of too much importance.[2] The three remaining are the tenancy in common, the joint tenancy, and the tenancy by the entirety. We shall take them up in turn.

Tenants in common have separate but undivided interests in the property; the interest of each is descendible and may be conveyed by deed or will. There are no survivorship rights between tenants in common. Example: *T* devises Blackacre "to *A* and *B*." *A* and *B* are tenants in common. If *A* conveys his

---

1. The concurrent and consecutive concepts can be and often are combined. *A* and *B* can have a concurrent life estate to last for their joint lives, with a remainder in *C*; or *A* and *B* can have concurrent interests in a remainder following a life estate in *C*.

2. The one of no importance is coparceny. At common law under the system of primogeniture the eldest son was the heir. If a decedent had only daughters, the daughters took as coparcenors. Coparceny was similar to, but not identical with, a tenancy in common. Primogeniture never took hold in the American colonies and was early eliminated, as was coparceny. See 2 American Law of Property §6.7 (1952). The common law concurrent interest of too much importance is the tenancy in partnership, which, as already noted, we leave to other courses. Today the common law of partnership has been largely superseded by the Uniform Partnership Act or other statutory partnership law.

interest to *C, B* and *C* are tenants in common. If *B* then dies intestate, *B*'s heir is a tenant in common with *C*. Each tenant in common owns an undivided share of the whole (a situation that, whatever its conceptual difficulties, gives rise to a host of practical ones).

Unlike tenants in common, *joint tenants* have the right of survivorship, the outstanding characteristic of a joint tenancy. The theory underlying this right is rather peculiar but still important in several instances. By a common law fiction, joint tenants together are regarded as a single owner; each tenant is seised *per my et per tout* (by the share or moiety and by the whole). In theory, then, each owns the undivided whole of the property; this being so, when one joint tenant dies *nothing passes* to the surviving joint tenant or tenants. Rather, the estate simply continues in survivors freed from the participation of the decedent, whose interest is extinguished.

Since the original notion was that all joint tenants were seised together as one owner, the common law insisted that their interests be equal in all respects. In particular, four "unities" were essential to a joint tenancy—time, title, interest, and possession. The meaning of each unity is as follows:

Time	The interest of each joint tenant must be acquired or vest at the same time.
Title	All joint tenants must acquire title by the same instrument or by a joint adverse possession. A joint tenancy can never arise by intestate succession or other act of law.
Interest	All must have equal undivided shares and identical interests measured by duration.
Possession	Each must have a right to possession of the whole. After a joint tenancy is created, however, one joint tenant can voluntarily give exclusive possession to the other joint tenant. (The unity of possession is essential to a tenancy in common as well; none of the other three unities is.)

At common law, and in many states today, if these four unities do not exist, a joint tenancy is not created; instead, a tenancy in common is created. Statutes in some jurisdictions abolish the requirement of the four unities and provide that a joint tenancy may be created simply by stating explicitly the intent to do so.

If the four unities exist at the time the joint tenancy is created but are later severed, the joint tenancy turns into a tenancy in common when the unities cease to exist. Hence, joint tenants can change their interests into a tenancy in common by a mutual agreement destroying one of the four unities. Indeed, any one joint tenant can convert a joint tenancy into a tenancy in common unilaterally by conveying his interest to a third party; this *severs* the joint tenancy as between the third party and his cotenants because it destroys one or more of the unities. (Which one or ones?)

If tenants in common or joint tenants cannot solve their problems by mutual agreement, any one of them can bring an action for judicial partition. In a partition action, a court will either physically partition the tract of land into separately owned parts or order the land sold and divide the proceeds among the tenants.

A *tenancy by the entirety* can be created only in husband and wife.[3] The tenancy by the entirety is like the joint tenancy in that the four unities (plus a fifth — the unity of marriage) are required, and the surviving tenant has the right of survivorship. However, husband and wife are considered to hold as one person at common law. They do not hold by the moieties; rather, both are seised of the entirety, *per tout et non per my*. As a result, neither husband nor wife can defeat the right of survivorship of the other by a conveyance of a moiety to a third party; only a conveyance by husband and wife together can do so. Neither husband nor wife, acting alone, has the right to judicial partition of property held as tenants by the entirety. Divorce terminates the tenancy by the entirety because it terminates the marriage, which is a requisite for a tenancy by the entirety; absent some agreement to the contrary, the parties usually become tenants in common.

The tenancy by the entirety exists today in fewer than half the states. Because the tenancy by the entirety gives rise to marital interests of importance in many states, we will be investigating it further in Section B of this chapter, where we treat marital property.

Presumptions. The discussion thus far has hinted at how the various sorts of concurrent interests are created; let us now be more explicit. The English common law, disliking division of land into smaller parcels (a policy also underlying primogeniture), favored joint tenancies over tenancies in common. If an instrument conveying property to two or more persons was ambiguous, a joint tenancy resulted. Today the situation is reversed; the presumption favoring joint tenancies has been abolished in all states (with an exception in a few states where the conveyance is to husband and wife). Usually, the abolition has been accomplished by statutes providing that a grant or devise to two or more persons creates a tenancy in common unless an intent to create a joint tenancy is expressly declared. Under such statutes, a conveyance "to *A* and *B* as joint tenants and not as tenants in common" will create a joint tenancy; something even a little bit less, such as "to *A* and *B* jointly," might not. Courts have sometimes thought a conveyance to *A* and *B* "jointly" merely indicates an intent to create some type of concurrent estate but not necessarily a joint tenancy. Some states require an express provision for survivorship in order to create a joint tenancy. Under these statutes, to create a joint tenancy it is necessary to say "to *A* and *B* as joint tenants with the right of survivorship." See Hoover v. Smith, 444 S.E.2d 546 (Va. 1994).[4] A few states have done

---

3. Several states have legislation permitting a tenancy by the entirety between unmarried persons prohibited from marrying each other.

4. On the other hand, in a few states it is dangerous to include expressly a right of survivorship. In Michigan, a grant "to *A* and *B* as joint tenants with full rights of survivorship" or "to *A* and *B* as joint tenants and to the survivor" creates a joint life estate in *A* and *B*, with a contingent remainder in the survivor (see Problem 3 below). Albro v. Allen, 454 N.W.2d 85 (Mich. 1990). So too in Kentucky. See Sanderson v. Saxon, 834 S.W.2d 676 (Ky. 1992).

away with the joint tenancy entirely. See William B. Stoebuck & Dale A. Whitman, The Law of Property 184 (3d ed. 2000).

What of conveyances to husband and wife? The common law presumed an intention to create a tenancy by the entirety, absent some clear indication to the contrary. The presumption still has considerable force in those states that retain the tenancy, though in some of these a conveyance to husband and wife will be presumed to create a tenancy in common or joint tenancy.

PROBLEMS AND NOTE

1. *O* conveys Blackacre "to *A*, *B*, and *C* as joint tenants." Subsequently, *A* conveys his interest to *D*. Then *B* dies intestate, leaving *H* as his heir. What is the state of the title? See Cortelyou v. Dinger, 310 N.Y.S.2d 764 (Sup. Ct. 1970). What if *B* had died leaving a will devising his interest to *H*?

2. *T* devises Blackacre "to *A* and *B* as joint tenants for their joint lives, remainder to the survivor." What interests are created by the devise? See Problem 3, page 283. How does a joint tenancy in fee simple differ?

3. *A* and *B* are planning to be married. Two weeks before the ceremony, they buy a house and take title "in *A* and *B* as tenants by the entirety." Several years after the marriage, *A* moves out of the house and conveys his interest in the house to his brother *C*. *C* brings an action to partition the property. What result? See Estate of Shelton, 796 N.E.2d 955 (Ohio App. 2003); Annot., 9 A.L.R.4th 1189 (1981).

4. In Germaine v. Delaine, 318 So. 2d 681 (Ala. 1975), the court was called upon to construe a deed to the grantees "jointly, as tenants in common, with equal rights and interest in said land, and to the survivor thereof, in fee simple. . . . To Have and to Hold the same unto the said parties hereto, equally, jointly, as tenants in common, with equal rights and interest for the period or term of their lives, and to the survivor thereof at the death of the other." The court held that the deed created a joint tenancy because it provided for survivorship.

Compare the approach of the court in Kipp v. Chips Estate, 732 A.2d 127 (Vt. 1999), involving a deed conveying "to Ervin W. Chips and June Kipp, joint tenants, and their heirs and assigns forever." This language appeared in the granting clause of the deed, the part that serves to transfer ownership. The habendum clause of the deed, the part that seeks to describe the type of title granted (see footnote 6, page 616), referred to the grantees as "tenants in common, their heirs and assigns." The court held that the deed created a tenancy in common. The granting clause of a deed is given priority over the habendum clause unless the language of the former is ambiguous, and the court thought it was. It expressed a joint tenancy, but also implied a tenancy in common because of the words "heirs and assigns forever." This additional language, the court concluded, suggested that upon the death of one of the grantees, the grantee's share should go to his or her heirs and assigns. That, of course, would be inconsistent with a joint tenancy's right of survivorship; hence the ambiguity, which the court resolved by resort to the tenancy in common language in the habendum clause, coupled with the modern presumption in favor of tenancies in common.

Apparently, the members of the court never learned (or later forgot) the difference between words of purchase and words of limitation. See page 218.

Avoidance of probate. Joint tenancies are popular, particularly between husband and wife, because a joint tenancy is the practical equivalent of a will but at the joint tenant's death probate of the property is avoided. Probate is the judicial supervision of the administration of the decedent's property that passes to others at the decedent's death: The probate court appoints an administrator or executor who collects the decedent's assets, pays debts and taxes, and distributes or changes title to the property to the beneficiaries. Probate is costly; administrators, lawyers, and court costs must be paid. And property may be tied up in probate for months, even years. A joint tenancy avoids probate because *no interest passes* on the joint tenant's death. Under the theory of joint tenancy, the decedent's interest vanishes at death, and the survivor's ownership of the whole continues without the decedent's participation. See also Note 2 on page 644 on avoiding probate by a revocable trust.

The idea that no interest passes at the death of a joint tenant, which shaped the historical development of the joint tenancy, was originally a clever ruse to bypass the medieval prohibition of wills of land. In order to pass land to a person other than the primogenitary heir, a landowner could enfeoff himself and his intended successor as joint tenants. When the landowner died, no interest passed by will from the landowner to the surviving tenant. See Anne L. Spitzer, Joint Tenancy with Right of Survivorship: A Legacy from Thirteenth Century England, 16 Texas Tech. L. Rev. 629 (1985).

A joint tenant cannot pass her interest in a joint tenancy by will. Inasmuch as the joint tenant's interest ceases at death, a joint tenant has no interest that can pass by will. Huff v. Metz, 676 So. 2d 264 (Miss. 1996).

The idea that a joint tenant's interest ceases at death also has important consequences for creditors. If a creditor acts during a joint tenant's life, the creditor can seize and sell the joint tenant's interest in property, severing the joint tenancy. If the creditor waits until after the joint tenant's death, the decedent joint tenant's interest has disappeared, and there is nothing the creditor can seize. See Rembe v. Stewart, 387 N.W.2d 313 (Iowa 1986) (criticizing but upholding the rule).

Although the theory that "nothing passes" at the joint tenant's death controls private law questions, it does not control federal estate taxation. Ignoring the fiction and looking at reality, Congress has provided that when a joint tenant dies, his share of the jointly held property is subject to federal estate taxation. If the joint tenants are husband and wife, one-half is subject to taxation when one spouse dies (though no taxes are paid on it because any amount of property passing to the surviving spouse qualifies for the marital deduction and passes tax-free). If the joint tenants are not husband and wife, when one joint tenant dies the portion of the value of the jointly held property attributable to the consideration furnished by the decedent is subject to federal estate taxation. See Internal Revenue Code §2040. Under most state inheritance taxes, the fractional share of a joint tenancy owned by the decedent is taxed; the federal who-furnished-the-consideration test is not followed.

Unequal shares. One of the four unities of a joint tenancy is equal shares. At common law if *A* owned a one-third share and *B* a two-thirds share, *A* and *B* could not hold as joint tenants. They would hold as tenants in common. This result is justifiable solely on historical grounds and makes no sense today. It is increasingly ignored by courts in situations where it counts. If *A* and *B* take title as joint tenants and *A* furnishes one-third of the purchase price and *B* two-thirds, and the parties intend the proceeds from sale of the joint tenancy property to be divided one-third and two-thirds if sold during their joint lives, a joint tenancy is created, and, if the property is sold, the court will divide the proceeds according to their intent. See Moat v. Ducharme, 555 N.E.2d 897 (Mass. App. 1990) (cohabitants with unequal contributions); Jezo v. Jezo, 127 N.W.2d 246 (Wis. 1964) (presumption of equal shares rebuttable by evidence of contrary intent).

There are other instances in which the law pays no attention to the requirement of unity of interest. In most states joint and survivor bank accounts are owned by the parties during life in proportion to the net contributions by each (see page 360). And, as stated above, Internal Revenue Code §2040 provides that a decedent joint tenant (other than a spouse) is deemed to own, and is taxed on, a fractional share of the property proportionate to the decedent's contributions.

2.   Severance of Joint Tenancies

Riddle v. Harmon

Court of Appeal of California, First District, 1980
162 Cal. Rptr. 530

POCHE, J. We must decide whether Frances Riddle, now deceased, unilaterally terminated a joint tenancy by conveying her interest from herself as joint tenant to herself as tenant in common. The trial court determined, via summary judgment quieting title to her widower, that she did not. The facts follow.

Mr. and Mrs. Riddle purchased a parcel of real estate, taking title as joint tenants. Several months before her death, Mrs. Riddle retained an attorney to plan her estate. After reviewing pertinent documents, he advised her that the property was held in joint tenancy and that, upon her death, the property would pass to her husband. Distressed upon learning this, she requested that the joint tenancy be terminated so that she could dispose of her interest by will. As a result, the attorney prepared a grant deed whereby Mrs. Riddle granted to herself an undivided one-half interest in the subject property. The document also provided that "The purpose of this Grant Deed is to terminate those joint tenancies formerly existing between the Grantor, Frances P. Riddle, and Jack C. Riddle, her husband. . . ." He also prepared a will disposing of Mrs. Riddle's interest in the property. Both the grant deed and will were executed on December 8, 1975. Mrs. Riddle died 20 days later.

The court below refused to sanction her plan to sever the joint tenancy and quieted title to the property in her husband. The executrix of the will of Frances Riddle appeals from that judgment.

The basic concept of a joint tenancy is that it is one estate which is taken jointly. Under the common law, four unities were essential to the creation and existence of an estate in joint tenancy: interest, time, title and possession. (Tenhet v. Boswell (1976) 18 Cal. 3d 150, 155, 133 Cal. Rptr. 10, 554 P.2d 330.) If one of the unities was destroyed, a tenancy in common remained. (Id.) Severance of the joint tenancy extinguishes the principal feature of that estate, the *jus accrescendi* or right of survivorship. This "right" is a mere expectancy that arises "only upon success in the ultimate gamble—survival—and then only if the unity of the estate has not theretofore been destroyed by voluntary conveyance . . . , by partition proceedings . . . , by involuntary alienation under an execution . . . , or by any other action which operates to sever the joint tenancy." (Id. at pp. 155-156, citations omitted.)

An indisputable right of each joint tenant is the power to convey his or her separate estate by way of gift or otherwise without the knowledge or consent of the other joint tenant and to thereby terminate the joint tenancy. (Delanoy v. Delanoy (1932) 216 Cal. 23, 26, 13 P.2d 513; Estate of Harris (1937) 9 Cal. 2d 649, 658, 72 P.2d 873; Walk v. Vencill (1947) 30 Cal. 2d 104, 108-109, 180 P.2d 351.) If a joint tenant conveys to a stranger and that person reconveys to the same tenant, then no revival of the joint tenancy occurs because the unities are destroyed. (Hammon v. McArthur (1947) 30 Cal. 2d 512, 183 P.2d 1; Comment, Severance of Joint Tenancy in California (1957) 8 Hastings L.J. 290, 291.) The former joint tenants become tenants in common.

At common law, one could not create a joint tenancy in himself and another by a direct conveyance. It was necessary for joint tenants to acquire their interests at the same time (unity of time) and by the same conveyancing instrument (unity of title). So, in order to create a valid joint tenancy where one of the proposed joint tenants already owned an interest in the property, it was first necessary to convey the property to a disinterested third person, a "strawman," who then conveyed the title to the ultimate grantees as joint tenants. This remains the prevailing practice in some jurisdictions. Other states, including California, have disregarded this application of the unities requirement "as one of the obsolete 'subtle and arbitrary distinctions and niceties of the feudal common law,' [and allow the creation of a valid joint tenancy without the use of a strawman]." (4A Powell on Real Property (1979) [¶] 616, p. 670, citation omitted.)

By amendment to its Civil Code,[5] California became a pioneer in allowing the *creation* of a joint tenancy by direct transfer. Under authority of Civil Code section 683, a joint tenancy conveyance may be made from a "sole owner to himself and others," or from joint owners to themselves and others as specified in the code. (See Bowman, Real Estate Law in Cal. (4th ed. 1975) p. 105.) The purpose of the amendment was to "avoid the necessity of making a conveyance through a dummy" in the statutorily enumerated situations. (Third Progress Rep. to the Legislature (Mar. 1955) p. 54, 2 Appen. to Sen. J. (1955 Reg. Sess.)). Accordingly, in California, it is no longer necessary to use a strawman to *create* a joint tenancy. (Donovan v. Donovan (1963) 223 Cal. App. 2d 691, 697, 36 Cal. Rptr. 225.) This court is now asked to reexamine whether a strawman is required to *terminate* a joint tenancy.

Twelve years ago, in Clark v. Carter (1968) 265 Cal. App. 2d 291, 295, 70 Cal. Rptr. 923, the Court of Appeal considered the same question and found the strawman to be indispensable. As in the instant case, the joint tenants in *Clark* were husband and wife. The day before Mrs. Clark died, she executed two documents without her husband's knowledge or consent: (1) a quitclaim deed conveying her undivided half interest in certain real property from herself as joint tenant to herself as tenant in common, and (2) an assignment of her undivided half interest in a deed of trust from herself as joint tenant to herself as tenant in common. These documents were held insufficient to sever the joint tenancy.

After summarizing joint tenancy principles, the court reasoned that

> [U]nder California law, a transfer of property presupposes participation by at least two parties, namely, a grantor and a grantee. Both are essential to the efficacy of a deed, and they cannot be the same person. A transfer of property requires that title be conveyed by one living person to another (Civ. Code, §1039.) . . .
>
> Foreign authority also exists to the effect that a person cannot convey to himself alone, and if he does so, he still holds under the original title.
>
> Similarly, it was the common law rule that in every property conveyance there be a grantor, a grantee, and a thing granted. Moreover, the grantor could not make himself the grantee by conveying an estate to himself. (*Clark*, supra, at pp. 295-296, citations omitted.)

That "two-to-transfer" notion stems from the English common law feoffment ceremony with livery of seisin. (Swenson & Degnan, Severance of Joint Tenancies (1954) 38 Minn. L. Rev. 466, 467.) If the ceremony took place upon the land being conveyed, the grantor (feoffor) would hand a symbol of the land, such as a lump of earth or a twig, to the grantee (feoffee). (Burby, Real Property (3d ed. 1966) p. 281.) In order to complete the investiture of seisin it was necessary that the feoffor completely relinquish possession of the land to the feoffee. (Moynihan,

---

5. Civil Code section 683, as amended in 1955, provides in relevant part that: "A joint interest is one owned by two or more persons in equal shares, by a title created by a single will or transfer, when expressly declared in the will or transfer to be a joint tenancy, or by transfer from a sole owner to himself and others, or from tenants in common or joint tenants to themselves or some of them, or to themselves or any of them and others, or from a husband and wife, when holding title as community property or otherwise to themselves or to themselves and others or to one of them and to another or others, when expressly declared in the transfer to be a joint tenancy, or when granted or devised to executors or trustees as joint tenants."

Preliminary Survey of the Law of Real Property (1940) p. 86.) It is apparent from the requirement of livery of seisin that one could not enfeoff oneself—that is, one could not be both grantor and grantee in a single transaction. Handing oneself a dirt clod is ungainly. Just as livery of seisin has become obsolete,[6] so should ancient vestiges of that ceremony give way to modern conveyancing realities.

"We are given to justifying our tolerance for anachronistic precedents by rationalizing that they have engendered so much reliance as to preclude their liquidation. Sometimes, however, we assume reliance when in fact it has been dissipated by the patent weakness of the precedent. Those who plead reliance do not necessarily practice it." (Traynor, No Magic Words Could Do It Justice (1961) 49 Cal. L. Rev. 615, 622-623.) Thus, undaunted by the *Clark* case, resourceful attorneys have worked out an inventory of methods to evade the rule that one cannot be both grantor and grantee simultaneously.

The most familiar technique for unilateral termination is use of an intermediary "strawman" blessed in the case of Burke v. Stevens (1968) 264 Cal. App. 2d 30, 70 Cal. Rptr. 87. There, Mrs. Burke carried out a secret plan to terminate a joint tenancy that existed between her husband and herself in certain real property. The steps to accomplish this objective involved: (1) a letter written from Mrs. Burke to her attorney directing him to prepare a power of attorney naming him as her attorney in fact for the purpose of terminating the joint tenancy; (2) her execution and delivery of the power of attorney; (3) her attorney's execution and delivery of a quitclaim deed conveying Mrs. Burke's interest in the property to a third party, who was an office associate of the attorney in fact; (4) the third party's execution and delivery of a quitclaim deed reconveying that interest to Mrs. Burke on the following day. The *Burke* court sanctioned this method of terminating the joint tenancy, noting at one point: "While the actions of the wife, from the standpoint of a theoretically perfect marriage, are subject to ethical criticism, and her stealthy approach to the solution of the problems facing her is not to be acclaimed, the question before the court is not what should have been done ideally in a perfect marriage, but whether the decedent and her attorneys acted in a legally permissible manner." (*Burke*, supra, at p. 34.)

Another creative method of terminating a joint tenancy appears in Reiss v. Reiss (1941) 45 Cal. App. 2d 740, 114 P.2d 718. There a trust was used. For the purpose of destroying the incident of survivorship, Mrs. Reiss transferred bare legal title to her son, as trustee of a trust for her use and benefit. The son promised to reconvey the property to his mother or to whomever she selected at any time upon her demand. (Id. at p. 746.) The court upheld this arrangement, stating, "We are of the opinion that the clearly expressed desire of Rosa Reiss to terminate the joint tenancy arrangement was effectively accomplished

---

6. It was not until 1845 that a statute was enacted in England making it possible for a freehold estate to be conveyed by grant deed. In America, livery of seisin was done away with long before legislative reforms were effected in the mother country. (Moynihan, op. cit. supra, at p. 87.) Maitland tells us that the physical acts involved in a feoffment grew out of a "mental incapacity, an inability to conceive that mere rights can be transferred." (Maitland, The Mystery of Seisin (1886) 2 L.Q. Rev. 481, 489.)

by the transfer of the legal title to her son for her expressed specific purpose of having the control and the right of disposition of her half of the property." (Id. at p. 747.)

In view of the rituals that are available to unilaterally terminate a joint tenancy, there is little virtue in steadfastly adhering to cumbersome feudal law requirements. "It is revolting to have no better reason for a rule of law than that so it was laid down in the time of Henry IV. It is still more revolting if the grounds upon which it was laid down have vanished long since, and the rule simply persists from blind imitation of the past." (Holmes, Collected Legal Papers (1920) p. 187.) Common sense as well as legal efficiency dictate that a joint tenant should be able to accomplish directly what he or she could otherwise achieve indirectly by use of elaborate legal fictions.

Moreover, this will not be the first time that a court has allowed a joint tenant to unilaterally sever a joint tenancy without the use of an intermediary. In Hendrickson v. Minneapolis Federal Sav. & L. Assn. (1968) 281 Minn. 462, 161 N.W.2d 688, decided one month after *Clark*, the Minnesota Supreme Court held that a tenancy in common resulted from one joint tenant's execution of a "Declaration of Election to Sever Survivorship of Joint Tenancy." No fictional transfer by conveyance and reconveyance through a strawman was required.[7]

Our decision does not create new powers for a joint tenant. A universal right of each joint tenant is the power to effect a severance and destroy the right of survivorship by conveyance of his or her joint tenancy interest to another "person." (Swenson & Degnan, supra, at p. 469.) "If an indestructible right of survivorship is desired—that is, one which may not be destroyed by one tenant—that may be accomplished by creating a joint life estate with a contingent remainder in fee to the survivor; a tenancy in common in fee simple with an executory interest in the survivor; or a fee simple to take effect in possession in the future." Id.

We discard the archaic rule that one cannot enfeoff oneself which, if applied, would defeat the clear intention of the grantor. There is no question but that the decedent here could have accomplished her objective—termination of the joint tenancy—by one of a variety of circuitous processes. We reject the rationale of the *Clark* case because it rests on a common law notion whose reason for existence vanished about the time that grant deeds and title companies replaced

---

7. In its reasoning the *Hendrickson* court recognized a policy disfavoring survivorship in Minnesota, noting that in modern times survivorship came to be regarded "as an 'odious thing' that too often deprived a man's heirs of their rightful inheritance [fn. omitted]." (*Hendrickson*, supra, at p. 690.) Construing the grant deed as effecting a termination of the joint tenancy will result in the concurrent estate becoming a tenancy in common. This outcome is consistent with California's statutorily decreed preference for recognizing tenancies in common. (See Civ. Code, §§683, 686; Tenhet v. Boswell, supra, 18 Cal. 3d 150, 157.) Contrary to the modern preference, at common law there was a presumption in favor of joint tenancy. This presumption was based on a desire to avoid the splitting of the feudal services due to the lord of the fee. (Moynihan, Preliminary Survey of the Law of Real Property (1940) p. 130.) Land was kept in larger tracts and thus facilitated the rendering of services to the lord. Tenancy in common, on the other hand, resulted in constant subdivision. (Swenson & Degnan, Severance of Joint Tenancies (1954) 38 Minn. L.R. 466, 503.) Another possible reason that joint tenancy was favored is that it is easier to rely on the loyalty of one man than two. (Id.) As the age of feudalism ended, the reasons for the presumption in favor of joint tenancies also ended. (Id.)

colorful dirt clod ceremonies as the way to transfer title to real property. One joint tenant may unilaterally sever the joint tenancy without the use of an intermediary device.

The judgment is reversed.

NOTES AND QUESTIONS

1. Is it fair to permit one joint tenant to sever the tenancy without giving notice to the other joint tenant? Should a deed such as the wife used in Riddle v. Harmon be effective without recordation? See In re Knickerbocker, 912 P.2d 969 (Utah 1996) (citing cases from many states agreeing with Riddle v. Harmon and some disagreeing); Cal. Civ. Code §683.2 (West 2012); N.Y. Real Prop. Law §240-c (McKinney 2012).

Suppose that the wife writes out the deed in her own handwriting: "I convey my interest in [Blackacre] to myself, to terminate the joint tenancy with my husband." Telling only her daughter of it, the wife puts the deed under some papers in her desk drawer. Subsequently, the husband dies, and the wife destroys the deed. What result? How would you, as lawyer for the husband's estate, find out these facts? See Samuel M. Fetters, An Invitation to Commit Fraud: Secret Destruction of Joint Tenant Survivorship Rights, 55 Fordham L. Rev. 173 (1986).

Compare a tenancy by the entirety, which cannot be severed by unilateral action of one spouse. It gives the spouses assurance that the survivor will take the property, unless both spouses act to destroy the survivorship rights.

2. As the court in Riddle notes, the modern trend is away from requiring adherence to the old four unities for purposes of creating joint tenancies and in favor of an intent test. The same is also true for purposes of severing joint tenancies. See, e.g., Estate of Johnson, 739 N.W.2d 493 (Iowa 2007); Chrystyan v. Feinberg, 510 N.E.2d 33 (Ill. App. 1987). See generally R.H. Helmholz, Realism and Formalism in the Severance of Joint Tenancies, 77 Neb. L. Rev. 1 (1998). Will a void deed be effective to sever a joint tenancy under an intent test? See Johnson, supra, 739 N.W.2d at 501.

3. Suppose A and B, joint tenants, die in a common disaster. The Uniform Simultaneous Death Act (USDA), enacted in various states, formerly provided that under circumstances where there is "no sufficient evidence" of the order of death, the jointly owned property would be distributed one-half as if A had survived, and one-half as if B had survived. This half-and-half approach "led to unfortunate litigation in which the representative of one of the individuals attempts, through the use of gruesome medical evidence, to prove that the one he or she represents survived the other by an instant or two." Prefatory Note to 1993 Revision of the USDA (providing examples we shall leave to the side). So the USDA was revised. Unless a governing instrument such as a will provides otherwise, the half-and-half approach is used unless there is clear and convincing evidence that one of the joint tenants survived the other by 120 hours. USDA §4 (1993).

If *A* murders *B*, Uniform Probate Code §2-803(c)(2) (2008) provides that the murder severs the joint tenancy and converts it into a tenancy in common. The killer loses his right of survivorship in the decedent's share.

Harms v. Sprague

Supreme Court of Illinois, 1984
473 N.E.2d 930

MORAN, J. Plaintiff, William H. Harms, filed a complaint to quiet title and for declaratory judgment in the circuit court of Greene County. Plaintiff had taken title to certain real estate with his brother John R. Harms, as a joint tenant, with full right of survivorship. The plaintiff named, as a defendant, Charles D. Sprague, the executor of the estate of John Harms and the devisee of all the real and personal property of John Harms. Also named as defendants were Carl T. and Mary E. Simmons, alleged mortgagees of the property in question. Defendant Sprague filed a counterclaim against plaintiff, challenging plaintiff's claim of ownership of the entire tract of property and asking the court to recognize his (Sprague's) interest as a tenant in common, subject to a mortgage lien. At issue was the effect the granting of a mortgage by John Harms had on the joint tenancy. Also at issue was whether the mortgage survived the death of John Harms as a lien against the property.

The trial court held that the mortgage given by John Harms to defendants Carl and Mary Simmons severed the joint tenancy. Further, the court found that the mortgage survived the death of John Harms as a lien against the undivided one-half interest in the property which passed to Sprague by and through the will of the deceased. The appellate court reversed, finding that the mortgage given by one joint tenant of his interest in the property does not sever the joint tenancy. Accordingly, the appellate court held that plaintiff, as the surviving joint tenant, owned the property in its entirety, unencumbered by the mortgage lien. (119 Ill. App. 3d 503.) Defendant Sprague filed a petition for leave to appeal in this court. (87 Ill. 2d R. 315.) Subsequently, defendants Carl and Mary Simmons petitioned this court to supplement Sprague's petition for leave to appeal. That motion was granted and the petition for leave to appeal was allowed.

Two issues are raised on appeal: (1) Is a joint tenancy severed when less than all of the joint tenants mortgage their interest in the property? and (2) Does such a mortgage survive the death of the mortgagor as a lien on the property?

A review of the stipulation of facts reveals the following. Plaintiff, William Harms, and his brother John Harms, took title to real estate located in Roodhouse, on June 26, 1973, as joint tenants. The warranty deed memorializing this transaction was recorded on June 29, 1973, in the office of the Greene County recorder of deeds.

Carl and Mary Simmons owned a lot and home in Roodhouse. Charles Sprague entered into an agreement with the Simmonses whereby Sprague was to purchase their property for $25,000. Sprague tendered $18,000 in cash and

signed a promissory note for the balance of $7,000. Because Sprague had no
security for the $7,000, he asked his friend, John Harms, to co-sign the note and
give a mortgage on his interest in the joint tenancy property. Harms agreed, and
on June 12, 1981, John Harms and Charles Sprague, jointly and severally, executed a promissory note for $7,000 payable to Carl and Mary Simmons. The note
states that the principal sum of $7,000 was to be paid from the proceeds of the
sale of John Harms' interest in the joint tenancy property, but in any event no
later than six months from the date the note was signed. The note reflects that
five monthly interest payments had been made, with the last payment recorded
November 6, 1981. In addition, John Harms executed a mortgage, in favor of the
Simmonses, on his undivided one-half interest in the joint tenancy property, to
secure payment of the note. William Harms was unaware of the mortgage given
by his brother.

John Harms moved from his joint tenancy property to the Simmons property
which had been purchased by Charles Sprague. On December 10, 1981, John
Harms died. By the terms of John Harms' will, Charles Sprague was the devisee
of his entire estate. The mortgage given by John Harms to the Simmonses was
recorded on December 29, 1981.

Prior to the appellate court decision in the instant case (119 Ill. App. 3d
503) no court of this State had directly addressed the principal question we are
confronted with herein — the effect of a mortgage, executed by less than all of
the joint tenants, on the joint tenancy. Nevertheless, there are numerous cases
which have considered the severance issue in relation to other circumstances surrounding a joint tenancy. All have necessarily focused on the four unities which
are fundamental to both the creation and the perpetuation of the joint tenancy.
These are the unities of interest, title, time, and possession. (Jackson v. O'Connell
(1961), 23 Ill. 2d 52, 55; Tindall v. Yeats (1946), 392 Ill. 502, 507.) The voluntary
or involuntary destruction of any of the unities by one of the joint tenants will
sever the joint tenancy. Van Antwerp v. Horan (1945), 390 Ill. 449, 451.

In a series of cases, this court has considered the effect that judgment liens
upon the interest of one joint tenant have on the stability of the joint tenancy. In
Peoples Trust & Savings Bank v. Haas (1927), 328 Ill. 468, the court found that
a judgment lien secured against one joint tenant did not serve to extinguish the
joint tenancy. As such, the surviving joint tenant "succeeded to the title in fee to
the whole of the land by operation of law." Id. at 471.

Citing to Haas for this general proposition, the court in Van Antwerp v.
Horan (1945), 390 Ill. 449, extended the holding in Haas to the situation where
a levy is made under execution upon the interest of the debtor joint tenant. The
court found that the levy was "not such an act as can be said to have the effect of
a divestiture of title . . . [so as to destroy the] identity of interest or of any other
unity which must occur before . . . the estate of joint tenancy has been severed
and destroyed." Id. at 455.

In yet another case involving the attachment of a judgment lien upon the
interest of a joint tenant, Jackson v. Lacey (1951), 408 Ill. 530, the court held
that the estate of joint tenancy had not been destroyed. As in Van Antwerp, the

judgment creditor had levied on the interest of the joint tenant debtor. In addition, that interest was sold by the bailiff of the municipal court to the other joint tenant, who died intestate before the time of redemption expired. While the court recognized that a conveyance, even if involuntary, destroys the unity of title and severs the joint tenancy, it held that there would be no conveyance until the redemption period had expired without a redemption. As such, title was not as yet divested and the estate in joint tenancy was unaltered.

Clearly, this court adheres to the rule that a lien on a joint tenant's interest in property will not effectuate a severance of the joint tenancy, absent the conveyance by a deed following the expiration of a redemption period. (See Johnson v. Muntz (1936), 364 Ill. 482.) It follows, therefore, that if Illinois perceives a mortgage as merely a lien on the mortgagor's interest in property rather than a conveyance of title from mortgagor to mortgagee, the execution of a mortgage by a joint tenant, on his interest in the property, would not destroy the unity of title and sever the joint tenancy.

Early cases in Illinois, however, followed the title theory of mortgages. In 1900, this court recognized the common law precept that a mortgage was a conveyance of a legal estate vesting title to the property in the mortgagee. (Lightcap v. Bradley (1900), 186 Ill. 510, 519.) Consistent with this title theory of mortgages, therefore, there are many cases which state, in dicta, that a joint tenancy is severed by one of the joint tenants mortgaging his interest to a stranger. (Lawler v. Byrne (1911), 252 Ill. 194, 196; Hardin v. Wolf (1925), 318 Ill. 48, 59; Partridge v. Berliner (1927), 325 Ill. 253, 258-59; Van Antwerp v. Horan (1945), 390 Ill. 449, 453; Tindall v. Yeats (1946), 392 Ill. 502, 511; Illinois Public Aid Com. v. Stille (1958), 14 Ill. 2d 344, 353 (personal property).) Yet even the early case of Lightcap v. Bradley, cited above, recognized that the title held by the mortgagee was for the limited purpose of protecting his interests. The court went on to say that "the mortgagor is the owner for every other purpose and against every other person. The title of the mortgagee is anomalous, and exists only between him and the mortgagor. . . ." Lightcap v. Bradley, 186 Ill. at 522-23.

Because our cases had early recognized the unique and narrow character of the title that passed to a mortgagee under the common law title theory, it was not a drastic departure when this court expressly characterized the execution of a mortgage as a mere lien in Kling v. Ghilarducci (1954), 3 Ill. 2d 455. In *Kling*, the court was confronted with the question of when a separation of title, necessary to create an easement by implication, had occurred. The court found that title to the property was not separated with the execution of a trust deed but rather only upon execution and delivery of a master's deed. The court stated:

> In some jurisdictions the execution of a mortgage is a severance, in others, the execution of a mortgage is not a severance. In Illinois the giving of a mortgage is not a separation of title, for the holder of the mortgage takes only a lien thereunder. After foreclosure of a mortgage and until delivery of the master's deed under the foreclosure sale, purchaser acquires no title to the land either legal or equitable. Title to land sold under mortgage foreclosure remains in the mortgagor or his grantee until the expiration of the redemption period and conveyance by the master's deed. [3 Ill. 2d 455, 460.]

Kling and later cases rejecting the title theory (Department of Transportation v. New Century Engineering & Development Corp. (1983), 97 Ill. 2d 343; Kerrigan v. Unity Savings Association (1974), 58 Ill. 2d 20; Mutual Life Insurance Co. of New York v. Chambers (1980), 88 Ill. App. 3d 952; Commercial Mortgage & Finance Co. v. Woodcock Construction Co. (1964), 51 Ill. App. 2d 61) do not involve the severance of joint tenancies. As such, they have not expressly disavowed the dicta of joint tenancy cases which have stated that the act of mortgaging by one joint tenant results in the severance of the joint tenancy. We find, however, that implicit in *Kling* and our more recent cases which follow the lien theory of mortgages is the conclusion that a joint tenancy is not severed when one joint tenant executes a mortgage on his interest in the property, since the unity of title has been preserved. As the appellate court in the instant case correctly observed: "If giving a mortgage creates only a lien, then a mortgage should have the same effect on a joint tenancy as a lien created in other ways." (119 Ill. App. 3d 503, 507.) Other jurisdictions following the lien theory of mortgages have reached the same result. People v. Nogarr (1958), 164 Cal. App. 2d 591, 330 P.2d 858; D.A.D., Inc. v. Moring (Fla. App. 1969), 218 So. 2d 451; American National Bank & Trust Co. v. McGinnis (Okla. 1977), 571 P.2d 1198; Brant v. Hargrove (Ariz. Ct. App. 1981), 129 Ariz. 475, 632 P.2d 978.

A joint tenancy has been defined as "a present estate in all the joint tenants, each being seized of the whole. . . ." (Partridge v. Berliner (1927), 325 Ill. 253, 257.) An inherent feature of the estate of joint tenancy is the right of survivorship, which is the right of the last survivor to take the whole of the estate. (In re Estate of Alpert (1983), 95 Ill. 2d 377, 381; Bonczkowski v. Kucharski (1958), 13 Ill. 2d 443, 451.) Because we find that a mortgage given by one joint tenant of his interest in the property does not sever the joint tenancy, we hold that the plaintiff's right of survivorship became operative upon the death of his brother. As such plaintiff is now the sole owner of the estate, in its entirety.

Further, we find that the mortgage executed by John Harms does not survive as a lien on plaintiff's property. A surviving joint tenant succeeds to the share of the deceased joint tenant by virtue of the conveyance which created the joint tenancy, not as the successor of the deceased. (In re Estate of Alpert (1983), 95 Ill. 2d 377, 381.) The property right of the mortgaging joint tenant is extinguished at the moment of his death. While John Harms was alive, the mortgage existed as a lien on his interest in the joint tenancy. Upon his death, his interest ceased to exist and along with it the lien of the mortgage. (Merchants National Bank v. Olson (1975), 27 Ill. App. 3d 432, 434.) . . .

For the reasons stated herein, the judgment of the appellate court is affirmed.

Judgment affirmed.

NOTES, QUESTIONS, AND PROBLEMS

1. The court in *Harms* takes a very formalistic approach to the question whether a mortgage severs a joint tenancy, with much turning on the difference between the title theory and lien theory of mortgages (on which see also footnote

17 on page 648). A more functional approach considers the likely intent of the party giving the mortgage. Did John Harms wish to have the right of survivorship disappear? Since a mortgage, as opposed to a conveyance, is an ambiguous sort of conveyance in this respect, it would seem to follow that a mortgage, absent any other evidence of intent, should not work a severance. But not all courts hold to this view.

If a mortgage does not sever a joint tenancy, then, as in Harms v. Sprague, the issue is whether the mortgage survives if the mortgagor is the first joint tenant to die. Here, a way to think about the correct answer, absent a statute that governs the question, is to ask whether the lender should take the risk of losing its security in making a loan to fewer than all joint tenants. If lenders do have to bear the risk, how might they protect themselves?

Here are a couple of related questions: First, if the court in *Harms* had held that the mortgage severed the joint tenancy, what would be the result if the note had been paid and the mortgage released during John Harms's life? Second, suppose that William Harms had died first, Sprague had not paid the note, and the Simmonses foreclosed the mortgage. Would the entire land be subject to the mortgage or only a one-half interest in it? See Brant v. Hargrove, 632 P.2d 978 (Ariz. App. 1981); B. Taylor Mattis, Joint Tenancy: Notice of Severance; Mortgages and Survivorship, 7 N. Ill. U. L. Rev. 41 (1987).

2. Questions of severance and survival arise with other sorts of conveyances that, like mortgages, fall short of granting a fee simple. Suppose A and B hold property as joint tenants, and that A conveys a life estate in the property to X, or leases the property to X. Is there a severance? If not, and A dies, does B take free and clear of, or subject to, the interests created by A? Again, the best approach is probably to think in terms of intent and risk bearing, as suggested in Note 1, but that approach is not always taken. Logically, for any kind of less-than-fee-simple conveyance (e.g., mortgage, life estate, lease), there are four possible outcomes, and you could probably find each represented in some judicial decisions. So say that A and B are joint tenants, and A conveys some interest less than a fee simple (just call it "the interest") to X. Then a court might hold that

— the conveyance of the interest severs the joint tenancy; X and B are tenants in common until the interest ends, and then A and B or their estates are tenants in common.
— the conveyance does not sever the joint tenancy; if B survives A, B takes free and clear of the interest; if A survives B, A is subject to the interest.
— the conveyance does not sever the joint tenancy, and if B survives A, B takes subject to the interest (becoming a tenant in common with X for the period of the interest); if B predeceases A, A is subject to the interest.
— the conveyance results in a partial or temporary severance: if A dies before B, proceed as in the first alternative above; if A survives B, proceed as in the second or third alternative; if X dies first, there is no severance and A and B remain joint tenants.

3. Joint tenants *A* and *B* sign a written agreement giving *B* the rentals from and possession of the land for her life. Does the agreement destroy the unity of possession? Upon *A*'s subsequent death, who owns the land? See Porter v. Porter, 472 So. 2d 630 (Ala. 1985); Tindall v. Yeats, 64 N.E.2d 903 (Ill. 1946).

4. *H* and *W*, owners of Blackacre in joint tenancy, are getting a divorce. They sign a divorce agreement providing that Blackacre will be sold and the proceeds divided equally between *H* and *W*. Before Blackacre is sold, *W* dies. Does *H* have survivorship rights in Blackacre? See Sondin v. Bernstein, 467 N.E.2d 926 (Ill. App. 1984); In re Estate of Violi, 482 N.E.2d 29 (N.Y. 1985).

A number of states have enacted statutes in recent years providing that divorce converts a joint tenancy between the former husband and wife into a tenancy in common.

3. Multiple-party Bank Accounts

Multiple-party accounts with financial institutions, including banks, generally take one of three forms — *joint* accounts ("*A* and *B*," or "*A* or *B*"), *savings account trusts*, called "Totten trusts" in some states ("*A*, in trust for *B*"), or *payable-on-death* (P.O.D.) accounts ("*A*, payable on death to *B*"). Of the three, joint accounts are the most common. Joint bank accounts have been the subject of much litigation. The primary reason is that the joint bank account is used by depositors with different intentions and for a variety of purposes. Suppose that *O* deposits $5,000 in a joint bank account with *O* and *A* as joint tenants. *O* may intend to make a present gift to *A* of one-half the sum deposited in addition to survivorship rights to the whole sum on deposit. Courts sometimes refer to this as a "true joint tenancy" bank account. Or *O* may intend to make a gift to *A* only of survivorship rights. This may be called a P.O.D. account and will likely be invalid unless there is a state statute expressly authorizing P.O.D. accounts (many states have such statutes). Or *O* may intend that *A* only have power to draw on the account to pay *O*'s bills and not have survivorship rights. This is often called a "convenience" account. The bank card signed by *O* and *A* usually says either *O* or *A* has the right to withdraw all money on deposit during their joint lives, and the balance goes to the survivor.

Why do you suppose banks usually do not offer depositors an account tailored to specific desires but instead suggest the all-purpose joint bank account? An account expressly giving *A* survivorship rights only is in reality a will; *A*'s name is put on the account solely for the purpose of passing the property at death. In some jurisdictions a P.O.D. account is not permitted because it is viewed as a testamentary instrument that is not signed and witnessed in accordance with the requirements of the Statute of Wills. Only in recent years have P.O.D accounts become legally acceptable, largely because of the influence of the Uniform Probate Code, which first authorized them in 1969 in its original version. In jurisdictions that do not permit P.O.D. accounts, depositors sometimes create a joint bank account with the intention that it be a P.O.D. account in disguise.

If *O* wants a convenience account, what *O* really intends is an account owned by *O* with a power in *A* to draw on the account during *O*'s life. Because a power of attorney expires at the death of the principal, many banks are wary of power-of-attorney accounts and prefer joint accounts. With a joint account, the bank is safe in paying all the money on deposit to any joint tenant or to the survivor. For the bank, a joint account has little risk.

Because the joint account is an all-purpose account, it invites litigation to establish the true intention of the depositor. The agreement signed with the bank, providing that the account belongs to the survivor, is, in most states, not controlling. It is viewed as intended merely to protect the bank if it makes payment to the survivor. It does not determine the realities of ownership between the joint tenants. After the death of the depositor, disappointed heirs may claim that the joint tenant's name was put on the account merely for the purpose of paying the decedent's bills; if they can establish this, the money in the account belongs to the decedent's estate and not to the surviving joint tenant. For an illustrative case, see Estate of Shea, 848 N.E.2d 185 (Ill. App. 2006).

A majority of jurisdictions holds that the surviving joint tenant takes the sum remaining on deposit in a joint account unless there is clear and convincing evidence that a convenience account was intended. The burden of proof is placed upon persons challenging the surviving joint tenant. In some jurisdictions, to prevent litigation, the presumption that survivorship rights were intended in a joint bank account is conclusive. See Wright v. Bloom, 635 N.E.2d 31 (Ohio 1994).

During the lifetime of the parties, litigation may arise over what present rights the parties to a joint account have in the sum on deposit. In most jurisdictions, during the lifetime of the parties the presumption is that the joint account belongs to the parties in proportion to the net contribution of each party. See Uniform Probate Code §6-211 (2008). Hence if *O* deposits $5,000 in a joint bank account with *A*, it is presumed that *O* does not intend a gift to *A* of $2,500 but intends *A* to have survivorship rights only. If *A* withdraws from this account without *O*'s permission or later ratification, *O* can force *A* to return the amount withdrawn. The presumption that *O* did not intend a gift to *A* can be overcome by clear and convincing evidence of a different intent. In a few jurisdictions, the parties to a joint account own, during the lifetime of the parties, equal fractional shares in the account (as in a joint tenancy in real property).

PROBLEMS

1. *O*, a widower, opens a joint bank account with his niece, *A*. *O* tells *A*, "I'll want your name on this account so that in case I am sick you can go and get the money for me." *O* dies. Is *A* entitled to the money in the bank account? See Franklin v. Anna Natl. Bank of Anna, 488 N.E.2d 1117 (Ill. App. 1986). Suppose that *O* also gives *A* a right of access to *O*'s safe deposit box by adding *A*'s name to the signature card giving access; the lease agreement signed with the bank

provides that the contents of the box are owned in joint tenancy with right of survivorship. The box contains $324,000 in U.S. savings bonds and $4,000 in cash. Is *A* entitled to the bonds and cash? See Newton County v. Davison, 709 S.W.2d 810 (Ark. 1986).

2. *H* and *W* and their son, *S*, open a joint savings account. *H* and *W* are in their sixties. The money deposited in the savings account comes from savings from *H*'s salary that *H* formerly had in a separate savings account. *H* dies. *W*, claiming that the entire amount in the savings account is hers, withdraws the balance. Does *S* have any rights to the money? See Allen v. Gordon, 429 So. 2d 369 (Fla. App. 1983).

3. *A* and *B* have a joint savings account of $40,000. How much of the account can *A*'s creditor reach? See Maloy v. Stuttgart Memorial Hosp., 872 S.W.2d 401 (Ark. 1994).

4. Relations Among Concurrent Owners

Suppose that *A* and *B* are the concurrent owners of a piece of property. What are their rights and liabilities as to the property and as to each other? In Swartzbaugh v. Sampson, at pages 376, 377, you will find the court making these announcements: "Each tenant owns an equal interest in all of the fee and each has an equal right to possession of the whole. . . . 'Neither a joint tenant nor a tenant in common can do any act to the prejudice of his cotenants in their estate.'" Even if these statements were not misleading, they would not be very helpful. If *A* cannot do as he wishes because it would prejudice *B*, then *B* in having her way harms *A*. "By definition, each tenant is entitled to possession of the entire parcel of land yet he cannot exercise that possession without coming into conflict with the reciprocal right of his cotenant." John E. Cribbet & Corwin W. Johnson, Principles of the Law of Property 112 (3d ed. 1989). The point was put more succinctly in Mastbaum v. Mastbaum, 9 A.2d 51, 55 (N.J. 1939), when the court observed that "Two men cannot plow the same furrow." How should the inherent conflict of reciprocal rights be resolved?

The question is an important one. We saw in Chapter 1 that communal ownership—and that is what we are dealing with here—encourages inefficient use of common property resources. See pages 40-50. Presumably, thoughtfully devised legal rules can help avoid inefficiency, but this can hardly be their sole objective. The rules governing co-ownership should also distribute in a fair manner the benefits and burdens of co-ownership. Keep efficiency and fairness in mind as we consider first the action of partition—the privilege of each co-owner to transform a concurrent estate into estates held in severalty—and next some of the rules that govern the sharing of benefits and burdens of ownership during the life of concurrent interests. (The latter rules, as you will see, are often applied in partition actions to take account of events occurring prior to partition; but the rules on the sharing of benefits and burdens are applicable independent of partition as well.)

a.   Partition

Concurrent owners might decide for any number of reasons to terminate a cotenancy. If they can agree on a division of the property or the proceeds from its sale, no problem arises; the termination can be accomplished through a voluntary agreement. But in the not unlikely event that such an arrangement is impossible, recourse to the equitable action of partition is necessary. The action is available to any joint tenant or tenant in common; it is unavailable to tenants by the entirety. The following materials explore some of the dimensions of partition.

Delfino v. Vealencis

Supreme Court of Connecticut, 1980
436 A.2d 27

HEALEY, J. The central issue in this appeal is whether the Superior Court properly ordered the sale, pursuant to General Statutes §52-500,[8] of property owned by the plaintiffs and the defendant as tenants in common.

The plaintiffs, Angelo and William Delfino, and the defendant, Helen C. Vealencis, own, as tenants in common, real property located in Bristol, Connecticut. The property consists of an approximately 20.5 acre parcel of land and the dwelling of the defendant thereon. The plaintiffs own an undivided 99/144 interest in the property, and the defendant owns a 45/144 interest. The defendant occupies the dwelling and a portion of the land, from which she operates a rubbish and garbage removal business.[9] Apparently, none of the parties is in actual possession of the remainder of the property. The plaintiffs, one of whom is a residential developer, propose to develop the property, upon partition, into forty-five residential building lots.

In 1978, the plaintiffs brought an action in the trial court seeking a partition of the property by sale with a division of the proceeds according to the parties' respective interests. The defendant moved for a judgment of in-kind partition[10]

---

8. General Statutes §52-500 states: "Sale of Real or Personal Property Owned by Two or More. Any court of equitable jurisdiction may, upon the complaint of any person interested, order the sale of any estate, real or personal, owned by two or more persons, when, in the opinion of the court, a sale will better promote the interests of the owners. The provisions of this section shall extend to and include land owned by two or more persons, when the whole or a part of such land is vested in any person for life with remainder to his heirs, general or special, or, on failure of such heirs, to any other person, whether the same, or any part thereof, is held in trust or otherwise. A conveyance made in pursuance of a decree ordering a sale of such land shall vest the title in the purchaser thereof, and shall bind the person entitled to the life estate and his legal heirs and any other person having a remainder interest in the lands; but the court passing such decree shall make such order in relation to the investment of the avails of such sale as it deems necessary for the security of all persons having any interest in such land."

9. The defendant's business functions on the property consist of the overnight parking, repair and storage of trucks, including refuse trucks, the repair, storage and cleaning of dumpsters, the storage of tools, and general office work. No refuse is actually deposited on the property.

10. Such a partition is authorized by General Statutes §52-495 which states: "Partition of Joint and Common Estates. Courts having jurisdiction of actions for equitable relief may, upon the complaint of any person interested, order partition of any real estate held in joint tenancy, tenancy in common or coparcenary, and may appoint a committee for that purpose, and may in like manner make partition of any real estate held by tenants

Helen Vealencis (right), her mother, and her brother, John

and the appointment of a committee to conduct said partition. The trial court, after a hearing, concluded that a partition in kind could not be had without "material injury" to the respective rights of the parties, and therefore ordered that the property be sold at auction by a committee and that the proceeds be paid into the court for distribution to the parties.

On appeal, the defendant claims essentially that the trial court's conclusion that the parties' interests would best be served by a partition by sale is not supported by the findings of subordinate facts, and that the court improperly considered certain factors in arriving at that conclusion. In addition, the defendant directs a claim of error to the court's failure to include in its findings of fact a paragraph of her draft findings.

General Statutes §52-495 authorizes courts of equitable jurisdiction to order, upon the complaint of any interested person, the physical partition of any real estate held by tenants in common, and to appoint a committee for that purpose.[11] When, however, in the opinion of the court a sale of the jointly owned property

---

in tail; and decrees aparting entailed estates shall bind the parties and all persons who thereafter claim title to such estate as heirs of their bodies."

11. If the physical partition results in unequal shares, a money award can be made from one tenant to another to equalize the shares. 4A Powell, Real Property ¶ 612, pp.653-54; 2 American Law of Property, Partition §6.26, p.113.

"will better promote the interests of the owners," the court may order such a sale under §52-500. See Kaiser v. Second National Bank, 123 Conn. 248, 256, 193 A. 761 (1937); Johnson v. Olmsted, 49 Conn. 509, 517 (1882).

It has long been the policy of this court, as well as other courts, to favor a partition in kind over a partition by sale. See Harrison v. International Silver Co., 78 Conn. 417, 420, 62 A. 342 (1905); Johnson v. Olmsted, supra; 2 American Law of Property, Partition §6.26, pp. 112-14; 4A Powell, Real Property ¶ 612, p.650; 59 Am. Jur. 2d, Partition §118, pp.864-65; 68 C.J.S., Partition §125. The first Connecticut statute that provided for an absolute right to partition by physical division was enacted in 1720; Statutes, 1796, p.258; the substance of which remains virtually unchanged today. Due to the possible impracticality of actual division, this state, like others, expanded the right to partition to allow a partition by sale under certain circumstances. See Penfield v. Jarvis, 175 Conn. 463, 470-71, 399 A.2d 1280 (1978); see also Restatement, 2 Property c. 11, pp.658-61. The early decisions of this court that considered the partition-by-sale statute emphasized that "[t]he statute giving the power of sale introduces . . . no new principles; it provides only for an emergency, when a division cannot be well made, in any other way. The Earl of Clarendon v. Hornby, 1 P. Wms., 446.4 Kent's Com., 365." Richardson v. Monson, 23 Conn. 94, 97 (1854); see Penfield v. Jarvis, supra, 471, 399 A.2d 1280; Harrison v. International Silver Co., 78 Conn. 417, 420, 62 A. 342 (1905); Vail v. Hammond, 60 Conn. 374, 379, 22 A. 954 (1891). The court later expressed its reason for preferring partition in kind when it stated: "[A] sale of one's property without his consent is an extreme exercise of power warranted only in clear cases." Ford v. Kirk, 41 Conn. 9, 12 (1874). See also 59 Am. Jur. 2d, Partition §118, p.865. Although under General Statutes §52-500 a court is no longer required to order a partition in kind even in cases of extreme difficulty or hardship; see Scovil v. Kennedy, 14 Conn. 349, 360-61 (1841); it is clear that a partition by sale should be ordered only when two conditions are satisfied: (1) the physical attributes of the land are such that a partition in kind is impracticable or inequitable; Johnson v. Olmsted, supra; and (2) the interests of the owners would better be promoted by a partition by sale. Kaiser v. Second National Bank, supra; see Gold v. Rosenfeld, Conn. (41 Conn. L.J., No. 4, p.18) (1979). Since our law has for many years presumed that a partition in kind would be in the best interests of the owners, the burden is on the party requesting a partition by sale to demonstrate that such a sale would better promote the owners' interests. Accord, 4A Powell, Real Property ¶ 612, p.651; 59 Am. Jur. 2d, Partition §118, p.865.

The defendant claims in effect that the trial court's conclusion that the rights of the parties would best be promoted by a judicial sale is not supported by the findings of subordinate facts. We agree.

Under the test set out above, the court must first consider the practicability of physically partitioning the property in question. The trial court concluded that due to the situation and location of the parcel of land, the size and area of the property, the physical structure and appurtenances on the property, and other factors,[12] a physical partition of the property would not be feasible. An examination of the subordinate findings of facts and the exhibits, however, demonstrates that the court erred in this respect.

It is undisputed that the property in question consists of one 20.5 acre parcel, basically rectangular in shape, and one dwelling, located at the extreme western end of the property. Two roads, Dino Road and Lucien Court, abut the property and another, Birch Street, provides access through use of a right-of-way. Unlike cases where there are numerous fractional owners of the property to be partitioned, and the practicability of a physical division is therefore drastically reduced; see, e.g., Penfield v. Jarvis, 175 Conn. 463, 464-65, 399 A.2d 1280 (1978); Lyon v. Wilcox, 98 Conn. 393, 394-95, 119 A. 361 (1923); Candee v. Candee, 87 Conn. 85, 89-90, 86 A. 758 (1913); in this case there are only two competing ownership interests: the plaintiffs' undivided 99/144 interest and the defendant's 45/144 interest. These facts, taken together, do not support the trial court's conclusion that a physical partition of the property would not be "feasible" in this case. Instead, the above facts demonstrate that the opposite is true: a partition in kind clearly would be practicable under the circumstances of this case.

Although a partition in kind is physically practicable, it remains to be considered whether a partition in kind would also promote the best interests of the parties. In order to resolve this issue, the consequences of a partition in kind must be compared with those of a partition by sale.

The trial court concluded that a partition in kind could not be had without great prejudice to the parties since the continuation of the defendant's business would hinder or preclude the development of the plaintiffs' parcel for residential purposes, which the trial court concluded was the highest and best use of the property. The court's concern over the possible adverse economic effect upon the plaintiffs' interest in the event of a partition in kind was based essentially on four findings: (1) approval by the city planning commission for subdivision of the parcel would be difficult to obtain if the defendant continued her garbage hauling business; (2) lots in a residential subdivision might not sell, or might sell at a lower price, if the defendant's business continued; (3) if the defendant were granted the one-acre parcel, on which her residence is situated and on which her business now operates, three of the lots proposed in the plaintiffs' plan to subdivide the property would have to be consolidated and would be lost; and (4) the proposed extension of one of the neighboring roads would have to be rerouted through one of the proposed building lots if a partition in kind were ordered. The trial court also found that the defendant's use of the portion of the property that she occupies is in violation of existing zoning regulations. The court presumably inferred from this finding that it is not likely that the defendant will be able to continue her rubbish hauling operations from this property in the future.

---

12. These other factors included the present use and the expected continued use by the defendant of the property, the property's zoning classification, and the plaintiffs' proposed subdivision plans. We consider these factors later in the opinion.

The court also premised its forecast that the planning commission would reject the plaintiffs' subdivision plan for the remainder of the property on the finding that the defendant's use was invalid. These factors basically led the trial court to conclude that the interests of the parties would best be protected if the land were sold as a unified unit for residential subdivision development and the proceeds of such a sale were distributed to the parties.

Before we consider whether these reasons are sufficient as a matter of law to overcome the preference for partition in kind that has been expressed in the applicable statutes and our opinions, we address first the defendant's assignment of error directed to the finding of subordinate facts relating to one of these reasons. The defendant claims that the trial court erred in finding that the defendant's use of a portion of the property is in violation of the existing zoning regulations, and in refusing to find that such use is a valid nonconforming use. . . . [The court concluded that there was insufficient evidence to support the trial court's finding that the defendant would be unable lawfully to continue her garbage hauling operation as a nonconforming use begun before the zoning ordinance was enacted.] We are left, then, with an unassailed finding that the defendant's family has operated a "garbage business" on the premises since the 1920s and that the city of Bristol has granted the defendant the appropriate permits and licenses each year to operate her business. There is no indication that this practice will not continue in the future.

Our resolution of this issue makes it clear that any inference that the defendant would probably be unable to continue her rubbish hauling activity on the property in the future is unfounded. We also conclude that the court erred in concluding that the city's planning commission would probably not approve a subdivision plan relating to the remainder of the property. Any such forecast must be carefully scrutinized as it is difficult to project what a public body will decide in any given matter. See Rushchak v. West Haven, 167 Conn. 564, 569, 356 A.2d 104 (1975). In this case, there was no substantial evidence to support a conclusion that it was reasonably probable that the planning commission would not approve a subdivision plan for the remainder of the property. Cf. Budney v. Ives, 156 Conn. 83, 90, 239 A.2d 482 (1968). Moreover, there is no suggestion in the statute relating to subdivision approval; see General Statutes §8-25; that the undeveloped portion of the parcel in issue, which is located in a residential neighborhood, could not be the subject of an approved subdivision plan notwithstanding the nearby operation of the defendant's business. The court's finding indicates that only garbage trucks and dumpsters are stored on the property; that no garbage is brought there; and that the defendant's business operations involve "mostly containerized . . . dumpsters, a contemporary development in technology which has substantially reduced the odors previously associated with the rubbish and garbage hauling industry." These facts do not support the court's speculation that the city's planning commission would not approve a subdivision permit for the undeveloped portion of the parties' property. See Rogers Co. v. F.W. Woolworth, 161 Conn. 6, 12, 282 A.2d 882 (1971); White v. Herbst, 128 Conn. 659, 661, 25 A.2d 68 (1942).

The court's remaining observations relating to the effect of the defendant's business on the probable fair market value of the proposed residential lots, the possible loss of building lots to accommodate the defendant's business and the rerouting of a proposed subdivision road, which may have some validity, are not dispositive of the issue. It is the interests of all of the tenants in common that the court must consider; see Lyon v. Wilcox, 98 Conn. 393, 395-96, 119 A. 361 (1923); 59 Am. Jur. 2d, Partition §118, p.865; and not merely the economic gain of one tenant, or a group of tenants. The trial court failed to give due consideration to the fact that one of the tenants in common has been in actual and exclusive possession of a portion of the property for a substantial period of time; that the tenant has made her home on the property; and that she derives her livelihood from the operation of a business on this portion of the property, as her family before her has for many years. A partition by sale would force the defendant to surrender her home and, perhaps, would jeopardize her livelihood. It is under just such circumstances, which include the demonstrated practicability of a physical division of the property, that the wisdom of the law's preference for partition in kind is evident.

As this court has many times stated, conclusions that violate "law, logic, or reason or are inconsistent with the subordinate facts" cannot stand. Russo v. East Hartford, 179 Conn. 250, 255, 425 A.2d 1282 (1979); Connecticut Coke Co. v. New Haven, 169 Conn. 663, 675, 364 A.2d 178, 185 (1975). Since the property in this case may practicably be physically divided, and since the interests of all owners will better be promoted if a partition in kind is ordered, we conclude that the trial court erred in ordering a partition by sale, and that, under the facts as found, the defendant is entitled to a partition of the property in kind.

There is error, the judgment is set aside and the case is remanded for further proceedings not inconsistent with this opinion.

NOTES, QUESTIONS, AND PROBLEMS

1. Although it is usually said, as in Delfino v. Vealencis, that partition in kind is preferred, the modern practice is to decree sales in partition actions in a great majority of cases, either because the parties all wish it or because courts are convinced that sale is the fairest method of resolving the conflict. In this connection, see Manel Baucells & Steven A. Lippman, Justice Delayed Is Justice Denied: A Cooperative Game Theoretic Analysis of Hold-Up in Co-Ownership, 22 Cardozo L. Rev. 1191, 1220-1243 (2001). In an appendix to their article, Baucells and Lippman provide a fascinating sketch of the history of the dispute in *Delfino*, examining events both before and after the lawsuit. They conclude that the physical partition resulting from the litigation left Helen Vealencis with the short end of the stick. She was awarded three lots, including the homestead at 311 Birch Street, for a total of approximately one acre, worth $72,000 altogether. This land appears as lot 135-1, located at the far left-hand-side of the 20.5-acre parcel inside the bold lines on Figure 5-1. Helen's award was further reduced by a requirement that she pay $26,000 in owelty to the Delfinos to compensate them for the

Figure 5-1
Subdivision plot plan for the 20.5-acre parcel

adverse impact of her garbage operation on their proposed subdivision. (Is this fair? Should Helen receive her fractional share of the total acreage as valued with the garbage hauling business on it? Suppose she went out of the garbage business a year later. Should the $26,000 be returned?) Thus Helen's net benefit was $46,000, less than one-fourth of what was due her for her 5/16 interest in the total value of the land.

The Delfinos received approximately 19 acres, which they sold some three years later for $725,000 to a developer who laid out a subdivision of 42 lots. Helen's lot was separated from the rest of the subdivision by a two-foot-wide strip of land made part of lots 39 and 40, depriving her land of access to Dino Road, with its water and sewage connections (see Figure 5-1). This strip also prevented Helen's garbage trucks from entering the subdivision, thus avoiding a loss in market value of the homes, but this was damage she had already paid for in the settlement! Helen's only access to her land was a one-rod (16.5 foot) easement over lot 9C on the figure. The Vealencis house today uses an artesian well and a septic tank.

Helen Vealencis died of a heart attack at age 55 in 1990, still running the garbage disposal business.

The authors of this eye-opening story detail the many uncertainties in valuing land in a physical partition. For a general discussion of the economic trade-offs involved in partition by sale versus partition in kind, see Thomas J. Miceli & C.F. Sirmans, Partition of Real Estate; or, Breaking Up Is (Not) Hard to Do, 29 J. Legal Stud. 783 (2000).

2. *By sale or in kind? A few more cases.* Ark Land Co. v. Harper, 599 S.E.2d 754 (W. Va. 2004), involved 75 acres of farm land and buildings owned by the Caudill family for almost a century. In 2001 Ark Land bought two-thirds of the property from family members; it wanted to purchase the rest from other Caudill heirs, but they refused to sell. So Ark Land sought partition by sale, planning, of course, to purchase the remaining interests by that means. The trial court granted the requested relief, thanks to evidence that partition in kind would add several million dollars in costs to the coal mining operations that Ark Land planned to conduct on the property. West Virginia's Supreme Court of Appeals reversed. Partition by sale, the court noted, can work hardship on owners unwilling to sell because they have emotional attachments to the land, as in the case of a homestead; money alone cannot compensate for the sentimental losses that sale would entail. The fact that the economic value of the property as a whole would be less if it were partitioned in kind is relevant but not dispositive, especially in cases of longstanding ownership coupled with emotional ties to the land.

A contrasting case is Johnson v. Hendrickson, 24 N.W.2d 914 (S.D. 1946). In 1904 Henry Bauman died intestate. His 160-acre farm passed one-third to his widow, Katie, and two-ninths to each of his three children. In 1908 Katie married Karl Hendrickson and had twin sons by him. The whole family lived in the homestead on a corner of the farm. The Bauman children grew up and left home. Karl and his sons bought an adjacent farm across the road from the family homestead. In 1944 Katie died, devising her one-third interest in the Bauman farm to Karl and his two sons.

The Bauman children brought an action for partition, requesting sale of the whole farm. Karl and his two sons asked for partition in kind, and particularly for allocation to them of the homestead where they lived, which was across the road from their adjacent farm. The court ordered a partition sale under a statute authorizing sale if physical partition "cannot be made without great prejudice to the owners."

The language of this statute means that a sale may be ordered if it appears to the satisfaction of the court that the value of the share of each cotenant, in case of partition, would be materially less than his share of the money equivalent that could probably be obtained for the whole. . . . Under the terms of the statute quoted above a sale is justified if it appears to the satisfaction of the court that the value of the land when divided into parcels is substantially less than its value when owned by one person. This land is now owned by six persons. The largest individual interest is two-ninths and the smallest is one-twelfth. Partition in kind would require the division of the land into not less than four parcels: Two-ninths to each of the three respondents, and one-third to appellants, collectively. It is a matter of common knowledge in this state that the division of this quarter section of land, located as it is, into four or more separate tracts would materially depreciate its value, both as to its salability and as to its use for agricultural purposes. The fact that it would be an advantage to appellants to have the farm partitioned according to their demands because of their ownership of adjoining land is immaterial. [24 N.W.2d at 916.]

The court gave no weight to the interest of Karl and his sons in remaining in the family homestead. See also Wizner v. Pavlin, 719 N.W.2d 770 (S.D. 2006).

In Gray v. Crotts, 293 S.E.2d 626 (N.C. 1982), one of the four cotenants argued that, upon physical partition, he should be awarded the part of the common property adjacent to his home. The court held that the property should be divided into four parcels of equal value, and then the cotenants should draw lots to determine who received which parcel. Why do courts not take into consideration the advantage to one cotenant of acquiring the portion of the tract adjacent to his other land?

3. *An alternative approach.* If a court orders partition, whether by sale or in kind, it might also order compensation (called owelty, as mentioned in Note 1) in order to make appropriate adjustments — say to compensate for the fact that partition in kind results in one cotenant getting a more valuable part than other cotenants, or that partition by sale yields a higher price than it otherwise would because one of the cotenants made certain valuable improvements. In some jurisdictions the principle behind this approach yields an alternative to standard partition in kind or by sale. If a court finds (1) that partition in kind is impractical or wasteful, and (2) that sale would not protect the interests of all parties, then the court may assign all of the property to one or more of the cotenants, provided they pay the other cotenant(s) compensation in an amount set by the court (and presumably equal to fair market value). See, e.g., Zimmerman v. Marsh, 618 S.E.2d 898 (S.C. 2005); Wilk v. Wilk, 795 A.2d 1191 (Vt. 2002).

4. There is considerable evidence that partition sales have worked to the disadvantage of poor black farmers who own "heir property," so-called because black farmers, perhaps distrustful of the legal system, commonly die intestate. Their heirs take the family farm as tenants in common, and after several generations the number of cotenants owning any particular farm can become unmanageably large. This makes farming difficult and black ownership vulnerable to partition sales. A buyer, usually white, purchases the interest of one of the cotenants and then seeks partition. The property is sold (the fractionated pattern of ownership makes division in kind impracticable), and the black families seldom have the resources to compete with white buyers. The pattern has contributed to a huge decline in black farm ownership over the last 80 years, and it continues. For discussion of the problem and various reforms (enacted or proposed), see Faith Rivers, Inequity in Equity: The Tragedy of Tenancy in Common for Heirs' Property Owners Facing Partition in Equity, 17 Temp. Pol. & Civ. Rts. L. Rev. 1 (2007) (discussing, among other remedies, the approach discussed in Note 3 above); Hanoch Dagan & Michael A. Heller, The Liberal Commons, 110 Yale L.J. 549, 603-623 (2001) (considering the problem in part by comparing American law to that of several other countries); Thomas W. Mitchell, From Reconstruction to Deconstruction: Undermining

Black Landownership, Political Independence, and Community Through Partition Sales of Tenancies in Common, 95 Nw. U. L. Rev. 505 (2001) (proposing, for example, majority rule by cotenants, restrictions on alienation, and improved legal services for low income farmers); Phyliss Craig-Taylor, Through a Colored Looking Glass: A View of Judicial Partition, Family Land Loss, and Rule Setting, 78 Wash. U. L.Q. 737 (2000) (proposing, for example, consent by a supermajority of cotenants before partition sale can be ordered, and a redemption period after sale).

5. Suppose that, before the decision in Delfino v. Vealencis, Helen Vealencis had conveyed to Superior Refuse Disposers, Inc., by a metes and bounds description, her undivided interest in the portion of the land devoted to the garbage removal business. Superior Refuse Disposers then took over her garbage business. Upon physical partition, would Superior Refuse Disposers be awarded the land devoted to the garbage business? See Kean v. Dench, 413 F.2d 1 (3d Cir. 1969) (A, cotenant with B, conveyed his undivided interest by metes and bounds to C; upon partition suit by C, the court awarded to C the land conveyed to C on the theory this did not prejudice or injure B); Landskroner v. McClure, 765 P.2d 189 (N.M. 1988) (dicta to same effect); 2 American Law of Property §6.10 (1952).

6. Partition obviously has much to do with fair and equitable treatment of the interests of cotenants. Has it anything to do with efficient use of the property involved?

7. A and B are heirs of their father, who owned one item both A and B very much want — his old rocking chair. They cannot agree who is to have the chair. A brings a partition action. What relief should the court award? See In re McDowell, 345 N.Y.S.2d 828 (Sur. Ct. 1973).

8. A and B own Blackacre as tenants in common. Each agrees in writing with the other never to bring an action to partition the land. A subsequently brings a partition action. What result? Suppose instead that the agreement provides for no partition until certain clouds on the title to the land are resolved in a pending lawsuit. Same result? On both questions, see Raisch v. Schuster, 352 N.E.2d 657 (Ohio App. 1975); see also Restatement (Second) of Property, Donative Transfers §4.5 (1983).

b. Sharing the Benefits and Burdens of Co-ownership

Concurrent owners might enter into an agreement concerning their rights and duties with respect to use, maintenance, and improvement of the property. These matters would then be governed by the law of contracts. Suppose, however, that there arises some problem not touched upon by the agreement or that the rights of third parties are in question or that there was never any agreement in the first place. Then there is a need for independent (property) rules to determine how the benefits and burdens of ownership are to be shared by the co-owners. The following materials explore some of these rules.

Spiller v. Mackereth

Supreme Court of Alabama, 1976
334 So. 2d 859

[John Spiller and Hettie Mackereth owned a building in downtown Tuscaloosa as tenants in common. When a lessee, Auto-Rite, which had been renting the building, vacated, Spiller entered and began using the structure as a warehouse. Mackereth then wrote a letter demanding that Spiller either vacate half of the building or pay half of the rental value, and, when Spiller did neither, she brought suit. The trial court awarded Mackereth $2,100 in rent. Spiller appealed.][13]

JONES, J. . . . On the question of Spiller's liability for rent, we start with the general rule that in absence of an agreement to pay rent or an ouster of a cotenant, a cotenant in possession is not liable to his cotenants for the value of his use and occupation of the property. Fundaburk v. Cody, 261 Ala. 25, 72 So. 2d 710, 48 A.L.R.2d 1295 (1954); Turner v. Johnson, 246 Ala. 114, 19 So. 2d 397 (1944). Since there was no agreement to pay rent, there must be evidence which establishes an ouster before Spiller is required to pay rent to Mackereth. The difficulty in this determination lies in the definition of the word "ouster." Ouster is a conclusory word which is used loosely in cotenancy cases to describe two distinct fact situations. The two fact situations are (1) the beginning of the running of the statute of limitations for adverse possession and (2) the liability of an occupying cotenant for rent to other cotenants. Although the cases do not acknowledge a distinction between the two uses of "ouster," it is clear that the two fact situations require different elements of proof to support a conclusion of ouster.

The Alabama cases involving adverse possession require a finding that the possessing cotenant asserted complete ownership of the land to support a conclusion of ouster. The finding of assertion of ownership may be established in several ways. Some cases find an assertion of complete ownership from a composite of activities such as renting part of the land without accounting, hunting the land, cutting timber, assessing and paying taxes and generally treating the land as if it were owned in fee for the statutory period. See Howard v. Harrell, 275 Ala. 454, 156 So. 2d 140 (1963). Other cases find the assertion of complete ownership from more overt activities such as a sale of the property under a deed purporting to convey the entire fee. Elsheimer v. Parker Bank & Trust Co., 237 Ala. 24, 185 So. 385 (1938). But whatever factual elements are present, the essence of the finding of an ouster in the adverse possession cases is a claim of absolute ownership and a denial of the cotenancy relationship by the occupying cotenant.

In the Alabama cases which adjudicate the occupying cotenant's liability for rent, a claim of absolute ownership has not been an essential element. The normal fact situation which will render an occupying cotenant liable to out of possession cotenants is one in which the occupying cotenant refuses a demand of the other cotenants to be allowed into use and enjoyment of the land, regardless of a

---

13. The facts have been slightly altered to eliminate extraneous issues. — EDS.

claim of absolute ownership. Judd v. Dowdell, 244 Ala. 230, 12 So. 2d 858 (1943); Newbold v. Smart, 67 Ala. 326 (1880).

The instant case involves a cotenant's liability for rent. Indeed, the adverse possession rule is precluded in this case by Spiller's acknowledgment of the cotenancy relationship as evidenced by filing the bill for partition. We can affirm the trial Court if the record reveals some evidence that Mackereth actually sought to occupy the building but was prevented from moving in by Spiller. To prove ouster, Mackereth's attorney relies upon the letter of November 15, 1973, as a sufficient demand and refusal to establish Spiller's liability for rent. This letter, however, did not demand equal use and enjoyment of the premises; rather, it demanded only that Spiller either vacate half of the building or pay rent. The question of whether a demand to vacate or pay rent is sufficient to establish an occupying cotenant's liability for rent has not been addressed in Alabama; however, it has been addressed by courts in other jurisdictions. In jurisdictions which adhere to the majority and Alabama rule of nonliability for mere occupancy, several cases have held that the occupying cotenant is not liable for rent notwithstanding a demand to vacate or pay rent. Grieder v. Marsh, 247 S.W.2d 590 (Tex. Civ. App. 1952); Brown v. Havens, 17 N.J. Super. 235, 85 A.2d 812 (1952).

There is a minority view which establishes liability for rents on a continued occupancy after a demand to vacate or pay rent. Re Holt's Estate, 14 Misc. 2d 971, 177 N.Y.S.2d 192 (1958). We believe that the majority view on this question is consistent with Alabama's approach to the law of occupancy by cotenants. As one of the early Alabama cases on the subject explains:

> Tenants in common are seized *per my et per tout*. Each has an equal right to occupy; and unless the one in actual possession denies to the other the right to enter, or agrees to pay rent, nothing can be claimed for such occupation. [Newbold v. Smart, supra.]

Thus, before an occupying cotenant can be liable for rent in Alabama, he must have denied his cotenants the right to enter. It is axiomatic that there can be no denial of the right to enter unless there is a demand or an attempt to enter. Simply requesting the occupying cotenant to vacate is not sufficient because the occupying cotenant holds title to the whole and may rightfully occupy the whole unless the other cotenants assert their possessory rights.

Besides the November 15 letter, Mackereth's only attempt to prove ouster is a showing that Spiller put locks on the building. However, there is no evidence that Spiller was attempting to do anything other than protect the merchandise he had stored in the building. Spiller testified that when Auto-Rite moved out they removed the locks from the building. Since Spiller began to store his merchandise in the building thereafter, he had to acquire new locks to secure it. There is no evidence that either Mackereth or any of the other cotenants ever requested keys to the locks or were ever prevented from entering the building because of the locks. There is no evidence that Spiller intended to exclude his cotenants by use of the locks. Again, we emphasize that as long as Spiller did not deny access to his cotenants, any activity of possession and occupancy of the building was consistent with his rights of ownership. Thus, the fact that Spiller placed locks on the building, without evidence that he intended to exclude the other cotenants, is insufficient to establish his liability to pay rent.

After reviewing all of the testimony and evidence presented at trial, we are unable to find any evidence which supports a legal conclusion of ouster. We are, therefore, compelled to reverse the trial Court's judgment awarding Mackereth $2,100 rental.

NOTES AND QUESTIONS

1. When a cotenant is in sole possession of concurrently owned property, the majority holds that, unless there has been an ouster, the cotenant in possession does not have to pay a proportionate share of the rental value to the cotenants out of possession. A few jurisdictions take the view that a cotenant in exclusive possession must pay rent to cotenants out of possession even in the absence of ouster. See Cohen v. Cohen, 106 N.E.2d 77 (Ohio 1952). Which view makes better sense?

For an illuminating and searching analysis of whether the cotenant in sole possession should pay rent to the other cotenants, which shows, among other things, that the majority rule is not nearly so clear in operation as it is in the stating, see Evelyn A. Lewis, Struggling with Quicksand: The Ins and Outs of Cotenant Possession Value Liability and a Call for Default Rule Reform, 1994 Wis. L. Rev. 331.

2. What constitutes an ouster? Does *Spiller* set too high a threshold? Would it be better to trigger liability for rental value rather quickly and easily, on grounds of fairness? Efficiency? Suppose a brother and sister inherit a house from their mother, and the sister moves in. The brother writes, as in *Spiller*, asking for rent. Should a refusal to pay, or even a failure to respond, amount to ouster? What if the sister's occupation makes occupation by the brother infeasible? Suppose a husband and wife own a home as joint tenants. The wife moves out because of abusive treatment by the husband. Ouster?

If the cotenants are holding the property for capital gain and neither wants to sell, what are the rights of the tenant out of possession against the tenant in sole possession in a jurisdiction following *Spiller*?

3. *Fiduciary duties.* Generally, cotenants are not fiduciaries with respect to each other. Each cotenant is expected to look after his or her interest. Nonetheless, in some situations the courts treat the cotenants as having fiduciary duties. If, for example, *A* and *B* are members of the same family (say brother and sister), courts may find that the relationship of familial trust and confidence requires that each act as a fiduciary with respect to the other.

A fiduciary duty is imposed most commonly in one of two situations. The first is where one cotenant buys concurrently owned property at a mortgage foreclosure or tax sale and then asserts a superior title against cotenants. Here courts normally compel the buyer to hold the superior title for the benefit of all the cotenants, provided they reimburse the buyer. See William B. Stoebuck & Dale A. Whitman, The Law of Property 210 (3d ed. 2000).

The second situation in which a fiduciary duty may arise involves a claim of adverse possession by the cotenant in exclusive possession. Where cotenants are kindred, courts often treat the cotenant in possession as a fiduciary, who can claim adverse possession only where his claim of sole ownership is so unequivocal and notorious as to put his cotenants on actual notice of a hostile claim. In any event, adverse possession against cotenants is not easily achieved. See, e.g., Ex parte Walker, 739 So. 2d 3 (Ala. 1999) (cotenant's redemption of property from tax sale in 1934, subsequent payment of all property taxes on the land, exclusive possession for more than half a century, demolition of old buildings, and harvesting of timber were insufficient to make out case for adverse possession against other cotenants).

See generally Alan M. Weinberger, Expanding the Fiduciary Relationship Bestiary: Does Concurrent Ownership Satisfy the Family Resemblance Test?, 24 Seton Hall L. Rev. 1767 (1994).

Swartzbaugh v. Sampson

Court of Appeal of California, Fourth District, 1936
54 P.2d 73

MARKS, J. This is an action to cancel two leases executed by John Josiah Swartzbaugh,[14] as lessor, to Sam A. Sampson, as lessee, of two adjoining parcels of land in Orange County. A motion for nonsuit was granted at the close of plaintiff's case and this appeal followed.

Defendant Swartzbaugh and plaintiff are husband and wife. They owned, as joint tenants with the right of survivorship, sixty acres of land in Orange County planted to bearing walnuts. In December, 1933, defendant Sampson started negotiations with plaintiff and her husband for the leasing of a small fraction of this land fronting on Highway 101 for a site for a boxing pavilion. Plaintiff at all times objected to making the lease and it is thoroughly established that Sampson knew she would not join in any lease to him.

The negotiations resulted in the execution of an option for a lease, dated January 5, 1934, signed by Swartzbaugh and Sampson. The lease, dated February 2, 1934, was executed by the same parties. A second lease of property adjoining the site of the boxing pavilion was signed by Swartzbaugh and Sampson. This was

14. "John J. Swartzbaugh is well known as one of the oldest and most extensive walnut growers in Orange County, and his splendid estate, in West Orange precinct, is a testimonial to his industry and good management. . . . [He was born in Maryland in 1858, married Lola Desirra Knott, daughter of an Ohio farmer, in 1887, and came to California in 1888.] Soon afterwards he purchased a squatter's claim in West Orange precinct, and made valuable improvements and additional purchases, being now the owner of one hundred and ten acres of good land. Ninety acres are devoted to the growing of walnuts, of which he has made a specialty for the past thirty years, and he has gained a high reputation for his ability and success in this line of effort.

". . . Mr. and Mrs. Swartzbaugh became the parents of nine children. . . . He belongs to the Garden Grove Walnut Association and is regarded by his associates as a man of sound and dependable judgment in practical things, while, socially, he is well liked by all with whom he comes in contact." 2 Mrs. J.E. Pleasants, History of Orange County, California, 193-194 (1931).—EDS.

also dated February 2, 1934, but probably was signed after that date. Plaintiff's name does not appear in any of the three documents and Sampson was advised that she would not sign any of them.

The walnut trees were removed from the leased premises. Sampson went into possession, erected his boxing pavilion and placed other improvements on the property.

Plaintiff was injured in February, 1934, and was confined to her bed for some time. This action was started on June 20, 1934. Up to the time of the trial plaintiff had received no part of the rental of the leased property. Sampson was in possession of all of it under the leases to the exclusion of plaintiff.

There is but one question to be decided in this case which may be stated as follows: Can one joint tenant who has not joined in the leases executed by her cotenant and another maintain an action to cancel the leases where the lessee is in exclusive possession of the leased property? This question does not seem to have been decided in California and there is not an entire uniformity of decision in other jurisdictions. In decisions on analogous questions where courts reached like conclusions they did not always use the same course of reasoning in reaching them. It seems necessary, therefore, that we consider briefly the nature of the estate in joint tenancy and the rights of the joint tenants in it. . . .

An estate in joint tenancy can be severed by destroying one or more of the necessary unities, either by operation of law, by death, by voluntary or certain involuntary acts of the joint tenants, or by certain acts or omissions of one joint tenant without the consent of the other. It seems to be the rule in England that a lease by one joint tenant for a term of years will effect a severance, at least during the term of the lease. (Napier v. Williams, [1911] 1 Ch. 361; Doe v. Read, 12 East, 57, 104 Reprint, 23; Roe v. Lonsdale, 12 East, 39, 104 Reprint, 16; Palmer v. Rich, [1897] 1 Ch. 134. See Thompson on Real Property, p.929, sec. 1715.) We have found no case in the United States where this rule has been applied. From the reasoning used and conclusions reached in many of the American cases its adoption in this country seems doubtful.

One of the essential unities of a joint tenancy is that of possession. Each tenant owns an equal interest in all of the fee and each has an equal right to possession of the whole. Possession by one is possession by all. Ordinarily one joint tenant out of possession cannot recover exclusive possession of the joint property from his cotenant. (Jamison v. Graham, 57 Ill. 94.) He can only recover the right to be let into joint possession of the property with his cotenant. He cannot eject his cotenant in possession. (Noble v. Manatt, 42 Cal. App. 496 [183 Pac. 823].)

Ordinarily one joint tenant cannot maintain an action against his cotenant for rent for occupancy of the property or for profits derived from his own labor. He may, however, compel the tenant in possession to account for rents collected from third parties. . . .

The case of Stark v. Barrett, 15 Cal. 361, discusses the rights of a grantee of one cotenant of a specific parcel of property. It is there said:

The case has been argued as though the question presented was to be determined by the rules of the common law, and in that view we have examined it. For its determination, considered by the common law, it is immaterial whether the grantees took the land embraced in their grant as joint tenants or as tenants in common. During the lives of the tenants, the rules regulating the transfer of their interest are substantially the same, whether they hold in joint tenancy or in common. Neither a joint tenant nor a tenant in common can do any act to the prejudice of his cotenants in their estate. This is the settled law, and hence a conveyance by one tenant of a parcel of a general tract, owned by several, is inoperative to impair any of the rights of his cotenants. The conveyance must be subject to the ultimate determination of their rights, and upon obvious grounds. One tenant cannot appropriate to himself any particular parcel of the general tract; as, upon a partition, which may be claimed by the cotenants at any time, the parcel may be entirely set apart in severalty to a cotenant. He cannot defeat this possible result whilst retaining his interest, nor can he defeat it by the transfer of his interest. He cannot, of course, invest his grantee with rights greater than he possesses. The grantee must take, therefore, subject to the contingency of the loss of the premises, if, upon the partition of the general tract, they should not be allotted to the grantor. Subject to this contingency, the conveyance is valid, and passes the interest of the grantor. And this, we consider the result of the several cases cited by the counsel of the appellants. They go to the extent that the conveyance can have no legal effect to the prejudice of the cotenant, not that it is absolutely void, that it is ineffectual against the assertion of his interest in a suit for partition of the general tract, but is good against all others. Until such partition, the grantee will be entitled to the use and possession as cotenant, in the parcel conveyed, with the other owners. . . .

It is a general rule that the act of one joint tenant without express or implied authority from or the consent of his cotenant cannot bind or prejudicially affect the rights of the latter. . . .

In the application of the foregoing rule the courts have imposed a limitation upon it which, in effect, is a qualification of its broad language. This perhaps is due to the nature of the estate which is universally held to be joint in enjoyment and several upon severance. This limitation arises in cases where one joint tenant in possession leases all of the joint property without the consent of his cotenant and places the lessee in possession. It seems to be based upon the theory that the joint tenant in possession is entitled to the possession of the entire property and by his lease merely gives to his lessee a right he, the lessor, had been enjoying, puts the lessee in the enjoyment of a right of possession which he, the lessor, already had and by so doing does not prejudicially affect the rights of the cotenant out of possession, it being conceded that the joint tenant not joining in the lease is not bound by its terms and that he can recover from the tenant of his cotenant the reasonable value of the use and enjoyment of his share of the estate, if the tenant under the lease refuses him the right to enjoy his moiety of the estate. (See Codman v. Hall, 9 Allen (91 Mass.) 335; Eagle Brewing Co. v. Netzel, 159 Ill. App. 375; Frans v. Young, 24 Iowa, 375.)

It has been held that each joint tenant, during the existence of the joint estate, has the right to convey, mortgage or subject to a mechanic's lien an equal share of the joint property. (People v. Varel, 351 Ill. 96, 184 N.E. 209.) It has also been held that one joint tenant in possession of personal property may pledge his interest in the property to another; that the pledgee's rights are valid to the extent of the pledgor's interest; that each joint tenant has an equal right of possession and so the pledgee has the same right of possession that the pledgor had; that the joint tenant out of possession can maintain no action against the pledgee that he could not maintain against the pledgor. . . .

In 2 Thompson on Real Property, page 929, section 1715, it is said: "One joint tenant may make a lease of the joint property, but this will bind only his share of it." The same rule is thus stated in 1 Landlord and Tenant, Tiffany, 405: "One of two or more joint tenants cannot, by making a lease of the whole, vest in the lessee more than his own share, since that is all to which he has an exclusive right. Such a lease is, however, valid as to his share."

The foregoing authorities support the conclusion that a lease to all of the joint property by one joint tenant is not a nullity but is a valid and supportable contract in so far as the interest of the lessor in the joint property is concerned. . . .

In the case of Lee Chuck v. Quan Wo Chong & Co., 91 Cal. 593, 28 Pac. 45, the plaintiff, a tenant in common, brought an action to oust defendant who was holding under a lease from another tenant in common. The Supreme Court reversed the judgment in favor of plaintiff and said: . . .

> One tenant in common may, "by either lease or license, . . . confer upon another person the right to occupy and use the property of the co-tenancy as fully as such lessor or licensor himself might have used or occupied it if such lease or license had not been granted. If either co-tenant expel such licensee or lessee, he is guilty of a trespass. If the lessee has the exclusive possession of the premises, he is not liable to any one but his lessor for the rent, unless the other co-tenants attempt to enter and he resists or forbids their entry, or unless, being in possession with them, he ousts or excludes some or all of them." (Freeman on Cotenancy and Partition, sec. 253.) There is no evidence tending to show that the defendant ever refused to allow the plaintiff to enjoy the use of the premises with him. The judgment does not confine the plaintiff's right of recovery to his own moiety, but provides that the plaintiff shall have and recover from defendant the restitution and possession of the premises described in the complaint. . . .

As far as the evidence before us in this case is concerned, the foregoing authorities force the conclusion that the leases from Swartzbaugh to Sampson are not null and void but valid and existing contracts giving to Sampson the same right to the possession of the leased property that Swartzbaugh had. It follows they cannot be cancelled by plaintiff in this action.

Plaintiff expresses the fear that as one of the leases runs for five years, with an option for an additional five years, she may lose her interest in the leased premises by prescription. It is a general rule that a lessee in possession of real property under a lease cannot dispute his landlord's title nor can he hold adversely to him while holding under the lease. If, as held in numerous cases, the lessee of one cotenant holds the possession of his lessor and that a cotenant in possession holds for the other cotenant and not adversely, Sampson would have great difficulty in establishing any holding adverse to plaintiff without a complete and definite ouster. As a general rule an adverse possessor must claim the property in fee and a lessee holding under a lease cannot avail himself of the claim of adverse possession. There are certain exceptions to this rule which do not seem to be applicable to this case. There is no showing that plaintiff ever demanded that

Sampson let her into possession of her moiety of the estate nor is there anything to indicate that he is holding adversely to her.

Judgment affirmed.

A petition by appellant to have the cause heard in the Supreme Court, after judgment in the District Court of Appeal, was denied by the Supreme Court on March 26, 1936.

NOTES AND QUESTIONS

1. At the trial in the principal case the plaintiff, Lola Desirra Swartzbaugh, testified that the land was set out in walnut trees by the Swartzbaughs in 1912; that she did not want the walnut trees taken out; that the rent payable by Sampson was $15 a month, which she regarded as too little when Sampson was to spend around $10,000 on building and equipping the boxing arena; that she had never received any part of the rent, and that she did not want prizefighting on her land because "women and liquor followed" and "I worked too hard for that place to have everybody against me bringing such a place there."

Mrs. Swartzbaugh also testified with respect to the signing of the lease by her husband on February 2, 1934:

A.   Mr. Swartzbaugh said it was an option or lease, but I am not sure which he said, because I felt so bad that I wasn't sure of anything, but I said "you had better take that to a lawyer, or see a lawyer before you sign anything like that. You don't know what it is," and Mr. Sampson said he read, or "I read it to him."

Q.   [Then what happened?]

A.   Well, when I saw Mr. Swartzbaugh go to the desk to sign it, I gathered up my crutches and left the room, fearing they would ask me—

A week or so later Mrs. Swartzbaugh telephoned Sampson that she was going to get an injunction against him and stop him. Sampson came to see her. Her daughter Arvilla and her son John were there. The meeting was inconclusive. John testified:

A.   . . . After mother objected and told him she would get an injunction against him and we would stop him, and I shook my fist in Sampson's face and said "you can't get away with it," and he said "forget it," and he started to tell about his previous experience [in conducting prizefighting] at Delhi and how orderly it was conducted and all [the fighters were] high school boys, and I told him to "come outside," and then I said "Sampson, get this straight, you are dealing with an old man in his dotage and my mother is lying in her bed, and nobody but a damned dirty rat would attempt to put this over," and he said "forget it, John, we will not say anything more about it," and Sampson left immediately after that, and the next time we heard anything from him, Sampson was working over there [cutting the trees and erecting the boxing pavilion] and my mother was on her back and in bed and couldn't get out an injunction.

Appellant's Opening Brief at 6-11, *Swartzbaugh v. Sampson*, 54 P.2d 73 (Cal. App. 1936).

2. Consider the remedies available to Mrs. Swartzbaugh.

(a) *Partition.* Mrs. Swartzbaugh could bring an action to partition the entire 60 acres or to partition the fraction leased to Sampson for the duration of the lease. If she brought an action to partition the fraction leased for a five-year term, with an option to renew for an additional five years, and the court ordered sale of the leasehold term, how would the court divide up the proceeds of the sale?

(b) *Ouster.* Another remedy for Mrs. Swartzbaugh is to enter, or try to enter, into possession with the lessee. If the lessee resists, the remedies of an ousted cotenant are then available. As the decision in the *Swartzbaugh* case points out, those remedies would allow Mrs. Swartzbaugh to recover from the lessee one-half the reasonable rental value of the leased land (a remedy called, for historical reasons, the recovery of mesne profits). Does the mere presence of the boxing pavilion work an ouster? If the lessee ousts Mrs. Swartzbaugh and becomes liable to her for one-half the fair rental value, is the lessee still liable to Mr. Swartzbaugh for the full amount of the agreed rental?

(c) *Accounting.* Mrs. Swartzbaugh can sue her husband for an accounting of the rents received by him. The Notes below discuss this and some related matters.

3. *Postscript.* In October 1934, John J. Swartzbaugh conveyed to his wife as her separate property all land he owned in Orange County, except the four acres leased to Sam Sampson. He conveyed his interest in the leased land to his daughter Ruth. Swartzbaugh died in 1943 after a long illness.

Sampson operated the boxing pavilion under the name "Orange County Athletic Club." In 1939, the Orange County Athletic Club was changed into a wrestling venue. Thereafter Mrs. Swartzbaugh had a change of heart. In January 1944, at the expiration of the 10-year lease, Mrs. Swartzbaugh and Ruth renewed the lease to Sampson for two years for $1,000 cash and a rent of $65 a month. Sampson was given the option of renewing this extended lease in 1945 for three more years at $100 a month.

The Swartzbaugh property is now part of the site of Angel Stadium, home of the Los Angeles Angels of Anaheim.

NOTES: ACCOUNTING FOR BENEFITS, RECOVERING COSTS

1. Concurrently owned property can yield a variety of benefits to the cotenants: rents realized from leases to third parties; profits realized from using the property for business purposes; value realized by one or more of the cotenants in occupying the property as a residence. Of course, concurrent ownership can also give rise to a variety of expenditures—for taxes and mortgage payments,

maintenance and repairs, improvements—and a cotenant making such expenditures might seek to recoup some or all of them through a partition action or an action for an accounting (brought independently or incident to a partition action) or an action for contribution from the other cotenants.

Accounting is an equitable proceeding, and, although the rules given below ordinarily apply, particular facts may compel a departure from the usual rules in order to be fair to the cotenants.

2. *Rents and profits.* In all states, a cotenant who collects from third parties rents and other payments arising from the co-owned land must account to cotenants for the amounts received, net of expenses. Thus, if one cotenant leases a farm to a third party, or executes a mineral lease, or cuts and sells timber, he must account for net rents, royalties, and other proceeds in excess of his share. See 2 American Law of Property §6.14 (1952).[15] Absent ouster, however, the accounting is usually based only on actual receipts, not fair market value. Suppose the lease signed by one cotenant claims to bind only that cotenant's share and not to give the lessee exclusive occupancy, and the agreed rent is equal to one-half the fair rental value. Would this affect the rights of the other cotenant to an accounting? See Annot., 51 A.L.R.2d 388, 407-408 (1957).

On payment of rent by a tenant in sole possession, see Spiller v. Mackereth, page 372, and the Notes and Questions that follow it.

3. *Taxes, mortgage payments, and other carrying charges.* A cotenant paying more than his share of taxes, mortgage payments, and other necessary carrying charges generally has a right to contribution from the other cotenants, at least up to the amount of the value of their share in the property. (Similarly, the cotenant paying more than his share receives a credit for the excess payments in an accounting or partition action.) The principle behind this result "is that the protection of the interest of each cotenant from extinction by a tax or foreclosure sale imposes on each the duty to contribute to the extent of his proportionate share the money required to make such payments." 2 American Law of Property, supra, §6.17 at 73-74. However, "[i]f the tenant who has paid taxes or interest has been in sole possession of the property, and the value of the use and enjoyment which he has had equals or exceeds such payments, no action in any form for contribution will lie against the others." Id. at 76.

The qualification just quoted is not uniformly applied. See Annot., supra, 51 A.L.R.2d at 455-459. Is it inconsistent with the principle behind the general rule? With the rule (followed in most jurisdictions) that a cotenant in possession need not account to cotenants out of possession for the reasonable rental value of the property?

4. *Repairs and improvements.* As to *necessary repairs*, some jurisdictions provide for contribution if the repairing cotenant gives notice to the other cotenants;

---

15. In some jurisdictions extraction of minerals or cutting of timber is deemed waste, even though such operations are permitted to the owners of a fee simple. See William B. Stoebuck & Dale A. Whitman, The Law of Property 206-207 (3d ed. 2000).

most, however, recognize no affirmative right to contribution from the other cotenants in the absence of an agreement. This is considered the rule by "weight of authority and of reason. . . ." 2 American Law of Property, supra, §6.18 at 77. The "reason" behind the rule is said to be that the questions "of how much should be expended on repairs, their character and extent, and whether as a matter of business judgment such expenditures are justified," are ones too uncertain for the law to settle. Id. at 78. Given this, how is it that the cotenant receives a credit for reasonable repairs in a partition or accounting action (subject to the same qualifications as apply to taxes and mortgage payments)?

Improvements. As with repairs, a cotenant has no right to contribution from other cotenants for expenditures for improvements; beyond this (and unlike the case of repairs), no credit for the cost of the improvements is given as such in an accounting or partition action. This does not mean, however, that an improving cotenant is always without means to recapture the costs or realize the value of improvements. The general rule is that the interests of the improver are to be protected if this can be accomplished without detriment to the interests of the other cotenants. Thus, if property is physically divided pursuant to a partition action, the improved portion is awarded to the improving cotenant if such a distribution would not diminish the interests of the other cotenants as they stood prior to the making of the improvements. If physical partition is impossible or would result in injustice to one of the cotenants, the property is sold and the proceeds distributed in such a way as to award to the improver the added value (if any) resulting from his improvements. See Graham v. Inlow, 790 S.W.2d 428 (Ark. 1990). An alternative remedy—where physical partition is possible but would jeopardize the interests of the improver by awarding improvements to cotenants who did not contribute to their cost—is to divide the property but order payment (called owelty) from noncontributing cotenants to the improver in an amount equal to the former's share of the enhanced value of the property resulting from the improvements. In an accounting for rents and profits, the improver is allowed all increments in value (if any) attributable to the improvements.

The various approaches discussed above pay heed only to the value of improvements, not their cost. In instances when "improvements" cost more than they yield in terms of increased sale or rental value (or, indeed, when they actually diminish value), the improver bears the full "downside" risk. When improvements increase value beyond their cost, the improver gets the full "upside"—the total increase in value—rather than being required to share it with the other cotenants. In a few cases, however, courts have limited recovery to the lesser of the value added by the improvement, or its cost; the downside, in short is borne by the improver, but the upside is shared by all the cotenants. Which is the better view? Should improvements be treated like repairs? Repairs like improvements?

For a comparative analysis of American and Continental law on the questions considered in these Notes, see Hanoch Dagan & Michael A. Heller, The Liberal Commons, 110 Yale L.J. 549, 611-620 (2001).

"They have this arrangement. He earns the money and she takes care of the house."

B. *Marital Interests*

Two different systems of marital property emerged from medieval Europe. One was a separate property system, which developed in England. Its fundamental principle is that husband and wife have separate property; ownership is given to the spouse who acquires the property. The other was the Continental system of community property. Community property rests on the notion that husband and wife are a marital partnership (a "community") and should share their acquisitions equally. In Europe, community property originated among the Germanic tribes and was carried by the Visigoths into Spain in the fifth century. Gradually, over hundreds of years, community property customs grew and spread throughout the continent of Europe but never took root in England. Under the pressure of a militaristic feudalism with a powerful king on top, the English royal judges suppressed any tendencies toward community property. The presumed necessities of the great lords dictated the effacement of the wife, which became the common law for all. See Charles Donahue, Jr., What Causes Fundamental Legal Ideas? Marital Property in England and France in the Thirteenth Century, 78 Mich. L. Rev. 59 (1979).

The common law marital property system was accepted in the large majority of American states. In eight states influenced by French or Spanish law (Arizona,

California, Idaho, Louisiana, Nevada, New Mexico, Texas, and Washington) and in two johnnies-come-lately (Wisconsin and Alaska), a community property system exists. In the late twentieth century, the common law marital property system came under pressure to reform itself so that the results resemble those reached under a community property system. The community property idea of treating husband and wife as an economic unit has more or less triumphed when spousal property is divided upon divorce, but it has less effect on division of property at the death of a spouse. Moreover, great differences between these marital property systems remain and cause complications when a couple moves from a common law property state to a community property state, or vice versa. See generally Mary Ann Glendon, The Transformation of Family Law (1989).

1.   The Common Law Marital Property System

Under the common law system of separate property, the property rights of each spouse are classified according to three categories: (1) rights during the marriage; (2) rights upon divorce; and (3) rights at death.

a.   During Marriage (The Fiction That Husband and Wife Are One)

> Now, although we act as one person, we are, in point of fact, two persons. . . .
> It is a legal fiction, and legal fictions are solemn things. . . .
> It's all very well to say we act as one person, but when you supply us with only one
> Ration between us, I should describe as a legal fiction carried a little too far. —
>
> *W.S. Gilbert,*
> The Gondoliers (1889)

The English marital property system, feudal in origin, mirrored the need of the patriarchal landed class to keep their estates intact and under the control of a single male. A married woman was to be supported and maintained for her entire life, but she was not entitled, by and large, to exercise powers of ownership. Her property relationship to her husband was one of dependency.

At the instant of marriage, a woman moved under her husband's protection or *cover* (becoming a *feme covert*). She ceased to be a legal person for the duration of the marriage. Husband and wife were regarded as one, and that one was the husband. Except for clothes and ornaments (known as the wife's *paraphernalia*), all personal property owned by the wife at the time of the marriage or acquired thereafter, including her earnings, became the property of the husband. Although the notion that husband and wife were one flesh was not pushed to the logical extreme of depriving the wife of title to her real property, the husband had the right of possession to all the wife's lands during marriage, including land acquired after marriage. That right, known as *jure uxoris*, was alienable by the husband and reachable by his creditors. In addition, the wife had the duty of rendering services within the home. In exchange for all this, and a marriage vow to obey her husband, the wife received the benefit of the husband's support and protection.[16]

Beginning with Mississippi in 1839, all common law property states had, by the end of the nineteenth century, enacted Married Women's Property Acts. These statutes removed the disabilities of coverture and gave a married woman, like a single woman, control over all her property. Such property was her separate property, immune from her husband's debts. The wife also gained control of all her earnings outside the home.

The Married Women's Property Acts, prompted by a desire to protect a wife's property from her husband's creditors, as well as to grant her legal autonomy, did not give the wife full equality. Husband and wife were expected to play complementary roles. The husband, employed outside the home, remained head of the family and owed his wife a duty of support; his wife, mistress of the household and in charge of rearing the children, owed him domestic services. Although the wife was given control over her property, it was unlikely that—as an unpaid homemaker—she would have much of that commodity. See Reva B. Siegel, The Modernization of Marital Status Law: Adjudicating Wives' Rights to Earnings, 1860-1930, 82 Geo. L.J. 2127 (1994).

PROBLEM

After having a stroke, *H*, anxious to avoid going into a nursing home or being cared for by professional nurses, entered into an agreement with *W*. *H* promised *W* that if *W* personally cared for him at home for the rest of his life, *H* would devise her certain property by will. In compliance with the agreement, *W* personally cared for *H* at home until his death. When he died, *H* devised the property promised *W* to his daughter by a prior marriage. Can *W* enforce the contract? See Borelli v. Brusseau, 16 Cal. Rptr. 2d 16 (Cal. App. 1993).

Sawada v. Endo

Supreme Court of Hawaii, 1977
561 P.2d 1291

MENOR, J. This is a civil action brought by the plaintiffs-appellants, Masako Sawada and Helen Sawada, in aid of execution of money judgments in their favor, seeking to set aside a conveyance of real property from judgment debtor Kokichi Endo to Samuel H. Endo and Toru Endo, defendants-appellees herein, on the ground that the conveyance as to the Sawadas was fraudulent.

---

16. At common law a husband was liable for the torts of his wife, for the law supposed that a wife acts under her husband's direction. "'If the law supposes that,' said Mr. Bumble, squeezing his hat emphatically in both hands, 'the law is a ass—a idiot. If that's the eye of the law, the law's a bachelor; and the worst I wish the law is, that his eye may be opened by experience—by experience.'" Charles Dickens, Oliver Twist, ch. 51, at 394 (Everyman Lib. ed. 1940).

On November 30, 1968, the Sawadas were injured when struck by a motor vehicle operated by Kokichi Endo. On June 17, 1969, Helen Sawada filed her complaint for damages against Kokichi Endo. Masako Sawada filed her suit against him on August 13, 1969. The complaint and summons in each case was served on Kokichi Endo on October 29, 1969.

On the date of the accident, Kokichi Endo was the owner, as a tenant by the entirety with his wife, Ume Endo, of a parcel of real property situate at Wahiawa, Oahu, Hawaii. By deed, dated July 26, 1969, Kokichi Endo and his wife conveyed the property to their sons, Samuel H. Endo and Toru Endo. This document was recorded in the Bureau of Conveyances on December 17, 1969. No consideration was paid by the grantees for the conveyance. Both were aware at the time of the conveyance that their father had been involved in an accident, and that he carried no liability insurance. Kokichi Endo and Ume Endo, while reserving no life interests therein, continued to reside on the premises.

On January 19, 1971, after a consolidated trial on the merits, judgment was entered in favor of Helen Sawada and against Kokichi Endo in the sum of $8,846.46. At the same time, Masako Sawada was awarded judgment on her complaint in the amount of $16,199.28. Ume Endo, wife of Kokichi Endo, died on January 29, 1971. She was survived by her husband, Kokichi. Subsequently, after being frustrated in their attempts to obtain satisfaction of judgment from the personal property of Kokichi Endo, the Sawadas brought suit to set aside the conveyance which is the subject matter of this controversy. The trial court refused to set aside the conveyance, and the Sawadas appeal.

The determinative question in this case is, whether the interest of one spouse in real property, held in tenancy by the entireties, is subject to levy and execution by his or her individual creditors. This issue is one of first impression in this jurisdiction.

A brief review of the present state of the tenancy by the entirety might be helpful. Dean Phipps, writing in 1951,[17] pointed out that only nineteen states and the District of Columbia continued to recognize it as a valid and subsisting institution in the field of property law. Phipps divided these jurisdictions into four groups. He made no mention of Alaska and Hawaii, both of which were then territories of the United States.

In the Group I states (Massachusetts, Michigan, and North Carolina) the estate is essentially the common law tenancy by the entireties, unaffected by the Married Women's Property Acts. As at common law, the possession and profits of the estate are subject to the husband's exclusive dominion and control. . . . In all three states, as at common law, the *husband* may convey the entire estate subject only to the possibility that the wife may become entitled to the whole estate upon surviving him. . . . As at common law, the obverse as to the wife does not hold true. Only in Massachusetts, however, is the estate in its entirety subject to levy by the husband's creditors. . . . In both Michigan and North Carolina, the use and

17. Phipps, Tenancy by Entireties, 25 Temple L.Q. 24 (1951).

income from the estate is not subject to levy during the marriage for the separate debts of either spouse. . . .

In the Group II states (Alaska, Arkansas, New Jersey, New York, and Oregon) the interest of the debtor spouse in the estate may be sold or levied upon for his or her separate debts, subject to the other spouse's contingent right of survivorship. . . . Alaska, which has been added to this group, has provided by statute that the interest of a debtor spouse in any type of estate, except a homestead as defined and held in tenancy by the entirety, shall be subject to his or her separate debts. . . .

In the Group III jurisdictions (Delaware, District of Columbia, Florida, Indiana, Maryland, Missouri, Pennsylvania, Rhode Island, Vermont, Virginia, and Wyoming) an attempted conveyance by either spouse is wholly void, and the estate may not be subjected to the separate debts of one spouse only. . . .

In Group IV, the two states of Kentucky and Tennessee hold that the contingent right of survivorship appertaining to either spouse is separately alienable by him and attachable by his creditors during the marriage. . . . The use and profits, however, may neither be alienated nor attached during coverture.

It appears, therefore, that Hawaii is the only jurisdiction still to be heard from on the question. Today we join that group of states and the District of Columbia which hold that under the Married Women's Property Acts the interest of a husband or a wife in an estate by the entireties is not subject to the claims of his or her individual creditors during the joint lives of the spouses. In so doing, we are placing our stamp of approval upon what is apparently the prevailing view of the lower courts of this jurisdiction.

Hawaii has long recognized and continues to recognize the tenancy in common, the joint tenancy, and the tenancy by the entirety, as separate and distinct estates. See Paahana v. Bila, 3 Haw. 725 (1876). That the Married Women's Property Act of 1888 was not intended to abolish the tenancy by the entirety was made clear by the language of Act 19 of the Session Laws of Hawaii, 1903 (now HRS §509-1); see also HRS §509-2. The tenancy by the entirety is predicated upon the legal unity of husband and wife, and the estate is held by them in single ownership. They do not take by moieties, but both and each are seized of the whole estate. Lang v. Commissioner of Internal Revenue, 289 U.S. 109 (1933).

A joint tenant has a specific, albeit undivided, interest in the property, and if he survives his cotenant he becomes the owner of a larger interest than he had prior to the death of the other joint tenant. But tenants by the entirety are each deemed to be seized of the entirety from the time of the creation of the estate. At common law, this taking of the "whole estate" did not have the real significance that it does today, insofar as the rights of the wife in the property were concerned. For all practical purposes, the wife had no right during coverture to the use and enjoyment and exercise of ownership in the marital estate. All she possessed was her contingent right of survivorship.

The effect of the Married Women's Property Acts was to abrogate the husband's common law dominance over the marital estate and to place the wife on a level of equality with him as regards the exercise of ownership over the whole estate. The tenancy was and still is predicated upon the legal unity of husband and wife, but the Acts converted it into a unity of equals and not of unequals as at common law. . . . No longer could the husband convey, lease, mortgage or otherwise encumber the property without her consent. The Acts confirmed her right to the use and enjoyment of the whole estate, and all the privileges that ownership of property confers, including the right to convey the property in its entirety, jointly with her husband, during the marriage relation. Jordan v. Reynolds, 105 Md. 288, 66 A. 37 (1907); Hurd v. Hughes, 12 Del. Ch. 188, 109 A. 418 (1920). They also had the effect of insulating the wife's interest in the estate from the separate debts of her husband. Jordan v. Reynolds, supra.

Neither husband nor wife has a separate divisible interest in the property held by the entirety that can be conveyed or reached by execution. Fairclaw v. Forrest, 76 U.S. App. D.C. 197, 130 F.2d 829 (1942). A joint tenancy may be destroyed by voluntary alienation, or by levy and execution, or by compulsory partition, but a tenancy by the entirety may not. The indivisibility of the estate, except by joint action of the spouses, is an indispensable feature of the tenancy by the entirety. Ashbaugh v. Ashbaugh, 273 Mo. 353, 201 S.W. 72 (1918); Newman v. Equitable Life Assur. Soc., 119 Fla. 641, 160 So. 745 (1935); Lang v. Commissioner of Internal Revenue, supra.

In Jordan v. Reynolds, supra, the Maryland court held that no lien could attach against entirety property for the separate debts of the husband, for that would be in derogation of the entirety of title in the spouses and would be tantamount to a conversion of the tenancy into a joint tenancy or tenancy in common. In holding that the spouses could jointly convey the property, free of any judgment liens against the husband, the court said:

> To hold the judgment to be a lien at all against this property, and the right of execution suspended during the life of the wife, and to be enforced on the death of the wife, would, we think, likewise encumber her estate, and be in contravention of the constitutional provision heretofore mentioned, protecting the wife's property from the husband's debts.
>
> It is clear, we think, if the judgment here is declared a lien, but suspended during the life of the wife, and not enforceable until her death, if the husband should survive the wife, it will defeat the sale here made by the husband and wife to the purchaser, and thereby make the wife's property liable for the debts of her husband. [66 A. at 39.]

In Hurd v. Hughes, supra, the Delaware court, recognizing the peculiar nature of an estate by the entirety, in that the husband and wife are the owners, not merely of equal interests but of the whole estate, stated:

> The estate [by the entireties] can be acquired or held only by a man and woman while married. Each spouse owns the whole while both live; neither can sell any interest except with the other's consent, and by their joint act; and at the death of either the other continues to own the whole, and does not acquire any new interest from the other. There can be no partition between them. From this is deduced the indivisibility and unseverability of the estate into two interests, and hence that the creditors of either spouse cannot during their joint lives reach by execution any interest which the debtor had in land so held. . . . One may have doubts as to whether the holding of land by entireties is advisable or in harmony with the spirit of the legislation in favor of married women; but when such an estate is created due effect must be given to its peculiar characteristics. [109 A. at 419.] . . .

We are not persuaded by the argument that it would be unfair to the creditors of either spouse to hold that the estate by the entirety may not, without the consent of both spouses, be levied upon for the separate debts of either spouse. No unfairness to the creditor is involved here. We agree with the court in Hurd v. Hughes, supra: "But creditors are not entitled to special consideration. If the debt arose prior to the creation of the estate, the property was not a basis of credit, and if the debt arose subsequently the creditor presumably had notice of the characteristics of the estate which limited his right to reach the property."[18] 12 Del. Ch. at 193, 109 A. at 420.

We might also add that there is obviously nothing to prevent the creditor from insisting upon the subjection of property held in tenancy by the entirety as a condition precedent to the extension of credit. Further, the creation of a tenancy by the entirety may not be used as a device to defraud existing creditors. In re Estate of Wall, 142 U.S. App. D.C. 187, 440 F.2d 215 (1971).

Were we to view the matter strictly from the standpoint of public policy, we would still be constrained to hold as we have done here today. In Fairclaw v. Forrest, supra, the court makes this observation: "The interest in family solidarity retains some influence upon the institution [of tenancy by the entirety]. It is available only to husband and wife. It is a convenient mode of protecting a surviving spouse from inconvenient administration of the decedent's estate and from the other's improvident debts. It is in that protection the estate finds its peculiar and justifiable function." 130 F.2d at 833.

It is a matter of common knowledge that the demand for single-family residential lots has increased rapidly in recent years, and the magnitude of the problem is emphasized by the concentration of the bulk of fee simple land in the hands of a few. The shortage of single-family residential fee simple property is critical and government has seen fit to attempt to alleviate the problem through legislation.[19] When a family can afford to own real property, it becomes their single most important asset. Encumbered as it usually is by a first mortgage, the fact remains that so long as it remains whole during the joint lives of the spouses, it is always available in its entirety for the benefit and use of the entire family. Loans for education and other emergency expenses, for example, may be obtained on the security of the marital estate. This would not be possible where a third party has become a tenant in common or a joint tenant with one of the spouses, or where the ownership of the contingent right of survivorship of one of the spouses in a third party has cast a cloud upon the title of the marital estate, making it virtually impossible to utilize the estate for these purposes.

If we were to select between a public policy favoring the creditors of one of the spouses and one favoring the interests of the family unit, we would not hesitate to choose the latter. But we need not make this choice for, as we pointed

18. This may be true for contract creditors, but is it true for tort creditors, like the Sawadas? — EDS.

19. For discussion of the Hawaii legislation designed to break the hold a few fee simple owners had on much Hawaii land, giving only leases to tenant-possessors, see Hawaii Housing Authority v. Midkiff, 467 U.S. 229, 233-234 (1984). — EDS.

out earlier, by the very nature of the estate by the entirety as we view it, and as other courts of our sister jurisdictions have viewed it, "[a] unilaterally indestructible right of survivorship, an inability of one spouse to alienate his interest, and, importantly for this case, a broad immunity from claims of separate creditors remain among its vital incidents." In re Estate of Wall, supra, 440 F.2d at 218.

Having determined that an estate by the entirety is not subject to the claims of the creditors of one of the spouses during their joint lives, we now hold that the conveyance of the marital property by Kokichi Endo and Ume Endo, husband and wife, to their sons, Samuel H. Endo and Toru Endo, was not in fraud of Kokichi Endo's judgment creditors. Cf. Jordan v. Reynolds, supra.

Affirmed.

KIDWELL, J., dissenting. . . . The majority reaches its conclusion by holding that the effect of the Married Women's Act was to equalize the positions of the spouses by taking from the husband his common law right to transfer his interest, rather than by elevating the wife's right of alienation of her interest to place it on a position of equality with the husband's. I disagree. I believe that a better interpretation of the Married Women's Acts is that offered by the Supreme Court of New Jersey in King v. Greene, 30 N.J. 395, 412, 153 A.2d 49, 60 (1959):

> It is clear that the Married Women's Act created an equality between the spouses in New Jersey, insofar as tenancies by the entirety are concerned. If, as we have previously concluded, the husband could alienate his right of survivorship at common law, the wife, by virtue of the act, can alienate her right of survivorship. And it follows, that if the wife takes equal rights with the husband in the estate, she must take equal disabilities. Such are the dictates of common equality. Thus, the judgment creditors of either spouse may levy and execute upon their separate rights of survivorship.

One may speculate whether the courts which first chose the path to equality now followed by the majority might have felt an unexpressed aversion to entrusting a wife with as much control over her interest as had previously been granted to the husband with respect to his interest. Whatever may be the historical explanation for these decisions, I feel that the resultant restriction upon the freedom of the spouses to deal independently with their respective interests is both illogical and unnecessarily at odds with present policy trends. Accordingly, I would hold that the separate interest of the husband in entireties property, at least to the extent of his right of survivorship, is alienable by him and subject to attachment by his separate creditors, so that a voluntary conveyance of the husband's interest should be set aside where it is fraudulent as to such creditors, under applicable principles of the law of fraudulent conveyances.

NOTES AND PROBLEMS

1. *Four different approaches.* As the court in Sawada v. Endo points out, various jurisdictions have taken various approaches regarding the effect of the Married Women's Property Acts on the tenancy by the entirety. Pushed by serious doubts

as to the constitutionality of unequal treatment of husband and wife in the common law tenancy by the entirety, and the modern movement to eradicate gender-based differences in the law, Massachusetts, Michigan, and North Carolina (the last three adherents to the classic tenancy by the entirety) have enacted legislation to give equal rights to husband and wife in a tenancy by the entirety. See Mass. Ann. Laws ch. 209, §§1, 1A (2012); Coraccio v. Lowell Five Cents Sav. Bank, 612 N.E.2d 650 (Mass. 1993) (interpreting statute to align Massachusetts with New York, except creditor of one spouse cannot seize and sell the couple's principal residence held by the entirety); see also Mich. Comp. Laws Ann. §557.71 (2012); N.C. Gen. Stat. §39-13.6 (2012) (aligning these states with the majority view).

These different approaches have important consequences for general creditors because a creditor can reach only such property as the debtor can voluntarily assign. In a majority of states a creditor of one spouse cannot reach a tenancy by the entirety because one spouse cannot assign his or her interest. Doubtless this exemption from creditors is one of the main reasons for the survival of the tenancy by the entirety. The tenancy serves to protect the family home as well as other property from transfer by one spouse and from creditors of one spouse. The tenancy by the entirety, where recognized, can be created in any amount of real property and, in many states, in any amount of personal property.

Sawada is discussed in Patricia A. Cain, Two Sisters vs. A Father and Two Sons: The Story of *Sawada v. Endo*, in Property Stories 99 (Gerald Korngold & Andrew P. Morriss eds. 2d ed. 2009).

For an insightful examination of the tenancy by the entirety, see John V. Orth, Reappraisals in the Law of Property 35-45 (2010).

2. *Taxes, taxes, taxes.* There is one creditor who can reach the interest of a debtor spouse in tenancy-by-the-entirety property: the IRS. In United States v. Craft, 535 U.S. 274 (2002), the United States Supreme Court held that a husband's interest in Michigan land that he and his wife owned as tenants by the entirety was "property" to which a federal tax lien could attach. The Court reached this result despite the fact that Michigan law bars creditors of one spouse from reaching any interest in tenancy-by-the-entirety property. The Court in *Craft* said that while state law delineates what rights a taxpayer has in property the government seeks to reach, federal law determines whether those rights qualify as property within the meaning of the federal tax lien statute. For a discussion, see Hanoch Dagan, The Craft of Property, 91 Cal. L. Rev. 1517 (2003).

Does *Craft* mean that the federal government can reach interests of one spouse in property owned as tenancy by the entirety under other federal statutes? In the past, courts have held that property owned by a bankrupt debtor in tenancy by the entirety is exempt from bankruptcy creditors if the debtor chooses the state law exemptions from creditors rather than the Bankruptcy Code exemptions and if applicable state law exempts the debtor spouse's interest. See In re Garner, 952 F.2d 232 (8th Cir. 1991). Does *Craft* change this result? At least one court has held that it does not. See Spears v. Boyd, 313 B.R. 212 (W.D. Mich. 2004) (limiting *Craft* to claims under federal tax liens; pre-*Craft* bankruptcy exemption rule applied).

Federal forfeiture law is another context in which arises the question whether tenancy-by-the-entirety property is reachable by the federal government. The Drug Abuse Prevention and Control Act provides for a civil forfeiture proceeding in rem. 21 U.S.C.A. §881. Upon proof that the property is used in an illegal drug transaction, the property itself is forfeited, except for any interest in an innocent owner. The act also provides (in §853) for criminal forfeiture of property by a person convicted of illegal drug activity. Each element of the criminal offense must be proved beyond a reasonable doubt. Criminal forfeiture is in personam; it is imposed as punishment and only the defendant's interest in the property is forfeited. The federal RICO statute also provides for criminal forfeiture of property used in dealing in drugs or acquired with funds from the activity. 18 U.S.C.A. §1963. Where a criminal defendant owns property as a joint tenant with an innocent party, federal criminal forfeiture will affect only the criminal defendant's interest. The balance of the cotenancy interest remains unaffected. See United States v. Pacheco, 393 F.3d 348 (2d Cir. 2004). Presumably, forfeiture effects a severance, and the innocent cotenant's interest is in tenancy in common.

The matter is more complicated in the case of tenants by the entirety, who do not hold by the share but only by the whole. In United States v. 1500 Lincoln Avenue, 949 F.2d 73 (3d Cir. 1991), *H* and *W* owned a pharmacy as tenants by the entirety. *H* illegally sold drugs out of the pharmacy. The federal government brought a civil forfeiture proceeding against him, conceding that *W* was an innocent owner. The question was whether part of the tenancy by the entirety is forfeited under these circumstances. If you begin by first defining the innocent co-owner's interest, *W*'s entire estate is protected, and *H* would forfeit nothing. On the other hand, if you begin by defining *H*'s interest first, then the government would take everything, leaving nothing for the innocent co-owner. The court held that the only forfeitable interest is *H*'s survivorship interest. That solution, the court said, best achieves the twin purposes of the statute, namely, to forfeit the guilty spouse's interest and to protect that of the innocent spouse.

In United States v. Lee, 232 F.3d 556 (7th Cir. 2000), Jack Lee was convicted of fraud and money laundering. The government sought to execute a forfeiture judgment against the home that he and his wife, Margaret, owned as tenants by the entirety. The court ruled against the government, distinguishing *1500 Lincoln Avenue* on the ground that the home had not been used for the husband's criminal activity, as the pharmacy had been. The court thought in such a case the innocent spouse deserved more protection.

Without the compelling need to seize unlawfully used property (or its derivatives), the interests of the innocent party become far more important. And from that perspective, it is plain that the Third Circuit's compromise substantially diminishes the innocent spouse's rights. In the hybrid arrangement that was approved in *1500 Lincoln Avenue*, Margaret would, as a practical matter, lose her right to control and manage the estate. The government would be Margaret Lee's co-tenant in a form of property ownership which requires both parties to participate in nearly every decision concerning the property. No mortgage would be possible without the signature of both tenants (since otherwise creditors would risk losing their entire investment at the death of one of the Lees). Margaret would need the government's approval to sell the property or to transfer the estate into a tenancy in common. Though she would be fully liable for taxes and other costs of homeownership in any tenancy by the entirety, in a normal tenancy by the entirety there would be a chance that her husband, also fully liable for the property, would contribute to those expenses. Because the government (as it admitted at oral argument) would not be there with its checkbook, she could do little more than sit by and hope that the estate would not fall into disrepair. We therefore conclude that the attributes of tenancy by the entirety recognized by Florida law here should not have been overridden by the district court, and the house should have been considered unavailable for a substitute asset order. [232 F.3d at 561-562.]

3. *H* and *W* owned their home in New York as tenants by the entirety. *H* abandoned *W*. *X*, a judgment creditor of *H*, levied on *H*'s interest in the dwelling and purchased it at execution sale. *X* demanded from *W* one-half the reasonable rental value of the house. *W* refused. What are *X*'s rights? See Lover v. Fennell, 179 N.Y.S.2d 1017 (Sup. Ct. 1958).

In New York, *X* steps into *H*'s shoes. Though the tenancy between *W* and *X* is labelled a "tenancy in common" (because a tenancy by the entirety can exist only between married persons), the rights of the parties are essentially the same as tenants by the entirety. Neither party can unilaterally sever the tenancy by partition. If *H* dies first, *W* owns the house free of *X*'s interest. If *W* dies first, *X* owns the house free of *W*'s interest. If *H* and *W* divorce, the tenancy becomes a tenancy in common in reality as well as in name, and *X*'s and *W*'s survivorship interests cease to exist. See V.R.W., Inc. v. Klein, 503 N.E.2d 496 (N.Y. 1986).

4. *Tenancy by the entirety in personalty.* At common law, a husband took title to all his wife's chattels and choses in action, and for this reason a tenancy by the entirety could not be created in personal property. Today many of the states recognizing the tenancy by the entirety permit it in personal as well as in real property.

Suppose that a jurisdiction recognizes the tenancy by the entirety only in real property. *H* and *W* own their home as tenants by the entirety. The house burns down, and *H* dies five days later. The insurance company is now ready to pay $100,000 on the policy insuring the house. To whom should the company pay the $100,000? See Regnante v. Baldassare, 448 N.E.2d 775 (Mass. App. 1983).

b. Termination of Marriage by Divorce

At common law, upon divorce property of the spouses remained the property of the spouse holding title. Property held by the spouses as tenants in common or as joint tenants remained in such co-ownership. Because the unity of marriage was severed by divorce, property held in tenancy by the entirety was converted into a tenancy in common. Inasmuch as the husband owed the wife a duty of support, a duty undertaken upon marriage, the wife was usually entitled to a continuation of support (called alimony), though it might be denied her if she was at fault.

The common law, then, placed great emphasis on the way title was held. Where the wage earner was the husband, probably most property other than the family home was held in the husband's name. The husband's wages (and what he bought with them) belonged to the husband unless he voluntarily made a gift to the wife. The common law largely ignored the wife's contribution of services in the home, although to some extent the wife was compensated by giving her continuing support in the form of alimony. Even considering rights to alimony and dower, the common law did not treat wives as (or even close to) equal partners with their husbands in the acquisition of assets during marriage.

In the last 30 years, dramatic changes have taken place in divorce law. Before 1970, divorce could be granted only if one party was found to have committed some marital fault, such as extreme cruelty or adultery. In 1970, California introduced no-fault divorce and in the years since, no-fault divorce has swept through the legislatures of almost every state. No-fault divorce brought with it changes in property division upon divorce. The common law division of property (according to how title is held) has been abrogated in every common law property state. Legislatures have replaced it with a rule of "equitable distribution." Under the rule of equitable distribution, property is divided by the court, in its discretion, on equitable principles. The concept of fault is sometimes expressly included, or ignored, or expressly excluded as a factor to guide equitable division.

Many equitable division statutes authorize a court to divide all property owned by the spouses, regardless of the time and manner of acquisition. Other statutes authorize a court to divide only "marital property." Marital property is defined in some states to include all property acquired during marriage by whatever means (earnings, gifts, or inheritances); in others it includes only property acquired from earnings of either spouse during marriage. This last approach is based on the principle underlying community property—that marriage is a partnership and property acquired from earnings of the spouses during marriage should be equally divided upon dissolution of the partnership.[20]

The idea that marriage involves a lifelong obligation of the husband to support the wife after divorce has also been discarded in modern divorce legislation. Alimony is largely viewed today as support for a limited period of time until the spouse can enter the job market and become self-sufficient (called "rehabilitative alimony").

In equitably dividing property, there is a movement toward equal distribution of marital property upon divorce. In some states equal division is required; in others it is only a presumptive rule.

In 2000, the American Law Institute adopted the Principles of the Law of Family Dissolution, which had been in gestation for more than ten years. This work is likely to be influential in firming up guidelines for equitable distribution. Professor Herma Hill Kay writes of the ALI Principles:

> The Principles are both imaginative and practical. The property division sections offer a redefinition of "marital" and "separate" property for use at dissolution that generally follows community property concepts. They steer a middle course between the "equitable division" and

---

20. On the community property system, which exists in 10 states, see pages 410-418.

"equal division" states by calling for a presumptive equal division of marital property subject to specified exceptions. They also provide for the gradual recharacterization in lengthy marriages of a portion of separate property into marital property.

"Maintenance" is renamed "Compensatory Spousal Payments" in the Principles and the draft draws on Professor Ira Mark Ellman's earlier work on alimony[21] in seeking to allocate financial losses that arise at the dissolution of marriage according to specified principles rather than simply basing income transfers on need and ability to pay. Five categories of compensable loss are recognized: (1) those arising from the loss of a higher living standard by the spouse with less wealth or earning capacity at the end of a marriage of significant duration; (2) those arising from the loss of earning capacity during marriage and continuing after dissolution because of one spouse's undertaking a disproportionate share of the care of children; (3) those arising from the loss of earning capacity during marriage and continuing after dissolution because of one spouse's caring for a sick, elderly, or disabled third party in fulfillment of a joint moral obligation; (4) those arising from the loss incurred by either spouse when the marriage is dissolved before that spouse "realizes a fair return from his or her investment in the other spouse's earning capacity"; and (5) an "unfairly disproportionate disparity between the spouses in their respective abilities to recover their pre-marital living standard after the dissolution of a short marriage." [Herma Hill Kay, From the Second Sex to the Joint Venture: An Overview of Women's Rights and Family Law in the United States During the Twentieth Century, 88 Cal. L. Rev. 2017, 2070 (2000).]

In re Marriage of Graham

Supreme Court of Colorado, 1978
574 P.2d 75

LEE, J. This case presents the novel question of whether in a marriage dissolution proceeding a master's degree in business administration (M.B.A.) constitutes marital property which is subject to division by the court. In its opinion in Graham v. Graham, Colo. App., 555 P.2d 527, the Colorado Court of Appeals held that it was not. We affirm the judgment.

The Uniform Dissolution of Marriage Act requires that a court shall divide marital property, without regard to marital misconduct, in such proportions as the court deems just after considering all relevant factors. The Act defines marital property as follows:

> For purposes of this article only, "marital property" means all property acquired by either spouse subsequent to the marriage except:
>
> (a) Property acquired by gift, bequest, devise, or descent;
> (b) Property acquired in exchange for property acquired prior to the marriage or in exchange for property acquired by gift, bequest, devise, or descent;
> (c) Property acquired by a spouse after a decree of legal separation; and
> (d) Property excluded by valid agreement of the parties. [Section 14-10-113(2), C.R.S. 1973.]

The parties to this proceeding were married on August 5, 1968, in Denver, Colorado. Throughout the six-year marriage, Anne P. Graham, wife and petitioner

---

21. See Ira Mark Ellman, The Theory of Alimony, 77 Cal. L. Rev. 1 (1989).

here, was employed full-time as an airline stewardess. She is still so employed. Her husband, Dennis J. Graham, respondent, worked part-time for most of the marriage, although his main pursuit was his education. He attended school for approximately three and one-half years of the marriage, acquiring both a bachelor of science degree in engineering physics and a master's degree in business administration at the University of Colorado. Following graduation, he obtained a job as an executive assistant with a large corporation at a starting salary of $14,000 per year.

The trial court determined that during the marriage petitioner contributed seventy percent of the financial support, which was used both for family expenses and for her husband's education. No marital assets were accumulated during the marriage. In addition, the Grahams together managed an apartment house and petitioner did the majority of housework and cooked most of the meals for the couple. No children were born during the marriage.

The parties jointly filed a petition for dissolution, on February 4, 1974, in Boulder County District Court. Petitioner did not make a claim for maintenance or for attorney fees. After a hearing on October 24, 1974, the trial court found, as a matter of law, that an education obtained by one spouse during a marriage is jointly-owned property to which the other spouse has a property right. The future earnings value of the M.B.A. to respondent was evaluated at $82,836 and petitioner was awarded $33,134 of this amount, payable in monthly installments of $100.[22]

The court of appeals reversed, holding that an education is not itself "property" subject to division under the Act, although it was one factor to be considered in determining maintenance or in arriving at an equitable property division.

I.

The purpose of the division of marital property is to allocate to each spouse what equitably belongs to him or her. See H. Clark, Domestic Relations §14.8. The division is committed to the sound discretion of the trial court and there is no rigid mathematical formula that the court must adhere to. Carlson v. Carlson, 178 Colo. 283, 497 P.2d 1006; Greer v. Greer, 32 Colo. App. 196, 510 P.2d 905. An appellate court will alter a division of property only if the trial court abuses its discretion. This court, however, is empowered at all times to interpret Colorado statutes.

---

22. The appellee's brief states that, at trial, an expert for the wife testified that an M.B.A. degree holder could expect to earn $178,000 more than the holder of a B.A. over his lifetime. The court discounted this to a present value of $82,836. The trial court awarded Anne 40 percent of $82,836, arrived at this way: Dennis pursued education 40 hours a week and worked part-time 20 hours a week, while Anne worked 40 hours a week. Thus Anne's contribution of the total time the couple invested in acquiring the M.B.A. degree was 40 percent. The trial court ordered Anne to be paid $33,134 over 27½ years at a rate of $100 a month. See Note, Graduate Degree Rejected as Marital Property Subject to Division Upon Divorce: *In re Marriage of Graham*, 11 Conn. L. Rev. 62, 65 n.12 (1978); Case Comment, 12 J. Marshall J. Prac. & Proc. 709, 713 n.27 (1979). Do you have any criticism of the trial court's valuation method?—EDS.

The legislature intended the term "property" to be broadly inclusive, as indicated by its use of the qualifying adjective "all" in section 14-10-113(2). Previous Colorado cases have given "property" a comprehensive meaning, as typified by the following definition: "In short it embraces anything and everything which may belong to a man and in the ownership of which he has a right to be protected by law." Las Animas County High School District v. Raye, 144 Colo. 367, 356 P.2d 237.

Nonetheless, there are necessary limits upon what may be considered "property," and we do not find any indication in the Act that the concept as used by the legislature is other than that usually understood to be embodied within the term. One helpful definition is "everything that has an exchangeable value or which goes to make up wealth or estate." Black's Law Dictionary 1382 (rev. 4th ed. 1968). In Ellis v. Ellis, Colo., 552 P.2d 506, this court held that military retirement pay was not property for the reason that it did not have any of the elements of cash surrender value, loan value, redemption value, lump sum value, or value realizable after death. The court of appeals has considered other factors as well in deciding whether something falls within the concept, particularly whether it can be assigned, sold, transferred, conveyed, or pledged, or whether it terminates on the death of the owner. In re Marriage of Ellis, 36 Colo. App. 234, 538 P.2d 1347, aff'd, Ellis v. Ellis, supra.

An educational degree, such as an M.B.A., is simply not encompassed even by the broad views of the concept of "property." It does not have an exchange value or any objective transferable value on an open market. It is personal to the holder. It terminates on death of the holder and is not inheritable. It cannot be assigned, sold, transferred, conveyed, or pledged. An advanced degree is a cumulative product of many years of previous education, combined with diligence and hard work. It may not be acquired by the mere expenditure of money. It is simply an intellectual achievement that may potentially assist in the future acquisition of property. In our view, it has none of the attributes of property in the usual sense of that term.

II.

Our interpretation is in accord with cases in other jurisdictions. We have been unable to find any decision, even in community property states, which appears to have held that an education of one spouse is marital property to be divided on dissolution. This contention was dismissed in Todd v. Todd, 272 Cal. App. 2d 786, 78 Cal. Rptr. 131 (Ct. App.), where it was held that a law degree is not a community property asset capable of division, partly because it "cannot have monetary value placed upon it." Similarly, it has been recently held that a person's earning capacity, even where enhanced by a law degree financed by the other spouse, "should not be recognized as a separate, particular item of property." Stern v. Stern, 66 N.J. 340, 331 A.2d 257.

Other cases cited have dealt only with related issues. For example, in awarding alimony, as opposed to dividing property, one court has found that an education is one factor to be considered. Daniels v. Daniels, 20 Ohio Op. 2d 458, 185

N.E.2d 773 (Ct. App.). In another case, the wife supported the husband while he went to medical school. Nail v. Nail, 486 S.W.2d 761 (Tex.). The question was whether the accrued goodwill of his medical practice was marital property, and the court held it was not, inasmuch as goodwill was based on the husband's personal skill, reputation, and experience. Contra, Mueller v. Mueller, 144 Cal. App. 2d 245, 301 P.2d 90; see Annot., 52 A.L.R.3d 1344.

III.

The trial court relied on Greer v. Greer, 32 Colo. App. 196, 510 P.2d 905, for its determination that an education is "property." In that case, a six-year marriage was dissolved in which the wife worked as a teacher while the husband obtained a medical degree. The parties had accumulated marital property. The trial court awarded the wife alimony of $150 per month for four years. The court of appeals found this to be proper, whether considered as an adjustment of property rights based upon the wife's financial contribution to the marriage, or as an award of alimony in gross. The court there stated that ". . . [i]t must be considered as a substitute for, or in lieu of, the wife's rights in the husband's property. . . ." We note that the court did not determine that the medical education itself was divisible property. The case is distinguishable from the instant case in that here there was no accumulation of marital property and the petitioner did not seek maintenance [alimony].

IV.

A spouse who provides financial support while the other spouse acquires an education is not without a remedy. Where there is marital property to be divided, such contribution to the education of the other spouse may be taken into consideration by the court. Greer v. Greer, supra. See also Carlson v. Carlson, 178 Colo. 283, 497 P.2d 1006. Here, we again note that no marital property had been accumulated by the parties. Further, if maintenance is sought and a need is demonstrated, the trial court may make an award based on all relevant factors. Section 14-10-114(2). Certainly, among the relevant factors to be considered is the contribution of the spouse seeking maintenance to the education of the other spouse from whom the maintenance is sought. Again, we note that in this case petitioner sought no maintenance from respondent.

The judgment is affirmed.

CARRIGAN, J. I respectfully dissent.

As a matter of economic reality the most valuable asset acquired by either party during this six-year marriage was the husband's increased earning capacity. There is no dispute that this asset resulted from his having obtained Bachelor of Science and Master of Business Administration degrees while married. These degrees, in turn, resulted in large part from the wife's employment which contributed about

70% of the couple's total income. Her earnings not only provided her husband's support but also were "invested" in his education in the sense that she assumed the role of breadwinner so that he would have the time and funds necessary to obtain his education.

The case presents the not-unfamiliar pattern of the wife who, willing to sacrifice for a more secure family financial future, works to educate her husband, only to be awarded a divorce decree shortly after he is awarded his degree. The issue here is whether traditional, narrow concepts of what constitutes "property" render the courts impotent to provide a remedy for an obvious injustice.

In cases such as this, equity demands that courts seek extraordinary remedies to prevent extraordinary injustice. If the parties had remained married long enough after the husband had completed his postgraduate education so that they could have accumulated substantial property, there would have been no problem. In that situation abundant precedent authorized the trial court, in determining how much of the marital property to allocate to the wife, to take into account her contributions to her husband's earning capacity. Greer v. Greer, 32 Colo. App. 196, 510 P.2d 905 (1973) (wife supported husband through medical school); In re Marriage of Vanet, 544 S.W.2d 236 (Mo. App. 1976) (wife was breadwinner while husband was in law school).

A husband's future income earning potential, sometimes as indicated by the goodwill value of a professional practice, may be considered in deciding property division or alimony matters, and the wife's award may be increased on the ground that the husband probably will have substantial future earnings. Todd v. Todd, 272 Cal. App. 2d 786, 78 Cal. Rptr. 131 (1969) (goodwill of husband's law practice); Golden v. Golden, 270 Cal. App. 2d 401, 75 Cal. Rptr. 735 (1969) (goodwill of husband's medical practice); Mueller v. Mueller, 144 Cal. App. 2d 245, 301 P.2d 90 (1956) (goodwill of husband's dental lab); In re Marriage of Goger, 27 Or. App. 729, 557 P.2d 46 (1976) (potential earnings of husband's dental practice); In re Marriage of Lukens, 16 Wash. App. 481, 558 P.2d 279 (1976) (goodwill of husband's medical practice indicated future earning capacity).

Similarly, the wife's contributions to enhancing the husband's financial status or earning capacity have been considered in awarding alimony and maintenance. Kraus v. Kraus, 159 Colo. 331, 411 P.2d 240 (1966); Shapiro v. Shapiro, 115 Colo. 505, 176 P.2d 363 (1946). The majority opinion emphasizes that in this case no maintenance was requested. However, the Colorado statute would seem to preclude an award of maintenance here, for it restricts the court's power to award maintenance to cases where the spouse seeking it is unable to support himself or herself. Section 14-10-114, C.R.S. 1973.[23]

While the majority opinion focuses on whether the husband's master's degree is marital "property" subject to division, it is not the degree itself which

---

23. Colo. Rev. Stat. §14-10-114(3) (2012) provides that in a proceeding for dissolution of marriage, the court may grant a maintenance order for either spouse only if it finds that the spouse seeking maintenance:

(a) Lacks sufficient property, including marital property apportioned to him, to provide for his reasonable needs; and

constitutes the asset in question. Rather it is the increase in the husband's earning power concomitant to that degree which is the asset conferred on him by his wife's efforts. That increased earning capacity was the asset appraised in the economist's expert opinion testimony as having a discounted present value of $82,000.

Unquestionably the law, in other contexts, recognizes future earning capacity as an asset whose wrongful deprivation is compensable. Thus one who tortiously destroys or impairs another's future earning capacity must pay as damages the amount the injured party has lost in anticipated future earnings. Nemer v. Anderson, 151 Colo. 411, 378 P.2d 841 (1963); Abram, Personal Injury Damages in Colorado, 35 Colo. L. Rev. 332, 338 (1963).

Where a husband is killed, the widow is entitled to recover for loss of his future support damages based in part on the present value of his anticipated future earnings, which may be computed by taking into account probable future increases in his earning capacity. See United States v. Sommers, 351 F.2d 354 (10th Cir. 1965); Good v. Chance, 39 Colo. App. 70, 565 P.2d 217 (1977).

The day before the divorce the wife had a legally recognized interest in her husband's earning capacity. Perhaps the wife might have a remedy in a separate action based on implied debt, quasi-contract, unjust enrichment, or some similar theory. See, e.g., Dass v. Epplen, 162 Colo. 60, 424 P.2d 779 (1967). Nevertheless, the law favors settling all aspects of a dispute in a single action where that is possible. Therefore I would affirm the trial court's award.

NOTES

1. *A different approach.* In Mahoney v. Mahoney, 453 A.2d 527 (N.J. 1982), the New Jersey court declined to recognize a professional degree as marital property. It found such an item too speculative to value. In addition, the court thought the idea of a spousal investment in human capital demeaned the concept of marriage. Instead, the court ordered that the working spouse be given "reimbursement alimony."

> To provide a fair and effective means of compensating a supporting spouse who has suffered a loss or reduction of support, or has incurred a lower standard of living, or has been deprived of a better standard of living in the future, the Court now introduces the concept of reimbursement alimony into divorce proceedings. The concept properly accords with the Court's belief that regardless of the appropriateness of permanent alimony or the presence or absence of marital property to be equitably distributed, there will be circumstances where a supporting spouse should be reimbursed for the financial contributions he or she made to the spouse's successful professional training. Such reimbursement alimony should cover *all* financial contributions towards the former spouse's education, including household expenses,

---

(b) Is unable to support himself through appropriate employment or is the custodian of a child whose condition or circumstances make it appropriate that the custodian not be required to seek employment outside the home.

Uniform Marriage and Divorce Act §308(a) is substantially identical. —EDS.

educational costs, school travel expenses and any other contributions used by the supported spouse in obtaining his or her degree or license . . . .

2. *The New York approach.* Almost all courts that have ruled on the issue agree with either *Graham* or *Mahoney.* New York is one of the exceptions. In O'Brien v. O'Brien, 489 N.E.2d 712 (N.Y. 1985), the court held that a husband's medical license constituted marital property within the meaning of the state's equitable distribution law. For an interesting discussion of *O'Brien,* see Ira Mark Ellman, *O'Brien v. O'Brien*: A Failed Reform, Unlikely Reformers, 27 Pace L. Rev. 949 (2007).

3. For more discussion, see Carolyn J. Frantz & Hanoch Dagan, Properties of Marriage, 104 Colum. L. Rev. 75, 106-112 (2004); Stewart E. Sterk, Restraints on Alienation of Human Capital, 79 Va. L. Rev. 383, 433-444 (1993); Erik V. Wicks, Professional Degree Divorces: Of Equity Positions, Equitable Distributions, and Clean Breaks, 45 Wayne L. Rev. 1975 (2000).

Elkus v. Elkus

Supreme Court of New York, Appellate Division, 1991
572 N.Y.S.2d 901

ROSENBERGER, J. In this matrimonial action, the plaintiff, Frederica von Stade Elkus, moved for an order determining, prior to trial, whether her career and/or celebrity status constituted marital property subject to equitable distribution. The parties have already stipulated to mutual judgments of divorce terminating their seventeen year marriage and to joint custody of their two minor children. The trial on the remaining economic issues has been stayed pending the outcome of this appeal from the order of the Supreme Court, which had determined that the enhanced value of the plaintiff's career and/or celebrity status was not marital property subject to equitable distribution. Contrary to the conclusion reached by the Supreme Court, we find that to the extent the defendant's contributions and efforts led to an increase in the value of the plaintiff's career, this appreciation was a product of the marital partnership, and, therefore, marital property subject to equitable distribution.

At the time of her marriage to the defendant on February 9, 1973, the plaintiff had just embarked on her career, performing minor roles with the Metropolitan Opera Company. During the course of the marriage, the plaintiff's career succeeded dramatically and her income rose accordingly. In the first year of the marriage, she earned $2,250. In 1989, she earned $621,878. She is now a celebrated artist with the Metropolitan Opera, as well as an international recording artist, concert and television performer. She has garnered numerous awards, and has performed for the President of the United States.

During the marriage, the defendant travelled with the plaintiff throughout the world, attending and critiquing her performances and rehearsals, and photographed her for album covers and magazine articles. The defendant was also the plaintiff's voice coach and teacher for ten years of the marriage. He states that he sacrificed his own career as a singer and teacher to devote himself to the plaintiff's career and to the lives of their young children, and that his efforts enabled the plaintiff to become one of the most celebrated opera singers in the world. Since the plaintiff's career and/or celebrity status increased in value during the marriage due in part to his contributions, the defendant contends that he is entitled to equitable distribution of this marital property.

The Supreme Court disagreed, refusing to extend the holding in O'Brien v. O'Brien, 66 N.Y.2d 576, 498 N.Y.S.2d 743, 489 N.E.2d 712, in which the Court of Appeals determined that a medical license constituted marital property subject to equitable distribution, to the plaintiff's career as an opera singer. The court found that since the defendant enjoyed a substantial life style during the marriage and since he would be sufficiently compensated through distribution of the parties' other assets, the plaintiff's career was not marital property.

There is a paucity of case law and no appellate authority in New York governing the issue of whether a career as a performing artist, and its accompanying celebrity status, constitute marital property subject to equitable distribution. The plaintiff maintains that since her career and celebrity status are not licensed, are not entities which are owned like a business, nor are protected interests which are subject to due process of law, they are not marital property. In our view, neither the Domestic Relations Law, nor relevant case law, allows for such a limited interpretation of the term marital property.

Domestic Relations Law §236[B][1][c] broadly defines marital property as property acquired during the marriage "regardless of the form in which title is held." In enacting the Equitable Distribution Law (L. 1980, ch. 281, §9), the Legislature created a radical change in the traditional method of distributing property upon the dissolution of a marriage (Price v. Price, 69 N.Y.2d 8, 14, 511 N.Y.S.2d 219, 503 N.E.2d 684). By broadly defining the term "marital property," it intended to give effect to the "economic partnership" concept of the marriage relationship (id. at 15, 511 N.Y.S.2d 219, 503 N.E.2d 684; Majauskas v. Majauskas, 61 N.Y.2d 481, 474 N.Y.S.2d 699, 463 N.E.2d 15). It then left it to the courts to determine what interests constitute marital property.

Things of value acquired during marriage are marital property even though they may fall outside the scope of traditional property concepts (O'Brien v. O'Brien, supra; Florescue, "Market Value," Professional Licenses and Marital Property: A Dilemma in Search of a Horn, 1982 N.Y. St. B.A. Fam. L. Rev. 13 (Dec.)). The statutory definition of marital property does not mandate that it be an asset with an exchange value or be salable, assignable or transferable. (Freed, Brandes and Weidman, "What is Marital Property?," NYLJ, December 5, 1990, p. 3, col. 1.) The property may be tangible or intangible (Id.).

Medical licenses have been held to enhance the earning capacity of their holders, so as to enable the other spouse who made direct or indirect contributions to their acquisition, to share their value as part of equitable distribution (O'Brien v. O'Brien, supra; Maloney v. Maloney, 137 A.D.2d 666, 524 N.Y.S.2d 758; Raff v. Raff, 120 A.D.2d 507, 501 N.Y.S.2d 707). A Medical Board Certification

(Savasta v. Savasta, 146 Misc. 2d 101, 549 N.Y.S.2d 544 (Sup. Ct. Nassau Co.)), a law degree (Cronin v. Cronin, 131 Misc. 2d 879, 502 N.Y.S.2d 368 (Sup. Ct. Nassau Co.)), an accounting degree (Vanasco v. Vanasco, 132 Misc. 2d 227, 503 N.Y.S.2d 480 (Sup. Ct. Nassau Co.)), a podiatry practice (Morton v. Morton, 130 A.D.2d 558, 515 N.Y.S.2d 499), the licensing and certification of a physician's assistant (Morimando v. Morimando, 145 A.D.2d 609, 536 N.Y.S.2d 701), a Masters degree in teaching (McGowan v. McGowan, 142 A.D.2d 355, 535 N.Y.S.2d 990) and a fellowship in the Society of Actuaries (McAlpine v. McAlpine, 143 Misc. 2d 30, 539 N.Y.S.2d 680 (Sup. Ct. Suffolk Co.)) have also been held to constitute marital property.

Although the plaintiff's career, unlike that of the husband in *O'Brien*, is not licensed, the *O'Brien* court did not restrict its holding to professions requiring a license or degree. In reaching its conclusion that a medical license constitutes marital property, the *O'Brien* court referred to the language contained in Domestic Relations Law §236 which provides that in making an equitable distribution of marital property,

> the court shall consider: . . . (6) any equitable claim to, interest in, or direct or indirect contribution made to the acquisition of such marital property by the party not having title, including joint efforts or expenditures and contributions and services as a spouse, parent, wage earner and homemaker, and *to the career or career potential* of the other party [and] (9) the impossibility or difficulty of evaluating any component asset or any interest in a business, corporation or profession (Domestic Relations Law §236[B][5][d][6], [9]) (emphasis added).

The court also cited §236[B][5][e] which provides that where equitable distribution of marital property is appropriate, but "the distribution of an interest in a business, corporation or profession would be contrary to law," the court shall make a distributive award in lieu of an actual distribution of the property (O'Brien v. O'Brien, supra, 66 N.Y.2d at 584).

The Court of Appeals' analysis of the statute is equally applicable here. "The words mean exactly what they say: that an interest in a profession or professional career potential is marital property which may be represented by direct or indirect contributions of the non-title-holding spouse, including financial contributions and nonfinancial contributions made by caring for the home and family" (Id.) Nothing in the statute or the *O'Brien* decision supports the plaintiff's contention that her career and/or celebrity status are not marital property. The purpose behind the enactment of the legislation was to prevent inequities which previously occurred upon the dissolution of a marriage. Any attempt to limit marital property to professions which are licensed would only serve to discriminate against the spouses of those engaged in other areas of employment. Such a distinction would fail to carry out the premise upon which equitable distribution is based, i.e., that a marriage is an economic partnership to which both parties contribute, as spouse, parent, wage earner or homemaker (Assembly Memorandum, 1980 N.Y. Legis. Ann., at 130; Governor's Memorandum of Approval, 1980 McKinney's Session Laws of N.Y., at 1863; O'Brien v. O'Brien, supra at 585).

In Golub v. Golub, 139 Misc. 2d 440, 527 N.Y.S.2d 946 (Sup. Ct. New York Co.), the Supreme Court agreed with the defendant husband that the increase in value in the acting and modeling career of his wife, Marisa Berenson, was marital property subject to equitable distribution as a result of his contributions thereto. Like Ms. von Stade, Ms. Berenson claimed that since her celebrity status was neither "professional" nor a "license," and, since her show business career was subject to fluctuation, it should not be considered "marital property."

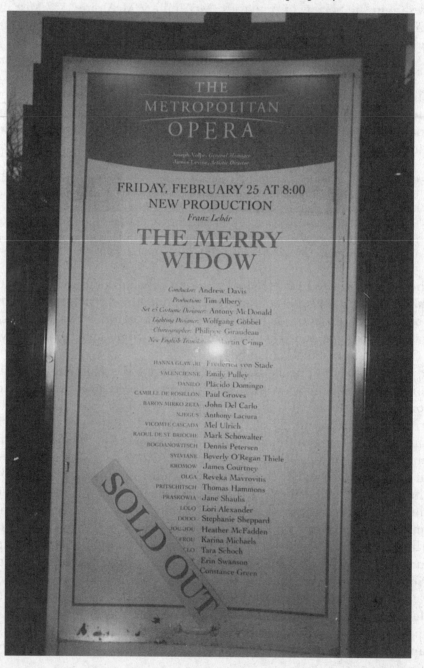

Frederica von Stade sells out the Met in 2000.

The court disagreed, concluding at p. 447, 527 N.Y.S.2d 946 that "the skills of an artisan, actor, professional athlete or any person whose expertise in his or her career has enabled him or her to become an exceptional wage earner should be valued as marital property subject to equitable distribution." (See, also, Getz v. Getz, NYLJ, March 2, 1989, p. 28, col. 6 [Sup. Ct. Westchester Co.].) As the *Golub* court found, it is the enhanced earning capacity that a medical license affords its holder that the *O'Brien* court deemed valuable, not the document itself. There is no rational basis upon which to distinguish between a degree, a license, or any other special skill that generates substantial income.

As further noted by the *Golub* court, there is tremendous potential for financial gain from the commercial exploitation of famous personalities. While the plaintiff insists that she will never be asked to endorse a product, this is simply speculation. More and more opportunities have presented themselves to her as she continues to advance in her career. The career of the plaintiff is unique, in that she has risen to the top in a field where success is rarely achieved.

Like the parties here, after Joe Piscopo and his wife married in 1973, they focused on one goal—the facilitation of his rise to stardom (Piscopo v. Piscopo, 231 N.J. Super. 576, 555 A.2d 1190, aff'd, 232 N.J. Super. 559, 557 A.2d 1040, certification denied, 117 N.J. 156, 564 A.2d 875). The defendant wife claimed that her husband's celebrity goodwill was a distributable asset and that she was entitled to a share in his excess earning capacity to which she contributed as homemaker, caretaker of their child, and sounding board for his artistic ideas.

Rejecting Mr. Piscopo's argument that celebrity goodwill is distinguishable from professional goodwill since professional goodwill had educational and regulatory requirements while celebrity goodwill requires ineffable talent, the court held that "it is the person with particular and uncommon aptitude for some specialized discipline whether law, medicine or entertainment that transforms the average professional or entertainer into one with measurable goodwill" (Piscopo v. Piscopo, supra at 555 A.2d 1191). We agree with the courts that have considered the issue, that the enhanced skills of an artist such as the plaintiff, albeit growing from an innate talent, which have enabled her to become an exceptional earner, may be valued as marital property subject to equitable distribution.

The plaintiff additionally contends that her career is not marital property because she had already become successful prior to her marriage to the defendant. As noted, supra, during the first year of marriage, the plaintiff earned $2,250. By 1989, her earnings had increased more than 275 fold. Further, in Price v. Price, supra, 69 N.Y.2d at 11, 511 N.Y.S.2d 219, 503 N.E.2d 684, the Court of Appeals held that

> under the Equitable Distribution Law an increase in the value of separate property of one spouse, occurring during the marriage and prior to the commencement of matrimonial proceedings, which is due in part to the indirect contributions or efforts of the other spouse as homemaker and parent, should be considered marital property (Domestic Relations Law §236[B][1][d][3]).

In this case, it cannot be overlooked that the defendant's contributions to plaintiff's career were direct and concrete, going far beyond child care and the like, which he also provided.

While it is true that the plaintiff was born with talent, and, while she had already been hired by the Metropolitan Opera at the time of her marriage to the defendant, her career, at this time, was only in the initial stages of development. During the course of the marriage, the defendant's active involvement in the plaintiff's career, in teaching, coaching, and critiquing her, as well as in caring for their children, clearly contributed to the increase in its value. Accordingly, to the extent the appreciation in the plaintiff's career was due to the defendant's efforts and contributions, this appreciation constitutes marital property.

In sum, we find that it is the nature and extent of the contribution by the spouse seeking equitable distribution, rather than the nature of the career, whether licensed or otherwise, that should determine the status of the enterprise as marital property. . . .

Accordingly, the order of the Supreme Court, New York County, entered September 26, 1990, which determined that the plaintiff's career and/or celebrity status was not "marital property" subject to equitable distribution, should be reversed, on the law, without costs, and the matter should be remitted to the Supreme Court for further proceedings.

All concur.

J. Thomas Oldham, Putting Asunder in the 1990s
80 Cal. L. Rev. 1091, 1121 (1992)

Could we keep the current system and add a new dimension for human capital accumulations during marriage? This is what New York state appears to be doing. Note, however, that this "double counts" wages earned by an employee, if (as is quite likely) the employee remarries. For example, in New York, one spouse may earn a medical degree during marriage. Upon divorce, the degree is included in the marital estate and its value is determined by the increased lifetime earning capacity that will be generated by that degree. If the educated spouse then remarries, the wages generated by the degree during the second marriage will be included in the second marital estate: no deduction is received for the amount included in the first marital estate. Under normal marital-partnership theory, property is deemed earned only once. As an illustration, assume that an employee works for forty years, during which time he has two twenty-year marriages. Half of the accumulated pension rights will be deemed part of the marital estate of the first marriage, and half will be part of the second marital estate. Similarly, if a lawyer-spouse works on a contingent fee case during the first marriage and settles the case during the second marriage, most courts would apportion the fee between both marriages in some manner, such as the relative amount of time spent on the case during the two marriages. By treating professional degrees and licenses earned during marriage as marital property, and by valuing the degree in terms of the lifetime earning capacity of the spouse, the New York system counts a professional's accumulations twice.

NOTES

1. *Professional goodwill.* Professional goodwill is a divisible marital asset in most jurisdictions, even in those that do not treat enhanced earning capacity from a professional degree as a marital asset subject to equitable distribution. In Dugan v. Dugan, 457 A.2d 1 (N.J. 1983), the court defined goodwill as "essentially reputation that will probably generate future business" and said:

> . . . [Goodwill] does not exist at the time professional qualifications and a license to practice are obtained. A good reputation is earned after accomplishment and performance. Field testing is an essential ingredient before goodwill comes into being. Future earning capacity per se is not goodwill. However, when that future earning capacity has been enhanced because reputation leads to probable future patronage from existing and potential clients, goodwill may exist and have value. When that occurs the resulting goodwill is property subject to equitable distribution. [457 A.2d at 6.]

See Grace G. Blumberg, Identifying and Valuing Goodwill at Divorce, 56 Law & Contemp. Probs. 217 (1993) (arguing celebrity goodwill generally is difficult to value, though some can be valued).

2. *Prenuptial agreements.* It is highly likely that before her second marriage Frederica von Stade entered into a prenuptial agreement with her prospective spouse. Such agreements are generally enforceable, provided the agreement is fair and reasonable *or*—or perhaps *and*—it is based upon full knowledge of each other's property. States have different standards for evaluating the enforceability of prenuptial agreements, and we leave this topic for you to study in courses on Trusts and Estates or Family Law.

c. Termination of Marriage by Death of One Spouse

(1) Common Law

The surviving spouse's rights at English common law reflected the desires of the landed class. Land should stay in the patriarchal family, but surviving spouses should be supported for their lives. The law accommodated these desires by the institutions of dower and curtesy.

With respect to personal property, the common law gave a surviving widow one-third if there were surviving issue and one-half otherwise.[24] A surviving widower took all his wife's personal property absolutely.

---

24. An exception was made for heirlooms, which were chattels that, by ancient custom, descended to the primogenitary heir under the rules applicable to real property. Heirlooms did not pass to the surviving spouse and the other children; nor could they be separated from the land by will. Heirlooms included the crown

Dower. Dower originally was a gift made by the bridegroom to the bride at the wedding; hence the importance of including in the marriage ceremony the words, "With all my worldly goods I thee endow." As time would have it, dower became fixed by law and was granted regardless of what was said at the wedding. The law gave dower to a surviving wife in all *freehold land of which her husband was seised during marriage and that was inheritable by the issue of husband and wife.* Thus any land owned in fee simple by the husband alone or as a tenant in common during marriage was subject to dower. Dower was a life estate in one-third of each parcel of qualifying land. In a feudal society that looked upon land as the resource to support a military state, dower was a generous concession to the widow of a rich man. But to the widow of a man who owned only a home and no farm acreage, dower (one-third for life) was small protection indeed.

Dower attaches to land at the moment of marriage, if the land is then owned, or thereafter when the land is acquired. It is "inchoate" until the husband dies. If the wife predeceases the husband, or they are divorced, her inchoate dower is extinguished. If she survives the husband, the wife becomes entitled to her dower in possession. After inchoate dower has attached, the husband is powerless to defeat it. Any purchaser from, or creditor of, the husband takes subject to it, unless the wife releases her dower.

Curtesy. At his wife's prior death, a widower was, at common law, entitled to a life estate in each piece of the wife's real property if certain conditions were fulfilled. This was known as curtesy or, more fully, an estate by the Curtesy of England. Curtesy, like dower, attached to all freehold land of which the wife was seised during marriage and that was inheritable by the issue of husband and wife. Unlike dower, however, curtesy did not attach to land unless issue of the marriage capable of inheriting the estate were born alive.

Dower and curtesy have been abolished in all but four American jurisdictions. In three of these, curtesy has been abolished and dower has been extended to husbands. Ark. Code Ann. §28-11-301 (2012); Ky. Rev. Stat. §§392.020, 392.080 (2012); Ohio Rev. Code Ann. §2103.02 (2012). In Michigan, curtesy has been abolished, but dower is still given to wives. Mich. Comp. Laws §558.1 (2012). The Michigan Court of Appeals has affirmed the constitutional validity of this dower statute. See In re Miltenberger Estate, 737 N.W.2d 513 (Mich. App. 2007), appeal granted, 741 N.W.2d 835 (Mich.), order granting leave to appeal vacated, 753 N.W.2d 219 (Mich. 2007). But see Boan v. Watson, 316 S.E.2d 401 (S.C. 1984), striking down a similar statute as violative of the Equal Protection Clause. In Iowa, dower has been replaced by a fractional fee simple interest in the decedent's lands owned during marriage. Iowa Code Ann. §§633.212, 633.238 (2012). In

---

jewels, title deeds, and, in some localities, the best bed. Co. Litt. 18b (1628). The evidence indicates that in Warwickshire, where Shakespeare lived, the best bed was an heirloom, going with the house to the new head of family. Hence Shakespeare, devising his house to his elder daughter Susanna, could, and did, bequeath only his second-best bed to his wife. See Robert Megarry & H.W.R. Wade, The Law of Real Property 547 (5th ed. 1984); O. Hood Phillips, Shakespeare and the Lawyers 16 (1972).

North Carolina dower has been abolished, but a ghost of it survives in the form of an elective share. N.C. Gen. Stat. §§29-4, 29-30 (2012).

The important consequence of dower in modern times is that both husband and wife must sign deeds to land to release dower, even though title is in only one of them.

PROBLEMS

1. During *O*'s marriage to *W*, *O* conveys Blackacre to *A* and *B* as joint tenants.

(a) *O* dies. Is *O*'s widow, *W*, entitled to dower?

(b) Suppose that *A* dies survived by his wife, *X*. Does *X* have a right to dower in Blackacre?

(c) *A* conveys his interest in Blackacre to *C*. *A* dies survived by his wife, *X*, who did not join in the deed to *C*. Is *X* entitled to dower in Blackacre? If *C* dies, is *C*'s widow, *Y*, entitled to dower in Blackacre?

2. *H* desires to purchase Brownacre. He wants to be able to deal with the property after the purchase without any interference from his wife. In what way should he take title to Brownacre in a jurisdiction that has common law dower?

(2)   The Modern Elective Share

After the Civil War, with the great growth in wealth in personal property (principally stocks and bonds) and the rise of a large class of urban renters, it appeared that dower and curtesy were no longer effective to protect the surviving spouse. Legislatures began to enact so-called forced share legislation, giving the surviving spouse an elective share in all property—real and personal—that the decedent spouse owned at death. The surviving spouse is not entitled only to support, as dower and curtesy provided, but to an ownership share in the decedent spouse's property. This is a form of deferred community property; one spouse does not receive a property interest in the other spouse's property during marriage, but only at the other spouse's death.

All common law property states except Georgia have elective-share statutes.[25] Under the conventional type of elective-share statute, the surviving spouse can renounce the will, if any, and elect to take a statutory share, which is usually one-half or one-third or some other fractional share.[26] By contrast, under the

---

25. Some states now have statutes providing inheritance, including elective share, rights for same-sex partners. See the discussion on page 439.

26. A spouse has a claim to a forced share whether married to the decedent for one hour or 50 years. In *Estate of Neiderhiser*, 2 Pa. D. & C.3d 302, 59 Westmoreland County L.J. 60 (1977), these facts occurred at the wedding ceremony. The groom answered "I will" to the question, "Wilt thou have this woman to be thy wife, etc."; the bride answered affirmatively to a similar question; the groom then placed a ring on the bride's finger, saying "With this ring I thee wed, In the name of the Father, and of the Son, and of the Holy Spirit. Amen." The minister began to pray and, during the prayer, the groom dropped dead; whereupon the minister cut the

Uniform Probate Code the surviving spouse is entitled to keep any property that the will devised to him or her. The value of such property is credited against the elective-share amount. See Uniform Probate Code §§2-204, 2-209 (2012). States retaining dower give the surviving spouse the right to elect dower or a statutory forced share; the statutory share is usually larger.

The elective share ordinarily applies only to property that the decedent spouse owns at death. The elective share usually does not apply to property held by the decedent and another in joint tenancy nor to life insurance proceeds. The elective share can be defeated by lifetime gifts of property, but a word of caution is appropriate here. Courts and statutes in many states permit the surviving spouse to set aside gifts made with the intent to defeat the elective share, or transfers when the donor spouse retained control (for example, a revocable trust). The law on this is subject to considerable variation from state to state. See Thomas P. Gallanis, Family Property Law: Wills, Trusts, and Future Interests 349-366 (5th ed. 2011).

For comprehensive discussion of dower and the modern elective share, see Ralph C. Brashier, Disinheritance and the Modern Family, 45 Case W. Res. L. Rev. 84, 89-113 (1994).

PROBLEM

H dies in a state that gives the surviving spouse an elective share of one-half of the decedent's property passing by will or intestacy. During his life *H* took out a life insurance policy in the face amount of $60,000 payable to *W*. *H* and *W* also bought a house, worth $60,000 at *H*'s death, and took title as joint tenants. *H* dies owning Blackacre worth $90,000, stocks and bonds worth $20,000, and a $10,000 savings account. *H*'s will bequeaths all his estate to his daughter by a first marriage, *D*. How is *H*'s estate distributed?

If you were advising *H* before he died, how would you advise him to carry out his wishes?

2. The Community Property System

a. Introduction

Eight states—Arizona, California, Idaho, Louisiana, Nevada, New Mexico, Texas, and Washington—have long had a system of community property traceable to French or Spanish influence among the early settlers in the South

---

ceremony short and pronounced the groom and bride man and wife. The court held that marriage is a contract and the contract becomes binding at the moment the couple exchange their vows (by saying "I will"); the subsequent pronouncement of the minister that they are man and wife is merely recognition of the marriage in a solemn way. The bride—made widow at her wedding—was entitled to a forced share in her husband's estate.

and West. Two states, Wisconsin and Alaska, have since joined them. In 1984 Wisconsin enacted the Uniform Marital Property Act, promulgated in 1983. Wis. Stat. Ann. §766.001 (2012). This act adopted community property principles, but avoided the term "community property" and used "marital property" instead. So Wisconsin must now be considered a community property state.[27] In 1998, Alaska enacted a statute providing that spouses may agree to hold their property as community. Alaska Stat. §34-77-030 (2012). Hence Alaska is now an "elective" community property state. Permitting couples to elect community property seems a sensible idea and is followed in many countries.

In Mexico and some European countries, spouses must elect at the time of marriage how they will hold their property. Three property regimes are usually available. They may choose (1) to hold all their property in separate ownership (as under the American common law system); (2) to hold property acquired from earnings as community property, and inherited property as separate property (the American community property system); or (3) to hold all their property from whatever source as community property (universal community property). A variation on the separate property option might include a provision that the surviving spouse takes a share of the decedent's property upon his or her death. Since the existence of optional marital property regimes within one foreign jurisdiction does not seem to have caused substantial difficulties, one wonders why married couples in the common law property states in this country are not given similar options.[28]

Although there are substantial differences in details among the community property states, the fundamental idea of community property is that *earnings* of each spouse during marriage should be owned equally in undivided shares by both spouses. For example, if the husband earns $1,000, one-half belongs to the wife. If the husband subsequently buys 10 shares of stock with the money, taking title in his name alone, the stock is marital property, and the wife owns one-half of it. The basic assumption is that both husband and wife contribute equally to the material success of the marriage, and thus each should own an equal share of property acquired during the marriage by their joint efforts. Community property includes earnings during marriage and the rents, profits, and fruits of earnings.[29] Whatever is bought with earnings is community property. All property that is not community is separate. Separate property is property acquired before marriage and property acquired during marriage by gift, devise, or descent. In Idaho, Louisiana, Texas, and Wisconsin, the income from all property—separate as well as community—is community property. In the other states the income from separate property retains its separate character.

27. The Internal Revenue Service has ruled that the provisions of the Wisconsin Marital Property Act establish community property for purposes of federal income taxation. Rev. Rul. 87-13, I.R.B. 1987-6, 4.

28. These choices are available in almost all American community property states because the spouses can make an agreement to hold their property in any one of these forms.

29. For extended treatment of community property, see William A. Reppy, Jr. & Cynthia A. Samuel, Community Property Regimes in the United States (7th ed. 2009); Grace G. Blumberg, Community Property in California (6th ed. 2012).

Property acquired or possessed during marriage by either husband or wife is presumed to be community property. This is a strong presumption and can be overcome only by a preponderance of the evidence. Where there has been a commingling of separate and community property, the party contending for separate property may have a very difficult tracing burden. Recitals in a deed prepared by one spouse that property is separate property are not controlling; otherwise a self-serving spouse could take his or her earnings and unilaterally convert them into separate property.

In most states the husband and wife can freely change ("transmute") the character of their property by written agreement and, in some states, by oral agreement. They can convert community property into separate property, or vice versa.

If marriage is terminated by divorce, some states require an equal division of community property. Other community property states authorize a divorce court to make equitable division of community property.

b. Community Property Compared with Common Law Concurrent Interests

None of the community property states recognizes dower or curtesy; none recognizes the tenancy by the entirety. These marital interests developed out of the subjugation of the wife to the husband at common law and were deemed inconsistent with the principles of a marital community based on sharing. However, a tenancy in common or a joint tenancy can be created between husband and wife in community property states. These concurrent estates are permitted as separate property, but husband and wife cannot simultaneously hold property both as community property and as a tenancy in common or a joint tenancy. These cotenancies have different characteristics from community property.

Community property, compared with tenancies in common and joint tenancies, has these significant differences:

Husband and wife. Community property can exist only between husband and wife, whereas a tenancy in common or a joint tenancy can exist between any two or more persons.

Conveyance of share. Unlike tenants in common or joint tenants, neither spouse acting alone can convey his or her *undivided* one-half share of community property, except to the other spouse. It follows from this principle that neither spouse can change community property into separate property without the consent of the other. A tenant in common or a joint tenant acting alone can convey his or her undivided share to a third party, can change the form of estate (for example, from a joint tenancy into a tenancy in common), and has the right to partition; all these actions are unavailable to an owner of community property acting alone.

At death. With respect to traditional community property, each spouse has the power to dispose by will of one-half the community property at death. There is no survivorship feature, as with joint tenancy. In most community property states, if a spouse dies intestate, his or her share of the community property passes to the surviving spouse. In a few states community property passes to the descendants of the decedent. In recent years several community property states have adopted statutes permitting the spouses to create a new form of community property: community property with a right of survivorship in the surviving spouse.

Sale after death. At the death of one spouse, the entire community property receives a "stepped-up" tax basis for federal income tax purposes. (The difference between "basis," which is usually what the item cost, and selling price is income to the taxpayer.) The new basis is the value of the property upon the date of the decedent's death. Internal Revenue Code §§1014(a), 1014(b)(6). Thus suppose that *H* and *W* buy a house for $100,000, taking title in community property. At *H*'s death several years later, the house is worth $300,000. The house receives a new tax basis of $300,000. If *W* thereafter sells the house for $325,000, *W* realizes taxable income of only $25,000. If *H* and *W* had taken title to the house as joint tenants, only *H*'s one-half would receive a stepped-up basis at *H*'s death, and *W*'s basis after *H*'s death would be $200,000 ($50,000 for her cost plus $150,000 for *H*'s stepped-up basis). When *W* sells the house for $325,000, she would realize $125,000 in taxable income. Hence there is a possible considerable income tax advantage in holding property as community property rather than in a common law concurrent ownership form.[30]

PROBLEM

H, married to *W*, saves $5,000 out of his earnings, which he deposits in a savings account in his name only. Subsequently, *H* withdraws the $5,000 and buys a lot, taking title in *H* and *W* as joint tenants. *H* then dies, devising all his separate and community property to his son, *S*. Who owns the lot?

c. Management of Community Property

In a tenancy in common or a joint tenancy each tenant separately can convey his or her undivided interest, but this cannot be done with community property. Because it can exist only between husband and wife and cannot be converted into separate property without the consent of both spouses, community property can be conveyed to a third person only as an undivided whole. As a result, special management problems arise. Can the husband or the wife or only both of them make a conveyance of community property? Prior to the 1960s, the husband was

---

30. This tax advantage may be secured by residents of a common law property state by creating a community property trust in Alaska with an Alaska resident as trustee. Alaska Stat. §34.77.100 (2012). It may also be secured by a couple changing their domicile to a community property state, such as California, then making an agreement to hold their property as community property, then moving back to the original state. Once the property becomes community property while the couple is domiciled in California, it stays community property when the couple moves out of California.

deemed to be manager of the community, but beginning in the late 1960s, all eight community property states enacted statutes giving the husband and wife equal management powers. These statutes, however, differ in many details. In most community property states either the husband or the wife, acting alone, has the power to manage community property, but in certain situations only one spouse may be empowered to manage. If title is in the name of only one spouse, for example, only that spouse may be able to manage the property. If a spouse is operating a business that is community property, exclusive control of the business may be given to that spouse. In most states, however, statutes require both spouses to join in transfers or mortgages of community real property. See J. Thomas Oldham, Management of the Community Estate During an Intact Marriage, 56 Law & Contemp. Probs. 99 (1993).

The manager of community property is a kind of fiduciary. The community property must be managed for the benefit of the community. Each spouse must act in good faith in exercising authority, but good judgment is not necessary. The manager can sell community personal property and, if joinder of the other spouse is not required by statute, community real property. Under the Spanish law of community property the manager (formerly the husband) could validly make reasonable gifts, for good cause, of community property. This law persists in some states, for example, Texas. In California and Washington any gift of community property by the managing spouse can be set aside by the other spouse. Any bona fide purchaser from the spouse having the right to manage is protected. Thus, if husband and wife are equal managers of an oil painting, either can sell it to a bona fide purchaser.

In most community property states liability to creditors follows management and control. The creditors of a managing spouse can reach whatever community property the creditor spouse is legally entitled to manage. Hence if the husband and wife are equal managers of the property, creditors of either the husband or the wife can reach the property.

PROBLEM

W.C. Fields, who married Harriett Fields in 1900, subsequently earned large sums of money as a movie star. All of these earnings were community property.[31] Although depicted on the screen as a skinflint, Fields bestowed handsome gifts of money upon various persons, including several "lady friends," without his wife's

---

31. Fields was long separated from his wife, but under the California law then applicable earnings were community property until divorce. This rule is still followed in most community property states. But today in three states—Arizona, California, and Washington—earnings cease to be community property at the time the spouses live separate and apart. This approach has created problems determining whether couples are living separate and apart. Can couples live separate and apart while still living under the same roof? See Marriage of Norviel, 126 Cal. Rptr. 2d 148 (Cal. App. 2002) (physical separation required but physical separation within same residence possible).

knowledge or consent. These gifts totaled $482,450. After Fields died in 1946,[32] his wife found out about these transfers and sued Fields's executor. She alleged that

> many of said donees are deceased and that those remaining alive reside at divers places, some of them away from the State of California, and that they have used up and dissipated the sums of money by way of gift transferred and set over to them as aforesaid, and would not be able to pay a judgment, if one were rendered against them for return to plaintiff of said gifts or some part thereof. Plaintiff is without any means of collecting in full from said donees those portions of said gifts which she is entitled to.

Should the court direct Fields's executor to pay Harriett Fields $241,225? See Fields v. Michael, 205 P.2d 402 (Cal. 1949).

d.   Mixing Community Property with Separate Property

When community property is mixed with separate property, the community property states are not all in agreement as to the consequences. This situation sometimes arises when property is acquired before marriage but part of the purchase price is paid after marriage with community funds. In this situation some states, including Texas, follow the "inception of right" rule, a few follow the "time of vesting" rule, and still others, including California, follow a pro rata apportionment. The differences are easily seen if you think of a house bought on an installment land contract by the wife paying one-third down before marriage, with the remaining two-thirds of the installments paid after marriage from community funds. Under the "inception of right" rule, the character of the property is determined at the time the wife signed the contract of purchase; the house is her separate property. The community is entitled only to a return of community payments plus interest. Under the "time of vesting" rule, title does not pass to the wife until all the installments are paid, and hence the house is community property. Under the pro rata sharing rule, the community payments "buy in" a pro rata share of the title.

---

32. Fields's estate, valued at around $800,000, was all community property since it had all been earned after his marriage to Harriett. In his will Fields left his wife and his son each $10,000, but Harriett, his wife, owned half of the $800,000 community property, and this attempt to cut her off with very little failed. After providing small legacies of a few hundred or a few thousand dollars for various friends and relatives, Fields left the residue of his property to establish an orphans' home to be called "the W.C. Fields College . . . where no religion of any sort is to be preached." See Robert L. Taylor, W.C. Fields 283 (1967). This final bequest came from a man who, playing Gus, wrote his own dialogue in the movie *Tillie and Gus* (1933):

Tillie. Do you like children?
Gus. I do if they're properly cooked.

Whatever Fields's motive in pitting his wife—a religious woman—against the orphans, her claims were satisfied first, leaving insufficient funds for an orphanage.

PROBLEMS

1. During marriage *H* takes out a $50,000 life insurance policy on his life, paying premiums out of his earnings. The named beneficiary is *H*'s son, *S*. At *H*'s death, who is entitled to the $50,000? Suppose that *H* had taken out the policy before marriage and that $3,000 in premiums had been paid before marriage and $7,000 in premiums had been paid after marriage from community funds. At *H*'s death who is entitled to the $50,000? See McCurdy v. McCurdy, 372 S.W.2d 381 (Tex. Civ. App. 1963).

2. During his marriage to *W*, *H* purchases land for $20,000, using $5,000 of his separate funds as a down payment and giving a note secured by a mortgage to the seller for the balance. *H* pays off the principal and interest of the note from community funds and then sells the land for $40,000. Who is entitled to the proceeds? Should the $5,000 be considered a gift to the community if title is taken in the name of *H* and *W* (that is, a voluntary contribution to the purchase price)? See Grace G. Blumberg, Community Property in California 196-246, 291-303 (6th ed. 2012); William A. Reppy, Jr. & Cynthia A. Samuel, Community Property in the United States 139-159 (7th ed. 2009).

3. Suppose *W* owns and operates a jewelry store before marriage. At marriage to *H* it is worth $100,000. Five years after marriage the jewelry store is sold for $250,000. Who is entitled to the proceeds? Should *W* receive $100,000 plus a fair rate of return on that sum for five years, and the community receive the rest? Or should the community receive a fair salary for *W*'s labors in the store over five years, and *W* receive the rest? In California the answer turns on whether the increase in value is primarily due to *W*'s personal activity and ability or due to the character of the investment in a jewelry store. Suppose that instead of managing a jewelry store, *W* manages her separate stock portfolio and increases its value to $250,000 after five years. What part of the increase is community? See Beam v. Bank of America, 490 P.2d 257 (Cal. 1971); see also Jensen v. Jensen, 665 S.W.2d 107 (Tex. 1984); J. Thomas Oldham, Separate Property Businesses That Increase in Value During Marriage, 1990 Wis. L. Rev. 585.

e. Migrating Couples

Whether property is characterized in accord with the community property system or in accord with the common law property system depends upon the domicile of the spouses when the property is acquired. Suppose that the wife earns $1,000 and buys a horse with it. If the parties are domiciled in New York, the horse belongs to the wife alone. If domiciled in Texas, the horse is community property. Once the property has been initially characterized, *the ownership does not change when the parties change their domicile* unless both parties consent to the change in ownership. If, after the wife earns the $1,000, the spouses move from New York to Texas, the horse remains the wife's separate property. On the other hand, if the parties had been domiciled in Texas when the wife earned the money, and then had moved from Texas to New York, the horse would remain community property unless the parties agreed to change the ownership to another form. Common law property states generally recognize community property when it is brought into the state from a community property state. This point is frequently overlooked by lawyers or real estate agents in common law property states who advise immigrating husbands and wives to take the proceeds from the sale of their house in a community property state and buy a new house as joint tenants or tenants by the entirety, thereby losing the tax advantage of community property (explained on page 413). See Stanley M. Johanson, The Migrating Client: Estate Planning for the Couple from a Community Property State, 9 U. Miami Inst. Est. Plan. ¶ 800 (1975).

Under traditional conflict-of-law rules, when a person dies, the law of the decedent's domicile at death governs the disposition of personal property, and the law where land is located governs the disposition of land. However, a number of common law property states have enacted the Uniform Disposition of Community Property Rights at Death Act. The act provides that real property located in the enacting state, purchased with or traceable to proceeds or income from community property, will be treated as community property on death. Hence, only half will be distributed through the decedent's estate. Aside from this statute, a move from a common law property state to a community property state may leave a nonworking spouse of a retired worker at a disadvantage. The nonworking spouse loses the protection of the elective share given by the common law property state and gains the protection of the law of the community property state. The community property laws in most states do not give the surviving spouse an elective share in the decedent spouse's property owned at death.[33] For example, if H, who owns land located in Texas, a community property state, but who is domiciled in Missouri, a separate property state, dies leaving a will that disinherits his spouse, W, the law-of-the-situs rule will prevent W from exercising her elective-share right as to the Texas land. See Singleton v. St. Louis Union Trust Co., 191 S.W.2d 143 (Tex. Civ. App. 1945).

PROBLEM

H and W marry and live in Ohio. From H's earnings during marriage, H accumulates personal property worth $500,000. Under Ohio law, W has, at H's death, an elective share of one-half of H's property. After retirement, H and W move to Texas, a community property state. H dies leaving a will devising all his property to a daughter by a prior marriage. Texas does not have an elective-share statute. What are W's rights? See Estate of Hanau v. Hanau, 730 S.W.2d 663 (Tex.

---

33. California attempts to put immigrating couples in somewhat the same marital property position as they would have been in had they been domiciled in California all along. Upon divorce or death of a spouse, one-half of that spouse's property that would have been community property had the couple been domiciled in California when the property was acquired belongs to the other spouse. This is called "quasi-community property." Cal. Prob. Code §§66, 6401 (2013). Idaho, Louisiana, and Washington have similar provisions.

1987). By moving to Texas, *W* lost the protection of the Ohio elective-share and gained no substitute protection. What advice would you give *W* before moving from Ohio?

3. Rights of Domestic Partners

Common law marriage, widely recognized in the nineteenth century when travel by horseback to the county courthouse to obtain a license might be an arduous or long-delayed journey, is now clearly recognized in only 10 states (Alabama, Colorado, Iowa, Kansas, Montana, Oklahoma, Rhode Island, South Carolina, Texas, and Utah) and the District of Columbia. To have a common law marriage, the cohabiting parties must manifest their intent to be husband and wife and hold themselves out to the public as husband and wife. If the jurisdiction recognizes common law marriage, the couple married by common law have the same rights as a couple married with license and ceremony. Common law marriage was abolished in most states because it "was thought to generate litigation and encourage perjured testimony about an agreement to marry by a cohabitant seeking the benefits of lawful marriage at the termination (either by death of the other cohabitant or by the couple's parting) of the relationship." William A. Reppy, Jr., Property and Support Rights of Unmarried Cohabitants: A Proposal for Creating a New Legal Status, 44 La. L. Rev. 1677, 1706 (1989). Other reasons given for the abolition of common law marriage include: (1) with the development of modern transportation and roads, it was no longer needed; (2) a certificated marriage made proof easy for government benefits, pensions, and property claims, which increased dramatically in the twentieth century; and (3) common law marriage dignified immorality among persons in the lower socio-economic class who were more likely than the well-off to enter into such an arrangement.

In the 1960s, many couples began to live together without holding themselves out as being married. Even common law marriage, where recognized, would not give property rights to persons not claiming to be married. The law of contracts was then brought into play in an attempt to give a partner (usually the female partner) some share in the gains accumulated during the cohabitation.

In a series of cases beginning more than 30 years ago, the status of an unmarried couple's property rights, including how their property is to be divided when one partner dies or the couple separates, was litigated under contract law theory. In California the supreme court broke new ground by holding that a contract for property division or support can be implied from the conduct of the parties. An express contract is not necessary. Marvin v. Marvin, 557 P.2d 106 (Cal. 1976). The California court was moved by the principles of unjust enrichment. "[T]he better approach is to presume . . . that the parties intended to deal fairly with each other." 557 P.2d at 121. "[T]he parties' intention can only be ascertained by a . . . searching inquiry into the nature of the relationship." 557 P.2d at 117, n.11. The *Marvin* doctrine has been received cautiously. "[C]ourts in other jurisdictions are far from stampeding to follow its lead." Mary Ann Glendon, The Transformation of Family Law 280 (1989). *Marvin* has been applied to same-sex couples. Whorton v. Dillingham, 248 Cal. Rptr. 405 (Cal. App. 1988).

The New York Court of Appeals rejected *Marvin*'s enforcement of an implied contract. In New York only a written or oral express contract to share earnings and assets between unmarried partners is enforceable. Morone v. Morone, 413 N.E.2d 1154 (N.Y. 1980). Illinois rejected enforcing any contract between unmarried cohabitants, express or implied. In Illinois a contract between unmarried partners to share acquisitions is unenforceable on the ground that this would, in effect, revive common law marriage, abolished by the legislature. Hewitt v. Hewitt, 394 N.E.2d 1204 (Ill. 1979).

The contract approach to the rights of domestic partners, with its reliance on the express or implied intent of the parties, has not produced what many regard as equitable results upon separation of the partners. Few domestic partners make express contracts to govern their relationship or its termination. And resort to implied agreements results in little predictability and stretching of contracts doctrine beyond recognition.

The American Law Institute's Principles of the Law of Family Dissolution, approved in 2002, adopts a different approach to domestic partners in §6. It is premised on the "principle that legal rights and obligations may arise from the *conduct of the parties with respect to one another*, even though they have created no formal document or agreement setting forth such an understanding." Id. §6.02 comment a (emphasis added). The same principle underlays common law marriage. Basically, the Principles require that domestic partners of the same or opposite sex share for a significant period of time a primary residence and a life together as a couple. Whether the persons shared life together as a couple is determined by reference to a detailed list of circumstances that indicate they shared life together. If the partnership terminates while both partners are living, the couple's property is divided according to the principles set forth for the division of marital property. If the partnership terminates at the death of one partner, the surviving partner's rights depend upon the state's law of intestate succession.

Varnum v. Brien

Supreme Court of Iowa, 2009
763 N.W.2d 862

[What follows is an edited version of a very long opinion.]

CADY, J. In this case, we must decide if our state statute limiting civil marriage to a union between a man and a woman violates the Iowa Constitution, as the district court ruled. On our review, we hold the Iowa marriage statute violates the equal protection clause of the Iowa Constitution. Therefore, we affirm the decision of the district court.

I.   Background Facts and Proceedings

This lawsuit is a civil rights action by twelve individuals who reside in six communities across Iowa. Like most Iowans, they are responsible, caring, and productive individuals. They maintain important jobs, or are retired, and are contributing, benevolent members of their communities. They include a nurse, business manager, insurance analyst, bank agent, stay-at-home parent, church organist and piano teacher, museum director, federal employee, social worker, teacher, and two retired teachers. Like many Iowans, some have children and others hope to have children. Some are foster parents. Like all Iowans, they prize their liberties and live within the borders of this state with the expectation that their rights will be maintained and protected—a belief embraced by our state motto.[34]

Despite the commonality shared with other Iowans, the twelve plaintiffs are different from most in one way. They are sexually and romantically attracted to members of their own sex. The twelve plaintiffs comprise six same-sex couples who live in committed relationships. Each maintains a hope of getting married one day, an aspiration shared by many throughout Iowa.

Unlike opposite-sex couples in Iowa, same-sex couples are not permitted to marry in Iowa. The Iowa legislature amended the marriage statute in 1998 to define marriage as a union between only a man and a woman.[35] Despite this law, the six same-sex couples in this litigation asked the Polk County recorder to issue marriage licenses to them. The recorder, following the law, refused to issue the licenses, and the six couples have been unable to be married in this state. Except for the statutory restriction that defines marriage as a union between a man and a woman, the twelve plaintiffs met the legal requirements to marry in Iowa.

As other Iowans have done in the past when faced with the enforcement of a law that prohibits them from engaging in an activity or achieving a status enjoyed by other Iowans, the twelve plaintiffs turned to the courts to challenge the statute. They seek to declare the marriage statute unconstitutional so they can obtain the array of benefits of marriage enjoyed by heterosexual couples, protect themselves and their children, and demonstrate to one another and to society their mutual commitment.

[The plaintiffs claimed in their lawsuit that the same-sex marriage ban violates certain liberty and equality rights under the Iowa Constitution, including the fundamental right to marry, as well as rights to privacy and familial association. Additionally, plaintiffs claimed the legislative and the executive actions unconstitutionally discriminated against them on several bases, including sexual orientation.

The case was presented to the district court by means of a summary judgment motion. The record was developed through witness affidavits and depositions,

---

34. The state motto of Iowa is: "Our liberties we prize and our rights we will maintain." It is inscribed on the Great Seal of Iowa and on our state flag. See Iowa Code §§1A.1, 1B.1 (2009).

35. Iowa Code section 595.2(1) provides "[o]nly a marriage between a male and a female is valid." All statutory references are to the 2009 Code of Iowa. While some statutes referenced here have been amended since this lawsuit originated, none of the amendments dictate the outcome of this case.

and included an explanation by some of the plaintiffs of the disadvantages and fears they face each day due to the inability to obtain a civil marriage in Iowa. Examples: The legal inability to make many life and death decisions affecting a partner, such as decisions about health care, burial arrangements, autopsies, and disposition of remains following death; the inability to share in a partner's state-provided health insurance, public employee pension benefits, and many private-employer-provided benefits and protections; the loss of various tax benefits, and numerous nongovernmental benefits of marriage that are common in daily life. Perhaps the ultimate disadvantage expressed by plaintiffs is the inability to obtain for themselves and for their children the personal and public affirmation that accompanies marriage.

The parties also explored the reasons for defining marriage in a way that denies these benefits to same-sex couples. The County offered five primary interests of society in support of the legislature's exclusive definition of marriage. The first three interests are broadly related to the advancement of child rearing. Specifically, the objectives centered on promoting procreation, promoting child rearing by a mother and a father within a marriage, and promoting stability in an opposite-sex relationship to raise and nurture children. The fourth interest raised by the County addressed the conservation of state resources, while the final reason concerned the governmental interest in promoting the concept and integrity of the traditional notion of marriage. Much of the testimony presented by the County was in the form of opinions by various individuals that same-sex marriage would harm the institution of marriage and also harm children raised in same-sex marriages.

The plaintiffs produced evidence that sexual orientation and gender have no effect on children raised by same-sex couples, and evidence that most scientific research repudiates the notion that children need opposite-sex parents or biological parents to grow into well-adjusted adults. Many leading organizations, including the American Academy of Pediatrics, the American Psychiatric Association, the American Psychological Association, the National Association of Social Workers, and the Child Welfare League of America, weighed the available research and supported the conclusion that gay and lesbian parents are as effective as heterosexual parents in raising children.

The district court concluded the statute was unconstitutional under the due process and equal protection clauses of the Iowa Constitution and granted summary judgment to the plaintiffs. It initially ordered the county recorder to begin processing marriage licenses for same-sex couples, but stayed the order during the pendency of an appeal.]

II. Standard of Review

Summary judgment is appropriate only when "there is no genuine issue as to any material fact and . . . the moving party is entitled to a judgment as a matter of law." Iowa R. Civ. P. 1.981(3). . . . We review the legal issues necessary for resolution of the constitutional claims presented within the context of the summary judgment proceeding de novo.

III.   Constitutional Separation of Powers

[The court affirmed its role to interpret the law, saying that this role includes the responsibility to determine if the law enacted by the legislative branch and enforced by the executive branch violates the Iowa Constitution.]

IV.   Equal Protection

A.   Background Principles

The primary constitutional principle at the heart of this case is the doctrine of equal protection. The concept of equal protection is deeply rooted in our national and state history, but that history reveals this concept is often expressed far more easily than it is practiced. . . . So, today, this court again faces an important issue that hinges on our definition of equal protection. This issue comes to us with the same importance as our landmark cases of the past. The same-sex-marriage debate waged in this case is part of a strong national dialogue centered on a fundamental, deep-seated, traditional institution that has excluded, by state action, a particular class of Iowans. This class of people asks a simple and direct question: How can a state premised on the constitutional principle of equal protection justify exclusion of a class of Iowans from civil marriage?

B.   Legal Tests to Gauge Equal Protection

The foundational principle of equal protection is expressed in article I, section 6 of the Iowa Constitution, which provides: "All laws of a general nature shall have a uniform operation; the general assembly shall not grant to any citizen or class of citizens, privileges or immunities, which, upon the same terms shall not equally belong to all citizens." . . . Like the Federal Equal Protection Clause found in the Fourteenth Amendment to the United States Constitution, Iowa's constitutional promise of equal protection " 'is essentially a direction that all persons similarly situated should be treated alike.' "[36] Racing Ass'n of Cent. Iowa v. Fitzgerald, 675 N.W.2d 1, 7 (Iowa 2004) [hereinafter *RACI II*] (quoting City of Cleburne v. Cleburne Living Ctr., 473 U.S. 432, 439 (1985)).

---

36. Plaintiffs' challenge to Iowa Code section 595.2 is based on the equal protection guarantee in the Iowa Constitution and does not implicate federal constitutional protections. Generally, we view the federal and state equal protection clauses as "identical in scope, import, and purpose." *Callender* [v. Skiles], 591 N.W.2d [182,] 187 [(Iowa 1999)]. At the same time, we have jealously guarded our right to "employ a different analytical framework" under the state equal protection clause as well as to independently apply the federally formulated principles. Racing Ass'n of Cent. Iowa v. Fitzgerald, 675 N.W.2d 1, 4-7 (Iowa 2004). Here again, we find federal precedent instructive in interpreting the Iowa Constitution, but we refuse to follow it blindly. . . .

Even in the zealous protection of the constitution's mandate of equal protection, courts must give respect to the legislative process and presume its enactments are constitutional. We understand that Iowa's tripartite system of government requires the legislature to make difficult policy choices, including distributing benefits and burdens amongst the citizens of Iowa. In this process, some classifications and barriers are inevitable. As a result, courts pay deference to legislative decisions when called upon to determine whether the Iowa Constitution's mandate of equality has been violated by legislative action. More specifically, when evaluating challenges based on the equal protection clause, our deference to legislative policymaking is primarily manifested in the level of scrutiny we apply to review legislative action.

In most cases, we apply a very deferential standard known as the "rational basis test." Under the rational basis test, "[t]he plaintiff has the heavy burden of showing the statute unconstitutional and must negate every reasonable basis upon which the classification may be sustained." Bierkamp v. Rogers, 293 N.W.2d 577, 579-80 (Iowa 1980). . . . Although the rational basis test is "deferential to legislative judgment, 'it is not a toothless one' in Iowa." [RACI II, 675 N.W.2d] at 9 (quoting Mathews v. de Castro, 429 U.S. 181 (1976)). . . . [T]he deference built into the rational basis test is not dispositive because this court engages in a meaningful review of all legislation challenged on equal protection grounds by applying the rational basis test to the facts of each case.

The constitutional guarantee of equal protection, however, demands certain types of statutory classifications must be subjected to closer scrutiny by courts. Thus, courts apply a heightened level of scrutiny under equal protection analysis when reasons exist to suspect "prejudice against discrete and insular minorities . . . which tends seriously to curtail the operation of those political processes ordinarily to be relied upon to protect minorities." United States v. Carolene Prods. Co., 304 U.S. 144, 152 n.4 (1938).

Under this approach, classifications based on race, alienage, or national origin and those affecting fundamental rights are evaluated according to a standard known as "strict scrutiny." Classifications subject to strict scrutiny are presumptively invalid and must be narrowly tailored to serve a compelling governmental interest.

A middle tier of analysis exists between rational basis and strict scrutiny. This intermediate tier has been applied to statutes classifying on the basis of gender or illegitimacy and requires the party seeking to uphold the statute to demonstrate the challenged classification is substantially related to the achievement of an important governmental objective. It is known as "intermediate scrutiny" or "heightened scrutiny,"[37] and groups entitled to this tier of review are often called "quasi-suspect" groups. To survive intermediate scrutiny, the law must not only further an important governmental interest and be substantially related to that

---

37. References to "heightened" scrutiny in this opinion are meant to be general; heightened scrutiny includes any judicial inquiry more searching than the rational basis test. References to "intermediate" scrutiny discuss a specific level of scrutiny between the rational basis test and strict scrutiny.

interest, but the justification for the classification must be genuine and must not depend on broad generalizations. United States v. Virginia, 518 U.S. 515, 533 (1996).

. . .

D. Similarly Situated People

The County seeks to undercut the plaintiffs' equal protection claim by asserting the plaintiffs are not similarly situated to heterosexuals. We consider this threshold argument before proceeding to the application of our equal protection test.

We begin by recognizing the constitutional pledge of equal protection does not prohibit laws that impose classifications. Many statutes impose classifications by granting special benefits or declaring special burdens, and the equal protection clause does not require all laws to apply uniformly to all people. Instead, equal protection demands that laws treat alike all people who are " 'similarly situated with respect to the legitimate purposes of the law.' " *RACI II*, 675 N.W.2d at 7 (quoting Coll. Area Renters & Landlord Ass'n v. City of San Diego, 50 Cal. Rptr. 2d 515, 520 (Cal. Ct. App. 1996)) (emphasis omitted).

This requirement of equal protection—that the law must treat all similarly situated people the same—has generated a narrow threshold test. . . . [I]f plaintiffs cannot show as a preliminary matter that they are similarly situated, courts do not further consider whether their different treatment under a statute is permitted under the equal protection clause. . . .

The County references this threshold test in this case and asserts the plaintiffs are not similarly situated to opposite-sex couples so as to necessitate further equal protection analysis because the plaintiffs cannot "procreate naturally." In other words, the County argues the statute does not treat similarly situated persons differently, but merely treats dissimilar persons differently.

In considering whether two classes are similarly situated, a court cannot simply look at the trait used by the legislature to define a classification under a statute and conclude a person without that trait is not similarly situated to persons with the trait. . . . [T]he similarly situated requirement cannot possibly be interpreted to require plaintiffs to be identical in every way to people treated more favorably by the law. No two people or groups of people are the same in every way, and nearly every equal protection claim could be run aground onto the shoals of a threshold analysis if the two groups needed to be a mirror image of one another. Such a threshold analysis would hollow out the constitution's promise of equal protection.

Thus, equal protection before the law demands more than the equal application of the classifications made by the law. The law itself must be equal. In other words, to truly ensure equality before the law, the equal protection guarantee requires that laws treat all those who are similarly situated with respect to the purposes of the law alike. . . . The purposes of the law must be referenced in order to meaningfully evaluate whether the law equally protects all people similarly situated with respect to those purposes. For these reasons, the trait asserted by the County is insufficient to support its threshold argument.

Nevertheless, we have said our marriage laws "are rooted in the necessity of providing an institutional basis for defining the fundamental relational rights and responsibilities of persons in organized society." Laws v. Griep, 332 N.W.2d 339, 341 (Iowa 1983). These laws also serve to recognize the status of the parties' committed relationship.

Therefore, with respect to the subject and purposes of Iowa's marriage laws, we find that the plaintiffs are similarly situated compared to heterosexual persons. Plaintiffs are in committed and loving relationships, many raising families, just like heterosexual couples. Moreover, official recognition of their status provides an institutional basis for defining their fundamental relational rights and responsibilities, just as it does for heterosexual couples. Society benefits, for example, from providing same-sex couples a stable framework within which to raise their children and the power to make health care and end-of-life decisions for loved ones, just as it does when that framework is provided for opposite-sex couples. . . .

E.   Classification Undertaken in Iowa Code Section 595.2

[The court concluded that the Iowa statute's ban on civil marriage between people of the same sex classifies on the basis of sexual orientation, even though the statute does not explicitly ban gays and lesbians from marrying (requiring, rather, that if they marry, they must marry someone of the opposite sex). By purposefully placing civil marriage outside the realistic reach of gay and lesbian individuals, the ban on same-sex civil marriages differentiates implicitly on the basis of sexual orientation.]

F.   Framework for Determining Appropriate Level of Judicial Scrutiny

Our determination that the marriage statute employs a sexual orientation-based classification does not, of course, control the outcome of our equal protection inquiry. Most statutes, one way or the other, create classifications. To determine if this particular classification violates constitutional principles of equal protection, we must next ask what level of scrutiny applies to classifications of this type. The County argues the more deferential rational basis test should apply, while plaintiffs argue closer scrutiny is appropriate. Although neither we nor the United States Supreme Court has decided which level of scrutiny applies to legislative classifications based on sexual orientation, numerous Supreme Court equal protection cases provide a general framework to guide our analysis under the Iowa Constitution. To say a general framework exists is not to say the Supreme Court has provided a precise formula for determining when legislative action is subject to a heightened form of scrutiny. Instead, the Supreme Court has expressed a number of general principles to assist in identifying the appropriate level of scrutiny. Classifications based on factors like race, alienage, national origin, sex, or illegitimacy are "so seldom relevant to achievement of any legitimate state interest that laws grounded in such considerations are deemed to reflect prejudice and antipathy." *Cleburne Living Ctr.*, 473 U.S. at 440. Rather than bearing some relationship to the burdened class's ability to contribute to society, such classifications often reflect irrelevant stereotypes. "For these reasons and because such discrimination is unlikely to be soon rectified by legislative means," laws based on these types of classifications must withstand more intense judicial scrutiny than other types of classifications. Id.

Instead of adopting a rigid formula to determine whether certain legislative classifications warrant more demanding constitutional analysis, the Supreme Court has looked to four factors[:] (1) the history of invidious discrimination against the class burdened by the legislation; (2) whether the characteristics that distinguish the class indicate a typical class member's ability to contribute to society; (3) whether the distinguishing characteristic is "immutable" or beyond the class members' control; and (4) the political power of the subject class. . . .

G. Determination of Appropriate Level of Scrutiny

Guided by the established framework, we next consider each of the four traditional factors and assess how each bears on the question of whether the constitution demands a more searching scrutiny be applied to the sexual-orientation based classification in Iowa's marriage statute.

1. History of Discrimination Against Gay and Lesbian People

The first consideration is whether gay and lesbian people have suffered a history of purposeful unequal treatment because of their sexual orientation. The County does not, and could not in good faith, dispute the historical reality that gay and lesbian people as a group have long been the victim of purposeful and invidious discrimination because of their sexual orientation. The long and painful history of discrimination against gay and lesbian persons is epitomized by the criminalization of homosexual conduct in many parts of this country until very recently. [The court provided other examples of historical discrimination against gays and lesbians, including dismissal from military service and continued victimization by hate crimes.]

In sum, this history of discrimination suggests any legislative burdens placed on lesbian and gay people as a class "are more likely than others to reflect deep-seated prejudice rather than legislative rationality in pursuit of some legitimate objective." Plyler v. Doe, 457 U.S. 202, 216 n.14. This observation favors an elevated scrutiny to uncover any such prejudice.

2. Sexual Orientation and the Ability to Contribute to Society

A second relevant consideration is whether the characteristic at issue—sexual orientation—is related to the person's ability to contribute to society. Heightened scrutiny is applied when the classification bears no relationship to a person's ability to contribute to society. The existence of this factor indicates the classification is likely based on irrelevant stereotypes and prejudice. A classification unrelated to a person's ability to perform or contribute to society typically reflects "prejudice and antipathy—a view that those in the burdened class are not as worthy or deserving as others" or "reflect[s] outmoded notions of the relative capabilities of persons with the characteristic." *Cleburne Living Ctr.*, 473 U.S. at 440-41.

Not surprisingly, none of the same-sex marriage decisions from other state courts around the nation have found a person's sexual orientation to be indicative of the person's general ability to contribute to society. More importantly, the Iowa legislature has recently declared as the public policy of this state that sexual orientation is not relevant to a person's ability to contribute to a number of societal institutions other than civil marriage. See Iowa Code §216.6 (employment); id. §216.7 (public accommodations); id. §216.8 (housing); id. §216.9 (education); id. §216.10 (credit practices). Significantly, we do not construe Iowa Code chapter 216 to allow marriage between persons of the same sex, a construction expressly forbidden in the Iowa Code. See id. §216.18A ("[Chapter 216] shall not be construed to allow marriage between persons of the same sex, in accordance with chapter 595."). Rather, we merely highlight the reality that chapter 216 and numerous other statutes and regulations demonstrate sexual orientation is broadly recognized in Iowa to be irrelevant to a person's ability to contribute to society. Those statutes and regulations reflect at least some measure of legislative and executive awareness that discrimination based on sexual orientation is often predicated on prejudice and stereotype and further express a desire to remove sexual orientation as an obstacle to the ability of gay and lesbian people to achieve their full potential. Therefore, we must scrutinize more closely those classifications that suggest a law may be based on prejudice and stereotype because laws of that nature are "incompatible with the constitutional understanding that each person is to be judged individually and is entitled to equal justice under the law." *Plyler*, 457 U.S. at 217 n.14. Thus, although we do not interpret chapter 216 to allow same-sex marriage, we rely on the legislative judgment underlying chapter 216 to determine the appropriate level of scrutiny when sexual orientation is the basis for a statutory classification. Based on Iowa statutes and regulations, it is clear sexual orientation is no longer viewed in Iowa as an impediment to the ability of a person to contribute to society.

3. *Immutability of Sexual Orientation*

The parties, consistent with the same-sex-marriage scholarship, opinions, and jurisprudence, contest whether sexual orientation is immutable or unresponsive to attempted change. The County seizes on this debate to argue the summary judgment granted by the district court in this case was improper because plaintiffs could not prove, as a matter of fact, that sexuality is immutable. This argument, however, essentially limits the constitutional relevance of mutability to those instances in which the trait defining the burdened class is absolutely impervious to change. To evaluate this argument, we must first consider the rationale for using immutability as a factor.

A human trait that defines a group is "immutable" when the trait exists "solely by the accident of birth," Frontiero v. Richardson, 411 U.S. 677, 686 (1973) (Brennan, J., plurality opinion), or when the person with the trait has no ability to change it. Immutability is a factor in determining the appropriate level of scrutiny because the inability of a person to change a characteristic that is used to justify different treatment makes the discrimination violative of the rather " 'basic concept of our system that legal burdens should bear some relationship to individual responsibility.' " *Frontiero*, 411 U.S. at 686 (Brennan, J., plurality opinion) (quoting Weber v. Aetna Cas. & Sur. Co., 406 U.S. 164 (1972)). Put another way, when a characteristic is immutable, different treatment based on this characteristic seems "all the more invidious and unfair." Nan D. Hunter, The Sex Discrimination Argument in Gay Rights Cases, 9 J.L. & Pol'y 397, 403 (2001). Additionally, immutability can relate to the scope and permanency of the barrier imposed on the group. Temporary barriers tend to be less burdensome on a group and more likely to actually advance a legitimate governmental interest. Consequently, such barriers normally do not warrant heightened scrutiny. The permanency of the barrier also depends on the ability of the individual to change the characteristic responsible for the discrimination. This aspect of immutability may separate truly victimized individuals from those who have invited discrimination by changing themselves so as to be identified with the group. . . .

Importantly, this background reveals courts need not definitively resolve the nature-versus-nurture debate currently raging over the origin of sexual orientation in order to decide plaintiffs' equal protection claims. The constitutional relevance of the immutability factor is not reserved to those instances in which the trait defining the burdened class is absolutely impossible to change. . . .

In this case, the County acknowledges sexual orientation is highly resistant to change. . . . Sexual orientation influences the formation of personal relationships between all people — heterosexual, gay, or lesbian — to fulfill each person's fundamental needs for love and attachment. . . . Sexual orientation is not the type of human trait that allows courts to relax their standard of review because the barrier is temporary or susceptible to self-help.

4.   Political Powerlessness of Lesbian and Gay People

As observed, the political power of the burdened class has been referenced repeatedly in Supreme Court cases determining the level of scrutiny to be applied to a given piece of legislation. Unfortunately, the Court has never defined what it means to be politically powerless for purposes of this analysis, nor has it quantified a maximum amount of political power a group may enjoy while still receiving the protection from unfair discrimination accompanying heightened scrutiny. The County points to the numerous legal protections gay and lesbian people have secured against discrimination, and the County argues those protections demonstrate gay and lesbian people are not a politically powerless class. The County's argument implies gay and lesbian people must be characterized by a complete, or nearly complete, lack of political power before courts should subject sexual-orientation-based legislative burdens to a heightened scrutiny.

Notwithstanding the lack of a mathematical equation to guide the analysis of this factor, a number of helpful general principles related to the political power of suspect classes can be culled from the Supreme Court's cases. First, these cases show absolute political powerlessness is not necessary to subject legislative burdens on a certain class to heightened scrutiny. For example, females enjoyed at least some measure of political power when the Supreme Court first heightened its scrutiny of gender classifications. . . .

Second, Supreme Court jurisprudence establishes that a group's current political powerlessness is not a prerequisite to enhanced judicial protection. . . .

While a more in-depth discussion of the history of the political-power factor is possible, we are satisfied, for the purpose of analyzing the Iowa Constitution, the political powerlessness factor of the level-of-scrutiny inquiry does not require a showing of absolute political powerlessness.

It is also important to observe that the political power of gays and lesbians, while responsible for greater acceptance and decreased discrimination, has done little to remove barriers to civil marriage. Although a small number of state legislatures have approved civil unions for gay and lesbian people without judicial intervention, no legislature has secured the right to civil marriage for gay and lesbian people without court order. The myriad statutes and regulatory protections against discrimination based on sexual orientation in such areas as employment, housing, public accommodations, and education have not only been absent in the area of marriage, but legislative bodies have taken affirmative steps to shore up the concept of traditional marriage by specifically excluding gays and lesbians. Like Iowa, over forty other states have passed statutes or constitutional amendments to ban same-sex marriages. Thus, although equal rights for gays and lesbians have been increasingly recognized in the political arena the right to civil marriage is a notable exception to this trend. Consequently, the specific right sought in this case has largely lacked any extensive political support and has actually experienced an affirmative backlash. We are convinced gay and lesbian people are not so politically powerful as to overcome the unfair and severe prejudice that history suggests produces discrimination based on sexual orientation. . . . These facts demonstrate, at the least, the political-power factor does not weigh against heightened judicial scrutiny of sexual-orientation based legislation.

5. *Classifications Based on Sexual Orientation Demand Closer Scrutiny*

. . .

The factors established to guide our determination of the level of scrutiny to utilize in our examination of the equal protection claim in this case all point to an elevated level of scrutiny. Accordingly, we hold that legislative classifications based on sexual orientation must be examined under a heightened level of scrutiny under the Iowa Constitution.

H.   Application of Heightened Scrutiny

Plaintiffs argue sexual orientation-based statutes should be subject to the most searching scrutiny. The County asserts Iowa's marriage statute, section 595.2, may be reviewed, at most, according to an intermediate level of scrutiny. Because we conclude Iowa's same-sex marriage statute cannot withstand intermediate scrutiny, we need not decide whether classifications based on sexual orientation are subject to a higher level of scrutiny. Thus, we turn to a discussion of the intermediate scrutiny standard.

1.   *Intermediate Scrutiny Standard*

"To withstand intermediate scrutiny, a statutory classification must be substantially related to an important governmental objective." Clark v. Jeter, 486 U.S. 456, 461 (1988). In applying an intermediate standard to review gender-based classifications, the Supreme Court has stated: "Focusing on the differential treatment or denial of opportunity for which relief is sought, the reviewing court must determine whether the proffered justification is 'exceedingly persuasive.'" *Virginia*, 518 U.S. at 532-33. To this end, courts evaluate whether the proffered governmental objectives are important and whether the statutory classification is "'substantially related to the achievement of those objectives.'" Id. at 533 (quoting Miss. Univ. for Women v. Hogan, 458 U.S. 718, 724 (1982)).

2.   *Statutory Classification: Exclusion of Gay and Lesbian People from Civil Marriage*

To identify the statutory classification, we focus on the "differential treatment or denial of opportunity for which relief is sought." Id. at 532-33 (considering "categorical exclusion" of women from institution of higher education). Plaintiffs bring this lawsuit complaining of their exclusion from the institution of civil marriage. In response, the County offers support for the legislature's decision to statutorily establish heterosexual civil marriage. Because the relevant focal point is the opportunity sought by the plaintiffs, the issue presented by this lawsuit is whether the state has "exceedingly persuasive" reasons for denying civil marriage to same-sex couples, not whether state sanctioned, heterosexual marriage is constitutional. Thus, the question we must answer is whether excluding gay and lesbian people from civil marriage is substantially related to any important governmental objective.

3.   *Governmental Objectives*

The County has proffered a number of objectives supporting the marriage statute. These objectives include support for the "traditional" institution of marriage, the optimal procreation and rearing of children, and financial considerations. The first step in scrutinizing a statutory classification can be to determine whether the objectives purportedly advanced by the classification are important. . . . Where we find, or can assume, the proffered governmental interests are sufficiently weighty to be called "important," the critical inquiry is whether these governmental objectives can fairly be said to be advanced by the legislative classification. . . .

a. Maintaining traditional marriage. First, the County argues the same-sex marriage ban promotes the "integrity of traditional marriage" by "maintaining the historical and traditional marriage norm ([as] one between a man and a woman)." This argument is straightforward and has superficial appeal. A specific tradition sought to be maintained cannot be an important governmental objective for equal protection purposes, however, when the tradition is nothing more than the historical classification currently expressed in the statute being challenged. When a certain tradition is used as both the governmental objective and the classification to further that objective, the equal protection analysis is transformed into the circular question of whether the classification accomplishes the governmental objective, which objective is to maintain the classification. . . .

This precise situation is presented by the County's claim that the statute in this case exists to preserve the traditional understanding of marriage. The governmental objective identified by the County—to maintain the traditional understanding of marriage—is simply another way of saying the governmental objective is to limit civil marriage to opposite-sex couples. Opposite-sex marriage, however, is the classification made under the statute, and this classification must comply with our principles of equal protection. Thus, the use of traditional marriage as both the governmental objective and the classification of the statute transforms the equal protection analysis into the question of whether restricting marriage to opposite-sex couples accomplishes the governmental objective of maintaining opposite-sex marriage.

This approach is, of course, an empty analysis. It permits a classification to be maintained " 'for its own sake.' " Moreover, it can allow discrimination to become acceptable as tradition and helps to explain how discrimination can exist for such a long time. If a simple showing that discrimination is traditional satisfies equal protection, previous successful equal protection challenges of invidious racial and gender classifications would have failed. Consequently, equal protection demands that [the classification (that is, the exclusion of gay persons from civil marriage) must advance a state interest that is separate from the classification itself].

. . . Thus, we must analyze the legislature's objective in maintaining the traditional classification being challenged.

The reasons underlying traditional marriage may include the other objectives asserted by the County, objectives we will separately address in this decision. However, some underlying reason other than the preservation of tradition must be identified. Because the County offers no particular *governmental* reason underlying the tradition of limiting civil marriage to heterosexual couples, we press forward to consider other plausible reasons for the legislative classification.

b. Promotion of optimal environment to raise children. Another governmental objective proffered by the County is the promotion of "child rearing by a father and a mother in a marital relationship which social scientists say with confidence is the optimal milieu for child rearing." This objective implicates the broader governmental interest to promote the best interests of children. The "best interests of children" is, undeniably, an important governmental objective. Yet, we first examine the underlying premise proffered by the County that the optimal environment for children is to be raised within a marriage of both a mother and a father.

Plaintiffs presented an abundance of evidence and research, confirmed by our independent research, supporting the proposition that the interests of children are served equally by same-sex parents and opposite-sex parents. On the other hand, we acknowledge the existence of reasoned opinions that dual-gender parenting is the optimal environment for children. These opinions, while thoughtful and sincere, were largely unsupported by reliable scientific studies. Even assuming there may be a rational basis at this time to believe the legislative classification advances a legitimate government interest, this assumed fact would not be sufficient to survive the equal protection analysis applicable in this case. In order to ensure this classification based on sexual orientation is not borne of prejudice and stereotype, intermediate scrutiny demands a closer relationship between the legislative classification and the purpose of the classification than mere rationality. Under intermediate scrutiny, the relationship between the government's goal and the classification employed to further that goal must be "substantial." In order to evaluate that relationship, it is helpful to consider whether the legislation is over-inclusive or under-inclusive. . . .

A statute is under-inclusive when the classification made in the statute [does not include all who are similarly situated with respect to the purpose of the law]. An under-inclusive statute means all people included in the statutory classification have the trait that is relevant to the aim of the statute, but other people with the trait are not included in the classification. A statute is over-inclusive when the classification made in the statute includes more persons than those who are similarly situated with respect to the purpose of the law. An over-inclusive statute [imposes a burden upon a wider range of individuals than are included in the class of those] with the trait relevant to the aim of the law. As the degree to which a statutory classification is shown to be over-inclusive or under-inclusive increases, so does the difficulty in demonstrating the classification substantially furthers the legislative goal.

We begin with the County's argument that the goal of the same-sex marriage ban is to ensure children will be raised only in the optimal milieu. In pursuit of this objective, the statutory exclusion of gay and lesbian people is both under-inclusive and over-inclusive. The civil marriage statute is under-inclusive because it does not exclude from marriage other groups of parents—such as child abusers, sexual predators, parents neglecting to provide child support, and violent felons—that are undeniably less than optimal parents. Such under-inclusion tends to demonstrate that the sexual-orientation-based classification is grounded in prejudice or "overbroad generalizations about the different talents, capacities, or preferences" of gay and lesbian people, rather than having a substantial relationship to some important objective. *See Virginia*, 518 U.S. at 533 (rejecting use of overbroad generalizations to classify). If the marriage statute was truly focused on optimal parenting, many classifications of people would be excluded, not merely gay and lesbian people.

. . . While a statute does not automatically violate equal protection merely by being under-inclusive, the degree of under-inclusion nonetheless indicates the substantiality of the relationship between the legislative means and end.

As applied to this case, it could be argued the same-sex marriage ban is just one legislative step toward ensuring the optimal environment for raising children. Under this argument, the governmental objective is slightly more modest. It seeks to reduce the number of same-sex parent households, nudging our state a step closer to providing the asserted optimal milieu for children. Even evaluated in light of this narrower objective, however, the ban on same-sex marriage is flawed.

The ban on same-sex marriage is substantially over-inclusive because not all same-sex couples choose to raise children. Yet, the marriage statute denies civil marriage to all gay and lesbian people in order to discourage the limited number of same-sex couples who desire to raise children. [In doing so, the legislature includes a consequential number of "individuals within the statute's purview who are not afflicted with the evil the statute seeks to remedy."]

At the same time, the exclusion of gay and lesbian people from marriage is under-inclusive, even in relation to the narrower goal of improving child rearing by limiting same-sex parenting. Quite obviously, the statute does not prohibit same-sex couples from raising children. Same-sex couples currently raise children in Iowa, even while being excluded from civil marriage, and such couples will undoubtedly continue to do so. Recognition of this under-inclusion puts in perspective just how minimally the same-sex marriage ban actually advances the purported legislative goal. A law so simultaneously over-inclusive and under-inclusive is not substantially related to the government's objective. In the end, a careful analysis of the over- and under-inclusiveness of the statute reveals it is less about using marriage to achieve an optimal environment for children and more about merely precluding gay and lesbian people from civil marriage. If the statute was truly about the best interest of children, some benefit to children derived from the ban on same-sex civil marriages would be observable. Yet, the germane analysis does not show how the best interests of children of gay and lesbian parents, who are denied an environment supported by the benefits of marriage under the statute, are served by the ban. Likewise, the exclusion of gays and lesbians from marriage does not benefit the interests of those children of heterosexual parents, who are able to enjoy the environment supported by marriage with or without the inclusion of same-sex couples.

The ban on same-sex civil marriage can only logically be justified as a means to ensure the asserted optimal environment for raising children if fewer children will be raised within same-sex relationships or more children will be raised in dual-gender marriages. Yet, the same-sex-marriage ban will accomplish these outcomes only when people in same-sex relationships choose not to raise children without the benefit of marriage or when children are adopted by dual-gender couples who would have been adopted by same-sex couples but for the same-sex civil marriage ban. We discern no substantial support for this proposition. These outcomes, at best, are minimally advanced by the classification. Consequently, a classification that limits civil marriage to opposite-sex couples is simply not substantially related to the objective of promoting the optimal environment to raise children. This conclusion suggests stereotype and prejudice, or some other unarticulated reason, could be present to explain the real objectives of the statute.

c. *Promotion of procreation.* The County also proposes that government endorsement of traditional civil marriage will result in more procreation. It points out that procreation is important to the continuation of the human race, and opposite-sex couples accomplish this objective because procreation occurs naturally within this group. In contrast, the County points out, same-sex couples can procreate only through assisted reproductive techniques, and some same-sex couples may choose not to procreate. While heterosexual marriage does lead to procreation, the argument by the County fails to address the real issue in our required analysis of the objective: whether exclusion of gay and lesbian individuals from the institution of civil marriage will result in more procreation? If procreation is the true objective, then the proffered classification must work to achieve that objective.

Conceptually, the promotion of procreation as an objective of marriage is compatible with the inclusion of gays and lesbians within the definition of marriage. Gay and lesbian persons are capable of procreation. Thus, the sole conceivable avenue by which exclusion of gay and lesbian people from civil marriage could promote more procreation is if the unavailability of civil marriage for same-sex partners caused homosexual individuals to "become" heterosexual in order to procreate within the present traditional institution of civil marriage. The briefs, the record, our research, and common sense do not suggest such an outcome. Even if possibly true, the link between exclusion of gay and lesbian people from marriage and increased procreation is far too tenuous to withstand heightened scrutiny. Specifically, the statute is significantly under-inclusive with respect to the objective of increasing procreation because it does not include a variety of groups that do not procreate for reasons such as age, physical disability, or choice. In other words, the classification is not substantially related to the asserted legislative purpose.

d. *Promoting stability in opposite-sex relationships.* A fourth suggested rationale supporting the marriage statute is "promoting stability in opposite sex relationships." While the institution of civil marriage likely encourages stability in opposite-sex relationships, we must evaluate whether excluding gay and lesbian people from civil marriage encourages stability in opposite-sex relationships. The County offers no reasons that it does, and we can find none. The stability of opposite-sex relationships is an important governmental interest, but the exclusion of same-sex couples from marriage is not substantially related to that objective.

e. *Conservation of resources.* The conservation of state resources is another objective arguably furthered by excluding gay and lesbian persons from civil marriage. The argument is based on a simple premise: couples who are married enjoy numerous governmental benefits, so the state's fiscal burden associated with civil marriage is reduced if less people are allowed to marry. In the common sense of the word, then, it is "rational" for the legislature to seek to conserve state resources by limiting the number of couples allowed to form civil marriages. By way of example, the County hypothesizes that, due to our laws granting tax benefits to married couples, the State of Iowa would reap less tax revenue if individual taxpaying gay and lesbian people were allowed to obtain a civil marriage. Certainly, Iowa's marriage statute causes numerous government benefits, including tax benefits, to be withheld from plaintiffs. Thus, the ban on same-sex marriages may conserve some state resources. Excluding any group from civil marriage—African-Americans, illegitimates, aliens, even red-haired individuals—would conserve state resources in an equally "rational" way. Yet, such classifications so obviously offend our society's collective sense of equality that courts have not hesitated to provide added protections against such inequalities.

One primary requirement of the equal protection clause is a more substantial relationship between the legislative goal and the means used to attain the goal. When heightened scrutiny is applicable, the means must substantially further the legislative end. Consequently, in this case, the sexual-orientation-based classification must substantially further the conservation-of-resources objective.

As observed in our analysis of the other reasons offered in support of the marriage statute, significant degrees of over-inclusion and under-inclusion shed light on the true relationship between exclusion of gay and lesbian people from civil marriage and the goal of conserving governmental resources. Exclusion of all same-sex couples is an extremely blunt instrument for conserving state resources through limiting access to civil marriage. In other words, the exclusion of same-sex couples is over-inclusive because many same-sex couples, if allowed to marry, would not use more state resources than they currently consume as unmarried couples. To reference the County's example, while many heterosexual couples who have obtained a civil marriage do not file joint tax returns—or experience any other tax benefit from marital status—many same-sex couples may not file a joint tax return either. The two classes created by the statute—opposite-sex couples and same-sex couples—may use the same amount of state resources. Thus, the two classes are similarly situated for the purpose of conserving state resources, yet the classes are treated differently by the law. In this way, sexual orientation is a flawed indicator of resource usage.

Just as exclusion of same-sex couples from marriage is a blunt instrument, however, it is also significantly undersized if the true goal is to conserve state resources. That is to say, the classification is under-inclusive. The goal of conservation of state resources would be equally served by excluding any similar-sized group from civil marriage. Indeed, under the County's logic, more state resources would be conserved by excluding groups more numerous than Iowa's estimated 5800 same-sex couples (for example, persons marrying for a second or subsequent time). Importantly, there is also no suggestion same-sex couples would use more state resources if allowed to obtain a civil marriage than heterosexual couples who obtain a civil marriage.

Such over-inclusion and under-inclusion demonstrates the trait of sexual orientation is a poor proxy for regulating aspiring spouses' usage of state resources. This tenuous relationship between the classification and its purpose demonstrates many people who are similarly situated with respect to the purpose of the law are treated differently. As a result, the sexual orientation-based classification does not substantially further the suggested governmental interest, as required by intermediate scrutiny.

4.   Conclusion

Having examined each proffered governmental objective through the appropriate lens of intermediate scrutiny, we conclude the sexual-orientation-based classification under the marriage statute does not substantially further any of the objectives. . . .

I.   Religious Opposition to Same-Sex Marriage

Now that we have addressed and rejected each specific interest advanced by the County to justify the classification drawn under the statute, we consider the reason for the exclusion of gay and lesbian couples from civil marriage left unspoken by the County: religious opposition to same-sex marriage. The County's silence reflects, we believe, its understanding this reason cannot, under our Iowa Constitution, be used to justify a ban on same-sex marriage.

While unexpressed, religious sentiment most likely motivates many, if not most, opponents of same-sex civil marriage and perhaps even shapes the views of those people who may accept gay and lesbian unions but find the notion of same-sex marriage unsettling. Consequently, we address the religious undercurrent propelling the same-sex marriage debate as a means to fully explain our rationale for rejecting the dual-gender requirement of the marriage statute.

It is quite understandable that religiously motivated opposition to same-sex civil marriage shapes the basis for legal opposition to same-sex marriage, even if only indirectly. Religious objections to same-sex marriage are supported by thousands of years of tradition and biblical interpretation. The belief that the "sanctity of marriage" would be undermined by the inclusion of gay and lesbian couples bears a striking conceptual resemblance to the expressed secular rationale for maintaining the tradition of marriage as a union between dual-gender couples, but better identifies the source of the opposition. Whether expressly or impliedly, much of society rejects same-sex marriage due to sincere, deeply ingrained — even fundamental — religious belief.

Yet, such views are not the only religious views of marriage. As demonstrated by amicus groups, other equally sincere groups and people in Iowa and around the nation have strong religious views that yield the opposite conclusion. This contrast of opinions in our society largely explains the absence of any religion-based rationale to test the constitutionality of Iowa's same-sex marriage ban. Our constitution does not permit any branch of government to resolve these types of religious debates and entrusts to courts the task of ensuring government *avoids* them. . . .

We, of course, have a constitutional mandate to protect the free exercise of religion in Iowa, which includes the freedom of a religious organization to define marriages it solemnizes as unions between a man and a woman. This mission to protect religious freedom is consistent with our task to prevent government from endorsing any religious view. State government can have no religious views, either directly or indirectly, expressed through its legislation. This proposition is the essence of the separation of church and state. As a result, civil marriage must be judged under our constitutional standards of equal protection and not under religious doctrines or the religious views of individuals. This approach does not disrespect or denigrate the religious views of many Iowans who may strongly believe in marriage as a dual-gender union, but considers, as we must, only the constitutional rights of all people, as expressed by the promise of equal protection for all. We are not permitted to do less and would damage our constitution immeasurably by trying to do more.

The only legitimate inquiry we can make is whether [the statute] is constitutional. If it is not, its virtues . . . cannot save it; if it is, its faults cannot be invoked to accomplish its destruction. If the provisions of the Constitution be not upheld when they pinch as well as when they comfort, they may as well be abandoned.

In the final analysis, we give respect to the views of all Iowans on the issue of same-sex marriage — religious or otherwise — by giving respect to our constitutional principles. These principles require that the state recognize both opposite-sex and same-sex civil marriage. Religious doctrine and views contrary to this principle of law are unaffected, and people can continue to associate with the religion that best reflects their views. A religious denomination can still define marriage as a union between a man and a woman, and a marriage ceremony performed by a minister, priest, rabbi, or other person ordained or designated as a leader of the person's religious faith does not lose its meaning as a sacrament or other religious institution. The sanctity of all religious marriages celebrated in the future will have the same meaning as those celebrated in the past. The only difference is civil marriage will now take on a new meaning that reflects a more complete understanding of equal protection of the law. This result is what our constitution requires.

J.   Constitutional Infirmity

We are firmly convinced the exclusion of gay and lesbian people from the institution of civil marriage does not substantially further any important governmental objective. The legislature has excluded a historically disfavored class of persons from a supremely important civil institution without a constitutionally sufficient justification. There is no material fact, genuinely in dispute, that can affect this determination.

We have a constitutional duty to ensure equal protection of the law. Faithfulness to that duty requires us to hold Iowa's marriage statute, Iowa Code section 595.2, violates the Iowa Constitution. To decide otherwise would be an abdication of our constitutional duty. If gay and lesbian people must submit to different treatment without an exceedingly persuasive justification, they are deprived of the benefits of the principle of equal protection upon which the rule of law is founded. Iowa Code section 595.2 denies gay and lesbian people the equal protection of the law promised by the Iowa Constitution.

V.   Remedy

Because our civil marriage statute fails to provide equal protection of the law under the Iowa Constitution, we must decide how to best remedy the constitutional violation. The sole remedy requested by plaintiffs is admission into the institution of civil marriage. The County does not suggest an alternative remedy. The high courts of other jurisdictions have remedied constitutionally invalid bans on same-sex marriage in two ways. Some courts have ordered gay and lesbian people to be allowed to access the institution of civil marriage. Other courts have allowed their state legislatures to create parallel civil institutions for same-sex couples.

Iowa Code section 595.2 is unconstitutional because the County has been unable to identify a constitutionally adequate justification for excluding plaintiffs from the institution of civil marriage. A new distinction based on sexual orientation would be equally suspect and difficult to square with the fundamental principles of equal protection embodied in our constitution. This record, our independent research, and the appropriate equal protection analysis do not suggest the existence of a justification for such a legislative classification that substantially furthers any governmental objective. Consequently, the language in Iowa Code section 595.2 limiting civil marriage to a man and a woman must be stricken from the statute, and the remaining statutory language must be interpreted and applied in a manner allowing gay and lesbian people full access to the institution of civil marriage.

VI. Conclusion

The district court properly granted summary judgment to plaintiffs. Iowa Code section 595.2 violates the equal protection provision of the Iowa Constitution. Our decision becomes effective upon issuance of procedendo.

AFFIRMED.
All justices concur.

NOTES AND QUESTIONS

1. *Opposing results.* State courts have hardly been uniform in their responses to constitutional challenges to statutes barring same-sex marriage. The supreme courts of Connecticut, Massachusetts, and New Mexico have struck down state prohibitions on same-sex marriage on state constitutional grounds. See Kerrigan v. Commr. of Public Health, 957 A.2d 407 (Conn. 2008); Goodridge v. Department of Public Health, 798 N.E.2d 941 (Mass. 2003); Griego v. Oliver, __ P.3d __, 2013 WL 6670704 (N.M. Dec. 19, 2013); see also Garden State Equality v. Dow, __ A.3d __, 2013 WL 5687193 (N.J. Oct. 18, 2013) (refusing to stay a lower court order holding that the state cannot prohibit same-sex marriage). Other state high courts, however, have upheld similar prohibitions. In Hernandez v. Robles, 855 N.E.2d 1 (N.Y. 2006), the New York Court of Appeals held that provisions of

New York's Domestic Relations Law limiting marriage to different-sex couples did not violate the due process or equal protection provisions of New York's constitution. The court reasoned that at least two grounds support the distinction drawn by the legislature. First, the legislature could rationally conclude that it is more important to promote stability in opposite-sex couples than in same-sex couples. "Heterosexual intercourse has a natural tendency to lead to the birth of children; homosexual intercourse does not." 855 N.E.2d at 7. Hence, the legislature could choose to offer an inducement in the form of marriage and its attendant benefits to opposite-sex couples who make a long-term commitment to each other. Second, the legislature could rationally conclude that it is better, all else being equal, for children to grow up with both a mother and a father. Any expansion of the traditional definition of marriage, the court concluded, should come from the legislature, not the courts.

The California Supreme Court's decision in In re Marriage Cases, 183 P.3d 384 (2008), had struck down California state laws limiting marriage to opposite-sex couples as violating the plaintiffs' privacy, due process, and equal protection rights under the state constitution. However, in November 2008, California voters passed Proposition 8, which added the following provision to the California state constitution: "Only marriage between a man and a woman is valid or recognized in California." Cal. Const., Art. I, §7.5 (2008). Two same-sex couples filed suit in federal court, challenging Proposition 8 on due process and equal protection grounds under the federal Constitution. The federal District Court declared Proposition 8 unconstitutional and enjoined state officials from enforcing it. On appeal, the Ninth Circuit held that the petitioners, the official proponents of the initiative, had standing to defend it, and affirmed on the merits. In 2013, the United States Supreme Court held that the petitioners lacked standing. It vacated the Ninth Circuit's judgment and remanded the case with instructions to dismiss the appeal for lack of jurisdiction. Hollingsworth v. Perry, 133 S. Ct. 2652 (2013). The upshot is that same-sex marriage is now legal in California.

Constitutional challenges to other states' bans on same-sex marriage are also working their way through the federal courts. See, e.g., Kitchen v. Herbert, ____ F. Supp. 2d ___, 2013 WL 6697874 (D. Utah Dec. 20, 2013) (invalidating state constitutional provisions and statutes that ban same-sex marriage), stayed pending appeal, 2014 WL 30367 (U.S. Jan. 6, 2014).

2. *Legislation and state constitutions.* State legislatures have been very active in this area. As of December 31, 2013, statutes in the District Columbia and at least a dozen states recognized same-sex marriage (Connecticut, Delaware, Hawaii, Illinois, Maine, Maryland, Minnesota, New Hampshire, New York, Rhode Island, Vermont, and Washington). Other states (such as Colorado, Nevada, New Jersey, Oregon, and Wisconsin) enacted statutes conferring some or all of the legal benefits and responsibilities of marriage to same-sex couples via non-marriage institutions like civil unions, reciprocal beneficiaries, or domestic partnerships.

A substantial number of states have constitutional provisions restricting marriage to different-sex couples. Among these states are Alabama, Alaska, Arizona, Arkansas, Florida, Georgia, Idaho, Kansas, Kentucky, Michigan, Missouri, Montana, North Dakota, Ohio, Oklahoma, South Carolina, South Dakota, Tennessee, Texas, Utah, Virginia, and Wisconsin.

Commentators have proposed model statutes extending inheritance rights to domestic partners, both same-sex and opposite-sex. See T.P. Gallanis, Inheritance Rights for Domestic Partners, 79 Tul. L. Rev. 55, 67 (2004); Lawrence W. Waggoner, Marital Property Rights in Transition, 59 Mo. L. Rev. 21 (1994). For a critical review of such proposals, see Lynn D. Wardle, Counting the Costs of Civil Unions: Some Potential Detrimental Effects on Family Law, 11 Widener J. Pub. L. 401 (2002).

3. *DOMA.* In 1996 Congress threw its weight solidly against recognition of same-sex unions, enacting the federal Defense of Marriage Act (DOMA), 28 U.S.C. §1738C. Section 2 of DOMA provides that no state shall be required under the Full Faith and Credit Clause of the Federal Constitution to give effect to a same-sex marriage contracted in another state. Additionally, §3 provided that for all federal purposes "the word 'marriage' means only a legal union between one man and one woman as husband and wife, and the word 'spouse' refers only to a person of the opposite sex who is a husband or a wife." The latter section means that same-sex married couples are deprived of social security, tax, and welfare benefits under federal law.

In 2013, the U.S. Supreme Court struck down §3 as a deprivation of equal liberty under the Fifth Amendment. United States v. Windsor, 133 S. Ct. 2675 (2013). The Court reasoned, in part:

> DOMA's unusual deviation from the usual tradition of recognizing and accepting state definitions of marriage here operates to deprive same-sex couples of the benefits and responsibilities that come with the federal recognition of their marriages. This is strong evidence of a law having the purpose and effect of disapproval of that class. The avowed purpose and practical effect of the law here in question are to impose a disadvantage, a separate status, and so a stigma upon all who enter into same-sex marriages made lawful by the unquestioned authority of the States.

This means that same-sex couples have the benefits of marriage under federal law so long as they were validly married under state law. As a result of the Court's decision, the petitioner, whose same-sex marriage was valid in New York, was entitled to the marital deduction under the federal estate tax for her deceased spouse's estate.

4. Suppose a Canadian lesbian married couple move to the United States. Will their marriage be recognized here? The traditional conflict of laws rule is that if a marriage is valid where contracted, it is valid everywhere. See In re Kandu, 315 B.R. 123 (W.D. Wash. 2004). See generally Restatement (Second) of Conflict of Laws §283 (1988); Uniform Marriage and Divorce Act §210 (1973); William Baude, Beyond DOMA: Choice of State Law in Federal Statutes, 64 Stan. L. Rev. 1371 (2012).

III

Leaseholds: The Law of Landlord and Tenant

Leaseholds — or nonfreeholds, or tenancies — are a part of the larger estates system considered in Part II. Like the freehold estates, leaseholds have roots that run deep into feudal times (hence the notion of a *tenant* who holds under a *landlord*). And again like freeholds, leaseholds have been fairly static over the years in terms of their formal characteristics. In terms of relations between landlord and tenant, however, there have been regular and significant developments. The most important of these, together with the body of conventional law in the background, make up the bulk of the next chapter. The chapter considers, step by step, the nature and incidents of leaseholds, and then concludes with a selective look at the persistent problem of affordable rental housing.

6

Tradition, Tension, and Change in Landlord-Tenant Law

A. The Leasehold Estates

Leaseholds, or tenancies, are the so-called nonfreehold estates briefly introduced in Chapter 3 (at page 244). The principal leaseholds are the term of years, the periodic tenancy, and the tenancy at will.[1] We consider them in turn.

1. The Term of Years

A term of years is an estate that lasts for some fixed period of time or for a period computable by a formula that results in fixing calendar dates for beginning and ending, once the term is created or becomes possessory. The period can be one day, two months, five years, or 3,000 years. These are all terms of years. At common law there was no limit on the number of years permitted, but in some American states statutes limit the duration of terms of years.[2] A term must be for a fixed period, but it can be terminable earlier upon the happening of some event or condition. Because a term of years states from the outset when it will terminate, no notice of termination is necessary to bring the estate to an end.

---

1. One could add the tenancy at sufferance to the list, though it is not really a tenancy at all. We consider it below.

Bear in mind that when any of the leasehold estates is created, a future interest—in the landlord or in a third party—necessarily arises. If the landlord has retained the right to possession at the end of the leasehold, the future interest is a reversion. If provision is made for some third party to take possession, ordinarily the future interest will be a remainder.

2. For example, in California leases of agricultural land cannot exceed 51 years, nor those of urban land 99 years, if any rent or service of some kind is reserved. Cal. Civ. Code §§717, 718 (West 2013). In many areas, though, very long leases are permitted. Yale University still receives annual rents from 999-year leases of Connecticut farmland executed in the 1700s. Fred Strebeigh, Yale's 999-Year Leases, Yale Alumni Mag., Dec. 1976, at 29. See also Trustees of First Presbyterian Church of Pittsburgh v. Oliver-Tyrone Corp., 375 A.2d 193 (Pa. Super. Ct. 1977) (999-year lease).

But for an example of a *really long* lease, consider the 10,000-year lease between Cincinnati College, the lessor, and the Young Men's Mercantile Library Association. The lease commenced on January 1, 1848, and is renewable "forever." Rent was an initial payment of $10,000. The private library housed in the leased property is still operating in Cincinnati, and the lease itself "can be viewed if one asks politely," says law professor Jorge L. Contreras, who very kindly provided us with the information above.

2. The Periodic Tenancy

A periodic tenancy is a lease for a period of some fixed duration that continues for succeeding periods until either the landlord or tenant gives notice of termination. Examples: "to *A* from month to month," or "to *B* from year to year." If notice is not given the period is automatically extended for another period. (These are examples of express periodic tenancies. As we shall see, periodic tenancies are often created by implication.)

Under common law rules, half a year's notice is required to terminate a year-to-year tenancy. For example, if *T* is a year-to-year tenant beginning January 1, 2010, *L* must receive notice of termination before July 1, 2010, or *T* can be held over for another period—until January 1, 2012. For any periodic tenancy of less than a year, notice of termination must be given equal to the length of the period, but not to exceed six months. The notice must terminate the tenancy on the final day of the period, not in the middle of the tenancy. Thus if a month-to-month tenant who began his tenancy on January 1 decided on March 20 to terminate, the earliest termination date would be April 30. In many states, statutes have shortened the length of notice required to terminate periodic tenancies and have permitted a month-to-month tenancy to be terminated at any time following 30 days' notice.

The death of the landlord or tenant has no effect on the duration of a term of years or periodic tenancy,[3] but it does on the tenancy at will.

PROBLEMS

1. On October 1, *L* leases Whiteacre "to *T* for one year, beginning October 1." On the following September 30, *T* moves out without giving *L* any notice. What are *L*'s rights? What if the lease had been "to *T* from year to year, beginning October 1"? What if the lease had been for no fixed term "at an annual rental of $24,000 payable $2,000 per month on the first of each month"?

2. *T*, a month-to-month tenant, notified *L* on November 16, 2012, that she would vacate as of November 30, 2012. *T* subsequently vacated on that date and paid no further rent to *L*. *L*, after reasonable efforts, finally relet the premises beginning April 1, 2013. The jurisdiction in question has no statute prescribing the method of terminating a month-to-month tenancy. *L* sues *T* for unpaid rent for the months of December 2012 and January through March 2013. What result? See S.D.G. v. Inventory Control Co., 429 A.2d 394 (N.J. Super. 1981).

---

3. But see Annot., 42 A.L.R.4th 963 (1985 & Supp. 2006), suggesting that courts sometimes terminate residential leaseholds upon the death of the tenant (absent statutes providing otherwise) on the ground that residential tenancies are "personal."

3. The Tenancy at Will

A tenancy at will is a tenancy of no fixed period that endures so long as both land-lord and tenant desire. If the lease provides that it can be terminated by one party, it is necessarily at the will of the other as well *if* a tenancy at will has been created. (Complications in this statement are examined in the *Garner* case, below.) Note, however, that a unilateral power to terminate a lease can be engrafted on a term of years or a periodic tenancy; for example, a lease by *L* to *T* for 10 years or until *L* sooner terminates creates a term of years determinable.

The tenancy at will ends, among other ways, when one of the parties ter-minates it. (It also ends, as suggested above, at the death of one of the parties.) Modern statutes ordinarily require a period of notice—say 30 days or a time equal to the interval between rent payments—in order for one party or the other to terminate a tenancy at will.[4]

Garner v. Gerrish

Court of Appeals of New York, 1984
473 N.E.2d 223

WACHTLER, J. The question on this appeal is whether a lease which grants the ten-ant the right to terminate the agreement at a date of his choice creates a deter-minable life tenancy on behalf of the tenant or merely establishes a tenancy at will. The courts below held that the lease created a tenancy at will permitting the current landlord to evict the tenant. We granted the tenant's motion for leave to appeal and now reverse the order appealed from.

In 1977 Robert Donovan owned a house located in Potsdam, New York. On April 14 of that year he leased the premises to the tenant Lou Gerrish. The lease was executed on a printed form and it appears that neither side was represented by counsel. The blanks on the form were filled in by Donovan who provided the names of the parties, described the property and fixed the rent at $100 a month. With respect to the duration of the tenancy the lease provides it shall continue "for and during the term of *quiet enjoyment* from the *first* day of *May*, 1977 which term will end— *Lou Gerrish has the privilege of termination [sic] this agreement at a date of his own choice*" (emphasis added to indicate handwritten and typewritten addi-tions to the printed form). The lease also contains a standard reference to the landlord's right of reentry if the rent is not timely paid, which is qualified by the handwritten statement: "Lou has thirty days grace for payment."

Gerrish moved into the house and continued to reside there, apparently without incident, until Donovan died in November of 1981. At that point David

---

4. How, in such jurisdictions, does the tenancy at will differ from a periodic tenancy? See 1 American Law of Property §§3.28, 3.31 (1952 & Supp. 1977). Note here, by the way, that if under a tenancy for no fixed period rent is reserved or paid periodically, a periodic tenancy—rather than a tenancy at will—arises in most jurisdic-tions by implication. See id. §3.25.

Garner, executor of Donovan's estate, served Gerrish with a notice to quit the premises. When Gerrish refused, Garner commenced this summary proceeding to have him evicted. Petitioner contended that the lease created a tenancy at will because it failed to state a definite term. In his answering affidavit, the tenant alleged that he had always paid the rent specified in the lease. He also contended that the lease granted him a tenancy for life, unless he elects to surrender possession during his lifetime.

The County Court granted summary judgment to petitioner on the ground that the lease is "indefinite and uncertain . . . as regards the length of time accorded respondent to occupy the premises. Although the writing specifies the date of commencement of the term, it fails to set forth the duration of continuance, and the date or event of termination." The court concluded that the original landlord leased the premises to the tenant "for a month-to-month term and that petitioner was entitled to terminate the lease upon the death of the lessor effective upon the expiration of the next succeeding monthly term of occupancy." In support of its decision the court quoted the following statement from our opinion in Western Transp. Co. v. Lansing, 49 N.Y. 499, 508: "A lease . . . for so long as the lessee shall please, is said to be a lease at will of both lessor and lessee."

The Appellate Division affirmed for the same reasons in a brief memorandum (99 A.D.2d 608, 471 N.Y.S.2d 717).

On appeal to our court, the parties concede that the agreement creates a lease. The only question is whether it should be literally construed to grant to the tenant alone the right to terminate at will, or whether the landlord is accorded a similar right by operation of law.

At early common law according to Lord Coke, "when the lease is made to have and to hold at the will of the lessee, this must be also at the will of the lessor" (1 Co. Litt., §55a). This rule was generally adopted in the United States during the 19th century and at one time was said to represent the majority view (see Ann., 137 A.L.R. 362, 367; 51C C.J.S., Landlord and Tenant, §167, p.475). However, it was not universally accepted (see, e.g., Effinger v. Lewis, 32 Pa. 367; Gunnison v. Evans, 136 Kan. 791, 18 P.2d 191; Thompson v. Baxter, 107 Minn. 122, 119 N.W. 797) and has been widely criticized, particularly in this century, as an antiquated notion which violates the terms of the agreement and frustrates the intent of the parties (1 Tiffany, Real Property [3d ed.], §159; 1 American Law of Real Property [Casner ed., 1952], §3.30; Schoshinski, American Law of Landlord and Tenant, §2.7; see, also, Restatement, Property 2d, Landlord and Tenant, §1.6).

It has been noted that the rule has its origins in the doctrine of livery of seisin (Tiffany, op. cit., §159; Effinger v. Lewis, supra), which required physical transfer of a clod of earth, twig, key or other symbol on the premises in the presence of witnesses, to effect a conveyance of a fee interest (23 Blackstone's Comm., pp.315, 316; Black's Law Dictionary [Fourth ed.], p.1084). Although this ceremony was not required for leases, which were generally limited to a specified term of years, it was necessary to create a life tenancy which was viewed as a fee interest. Thus, if a lease granting a tenant a life estate was not accompanied by livery of seisin, the intended conveyance would fail and a mere tenancy at will would result. The corollary to Lord Coke's comment is that the grant of a life estate would be enforceable if accompanied by livery of seisin and the other requisites for a conveyance. Because such a tenancy was terminable at the will of the grantee, there was in fact no general objection at common law to a tenancy at the will of the tenant. The express terms of a lease granting a life tenancy would fail, and a tenancy at will would result, only when livery of seisin, or any other requirement for a conveyance, had not been met. . . .

Because livery of seisin, like the ancient requirement for a seal, has been abandoned, commentators generally urge that there is no longer any reason why a lease granting the tenant alone the right to terminate at will, should be converted into a tenancy at will terminable by either party. . . . The Restatement adopts this view and provides the following illustration: "*L* leases a farm to *T* for as long as *T* desires to stay on the land." The lease creates a determinable life estate in *T*, terminable at *T*'s will or on his death. (Restatement, Property 2d, Landlord and Tenant, §1.6, Comment g, Illustration 6.) This rule has increasingly gained acceptance in courts which have closely examined the problem. . . .

In the case now before us, the lease . . . simply grants a personal right to the named lessee, Lou Gerrish, to terminate at a date of his choice, which is a fairly typical means of creating a life tenancy terminable at the will of the tenant. . . . Thus the lease will terminate, at the latest, upon the death of the named lessee. The fact that it may be terminated at some earlier point, if the named tenant decides to quit the premises, does not render it indeterminate. Leases providing for termination upon the occurrence of a specified event prior to the completion of an otherwise fixed term, are routinely enforced even when the event is within the control of the lessee.

In sum, the lease expressly and unambiguously grants to the tenant the right to terminate, and does not reserve to the landlord a similar right. To hold that such a lease creates a tenancy terminable at the will of either party would violate the terms of the agreement and the express intent of the contracting parties.

Accordingly, the order of the Appellate Division should be reversed and the petition dismissed.

QUESTION AND PROBLEMS

1. Does the decision in *Garner* violate the *numerus clausus* principle discussed earlier at pages 221-222? Consider the following from Thomas W. Merrill & Henry E. Smith, Optimal Standardization in the Law of Property: The *Numerus Clausus* Principle, 110 Yale L.J. 1, 22-23 (2000):

> [O]ne issue implicating [the *numerus clausus*] doctrine that has arisen in several jurisdictions concerns the proper construction of an instrument that purports to grant a lease of property for the life of the tenant. Under the system of estates in land, there is no such thing as a "lease for life." One can create a life estate. And one can create a lease. But a lease must be either a term of years, a periodic tenancy, a tenancy at will, or a tenancy at sufferance. Thus, courts confronted with an instrument purporting to create a "lease for life" have typically asked which common-law box best matches the grantor's intentions: a life estate or a tenancy at will. Yet there

is no evidence in these decisions that the courts are aware that they are applying a foundational precept of property law. . . .

A . . . New York case [here referring to *Garner*] confronting the lease-for-life problem suggests that courts in the future may simply defer to the parties' intention to create a new type of leasehold. The opinion attacked the argument in favor of the tenancy at will—the harsh application of the *numerus clausus*—as being grounded in the "antiquated notion" that a life estate cannot be created without livery of seisin. This outcome was also condemned as "violat[ing] the terms of the agreement and frustrat[ing] the intent of the parties." As to whether the court was willing to follow the intent of the parties to the point of recognizing a new type of estate—a lease for life—the decision is ambiguous. Near the end of the opinion, the court characterized the interest as a "life tenancy terminable at the will of the tenant," which sounds like a life estate. . . . Thus, the result that the court ultimately reached may have been to hold that the instrument created a life estate, which would be consistent with the *numerus clausus*. However, the court also noted that both parties agreed that the instrument created a lease, and it, too, spoke of the interest as a lease. This characterization, plus the court's condemnation of "antiquated notion[s]" about established forms of property and its insistence on resolving the issue in terms of the parties' intent, could mean that the court saw no problem with enforcing the instrument in accordance with its terms, as a "lease for life."

2. *L* leases Orangeacre "to *T* for as many years as *L* desires." What estate does *T* have? See Restatement (Second) of Property, Landlord and Tenant §1.6 comment g (1977).

3. For rent payments of $500 a month *L* leases Greenacre "to *T* for the duration of the war." What estate does *T* have? What difference does it make? National Bellas Hess, Inc. v. Kalis, 191 F.2d 739 (8th Cir. 1951); Smith's Transfer & Storage Co. v. Hawkins, 50 A.2d 267 (D.C. 1946).

Philpot v. Field, 633 S.W.2d 546 (Tex. Civ. App. 1982), involved a lease to *T* for a term of 20 years and so long thereafter as *T* used the premises for particular purposes. Thereafter the premises were used continuously by *T* for the particular purposes. *L*, sometime after the expiration of the 20-year term, wished to terminate the lease. *L* argued that because the lease had an uncertain term, it was a tenancy at will terminable by either party once the 20 years expired. The court held otherwise, saying:

> Although there is no definite ending date after the 20 year term, that date is tied to the cessation of the use of the land for certain definitely ascertainable purposes. Common sense, logic and the trend in the law support this decision. It appears that the parties intended to create a perpetual right to lease the land. When the parties' intent is made clear, courts should enforce the agreement as written, even though perpetual rights are not favored. . . .
>
> No legitimate reason exists for us to hold that the parties cannot freely and intelligently lease land for so long as a certain definite use is made of the land. Although [*T*] can terminate this lease when he desires by his voluntary choice, this lease does not create a tenancy at will terminable at the will of either party. [633 S.W.2d at 548.]

See also Myers v. East Ohio Gas Co., 364 N.E.2d 1369 (Ohio 1977), holding that "leases which clearly and unambiguously terminate at the will of only one party are to be controlled by their express terms." But ambiguous leases—"those leases which do not clearly state whether they are terminable at the will of one or both parties"—are subject to a rebuttable presumption that they are at the will of both. Id. at 1373. The lease in *Myers* was similar to the lease in *Philpot*. The court found it unambiguous and enforced it according to its terms.

4.   The Tenancy at Sufferance: Holdovers

The so-called tenancy at sufferance arises when a tenant remains in possession (holds over) after termination of the tenancy. Common law rules give the landlord confronted with a holdover essentially two options—eviction (plus damages), or consent (express or implied) to the creation of a new tenancy. Some jurisdictions have changed these rules. Complications arise in any event.

Suppose, for example, that a tenant holds over after the end date of a one-year term, sends the landlord a check for the usual monthly rental payment, and the landlord cashes it. Since the landlord has elected not to evict, there appears to be a new tenancy. But of what sort? The answer varies, depending on the jurisdiction. In most, holding over gives rise to a periodic tenancy, in the balance, it results in a term. As to the basis for the length of the period or term, on one view it is the length of the original period or term, with the maximum length limited in either case to one year. Other courts base length (again limited to no more than a year) on the way rent was computed in the original lease. This is not so straightforward as it sounds. A lease might state (the technical term is "reserve") an annual rent of, say, $12,000, but call for it to be paid in installments of $1,000 at the beginning of each month. So is there a new term of one month (or a new periodic tenancy of month-to-month), or is there instead a new term of one year (or a new periodic tenancy of year-to-year)? Again, it depends on the jurisdiction.

These points aside, the tenancy resulting from holding over is usually subject to the same terms and conditions (the amount of rent, the duty to repair, and so forth) as those in the original lease, unless the parties agree otherwise or unless some term or condition is regarded as inconsistent with the new situation.

Many states have adopted legislation to deal with holdovers, but in widely varying ways. Some statutes specify the length of the holdover tenancy. See, e.g., Cal. Civ. Code §1945 (West 2013) ("not exceeding one month when the rent is payable monthly, nor in any case one year"); Aviel v. Ng, 74 Cal. Rptr. 3d 200, 209 (Cal. App. 2008) (acceptance of rent from tenant of foreclosed property leads to month-to-month tenancy). Others, probably only a few, convert the holdover tenancy into a tenancy at will and provide that the tenant shall be liable for the reasonable value of use and occupation—even though this may be less than the rent agreed upon in the original lease! Such, at least, is one judicial interpretation. See Townsend v. Singleton, 183 S.E.2d 893 (S.C. 1971). Still other statutes provide that landlords may demand double rent from holdover tenants.

Given the common law approach to holdovers, and the various legislative alternatives, which do you prefer? In thinking about the question, consider that conventional common law holdover doctrine is said to be for the benefit of tenants as a class because it secures to the incoming tenants the possession of the premises on the date bargained for, and . . . since leases . . . tend to begin and end at certain periods and property values are based on continuity of rental income, it is socially and economically important for the landlord to be able to deliver possession on a stipulated date. While this is true, the penalty imposed on the tenant frequently is out of all proportion to the injury to the landlord or the incoming tenant. [1 American Law of Property, supra, §3.33 at 238.][5]

B.   The Lease

An arrangement that resembles a lease—indeed, an arrangement explicitly declaring itself, in writing, to be a "lease"—might nevertheless be held by the courts to amount to something else, such as a license (see the discussion of licenses at page 820), or a life estate (see page 226).[6] Suppose, for example, that A (1) "rents" from B the right to erect a billboard on land owned by B; (2) contracts with B to install and operate a cosmetics concession in B's department store; (3) is allowed to farm B's land, the consideration being that A will share the crops with B; (4) rents a room for two months in B's rustic country inn; (5) works for B and is given a room in B's house as partial compensation. Do these examples involve leases—or something else? See generally 1 American Law of Property §§3.3-3.8 (1952 & Supp. 1977), discussing the many considerations that bear on the question (such as the intention of the parties, the number of restrictions on use, the exclusivity of possession, the degree of control retained by the granting party, the presence or absence of incidental services, and so on).

Putting aside obvious instances like that suggested in footnote 6, why might it matter whether any given arrangement amounts to a lease, as opposed to something else? The answer, for now, has to be limited to a pretty empty generalization: It matters primarily whether or not an arrangement amounts to a lease

---

5. For the sake of tenants, courts commonly soften the application of holdover doctrine by various means. Say a tenant vacates leased premises in a timely fashion but leaves some office equipment behind. Is the tenant liable as a holdover? Perhaps not. See Caserta v. Action for Bridgeport Community, 377 A.2d 856 (Conn. Super. 1976) (no holdover, because the equipment did not interfere with the landlord's use of the premises). Or say a tenant stays on after the end of the term because her doctor has advised her that it would be dangerous, for the time being, to move her very ill child. Is the tenant liable as a holdover? Probably not. See Herter v. Mullen, 53 N.E. 700 (N.Y. 1899) (no holdover, because the tenant did not stay on voluntarily).

6. Or a loan, even though the document in question speaks in terms of a lease and looks and acts like one. See, e.g., In re Pittsburgh Sports Associates Holding Co., 239 B.R. 75 (Bankr. W.D. Pa. 1999), involving the Pittsburgh Penguins bankruptcy. One reason the bankruptcy judge gave for finding a loan rather than a lease was that the agreement in question was to expire on September 1, 2012, unless terminated earlier. "Such an indefinite term," the judge said, "is inconsistent with the requirement that a lease be for a 'prescribed period.'" 239 B.R. at 85. But you have learned that the judge is wrong. Recall the discussion of the term of years at page 443. Similarly, an arrangement that does not announce itself as a lease might still be regarded as one. See, e.g., Township of Sandyston v. Angerman, 341 A.2d 682 (N.J. Super. 1975), involving an agreement between the Angermans and the U.S. Department of the Interior. By the terms of the agreement, the Angermans were given exclusive possession of a single family dwelling and adjoining land located in a national recreation area; no rent was called for, but the Angermans were obligated to restore and maintain the dwelling and watch for forest fires in the area. A New Jersey statute subjected leaseholds to a municipal tax. The Angermans claimed that their arrangement with the Department of the Interior was a license, not a lease, and hence not subject to the leasehold tax. They lost.

because leases give rise to the landlord-tenant relationship, which carries with it certain incidents—certain rights and duties and liabilities and remedies—that do not attach to other relationships. Those incidents are the chief concern of the balance of this chapter.

Conveyance versus contract. Here is another question you will see playing a part in much of the material that follows: Is a lease a *conveyance* or a *contract?* Actually, of course, it is both. A lease transfers a possessory interest in land, so it is a conveyance that creates property rights. But it is also the case that leases usually contain a number of promises (or covenants, which originally referred to promises under seal)—such as a promise by the tenant to pay rent or a promise by the landlord to provide utilities—so the lease is a contract, too, thus creating contract rights.[7]

Historically, it was lease-as-conveyance that the courts tended to stress, but over the last several decades this has changed, to some degree, in favor of a view emphasizing the contractual nature of leases. The objective of the new orientation has been to reform the "property law" of landlord and tenant by importing into it much of the modern law of contracts. Some commentators have found the move unnecessary, or even counterproductive;[8] others argue that it still has far to go.[9] In any event, it is a fact that courts today commonly rely, explicitly, on contract principles to reshape the law of leases with respect to such questions as the following: (1) Are the covenants in leases "mutually dependent," such that (as in contract doctrine) a material breach by one party excuses further performance by the other party, even if the lease does not so provide? Suppose, for example, that the landlord breaches a promise to repair. Does the tenant's obligation to pay rent cease? If the tenant defaults in rent payments, may the landlord terminate the lease, absent a provision allowing him to do so? (2) If the leased premises are destroyed, is the tenant still liable for rent (again, notwithstanding the absence of any relevant provision in the lease)? (3) If the tenant wrongfully abandons the leased premises, must the landlord take steps to mitigate (reduce) the damages, say by searching for a suitable new tenant?[10] (4) Is a warranty of quality—that the leased premises are habitable or fit for their purpose—to be

---

7. Though leaseholds eventually came to be recognized as interests in land, they were and still are classified, like contractual interests, as personal property. Their peculiar origin is indicated by their old-fashioned name, chattels real. Chattel suggests personal property; real suggests a connection with land. The reasons for classifying a lessee's interest as personal property have generally disappeared, but the classification can nevertheless be of some significance. For discussion, see 1 American Law of Property, supra, §3.12.

8. See, e.g., Edward Chase, The Property-Contract Theme in Landlord and Tenant Law: A Critical Commentary on Schoshinski's American Law of Landlord and Tenant, 13 Rutgers L.J. 189 (1982); John A. Humbach, The Common-Law Conception of Leasing: Mitigation, Habitability, and Dependence of Covenants, 60 Wash. U. L.Q. 1213 (1983).

Understand that contract principles have always governed agreements to make a lease, though it can sometimes be difficult to tell whether a particular transaction amounts to a lease (but one to commence in the future), or rather to an agreement to make a lease. See generally 1 American Law of Property, supra, §3.17.

9. See, e.g., Robert H. Kelley, Any Reports of the Death of the Property Law Paradigm for Leases Have Been Greatly Exaggerated, 41 Wayne L. Rev. 1563 (1995). For an economic analysis (stressing information costs) of the choice between property and contract in several areas of property, see Thomas W. Merrill & Henry E. Smith, The Property/Contract Interface, 101 Colum. L. Rev. 773 (2001) (on landlord-tenant law in particular, see id. at 820-833).

10. Usually, of course, the landlord will wish to re-rent as soon as possible in any event, for the sake of cash flow and protection of the premises. But see Sommer v. Kridel, reproduced on page 492.

implied in leases? We shall be addressing questions like these in subsequent sections of this chapter.

The Statute of Frauds. Every state has a Statute of Frauds (intended to prevent just that) patterned in one way or another after the English Statute of Frauds enacted in the seventeenth century. Commonly, the American statutes provide that leases for more than one year must be in writing. All but a few jurisdictions permit oral leases for a term less than a year; those that do not usually hold that entry under an oral lease plus payment of rent creates a periodic tenancy that is not subject to the Statute. For a discussion of the consequences of failure to comply with the statutory requirements, see 1 American Law of Property, supra, §§3.18-3.21; see also pages 570-576.

Form leases and the question of "bargaining power." The written lease can be a long document. Unlike a deed, by which (in the usual case) all of the seller's interest is conveyed to the buyer forever, a lease contemplates a continuing relationship between landlord and tenant. Thus deeds are commonly brief, whereas leases can be wordy, full of clauses to handle various contingencies.

Quite typically, landlords use form leases—standardized documents offered to all tenants on a take-it-or-leave-it basis, with no negotiation over terms. Does this indicate that tenants lack bargaining power, such that harsh terms can be forced upon them by landlords? Not necessarily. Consider the following, addressing form contracts generally:

> It is an easy step from the observation that there is no negotiation to the conclusion that the purchaser lacked a free choice and therefore should not be bound. But there is an innocent explanation for these so-called "contracts of adhesion": the seller is trying to avoid the costs of negotiating and drafting a separate agreement with each purchaser. Those costs, of which probably the largest is the cost of supervising the employees and agents who engage in the actual contract negotiations on the company's behalf, are likely to be high for a large company that has many contracts.
>
> Consistent with the innocent explanation, large and sophisticated buyers, as well as individual consumers, often make purchases pursuant to printed form contracts. . . .
>
> The sinister explanation for the form contract is that the seller refuses to dicker separately with each purchaser because the buyer has no choice but to accept the seller's terms. But if one seller offers unattractive terms, won't a competing seller, wanting sales for himself, offer more attractive terms, the process continuing until the terms are optimal? All the firms in the industry may find it economical to use standard contracts and refuse to negotiate with purchasers. But what is important is not whether there is haggling in every transaction but whether competition forces sellers to incorporate in their standard contracts terms that protect the purchasers.
>
> Under monopoly, by definition, the buyer has no good alternatives to dealing with the seller, who is therefore in a position to insist on terms that in a competitive market would be bettered by another seller. [Richard A. Posner, Economic Analysis of Law 144 (8th ed. 2011).]

On this view, the underlying problem is not form leases but monopoly power—created, say, by a shortage of rental housing.[11] What, then, should be the remedy? The courts can respond by policing lease terms on grounds of "unequal

---

11. If there is a glut, tenants will have enhanced "bargaining power." Form leases might still be used, but their terms—especially terms regarding the amount of rent—are likely to be attractive to tenants.

bargaining power" (a theme you will see running throughout this chapter), but this case-by-case approach is thought by some to be insufficient. See, e.g., Curtis J. Berger, Hard Leases Make Bad Law, 74 Colum. L. Rev. 791 (1974), calling instead for statutory reform—legislation requiring full disclosure of landlords' and tenants' duties, rights, and remedies. A more far-reaching approach would rely on statutory leases setting out prescribed terms and conditions.[12]

Given the assumption of market (monopoly) power, would not landlords respond to any of the foregoing measures by increasing the rents they charged? Rent controls could then be considered, but they might aggravate the underlying housing shortage. See pages 534-536.

C. Selection of Tenants (Herein of Unlawful Discrimination)

Landlords, once free to discriminate as they wished in selecting tenants—whether on grounds of race, gender, national origin, or whatever—are today constrained in a number of respects. Perhaps the most significant constraints (but not, as we shall see, the only ones) are imposed by the federal Fair Housing Act, 42 U.S.C.A §§3601-3619, 3631, originally enacted in 1968 and amended several times since. Portions of the legislation provide as follows:

§3603. [Exemptions]

(a) Application to certain described dwellings

Subject to the provisions of subsection (b) of this section and section 3607 of this title [section 3607 exempts religious organizations and private clubs under certain circumstances, and also states that provisions regarding familial status do not apply to housing for older persons], the prohibitions against discrimination in the sale or rental of housing set forth in section 3604 of this title shall apply. . . .

(b) Exemptions

Nothing in section 3604 of this title (other than subsection (c)) shall apply to—

(1) any single family house sold or rented by an owner: *Provided,* That such private individual owner does not own more than three such single family houses at any one time. . . . *Provided further,* That after December 31, 1969, the sale or rental of any such single family house shall be excepted from the application of this subchapter only if such house is sold or rented (A) without the use in any manner of the sales or rental facilities or the sales or rental services of any real estate broker, agent, or salesman, or of such facilities or services of any person in the business of selling or renting dwellings, or of any employee or agent of any such broker, agent, salesman, or person and (B) without the publication, posting or mailing, after notice, of any advertisement or written notice in violation of section 3604(c) of this title; but nothing in this proviso shall prohibit the use of attorneys, escrow agents, abstractors, title companies, and other such professional assistance as necessary to perfect or transfer the title, or

---

12. See, e.g., Allen R. Bentley, An Alternative Residential Lease, 74 Colum. L. Rev. 836 (1974). Statutory leases can be problematic if landlords have political power as well as market power. See Note, Standard Form Leases in Wisconsin, 1966 Wis. L. Rev. 583, describing a program that allowed Wisconsin real estate brokers to use form leases only if the forms were issued or approved by the Wisconsin Real Estate Commission. The Commission, charged by legislation to "safeguard the interests of the public," nevertheless approved standard forms that contained provisions and clauses in conflict with state policy; the forms were "landlords' leases." Id. at 585, 592.

(2) rooms or units in dwellings containing living quarters occupied or intended to be occupied by no more than four families living independently of each other, if the owner actually maintains and occupies one of such living quarters as his residence. . . .

§3604. Discrimination in the Sale or Rental of Housing and Other Prohibited Practices

As made applicable by section 3603 of this title and except as exempted by sections 3603(b) and 3607 of this title, it shall be unlawful—

(a) To refuse to sell or rent after the making of a bona fide offer, or to refuse to negotiate for the sale or rental of, or otherwise make unavailable or deny, a dwelling to any person because of race, color, religion, sex, familial status, or national origin.

(b) To discriminate against any person in the terms, conditions, or privileges of sale or rental of a dwelling, or in the provision of services or facilities in connection therewith, because of race, color, religion, sex, familial status, or national origin.

(c) To make, print, or publish, or cause to be made, printed, or published any notice, statement, or advertisement, with respect to the sale or rental of a dwelling that indicates any preference, limitation, or discrimination based on race, color, religion, sex, handicap, familial status, or national origin, or an intention to make any such preference, limitation, or discrimination. . . .

(f)(1) To discriminate in the sale or rental, or to otherwise make unavailable or deny, a dwelling to any buyer or renter because of a handicap . . .

(2) To discriminate against any person in the terms, conditions, or privileges of sale or rental of a dwelling, or in the provision of services or facilities in connection with such dwelling, because of a handicap . . .

(3) For purposes of this subsection, discrimination includes—

(A) a refusal to permit, at the expense of the handicapped person, reasonable modifications of existing premises occupied or to be occupied by such person if such modifications may be necessary to afford such person full enjoyment of the premises except that, in the case of a rental, the landlord may where it is reasonable to do so condition permission for a modification on the renter agreeing to restore the interior of the premises to the condition that existed before the modification, reasonable wear and tear excepted;

(B) a refusal to make reasonable accommodations in rules, policies, practices, or services, when such accommodations may be necessary to afford such person equal opportunity to use and enjoy a dwelling; or

(C) in connection with the design and construction of covered multifamily dwellings for first occupancy after the date that is 30 months after September 13, 1988, a failure to design and construct those dwellings in such a manner that [common and public areas of the dwellings are readily accessible to handicapped persons, doors within the dwellings are wide enough for wheelchairs, and other features of "adaptive design," such as easily reached light switches, are provided].

NOTES AND QUESTIONS

1. Portions of the Fair Housing Act not set out above prohibit discrimination in the financing of housing and in the provision of brokerage services. Anyone injured by a discriminatory practice may commence a civil suit for injunctive relief and damages (including punitive damages). Other enforcement measures include conference and conciliation proceedings, suits by the U.S. Attorney General, and criminal penalties.

2. Attempts by the federal government to combat discrimination, *racial* discrimination in particular, date back to adoption of the Fourteenth Amendment

and its guarantee of equal protection. The Fourteenth Amendment prohibits only state (not private) action, but the Supreme Court's decision in Shelley v. Kraemer, 334 U.S. 1 (1948), effectively eliminated at least some private discrimination as well. (In *Shelley*, the Court held that state courts could not enforce racially restrictive land use agreements entered into by neighbors.) Much earlier, a section of the Civil Rights Act of 1866, 42 U.S.C.A. §1982, had promised to do more, at least with respect to property transactions. It provided:

> All citizens of the United States shall have the same right, in every State and Territory, as is enjoyed by white citizens thereof to inherit, purchase, lease, sell, hold, and convey real and personal property.

This measure had essentially no impact on private housing discrimination during the first century of its life, but the situation changed with Jones v. Alfred H. Mayer Co., 392 U.S. 409 (1968), decided the same year the original Fair Housing Act became law. In *Jones*, the Court held that the 1866 provision bars *all* racial discrimination, private and public, in the sale or rental of property. The 1866 law is narrower than the Fair Housing Act in that it reaches only racial discrimination, does not deal with discrimination in the provision of services and facilities, and does not prohibit discriminatory advertising; it is broader, however, in that it is not limited to dwellings and contains none of the exemptions found in the Fair Housing Act.[13]

Someone claiming discrimination has two avenues for proving a violation of the Fair Housing Act. The first is to show disparate treatment, which can be done with testimony or written records showing that the landlord, seller, real estate agent, or government agency intended to discriminate against her. In many instances, however, there is no direct evidence to demonstrate an intent to discriminate. A plaintiff can still show disparate treatment by setting forth a prima facie case of discrimination by circumstantial evidence. The plaintiff must show that she is a member of a protected class, that she qualified for the housing at issue, that she was rejected, and that the housing remained available after the rejection or was given to someone who was not a member of the protected class. At this point, the defendant must give a legitimate, non-discriminatory reason for the denial. If the defendant is able to offer this reason, then the plaintiff can still win by showing that the reason was pretextual and not the real reason for the denial. See, e.g., Robert Schwemm, Housing Discrimination Law and Litigation §10:2 (2012).

Virtually every federal circuit court of appeals in the nation has held that plaintiffs can also prove a discrimination claim through a "disparate impact" framework, although the specific tests they employ vary. A disparate impact claim challenges a facially non-discriminatory practice that has the effect of disproportionately

---

13. The 1866 legislation was broader in another important respect as well: It had no cap on damages, whereas the Fair Housing Act as originally enacted limited punitive damages to $1,000. Subsequent amendments did away with the limitation.

burdening members of a protected group. Under one type of disparate impact framework, once the plaintiff establishes a prima facie case by showing that some policy or practice of the landlord had a disproportionate effect or burden on a protected class, the burden shifts to the defendant to prove that he had a legitimate, non-discriminatory reason for his actions and that "no alternative course of action could be adopted that would enable that interest to be served with less impact." Resident Advisory Bd. v. Rizzo, 564 F.2d 126, 148-149 (3d Cir. 1977); see also Betsy v. Turtle Creek Associates, 736 F.2d 983, 988-989 (4th Cir. 1984); Huntington Branch NAACP v. Town of Huntington, 844 F.2d 926, 936 (2d Cir. 1988), aff'd in part, 488 U.S. 15 (1988). If the defendant alleges a rationale to support the practice, the plaintiff can still win by showing that there is an alternative course to achieve the legitimate interest. The disparate impact approach to Fair Housing has been used to invalidate landlord restrictions on family composition, zoning laws, and a multitude of other practices that disproportionately affect protected groups. For examples, see Schwemm, supra, at §10:6. In its 2013-2014 Term, the Supreme Court agreed to hear a challenge to the use of disparate impact in Fair Housing Act cases, Township of Mount Holly v. Mt. Holly Gardens Citizens in Action, but the case settled before oral argument.

In contrast to the foregoing, claims under the Civil Rights Act of 1866 probably do require proof of intentional or purposeful discrimination. On the use of testers to show discrimination, see Teresa Coleman Hunter & Gary L. Fischer, Fair Housing Testing—Uncovering Discriminatory Practices, 28 Creighton L. Rev. 1127 (1995).

3. Mrs. Murphy[14] has an apartment to rent in her home. She puts the following advertisement in a local newspaper:

> *For rent:* Furnished basement apartment in private white home. Call 376-7410.

An African American couple applies and is rejected by Mrs. Murphy because of race. Are there any violations of 42 U.S.C. §1982 or §3604? See United States v. Hunter, 459 F.2d 205 (4th Cir. 1972) (discriminatory advertisement). Suppose the advertisement had not contained the word "white." What result? See Bush v. Kaim, 297 F. Supp. 151 (N.D. Ohio 1969) (discussing discriminatory actions). Suppose the advertisement had not said "in private white home," but had said "rented only to persons speaking Polish, German, or Swedish." What result? See Holmgren v. Little Village Community Reporter, 342 F. Supp. 512 (N.D. Ill. 1971) (discrimination based on national origin).[15]

---

14. Why "Mrs. Murphy"? The answer has to do with the exemptions set forth in §3603(b) of the Fair Housing Act. During congressional deliberations on the act, the exemptions were discussed in terms of "an imagined 'Mrs. Murphy's boardinghouse,' run by a Mrs. Murphy who did not wish to rent to Blacks." Diane J. Klein & Charles Doskow, Housingdiscrimination.Com?: The Ninth Circuit (Mostly) Puts Out the Welcome Mat for Fair Housing Suits Against Roommate-Matching Websites, 38 Golden Gate U. L. Rev. 329, 334 n.17 (2008).

15. See also Judy Pasternak, Housing Bias with a Twist, L.A. Times, Feb. 7, 1991, at A1 ("Complaints are increasing about immigrant landlords who close the door to renters who are not from their homeland. . . . Patricia Leigh felt the stinging suspicion that she was a victim of racism. It was an odd, unsettling thought for a white American.").

Suppose Mrs. Murphy discriminates *against,* say, German people in renting the apartment in her home. This would not violate the Fair Housing Act. (Do you see why?) Would it violate the Civil Rights Act of 1866, 42 U.S.C.A §1982? See Shaare Tefila Congregation v. Cobb, 481 U.S. 615 (1987) (taking "race" to mean what it meant in 1866).

Suppose that *L* places the following advertisement in a campus newspaper: "Wanted: Female to share 2-bdrm. 2-bath apt. near campus. $500/mo. plus half utilities. Call Pat at 917-4513." Does this ad violate the federal Fair Housing Act? May *L* discriminate in this fashion? See Fair Housing Council of San Fernando Valley v. Roommate.com, LLC, 666 F.2d 1216 (9th Cir. 2012), holding that the act does not apply to the sharing of living units. A newspaper publishers' association has compiled a catalog of "taboo, troublesome, and safe words" for real estate advertisements. Such expressions as able-bodied, bachelor, near churches, couples only, empty nesters, exclusive, executive, responsible, and no smokers are part of a long list of unacceptable terms. It is acceptable to mention a location near bus lines, to say a credit check is required, to say no drugs or drinking (but not no alcoholics), to refer to school districts, to mention a senior discount, or the presence of a nursery. Caution is advised with respect to statements like fisherman's retreat, no gays, no lesbians, handyman's dream, prestigious, nanny's room, quality neighborhood, and secure. See Kirsten Lagatree, Fighting Words: Effort to Avoid Housing Discrimination Has Changed the Way Realty Ads Are Written, L.A. Times, Feb. 12, 1995, at K1 (real estate section).

Would a "housing for rent" notice posted on Craigslist stating "No Minorities" violate §3604(c)? See Chicago Lawyers' Committee for Civil Rights Under Law, Inc. v. Craigslist, 519 F.3d 666, 672 (7th Cir. 2008) (holding that on-line services are immunized by §230(c)(1) of the Communications Decency Act of 1996).

Suppose the owner of a large apartment complex reserves a certain number of units exclusively for white applicants, the objective being to guard against "white flight" and thus maintain integrated housing conditions. Does the practice violate the Fair Housing Act? See United States v. Starrett City Associates, 840 F.2d 1096 (2d Cir. 1988); Raso v. Lago, 135 F.3d 11 (1st Cir. 1998); Note, Integration as a Two-Way Street, 108 Yale L.J. 479 (1988).

4. *Discrimination on grounds other than race, religion, or national origin.* As originally enacted in 1968, the Fair Housing Act did not prohibit discrimination on the grounds of sex, handicap, or familial status. Sex discrimination was added to the Act in 1974; amendments in 1988 added the prohibitions regarding familial status and handicapped persons. The discussion below suggests how the courts have resolved common allegations involving these sorts of discrimination.

Discrimination based on family status, and on sex.

(a) Landlords, a retired couple, have eight single family houses for rent. They limit the number of occupants in each house, depending upon its size, number of bedrooms, layout, and yard size. Their business strategy is to maintain their houses well and to rent them for slightly below market in order to give tenants an incentive to stay, thereby avoiding turnover. One of their houses is a 1,200-square-foot house, consisting of a living room, master bedroom, another

10 × 10 bedroom, two baths, a den opening directly into the living room (which could be used as a bedroom), and very little yard. The landlords limit occupancy of this house to four persons and refuse to rent to a couple with three children. See Pfaff v. H.U.D., 88 F.3d 739 (9th Cir. 1996) (even if the numerical occupancy limitations have a disparate impact on families with children, they could be justified on the ground of maintaining the economic value of the property).

(b) *L* regularly rents one-bedroom apartments to households consisting of two adults, and two-bedroom apartments to households of two adults and two children, but will not rent one-bedroom units to one adult and one child, nor two-bedroom units to one adult and three children. See Glover v. Crestwood Lake Section 1 Holding Corps., 746 F. Supp. 301 (S.D.N.Y. 1990) (practice described violates prohibition against discrimination based on familial status).

(c) *L* refuses to rent to a heterosexual couple because they are unmarried. See James A. Kushner, Fair Housing Amendments Act of 1988: The Second Generation of Fair Housing, 42 Vand. L. Rev. 1049, 1106-1107 (1989) (refusal to rent to unmarried couples is clearly not covered by the act unless it can be demonstrated to have a disproportionate racial, ethnic, religious, or gender-based impact).

(d) *L* refuses to rent to a gay couple because he objects to the partners' sexual orientation. See Kushner, supra, at 1108 (the act does not prohibit sexual-orientation discrimination).

(e) *L* rents to a single woman and then, several weeks into the tenancy, begins harassing her with demands for sexual favors. See Grieger v. Sheets, 689 F. Supp. 835 (N.D. Ill. 1988) (holding that acts like those described violate the Fair Housing Act); Robert G. Schwemm & Rigel C. Oliveri, A New Look at Sexual Harassment Under the Fair Housing Act: The Forgotten Role of Section 3604(c), 2002 Wis. L. Rev. 771 (arguing that federal appellate cases reflect an unduly narrow view of what constitutes prohibited sexual harassment, and suggesting that litigation based on §3604(c) would be more effective).

Discrimination based on handicap. "Handicap" is defined by §3602(h) of the Fair Housing Act, which states that the term means "a physical or mental impairment which substantially limits one or more of [the handicapped person's] major life activities, a record of having such an impairment, or being regarded as having such an impairment, but such term does not include current, illegal use of or addiction to a controlled substance." Proposed amendments that would have excluded alcoholism and infectious, contagious, and communicable diseases from the definition failed to pass.[16]

(f) Referring to (d) above, suppose that *L* refuses to rent to the gay couple because of a fear of AIDS? See Baxter v. City of Belleville, 720 F. Supp. 720, 728 (S.D. Ill. 1989) (people with AIDS have a "handicap" for purposes of the act, so refusing to rent to someone out of fear or knowledge that the person has AIDS is prohibited).

---

16. Regarding the meaning of "handicap," one odd provision did become law: the term does not include transvestism. See Note on Transvestism set out under §3602. "By adopting this provision, Congress was likely reacting [to a 1986 case] in which a district court held that . . . transvestites are 'handicapped'" within the meaning of the federal Rehabilitation Act. Recent Developments, 24 Harv. C.R.-C.L. L. Rev. 249, 252 (1989).

(g) *L* wants to evict *T* because *T* has a mental disability that results in seemingly threatening behavior. See Roe v. Housing Authority of the City of Boulder, 909 F. Supp. 814 (D. Colo. 1995) (dwellings need not be made available to people whose condition would create a direct threat to the health and safety of others or result in substantial damage to property, but landlords must try to make reasonable accommodations).

(h) *L*, owner of an apartment building with a no-pets policy, refuses to allow *T* to have a dog in her apartment; *T* has a schizoid personality disorder and depends on the dog as a companion. See Stevens v. Hollywood Towers & Condo Assn., 836 F. Supp. 2d 800 (N.D. Ill. 2011) (allowing exception to no-pet policy for emotional support dog); H.U.D. v. Riverbay, 1994 WL 497536 (H.U.D. Admin. Law J.), 1995 WL 108212 (no-pets policy would prevail only if there were no reasonable way to accommodate the type of pet in question or if the tenant did not in fact need the pet).

5. *State and local legislation.* Many states and localities prohibit discrimination in the sale or leasing of housing. State and local measures may not, of course, operate to narrow the rights and remedies available under federal law, but they may and sometimes do have a broader reach, covering, for example, discrimination based on age, sexual orientation, marital status—and, at least in Austin, Texas, status as a student! Once again, the discussion below suggests the range of problems and judicial responses.

(a) *L* owns an apartment building in an area where state and local law forbid discrimination on the basis of marital status. *L* refuses because of religious convictions to rent a unit to an unmarried couple and argues that to enforce the state and local measures would constitute an unconstitutional interference with his right to free exercise of religion. What result? See Smith v. Fair Employment & Housing Commission, 913 P.2d 909 (Cal. 1996); Swanner v. Anchorage Equal Rights Commission, 874 P.2d 274 (Alaska 1994) (*Smith* and *Swanner* both held that the freedom of religion clause of the Constitution does not exempt landlords from complying with a neutral law of general applicability); Anthony J. Vlatas, Note, The Religious Landlord and the Conflict Between Free Exercise Rights and Housing Discrimination Laws—Which Interest Prevails?, 47 Hastings L.J. 1669 (1996).

(b) New York legislation prohibits discrimination on the basis of race, creed, color, national origin, gender, sexual orientation, disability, or marital status. *L* refuses to rent an apartment to *T*, a divorced black woman, who subsequently brings suit claiming unlawful discrimination. *L* testifies that his refusal was motivated only by the fact that *T* is a lawyer. He finds lawyers to be troublesome tenants, and he prefers to rent to passive people who are not attuned to their legal rights. What result? See Kramarsky v. Stahl Management, 401 N.Y.S.2d 943 (Sup. Ct. 1977) (holding for landlord because his testimony was credible and the state legislation does not prohibit discrimination against lawyers); see also Verne G. Kopytoff, A Developer Balks at Selling to a Lawyer, N.Y. Times, Sept. 12, 1999, reporting on a similar case of discrimination against a lawyer in Bakersfield, California, and pointing out that only a few cities have laws that protect buyers and tenants based on their profession. "One is New York City, which passed a law in 1986 prohibiting discrimination based on profession after lawyers, among others, complained that landlords had refused to rent them apartments."

How would *T* fare under the federal Fair Housing Act?[17]

6. *Who pays the piper?* The Fair Housing Act provides for the award of reasonable attorneys' fees to successful aggrieved parties from losing landlords. 42 U.S.C.A. §3613(c)(2). Award of attorneys' fees in FHA cases, which is contrary to the usual rule in civil litigation, has the purpose of encouraging victims of discrimination to seek judicial relief. Award of attorneys' fees to defendants who prevail is permitted only if the complaint is frivolous or in bad faith. See Sassower v. Field, 973 F.2d 75 (2d Cir. 1992) ($93,350 in attorneys' fees awarded against vexatious lawyer-complainant who conducted case in bad faith). Congress believed that vindication of fair housing claims would be discouraged by awards to defendants.

Defendant landlords may, however, recover attorneys' fees in some cases from HUD under the Equal Access to Justice Act, enacted in 1980. Under this act, in a suit by or against the government enforcing a statute, the prevailing party other than the government is entitled to attorneys' fees from the government except where the government position is "substantially justified" or when special circumstances make an award unjust.

7. *How prevalent is housing discrimination today?* For obvious reasons, it is difficult to get a good approximation of the extent of discrimination in the housing market. Most survey respondents who have committed acts of discrimination are unlikely to reveal their identities to a stranger. In addition, protected parties may experience housing discrimination by being shown fewer housing units, being steered to certain neighborhoods, or being told a unit has been taken off the market, and never know for sure that they have been treated in an unfavorable way. The "state of the art" in measuring housing discrimination is matched-pair testing. Two testers are sent out to housing providers, realtors, and lenders with identical fictitious backgrounds, with one exception—their membership in a protected group. If the two testers encounter differential treatment, discrimination can be inferred. The most recent large-scale, matched-pair testing study was released in 2013. According to the study, while the most blatant forms of discrimination have declined sharply over the past four decades, African Americans, Hispanics, and Asians still experience more subtle forms of disparate treatment compared to whites. For example, African-American renters who contact real estate agents learn about 11.4 percent fewer housing units than equally qualified

---

17. Landlords routinely use services that provide information on the credit standing of prospective tenants. Beyond this, "[i]n some housing markets, a landlord can purchase from a commercial data bank a report detailing a prospective tenant's prior involvement in housing litigation." Robert C. Ellickson, Order Without Law: How Neighbors Settle Disputes 277 (1991), citing Pam Belluck, Tenants Cry Foul as Screening Companies Help Landlords Spot "Problem" Applicants, Wall St. J., Dec. 27, 1985, at 13; see also Lior Jacob Strahilevitz, Information and Exclusion 135-138 (2011) (discussing landlords' use of tenant background checks and a thwarted effort by California's government to curtail such use). For more discussion of tenant screening, see Note 1 on page 488.

whites. The disparities among Hispanic and Asian renters are 12.5 percent and 9.8 percent, respectively. See U.S. Dept. of HUD, Housing Discrimination Against Racial and Ethnic Minorities 2012 xv (2013). With respect to home buyers, African Americans learn about 17.0 percent fewer homes and Asians 15.5 percent fewer. The results for Hispanics were statistically insignificant. See id. at xvii.

8. On housing discrimination law generally, see James A. Kushner, Fair Housing: Discrimination in Real Estate, Community Development and Revitalization (2d ed. 1995); Michael H. Schill, Implementing the Federal Fair Housing Act, in Fragile Rights Within Cities: Government, Housing, and Fairness 143 (John Goering ed. 2007); Robert G. Schwemm, Housing Discrimination: Law and Litigation (1996). On the Fair Housing Act in particular, see Symposium, The Fair Housing Act After 40 Years: Continuing the Mission to Eliminate Housing Discrimination and Segregation, 41 Ind. L. Rev. 507 (2008).

D.   Delivery of Possession

Suppose that L and T have entered into a lease to begin on the first of January. On that date T arrives at the premises, ready to take possession, only to find a former tenant holding over. Is this L's problem, or T's? Could there be any question?

Hannan v. Dusch

Supreme Court of Appeals of Virginia, 1930
153 S.E. 824

PRENTIS, C.J., delivered the opinion of the court. The declaration filed by the plaintiff, Hannan, against the defendant, Dusch, alleges that Dusch had on August 31, 1927, leased to the plaintiff certain real estate in the city of Norfolk, Virginia, therein described, for fifteen years, the term to begin January 1, 1928, at a specified rental; that it thereupon became and was the duty of the defendant to see to it that the premises leased by the defendant to the plaintiff should be open for entry by him on January 1, 1928, the beginning of the term, and to put said petitioner in possession of the premises on that date; that the petitioner was willing and ready to enter upon and take possession of the leased property, and so informed the defendant; yet the defendant failed and refused to put the plaintiff in possession or to keep the property open for him at that time or on any subsequent date; and that the defendant suffered to remain on said property a certain tenant or tenants who occupied a portion or portions thereof, and refused to take legal or other action to oust said tenants or to compel their removal from the property so occupied. Plaintiff alleged damages which he had suffered by reason of this alleged breach of the contract and deed, and sought to recover such damages in the action. There is no express covenant as to the delivery of the premises nor for the quiet possession of the premises by the lessee. . . .

The single question of law therefore presented in this case is whether a landlord, who without any express covenant as to delivery of possession leases property to a tenant, is required under the law to oust trespassers and wrongdoers so as to have it open for entry by the tenant at the beginning of the term — that is, whether without an express covenant there is nevertheless an implied covenant to deliver possession. . . .

It seems to be perfectly well settled that there is an implied covenant in such cases on the part of the landlord to assure to the tenant the legal right of possession — that is, that at the beginning of the term there shall be no legal obstacle to the tenant's right of possession. This is not the question presented. Nor need we discuss in this case the rights of the parties in case a tenant rightfully in possession under the title of his landlord is thereafter disturbed by some wrongdoer. In such case the tenant must protect himself from trespassers, and there is no obligation on the landlord to assure his quiet enjoyment of his term as against wrongdoers or intruders.

Of course, the landlord assures to the tenant quiet possession as against all who rightfully claim through or under the landlord.

The discussion then is limited to the precise legal duty of the landlord in the absence of an express covenant, in case a former tenant, who wrongfully holds over, illegally refuses to surrender possession to the new tenant. This is a question about which there is a hopeless conflict of authorities. . . .

It is conceded by all that the two rules, one called the English rule, which implies a covenant requiring the lessor to put the lessee in possession, and that called the American rule, which recognizes the lessee's legal right to possession, but implies no such duty upon the lessor as against wrongdoers, are irreconcilable.

The English rule is that in the absence of stipulations to the contrary, there is in every lease an implied covenant on the part of the landlord that the premises shall be open to entry by the tenant at the time fixed by the lease for the beginning of his term. . . .

It must be borne in mind, however, that the courts which hold that there is such an implied covenant do not extend the period beyond the day when the lessee's term begins. If after that day a stranger trespasses upon the property and wrongfully obtains or withholds possession of it from the lessee, his remedy is against the stranger and not against the lessor.

It is not necessary for either party to involve himself in uncertainty, for by appropriate covenants each may protect himself against any doubt either as against a tenant then in possession who may wrongfully hold over by refusing to deliver the possession at the expiration of his own term, or against any other trespasser. . . .

As has been stated, the lessee may also protect himself by having his lessor expressly covenant to put him in possession at a specified time, in which case, of course, the lessor is liable for breach of his covenant where a trespasser goes into possession, or wrongfully holds possession, and thereby wrongfully prevents the lessee from obtaining possession. . . .

A case which supports the English rule is Herpolsheimer v. Christopher, 76 Neb. 352, 107 N.W. 382, 111 N.W. 359, 9 L.R.A. (N.S.) 1127, 14 Ann. Cas. 399 note. In that case the court gave these as its reasons for following the English rule:

> We deem it unnecessary to enter into an extended discussion, since the reasons pro and con are fully given in the opinions of the several courts cited. We think, however, that the English rule is most in consonance with good conscience, sound principle, and fair dealing. Can it be supposed that the plaintiff in this case would have entered into the lease if he had known at the time that he could not obtain possession on the 1st of March, but that he would be compelled to begin a lawsuit, await the law's delays, and follow the case through its devious turnings to an end before he could hope to obtain possession of the land he had leased? Most assuredly not. It is unreasonable to suppose that a man would knowingly contract for a lawsuit, or take the chance of one. Whether or not a tenant in possession intends to hold over or assert a right to a future term may nearly always be known to the landlord, and is certainly much more apt to be within his knowledge than within that of the prospective tenant. Moreover, since in an action to recover possession against a tenant holding over, the lessee would be compelled largely to rely upon the lessor's testimony in regard to the facts of the claim to hold over by the wrongdoer, it is more reasonable and proper to place the burden upon the person within whose knowledge the facts are most apt to lie. We are convinced, therefore, that the better reason lies with the courts following the English doctrine, and we therefore adopt it, and hold that, ordinarily, the lessor impliedly covenants with the lessee that the premises leased shall be open to entry by him at the time fixed in the lease as the beginning of the term.

In commenting on this line of cases, Mr. Freeman says [in a note on the subject in 134 Am. St. Rep. 916 (1909)]:

> The above rule practically prohibits the landlord from leasing the premises while in the possession of a tenant whose term is about to expire, because notwithstanding the assurance on the part of the tenant that he will vacate on the expiration of his term, he may change his mind and wrongfully hold over. It is true that the landlord may provide for such a contingency by suitable provisions in the lease to the prospective tenant, but it is equally true that the prospective tenant has the privilege of insisting that his prospective landlord expressly agree to put him in possession of the premises if he imagines there may be a chance for a lawsuit by the tenant in possession holding over.

So let us not lose sight of the fact that under the English rule a covenant which might have been but was not made is nevertheless implied by the court, though it is manifest that each of the parties might have provided for that and for every other possible contingency relating to possession by having express covenants which would unquestionably have protected both.

Referring then to the American rule: Under that rule, in such cases,

> the landlord is not bound to put the tenant into actual possession, but is bound only to put him in legal possession, so that no obstacle in the form of superior right of possession will be interposed to prevent the tenant from obtaining actual possession of the demised premises. . . .

This quoted language is Mr. Freeman's. . . .

So that, under the American rule, where the new tenant fails to obtain possession of the premises only because a former tenant wrongfully holds over, his remedy is against such wrongdoer and not against the landlord—this because the landlord has not covenanted against the wrongful acts of another and should not be held responsible for such a tort unless he has expressly so contracted. This accords with the general rule as to other wrongdoers, whereas the English rule appears to create a specific exception against lessors. It does not occur to us now that there is any other instance in which one clearly without fault is held responsible for the independent tort of another in which he has neither participated nor concurred and whose misdoings he cannot control. . . .

For the reasons which have been so well stated by those who have enforced the American rule, our judgment is that there is no error in the judgment complained of. . . .

Affirmed.

NOTES AND QUESTIONS

1. Case law on the matter of delivery of possession remains divided, with substantial support for both the English and the American rule. Restatement (Second) of Property, Landlord and Tenant §6.2 (1977) adopts the English rule, as does the Uniform Residential Landlord and Tenant Act (URLTA) §2.103. The former permits the parties to agree otherwise; the latter, it appears, does not (see URLTA §1.403).

2. Under the American rule, the tenant's remedies are against the person wrongfully in possession: He may sue to recover possession and damages. As to remedies under the English rule, see Restatement (Second) of Property, Landlord and Tenant, supra, §6.2 Reporter's Note at 246:

> It is well established that upon the landlord's default, the tenant may terminate the lease and sue for damages. . . . If the third party is in possession of only a part of the premises, the tenant may take possession of the remainder with an appropriate abatement in rent and damages. . . . Where the tenant's entry into possession is delayed beyond the date on which the term was to begin, he is not obligated to pay rent for the portion of the term during which he was kept out of possession and may collect appropriate damages. . . . See also 1 American Law of Property §3.37 (A.J. Casner ed. 1952) on the right of the tenant to continue the lease and sue for damages.
>
> It is well established that the tenant may go directly against the third party to recover possession or damages.

3. It has been said that the "American rule seems to be founded on the argument that the tenant has sufficient legal and equitable remedies available to protect himself against the third party wrongfully in possession and a greater incentive to use them than the landlord would have." Restatement (Second) of Property, Landlord and Tenant, supra, §6.2 Reporter's Note at 245. What policies support the English rule? See id., comment a at 236-237.

As suggested in the *Hannan* case, both the American rule and the English rule are so-called default rules (as opposed to mandatory rules), meaning that the parties are free to change the delivery obligation by agreement between themselves. Given this, why does it matter what the rule happens to be in the first instance?

PROBLEMS

1. *T* leases from *L* a large piece of open land to be used for hunting and trapping. After paying a year's rent in advance, *T* finds out that there is no public access to the land. Neighboring landowners refuse to give *T* ingress and egress. The jurisdiction follows the English rule. Has *L* satisfied the duty imposed by that rule? See Moore v. Cameron Parish School Bd., 511 So. 2d 62 (La. App. 1987). On landlocked parcels generally, see pages 833-839.

2. *L* and *T* execute a lease for a specified term. *T* takes possession and pays rent for several months. *T* then learns that *L* had earlier leased the premises to another tenant for the same term. *T* remains in possession but stops paying rent. *L* sues *T* for unpaid rent; *T* counterclaims for rent already paid. What result? See Campbell v. Hensley, 450 S.W.2d 501 (Ky. 1970).

E.   *Subleases and Assignments*

Ernst v. Conditt

Court of Appeals of Tennessee, 1964
390 S.W.2d 703

CHATTIN, J. Complainants, B. Walter Ernst and wife, Emily Ernst, leased a certain tract of land in Davidson County, Tennessee, to Frank D. Rogers on June 18, 1960, for a term of one year and seven days, commencing on June 23, 1960.

Rogers went into possession of the property and constructed an asphalt race track and enclosed the premises with a fence. He also constructed other improvements thereon such as floodlights for use in the operation of a Go-Cart track.

We quote these paragraphs of the lease pertinent to the question for consideration in this controversy:

> 3. Lessee covenants to pay as rent for said leased premises the sum of $4,200 per annum, payable at the rate of $350 per month or 15% of all gross receipts, whether from sales or services occurring on the leased premises, whichever is the larger amount. The gross receipts shall be computed on a quarterly basis and if any amount in addition to the $350 per month is due, such payment shall be made immediately after the quarterly computation. All payments shall be payable to the office of Lessors' agent, Guaranty Mortgage Company, at 316 Union Street, Nashville, Tennessee, on the first day of each month in advance. Lessee shall have the first right to refusal in the event Lessors desire to lease said premises for a period of time commencing immediately after the termination date hereof. . . .
>
> 5. Lessee shall have no right to assign or sublet the leased premises without prior written approval of Lessors. In the event of any assignment or sublease, Lessee is still liable to perform the covenants of this lease, including the covenant to pay rent, and nothing herein shall be construed as releasing Lessee from his liabilities and obligations hereunder. . . .

9. Lessee agrees that upon termination of this contract, or any extensions or renewals thereof, that all improvements above the ground will be moved at Lessee's expense and the property cleared. This shall not be construed as removing or digging up any surface paving; but if any pits or holes are dug, they shall be leveled at Lessors' request.

Rogers operated the business for a short time. In July, 1960, he entered into negotiations with the defendant, A.K. Conditt, for the sale of the business to him. During these negotiations, the question of the term of the lease arose. Defendant desired a two-year lease of the property. He and Rogers went to the home of complainants and negotiated an extension of the term of the lease which resulted in the following amendment to the lease, and the sublease or assignment of the lease as amended to Conditt by Rogers:

By mutual consent of the parties, the lease executed the 18th day of June 1960, between B. Walter Ernst and wife, Emily H. Ernst, as Lessors, and Frank D. Rogers as Lessee, is amended as follows:

1. Paragraph 2 of said lease is amended so as to provide that the term will end July 31, 1962 and not June 30, 1961.

2. The minimum rent of $350 per month called for in paragraph 3 of said lease shall be payable by the month and the percentage rental called for by said lease shall be payable on the first day of the month following the month for which the percentage is computed. In computing gross receipts, no deduction or credit shall be given the Lessee for the payment of sales taxes or any other assessments by governmental agencies.

3. Lessee agrees that on or prior to April 1, 1961, the portion of the property covered by this lease, consisting of about one acre, which is not presently devoted to business purposes will be used for business purposes and the percentage rent called for by paragraph 3 of the original lease will be paid on the gross receipts derived therefrom. In the event of the failure of the Lessee to devote the balance of said property to a business purpose on or before April 1, 1961, then this lease shall terminate as to such portion of the property.

4. Lessee agrees to save the Lessor harmless for any damage to the property of the lessor, whether included in this lease or not, which results from the use of the leased property by the Lessee or its customers or invitees. Lessee will erect or cause to be erected four (4) "No Parking" signs on the adjoining property of the Lessor not leased by it.

5. Lessor hereby consents to the subletting of the premises to A.K. Conditt, but upon the express condition and understanding that the original Lessee, Frank D. Rogers, will remain personally liable for the faithful performance of all the terms and conditions of the original lease and of this amendment to the original lease.

Except as modified by this amendment, all terms and conditions of the original lease dated the 18th day of June, 1960, by and between the parties shall remain in full force and effect.

In witness whereof the parties have executed this amendment to lease on this the 4 day of August, 1960.

B. Walter Ernst
Emily H. Ernst
Lessors
Frank D. Rogers
Lessee

For value received and in consideration of the promise to faithfully perform all conditions of the within lease as amended, I hereby sublet the premises to A.K. Conditt upon the understanding that I will individually remain liable for the performance of the lease.

This 4 day of Aug, 1960.

Frank D. Rogers
Frank D. Rogers

The foregoing subletting of the premises is accepted, this the 4 day of Aug, 1960.

A.K. Conditt
A.K. Conditt

Conditt operated the Go-Cart track from August until November, 1960. He paid the rent for the months of August, September and October, 1960, directly to complainants. In December, 1960, complainants contacted defendant with reference to the November rent and at that time defendant stated he had been advised he was not liable to them for rent. However, defendant paid the basic monthly rental of $350.00 to complainants in June, 1961. This was the final payment received by complainants during the term of the lease as amended. The record is not clear whether defendant continued to operate the business after the last payment of rent or abandoned it. Defendant, however, remained in possession of the property until the expiration of the leasehold.

On July 10, 1962, complainants, through their Attorneys, notified Conditt by letter the lease would expire as of midnight July 31, 1962, and they were demanding a settlement of the past due rent and unless the improvements on the property were removed by him as provided in paragraph 9 of the original lease, then, in that event, they would have same removed at his expense. Defendant did not reply to this demand.

On August 1, 1962, complainants filed their bill in this cause seeking a recovery of $2,404.58 which they alleged was the balance due on the basic rent of $350.00 per month for the first year of the lease and the sum of $4,200.00, the basic rent for the second year, and the further sum necessary for the removal of the improvements constructed on the property.

The theory of the bill is that the agreement between Rogers, the original lessee, and the defendant, Conditt, is an assignment of the lease; and, therefore, defendant is directly and primarily liable to complainants.

The defendant by his answer insists the agreement between Rogers and himself is a sublease and therefore Rogers is directly and primarily liable to complainants.

The Chancellor heard the matter on the depositions of both complainants and three other witnesses offered in behalf of complainants and documentary evidence filed in the record. The defendant did not testify nor did he offer any evidence in his behalf.

The Chancellor found the instrument to be an assignment. A decree was entered sustaining the bill and entering judgment for complainants in the sum of $6,904.58 against defendant.

Defendant has appealed to this Court and has assigned errors insisting the Chancellor erred in failing to hold the instrument to be a sublease rather than an assignment.

To support his theory the instrument is a sublease, the defendant insists the amendment to the lease entered into between Rogers and complainants was for the express purpose of extending the term of the lease and obtaining the consent of the lessors to a "subletting" of the premises to defendant. That by the use of the words "sublet" and "subletting" no other construction can be placed on the amendment and the agreement of Rogers and the acceptance of defendant attached thereto.

Further, since complainants agreed to the subletting of the premises to defendant "upon the express condition and understanding that the original lessee, Frank D. Rogers, will remain personally liable for the faithful performance of all the terms and conditions of the original lease and this amendment to the original lease," no construction can be placed upon this language other than it was the intention of complainants to hold Rogers primarily liable for the performance of the original lease and the amendment thereto. And, therefore, Rogers, for his own protection, would have the implied right to re-enter and perform the lease in the event of a default on the part of the defendant. This being true, Rogers retained a reversionary interest in the property sufficient to satisfy the legal distinction between a sublease and an assignment of a lease.

It is then urged the following rules of construction of written instruments support the above argument:

> Where words or terms having a definite legal meaning and effect are knowingly used in a written instrument the parties thereto will be presumed to have intended such words or terms to have their proper legal meaning and effect, in the absence of any contrary intention appearing in the instrument. [12 Am. Jur., Contracts, Section 238.]
>
> Technical terms or words of art will be given their technical meaning unless the context, or local usage shows a contrary intention. [3 Williston on Contracts, Section 68, Sub S. 2.]

As stated in complainants' brief, the liability of defendant to complainants depends upon whether the transfer of the leasehold interest in the premises from Rogers is an assignment of the lease or a sublease. If the transfer is a sublease, no privity of contract[18] exists between complainants and defendant; and, therefore, defendant could not be liable to complainants on the covenant to pay rent and the expense of the removal of the improvements. But, if the transfer is an assignment of the lease, privity of contract does exist between complainants and defendant; and defendant would be liable directly and primarily for the amount of the judgment. . . .

The general rule as to the distinction between an assignment of a lease and a sublease is an assignment conveys the whole term, leaving no interest nor reversionary interest in the grantor or assignor. Whereas, a sublease may be generally defined as a transaction whereby a tenant grants an interest in the leased premises less than his own, or reserves to himself a reversionary interest in the term.

---

18. In this and the next sentence, substitute the words "privity of estate" where the opinion reads "privity of contract." Privity of estate is what the court means to say; the materials on pages 471-472 explore the distinction between the two concepts.—EDS.

The common law distinction between an assignment of a lease and a sublease is succinctly stated in the case of Jaber v. Miller, 219 Ark. 59, 239 S.W.2d 760: "If the instrument purports to transfer the lessee's estate for the entire remainder of his term it is an assignment, regardless of its form or the parties' intention. Conversely, if the instrument purports to transfer the lessee's estate for less than the entire term—even for a day less—it is a sublease, regardless of its form or of the parties' intention."

The modern rule which has been adopted in this State for construing written instruments is stated in the case of City of Nashville v. Lawrence, 153 Tenn. 606, 284 S.W. 882: "The cardinal rule to be followed in this state, in construing deeds and other written instruments, is to ascertain the intention of the parties."

In Williams v. Williams, 84 Tenn. 164, 171, it was said: "We have most wisely abandoned technical rules in the construction of conveyances in this State, and look to the intention of the instrument alone for our guide, that intention to be arrived at from the language of the instrument read in the light of the surrounding circumstances." . . .

It is our opinion under either the common law or modern rule of construction the agreement between Rogers and defendant is an assignment of the lease.

The fact that Rogers expressly agreed to remain liable to complainants for the performance of the lease did not create a reversion nor a right to re-enter in Rogers either express or implied. The obligations and liabilities of a lessee to a lessor, under the express covenants of a lease, are not in anywise affected by an assignment or a subletting to a third party, in the absence of an express or implied agreement or some action on his part which amounts to a waiver or estops him from insisting upon compliance with the covenants. This is true even though the assignment or sublease is made with the consent of the lessor. By an assignment of a lease the privity of estate between the lessor and lessee is terminated, but the privity of contract between them still remains and is unaffected. Neither the privity of estate or contract between the lessor and lessee are affected by a sublease. 32 Am. Jur., Landlord and Tenant, Sections 356, 413, pages 310, 339.

Thus the express agreement of Rogers to remain personally liable for the performance of the covenants of the lease created no greater obligation on his part or interest in the leasehold, other than as set forth in the original lease.

The argument that since the agreement between Rogers and defendant contains the words, "sublet" and "subletting" is conclusive the instrument is to be construed as a sublease is, we think, unsound.

> A consent to sublet has been held to include the consent to assign or mortgage the lease; and a consent to assign has been held to authorize a subletting. [51 C.J.S. Landlord and Tenant §36, page 552.]

Prior to the consummation of the sale of the Go-Cart business to defendant, he insisted upon the execution of the amendment to the lease extending the term of the original lease. For value received and on the promise of the defendant to perform all of the conditions of the lease as amended, Rogers parted with his entire interest in the property. Defendant went into possession of the property and paid the rent to complainants. He remained in possession of the property for the entire term. By virtue of the sale of the business, defendant became the owner of the improvements with the right to their removal at the expiration of the lease.

Rogers reserved no part or interest in the lease; nor did he reserve a right of re-entry in event of a breach of any of the conditions or covenants of the lease on the part of defendant.

It is our opinion the defendant, under the terms of the agreement with Rogers, had a right to the possession of the property for the entire term of the lease as amended, including the right to remove the improvements after the expiration of the lease. Rogers merely agreed to become personally liable for the rent and the expense of the removal of the improvements upon the default of defendant. He neither expressly, nor by implication, reserved the right to re-enter for a condition broken by defendant.

Thus, we are of the opinion the use of the words, "sublet" and "subletting" is not conclusive of the construction to be placed on the instrument in the case; it plainly appearing from the context of the instrument and the facts and circumstances surrounding the execution of it the parties thereto intended an assignment rather than a sublease.

It results that the assignments are overruled and the decree of the Chancellor is affirmed with costs.

NOTES AND PROBLEMS

1. *Sublease or assignment?* The *Ernst* case indicates the two ways in which courts have gone about distinguishing between a sublease and an assignment. The first (and most commonly used) approach is formalistic: an *assignment* arises when the lessee transfers his entire interest under the lease—when, that is, he transfers the right to possession for the duration of the term. If the lessee transfers anything less than his entire interest (if two years remain on the lease and the lessee transfers for a term of one year), a *sublease* results. In the latter case, the lessee is said to have retained a reversion; the right to possession goes back (reverts) to him at the end of the period designated in the transfer. (Compare the analogous reversion in the landlord discussed in footnote 1 on page 443.) Suppose the lessee transfers all of his interest in some physical part of the premises; is this a sublease or a partial assignment? Most courts, quite correctly, say the latter. Suppose the lessee transfers his entire interest, but the instrument of transfer provides that if the transferee breaches any obligation of the lease, the original lessee may terminate the arrangement and retake possession (such a provision is called a power of termination or right of re-entry). A substantial minority of jurisdictions finds a sublease in this situation.

The second (and less common) approach to the sublease-assignment problem considers the intention of the parties. The actual words used—*sublease* or *assignment*—are not conclusive (witness the *Ernst* case), though they may be persuasive (except in those cases, hardly unheard of, when both terms are used). Indeed, one occasionally gets the impression that courts claiming to honor the intention of the parties are in fact doing nothing more than inferring that "intention" from use of the words *sublease* or *assignment*, without the slightest basis for assuming that the parties knew the consequences of what they were saying. See, e.g., Jaber v. Miller, 239 S.W.2d 760 (Ark. 1951).

Whether sublease or assignment, what happens if the primary lease between the landlord and the original tenant is prematurely terminated? It depends. If the landlord exercises a power to forfeit the primary lease because of some breach by the original tenant, then the landlord is entitled to possession as against sublessees and assignees. But if the original tenant merely gives up the primary lease voluntarily—"surrenders" it, see page 499—the rights of possession of sublessees and assignees remain intact. In the case of a sublease, for example, surrender by the original tenant (the sublessor) leaves the sublessee holding of the landlord. They are in privity of estate. See, e.g., Parris-West Maytag Hotel Corp. v. Continental Amusement Co., 168 N.W.2d 735 (Iowa 1969).

2. *Privity of estate and privity of contract.* As indicated in *Ernst* (and the corrections set out in footnote 18), leases typically give rise to both privity of contract and privity of estate (the two concepts come up again in Chapter 10, in the context of covenants running with the land). *Privity* denotes a voluntary transactional relationship between two or more people or entities. With respect to leases of real property, the two types of privity reflect the dual nature of a lease as a contract and as a conveyance (recall the discussion on page 451). Whether oral or in writing, the lease between the landlord and the original tenant amounts to a conveyance of a right of possession from the former to the latter, and that conveyance creates between the landlord and the tenant the so-called privity of *estate*. If the lease also contains promises by one party to the other (and leases almost always do), those promises create what is called privity of *contract*. None of this is of much interest in cases where there has not been a transfer of the lease from the original tenant to a third party. But if the original tenant has transferred to a third party, *T1*, who subsequently breaches some provision in the lease, then matters are more complicated. The rights and liabilities of the various parties (*L*, *T*, *T1*) will turn on the promises, if any, between *L* and *T* in the original lease, and on whether or not *T1* "assumed" those promises upon the transfer of the lease by stating that she would be liable for them. If *T1* did assume, then she is liable on a privity of contract theory. If *T1* did not assume, then she is only liable to parties with whom she is in privity of estate—liable for rent, and also for damages resulting from breaches of certain kinds of promises that are said to "touch and concern" the rented premises.

But enough with the abstractions. The points are much better illustrated by way of concrete problems, as below.

3. *The consequences.* Suppose that:

(a) *L* leases to *T* for a term of three years at a monthly rent of $1,000. One year later *T* "subleases, transfers, and assigns" to *T1* for "a period of one year from date." Thereafter neither *T* nor *T1* pays rent to *L*. What rights has *L* against *T*?

Against *T1?* See 1 American Law of Property §§3.57, 3.62 (1952 & Supp. 1977). Compare Ky. Rev. Stat. Ann. §383.010(5) (LexisNexis 2012). Suppose in the instrument of transfer there was a covenant (promise) whereby *T1* "agreed to pay the rents" reserved in the head lease. What effect might this have on *L*'s rights? See Restatement (Second) of Property, Landlord and Tenant, §16.1 comment c at 120-121 (1977):

> At the time a transfer of an interest in the leased property is made, the transferor may exact a promise from the transferee that he will perform the promises in the lease which were made by the transferor. The exaction of such a promise does not relieve the transferor of liability on his promises. It does give him a direct remedy against his transferee if the transferee fails to perform the promises, which remedy will continue to be available even after the transferee has transferred the interest to someone else. If the holder of the benefits of the promises made by the transferor acquires enforcement rights as a third party beneficiary against the transferee by virtue of the transferee's promise to the transferor, then the transferee is in privity of contract with such third party beneficiary and a subsequent transfer by the transferee of an interest in the leased property will not affect that privity of contract liability.

(b) *L* leases to *T* for a term of three years at a monthly rent of $1,000; the lease provides that "*T* hereby covenants to pay said rent in advance on the first of each month." The lease also provides that "*T* shall not sublet or assign without the permission of *L*." Six months later *T*, with the permission of *L*, transfers to *T1* for the balance of the term. Thereafter *T1* pays the rent directly to *L* for several months, then defaults. *L* sues *T* for the rent due. What result, and why? See South Bay Center, Inc. v. Butler, Herrick & Marshall, 250 N.Y.S.2d 863 (Sup. Ct. 1964); Buck v. J.M. McEntee & Sons, 275 P.2d 984 (Okla. 1954).

(c) *L* leases to *T* for a term of three years at a monthly rent of $1,000; in the lease "*T* covenants to pay the rent in advance on the first of each month" and also "covenants to keep the leased premises in good repair." Six months later *T* assigns her entire interest to *T1*, who agrees in the instrument of assignment to "assume all the covenants in the lease" between *L* and *T*; three months later *T1* assigns his entire interest to *T2*, and three months after that *T2* assigns his entire interest to *T3*. *T3* defaults on rent payments and fails to keep the premises in good repair. *L* sues *T, T1, T2,* and *T3*. What are the liabilities of the four tenants to *L* and as among themselves? See 1 American Law of Property, supra, §3.61; 2 id. §§9.4, 9.5.[19]

4. Notice that the prime lease in the *Ernst* case contained a provision (paragraph 5 of the lease) prohibiting assignment or sublease without the lessors' approval. Suppose instead there had been no such provision, or suppose the provision had gone on to state that "lessors' approval shall not be unreasonably withheld." What in each case would be the rights of the parties? Consider the following materials.

---

19. According to the opinion in the *Ernst* case, the defendant's liability depended upon whether the transfer in question was an assignment or a sublease. Having worked through the Problems thus far, can you see grounds for disagreeing with that statement?

Kendall v. Ernest Pestana, Inc.

Supreme Court of California, 1985
709 P.2d 837

BROUSSARD, J. This case concerns the effect of a provision in a commercial lease[20] that the lessee may not assign the lease or sublet the premises without the lessor's prior written consent. The question we address is whether, in the absence of a provision that such consent will not be unreasonably withheld, a lessor may unreasonably and arbitrarily withhold his or her consent to an assignment.[21] This is a question of first impression in this court. . . .

The allegations of the complaint may be summarized as follows. The lease at issue is for 14,400 square feet of hangar space at the San Jose Municipal Airport. The City of San Jose, as owner of the property, leased it to Irving and Janice Perlitch, who in turn assigned their interest to respondent Ernest Pestana, Inc. Prior to assigning their interest to respondent, the Perlitches entered into a 25-year sublease with one Robert Bixler commencing on January 1, 1970. The sublease covered an original five-year term plus four 5-year options to renew. The rental rate was to be increased every 10 years in the same proportion as rents increased on the master lease from the City of San Jose. The premises were to be used by Bixler for the purpose of conducting an airplane maintenance business.

Bixler conducted such a business under the name "Flight Services" until, in 1981, he agreed to sell the business to appellants Jack Kendall, Grady O'Hara and Vicki O'Hara. The proposed sale included the business and the equipment, inventory and improvements on the property, together with the existing lease. The proposed assignees had a stronger financial statement and greater net worth than the current lessee, Bixler, and they were willing to be bound by the terms of the lease.

The lease provided that written consent of the lessor was required before the lessee could assign his interest, and that failure to obtain such consent rendered the lease voidable at the option of the lessor. Accordingly, Bixler requested consent from the Perlitches' successor-in-interest, respondent Ernest Pestana, Inc. Respondent refused to consent to the assignment and maintained that it had an absolute right arbitrarily to refuse any such request. The complaint recites that respondent demanded "increased rent and other more onerous terms" as a condition of consenting to Bixler's transfer of interest.

The proposed assignees brought suit for declaratory and injunctive relief and damages seeking, inter alia, a declaration "that the refusal of Ernest Pestana, Inc. to consent to the assignment of the lease is unreasonable and is an unlawful restraint on the freedom of alienation. . . ." The trial court sustained a demurrer to the complaint without leave to amend and this appeal followed.

---

20. We are presented only with a commercial lease and therefore do not address the question whether residential leases are controlled by the principles articulated in this opinion.

21. Since the present case involves an assignment rather than a sublease, we will speak primarily in terms of assignments. However, our holding applies equally to subleases. . . .

The law generally favors free alienability of property, and California follows the common law rule that a leasehold interest is freely alienable. Contractual restrictions on the alienability of leasehold interests are, however, permitted. "Such restrictions are justified as reasonable protection of the interests of the lessor as to who shall possess and manage property in which he has a reversionary interest and from which he is deriving income." (Schoshinski, American Law of Landlord and Tenant (1980) §8:15, at pp. 578-579. See also 2 Powell on Real Property, ¶ 246[1], at p. 372.97.)

The common law's hostility toward restraints on alienation has caused such restraints on leasehold interests to be strictly construed against the lessor. . . . This is particularly true where the restraint in question is a "forfeiture restraint," under which the lessor has the option to terminate the lease if an assignment is made without his or her consent. . . .

Nevertheless, a majority of jurisdictions have long adhered to the rule that where a lease contains an approval clause (a clause stating that the lease cannot be assigned without the prior consent of the lessor), the lessor may arbitrarily refuse to approve a proposed assignee no matter how suitable the assignee appears to be and no matter how unreasonable the lessor's objection. . . . The harsh consequences of this rule have often been avoided through application of the doctrines of waiver and estoppel, under which the lessor may be found to have waived (or be estopped from asserting) the right to refuse consent to assignment.

The traditional majority rule has come under steady attack in recent decades. A growing minority of jurisdictions now hold that where a lease provides for assignment only with the prior consent of the lessor, such consent may be withheld *only where the lessor has a commercially reasonable objection to the assignment,* even in the absence of a provision in the lease stating that consent to assignment will not be unreasonably withheld. (See Rest. 2d Property, §15.2(2) (1977); 21 A.L.R.4th 188 (1983).)

For the reasons discussed below, we conclude that the minority rule is the preferable position. . . .

The impetus for change in the majority rule has come from two directions, reflecting the dual nature of a lease as a conveyance of a leasehold interest and a contract. (See Medico-Dental etc. Co. v. Horton & Converse (1942) 21 Cal. 2d 411, 418, 132 P.2d 457.) The policy against restraints on alienation pertains to leases in their nature as *conveyances.* Numerous courts and commentators have recognized that "[i]n recent times the necessity of permitting reasonable alienation of commercial space has become paramount in our increasingly urban society." (Schweiso v. Williams [(1984) 150 Cal. App. 3d 883, 887, 198 Cal. Rptr. 238.]) . . .

In Cohen v. Ratinoff [(1983) 147 Cal. App. 3d 321, 195 Cal. Rptr. 84], the court examined the reasonableness of the restraint created by an approval clause in a lease:

Because the lessor has an interest in the character of the proposed commercial assignee, we cannot say that an assignment provision requiring the lessor's consent to an assignment is inherently repugnant to the leasehold interest created. We do conclude, however, that *if such an assignment provision is implemented in such a manner that its underlying purpose is perverted by the arbitrary or unreasonable withholding of consent, an unreasonable restraint on alienation is established.* [147 Cal. App. 3d at p. 329, 195 Cal. Rptr. 84, italics added.]

One commentator explains as follows:

The common-law hostility to restraints on alienation had a large exception with respect to estates for years. A lessor could prohibit the lessee from transferring the estate for years to whatever extent he might desire. It was believed that the objectives served by allowing such restraints outweighed the social evils implicit in the restraints, in that they gave to the lessor a needed control over the person entrusted with the lessor's property and to whom he must look for the performance of the covenants contained in the lease. Whether this reasoning retains full validity can well be doubted. Relationships between lessor and lessee have tended to become more and more impersonal. Courts have considerably lessened the effectiveness of restraint clauses by strict construction and liberal applications of the doctrine of waiver. With the shortage of housing and, in many places, of commercial space as well, the allowance of lease clauses forbidding assignments and subleases is beginning to be curtailed by statutes. [2 Powell, supra, ¶ 246[1], at pp. 372.97-372.98.]

The Restatement Second of Property adopts the minority rule on the validity of approval clauses in leases: "A restraint on alienation without the consent of the landlord of a tenant's interest in leased property is valid, *but the landlord's consent to an alienation by the tenant cannot be withheld unreasonably,* unless a freely negotiated provision in the lease gives the landlord an absolute right to withhold consent." (Rest. 2d Property, §15.2(2) (1977), italics added.)[22] A comment to the section explains:

The landlord may have an understandable concern about certain personal qualities of a tenant, particularly his reputation for meeting his financial obligations. The preservation of the values that go into the personal selection of the tenant justifies upholding a provision in the lease that curtails the right of the tenant to put anyone else in his place by transferring his interest, but this justification does not go to the point of allowing the landlord arbitrarily and without reason to refuse to allow the tenant to transfer an interest in leased property. [Id., com. a.]

Under the Restatement rule, the lessor's interest in the character of his or her tenant is protected by the lessor's right to object to a proposed assignee on reasonable commercial grounds. (See id., reporter's note 7 at pp. 112-113.) The lessor's interests are also protected by the fact that the original lessee remains liable to the lessor as a surety even if the lessor consents to the assignment and the assignee expressly assumes the obligations of the lease. . . .

The second impetus for change in the majority rule comes from the nature of a lease as a *contract*. As the Court of Appeal observed in Cohen v. Ratinoff, supra, "[s]ince Richard v. Degan & Brody, Inc. [espousing the majority rule] was decided, . . . there has been an increased recognition of and emphasis on the

---

22. This case does not present the question of the validity of a clause absolutely prohibiting assignment, or granting absolute discretion over assignment to the lessor. We note that under the Restatement rule such a provision would be valid if freely negotiated.

duty of good faith and fair dealing inherent in every contract." (Id., 147 Cal. App. 3d at p. 329, 195 Cal. Rptr. 84.) Thus, "[i]n every contract there is an implied covenant that neither party shall do anything which will have the effect of destroying or injuring the right of the other party to receive the fruits of the contract. . . ." (Universal Sales Corp. v. Cal. etc. Mfg. Co. (1942) 20 Cal. 2d 751, 771, 128 P.2d 665. . . .) "[W]here a contract confers on one party a discretionary power affecting the rights of the other, a duty is imposed to exercise that discretion in good faith and in accordance with fair dealing." (Cal. Lettuce Growers v. Union Sugar Co. (1955) 45 Cal. 2d 474, 484, 289 P.2d 785. See also, Larwin-Southern California, Inc. v. J.G.B. Inv. Co. (1979) 101 Cal. App. 3d 626, 640, 162 Cal. Rptr. 52.) Here the lessor retains the discretionary power to approve or disapprove an assignee proposed by the other party to the contract; this discretionary power should therefore be exercised in accordance with commercially reasonable standards. . . .[23]

Under the minority rule, the determination whether a lessor's refusal to consent was reasonable is a question of fact. Some of the factors that the trier of fact may properly consider in applying the standards of good faith and commercial reasonableness are: financial responsibility of the proposed assignee; suitability of the use for the particular property; legality of the proposed use; need for alteration of the premises; and nature of the occupancy, i.e., office, factory, clinic, etc.

Denying consent solely on the basis of personal taste, convenience or sensibility is not commercially reasonable. Nor is it reasonable to deny consent "in order that the landlord may charge a higher rent than originally contracted for." (Schweiso v. Williams, supra, 150 Cal. App. 3d at p. 886, 198 Cal. Rptr. 238.) This is because the lessor's desire for a better bargain than contracted for has nothing to do with the permissible purposes of the restraint on alienation—to protect the lessor's interest in the preservation of the property and the performance of the lease covenants. "'[T]he clause is for the protection of the landlord *in its ownership and operation of the particular property*—not for its general economic protection.'" (Ringwood Associates v. Jack's of Route 23, Inc. [(1977) 153 N.J. Super. 294, 379 A.2d 508, 512], quoting Krieger v. Helmsley-Spear, Inc. (1973) 62 N.J. 423, 302 A.2d 129, italics added.)

In contrast to the policy reasons advanced in favor of the minority rule, the majority rule has traditionally been justified on three grounds. Respondent raises a fourth argument in its favor as well. None of these do we find compelling.

First, it is said that a lease is a conveyance of an interest in real property, and that the lessor, having exercised a personal choice in the selection of a tenant and provided that no substitute shall be acceptable without prior consent, is under no obligation to look to anyone but the lessee for the rent. This argument is based

---

23. Some commentators have drawn an analogy between this situation and the duties of good faith and reasonableness implied in all transactions under the Uniform Commercial Code. (U. Com. Code §§1-203, 2-103(b); see also U. Com. Code §1-102, com. 1 [permitting application of the U. Com. Code to matters not expressly within its scope].) See Comment, The Approval Clause in a Lease: Toward a Standard of Reasonableness 17 U.S.F. L. Rev. 681, 695 (1983); see also Levin, Withholding Consent to Assignment: The Changing Rights of the Commercial Landlord, 30 De Paul L. Rev. 109, 136 (1980).

on traditional rules of conveyancing and on concepts of freedom of ownership and control over one's property.

A lessor's freedom at common law to look to no one but the lessee for the rent has, however, been undermined by the adoption in [many jurisdictions] of a rule that lessors—like all other contracting parties—have a duty to mitigate damages upon the lessee's abandonment of the property by seeking a substitute lessee. Furthermore, the values that go into the personal selection of a lessee are preserved under the minority rule in the lessor's right to refuse consent to assignment on any commercially reasonable grounds. Such grounds include not only the obvious objections to an assignee's financial stability or proposed use of the premises, but a variety of other commercially reasonable objections as well. (See, e.g., Arrington v. Walter E. Heller Intl. Corp. (1975) 30 Ill. App. 3d 631, 333 N.E.2d 50 [desire to have only one "lead tenant" in order to preserve "image of the building" as tenant's international headquarters]; Warmack v. Merchants Natl. Bank of Fort Smith (Ark. 1981) 612 S.W.2d 733 [desire for good "tenant mix" in shopping center]; List v. Dahnke (Col. App. 1981) 638 P.2d 824 [lessor's refusal to consent to assignment of lease by one restaurateur to another was reasonable where lessor believed proposed specialty restaurant would not succeed at that location].) The lessor's interests are further protected by the fact that the original lessee remains a guarantor of the performance of the assignee. . . .

The second justification advanced in support of the majority rule is that an approval clause is an unambiguous reservation of absolute discretion in the lessor over assignments of the lease. The lessee could have bargained for the addition of a reasonableness clause to the lease (i.e., "consent to assignment will not be unreasonably withheld"). The lessee having failed to do so, the law should not rewrite the parties' contract for them. . . .

Numerous authorities have taken a different view of the meaning and effect of an approval clause in a lease, indicating that the clause is not "clear and unambiguous," as respondent suggests. As early as 1940, the court in Granite Trust Bldg. Corp. v. Great Atlantic & Pacific Tea Co. [(D. Mass. 1940)] 36 F. Supp. 77, examined a standard approval clause and stated: "It would seem to be the better law that when a lease restricts a lessee's rights by requiring consent before these rights can be exercised, *it must have been in the contemplation of the parties that the lessor be required to give some reason for withholding consent.*" (Id., at p. 78, italics added.) . . .

In light of . . . the increasing number of jurisdictions that have adopted the minority rule in the last 15 years, the assertion that an approval clause "clearly and unambiguously" grants the lessor absolute discretion over assignments is untenable. It is not a rewriting of a contract, as respondent suggests, to recognize the obligations imposed by the duty of good faith and fair dealing, which duty is implied by law in every contract.

The third justification advanced in support of the majority rule is essentially based on the doctrine of stare decisis. It is argued that the courts should not depart from the common law majority rule because "many leases now in effect covering a substantial amount of real property and creating valuable property rights were carefully prepared by competent counsel in reliance upon the majority viewpoint." (Gruman v. Investors Diversified Services [(1956) 247 Minn. 502, 78 N.W.2d 377, 381].) As pointed out above, however, the majority viewpoint has been far from universally held and has never been adopted by this court. Moreover, the trend in favor of the minority rule should come as no surprise to observers of the changing state of real property law in the 20th century. The minority rule is part of an increasing recognition of the contractual nature of leases and the implications in terms of contractual duties that flow therefrom. We would be remiss in our duty if we declined to question a view held by the majority of jurisdictions simply because it is held by a majority. . . .

A final argument in favor of the majority rule is advanced by respondent and stated as follows: "Both tradition and sound public policy dictate that the lessor has a right, under circumstances such as these, to realize the increased value of his property." Respondent essentially argues that any increase in the market value of real property during the term of a lease properly belongs to the lessor, not the lessee. We reject this assertion. . . . Respondent here is trying to get *more* than it bargained for in the lease. A lessor is free to build periodic rent increases into a lease, as the lessor did here. . . . Any increased value of the property beyond this "belongs" to the lessor only in the sense, as explained above, that the lessor's reversionary estate will benefit from it upon the expiration of the lease. We must therefore reject respondent's argument in this regard. . . .[24]

In conclusion, both the policy against restraints on alienation and the implied contractual duty of good faith and fair dealing militate in favor of adoption of the rule that where a commercial lease provides for assignment only with the prior consent of the lessor, such consent may be withheld only where the lessor has a commercially reasonable objection to the assignee or the proposed use. Under this rule, appellants have stated a cause of action against respondent Ernest Pestana, Inc.

[Two justices dissented in *Kendall*, on the ground that the provisions of the agreement between the parties should be respected, especially because the lessor had relied upon the rule existing at the time of the lease. In the view of the dissent, the legislature had implicitly endorsed the common law rule overturned in *Kendall*; it was up to the legislature, not the court, to change the rule, and any change should be prospective only.]

NOTES AND QUESTIONS

1. Legislation enacted in California in 1989 codifies the holding in *Kendall* and resolves certain questions about the case, including the matter of retroactivity (*Kendall* is made applicable only to restrictions on transfer executed on or

24. Amicus Pillsbury, Madison & Sutro request that we make clear that, "whatever principle governs in the absence of express lease provisions, nothing bars the parties to commercial lease transactions from making their own arrangements respecting the allocation of appreciated rentals if there is a transfer of the leasehold." This principle we affirm; we merely hold that the clause in the instant lease established no such arrangement.

after September 23, 1983 — the date of Cohen v. Ratinoff, cited by the court in *Kendall*). See Cal. Civ. Code §§1995.010-1995.270 (West 2013).

Notice the statement in footnote 22 on page 475. Section 1995.230 of the foregoing legislation provides: "A restriction on transfer of a tenant's interest in a lease may absolutely prohibit transfer." A Law Revision Commission Comment appearing after the section states that it "settles the question raised in *Kendall* . . . of the validity of a clause absolutely prohibiting assignment or sublease."

Notice also footnote 24 on page 478. In Carma Dev. v. Marathon Dev. California, Inc., 826 P.2d 710 (Cal. 1992), the court considered and upheld a so-called termination and recapture clause in a commercial lease entered into by "sophisticated commercial entities operating at arm's length and assisted by competent counsel." The clause provided: (1) that the tenant, before entering into any sublease or assignment, was to give the landlord written notice identifying the intended assignee or sublessee and specifying the terms of the intended transfer; (2) that the landlord could then terminate its lease with the tenant and, if the landlord elected to do so, enter into a new lease with the intended assignee or sublessee; and (3) that the tenant was not entitled to any profit realized by the landlord in consequence of the termination and reletting. The court held the clause valid under *Kendall* and the new legislation alike, notwithstanding another lease provision stating that the landlord's consent to any sublease or assignment was not to be unreasonably withheld.

2. Should the rule in *Kendall* apply to residential leases? The opinion in the case leaves the question open (see footnote 20 on page 473), and the California legislation discussed above is limited to leases for other than residential purposes, Cal. Civ. Code §1995.010, because, according to a Law Revision Commission Comment following that section, "residential real property leases involve different public policies than commercial real property leases."

See in this respect Slavin v. Rent Control Bd. of Brookline, 548 N.E.2d 1226, 1228-1229 (Mass. 1990):

[N]o State court has acted to create a reasonableness requirement in a case involving only a residential lease. . . .

[An important] concern that appears to have motivated the commercial lease decisions is a desire to limit restraints on alienation in light of the fact that "the necessity of reasonable alienation of commercial building space has become paramount in our ever-increasing urban society." . . . [W]e are not persuaded that there is such a "necessity of reasonable alienation of [residential] building space" that we ought to impose on residential landlords a reasonableness requirement to which they have not agreed. We are mindful that valid arguments in support of such a rule can be made, but there are also valid counter-arguments, not the least of which is that such a rule would be likely to engender a plethora of litigation about whether the landlord's withholding of consent was reasonable. The question is one of public policy which, of course, the Legislature is free to address. We note that the Legislature has spoken in at least four States [Alaska, Delaware, Hawaii, and New York].[25]

25. In light of this language, one might think that the Supreme Judicial Court of Massachusetts would follow *Kendall* with respect at least to commercial leases. Not so! See Merchants Row Corp. v. Merchants Row, Inc.,

Do the court's reasons for not extending the reasonableness requirement to residential leases strike you as persuasive? Are there any other justifications for not requiring landlords of residential buildings to act reasonably in approving or rejecting subleases and assignments? Should it matter whether the apartments or homes are rent-regulated (as in the case of *Slavin*)? How about whether the building is occupied by the landlord?

The opinions in *Kendall* and *Slavin* mention concerns about restraints on alienability as arguments against allowing landlords to reject assignments and subleases arbitrarily. Recall from the discussion in Chapter 3 (at pages 232-233) that restraints on alienability are disfavored for a number of reasons, including the concern that such restraints will keep land from moving to its highest and best uses. Is it very likely that if the court in *Kendall* had allowed Pestana to reject the assignment arbitrarily, the leased property would not have found its way to its most efficient use (presumably by Kendall)?

3. Notice the mention in *Kendall* (at page 477) of the landlord's duty to mitigate damages. In some jurisdictions the courts follow the common law rule that a landlord may arbitrarily and unreasonably refuse permission to sublet or assign (unless, of course, the lease provides to the contrary) but go on to say that if the tenant thereafter abandons the premises, the landlord is under a duty to mitigate damages. Is this any different than saying that a landlord may not unreasonably and arbitrarily refuse permission to sublet or assign? Cf. Vasquez v. Carmel Shopping Center Co., 777 S.W.2d 532 (Tex. App. 1989). (We look more closely at abandonment and mitigation beginning at page 492.)

PROBLEMS

1. Suppose the following situations arise in a jurisdiction following the rule in *Kendall*, or in any jurisdiction under a lease providing that "there shall be no sublease or assignment without landlord's consent, and such consent shall not be unreasonably withheld." What result?

(a) *L* leases to *T* for a term of five years. After two years, *T* wishes to transfer the lease to *T1*. *L* refuses consent because *T1* is a tenant in another of *L*'s buildings under a lease that is about to expire; *L* and *T1* have been actively negotiating a new lease, and *L* wants to avoid losing *T1* as a tenant in the other building. See Krieger v. Helmsley-Spear, Inc., 302 A.2d 129 (N.J. 1973), cited with apparent approval in *Kendall* at page 476.

Suppose instead that *T1* is not already a tenant of *L*, but rather is a prospective tenant who wants to use the leased property for a business that will compete

---

587 N.E.2d 788, 789 (Mass. 1992). For another case rejecting the rule in *Kendall*, see First Federal Sav. Bank v. Key Markets, Inc., 559 N.E.2d 600 (Ind. 1990).

In contrast to the foregoing, several states have followed *Kendall* in the case of commercial leases. See Van Sloun v. Agons Bros., Inc., 778 N.W.2d 174, 180 (Iowa 2010); Newman v. Hinky Dinky Omaha-Lincoln, Inc., 427 N.W.2d 50 (Neb. 1988); Julian v. Christopher, 575 A.2d 735, 740 (Md. 1990).

On *Kendall*, see Alex M. Johnson, Jr., Correctly Interpreting Long-Term Leases Pursuant to Modern Contract Law: Toward a Theory of Relational Leases, 74 Va. L. Rev. 751 (1988).

with L's business in the same area. See Norville v. Carr-Gottstein Foods Co., 84 P.3d 996 (Ala. App. 2004); Pay 'N Pak Stores, Inc. v. Superior Court, 258 Cal. Rptr. 816 (Cal. App. 1989).

(b) L, a Christian evangelical organization, owns a building that it uses as its headquarters. No religious services are held in the building. L leases space in the building to T for a term of three years. After one year, T wishes to transfer the lease to $T1$, an organization that proposes to use the leased space as a counseling center providing information on birth control and abortion. L refuses consent on the sole ground that it is fundamentally opposed to the aims and activities of $T1$. See American Book Co. v. Yeshiva Univ. Dev. Found., 297 N.Y.S.2d 156 (Sup. Ct. 1969).[26]

(c) What if in any given situation L demands a fee in exchange for consenting to a transfer of the lease? See Giordano v. Miller, 733 N.Y.S.2d 94 (App. Div. 2001).

2. Suppose a jurisdiction following the majority rule and a lease providing that L may terminate if T transfers without the necessary consent. Unlike the situation in Problem 1, however, the lease prohibits only assignment without L's permission. T wishes to assign to $T1$, but L—because she wishes to rent to $T1$ on her own for a higher rent—refuses consent. T then transfers the lease to $T1$ for the remainder of the original term, minus one day. L brings suit to terminate the head lease with T (which would terminate $T1$'s tenancy as well), arguing that the form of the transaction should be disregarded, that it was a subterfuge, that the parties clearly intended the transfer to be an assignment, and that the assignment was made without L's consent. What result? See page 470 and Walgreen Arizona Drug Co. v. Plaza Center Corp., 647 P.2d 643 (Ariz. 1982).

3. L leases to T for a term of five years at a monthly rent of $900; in the lease, T covenants to pay the rent and further covenants not to sublet or assign without L's permission. Thereafter T, with L's permission, assigns to $T1$ ($T1$ does not expressly assume the obligations of the lease); then $T1$ assigns to $T2$ without first obtaining L's permission. $T2$ defaults in rent payments, and L sues $T1$ for the amount due. What result? See Restatement (Second) of Property, Landlord and Tenant §16.1 comment g at 125 (1977) (expressing disapproval of the so-called Rule in Dumpor's Case, 4 Coke 119b, 76 Eng. Rep. 1110 (K.B. 1578), "which would terminate the prohibition against assignment when the landlord consents to an assignment unless he specifically reserves the right to prohibit future assignments").

4. L leases a building to T (a company that makes computers) for a period of 10 years; a clause in the lease states that T shall not transfer the lease without the permission of L. T subsequently merges into a corporation, ABC. Does the merger result in a transfer of the lease that triggers the permission requirement? Does it matter whether T and ABC are related (e.g., as parent and subsidiary)? Cf.

---

26. Is it never "commercially reasonable" to deny consent to a transfer "solely on the basis of personal taste, convenience or sensibility," as the court in *Kendall* puts it at page 476? See the discussion of leases in housing cooperatives at pages 938-940.

Brentsun Realty Corp. v. D'Urso Supermarkets, Inc., 582 N.Y.S.2d 216 (App. Div. 1992) (merger into subsidiary not deemed to constitute an assignment under lease); Pacific First Bank v. New Morgan Park Corp., 876 P.2d 761 (Or. 1994) (merger into subsidiary effected transfer requiring landlord's consent, which could be withheld at his sole discretion); Standard Operations, Inc. v. Montague, 758 S.W.2d 442 (Mo. 1988) (merger not considered an assignment under lease). If a court were to require *T* to get the approval of *L*, and the applicable rule is that announced in the *Kendall* case, what considerations might *L* be obliged, or allowed, to take into account?

Suppose that instead of a merger, *T* changes its ownership (but not its name) by sale of its stock to *ABC*. Would the sale constitute a transfer of the lease with *L*? Compare Branmar Theatre Co. v. Branmar, Inc., 264 A.2d 526 (Del. Ch. 1970) (not an assignment when lease does not address sale of stock), with Zona, Inc. v. Soho Centrale LLC, 704 N.Y.S.2d 38 (App. Div. 2000) (deemed an assignment in violation of lease term requiring permission when more than 25 percent of beneficial ownership is transferred). See generally Joshua Stein, Assignment and Subletting Restrictions in Leases and What They Mean in the Real World, 44 Real Prop., Tr. & Est. L.J. 1 (2009); William G. Coskran, Assignment and Sublease Restrictions: The Tribulations of Leasehold Transfers, 22 Loy. L.A. L. Rev. 405 (1989).

F.   The Tenant Who Defaults

Suppose a tenant *in possession* has defaulted—say by failing to pay rent or observe some other lease obligation—or is holding over after the termination of the lease (see pages 449-450), and the landlord wishes to recover possession. Or suppose the tenant has *abandoned* the premises prior to the end of the tenancy, perhaps owing some back rent. What, in each case, may the landlord do? Consider the following materials.

1.   The Tenant in Possession

Berg v. Wiley

Supreme Court of Minnesota, 1978
264 N.W.2d 145

ROGOSHESKE, J. Defendant landlord, Wiley Enterprises, Inc., and defendant Rodney A. Wiley (hereafter collectively referred to as Wiley) appeal from a judgment upon a jury verdict awarding plaintiff tenant, A Family Affair Restaurant, Inc., damages for wrongful eviction from its leased premises. The issues for review are whether the evidence was sufficient to support the jury's finding that the tenant did not abandon or surrender the premises and whether the trial court erred in finding Wiley's reentry forcible and wrongful as a matter of law. We hold that the jury's verdict is supported by sufficient evidence and that the trial court's determination of unlawful entry was correct as a matter of law, and affirm the judgment.

On November 11, 1970, Wiley as lessor and tenant's predecessor in interest as lessee executed a written lease agreement letting land and a building in Osseo, Minnesota, for use as a restaurant. The lease provided a 5-year term beginning December 1, 1970, and specified that the tenant agreed to bear all costs of repairs and remodeling, to "make no changes in the building structure" without prior written authorization from Wiley, and to "operate the restaurant in a lawful and prudent manner." Wiley also reserved the right "at [his] option [to] retake possession" of the premises "[s]hould the Lessee fail to meet the conditions of this Lease."[27] In early 1971, plaintiff Kathleen Berg took assignment of the lease from the prior lessee, and on May 1, 1971, she opened "A Family Affair Restaurant" on the premises. In January 1973, Berg incorporated the restaurant and assigned her interest in the lease to "A Family Affair Restaurant, Inc." As sole shareholder of the corporation, she alone continued to act for the tenant. [The prior lessee referred to by the court was Phillip Berg, Kathleen's brother, who ran a pool hall and served low-alcohol beer and small meals on the leased premises from December 1, 1970 (when the lease began), until February 20, 1971 (when Phillip assigned to Kathleen with the consent of Wiley). Kathleen then began remodeling the premises to make them suitable for a restaurant.]

The present dispute has arisen out of Wiley's objection to Berg's continued remodeling of the restaurant without procuring written permission and her consequent operation of the restaurant in a state of disrepair with alleged health code violations. Strained relations between the parties came to a head in June and July 1973. In a letter dated June 29, 1973, Wiley's attorney charged Berg with having breached lease items 5 and 6 by making changes in the building structure without written authorization and by operating an unclean kitchen in violation of health regulations. The letter demanded that a list of eight remodeling items be completed within 2 weeks from the date of the letter, by Friday, July 13, 1973, or Wiley would retake possession of the premises under lease item 7. Also, a June 13 inspection of the restaurant by the Minnesota Department of Health had produced an order that certain listed changes be completed within specified time limits in order to comply with the health code. The major items on the inspector's list, similar to those listed by Wiley's attorney, were to be completed by July 15, 1973.

27. The provisions of the lease pertinent to this case provide:

Item #5 The Lessee will make no changes to the building structure without first receiving written authorization from the Lessor. The Lessor will promptly reply in writing to each request and will cooperate with the Lessee on any reasonable request.
Item #6 The Lessee agrees to operate the restaurant in a lawful and prudent manner during the lease period.
Item #7 Should the Lessee fail to meet the conditions of this Lease the Lessor may at their [sic] option retake possession of said premises. In any such event such act will not relieve Lessee from liability for payment [of] the rental herein provided or from the conditions or obligations of this lease.

During the 2-week deadline set by both Wiley and the health department, Berg continued to operate the restaurant without closing to complete the required items of remodeling. The evidence is in dispute as to whether she intended to permanently close the restaurant and vacate the premises at the end of the 2 weeks or simply close for about 1 month in order to remodel to comply with the health code. At the close of business on Friday, July 13, 1973, the last day of the 2-week period, Berg dismissed her employees, closed the restaurant, and placed a sign in the window saying "Closed for Remodeling." Earlier that day, Berg testified, Wiley came to the premises in her absence and attempted to change the locks. When she returned and asserted her right to continue in possession, he complied with her request to leave the locks unchanged. Berg also testified that at about 9:30 p.m. that evening, while she and four of her friends were in the restaurant, she observed Wiley hanging from the awning peering into the window. Shortly thereafter, she heard Wiley pounding on the back door demanding admittance. Berg called the county sheriff to come and preserve order. Wiley testified that he observed Berg and a group of her friends in the restaurant removing paneling from a wall. Allegedly fearing destruction of his property, Wiley called the city police, who, with the sheriff, mediated an agreement between the parties to preserve the status quo until each could consult with legal counsel on Monday, July 16, 1973.

Wiley testified that his then attorney advised him to take possession of the premises and lock the tenant out. Accompanied by a police officer and a locksmith, Wiley entered the premises in Berg's absence and without her knowledge on Monday, July 16, 1973, and changed the locks. Later in the day, Berg found herself locked out. The lease term was not due to expire until December 1, 1975. The premises were re-let to another tenant on or about August 1, 1973. Berg brought this damage action against Wiley and three other named defendants, including the new tenant, on July 27, 1973. A second amended complaint sought damages for lost profits, damage to chattels, intentional infliction of emotional distress, and other tort damages based upon claims in wrongful eviction, contract, and tort. Wiley answered with an affirmative defense of abandonment and surrender and counterclaimed for damage to the premises and indemnification on mechanics lien liability incurred because of Berg's remodeling. At the close of Berg's case, all defendants other than Rodney A. Wiley and Wiley Enterprises, Inc., were dismissed from the action. Only Berg's action for wrongful eviction and intentional infliction of emotional distress and Wiley's affirmative defense of abandonment and his counterclaim for damage to the premises were submitted by special verdict to the jury. With respect to the wrongful eviction claim, the trial court found as a matter of law that Wiley did in fact lock the tenant out, and that the lockout was wrongful.

The jury, by answers to the questions submitted, found no liability on Berg's claim for intentional infliction of emotional distress and no liability on Wiley's counterclaim for damages to the premises, but awarded Berg $31,000 for lost profits and $3,540 for loss of chattels resulting from the wrongful lockout. The jury also specifically found that Berg neither abandoned nor surrendered the premises. . . .

On this appeal, Wiley seeks an outright reversal of the damages award for wrongful eviction, claiming insufficient evidence to support the jury's finding of no abandonment or surrender and claiming error in the trial court's finding of wrongful eviction as a matter of law.

The first issue before us concerns the sufficiency of evidence to support the jury's finding that Berg had not abandoned or surrendered the leasehold before being locked out by Wiley. Viewing the evidence to support the jury's special verdict in the light most favorable to Berg, as we must, we hold it amply supports the jury's finding of no abandonment or surrender of the premises. While the evidence bearing upon Berg's intent was strongly contradictory, the jury could reasonably have concluded, based on Berg's testimony and supporting circumstantial evidence, that she intended to retain possession, closing temporarily to remodel. Thus, the lockout cannot be excused on the ground that Berg abandoned or surrendered the leasehold.

The second and more difficult issue is whether Wiley's self-help repossession of the premises by locking out Berg was correctly held wrongful as a matter of law.

Minnesota has historically followed the common-law rule that a landlord may rightfully use self-help to retake leased premises from a tenant in possession without incurring liability for wrongful eviction provided two conditions are met: (1) The landlord is legally entitled to possession, such as where a tenant holds over after the lease term or where a tenant breaches a lease containing a reentry clause; and (2) the landlord's means of reentry are peaceable. Mercil v. Broulette, 66 Minn. 416, 69 N.W. 218 (1896). Under the common-law rule, a tenant who is evicted by his landlord may recover damages for wrongful eviction where the landlord either had no right to possession or where the means used to remove the tenant were forcible, or both.

Wiley contends that Berg had breached the provisions of the lease, thereby entitling Wiley, under the terms of the lease, to retake possession, and that his repossession by changing the locks in Berg's absence was accomplished in a peaceful manner. In a memorandum accompanying the post-trial order, the trial court stated two grounds for finding the lockout wrongful as a matter of law: (1) It was not accomplished in a peaceable manner and therefore could not be justified under the common-law rule, and (2) any self-help reentry against a tenant in possession is wrongful under the growing modern doctrine that a landlord must always resort to the judicial process to enforce his statutory remedy against a tenant wrongfully in possession. Whether Berg had in fact breached the lease and whether Wiley was hence entitled to possession was not judicially determined. That issue became irrelevant upon the trial court's finding that Wiley's reentry was forcible as a matter of law because even if Berg had breached the lease, this could not excuse Wiley's nonpeaceable reentry. The finding that Wiley's reentry was forcible as a matter of law provided a sufficient ground for damages, and the issue of breach was not submitted to the jury.

In each of our previous cases upholding an award of damages for wrongful eviction, the landlord had in fact been found to have no legal right to possession.

In applying the common-law rule, we have not before had occasion to decide what means of self-help used to dispossess a tenant in his absence will constitute a nonpeaceable entry, giving a right to damages without regard to who holds the legal right to possession. Wiley argues that only actual or threatened violence used against a tenant should give rise to damages where the landlord had the right to possession. We cannot agree.

It has long been the policy of our law to discourage landlords from taking the law into their own hands, and our decisions and statutory law have looked with disfavor upon any use of self-help to dispossess a tenant in circumstances which are likely to result in breaches of the peace. We gave early recognition to this policy in Lobdell v. Keene, 85 Minn. 90, 101, 88 N.W. 426, 430 (1901), where we said:

> The object and purpose of the legislature in the enactment of the forcible entry and unlaw-ful detainer statute was to prevent those claiming a right of entry or possession of lands from redressing their own wrongs by entering into possession in a violent and forcible manner. All such acts tend to a breach of the peace, and encourage high-handed oppression. The law does not permit the owner of land, be his title ever so good, to be the judge of his own rights with respect to a possession adversely held, but puts him to his remedy under the statutes.

To facilitate a resort to judicial process, the legislature has provided a summary procedure in Minn. St. 566.02 to 566.17 whereby a landlord may recover posses-sion of leased premises upon proper notice and showing in court in as little as 3 to 10 days. As we recognized in Mutual Trust Life Ins. Co. v. Berg, 187 Minn. 503, 505, 246 N.W. 9, 10 (1932), "[t]he forcible entry and unlawful detainer statutes were intended to prevent parties from taking the law into their own hands when going into possession of lands and tenements. . . ." To further discourage self-help, our legislature has provided treble damages for forcible evictions, §§557.08 and 557.09, and has provided additional criminal penalties for intentional and unlawful exclusion of a tenant, §504.25. In Sweeney v. Meyers, 199 Minn. 21, 270 N.W. 906 (1937), we allowed a business tenant not only damages for lost profits but also punitive damages against a landlord who, like Wiley, entered in the ten-ant's absence and locked the tenant out.

In the present case, as in *Sweeney*, the tenant was in possession, claiming a right to continue in possession adverse to the landlord's claim of breach of the lease, and had neither abandoned nor surrendered the premises. Wiley, well aware that Berg was asserting her right to possession, retook possession in her absence by picking the locks and locking her out. The record shows a history of vigorous dispute and keen animosity between the parties. Upon this record, we can only conclude that the singular reason why actual violence did not erupt at the moment of Wiley's changing of the locks was Berg's absence and her subsequent self-restraint and resort to judicial process. Upon these facts, we can-not find Wiley's means of reentry peaceable under the common-law rule. Our long-standing policy to discourage self-help which tends to cause a breach of the peace compels us to disapprove the means used to dispossess Berg. To approve this lockout, as urged by Wiley, merely because in Berg's absence no actual violence erupted while the locks were being changed, would be to encourage all future tenants, in order to protect their possession, to be vigilant and thereby set the stage for the very kind of public disturbance which it must be our policy to discourage. . . .

We recognize that the growing modern trend departs completely from the common-law rule to hold that self-help is never available to dispossess a tenant who is in possession and has not abandoned or voluntarily surrendered the premises. Annotation, 6 A.L.R.3d 177, 186; 76 Dickinson L. Rev. 215, 227. This growing rule is founded on the recognition that the potential for violent breach of peace inheres in any situation where a landlord attempts by his own means to remove a tenant who is claiming possession adversely to the landlord. Courts adopting the rule reason that there is no cause to sanction such potentially disruptive self-help where adequate and speedy means are provided for removing a tenant peacefully through judicial process. At least 16 states[28] have adopted this modern rule, holding that judicial proceedings, including the summary procedures provided in those states' unlawful detainer statutes, are the exclusive remedy by which a landlord may remove a tenant claiming possession. . . .

While we would be compelled to disapprove the lockout of Berg in her absence under the common-law rule as stated, we approve the trial court's reasoning and adopt as preferable the modern view represented by the cited cases. To make clear our departure from the common-law rule for the benefit of future landlords and tenants, we hold that, subsequent to our decision in this case, the only lawful means to dispossess a tenant who has not abandoned nor voluntarily surrendered but who claims possession adversely to a landlord's claim of breach of a written lease is by resort to judicial process. . . .

Applying our holding to the facts of this case, we conclude, as did the trial court, that because Wiley failed to resort to judicial remedies against Berg's holding possession adversely to Wiley's claim of breach of the lease, his lockout of Berg was wrongful as a matter of law. The rule we adopt in this decision is fairly applied against Wiley, for it is clear that, applying the older common-law rule to the facts and circumstances peculiar to this case, we would be compelled to find the lockout nonpeaceable for the reasons previously stated. The jury found that the lockout caused Berg damage and, as between Berg and Wiley, equity dictates that Wiley, who himself performed the act causing the damage, must bear the loss.

Affirmed.

---

28. Annotation, 6 A.L.R.3d 177, 186, Supp. 13, shows this modern rule to have been adopted in California, Connecticut, Delaware, Florida, Georgia, Illinois, Indiana, Louisiana, Nebraska, North Carolina, Ohio, Tennessee, Texas, Utah, Vermont, and Washington.

We have examined the summary statutory procedures for repossession held exclusive in these other states and we find them comparable and on the whole no speedier than the summary judicial procedures by which a landlord may regain possession in as little as 3 to 10 days under Minn. St. §§566.02 to 566.17.

NOTES AND QUESTIONS

1. Under the common law, a landlord entitled to possession could resort to self-help without fear of civil liability—so long as he used no more force than reasonably necessary. Criminal prosecution was nevertheless a possibility; forcible entry was a common law crime. Thus the civil and criminal systems were a bit at odds.[29] The modern view (and majority rule) on self-help appears to be that in *Berg v. Wiley.* See Adam B. Badawi, Self-Help and the Rules of Engagement, 29 Yale J. on Reg. 1, 24 (2012) (virtually all states prohibit self-help in residential settings; a dozen recognize a right to use peaceable self-help in commercial settings); Randy D. Gerchick, Comment, No Easy Way Out: Making the Summary Eviction Process a Fairer and More Efficient Alternative to Landlord Self-Help, 41 UCLA L. Rev. 759, 777 (1994) (self-help banned by majority of states). Where self-help is allowed, of course, there still arises the difficult issue of just what constitutes reasonable or permissible force. Here the courts have tended to be rather strict, so that self-help may be a theoretical but not a practical alternative.

Are limitations on self-help evictions a good thing for tenants? Consider the following:

> The movement to prohibit self-help evictions by landlords has long had a few critics, with the most prominent ones suggesting that landlords would pass the high costs of judicially evicting deadbeat tenants onto the tenants who paid their bills on time. Some passing on of these costs undoubtedly occurs, but the [rise of commercial data brokers] suggests a deeper criticism of the prohibitions on landlord self-help. Eviction via self-help typically creates no public records. Courts are not involved in a self-help eviction, and a landlord has no economic incentive to report such a dispossession to a credit bureau or any other information broker. Evictions via summary proceedings, on the other hand, necessarily generate public records, and it is those public records that will prove so damaging to tenants the next time they try to rent an apartment. From the perspective of facilitating tenant rehabilitation and second chances, a law prohibiting self-help by landlords will prove counterproductive. Many tenants who have trouble making rent payments will fail to appreciate the reputational repercussions of involvement in summary proceedings. For these tenants, the law's prohibition on self-help can be a particularly raw deal. This is a point overlooked by defenders of the prohibition on self-help. [Lior Jacob Strahilevitz, Reputation Nation: Law in an Era of Ubiquitous Personal Information, 102 Nw. U. L. Rev. 1667, 1679-1680 (2008).]

2. *Berg* involved a commercial lease, but the court's reasoning would appear to apply to all leases, residential and commercial alike. See also Simpson v. Lee, 499 A.2d 889 (D.C. App. 1985) (self-help prohibited in either instance). In some jurisdictions, the prohibition on self-help applies only to residential leases. Is there any reason to treat the two situations differently? See Case Note, 60 N.C.

---

29. And may still be so today—to some degree. See, e.g., Restatement (Second) of Property, Landlord and Tenant §14.1 Statutory Note at 5 (1977): "If a person makes a 'forcible' entry by using self-help, he will probably be subject to criminal liability; yet he may be entitled to retain possession of the premises which he has obtained through such force. If the law permits the party entitled to possession to keep the premises, the . . . tenant may be uninterested in pressing criminal charges against the party using self-help. Thus, in practice, such a jurisdiction may still permit self-help." But might not the tenant be interested in remedies other than regaining possession? See Berg v. Wiley and Annot., 6 A.L.R.3d 177, 182, 199-237 (1966).

L. Rev. 885, 891-892 (1982) (loss of residence has greater psychological impact than loss of possession of place of business, and the need for immediate replacement of commercial space is less vital; moreover, in the commercial setting there is more likely to be equal bargaining power between the parties); see also Watson v. Brown, 686 P.2d 12 (Haw. 1984) (permits self-help in commercial tenancies, because of equality of bargaining power; expresses no opinion as to residential tenancies). Of what relevance is equal bargaining power?

In *Berg*, item 7 of the lease might be read to permit self-help by the landlord. Should such a provision make a difference in a jurisdiction otherwise prohibiting self-help? Courts appear to split on this question, but the Restatement view is that the prohibition cannot be contracted away. See Restatement (Second) of Property, Landlord and Tenant §§14.2-14.3 (1977).

3. Contrast the customary prohibition on self-help in the context of real property with the situation regarding personal property, in which creditors are often permitted to use self-help to recover possession, even to the extent of trespassing, provided that entry is not forcible. Why this difference? See Badawi, supra, at 25-30.

4. Should self-help repossession by a landlord be subject to constitutional attack on the ground that it denies the tenant due process of law? Apparently no decision has ever held to that effect, although a number of state courts have invalidated a related self-help remedy—distraint, or distress for rent—on due process grounds. See Restatement (Second) of Property, Landlord and Tenant §12.1 Reporter's Note at 429; id. §14.1 Statutory Note at 6-7. Under the common law remedy of distress for rent (abolished in some states by statute), a landlord could seize a defaulting tenant's property found on the premises and retain it until payment of overdue rent, all without prior hearing. The absence of a prior hearing has proved the vulnerable point in cases invalidating modern analogues of this procedure. See also Soldal v. Cook County, 506 U.S. 56 (1992) (Fourth Amendment protects against unreasonable seizures, by or with the assistance of public officials, of tenant's property prior to eviction order required under state law); Revis v. Meldrum, 489 F.3d 273 (6th Cir. 2007) (noting that due process has long required notice and an opportunity to be heard before eviction).

5. In recent years, nonprofit social service organizations have sponsored the construction of residential facilities for their clientele. In some instances these housing developments have on-site social services and extensive rules governing behavior. Often they serve vulnerable groups such as battered women, recovering substance abusers, or the elderly. The housing provided is usually temporary and transitional rather than permanent. When residents fail to pay the charges for their rooms or otherwise violate rules, must the owners seek an eviction order from a court or can they use self-help repossession (e.g., change the locks)? The answer depends in part upon whether a court defines the situation as one amounting to a landlord-tenant relationship. Compare Higdon v. Sign of the Cross Housing, Inc., 803 N.E.2d 876 (Ohio Mun. Ct. 2003) (operator of shelter for low income persons with maximum stay of 180 days could not change the locks without going to court), and Serreze v. YWCA of Western Massachusetts, 572 N.E.2d 581 (Mass.

App. 1991) (managers of transitional living program for battered women could not change locks of apartments), with Ann Arbor Tenants Union v. Ann Arbor YMCA, 581 N.W.2d 794 (Mich. App. 1998) (relationship of owner and resident of single room occupancy residence is not that of landlord-tenant but instead of hotel and guest and therefore not subject to forcible detainer act), and Parker v. Salvation Army, 971 N.E.2d 995, 998 (Ohio. App. 2012) (emergency shelters are not subject to landlord-tenant laws). See generally Matthew R. Hays, Crusading for the Helpless or Biting the Hand That Feeds? Applying Landlord-Tenant Law to Residents of Shelters, 83 Notre Dame L. Rev. 443 (2007). Do the arguments against self-help repossession for traditional tenancies apply with equal force to non-traditional housing arrangements such as transitional shelters? Should the technical categories of "landlord" and "tenant" determine the rights of occupants to be free from self-help repossession?

NOTES: SUMMARY PROCEEDINGS — PURPOSE AND PROBLEMS

1. *Summary proceedings.* At one time, self-help was a very important remedy for the landlord who sought to recover possession of leased premises, because the only alternative was a cumbersome, time-consuming, common law procedure called ejectment (which still exists today, with statutory modifications). The time and expense associated with ejectment ill served the landlord's needs; self-help, on the other hand, was seen as problematic from the viewpoint of landlords, tenants, and society generally. A response to this mix of shortcomings began to develop in the nineteenth century—legislative provision for summary proceedings (sometimes called forcible entry and detainer statutes). Today every state provides some form of summary proceeding. For background, description, and discussion of the variety of provisions, see Restatement (Second) of Property, Landlord and Tenant §12.1 Statutory Note at 399-405 (1977); id. §14.1 Statutory Note at 3-11.

Summary proceedings are intended to be just what the name implies—a quick and efficient means by which to recover possession (and, in some jurisdictions, rent) after termination of a tenancy. To promote quickness, the typical statute requires only a few days' notice to the tenant prior to bringing an eviction action, and the range of issues subject to litigation is kept narrow. It is difficult to generalize about the latter point other than to say that any matter extrinsic to the issue of possession is normally excluded (for example, a tenant may not claim an earlier unrelated debt owed by the landlord as a setoff for past due rent). As we shall see later in this chapter, a number of jurisdictions are beginning to provide that failure by a landlord to maintain leased premises in a habitable condition justifies certain "self-help" measures by a tenant, including rent withholding. It seems quite logical, then, to permit a tenant to raise the condition of the premises as a defense to a summary eviction action brought for nonpayment of rent—the defense appears to go, after all, to the issue of the right to possession. Many states so provide, but not all do, and the U.S. Supreme

Court has held that a failure to do so does not violate due process. Lindsey v. Normet, 405 U.S. 56 (1972).[30]

2. *Problems.* Courts have regularly relied on the availability of summary proceedings as one reason to abrogate the common law remedy of self-help. After all, if a quick and economical remedy is available to the landlord, why court the troubles to which self-help is thought to give rise? The difficulty is that typical summary eviction procedures can be time-consuming and expensive, even if uncontested. See, e.g., U.S. G.A.O., District of Columbia: Information on Court-Ordered Tenant Evictions 2 (Dec. 1990), reporting that an average of 114 days elapsed from the date landlords requested evictions to the date they were accomplished.[31] Delay occurred for a variety of reasons: stay of eviction orders when tenants agreed (but subsequently failed) to pay the rent due; trials; failure of the marshal to evict on bad weather days, holidays, and weekends; a shortage of marshals; landlords' failure to comply with arrangements agreed upon with the marshals (for example, failure to have movers at the eviction sites).

Current institutional arrangements for adjudicating landlord-tenant disputes, particularly in the nation's larger cities, have attracted criticism from landlords and tenants alike. Landlord advocates complain that judges drag out summary proceedings because the judges are biased in favor of tenants; tenant advocates argue that tenants are unable to effectively represent themselves in litigation, yet have insufficient resources to retain lawyers. For both sides of the story, see, e.g., Chester Hartman & David Robinson, Evictions: The Hidden Housing Problem, 14 Housing Policy Debate 461 (2003), speaking on behalf of tenants; and the reply by Leonore Monello Schloming & Skip Schloming, id. at 529. Studies of housing courts in major cities show that the vast majority of tenants are unrepresented and often default.[32] According to one study, which randomly assigned tenants in

30. As we shall see later, many jurisdictions today prohibit "retaliatory eviction"—eviction motivated by a landlord's desire to retaliate against a tenant who has, for example, withheld rent payments because of the condition of the leased premises. While retaliatory eviction can usually be asserted by a tenant as a defense in a summary proceeding, Lindsey v. Normet implies that this need not be the case.

A related point: Some five million American households live in housing owned or subsidized by federal and state public authorities. A bit more on government housing programs later (see Note 4 on page 537), but understand for now that in some instances the rights of tenants in subsidized housing go far beyond those of tenants living in non-subsidized leased residences. For example, the Fourteenth Amendment to the United States Constitution provides in part that states shall not "deprive any person of life, liberty or property, without due process of law. . . ." Public housing tenants are deemed to have a property interest in their housing, and courts have ruled that the Due Process Clause entitles them to a hearing before their leases can be terminated. See, e.g., Caulder v. Durham Housing Authority, 433 F.2d 998 (4th Cir. 1970); Escalera v. New York City Housing Authority, 425 F.2d 853 (2d Cir. 1970). Similar rights have been extended to tenants in privately owned housing subsidized by the government. See, e.g., Simmons v. Drew, 716 F.2d 1160 (7th Cir. 1983) (tenant entitled to hearing before being terminated from rent assistance program); Jeffries v. Georgia Residential Finance Authority, 678 F.2d 919, 925 (11th Cir. 1982) (Section 8 tenants have constitutionally protected rights). The rules governing pre-termination notice and grievance procedures are now set forth in federal statutes and regulations. See 42 U.S.C. §1437d. Negative determinations can be challenged in court.

31. But the 114-day average is nothing compared to the summary process that took two years in Hodge v. Klug, 604 N.E.2d 1329 (Mass. App. 1992).

32. See, e.g., Laura Abel et al., Results from Three Surveys of Tenants Facing Eviction in New York City Housing Court (Brennan Center for Justice at NYU School of Law, 2007) (of 1,767 tenants in New York City Housing Court who provided information on legal representation, at least 76 percent had no lawyer); Lawyers Committee for Better Housing, No Time for Justice: A Study of Chicago's Eviction Court (2003) (of 763 cases

New York City's Housing Court into represented and unrepresented groups, tenants with lawyers fared significantly better than those who were unrepresented.[33]

Would expanded access to attorneys for tenants facing eviction improve the housing conditions of low income families in the United States? See Michael H. Schill, Comment on Chester Hartman and David Robinson's "Evictions: The Hidden Housing Problem"—Protection or Protraction?, id. at 503, 508 (2003), suggesting that more lawyers for tenants without other reforms could lead to greater delays and burdens on housing providers.

NOTE: LANDLORD'S REMEDIES IN ADDITION TO EVICTION

Usually, a landlord will want to do more than simply terminate the lease and evict the defaulting tenant in possession, because, for example, back rent may be due, the rent set in the lease may exceed what the landlord can obtain on a reletting, the leased premises may have been damaged in some way, and so on. But the remedies available in these and related instances are essentially the same as the remedies landlords might pursue against tenants who have abandoned possession. Accordingly, we defer them until the end of the next section.

2.   The Tenant Who Has Abandoned Possession

Sommer v. Kridel

Supreme Court of New Jersey, 1977
378 A.2d 767

PASHMAN, J. We granted certification in these cases to consider whether a landlord seeking damages from a defaulting tenant is under a duty to mitigate damages by making reasonable efforts to re-let an apartment wrongfully vacated by the tenant. Separate parts of the Appellate Division held that, in accordance with their respective leases, the landlords in both cases could recover rents due under the leases regardless of whether they had attempted to re-let the vacated apartments. Although they were of different minds as to the fairness of this result, both parts agreed that it was dictated by Joyce v. Bauman, 113 N.J.L. 438, 174 A. 693 (E.&A. 1934), a decision by the former Court of Errors and Appeals. We now reverse and hold that a landlord does have an obligation to make a reasonable effort to

---

observed, only 4 percent had lawyers representing both parties; tenants were represented by attorneys only 5 percent of the time in hearings).

33. Caroll Seron et al., The Impact of Legal Counsel on Outcomes for Poor Tenants in New York City's Housing Court: Results of a Randomized Experiment, 35 Law & Socy. Rev. 419 (2001) (tenants represented by lawyers had a 21.5 percent probability of having a judgment issued against them, compared to a 50.6 percent probability for unrepresented tenants).

mitigate damages in such a situation. We therefore overrule Joyce v. Bauman to the extent that it is inconsistent with our decision today.

Sommer v. Kridel

The case was tried on stipulated facts. On March 10, 1972 the defendant, James Kridel, entered into a lease with the plaintiff, Abraham Sommer, owner of the "Pierre Apartments" in Hackensack, to rent apartment 6-L in that building.[34] The term of the lease was from May 1, 1972 until April 30, 1974, with a rent concession for the first six weeks, so that the first month's rent was not due until June 15, 1972.

One week after signing the agreement, Kridel paid Sommer $690. Half of that sum was used to satisfy the first month's rent. The remainder was paid under the lease provision requiring a security deposit of $345. Although defendant had expected to begin occupancy around May 1, his plans were changed. He wrote to Sommer on May 19, 1972, explaining

> I was to be married on June 3, 1972. Unhappily the engagement was broken and the wedding plans cancelled. Both parents were to assume responsibility for the rent after our marriage. I was discharged from the U.S. Army in October 1971 and am now a student. I have no funds of my own, and am supported by my stepfather.
>
> In view of the above, I cannot take possession of the apartment and am surrendering all rights to it. Never having received a key, I cannot return same to you.
>
> I beg your understanding and compassion in releasing me from the lease, and will of course, in consideration thereof, forfeit the 2 months' rent already paid.
>
> Please notify me at your earliest convenience.

Plaintiff did not answer the letter.

Subsequently, a third party went to the apartment house and inquired about renting apartment 6-L. Although the parties agreed that she was ready, willing and able to rent the apartment, the person in charge told her that the apartment was not being shown since it was already rented to Kridel. In fact, the landlord did not re-enter the apartment or exhibit it to anyone until August 1, 1973. At that time it was rented to a new tenant for a term beginning on September 1, 1973. The new rental was for $345 per month with a six week concession similar to that granted Kridel.

Prior to re-letting the new premises, plaintiff sued Kridel in August 1972, demanding $7,590, the total amount due for the full two-year term of the lease. Following a mistrial, plaintiff filed an amended complaint asking for $5,865, the amount due between May 1, 1972 and September 1, 1973. The amended complaint included no reduction in the claim to reflect the six week concession provided for in the lease or the $690 payment made to plaintiff after signing the agreement. Defendant filed an amended answer to the complaint, alleging that

---

34. Among other provisions, the lease prohibited the tenant from assigning or transferring the lease without the consent of the landlord. If the tenant defaulted, the lease gave the landlord the option of re-entering or re-letting, but stipulated that failure to re-let or to recover the full rental would not discharge the tenant's liability for rent.

The Pierre Apartments
Hackensack

plaintiff breached the contract, failed to mitigate damages and accepted defendant's surrender of the premises. . . .

The trial judge ruled in favor of the defendant. Despite his conclusion that the lease had been drawn to reflect "the 'settled law' of this state," he found that "justice and fair dealing" imposed upon the landlord the duty to attempt to re-let the premises and thereby mitigate damages. He also held that plaintiff's failure to make any response to defendant's unequivocal offer of surrender was tantamount to an acceptance, thereby terminating the tenancy and any obligation to pay rent. . . . The Appellate Division reversed in a per curiam opinion.

Riverview Realty Co. v. Perosio

This controversy arose in a similar manner. On December 27, 1972, Carlos Perosio entered into a written lease with plaintiff Riverview Realty Co. The agreement covered the rental of apartment 5-G in a building owned by the realty company at 2175 Hudson Terrace in Fort Lee. As in the companion case, the lease prohibited the tenant from subletting or assigning the apartment without the consent of the landlord. It was to run for a two-year term, from February 1, 1973 until January 31, 1975, and provided for a monthly rental of $450. The defendant took possession of the apartment and occupied it until February 1974. At that time he vacated the premises, after having paid the rent through January 31, 1974.

The landlord filed a complaint on October 31, 1974, demanding $4,500 in payment for the monthly rental from February 1, 1974 through October 31, 1974. Defendant answered the complaint by alleging that there had been a valid

River View Towers
2175 Hudson Terrace
Fort Lee

surrender of the premises and that plaintiff failed to mitigate damages. The trial court granted the landlord's motion for summary judgment against the defendant, fixing the damages at $4,050 plus $182.25 interest.[35]

The Appellate Division affirmed the trial court holding that it was bound by prior precedents, including Joyce v. Bauman, supra.

As the lower courts in both appeals found, the weight of authority in this State supports the rule that a landlord is under no duty to mitigate damages caused by a defaulting tenant. . . . This rule has been followed in a majority of states, and has been tentatively adopted in the American Law Institute's Restatement of Property. Restatement (Second) of Property, §11.1(3) (Tent. Draft No. 3, 1975).

Nevertheless, while there is still a split of authority over this question, the trend among recent cases appears to be in favor of a mitigation requirement. . . .

The majority rule is based on principles of property law which equate a lease with a transfer of a property interest in the owner's estate. Under this rationale the lease conveys to a tenant an interest in the property which forecloses any control by the landlord; thus, it would be anomalous to require the landlord to concern himself with the tenant's abandonment of his own property. Wright v. Baumann, 239 Or. 410, 398 P.2d 119, 120-21, 21 A.L.R.3d 527 (1968).

35. The trial court noted that damages had been erroneously calculated in the complaint to reflect ten months' rent. As to the interest awarded to plaintiff, the parties have not raised this issue before this Court. Since we hold that the landlord had a duty to attempt to mitigate damages, we need not reach this question.

For instance, in Muller v. Beck, [94 N.J.L. 311, 110 A. 831 (Sup. Ct. 1920)], where essentially the same issue was posed, the court clearly treated the lease as governed by property, as opposed to contract, precepts.[36] The court there observed that the "tenant had an estate for years, but it was an estate qualified by this right of the landlord to prevent its transfer," 94 N.J.L. at 313, 110 A. at 832, and that "the tenant has an estate with which the landlord may not interfere." Id. at 314, 110 A. at 832. Similarly, in Heckel v. Griese, [12 N.J. Misc. 211, 171 A. 148 (Sup. Ct. 1934)], the court noted the absolute nature of the tenant's interest in the property while the lease was in effect, stating that "when the tenant vacated, . . . no one, in the circumstances, had any right to interfere with the defendant's possession of the premises." 12 N.J. Misc. at 213, 171 A. at 148, 149. Other cases simply cite the rule announced in Muller v. Beck, supra, without discussing the underlying rationale. . . .

Yet the distinction between a lease for ordinary residential purposes and an ordinary contract can no longer be considered viable. . . . This Court has taken the lead in requiring that landlords provide housing services to tenants in accordance with implied duties which are hardly consistent with the property notions expressed in Muller v. Beck, supra, and Heckel v. Griese, supra. See Braitman v. Overlook Terrace Corp., 68 N.J. 368, 346 A.2d 76 (1975) (liability for failure to repair defective apartment door lock); Berzito v. Gambino, 63 N.J. 460, 308 A.2d 17 (1973) (construing implied warranty of habitability and covenant to pay rent as mutually dependent); Marini v. Ireland, 56 N.J. 130, 265 A.2d 526 (1970) (implied covenant to repair); Reste Realty Corp. v. Cooper, 53 N.J. 444, 251 A.2d 268 (1969) (implied warranty of fitness of premises for leased purpose). . . .

Application of the contract rule requiring mitigation of damages to a residential lease may be justified as a matter of basic fairness.[37] Professor McCormick first commented upon the inequity under the majority rule when he predicted in 1925 that eventually

> the logic, inescapable according to the standards of a "jurisprudence of conceptions" which permits the landlord to stand idly by the vacant, abandoned premises and treat them as the property of the tenant and recover full rent, will yield to the more realistic notions of social advantage which in other fields of the law have forbidden a recovery for damages which the plaintiff by reasonable efforts could have avoided. [McCormick, The Rights of the Landlord Upon Abandonment of the Premises by the Tenant, 23 Mich. L. Rev. 211, 221-22 (1925).]

Various courts have adopted this position.

The pre-existing rule cannot be predicated upon the possibility that a landlord may lose the opportunity to rent another empty apartment because he must first rent the apartment vacated by the defaulting tenant. Even where the breach

---

36. It is well settled that a party claiming damages for a breach of contract has a duty to mitigate his loss . . . .

37. We see no distinction between the leases involved in the instant appeals and those which might arise in other types of residential housing. However, we reserve for another day the question of whether a landlord must mitigate damages in a commercial setting. Cf. Kruvant v. Sunrise Market, Inc., 58 N.J. 452, 456, 279 A.2d 104 (1971), modified on other grounds, 59 N.J. 330, 282 A.2d 746 (1971).

occurs in a multi-dwelling building, each apartment may have unique qualities which make it attractive to certain individuals. Significantly, in Sommer v. Kridel, there was a specific request to rent the apartment vacated by the defendant; there is no reason to believe that absent this vacancy the landlord could have succeeded in renting a different apartment to this individual.

We therefore hold that antiquated real property concepts which served as the basis for the pre-existing rule, shall no longer be controlling where there is a claim for damages under a residential lease. Such claims must be governed by more modern notions of fairness and equity. A landlord has a duty to mitigate damages where he seeks to recover rents due from a defaulting tenant.

If the landlord has other vacant apartments besides the one which the tenant has abandoned, the landlord's duty to mitigate consists of making reasonable efforts to re-let the apartment. In such cases he must treat the apartment in question as if it was one of his vacant stock.

As part of his cause of action, the landlord shall be required to carry the burden of proving that he used reasonable diligence in attempting to re-let the premises. We note that there has been a divergence of opinion concerning the allocation of the burden of proof on this issue. While generally in contract actions the breaching party has the burden of proving that damages are capable of mitigation, see Sandler v. Lawn-A-Mat Chem. & Equip. Corp., 141 N.J. Super. 437, 455, 358 A.2d 805 (App. Div. 1976); McCormick, Damages, §33 at 130 (1935), here the landlord will be in a better position to demonstrate whether he exercised reasonable diligence in attempting to re-let the premises. Cf. Kulm v. Coast to Coast Stores Central Org., 248 Or. 436, 432 P.2d 1006 (1967) (burden on lessor in contract to renew a lease).

The Sommer v. Kridel case presents a classic example of the unfairness which occurs when a landlord has no responsibility to minimize damages. Sommer waited 15 months and allowed $4,658.50 in damages to accrue before attempting to re-let the apartment. Despite the availability of a tenant who was ready, willing and able to rent the apartment, the landlord needlessly increased the damages by turning her away. While a tenant will not necessarily be excused from his obligations under a lease simply by finding another person who is willing to rent the vacated premises, see, e.g., Regent v. Dempsey-Tegler & Co., 70 Ill. App. 2d 32, 216 N.E.2d 500 (Ill. App. 1966) (new tenant insisted on leasing the premises under different terms); Edmands v. Rust & Richardson Drug Co., 191 Mass. 123, 77 N.E. 713 (1906) (landlord need not accept insolvent tenant), here there has been no showing that the new tenant would not have been suitable. We therefore find that plaintiff could have avoided the damages which eventually accrued, and that the defendant was relieved of his duty to continue paying rent. Ordinarily we would require the tenant to bear the cost of any reasonable expenses incurred by a landlord in attempting to re-let the premises, . . . but no such expenses were incurred in this case.

In Riverview Realty Co. v. Perosio, no factual determination was made regarding the landlord's efforts to mitigate damages, and defendant contends that plaintiff never answered his interrogatories. Consequently, the judgment is reversed and the case remanded for a new trial. Upon remand and after discovery has been completed, R. 4: 17 et seq., the trial court shall determine whether plaintiff attempted to mitigate damages with reasonable diligence, . . . and if so, the extent of damages remaining and assessable to the tenant. As we have held above, the burden of proving that reasonable diligence was used to re-let the premises shall be upon the plaintiff.

In assessing whether the landlord has satisfactorily carried his burden, the trial court shall consider, among other factors, whether the landlord, either personally or through an agency, offered or showed the apartment to any prospective tenants, or advertised it in local newspapers. Additionally, the tenant may attempt to rebut such evidence by showing that he proffered suitable tenants who were rejected. However, there is no standard formula for measuring whether the landlord has utilized satisfactory efforts in attempting to mitigate damages, and each case must be judged upon its own facts. Compare Hershorin v. La Vista, Inc., 110 Ga. App. 435, 138 S.E.2d 703 (App. 1964) ("reasonable effort" of landlord by showing the apartment to all prospective tenants); Carpenter v. Wisniewski, 139 Ind. App. 325, 215 N.E.2d 882 (App. 1966) (duty satisfied where landlord advertised the premises through a newspaper, placed a sign in the window, and employed a realtor); Re Garment Center Capitol, Inc., 93 F.2d 667, 115 A.L.R. 202 (2 Cir. 1938) (landlord's duty not breached where higher rental was asked since it was known that this was merely a basis for negotiations); Foggia v. Dix, 265 Or. 315, 509 P.2d 412, 414 (1973) (in mitigating damages, landlord need not accept less than fair market value or "substantially alter his obligations as established in the pre-existing lease"); with Anderson v. Andy Darling Pontiac, Inc., 257 Wis. 371, 43 N.W.2d 362 (1950) (reasonable diligence not established where newspaper advertisement placed in one issue of local paper by a broker); Scheinfeld v. Muntz T.V., Inc., 67 Ill. App. 2d 8, 214 N.E.2d 506 (Ill. App. 1966) (duty breached where landlord refused to accept suitable subtenant); Consolidated Sun Ray, Inc. v. Oppenstein, 335 F.2d 801, 811 (8 Cir. 1964) (dictum) (demand for rent which is "far greater than the provisions of the lease called for" negates landlord's assertion that he acted in good faith in seeking a new tenant).

The judgment in Sommer v. Kridel is reversed. In Riverview Realty Co. v. Perosio, the judgment is reversed and the case is remanded to the trial court for proceedings in accordance with this opinion.

NOTES AND QUESTIONS

1. *About the plaintiff James Kridel.* Ezra Rosser, a law professor at American University Washington College of Law, interviewed James Kridel and kindly reported to us the following:

Kridel was a law student at the time his problems arose; once he graduated he worked on his case after hours at the firm that hired him. The litigation consumed seven years and about $500,000 in fees; the cost to print the briefs on appeal exceeded the $800 the case could have been settled for at the outset. After Kridel lost at one stage in the appeals process, a local newspaper wrote a story about Sommer v. Kridel with the title "Engagement Broke But Not Lease." A lengthy brief Kridel submitted relied in part on an Oregon case, prompting his adversary to dismiss the case as being from Oregon, "a state whose principal industries are logging and salmon." When Kridel eventually won (based in part on the Oregon case), he sent that lawyer a salmon and some wood wrapped in a copy of the court's ruling; the lawyer responded by sending back the message "touché." One of the justices hearing Kridel's appeal had to recuse himself because his son had been in the army with Kridel and was going to lend money to Kridel if Kridel lost his case (the justice figured his son would borrow the funds from him!). A grandson of Justice Pashman, the author of the opinion in the case, ended up being a tenant of Kridel's.

2. Various justifications are given for the rule, forsaken in the *Sommer* case, that a landlord is under no obligation to mitigate damages in the event of abandonment by a tenant: The tenant cannot by his own wrongdoing impose a duty on the landlord; the tenant has "purchased" an interest in real estate (and, presumably, is stuck with it); the landlord should not be forced into a personal relationship with a new tenant he does not wish to accept; the landlord should not be required to seek out new tenants "continually." See Annot., 75 A.L.R.5th 1, 42-62 (2000). The Restatement offers another consideration in support of its surprising position against a duty of mitigation: "Abandonment of property is an invitation to vandalism, and the law should not encourage such conduct by putting a duty of mitigation of damages on the landlord." Restatement (Second) of Property, Landlord and Tenant §12.1 comment i at 392 (1977). Are any of these points compelling?

Yet another justification for the no-mitigation rule arises from a line of cases suggesting that efforts on the part of a landlord to mitigate damages by reletting abandoned premises might be held to constitute an unwilling acceptance of the surrender offered by the defaulting tenant. See, e.g., Ex parte Kaschak, 681 So. 2d 197 (Ala. 1996).

Surrender is a term of art, one that connotes quite neatly a tenant's offer to end a tenancy—"here, I give up." Surrender terminates a lease, provided, of course, that the landlord accepts the tenant's offer. If he does—if the surrender is effected—this extinguishes the lessee's liability for future rent,[38] but not for accrued rent or for past breaches of other covenants. 1 American Law of Property §3.99 at 390 (1952).

Surrender may, of course, come about explicitly—tenant expressly offers, landlord expressly accepts. In such event, and if the Statute of Frauds is complied with, the lease is unambiguously terminated. Our concern here, though, is with an implied offer and, more particularly, an implied acceptance. Suppose, then,

---

38. Be cautioned that this statement does not necessarily mean what you probably think it does. To say a lessee is no longer liable for future *rent* after a surrender does not necessarily mean that there is no liability for *damages* equal to the landlord's loss of the value of the remaining portion of the original lease. This is a matter that we take up in the Notes beginning on page 502. See especially footnote 43 on page 503.

that tenant abandons—an implied offer of surrender.[39] What acts of the landlord might be regarded as an acceptance? The answer to this question is generally said to turn on the intent of the landlord in retaking possession, without regard to whether the tenant is on notice that any reletting is on the tenant's account (the Restatement would require notice; see Restatement (Second) of Property, Landlord and Tenant, supra, §12.1). Under the intent test, one considers whether the landlord's actions are inconsistent with or repugnant to continuation of the original lease. The length of the new tenancy, whether alterations have been made, the new rent, and similar factors will be suggestive but not conclusive.

The upshot of the common law rule, still followed in some jurisdictions, is that a landlord may but need not mitigate.[40] What happens if the landlord relets, on the tenant's account, for less than the fair rental value and also less than the original rent? If the landlord relets for more than the original rent? Suppose the tenant abandons, and the landlord notifies him, as the law in the jurisdiction permits, that he intends to relet on the tenant's account. The landlord then finds a new tenant willing to pay more than the original rent, revokes the notice to the original tenant and accepts his surrender, and relets at the higher amount. Who is entitled to the excess rent?

3. Although *Sommer* refers to the no-mitigation rule as the majority rule, according to an opinion by the Supreme Court of Texas, 42 states and the District of Columbia hold that landlords have a duty to mitigate damages. See Austin Hill Country Realty, Inc. v. Palisades Plaza, Inc., 948 S.W.2d 293 (Tex. 1997). A subsequent survey, however, suggests a smaller number, but still a majority. See Stephanie G. Flynn, Duty to Mitigate Damages Upon a Tenant's Abandonment, 34 Real Prop., Prob. & Tr. J. 721 (2000). In any event, not all of these jurisdictions apply the duty across the board; some apply it only to commercial leases and others only to residential leases. Are there any reasons to find a duty in the one case but not the other?

The justifications for the duty to mitigate are pertinent to the question. The opinion in *Sommer* mentions "modern notions of fairness and equity." Considerations of efficiency also enter in. The court in the *Austin Hill* case, for example, observed that the old common law rule (no duty to mitigate) "encourages both economic and physical waste. . . . A mitigation requirement thus returns the property to productive use rather than allowing it to remain idle." Relatedly, it helps prevent property damage. "If the landlord is encouraged to let the property remain unoccupied, 'the possibility of physical damage to the property through accident or vandalism is increased.'" 948 S.W.2d at 298. (Compare

---

39. "An abandonment of the leased property by the tenant occurs when he vacates the leased property without justification and without any present intention of returning and he defaults in the payment of rent." Restatement (Second) of Property, Landlord and Tenant, supra, §12.1 comment i at 392. See generally Annot., 84 A.L.R.4th 183 (1991).

40. "[T]he landlord has the option of (1) terminating the lease, (2) obtaining another tenant while holding the original tenant liable for any deficiency that may occur, or (3) permitting the premises to remain vacant while collecting the agreed-upon rent from the original tenant." Crolley v. Crow-Childress-Mobley No. 2, 379 S.E.2d 202, 204 (Ga. App. 1989).

in this connection the Restatement's views about vandalism, mentioned in Note 2 above.)

The court in *Sommer* held that a landlord must treat abandoned premises as part of his "vacant stock" (page 497); presumably, then, the landlord must make at least the same effort to rent the abandoned premises as he makes to rent other vacant units. Is this justified by the rationale that the rent the landlord "receives from the substitute tenant is . . . a gain *enabled* by the breach of contract by the first tenant"? See Richard A. Posner, Economic Analysis of Law 153-154 (8th ed. 2011).[41]

4. Notwithstanding the pronounced pro-mitigation trend noted in *Austin Hill*, New York's highest court has opted to stick with the old common law rule, even if it is an inferior rule, reasoning that "[p]arties who engage in commercial transactions based on prevailing law must be able to rely on the stability of such precedents." Holy Properties v. Kenneth Cole Productions, Inc., 661 N.E.2d 694, 696 (N.Y. 1995). Subsequent to the decision in *Holy Properties*, lower New York courts differed about whether the decision was limited to commercial leases, but the matter was put to rest in Rios v. Carrillo, 861 N.Y.S.2d 129 (App. Div. 2008) (extending *Holy Properties* to residential leases). See 30 Holding Corp. v. Diaz, 775 N.Y.S.2d 807 (Sup. Ct. 2004) (residential landlords must mitigate); Whitehouse Estates v. Post, 662 N.Y.S.2d 982 (Sup. Ct. 1997) (residential landlords have no obligation to mitigate).

5. What are the consequences of a landlord's failure to mitigate? May he recover no rent subsequent to an abandonment, or may he recover the difference between the agreed rent and the amount of loss that could reasonably have been avoided? There is authority for each alternative. See, e.g., URLTA §4.208 (failure by landlord to use reasonable efforts terminates rental agreement); *Austin Hill*, supra, 948 S.W.2d at 299 (landlord's failure to use reasonable efforts to mitigate bars recovery "only to the extent that damages reasonably could have been avoided").

The court in *Austin Hill* held that "the tenant properly bears the burden of proof to demonstrate that the landlord has mitigated or failed to mitigate damages." A contrary (and probably minority) view is expressed in Snyder v. Ambrose, 639 N.E.2d 639 (Ill. App. 1994) (burden of proving mitigation is on the landlord).

---

41. See also Thomas A. Lucarelli, Note, Application of the Avoidable Consequence Rule to the Residential Leasehold Agreement, 57 Fordham L. Rev. 425, 442-443 (1988) (discussing the lost-volume problem). In one of the lower appellate court decisions reversed in *Sommer* the court remarked that the doctrine of mitigation "cuts both ways. Why should plaintiff be compelled to lease defendant's apartment in order to mitigate defendant's damages when he has other empty apartments being held for rent? We know of no sound reason, legal or equitable, why plaintiff should be required to suffer in order to mitigate defendant's damages." 378 A.2d at 777. Nevertheless, most courts adhere to the principle applied in *Sommer*. An example is Centerline Investment Co. v. Tri-Cor Industries, Inc., 80 S.W.3d 499 (Mo. App. 2002), where the landlord mitigated damages by letting the abandoned premises to another of its tenants, then sought from the defaulting tenant the rent that would have been paid by the other tenant on the other premises. The court denied recovery, but indicated that the remedy might be allowed in cases where the landlord first gave notice to the defaulting tenant and obtained its consent to the move.

6. If in a given jurisdiction landlords have the obligation to mitigate, should the rule be mandatory, or rather should it be a so-called default rule around which the parties may contract in the lease? (It appears that the parties in *Sommer* attempted to do just that; see the lease provision discussed in footnote 34 on page 493.) A North Carolina appellate court has held that a no-mitigation clause in the lease foreclosed the tenant owner of a bagel shop from claiming an offset against unpaid rent based on the landlord's failure to mitigate damages. Sylva Shops Ltd. Partnership v. Hibbard, 623 S.E.2d 785 (N.C. App. 2006). The parties were free to contract around the state's mitigation requirement, the court said, because doing so did not violate public policy, and because no "inequality of bargaining power" was alleged by the tenant. "Ultimately, if the rent is too high or the provisions unacceptable to the lessee, a prospective commercial tenant can always look for another location." 623 S.E.2d at 791. Should a court enforce a no-mitigation clause if the lease also allows the landlord to withhold consent to assignments and subleases in its sole discretion? See *Sylva Shops*, 623 S.E.2d at 792, and recall Note 3 on page 480. Should a no-mitigation clause be allowed in residential leases?

NOTES: LANDLORD'S REMEDIES AND SECURITY DEVICES

Thus far we have considered the means available to a landlord to terminate a tenancy and regain the leased premises from a defaulting tenant (Section F1), and the question of a landlord's duty to mitigate damages (Section F2). These Notes address some related matters.

1. *Rent and damages.* Suppose the tenant has failed to pay rent when due or has breached some other lease obligation. Putting aside the question of a tenant's defenses (some of which will be suggested in Section G1), the landlord's right to sue for back rent and for damages occasioned by the tenant's breach of lease obligations is straightforward. If the tenant is in possession, the landlord may also terminate the lease and recover possession.[42]

---

42. Matters were not always so simple. At common law, the failure by the tenant to pay rent or perform some other lease obligation did not of itself permit the landlord to terminate the lease; the landlord's remedy, rather, was to sue for the rent due. This is another way of saying that the obligations of landlord and tenant were regarded as independent, such that a material breach by one party usually did *not* excuse performance by the other absent some language in the lease providing otherwise. Modern contract law is to the contrary, and (as mentioned earlier on page 451) the law of landlord and tenant is coming to be so as well.

In response to the common law rule, landlords began putting "forfeiture" clauses in leases. Wording could be very important: If the clause were phrased so as to end the lease automatically in the event of the tenant's breach, the landlord could resort to the sort of summary proceedings discussed in the Note on page 490; if, on the other hand, the clause merely gave the landlord an election in the event of breach, eviction could only be accomplished through the cumbersome ejectment remedy. See Stephen Ross, Converting Nonpayment to Holdover Summary Proceedings: The New York Experience with Conditional Limitations Based upon Nonpayment of Rent, 15 Fordham Urb. L.J. 289, 300 n.66 (1987). Most jurisdictions today have done away with the common law technicalities; summary proceedings are usually available regardless of the wording of the forfeiture clause, or even without such a clause, at least for some kinds of breach (in particular, the tenant's failure to pay rent). By and large, this reform has been accomplished by statute, but in a few states the courts have simply changed the old common law rules. An example is Cain Partnership, Ltd. v. Pioneer Investment Services, 914 S.W.2d 452 (Tenn. 1996).

Suppose that the landlord also wishes—in addition to collecting past rent and damages, and in addition to terminating the lease and evicting the tenant—to recover damages equal to the difference (reduced to present value) between the rent reserved in the lease for the unexpired term and the reasonable rental value of the premises for that period. Is there such a remedy?

The question has to do with the doctrine of anticipatory breach familiar to contract law. In some jurisdictions, at least, the remedy is made available by statute. See, e.g., Cal. Civ. Code §1951.2(a)(3) (West 2012) (if landlord terminates because of a breach of the lease, he may recover—in addition to back rent and other damages—the present value "of the amount by which the unpaid rent for the balance of the term . . . exceeds the amount of such rental loss that the lessee proves could be reasonably avoided," provided the lease either expresses such a remedy or the landlord has relet in mitigation; notice that the doctrine of anticipatory breach has mitigation built into its damage formula). Absent such a statute, it appears that the anticipatory breach remedy is generally unavailable, at least as to a failure to pay rent.[43] In the case of a tenant's abandonment, however, repudiation is clear-cut, and here anticipatory breach will apply if the jurisdiction in question extends that contract doctrine to leases. (This, then, is a remedy in addition to those listed in footnote 40 on page 500, and its mention should clarify the ambiguity raised in footnote 38 on page 499.) For an overview, see Sarajane Love, Landlord's Remedies When the Tenant Abandons: Property, Contract, and Leases, 30 U. Kan. L. Rev. 533 (1982).

2. *Security devices.* There is an old saw that a landlord's best security is judicious selection of tenants. Most landlords want more, and they have over the years developed a number of techniques to protect themselves in the event of a tenant's default. The following summary highlights the most important of these.

(a) *Security deposits.* The first security device that occurs to most people is, we suspect, the security deposit—simply because most people have had (probably unpleasant) experience with it. The purposes of such deposits—to protect the landlord in the event a tenant defaults in rent, damages the premises, or otherwise breaches the lease—are straightforward, but there is some evidence that things get bent in practice. In principle, the landlord is obliged to return to the tenant, upon termination of the lease, the deposit less any amounts necessary to compensate for defaults by the tenant. In practice, the landlord has an incentive to imagine all sorts of reasons why he should be entitled to retain the deposit, and with money in hand he has leverage that permits abuse. This, at least, is the central concern; justified or not, it has led to a good deal of reform—most of it statutory. The following provisions are typical: limits are placed on the amount of deposits (e.g., two months' rent); deposits create a trust relationship; deposits

---

43. But see Lennon v. U.S. Theatre Corp., 920 F.2d 996, 1000 (D.C. Cir. 1990) (under District of Columbia law, termination—including termination by acceptance of surrender or by re-entry for nonpayment—forecloses landlord's right to collect rent but does not eliminate an otherwise applicable right to damages; a lease covenant providing for tenant liability for lost rent after landlord's re-entry creates a right to damages, subject to a mitigation requirement).

must be placed in a trust or escrow account; deposits are not to be commingled with other funds; the tenant's claim to a deposit is made prior to other creditors, including, in some instances, a trustee in bankruptcy; the landlord must pay interest on deposits; the landlord must submit an itemized list of deductions from a deposit; penalties are levied for violations (e.g., double or treble the amount of the deposit, or some fixed sum).

(b) *Other techniques.* Landlords have tried in various ways, and with some success, to avoid the legal strictures on security deposits. Thus a lease might characterize a payment as "consideration" or a "bonus" for execution of the lease, an approach that tends to work so long as there is no provision for return of the payment upon termination. Designating the payment "advance rent" has been even more successful; a number of jurisdictions permit the landlord to retain such a deposit on termination for default, sometimes relying on the theory that rent is nonapportionable. Finally, a deposit may be characterized as "liquidated damages." This technique might be tolerated when the amount in question is reasonable and especially when actual damages are difficult to determine. Most often, though, the "liquidated damages" are regarded as an unenforceable penalty. A liquidated damages clause is not ideal from the landlord's standpoint in any event. With such a clause, once default has occurred the tenant has little incentive to minimize damages. If the landlord attempts to guard against this shortcoming with a provision allowing him to hold the tenant for damages over and above the deposit, the likelihood is that the liquidated damages will be regarded as a penalty.

A final device worth mention is rent acceleration—a provision that upon the tenant's default, all rent for the entire term is due and payable. Rent acceleration is accepted by a majority of courts, at least with regard to default in rent payments as opposed to other breaches. If rent is accelerated, the landlord usually cannot take possession as well.[44]

G.   Duties, Rights, and Remedies (Especially Regarding the Condition of the Leased Premises)

Leases give rise to a rather obvious problem. Once a lease is entered into, the landlord has an incentive to neglect everyday repairs because the costs of neglect are borne primarily by tenants. Tenants, in turn, have an incentive to neglect maintenance, especially toward the end of the term, because the costs of neglect will soon shift to the landlord. How might the law deal with these difficulties? That question is the subject of this section.

---

44. The result might be otherwise if the lease expressly provides that the landlord may terminate and hold the tenant liable for all the future rent. See, e.g., Nylen v. Park Doral Apts., 535 N.E.2d 178 (Ind. App. 1989) (lease of school-year residence to students).

1. Landlord's Duties; Tenant's Rights and Remedies

The early common law was hardheaded, and hardhearted, about a tenant's rights and remedies. The law implied covenants concerning title and possession (see pages 461-465), but not concerning the condition of the premises. Absent some clause in the lease providing otherwise, the tenant took the premises "as is," and landlords were under no obligation to warrant their fitness.

Given the culture in which the early common law rules developed, perhaps they made some sense. In any event, as the culture changed, largely in the direction of urbanization and specialization, so too did the common law—but begrudgingly, usually in the language of exceptions and qualifications rather than the bold rhetoric of reform, and often with statutory prodding. The process of change began well over a century ago and led to the development of a body of conventional doctrine that was, for a long time, very stable. But with the 1960s there began a period of sweeping reform—most of it at first concerned with residential tenancies, much of it initiated by courts rather than legislatures—the implications and merits of which are still matters of dispute. The reforms have not so much replaced conventional doctrine as riddled it. A given jurisdiction might adopt one new reform but not another, or limit what it adopts to residential tenancies. A useful understanding of this area of landlord-tenant relations thus requires some attention to the older rules as well as the newer ones.

Disputes between landlord and tenant regarding the condition of the premises arise in essentially two ways. First, the tenant might wish to vacate, or to stay but pay less (or no) rent. Second, the tenant (or an invitee of the tenant) might be injured by allegedly defective premises and claim damages against the landlord in tort. The materials below concentrate on the first sort of dispute, but give some attention to the second as well.

a. Quiet Enjoyment and Constructive Eviction

Village Commons, LLC v. Marion County Prosecutor's Office

Court of Appeals of Indiana, 2008
882 N.E.2d 210

RILEY, J. Appellants-Plaintiffs, Village Commons, LLC and Rynalco, Inc. (collectively, Landlord), appeals the trial court's judgment in favor of the Appellees-Defendants, Marion County Prosecutor's Office and Carl Brizzi, in his official capacity as Marion County Prosecutor (collectively, MCPO). We affirm.

Landlord raises three issues for our review: (1) Whether the exclusive-remedy provision of the lease between Landlord and the MCPO barred the MCPO from asserting that it was evicted by acts or omissions of the Landlord; (2) Whether the trial court's findings that the MCPO was both actually evicted and constructively evicted were clearly erroneous; and (3) Whether a provision limiting the MCPO's time to sue barred the MCPO's defenses and counterclaims.

Facts and Procedural History

On June 2, 1999, then Marion County Prosecutor Scott C. Newman executed a lease on behalf of the MCPO with Lombard Associate Limited Partnership (Lombard) to lease the basement of the Victoria Centre in Indianapolis, Indiana (the Lease). Sometime thereafter, Lombard sold the Victoria Centre to Landlord and assigned the Lease to Landlord. The MCPO's Grand Jury Division used the leased premises as its office and evidence storage space.

Pursuant to the provisions of the Lease, the MCPO was to rent 9,356 square feet of lower level space in the Victoria Centre for a period of seven years and five months, commencing on August 1, 1999. The payment obligations increased over time, beginning with zero dollars owed per month for the first five months, increasing to $8,576.33 per month for months seventy-eight through eighty-nine of the lease term.

Under the Lease provisions, Landlord was required to maintain all equipment used in common with other tenants—such as elevators, plumbing, heating and similar equipment—and to maintain the premises in good order, condition and repair. In the event of breach by Landlord, the lease provided that the MCPO could "sue for injunctive relief or to recover damages for any loss resulting from the breach, but [it] shall not be entitled to terminate this Lease or withhold, set-off or abate any rent due thereunder."

Beginning in 2001, there was a series of water intrusions from the outside and leaks from building equipment, which damaged property secured by the MCPO and affected the areas that the MCPO occupied or used. On March 11, 2001, there was a leak in the restroom area. On June 25, 2001, there was a leak in the MCPO's evidence room. On August 2, 2001, there was leak in what the MCPO refers to as its war room, a room that extends out from the building underneath a sidewalk adjacent to the building. On August 16, 2001, there was leak in the electrical conduit. On August 24 and 28, 2001, Landlord took an inventory of water spots on ceiling tiles and other water damage throughout the MCPO's leased area and noted several spots and other damage that had been caused by sweating pipes or leaks. On August 28 and September 10, 2001, leaks were again noted in the war room, which were either caused by cracks in the sidewalk or steam from Indianapolis Power and Light's underground pipes.

As a result of repeated water intrusions in the war room, Landlord hired Indoor Air Management (IAM) to conduct microbiological sampling and visual inspections. IAM reported visual signs of water damage in the war room and along dry wall. Landlord caulked and sprayed sealant on the sidewalk above the war room on several occasions, but these actions did not stop the leaking. The drywall was scheduled to be repaired, but another leak delayed the work. Landlord sought an estimate to remove and re-pour the concrete sidewalk above the war room on October 11, 2001. However, Landlord elected not to perform this work due to the estimated costs.

Another leak was discovered outside of an office on January 22, 2002, and was noticeably worse on January 29, 2002. On Memorial Day 2002, the main water supply pipe in the building's air conditioning system broke causing a leak in the evidence room. Approximately seventy boxes of evidence were damaged. The MCPO had to dedicate several person-hours to attend to the damaged evidence. On June 10, 2002, Mold Remediation Services (MRS) inspected the damaged evidence room and detected mold spores. MRS provided Landlord a quoted price for recommended work to address the microbial contamination. However, due to the estimated cost of the remediation services, Landlord did not hire MRS, but rather permitted its maintenance man to perform demolition and replace drywall. Landlord's maintenance man did not perform several of the tasks recommended by MRS.

On July 17, 2002, nearly one year after the original leak in the war room, Landlord's maintenance man again replaced ceiling tiles that showed signs of water damage. On July 19, 2002, IAM performed microbiological testing in the main evidence room, hallway, conference room and office of the Chief Deputy Prosecutor of the Grand Jury Division, Mark Hollingsworth (Hollingsworth). IAM informed the MCPO that additional demolition was necessary and that the boxes that were damaged should be discarded because of microbiological contamination.

On July 31, 2002, a new leak caused by the HVAC system was discovered in the break room. On August 2, 2002, IAM reported that moisture readings collected from drywall in the closet area were elevated. A wall in the war room had visible signs of water damage. Also, different types of mold spores were present inside the premises than those found outdoors. Surface testing reported excessive fungal growth. IAM recommended several actions to deal with the moisture and microbiological problems, many of which were previously recommended by MRS.

Landlord spoke with IAM and was advised regarding the possibility of allergic reactions for certain people to mold contamination. However, after this meeting Landlord advised the MCPO there were no health risks presented by the building conditions. At least one of the MCPO employees complained of suffering from unusual coughing and sneezing for a prolonged period of time. Another of the MCPO employees experienced headaches while working at the leased premises. The employee reported his symptoms to a physician, was reassigned outside of the leased premises, and the symptoms subsided. On August 13, 2002, Landlord and the MCPO met with an IAM employee to discuss IAM's report. IAM's employee explained to the MCPO there was an elevated mold count, but not the type of mold that requires a building to be quarantined.

On October 10, 2002, Hollingsworth instructed an employee to make daily inspections. The employee reported to Hollingsworth that there were moisture problems in three of the four rooms the MCPO Grand Jury Division used to store evidence. Landlord sent a letter to the MCPO on October 14, 2002, suggesting the MCPO move evidence that it was storing and other materials away from parts of the premises that were vulnerable to water damage. On November 25, 2002, there was a sewage leak in Hollingsworth's office. On January 9, 2003, a water intrusion was discovered in the women's restroom, causing it to be closed for approximately three weeks. The phone system for the MCPO Grand Jury Division went out on January 27, 2003, and MCPO employees took photographs of water damage on the phone board. On January 28, 2003, a major water intrusion was discovered in the main evidence room. An employee photographed a stream of water pouring from the ceiling.

On January 30, 2003, the MCPO elected to vacate the leased premises, and moved to a location where another of the MCPO's divisions was located. Also, January 2003, was the last month that the MCPO paid rent to Landlord, leaving three years and eleven months, or $380,477.37, unpaid according to the terms of the Lease.

On February 23, 2004, Landlord filed a Complaint against the MCPO, alleging that the MCPO breached the Lease, and sought the damages provided under the Lease. The MCPO filed its answer on April 14, 2004, asserting affirmative defenses and a counterclaim premised on a wrongful eviction theory. In its counterclaim, MCPO initially alleged that it had been constructively evicted in January 2003. On July 18, 2005, the MCPO sought leave to amend its counterclaim, stating that the January 2003 allegation had been an error in dates. To correct that error in the amended counterclaim, the MCPO changed an allegation that it was constructively evicted in August 2002.

On January 9 through 11, 2007, the trial court held a bench trial. Thereafter, the parties submitted proposed findings of fact and conclusions of law pursuant to Ind. Trial Rule 52(C). The trial court's judgment held that: (1) the MCPO's defenses and counterclaim were not barred by the Lease's exclusive-remedy provisions; (2) the MCPO was "actually" evicted in October 2002 and then "constructively" evicted in January 2003; and (3) assuming the Landlord could recover against the MCPO, the Landlord did not mitigate its damages reasonably. MCPO was awarded $7,664 and costs on its wrongful eviction counterclaim.

Discussion and Decision

Exclusive-Remedy Provision

Landlord argues that the trial court's judgment is clearly erroneous because it ignored the exclusive-remedy provision of the Lease by concluding that the MCPO had been constructively evicted. Specifically, Landlord argues that the exclusive-remedy provision is permissible under Indiana law and the trial court erred by granting MCPO a remedy prohibited by that provision. Indiana courts have recognized the contractual nature of leases and the applicability of the law of contracts to leases. The construction of a written contract is a question of law. When interpreting a contract, our paramount goal is to ascertain and effectuate the intent of the parties. This requires the contract to be read as a whole, and the language construed so as not to render any words, phrases, or terms ineffective or meaningless. Id. Where the terms of a contract are clear and unambiguous, we will not construe the contract or look at extrinsic evidence, but will apply the contractual provisions.

The provision of the Lease which Landlord refers to as the exclusive-remedy provision, provides as follows:

> Section 15.04. Default by Landlord and Remedies by Tenant. It shall be a default under and breach of this Lease by Landlord if it shall fail to perform or observe any term, condition, covenant or obligation required to be performed or observed by it under this Lease for a period of thirty (30) days after notice thereof from Tenant; provided, however, that if the term, condition, covenant or obligation to be performed by Landlord is of such nature that the same cannot reasonably be performed within such thirty-day period, such default shall be deemed to have been cured if Landlord commences such performance within said thirty-day period and thereafter diligently undertakes to complete the same, and further failure to perform or observe any term, condition, covenant or obligation under this Lease is due to causes beyond the reasonable control of Landlord. Upon the occurrence of any such default, Tenant may sue for injunctive relief or to recover damages for any loss resulting from the breach, but Tenant shall not be entitled to terminate this Lease or withhold, setoff or abate any rent due thereunder.

Landlord encourages us to conclude that the remedy provision of the Lease is exclusive and bars any other remedy, such as the one utilized by the trial court . . . . [W]e conclude from the unambiguous language of the Lease that the MCPO did not have the right to terminate the Lease or withhold, setoff, or abate any rent due. However, this determination is not dispositive of the dispute before us.

Eviction

The trial court found that the MCPO was actually evicted from the leased premises beginning in October of 2002, and was then constructively evicted as of January 28, 2003, due to repeated and un-remedied water intrusions. In explaining the theories of eviction, our supreme court stated the following:

> Eviction is either *actual* or *constructive*, actual when the tenant is deprived of the occupancy of some part of the demised premises, and constructive when the lessor, without intending to oust the lessee, does an act by which the latter is deprived of the beneficial enjoyment of some part of the premises, in which case the tenant has his right of election, to quit, and avoid the lease and rent, or abide the wrong and seek his remedy in an action for the trespass. But in every case of constructive eviction the tenant must quit the premises if he would relieve himself from liability to pay rent; and whether or not he is justifiable in so quitting is a question for the jury. [Talbott v. English, 156 Ind. 299, 307-308, 59 N.E. 857, 860 (1901).]

In further explaining the nature of actual eviction and the effects thereof on the obligations of a tenant, the *Talbott* court stated:

> It may be said that in every lease there is an implied covenant that the tenant shall have the right of possession, occupancy, and beneficial use of every portion of the leased premises. The tenant is regarded as having hired the use of the property as an entirety, and therefore if the

landlord, after the grant, deprives the tenant of the possession and enjoyment of any part of the premises, the landlord shall not be entitled to any part of the rent during the time he thus deprives the tenant of this rights. The landlord may not apportion the rent by his own wrong. [Id. at 859.]

We have more recently articulated this concept by stating: "The general rule is that a tenant will be relieved of any obligation to pay further rent if the landlord deprives the tenant of possession and beneficial use and enjoyment of any part of the demised premises by actual eviction. . . . Stated differently, after termination *the lease and all liability under it for future rent are extinguished*." Gigax v. Boone Village Ltd. Partnership, 656 N.E.2d 854, 858 (Ind. Ct. App. 1995) (emphasis in original).

In [Sigsbee v. Swathwood, 419 N.E.2d 789, 796 (Ind. Ct. App. 1981], we summarized the theory of constructive eviction by explaining: "If an act or omission by the lessor materially deprives the lessee of the beneficial use or enjoyment of the lease property, the lessee may elect to abandon the property and avoid further obligations under the lease. If the lessee so elects, the abandonment of the property must occur within a reasonable time after the act or omission." Thus, if a landlord commits acts or omissions sufficient to actually evict the tenant, the tenant is no longer obligated to pay rent. And likewise, if a landlord commits acts or omissions sufficient to constructively evict the tenant, and the tenant leaves within a reasonable period, the tenant is no longer obligated to pay rent under the lease.

Here, the trial court concluded that "it would be contrary to public policy to permit a landlord to completely eliminate a Tenant's remedy of constructive eviction if conditions are such that the leased property is unusable." However, we find that it is unnecessary to resort to a consideration of public policy to determine this dispute since the unambiguous terms of the exclusive-remedy provision did not prohibit Landlord from evicting the MCPO. The exclusive-remedy provision limited only the MCPO's ability to "terminate this Lease or withhold, setoff or abate any rent due thereunder." Upon the occurrence of eviction, either actual or constructive, it is the lessor's act or omission that ends the obligation to pay rent, not the lessee. Therefore, since we conclude below that the trial court's findings that the MCPO had been wrongfully evicted were not clearly erroneous, we hold that it was the Landlord's own act or omission that resulted in extinguishing MCPO's future rent payment obligations.

MCPO Was Wrongfully Evicted

Landlord contends that the trial court erred when it found that the MCPO had been evicted. Specifically, Landlord argues that the uncontroverted testimony, largely by the MCPO's own witnesses, contradict the findings and conclusions entered by the trial court, and therefore are clearly erroneous and should be reversed.

In reviewing the record, we observe that the trial court concluded that Landlord actually evicted the MCPO in October of 2002 when "Landlord informed the [MCPO] to refrain from using those portions of the leased space 'most vulnerable to water.'" We also observe the trial court concluded the MCPO was "constructively evicted as of January 28, 2003, due to repeated un-remedied water intrusions."

As we stated above, actual eviction occurs when a tenant is deprived of a material part of the leased premises, and constructive eviction occurs when an interference with possession so serious that it deprives the lessee of the beneficial enjoyment of the leased premises. When a transitory and fleeting interference by the lessor with the lessee's possession occurs, there is no eviction, but a mere trespass, for which the lessee is entitled to damages.

In challenging the trial court's conclusion of eviction, . . . Landlord argues that testimony by employees or agents of the MCPO, stating that each incident of water intrusions and related problems were temporary or eventually fixed, is uncontroverted evidence which shows that the trial court's findings of both actual and constructive eviction are clearly erroneous. To the contrary, when reviewing the record, we find substantial evidence supporting the trial court's findings that the water intrusions were recurring, which in turn supports a finding that they were not transitory or fleeting. Moreover, it was Landlord who suggested to the MCPO that it should move evidence and materials out of areas of the leased premises that were vulnerable to water, showing the Landlord's acknowledgement that water leaks would recur. Additionally, this evidence supports the trial court's findings that the MCPO was deprived of a material part of the leased premises by these water intrusions and related problems . . . .

Affirmed.

NOTES AND QUESTIONS

1. *The covenant of quiet enjoyment.* As the court notes in the *Village Commons* case, "in every lease there is an implied covenant that the tenant shall have the right of possession, occupancy, and beneficial use of every portion of the leased premises." (See page 509, quoting from an earlier decision.) Originally, this covenant of quiet enjoyment, as it is customarily called, was developed to protect a tenant against wrongful eviction by the landlord or someone claiming under the landlord. The common law at one time viewed all promises in leases—a promise, say, on the part of the landlord to keep the premises in repair—as independent, such that a breach by the landlord gave the tenant a cause of action for damages, but not the right to suspend rent payments or to terminate the tenancy, but with this exception: In the event of a wrongful eviction, the tenant could treat the lease and the obligation to pay rent as terminated. Expressed in terms of contract doctrine, the tenant's obligation was dependent on not being evicted by the landlord.

Early on, the covenant of quiet enjoyment was held to be breached only by wrongful physical eviction, but with time it was expanded to include other landlord breaches that interfered with tenants' beneficial enjoyment of the leased premises. This was obviously sensible—otherwise landlords could simply make tenants miserable, without actually ousting them—but it was also obviously limited, at least in theory. The early common law, remember, imposed on landlords no duty to provide suitable premises. See page 505. As a matter of principle, then, the implied covenant of quiet enjoyment would be breached only when the landlord's conduct had "the effect of depriving the lessee of the beneficial use of the demised premises, whether by positive acts of interference or by withholding something essential to full enjoyment *and included within the terms of the lease.*" 1 American Law of Property, supra, §3.51 at 280 (emphasis added). But given the absence of a common law duty on the landlord's part, what if anything would be "included within the terms of the lease"?

One clear answer is that an explicit clause in the lease, or a statutory requirement, might express certain landlord obligations (to provide heat, for example, to make repairs, and so on). And the common law gradually developed exceptions to the general no-landlord-duty rule. An early exception concerned short-term leases of furnished dwellings, as to which landlords had an implied duty to make and keep the premises habitable. Additional exceptions developed such that landlords had the duty to disclose latent defects in the premises that existed at the time the lease was entered into, were or should have been known by the landlord, and were not apparent on reasonable inspection by the tenant; to maintain common areas used by all the tenants in a building; to undertake carefully any repairs the landlord promised or volunteered to make; to abstain from fraudulent misrepresentations as to the condition of the leased premises; and, in some jurisdictions, to abate immoral conduct and other nuisances that occurred on property owned by the landlord if they affected the leased premises.

You should see that there was no problem of landlord duty in the *Village Commons* case, because the lease in the case expressly required the landlord to maintain all equipment used in common with other tenants and to maintain the premises in good order, condition, and repair. It seems to be increasingly the case, however, that no such lease provisions are required, and no common law exceptions need be brought into play, in order to pin liability on landlords. Instead, the covenant of quiet enjoyment is taken to create, of itself, a duty upon the part of landlords to provide suitable premises. See, e.g., Reste Realty Corp. v. Cooper, 251 A.2d 268 (N.J. 1969); Max P. Rapacz, Origin and Evolution of Constructive Eviction in the United States, 1 DePaul L. Rev. 69 (1951).

2. *The idea of constructive eviction.* As noted above, the lease obligations of a tenant are dependent on not being wrongfully evicted by the landlord. Just what does "eviction" mean? As explained in the *Village Commons* case (see page 509), eviction might mean being physically removed or kept out by the landlord, in which case there is an *actual* eviction. But further to aid the cause of tenants, courts developed the idea of *constructive* eviction. If (a) the condition of the leased premises amounts to a breach of the covenant of quiet enjoyment, and (b) if the breach is so substantial as to justify the tenant absenting the premises, and (c) if the tenant thereafter leaves within a reasonable time, then it was *as though* the tenant has been evicted (the eviction was "constructive"—recall footnote 17 on

page 32). And once evicted, of course, the tenant is relieved of the obligation to pay rent. Q.E.D.

3. *Other tenant remedies.* It has been said that the doctrine of constructive eviction "serves as a substitute for dependency of covenants [recall the discussion on page 451]." 1 American Law of Property §3.11 at 204 (1952). That statement, however, is not quite accurate. Suppose a landlord's breach is significant, but not so substantial as to amount to a constructive eviction. In such an instance, conventional constructive eviction doctrine does not entitle the tenant to vacate. If, however, the more general contract doctrine of dependence of covenants applies, vacation might be allowed. And courts in a handful of states have made this move. See, for example, Wesson v. Leone Enterprises, 774 N.E.2d 611 (Mass. 2002), adopting the principle of dependent covenants and holding that a tenant was justified in vacating the premises when the landlord committed a breach that was "major" but not so substantial as to amount to a constructive eviction.

Judicial decisions sometimes say that an eviction, actual or constructive, is necessary to constitute a *breach* of the covenant of quiet enjoyment, but they are incorrect. For discussion, see Moe v. Sprankle, 221 S.W.2d 712 (Tenn. App. 1948). The view that eviction is necessary reflects conceptual confusion between a breach of the implied covenant on the one hand and the remedies available for its breach on the other—a confusion that probably relates back to the early common law notion that a breach occurred only in cases of actual ouster. Once the covenant of quiet enjoyment was broadened beyond that notion, it should have been understood that actionable interference by the landlord could be remedied other than by the tenant's vacating the premises. So the tenant should be, and usually is, able to stay in possession and sue for damages equal to the difference between the value of the property with and without the breach. See Echo Consulting Services, Inc. v. North Conway Bank, 669 A.2d 227 (N.H. 1995) (if breach is not so substantial as to work a constructive eviction, tenant may stay in possession and sue for compensatory damages); Stevan v. Brown, 458 A.2d 466 (Md. App. 1983) (same).

4. *Partial eviction—actual and constructive.* The conventional rule holds that where a landlord commits an *actual eviction*, even though from a *part* of the premises only, the tenant is relieved of *all* liability for rent notwithstanding continued occupation of the balance. The landlord, it is said, may not apportion his wrong. (See *Village Commons* at pages 509-510.) Restatement (Second) of Property, Landlord and Tenant §6.1 (1977) rejects this rule and provides that the tenant may receive an abatement in the rent but may not withhold all rent. Some states follow this approach to a degree, in the case of a landlord intrusion so minimal as to fall short of an "eviction." See, e.g., Eastside Exhibition Corp. v. 210 East 86th Street Corp., 965 N.E.2d 246 (N.Y. 2012).

Suppose a state follows the conventional rule stated above. In such a jurisdiction, is a tenant relieved of the obligation to pay rent when there is not an actual but rather a *constructive* partial eviction—say when some breach by the landlord makes only a part, but not all, of the premises uninhabitable—even though the tenant remains in undisturbed possession of the balance? In most jurisdictions the answer is no. See, e.g., Brine v. Bergstrom, 480 P.2d 783 (Wash. App. 1971). Some years ago the lower courts in New York went back and forth on the question. See Minjak Co. v. Randolph, 528 N.Y.S.2d 554 (Sup. Ct. 1988) (accepting theory); Zweighaft v. Remington, 66 Misc. 2d 261, (Civ. Ct. 1971) (rejecting theory); East Haven Assocs., Inc. v. Gurian, 64 Misc. 2d 276 (Civ. Ct. 1970) (accepting the theory of constructive partial eviction).

PROBLEMS

1. *T* is a tenant at will of *L*. *L* causes a nuisance that interferes with *T*'s business on the leased premises. *T* vacates, rents equivalent space at a higher rent, and subsequently sues for damages on a theory of constructive eviction arising from a breach of the covenant of quiet enjoyment. What result? Cf. Kent v. Humphries, 281 S.E.2d 43 (N.C. 1981).

2. In each of the following cases, *T*, who has a term of years, vacates the leased premises prior to the end of the term and stops paying rent. In a subsequent suit by *L* for unpaid rent, *T* asserts a defense of constructive eviction, claiming that *L* breached the covenant of quiet enjoyment. What result on the facts described below?

(a) *L* fails to control excessive noise made by neighboring tenants of *T*. See Blackett v. Olanoff, 358 N.E.2d 817 (Mass. 1977); JMB Properties Urban Co. v. Paolucci, 604 N.E.2d 967 (Ill. App. 1992). In the *JMB* case, the court ducked the excessive noise issue by holding that in any event the tenant had not vacated the leased premises within a reasonable time, as required by constructive eviction doctrine (the tenant waited over five years). This illustrates one of the risks taken by tenants who vacate claiming constructive eviction, especially in jurisdictions that require tenants to give landlords notice of the alleged breach and time to correct it. Other risks include the chance that a court will find the landlord had no duty regarding the condition in question, or that the landlord's breach was not sufficiently substantial as to work a constructive eviction. If in any of these circumstances the tenant guesses wrong about how a court will rule, the tenant's constructive eviction defense vanishes and the tenant is liable for rent due but unpaid under the lease.

What if the disturbance in question is not noise but cigarette smoke seeping from neighboring units into the unit of a nonsmoking tenant? According to an article in the National Law Journal, courts in several states have found such second-hand smoke to be a breach of the covenant of quiet enjoyment. Stefanie Shaffer, Lighting Up in Your Condo? Think Again, Natl. L.J., July 4, 2005, at 6. Compare DeNardo v. Corneloup, 163 P.3d 956 (Alaska 2007), with Merrill v. Bosser, 2005 WL 5680219 (Fla. Cir. Ct.), and Upper East Lease Associates, LLC v. Cannon, 924 N.Y.S.2d 312 (Dist. Ct. 2011).

(b) The building in which *T* leases an apartment from *L* has been the site of criminal activity—acts of burglary and vandalism by unknown third parties. *L* installs deadbolt locks on all entrance doors and hires private security guards, but the problems continue. See Charlotte Eastland Mall, L.L.C. v. Sole Survivor, Inc., 608 S.E.2d 70 (N.C. App. 2004); Sciascia v. Riverpark Apts., 444 N.E.2d 40 (Ohio App. 1981); Annot., 43 A.L.R.5th 207 (1996).

(c) The office space leased by *T*, a gynecologist whose practice includes performing elective abortions, has been the target of ongoing demonstrations by anti-abortion protesters. During the protests, singing and chanting demonstrators picket in the parking lot and inner lobby. They approach patients to speak to them, distribute literature, discourage patients from entering, and accuse *T* of "killing babies." Despite many months of complaints by *T*, *L* has done essentially nothing. See Fidelity Mutual Life Ins. Co. v. Kaminsky, 768 S.W.2d 818 (Tex. App. 1989).

NOTE: THE ILLEGAL LEASE

In Brown v. Southall Realty Co., 237 A.2d 834 (D.C. App. 1968), the landlord sued to evict for nonpayment of rent. In defense, the tenant argued that no rent was due under the lease because the unsafe and unsanitary conditions of the leased premises violated the housing code. The court agreed, holding that the lease was an illegal contract made in violation of statutory prohibitions and therefore unenforceable. In a quick series of subsequent decisions, the court sketched out the contours of the illegal lease doctrine. It does not apply if code violations develop *after* the making of the lease. Saunders v. First Natl. Realty Corp., 245 A.2d 836 (D.C. App. 1968). Minor technical violations do not render a lease illegal, nor do violations of which the landlord had neither actual nor constructive notice. Diamond Hous. Corp. v. Robinson, 257 A.2d 492 (D.C. App. 1969). A tenant under an illegal lease is a tenant at sufferance, and the landlord is entitled to the reasonable rental value of the premises, given their condition. William J. Davis, Inc. v. Slade, 271 A.2d 412 (D.C. App. 1970).

From the tenant's point of view, the chief attraction of the illegal lease defense was the leverage it provided: Unlike a claim based on quiet enjoyment and constructive eviction, the tenant could withhold rent and still stave off the landlord's inevitable action to evict for nonpayment. Alas for tenants, however, it appears that the doctrine is a dead letter. See William B. Stoebuck & Dale A. Whitman, The Law of Property 299 (3d ed. 2000). But it did anticipate a development that was soon to follow and to which we now turn.

b. The Implied Warranty of Habitability

Hilder v. St. Peter

Supreme Court of Vermont, 1984
478 A.2d 202

BILLINGS, C.J. Defendants appeal from a judgment rendered by the Rutland Superior Court. The court ordered defendants to pay plaintiff damages in the amount of $4,945.00, which represented "reimbursement of all rent paid and additional compensatory damages" for the rental of a residential apartment over a fourteen month period in defendants' Rutland apartment building. Defendants filed a motion for reconsideration on the issue of the amount of damages awarded to the plaintiff, and plaintiff filed a cross-motion for reconsideration of the court's denial of an award of punitive damages. The court denied both motions. On appeal, defendants raise three issues for our consideration: first, whether the court correctly calculated the amount of damages awarded the plaintiff; secondly, whether the court's award to plaintiff of the entire amount of rent paid to defendants was proper since the plaintiff remained in possession of the apartment for the entire fourteen month period; and finally, whether the court's finding that defendant Stuart St. Peter acted on his own behalf and with the apparent authority of defendant Patricia St. Peter was error.

The facts are uncontested. In October, 1974, plaintiff began occupying an apartment at defendants' 10-12 Church Street apartment building in Rutland with her three children and new-born grandson.[45] Plaintiff orally agreed to pay defendant Stuart St. Peter $140 a month and a damage deposit of $50; plaintiff paid defendant the first month's rent and the damage deposit prior to moving in. Plaintiff has paid all rent due under her tenancy. Because the previous tenants had left behind garbage and items of personal belongings, defendant offered to refund plaintiff's damage deposit if she would clean the apartment herself prior to taking possession. Plaintiff did clean the apartment, but never received her deposit back because the defendant denied ever receiving it. Upon moving into the apartment, plaintiff discovered a broken kitchen window. Defendant promised to repair it, but after waiting a week and fearing that her two year old child might cut herself on the shards of glass, plaintiff repaired the window at her own expense. Although defendant promised to provide a front door key, he never did. For a period of time, whenever plaintiff left the apartment, a member of her family would remain behind for security reasons. Eventually, plaintiff purchased and installed a padlock, again at her own expense. After moving in, plaintiff discovered that the bathroom toilet was clogged with paper and feces and would flush only by dumping pails of water into it. Although plaintiff repeatedly complained about the toilet, and defendant promised to have it repaired, the toilet remained clogged and mechanically inoperable throughout the period of plaintiff's tenancy. In addition, the bathroom light and wall outlet were inoperable. Again, the defendant agreed to repair the fixtures, but never did. In order to have light in the bathroom, plaintiff attached a fixture to the wall and connected it to an extension cord that was plugged into an adjoining room. Plaintiff also discovered that water leaked from the water pipes of the upstairs apartment down the ceilings and walls of both

---

45. Between October, 1974, and December, 1976, plaintiff rented apartment number 1 for $140.00 monthly for 18 months, and apartment number 50 for $125.00 monthly for 7 months.

her kitchen and back bedroom. Again, defendant promised to fix the leakage, but never did. As a result of this leakage, a large section of plaster fell from the back bedroom ceiling onto her bed and her grandson's crib. Other sections of plaster remained dangling from the ceiling. This condition was brought to the attention of the defendant, but he never corrected it. Fearing that the remaining plaster might fall when the room was occupied, plaintiff moved her and her grandson's bedroom furniture into the living room and ceased using the back bedroom. During the summer months an odor of raw sewage permeated plaintiff's apartment. The odor was so strong that the plaintiff was ashamed to have company in her apartment. Responding to plaintiff's complaints, Rutland City workers unearthed a broken sewage pipe in the basement of defendants' building. Raw sewage littered the floor of the basement, but defendant failed to clean it up. Plaintiff also discovered that the electric service for her furnace was attached to her breaker box, although defendant had agreed, at the commencement of plaintiff's tenancy, to furnish heat.

In its conclusions of law, the court held that the state of disrepair of plaintiff's apartment, which was known to the defendants, substantially reduced the value of the leasehold from the agreed rental value, thus constituting a breach of the implied warranty of habitability. The court based its award of damages on the breach of this warranty and on breach of an express contract. Defendant argues that the court misapplied the law of Vermont relating to habitability because the plaintiff never abandoned the demised premises and, therefore, it was error to award her the full amount of rent paid. Plaintiff counters that, while never expressly recognized by this Court, the trial court was correct in applying an implied warranty of habitability and that under this warranty, abandonment of the premises is not required. Plaintiff urges this Court to affirmatively adopt the implied warranty of habitability.

Historically, relations between landlords and tenants have been defined by the law of property. Under these traditional common law property concepts, a lease was viewed as a conveyance of real property. See Note, Judicial Expansion of Tenants' Private Law Rights: Implied Warranties of Habitability and Safety in Residential Urban Leases, 56 Cornell L.Q. 489, 489-90 (1971) (hereinafter cited as Expansion of Tenants' Rights). The relationship between landlord and tenant was controlled by the doctrine of caveat lessee; that is, the tenant took possession of the demised premises irrespective of their state of disrepair. Love, Landlord's Liability for Defective Premises: Caveat Lessee, Negligence, or Strict Liability?, 1975 Wis. L. Rev. 19, 27-28. The landlord's only covenant was to deliver possession to the tenant. The tenant's obligation to pay rent existed independently of the landlord's duty to deliver possession, so that as long as possession remained in the tenant, the tenant remained liable for payment of rent. The landlord was under no duty to render the premises habitable unless there was an express covenant to repair in the written lease. Expansion of Tenants' Rights, supra, at 490. The land, not the dwelling, was regarded as the essence of the conveyance.

10-12 Church Street
Rutland, Vermont, 1999

An exception to the rule of caveat lessee was the doctrine of constructive eviction. Lemle v. Breeden, 51 Haw. 426, 430, 462 P.2d 470, 473 (1969). Here, if the landlord wrongfully interfered with the tenant's enjoyment of the demised premises, or failed to render a duty to the tenant as expressly required under the terms of the lease, the tenant could abandon the premises and cease paying rent.

Beginning in the 1960's, American courts began recognizing that this approach to landlord and tenant relations, which had originated during the Middle Ages, had become an anachronism in twentieth century, urban society. Today's tenant enters into lease agreements, not to obtain arable land, but to obtain safe, sanitary and comfortable housing.

> [T]hey seek a well known package of goods and services—a package which includes not merely walls and ceilings, but also adequate heat, light and ventilation, serviceable plumbing facilities, secure windows and doors, proper sanitation, and proper maintenance. [Javins v. First National Realty Corp., 428 F.2d 1071, 1074 (D.C. Cir.), cert. denied, 400 U.S. 925 (1970).]

Not only has the subject matter of today's lease changed, but the characteristics of today's tenant have similarly evolved. The tenant of the Middle Ages was a farmer, capable of making whatever repairs were necessary to his primitive dwelling. Additionally, "the common law courts assumed that an equal bargaining position existed between landlord and tenant. . . ." Note, The Implied Warranty of Habitability: A Dream Deferred, 48 UMKC L. Rev. 237, 238 (1980) (hereinafter cited as A Dream Deferred).

In sharp contrast, today's residential tenant, most commonly a city dweller, is not experienced in performing maintenance work on urban, complex living units. The landlord is more familiar with the dwelling unit and mechanical equipment attached to that unit, and is more financially able to "discover and cure" any faults and break-downs. Confronted with a recognized shortage of safe, decent housing, today's tenant is in an inferior bargaining position compared to that of the landlord. Park West Management Corp. v. Mitchell, 47 N.Y.2d 316, 324-25, 391 N.E.2d 1288, 1292, 418 N.Y.S.2d 310, 314, cert. denied, 444 U.S. 992 (1979). Tenants vying for this limited housing are "virtually powerless to compel the performance of essential services." Id. at 325, 391 N.E.2d at 1292, 418 N.Y.S.2d at 314.

In light of these changes in the relationship between tenants and landlords, it would be wrong for the law to continue to impose the doctrine of caveat lessee on residential leases. . . .

Therefore, we now hold expressly that in the rental of any residential dwelling unit an implied warranty exists in the lease, whether oral or written, that the landlord will deliver over and maintain, throughout the period of the tenancy, premises that are safe, clean and fit for human habitation. This warranty of habitability is implied in tenancies for a specific period or at will. Additionally, the implied warranty of habitability covers all latent and patent defects in the essential facilities of the residential unit.[46] Essential facilities are "facilities vital to the use of the premises for residential purposes. . . ." Kline v. Burns, 111 N.H. 87, 92, 276 A.2d 248, 252 (1971). This means that a tenant who enters into a lease agreement with knowledge of any defect in the essential facilities cannot be said to have assumed the risk, thereby losing the protection of the warranty. Nor can this implied warranty of habitability be waived by any written provision in the lease or by oral agreement.

In determining whether there has been a breach of the implied warranty of habitability, the courts may first look to any relevant local or municipal housing code; they may also make reference to the minimum housing code standards enunciated in 24 V.S.A. §§5003(c)(1)-5003(c)(5). A substantial violation of an applicable housing code shall constitute prima facie evidence that there has been a breach of the warranty of habitability. "[O]ne or two minor violations standing alone which do not affect" the health or safety of the tenant, shall be considered de minimis and not a breach of the warranty. In addition, the landlord will not be liable for defects caused by the tenant.

However, these codes and standards merely provide a starting point in determining whether there has been a breach. Not all towns and municipalities have housing codes; where there are codes, the particular problem complained of may not be addressed. In determining whether there has been a breach of the implied

---

46. The warranty also covers those facilities located in the common areas of an apartment building or duplex that may affect the health or safety of a tenant, such as common stairways, or porches. . . .

warranty of habitability, courts should inquire whether the claimed defect has an impact on the safety or health of the tenant.

In order to bring a cause of action for breach of the implied warranty of habitability, the tenant must first show that he or she notified the landlord "of the deficiency or defect not known to the landlord and [allowed] a reasonable time for its correction." King v. Moorehead, 495 S.W.2d [65, 76 (Mo. App. 1973)].

Because we hold that the lease of a residential dwelling creates a contractual relationship between the landlord and tenant, the standard contract remedies of rescission, reformation and damages are available to the tenant when suing for breach of the implied warranty of habitability. The measure of damages shall be the difference between the value of the dwelling as warranted and the value of the dwelling as it exists in its defective condition. In determining the fair rental value of the dwelling as warranted, the court may look to the agreed upon rent as evidence on this issue. . . .

We also find persuasive the reasoning of some commentators that damages should be allowed for a tenant's discomfort and annoyance arising from the landlord's breach of the implied warranty of habitability. See Moskovitz, The Implied Warranty of Habitability: A New Doctrine Raising New Issues, 62 Cal. L. Rev. 1444, 1470-73 (1974) (hereinafter cited as A New Doctrine); A Dream Deferred, supra, at 250-51. Damages for annoyance and discomfort are reasonable in light of the fact that

> the residential tenant who has suffered a breach of the warranty . . . cannot bathe as frequently as he would like or at all if there is inadequate hot water; he must worry about rodents harassing his children or spreading disease if the premises are infested; or he must avoid certain rooms or worry about catching a cold if there is inadequate weather protection or heat. Thus, discomfort and annoyance are the common injuries caused by each breach and hence the true nature of the general damages the tenant is claiming. [Moskovitz, A New Doctrine, supra, at 1470-71.]

Damages for discomfort and annoyance may be difficult to compute; however, "[t]he trier [of fact] is not to be deterred from this duty by the fact that the damages are not susceptible of reduction to an exact money standard." Vermont Electric Supply Co. v. Andrus, 132 Vt. 195, 200, 315 A.2d 456, 459 (1974).

Another remedy available to the tenant when there has been a breach of the implied warranty of habitability is to withhold the payment of future rent.[47] The burden and expense of bringing suit will then be on the landlord who can better afford to bring the action. In an action for ejectment for nonpayment of rent, 12 V.S.A. §4773, "[t]he trier of fact, upon evaluating the seriousness of the breach and the ramification of the defect upon the health and safety of the tenant, will abate the rent at the landlord's expense in accordance with its findings." A Dream Deferred, supra, at 248. The tenant must show that: (1) the landlord

---

47. Because we hold that the tenant's obligation to pay rent is contingent on the landlord's duty to provide and maintain a habitable dwelling, it is no longer necessary for the tenant to first abandon the premises; thus, the doctrine of constructive eviction is no longer a viable or needed defense in an action by the landlord for unpaid rent. . . .

had notice of the previously unknown defect and failed, within a reasonable time, to repair it; and (2) the defect, affecting habitability, existed during the time for which rent was withheld. See A Dream Deferred, supra, at 248-50. Whether a portion, all or none of the rent will be awarded to the landlord will depend on the findings relative to the extent and duration of the breach.[48] Javins v. First National Realty Corp., supra, 428 F.2d at 1082-83. Of course, once the landlord corrects the defect, the tenant's obligation to pay rent becomes due again.

Additionally, we hold that when the landlord is notified of the defect but fails to repair it within a reasonable amount of time, and the tenant subsequently repairs the defect, the tenant may deduct the expense of the repair from future rent. 11 Williston on Contracts §1404 (3d ed. W. Jaeger 1968); Marini v. Ireland, 56 N.J. 130, 146, 265 A.2d 526, 535 (1970).

In addition to general damages, we hold that punitive damages may be available to a tenant in the appropriate case. Although punitive damages are generally not recoverable in actions for breach of contract, there are cases in which the breach is of such a willful and wanton or fraudulent nature as to make appropriate the award of exemplary damages. A willful and wanton or fraudulent breach may be shown "by conduct manifesting personal ill will, or carried out under circumstances of insult or oppression, or even by conduct manifesting . . . a reckless or wanton disregard of [one's] rights. . . ." Sparrow v. Vermont Savings Bank, 95 Vt. 29, 33, 112 A. 205, 207 (1921). When a landlord, after receiving notice of a defect, fails to repair the facility that is essential to the health and safety of his or her tenant, an award of punitive damages is proper. 111 East 88th Partners v. Simon, 106 Misc. 2d 693, 434 N.Y.S.2d 886, 889 (N.Y. Civ. Ct. 1980). . . .

In the instant case, the trial court's award of damages, based in part on a breach of the implied warranty of habitability, was not a misapplication of the law relative to habitability. Because of our holding in this case, the doctrine of constructive eviction, wherein the tenant must abandon in order to escape liability for rent, is no longer viable. When, as in the instant case, the tenant seeks, not to escape rent liability, but to receive compensatory damages in the amount of rent already paid, abandonment is similarly unnecessary. Under our holding, when a landlord breaches the implied warranty of habitability, the tenant may withhold future rent, and may also seek damages in the amount of rent previously paid.

In its conclusions of law the trial court stated that the defendants' failure to make repairs was compensable by damages to the extent of reimbursement of all rent paid and additional compensatory damages. The court awarded plaintiff a total of $4,945.00; $3,445.00 represents the entire amount of rent plaintiff paid, plus the $50.00 deposit. This appears to leave $1,500.00 as the "additional compensatory damages." However, although the court made findings which clearly

---

48. Some courts suggest that, during the period rent is withheld, the tenant should pay the rent, as it becomes due, into legal custody. See, e.g., Javins v. First National Realty Corp., supra, 428 F.2d at 1083 n.67; see also King v. Moorehead, supra, 495 S.W.2d at 77 (*King* requires the deposit of the rent into legal custody pending the litigation). Such a procedure assures the availability of that portion, if any, of the rent which the court determines is due to the landlord. King v. Moorehead, supra, 495 S.W.2d at 77; see A Dream Deferred, supra, at 248-250.

demonstrate the appropriateness of an award of compensatory damages, there is no indication as to how the court reached a figure of $1,500.00. It is "crucial that this Court and the parties be able to determine what was decided and how the decision was reached." Fox v. McLain, 142 Vt. 11, 16, 451 A.2d 1122, 1124 (1982).

Additionally, the court denied an award to plaintiff of punitive damages on the ground that the evidence failed to support a finding of willful and wanton or fraudulent conduct. The facts in this case, which defendants do not contest, evince a pattern of intentional conduct on the part of defendants for which the term "slumlord" surely was coined. Defendants' conduct was culpable and demeaning to plaintiff and clearly expressive of a wanton disregard of plaintiff's rights. The trial court found that defendants were aware of defects in the essential facilities of plaintiff's apartment, promised plaintiff that repairs would be made, but never fulfilled those promises. The court also found that plaintiff continued, throughout her tenancy, to pay her rent, often in the face of verbal threats made by defendant Stuart St. Peter. These findings point to the "bad spirit and wrong intention" of the defendants, Glidden v. Skinner, 142 Vt. 644, 648, 458 A.2d 1142, 1144 (1983), and would support a finding of willful and wanton or fraudulent conduct, contrary to the conclusions of law and judgment of the trial judge. However, the plaintiff did not appeal the court's denial of punitive damages, and issues not appealed and briefed are waived.

We find that defendants' third claimed error, that the court erred in finding that both defendant Stuart St. Peter and defendant Patricia St. Peter were liable to plaintiff for the breach of the implied warranty of habitability, is meritless. Both defendants were named in the complaint as owners of the 10-12 Church Street apartment building. Plaintiff's complaint also alleged that defendant Stuart St. Peter acted as agent for defendant Patricia St. Peter. Defendants failed to deny these allegations; under V.R.C.P. 8(d) these averments stand as admitted.

Affirmed in part; reversed in part and remanded for hearing on additional compensable damages, consistent with the views herein.

NOTES, QUESTIONS, AND PROBLEMS

1. *The implied warranty of habitability and other legal doctrines.* The implied warranty of habitability does *not* render pointless the doctrines of quiet enjoyment, constructive eviction, and illegal leases considered earlier. First of all, a small number of jurisdictions have yet to adopt the warranty. See, e.g., Hall v. Lunsford, 732 S.W.2d 141 (Ark. 1987). Second, the warranty, even where generally applicable, commonly does not apply across the board to all residential leases; single family residences might be excluded, for example, or agricultural leases, or long-term leases. So too for casual leases by non-merchant landlords, as when a law professor goes off on sabbatical and rents her house to a visitor. See, e.g., Zimmerman v. Moore, 441 N.E.2d 690 (Ind. App. 1982) (single family home rented by non-merchant landlord). Third, a majority of jurisdictions have declined to extend the idea to an implied warranty of fitness or suitability

for purpose in commercial leases. For discussion, see Anthony J. Vlatas, Note, An Economic Analysis of Implied Warranties of Fitness in Commercial Leases, 94 Colum. L. Rev. 658 (1994), suggesting that efficiency would be advanced by implying such a warranty, unless the parties agree otherwise; see also Daniel B. Bogart, Good Faith and Fair Dealing in Commercial Leasing: The Right Doctrine in the Wrong Transaction, 41 J. Marshall L. Rev. 275, 297-306 (2008).[49]

2. *Standard and breach of the warranty.* The standard of the implied warranty of habitability, and the shortcomings that amount to breaches of the standard, appear to vary among jurisdictions, but the differences are probably more nominal than real when it comes to actual cases. Generally speaking, an "adequate standard of habitability" has to be met, and a breach occurs when the leased premises are "uninhabitable" in the eyes of a reasonable person. Housing code provisions and their violation are compelling but usually not conclusive.

In short, the objective is safe and healthy housing; substantial compliance is required. But this means something more than merely avoiding slum conditions. For example, continued loud noise in an apartment building might be a breach. See, e.g., Millbridge Apts. v. Linden, 376 A.2d 611 (N.J. Dist. Ct. 1977). So too for failure of a central air conditioning system. See, e.g., Park Hill Terrace Assocs. v. Glennon, 369 A.2d 938 (N.J. App. Div. 1977). So too for bedbugs. See, e.g., Bender v. Green, 874 N.Y.S.2d 786 (Civ. Ct. 2009); Ludlow Properties, LLC v. Young, 780 N.Y.S.2d 853 (N.Y. City Civ. Ct. 2004). And second-hand smoke. See, e.g., Poyck v. Bryant, 820 N.Y.S.2d 774 (N.Y. City Civ. Ct. 2006).

3. *Remedies for breach.* The implied warranty of habitability is based largely on contractual principles, and a number of cases agree with *Hilder* that in the case of breach a tenant may avail himself of all the basic contract remedies — damages, rescission, and reformation. There are some unique aspects of the tenant's remedies, however. Moreover, the remedies vary with the circumstances and also from jurisdiction to jurisdiction.

As to circumstances, the posture of the *Hilder* case is one possibility: a tenant who has paid rent and remained in possession later sues for reimbursement and damages, claiming breach of the implied warranty of habitability. Perhaps more typical is the tenant who remains in possession but withholds rent. The landlord sues for possession and back rent, whereupon the tenant asserts breach of the warranty as a defense. Virtually all jurisdictions permit the tenant to raise the defense in a summary eviction action. If the tenant is successful, rent is reduced

---

49. Most jurisdictions agree with *Hilder* that the implied warranty of habitability cannot be waived, but a few might permit a "knowing" waiver by the tenant if "bargaining power" is essentially "equal." See Restatement (Second) of Property, Landlord and Tenant §5.6 (1977); P.H. Investment v. Oliver, 818 P.2d 1018 (Utah 1991) (waiver must be express and specific). Consistent with this, most jurisdictions apply the warranty even to patent defects, though a few appear to exclude them at least so long as they do not violate housing code provisions. Why might it be that the warranty of habitability is typically a mandatory rule, rather than a default rule? For one perspective, see Thomas W. Merrill & Henry E. Smith, The Property/Contract Interface, 101 Colum. L. Rev. 773, 827 (2001) ("given the landlord's superior information about the law and the facts regarding the quality of the premises, and the low probability that it will be cost effective for tenants to acquire sufficient information to negotiate over the issue, arguably it makes sense to interpose minimum standards of quality and make those standards nonwaivable").

partially or totally (depending on the degree of breach), and the tenant may retain possession if he pays whatever reduced amount is determined.[50] Whether viewed as a rent reduction or a setoff or a counterclaim for damages, the practical result is the same: The tenant may withhold rent, retain possession, and have the agreed rent reduced by virtue of the landlord's breach.

While there is general agreement on these points, there is considerable disagreement about how to calculate the rent reduction or damages. In *Hilder*, for example, the court said that damages "shall be the difference between the value of the dwelling as warranted and the value of the dwelling as it exists in its defective condition." The agreed rent is evidence of "fair rental value as warranted." (See page 520.) Was the apartment in *Hilder* worthless?

Some other jurisdictions say damages are "the difference between the agreed rent and the fair rental value of the premises as they were during their occupancy in the unsafe, unsanitary or unfit condition." Kline v. Burns, 276 A.2d 248, 252 (N.H. 1971). Still other states use a percentage-diminution approach: The agreed rent is reduced by a percentage equal to the percentage of lease-value lost by the tenant in consequence of the landlord's breach. How do these differ from the approach in *Hilder*? What problems can you see in each of the various methods of calculation?

Other remedies. The foregoing comments address a tenant's right to assert breach of the implied warranty of habitability as a *defense* justifying rent withholding, retention of possession, and rent abatement; or to stay in possession, pay rent, and bring an *affirmative cause of action* for damages—presumably measured on one of the bases (depending on the jurisdiction) described above. The tenant may also terminate the lease and sue for damages. In any of these cases, special and consequential damages should also be recoverable—and perhaps, on occasion, punitive damages as well. See, e.g., Morris v. Flaig, 511 F. Supp. 2d 282 (E.D.N.Y. 2007) (upholding jury's award of punitive damages for violation of implied warranty of habitability).

One reason why damages for breach of the implied warranty of habitability is complicated has to do with the warranty's origins: it derives from both contract and tort law, each of which typically uses its own distinct damage measures. Compare Johnson v. Scandia Assocs., Inc., 717 N.E.2d 24 (Ind. 1999) (contract), with Scott v. Garfield, 912 N.E.2d 1000, 1005 (Mass. 2009) (contract and tort).

The equitable remedy of specific performance—in the form of injunctive relief against violations of the warranty—has been mentioned in dicta, but tenants tend to ignore it. See Mary Marsh Zulock, If You Prompt Them, They Will Rule: The Warranty of Habitability Meets the New Court Information Systems, 40 J. Marshall L. Rev. 425 (2007). Another equitable remedy, application of rent to

---

50. Courts in several jurisdictions hold that, notwithstanding breach of warranty by the landlord, the tenant cannot defend an eviction action for nonpayment of rent unless the landlord's breach is so substantial as to have totally abated the rent (or unless, in the event a partial abatement is justified, the tenant has managed to calculate the amount to be abated and tendered the balance to the landlord!). See Foisy v. Wyman, 515 P.2d 160 (Wash. 1973).

repairs, has existed in some states for many years in the form of repair-and-deduct statutes. Several cases have adopted the remedy in the event of breach of the implied warranty of habitability. See, e.g., Marini v. Ireland, 265 A.2d 526 (N.J. 1970); see also Restatement (Second) of Property, Landlord and Tenant, supra, §11.2, and the *Hilder* case at page 521.

4. Consider the following problems:

(a) *L* owns a high rise apartment building. *L*'s entire maintenance and janitorial staff goes on strike for two weeks. The building's incinerators are inoperative as a consequence of the strike; tenants must take their garbage to the curb in paper bags supplied by *L*. City sanitation workers refuse to cross the striking employees' picket lines. Trash piles up to the height of the building's first-floor windows. The garbage exudes noxious odors and results in a declaration of a health emergency by the city. Routine maintenance and extermination service is not performed during the strike, and rats and vermin become a problem. Has *L* breached the implied warranty of habitability? See Park West Management Corp. v. Mitchell, 391 N.E.2d 1288 (N.Y. 1979).

(b) *T* resides in a fancy apartment building on Manhattan's "fashionable" Upper East Side and pays a high rent for the privilege. *T*'s lease provides for a lot of fancy amenities: an attendant at the door, an elevator, a swimming pool and gym in the apartment building, and so on. State law requires that leased dwellings be fit for habitation, safe and healthy, and in accord with "the uses reasonably intended by the parties." Does the quoted language extend the implied warranty of habitability so as to encompass the services and amenities that *T* reasonably expected to get according to the terms of his lease? Why might it matter? See Solow v. Wellner, 658 N.E.2d 1005 (N.Y. 1995).

(c) *L* leases an apartment to *X*, a registered sex offender. *T*, who had already leased an adjacent apartment for a one-year term, learns of the lease to *X* and notifies *L* in writing that she wants *L* to terminate her tenancy. When *L* does not respond, *T* vacates and sues for return of her security deposit; *L* counterclaims for the balance of the rent due on the original lease. Did *L*, by leasing to *X*, breach the implied warranty of habitability? Is *T* free to vacate in any event? See Knudsen v. Lax, 842 N.Y.S.2d 341 (Co. Ct. 2007).

(d) *L* offers a small run-down house for rent at $100 per month. *T* inspects the premises, finds a number of defects, and tells *L* that she will take the place as is, "but only at $50 a month because that's all it's worth in its condition." *L* agrees and *T* takes possession; subsequently she fails to pay any rent. In an eviction suit by *L*, may *T* assert breach of the implied warranty of habitability as a defense (and what are *T*'s damages)? See Haddad v. Gonzalez, 576 N.E.2d 658, 668 (Mass. 1991); Foisy v. Wyman, 515 P.2d 160 (Wash. 1973).

5. Compared to quiet enjoyment, constructive eviction, and illegal lease doctrine, what are the advantages of the implied warranty of habitability from the tenant's point of view? Should tenants regard the warranty theory as risk-free? More generally, is the warranty a good thing for tenants? (We return to this last question in Section H. See pages 536-537.)

NOTE: RETALIATORY EVICTION

Conventional common law doctrine gave landlords virtually unlimited free-dom to terminate periodic tenancies and tenancies at will upon proper notice and to refuse to renew expired terms of years. The landlord's reasons were irrelevant and could be malevolent. This feature of the common law could eas-ily undermine such reforms as the implied warranty of habitability: Landlords could cope with expanding tenant rights simply by getting rid of tenants who exercised them, at the same time giving a message to tenants who were thinking of doing so. So something had to change, and it did. Most jurisdictions today, whether by statute or judicial decision, forbid retaliatory action by landlords rent-ing residential space (few if any extend the prohibition to commercial leases). See generally Restatement (Second) of Property, Landlord and Tenant §§14.8, 14.9 and Commentary (1977). A fairly common approach is to create a rebut-table presumption of retaliatory purpose if the landlord seeks to terminate a ten-ancy, increase rent, or decrease services within some given period (commonly anywhere from 90 to 180 days) after a good-faith complaint or other action by a tenant based on the condition of the premises. Retaliatory acts beyond the stated period are also usually prohibited, but the tenant bears the burden of proof. Compare the following from Building Monitoring Systems, Inc. v. Paxton, 905 P.2d 1215, 1219 (Utah 1995):

> An alternative approach has been explored by New York courts. These courts have recog-nized that a tenant may be evicted anytime after repairs have been made but that courts "should be generous in allowing the tenant sufficient time, without the pressure normally exerted in a holdover eviction proceeding, to find other suitable housing." . . . We agree. Once repairs have been made, a landlord may serve the tenant with an eviction notice and bring an unlawful detainer action without proffering evidence of intent. However, because the unlawful detainer action may still be tainted with an unlawful motive, the burden is on the landlord to show that he has given the tenant a reasonable opportunity to procure other housing.

Bear in mind that a landlord's freedom to terminate tenancies is constrained by more than retaliatory eviction prohibitions, such as antidiscrimination mea-sures (see pages 453-461) and rent control laws (in the few areas where they exist; see pages 534-536). "Some landlords, however, have experienced even greater restriction of their common law rights. New Jersey, for example, permits the land-lord to evict a tenant at the end of the lease term only for 'good cause' "—fail-ure to pay rent, property destruction, and so on. See Edward H. Rabin, The Revolution in Residential Landlord-Tenant Law: Causes and Consequences, 69 Cornell L. Rev. 517, 534-535 (1984).

NOTE AND PROBLEMS: LANDLORD'S TORT LIABILITY

The common law held landlords liable for tenant injuries (and perhaps for injuries to third parties on the leased premises) only when the landlord negligently breached the limited duties that arise from the handful of exceptions introduced earlier in connection with our discussion of quiet enjoyment and constructive eviction. See Note 1 on pages 511-512. Here again, however, matters have changed somewhat in the last several decades, partly in response to the development of the implied warranty of habitability. A few jurisdictions have cited the warranty as a reason to impose a general standard of care—a negligence standard—on landlords under all circumstances. The leading case is Sargent v. Ross, 308 A.2d 528 (N.H. 1973); see also, e.g., Joiner v. Haley, 777 So. 2d 50 (Miss. App. 2001) (warranty creates a duty to use reasonable care). But see Isbell v. Commercial Investment Assocs., Inc., 644 S.E.2d 72 (Va. 2007). The California Supreme Court at first went further, holding landlords strictly liable for injuries caused by latent defects in the leased premises; 10 years later, however, the court reversed itself. See Becker v. IRM Corp., 698 P.2d 116 (Cal. 1985) (strict liability); Peterson v. Superior Court (Paribas), 899 P.2d 905 (Cal. 1995) (overruling *Becker*). Although the majority of jurisdictions do not impose strict liability, there is a trend in the direction of recognizing a general duty of care on the part of landlords. See, e.g., Miller v. David Grace, Inc., 212 P.3d 1223 (Okla. 2009); Merrill v. Jansma, 86 P.3d 270 (Wyo. 2004). Suppose, in a jurisdiction that recognizes only the conventional common law exceptions, that:

1. *L* leases land to *T* for a term of one year, knowing that *T* intends to use the land to board and rent horses and to operate a riding trail. *T* holds over at the end of the term and becomes a month-to-month tenant, from the first till the last of each month. On a rainy Fourth of July a customer of *T*'s is injured when her horse slips on a soft, narrow riding trail and falls on top of her. Is *L* liable? See Pritchett v. Rosoff, 546 F.2d 463 (2d Cir. 1976); see also Stone v. Center Trust Retail Props, Inc., 77 Cal. Rptr. 3d 556 (Cal. App. 2008); Humphrey v. Byron, 850 N.E.2d 1044 (Mass. 2006).

2. *L* leases a farm to the father of the plaintiff, a young boy badly injured when he becomes entangled in a silage auger in the barn. Is *L* liable? See Thomas v. Shelton, 740 F.2d 478 (7th Cir. 1984).

3. *L* leases a unit in an apartment building to the parents of the plaintiff, a little girl badly injured when she is struck by boys racing their bikes in a parking lot owned by *L* and used by his tenants. The parking lot has no speed bumps. Is *L* liable? See Jackson v. Ray Kruse Constr. Co., 708 S.W.2d 664 (Mo. 1986). Compare Kuzmicz v. Ivy Hill Apts., 688 A.2d 1018 (N.J. 1997) (no liability when landlord didn't own parking lot and didn't derive economic benefit from it).

Suppose the little girl is injured on the street, *off L*'s property (which has no fence around it). Is *L* liable? Compare Udy v. Calvary Corp., 780 P.2d 1055 (Ariz. App. 1989), with Brooks v. Eugene Burger Management Corp., 264 Cal. Rptr. 756 (Cal. App. 1989).

4. *L* leases a unit in an apartment building to the *T*s, a married couple. A parking garage adjacent to the building, and owned by *L*, is available for use by tenants. Parking there one evening, the *T*s are attacked and badly injured by three men who are never caught. Is *L* liable? See Feld v. Merriam, 485 A.2d 742 (Pa. 1984). Suppose the *T*s are attacked by other tenants (or their guests) of *L*. Is *L* liable? See Castaneda v. Olsher, 162 P.3d 610 (Cal. 2007); Todd v. Pink Oak Greene, 75 S.W.3d 658 (Tex. App. 2002).

5. Would it matter if in any of the foregoing the lease in question provided as follows? "Lessor shall not be liable to tenant or to any other person or to any property for damage or injury occurring on or owing to the condition of the leased premises, or any part thereof, or in the common areas thereof, and tenant agrees to hold lessor harmless from any claims for damages no matter how caused." See generally Karen A. Read, Public Policy Violations or Permitted Provisions? The Validity of Exculpatory Provisions in Residential Leases, 62 Mo. L. Rev. 897 (1997); William K. Jones, Private Revision of Public Standards: Exculpatory Agreements in Leases, 63 N.Y.U. L. Rev. 717 (1988). See also Lewis Operating Corp. v. Super. Ct., 132 Cal. Rptr. 3d 849 (Cal. App. 2011) (upholding narrowly drawn release confined to health club on premises).

2. Tenant's Duties; Landlord's Rights and Remedies

Having considered above how the law deals with a landlord's incentives to neglect the condition of the leased premises, we turn now—very briefly—to the flip side of the matter. Tenants too, after all, have reasons to shirk when it comes to maintenance and repair.

Actually, we have already considered some of the relevant doctrine.[51] Recall, for example, the law of *waste*, which can come into play whenever property ownership is divided such that two or more persons have consecutive rights to possession (as with present and future interests). The relationship of landlord and tenant is an instance, and our earlier discussion (in Note 4 on page 241) suggests the nature of the tenant's duties. A dated but still accurate statement is that the duty not to commit waste is breached if a tenant makes "such a change as to affect a vital and substantial portion of the premises; as would change its characteristic appearance; the fundamental purpose of the erection; or the uses contemplated, or a change of such a nature, as would affect the very realty itself, extraordinary in scope and effect, or unusual in expenditure." Pross v. Excelsior Cleaning & Dyeing Co., 179 N.Y.S. 176, 179-180 (Mun. Ct. 1919). So not every alteration made by a tenant amounts to waste. The degree of effect on the use and value of the leased premises is relevant, as is its permanence; so too should be the length of the term remaining at the time the tenant makes the changes in question. (Do you see why?)

There is no bright line that distinguishes waste from lawful activities. For example, in Rumiche Corp. v. Eisenreich, 352 N.E.2d 125 (N.Y. 1976), the tenant replaced a defective ceiling with sheetrock that did not meet code requirements, installed a light fixture and light switch, attached a wooden closet to a wall, and put a frame around a window. The court, quoting the language from the *Pross* case set out above, found no waste; a dissenting judge thought otherwise because

---

51. Including doctrine on the landlord's remedies in the event of tenant default. Recall the general treatment of this topic in Section F.

there were substantial and material changes in the structure of the leased premises, and because at least one of the changes was not up to code.

Suppose in a case like *Rumiche* that the tenant subsequently moves from the apartment and takes along some of the improvements—say, the light fixture and the window frame. Obviously the tenant might be liable for waste if removal results in substantial damage, but suppose it does not. Might the tenant be liable anyway, and for what? See Kane v. Timm, 527 P.2d 480 (Wash. App. 1974); Ray A. Brown, The Law of Personal Property §§16.1-16.5, 16.8-16.10 (Walter B. Raushenbush 3d ed. 1975) (discussing the law of *fixtures*). Or suppose the tenant agrees in the lease not to make any alterations in the premises without the landlord's consent, then does so without consent. Is this a breach? The cases are mixed. See, e.g., *Rumiche*, supra (making alterations without permission violates agreement); Garland v. Titan West Assocs., 543 N.Y.S.2d 56 (App. Div. 1989) (no breach absent alterations that would amount to waste independent of agreement; in other words, the agreement is read as simply restating the law of waste).

The *Rumiche* case involved acts of voluntary waste, arising from affirmative actions, as opposed to involuntary or permissive waste arising from a failure to act. Permissive waste provided the foundation of the tenant's *duty to repair*. See, e.g., 1 American Law of Property §3.78 at 347 (1952 & Supp. 1977):

> The tenant . . . had an implied duty at common law to make minor repairs, a duty which arose out of his duty not to commit waste. The duty was to make such repairs as would keep the buildings windtight and watertight, thus preserving the property in substantially the same condition as at the commencement of the term, ordinary wear excepted. So the tenant was required to replace broken windows and doors, repair a leaking roof, and restore boards on the side of a building. He was not required to rebuild or restore a building, or any substantial part thereof, that had been destroyed by fire or other casualty or become so dilapidated from ordinary wear that it had to be torn down. Nor was he under any obligation to correct defects existing at the commencement of his lease.[52]

It is a common view today that the tenant's implied duty to repair no longer makes sense, the argument being that landlords, not tenants, are generally in the best position to maintain the property. See, e.g., id. at 347-348. The implied warranty of habitability—which essentially negates the tenant's duty to repair—is based in part on this view, but bear in mind that the warranty does not apply across the board to all residential leases and seldom extends to commercial leases. See Note 1 on page 522.

In what respects, then, might a commercial tenant's duty to repair be altered by a covenant in the lease? The answer depends considerably on the language of the agreement in question. A covenant that excepts "fair wear and tear" amounts to no more than the common law duty. Slightly different wording (say "to keep in good repair") might be found to enlarge the tenant's obligations, and a number of vexing interpretive problems can arise. For instance, a bald promise to

---

52. Was the *landlord* under any obligation to correct defects existing at the outset of the tenancy? Recall the discussion in Note 1 on page 511.—EDS.

repair that contains no qualifications whatsoever *may* give rise to a duty to repair whatever the cause of the damage and even if repair entails rebuilding an entire structure. On the other hand, statutes in a number of jurisdictions abrogate the latter part of this rule absent an express promise to rebuild, and some courts, perhaps a majority, reach the same result by holding that "repair" does not mean "rebuild." See Amoco Oil Co. v. Jones, 467 N.W.2d 357 (Minn. App. 1991); Restatement (Second) of Property, Landlord and Tenant §13.1 Reporter's Note at 504-505 (1977).

Explicit covenants to repair regularly except, in addition to fair wear and tear, damage by fire or other casualty. The current trend appears to be that the exception relieves the tenant from liability even with regard, say, to fire damage brought about by the tenant's negligence. See, e.g., Belden Mfg. Co. v. Chicago Threaded Fasteners, Inc., 228 N.E.2d 532 (Ill. App. 1967) (clause exculpates lessee; statute voiding exculpatory clauses applies only to landlords); Stein v. Yarnell-Todd Chevrolet, Inc., 241 N.E.2d 439 (Ill. 1969) (tenant relieved of liability for negligence despite the fact that clause in lease excepted only fire or other casualty *beyond lessee's control*). Compare U.S. Fidelity & Guaranty Co. v. Let's Frame It, Inc., 759 P.2d 819 (Colo. App. 1988) (fire damage exception held inapplicable to fire caused by tenant's negligence when other lease provisions required tenant to repair damage resulting from its negligence).

Whether or not there is a covenant to repair, must a tenant continue to pay rent after the leased premises have been destroyed? The common law usually answered in the affirmative, unless the lease provided otherwise, on the theory "that although a building may be an important element of consideration for the payment of rent, the interest in the soil remains to support the lease despite destruction of the building." Albert M. Greenfield & Co. v. Kolea, 380 A.2d 758, 759 (Pa. 1976). But what if the lease covers only a portion of a building, which is subsequently destroyed? Here an exception was made to the general rule, because the tenant never had any "interest in the soil" in the first place. The building, since destroyed, was the only consideration for the lease. The court in *Greenfield* seized on this reasoning in the service of a second exception, based on the contract theory of frustration of purpose (or impossibility of performance): "[W]hen the building was destroyed by fire it became impossible for the [landlord] to furnish the agreed consideration. . . . It is also obvious that the purpose of the lease with respect to the [tenant] was frustrated." 380 A.2d at 759-760. Accidental destruction of the building excused both parties from further performance of their obligations under the lease. In many jurisdictions the same results are achieved by legislation.[53]

---

53. If a provision in the lease clearly suggests that the tenant must pay rent even if the premises are damaged or destroyed, then courts are likely to defer to that explicit allocation of risk. See Portnoy v. Omnicare Pharmaceutics, 2004 WL 1535780 (E.D. Pa. June 25, 2004).

H. The Problem of Decent Affordable Housing

Finding affordable housing of decent quality is a challenge to many Americans, not just—but obviously most especially—the poor. The implied warranty of habitability and allied reforms, studied above, aimed to improve the situation. But wouldn't landlords, in response to the higher costs imposed on them by such measures, simply increase the rents they charge, such that housing might be more decent but even less affordable? Could rent controls help allay this problem? What about government-assisted housing programs?

These are large and contentious questions, much beyond the scope of a basic course in property law. The materials that follow are just an introduction, meant to suggest the central points in an ongoing debate.

Chicago Board of Realtors, Inc. v. City of Chicago

United States Court of Appeals, Seventh Circuit, 1987
819 F.2d 732

[In 1986, the Chicago City Council enacted a Residential Landlord and Tenant Ordinance. The ordinance was not a rent control measure; rather, it essentially codified the implied warranty of habitability and, beyond that, established new landlord responsibilities and tenant rights in respects described below. A group of property owners challenged the constitutionality of the ordinance. . . . The district court denied a motion for a preliminary injunction, concluding that the plaintiff property owners did not have a reasonable likelihood of prevailing on the merits.

The plaintiffs appealed. . . . The court of appeals affirmed in an opinion by Cudahy, J., holding, among other things, that the ordinance was sufficiently specific and—giving due deference to the legislative judgment—sufficiently reasonable in light of its stated purpose to promote public health, safety, and welfare.

Of interest to us here is not the constitutional analysis in Judge Cudahy's opinion but the policy analysis in a separate opinion filed in the case, an opinion that moved Judge Cudahy to say: "the economic critique of the Ordinance contained in the separate opinion has not been litigated here and is, at best, superfluous." 819 F.2d at 737 n.2. That "critique" follows.]

POSNER, J.,[54] with whom Easterbrook, J., joins. We agree with Judge Cudahy's opinion as far as it goes, and we therefore join it. But in our view it does not go far enough. It makes the rejection of the appeal seem easier than it is, by refusing to acknowledge the strong case that can be made for the unreasonableness

---

54. Far more opinions by Judge Posner have been selected by casebook editors for inclusion in their casebooks than those of any other judge. Why do you suppose this is so? See Mitu Gulati & Veronica Sanchez, Giants in a World of Pygmies? Testing the Superstar Hypothesis with Judicial Opinions in Casebooks, 87 Iowa L. Rev. 1141 (2002) (suggesting reasons why even reputedly liberal academics choose the opinions of reputedly conservative judges like Judge Posner and his colleague on the Seventh Circuit, Judge Easterbrook, who came in second to Posner).—EDS.

of the ordinance. . . . So we are led to write separately, and since this separate opinion commands the support of two members of this panel, it is also a majority opinion.

The new ordinance rewrites present and future leases of apartments in Chicago to give tenants more legal rights than they would have without the ordinance. It requires the payment of interest on security deposits; requires that those deposits be held in Illinois banks; allows (with some limitations) a tenant to withhold rent in an amount reflecting the cost to him of the landlord's violating a term in the lease; allows a tenant to make minor repairs and subtract the reasonable cost of the repair from his rent; forbids a landlord to charge a tenant more than $10 a month for late payment of rent (regardless of how much is owing); and creates a presumption (albeit rebuttable) that a landlord who seeks to evict a tenant after the tenant has exercised rights conferred by the ordinance is retaliating against the tenant for the exercise of those rights.

The stated purpose of the ordinance is to promote public health, safety, and welfare and the quality of housing in Chicago. It is unlikely that this is the real purpose, and it is not the likely effect. Forbidding landlords to charge interest at market rates on late payment of rent could hardly be thought calculated to improve the health, safety, and welfare of Chicagoans or to improve the quality of the housing stock. But it may have the opposite effect. The initial consequence of the rule will be to reduce the resources that landlords devote to improving the quality of housing, by making the provision of rental housing more costly. Landlords will try to offset the higher cost (in time value of money, less predictable cash flow, and, probably, higher rate of default) by raising rents. To the extent they succeed, tenants will be worse off, or at least no better off. Landlords will also screen applicants more carefully, because the cost of renting to a deadbeat will now be higher; so marginal tenants will find it harder to persuade landlords to rent to them. Those who do find apartments but then are slow to pay will be subsidized by responsible tenants (some of them marginal too), who will be paying higher rents, assuming the landlord cannot determine in advance who is likely to pay rent on time. Insofar as these efforts to offset the ordinance fail, the cost of rental housing will be higher to landlords and therefore less will be supplied—more of the existing stock than would otherwise be the case will be converted to condominia and cooperatives and less rental housing will be built.

The provisions of the ordinance requiring that interest on security deposits be paid and that those deposits be kept in Illinois banks are as remote as the provision on late payment from any concern with the health or safety of Chicagoans, the quality of housing in Chicago, or the welfare of Chicago as a whole. Their only apparent rationale is to transfer wealth from landlords and out-of-state banks to tenants and local banks—making this an unedifying example of class legislation and economic protectionism rolled into one. However, to the extent the ordinance seeks to transfer wealth from landlords to tenants it could readily be undone by a rent increase; the ordinance puts no cap on rents. Cf. Coase, The Problem of Social Cost, 3 J. Law & Econ. 1 (1960).

The provisions that authorize rent withholding, whether directly or by subtracting repair costs, may seem more closely related to the stated objectives of the ordinance; but the relation is tenuous. The right to withhold rent is not limited to cases of hazardous or unhealthy conditions. And any benefits in safer or healthier housing from exercise of the right are likely to be offset by the higher costs to landlords, resulting in higher rents and less rental housing.

The ordinance is not in the interest of poor people. As is frequently the case with legislation ostensibly designed to promote the welfare of the poor, the principal beneficiaries will be middle class people. They will be people who buy rather than rent housing (the conversion of rental to owner housing will reduce the price of the latter by increasing its supply); people willing to pay a higher rental for better-quality housing; and (a largely overlapping group) more affluent tenants, who will become more attractive to landlords because such tenants are less likely to be late with the rent or to abuse the right of withholding rent—a right that is more attractive, the poorer the tenant. The losers from the ordinance will be some landlords, some out-of-state banks, the poorest class of tenants, and future tenants. The landlords are few in number (once owner-occupied rental housing is excluded—and the ordinance excludes it). Out-of-staters can't vote in Chicago elections. Poor people in our society don't vote as often as the affluent. See Filer, An Economic Theory of Voter Turnout 81 (Ph.D. thesis, Dept. of Econ., Univ. of Chi., Dec. 1977); Statistical Abstract of the U.S., 1982-83, at pp. 492-93 (tabs. 805, 806). And future tenants are a diffuse and largely unknown class. In contrast, the beneficiaries of the ordinance are the most influential group in the city's population. So the politics of the ordinance are plain enough, cf. DeCanio, Rent Control Voting Patterns, Popular Views, and Group Interests, in Resolving the Housing Crisis 301, 311-12 (Johnson ed. 1982), and they have nothing to do with either improving the allocation of resources to housing or bringing about a more equal distribution of income and wealth.

A growing body of empirical literature deals with the effects of governmental regulation of the market for rental housing. The regulations that have been studied, such as rent control in New York City and Los Angeles, are not identical to the new Chicago ordinance, though some—regulations which require that rental housing be "habitable"—are close. The significance of this literature is not in proving that the Chicago ordinance is unsound, but in showing that the market for rental housing behaves as economic theory predicts: if price is artificially depressed, or the costs of landlords artificially increased, supply falls and many tenants, usually the poorer and the newer tenants, are hurt. See, e.g., Olsen, An Econometric Analysis of Rent Control, 80 J. Pol. Econ. 1081 (1972); Rydell et al., The Impact of Rent Control on the Los Angeles Housing Market, ch. 6 (Rand Corp. N-1747-LA, Aug. 1981); Hirsch, Habitability Laws and the Welfare of Indigent Tenants, 61 Rev. Econ. & Stat. 263 (1981). The single proposition in economics from which there is the least dissent among American economists is that "a ceiling on rents reduces the quantity and quality of housing available." Frey et al., Consensus and Dissension Among Economists: An Empirical Inquiry, 74 Am. Econ. Rev. 986, 991 (1984) (tab. 2). . . .

NOTES

1. *Mixed accounts.* At the beginning of the twentieth century, slums were a pressing problem, especially in large cities, where immigrants crowded into tenements that lacked sufficient sanitary facilities, light and air, and space. Programs such as New York City's pathbreaking Tenement House Act of 1901 aimed to improve the situation, but not out of altruism alone. Slums brought with them such dangers as disease and fire, threats not just to tenement dwellers but to the general public as well. See generally Roy Lubove, The Progressives and the Slums: Tenement House Reform in New York City 1890-1917 (1974). Since the time of those early programs, many other measures to improve the quality and reduce the cost of housing for low and moderate income Americans have been put in place, and debate about purpose and effect have usually followed on their heels, as witness the views of Judges Posner and Easterbrook (both of whom were once full-time faculty members at the University of Chicago Law School). Many people who have studied the matter agree with their views on such measures as the Chicago ordinance, or the implied warranty of habitability, or rent controls (notice that Posner and Easterbrook question all of these on essentially the same grounds). On the other hand, many other people disagree.[55] Unhappily for the student, though, the vast literature bearing on the debate—a literature that we merely sample here—is unlikely to lead a disinterested observer to firm conclusions one way or the other.

2. *Rent controls.* Posner and Easterbrook pretty much capture the case against rent controls. Virtually all economists, as they point out right at the end of their analysis, regard rent regulation as counterproductive. Virtually all *American* economists, that is. Fewer than 2 percent of them dissented from the propositions stated by Posner and Easterbrook. But almost 44 percent of French economists did, along with almost 20 percent of Swiss economists and 11 percent of Austrian economists, down to 6 percent of German economists. See page 991 (table 2) of the article by Frey et al. cited by Posner and Easterbrook.

A thorough study of rent controls, published by the Urban Land Institute, is Anthony Downs, Residential Rent Controls: An Evaluation (1988). Among Downs's principal conclusions are these:

> As a general rule, residential rent regulation makes economic sense if, and only if, two conditions occur simultaneously in the market and are both expected to last for some time. Demand for rental units must rise sharply at the same time that new construction of such units has been legally restricted in order to conserve resources—as during wartime. In the absence of these conditions, rent controls are neither an appropriate nor an effective response to perceived housing shortages. On the contrary, they generally exacerbate such shortages. . . .
>
> As a general rule, the more an ordinance intrudes upon the market conditions that would otherwise prevail, the more likely it is to cause dislocations in a housing market. Conversely, less intrusive rent regulations appear to cause less severe dislocations. . . .

---

55. See, e.g., Lior Jacob Strahilevitz, Don't Try This at Home: Posner as Political Economist, 74 U. Chi. L. Rev. 1873 (2007) (arguing that the opinion in the *Chicago Board of Realtors* case was based on faulty assumptions).

... Much evidence indicates that all rent controls, even temperate controls, transfer income from owners to tenants or between various classes of tenants. In addition, many of the short-term benefits of rent controls (reduced rents) aid affluent rather than poor households, and some of the costs (reduced access to vacant units) must be borne by very poor households. Where rent is eliminated as a basis for distinguishing among potential tenants, owners often use other factors such as credit-worthiness, race, sex, or ethnicity in allocating scarce rental units—even though most such discrimination is illegal. [Id. at 1-2.][56]

Defenders of rent control respond to such conclusions in two different ways, arguing either that they are unreliable or largely irrelevant. An example of the first approach is John I. Gilderbloom & Richard P. Appelbaum, Rethinking Rental Housing (1988). Finding "little research that systematically examines the differences between restrictive, moderate, and strong rent controls in cities across the United States," the authors undertook "a comprehensive review of studies by economists, political scientists, planners, and sociologists. Such a review suggests that neither moderate nor strong forms of control have caused a decline in either the quality or supply of the rental stock. Although such findings do not, of course, prove that rent controls are without deleterious effect, they provide no warrant for drawing the conventional conclusions." Id. at 134. They add: "Rent control has *not*, however, brought average rents down to affordable levels." Id. at 149; see also Note, Reassessing Rent Control: Its Economic Impact in a Gentrifying Housing Market, 101 Harv. L. Rev. 1835 (1988) (arguing that the conclusions of economists about rent controls have little application to gentrifying markets; controls in such markets will not lead to abandonment, conversion, inadequate maintenance, or a decrease in future construction, but will reduce the social costs of poverty by increasing the supply of low income housing); Richard Arnott, Time for Revisionism on Rent Control?, 9 J. Econ. Perspectives 99 (1995) (suggesting that moderate rent regulation may be beneficial in certain markets, particularly those dominated by a firm with considerable market power).[57]

---

56. "The conclusion of this study," Downs adds, "is that the social and economic costs and disadvantages of rent controls—especially over the long run—almost always outweigh any perceived short-term benefits they provide, in the absence of the two justifying conditions described earlier." Id. at 2.

On rent control and discrimination, a point mentioned by Downs, see also James A. Kushner, The Fair Housing Amendments Act of 1988: The Second Generation of Fair Housing, 42 Vand. L. Rev. 1049, 1056 (1989): "In a very tight, rent-controlled rental market, landlords may be successful in renting solely through word of mouth advertising and referrals by current tenants or relatives—a scheme that carries extreme discriminatory impact."

57. In addition to theoretical criticisms of rent regulation, there is also empirical evidence. One survey of the literature finds that the transfer efficiency (the ratio of tenant benefits to landlord costs) of controls is less than 100 percent, suggesting that rent regulation leads to a reduction in allocative efficiency. Although typical tenant incomes in rent-controlled housing are somewhat lower than those of landlords, the differences are not great. Rent regulations are also associated with higher housing depreciation. See Stephen Malpezzi & Benjt Turner, A Review of the Empirical Evidence on the Costs and Benefits of Rent Control, 10 Swedish Econ. Poly. Rev. 11 (2003). Within a jurisdiction, rent controls are often criticized for being poorly targeted. Stories are legion of wealthy widows living in six-bedroom apartments on Park Avenue. A study of New York City's situation estimates that about 20 percent of controlled units are, in terms of intended beneficiaries, in the "wrong" hands. See Edward L. Glaeser & Erzo F.P. Luttmer, The Misallocation of Housing Under Rent Control, 93 Am. Econ. Rev. 1027 (2003).

An example of the second approach is Margaret J. Radin, Residential Rent Control, 15 Phil. & Pub. Affairs 350 (1986), who wonders whether economists have overlooked important nonutilitarian considerations that might "trump" the conventional analysis. Radin knows that existing tenants are usually the primary beneficiaries of most rent controls, but perhaps that's the whole point: Rent controls "make it possible for existing tenants to stay where they are, with roughly the same proportion of their income going to rent as they have become used to," a result that might be more justified in some circumstances than in others. From a moral point of view, then, judgments about rent controls must turn very much on context. Id. at 352-353. They might be justified in the easy case where a landlord is earning monopoly rents, for example, but not where the landlord lives on the premises and rents a portion to commercial tenants or transients who are not maintaining a home. (The home counts for much in Radin's analysis.) See also Mark Kelman, On Democracy-Bashing: A Skeptical Look at the Theoretical and "Empirical" Practice of the Public Choice Movement, 74 Va. L. Rev. 199, 271-273 (1988) (rent control and community); William H. Simon, Social-Republican Property, 38 UCLA L. Rev. 1355, 1361 (1991) ("the social-republican argument sees rent control as protecting against loss of membership in the community"). For commentary on non-economic arguments in favor of rent regulation, see Walter Block, A Critique of the Legal and Philosophical Case for Rent Control, 40 J. Bus. Ethics 75 (2002).

It bears mention, in concluding this little discussion, that rent control outside New York City is withering. Massachusetts, for example, essentially abolished rent control in late 1994, and California weakened its program in 1995-1996. A study of what happened after rent control ended in three Massachusetts cities — Boston, Brookline, and Cambridge — suggests that rent regulation there led to a decrease in rental units and housing quality. See David P. Sims, Out of Control: What Can We Learn from the End of Massachusetts Rent Control, 61 J. Urb. Econ. 129 (2007). The lifting of rent controls also had a spillover effect on the unregulated rental housing market. Can you guess what it was? See David Autor, Christopher J. Palmer & Parag A. Pathak, Housing Market Spillovers: Evidence from the End of Rent Control in Cambridge, Massachusetts, NBER Working Paper 18125 (June 2012).

3. *The implied warranty of habitability.* The debate here is much the same as the rent control debate, in virtually every respect. A very large literature examines the warranty and related reforms (illegal lease doctrine, prohibition of retaliatory evictions) and reaches conclusions similar to — and mixed like — the conclusions regarding rent controls. See, for example, the review of the theoretical and empirical literature in Roger A. Cunningham, The New Implied and Statutory Warranties of Habitability in Residential Leases: From Contract to Status, 16 Urb. L. Ann. 3 (1979). Subsequent research has not changed matters. Thus there are arguments that the reforms are beneficial, from the standpoint of low income tenants, under various circumstances. See, e.g., Duncan Kennedy, The Effect of the Warranty of Habitability on Low Income Housing: "Milking" and Class Violence,

15 Fla. St. U. L. Rev. 484 (1987) (selective enforcement of the implied warranty could increase supply more than it decreases it, thus reducing rent levels for poor tenants). But, again, there are responses questioning the assumptions of the pro-reform literature, or finding that the reforms have had little effect in practice. See, e.g., Richard A. Posner, Economic Analysis of Law 645-648 (8th ed. 2011). For an interesting analysis of the limitations of the implied warranty of habitability in protecting tenants, see David A. Super, The Rise and Fall of the Implied Warranty of Habitability, 99 Cal. L. Rev. 389 (2011). See also Michael A. Brower, The "Backlash" of the Implied Warranty of Habitability: Theory vs. Analysis, 60 DePaul L. Rev. 849 (2011) (regression analysis suggests that the implied warranty of habitability caused rents to increase, but it is still possible that tenants benefitted as a class).

One can, of course, make a normative or moral argument on behalf of tenant reforms like the implied warranty of habitability. See, e.g., Joseph W. Singer, The Reliance Interest in Property, 40 Stan. L. Rev. 614, 659-663, 679-684 (1988). Some would reply that the moral argument wrongly blames landlords for, and burdens them with, a social problem that is not of their making.[58]

4. *Government housing programs.* The vast majority of rental housing in the United States is owned by private sector landlords. Nevertheless, in 2009, over 1.1 million households lived in publicly owned housing, close to 2.2 million received housing vouchers, and an additional 3.8 million lived in private housing built with federal subsidies or tax credits. See Alex F. Schwartz, Housing Policy in the United States 9 (2010). Government housing programs have aimed to provide decent, affordable housing to low and moderate income families, to eliminate blight, and to redevelop neighborhoods. Conventional public housing began with the federal Housing Act of 1937 (which had the additional aim of putting people to work after the Great Depression). Public housing is typically owned and operated by local public housing authorities (governmental agencies created pursuant to state legislation); most of the housing was financed by the federal government and built between 1949 and 1974.

Public housing was controversial from the outset, initially because it competed with private market housing and, since the mid-1970s, because it concentrated the poor in racially segregated communities. See, e.g., Arnold R. Hirsch, Making the Second Ghetto: Race and Housing in Chicago 1940-1960 (1983); Michael H. Schill, Distressed Public Housing: Where Do We Go from Here?, 60 U. Chi. L. Rev. 497 (1993); Sudhir A. Venkatesh, American Project: The Rise and Fall of a Modern Ghetto (2000). The major alternative to public housing is the housing voucher, which enables families to rent housing in the private

---

58. Thanks perhaps in part to reforms like the implied warranty of habitability, affordability, as opposed to quality, is the foremost housing problem in the United States today. In 2003, only 3.1 percent of all renters lived in severely substandard dwellings, with another 7.5 percent in dwellings with moderate problems. In contrast, 22.6 percent of all households faced severe affordability problems (defined as rent in excess of 50 percent of income). See Alex F. Schwartz, Housing Policy in the United States: An Introduction 16-29 (2006).

sector using vouchers issued by the government. Economists and some sociologists were among the first to support housing vouchers as an alternative to public housing. Can you see why? See Edgar O. Olsen, Housing Programs for Low-Income Households, in Means-Tested Transfer Programs in the United States 365 (Robert Moffitt ed. 2003); Margery Austin Turner, Moving Out of Poverty: Expanding Mobility and Choice Through Tenant-Based Housing Assistance, 9 Housing Policy Debate 373 (1998).

By the 1990s, public housing developments experienced high rates of unemployment, crime, drug abuse, and physical deterioration. One response to the problems was legislation authorizing local public housing authorities to expedite termination proceedings for tenants engaged in drug-related or other violent criminal activity, and to evict residents who allowed their apartments to be used for drug-related activity even if they had no role in or even knowledge of it. See Anti-Drug Abuse Act of 1988, 42 U.S.C. §11901, upheld by H.U.D. v. Rucker, 535 U.S. 125 (2002).[59]

A second response to the problems of severely distressed public housing was the demolition of many projects throughout the nation. As of 2013, over 150,000 units had been eliminated. See Lawrence J. Vale, Purging the Poorest: Public Housing and the Design Politics of Twice-Cleared Communities 22 (2013). Tenants were either relocated to mixed income developments, where they would presumably benefit from contact with higher income, more stable residents, or they were provided with vouchers for use in the private rental market. While the physical condition of some neighborhoods that were once home to public housing developments has improved as a result of their demolition, there are concerns about implementation of the demolition program. Some analysts are skeptical about the wisdom of housing the poor in mixed income environments. See Robert C. Ellickson, The False Promise of the Mixed-Income Housing Project, 57 UCLA L. Rev. 983 (2010). Others feel that the former residents were ill equipped to relocate and that public housing authorities failed to assist them appropriately. See, e.g., Edward G. Goetz, New Deal Ruins: Race, Economic Justice, and Public Housing Policy (2013); Susan Popkin, The CHA's Plan for Transformation: How Have Residents Fared? (Urban Institute, August 2010). See also Brian A. Jacob, Public Housing, Housing Vouchers, and Student Achievement: Evidence from Public Housing Demolitions in Chicago, 94 Am. Econ. Rev. 233 (2004) (a study of Chicago's once notorious and now demolished Cabrini Green, Robert Taylor Homes, and Ida B. Wells Homes).

5. *Renting versus owning.* In addition to rent regulation and housing subsidies, government affects the housing market in many other ways. Indeed, increasing

---

59. In *Rucker,* the Oakland Housing Authority sought to evict four tenants including the named party, Pearlie Rucker, a woman who had lived in the apartment with her disabled daughter. According to the facts of the case, drugs were found on the person of her daughter approximately three blocks from her home. 535 U.S. at 127. Ms. Rucker claimed that she did not know about her daughter's drug use. The Court nevertheless upheld her eviction from public housing.

homeownership has been one of the primary objectives of federal housing and tax policy since World War II. The homeownership rate among Americans rose from 44 percent in 1940 to an all-time high of 69.2 percent in 2004. See Alex F. Schwartz, Housing Policy in the United States 19 (2d ed. 2010). By 2013, after the burst of the housing bubble and recession, the homeownership rate had declined to 65 percent. See U.S. Dept. of Commerce, Residential Vacancies and Homeownership in the First Quarter 2013 (Apr. 30, 2013). Among the policies fueling the ownership increase are the subsidies to homeownership contained in the U.S. Tax Code. For example, mortgage loan interest is generally deductible from taxable income, at least for loan amounts up to $1 million. 26 U.S.C. §163(h)(3)(B)(ii). Similarly, subject to several limitations, property taxes are also deductible. 26 U.S.C. §164(a). In addition, up to $500,000 of gain from the sale of a principal residence ($250,000 for single taxpayers) is excluded from taxation. 26 U.S.C. §121. Perhaps most important, homeowners are not required to pay tax on the imputed income they receive from living in a house. When compared to tenants whose rental payments are taxed to their landlords, this creates an asymmetric advantage. See Edward L. Glaeser & Joseph Gyourko, Rethinking Federal Housing Policy 88-99 (2008); James Poterba & Todd Sinai, Tax Expenditures for Owner-Occupied Housing: Deductions for Property Taxes and Mortgage Interest and the Exclusion of Imputed Rental Income, 98 Am. Econ. Rev. 84 (2008). In addition to tax benefits, the federal government has also sought to make capital to purchase homes plentiful and cheap through the secondary mortgage market. See pages 645-646. In 2008, the "American dream" of homeownership became a nightmare for many. The Great Recession that burst the housing bubble revealed that many households had stretched too far and purchased homes they could not afford. As of mid-2013, over 4.4 million homes have been foreclosed upon, exposing their owners to eviction and the loss of life savings. See Leah Schnurr, Completed Foreclosures Hold Steady in April: CoreLogic, Reuters, May 29, 2013, available at http://www.reuters.com/article/2013/05/29/us-usa-housing-corelogic-idUSBRE94S0JI20130529.

The mortgage meltdown has caused many to wonder whether government policies favoring homeownership are misguided, particularly with respect to families who earn modest incomes. Unquestionably, though, homeownership entails many potential benefits for both neighborhoods and individuals. Can you identify what some of these benefits might be? See N. Edward Coulsen & Herman Li, Measuring the External Benefits of Homeownership, 77 J. Urb. Econ. 57 (2013); Christopher E. Herbert & Eric S. Belsky, The Homeownership Experience of Low-Income and Minority Households: A Review and Synthesis of the Literature, 10 Cityscape: A Journal of Policy Development and Research 4-59 (2008). Indeed, some research even suggests that the children of homeowners do better in schools than children of renters. See, e.g., Donald R. Haurin, Toby Parcel & Jean Haurin, Does Homeownership Affect Child Outcomes?, 30 R.E. Econ. 635 (2002). Other research suggests these results may be partly attributable to selection problems. See Scott Holupka & Sandra J. Newman, The Effects of Homeownership on Children's Outcomes: Real Effects or Self-Selection?, 40 R.E. Econ. 566 (2012).

To the extent that homeownership does indeed generate benefits, is there a way to minimize the risks it imposes on homeowners? For an interesting analysis of some alternatives, see Lee Anne Fennell, The Unbounded Home (2009); Lee Anne Fennell, Homeownership 2.0, 102 Nw. U. L. Rev. 1047 (2008).

IV
Transfers of Land

By now you should understand the premium that the legal system puts on alienability, on the easy transfer and exchange of property rights. Generally speaking, free and voluntary exchange permits resources, land included, to move to higher valued uses. But free here means unfettered, not costless. Exchange is never costless because it takes place in a world full of friction and imperfect information. Transferors and transferees must search out mutually beneficial opportunities for exchange, must negotiate and enforce agreements, must confront risk and uncertainty, must obtain and secure that elusive thing called title. Presumably, the law strives to reduce these burdens—these transaction costs—but how well it succeeds is a matter of dispute, in the case of land transfers in particular. There is little question that the cost (including time expended) of transferring land ownership is greater per dollar value than the cost of transferring ownership of stocks or automobiles or diamond rings. Why?

The reasons should become apparent in the next two chapters, which focus on inter vivos transfers of land. A comprehensive survey would include transfers at death as well, but transfers at death involve the application of a separate body of doctrines taught in advanced courses in decedents' estates. Thus they are largely excluded here. So are involuntary transfers, already considered in Part I's study of conquest and adverse possession and to be considered again in Part V's examination of zoning and the taking of property by government action.

A. Introduction to Buying and Selling Real Estate

While most real estate transactions share many elements in common, each deal presents its own complications and challenges. The following example illustrates the steps that will take place as Robert and Elizabeth Byar (which is to say, of course, Bob and Betty Byar) go about buying a home. The first step for the Byars is to assess how much they can afford to pay, given their income and savings (lenders frequently require borrowers to contribute 10 to 20 percent of the purchase price as a down payment). The Byars might also contact a mortgage bank or financial institution to pre-qualify for a loan. Then the search for properties will begin, perhaps with the Byars using an Internet site such as www.realtor.com to learn about the market. But eventually, if they are like most home buyers, the Byars will consult a broker with access to Multiple Listing Service (MLS) listings and happy to show a variety of homes. The commission for the broker will typically be paid for by the seller (see pages 562-563).

Once the Byars find a house they want to buy, they'll begin negotiating a purchase and sale agreement. Usually it's best to hire an attorney to do this, but in some states brokers are permitted to provide the service. In any event, the agreement will probably be done in terms of a form contract such as the one on pages 544-558, which we will be referring to from time to time. The contract will set forth the legal description of the property, its price, provision for an earnest money deposit, and the date for the closing or settlement (the transfer of title).

Real estate contracts are almost always executory, meaning that title is not transferred immediately upon signing the agreement, because both buyers and seller must do certain things during the time between the contract and closing. The buyer will need to obtain a title search to satisfy herself and her lender that the seller can convey good title to the property. The title search is conducted by a title company in some states, by attorneys in others. Most contracts of sale also contain a mortgage contingency, which provides that if the purchaser cannot obtain a mortgage loan within a given time, she can rescind the contract and get back her deposit. For an example of a mortgage contingency clause, see paragraph 11 in the form contract. A second contingency found in many contracts is a clause allowing the buyer to obtain an inspection of the property and rescind the contract if the cost of remedying the problem exceeds some threshold. See paragraph 10 of the form contract. Sometimes this clause is the most heatedly negotiated part of the sales contract. (Can you see why?)

After the contract has been signed by both parties, either the Byars or the seller will order the title search. The Byars will also typically have an inspector visit the property and apply for a mortgage loan. The title company or lawyer who does the search will provide an abstract of title that will list any encumbrances (such as existing mortgages, liens, rights of way) as well as a listing of the preceding owners of the property. Assuming that the title abstract turns up nothing troubling, the transaction moves forward. If the Byars' application for a mortgage is approved by the lender, they are issued a mortgage commitment that is good for a specified period—typically a couple of months. If all of the other contingencies are satisfied, the Byars and their seller proceed to the closing and transfer of title.

In many states (New York, for example) the transfer of the deed takes place with all parties physically present; in some other states (California, for example) transfer is handled by a third-party escrow agent. The lender provides the proceeds of the loan to the seller, who uses that money and the additional funds paid by the Byars to (1) pay off any existing loans on the property, (2) pay the real estate brokers their commission, (3) pay the legal fees and other fees (such as title insurance) he has agreed to take care of, and (4) pockets the remaining proceeds. At the same time the lender advances the funds for the purchase, the seller transfers title to the property to the Byars by giving them a deed; they sign a promissory note for the loan; they execute a mortgage or deed of trust in favor of the lender and pay fees for the services provided by their lawyer, the title company, and any other parties involved in the transaction. In most instances, a title insurance company will record the deed and mortgage at the County Clerk's office. The company also will issue a policy of title insurance, which promises to defend against any adverse claims and pay a fixed amount if the title is later found to be flawed or unmarketable. The Byars are now the proud owners of a new home.

MULTI-BOARD RESIDENTIAL REAL ESTATE CONTRACT 5.0

1. THE PARTIES: Buyer and Seller are hereinafter referred to as the "Parties".

Buyer(s)_____ Seller(s)_____
     (Please Print)   (Please Print)

If Dual Agency applies, complete Optional Paragraph 41.

2. THE REAL ESTATE: Real Estate shall be defined as the Property, all improvements, the fixtures and Personal Property included therein. Seller agrees to convey to Buyer or to Buyer's designated grantee, the Real Estate with the approximate lot size or acreage of _____ commonly known as:

_____

Address   City   State   Zip

_____

County Unit # (if applicable) Permanent Index Number(s) of Real Estate
If Condo/Coop/Townhome Parking Is Included: # of space(s) ____; identified
as Space(s) #_____; **(check type)** ☐ deeded space ☐ limited common
element ☐ assigned space.

3. FIXTURES AND PERSONAL PROPERTY: All of the fixtures and included
Personal Property are owned by Seller and to Seller's knowledge are in operating condition on the Date of Acceptance, unless otherwise stated herein. Seller
agrees to transfer to Buyer all fixtures, all heating, electrical, plumbing and well
systems together with the following items of Personal Property by Bill of Sale at
Closing:

[*Check or enumerate applicable items*]

_____ Refrigerator _____ Central Air Conditioning _____ Central Humidifier
_____ Light Fixtures, as they exist _____ Oven/Range/Stove _____ Window
Air Conditioners _____ Water Softener (owned) _____ Microwave _____
Built-in or _____ Ceiling Fan(s) _____ Sump Pumps _____ All Window
Treatments and Attached Shelving and Hardware _____ Dishwasher _____
Intercom System _____ Electronic or Media _____ Existing Storms & Air
Filter Screens _____ Garbage Disposal _____ TV Antenna System _____
Central Vac & Equipment _____ Washer _____ Fireplace Screens/Doors/
Grates _____ Trash Compactor _____ Satellite Dish _____ Outdoor Shed
_____ Security System (owned) _____ Fireplace Gas Logs _____ Garage
Door Opener with Transmitters _____ Invisible Fence System, Collars & Box
_____ Dryer _____ Planted Vegetation _____ Gas Grill _____ Attached
Gas _____ Outdoor Playsets _____ All Tacked Down Carpeting _____
Carbon Monoxide Detectors

Other items included:

_____

Other items NOT included:

Seller warrants to Buyer that all fixtures, systems and Personal Property included
in this Contract shall be in operating condition at Possession, except:

_____.

A system or item shall be deemed to be in operating condition if it performs the
function for which it is intended, regardless of age, and does not constitute a
threat to health or safety.

Home Warranty ☐ shall ☐ not be included at a Premium not to exceed $_____.

4. PURCHASE PRICE: Purchase Price of $_____ shall be paid
as follows: Initial earnest money of $_____ by ☐ check, ☐ cash
OR ☐ note due on _____, 20____ to be increased to a total of
$_____ by _____, 20____. The earnest money shall

be held by the [*check one*] ☐ Seller's Broker ☐ Buyer's Broker as "Escrowee", in trust for the mutual benefit of the Parties. The balance of the Purchase Price, as adjusted by prorations, shall be paid at Closing by wire transfer of funds, or by certified, cashier's, mortgage lender's or title company's check (provided that the title company's check is guaranteed by a licensed title insurance company).

5. CLOSING: Closing or escrow payout shall be on _____, 20_____ or at such time as mutually agreed by the Parties in writing. Closing shall take place at the escrow office of the title company (or its issuing agent) that will issue the Owner's Policy of Title Insurance, situated nearest the Real Estate or as shall be agreed mutually by the Parties.

6. POSSESSION: Unless otherwise provided in Paragraph 39, Seller shall deliver possession to Buyer at the time of Closing. Possession shall be deemed to have been delivered when Seller has vacated the Real Estate and delivered keys to the Real Estate to Buyer or to the office of the Seller's Broker.

7. STATUTORY DISCLOSURES: If applicable, prior to signing this Contract, Buyer [*check one*] ☐ has ☐ has not received a completed Illinois Residential Real Property Disclosure Report; [*check one*] ☐ has ☐ has not received the EPA Pamphlet, "Protect Your Family From Lead in Your Home"; [*check one*] ☐ has ☐ has not received a Lead-Based Paint Disclosure; [*check one*] ☐ has ☐ has not received the IEMA Pamphlet "Radon Testing Guidelines for Real Estate Transactions"; [*check one*] ☐ has ☐ has not received the Disclosure of Information on Radon Hazards.

8. PRORATIONS: Proratable items shall include, without limitation, rents and deposits (if any) from tenants; Special Service Area or Special Assessment Area tax for the year of Closing only; utilities, water and sewer; and Homeowner or Condominium Association fees (and Master/Umbrella Association fees, if applicable). Accumulated reserves of a Homeowner/Condominium Association(s) are not a proratable item. Seller represents that as of the Date of Acceptance Homeowner/Condominium Association(s) fees are $_____ per _____ (and, if applicable, Master/Umbrella Association fees are $_____ per _____). Seller agrees to pay prior to or at Closing any special assessments (by any association or governmental entity) confirmed prior to the Date of Acceptance. Installments due after the year of Closing for a Special Assessment Area or Special Service Area shall not be a proratable item and shall be payable by Buyer. The general Real Estate taxes shall be prorated as of the date of Closing based on _____% of the most recent ascertainable full year tax bill. All prorations shall be final as of Closing, except as provided in Paragraph 20. If the amount of the most recent ascertainable full year tax bill reflects a homeowner, senior citizen or other exemption, a senior freeze or senior deferral, then Seller has submitted or will submit in a timely manner all necessary documentation to the appropriate governmental entity, before or after closing, to preserve said exemption(s).

9. ATTORNEY REVIEW: Within five (5) Business Days after the Date of Acceptance, the attorneys for the respective Parties, by Notice, may:

(a) Approve this Contract; or

(b) Disapprove this Contract, which disapproval shall not be based solely upon the Purchase Price; or

(c) Propose modifications except for the Purchase Price. If within ten (10) Business Days after the Date of Acceptance written agreement is not reached by the Parties with respect to resolution of the proposed modifications, then either Party may terminate this Contract by serving Notice, whereupon this Contract shall be null and void; or

(d) Propose suggested changes to this Contract. If such suggestions are not agreed upon, neither Party may declare this Contract null and void and this Contract shall remain in full force and effect.

Unless otherwise specified, all Notices shall be deemed made pursuant to Paragraph 9(c). If Notice is not served within the time specified herein, the provisions of this paragraph shall be deemed waived by the Parties and this Contract shall remain in full force and effect.

10. PROFESSIONAL INSPECTIONS AND INSPECTION NOTICES: Buyer may conduct at Buyer's expense (unless otherwise provided by governmental regulations) a home, radon, environmental, lead-based paint and/or lead-based paint hazards (unless separately waived), and/or wood destroying insect infestation inspection of the Real Estate by one or more licensed or certified inspection service(s).

(a) Buyer agrees that minor repairs and routine maintenance items of the Real Estate do not constitute defects and are not a part of this contingency. **The fact that a functioning major component may be at the end of its useful life shall not render such component defective for purposes of this paragraph.** Buyer shall indemnify Seller and hold Seller harmless from and against any loss or damage caused by the acts or negligence of Buyer or any person performing any inspection. The home inspection shall cover only the major components of the Real Estate, including but not limited to central heating system(s), central cooling system(s), plumbing and well system, electrical system, roof, walls, windows, ceilings, floors, appliances and foundation. A major component shall be deemed to be in operating condition if it performs the function for which it is intended, regardless of age, and does not constitute a threat to health or safety. If radon mitigation is performed, Seller shall pay for any retest.

(b) Buyer shall serve Notice upon Seller or Seller's attorney of any defects disclosed by any inspection for which Buyer requests resolution by Seller, together with a copy of the pertinent pages of the inspection reports within five (5) Business Days (ten (10) calendar days for a lead-based paint and/or lead-based paint hazard inspection) after the Date of Acceptance. If within ten (10) Business Days after the Date of Acceptance written agreement is not reached by the Parties with respect to resolution of all inspection issues, then either Party may terminate this Contract by serving Notice to the other Party, whereupon this Contract shall be null and void.

(c) Notwithstanding anything to the contrary set forth above in this paragraph, in the event the inspection reveals that the condition of the Real Estate is unacceptable to Buyer and Buyer serves Notice to Seller within five (5) Business Days after the Date of Acceptance, this Contract shall be null and void.

(d) Failure of Buyer to conduct said inspection(s) and notify Seller within the time specified operates as a waiver of Buyer's right to terminate this Contract under this Paragraph 10 and this Contract shall remain in full force and effect.

11. MORTGAGE CONTINGENCY: This Contract is contingent upon Buyer obtaining a firm written mortgage commitment (except for matters of title and survey or matters totally within Buyer's control) on or before _____, 20____ for a [*check one*] ☐ fixed ☐ adjustable; [*check one*] ☐ conventional FHA/VA (if FHA/VA is chosen, complete Paragraph 35) ☐ other_____ loan of ____% of Purchase Price, plus private mortgage insurance (PMI), if required. The interest rate (initial rate, if applicable) shall not exceed ____% per annum, amortized over not less than _____ years. Buyer shall pay loan origination fee and/or discount points not to exceed ____% of the loan amount. Buyer shall pay the cost of application, usual and customary processing fees and closing costs charged by lender. (Complete Paragraph 33 if closing cost credits apply.) Buyer shall make written loan application within five (5) Business Days after the Date of Acceptance. **Failure to do so shall constitute an act of Default under this Contract. If Buyer, having applied for the loan specified above, is unable to obtain such loan commitment and serves Notice to Seller within the time specified, this Contract shall be null and void. If Notice of inability to obtain such loan commitment is not served within the time specified, Buyer shall be deemed to have waived this contingency and this Contract shall remain in full force and effect. Unless otherwise provided in Paragraph 31, this Contract shall not be contingent upon the sale and/or closing of Buyer's existing real estate. Buyer shall be deemed to have satisfied the financing conditions of this paragraph if Buyer obtains a loan commitment in accordance with the terms of this paragraph even though the loan is conditioned on the sale and/or closing of Buyer's existing real estate.** If Seller at Seller's option and expense, within thirty (30) days after Buyer's Notice, procures for Buyer such commitment or notifies Buyer that Seller will accept a purchase money mortgage upon the same terms, this Contract shall remain in full force and effect. In such event, Seller shall notify Buyer within five (5) Business Days after Buyer's Notice of Seller's election to provide or obtain such financing, and Buyer shall furnish to Seller or lender all requested information and shall sign all papers necessary to obtain the mortgage commitment and to close the loan.

12. HOMEOWNER INSURANCE: This Contract is contingent upon Buyer obtaining evidence of insurability for an Insurance Service Organization HO-3 or equivalent policy at standard premium rates within ten (10) Business Days after the Date of Acceptance. If Buyer is unable to obtain evidence of insurability and serves Notice with proof of same to Seller within the time specified, this Contract shall be null and void. If Notice is not served within the time specified, Buyer shall be deemed to have waived this contingency and this Contract shall remain in full force and effect.

13. FLOOD INSURANCE: Unless previously disclosed in the Illinois Residential Real Property Disclosure Report, Buyer shall have the option to declare this Contract null and void if the Real Estate is located in a special flood hazard area which requires Buyer to carry flood insurance. **If Notice of the option to declare this Contract null and void is not given to Seller within ten (10) Business Days after the Date of Acceptance or by the Mortgage Contingency deadline date described in Paragraph 11 (whichever is later), Buyer shall be deemed to have waived such option and this Contract shall remain in full force and effect.** Nothing herein shall be deemed to affect any rights afforded by the Residential Real Property Disclosure Act.

    14. CONDOMINIUM/COMMON INTEREST ASSOCIATIONS: (If applicable) The Parties agree that the terms contained in this paragraph, which may be contrary to other terms of this Contract, shall supersede any conflicting terms.

    (a) Title when conveyed shall be good and merchantable, subject to terms, provisions, covenants and conditions of the Declaration of Condominium/ Covenants, Conditions and Restrictions and all amendments; public and utility easements including any easements established by or implied from the Declaration of Condominium/Covenants, Conditions and Restrictions or amendments thereto; party wall rights and agreements; limitations and conditions imposed by the Condominium Property Act; installments due after the date of Closing of general assessments established pursuant to the Declaration of Condominium/ Covenants, Conditions and Restrictions.

    (b) Seller shall be responsible for payment of all regular assessments due and levied prior to Closing and for all special assessments confirmed prior to the Date of Acceptance.

    (c) Buyer has, within five (5) Business Days from the Date of Acceptance, the right to demand from Seller items as stipulated by the Illinois Condominium Property Act, if applicable, and Seller shall diligently apply for same. This Contract is subject to the condition that Seller be able to procure and provide to Buyer, a release or waiver of any option of first refusal or other pre-emptive rights of purchase created by the Declaration of Condominium/Covenants, Conditions and Restrictions within the time established by the Declaration of Condominium/ Covenants, Conditions and Restrictions. In the event the Condominium Association requires the personal appearance of Buyer and/or additional documentation, Buyer agrees to comply with same.

    (d) In the event the documents and information provided by Seller to Buyer disclose that the existing improvements are in violation of existing rules, regulations or other restrictions or that the terms and conditions contained within the documents would unreasonably restrict Buyer's use of the premises or would result in financial obligations unacceptable to Buyer in connection with owning the Real Estate, then Buyer may declare this Contract null and void by giving Seller Notice within five (5) Business Days after the receipt of the documents and information required by Paragraph 14(c), listing those deficiencies which are unacceptable to Buyer. If Notice is not served within the time specified, Buyer shall be deemed to have waived this contingency, and this Contract shall remain in full force and effect.

    (e) Seller shall not be obligated to provide a condominium survey.

(f) Seller shall provide a certificate of insurance showing Buyer and Buyer's mortgagee, if any, as an insured.

15. THE DEED: Seller shall convey or cause to be conveyed to Buyer or Buyer's designated grantee good and merchantable title to the Real Estate by recordable general Warranty Deed, with release of homestead rights, (or the appropriate deed if title is in trust or in an estate), and with real estate transfer stamps to be paid by Seller (unless otherwise designated by local ordinance). Title when conveyed will be good and merchantable, subject only to: general real estate taxes not due and payable at the time of Closing; covenants, conditions and restrictions of record; and building lines and easements, if any, provided they do not interfere with the current use and enjoyment of the Real Estate.

16. TITLE: At Seller's expense, Seller will deliver or cause to be delivered to Buyer or Buyer's attorney within customary time limitations and sufficiently in advance of Closing, as evidence of title in Seller or Grantor, a title commitment for an ALTA title insurance policy in the amount of the Purchase Price with extended coverage by a title company licensed to operate in the State of Illinois, issued on or subsequent to the Date of Acceptance, subject only to items listed in Paragraph 15. The requirement to provide extended coverage shall not apply if the Real Estate is vacant land. The commitment for title insurance furnished by Seller will be conclusive evidence of good and merchantable title as therein shown, subject only to the exceptions therein stated. If the title commitment discloses any unpermitted exceptions or if the Plat of Survey shows any encroachments or other survey matters that are not acceptable to Buyer, then Seller shall have said exceptions, survey matters or encroachments removed, or have the title insurer commit to either insure against loss or damage that may result from such exceptions or survey matters or insure against any court-ordered removal of the encroachments. If Seller fails to have such exceptions waived or insured over prior to Closing, Buyer may elect to take the title as it then is with the right to deduct from the Purchase Price prior encumbrances of a definite or ascertainable amount. Seller shall furnish Buyer at Closing an Affidavit of Title covering the date of Closing, and shall sign any other customary forms required for issuance of an ALTA Insurance Policy.

17. PLAT OF SURVEY: Not less than one (1) Business Day prior to Closing, except where the Real Estate is a condominium (see Paragraph 14) Seller shall, at Seller's expense, furnish to Buyer or Buyer's attorney a Plat of Survey that conforms to the current Minimum Standards of Practice for boundary surveys, is dated not more than six (6) months prior to the date of Closing, and is prepared by a professional land surveyor licensed to practice land surveying under the laws of the State of Illinois. The Plat of Survey shall show visible evidence of improvements, rights of way, easements, use and measurements of all parcel lines. The land surveyor shall set monuments or witness corners at all accessible corners of the land. All such corners shall also be visibly staked or flagged. The Plat of Survey shall include the following statement placed near the professional land surveyor seal and signature: "This professional service conforms to the current Illinois Minimum Standards for a boundary survey." A Mortgage Inspection, as defined, is not a boundary survey and is not acceptable.

18. ESCROW CLOSING: At the election of either Party, not less than five (5) Business Days prior to Closing, this sale shall be closed through an escrow with the lending institution or the title company in accordance with the provisions of the usual form of Deed and Money Escrow Agreement, as agreed upon between the Parties, with provisions inserted in the Escrow Agreement as may be required to conform with this Contract. The cost of the escrow shall be paid by the Party requesting the escrow. If this transaction is a cash purchase (no mortgage is secured by Buyer), the Parties shall share the title company escrow closing fee equally.

19. DAMAGE TO REAL ESTATE OR CONDEMNATION PRIOR TO CLOSING: If prior to delivery of the deed the Real Estate shall be destroyed or materially damaged by fire or other casualty, or the Real Estate is taken by condemnation, then Buyer shall have the option of either terminating this Contract (and receiving a refund of earnest money) or accepting the Real Estate as damaged or destroyed, together with the proceeds of the condemnation award or any insurance payable as a result of the destruction or damage, which gross proceeds Seller agrees to assign to Buyer and deliver to Buyer at Closing. Seller shall not be obligated to repair or replace damaged improvements. The provisions of the Uniform Vendor and Purchaser Risk Act of the State of Illinois shall be applicable to this Contract, except as modified by this paragraph.

20. REAL ESTATE TAX ESCROW: In the event the Real Estate is improved, but has not been previously taxed for the entire year as currently improved, the sum of three percent (3%) of the Purchase Price shall be deposited in escrow with the title company with the cost of the escrow to be divided equally by Buyer and Seller and paid at Closing. When the exact amount of the taxes to be prorated under this Contract can be ascertained, the taxes shall be prorated by Seller's attorney at the request of either Party and Seller's share of such tax liability after proration shall be paid to Buyer from the escrow funds and the balance, if any, shall be paid to Seller. If Seller's obligation after such proration exceeds the amount of the escrow funds, Seller agrees to pay such excess promptly upon demand.

21. SELLER REPRESENTATIONS: Seller represents that with respect to the Real Estate Seller has no knowledge of nor has Seller received written notice from any governmental body regarding:

(a) zoning, building, fire or health code violations that have not been corrected;

(b) any pending rezoning;

(c) boundary line disputes;

(d) any pending condemnation or Eminent Domain proceeding;

(e) easements or claims of easements not shown on the public records;

(f) any hazardous waste on the Real Estate;

(g) any improvements to the Real Estate for which the required permits were not obtained;

(h) any improvements to the Real Estate which are not included in full in the determination of the most recent tax assessment; or

(i) any improvements to the Real Estate which are eligible for the home improvement tax exemption.

Seller further represents that:

1. There [*check one*] ☐ is ☐ is not a pending or unconfirmed special assessment affecting the Real Estate by any association or governmental entity payable by Buyer after date of Closing.

2. The Real Estate [*check one*] ☐ is ☐ is not located within a Special Assessment Area or Special Service Area, payments for which will not be the obligation of Seller after the year in which the Closing occurs.

If any of the representations contained herein regarding a Special Assessment Area or Special Service Area are unacceptable to Buyer, Buyer shall have the option to declare this Contract null and void. If Notice of the option to declare this Contract null and void is not given to Seller within ten (10) Business Days after the Date of Acceptance or by the Mortgage Contingency deadline date described in Paragraph 11 (whichever is later), Buyer shall be deemed to have waived such option and this Contract shall remain in full force and effect. Seller's representations contained in this paragraph shall survive the Closing.

22. CONDITION OF REAL ESTATE AND INSPECTION: Seller agrees to leave the Real Estate in broom clean condition. All refuse and personal property that is not to be conveyed to Buyer shall be removed from the Real Estate at Seller's expense prior to delivery of Possession. Buyer shall have the right to inspect the Real Estate, fixtures and included Personal Property prior to Possession to verify that the Real Estate, improvements and included Personal Property are in substantially the same condition as of the Date of Acceptance, normal wear and tear excepted.

23. MUNICIPAL ORDINANCE, TRANSFER TAX, AND GOVERNMENTAL COMPLIANCE:

(a) Parties are cautioned that the Real Estate may be situated in a municipality that has adopted a pre-closing inspection requirement, municipal Transfer Tax or other similar ordinances. Transfer taxes required by municipal ordinance shall be paid by the party designated in such ordinance.

(b) Parties agree to comply with the reporting requirements of the applicable sections of the Internal Revenue Code and the Real Estate Settlement Procedures Act of 1974, as amended.

24. BUSINESS DAYS/HOURS: Business Days are defined as Monday through Friday, excluding Federal holidays. Business Hours are defined as 8:00 A.M. to 6:00 P.M. Chicago time.

25. FACSIMILE OR DIGITAL SIGNATURES: Facsimile or digital signatures shall be sufficient for purposes of executing, negotiating, and finalizing this Contract.

26. DIRECTION TO ESCROWEE: In every instance where this Contract shall be deemed null and void or if this Contract may be terminated by either Party, the following shall be deemed incorporated: "and earnest money refunded to Buyer upon written direction of the Parties to Escrowee or upon entry of an order by a court of competent jurisdiction." There shall be no disbursement of earnest money unless Escrowee has been provided written direction from Seller and Buyer. Absent a direction relative to the disbursement of earnest money within a reasonable period of time, Escrowee may deposit funds with the Clerk of the Circuit Court by the filing of an action in the nature of Interpleader. Escrowee shall be reimbursed from the earnest money for all costs, including reasonable attorney fees, related to the filing of the Interpleader action. Seller and Buyer shall indemnify and hold Escrowee harmless from any and all conflicting claims and demands arising under this paragraph.

. . .

28. PERFORMANCE: Time is of the essence of this Contract. In any action with respect to this Contract, the Parties are free to pursue any legal remedies at law or in equity and the prevailing Party in litigation shall be entitled to collect reasonable attorney fees and costs from the non-Prevailing Party as ordered by a court of competent jurisdiction.

29. CHOICE OF LAW/GOOD FAITH: All terms and provisions of this Contract including but not limited to the Attorney Review and Professional Inspection Paragraphs shall be governed by the laws of the State of Illinois and are subject to the covenant of good faith and fair dealing implied in all Illinois contracts.

30. OTHER PROVISIONS: This Contract is also subject to those OPTIONAL PROVISIONS initialed by the Parties and the following attachments, if any:

_____.

OPTIONAL PROVISIONS (Applicable ONLY if initialed by all Parties)

31. SALE OF BUYER'S REAL ESTATE:

[Initials]

(A) REPRESENTATIONS ABOUT BUYER'S REAL ESTATE: Buyer represents to Seller as follows:

(1) Buyer owns real estate commonly known as (address):

_____.

(2) Buyer [*check one*] ☐ has ☐ has not entered into a contract to sell said real estate.

If Buyer has entered into a contract to sell said real estate, that contract:

(a) [*check one*] ☐ is ☐ is not subject to a mortgage contingency.

(b) [*check one*] ☐ is ☐ is not subject to a real estate sale contingency.

(c) [*check one*] ☐ is ☐ is not subject to a real estate closing contingency.

(3) Buyer [*check one*] ☐ has ☐ has not listed said real estate for sale with a licensed real estate broker and in a local multiple listing service.

(4) If Buyer's real estate is not listed for sale with a licensed real estate broker and in a local multiple listing service, Buyer [*check one*]

(a) ☐ Shall list said real estate for sale with a licensed real estate broker who will place it in a local multiple listing service within five (5) Business Days after the Date of Acceptance. [For information only] Broker: _____

Broker's Address: _____ Phone: _____.

(b) ☐ Does not intend to list said real estate for sale.

(B) CONTINGENCIES BASED UPON SALE AND/OR CLOSE OF BUYER'S REAL ESTATE:

(1)   This Contract is contingent upon Buyer having entered into a contract for the sale of Buyer's real estate that is in full force and effect as of _____, 20___. Such contract should provide for a closing date not later than the Closing Date set forth in this contract. **If Notice is served on or before the date set forth in this subparagraph that Buyer has not procured a contract for the sale of Buyer's real estate, this Contract shall be null and void. If notice that Buyer has not procured a contract for the sale of Buyer's real estate is not served on or before the close of business on the date set forth in this subparagraph, Buyer shall be deemed to have waived all contingencies contained in this Paragraph 31, and this Contract shall remain in full force and effect.** (If this paragraph is used, then the following paragraph **must** be completed.)

(2)   In the event Buyer has entered into a contract for the sale of Buyer's real estate as set forth in Paragraph 31(B)(1) and that contract is in full force and effect, or has entered into a contract for the sale of Buyer's real estate prior to the execution of this Contract, this Contract is contingent upon Buyer closing the sale of Buyer's real estate on or before _____, 20____. **If Notice that Buyer has not closed the sale of Buyer's real estate is served before the close of business on the next Business Day after the date set forth in the preceding sentence, this Contract shall be null and void. If Notice is not served as described in the preceding sentence, Buyer shall be deemed to have waived all contingencies contained in this Paragraph 31, and this Contract shall remain in full force and effect.**

(3)   If the contract for the sale of Buyer's real estate is terminated for any reason after the date set forth in Paragraph 31(B)(1) (or after the date of this Contract if no date is set forth in Paragraph 31(B)(1)), Buyer shall, within three (3) Business Days of such termination, notify Seller of said termination. **Unless Buyer, as part of said Notice, waives all contingencies in Paragraph 31 and complies with Paragraph 31(D), this Contract shall be null and void as of the date of Notice. If Notice as required by this subparagraph is not served within the time specified, Buyer shall be in default under the terms of this Contract.**

(C) SELLER'S RIGHT TO CONTINUE TO OFFER REAL ESTATE FOR SALE: During the time of this contingency, Seller has the right to continue to show the Real Estate and offer it for sale subject to the following:

(1) If Seller accepts another bona fide offer to purchase the Real Estate while the contingencies expressed in Paragraph 31(B) are in effect, Seller shall notify Buyer in writing of same. Buyer shall then have _____ hours after Seller gives such Notice to waive the contingencies set forth in Paragraph 31(B), subject to Paragraph 31(D).

(2) Seller's Notice to Buyer (commonly referred to as a "kick-out" Notice) shall be in writing and shall be served on Buyer, not Buyer's attorney or Buyer's real estate agent. Courtesy copies of such "kick-out" Notice should be sent to Buyer's attorney and Buyer's real estate agent, if known. Failure to provide such courtesy copies shall not render Notice invalid. Notice to any one of a multiple-person

Buyer shall be sufficient Notice to all Buyers. Notice for the purpose of this sub-paragraph only shall be served upon Buyer in the following manner:

(a) By personal delivery effective at the time and date of personal delivery; or

(b) By mailing to the addresses recited herein for Buyer by regular mail and by certified mail. Notice shall be effective at 10:00 A.M. on the morning of the second day following deposit of Notice in the U.S. Mail; or

(c) By commercial overnight delivery (e.g., FedEx). Notice shall be effective upon delivery or at 4:00 P.M. Chicago time on the next delivery day following deposit with the overnight delivery company, whichever first occurs.

(3) If Buyer complies with the provisions of Paragraph 31(D) then this Contract shall remain in full force and effect.

(4) If the contingencies set forth in Paragraph 31(B) are NOT waived in writing within said time period by Buyer, this Contract shall be null and void.

(5) Except as provided in Paragraph 31(C)(2) above, all Notices shall be made in the manner provided by Paragraph 27 of this Contract.

(6) Buyer waives any ethical objection to the delivery of Notice under this paragraph by Seller's attorney or representative.

(D) WAIVER OF PARAGRAPH 31 CONTINGENCIES: Buyer shall be deemed to have waived the contingencies in Paragraph 31(B) when Buyer has delivered written waiver and deposited with the Escrowee additional earnest money in the amount of $_____ in the form of a cashier's or certified check within the time specified. **If Buyer fails to deposit the additional earnest money within the time specified, the waiver shall be deemed ineffective and this Contract shall be null and void.**

(E) BUYER COOPERATION REQUIRED: Buyer authorizes Seller or Seller's agent to verify representations contained in Paragraph 31 at any time, and Buyer agrees to cooperate in providing relevant information.

32. CANCELLATION OF PRIOR REAL ESTATE CONTRACT: In the event either Party has entered into a prior real estate contract, this Contract shall be subject to written cancellation of the prior contract on or before _____, 20____. **In the event the prior contract is not cancelled within the time specified, this Contract shall be null and void. Seller's notice to the purchaser under the prior contract should not be served until after Attorney Review and Professional Inspections provisions of this Contract have expired, been satisfied or waived.**

33. CREDIT AT CLOSING: Provided Buyer's lender permits such credit to show on the HUD-1 Settlement Statement, **and if not, such lesser amount as the lender permits,** Seller agrees to credit to Buyer at Closing $_____ to be applied to prepaid expenses, closing costs or both.

34. INTEREST BEARING ACCOUNT: Earnest money (with a completed W-9 and other required forms), shall be held in a federally insured interest bearing account at a financial institution designated by Escrowee. All interest earned on the earnest money shall accrue to the benefit of and be paid to Buyer. **Buyer shall be responsible for any administrative fee (not to exceed $100) charged for setting up the account.** In anticipation of Closing, the Parties direct Escrowee to close the account no sooner than ten (10) Business Days prior to the anticipated Closing date.

35. VA OR FHA FINANCING: If Buyer is seeking VA or FHA financing, this provision shall be applicable: **Required FHA or VA amendments and disclosures shall be attached to this Contract**. If VA, the Funding Fee, or if FHA, the Mortgage Insurance Premium (MIP) shall be paid by Buyer and [*check one*] ☐ shall ☐ shall not be added to the mortgage loan amount.

36. INTERIM FINANCING: This Contract is contingent upon Buyer obtaining a written commitment for interim financing on or before _____, 20____ in the amount of $_____. **If Buyer is unable to secure the interim financing commitment and gives Notice to Seller within the time specified, this Contract shall be null and void. If Notice is not served within the time specified, this provision shall be deemed waived by the Parties and this Contract shall remain in full force and effect.**

37. WELL AND/OR SEPTIC/SANITARY INSPECTIONS: Seller shall obtain at Seller's expense a well water test stating that the well delivers not less than five (5) gallons of water per minute and including a bacteria and nitrate (and lead test for FHA loans) and/or a septic report from the applicable County Health Department, a Licensed Environmental Health Practitioner, or a licensed well and septic inspector, each dated not more than ninety (90) days prior to Closing, stating that the well and water supply and the private sanitary system are in proper operating condition with no defects noted. Seller shall remedy any defect or deficiency disclosed by said report(s) prior to Closing, provided that if the cost of remedying a defect or deficiency and the cost of landscaping together exceed $3,000.00, and if the Parties cannot reach agreement regarding payment of such additional cost, this Contract may be terminated by either Party. Additional testing recommended by the report shall be obtained at Seller's expense. If the report recommends additional testing after Closing, the Parties shall have the option of establishing an escrow with a mutual cost allocation for necessary repairs or replacements, or either Party may terminate this Contract prior to Closing. Seller shall deliver a copy of such evaluation(s) to Buyer not less than one (1) Business Day prior to Closing.

38. WOOD DESTROYING INFESTATION: Notwithstanding the provisions of Paragraph 10, within ten (10) Business Days after the Date of Acceptance, Seller at Seller's expense shall deliver to Buyer a written report, dated not more than six (6) months prior to the date of Closing, by a licensed inspector certified by the appropriate state regulatory authority in the subcategory of termites, stating that there is no visible evidence of active infestation by termites or other wood destroying insects. Unless otherwise agreed between the Parties, if the report discloses evidence of active infestation or structural damage, Buyer has the option within five (5) Business Days of receipt of the report to proceed with the purchase or declare this Contract null and void.

39. POST-CLOSING POSSESSION: Possession shall be delivered no later than 11:59 P.M. on the date that is _____ days after the date of Closing ("the Possession Date"). Seller shall be responsible for all utilities, contents and liability insurance, and home maintenance expenses until delivery of possession. Seller shall deposit in escrow at Closing with _____, [*check one*] ☐ one percent (1%) of the Purchase Price or ☐ the sum of $_____ to be paid by Escrowee as follows:

(a) The sum of $_____ per day for use and occupancy from and including the day after Closing to and including the day of delivery of Possession, if on or before the Possession Date;

(b) The amount per day equal to three (3) times the daily amount set forth herein shall be paid for each day after the Possession Date specified in this paragraph that Seller remains in possession of the Real Estate; and

(c) The balance, if any, to Seller after delivery of Possession and provided that the terms of Paragraph 22 have been satisfied. Seller's liability under this paragraph shall not be limited to the amount of the possession escrow deposit referred to above. Nothing herein shall be deemed to create a Landlord/Tenant relationship between the Parties.

40. "AS IS" CONDITION: This Contract is for the sale and purchase of the Real Estate in its "As Is" condition as of the Date of Offer. Buyer acknowledges that no representations, warranties or guarantees with respect to the condition of the Real Estate have been made by Seller or Seller's Designated Agent other than those known defects, if any, disclosed by Seller. Buyer may conduct an inspection at Buyer's expense. **In that event, Seller shall make the Real Estate available to Buyer's inspector at reasonable times. Buyer shall indemnify Seller and hold Seller harmless from and against any loss or damage caused by the acts or negligence of Buyer or any person performing any inspection. In the event the inspection reveals that the condition of the Real Estate is unacceptable to Buyer and Buyer so notifies Seller within five (5) Business Days after the Date of Acceptance, this Contract shall be null and void. Failure of Buyer to notify Seller or to conduct said inspection operates as a waiver of Buyer's right to terminate this Contract under this paragraph and this Contract shall remain in full force and effect.** Buyer acknowledges that the provisions of Paragraph 10 and the warranty provisions of Paragraph 3 do not apply to this Contract.

41. CONFIRMATION OF DUAL AGENCY: The Parties confirm that they have previously consented to _____ (Licensee) acting as a Dual Agent in providing brokerage services on their behalf and specifically consent to Licensee acting as a Dual Agent with regard to the transaction referred to in this Contract.

42. SPECIFIED PARTY APPROVAL: This Contract is contingent upon the approval of the Real Estate by _____ Buyer's Specified Party, within five (5) Business Days after the Date of Acceptance. In the event Buyer's Specified Party does not approve of the Real Estate and Notice is given to Seller within the time specified, this Contract shall be null and void. If Notice is not served within the time specified, this provision shall be deemed waived by the Parties and this Contract shall remain in full force and effect.

43. MISCELLANEOUS PROVISIONS: Buyer's and Seller's obligations are contingent upon the Parties entering into a separate written agreement consistent with the terms and conditions set forth herein, and with such additional terms as either Party may deem necessary, providing for one or more of the following: [*check applicable boxes*]

☐ Articles of Agreement for Deed or Purchase Money Mortgage ☐ Assumption of Seller's Mortgage ☐ Commercial/Investment ☐ Cooperative Apartment ☐ New Construction ☐ Short Sale ☐ Tax-Deferred Exchange ☐ Vacant Land.

QUESTIONS AND PROBLEMS

1. Read the Multi-Board Residential Real Estate Contract carefully. The contract does not disclose the seller's marital status. Why might the buyer want to know this?

The contract does not indicate whether the buyers intend to take title as joint tenants or tenants in common or tenants by the entireties. At the time the contract is executed, the buyers have equitable title and can enforce the contract by specific performance. If the seller tries to back out of the contract, and one of the buyers dies and the surviving buyer sues, would it matter what form of title the buyers intended to take?

Paragraph 15 of the Multi-Board Residential Real Estate Contract states that the seller shall convey "good and merchantable title" to the property. This is the most important phrase in the entire purchase agreement. The usual contract of sale requires the seller to furnish "marketable title." Is "good and merchantable title" satisfied by a title based on adverse possession?

Another question about Paragraph 15. Suppose there is a recorded covenant restricting the land to a house of Georgian style or, if it is a vacant lot, a recorded easement cutting diagonally across the property. Is the buyer bound by the contract?

2. *A* wants to buy a house in a new development from the developer. The house is in the course of construction. The developer offers a standard form contract with this provision:

> The house will be completed substantially similar to a model house [the model house being identified]. But the builder may make substitution of material whenever the builder shall find it necessary or expedient and may make changes in construction the seller may find necessary.
>
> The contract is conditioned on the ability of the seller to complete construction at current prices of material and labor. Otherwise, the seller may return the down payment and cancel the contract.
>
> If completion of construction is delayed because of inclement weather, strikes, or for other reasons, the seller's time to perform is extended for a period commensurate with such delay.

Would you advise *A* to accept such a provision? Remember that a principle of modern contract law is that each party has an implied duty of good faith and fair dealing. See Milton R. Friedman, 1 Friedman on Contracts and Conveyances of Real Property §1.7 (James Charles Smith ed. 7th ed. 2005).

B. Real Estate Brokers

Real estate brokers are often hired by sellers of property to attract prospective buyers and facilitate real estate transactions. Brokers do this in a number of ways: by marketing a seller's property, listing residential properties on a multiple listing service (MLS), negotiating purchase agreements, serving as an intermediary between buyers and sellers, participating in physical inspections of the property, assisting in arranging financing, and engaging in many other essential activities. Residential brokers are licensed by the state and typically receive a commission, usually ranging from 5 to 6 percent of the actual purchase price, as compensation for their services.

Most sellers enlist brokers to help sell their property. In a listing agreement, the seller authorizes the broker to locate a buyer on the seller's behalf. Traditionally, only sellers hired brokers, but recent decades have seen an interesting development: the increased use of buyers' brokers.

Licari v. Blackwelder

Appellate Court of Connecticut, 1988
539 A.2d 609

BIELUCH, J. This is an appeal by the defendants from the judgment of the trial court awarding damages to the plaintiffs for breach of the defendants' duty as real estate brokers to find a buyer for the plaintiffs' property at the best possible price, and for acting improperly in dealing for themselves to the financial loss of the plaintiffs. The defendants claim that certain of the court's factual findings were not substantiated by sufficient evidence, and that some of the court's conclusions were not only unsupported by the facts of the case, but also were irrelevant to the cause of action brought by the plaintiffs and therefore were not issues properly before the court. Our review of the transcript and record in this case reveals that the court had before it sufficient evidence on which to base its findings, and that the court's conclusions were fully supported by the facts and the law and were relevant to the issues presented. We therefore find no error.

The trial court found the following facts. The six plaintiffs are brothers and sisters who inherited from their parents the family home and property in question located in Westport. The plaintiffs, whom the court found to be "unsophisticated lay people with no extensive dealings in real estate," decided to sell the property in 1978. The plaintiffs had no real knowledge as to the actual or potential value of their inherited real estate, which was located in a neighborhood of mixed residential and commercial properties at a time of changing property values. Upon the recommendation of a neighbor, the plaintiffs contacted Robert Schwartz, a Norwalk real estate broker, for guidance and assistance in the sale of their property.

Schwartz consulted with the real estate agency of the defendants Donald Blackwelder and Hannah Opert, Westport brokers experienced as to the marketing and values of property in the area of the plaintiffs' home. The defendants and Schwartz discussed several prospective clients generated by the defendants who might be interested in various listings held by Schwartz. The defendants and Schwartz also agreed to a "co-broke arrangement" under which they would share the real estate listings and divide the commissions evenly if one of the defendants' prospective clients purchased real estate listed by Schwartz. Thereafter, Opert asked Schwartz to secure a listing on the plaintiffs' property so that it could be shown to a prospective buyer. On October 18, 1978, Schwartz obtained an exclusive twenty-four hour right to sell the plaintiffs' real estate at a price of $125,000, and the property was immediately shown to the defendants' prospective buyer by a sales agent employed by Schwartz.

Within the twenty-four hour listing period obtained by Schwartz, the defendants made their own offer of $115,000 for the plaintiffs' property, which was accepted by the plaintiffs. The defendants did not negotiate on behalf of or for the plaintiffs with the potential buyer secured by them, and did not allow for a reasonable period of time to expire for such negotiations before they made their own personal offer. The defendants also did not disclose to the plaintiffs their understanding of the potential value that the plaintiffs' property might have to other buyers. The plaintiffs, therefore, believed that they had sold their property at its true market value. On December 29, 1978, the plaintiffs transferred title to the premises to the defendants upon payment of $115,000 as follows: cash in the amount of $11,500 and a purchase money mortgage in the amount of $103,500 from the purchasers.

The plaintiffs were led to believe that the defendants would occupy and use the property. The defendants neither took possession nor contracted for any improvements to the property. Instead, immediately upon signing the contract to buy the plaintiffs' property for $115,000, the defendant Opert contracted on behalf of her partnership to sell the home to another buyer for the price of $160,000. This potential buyer, a neighbor of the plaintiffs, was previously known by them to be interested in the property, but the plaintiffs had instructed Schwartz not to contact him. Title from the defendants passed to this buyer on January 4, 1979, six days after its purchase from the plaintiffs, for $160,000, a gain to the defendants of $45,000 on their cash investment of $11,500. Their purchase money mortgage held by the plaintiffs for six days was paid and released at the second title transfer.

The plaintiffs' revised complaint in two counts claimed first, that the defendants breached their duty to the plaintiffs by withholding from them information of other negotiations with potential buyers for the purchase of the plaintiffs' property at a higher price, and second, that the defendants intentionally misrepresented the identities of the serious prospective buyers in order to mislead the plaintiffs into selling the property to the defendants at a lower price.

The court, from the testimony and exhibits offered during the trial, found that "the more credible and weightier evidence support[ed] an ultimate fact conclusion that the defendants were obligated to act on behalf of the best interest of the plaintiffs." This obligation, the court concluded, "imposed upon the defendants the duty to find a buyer for the property at the best price to the plaintiffs based upon the defendants' knowledge, advice and information concerning all material facts affecting the property in question." The court also found that the defendants not only breached a duty they owed to their own prospective client, but that "they also acted incorrectly in dealing for themselves at the expense of the plaintiffs." The defendants' obligation to the plaintiffs, the court held, was the result of the defendants' relationship with Schwartz, the listing broker with whom they had an agreement "to split Mr. Schwartz's commission on the sale to the defendants." Although it found that the plaintiffs had not proven any actual fraud, the court did find that the defendants' failure to use "reasonable efforts on behalf of the plaintiffs," and their own personal offer without disclosure of material facts affecting the plaintiffs' property rendered the defendants' "clear profit" of $45,000 "unconscionable."

The defendants appeal from the judgment rendered in favor of the plaintiffs awarding $45,000 plus legal interest from January 4, 1979, with taxable costs. . . .

The defendants . . . maintain that the court erred in its findings as to the manner in which they breached their duty to the plaintiffs. Specifically, the defendants argue that because the grounds for the plaintiffs' complaint were limited to allegations that the defendants breached a duty to disclose prior negotiations and offers on the plaintiffs' property, and that the defendants had misrepresented the identities of other potential buyers in order to induce the plaintiffs to sell to them, the court's findings went beyond these specific allegations. We do not agree.

The facts found by the court were sufficient to support its conclusion that the defendants had breached a duty owed to the plaintiffs, and that they had intentionally misrepresented certain facts to induce the plaintiffs to sell their property to them. Once the court had made these requisite threshold findings of fact, the law of this state and general principles of law support its conclusions based on these findings, contrary to the assertion of the defendants.

A real estate broker is a fiduciary. Kurtz v. Farrington, 104 Conn. 257, 269, 132 A.540 (1926). As such, he is required to exercise fidelity and good faith, and "cannot put himself in a position antagonistic to his principal's interest"; Ritch v. Robertson, 93 Conn. 459, 463, 106 A. 509 (1919); by fraudulent conduct, acting adversely to his client's interests, or by failing to communicate information he may possess or acquire which is or may be material to his principal's advantage. A real estate broker acting as a subagent with the express permission of another broker who has the listing of the property to be sold is under the same duty as the primary broker to act in the utmost good faith. Robertson v. Chapman, 152 U.S. 673 (1893); see 12 Am. Jur. 2d 837-38, Brokers §84.

This rule requiring a broker, or his subagent, to act with the utmost good faith towards his principal places him under a legal obligation to make a full, fair and prompt disclosure to his employer of all facts within his knowledge which are, or may be material to the matter in connection with which he is employed, which might affect his principal's rights and interests, or his action in relation to the subject matter of the employment, or which in any way pertains to the discharge of the agency which the broker has undertaken. Upon hearing that a more advantageous sale or exchange can be made, the facts concerning which are unknown to the principal, the broker has the duty to communicate these facts to the principal before making the sale. A failure to do so renders the broker liable to the principal for whatever loss the latter may suffer as a consequence thereof and precludes recovery of a commission for his services. 12 Am. Jur. 2d 842, Brokers §89.

Our state has codified these principles of law in its real estate licensing law; General Statutes §§20-311 through 20-329bb; and in the regulations it has promulgated concerning the conduct of real estate brokers and salespersons. Regs., Conn. State Agencies §§20-328-1 through 20-328-18. Section 20-320 of the General Statutes provides for the suspension or revocation of a real estate license, as well as the levy of a fine, where a broker or salesperson has violated the code of conduct generally set out in the statute. Included in the proscribed conduct are the following: "(1) Making any material misrepresentation; (2) making any false promise of a character likely to influence, persuade or induce; (3) acting for more than one party in a transaction without the knowledge of all parties for whom he acts . . . [and] (11) any act or conduct which constitutes dishonest, fraudulent or improper dealings."

The trial court did not err in finding that the essential claims of breach of duty and intentional misrepresentation set out in the plaintiffs' complaint were proven by the facts presented, nor in finding that the conduct of the defendants entitled the plaintiffs to an award of damages. The defendants' conduct fell within the proscriptions of the general principles of law regarding the fiduciary relationship of a broker to his principal, as well as of the code of conduct required by the law of this state in General Statutes §20-320.

There is no error.

NOTES AND PROBLEM

1. *Brokers' duties in the traditional brokerage arrangement.* In the traditional regime, real estate brokers represent sellers; this is the case as to listing brokers, who contract with the seller to sell the property, and selling brokers, who introduce the buyer to the seller's property. Thomas J. Miceli et al., Restructuring Agency Relationships in the Real Estate Brokerage Industry: An Economic Analysis, 20 J. Real Est. Res. 31, 32-33 (2000) (hereinafter Miceli et al., Restructuring Agency Relationships). By entering into a listing contract with the listing broker, the seller empowers the broker to serve as the seller's agent in selling the property. Separate from listing brokers, selling brokers have a more indirect relationship with the seller, and receive their compensation by splitting the listing broker's commission. Commonly a prospective buyer initiates the relationship with a selling broker, who then introduces the buyer to sellers and to listing brokers. Ronald B. Brown et al., Real Estate Brokerage: Recent Changes in Relationships and a

Proposed Cure, 29 Creighton L. Rev. 25, 35 (1995); Ronald B. Brown & Joseph M. Grohman, Real Estate Brokers: Shouldering New Burdens, 11 Prob. & Prop. 14, 14-15 (1997).

Selling brokers often work with prospective buyers over long periods of time and develop personal relationships with them. This is probably why, according to one survey, about three-fourths of buyers believed that the selling broker they had been working with was representing them and not the seller. See U.S. Federal Trade Commission, The Residential Real Estate Brokerage Industry: A Staff Report by the Los Angeles Regional Office 69 (1983). In traditional brokerage relationships, however, a listing broker's sole duties owe to the seller, and so too for a selling broker, whose legal relationship is that of a subagent.

As discussed in the *Licari* case, brokers owe their principals certain fiduciary duties and are expected to adhere to high ethical and professional standards. While brokers have to deal fairly with both buyers and sellers, they must work entirely on behalf of their principals (in this case, sellers). Specifically, brokers owe their principals a "fiduciary duty to act loyally for the principal's benefit in all matters connected with the agency relationship." Restatement (Third) of Agency §8.01 (2006). Brokers' actions cannot diverge from their clients' interests or expectations. Further, part of a broker's duty is to follow the principal's directives. Sellers normally want to sell their property for the highest price the market will bear, so the duties of listing and selling brokers, in particular the duty of loyalty and good faith, include an obligation to maximize the sale price. Selling brokers even have the duty to report to the seller any information that the buyer shares with the selling broker. Brokers who breach the duty of loyalty and good faith risk losing their broker's license and risk financial liability as well.

The central problem in the traditional residential brokerage arrangement derives from subagency. Since the listing and selling broker are both the seller's agents, the buyer lacks representation in the deal. The subagency relationship can be misleading because, as mentioned above, buyers often mistakenly believe that the selling broker is working on the buyer's behalf. Buyers can become disillusioned with the process when they discover that the selling broker has divulged the buyer's private conversations to the seller, because the selling broker's duties were contrary to what the buyer expected.

So here is a problem. Suppose that selling broker *B* spends several months working with *P*, who is looking for a residence with a white picket fence and a swimming pool. To guide the search, *P* tells *B* that she is unwilling to spend any more than $870,000. *B* then starts a search for appropriate properties, diligently scanning the MLS listings. *B* subsequently finds a house with an asking price of $899,000. *P* falls in love with the house and wants to begin negotiations to buy it as soon as possible. *B* has never met the listing broker or the owner of the house. Does *B* have a duty to inform the owner or the listing broker how much *P* is willing to pay?

2. *Alternatives and supplements to traditional brokerage arrangements.* The majority of states adhere to the traditional view of broker duties to sellers, but its shortcomings have led to various alternative arrangements and disclosure requirements.

Buyers' brokers. A relatively recent but increasingly common practice in residential real estate transactions is for prospective buyers to hire their own agents (buyers' brokers) to help conduct their search for real estate.

Buyers' brokers owe fiduciary duties to prospective purchasers. Brown et al., supra, at 44. Buyers' brokers perform a wide range of services — narrowing property searches to particular areas and price ranges, reviewing past sales records and current property on the market, showing buyers property that conforms to their search criteria, helping arrange for physical inspection of the property, preparing offers and counteroffers, facilitating buyer consultations with other experts in aspects of real estate transactions, assisting buyers in the escrow process.

Prospective buyers seldom compensate buyers' brokers directly. Instead, buyers' brokers typically share the commission earned by the listing agent when the property is purchased. However, since buyers' brokers are not in privity with the listing broker or the seller, listing agents are not compelled to share their commissions with buyers' brokers. See, e.g., Brown & Grohman, supra, at 16.

An example of the move toward (and regulation of) buyers' brokerage is a 1994 Georgia real estate agency law eliminating automatic subagency and requiring agents to disclose to prospective purchasers the full scope of diverse agency relationships available to them, including buyer's agency. See Ga. Code Ann. §10-6A-10(1) (LexisNexis 2012). Economic theory would predict that the shift from seller's agency to buyer's agency would enhance buyers' bargaining power and possibly improve efficiency because buyers would reveal more information to their brokers than would otherwise be the case. See Christopher Curran & Joel Schrag, Does It Matter Whom an Agent Serves? Evidence from Recent Changes in Real Estate Agency Law, 43 J.L. & Econ. 265, 266 (2000). Curran and Schrag found that after passage of the Georgia law, prices generally fell, as did the average time needed to sell a house. Id. They also found that a majority of buyers in Georgia have since opted to hire buyers' brokers. Id. at 270.

Dual agents. Brokers' duties become complicated if both the buyer and seller in a transaction hire the same person. A broker in this situation is referred to as a dual agent and owes both the buyer and seller the same duty of loyalty and good faith. Dual agency can be risky for both buyers and sellers because the broker cannot be exclusively loyal to any one party. In spite of this danger, many states permit dual agency on the conditions that the dual agent reveals her dual agency to both the buyer and seller early on and that both parties approve the arrangement. Restatement (Third) of Agency §8.06(2)(b)(i) (2006).

Disclosure requirements. The law in some states requires brokers to disclose to buyers, in writing, that they are the seller's agent and not the buyer's. See, e.g., Cal. Civ. Code §2079.17 (West 2012); Ga. Code Ann. §10-6A-10(2) (LexisNexis 2012). The purpose of the disclosure requirement is to make sure that buyers understand whether their broker represents them, or represents the seller. It may also have the effect of encouraging buyers to use buyers' brokers. Miceli et al., Restructuring Agency Relationships, supra, at 39.

In many states, brokers must also disclose to the buyer any material defects known by the broker and unknown to the buyer. In Easton v. Strassburger, 199

Cal. Rptr. 383 (Cal. App. 1984), the court went one step further and held that brokers have a duty to diligently inspect the property for any hidden defects of which buyer or broker were unaware and disclose any such defects to the buyer. In response to pressure from the California Association of Realtors, a group that was looking to shield its members from greater duties, the California legislature enacted Cal. Civ. Code §2079 (West 2013). The provision clarifies the meaning of *Easton* in that brokers' duties to disclose defects are confined to any defects that could be discovered from "diligent visual inspection." Although few courts outside of California have adopted the *Easton* holding, many state legislatures have responded with laws requiring owners to disclose defects. For a summary of the literature on state disclosure requirements, see Nancy A. Allen, Digest of Selected Articles, 36 Real Est. L.J. 386 (2007); see also Thomas J. Miceli et al., Evolving Property Condition Disclosure Duties: Caveat Procurator?, 39 Real Est. L.J. 464 (2011) (discussing *Easton* and the economics of disclosure).

A small but growing empirical literature exists to analyze whether the legal duties of brokers to their principals are translated into action and whether disclosure laws have an impact. For example, one study in Hawaii examined whether the enactment of a state disclosure law had an impact on sales prices of properties sold by dual agents. The results indicated that the frequency of dual agency declined in the post-legislative period. They also suggested that dual agency led to reduced sales prices, but that the influence was smaller after the legislation was enacted. See J'Noel Gardiner et al., The Impact of Dual Agency, 35 J. Real Est. Fin. & Econ. 39 (2007). Another study found evidence suggesting that selling agents may act in ways to benefit buyers. See Royce de R. Barondes et al., Examining Compliance with Fiduciary Duties: A Study of Real Estate Agents, 84 Or. L. Rev. 681 (2005). See also Jonathan A. Wiley & Leonard V. Zumpano, Agency Disclosure in the Real Estate Transaction and the Impact of Related State Policies, 31 Real Est. Res. 265 (2009) (discussing differences among states on disclosure).

3. *Multiple listing services, price fixing, and antitrust issues.* An MLS is a "facility of cooperation" that allows brokers and appraisers to share residential listing information, for a fee, on one main database. (Unlike the residential market, there is no MLS-type database for commercial properties. Miceli et al., Restructuring Agency Relaionships, supra, at 38.) Brokers submit listings to the MLS, which are then disseminated either on the Internet or in hard copy to other brokers. Only brokers and appraisers can list on the MLS, which gives rise to antitrust concerns (discussed in this Note below).

Within an individual listing on the MLS, a broker or appraiser can expect to find a photograph of the property, information regarding square footage and lot size, the number of rooms, asking price, location, and other relevant information. The MLS is advantageous to buyers and sellers alike. It provides the most efficient way for a prospective buyer to scan the market, since brokers can search the MLS on behalf of buyers and find an exhaustive compilation of nearly every property for sale within a given area. The MLS also provides maximum exposure for the sellers and is the chief method through which a listing agent markets a property.

A lingering criticism regarding the real estate industry stems from concerns about potential antitrust violations and price fixing. Brokers are prohibited from fixing commission rates. Brokers typically receive (and often share) a commission rate of 5 to 6 percent of the purchase price. There is a widespread belief that brokers fix commission rates, and some studies suggest that the optimal commission rate may be lower than the 5 to 6 percent figure. See, e.g., Lynn M. Fisher & Abdullah Yavas, A Case for Percentage Commission Contracts: The Impact of a "Race" Among Agents, 40 J. Real Est. Fin. & Econ. 1, 12 (2010); Paul Anglin & Richard Arnott, Are Brokers' Commission Rates on Home Sales Too High? A Conceptual Analysis, 27 Real Est. Econ. 719, 741 (1999). Courts have concluded that it is a per se violation of state antitrust laws for brokers to agree to fix commission rates. See Vitauts M. Gulbis, Annotation, Application of State Antitrust Laws to Activities or Practices of Real-Estate Agents or Associations, 22 A.L.R.4th 103 (2004); State v. Heritage Realty of Vermont, 407 A.2d 509 (Vt. 1979). A California court has held that the uniformity of commission rates among a board of brokers is enough circumstantial evidence to permit an inference of collusive price fixing. People v. Natl. Assn. of Realtors, 174 Cal. Rptr. 728 (Cal. App. 1981). Despite recent consolidation in many cities, the residential brokerage industry remains highly decentralized. For example, in 2012 there were 1,379 local associations and 999,824 National Association of Realtors members in the United States. NAR Membership Statistics, Historic Report, 1908-Present, National Association of Realtors, available at http://www.realtor.org/membership/historic-report. Still, the ubiquity of the MLS system outside of New York City (see Jay Romano, These Days, You Can Call It Real E-state, N.Y. Times, Mar. 12, 2000, §11 at 1) provides a means to fix prices.

Access to a multiple listing service is generally limited to MLS members, a restriction that raises antitrust concerns because it hinders the ability of brokers who are not real estate board members to conduct business. In Collins v. Main Line Bd. of Realtors, 304 A.2d 493 (Pa. 1973), the court held that an MLS that denied access to nonmember brokers was an illegal restraint of trade. See also Marin County Bd. of Realtors, Inc. v. Palsson, 549 P.2d 833 (Cal. 1976), holding that exclusion of part-time brokers from the MLS system was a violation of California's Cartwright Act as well as an illegal restraint of trade. The structure of broker compensation has been criticized for encouraging anti-competitive behavior and skewing broker behavior in ways that may not benefit home sellers and buyers. See Thomas J. Miceli et al., Is the Compensation Model for Real Estate Brokers Obsolete?, 35 J. Real Est. Fin. & Econ. 7 (2007). In recent years, a number of reduced-fee real estate agencies have emerged, such as Redfin and ZipRealty. These agencies typically use the Internet to advertise properties and usually offer a home seller the option of choosing from an array of marketing services at prices lower than those of traditional brokerage firms. See, e.g., Annette Haddad, Don't Be Afraid to Sell Home Alone, L.A. Times, Sept. 16, 2007. Traditional real estate brokers sought to limit the growth of some of these "discount" brokerages by denying them access to MLS listings. In 2008, the Justice Department settled an antitrust suit it filed against the NAR and obtained an agreement that the MLS listings would be made available. See United States v. Natl. Assn. of Realtors, Civ. Action No. 05-C-5140 (Final Judgment dated Nov. 18, 2008). See also Realcomp II, Ltd. v. F.T.C., 635 F.3d 815, 836 (6th Cir. 2011) (MLS rules restricting sharing of non-traditional listings had anti-competitive effects and violated federal law).

4. *The economics of real estate brokerage.* Brokers exist because there is a scarcity of information in the market for real property. See John D. Benjamin et al., What Do We Know About Real Estate Brokerage?, 20 J. Real Est. Res. 5, 23 (2000). Sellers are sporadic actors in the property market who normally want to sell for as much as they can as fast as they can; they rely on brokers to provide expert advice and information to fulfill their goals. Miceli et al., Restructuring Agency Relationships, supra, at 35; John R. Knight, Listing Price, Time on Market, and Ultimate Selling Price: Causes and Effects of Listing Price Changes, 30 Real Est. Econ. 213, 213 (2002). Moreover, there is a need for brokers because real estate is not the same as widgets. Each piece of property is unique and it takes significant amounts of time to collect information regarding the real estate market. Because buyers and sellers tend not to enter into these transactions often and because the value of each transaction is so high, it makes economic sense to have specialists develop information rather than reinvent the wheel each time an individual enters the market. But the rise of the Internet threatens the role of real estate brokers. Miceli et al., Restructuring Agency Relationships, supra, at 40. With property frequently listed on-line, buyers and sellers are able to some considerable degree to do their own searches without the use of a broker. If brokers were to lose their role as matchmakers for buyers and sellers, their principal function would be reduced to mere oversight of negotiations about price and the terms of sales contracts. Broker compensation would undoubtedly decline, and brokers would risk losing a portion of their business to attorneys, mortgage lenders, and title companies. Id. at 41. The good news for brokers is that some—but considerably less—business would remain, with much of the demand coming from wealthy buyers and sellers, and from people moving into a new region or out of a familiar one. See Benjamin et al., supra, at 6.

5. *Types of listings.* A listing agreement, or listing, is an employment contract between a real estate broker and a seller. The contracts are usually in writing; in some states they must be. If the broker satisfies the obligations set forth in the listing, the seller pays the broker a commission, usually a percentage of the price at which the property sold.

Listing agreements typically include a description of the property, the seller's asking price, the names of the owner(s) and broker, and the duration of the broker's contract. There are various types of listings between sellers and brokers, and, within each type of listing, there are also competing rights and incentives:

(a) *Open listing.* This is the least protective listing that a broker can secure, because the seller retains the right to sell the property herself or use a different broker without paying the open listing broker a commission. A broker earns a commission only if she is first to procure an offer from a ready, willing, and able buyer who either matches the terms set forth in the listing or includes terms acceptable to the seller. See Bedard v. Pellon, 606 A.2d 205 (Me. 1992); Mapes v. City Council of City of Walsenburg, 151 P.3d 574 (Colo. App. 2006). Open listings do not typically have set termination dates.

(b) *Exclusive-agency listing.* This listing agreement permits only one broker, the exclusive agent, to sell the property for a specified period of time. The exclusive agent earns a commission for the sale of the property if she secures a buyer, or even if a separate broker secures a buyer. Brokers prefer exclusive-agency listings to open listings because they do not have to compete with other brokers during the period of the exclusive listing. Exclusive-agency listings also may appeal to owners, because an owner can avoid paying the exclusive agent a commission if the owner directly sells the property herself. See Fearick v. Smugglers Cove, Inc., 379 So. 2d 400 (Fla. App. 1980).

(c) *Exclusive-right-to-sell listing.* This is the most protective listing that a broker can secure. Under an exclusive right to sell listing, the owner must pay that broker if *any* buyer purchases the property during the specified duration of the listing, no matter who found the purchaser.

The vast majority of listing agreements for residential properties are exclusive rights to sell. It is easy to see why a broker would prefer this arrangement. But why might a seller also prefer it? If you were a seller of real estate, which type of listing agreement would you prefer? See, e.g., Stephanie Councilman, The Requirement of Statute of Frauds for Real Estate Brokers to Receive Commissions and the Festering Minority View of Equity, 10 Tex. Wesleyan L. Rev. 441, 446 (2004).

6. *Unauthorized practice of law.* The issues here reflect a tension between attorneys and real estate brokers. Traditionally, brokers have been prohibited from drafting legal documents, offering legal advice, or carrying out property closings. See, e.g., Duncan & Hill Realty, Inc. v. Dept. of State, 405 N.Y.S.2d 339 (App. Div. 1978); People ex rel. Illinois State Bar Assn. v. Schafer, 87 N.E.2d 773 (Ill. 1949). A broker who performs any of these services may be found to have engaged in the unauthorized practice of law. See, e.g., In re UPL Advisory Opinion 2003-2, 588 S.E.2d 741 (Ga. 2003). In many jurisdictions, however, brokers are permitted to fill in the blanks on simple or standardized legal forms on the ground that such acts are incidental to a broker's usual tasks.

Advocates of increased realtor participation contend that reducing the influence of attorneys in real estate transactions will reduce transaction costs and benefit buyers and sellers. On the other hand, supporters of increased attorney participation argue that only attorneys are properly trained and capable of understanding and managing the legal intricacies involved in real estate transactions.

In recent years, the permissible role of brokers has expanded. For example, the Supreme Court of New Jersey has allowed brokers greater freedom to conduct tasks (specifically, closings) that were once carried out exclusively by attorneys. The court reasoned that "the public interest would not be disserved by allowing the parties, after advance written notice of their right to retain counsel and the risk of not doing so, to choose to proceed without a lawyer" and that the "public interest does not require that the protection of counsel be forced upon the parties against their will." In re Opinion No. 26 of the Comm. on the Unauthorized Practice of Law, 654 A.2d 1344 (N.J. 1995). In addition, some cases (such as *Duncan & Hill*, 405 N.Y.S.2d at 701) have suggested that an attorney approval clause in a contract can protect brokers from unauthorized practice of law. See Bryan Porter, Comment, Bad Faith and Attorney Approval Clause: Breach, or Moot Point?, 34 J. Legal Prof. 399 (2010) (discussing various interpretations of clause).

7. *When a commission is due.* The traditional rule is that a broker earns a commission upon bringing to the seller a buyer who is ready, willing, and able. A ready, willing, and able purchaser is typically construed to mean someone who expresses a desire to buy the property by making an offer for the specified asking price (or some other price that the owner finds acceptable) and has sufficient assets to proceed with the successful purchase of the property. The traditional rule advantages brokers because the broker is entitled to earn a commission even if the sale fails to close. See, e.g., Coldwell Banker Village Green Realty v. Pillsworth, 818 N.Y.S.2d 868 (App. Div. 2006); Sowash v. Garrett, 630 P.2d 8 (Alaska 1981). Under the traditional rule, the broker is entitled to a commission if the seller defaults *and also* if the buyer defaults. See, e.g., Chicago Title Agency of Las Vegas, Inc. v. Schwartz, 851 P.2d 419 (Nev. 1993); Fairbourn Commercial, Inc. v. American Housing Partners, Inc., 94 P.3d 292 (Utah 2004); Nelson v. Rosenblum Co., 182 N.W.2d 666 (Minn. 1970). The seller owes the broker a commission even if the buyer cannot obtain financing. See, e.g., Winston v. Minkin, 216 N.W.2d 38 (Wis. 1974). But the owner can circumvent the dangers of the traditional rule through contract. If the parties agree to make the commission conditional—on the actual sale of the property, for instance—the broker only earns her commission when the condition is fulfilled. See, e.g., Norma Reynolds Realty, Inc. v. Edelman, 817 N.Y.S.2d 85 (App. Div. 2006); Shumaker v. Lear, 345 A.2d 249 (Pa. App. 1975). See also Roger Bernhardt & Dale A. Whitman, When Is a Commission Due? Problems with Broker Listing Agreements, 27 Prob. & Prop. 30 (2013) (discussing the traditional rule).

A minority view holds that a broker is not entitled to a commission until the property sale closes. In Ellsworth Dobbs, Inc. v. Johnson, 236 A.2d 843 (N.J. 1967), the New Jersey Supreme Court concluded that if a buyer defaults because she changed her mind or was unable to secure proper financing, then the broker has not found a ready, willing, and able buyer and has therefore not earned a commission. Similar to the majority approach, however, the minority view holds that the broker is still entitled to a commission if the seller, through her own frustrating conduct, does not act in good faith and backs out of the agreement before closing. See, e.g., Drake v. Hosley, 713 P.2d 1203 (Alaska 1986).

The custom in the industry is that brokers are not actually paid their commissions until closing, reflecting the reality that most sellers pay the broker with proceeds from the sale of the property. Even though the majority of jurisdictions adhere to the traditional rule, most brokers decline to pursue a commission when a transaction fails to close, no doubt because they want to maintain friendly relations with their clients, both to encourage repeat business and to get referrals.

A potential problem rises as the end of a listing agreement term draws near. Brokers are no doubt tempted to consummate a deal at almost any price, since if a listing expires without a sale, any right to a commission is forgone. At the same time, however, brokers might resist the temptation in hopes that the owner will renew the broker's listing agreement, thereby giving the broker another chance to sell the property at its highest value.

C.   The Contract of Sale

1.   The Statute of Frauds

The Statute of Frauds, enacted in 1677 under the title "An Act for the Prevention of Frauds and Perjuries," sought to make people more secure in their property and their contracts by making deceitful claims unenforceable. The Statute dealt with diverse subjects, but two provisions were of particular importance for the law of real property. First, sections 1 to 3 provided that, except for leases for less than three years, no interest in land could be created or transferred except by an instrument in writing signed by the party to be bound thereby. Second, section 4 provided that no action shall be brought "upon any contract or sale of lands . . . or any interest in or concerning them . . . unless the agreement upon which such action shall be brought or some memorandum or note thereof shall be in writing, and signed by the party to be charged therewith."

The provisions of the English Statute of Frauds have been generally re-enacted in the United States. The courts, however, when not confined by express language, have treated the Statute of Frauds as a principle rather than as a statute. Frequently, in discussing the Statute, they do not cite or quote any statutory text. As a consequence, most law relating to the Statute of Frauds is judge-made law, not statutory. Some judges, believing the requirements wise and salutary, are quite strict in enforcing the Statute. Others have relaxed the requirements, giving effect to oral agreements under circumstances when fraud seems unlikely or unfairness results. Even within a single jurisdiction there is likely to be no consistent view on the necessity for a written instrument; judges may enforce some types of oral agreements while rejecting others.

To satisfy the Statute of Frauds a memorandum of sale must, at a minimum, be signed by the party to be bound, describe the real estate, and state the price. When a price has been agreed upon, most courts regard it as an essential term that must be set forth. But if no price was agreed upon, a court may imply an agreement to pay a reasonable price. Under Uniform Land Transactions Act §2-203 (1978), the parties may enter into a binding contract without having agreed on the price. However, the agreement is not enforceable unless the parties refer to price and indicate the method they intend to use in fixing it. A contract for sale at "fair market value" is enforceable. Goodwest Rubber Corp. v. Munoz, 216 Cal. Rptr. 604 (Cal. App. 1985). In some states, the memorandum must contain, in addition to the above, all the material or essential terms of the agreement, but given the extensive litigation, no accurate simple summary of "material terms" is possible. House of Prayer: Renewal & Healing Ctr. of Yuba City v. Evangelical Assn. for India, 7 Cal. Rptr. 3d 24 (Cal. App. 2003).

Exceptions to the Statute of Frauds. Courts have created two principal exceptions to the Statute of Frauds: *part performance* and *estoppel.* Part performance allows the specific enforcement of oral agreements when particular acts have been performed by one of the parties to the agreement. Acts held to constitute part performance vary from jurisdiction to jurisdiction, depending primarily on how the court views the theoretical basis for the doctrine of part performance. One theory is that the acts of the parties substantially satisfy the evidentiary requirements of the Statute. Hence if the acts make sense only as having been performed pursuant to the oral contract ("unequivocally referable to a contract of sale"), they constitute part performance. Such acts include the buyer's taking possession *and* paying all or part of the purchase price or making valuable improvements. Another theory of part performance is that it is a doctrine used to prevent injurious reliance on the contract; if the plaintiff shows that he would suffer irreparable injury if the contract were not enforced, then the buyer's taking of possession alone is sufficient to set the court in motion. The doctrine of part performance originated in equity in suits for specific performance and in most jurisdictions does not apply to actions at law for damages. In a few states, acts of part performance are not recognized. See William B. Stoebuck & Dale A. Whitman, The Law of Property 719 (3d ed. 2000).

Estoppel applies when unconscionable injury would result from denying enforcement of the oral contract after one party has been induced by the other seriously to change his position in reliance on the contract. Estoppel may also apply when unjust enrichment would result if a party who has received the benefits of the other's performance were allowed to rely upon the Statute. Estoppel, though originating in equity, has long been recognized as a defense in law. See Stewart E. Sterk, Estoppel in Property Law, 77 Neb. L. Rev. 756, 759-769 (1998).

Hickey v. Green

Appeals Court of Massachusetts, 1982
442 N.E.2d 37, rev. denied,
445 N.E.2d 156 (1983)

CUTTER, J. This case is before us on a stipulation of facts (with various attached documents). A Superior Court judge has adopted the agreed facts as "findings." We are in the same position as was the trial judge (who received no evidence and saw and heard no witnesses).

Mrs. Gladys Green owns a lot (Lot S) in the Manomet section of Plymouth. In July, 1980, she advertised it for sale. On July 11 and 12, Hickey and his wife discussed with Mrs. Green purchasing Lot S and "orally agreed to a sale" for $15,000. Mrs. Green on July 12 accepted a deposit check of $500, marked by Hickey on the back, "Deposit on Lot . . . Massasoit Ave. Manomet . . . Subject to Variance from Town of Plymouth." Mrs. Green's brother and agent "was under the impression that a zoning variance was needed and [had] advised . . . . Hickey to write" the quoted language on the deposit check. It turned out, however, by July 16 that no variance would be required. Hickey had left the payee line of the deposit check blank, because of uncertainty whether Mrs. Green or her brother was to receive the check, and asked "Mrs. Green to fill in the appropriate name." Mrs. Green held the check, did not fill in the payee's name, and neither cashed nor endorsed it. Hickey "stated to Mrs. Green that his intention was to sell his home and build on Mrs. Green's lot."

"Relying upon the arrangements . . . with Mrs. Green," the Hickeys advertised their house on Sachem Road in newspapers on three days in July, 1980, and agreed with a purchaser for its sale and took from him a deposit check for $500 which they deposited in their own account.[1] On July 24, Mrs. Green told Hickey that she "no longer intended to sell her property to him" but had decided to sell to another for $16,000. Hickey told Mrs. Green that he had already sold his house and offered her $16,000 for Lot S. Mrs. Green refused this offer.

The Hickeys filed this complaint seeking specific performance. Mrs. Green asserts that relief is barred by the Statute of Frauds contained in G.L. c. 259 §1. The trial judge granted specific performance.[2] Mrs. Green has appealed.

The present rule applicable in most jurisdictions in the United States is succinctly set forth in Restatement (Second) of Contracts, §129 (1981). The section reads,

A contract for the transfer of an interest in land may be specifically enforced notwithstanding failure to comply with the Statute of Frauds if it is established that the party seeking enforcement, in *reasonable reliance on the contract* and on the continuing assent of the party against whom enforcement is sought, *has so changed his position that injustice can be avoided only by specific enforcement* (emphasis supplied).[3]

The earlier Massachusetts decisions laid down somewhat strict requirements for an estoppel precluding the assertion of the Statute of Frauds. See, e.g., Glass v. Hulbert, 102 Mass. 24, 31-32, 43-44 (1869); Davis v. Downer, 210 Mass. 573, 576-577, 97 N.E. 90 (1912); Hazelton v. Lewis, 267 Mass. 533, 538-540, 166 N.E.

1. On the back of the check was noted above the Hickeys' signatures endorsing the check "Deposit on Purchase of property at Sachem Rd. and First St., Manomet, Ma. Sale price, $44,000."

2. The judgment ordered Mrs. Green to convey Lot S to the Hickeys but, probably by inadvertence, it failed to include an order that it be conveyed only upon payment by the grantees of the admittedly agreed price of $15,000.

3. Comments a and b to §129, read (in part): "a. . . . This section restates what is widely known as the 'part performance doctrine.' Part performance is not an accurate designation of such acts as taking possession and making improvements when the contract does not provide for such acts, but such acts regularly bring the doctrine into play. The doctrine is contrary to the words of the Statute of Frauds, but it was established by English courts of equity soon after the enactment of the Statute. Payment of purchase-money, without more, was once thought sufficient to justify specific enforcement, but a contrary view now prevails, since in such cases restitution is an adequate remedy. . . . Enforcement has . . . been justified on the ground that repudiation after 'part performance' amounts to a 'virtual fraud.' A more accurate statement is that courts with equitable powers are vested by tradition with what in substance is a dispensing power based on the promisee's reliance, *a discretion to be exercised with caution* in the light of all the circumstances . . . [emphasis supplied].

"b. . . . Two distinct elements enter into the application of the rule of this Section: first, the extent to which the evidentiary function of the statutory formalities is fulfilled by the conduct of the parties; second, the reliance of the promisee, providing a compelling substantive basis for relief in addition to the expectations created by the promise."

876 (1929); Andrews v. Charon, 289 Mass. 1, 5-7, 193 N.E. 737 (1935), where specific performance was granted upon a consideration of "the effect of all the facts in combination"; Winstanley v. Chapman, 325 Mass. 130, 133, 89 N.E.2d 506 (1949); Park, Real Estate Law, §883 (1981). . . . Frequently there has been an actual change of possession and improvement of the transferred property, as well as full payment of the full purchase price, or one or more of these elements.

It is stated in Park, Real Estate Law, §883, at 334, that the "more recent decisions . . . indicate a trend on the part of the [Supreme Judicial C]ourt to find that the circumstances warrant specific performance." This appears to be a correct perception. See Fisher v. MacDonald, 332 Mass. 727, 729, 127 N.E.2d 484 (1955), where specific performance was granted upon a showing that the purchaser "was put into possession and . . . [had] furnished part of the consideration in money and services"; Orlando v. Ottaviani, 337 Mass. 157, 161-162, 148 N.E.2d 373 (1958), where specific performance was granted to the former holder of an option to buy a strip of land fifteen feet wide, important to the option holder, and the option had been surrendered in reliance upon an oral promise to convey the strip made by the purchaser of a larger parcel of which the fifteen-foot strip was a part; Cellucci v. Sun Oil Co., 2 Mass. App. 722, 727-728, 320 N.E.2d 919 (1974), aff'd, 368 Mass. 811, 331 N.E.2d 813 (1975). . . .

The present facts reveal a simple case of a proposed purchase of a residential vacant lot, where the vendor, Mrs. Green, knew that the Hickeys were planning to sell their former home (possibly to obtain funds to pay her) and build on Lot S. The Hickeys, relying on Mrs. Green's oral promise, moved rapidly to make their sale without obtaining any adequate memorandum of the terms of what appears to have been intended to be a quick cash sale of Lot S. So rapid was action by the Hickeys that, by July 21, less than ten days after giving their deposit to Mrs. Green, they had accepted a deposit check for the sale of their house, endorsed the check, and placed it in their bank account. Above their signatures endorsing the check was a memorandum probably sufficient to satisfy the Statute of Frauds under A.B.C. Auto Parts, Inc. v. Moran, 359 Mass. 327, 329-331, 268 N.E.2d 844 (1971). Cf. Guarino v. Zyfers, 9 Mass. App. 874, 401 N.E.2d 857 (1980). At the very least, the Hickeys had bound themselves in a manner in which, to avoid a transfer of their own house, they might have had to engage in expensive litigation. No attorney has been shown to have been used either in the transaction between Mrs. Green and the Hickeys or in that between the Hickeys and their purchaser.

There is no denial by Mrs. Green of the oral contract between her and the Hickeys. This, under §129 of the Restatement, is of some significance.[4] There can be no doubt (a) that Mrs. Green made the promise on which the Hickeys so

---

4. Comment d of Restatement (Second) of Contracts, §129, reads: "d. . . . Where specific enforcement is rested on a transfer of possession plus either part payment of the price or the making of improvements, it is commonly said that the action taken by the purchaser must be unequivocally referable to the oral agreement. But this requirement is not insisted on *if the making of the promise is admitted or is clearly proved*. The promisee *must act in reasonable reliance on the promise, before the promisor has* repudiated it, and the action must be such that the remedy of restitution is inadequate. If these requirements are met, *neither taking of possession nor payment of money nor the making of improvements is essential*. . . ." (emphasis supplied).

promptly relied, and also (b) she, nearly as promptly, but not promptly enough, repudiated it because she had a better opportunity. The stipulated facts require the conclusion that in equity Mrs. Green's conduct cannot be condoned. This is not a case where either party is shown to have contemplated the negotiation of a purchase and sale agreement. If a written agreement had been expected, even by only one party, or would have been natural (because of the participation by lawyers or otherwise), a different situation might have existed. It is a permissible inference from the agreed facts that the rapid sale of the Hickeys' house was both appropriate and expected. These are not circumstances where negotiations fairly can be seen as inchoate. Compare Tull v. Mister Donut Development Corp., 7 Mass. App. 626, 630-632, 389 N.E.2d 447 (1979).

We recognize that specific enforcement of Mrs. Green's promise to convey Lot S may well go somewhat beyond the circumstances considered in the *Fisher* case, 332 Mass. 727, and in the *Orlando* case, 337 Mass. 157, 148 N.E.2d 373, where specific performance was granted. It may seem (perhaps because the present facts are less complicated) to extend the principles stated in the *Cellucci* case (see esp. 2 Mass. App. at 728, 320 N.E.2d 919). We recognize also the cautionary language about granting specific performance in comment a to §129 of the Restatement (see footnote 3, supra). No public interest behind G.L. c. 259 §1, however, in the simple circumstances before us, will be violated if Mrs. Green fairly is held to her precise bargain by principles of equitable estoppel, subject to the considerations mentioned below.

Over two years have passed since July, 1980, and over a year since the trial judge's findings were filed on July 6, 1981. At that time, the principal agreed facts of record bearing upon the extent of the injury to the Hickeys (because of their reliance on Mrs. Green's promise to convey Lot S) were those based on the Hickeys' new obligation to convey their house to a purchaser. Performance of that agreement had been extended to May 1, 1981. If that agreement has been abrogated or modified since the trial, the case may take on a different posture. If enforcement of that agreement still will be sought, or if that agreement has been carried out, the conveyance of Lot S by Mrs. Green should be required now.

The case, in any event, must be remanded to the trial judge for the purpose of amending the judgment to require conveyance of Lot S by Mrs. Green only upon payment to her in cash within a stated period of the balance of the agreed price of $15,000. The trial judge, however, in her discretion and upon proper offers of proof of counsel, may reopen the record to receive, in addition to the presently stipulated facts, a stipulation or evidence concerning the present status of the Hickeys' apparent obligation to sell their house. If the circumstances have changed, it will be open to the trial judge to require of Mrs. Green, instead of specific performance, only full restitution to the Hickeys of all costs reasonably caused to them in respect of these transactions (including advertising costs, deposits, and their reasonable costs for this litigation) with interest. The case is remanded to the Superior Court Department for further action consistent with this opinion. The Hickeys are to have costs of this appeal.

So ordered.

NOTES AND PROBLEMS

1. In Walker v. Ireton, 559 P.2d 340 (Kan. 1977), the buyer entered into an oral contract to purchase a farm for $30,000. The preparation of a written contract was discussed; the seller said he wanted first to see his accountant to find out how to take the money. Several discussions later the buyer asked the seller to put the agreement in writing; the seller said that was not needed because he was honest. The buyer gave the seller a check for $50 as a down payment, which the seller never cashed. Relying on the contract, the buyer sold his other farm, though he did not tell the seller of his intention to sell it or of the sale until after the other farm had been sold.

The seller changed his mind and backed out of the oral contract. The court refused to grant specific performance. The delivery of the check was not sufficient part performance to remove the defense of the Statute of Frauds. The sale of the other farm did not constitute sufficient reliance on the oral contract because it was not within the contemplation and understanding of the parties and not foreseeable by the seller. Compare *Walker* with Beaver v. Brumlow, 231 P.3d 628 (N.M. App. 2010) (purchase of mobile home and placement on land considered sufficient performance).

2. *O*, owner of Blackacre, executes and delivers a deed of Blackacre to her daughter *A* as a gift. The deed is not recorded. Subsequently *O* tells *A* that she would like Blackacre back, and *A*, a dutiful daughter, hands the deed back to *O* and says, "The land is yours again." *O* tears up the deed. Who owns Blackacre?

Suppose that, instead of as above, *O* executes and delivers a deed to her daughter conveying Blackacre to *O* and *A* as joint tenants. The deed is not recorded. Subsequently, *A* tells *O* she would like her son *B* to have her interest, and *O* agrees. To save the recording tax on two deeds, *A* "whites out" her name on the deed and replaces it with *B*'s name. This deed is then recorded. *O* dies. Who owns Blackacre? See Mann v. Mann, 677 So. 2d 62 (Fla. App. 1996).

3. For a detailed analysis of forms of real estate sales contracts, both simple and complex, see Lucy A. Marsh, Real Property Transactions 168-223 (1992).

NOTE: THE STATUTE OF FRAUDS AND ELECTRONIC TRANSACTIONS

The Statute of Frauds requires that transfers of interests in land be in writing. But thanks to the increasing use of such electronic media as email and the Internet, legal scholars and legislators alike have had to confront a nice question regarding the Statute of Frauds: What constitutes a writing?

In 2000, Congress enacted The Electronic Signatures in Global and National Commerce Act, commonly known as E-sign, to address the issue. E-sign provides that "a signature, contract, or other record . . . may not be denied legal effect, validity, or enforceability solely because it is in electronic form." 15 U.S.C §7001(a)(1). Section 7006(5) defines an electronic signature as "an electronic sound, symbol, or process, attached to or logically associated with a contract or other record and executed or adopted by a person with the intent to sign the record." 15 U.S.C. §7006(5).[5]

There is increasing litigation regarding electronic transactions and contracts for the sale of land. In 2001, a lower court in Massachusetts held that where the purchaser and vendor in a real estate transaction exchanged several emails, which included the address of the property to be sold, purchase price, deposit amount, closing date, additional terms, provisions for an inspection, and which were signed with the type-written name of the sender at the bottom of every email, these emails as a group were sufficient to constitute a "written document" and satisfy the Statute of Frauds. Shattuck v. Klotzback, 2001 WL 1839720 (Mass. Super. Ct. Dec. 11, 2001); see also Rosenfeld v. Zerneck, 776 N.Y.S.2d 458 (Sup. Ct. 2004) (holding that had the emails exchanged by the parties contained deposit information in addition to other contract terms, the Statute of Frauds would have been satisfied); Dittman v. Cerone, 2013 WL 5970356 (Tex. App. Oct. 31, 2013) (emails sufficient for Statute of Frauds). But not all courts have been so receptive. In dicta, another lower court in Massachusetts noted that "Emails . . . by their quick and casual nature, tend to lack in many instances the cautionary and memorializing functions a traditional signed writing serves under the statute of frauds." Singer v. Adamson, 2003 WL 23641985, at *5 (Mass. Land. Ct. Dec. 24, 2003), aff'd, 837 N.E.2d 313 (Mass. App. 2005) (ruling that emails did not contain sufficient specificity to constitute a contract). While the emails exchanged in *Shattuck* did have greater specificity than those in *Singer*, the court in *Singer* seemed to take a generally skeptical view of the validity of email exchanges under the Statute of Frauds. Compare Vista Developers Corp. v. VFP Realty LLP, 847 N.Y.S.2d 416 (Sup. Ct. 2007), with Naldi v. Grunberg, 908 N.Y.S.2d 639 (App. Div. 2010). Some commentators agree, arguing that E-sign and similar statutes have detrimentally weakened the Statute of Frauds by eliminating the role it played in ensuring that those engaging in real estate transactions "think twice" before being formally bound. Moreover, lax requirements regarding what constitutes an "electronic signature" could increase the possibility of electronic forgeries. Patrick A. Randolph, Jr., Has E-Sign Murdered the Statute of Frauds?, 15 Prob. & Prop. 23 (2001).

Issues regarding the Statute of Frauds and electronic transactions are far from solved, and are likely to grow as technology advances and more and more people get computer savvy.

2.   Marketable Title

An implied condition of a contract of sale of land is that the seller must convey to the buyer a "marketable title." If the seller cannot convey a marketable title, the

---

5. Forty-seven states have enacted the Uniform Electronic Transactions Act (UETA), which is similar to E-sign. See Brian Henry & Mary Dunn, Forming Real Estate Contracts Electronically: An Evaluation of Relevant Law, 38 Mich. Real Prop. Rev. 143, 144 (2011-2012). New York has enacted similar legislation. The New York statute carves out an exception for real property contracts and therefore requires a more traditional form of a writing. See Gerald J. Ferguson & Manuel Campos Galvan, Enforcing Electronic Contracts in the Americas, 15 Intl. L. Practicum 42, 43 (2007).

buyer is entitled to rescind the contract. Marketable title is "a title not subject to such reasonable doubt as would create a just apprehension of its validity in the mind of a reasonable, prudent and intelligent person, one which such persons, guided by competent legal advice, would be willing to take and for which they would be willing to pay fair value." Seligman v. First Natl. Invs., Inc., 540 N.E.2d 1057, 1060 (Ill. App. 1989). See also Mellinger v. Ticor Title Ins. Co. of California, 113 Cal. Rptr. 2d 357 (Cal. App. 2001).

Lohmeyer v. Bower

Supreme Court of Kansas, 1951
227 P.2d 102

[In May 1949, Dr. K.L. Lohmeyer entered into a contract to buy from the Bowers lot number 37 in the Berkley Hills Addition to the city of Emporia. The contract provided that the Bowers would convey

> By Warranty Deed with an abstract of title, certified to date showing good merchantable title or an Owners Policy of Title Insurance in the amount of the sale price, guaranteeing said title to party of the second part [Dr. Lohmeyer], free and clear of all encumbrances except special taxes subject, however, to all restrictions and easements of record applying to this property, it being understood that the first party shall have sufficient time to bring said abstract to date or obtain Report for Title Insurance and to correct any imperfections in the title if there be such imperfections.

The abstract of title showed that the original subdivider of the Berkley Hills Addition had, in 1926, imposed a restrictive covenant on lot 37 requiring any house erected on lot 37 to be two stories in height. Lot 37 had a one-story house on it.

Dr. Lohmeyer gave the abstract of title to a lawyer to examine, and from the lawyer Dr. Lohmeyer learned that the city of Emporia had a zoning ordinance providing that no frame building could be erected within three feet of a side or rear lot line. The frame house on lot 37 was located within 18 inches of the north line of the lot in violation of the ordinance. The Bowers had, in 1946, moved the house, which had been built elsewhere, onto lot 37. When Dr. Lohmeyer brought the zoning violation to the attention of the Bowers, they offered to purchase and convey to Lohmeyer two feet along the entire north side of lot 37. Dr. Lohmeyer refused their offer.

Dr. Lohmeyer brought suit to rescind the contract and demanded return of his earnest money. The Bowers answered, contesting Lohmeyer's right to rescind, and by cross-complaint asked specific performance of the contract. The trial court rendered judgment for the Bowers and decreed specific performance of the contract. Dr. Lohmeyer appealed from that judgment.]

PARKER, J. . . . From what has been heretofore related, since resort to the contract makes it clear appellees agreed to convey the involved property with an abstract of title showing good merchantable title, free and clear of all

**The house on lot 37, Berkley Hills Addition,
which Dr. Lohmeyer backed out of buying, 1990.**

encumbrances, it becomes apparent the all decisive issue presented by the pleadings and the stipulation is whether such property is subject to encumbrances or other burdens making the title unmerchantable and if so whether they are such as are excepted by the provision of the contract which reads "subject however, to all restrictions and easements of record applying to this property."

Decision of the foregoing issue can be simplified by directing attention early to the appellant's position. Conceding he purchased the property subject to all restrictions of record he makes no complaint of the restrictions contained in the declaration forming a part of the dedication of Berkley Hills Addition nor of the ordinance restricting the building location on the lot but bases his right to rescission of the contract solely upon presently existing violations thereof. This, we may add, limited to restrictions imposed by terms of the ordinance relating to the use of land or the location and character of buildings that may be located thereon, even in the absence of provisions in the contract excepting them, must necessarily be his position for we are convinced, although it must be conceded there are some decisions to the contrary, the rule supported by the better reasoned decisions, indeed if not by the great weight of authority, is that municipal restrictions of such character, existing at the time of the execution of a contract for the sale of real estate, are not such encumbrances or burdens on title as may be availed of by a vendee to avoid his agreement to purchase on the ground they render his title unmerchantable. For authorities upholding this conclusion see Hall v. Risley & Heikkila, 188 Or. 69, 213 P.2d 818; Miller v. Milwaukee Odd Fellows Temple, 206 Wis. 547, 240 N.W. 193; Wheeler v. Sullivan, 90 Fla. 711, 106 So. 876; Lincoln Trust Co. v. Williams Bldg. Corp., 229 N.Y. 313, 128 N.E. 209;

Maupin on Marketable Title to Real Estate, (3rd Ed.) 384 §143; 175 A.L.R. anno. 1056 §2; 57 A.L.R. anno. 1424 §11(c); 55 Am. Jur. 705 §205; 66 C.J. 860, 911 §§531, 591.

On the other hand there can be no question the rule respecting restrictions upon the use of land or the location and type of buildings that may be erected thereon fixed by covenants or other private restrictive agreements, including those contained in the declaration forming a part of the dedication of Berkley Hills Addition, is directly contrary to the one to which we have just referred. Such restrictions, under all the authorities, constitute encumbrances rendering the title to land unmerchantable. . . .

There can be no doubt regarding what constitutes a marketable or merchantable title in this jurisdiction. This court has been called on to pass upon that question on numerous occasions. See our recent decision in Peatling v. Baird, 168 Kan. 528, 213 P.2d 1015, and cases there cited, wherein we held:

A marketable title to real estate is one which is free from reasonable doubt, and a title is doubtful and unmarketable if it exposes the party holding it to the hazard of litigation.

To render the title to real estate unmarketable, the defect of which the purchaser complains must be of a substantial character and one from which he may suffer injury. Mere immaterial defects which do not diminish in quantity, quality or value the property contracted for, constitute no ground upon which the purchaser may reject the title. Facts must be known at the time which fairly raise a reasonable doubt as to the title; a mere possibility or conjecture that such a state of facts may be developed at some future time is not sufficient.

Under the rule just stated, and in the face of facts such as are here involved, we have little difficulty in concluding that the violation of section 5-224 of the ordinances of the city of Emporia as well as the violation of the restrictions imposed by the dedication declaration so encumber the title to lot 37 as to expose the party holding it to the hazard of litigation and make such title doubtful and unmarketable. It follows, since, as we have indicated, the appellees had contracted to convey such real estate to appellant by warranty deed with an abstract of title showing good merchantable title, free and clear of all encumbrances, that they cannot convey the title contracted for and that the trial court should have rendered judgment rescinding the contract. This, we may add is so, notwithstanding the contract provides the conveyance was to be made subject to all restrictions and easements of record for, as we have seen, it is the violation of the restrictions imposed by both the ordinance and the dedication declaration, not the existence of those restrictions, that render the title unmarketable. The decision just announced is not without precedent or unsupported by sound authority. . . .

Finally appellees point to the contract which, it must be conceded, provides they shall have time to correct imperfections in the title and contend that even if it be held the restrictions and the ordinance have been violated they are entitled to time in which to correct those imperfections. Assuming, without deciding, they might remedy the violation of the ordinance by buying additional ground the short and simple answer to their contention with respect to the violation of the restrictions imposed by the dedication declaration is that any changes in the house would compel the purchaser to take something that he did not contract to buy.

Conclusions heretofore announced require reversal of the judgment with directions to the trial court to cancel and set aside the contract and render such judgment as may be equitable and proper under the issues raised by the pleadings.

It is so ordered.

NOTES AND QUESTIONS

1. Look at the contract Dr. Lohmeyer signed. Would you have advised Dr. Lohmeyer not to sign it? First, the contract provides that Lohmeyer agrees to take the property subject to all restrictions and easements on record. Second, it provides that the sellers must provide Lohmeyer "with an abstract of title, certified to date showing good merchantable title *or* an Owners Policy of Title Insurance." Suppose that a title insurance company, of which you will learn more in Chapter 8, agreed to issue a policy of title insurance on the property, guaranteeing title, even though the title is legally unmarketable. Would Lohmeyer be entitled to rescind the contract? See Creative Living, Inc. v. Steinhauser, 355 N.Y.S.2d 897 (App. Div. 1974), aff'd without opinion, 365 N.Y.S.2d 987 (App. Div. 1975) (contract provided seller shall have a title such as a title insurer would insure; "[t]his provision in the contract made the title company the final judge of title and when the title company was prepared to insure title in accordance with the contract no further requirement had to be met"); see also Nelson v. Anderson, 676 N.E.2d 735 (Ill. App. 1997) (holding that agreement by insurance company that it would insure purchaser, as well as future purchasers from the purchaser, against the defect did not make the title marketable).

What is the function of the concept of "marketable title"? Why do courts not rule that the seller must produce a complete chain of title from an unimpeachable source (a sovereign) and prove that no encumbrance exists? See William B. Stoebuck & Dale A. Whitman, The Law of Property 775-784 (3d ed. 2000).

Why do public restrictions on land use, such as zoning or wetlands designations, make title unmarketable only if they are violated (see Truck South, Inc. v. Patel, 528 S.E.2d 424 (S.C. 2000) (wetlands); War Eagle, Inc. v. Belair, 694 S.E.2d 497 (N.C. App. 2010) (zoning); Wolf v. Commonwealth Land Title Ins. Co., 690 N.Y.S.2d 880 (App. Div. 1999) (zoning)), whereas private covenants make title unmarketable whether or not they are violated? See Allison Dunham, The Effect on Title of Violations of Building Covenants and Zoning Ordinances, 27 Rocky Mtn. L. Rev. 255 (1955); Michael J. Gamson & J. David Reitzel, Zoning Restrictions and Marketability of Title, 35 Real Est. L.J. 257 (2006); George P. Stephan, Comment, Public Land Use Regulations and Marketability of Title, 1958 Wis. L. Rev. 128.

2. Suppose there is a recorded sewage easement or easement for utility poles across the property. Does this make title unmarketable? Should it matter whether

the easement is visible, or whether the easement diminishes or enhances the value of the property? See Rhodes v. Astro-Pac, Inc., 363 N.E.2d 347 (N.Y. 1977) (easement is an encumbrance, even though it does not diminish value of property); Ziskind v. Bruce Lee Corp., 307 A.2d 377 (Pa. Super. Ct. 1973) (knowledge of easement irrelevant; title unmarketable); Ludke v. Egan, 274 N.W.2d 641 (Wis. 1979) (easement known to purchaser, or open and obvious, does not make title unmarketable).

3. In Sinks v. Karleskint, 474 N.E.2d 767 (Ill. App. 1985), the purchasers of a 40-acre tract alleged that title was not marketable because the tract had no legal access, which the purchasers knew. The court held the title was marketable. The court reasoned that lack of access affects market value, not marketability of title. A title is marketable, said the court, if the seller has a fee simple, the title is free from any encumbrances, and the buyer is entitled to possession. The fact that the buyer may not be able to reach the property does not make title legally unmarketable. The court further held that, even if lack of access were a title defect, the purchaser entered the contract with knowledge of lack of access and had waived such a defect. See also Campbell v. Summit Plaza Associates, 192 P.3d 465 (Colo. App. 2008). Not all courts would agree with *Sinks* or *Campbell.* See Loveland Essential Group, LLC v. Grommon Farms, Inc., 251 P.3d 1109 (Colo. App. 2010) (knowledge of encumbrance does not preclude action for breach); Janian v. Barnes, 742 N.Y.S.2d 445 (App. Div. 2002) (lack of legal access renders title unmarketable). For more on the problem of landlocked property, see pages 833-842.

4. It has been held that the presence of hazardous waste on the property does not render the title unmarketable. HM Holdings, Inc. v. Rankin, 70 F.3d 933 (7th Cir. 1995); Humphries v. Ables, 789 N.E. 2d 1025 (Ind. App. 2003); Vandervort v. Higginbotham, 634 N.Y.S.2d 800 (App. Div. 1995); Pamela A. Harbeson, Comment, Toxic Clouds on Titles, 19 B.C. Envtl. Aff. L. Rev. 355 (1991).

NOTE: EQUITABLE CONVERSION

Both purchasers and sellers of real property are normally entitled to specific performance as a remedy for the other's breach of contract (see page 612). The doctrine of equitable conversion, simply put, is that if there is a specifically enforceable contract for the sale of land, equity regards as done that which ought to be done. The buyer is viewed in equity as the owner from the date of the contract (thus having the "equitable title"); the seller has a claim for money secured by a vendor's lien on the land. The seller is also said to hold the legal title as trustee for the buyer.

Risk of loss. Equitable conversion has been used by some courts to determine whether the seller or the purchaser takes the loss when the premises are destroyed between signing the contract of sale and the closing, and the contract has no provision allocating the risk of loss. Paine v. Meller, 31 Eng. Rep. 1088 (Ch. 1801), held that from the time of the contract of sale of real estate the burden of fortuitous loss is on the purchaser, even though the seller retains possession. This result was said to follow from equitable conversion, treating the purchaser as owner. Most courts are thought to follow this view. Some courts, however, have declined to apply equitable conversion and have held that the loss is on the seller until legal title is conveyed. In Massachusetts, the risk of loss is on the seller if the loss is substantial and the terms of the contract show that the building constituted an important part of the subject matter of the contract; if the loss is not substantial, either party can enforce the contract, though an abatement in purchase price may be given. In some other states, the risk of loss is placed on the party in possession, the view also taken by the Uniform Vendor and Purchaser Act (1935). See, e.g., Brush Grocery Kart, Inc. v. Sure Fine Market, Inc., 47 P.3d 680 (Colo. 2002). If the purchaser has the risk of loss, and the seller has insurance, in most states the seller holds the insurance proceeds as trustee for the buyer. See Bryant v. Willison Real Estate Co., 350 S.E.2d 748 (W. Va. 1986) (discussing the law of many states); William B. Stoebuck & Dale A. Whitman, The Law of Property 792-797 (3d ed. 2000). Which rule is likely to promote economic efficiency—equitable conversion or an approach such as the one adopted in Massachusetts? Obviously, to avoid litigation, the parties should include a provision regarding risk of loss in the contract of sale and buy insurance accordingly.

Inheritance. Equitable conversion has been applied in situations when one of the parties to a contract for the sale of land dies and the issue arises whether the decedent's interest is real property or personal property. If equitable conversion has occurred, the seller's interest is personal property (right to the purchase price), and the buyer is treated as owner of the land. Thus suppose that *O*, owner of Blackacre, contracts to sell Blackacre to *A* for $10,000. Before closing, *O* dies intestate. By the applicable intestacy statute, *B* succeeds to *O*'s real property, and *C* succeeds to *O*'s personal property. Under equitable conversion, *C* is entitled to the $10,000 when it is paid. See also In re Estate of Pickett, 879 So. 2d 467 (Miss. App. 2004); Shay v. Penrose, 185 N.E.2d 218 (Ill. 1962); Coe v. Hays, 661 A.2d 220 (Md. App. 1995).

3. The Duty to Disclose Defects

Stambovsky v. Ackley

New York Supreme Court, Appellate Division
First Department, 1991
572 N.Y.S.2d 672

RUBIN, J. Plaintiff, to his horror, discovered that the house he had recently contracted to purchase was widely reputed to be possessed by poltergeists, reportedly seen by defendant seller and members of her family on numerous occasions over the last nine years. Plaintiff promptly commenced this action seeking rescission of the contract of sale. Supreme Court reluctantly dismissed the complaint, holding that plaintiff has no remedy at law in this jurisdiction.

The unusual facts of this case, as disclosed by the record, clearly warrant a grant of equitable relief to the buyer who, as a resident of New York City, cannot be expected to have any familiarity with the folklore of the Village of Nyack. Not being a "local," plaintiff could not readily learn that the home he had contracted to purchase is haunted. Whether the source of the spectral apparitions seen by defendant seller are parapsychic or psychogenic, having reported their presence in both a national publication (Reader's Digest) and the local press (in 1977 and 1982, respectively), defendant is estopped to deny their existence and, as a matter of law, the house is haunted. More to the point, however, no divination is required to conclude that it is defendant's promotional efforts in publicizing her close encounters with these spirits which fostered the home's reputation in the community. In 1989, the house was included in a five-home walking tour of Nyack and described in a November 27th newspaper article as "a riverfront Victorian (with ghost)." The impact of the reputation thus created goes to the very essence of the bargain between the parties, greatly impairing both the value of the property and its potential for resale. The extent of this impairment may be presumed for the purpose of reviewing the disposition of this motion to dismiss the cause of action for rescission (Harris v. City of New York, 147 A.D.2d 186, 188-189) and represents merely an issue of fact for resolution at trial.

While I agree with Supreme Court that the real estate broker, as agent for the seller, is under no duty to disclose to a potential buyer the phantasmal reputation of the premises and that, in his pursuit of a legal remedy for fraudulent misrepresentation against the seller, plaintiff hasn't a ghost of a chance, I am nevertheless moved by the spirit of equity to allow the buyer to seek rescission of the contract of sale and recovery of his down payment. New York law fails to recognize any remedy for damages incurred as a result of the seller's mere silence, applying instead the strict rule of caveat emptor. Therefore, the theoretical basis for granting relief, even under the extraordinary facts of this case, is elusive if not ephemeral.

"Pity me not but lend thy serious hearing to what I shall unfold" (William Shakespeare, Hamlet, Act I, Scene V [Ghost]).

From the perspective of a person in the position of plaintiff herein, a very practical problem arises with respect to the discovery of a paranormal phenomenon: "Who you gonna' call?" as a title song to the movie "Ghostbusters" asks. Applying the strict rule of caveat emptor to a contract involving a house possessed by poltergeists conjures up visions of a psychic or medium routinely accompanying the structural engineer and Terminix man on an inspection of every home subject to a contract of sale. It portends that the prudent attorney will establish an escrow account lest the subject of the transaction come back to haunt him and his client—or pray that his malpractice insurance coverage extends to supernatural disasters. In the interest of avoiding such untenable consequences, the notion that a haunting is a condition which can and should be ascertained upon reasonable inspection of the premises is a hobgoblin which should be exorcised from the body of legal precedent and laid quietly to rest.

It has been suggested by a leading authority that the ancient rule which holds that mere nondisclosure does not constitute actionable misrepresentation "finds proper application in cases where the fact undisclosed is patent, or the plaintiff has equal opportunities for obtaining information which he may be expected to utilize, or the defendant has no reason to think that he is acting under any misapprehension" (Prosser, Torts §106, at 696 (4th ed. 1971)). However, with respect to transactions in real estate, New York adheres to the doctrine of caveat emptor and imposes no duty upon the vendor to disclose any information concerning the premises (London v. Courduff, 141 A.D.2d 803) unless there is a confidential or fiduciary relationship between the parties (Moser v. Spizzirro, 31 A.D.2d 537, aff'd 25 N.Y.2d 941; IBM Credit Fin. Corp. v. Mazda Motor Mfg. [USA] Corp., 152 A.D.2d 451) or some conduct on the part of the seller which constitutes "active concealment" (see, 17 E. 80th Realty Corp. v. 68th Assocs., 173 A.D.2d 245 (dummy ventilation system constructed by seller); Haberman v. Greenspan, 82 Misc. 2d 263 (foundation cracks covered by seller)). Normally, some affirmative misrepresentation (e.g., Tahini Invs. v. Bobrowsky, 99 A.D.2d 489 (industrial waste on land allegedly used only as farm); Jansen v. Kelly, 11 A.D.2d 587 (land containing valuable minerals allegedly acquired for use as campsite)) or partial disclosure (Junius Constr. Corp. v. Cohen, 257 N.Y. 393 (existence of third unopened street concealed); Noved Realty Corp. v. A.A.P. Co., 250 A.D. 1 (escrow agreements securing lien concealed)) is required to impose upon the seller a duty to communicate undisclosed conditions affecting the premises (contra, Young v. Keith, 112 A.D.2d 625 (defective water and sewer systems concealed)).

Caveat emptor is not so all-encompassing a doctrine of common law as to render every act of nondisclosure immune from redress, whether legal or equitable. . . . Where fairness and common sense dictate that an exception should be created, the evolution of the law should not be stifled by rigid application of a legal maxim.

The doctrine of caveat emptor requires that a buyer act prudently to assess the fitness and value of his purchase and operates to bar the purchaser who fails to exercise due care from seeking the equitable remedy of rescission (see, e.g., Rodas v. Manitaras, 159 A.D.2d 341). . . . It should be apparent, however, that the most meticulous inspection and search would not reveal the presence of poltergeists at the premises or unearth the property's ghoulish reputation in the community. Therefore, there is no sound policy reason to deny plaintiff relief for failing to discover a state of affairs which the most prudent purchaser would not be expected to even contemplate (see, Da Silva v. Musso, 53 N.Y.2d 543, 551).

The case law in this jurisdiction dealing with the duty of a vendor of real property to disclose information to the buyer is distinguishable from the matter under review. The most salient distinction is that existing cases invariably deal with the physical condition of the premises (e.g., London v. Courduff, supra) (use as a landfill); Perin v. Mardine Realty Co., 5 A.D.2d 685, aff'd 6 N.Y.2d 920 (sewer line crossing adjoining property without owner's consent), defects in title (e.g., Sands v. Kissane, 282 A.D. 140 (remainderman)), liens against the property (e.g., Noved Realty Corp. v. A.A.P. Co., supra), expenses or income (e.g., Rodas v. Manitaras, supra (gross receipts)) and other factors affecting its operation. No case has been brought to this court's attention in which the property value was impaired as the result of the reputation created by information disseminated to the public by the seller (or, for that matter, as a result of possession by poltergeists).

Where a condition which has been created by the seller materially impairs the value of the contract and is peculiarly within the knowledge of the seller or unlikely to be discovered by a prudent purchaser exercising due care with respect to the subject transaction, nondisclosure constitutes a basis for rescission as a matter of equity. Any other outcome places upon the buyer not merely the obligation to exercise care in his purchase but rather to be omniscient with respect to any fact which may affect the bargain. No practical purpose is served by imposing such a burden upon a purchaser. To the contrary, it encourages predatory business practice and offends the principle that equity will suffer no wrong to be without a remedy.

Defendant's contention that the contract of sale, particularly the merger or "as is" clause, bars recovery of the buyer's deposit is unavailing. Even an express

". . . as a matter of law, the house is haunted."

AP/Wide World Photos

disclaimer will not be given effect where the facts are peculiarly within the knowledge of the party invoking it (Danaan Realty Corp. v. Harris, 5 N.Y.2d 317, 322; Tahini Invs. v. Bobrowsky, supra). Moreover, a fair reading of the merger clause reveals that it expressly disclaims only representations made with respect to the physical condition of the premises and merely makes general reference to representations concerning "any other matter or things affecting or relating to the aforesaid premises." As broad as this language may be, a reasonable interpretation is that its effect is limited to tangible or physical matters and does not extend to paranormal phenomena. Finally, if the language of the contract is to be construed as broadly as defendant urges to encompass the presence of poltergeists in the house, it cannot be said that she has delivered the premises "vacant" in accordance with her obligation under the provisions of the contract rider. . . .

In the case at bar, defendant seller deliberately fostered the public belief that her home was possessed. Having undertaken to inform the public-at-large, to whom she has no legal relationship, about the supernatural occurrences on her property, she may be said to owe no less a duty to her contract vendee. It has been remarked that the occasional modern cases which permit a seller to take unfair advantage of a buyer's ignorance so long as he is not actively misled are "singularly unappetizing" (Prosser, Torts §106, at 696 (4th ed. 1971)). Where, as here, the seller not only takes unfair advantage of the buyer's ignorance but has created and perpetuated a condition about which he is unlikely to even inquire, enforcement of the contract (in whole or in part) is offensive to the court's sense of equity. Application of the remedy of rescission, within the bounds of the narrow exception to the doctrine of caveat emptor set forth herein, is entirely appropriate to relieve the unwitting purchaser from the consequences of a most unnatural bargain.

Accordingly, the judgment of the Supreme Court, New York County, entered April 9, 1990, which dismissed the complaint pursuant to CPLR 3211(a)(7), should be modified, on the law and the facts, and in the exercise of discretion, and the first cause of action seeking rescission of the contract reinstated, without costs.

SMITH, J., dissenting. . . . [I]f the doctrine of caveat emptor is to be discarded, it should be for a reason more substantive than a poltergeist. The existence of a poltergeist is no more binding upon the defendants than it is upon this court.

Johnson v. Davis

Supreme Court of Florida, 1985
480 So. 2d 625

ADKINS, J. [The Davises entered into a contract to buy the Johnsons' home for $310,000. The Johnsons knew that the roof leaked, but they affirmatively represented to the Davises that there were no problems with the roof. After the Davises made a $31,000 deposit, the Johnsons vacated the home. Several days later, following a heavy rain, Mrs. Davis entered the home and discovered water "gushing" in from around the windows and from the ceiling in two rooms. The Davises brought an action for rescission of the contract and return of their deposit. The court held that the affirmative representation that the roof was sound was a false representation, entitling the Davises to rescind. Then the court turned to an alternative ground for the judgment.]

In determining whether a seller of a home has a duty to disclose latent material defects to a buyer, the established tort law distinction between misfeasance and nonfeasance, action and inaction must carefully be analyzed. The highly individualistic philosophy of the earlier common law consistently imposed liability upon the commission of affirmative acts of harm, but shrank from converting the courts into an institution for forcing men to help one another. This distinction is deeply rooted in our case law. Liability for nonfeasance has therefore been slow to receive recognition in the evolution of tort law.

In theory, the difference between misfeasance and nonfeasance, action and inaction is quite simple and obvious; however, in practice it is not always easy to draw the line and determine whether conduct is active or passive. That is, where failure to disclose a material fact is calculated to induce a false belief, the distinction between concealment and affirmative representations is tenuous. Both proceed from the same motives and are attended with the same consequences; both are violative of the principles of fair dealing and good faith; both are calculated to produce the same result; and, in fact, both essentially have the same effect.

Still there exists in much of our case law the old tort notion that there can be no liability for nonfeasance. The courts in some jurisdictions, including Florida, hold that where the parties are dealing at arm's length and the facts lie equally open to both parties, with equal opportunity of examination, mere nondisclosure does not constitute a fraudulent concealment. . . .

These unappetizing cases are not in tune with the times and do not conform with current notions of justice, equity and fair dealing. One should not be able to stand behind the impervious shield of caveat emptor and take advantage of another's ignorance. . . . Thus, the tendency of the more recent cases has been to restrict rather than extend the doctrine of caveat emptor. The law appears to be working toward the ultimate conclusion that full disclosure of all material facts must be made whenever elementary fair conduct demands it.

The harness placed on the doctrine of caveat emptor in a number of other jurisdictions has resulted in the seller of a home being liable for failing to disclose material defects of which he is aware. This philosophy was succinctly expressed in Lingsch v. Savage, 213 Cal. App. 2d 729, 29 Cal. Rptr. 201 (1963):

> It is now settled in California that where the seller knows of facts materially affecting the value or desirability of the property which are known or accessible only to him and also knows that such facts are not known to or within the reach of the diligent attention and observation of the buyer, the seller is under a duty to disclose them to the buyer.

In Posner v. Davis, 76 Ill. App. 3d 638, 32 Ill. Dec. 186, 395 N.E.2d 133 (1979), buyers brought an action alleging that the sellers of a home fraudulently concealed certain defects in the home which included a leaking roof and basement flooding. Relying on *Lingsch*, the court concluded that the sellers knew of and failed to disclose latent material defects and thus were liable for fraudulent concealment. Id. 32 Ill. Dec. at 190, 395 N.E.2d at 137. Numerous other jurisdictions have followed this view in formulating law involving the sale of homes. See Flakus v. Schug, 213 Neb. 491, 329 N.W.2d 859 (1983) (basement flooding); Thacker v. Tyree, 297 S.E.2d 885 (W. Va. 1982) (cracked walls and foundation problems); Maguire v. Masino, 325 So. 2d 844 (La. Ct. App. 1975) (termite infestation); Weintraub v. Krobatsch, 64 N.J. 445, 317 A.2d 68 (1974) (roach infestation); Cohen v. Vivian, 141 Colo. 443, 349 P.2d 366 (1960) (soil defect).

We are of the opinion, in view of the reasoning and results in *Lingsch, Posner* and the aforementioned cases decided in other jurisdictions, that the same philosophy regarding the sale of homes should also be the law in the state of Florida. Accordingly, we hold that where the seller of a home knows of facts materially affecting the value of the property which are not readily observable and are not known to the buyer, the seller is under a duty to disclose them to the buyer. This duty is equally applicable to all forms of real property, new and used.

. . . Thus, we . . . find that the Johnsons' fraudulent concealment . . . entitles the Davises to the return of the . . . deposit payment plus interest. We further find that the Davises should be awarded costs and fees. It is so ordered.

NOTES AND QUESTIONS

1. In Harding v. Willie, 458 N.W.2d 612 (Iowa App. 1990), when the buyer inquired about a crack in the ceiling, the seller stated there was "absolutely no problem" with the roof because the leak had been fixed. Later the buyer found new evidence of leaking and elected to rescind the contract, either because of fraud or mutual mistake. The court permitted rescission, reasoning that when the seller stated there was "absolutely no problem" with the roof, he either knew it still leaked, which was fraud, or thought the roof had been repaired and no longer leaked, which led to a mutual mistake of fact (that the roof would not leak).

2. An increasing majority of states puts on the seller the duty to disclose all known defects, equating nondisclosure with fraud or misrepresentation. Caveat emptor is steadily being eroded. When the seller breaches this duty, the buyer can rescind the contract or sue for damages after the closing. What should the seller's state of mind be for a buyer to maintain a successful action for nondisclosure? Compare Nystrom v. Cabada, 652 So. 2d 1266 (Fla. App. 1995), with Jensen v. Bailey, 76 So. 3d 980, 983 (Fla. App. 2011).

In most states statutes have been enacted requiring the seller to deliver to prospective buyers a written statement disclosing facts about the property. The statutes set forth detailed information forms. The forms vary, but the required disclosure may include known significant structural defects, soil problems, underground sewage or storage tanks, presence of hazardous materials, alterations or repairs made without necessary permits, violations of building codes or zoning ordinances, and encroachments by neighbors. See, e.g., Cal. Civ. Code §1102.6 (West Supp. 2013); Wis. Stat. Ann. §709.03 (West Supp. 2012). For a comprehensive discussion of these statutes, see George Lefcoe, Property Condition Disclosure Forms: How the Real Estate Industry Eased the Transition from Caveat Emptor to "Seller Tell All," 39 Real Prop., Prob. & Tr. J. 193 (2004); Robert M. Washburn, Residential Real Estate Disclosure Legislation, 44 DePaul L. Rev. 381 (1995). Some statutes apply only to residential sellers and not to sellers of commercial property. See Kathleen M. Tocho, Commercial Real Estate Buyer Beware: Sellers May Have the Right to Remain Silent, 70 S. Cal. L. Rev. 1571 (1997).

In each jurisdiction requiring disclosure, the defect must be "material" to be actionable. One of two tests of materiality is applied: (1) An objective test of whether a reasonable person would attach importance to it in deciding to buy, or (2) a subjective test of whether the defect "affects the value or desirability of the property to the buyer."

In California, the seller must disclose, among other things, any "neighborhood noise problems or other nuisances." In Alexander v. McKnight, 9 Cal. Rptr. 2d 453 (Cal. App. 1992), the McKnights were bad neighbors. In violation of subdivision covenants, they constructed a deck and two-story cabana in their backyard. They staged late-night basketball games, parked too many cars on their property, and, after complaints by neighbors, poured motor oil on the roof of their house. The Alexanders, who lived next door, sued for an injunction against the nuisances and for damages. The trial court enjoined all the objectionable behavior and awarded the Alexanders $24,000 damages on this theory: Since the Alexanders would have to disclose to prospective buyers that the McKnights were difficult neighbors, the Alexanders' property would sell for $24,000 less because of the McKnights' conduct. On appeal, the appellate court agreed that the Alexanders would be legally required to disclose the offensive and noisy activities of the McKnights, if the McKnights were still living in the neighborhood.

> The fact that a neighborhood contains an overly hostile family who delights in tormenting their neighbors with unexpected noises or unending parties is not a matter which will ordinarily come to the attention of a buyer viewing the property at a time carefully selected by the seller to correspond with an anticipated lull in the "festivities." [9 Cal. Rptr. 2d at 456.]

However, the court reversed the award of damages as premature. The court assumed that the McKnights would comply with the court order and cease the objectionable activity. If the McKnights failed to comply or found other ways to offend their neighbors, so that the economic loss was not eliminated, the Alexanders could then enforce the existing judgment by an action for damages.

In Shapiro v. Sutherland, 76 Cal. Rptr. 2d 101 (Cal. App. 1998), the seller, who had had considerable trouble with a noisy family next door, checked "No neighborhood noise problems" on the statutory disclosure form. The court held the seller was liable to a subsequent buyer who was shown the disclosure form and bought in reliance on it.

Because of increasing litigation over seller's failure to disclose, many residential sale contracts prepared by brokers contain a provision that any dispute or claim arising from failure to disclose shall be arbitrated and not sued upon. Is this enforceable? Is it a contract of adhesion if contained in standard sale forms routinely signed by buyers with the broker's guidance? See Johnson v. Siegel, 101 Cal. Rptr. 2d 412 (Cal. App. 2000) (enforceable); State ex rel. Vincent v. Schneider, 194 S.W.3d 853 (Mo. 2006) (enforceable); TMI, Inc. v. Brooks, 225 S.W.3d 783 (Tex. App. 2007) (enforceable). May a purchaser waive his right to disclosure? See Deptula v. Simpson, 164 P.3d 640 (Alaska 2007).

3. Partly in response to cases finding sellers liable for failing to disclose conditions that "stigmatized" properties (see, e.g., Reed v. King, 193 Cal. Rptr. 130 (Cal. App. 1983)), several states have enacted statutes shielding sellers from a failure to disclose psychological or prejudicial factors that might affect market value, such as a murder within the house or that a former occupant died of AIDS. These statutes are known as stigma statutes. See, e.g., N.Y. Real Prop. Law §443(a) (McKinney Supp. 2013); see also Stuart C. Edmiston, Comment, Secrets Worth Keeping: Toward a Principled Basis for Stigmatized Property Disclosure Statutes, 58 UCLA L. Rev. 281 (2010); Florise R. Neville-Ewell, Residential Real Estate Transactions: The AIDS Influence, 5 Hofstra Prop. L.J. 301 (1993).

Consider common law or statutory rules modifying caveat emptor to require disclosure on the part of sellers of real property. Are they wealth-maximizing? For two approaches to this question—one theoretical and the other empirical—see Alex M. Johnson, Jr., An Economic Analysis of the Duty to Disclose Information: Lessons Learned from the Caveat Emptor Doctrine, 45 San Diego L. Rev. 79 (2008); Anupam Nanda & Stephen L. Ross, The Impact of Property Condition Disclosure Laws on Housing Prices: Evidence from an Event Study Using Propensity Scores, 45 J. Real Est. Fin. & Econ. 88 (2012).

Under Megan's Law, enacted in several states, certain convicted sex offenders are required to register with a local police station. The local chief of police must notify the community of the registrant's presence in the community. See Doe v. Poritz, 662 A.2d 367 (N.J. 1995). Suppose that the seller is aware that a convicted sex offender is living in the vicinity. Must the seller disclose that information? Does the seller or the broker have a duty to inquire at the local police station? If so, is there a duty also to report discovered mass murderers and ordinary felons living nearby? See Thomas D. Larson, Comment, To Disclose or Not to Disclose: The Dilemma of Homeowners and Real Estate Brokers Under Wisconsin's "Megan's Law," 81 Marq. L. Rev. 1161 (1998). If the buyer has a lawyer, the lawyer may write into the contract of sale a requirement that the seller disclose whether the seller has been notified of any sex offender living nearby. See also Shelly Ross Saxer, "Am I My Brother's Keeper?": Requiring Landowner Disclosure of the Presence of Sex Offenders and Other Criminal Activity, 80 Neb. L. Rev. 522 (2001).

4. *Broker's duty to disclose.* One of the reasons so many states have passed statutes requiring sellers to disclose defects is the political pressure brought to bear on legislators by real estate brokers. See Lefcoe, supra, at 193. In recent years, brokers have been subjected to liability under a number of theories. They have

been found liable for fraud for either intentionally or negligently misrepresenting the condition of a property. See Powell v. Wold, 362 S.E.2d 796 (N.C. App. 1987) (intentional misrepresentation); Bloor v. Fritz, 180 P.3d 805 (Wash. App. 2008) (negligent misrepresentation); Tennant v. Lawton, 615 P.2d 1305 (Wash. App. 1980) (negligent misrepresentation). Innocent misrepresentations by brokers—non-negligently repeating statements made by their sellers to prospective buyers—have also led to liability. See Bevins v. Ballard, 655 P.2d 757 (Alaska 1982), subsequently reversed by statute as noted in Amyot v. Luchini, 932 P.2d 244 (Alaska 1997). Perhaps the straw that broke the camel's back was a decision by an intermediate appellate court in California holding that brokers could be held liable for negligently failing to uncover defects in a property's driveway that caused landslides. See Easton v. Strassburger, 199 Cal. Rptr. 383 (Cal. App. 1984). To protect themselves against lawsuits, brokers promoted seller disclosure laws.

On the broker's liability for misrepresentations or failure to disclose, see Paul Meyer, Illinois Real Estate Brokers: The Duties of Disclosure and Accuracy, 23 Loy. U. Chi. L.J. 241 (1992); Diane M. Allen, Annotation, Real-Estate Broker's Liability to Purchaser for Misrepresentation or Nondisclosure of Physical Defects in Property Sold, 46 A.L.R.4th 546 (2005).

5. *Disclosure of hazardous waste disposal.* In 1980 Congress enacted the Comprehensive Environmental Response, Compensation, and Liability Act (CERCLA), 42 U.S.C. §§9601-9675. CERCLA imposes strict liability for cleanup costs of a hazardous waste site upon any *current owner* or operator of a site containing hazardous waste, any *prior owner* or operator of the site at the time it was contaminated, any generator of hazardous waste, and transporters of hazardous substances. 42 U.S.C. §9607(a). The principal implementing agency of CERCLA is the U.S. Environmental Protection Agency (EPA). At the time CERCLA was enacted, Congress appropriated a "superfund" of $1.6 billion to be used to pay for cleanup costs of sites contaminated with hazardous wastes. The EPA is authorized to use this money to clean up contaminated sites. Then it sues the responsible parties to recover its costs. The cleanup costs of hazardous waste sites can run into the millions of dollars, and the liability of owners can be staggering.

CERCLA was amended in 2002 to establish a "bona fide prospective purchaser" defense. 42 U.S.C. §9601(40). The defense is available provided that the release of hazardous materials took place before the purchaser bought the property, that the purchaser "made all appropriate inquiries into the previous ownership and uses" of the property, and that the purchaser "exercises appropriate care with respect to hazardous substances found at the facility. . . ."

Purchasers of contaminated property held liable under CERCLA may sue their sellers for contribution. See, e.g., Sherwin-Williams Co. v. Artra Group, Inc., 125 F. Supp. 2d 739 (D. Md. 2001); Volunteers of America of W. New York v. Heinrich, 90 F. Supp. 2d 252 (W.D.N.Y. 2000).

As a result of CERCLA, cautious buyers have spawned a fast-growing environmental assessment industry to discover possible contamination before closing a deal. Buyers want to know about all previous owners and occupants of the property as well as the uses to which the property has been put. Physical tests are used to discover contamination. See Casey Cohn, The Brownfields Revitalization and Environmental Restoration Act: Landmark Reform or a "Trap for the Unwary"?, 12 N.Y.U. Envtl. L.J. 672 (2004); Judith G. Tracy, Beyond Caveat Emptor: Disclosure to Buyers of Contaminated Land, 10 Stan. Envtl. L.J. 169 (1991).

In Strawn v. Canuso, 657 A.2d 420 (N.J. 1995), the court held that the builder and selling brokers of new homes had the duty to disclose to potential buyers the existence of a landfill nearby that was suspected of containing toxic waste. The court said that professional sellers and brokers have a duty to disclose off-site as well as on-site conditions that are of sufficient materiality to affect the habitability, use, or enjoyment of the property and, therefore, render the property substantially less desirable or valuable to the objectively reasonable buyer. Although this duty appears to call for very broad disclosure, the court limited it somewhat by this comment.

> We do not hold that sellers and brokers have a duty to investigate or disclose transient social conditions in the community that arguably affect the value of the property. In the absence of a purchaser communicating specific needs, builders and brokers should not be held to decide whether the changing nature of a neighborhood, the presence of a group home, or the existence of a school in decline are facts material to the transaction. Rather we root in the land the duty to disclose off-site conditions that are material to the transaction. [657 A.2d at 431.]

Within six months of the Supreme Court's decision in *Strawn*, the New Jersey legislature passed the New Residential Construction Off-Site Conditions Disclosure Act, N.J. Stat. Ann. §§46:3C-1 to 46:3C-12 (West 2012). The act effectively immunizes sellers of new homes from liability for nondisclosure of off-site conditions, provided they give buyers notice that lists of these conditions are available in the municipal clerk's office. Despite the immunity, the act permits buyers to maintain lawsuits based upon violations of certain statutes. The immunity provision is interpreted in Nobrega v. Edison Glen Assocs., 743 A.2d 864 (N.J. App. 2000).

In Haberstick v. Gordon A. Gundaker Real Estate Co., Inc., 921 S.W.2d 104 (Mo. App. 1996), the court held that real estate brokers have a duty to disclose to purchasers the possible presence of hazardous wastes on adjacent property. The court upheld awards of both actual and punitive damages for nondisclosure. See Florrie Young Roberts, Off-Site Conditions and Disclosure Duties: Drawing the Line at the Property Line, 2006 BYU L. Rev. 957; Serena M. Williams, When Daylight Reveals Neighborhood Nightmares: The Duty of Builders and Developers to Disclose Off-Site Environmental Conditions, 12 J. Nat. Resources & Envtl. L. 1 (1997); Annot., 12 A.L.R.5th 630 (1993).

Should the seller and broker have a duty to disclose other known off-site conditions that materially affect the value of the property, such as crimes or drug-dealing in the neighborhood?

6. Generally, an "as is" clause in a sales contract will be upheld if the defects are reasonably discoverable and there is no fraud. But if there is a fraudulent representation or concealment of information by the seller, the buyer usually is not bound by the "as is" clause. See Prudential Ins. Co. v. Jefferson Assocs., Ltd.,

896 S.W.2d 156 (Tex. 1995); Snyder v. Lovercheck, 992 P.2d 1079 (Wyo. 1999) (analyzing cases from many jurisdictions). But cf. Benton v. Clegg Land Co., Ltd., 99 So. 3d 872 (Ala. Civ. App. 2012) (enforcing "as is" clause despite misrepresentation). What if the defects in a property were not disclosed in the mandated disclosure form and were reasonably discoverable? See Burgess v. Fendi, 263 S.W.3d 578 (Ark. App. 2007).

NOTE: MERGER

An old doctrine says that when a buyer accepts a deed, the buyer is deemed to be satisfied that all the contractual obligations have been met. Thus the contract merges into the deed, and the deed is deemed the final act of the parties expressing the terms of their agreement. The buyer can no longer sue the seller on promises in the contract of sale not contained in the deed, but must sue the seller on the warranties, if any, contained in the deed. There are recognized exceptions to the doctrine, such as fraud and contractual promises deemed collateral to the deed. The merger doctrine principally applies to questions of title or quantity of land. If a contract, for instance, calls for marketable title, and the buyer accepts a deed with no warranties, the buyer cannot thereafter upon discovery of a title defect sue on the contract provision requiring the seller to furnish marketable title. See James v. McCombs, 936 P.2d 520 (Alaska 1997).

The merger doctrine is now in disfavor and is becoming riddled with exceptions when the buyer does not intend to discharge the seller's contractual obligations by acceptance of the deed. The usual way of avoiding the doctrine is to say the particular obligation of the seller is an independent or collateral obligation. See Lawrence Berger, Merger by Deed—What Provisions of a Contract for the Sale of Land Survive the Closing?, 21 Real Est. L.J. 22 (1992); Abi-Najm v. Concord Condominium, LLC, 699 S.E.2d 483 (Va. 2010); Neppl v. Murphy, 736 N.E.2d 1174 (Ill. App. 2000); Davis v. Tazewell Place Assocs., 492 S.E.2d 162 (Va. 1997) (seller's contract to construct townhouse in good and workmanlike manner was collateral to the sale of the property and did not merge with the deed at closing).

The seller and buyer may bargain about what contract warranties survive the closing, and so provide in the contract. But a provision that no warranties survive closing is not valid if the seller has misrepresented a material fact or committed fraud.

4. The Implied Warranty of Quality

Recall the implied warranty of habitability in landlord-tenant law. (See pages 515-525.) Sales of real estate may also give rise to a similar warranty. Suits on the warranty can arise only after the closing has taken place and the plaintiff has accepted the deed. Nonetheless, because such suits are closely connected with suits against the seller for nondisclosure, we take up the implied warranty of quality at this point.

Lempke v. Dagenais

Supreme Court of New Hampshire, 1988
547 A.2d 290

THAYER, J. This is an appeal from the Trial Court's dismissal of the plaintiffs' complaint alleging breach of implied warranty of workmanlike quality and negligence. The primary issue before this court is whether a subsequent purchaser of real property may sue the builder/contractor on the theory of implied warranty of workmanlike quality for latent defects which cause economic loss, absent privity of contract.

We hold that privity of contract is not necessary for a subsequent purchaser to sue a builder or contractor under an implied warranty theory for latent defects which manifest themselves within a reasonable time after purchase and which cause economic harm. Accordingly, we reverse the dismissal by the trial court, and remand.

In 1977, the plaintiffs' predecessors in title contracted with the defendant, Dagenais, to build a garage. In April, 1978, within six months after the garage's construction, the original owners sold the property to plaintiffs, Elaine and Larry Lempke. Shortly after they purchased the property, the plaintiffs began to notice structural problems with the garage—the roof line was uneven and the roof trusses were bowing out. The plaintiffs contend that the separation of the trusses from the roof was a latent defect which could not be discovered until the separation and bowing became noticeable from the exterior of the structure. Fearing a cave-in of the roof, the plaintiffs contacted the defendant and asked him to repair the defects. The defendant initially agreed to do so, but never completed the necessary repairs. The plaintiffs then brought suit against the builder. In turn, the builder filed a motion to dismiss, which the superior court granted based on our holding in Ellis v. Morris, 128 N.H. 358, 513 A.2d 951 (1986). This appeal followed.

The plaintiffs set forth three claims in their brief: one for breach of implied warranty of workmanlike quality; one for negligence; and one, in the alternative, for breach of assigned contract rights. We need address only the first two claims.

We have previously denied aggrieved subsequent purchasers recovery in tort for economic loss and denied them recovery under an implied warranty theory for economic loss. See Ellis v. Morris, supra. The court in *Ellis* acknowledged the problems a subsequent purchaser faces, but declined to follow the examples of those cases which allow recovery. 128 N.H. at 361, 513 A.2d at 952. The policy arguments relied upon in *Ellis* for precluding tort recovery for economic loss, in these circumstances, accurately reflect New Hampshire law and present judicial scholarship, see generally Bertschy, Negligent Performance of Service Contracts and Economic Loss, 17 J. Mar. L. Rev. 246 (1984) (hereinafter Negligent Performance) and, as such, remain controlling on the negligence claim. However, the denial of relief to subsequent purchasers on an implied warranty theory was predicated on the court's adherence to the requirement of privity in a contract action and on the fear that to allow recovery without privity would impose unlimited liability on builders and contractors. Thus we need only discuss the implied warranty issue.

I. Privity

This case affords us an opportunity to review and reassess the issue of privity as it relates to implied warranties of workmanlike quality. In Norton v. Burleaud, 115 N.H. 435, 342 A.2d 629 (1975), this court held that an implied warranty of workmanlike quality applied between the builder of a house and the first purchaser. The Norton court so held based on the facts before it, and did not explicitly or impliedly limit the benefit of implied warranties solely to the first purchaser. The question before us today is whether this implied warranty may be relied upon by subsequent purchasers and, if so, whether recovery may be had for solely economic loss.

There has been much judicial debate on the basis of implied warranty. Some courts find that it is premised on tort concepts. See, e.g., LaSara Grain v. First National Bank of Mercedes, 673 S.W.2d 558, 565 (Tex. 1984) ("implied warranties are created by operation of law and are grounded more in tort than contract"); Berman v. Watergate West, Inc., 391 A.2d 1351 (D.C. App. 1978).

Other courts find that implied warranty is based in contract. See, e.g., Redarowicz v. Ohlendorf, 92 Ill. 2d 171, 183, 65 Ill. Dec. 411, 417, 441 N.E.2d 324, 330 (1982) (Implied warranty extended to subsequent purchaser, who purchased house from original owner within first year, for policy reason. Plaintiff could recover under implied warranty theory for cracks in basement, chimney and adjoining wall separating, water leakage in basement, but no recovery in negligence for economic harm.); Aronsohn v. Mandara, 98 N.J. 92, 484 A.2d 675 (1984) (suit for implied warranty of habitability for structurally unsound patio); Cosmopolitan Homes, Inc. v. Weller, 663 P.2d 1041 (Colo. 1983) (en banc) (implied warranty arises from contractual relationship).

Other authorities find implied warranty neither a tort nor a contract concept, but "a freak hybrid born of the illicit intercourse of tort and contract. . . . Originally sounding in tort, yet arising out of the warrantor's consent to be bound, it later ceased necessarily to be consensual, and at the same time came to lie mainly in contract." Prosser, The Assault Upon the Citadel, 69 Yale L.J. 1099, 1126 (1960); accord Scott v. Strickland, 10 Kan. App. 2d 14, 18, 691 P.2d 45, 50 (1984) (discussing first purchaser, court found implied warranty could be tort or contract); Edmeades, The Citadel Stands: The Recovery of Economic Loss in American Products Liability, 27 Case W. Res. L. Rev. 647, 662 (1977).

Regardless of whether courts have found the implied warranty to be based in contract or tort, many have found that it exists independently, imposed by operation of law, the imposition of which is a matter of public policy. See 67A Am. Jur.

2d §690 ("Implied warranties arise by operation of law and not by agreement of the parties, their purpose being to protect the buyer from loss. . . ."); Elliott v. Lachance, 109 N.H. 481, 483, 256 A.2d 153, 155 (1969) ("Such warranties [referring to UCC merchantability] are not created by agreement . . . but are said to be imposed by law on the basis of public policy."); Richards v. Powercraft Homes, Inc., 139 Ariz. 242, 678 P.2d 427 (1984) (en banc) (Warranty of workmanlike quality and habitability is imposed by law. Homeowners were entitled to recover for breach of implied warranty of workmanlike quality for damages such as cracking, separation of floors from walls, regardless of privity, so long as no substantial change occurred to structure.); Terlinde v. Neely, 275 S.C. 395, 271 S.E.2d 768 (1980) (Subsequent purchaser can rely on theories of implied warranty and negligence for cracks in structure, ill-fitting doors, etc. Court allowed recovery on both theories as a matter of public policy, holding builder to industry standards.); Barnes v. Mac Brown & Co., Inc., 264 Ind. 227, 342 N.E.2d 619 (1976) (Implied warranty extended to second purchaser for latent defects which caused economic harm. Implied warranty of fitness is to real property what implied warranty of merchantability is to personal property.); Redarowicz, 92 Ill. 2d at 183, 65 Ill. Dec. at 417, 441 N.E.2d at 330 ("While the warranty of habitability has its roots in the execution of the contract . . . we emphasize that it exists independently.") (Citations omitted.); Petersen v. Hubschman Const. Co., 76 Ill. 2d 31, 38, 27 Ill. Dec. 746, 749, 389 N.E.2d 1154, 1157 (1979) ("implied warranty . . . is a judicial innovation . . . used to avoid the harshness of caveat emptor. . . ."); George v. Veach, 67 N.C. App. 674, 677, 313 S.E.2d 920, 922 (1984) ("An implied warranty arises by operation of law. . . ."); Woodward v. Chirco Const. Co., Inc., 141 Ariz. 514, 687 P.2d 1269 (1984) (en banc); Nastri v. Wood, 142 Ariz. 439, 690 P.2d 158 (1984).

We continue to agree with our statement in *Elliott*, supra at 483-84, 256 A.2d at 155, that

[implied] warranties are not created by an agreement . . . between the parties but are said to be imposed by law on the basis of public policy. They arise by operation of law because of the relationship between the parties, the nature of the transaction, and the surrounding circumstances,

and agree with other courts that find implied warranties, in circumstances similar to those presented here, to be creatures of public policy "that ha[ve] evolved to protect purchasers of . . . homes upon the discovery of latent defects," *Redarowicz*, 92 Ill. 2d at 183, 65 Ill. Dec. at 417, 441 N.E.2d at 330, and that, regardless of their theoretical origins, "exist independently." Id.

There are jurisdictions which have refused to extend the implied warranty to subsequent purchasers, finding privity necessary. . . .

However, numerous jurisdictions have now found privity of contract unnecessary for implied warranty. See, e.g., Tusch Enterprises v. Coffin, 113 Ida. 37, 740 P.2d 1022 (1987) (Subsequent purchasers who suffer purely economic damages from latent defects manifested within a reasonable time may maintain an action in implied warranty without privity, but not in negligence.); Richards v.

Powercraft Homes, Inc., 139 Ariz. 242, 678 P.2d 427; Nastri v. Wood, 142 Ariz. 439, 690 P.2d 158; Reichelt v. Urban Investment & Development Co., 577 F. Supp. 971 (N.D. Ill., E.D. 1984); Aronsohn v. Mandara, 98 N.J. 92, 484 A.2d 675 (Subsequent purchasers could sue, on negligence and implied warranty of habitability, for defective construction of patio and recover for economic damages.); Bridges v. Ferrell, 685 P.2d 409 (Okl. App. 1984); Keyes v. Guy Baily Homes, Inc., 439 So. 2d 670 (Miss. 1983) (Overruling earlier Mississippi cases preventing recovery. Subsequent purchaser can now sue builder for breach of implied warranty of good workmanship for latent defects resulting in financial losses. The Court reasoned that an innocent purchaser should not suffer when the builder failed to construct the building in a workmanlike manner.); Briarcliffe West v. Wiseman Const. Co., 118 Ill. App. 3d 163, 73 Ill. Dec. 503, 454 N.E.2d 363 (1983) (implied warranty extended to subsequent purchaser of vacant common lot who discovers latent defect within reasonable time); Gupta v. Ritter Homes, Inc., 646 S.W.2d 168 (Tex. 1983) (implied warranty of habitability and good workmanship implicit in contract and automatically assigned to subsequent purchaser); Redarowicz v. Ohlendorf, 92 Ill. 2d 171, 65 Ill. Dec. 411, 441 N.E.2d 324; Elden v. Simmons, 631 P.2d 739 (Okl. 1981) (Suit for damages resulting from cracking, buckling; implied warranty of habitability and workmanlike manner does not necessarily terminate upon transfer of title. Court analogized situation similar to the UCC and reasoned that buyers were in chain of title.); Blagg v. Fred Hunt Co., 272 Ark. 185, 612 S.W.2d 321 (1981); Hermes v. Staiano, 181 N.J. Super. 424, 437 A.2d 925 (1981) (subsequent purchasers could recover for buckling foundation on theory of implied warranty and strict liability); Terlinde v. Neely, 275 S.C. 395, 271 S.E.2d 768; Wagner Construction Co., Inc. v. Noonan, 403 N.E.2d 1144 (Ind. App. 1st Dist. 1980) (subsequent purchasers could maintain suit in implied warranty for damages resulting from septic system backup); Moxley v. Laramie Builders, Inc., 600 P.2d 733 (Wyo. 1979) (Subsequent purchasers could sue on an implied warranty and negligence theories for latent defects in electric system.); Berman v. Watergate West, Inc., 391 A.2d 1351; Barnes v. Mac Brown & Co. Inc., 264 Ind. 227, 342 N.E.2d 619. . . .

In keeping with judicial trends and the spirit of the law in New Hampshire, we now hold that the privity requirement should be abandoned in suits by subsequent purchasers against a builder or contractor for breach of an implied warranty of good workmanship for latent defects. "To require privity between the contractor and the home owner in such a situation would defeat the purpose of the implied warranty of good workmanship and could leave innocent homeowners without a remedy. . . ." Aronsohn, 98 N.J. at 102, 484 A.2d at 680.

Numerous practical and policy reasons justify our holding. The essence of implied warranty is to protect innocent buyers. As such, this principle, which protects first purchasers as recognized by Norton v. Burleaud, 115 N.H. 435, 342 A.2d 629, is equally applicable to subsequent purchasers. The extension of this principle is based on "sound legal and policy considerations." Terlinde, 275 S.C. at 397, 271 S.E.2d at 769. The mitigation of caveat emptor should not be frustrated by the intervening ownership of the prior purchasers. As a general principle, "[t]he contractor should not be relieved of liability for unworkmanlike construction simply because of the fortuity that the property on which he did the construction has changed hands." *Aronsohn*, supra at 102, 484 A.2d at 680. . . .

First, "[c]ommon experience teaches that latent defects in a house will not manifest themselves for a considerable period of time . . . after the original purchaser has sold the property to a subsequent unsuspecting buyer." *Terlinde*, 275 S.C. at 398, 271 S.E.2d at 769.

Second, our society is rapidly changing.

> We are an increasingly mobile people; a builder-vendor should know that a house he builds might be resold within a relatively short period of time and should not expect that the warranty will be limited by the number of days that the original owner holds onto the property. [*Redarowicz*, 92 Ill. 2d at 185, 65 Ill. Dec. at 417, 441 N.E.2d at 330.]

Furthermore, "the character of society has changed such that the ordinary buyer is not in a position to discover hidden defects. . . ." *Terlinde*, supra at 397, 271 S.E.2d at 769; *Redarowicz*, supra at 184, 65 Ill. Dec. at 417, 441 N.E.2d at 330 (citation omitted).

Third, like an initial buyer, the subsequent purchaser has little opportunity to inspect and little experience and knowledge about construction. "Consumer protection demands that those who buy homes are entitled to rely on the skill of a builder and that the house is constructed so as to be reasonably fit for its intended use." *Moxley*, 600 P.2d at 735; accord *Wagner Const. Co., Inc.*, 403 N.E.2d 1144, 1147.

Fourth, the builder/contractor will not be unduly taken unaware by the extension of the warranty to a subsequent purchaser. "The builder already owes a duty to construct the home in a workmanlike manner. . . ." *Keyes*, 439 So. 2d at 673. And extension to a subsequent purchaser, within a reasonable time, will not change this basic obligation.

Fifth, arbitrarily interposing a first purchaser as a bar to recovery "might encourage sham first sales to insulate builders from liability." *Richards*, 139 Ariz. at 245, 678 P.2d at 430.

Economic policies influence our decision as well. "[B]y virtue of superior knowledge, skill, and experience in the construction of houses, a builder-vendor is generally better positioned than the purchaser to . . . evaluate and guard against the financial risk posed by a [latent defect]. . . ." George v. Veach, 67 N.C. App. 674, 313 S.E.2d 920, 923 (1984). . . .

As the *Moxley* court stated: the "purpose of [an] [implied] warranty is to protect innocent purchasers and hold builders accountable for their work . . . [and] any reasoning which would arbitrarily interpose a first buyer as an obstruction to someone equally as deserving of recovery is incomprehensible." 600 P.2d 736.

This court, as well, does not find it logical to limit protection arbitrarily to the first purchaser. Most purchasers do not have the expertise necessary to discover latent defects, and they need to rely on the skill and experience of the builder. After all, the effect of a latent defect will be equally debilitating to a subsequent purchaser as to a first owner, and the builder will be "just as unable to justify the improper or substandard work." *Richards*, 139 Ariz. at 245, 678 P.2d at 430; accord *Gupta*, 646 S.W.2d at 169.

Not only do policy and economic reasons convince us that a privity requirement in this situation is unwarranted, but analogous situations show us the soundness of this extension. Public policy has compelled a change in the law of personal property and goods, as witnessed by the adoption of UCC. The logic which compelled this change is equally persuasive for real property. . . . As one law review commentator said: the "[a]pplication of such a warranty is similar to that of implied warranty of fitness and merchantability under the Uniform Commercial Code." Comment, Builder's Liability for Latent Defects in Used Homes, 32 Stan. L. Rev. 607 (1980) (author urged that regardless of method employed, liability for latent defects occurring within a reasonable time should be placed on builder). . . .

II. *Economic Loss*

Finally, we address the issue of whether we should allow recovery for purely economic harm, which generally is that loss resulting from the failure of the product to perform to the level expected by the buyer and is commonly measured by the cost of repairing or replacing the product. See Comment, Manufacturers' Liability to Remote Purchasers for "Economic Loss" Damages—Tort or Contract?, 114 U. Pa. L. Rev. 539, 541 (1966) (hereinafter Remote Purchaser); Bertschy, Negligent Performance, 17 J. Mar. L. Rev. at 264-70. Much theoretical debate has taken place on whether to allow economic recovery and whether tort or contract is the most appropriate vehicle for such recovery.

It is clear that the majority of courts do not allow economic loss recovery in tort, but that economic loss is recoverable in contract, see Remote Purchaser, 114 U. Pa. L. Rev. 539; Negligent Performance, 17 J. Mar. L. Rev. 246; Note, Economic Loss in Products Liability Jurisprudence, 66 Colum. L. Rev. 917 (1966). . . . However, what is less clear is whether courts allow recovery for economic loss on an implied warranty theory, without privity, in situations such as ours. Some courts do not. Other courts implicitly allow recovery for economic loss, see, e.g., *Moxley*, 600 P.2d 733 (electrical wire defective); *Terlinde*, 275 S.C. 395, 271 S.E.2d 768 (ill-fitting doors, cracking); *Richards*, 139 Ariz. 242, 678 P.2d 427 (separation of walls); *Elden*, 631 P.2d 739 (faulty bricks); *Nastri*, 142 Ariz. 439, 690 P.2d 158; and other courts that have dealt directly with the issue of economic harm in implied warranty have found that an aggrieved party can recover. . . .

The courts which have allowed economic loss recovery in situations similar to ours have done so basically because the line between property damage and economic loss is not always easy to draw. . . .

We agree with the courts that allow economic recovery in implied warranty for subsequent purchasers, finding as they have that "the contention that a distinction should be drawn between mere 'economic loss' and personal injury is without merit."

Why there should be a difference between an economic loss resulting from injury to property and an economic loss resulting from personal injury has not been revealed to us. When one is personally injured from a defect, he recovers mainly for his economic loss. Similarly, if a wife loses a husband because of injury resulting from a defect in construction, the measure of damages is totally economic loss. We fail to see any rational reason for such a distinction.

If there is a defect in a stairway and the purchaser repairs the defect and suffers an economic loss, should he fail to recover because he did not wait until he or some member of his family fell down the stairs and broke his neck? Does the law penalize those who are alert and prevent injury? Should it not put those who prevent personal injury on the same level as those who fail to anticipate it? [*Barnes*, 264 Ind. at 230, 342 N.E.2d at 621.]

The vendee has a right to expect to receive that for which he has bargained. . . .

III.   Limitations

We are, however, aware of the concerns that this court in *Ellis* raised about unlimited liability. As with any rule, there must be built-in limitations, which in this case would act as a barrier to the possibility of unlimited liability.

Therefore, our extension of the implied warranty of workmanlike quality is not unlimited; it does not force the builder to act as an insurer, in all respects, to a subsequent purchaser. Our extension is limited to *latent* defects "which become manifest after the subsequent owner's purchase and which were not discoverable had a reasonable inspection of the structure been made prior to the purchase." *Richards*, 139 Ariz. at 245, 678 P.2d at 430.

The implied warranty of workmanlike quality for latent defects is limited to a reasonable period of time. *Terlinde*, 275 S.C. at 398, 271 S.E.2d at 769; *Redarowicz*, 92 Ill. 2d at 185, 65 Ill. Dec. at 418, 441 N.E.2d at 331. "The length of time for latent defects to surface, so as to place subsequent purchasers on equal footing, should be controlled by the standard of reasonableness and not an arbitrary time limit created by the Court." *Terlinde*, supra at 398, 271 S.E.2d at 769; accord *Barnes*, 264 Ind. at 229, 342 N.E.2d at 621; *Blagg*, 272 Ariz. at 187, 612 S.W.2d at 322.

Furthermore, the plaintiff still has the burden to show that the defect was caused by the defendant's workmanship, *Barnes*, supra at 230, 342 N.E.2d at 621; and defenses are also available to the builder. "The builder . . . can demonstrate that the defects were not attributable to him, that they are the result of age or ordinary wear and tear, or that previous owners have made substantial changes." *Richards*, 139 Ariz. at 245, 678 P.2d at 430.

Finally, we want to clarify that the duty inherent in an implied warranty of workmanlike quality is to perform in "a workmanlike manner and in accordance with accepted standards." Norton v. Burleaud, 115 N.H. at 436, 342 A.2d at 630. "The law recognizes an implied warranty that the contractor or builder will use the customary standard of skill and care." Kenney v. Medlin Const. & Realty Co., 68 N.C. App. 339, 343, 315 S.E.2d 311, 314 (1984); accord *Nastri*, 142 Ariz. at 444, 690 P.2d at 163.

In conclusion, to the extent Ellis v. Morris, 128 N.H. 358, 513 A.2d 951 (1986) suggests otherwise, we overrule it, and therefore reverse and remand this case for further proceedings.

Reversed and remanded.

SOUTER, J. [now retired from the United States Supreme Court], dissenting. Because I am not satisfied that there is an adequate justification to repudiate the rationale unanimously adopted by this court a mere two years ago in Ellis v. Robert C. Morris, Inc., 128 N.H. 358, 513 A.2d 951 (1986), I respectfully dissent.

NOTES AND QUESTIONS

1. Caveat emptor in the sale of real estate by a vendor-builder is, if not yet dead, certainly moribund. Almost all of the modern cases imply a warranty of quality or skillful construction in connection with the sale of homes. See William B. Stoebuck & Dale A. Whitman, The Law of Property 934-935 (3d ed. 2000). But what about commercial properties? Should sellers of retail stores, bank buildings, and warehouse buildings be subject to the implied warranty? Compare Hodgson v. Chin, 403 A.2d 942 (N.J. App. Div. 1979), with Hayden Bus. Ctr. Condos. Assn. v. Pegasus Dev. Corp., 105 P.3d 157 (Ariz. App. 2005). See also D. Andrew Gaona, Comment, Privity No More: Implied Warranty Rights of Subsequent Purchasers of Commercial Property in Arizona, 41 Ariz. St. L.J. 877 (2009).

2. As discussed in *Lempke*, the modern trend is toward eliminating the privity requirement for subsequent purchasers of real property to sue home builders for breach of quality. For example, in 2008, the Supreme Court of Iowa cited *Lempke* in Speight v. Walters Dev. Co., Ltd., 744 N.W.2d 108, 113 (Iowa 2008), in reversing the grant of summary judgment to a builder who alleged lack of privity. See also Elizabeth Murphy, Note, The Current State of Caveat Emptor in Alabama Real Estate Sales, 60 Ala. L. Rev. 499, 504 (2009) (at least 16 jurisdictions allow subsequent purchasers of a home to sue builders for breach of implied warranty).

3. Uniform Land Transactions Act §2-309(b) (1978) provides for two implied warranties against persons who are in "the business of selling" real estate: (1) a warranty of suitability and (2) a warranty of quality. What is the difference? The warranty of suitability arises in the case of used as well as new buildings, whereas the warranty of quality applies only to new construction. The warranty of quality is broader than the warranty of suitability in that defects may not be so serious as to make property unsuitable for its intended purpose, but may nonetheless breach the warranty of quality. See Evans v. J. Stiles, Inc., 689 S.W.2d 399 (Tex. 1985).

Uniform Land Transactions Act §2-311 provides that the warranties implied by law may be excluded or modified by agreement of the parties, or by including such expressions as "as is," *except* no general disclaimer is effective with respect to a buyer of a home in which the buyer intends to live. A seller may disclaim liability to such a buyer only for a specific defect and then only if the specific defect entered into and became a part of the basis of the bargain.

Uniform Land Transactions Act §2-312(b) provides that, notwithstanding any contrary agreement, the warranty of quality runs with the land to subsequent buyers. Thus a waiver by the first buyer could not prevent a subsequent buyer from suing the builder on the warranty.

Uniform Land Transactions Act §2-521 provides for a six-year statute of limitations that begins to run, regardless of the buyer's lack of knowledge of the breach, when the buyer to whom the warranty is first made enters into possession. Six years is the usual amount of time allowed for suit on an express warranty; the idea underlying the Uniform Act is that the statute of limitations applicable to express warranties should apply to implied warranties.

Although no state has yet adopted the Uniform Land Transactions Act, the act is likely to be influential on judicial decisions regarding implied warranties of quality and suitability. See Ronald B. Brown, Symposium: Whatever Happened to the Uniform Land Transactions Act?, 20 Nova L. Rev. 1017 (1996).

New York has enacted a housing merchant warranty statute. N.Y. Gen. Bus. Law §777 (McKinney 2012). The statute implies a warranty that the house was built in a "skillful manner" in all contracts for sales of new homes, in addition to any express warranties the builder may make. The statutory warranty covers material defects for six years after the warranty date.

4. A warranty of quality is not normally implied where the seller is not a "merchant of housing," that is, a builder, subdivider, or commercial vendor. See Stevens v. Bouchard, 532 A.2d 1028 (Me. 1987). This is true even when the seller acted as his own general contractor. See Thompson v. Miles, 2011 WL 7639708 (D. Me. Dec. 30, 2011). Compare the treatment of the non-merchant landlord discussed in Note 1 on page 522. Suits against a person who sells his home to another ordinarily must be based on fraud, misrepresentation, or failure to disclose.

5. Should purchasers of new homes be able to waive the implied warranty of quality? See Briarcliffe W. Townhouse Owners Assn. v. Wiseman Constr. Co., 480 N.E.2d 833 (Ill. App. 1985); Tibbitts v. Openshaw, 425 P.2d 160 (Utah 1967); Welwood v. Cypress Creek Estates, Inc., 205 S.W.3d 722 (Tex. App. 2006); Jones v. Centex Homes, 967 N.E.2d 1199 (Ohio 2012). Recall that tenants cannot waive the implied warranty of habitability. (See footnote 49 on page 523.) Do the same policies behind that prohibition apply to home buyers?

5. Remedies for Breach of the Sales Contract

In the event that the contract for sale is breached, three remedies are available to the nondefaulting party, whether the buyer or the seller: (1) damages, (2) retention of the deposit (sellers) or restitution of the deposit (buyers), or (3) specific performance of the contract. Generally, the winner may elect which remedy he or she prefers.

Jones v. Lee

Court of Appeals of New Mexico, 1998
971 P.2d 858

DONNELLY, J. Ihn P. Lee and Philomena Lee (Buyers) appeal from judgments determining that they breached a contract to purchase an Albuquerque, New Mexico, residence and awarding compensatory and punitive damages to Sam P. Jones and Sharon A. Jones (Sellers). . . . Following negotiations between the parties, on June 25, 1994, Buyers entered into a written real estate contract wherein they agreed to purchase Sellers' residence for $610,000. Sellers had listed the property for sale with Metro 100 Realtors. The purchase agreement entered into between Buyers and Sellers also listed Broker-Agents as Sellers' agents. Several weeks after signing the purchase agreement and tendering $6000 in earnest money, Buyers informed Sellers they were unable to consummate the agreement because of financial reasons. Buyers submitted a proposed termination agreement, dated August 23, 1994, to Sellers, whereby Buyers offered to void the contract in return for forfeiting their $6000 earnest money deposit.

Sellers rejected the proposed termination agreement and when it became clear that Buyers were not going to honor the purchase agreement, Sellers relisted the property for sale. Sellers ultimately sold the property in November 1994 to another purchaser for $540,000, $70,000 below the contract price originally agreed upon by the defaulting Buyers.

On April 12, 1995, Sellers filed suit against Buyers, seeking damages for breach of the real estate purchase agreement. . . . [The trial court awarded the sellers $70,000 in damages. Additionally, the trial court awarded the sellers special damages and punitive damages, for a total award of $157,118.94.]

I. Applicability and Measure of Damages

Buyers argue that the trial court erred in awarding compensatory and special damages to Sellers and that it utilized an incorrect measure in calculating the amount of damages to be awarded. On appeal, a reviewing court will not overturn the trial court's findings of fact or award of damages if there is substantial and competent evidence to support such determination, or unless it is clearly demonstrated that the trial court employed an incorrect measure of damages.

If a purchaser defaults on a contract to purchase realty, as a general rule, the seller has three alternative remedies. The sellers may (1) seek relief in equity for rescission, (2) offer to perform and bring an action for specific performance, or (3) elect to retain the realty and file suit seeking an award of damages. See Van Moorlehem v. Brown Realty Co., 747 F.2d 992, 994 (10th Cir. 1984). Here, Sellers elected to sue for damages. Where a party elects to sue for damages resulting from a breach of land sale contract, the burden is on that party to present competent evidence to support such claim for damages. The rationale underlying the award of damages in a breach of contract case is to compensate the non-defaulting party with just compensation commensurate with his or her loss.

Buyers accurately note that New Mexico follows the "loss of the bargain" rule in determining damages resulting from a purchaser's breach of a contract to buy realty. See Aboud v. Adams, 84 N.M. 683, 688-89, 507 P.2d 430, 435-36 (1973). The "loss of the bargain" rule . . . has been reaffirmed by our Supreme Court in Hickey v. Griggs, 106 N.M. 27, 30, 738 P.2d 899, 902 (1987). In *Hickey* the Court stated that when a purchaser breaches an executory real estate contract, the "vendor's measure of damages is the difference between the purchase price and the market value of the property at the time of the breach." *Hickey*, 106 N.M. at 30, 738 P.2d at 902.

Buyers argue that the trial court erred in calculating compensatory damages of $70,000 solely by determining the difference between the contract price agreed upon by the parties and the subsequent resale price of the property, without determining the fair market value of the property at the time of the breach. The parties stipulated that the fair market value on August 23, 1994, was $610,000; thus, Buyers argue that Sellers did not sustain any compensatory damages because "at the time of the breach . . . they held property worth exactly the same amount as the contract price[.]"

Buyers are correct that in order to apply the loss of the bargain rule, the trial court must determine the value of the property at the time of the breach and compare that amount with the contract price. *Aboud*, 84 N.M. at 689, 507 P.2d at 436; see also 5 Arthur L. Corbin, Corbin on Contracts §1098A, at 535 (1964) (where purchaser defaults on purchase of realty, "the vendor's damages are the full contract price minus the market value of the land at date of breach and also minus any payment received").

. . . Where the market value at the time of the breach is the same as the contract price, the sellers are generally limited to the recovery of only nominal damages or forfeiture of any earnest money, unless the sellers have established that they have also incurred special damages resulting from such breach.

In the instant case, like *Aboud*, there was no finding determining the date of breach or the market value of the property at the time of the breach. These determinations are essential factors in applying the loss of the bargain rule and in calculating the amount of general damages resulting from a purchaser's breach of a real estate contract. Thus, we conclude that the cause must be remanded for adoption of express findings of fact in accordance with the rule.

. . . As indicated in *Aboud*, 84 N.M. at 689, 507 P.2d at 436, a subsequent sale of land may be considered evidence of the market value at the time of breach and should be considered with other evidence bearing on the issue. It is unclear from the appellate record, including our questioning and the attorneys' answers at oral argument, for what purpose and to what effect the parties agreed to the stipulation before the trial court concerning market value. It shall be for the trial court on remand to determine what effect to give the stipulation and to otherwise determine the market value at the time of breach, to compare that to the contract sale price, and to calculate general damages, if any.

II.   Award of Special Damages

Buyers also challenge the trial court's award of special damages. Special damages may be awarded by the fact finder in a breach of contract case if the damages are shown to have resulted as the natural and probable consequence of the breach and, at the time of the formation of the contract, the breaching party reasonably knew or should have anticipated from the facts and circumstances that the damages would probably be incurred.

1.   Solar System and Heating Warranty

Buyers challenge the trial court's special damages award of $1433 for an inspection of the solar system, $126 for a consultation on the solar system, and $300 for a heating warranty incident to the resale of the residence. The trial court found that these damages were reasonably foreseeable by a person in Buyers' situation when the contract was formed. We agree. Whether a situation is reasonably foreseeable is generally a question of fact to be determined by the fact finder from the evidence and circumstances.

. . . [T]he contract contemplated that an inspection would be made of the solar and heating systems, and these are major components of the residence, there was evidence in the record from which the trial court could reasonably determine that inspection of these systems and consultation with a specialist concerning such systems would be a reasonably foreseeable requirement imposed by a future purchaser. Similarly, our review of Paragraph 10 of the real estate sales agreement indicates the existence of evidence from which the trial court could find that Sellers may be required to pay for a heating warranty from a future purchaser. Paragraph 10 is a paragraph in the form contract indicating a list of warranties, the costs of which are sometimes borne by the sellers. The existence of this list in the contract is evidence upon which the trial court could find that the cost of the warranty was reasonably foreseeable.

2.   Interest

After Buyers' default, Sellers relisted the property for sale and continued making payments on the first and second mortgages on the property until the subsequent sale. Sellers presented evidence that the interest payments on the mortgages totaled $4500. The trial court found that the mortgage interest that Sellers continued to pay on their residence following the breach by Buyers was foreseeable. However, the trial court acknowledged that Sellers enjoyed the benefit of the continued occupancy of the residence and therefore reduced this award of interest by one-half.

The trial court correctly determined that Sellers may be entitled to damages resulting from the payment of mortgage interest due to Buyers' breach of contract to purchase realty because such damages were reasonably foreseeable. Where a buyer defaults on a residential purchase agreement, thus forcing the seller to replace the property on the market for sale, the lapse of time between the original closing date and a subsequent sale may give rise to the incurring of special damages by the seller. See Shaeffer v. Kelton, 95 N.M. 182, 187, 619 P.2d 1226, 1231 (1980) (after default by purchaser plaintiff may recover interest payments on construction loan for period plaintiff sought to locate another buyer). . . .

III. Award of Punitive Damages

The trial court awarded punitive damages against Buyers for their conduct in attempting to persuade Sellers to agree to terminate the contract. The trial court found, among other things: Buyers and their family members engaged in acts of extremely poor judgment toward Sellers in their efforts to persuade Sellers to agree to a termination of the contract. One of these acts, Buyers' and their son's attempting to contact Mrs. Jones at her house, reasonably frightened Mrs. Jones but did not intimidate Sellers into agreeing to termination of the contract. Buyers made misrepresentations of fact regarding their financial situation in their efforts to persuade [Sellers] to agree to a termination of the contract.

At the time of their breach of the contract, Buyers had approximately $577,000 in a checking account, and earned income of more than $16,000.00 per month, plus bonuses. Buyers' failure to consummate the contract to purchase was wanton, utterly reckless and in utter disregard of their contractual obligations, and was sufficient to warrant the imposition of punitive damages. [Buyers'] conduct evidenced such a cavalier attitude toward their own obligations and the harm inflicted on [Sellers] as to establish their intent to harm Sellers. . . .

Kutzin v. Pirnie

Supreme Court of New Jersey, 1991
591 A.2d 932

CLIFFORD, J. . . . On September 1, 1987, defendants, Duncan and Gertrude Pirnie, and plaintiffs, Milton and Ruth Kutzin, signed a contract for the sale of the Kutzins' house in Haworth for $365,000. The contract, which is the standard-form real-estate sales contract adopted by the New Jersey Association of Realtors, had been prepared by Weichert Realtors (Weichert), the sellers' real-estate agent. Under its terms, the Pirnies agreed to pay a partial deposit of $1,000 on signing the contract and the remainder of the deposit, $35,000, within seven days. In compliance therewith, the Pirnies made out a check for $1,000 to the trust account of Russo Real Estate (Russo), their real-estate agent. The contract does not contain a "forfeiture" or "liquidated damages" clause; with reference to the disposition of the deposit should the sale not take place, the contract merely states, "If this contract is voided by either party, the escrow monies shall be disbursed pursuant to the written direction of both parties."

. . . The trial court ruled that the parties had entered into a binding contract that had not been rescinded either by agreement or pursuant to the attorney-review clause. Consequently, the court held that the sellers were entitled to $17,325 in damages. That amount consisted of the $12,500 difference between the $365,000 the Pirnies had contracted to pay and the $352,500 for which the house eventually sold; $3,825 in utilities, real-estate taxes, and insurance expenses the Kutzins had incurred during the six-month period between the originally-anticipated closing date and the date of actual sale; and $1,000 the Kutzins had paid for a new basement carpet, which their realtor had recommended they buy to enhance the attractiveness of their house to prospective buyers. The court denied recovery of interest the Kutzins contended they would have earned on the purchase price had the sale to the Pirnies gone through. It also refused to award damages for the increased capital-gains tax the Kutzins had paid as a result of the breach. The court ordered the Kutzins to return the $18,675 balance of the deposit to the Pirnies.

On appeal, the Kutzins argued that they should recover the lost interest and the increased capital-gains tax they had incurred, or, alternatively, that they should be allowed to retain the deposit. On cross-appeal the Pirnies claimed entitlement to the entire deposit, again asserting that the contract had been validly rescinded. In an unreported opinion, the Appellate Division found that the contract between the parties "was enforceable according to its terms" but that "the Kutzins' claims to compensation for their allegedly increased tax liability and lost interest were too speculative to be compensable." The court then noted that "the Kutzins' loss as determined by the trial court was less than the Pirnies' $36,000 deposit," and concluded that "the Kutzins are entitled to retain the [entire] deposit, but they may not recover any additional amount as damages."

. . . The issue of whether a seller should be entitled to retain a deposit when a buyer breaches a contract that does not contain a liquidated-damages or forfeiture clause has long troubled courts. As Professor Williston has observed, "Few questions in the law have given rise to more discussion and difference of opinion than that concerning the right of one who has materially broken his contract without legal excuse to recover for such benefit [here, the deposit] as he may have conferred on the other party. . . ." 12 S. Williston, A Treatise on the Law of Contracts §1473 at 220 (3d ed. 1961) (Williston).

"[T]he common-law rule, which has been very generally followed, [was] that where the vendee of real property makes a part payment on the purchase price, but fails to fulfill the contract without lawful excuse, he cannot recover the payment . . . even though the vendor may have made a profit by reason of the default." Quillen v. Kelley, 216 Md. 396, 401-02, 140 A.2d 517, 520 (1958).

New Jersey traditionally has adhered to the common-law rule. As the Appellate Division stated in Oliver v. Lawson, 92 N.J. Super. 331, 333, 223 A.2d 355 (1966) . . . , "It has heretofore generally been held in New Jersey that . . . the defaulting buyer may not recover his deposit, irrespective of the actual damages suffered by the seller and regardless of whether the contract contains a forfeiture provision or not."

. . . [T]he Appellate Division held that the Kutzins are entitled to retain the deposit even though the court was "sympathetic to the trial judge's ruling that the Pirnies were entitled to the return of the balance of their $36,000 contract deposit in excess of the Kutzins' actual damages."

Despite the ample authority supporting the Appellate Division's disposition of the damages question, "there has been a growing recognition of the injustice that often results from the application of the rule permitting total forfeiture of part payments under a contract of sale." Great United Realty Co. v. Lewis, 203 Md. 442, 448, 101 A.2d 881, 883 (1954).

Professor Corbin led the movement favoring departure from the strict common-law rule. In The Right of a Defaulting Vendee to the Restitution of Instalments Paid, 40 Yale L.J. 1013, 1013 (1931) (Defaulting Vendee), he stated: "[where there is] proper evidence that the defendant is holding an amount of money as a penalty rather than as compensation for injury, he should be given judgment for restitution of that amount." Id. at 1025-26 (footnote omitted). He then concluded that

> [t]he cases denying restitution can . . . be justified on one or more of the following grounds: (1) The defendant has not rescinded and remains ready and willing to perform, and still has a right to specific performance by the vendee; (2) the plaintiff has not shown that the injury caused by his breach is less than the installments received by the defendant; (3) there is an express provision that the money may be retained by the vendor and the facts are such as to make this a genuine provision for liquidated damages, and not one for a penalty or forfeiture. If the facts are such that none of these justifications exists, restitution should be allowed. [Id. at 1032-33.]

. . . Section 374(1) of the Restatement (Second) of Contracts is based on section 357 [of the Restatement] but "is more liberal in allowing recovery in accord with the policy behind Uniform Commercial Code §2-718(2)." Restatement (Second) of Contracts §374 reporter's note (1981). That section sets forth the rule as follows:

> [I]f a party justifiably refuses to perform on the ground that his remaining duties of performance have been discharged by the other party's breach, the party in breach is entitled to restitution for any benefit that he has conferred by way of part performance or reliance in excess of the loss that he has caused by his own breach. [Id. §374(1).]

. . . Since publication of the first Restatement of Contracts in 1932, few courts have followed the common-law rule refusing restitution. The Restatement approach of allowing recovery "has steadily increased in favor and probably represents the weight of authority." 12 Williston, supra, §1473 at 222. In 1941 the Supreme Court of Rhode Island, in the context of a suit to recover a deposit by a buyer who had breached a real-estate contract, stated the common-law rule but recognized an "exception" allowing recovery for a defaulting vendee in the absence of a liquidated-damages clause "in certain instances where a person has received from another a benefit the retention of which would be unjust under some legal principle or situation which equity has established or recognized." Seekins v. King, 66 R.I. 105, 110, 17 A.2d 869, 871. By 1953 the Supreme Court of

Wisconsin was able to state that its holding was "in accord with the trend of modern decisions which recognize that when the result of retention of moneys paid upon a contract by a vendee who later repudiates his obligation is a clear unjust enrichment of the vendor, the vendor may be required to return such part of the payments as exceeds the loss which the vendee's default causes him." Schwartz v. Syver, 264 Wis. 526, 531, 59 N.W.2d 489, 492. And in Wilkins v. Birnbaum, 278 A.2d 829, 831 (1971), the Supreme Court of Delaware recognized that "a defaulting buyer [who] can prove that the deposit exceeds in amount the actual damages resulting from the breach [can] recover back the excess, but the burden of proving this is placed on him."

The leading New Jersey case is Oliver v. Lawson, supra, 92 N.J. Super. 331, 223 A.2d 355, in which the court permitted the seller to retain the breaching buyer's $20,000 deposit on a $215,000 contract even though the seller had sold the property at no significant loss. After recognizing that New Jersey follows the strict common-law rule, the court acknowledged that "[p]laintiffs argue that the more modern view would allow the seller to retain only so much of the deposit as would compensate him for his actual damage sustained. . . ."

The court in *Oliver* then denied recovery to the breaching buyers, stating that "[t]hey failed to present any adequate proof of an unjust enrichment." Id. at 336, 223 A.2d 355. . . .

With the issue squarely presented in this case, we overrule those New Jersey cases adhering to the common-law rule and adopt the modern approach set forth in section 374(1) of the Restatement (Second) of Contracts. In Professor Williston's words, "to deny recovery [in this situation] often gives the [seller] more than fair compensation for the injury he has sustained and imposes a forfeiture (which the law abhors) on the [breaching buyer]." 12 Williston, supra, §1473 at 222. The approach that we adopt is suggested to have the added benefit of promoting economic efficiency: penalties deter "efficient" breaches of contract "by making the cost of the breach to the contract breaker greater than the cost of the breach to the victim." R. Posner, Economic Analysis of Law §4.10 at 116 (3d ed. 1986).

We conclude that the Pirnies are entitled, under the Restatement formulation of damages, to restitution for any benefit that they conferred by way of part performance or reliance in excess of the loss that they caused by their own breach. See Restatement (Second) of Contracts, supra, §374(1). We stress, however, that "[o]ne who charges an unjust enrichment has the burden of proving it." Oliver v. Lawson, supra, 92 N.J. Super. at 336, 223 A.2d 355.

The trial court found that the Kutzins had suffered $17,325 in damages, a figure that we accept because it is not challenged in this Court. The Pirnies' deposit of $36,000 exceeded the injury caused by their breach by $18,675, and they are thus entitled to recovery of that amount. Our holding is not affected by the fact that the $36,000 deposit was less than ten percent of the $365,000 purchase price. Cf. Krupnick v. Guerriero, 589 A.2d 620, 624 (N.J. Super. 1990) ("As a general rule a defaulting buyer may not recover a deposit which does not materially exceed 10%. . . ."). Whenever the breaching buyer proves that the deposit exceeds the seller's actual damages suffered as a result of the breach, the buyer may recover the difference.

To ensure that our opinion not be misread, we emphasize that the contract at issue does not contain a forfeiture or liquidated-damages clause; it merely states, "If this contract is voided by either party, the escrow monies shall be disbursed pursuant to the written direction of both parties." The contract is otherwise silent on the subject of what would happen to the deposit were the sale not to occur. Had the contract contained a liquidated-damages clause, this case would have been governed by section 374(2) of the Restatement (Second) of Contracts, which states:

> To the extent that, under the manifested assent of the parties, a party's performance is to be retained in the case of breach, that party is not entitled to restitution if the value of the performance as liquidated damages is reasonable in the light of the anticipated loss caused by the breach and the difficulties of proof of loss.

Although we do not consider the validity or enforceability of a liquidated-damages clause in this case, we are reminded of Professor Corbin's warning: "Penalties and forfeitures are not favored; and calling an outrageous penalty by the more kindly name of liquidated damages does not absolve it from its sin." Defaulting Vendee, supra, 40 Yale L.J. at 1016; cf. Central Steel Drum Co. v. Gold Cooperage, Inc., 491 A.2d 49 (N.J. Super. 1985) (considering validity of liquidated-damages clause).

We . . . hold that the Kutzins cannot retain the entire deposit as damages. The Pirnies are entitled to restitution of their deposit less the amount of the injury to the Kutzins caused by the Pirnies' breach. To allow retention of the entire deposit would unjustly enrich the Kutzins and would penalize the Pirnies contrary to the policy behind our law of contracts.

The judgment of the Appellate Division is modified to reinstate the trial court's damage award.

As modified the judgment is:

Affirmed.

NOTES AND QUESTIONS

1. *Damages and timing.* As noted in *Jones*, the general rule for a party seeking damages for breach of a contract to convey real estate is the difference between the contract price and the fair market value at the time of breach. See, e.g., White v. Farrell, 20 N.Y.3d 487 (N.Y. 2013); Kirkpatrick v. Strosberg, 894 N.E.2d 781 (Ill. App. 2008). This rule, however, might only protect the expectations of the parties in a static market. Because of the inequity that can result in calculating damages at the time of a buyer's breach in a real estate market that is rapidly declining, making it more difficult for the nondefaulting seller to find a new buyer, some courts have allowed damages to be calculated on the date the property is re-sold. Kuhn v. Spatial Design, Inc., 585 A.2d 967, 971 (N.J. App. 1991). In

this respect the court in *Kuhn* adopted the essence of the Uniform Commercial Code—which applies only to sales of goods—regarding sellers' damages. See, e.g., Gerald Korngold, Seller's Damages from a Defaulting Buyer of Realty: The Influence of the Uniform Land Transactions Act on the Courts, 20 Nova L. Rev. 1069 (1996).

The common law rule for buyer's damages upon breach by seller is also based on the value of a property at the time of breach, minus the contract price. Though it is not commonly done, buyers can also argue that their damages should be calculated at the time of the defaulting vendor's re-sale of the property, so that the buyer (rather than the defaulting seller) recoups any profit. See Coppola Enters., Inc. v. Alfone, 506 So. 2d 1180 (Fla. App. 1987) (holding that buyer's damages should include the vendor's subsequent profit from re-sale of the property).

2. *Retention of deposit.* The holding in *Kutzin*—that defaulting buyers are entitled to restitution of the deposit money in excess of damages incurred—is a minority view. The general rule, as the *Kutzin* court recognizes, holds that when a buyer breaches a contract to purchase land, the seller may elect to retain the down payment, because of "the difficulty of estimating actual damages and the general acceptance of the traditional 10% down payment as a reasonable amount," even if the sales contract has no liquidated damages provision. See Maxton Builders, Inc. v. Lo Galbo, 502 N.E.2d 184, 189 (N.Y. 1986). If the seller does elect to retain the deposit, most courts hold that she is limited to deposit money totaling 10 percent of the contract price or less. See James O. Pearson, Jr., Annotation, Modern Status of Defaulting Vendee's Right to Recover Contractual Payments Withheld by Vendor as Forfeited, 4 A.L.R.4th 993 §3 (1981). However, one New York opinion allowed the nondefaulting seller to keep a deposit of 25 percent where there was no evidence of a disparity of bargaining power, duress, fraud, illegality or mutual mistake by the parties. Uzan v. 845 UN Ltd. Pship., 778 N.Y.S.2d 171 (App. Div. 2004). The holding in *Uzan* might be attributable to its unique fact situation: the defaulting buyer contracted to buy penthouse condominiums on top of Trump Tower, pulled out after 9/11, and claimed that Trump had prior knowledge of the danger to the top floor residents in such a prominent building.

Most courts limit the retention-of-deposit remedy to 10 percent of the contract price (or less) to avoid imposing a penalty on the breaching party. Efficient breach theory suggests that when the cost of breach (damages) is less than the potential gain from breach (due to changing market conditions), breach of the contract is the economically efficient result. The theory depends on damages being reasonably certain and foreseeable. If excessive damages are imposed—whether by way of deposit retention or liquidated damages clauses—then the cost of breach is large, perhaps inducing parties to stay in economically inefficient contracts. This rationale was extended in *Kutzin* to include deposits not in excess of 10 percent.

Many real estate sales contracts do contain liquidated damages clauses. "It has long been the law that when contracting parties stipulate the amount of damage that shall be paid in the event of breach of contract, such stipulation is generally enforceable, so long as the stipulated amount is not disproportionate to the damage actually sustained." Hutcheson v. Gleave, 632 P.2d 815, 817 (Utah 1981);

see also Cegers v. United States, 7 Cl. Ct. 615, 620 (1985); Warner v. Rasmussen, 704 P.2d 559, 561 (Utah 1985); Taylor v. Sanders, 353 S.E.2d 745, 746-747 (Va. 1987).

While sellers electing to retain the deposit money as a remedy are normally limited to 10 percent of the contract price, sellers electing to retain the deposit money in the presence of a liquidated damages clause have more leeway. For example, a district court in Florida upheld a liquidated damages clause totaling 13.3 percent of the contract price. See Hooper v. Breneman, 417 So. 2d 315, 317 (Fla. App. 1982). Even more extreme, a New Hampshire court upheld a liquidated damages sum equal to 22 percent of the contract price, noting that other courts had recognized the validity of clauses equaling 25 percent, 42 percent, and even 500 percent(!) of the contract price so long as these sums were a reasonable estimate of damages at the time of contracting. Shallow Brook Assocs. v. Dube, 599 A.2d 132, 137-138 (N.H. 1991).

Buyers have a parallel remedy for breach by the seller: restitution of their deposit money. See Slattery v. Maykut, 405 A.2d 76 (Conn. 1978); Kim v. Conway & Forty, Inc., 772 S.W.2d 723, 726-727 (Mo. App. 1989). But injured buyers rarely elect restitution as their sole remedy, because restitution alone is likely to fall short of the value of the property to the buyer—the buyer's expectation damages.

3. *Specific performance.* Specific performance—a judicial order that a breached contract be fulfilled as originally agreed—is relatively unusual in the case of contracts for the sale of goods, but very common in the case of contracts for the sale of land; an aggrieved seller or buyer of land is broadly entitled to elect that remedy. See, e.g., Wiggins v. Shewmake, 374 N.W.2d 111 (S.D. 1985). Behind this general rule is the thought that each piece of real estate is unique, making damages an inadequate remedy. A disappointed buyer who bargained for a singular piece of property of special appeal wants the land itself. A disappointed seller who finally found someone on whom to unload a singularly unattractive piece wants to be rid of the land. In neither case will a mere award of money do. See, e.g., Turley v. Ball Assocs. Ltd., 641 P.2d 286 (Colo. App. 1981); O'Halloran v. Oechslie, 402 A.2d 67 (Me. 1979). But some courts have begun to depart from this general practice, applying ordinary contract (damages) remedies in appropriate cases. For example, the court in Lakshman v. Vecchione, 430 N.E.2d 199 (Ill. App. 1981), held that a grant of specific performance is not a matter of absolute right, but rather in discretion of the trial court. See also Wolf v. Anderson, 334 N.W.2d 212 (N.D. 1983). On this view, parties who wish to elect the remedy of specific performance have to prove that money damages would be an inadequate remedy.

For a recent critique of the presumption that specific performance is a remedy for breach of real estate contracts, see Tanya D. Marsh, Sometimes Blackacre Is a Widget: Rethinking Commercial Real Estate Contract Remedies, 88 Neb. L. Rev. 635 (2010).

Courts have been particularly hesitant to award specific performance to condominium sellers automatically, presumably based upon the absence of uniqueness among homes in a development. See Centex Homes Corp. v. Boag, 320 A.2d 194 (N.J. Ch. 1974). Though *Centex* provides a theoretical basis for undermining the availability of specific performance, it is still a minority opinion. For example, Giannini v. First Natl. Bank of Des Plaines, 483 N.E.2d 924, 933 (Ill. App. 1985), upheld the availability of specific performance for condominium purchasers, concluding that "where land, or any estate therein, is the subject matter of the agreement, the inadequacy of the legal remedy is well settled, and the equitable jurisdiction is firmly established." See also Schwinder v. Austin Bank of Chicago, 809 N.E.2d 180 (Ill. App. 2004); Pruitt v. Graziano, 521 A.2d 1313 (N.J. App. Div. 1987); Prospect Enterprises, LLC v. Ruff, 2011 WL 2683004 (C.D. Ill. July 11, 2011).

In the vast majority of cases undermining the presumed availability of specific performance, it is the seller who is seeking specific performance. Do you see why? For one view, see Curtis J. Berger, The Influence of Law and Economics on Real Estate Contract Enforcement, in Equity and Contemporary Legal Developments 173, 188-189 (Stephen Goldstein ed. 1992). For a critique of the specific performance remedy in real estate transactions, see Jason Kirwan, Note, Appraising a Presumption: A Modern Look at the Doctrine of Specific Performance in Real Estate Contracts, 47 Wm. & Mary L. Rev. 697 (2005).

4. *Seller's breach due to title defect.* There is a breach if the seller in a real estate contract is unable to convey marketable title as stipulated in the agreement. But in this setting, nearly half the jurisdictions in the United States follow the English rule (sometimes referred to as the *Flureau* rule, after Flureau v. Thornhill, 96 Eng. Rep. 635 (Common Pleas 1176)) and "limit the buyer's recovery to his down payment plus interest and reasonable expenses incurred in investigating the title; only if the seller has acted in bad faith or has assumed the risk of a failure to secure title will he be liable for ordinary contract damages." Large v. Gregory, 417 N.E.2d 1160, 1163 (Ind. App. 1981). See Robert N. Leavell et al., Cases and Materials on Equitable Remedies, Restitution and Damages 1203-1204 (8th ed. 2011). The American rule, which is gradually becoming the dominant position, allows the purchaser to recover expectation (benefit-of-the-bargain) damages, plus any other reasonably foreseeable special damages. Donovan v. Bachstadt, 453 A.2d 160, 163-164 (N.J. 1982); see also Basiliko v. Pargo Corp., 532 A.2d 1346 (D.C. 1987); Burgess v. Arita, 704 P.2d 930 (Haw. App. 1985). The English rule developed in response to uncertainties regarding English title to land in the eighteenth and nineteenth centuries. American recording systems, while by no means perfect, are much more reliable, leading many commentators to conclude that there is no good reason to deprive innocent purchasers from recovering damages, "irrespective of the good or bad faith of the seller." *Donovan,* 453 A.2d at 164.

Purchasers may, if they wish, elect to sue for specific performance of the contract despite title defects. See, e.g., Arensberg v. Drake, 693 S.W.2d 588, 592 (Tex. App. 1985) ("when a vendor has contracted to convey a greater interest in property than he has power to convey, the purchaser, if he chooses, is entitled to have the contract specifically performed, as far as the vendor can perform it"). A purchaser electing specific performance is also entitled to an abatement in price to reflect the decreased value of the property with the title defect. See Wittick v. Miles, 545 P.2d 121 (Or. 1972).

5. *Time-of-the-essence clauses.* Unless the parties expressly provide that "time is of the essence," a court will give the parties a reasonable time for performance, and either party can fix the time for performance by giving notice to the other, provided the notice leaves a reasonable time for rendering performance. See DeMattia v. Mauro, 860 A.2d 262 (Conn. App. 2004); Sohayegh v. Oberlander, 547 N.Y.S.2d 98 (App. Div. 1989). Notice that paragraphs 5 and 28 of the Residential Real Estate Contract (see pages 546, 553) provide for a closing date as well as a time-of-the-essence clause. Under what circumstances might a seller or purchaser want the contract to include such a clause? See Mindy H. Stern, 2007-2008 Survey of New York Law: Time of the Essence in Real Estate Contracts of Sale—Lore and Law, 59 Syracuse L. Rev. 1011 (2009).

6. As illustrated by the cases in this section on remedies for breach of a contract to convey real property, the law governing real estate is not governed by the sort of uniform rules applied to the sale of goods under the Uniform Commercial Code, which explicitly exempts real property from its scope. In 1975, the National Conference of Commissioners on Uniform State Laws proposed the Uniform Land Transactions Act, a uniform set of rules to govern real estate transactions. ULTA has not been widely adopted, and law governing real estate conveyancing, title, and mortgage lending continues to vary widely among the states. Ronald B. Brown, Whatever Happened to the Uniform Land Transactions Act?, 20 Nova L. Rev. 1017 (1996). But judges do sometimes look to the Uniform Commercial Code as persuasive authority. See, e.g., Desouza v. Lauderdale, 928 So. 2d 1035 (Ala. App. 2005) (disclaimer of implied warranty of merchantability); Conference Ctr. Ltd. v. TRC, 455 A.2d 857 (Conn. 1983) (commercial insecurity).

Why so much resistance to a uniform approach to real estate transactions, given the striking success of the UCC, dealing with goods (personal property) throughout the United States? Compare Michael Madison, The Real Properties of Contract Law, 82 B.U. L. Rev. 405 (2002), with Michael H. Schill, The Impact of the Capital Markets on Real Estate Law and Practice, 32 J. Marshall L. Rev. 269 (1999).

D. The Deed

1. Warranties of Title

Over the long course of English and American law, various types of deeds developed. The earliest deed of historical interest is the charter of feoffment. This deed, which evidenced the fact and terms of a feoffment, was used from the Norman Conquest until the middle of the sixteenth century. The charter of feoffment passed out of fashion after the Statute of Uses (1536) made it possible to convey a legal interest in land by a bargain and sale deed without livery of seisin (see page 243). It was far more convenient to deliver a deed to the grantee in the solicitor's office than to go out on the land (perhaps many miles away) and perform the ceremony of livery of seisin. In 1677, the Statute of Frauds was enacted requiring a written instrument for the conveyance of an interest in land and abolishing livery of seisin.

In the several hundred years since, a number of different kinds of deeds came into use, each designed to transfer a particular type of interest in land. It was only in the nineteenth century that these old forms of deeds became obsolete, replaced by the modern deed. In the process of evolving one deed out of many, either because the scrivener was being paid by the word or the lawyer was overly cautious, all of the words of transfer used in earlier kinds of deeds were incorporated into one deed. A deed might contain this all-embracing language: "By these presents the grantor does give, grant, bargain, sell, remise, demise, release, and convey unto the grantee, and to his heirs and assigns forever, all that parcel of land described as follows." This lawyer's habit of coupling well-worn words represents, according to Professor Mellinkoff, "the lawyer's gamble on venial repetition against mortal omission. . . . The great mass of these coupled synonyms are simply redundancies, furnishing opportunity for argument that something beyond synonymy was intended." David Mellinkoff, Dictionary of American Legal Usage 129 (1992). "Grant, bargain, and sell," as well as longer couplings, says this doyen of the plain language movement, is "an archaic form, awaiting only interment. *Grant* is sufficient." Id. at 274.

To wean lawyers away from verbosity, many states have by statute provided a short form of deed that may be used. The short form deed contains all the essential elements required in order for an instrument to be a conveyance: grantor, grantee, words of grant, description of the land involved, signature of the grantor, and, sometimes, attestation or acknowledgment. It is a matter of local custom whether statutory short form deeds or more elaborate instruments are used.

Currently in general use in the United States are three types of deeds: general warranty deed, special warranty deed, and quitclaim deed. A *general warranty deed* warrants title against all defects in title, whether they arose before or after the grantor took title. A *special warranty deed* contains warranties only against the grantor's own acts but not the acts of others. Thus if the defect is a mortgage on the land executed by the grantor's predecessors in ownership, the grantor is not liable. A *quitclaim deed* contains no warranties of any kind. It merely conveys whatever title the grantor has, if any, and if the grantee of a quitclaim deed takes nothing by the deed, the grantee cannot sue the grantor.

Here is a general warranty deed:

GENERAL WARRANTY DEED

I, John Doe, grant to Nancy Roe and her heirs and assigns forever, for $10 and other good and valuable consideration, the following real estate situated in _____County, State of _____, described as follows:

[Insert description of land]

To have and to hold[6] the premises, with all the privileges and appurtenances belonging thereunto, to the use of the grantee and her heirs and assigns forever.

The grantor, for himself and his heirs and assigns, covenants (1) that the grantor is lawfully seized in fee simple of the premises, (2) that he has a good right to convey the fee simple, (3) that the premises are free from all encumbrances, (4) that the grantor and his heirs and assigns will forever warrant and defend the grantee and her heirs and assigns against every person lawfully claiming the premises or any part thereof, (5) that the grantor and his heirs and assigns will guarantee the quiet enjoyment of the premises to the grantee and her heirs and assigns, and (6) that the grantor and his heirs and assigns will, on demand of the grantee or her heirs or assigns, execute any instrument necessary for the further assurance of the title to the premises that may be reasonably required.

Dated this _____ day of _____, 20_____.

John Doe

_____

[signature of grantor]

Acknowledgment[7]

State of

County of

I hereby certify that on this day before me, a notary public, personally appeared the above named John Doe, who acknowledged that he voluntarily signed the foregoing instrument on the day and year therein mentioned.

In testimony whereof, I hereunto subscribe my name and affix my official seal on this _____ day of _____, 20_____.

[*signature of notary*]

Notary Public in and for

_____County,

State of_____

My commission

expires_____

---

6. The clause beginning "To have and to hold" is known as the *habendum clause* (after the Latin *habendum et tenendum*). (Early deeds were written in Latin, the language of clerks (clerics).) The habendum clause had the function in feudal times of declaring of which lord the land was held and by what services. Modern deeds usually contain a habendum clause, which is unnecessary but may function to limit the estate granted in some way. See Robert G. Natelson, Modern Law of Deeds to Real Property §§9.1-9.10 (1992).

7. In almost all states, a deed signed by the grantor, and delivered, is valid without an acknowledgment before a notary public. However, in order for the deed to be recorded in the courthouse, giving notice to the world of the grantee's interest, the deed must be acknowledged by the grantor (in some states, witnessing is permitted in place of acknowledgment). Therefore, as a matter of practice, all deeds prepared by professionals are acknowledged.

NOTES AND QUESTIONS: THE DEED

1. *Consideration.* It is customary to state in a deed that some consideration was paid by the grantee, in order to raise a presumption that the grantee is a bona fide purchaser entitled to the protection of the recording acts against prior unrecorded instruments. See page 694. It is neither customary nor necessary to state the exact consideration given. Do you see why?

Some years ago the federal government levied a documentary stamp tax on deeds conveying land to a purchaser. When the tax was repealed, many state legislatures, at the instigation of real estate brokers who wanted to learn the sales price by counting the tax stamps, imposed state documentary stamp taxes. Can you imagine why a purchaser might affix more tax stamps to a deed than are required? Might not?

2. *Description of tract.* A deed must contain a description of the parcel of land conveyed that locates the parcel by describing its boundaries. Customary methods of description include (1) reference to natural or artificial monuments and, from the starting point, reference to directions and distances ("metes and bounds"); (2) reference to a government survey, recorded plat, or some other record; and (3) reference to the street and number or the name of the property.

There are many cases, particularly old ones, litigating the correct boundaries of a tract of land. When this country was settled, deed descriptions of land were very informal. They might refer to "Hester Quinn's farm" or to a tract "beginning at the old oak tree near the road and running 30 feet north, thence 70 feet east to the creek, thence south along the creek to an iron post, thence back to the beginning." In time, the reference points frequently disappeared.[8]

Then too, the descriptions were sometimes conflicting. Using the monuments referred to in the deed might yield a tract of different dimensions than would be produced by using the metes and bounds description in the deed. Ultimately, courts laid down a hierarchy of rules to decide cases of conflicting descriptions: Natural monuments (e.g., trees) prevail over artificial monuments (e.g., surveyor's stakes), which prevail over references to adjacent boundaries (e.g., "to Hunter's property line"), which prevail over directions (e.g., northwest), which prevail over distances (e.g., 30 feet), which prevail over area (e.g., 5 acres), which prevails over place names (e.g., "the Quinn farm"). These rules were designed to discover the intent of the parties, who probably relied more on specific, visible landmarks than on measurements of the eye. The hierarchy of precedence is not inflexible, however, and conflicts in boundary descriptions in a deed tend to be resolved on the particular facts of a case.

---

8. *Water boundaries.* When natural forces gradually shift a river and cause the adjacent land to recede or to advance by the build-up of new soil, there has been an *accretion.* With accretion, the owner of the adjacent land gains or loses land as the water boundary gradually shifts. If there is a sudden change in the course of a river (as after a flood), the process is called *avulsion,* not accretion, and the boundaries do not change. See 3 American Law of Property §15.27 (1952); see also *Stop the Beach,* discussed infra at 1222.

3. *Seal.* An old saw says a deed to land is effective when it is signed, sealed, and delivered. The requirement of a signed document was initiated by the Statute of Frauds in 1677. The requirement of sealing is older, going back to the Norman Conquest, when a seal replaced the sign of the cross[9] on documents. If a person had no seal, he borrowed someone else's. At common law a "deed" was defined as a sealed instrument; a sealed instrument was required for the conveyance of a freehold. Most state legislatures have abolished the distinction between sealed and unsealed instruments. Where still extant, the requirement of a seal on transfers of real property is formal in the purest sense. Almost anything can be a seal: the word *seal,* the initials L.S. (standing for *locus sigilli,* the place of the seal), a ribbon, a scrawl, a scratch.

4. *Forgery and fraud.* A forged deed is void. The grantor whose signature is forged to a deed prevails over all persons, including subsequent bona fide purchasers from the grantee who do not know the deed is forged.

On the other hand, most courts hold that a deed procured by fraud is voidable by the grantor in an action against the grantee, but a subsequent bona fide purchaser from the grantee who is unaware of the fraud prevails over the grantor. The grantor, having introduced the deed into the stream of commerce, made it possible for a subsequent innocent purchaser to suffer loss. As between two innocent persons, one of whom must suffer by the act of the fraudulent third party, the law generally places the loss on the person who could have prevented the loss to the other. McCoy v. Love, 382 So. 2d 647 (Fla. 1979), illustrates this. In the case, one B.G. Russell sought to buy certain mineral interests from Mary Elliott, "a totally illiterate 87-year-old widow." Mrs. Elliott agreed to sell Russell the mineral rights in 2 of 15 acres that she owned, but, unknown to her, the deed prepared by Russell and that Mrs. Elliott signed by her mark conveyed to him a much larger interest. Russell recorded his deed and promptly conveyed his interest to Love, who recorded. Oil was then found under the land. The court held that a deed procured by fraud, unlike a forged deed, is effectual to pass title to a bona fide purchaser. It remanded the case to determine if Love was a bona fide purchaser. If so, Love would prevail.

Determining the line between forgery and fraud is not always easy. See Sheffield v. Andrews, 679 So. 2d 1052 (Ala. 1996) (holding that a signature procured by deceiving the grantor into signing the instrument in ignorance of its true character is considered forged; $1 million punitive damages assessed); see also Delsas ex rel. Delsas v. Centex Home Equity Co., LLC, 186 P.3d 141 (Colo. App. 2008) (distinguishing between fraud in factum and fraud in the inducement).

5. *Indenture and deed poll.* In the days before typewriters and carbon paper, and centuries before Xerox, lawyers were faced with the problem of providing duplicate copies of deeds in certain instances when both the grantor and grantee wanted a copy (for example, in case of a mortgage). They found the solution in an *indenture.* The deed was written out twice on a single sheet of parchment

---

9. The sign of the cross is the ancestral form of signing by the mark X.

(usually made from sheepskin stretched, scraped, and scoured) and signed at the end of each copy by both grantor and grantee. The parchment was then cut into two pieces in an irregular line, leaving a sawtooth or indented edge. The two halves, forming two separate deeds, one for the grantor and one for the grantee, could be fitted together to show their genuineness.

An indenture is to be contrasted with a *deed poll*, which is signed only by the grantor. It was called a deed poll because the top was not indented but polled or shaved even.

Indentures were rarely used in the United States because, from earliest times, every state had a recording system in which the county clerk copied the deed into the public records by hand, thus providing an official copy for the interested parties. We take up the recording system in the next chapter.

Do you see how the phrase "indentured servant" arose?

6. Suppose the grantor has given the buyer a special warranty deed. During the period the grantor owned the land, *A* got title to the land by adverse possession. Is the grantor liable to the grantee on the special warranties? Greenberg v. Sutter, 661 N.Y.S.2d 933 (Sup. Ct. 1997); cf. Egli v. Troy, 602 N.W.2d 329 (Iowa 1999).

7. A study of over 37,000 home sales in 5 Midwestern metropolitan areas found that the type of deed one has correlates strongly with sales price. For example, a home selling with a general warranty deed sells for double the price of a home selling with a quitclaim deed. A house with a limited warranty deed sells at a 19 percent discount compared to one with a general warranty deed. See David M. Brasington & Robert F. Sarama, Jr., Deed Types, House Prices and Mortgage Interest Rates, 36 Real Est. Econ. 587 (2008).

Read closely the warranty clause of the general warranty deed set forth on page 616, and you will see that it contains six express warranties:

1. *A covenant of seisin*—The grantor warrants that he owns the estate that he purports to convey.

2. *A covenant of right to convey*—The grantor warrants that he has the right to convey the property. In most instances this covenant serves the same purpose as the covenant of seisin, but it is possible for a person who has seisin not to have the right to convey (e.g., a trustee may have legal title but be forbidden by the trust instrument to convey it).

3. *A covenant against encumbrances*—The grantor warrants that there are no encumbrances on the property. Encumbrances include, among other items, mortgages, liens, easements, and covenants.

4. *A covenant of general warranty*—The grantor warrants that he will defend against lawful[10] claims and will compensate the grantee for any loss that the grantee may sustain by assertion of superior title.

---

10. Carefully note the word *lawful*. The grantor is not liable for legal fees incurred by the grantee in *successfully* defending title, because the third party's losing claim is not lawful. The grantor is liable for the grantee's

5. *A covenant of quiet enjoyment*—The grantor warrants that the grantee will not be disturbed in possession and enjoyment of the property by assertion of superior title. This covenant is, for all practical purposes, identical with the covenant of general warranty and is often omitted from general warranty deeds.

6. *A covenant of further assurances*—The grantor promises that he will execute any other documents required to perfect the title conveyed.

Observe that the first three covenants are phrased in the present tense and are called *present covenants*. The last three covenants are phrased in the future tense and are called *future covenants*. The distinction is this: A present covenant is broken, if ever, at the time the deed is delivered. Either the grantor owns the property at that time, or he does not; either there are existing encumbrances at that time, or there are none. A future covenant promises that the grantor will do some future act, such as defending against claims of third parties or compensating the grantee for loss by virtue of failure of title. A future covenant is not breached until the grantee or his successor is evicted from the property, buys up the paramount claim, or is otherwise damaged.

The statute of limitations begins to run on a breach of a present covenant at the date of delivery of the deed. It begins to run on a future covenant at the time of eviction or when the covenant is broken in the future.

Brown v. Lober

Supreme Court of Illinois, 1979
389 N.E.2d 1188

[In 1947, the owner of 80 acres of land conveyed it to William and Faith Bost, reserving a two-thirds interest in the mineral rights. In 1957, the Bosts conveyed the 80-acre tract to James R. Brown and his wife by a general warranty deed containing no exceptions. In 1974, the Browns contracted to sell the mineral rights to Consolidated Coal Co. for $6,000, but upon finding that the Browns owned only one-third of the mineral rights the parties had to renegotiate the contract to provide for payment of $2,000 for one-third of the mineral rights. The prior grantor had never made any attempt to exercise his mineral rights. The 10-year statute of limitations barred a suit on the present covenants, so the Browns sued the executor of the Bosts, who had died, seeking $4,000 damages for breach of the covenant of quiet enjoyment. The trial court ruled in favor of the defendant. The appellate court reversed, and the case is now before the supreme court.]

UNDERWOOD, J. . . . The question is whether plaintiffs have alleged facts sufficient to constitute a constructive eviction. They argue that if a covenantee fails in his effort to sell an interest in land because he discovers that he does not own

---

legal fees only if the grantee loses to a superior lawful claim. See Black v. Patel, 594 S.E.2d 162 (S.C. 2004); McDonald v. Delhi Sav. Bank, 440 N.W.2d 839 (Iowa 1989).

In some jurisdictions, the grantee can recover legal fees for an unsuccessful defense only if the grantee gives the grantor notice of the suit and demands that the grantor defend title. See Gaede v. Stansberry, 779 N.W.2d 746 (Iowa 2010).

what his warranty deed purported to convey, he has suffered a constructive eviction and is thereby entitled to bring an action against his grantor for breach of the covenant of quiet enjoyment. We think that the decision of this court in Scott v. Kirkendall, 88 Ill. 465 (1878), is controlling on this issue and compels us to reject plaintiffs' argument.

In *Scott*, an action was brought for breach of the covenant of warranty by a grantee who discovered that other parties had paramount title to the land in question. The land was vacant and unoccupied at all relevant times. This court, in rejecting the grantee's claim that there was a breach of the covenant of quiet enjoyment, quoted the earlier decision in Moore v. Vail, 17 Ill. 185, 191 (1855): "Until that time, (the taking possession by the owner of the paramount title,) he might peaceably have entered upon and enjoyed the premises, without resistance or molestation, which was all his grantors covenanted he should do. They did not guarantee to him a perfect title, but the possession and enjoyment of the premises." 88 Ill. 465, 468.

Relying on this language in *Moore*, the *Scott* court concluded:

> We do not see but what this fully decides the present case against the appellant. It holds that the mere existence of a paramount title does not constitute a breach of the covenant. That is all there is here. There has been no assertion of the adverse title. The land has always been vacant. Appellant could at any time have taken peaceable possession of it. He has in no way been prevented or hindered from the enjoyment of the possession by any one having a better right. It was but the possession and enjoyment of the premises which was assured to him, and there has been no disturbance or interference in that respect. True, there is a superior title in another, but appellant has never felt "its pressure upon him." [88 Ill. 465, 468-469.]

Admittedly, *Scott* dealt with surface rights while the case before us concerns subsurface mineral rights. We are, nevertheless, convinced that the reasoning employed in *Scott* is applicable to the present case. While plaintiffs went into possession of the surface area, they cannot be said to have possessed the subsurface minerals. "Possession of the surface does not carry possession of the minerals. . . . To possess the mineral estate, one must undertake the actual removal thereof from the ground or do such other act as will apprise the community that such interest is in the exclusive use and enjoyment of the claiming party." Failoni v. Chicago & North Western Ry. Co., 30 Ill. 2d 258, 262, 195 N.E.2d 619, 622 (1964).

Since no one has, as yet, undertaken to remove the coal or otherwise manifested a clear intent to exclusively "possess" the mineral estate, it must be concluded that the subsurface estate is "vacant." As in *Scott*, plaintiffs "could at any time have taken peaceable possession of it. [They have] in no way been prevented or hindered from the enjoyment of the possession by any one having a better right." (88 Ill. 465, 468.) Accordingly, until such time as one holding paramount title interferes with plaintiffs' right of possession (e.g., by beginning to mine the coal), there can be no constructive eviction and, therefore, no breach of the covenant of quiet enjoyment.

What plaintiffs are apparently attempting to do on this appeal is to extend the protection afforded by the covenant of quiet enjoyment. However, we decline to expand the historical scope of this covenant to provide a remedy where another of the covenants of title is so clearly applicable. As this court stated in Scott v. Kirkendall, 88 Ill. 465, 469 (1878): "To sustain the present action would be to confound all distinction between the covenant of warranty and that of seisin, or of right to convey. They are not equivalent covenants. An action will lie upon the latter, though there be no disturbance of possession. A defect of title will suffice. Not so with the covenant of warranty, or for quiet enjoyment, as has always been held by the prevailing authority." The covenant of seisin, unquestionably, was breached when the Bosts delivered the deed to plaintiffs, and plaintiffs then had a cause of action. However, despite the fact that it was a matter of public record that there was a reservation of a two-thirds interest in the mineral rights in the earlier deed, plaintiffs failed to bring an action for breach of the covenant of seisin within the 10-year period following delivery of the deed. The likely explanation is that plaintiffs had not secured a title opinion at the time they purchased the property. . . . Plaintiffs' oversight, however, does not justify us in overruling earlier decisions in order to recognize an otherwise premature cause of action. The mere fact that plaintiffs' original contract with Consolidated had to be modified due to their discovery that paramount title to two-thirds of the subsurface minerals belonged to another is not sufficient to constitute the constructive eviction necessary to a breach of the covenant of quiet enjoyment.

Accordingly, the judgment of the appellate court is reversed, and the judgment of the circuit court of Montgomery County is affirmed.

Holding for Defendant

QUESTIONS

1. Suppose that the Browns buy up the two-thirds interest in the minerals for $10,000 and then sue the Bosts' executor on the covenant of general warranty. Can they recover?

2. Suppose that the buyer has knowledge of an encumbrance on the property when he accepts a general warranty deed. Is the covenant against encumbrances breached?

> There is considerable conflict among the authorities as to whether or not a visible or known easement is excepted from a covenant against encumbrances. A distinction is made in some cases between encumbrances which affect the title and those which simply affect the physical condition of the land. In the first class, it is universally held that the encumbrances are included in the covenant, regardless of the knowledge of the grantee. Those encumbrances relating to physical conditions of the property have, in many instances, been treated as excluded from the covenant. Some of these cases are decided upon the theory that, whenever the actual physical conditions of the realty are apparent, and are in their nature permanent and irremediable, such conditions are within the contemplation of the parties when contracting, and are therefore not included in a general covenant against encumbrances.
>
> There seems to be a tendency toward the proposition that certain visible public easements, such as highways and railroad rights of way, in open and notorious use at the time of the conveyance, do not breach a covenant against encumbrances. However, it still seems to be the general rule, particularly in those cases involving private rights of way, that an easement which is a burden upon the estate granted and which diminishes its value constitutes a breach of the covenant

against encumbrances in the deed, regardless of whether the grantee had knowledge of its existence or that it was visible and notorious.

Certainly, if the deed contains anything which would indicate that a known encumbrance was not intended to be within the covenant, the purchaser cannot complain that such an encumbrance was a breach of the covenant. However, with the possible exception of public easements that are apparent and in their nature permanent and irremediable, mere knowledge of the encumbrance is not sufficient to exclude it from the operation of the covenant. The intention to exclude an encumbrance should be manifested in the deed itself, for a resort to oral or other extraneous evidence would violate settled principles of law in regard to deeds. [Jones v. Grow Inv. & Mortgage Co., 358 P.2d 909, 910-911 (Utah 1961).]

3. Katarzyna and Adolph Lewicki conveyed a lot they owned to Adam Marszalkowski by general warranty deed. Adam did not go into possession. The Lewickis continued to use the lot to mow hay, grow oats, maintain a garden, and feed cattle. Some 40 years later, Adam's grandchildren converted the lot into a baseball field. The Lewickis claim title by adverse possession. Judgment for whom? Lewicki v. Marszalkowski, 455 A.2d 307 (R.I. 1983); see also Carrozza v. Carrozza, 944 A.2d 161 (R.I. 2008); Hood v. Denny, 555 S.W.2d 337 (Mo. App. 1977).

Frimberger v. Anzellotti

Appellate Court of Connecticut, 1991
594 A.2d 1029

LAVERY, J. The defendant appeals from the judgment of the trial court awarding the plaintiff damages for breach of the warranty against encumbrances and innocent misrepresentation of real property that the defendant conveyed to the plaintiff by warranty deed.

The defendant claims that the court was incorrect (1) in finding that she had misrepresented the property and that the plaintiff had relied on that misrepresentation to his detriment, (2) in finding that she breached the warranty deed covenant against encumbrances, and (3) in awarding damages for diminution of value to the property caused by a wetlands violation as well as damages for costs of correcting that violation. We agree with the defendant and reverse the decision of the trial court.

The record and memorandum of decision disclose the following facts. In 1978, the defendant's brother and predecessor in title, Paul DiLoreto, subdivided a parcel of land located in Old Saybrook for the purpose of constructing residences on each of the two resulting parcels. The property abuts a tidal marshland and is, therefore, subject to the provisions of General Statutes §22a-28 et seq.

DiLoreto built a bulkhead and filled that portion of the subject parcel immediately adjacent to the wetlands area, and then proceeded with the construction of a dwelling on the property. On February 21, 1984, DiLoreto transferred the subject property to the defendant by quit claim deed. On December 31, 1985, the defendant conveyed the property to the plaintiff by warranty deed, free and clear of all encumbrances but subject to all building, building line and zoning restrictions as well as easements and restrictions of record.

During the summer of 1986, the plaintiff decided to perform repairs on the bulkhead and the filled area of the property. The plaintiff engaged an engineering firm which wrote to the state department of environmental protection (DEP) requesting a survey of the tidal wetlands on the property. On March 14, 1986, working with the plaintiff's engineers, the DEP placed stakes on the wetlands boundary and noted that there was a tidal wetlands violation on the property. In a letter to the plaintiff dated April 10, 1986, the DEP confirmed its findings and indicated that in order to establish the tidal wetlands boundary, as staked for regulatory purposes, the plaintiff must provide DEP with an A-2 survey of the property. At some point after April, 1986, and before March, 1988, the plaintiff engaged a second group of engineers who met with DEP officials and completed an A-2 survey.

On March 28, 1988, members of the DEP water resources unit met with the plaintiff's new engineers to stake out the wetlands boundary again. On April 13, 1988, as confirmation of that meeting, Denis Cunningham, the assistant director of the DEP water resources unit, wrote to the plaintiff to advise him that the filled and bulkheaded portion of the property, and possibly the northwest corner of the house were encroaching on the tidal wetlands boundary, thereby creating a violation of General Statutes §22a-30. This letter suggested that to correct the violation, the plaintiff would have to submit an application to DEP demonstrating the necessity of maintaining the bulkhead and fill within the tidal wetlands. Instead of filing the application, the plaintiff filed the underlying lawsuit against the defendant, claiming damages for breach of the warranty against encumbrances and innocent misrepresentation.

The trial court determined that the area has been filled without obtaining the necessary permits required under General Statutes §22a-32. The court found that the defendant had breached the warranty against encumbrances and had innocently misrepresented the condition of the property by allowing the plaintiff to purchase the property in reliance on the defendant's warranty against encumbrances. The court awarded the plaintiff damages and costs in the amount of $47,792.60, a figure that included the costs to correct the wetlands violation as well as the diminution of value of the property caused by the wetlands violation. The defendant brought the present appeal.

This appeal turns on a determination of whether an alleged latent violation of a land use statute or regulation, existing on the land at the time title is conveyed, constitutes an encumbrance such that the conveyance breaches the grantor's covenant against encumbrances. An encumbrance is defined as "every right to or interest in the land which may subsist in third persons, to the diminution of the value of the land, but consistent with the passing of the fee by the conveyance." H. Tiffany, Real Property (1975) §1002; Aczas v. Stuart Heights, Inc., 154 Conn. 54, 60, 221 A.2d 589 (1966). All encumbrances may be classed as either (1) a pecuniary charge against the premises, such as mortgages, judgment liens, tax liens, or assessments, or (2) estates or interests in the property less than the fee, like leases, life estates or dower rights, or (3) easements or servitudes on the land, such as rights of way, restrictive covenants and profits. H. Tiffany, supra,

§§1003-1007. It is important to note that the covenant against encumbrances operates in praesenti and cannot be breached unless the encumbrance existed at the time of the conveyance. Id.

The issue of whether a latent violation of a restrictive land use statute or ordinance, that exists at the time the fee is conveyed, constitutes a breach of the warranty deed covenant against encumbrances has not been decided in Connecticut. There is, however, persuasive and authoritative weight in the legal literature and the case law of other jurisdictions to support the proposition that such an exercise of police power by the state *does not* affect the marketability of title and should not rise to the level of an encumbrance. See, e.g., Domer v. Sleeper, 533 P.2d 9 (Alaska 1975) (latent building code violation not an encumbrance); McCrae v. Giteles, 253 So. 2d 260, 261 (Fla. App. 1971) (violation of housing code noticed and known by vendor not an encumbrance); Monti v. Tangora, 99 Ill. App. 3d 575, 54 Ill. Dec. 732, 425 N.E.2d 597 (1981) (noticed building code violations not an encumbrance); Silverblatt v. Livadas, 340 Mass. 474, 164 N.E.2d 875 (1960) (contingent or inchoate lien which might result from building code violation not an encumbrance); Fahmie v. Wulster, 81 N.J. 391, 408 A.2d 789 (1979) (discussed infra); Woodenbury v. Spier, 122 App. Div. 396, 106 N.Y.S. 817 (1907) (a lis pendens filed to enforce housing code violations after conveyance not an encumbrance); Stone v. Sexsmith, 28 Wash. 2d 947, 184 P.2d 567 (1947).

Of the cases cited from other jurisdictions, Fahmie v. Wulster, supra, provides the closest factual analogue to the case before us. In *Fahmie*, a closely held corporation that originally owned certain property requested permission from the New Jersey bureau of water to place a nine foot diameter culvert on the property to enclose a stream. The bureau required instead that a sixteen and one-half foot diameter culvert should be installed. The corporation went ahead with its plan and installed the nine foot culvert.

The property was later conveyed to Wulster, the titular president of the corporation, who had no knowledge of the installation of the nine foot culvert. Nine years after the installation of the culvert, Wulster conveyed the property, by warranty deed, to Fahmie.

In anticipation of the subsequent resale of the property, Fahmie made application to the New Jersey economic development commission, division of water policy and supply, to make additional improvements to the stream and its banks. It was then that the inadequate nine foot culvert was discovered, and the plaintiff was required to replace it with a sixteen and one-half foot diameter pipe. Fahmie sued Wulster for the cost to correct the violation claiming a breach of the deed warranty against encumbrances.

The New Jersey Supreme Court concluded that it was generally the law throughout the country that a claim for breach of a covenant against encumbrances cannot be predicated on the necessity to repair or alter the property to conform with land use regulations. By so doing, the *Fahmie* court refused to expand the concept of an encumbrance to include structural conditions existing on the property that constitute violations of statute or governmental regulation. The court concluded that such a conceptual enlargement of the covenant against encumbrances would create uncertainty and confusion in the law of conveyancing and title insurance because neither a title search nor a physical examination of the premises would disclose the violation. The New Jersey court went on to state that "[t]he better way to deal with violations of governmental regulations, their nature and scope being as pervasive as they are, is by contract provisions which can give the purchaser full protection [in such situations]." 81 N.J. at 397, 408 A.2d 789.

The case before us raises the same issues as those raised in *Fahmie*. Here, the court found that in 1978 the wetlands area was filled without a permit and in violation of state statute. The alleged violation was unknown to the defendant, was not on the land records and was discovered only after the plaintiff attempted to get permission to perform additional improvements to the wetlands area.

Although the DEP first advised the plaintiff of the alleged violation in 1986, it did not bring any action to compel compliance with the statute. Rather, it suggested that the violation may be corrected by submitting an application to DEP. As of the date of trial, the plaintiff had not made such an application, there had been no further action taken by the DEP to compel compliance, and no administrative order was ever entered from which the plaintiff could appeal. Thus, the plaintiff was never required by DEP to abate the violation or restore the wetlands.

Our Supreme Court has stated that for a deed to be free of all encumbrances there must be marketable title that can be sold "at a fair price to a reasonable purchaser or mortgaged to a person of reasonable prudence as a security for the loan of money." Perkins v. August, 109 Conn. 452, 456, 146 A. 831 (1929). To render a title unmarketable, the defect must present a real and substantial probability of litigation or loss at the time of the conveyance. Frank Towers Corporation v. Laviana, 140 Conn. 45, 53, 97 A.2d 567 (1953). Latent violations of state or municipal land use regulations that do not appear on the land records, that are unknown to the seller of the property, as to which the agency charged with enforcement has taken no official action to compel compliance at the time the deed was executed, and that have not ripened into an interest that can be recorded on the land records do not constitute an encumbrance for the purpose of the deed warranty. Monti v. Tangora, 99 Ill. App. 3d 575, 581-582, 54 Ill. Dec. 732, 425 N.E.2d 597 (1981). Although, under the statute, DEP could impose fines or restrict the use of the property until it is brought into compliance, such a restriction is not an encumbrance. Silverblatt v. Livadas, 340 Mass. 474, 479, 164 N.E.2d 875 (1960); Gaier v. Berkow, 90 N.J. Super. 377, 379, 217 A.2d 642 (1966).

Because the plaintiff never actually filed the application, any damages that he may have suffered were speculative. The court based its assessment of damages on a *proposed* application and the anticipated costs of complying with that *proposed* application. The fact that the alleged violation was first noted by DEP only after the plaintiff made requests to rework the bulkhead and filled area, leads us to the conclusion that no litigation or loss was imminent. This position is confirmed by the fact that, as of the date of trial, no order was entered by DEP to compel the plaintiff to rectify the violative condition and no application was made by the plaintiff to gain approval of existing conditions.

We adopt the reasoning of Fahmie v. Wulster, supra, and hold that the concept of encumbrances cannot be expanded to include latent conditions on property that are in violation of statutes or government regulations. To do so would create uncertainty in the law of conveyances, title searches and title insurance. The parties to a conveyance of real property can adequately protect themselves from such conditions by including protective language in the contract and by insisting on appropriate provisions in the deed. As the Illinois Appellate Court held in Monti v. Tangora, supra, 99 Ill. App. 3d at 582, 54 Ill. Dec. 732, 425 N.E.2d 597, "[t]he problem created by the existence of code violations is not one to be resolved by the courts, but is one that can be handled quite easily by the draftsmen of contracts for sale and of deeds. All that is required of the law on this point is that it be certain. Once certainty is achieved, parties and their draftsmen may place rights and obligations where they will. It is the stability in real estate transactions that is of paramount importance here." Id.

The plaintiff in this case is an attorney and land developer who had developed waterfront property and was aware of the wetlands requirement. He could have protected himself from any liability for wetlands violations either by requiring an A-2 survey prior to closing or by inserting provisions in the contract and deed to indemnify himself against potential tidal wetlands violations or violations of other environmental statutes.

We disagree as well with the court's finding of innocent misrepresentation. The elements of innocent misrepresentation are (1) a representation of material fact (2) made for the purpose of inducing the purchase, (3) the representation is untrue, and (4) there is justifiable reliance by the plaintiff on the representation by the defendant and (5) damages. Johnson v. Healy, 176 Conn. 97, 405 A.2d 54 (1978). From the evidence adduced at trial, *no* representation was made relating to the wetlands area. The court relied exclusively on the warranty against encumbrances as the "assertion" that the property was free and clear of all encumbrances as the material fact misrepresented. Because we have held that the warranty of a covenant against encumbrances was not violated, no misrepresentation was made.

The judgment is reversed as to the award of damages for breach of the warranty against encumbrances and for innocent misrepresentation of real property, and the case is remanded with direction to render judgment in favor of the defendant on those issues.

NOTES, QUESTIONS, AND PROBLEMS

1. Is the definition of "encumbrance" the same in a suit alleging breach of the covenant against encumbrances as in a suit on a contract of sale alleging unmarketable title? See Lohmeyer v. Bower, page 577. Compare 3 American Law of Property §12.128 with §11.49 (1952).

2. Compare Bianchi v. Lorenz, 701 A.2d 1037 (Vt. 1997), with *Frimberger.* In *Bianchi* the sellers' contractor, in building their house, constructed a septic system not complying with the building code. The contractor never obtained a certificate of lawful completion nor a certificate of occupancy from the city.

The sellers relied upon the contractor and did not know of his violations. They moved into the house without obtaining a certificate of occupancy. Two years later the sellers sold the house to the buyers. Six months after the sale, major septic problems appeared, which cost the buyers $40,000 to repair. The buyers sued for breach of the covenant against encumbrances. The court ruled for the buyers. It held that any substantial violation of municipal ordinances is an encumbrance in violation of the deed covenants if the seller — either the builder or a subsequent owner — can determine from municipal records that the property violates local zoning or building regulations at the time of the conveyance. See also New England Fed. Credit Union v. Stewart Title Guarantee. Co., 765 A.2d 450 (Vt. 2000) (interpreting *Bianchi* to refer to matters of record that would give constructive notice of violation).

For a critique of *Frimberger,* see Jessica P. Wilde, Comment, Violations of Zoning Ordinances, the Covenant Against Encumbrances, and Marketability of Title: How Purchasers Can Be Better Protected, 23 Touro L. Rev. 199, 219-225 (2007).

3. Suppose that *B* discovers that hazardous waste was deposited on the land many years ago by *X* Corporation, which conveyed the land to *A*. *X* Corporation is now out of business. *A*, unaware of the contamination, had conveyed the land by general warranty deed to *B*. What are *B*'s remedies? If the EPA comes in, cleans up the land, and sues *B* to recover the costs, is *A* liable to *B* for the costs?

4. The measure of damages for breach of a covenant of seisin is the return of all or a portion of the purchase price. For example, if *A* buys a tract of 100 acres, and title fails as to 20 acres, *A* is entitled to the return of one-fifth of the purchase price (and not to the market value of 20 acres of land). If *A* struck a particularly good bargain, and the market value is significantly higher than *A* paid, *A* does not get the benefit of her bargain.

The measure of damages for breach of a covenant against encumbrances is different. If the encumbrance is easily removable (for example, a mortgage), the measure of damages is the cost of removal. If the encumbrance is not easily removable (for example, a restrictive covenant or easement), the measure of damages is the difference in value between the land with the encumbrance and without the encumbrance. In all cases damages are limited by the total price received by the warrantor.

The measure of damages for breach of a covenant against encumbrances generally follows the rules of contract law by putting the grantee in as good a position as if the covenant or warranty had not been breached, thus giving the grantee the benefit of her bargain. Why does not the measure of damages for breach of a covenant of seisin do this? See William B. Stoebuck & Dale A. Whitman, The Law of Property 913-917 (3d ed. 2000).

Future covenants run with the land to all successors in interest of the grantee. Hence if *A* gives a general warranty deed to *B*, and *B* sells to *C*, *A* is liable to *C* on any of the future covenants in *A*'s deed. If the paramount owner, *O*, evicts *C*, *A* is liable to *C* on the covenants of general warranty and quiet enjoyment.

A present covenant, if not breached when the deed is delivered, can never be broken, and it is senseless to say it either runs or does not run with the land. It can never be sued upon. On the other hand, if a present covenant is breached when the deed is delivered, the grantee no longer has a covenant but, instead, has a cause of action for breach of the covenant. Under the older common law view, which objected to assignment of choses in action, the cause of action was not impliedly assigned. Thus *C* could not sue *A* for breach of a covenant of seisin. This view is still adhered to in a majority of states. In a number of states, however, a different view is now taken. The chose in action of *B* against *A* can be, and is impliedly, assigned to *C* when *B* sells the land to *C*. Under this latter view *C* can sue *A* for breach of the covenant of seisin. Rockafellor v. Gray explains this in greater detail.

Rockafellor v. Gray

Supreme Court of Iowa, 1922
191 N.W. 107

FAVILLE, J. On October 14, 1907, one Doffing conveyed to the plaintiff, by warranty deed, the 80 acres of land in controversy in this action. At that time there was outstanding a certain mortgage to one Gray of $500 against said land, which the grantee in said deed assumed and agreed to pay. Subsequently foreclosure proceedings were instituted upon said mortgage, and the same culminated in a sheriff's deed, which was executed and delivered to the appellant Connelly on February 23, 1911. On April 20, 1911, Connelly conveyed said premises to one Dixon. The said deed contained the usual covenants of warranty and recited a consideration of $4,000. On June 26, 1911, Dixon in turn conveyed the premises to Hansen & Gregerson by a special warranty deed which recited a consideration of $7,000. On August 15, 1918, the plaintiff, who was the original grantee from Doffing, brought this suit to vacate and set aside the foreclosure sale under said mortgage, on the ground that the same was void because no jurisdiction had been acquired of the plaintiff in said action. On January 13, 1920, Hansen & Gregerson filed their cross-petition. Connelly, who acquired the title by sheriff's deed, as well as Hansen & Gregerson, the present owners, were made parties to said action. Hansen & Gregerson, in their cross-petition against Connelly, prayed that in the event the plaintiff was successful in vacating and setting aside the sheriff's deed that they have judgment against the remote grantor Connelly upon the covenants in his deed to Dixon, their immediate grantor. The court entered a decree in favor of the plaintiff adjudging that the said foreclosure proceedings were invalid and void, and that the sheriff's deed to Connelly should be vacated and set aside, and upon the cross-petition of Hansen & Gregerson entered judgment against Connelly on the covenant of seizin in his deed for the amount of $4,000 and interest, being the consideration recited in the deed from Connelly to Dixon, with interest from the date of the deed from Dixon to Hansen & Gregerson. From this portion of the decree Connelly prosecutes this appeal and the questions presented for our consideration are only those that arise between Connelly, the remote grantor, and Hansen & Gregerson, the remote grantees, in the chain of title.

The first question for our determination is whether or not the covenant of seizin runs with the land in this state, so that an action thereon may be maintained by a remote grantee. In Brandt v. Foster, 5 Iowa 287, we announced the rule that a covenant of seizin is a covenant for the title, and that if, at the time of the conveyance, the grantor did not own the land the covenant is broken immediately, and that it is not necessary, in order to recover, to allege or prove an ouster or eviction.

In Schofield v. Iowa Homestead Co., 32 Iowa 317, 7 Am. Rep. 197, the precise question now presented was before us. The opinion contains a full discussion of the proposition. The court recognized the division among the authorities and also that a majority of American courts recognize that the covenant of seizin does not run with the land. This court expressly, at that time (1871), adopted the English rule, holding that the covenant of seizin runs with the land, and is broken the instant the conveyance is delivered, and then becomes a chose in action held by the covenantee in the deed, and that a deed by said first covenantee operates as an assignment of such chose in action to a remote grantee, who can maintain an action thereon against the grantor in the original deed. This case has withstood all subsequent assaults upon it, and the rule therein announced has become thoroughly imbedded in the jurisprudence of this state. It is a rule of property, and we are disposed to adhere to it, regardless of any views we may entertain as to the soundness of the rule as originally announced. It is too well established for us to now consider any repudiation of it. . . .

However, another question confronts us, and that is the contention that the original covenantee, never having been in possession of the premises, that the covenant of seizin could not run with the land. Some of the courts which recognize the rule that the covenant of seizin runs with the land appear to base the holding upon the fact of the grantee having had possession under the deed. It is the theory that seizin in fact is what carries the covenant of seizin and causes it to run with the land. See Mecklem v. Blake, 22 Wis. 495, 99 Am. Dec. 68. This, however, is not the reason for the rule that the covenant of seizin runs with the land to a remote grantee, as recognized by this court. In the *Schofield* case, speaking by Mr. Justice Beck, this court said:

> What legal principle would be violated by holding that the deed from the first grantee operates as an assignment of this chose in action? Deeds under the laws of this state have been reduced to forms of great simplicity. Intricate technicalities have been pruned away, and they are now as brief and simple in form as a promissory note. All choses in action, as I have just remarked, may be assigned and transferred. The covenant of seizin (if it be held that such a covenant exists in a deed of the form authorized by the laws of this state), as we have seen, is intended to secure indemnity for the deprivation of the title and enjoyment of the lands conveyed. Why not brush away the "technical scruples" gathered about the covenant of seizin, as we have the like technical and cumbrous forms of the instrument itself, and enforce it for the benefit of the party who is really injured by its breach, even though, in so doing, we find it necessary to hold that a chose in action is assigned and transferred by the operation of the deed?

In the case at bar the evidence shows that the original grantor, Connelly, never had possession of the premises in question, nor did his grantee Dixon, who conveyed to the appellees Hansen & Gregerson. Neither Connelly nor Dixon paid any attention to the land. They never were in possession, nor leased the same, nor paid any taxes thereon. If in every case it must be held that the covenant of seizin only runs with the land where the original covenantee takes possession before conveyance by him to another, then it could not be said to run with the land in this case. The original covenantee, Dixon, did not take possession of the land and had no such possession when he conveyed to the appellees Hansen & Gregerson. The evidence tends to show that the latter never had actual possession of the premises. If the covenant of seizin runs with the land to a remote grantee, under the theory that subsequent deeds operate as an assignment of the chose in action that accrued to the first grantee, then there is no logical reason why the remote grantee, claiming by conveyance under the original grantee, cannot maintain the action whether or not he ever had actual possession of the land. The rights of the remote grantee are acquired by conveyance (assignment) and not by virtue of actual possession of the premises. The grantor (appellant Connelly) had neither title to nor possession of the premises at the time he executed and delivered his deed to Dixon on April 20, 1911. Dixon thereupon had a right of action against Connelly for the breach of the covenant of seizin. This right of action, under our holding in Schofield v. Iowa Homestead Co., supra, passed by assignment to the appellees Hansen & Gregerson by the deed which Dixon executed and delivered to them June 26, 1918. These grantees asserted their claim for breach of appellant's deed within the 10-year period from the date of the execution and delivery of the original deed from Connelly to Dixon, and were entitled to maintain said action and to recover against the remote grantor Connelly.

A question is raised as to the amount of the recovery of the appellees Hansen & Gregerson against Connelly. The court allowed recovery in the amount of the consideration recited in the deed from Connelly to his grantee Dixon, with interest thereon from the date of the execution of the deed from Dixon to Hansen & Gregerson. This was in accordance with the general rule in cases of a breach of the covenant of seizin.

In Brandt v. Foster, supra, we held that—

> If, at the time of the conveyance, the grantor does not own the land, the covenant is broken immediately. . . . The measure of damages for breach of this covenant is the consideration money and interest, upon the ground that this is the actual loss. If the grantee, however, has lost less, he is limited to the amount of injury sustained. . . . The consideration money with interest is the extent to which damages can, under any circumstances, be recovered, upon this covenant. As a general rule, this is the standard. They may, under some circumstances, fall below, but can never exceed.

In Shorthill v. Ferguson, 44 Iowa 249, we said: "Parol proof of consideration to contradict that expressed in the deed is admissible as between the original parties, but it is not admissible in a suit against the original grantor by one to whom his grantee has transferred the land." . . .

In Foshay v. Shafer, 116 Iowa 302, 89 N.W. 1106, we held that where the covenantee had been given possession the breach of the covenant of seizin did not entitle him to recover substantial damages until some positive injury had been suffered; and held that no more than nominal damages could be recovered so long as the grantee remains in possession, without actual injury.[11] See, also, Greenvault v. Davis, 4 Hill (N.Y.) 643.

Appellant contends that if it is held that the covenant of seizin is breached immediately upon the execution and delivery of the original deed to the immediate grantee where the grantor has no title, and that the rights of the grantee pass by assignment to a remote grantee by mesne conveyances, that the measure of damages in an action by the remote grantee would be the same as the damages which the original grantee could have recovered against the grantor. It must be conceded that there is much force in this contention of the appellant. If the consideration recited in the original deed could be attacked between the original grantor and his immediate grantee, and if a conveyance by the first grantee operates as an assignment of a chose in action for breach of the covenant of seizin to a remote grantee, it can well be argued that the remote grantee can in no event recover any greater amount than could the immediate grantee. . . . In this case it is the contention of the appellant that while the deed from him to his immediate grantee Dixon recites a consideration of $4,000 that in truth and in fact there was no consideration, or at least it was merely a nominal one, and it is his contention that the remote grantees Hansen & Gregerson can recover against him no greater amount than Dixon could have recovered.

Just what would be our ruling on this question, if it were one of first impression, we do not need to determine. We regard the question as settled by our previous decisions, and are bound by the rule of stare decisis. We have recognized and announced the rule that, as between the original parties parol proof of the actual consideration is admissible to contradict the recitals of a deed, but that such evidence is not admissible in a suit by a remote grantee against the original grantor. See cases supra. The remote grantee, in purchasing the premises, had a right to rely upon the fact that the original grantor in a prior deed was bound by the covenants of warranty and of seizin therein, and had a right to take into account the consideration recited in such prior deed in purchasing the premises. In this case Hansen & Gregerson, from an examination of the record, would have been apprised of the fact that the appellant had executed and delivered to his grantee Dixon a warranty deed containing the covenant of seizin and that said deed recited a consideration of $4,000. They likewise had a right to rely upon the law of this state that said covenant of said deed ran with the land and inured to their benefit. It is to be presumed that they took these matters into consideration in purchasing from Dixon. As to them, the original grantor is estopped to claim that the consideration recited in said deed is in fact less than the recitals therein

11. In Hilliker v. Rueger, 126 N.E. 266 (N.Y. 1920), the court allowed the warrantee to recover a proportionate part of the purchase price *and* remain in possession of the acreage to which title had failed (the holder of superior title had not yet appeared to claim possession). Which view is more sound? — EDS.

contained. This is the rule as to the covenant of warranty and applies in this state equally to the covenant of seizin. In no event could the remote grantee recover from the remote grantor a greater amount than the consideration recited in the original deed between the remote grantor and his immediate grantee.

In this instance the recovery of Hansen & Gregerson against the appellant Connelly is limited to $4,000, the consideration recited in the deed from Connelly to his grantee Dixon. Hansen & Gregerson are entitled to interest on this amount from the date of their deed from Dixon. The recited consideration in the deed from Dixon to Hansen & Gregerson is $7,000. The evidence tends to show that this consideration was in fact paid by Hansen & Gregerson to Dixon. The amount of the recovery of Hansen & Gregerson, as before stated, is limited to the consideration recited in the deed from the original grantor to his immediate grantee, even though the remote grantee paid a larger consideration. Whether or not the remote grantee could recover from the remote grantor the amount of the consideration recited in the original deed between the remote grantor and his immediate grantee, in the event that the remote grantee had paid his grantor a less sum than the consideration recited in said original deed, is not before us, and we express no opinion thereon. . . .

The decree of the lower court was in accordance with the rules herein announced, and was correct.

The decree of the district court should be in all respects affirmed.

NOTES AND PROBLEMS

1. In Rockafellor v. Gray, why did Hansen & Gregerson not sue on the future covenants of warranty and quiet enjoyment, which do run with the land? There are two explanations. First, for a covenant to "run with the land" to a successor claimant, the covenantee must convey to the successor either title or possession, some "thing" to which the covenant can "attach" and with which it can "run." In the case, Dixon (the covenantee) transferred neither title nor possession to Hansen & Gregerson; both were in Rockafellor. Second, future covenants of warranty and quiet enjoyment are intended to secure compensation to the purchaser when his quiet possession is disturbed. These covenants are not breached unless the covenantee or his assigns are prevented from taking complete possession or are actually or constructively evicted by a person having paramount title. 3 American Law of Property §12.129 (1952).

Observe that the Iowa court, in quoting from the *Schofield* case, is careful to say that Hansen & Gregerson can sue on the covenant of seisin because the chose in action arising from its breach was assigned to them, not because the covenant runs with title or possession (seisin in fact).

2. By general warranty deed *A* conveys Blackacre to *B* for $20,000. *B* conveys Blackacre to *C* for $15,000. *O*, the true owner, ousts *C*. The jurisdiction holds that present covenants are breached, if at all, when made, and the chose in action is not assigned to subsequent grantees.

(a) The deed from *B* to *C* is a quitclaim deed. How much, if anything, can *B* recover from *A*?

(b) The deed from *B* to *C* is a general warranty deed. *C* has not sued *B* nor settled with him. How much, if anything, can *B* recover from *A*?

(c) The deed from *B* to *C* is a general warranty deed. *C* sues *B* and recovers $15,000. How much, if anything, can *B* recover from *A*?

(d) Would your answers be different if the jurisdiction follows the view of Rockafellor v. Gray?

3. By general warranty deed *A* conveys Whiteacre to *B* for $15,000. By quitclaim deed *B* conveys Whiteacre to *C* for $12,000. By general warranty deed *C* conveys Whiteacre to *D* for $20,000. *O*, the true owner, ousts *D* at a time that the land is worth $24,000. Advise *D* and *C* as to how much they can recover on the warranties.

4. How effective is a warranty deed in protecting the purchaser against defects in title? Consider the following:

(a) The maximum recovery on a warranty is the consideration received by the covenantor, plus incidental damages such as out-of-pocket expenses incurred in examining title or defending the title against a successful direct attack. Suppose that *B* purchases Blackacre from *A* for $10,000, and 20 years later, when paramount title is asserted by *O*, Blackacre is worth $125,000. Should *A* or *B* bear the risk of loss for increase in value?

(b) Most states have statutes authorizing a decedent's personal representative to publish notice to creditors of the decedent's death in a local newspaper and barring claims not presented to the personal representative within a specified period thereafter. These statutes, varying in detail, are thought necessary to permit distribution of the decedent's assets free and clear to the beneficiaries. Iowa Code Ann. §633.410 (West Supp. 2013) generally bars all claims not presented within four months after publication of the notice to creditors.

Suppose that in Rockafellor v. Gray the defendant Connelly had died in 1915 and no claim had been filed against his estate by Hansen & Gregerson within four months of publication of a creditors' notice. What result? See Arthur R. Gaudio, Title Covenants for the Iowa Homeowner—Some Good News and Much Bad News, 23 Drake L. Rev. 1, 9-13 (1973).

(c) Judgments against the covenantor may be uncollectible because the covenantor is insolvent or owns no property, or the covenantor's property is fully within statutory exemptions to creditors' claims or is fully covered by a mortgage.

NOTE: ESTOPPEL BY DEED

Suppose that a grantor conveys land to a grantee that the grantor does not own, and the grantor warrants the title to the land. If the grantor *subsequently* acquires title to the land, the grantor is estopped to deny that he had title at the time of the deed and that title passed to the grantee. Since the grantee could sue the grantor on the warranty, when the grantor later acquires title, and compel the delivery of a new conveyance, the law eliminates the necessity of a lawsuit and automatically passes the subsequently acquired title to the grantee.

Estoppel by deed originated in cases involving warranty deeds, but it has been extended by courts to quitclaim deeds if the deed represents that the grantor had title. See William B. Stoebuck & Dale A. Whitman, The Law of Property 841 (3d ed. 2000).

2.   Delivery

To be effective, a deed must be delivered with the intent that it be presently operative. Delivery is rarely an issue in commercial transactions. Either the grantor hands the deed to the grantee upon receipt of the purchase price, or the grantor puts the deed in the hands of a third party (an escrow agent) who hands over the deed upon closing the transaction. In the first case, the grantor intends to make an immediate transfer of title to the grantee. In the second, the grantor intends to transfer title when all conditions are fulfilled. If there is an enforceable contract of sale, the escrow agent is the agent of both the grantor and grantee. The grantor cannot recall the deed from the agent. When the agent delivers the deed to the grantee, if necessary to carry out the parties' intent and do equity, the title of the grantee will "relate back" to the date the grantor handed the deed to the agent. For example, if the grantor dies before the escrow agent delivers the deed, the delivery of the deed by the agent is treated as if it occurred before the grantor's death. By this fiction the rule that a will is required to pass title at death is avoided. Title is regarded as having been transferred to the grantee during the grantor's life.

Problems involving delivery usually arise in donative transactions, to which we now turn our attention.

Sweeney v. Sweeney

Supreme Court of Errors of Connecticut, 1940
11 A.2d 806

JENNINGS, J. Maurice Sweeney, plaintiff's intestate, hereinafter called Maurice, deeded his farm to his brother John M. Sweeney, hereinafter called John, and the deed was recorded. John deeded the property back to Maurice. This deed is unrecorded and was accidentally burned. The question to be decided is whether the second deed was delivered and if so, whether or not a condition claimed to be attached to the delivery is operative. This must be determined on the finding. The following statement includes such changes therein as are required by the evidence:

The plaintiff is the widow and administratrix of Maurice but had not lived with him for the twenty years preceding his death in September, 1938, at the age of seventy-three years. Maurice lived on a tract of land of some hundred and thirty-five acres which he owned in East Hampton, where he ran a tavern. John assisted him in running the tavern to some extent. On February 2, 1937, Maurice and John went to the town clerk's office in East Hampton pursuant to an appointment made the preceding day. Maurice requested the town clerk to draw a deed of his East Hampton property to John and this was done. At the same time he requested that a deed be prepared from John to himself so that he, Maurice, would be protected if John predeceased him. Both deeds were duly executed. The first was left for recording and the second was taken away by Maurice and never recorded. A week or two later Maurice took to John the recorded deed and a week or two after that took the unrecorded deed to John's house. John kept both deeds and gave the second deed to his attorney after the institution of this action. It was destroyed when the latter's office was burned. After the execution of the deeds, Maurice continued to occupy the property, paid the fixed charges, received the rents and exercised full dominion over it until his death. In April, 1937, Maurice made a written lease to Ernest Myers of a portion of the premises and on June 18, 1938, a written lease to Frank and Esther Fricke for twenty years. The first lease is lost but the second was recorded. The defendant never collected any money from tenants or paid any fixed charges or repairs prior to the death of Maurice. On these facts the trial court concluded that there was no intention to make present delivery of John's deed to Maurice, that there was no delivery or acceptance thereof, that it was not intended to operate until John's death and rendered judgment for the defendant.

This deed was, in effect, manually delivered. Maurice continued to occupy the property and exercised full dominion over it without interference by John. It follows that all the essentials of a good delivery were present unless there is something in the contentions of John which defeats this result. He claims that there was no intention on his part to make present delivery.

It is, of course, true that physical possession of a duly executed deed is not conclusive proof that it was legally delivered. McDermott v. McDermott, 97 Conn. 31, 34, 115 Atl. 638. This is so under some circumstances even where there has been a manual delivery. Hotaling v. Hotaling, 193 Cal. 368, 381, 224 Pac. 455, 56 A.L.R. 734, and note p. 746. Delivery must be made with the intent to pass title if it is to be effective. Porter v. Woodhouse, 59 Conn. 568, 575, 22 Atl. 299; McDermott v. McDermott, supra.

The deed having been in effect actually delivered to Maurice, the execution of the attestation clause was prima facie proof that the deed was delivered. New Haven Trust Co. v. Camp, 81 Conn. 539, 542, 71 Atl. 788. There is a rebuttable presumption that the grantee assented since the deed was beneficial to him. Moore v. Giles, 49 Conn. 570, 573. No fact is found which militates against this presumption. Where deeds are formally executed and delivered, these presumptions can be overcome only by evidence that no delivery was in fact intended. Loughran v. Kummer, 297 Pa. St. 179, 183, 146 Atl. 534; Cragin's Estate, 274 Pa. St. 1, 5, 117 Atl. 445; Stewart v. Silva, 192 Cal. 405, 409, 221 Pac. 191. The only purpose in making the deed expressed by either party was the statement by Maurice that it was to protect him in case John predeceased him. Since this purpose would have been defeated had there been no delivery with intent to pass title, this conclusively establishes the fact that there was a legal delivery.

The defendant next claims that if there was a delivery, it was on condition and that the condition (the death of John before that of Maurice) was not and cannot be fulfilled. This claim is not good because the delivery was to the grantee. "A conditional delivery is and can only be made by placing the deed in the hands of a third person to be kept by him until the happening of the event upon the happening of which the deed is to be delivered over by the third person to the grantee." Porter v. Woodhouse, supra, 574; Raymond v. Smith, 5 Conn. 555, 559. Conditional delivery to a grantee vests absolute title in the latter. As is pointed out in the *Loughran* case, supra, this is one of the instances where a positive rule of law may defeat the actual intention of the parties. The safety of real estate titles is considered more important than the unfortunate results which may follow the application of the rule in a few individual instances. To relax it would open the door wide to fraud and the fabrication of evidence. Although the doctrine has been criticized (2 Tiffany, Real Property [2d ed.] p. 1764; 5 Wigmore, Evidence [2d ed.] §§2405, 2408) no material change has been noted in the attitude of the courts in this country.

The finding does not support the conclusion. The finding shows a delivery and, even if a conditional delivery is assumed, the condition is not good for the reasons stated. Since a new trial is necessary, the one ruling on evidence made a ground of appeal is noticed. The town clerk was permitted to testify to certain statements made by Maurice when the deed was drafted. Parol evidence is not admissible to vary the terms of the deed but may be received to show the use that was to be made of it. Fisk's Appeal, 81 Conn. 433, 437, 71 Atl. 559. The ruling was correct as showing the circumstances surrounding delivery.

There is error and a new trial is ordered.

NOTES AND QUESTIONS

1. At the time of Maurice Sweeney's death, Conn. Gen. Stat. §5156 (1930) gave the surviving spouse an elective share of a life estate in one-third of decedent's property in his probate estate.[12] Dower had long been abolished. If decedent died intestate, as Maurice did, §5156 gave his surviving spouse one-third absolutely; if no issue or parent of the decedent survived, §5156 gave the surviving spouse all of the estate of the decedent. From the facts it appears that Maurice was survived by his estranged wife Maria and his brother John. If so, under Connecticut law Maria took all of Maurice's property.

Maurice Sweeney failed to carry out his wish that John have the land if John survived him. What would you have recommended had Maurice consulted you before engaging in the sleight-of-hand business with the two deeds?

---

12. The rights of a surviving spouse under Connecticut's present law are substantially the same as those set forth in this paragraph. See Conn. Gen. Stat. Ann. §§45a-436, 45a-437 (West 2013).

2. The *Sweeney* case represents the prevailing view, though there are two other solutions courts have reached.

(a) *No delivery.* When the deed is handed over to the grantee but the extrinsic evidence shows that the deed is to "take effect" at the death of the grantor, a few courts have held that there is no delivery and that the transfer is testamentary and void. See William B. Stoebuck & Dale A. Whitman, The Law of Property 830 (3d ed. 2000).

(b) *Delivery good and condition enforced.* Chillemi v. Chillemi, 78 A.2d 750 (Md. 1951), rejected the *Sweeney* rule, on particularly compelling facts. *H*, going overseas on a dangerous military mission, delivered a deed to *W* with oral instructions that if *H* was killed, *W* was to record the deed, and if *H* returned from the mission, the deed was to be returned to *H* and destroyed. One month after *H*'s return, and following considerable marital squabbling, *W* recorded the deed. The court upheld the oral conditions and annulled the deed, saying:

> The ancient rule that the mere transfer of a deed from the grantor to the grantee overrides the grantor's explicit declaration of intention that the deed shall not become operative immediately is a relic of the primitive formalism which attached some peculiar efficacy to the physical transfer of the deed as a symbolical transfer of the land. . . . In England in ancient times there could be no change of possession of land until a livery of seisin had taken place. A knife was produced and a piece of turf was cut, and the turf was handed over to the new owner. Later, under the Roman influence, the written document came into use. These documents, which few people had the art to manufacture, were regarded with mystical awe. Just as the sod had been taken up from the ground to be delivered, so the document was laid upon the ground and then solemnly lifted and delivered as a symbol of ownership. In this way the principle developed that the delivery of the deed was the mark of finality. . . .
>
> But there is actually no logical reason why a deed should not be held in escrow by the grantee as well as by any other person. . . . After all, conditional delivery is purely a question of intention, and it is immaterial whether the instrument, pending satisfaction of the condition, is in the hands of the grantor, the grantee, or a third person. After the condition is satisfied, there is an operative conveyance which is considered as having been delivered at the time of the conditional delivery, for the reason that it was then that it was actually delivered, although the ownership does not pass until the satisfaction of the condition. [78 A.2d at 753.]

Blancett v. Blancett, 102 P.3d 640 (N.M. 2004), rejects a per se rule against conditional deliveries of deeds. Instead the court holds that physical delivery creates a rebuttable presumption of a present transfer.

3. Seller is ready to deliver a deed to buyer, but buyer does not yet have the money. Seller says to buyer, "I'll give you this deed now on condition that you pay me by the first of next month." Buyer takes the deed and records, but subsequently does not pay. If the *Sweeney* case is followed, what is seller's remedy? Compare Gilbert ex rel. Roberts v. Rainey, 71 S.W.3d 66 (Ark. App. 2002), with State ex rel. Pai v. Thom, 563 P.2d 982 (Haw. 1977).

NOTE: DELIVERY WITHOUT HANDING OVER

To deliver a deed of land, it is not necessary that the deed be "handed over" to the grantee. "Delivery" means no more than an act that evinces an intent to be immediately bound by the transfer. The act can be, of course, handing over the document to the grantee, but it can also be the grantor's declaration, express or implied, that he is bound by his deed. The traditional view was put by Sir Edward Coke with his usual felicity: "As a deed may be delivered to the party without words, so may a deed be delivered by words without any act of delivery." 1 Co. Litt. 36A.

The most common case of delivery without manual tradition arises when the grantor executes a deed and places it in a safe deposit box, usually with the thought that the grantee will "take" the land at the grantor's death. If the grantor intends to pass title or a future interest to the grantee *now*, there has been a delivery even though possession may be postponed until the grantor's death. See Lucero v. Lucero, 2011 WL 6016981 (N.M. App. Nov. 1, 2011) (holding that grantor who gave key to safety deposit box containing will to someone to give to grantee supported presumption of delivery). On the other hand, if the grantor intends that no interest should arise until death, no delivery during life has taken place; the deed cannot take legal effect at death because the grantor intended it to be a will, not a deed, and the instrument is not executed with two witnesses in accordance with the Statute of Wills. Laypersons often do not know of the sharp distinction the law draws between an *inter vivos transfer of land*, requiring the delivery of a signed instrument, and a *transfer at death*, requiring an instrument complying with the Statute of Wills.

Rosengrant v. Rosengrant

Court of Appeals of Oklahoma, 1981
629 P.2d 800

BOYDSTON, J. This is an appeal by J.W. (Jay) Rosengrant from the trial court's decision to cancel and set aside a warranty deed which attempted to vest title in him to certain property owned by his aunt and uncle, Mildred and Harold Rosengrant. The trial court held the deed was invalid for want of legal delivery. We affirm that decision.

Harold and Mildred were a retired couple living on a farm southeast of Tecumseh, Oklahoma.[13] They had no children of their own but had six nieces

---

13. Tecumseh, Oklahoma (pop. 6,457), is named after the great Shawnee chief Tecumseh, the most formidable Indian adversary of white expansion across the Appalachians. A powerful orator and magnetic leader, Tecumseh held—and preached, to tribes from Canada to Florida—that the Great Spirit had given the North American continent to the Indian people, as their common property, and that no tribe could sell the part of the commons it used without the consent of all the tribes. He denounced chiefs of the tribes in Indiana who purported to sell three million acres to the United States for $7,000 and an annuity of $1,750, land upon which half a dozen other tribes were living. When General William Henry Harrison, governor of the Territory of Indiana, would not cancel these land-sale treaties, which Tecumseh called fraudulent, Tecumseh went to war to void them. Tecumseh was killed in 1813 in a great battle with United States forces led by General Harrison. "Within mere minutes [of Tecumseh's death] the Indians had melted away and a weird stillness settled over the battlefield. They had lost the war. They had lost their homelands. They had lost their cause. *They had lost Tecumseh!*" Allan W. Eckert, A Sorrow in Our Heart: The Life of Tecumseh 678 (1992).

After Tecumseh's death, the Shawnees moved from Ohio and Indiana across the Mississippi. Remnants of the tribe settled on land reserved for them in the Indian Territory, now Oklahoma. The reservations were broken up by the federal government at the end of the nineteenth century, all tribal lands allotted to individual

and nephews through Harold's deceased brother. One of these nephews was Jay Rosengrant. He and his wife lived a short distance from Harold and Mildred and helped the elderly couple from time to time with their chores.

In 1971, it was discovered that Mildred had cancer. In July, 1972, Mildred and Harold went to Mexico to obtain Laetrile treatments accompanied by Jay's wife. Jay remained behind to care for the farm.

Shortly before this trip, on June 23, 1972, Mildred had called Jay and asked him to meet her and Harold at Farmers and Merchants Bank in Tecumseh. Upon arriving at the bank, Harold introduced Jay to his banker, J.E. Vanlandengham, who presented Harold and Mildred with a deed to their farm which he had prepared according to their instructions. Both Harold and Mildred signed the deed and informed Jay that they were going to give him "the place," but that they wanted Jay to leave the deed at the bank with Mr. Vanlandengham and when "something happened" to them,[14] he was to take it to Shawnee and record it and "it" would be theirs. Harold personally handed the deed to Jay to "make this legal." Jay accepted the deed and then handed it back to the banker who told him he would put it in an envelope and keep it in the vault until he called for it.

In July, 1974, when Mildred's death was imminent, Jay and Harold conferred with an attorney concerning the legality of the transaction. The attorney advised them it should be sufficient but if Harold anticipated problems he should draw up a will.

In 1976, Harold discovered he had lung cancer. In August and December, 1977, Harold put $10,000 into two certificates of deposit in joint tenancy with Jay.

Harold died January 28, 1978. On February 2, Jay and his wife went to the bank to inventory the contents of the safety deposit box. They also requested the envelope containing the deed which was retrieved from the collection file of the bank.

Jay went to Shawnee the next day and recorded the deed.

The petition to cancel and set aside the deed was filed February 22, 1978, alleging that the deed was void in that it was never legally delivered and alternatively that since it was to be operative only upon recordation after the death of the grantors it was a testamentary instrument and was void for failure to comply with the Statute of Wills.

The trial court found the deed was null and void for failure of legal delivery. The dispositive issue raised on appeal is whether the trial court erred in so ruling. We hold it did not and affirm the judgment.

The facts surrounding the transaction which took place at the bank were uncontroverted. It is the interpretation of the meaning and legal result of the transaction which is the issue to be determined by this court on appeal.

In cases involving attempted transfers such as this, it is the grantor's intent at the time the deed is delivered which is of primary and controlling importance. It

---

Indians (100 to 160 acres each), and the surplus opened to white settlement. As of 2010, 1,069 residents of Tecumseh, Oklahoma, were Native American. — EDS.

14. Common euphemism meaning their deaths.

is the function of this court to weigh the evidence presented at trial as to grantor's intent and unless the trial court's decision is clearly against the weight of the evidence, to uphold that finding.

The grantor and banker were both dead at the time of trial. Consequently, the only testimony regarding the transaction was supplied by the grantee, Jay. The pertinent part of his testimony is as follows:

A. (A)nd was going to hand it back to Mr. Vanlandingham (sic), and he wouldn't take it.

Q. What did Mr. Vanlandingham (sic) say?

A. Well, he laughed then and said that "We got to make this legal," or something like that. And said, "You'll have to give it to Jay and let Jay give it back to me."

Q. And what did Harold do with the document?

A. He gave it to me.

Q. Did you hold it?

A. Yes.

Q. Then what did you do with it?

A. Mr. Vanlandingham (sic), I believe, told me I ought to look at it.

Q. And you looked at it?

A. Yes.

Q. And then what did you do with it?

A. I handed it to Mr. Vanlandingham (sic).

Q. And what did he do with the document?

A. He had it in his hand, I believe, when we left.

Q. Do you recall seeing the envelope at any time during this transaction?

A. I never saw the envelope. But Mr. Vanlandingham (sic) told me when I handed it to him, said, "Jay, I'll put this in an envelope and keep it in a vault for you until you call for it." . . .

A. Well, Harold told me while Mildred was signing the deed that they were going to deed me the farm, but they wanted me to leave the deed at the bank with Van, and that when something happened to them that I would go to the bank and pick it up and take it to Shawnee to the court house and record it, and it would be mine.

When the deed was retrieved, it was contained in an envelope on which was typed: "J.W. Rosengrant or Harold H. Rosengrant."

The import of the writing on the envelope is clear. It creates an inescapable conclusion that the deed was, in fact, retrievable at any time by Harold before his death. The bank teller's testimony as to the custom and usage of the bank leaves no other conclusion but that at any time Harold was free to retrieve the deed. There was, if not an expressed, an implied agreement between the banker and Harold that the grant was not to take effect until two conditions occurred—the death of both grantors and the recordation of the deed.

In support of this conclusion conduct relative to the property is significant and was correctly considered by the court. Evidence was presented to show that after the deed was filed Harold continued to farm, use and control the property. Further, he continued to pay taxes on it until his death and claimed it as his homestead.

Grantee confuses the issues involved herein by relying upon grantors' goodwill toward him and his wife as if it were a controlling factor. From a fair review of the record it is apparent Jay and his wife were very attentive, kind and helpful to this elderly couple. The donative intent on the part of grantors is undeniable. We believe they fully intended to reward Jay and his wife for their kindness. Nevertheless, where a grantor delivers a deed under which he reserves a right of retrieval and attaches to that delivery the condition that the deed is to become operative only after the death of grantors and further continues to use the property as if no transfer had occurred, grantor's actions are nothing more than an attempt to employ the deed as if it were a will. Under Oklahoma law this cannot be done. The ritualistic "delivery of the deed" to the grantee and his redelivery of it to the third party for safe keeping created under these circumstances only a symbolic delivery. It amounted to a pro forma attempt to comply with the legal aspects of delivery. Based on all the facts and circumstances the true intent of the parties is expressed by the notation on the envelope and by the later conduct of the parties in relation to the land. Legal delivery is not just a symbolic gesture. It necessarily carries all the force and consequence of absolute, outright ownership at the time of delivery or it is no delivery at all.[15]

The trial court interpreted the envelope literally. The clear implication is that grantor intended to continue to exercise control and that the grant was not to take effect until such time as both he and his wife had died and the deed had been recorded. From a complete review of the record and weighing of the evidence we find the trial court's judgment is not clearly against the weight of the evidence. Costs of appeal are taxed to appellant.

BRIGHTMIRE, J., concurring specially. In a dispute of this kind dealing with the issue of whether an unrecorded deed placed in the custody of a third party is a valid conveyance to the named grantee at that time or is deposited for some other reason, such as in trust or for a testamentary purpose, the fact finder often has a particularly tough job trying to determine what the true facts are.

The law, on the other hand, is relatively clear. A valid in praesenti conveyance requires two things: (1) actual or constructive delivery of the deed to the

---

15. In Anderson v. Mauk, 67 P.2d 429 (Okla. 1937), the court stated:

It is the established law in this jurisdiction that when the owner of land executes a deed during his lifetime and delivers the same to a third party (who acts as a depository rather than an agent of the property owner) with instructions to deliver the deed to the grantee therein named upon his death, intending at the time of delivery to forever part with all lawful right and power to retake or repossess the deed, or to thereafter control the same, the delivery to the third party thus made is sufficient to operate as a valid conveyance of real estate.

grantee or to a third party; and (2) an intention by the grantor to divest himself of the conveyed interest. Here the trial judge found there was no delivery despite the testimony of Jay Rosengrant to the contrary that one of the grantors handed the deed to him at the suggestion of banker J.E. Vanlandengham.

So the question is, was the trial court bound to find the facts to be as Rosengrant stated? In my opinion it was not for several reasons. Of the four persons present at the bank meeting in question only Rosengrant survives which, when coupled with the self-serving nature of the nephew's statements, served to cast a suspicious cloud over his testimony. And this, when considered along with other circumstances detailed in the majority opinion, would have justified the fact finder in disbelieving it. I personally have trouble with the delivery testimony in spite of the apparent "corroboration" of the lawyer, Jeff Diamond. The only reason I can see for Vanlandengham suggesting such a physical delivery would be to assure the accomplishment of a valid conveyance of the property at that time. But if the grantors intended that then why did they [not] simply give it to the named grantee and tell him to record it? Why did they go through the delivery motion in the presence of Vanlandengham and then give the deed to the banker? Why did the banker write on the envelope containing the deed that it was to be given to either the grantee "or" a grantor? The fact that the grantors continued to occupy the land, paid taxes on it, offered to sell it once and otherwise treated it as their own justifies an inference that they did not make an actual delivery of the deed to the named grantee. Or, if they did, they directed that it be left in the custody of the banker with the intent of reserving a de facto life estate or of retaining a power of revocation by instructing the banker to return it to them if they requested it during their lifetimes or to give it to the named grantee upon their deaths. In either case, the deed failed as a valid conveyance.

I therefore join in affirming the trial court's judgment.

NOTES AND QUESTIONS

1. What was crucial to the finding of no delivery in *Rosengrant*: the reservation of a de facto life estate, retention of a power to revoke, or the instruction that the deed be delivered on the grantors' deaths? See Sargent v. Baxter, 673 So. 2d 979 (Fla. App. 1996), holding no delivery on similar facts.

In Vasquez v. Vasquez, 973 S.W.2d 330 (Tex. App. 1998), the grantor delivered a deed to her lawyer to be kept secret from the grantee and to be delivered to the grantee upon the grantor's death. The court found that the grantor made delivery without a reservation to recall, even though her lawyer said he would have returned the deed to the grantor if she had requested it. Compare *Vasquez* with In re Padezanin, 937 A.2d 475 (Pa. Super. Ct. 2007), in which the court found no delivery had occurred when decedent gave deeds to a third party telling him, "these deeds [are] for my girls, take them someplace safe."

Suppose the deed to Jay Rosengrant had had a clause in it providing that it could be revoked by the grantors and that the deed had been handed over to

Jay by the grantors. Would the deed be valid? Deeds with an express revocation clause are valid in some jurisdictions (see St. Louis County Natl. Bank v. Fielder, 260 S.W.2d 483 (Mo. 1953)), but invalid in others. Butler v. Sherwood, 188 N.Y.S. 242 (App. Div. 1921), aff'd 135 N.E. 957 (N.Y. 1922), is the leading case holding deeds with an express revocation clause invalid.

2. *Revocable trusts.* Harold and Mildred Rosengrant wanted to avoid probate. They thought they could accomplish their plan without a will; they failed. What should they have done?

They should have established a revocable trust of their farm. A revocable deed of land may be invalid, but a revocable trust is valid in all states. Here's how it works: Harold and Mildred sign a declaration of trust providing that they hold their farm in trust, retaining the right to possession and to all rents and profits of the farm for their joint lives and the life of the survivor, and on their deaths the title to the farm is to pass to Jay. They also retain the right to revoke the trust and reclaim legal title for themselves. They need not deliver the trust instrument to Jay, but should keep it in a secure place. Harold and Mildred do not have to record the trust instrument in the county recorder's office, but recordation is convincing evidence that they intend the trust instrument to be effective. Once Harold and Mildred have signed the trust instrument with the intent of creating a trust, the legal title to the farm is held by Harold and Mildred as trustees. The equitable or beneficial interests are: life estate in Harold and Mildred for the life of the survivor, remainder in Jay upon their deaths. Since they have retained a power of revocation, at any time during their lives they can change their minds and revoke the trust. The trust instrument may also provide that the survivor can revoke the trust.

The revocable trust avoids probate because Jay need not go to probate court to get legal title changed to him at the deaths of Harold and Mildred. Probate is necessary only when the beneficiary is not entitled to property under some valid inter vivos instrument and must get legal title changed to the beneficiary at the owner's death. Jay's document of title is the trust instrument, which he can record after the deaths of Harold and Mildred if they have not recorded it during their lives.

Why is a revocable trust valid whereas, in some jurisdictions, a revocable deed is not? At law, courts focus on whether the deed has been delivered and whether the grantor has lost dominion and control. In equity, to create a valid trust (revocable or irrevocable), the grantor need only manifest an intent to create a trust and, if land is involved, sign a written instrument to satisfy the Statute of Frauds. Delivery of a declaration of trust is not required if the grantor is the trustee.

A revocable trust functions very much like a will, but avoids probate. Revocable trusts are popular with people who want to pass property at death without the cost, delay, and publicity of probate. For discussions of transfer-on-death deeds and the use of revocable trusts, see Susan N. Gary, Transfer-on-Death Deeds: The Nonprobate Revolution Continues, 41 Real Prop., Prob. & Tr. J. 529 (2006); David Major, Comment, Revocable Transfer on Death Deeds: Cheap, Simple and Has California's Trusts & Estates Attorneys Heading for the Hills, 49 Santa

Clara L. Rev. 285 (2009). In 2009, the Uniform Law Commissioners approved the Uniform Real Property Transfer on Death Act. See Dennis M. Horn & Susan N. Gary, Death Without Probate: TOD Deeds — The Latest Tool in the Toolbox, 24 Prob. & Prop. 13 (2010). At least six states have enacted the provision. See Shelby D. Green, Keeping Current: Property, 26 Prob. & Prop. 45 (2012).

3. Refer back to Question 1 on page 637, which asks what advice you would have given Maurice Sweeney. Connecticut is one of the few states where Maurice Sweeney can put his property in a revocable trust and remove it from his wife's forced share, which applies only to the decedent's probate estate. Cherniack v. Home Natl. Bank, 198 A.2d 58 (Conn. 1964). See Alan Newman, Revocable Trusts and the Law of Wills: An Imperfect Fit, 43 Real Prop., Tr. & Est. L.J. 523 (2008) (describing efforts to change rule in Oregon and Ohio).

4. Take a look at footnote 15 in the *Rosengrant* case. A grantor can hand a deed to a third party with oral instructions to deliver the deed to the grantee upon the grantor's death. Why are oral instructions to a third party given effect but not oral instructions to the grantee, as in Sweeney v. Sweeney?

E.   *Financing Real Estate Transactions*

1.   Introduction to Mortgages and the Mortgage Market

Most people cannot pay all cash when buying real estate. Those who can pay all cash may choose for tax reasons (see page 539) not to and instead substitute debt for equity. Ordinarily the buyer will make a down payment of a small fraction of the purchase price and borrow the rest of the money needed. Let us assume that Bob and Betty Byar, looking for a house, find "just what they want" at a price of $200,000. They cannot pay that amount in cash and must borrow a large portion of it. Where can they borrow the money and under what terms? Herein we treat moneylending and mortgages.

Over the past three decades, the market for home loan mortgage financing has been dramatically transformed. Until the mid-1980s, a couple such as the Byars would go to a local savings and loan association and borrow money to purchase their home. The association would make the loan from money in customer savings accounts, would secure the loan with a mortgage, and would hold the promissory note and the mortgage until the loan was fully repaid or otherwise terminated. Thus, the flow of mortgage money was geographically constrained, with some areas—particularly rapidly growing areas—facing shortages of funds and relatively high interest rates.

The walls that segmented mortgage markets by state or locality began to crack a bit when Congress established the Federal National Mortgage Association (Fannie Mae) in 1938 and the Federal Home Loan Mortgage Corporation (Freddie Mac) in 1970. These government-sponsored enterprises were created to establish a secondary market in which mortgages could be bought and sold much like stocks, thereby evening out credit flows across the nation. In the 1980s,

Fannie Mae and Freddie Mac were instrumental in creating mortgage-backed securities (MBS). Hundreds of mortgage loans were purchased and pooled together; securities representing the pool were issued to investors, who received payments of principal and interest as they were made by homeowners. The securities, typically guaranteed by Fannie Mae and Freddie Mac, appealed to many investors who would otherwise have found home mortgage loans unattractive investments, thereby increasing the supply of capital and reducing interest rates. For loans that did not meet the credit requirements or size limitations of Fannie Mae and Freddie Mac, similar MBS markets were created by private investors and investment banks. They were often called "private label" MBS. For a description of the transformation of the secondary mortgage market, see Michael H. Schill, Uniformity or Diversity: Residential Real Estate Finance Law in the 1990s and the Implications of Changing Financial Markets, 64 S. Cal. L. Rev. 1261 (1991). We shall return to Fannie Mae and Freddie Mac later, in connection with our discussion of the recent mortgage crisis.

The growth of an efficient secondary mortgage market was accompanied by a change in the types of mortgage loans offered to borrowers. For years, the only type in the United States was a fully amortizing fixed interest rate mortgage. With this type of loan, borrowers make a constant payment each month that includes both a component for interest and one for principal. The amount of each payment stays the same for the life of the loan—typically 15 to 30 years—but as the principal is gradually paid off, the part of each payment attributable to interest declines and the part attributable to principal increases (do you see why?). At the end of the loan term the debt is completely paid off.

In the early 1980s, when interest rates on home mortgage loans went up to 16 percent and more, financial institutions began to experiment with adjustable rate loans. Such loans, still widely used, feature an initial below-market interest rate that gradually increases according to an index based on debt issued by the Federal Reserve Bank. Typically, an adjustable rate mortgage loan can go up or down by a limited amount each year and has a lifetime cap.

Beginning in the late 1990s, there has been tremendous and sometimes convulsive change in the home loan mortgage market. Increasing automation, the growth of the secondary mortgage market, the increasing detachment between origination and investment in mortgage debt, a desire to extend homeownership to underserved groups, and increasing competition in the industry led to a profusion of mortgage instruments. Only three decades ago, home mortgage lending was a "one size fits all" industry where would-be borrowers either qualified for a loan or did not, and if they did were given a standard fixed rate or adjustable rate loan at a set interest rate. But by 2005, risk-based lending was in full swing and seemingly no matter how risky one's profile, a mortgage loan of some sort could be obtained . . . at a price.

This increasingly risky segment of the mortgage market is often categorized as the subprime market or the Alt-A market. The prime market provides loans to people with high credit scores, fairly typical loan-to-value ratios of 80 or 90 percent, and characteristics that meet standard underwriting criteria. The subprime and Alt-A markets, on the other hand, made loans available to people with low credit scores and sometimes unverifiable income. Loan instruments often combined low "teaser" rates for two years with much higher rates for the remainder of the term. Oftentimes, borrowers were allowed to borrow 100 percent or more of the value of the properties they were purchasing. In some instances, they paid less than the full interest accruing on the debt, which led to the growth rather than the decline of mortgage principal (sometimes referred to as "negative amortization"). As described later in this chapter, the economic slowdown and then the deep recession that the United States experienced beginning in 2007 led this house of cards to collapse and resulted in unprecedented waves of mortgage default and foreclosure, the collapse and bailout of Fannie Mae and Freddie Mac and, ultimately, the deepest recession since the Great Depression of the 1930s.

Now, back to the Byars. Upon identifying the house they want to purchase and the type of mortgage loan that is most suitable,[16] Bob and Betty apply for a loan. The lender checks their credit rating, earnings, and job security to determine if they are an acceptable credit risk. If the loan is approved, the lender will issue its commitment to provide financing on specified terms within a specified period. It will require security in the form of a mortgage on the property purchased. Generally the lender will set the terms and requirements of the mortgage with strict inflexibility; the buyer is asked to sign a "standard form" used in the jurisdiction.

Although real estate credit markets have been generally integrated into the national capital market, and mortgages, after being originated by local lenders, are sold on the secondary mortgage market to capital investors more or less as just another form of investment, mortgage law has proved highly resistant to uniformity. The following typical transaction is common to each of the states, but significant variations in the law and practices exist in every state.

To borrow the money from the lender, the borrower must give the lender a *note* and a *mortgage*. Let us assume that the lender will lend Bob and Betty Byar $150,000 toward the purchase of the house costing $200,000.

The Byars will execute a promissory note that creates personal liability. However, in case of default the lender will want to be able to reach, with priority over other creditors of the borrowers, some specific property. To secure the note the lender will require Bob and Betty Byar to execute a mortgage on the property they are buying. The Byars are the *mortgagors*, the lender is the *mortgagee*. If the Byars fail to pay their note or do not otherwise perform their obligations, the lender, either at private sale or under judicial supervision, depending on the jurisdiction, can have the property sold ("foreclose the mortgage") and apply the proceeds of sale to the amount due on the note.

The mortgagor's interest in the property is known as the "equity," a shortened form of "equity of redemption," which also pays linguistic homage to the

---

16. In recent years, prospective home purchasers are increasingly obtaining prequalification from lenders to facilitate swift consummation of sales contracts.

generations of chancellors who have been moved to protect debtors from over-reaching moneylenders. The early classic form of the mortgage, which came into common use in the fourteenth century, was a deed in fee simple given to the moneylender by the borrower, with a condition subsequent clause providing that if the borrower paid back the sum owed on the day due, the deed would become void.[17] If the borrower did not pay the sum due on the very day set, the money-lender owned the land in fee simple absolute; the defeasance clause could no longer become operative. As the land was almost always worth more than the debt, the lender received a windfall. The chancellor, believing that prompt payment was not of sufficient importance to justify the debtor losing the property when the lender could be compensated by an award of money, moved to protect the debtor. At first the chancellor permitted the borrower, by paying the sum due, to redeem the property after the time set only when a great injustice would occur. But by the seventeenth century the right of the mortgagor to redeem after the day set had become a matter of course and right. The right of redemption was given to all mortgagors and continued until it was cut off by the chancellor.

The possibility of redemption after the time set meant that the lender could not rest safe in his possession after default by the debtor. The lender had title to the land, but the mortgagor could redeem at any time. To remedy this, the chancellor permitted the mortgagor's right of redemption to be foreclosed. This was accomplished at first by a *strict foreclosure*, a proceeding in which the mortgagor was ordered to pay within a given period or be forever barred. Later, a different approach came to be used, whereby the right of redemption was barred by a judicial proceeding determining the amount of the debt and ordering a *foreclosure sale*. The foreclosure decree directed an officer of the court to sell the land at a public sale, conveying title to the property to the purchaser and, from the proceeds of sale, paying the debt to the lender and paying any amount exceeding the debt to the borrower. If the land did not bring enough to satisfy the debt, the mortgagee could recover a judgment for the deficiency against the mortgagor (subject to antideficiency legislation, which we will discuss later). The foreclosure sale became standard practice in most American states; in some jurisdictions there are variations on it.

So far we have recounted how the *courts* stepped in to protect borrowers from overreaching lenders. They ended up requiring a lawsuit ordering foreclosure sale of the property, cutting off the borrower's *equity of redemption*. Even this was not deemed enough protection of debtors by legislators, who in about half the states passed statutes giving the mortgagor a *statutory* right to buy back

---

17. Under this form of mortgage the mortgagee takes legal title to the land; the mortgagor has only the equity of redemption. This approach is still retained in about a dozen states and is called the "title theory" of mortgages. Most states subscribe to the "lien theory," which disregards the form and holds that the mortgagor keeps legal title and the mortgagee has only a lien on the property. Although this distinction used to count for a lot, the differences in practical application between "title theory" and "lien theory" states have almost entirely disappeared because title theory states have come to see that title passes to the mortgagee only for purposes of securing the debt and have interpreted the mortgage accordingly. See Ann M. Burkhart, Freeing Mortgages of Merger, 40 Vand. L. Rev. 283, 322-329 (1987); Restatement (Third) of Property, Mortgages §4.1 (1997). But cf. severance of a joint tenancy by one tenant giving a mortgage (pages 354-358).

the title from the purchaser at a judicial foreclosure sale for the sales price (plus costs) within a specified period *after* the foreclosure sale (ranging from three months to two years). These statutes were usually enacted in periods of depression or collapse of land values. Carefully distinguish the *judicially* created right to redeem *from the mortgagee* (the equity of redemption), on the one hand, and the *statutory* right to redeem from the *purchaser* at foreclosure sale, on the other hand. The statutory right does not come into play until the borrower's equity is extinguished at foreclosure sale. See Grant S. Nelson & Dale A. Whitman, Real Estate Finance Law §§8.4-8.8 (5th ed. 2007); see also Matthew J. Baker et al., An Economic Theory of Mortgage Redemption Laws, 36 Real Est. Econ. 31 (2008).

Quite naturally, lawyers for lenders cast about for a way to avoid judicial foreclosure (which requires a costly and time-consuming lawsuit) and, where enacted, the statutory right of redemption from foreclosure sale. They sought a way for the lender to sell the land and be paid soon after default. They found this in the form of a *deed of trust*, which is recognized in a majority of jurisdictions. See Nelson & Whitman, supra, §§1.6, 7.19. Under a deed of trust, the borrower conveys title to the land to a person (who is usually a third person but may be the lender) to hold in trust to secure payment of the debt to the lender. In a deed of trust, the trustee is given the power to sell the land without going to court if the borrower defaults. (A mortgage that is not a deed of trust may also have a power of sale incorporated into it.) Although, virtually all states that recognize power of sale foreclosures specify procedural safeguards including notice and public sale, this method of foreclosure is quicker and less costly than judicial foreclosure. Except for the power to foreclose without resort to judicial sale, the deed of trust is treated in almost all significant respects as a mortgage.

As with the sale of real property, the financing of real property transactions is not subject to uniform law. Just as Article 2 of the UCC does not apply to real estate sales contracts, Article 9, which governs the financing of personal property, does not apply to real property (aside from fixtures). But the growth of the secondary mortgage market and the integration of real estate credit markets with general capital markets has led to pressure for uniform national law (can you see why?). Given the refusal by the overwhelming number of states to adopt proposals such as the Uniform Land Transactions Act, the federal government has increasingly preempted state and local regulations and supplanted them with federal law. See, e.g., Depository Institutions Deregulation and Monetary Control Act, 12 U.S.C. §1735f-7 (preempting state usury laws); Garn-St. Germain Depository Institutions Act of 1982, 12 U.S.C. §1701j-3 (preempting state interferences with enforcement of due-on-sale clauses). For arguments for and against a uniform national mortgage law, compare Grant S. Nelson & Dale A. Whitman, Reforming Foreclosure: The Uniform Nonjudicial Foreclosure Act, 53 Duke L.J. 1399 (2004), with Michael H. Schill, Uniformity or Diversity: Residential Real Estate Finance Law in the 1990s and Its Implications of Changing Financial Markets, 64 S. Cal. L. Rev. 1261 (1991).

The collapse of the mortgage market that occurred after 2007, the bailouts of Fannie Mae and Freddie Mac, and the difficulties courts faced with an avalanche of foreclosures (see pages 659-686) have reignited the debate over whether mortgage law should become "federalized." How has the case become stronger? See Grant S. Nelson, Confronting the Mortgage Meltdown: A Brief for the Federalization of State Mortgage Foreclosure Law, 37 Pepp. L. Rev. 583 (2010); Helen Mason, No One Saw It Coming—Again Systemic Risk and State Foreclosure Proceedings: Why a National Uniform Foreclosure Law Is Necessary, 67 U. Miami L. Rev. 41 (2012).

To conclude this introduction, let us return to our hypothetical couple, Bob and Betty Byar. The Byars purchase the house they want for $200,000. They make a down payment of $20,000 patched together from several sources, including savings and family help. They borrow $150,000 from a bank and give the bank a note secured by a mortgage on the house, and give the seller a note secured by a second mortgage for $30,000. The second mortgagee is subject to the prior rights of the first mortgagee; if the sum brought upon foreclosure sale is insufficient to pay off both the first and second mortgages, the first mortgage is paid off first. Because of this increased risk, a second mortgage usually carries a higher interest rate than a first mortgage. Perhaps at some future time the Byars will take out a home equity loan and give a financing institution a third mortgage.

PROBLEMS AND NOTES

1. The Byars purchase the house and finance the purchase as stated above. Subsequently, the Byars default on payments of the note secured by the first mortgage and the bank forecloses. At the foreclosure sale, the house brings $100,000. How should this be distributed? What if the sale price at foreclosure was $160,000?

Suppose the Byars had defaulted on payments of the note secured by the second mortgage, but had kept paying the note given to the bank. What would be the rights of the second mortgagee?

2. *Deficiency judgments.* If the house brings $100,000 on foreclosure sale, and the mortgage debt is $140,000, can the mortgagee obtain a deficiency judgment for $40,000 against the borrower? The answer may turn on whether $100,000, the proceeds of sale, is a fair price for the property and hence the appropriate amount to credit against the debt. If foreclosure is through a judicial proceeding, the sale price is ordinarily not challengeable (unless it shocks the conscience of the court), and the amount realized is applied to the debt. The mortgagee is entitled to a deficiency judgment for the difference, collectible out of the general assets of the borrower. When the foreclosure is by private sale, however, courts may scrutinize the sale more closely to assure that the mortgagee acted fairly, and may deny a deficiency judgment when there are sufficient grounds to set the sale aside. Thus if the mortgagee is interested in obtaining a deficiency judgment against the borrower, judicial foreclosure is the prudent route. See Grant S. Nelson & Dale A. Whitman, Real Estate Finance Law §8.1 (5th ed. 2007).

3. *Antideficiency statutes.* Many states have enacted legislation designed to protect some borrowers from deficiency judgments.

> Some states prohibit deficiency judgments if the mortgagor has used the proceeds of the loan to purchase a residence. Other states prohibit deficiency judgments only when a particular type of foreclosure process is utilized, most commonly power of sale foreclosure. A number of states permit mortgagees to sue mortgagors for deficiency judgments, but regulate how the judgment can be obtained and the amount of the judgment. Some states require that mortgagees seek deficiency judgments at the same time they foreclose a mortgage; others limit the amount of the deficiency judgment to the difference between the principal balance and the property's fair market value at the time of foreclosure, rather than the difference between the principal balance and the high bid at the foreclosure sale. [Michael H. Schill, An Economic Analysis of Mortgagor Protection Laws, 77 Va. L. Rev. 489, 494-495 (1991).]

Dean Schill reconceptualizes the mortgagor protection laws (including the statutory right to redeem and antideficiency legislation) as a form of insurance against the adverse effects of default and foreclosure. He suggests that a compulsory insurance program would be more efficient in ameliorating the adverse effects of foreclosure than the existing mortgagor protection laws.

2. Mortgage Foreclosure

Murphy v. Fin. Dev. Corp.

Supreme Court of New Hampshire, 1985
495 A.2d 1245

DOUGLAS, J. The plaintiffs brought this action seeking to set aside the foreclosure sale of their home, or, in the alternative, money damages. The Superior Court (Bean, J.), adopting the recommendation of a Master (R. Peter Shapiro, Esq.), entered a judgment for the plaintiffs in the amount of $27,000 against two of the defendants, Financial Development Corporation and Colonial Deposit Company (the lenders).

The plaintiffs purchased a house in Nashua in 1966, financing it by means of a mortgage loan. They refinanced the loan in March of 1980, executing a new promissory note and a power of sale mortgage, with Financial Development Corporation as mortgagee. The note and mortgage were later assigned to Colonial Deposit Company.

In February of 1981, the plaintiff Richard Murphy became unemployed. By September of 1981, the plaintiffs were seven months in arrears on their mortgage payments, and had also failed to pay substantial amounts in utility assessments and real estate taxes. After discussing unsuccessfully with the plaintiffs proposals for revising the payment schedule, rewriting the note, and arranging alternative financing, the lenders gave notice on October 6, 1981, of their intent to foreclose.

During the following weeks, the plaintiffs made a concerted effort to avoid foreclosure. They paid the seven months' mortgage arrearage, but failed to pay some $643.18 in costs and legal fees associated with the foreclosure proceedings. The lenders scheduled the foreclosure sale for November 10, 1981, at the site of the subject property. They complied with all of the statutory requirements for notice. See RSA 479:25.

At the plaintiffs' request, the lenders agreed to postpone the sale until December 15, 1981. They advised the plaintiffs that this would entail an additional cost of $100, and that the sale would proceed unless the lenders received payment of $743.18, as well as all mortgage payments then due, by December 15. Notice of the postponement was posted on the subject property on November 10 at the originally scheduled time of the sale, and was also posted at the Nashua City Hall and Post Office. No prospective bidders were present for the scheduled sale.

In late November, the plaintiffs paid the mortgage payment which had been due in October, but made no further payments to the lenders. An attempt by the lenders to arrange new financing for the plaintiffs through a third party failed when the plaintiffs refused to agree to pay for a new appraisal of the property. Early on the morning of December 15, 1981, the plaintiffs tried to obtain a further postponement, but were advised by the lenders' attorney that it was impossible unless the costs and legal fees were paid.

At the plaintiffs' request, the attorney called the president of Financial Development Corporation, who also refused to postpone the sale. Further calls by the plaintiffs to the lenders' office were equally unavailing.

The sale proceeded as scheduled at 10:00 A.M. on December 15, at the site of the property. Although it had snowed the previous night, the weather was clear and warm at the time of the sale, and the roads were clear. The only parties present were the plaintiffs, a representative of the lenders, and an attorney, Morgan Hollis, who had been engaged to conduct the sale because the lenders' attorney, who lived in Dover, had been apprehensive about the weather the night before. The lenders' representative made the only bid at the sale. That bid of $27,000, roughly the amount owed on the mortgage, plus costs and fees, was accepted and the sale concluded.

Later that same day, Attorney Hollis encountered one of his clients, William Dube, a representative of the defendant Southern New Hampshire Home Traders, Inc. (Southern). On being informed of the sale, Mr. Dube contacted the lenders and offered to buy the property for $27,000. The lenders rejected the offer and made a counter offer of $40,000. Within two days a purchase price of $38,000 was agreed upon by Mr. Dube and the lenders and the sale was subsequently completed.

The plaintiffs commenced this action on February 5, 1982. The lenders moved to dismiss, arguing that any action was barred because the plaintiffs had failed to petition for an injunction prior to the sale. The master denied the motion. After hearing the evidence, he ruled for the plaintiffs, finding that the lenders had "failed to exercise good faith and due diligence in obtaining a fair price for the subject property at the foreclosure sale...."

The master also ruled that Southern was a bona fide purchaser for value, and thus had acquired legal title to the house. That ruling is not at issue here. He assessed monetary damages against the lenders equal to "the difference between the fair market value of the subject property on the date of the foreclosure and the price obtained at said sale."

Having found the fair market value to be $54,000, he assessed damages accordingly at $27,000. He further ruled that "[t]he bad faith of the 'Lenders' warrants an award of legal fees." The lenders appealed. . . .

The . . . issue before us is whether the master erred in concluding that the lenders had failed to comply with the often-repeated rule that a mortgagee executing a power of sale is bound both by the statutory procedural requirements *and* by a duty to protect the interests of the mortgagor through the exercise of good faith and due diligence. . . .

The master found that the lenders, throughout the time prior to the sale, "did not mislead or deal unfairly with the plaintiffs." They engaged in serious efforts to avoid foreclosure through new financing, and agreed to one postponement of the sale. The basis for the master's decision was his conclusion that the lenders had failed to exercise good faith and due diligence in obtaining a fair price for the property.

This court's past decisions have not dealt consistently with the question whether the mortgagee's duty amounts to that of a fiduciary or trustee. Compare Pearson v. Gooch, 69 N.H. 208, 209, 40 A. 390, 390-91 (1897) and Merrimack Industrial Trust v. First National Bank of Boston, 121 N.H. 197, 201, 427 A.2d 500, 504 (1981) (duty amounts to that of a fiduciary or trustee), with Silver v. First National Bank, 108 N.H. 390, 391, 236 A.2d 493, 494-95 (1967) and Proctor v. Bank of N.H., 123 N.H. 395, 400, 464 A.2d 263, 266 (1983) (duty does not amount to that of a fiduciary or trustee). This may be an inevitable result of the mortgagee's dual role as seller and potential buyer at the foreclosure sale, and of the conflicting interests involved. See Wheeler v. Slocinski, 82 N.H. 211, 214, 131 A. 598, 600 (1926).

We need not label a duty, however, in order to define it. In his role as a seller, the mortgagee's duty of good faith and due diligence is essentially that of a fiduciary. Such a view is in keeping with "[t]he 'trend . . . towards liberalizing the term [fiduciary] in order to prevent unjust enrichment.'" Lash v. Cheshire County Savings Bank, Inc., 124 N.H. 435, 438, 474 A.2d 980, 981 (1984) (quoting Cornwell v. Cornwell, 116 N.H. 205, 209, 356 A.2d 683, 686 (1976)).

A mortgagee, therefore, must exert every reasonable effort to obtain "a fair and reasonable price under the circumstances," Reconstruction Finance Corp. v. Faulkner, 101 N.H. 352, 361, 143 A.2d 403, 410 (1958), even to the extent, if necessary, of adjourning the sale or of establishing "an upset price below which he will not accept any offer." Lakes Region Fin. Corp. v. Goodhue Boat Yard, Inc., 118 N.H. 103, 107, 382 A.2d 1108, 1111 (1978).

What constitutes a fair price, or whether the mortgagee must establish an upset price, adjourn the sale, or make other reasonable efforts to assure a fair price, depends on the circumstances of each case. Inadequacy of price alone is not sufficient to demonstrate bad faith unless the price is so low as to shock the judicial conscience. Mueller v. Simmons, 634 S.W.2d 533, 536 (Mo. App. 1982);

Rife v. Woolfolk, 289 S.E.2d 220, 223 (W. Va. 1982); Travelers Indem. Co. v. Heim, 218 Neb. 326, 352 N.W.2d 921, 923-24 (1984).

We must decide, in the present case, whether the evidence supports the finding of the master that the lenders failed to exercise good faith and due diligence in obtaining a fair price for the plaintiffs' property.

We first note that "[t]he duties of good faith and due diligence are distinct. . . . One may be observed and not the other, and any inquiry as to their breach calls for a separate consideration of each." Wheeler v. Slocinski, 82 N.H. at 213, 131 A. at 600. In order "to constitute bad faith there must be an intentional disregard of duty or a purpose to injure." Id. at 214, 131 A. at 600-01.

There is insufficient evidence in the record to support the master's finding that the lenders acted in bad faith in failing to obtain a fair price for the plaintiffs' property. The lenders complied with the statutory requirements of notice and otherwise conducted the sale in compliance with statutory provisions. The lenders postponed the sale one time and did not bid with knowledge of any immediately available subsequent purchaser. Further, there is no evidence indicating an intent on the part of the lenders to injure the mortgagor by, for example, discouraging other buyers.

There is ample evidence in the record, however, to support the master's finding that the lenders failed to exercise due diligence in obtaining a fair price. "The issue of the lack of due diligence is whether a reasonable man in the [lenders'] place would have adjourned the sale," id. at 215, 131 A. at 601, or taken other measures to receive a fair price.

In early 1980, the plaintiffs' home was appraised at $46,000. At the time of the foreclosure sale on December 15, 1981, the lenders had not had the house reappraised to take into account improvements and appreciation. The master found that a reasonable person in the place of the lenders would have realized that the plaintiffs' equity in the property was at least $19,000, the difference between the 1980 appraised value of $46,000 and the amount owed on the mortgage totaling approximately $27,000.

At the foreclosure sale, the lenders were the only bidders. The master found that their bid of $27,000 "was sufficient to cover all monies due and did not create a deficiency balance" but "did not provide for a return of any of the plaintiffs' equity."

Further, the master found that the lenders "had reason to know" that "they stood to make a substantial profit on a quick turnaround sale." On the day of the sale, the lenders offered to sell the foreclosed property to William Dube for $40,000. Within two days after the foreclosure sale, they did in fact agree to sell it to Dube for $38,000. It was not necessary for the master to find that the lenders knew of a specific potential buyer before the sale in order to show lack of good faith or due diligence as the lenders contend. The fact that the lenders offered the property for sale at a price sizably above that for which they had purchased it, only a few hours before, supports the master's finding that the lenders had reason to know, at the time of the foreclosure sale, that they could make a substantial profit on a quick turnaround sale. For this reason, they should have taken more measures to ensure receiving a higher price at the sale.

While a mortgagee may not always be required to secure a portion of the mortgagor's equity, such an obligation did exist in this case. The substantial amount of equity which the plaintiffs had in their property, the knowledge of the lenders as to the appraised value of the property, and the plaintiffs' efforts to forestall foreclosure by paying the mortgage arrearage within weeks of the sale, all support the master's conclusion that the lenders had a fiduciary duty to take more reasonable steps than they did to protect the plaintiffs' equity by attempting to obtain a fair price for the property. They could have established an appropriate upset price to assure a minimum bid. They also could have postponed the auction and advertised commercially by display advertising in order to assure that bidders other than themselves would be present.

Instead, as Theodore DiStefano, an officer of both lending institutions testified, the lenders made no attempt to obtain fair market value for the property but were concerned *only* with making themselves "whole." On the facts of this case, such disregard for the interests of the mortgagors was a breach of duty by the mortgagees.

Although the lenders *did* comply with the statutory requirements of notice of the foreclosure sale, these efforts were not sufficient in this case to demonstrate due diligence. At the time of the initially scheduled sale, the extent of the lenders' efforts to publicize the sale of the property was publication of a legal notice of the mortgagees' sale at public auction on November 10, published once a week for three weeks in the Nashua Telegraph, plus postings in public places. The lenders did not advertise, publish, or otherwise give notice to the general public of postponement of the sale to December 15, 1981, other than by posting notices at the plaintiffs' house, at the post office, and at city hall. That these efforts to advertise were ineffective is evidenced by the fact that no one, other than the lenders, appeared at the sale to bid on the property. This fact allowed the lenders to purchase the property at a minimal price and then to profit substantially in a quick turnaround sale.

We recognize a need to give guidance to a trial court which must determine whether a mortgagee who has complied with the strict letter of the statutory law has nevertheless violated his additional duties of good faith and due diligence. A finding that the mortgagee had, or should have had, knowledge of his ability to get a higher price at an adjourned sale is the most conclusive evidence of such a violation.

More generally, we are in agreement with the official Commissioners' Comment to section 3-508 of the Uniform Land Transactions Act:

> The requirement that the sale be conducted in a reasonable manner, including the advertising aspects, requires that the person conducting the sale use the ordinary methods of making buyers aware that are used when an owner is voluntarily selling his land. Thus an advertisement in the portion of a daily newspaper where these ads are placed or, in appropriate cases such as the sale of an industrial plant, a display advertisement in the financial sections of the daily newspaper may be the most reasonable method. In other cases employment of a professional real estate agent may be the more reasonable method. It is unlikely that an advertisement in a legal publication among other legal notices would qualify as a commercially reasonable method of sale advertising. [13 Uniform Laws Annotated 704 (West 1980).]

As discussed above, the lenders met neither of these guidelines.

While agreeing with the master that the lenders failed to exercise due diligence in this case, we find that he erred as a matter of law in awarding damages equal to "the difference between the fair market value of the subject property . . . and the price obtained at [the] sale."

Such a formula may well be the appropriate measure where *bad faith* is found. See Danvers Savings Bank v. Hammer, 122 N.H. 1, 5, 440 A.2d 435, 438 (1982). In such a case, a mortgagee's conduct amounts to more than mere negligence. Damages based upon the *fair market value*, a figure in excess of a *fair* price, will more readily induce mortgagees to perform their duties properly. A "fair" price may or may not yield a figure close to fair market value; however, it will be that price arrived at as a result of due diligence by the mortgagee.

Where, as here, however, a mortgagee fails to exercise due diligence, the proper assessment of damages is the difference between a fair price for the property and the price obtained at the foreclosure sale. We have held, where lack of due diligence has been found, that "the test is not 'fair market value' as in eminent domain cases nor is the mortgagee bound to give credit for the highest possible amount which might be obtained under different circumstances, as at an owner's sale." Silver v. First National Bank, 108 N.H. 390, 392, 236 A.2d 493, 495 (1967) (quoting Reconstruction Finance Corp. v. Faulkner, 101 N.H. 352, 361, 143 A.2d 403, 410 (1958)) (citation omitted). Accordingly, we remand to the trial court for a reassessment of damages consistent with this opinion.

Because we concluded above that there was no "bad faith or obstinate, unjust, vexatious, wanton, or oppressive conduct," on the part of the lenders, we see no reason to stray from our general rule that the prevailing litigant is not entitled to collect attorney's fees from the loser. Harkeem v. Adams, 117 N.H. 687, 688, 377 A.2d 617, 617 (1977). Therefore, we reverse this part of the master's decision.

Reversed in part; affirmed in part; remanded.

Grant S. Nelson & Dale A. Whitman, Real Estate Finance Law §7.21 at 640-641

(5th ed. 2007)

All jurisdictions adhere to the recognized rule that mere inadequacy of the foreclosure sale price will not invalidate a sale, absent fraud, unfairness or other irregularity. Courts generally articulate two main standards for invalidating a foreclosure sale based on price. First, many courts state that inadequacy of the sale price is an insufficient ground unless it is so gross as to shock the conscience of the court, warranting an inference of fraud or imposition. Second, another significant group of courts require that, in the absence of some other defect in the foreclosure process, the price must be "grossly inadequate" before a sale may be invalidated. . . .

Under either the "shock the conscience" or "grossly inadequate" standards, unless other foreclosure defects exist, it is extremely difficult to get a sale set aside on mere price inadequacy. While some courts have found that sales for one-seventh and one-sixtieth of fair market value "shock the conscience," one commentator has noted with respect to his jurisdiction that "such sales have been upheld where the price paid for the property was only one-half, one-third, one-fourth, one-fifth, or even one-twentieth of its reasonable value." On the other hand, where other factors are present, such as chilled bidding, unusual hour of sale or any other indicia of unfairness, courts do set sales aside. For example, in a case where the mortgaged real estate sold for 3% of the fair market value, the court set aside the sale because of the additional factor that the mortgagee had informed the mortgagor of the incorrect sale date.

NOTES AND QUESTIONS

1. In the *Murphy* case, how can the mortgagee determine an appropriate upset price? Specifically, what should the lenders have done to receive a higher bid? See Pamela Giss, Comment, An Efficient and Equitable Approach to Real Estate Foreclosure Sales: A Look at the New Hampshire Rule, 40 St. Louis U. L.J. 929 (1996).

2. The *Murphy* case is unusual in that courts typically uphold foreclosure sales despite low prices in the absence of procedural irregularity that is prejudicial or that chilled bidding. See, e.g., Lo v. Jensen, 106 Cal. Rptr. 2d 443 (Cal. App. 2001); Lona v. Citibank, N.A., 134 Cal. Rptr. 3d 622 (Cal. App. 2011). The recent spate of procedural irregularities among mortgage servicers (see pages 680-681) may have sensitized courts with respect to the importance of procedural integrity in mortgage foreclosure proceedings. There have been a number of cases setting aside judgments based upon mistakes. See, e.g., Millennium Rock Mortgage, Inc. v. T.D. Service Co., 102 Cal. Rptr. 3d 544 (Cal. App. 2009) (disparity between legal description and address); CitiMortgage, Inc. v. Synuria, 86 So. 3d 1237 (Fla. App. 2012) (bank did not have agent at foreclosure sale). Also, in Lost Mountain Dev. Co. v. King, 2006 WL 3740791 (Tenn. App. Dec. 19, 2006), the court scrutinized a sale particularly stringently because of the deficiency judgment. What constitutes chilled bidding? For one view, see Justin Lischak Earley, Chilling the Bidding, 5 J. Marshall L.J. 99 (2011).

3. If the foreclosure sale is defective, what are the borrower's remedies? Can the title of the purchaser at the sale be set aside? See Grant S. Nelson & Dale A. Whitman, Real Estate Finance Law §7.22 (5th ed. 2007). The avalanche of mortgage foreclosures that began in 2007 has spawned renewed interest in the subject of mortgage foreclosure and its reform. See, e.g., Aaron Byrkit, Reforming Foreclosure Disposition: A Tool for Tempering the Financial Meltdown, 63 Consumer Fin. L. Q. Rep. 275 (2009).

4. Why is the mortgagee frequently the only bidder at a foreclosure sale? See Nelson & Whitman, supra, at §8.8. What reform of the foreclosure sale system would bring a higher sale price?

5. Since the mid-1960s, federal housing policy has increasingly tried to increase the rate of homeownership among low and moderate income households in general and among racial and ethnic minorities in particular. See page 534. Among the laws enacted by Congress to promote greater access to credit are the Fair Housing Act of 1968, 42 U.S.C. §§3601-3619 (outlawing discrimination in housing based on race, sex, national origin, religion, color, disability, or familial status; see pages 453-454); Home Mortgage Disclosure Act of 1975, 12 U.S.C. §§2801-2810 (requiring regulated mortgage lenders to disclose information about applicants for home mortgage loans); Community Reinvestment Act, 12 U.S.C. §§2901-2907 (mandating that federally regulated financial institutions meet the credit needs of their communities); and Federal Housing Enterprises Financial Safety and Soundness Act of 1992, 12 U.S.C. §§4561-4567 (establishing affordable housing goals for Fannie Mae and Freddie Mac).

These laws may have contributed to the growth of the subprime mortgage market over the course of the last two decades. Indeed, some borrowers were targeted by unscrupulous lenders and offered loans with extremely high interest rates and fees (points). In addition, some groups, particularly the elderly, were repeatedly induced to refinance their loans, causing them to reduce the equity in their homes (sometimes called equity stripping) and to pay pyramiding fees. These predatory practices—often targeted at elderly and minority persons—caused many borrowers to lose their homes to foreclosure even before the housing market collapsed. See U.S. Dept. of Housing and Urban Development & U.S. Dept. of Treasury, Curbing Predatory Home Mortgage Lending: A Joint Report (2000).

Because a large proportion of home mortgage loans are sold into the secondary mortgage market, most equitable defenses are unavailable to homeowners as a result of the holder-in-due-course doctrine. See Baher Azmy & David Reiss, Modeling a Response to Predatory Lending: The New Jersey Home Ownership Security Act of 2002, 35 Rutgers L.J. 645, 668 (2004); Kurt Eggert, Held Up in Due Course: Predatory Lending, Securitization, and the Holder-in-Due-Course Doctrine, 35 Creighton L. Rev. 503 (2002); Alex M. Johnson, Jr., Preventing a Return Engagement: Eliminating the Mortgage Purchasers' Status as a Holder-in-Due Course: Properly Aligning Incentives Among the Parties, 37 Pepp. L. Rev. 529 (2010); Kurt Eggert, Not Dead Yet: The Surprising Survival of Negotiability, 66 Ark. L. Rev. 145 (2013). Congress passed the Home Ownership and Equity Protection Act of 1994, 15 U.S.C. §1639, to regulate certain "high cost" home mortgage loans. Under HOEPA, certain protections are triggered when a home loan has particularly high interest rates or fees. In response to perceived weaknesses in HOEPA, several states have enacted laws to regulate predatory lending practices and, in some instances, establish liability for purchasers of loans through the secondary mortgage market. See, e.g., Ga. Code Ann. §§7-6A-1 to 7-6A-13 (LexisNexis 2012); N.C. Gen. Stat. §§24-1.1E to 24-10.2 (LexisNexis 2012). In response, the U.S. Comptroller of the Currency has sought to preempt some of these state laws as inconsistent with HOEPA. For a description of the controversy and its implications, see Nicholas Bagley, Note, The Unwarranted Regulatory Preemption of Predatory Lending Laws, 79 N.Y.U. L. Rev. 2274 (2004); Kathleen C. Engel &

Patricia A. McCoy, Federal Preemption and Consumer Financial Protection: Past and Future, 31 No. 3 Banking & Fin. Services Poly. Rep. 25 (2012).

In 2010, Congress revisited the problem of mortgage lending risk in the Dodd-Frank Wall Street Reform and Consumer Protection Act, Pub. L. No. 111-203, 124 Stat. 1376 et seq. (codified as amended in scattered sections of the U.S.C.). For a description of the provisions of the act regulating lending, see page 683.

6. *Deeds in lieu of foreclosure.* Mortgage foreclosure can be an extremely costly proposition for borrowers and lenders alike. In instances where a borrower cannot repay its debt, it can frequently avoid foreclosure by tendering its deed to the lender in lieu of foreclosure. In most instances, the lender will agree to give up any claim for a deficiency judgment. When a mortgagor cannot pay its debt and the property's value is above the amount of the loan, he or she can always sell the property and pay off the loan. Similarly, when the debt is greater than the loan, he or she can offer a deed in lieu of foreclosure. Why would the parties ever go to the expense and trouble of foreclosure?

7. *Transfer by the mortgagor.* Notwithstanding any agreement to the contrary, the mortgagor can transfer his interest in the land by sale, mortgage, or otherwise. The transfer will not, however, shake off the mortgage. The land remains subject to the mortgage in the hands of the transferee.

The purchaser of the equity may buy the mortgagor's equity either "subject to the mortgage" or "assuming the mortgage." If the purchaser takes subject to the mortgage, the purchaser does not assume any personal liability for the mortgage debt, for which the mortgagor remains liable. But the purchaser agrees, as between himself and the mortgagor, that the debt is to be satisfied out of the land; if the debt is not paid, the land will be sold and the debt paid from the proceeds. If the purchaser assumes the mortgage, the purchaser promises to pay off the mortgage debt. This promise does not relieve the mortgagor of the duty to pay the mortgagee, unless the lender consents to this change in the contract, but it gives the mortgagor the right to pay the debt and sue the assuming purchaser for reimbursement. The mortgagee can enforce the promise made by the purchaser of the equity in assuming the mortgage.

Although the mortgagor can transfer his interest, the mortgage contract may contain an acceleration clause that enables the mortgagee, upon transfer of the mortgagor's equity, to declare the whole amount of the mortgage debt due and, upon failure to pay, to foreclose. By enforcing the acceleration clause, thus requiring the new purchaser of the equity to refinance, the lender may use a due-on-sale clause to increase the loan interest rate to current rates upon transfer of the property.

3.   The Mortgage Crisis and the Great Recession

The changes in the mortgage market described earlier (see pages 645-647) were a contributing factor to the housing "bubble" that affected the United States in the first decade of the twenty-first century. According to the widely cited 20-city Case-Shiller repeat sales housing price index, from 2001 to 2006 house prices skyrocketed by 70 percent in real terms. Over the next five years, they fell back to earth, declining by over 40 percent. See Edward L. Glaeser & Todd Sinai, Postmortem for a Housing Crash, in Housing and the Financial Crisis 1 (Edward L. Glaeser & Todd Sinai eds. 2013). A complete understanding of the housing bubble may never be achieved, but the combination of historically low interest rates, "irrational exuberance," and diminishing credit quality seem to be the primary culprits. Old underwriting principles such as minimum down payments, income verifications, and careful appraisal policies were abandoned as borrowers frequently purchased homes they could not afford, either for their own use or as speculative investments. As the economy slowed and interest rates increased, borrowers increasingly had trouble making payments, and defaults rose. The wave of foreclosures that occurred further depressed prices, leaving many homeowners with homes worth less than their mortgage loan balances. These owners were unable to sell their homes and, with no equity left, many stopped paying their mortgages to avoid "throwing good money after bad." This magnified the foreclosure problem and, in turn, intensified the decline in prices. Before prices started stabilizing in 2012, more than 5 million homeowners had lost their homes to foreclosure and an additional 11 million (one out of every four households with a mortgage) were underwater.

Why did lenders make loans to borrowers who could not afford them and why did borrowers ultimately want these loans? Clearly, the low interest rate environment maintained by the Federal Reserve Bank provided many investors with an incentive to seek out vehicles that would provide higher rates of return for their money. Mortgage-backed securities (MBS) became one of these investments and were pursued by everyone from individual investors and hedge funds to pension funds and government-sponsored enterprises such as Fannie Mae and Freddie Mac. Loan originators came under great pressure to increase their volumes of loans to feed the MBS pipeline, leading to deterioration in quality and more and more subprime and Alt-A (no documentation)[18] loans. The number of subprime mortgages originated almost doubled from 1.1 million in 2003 to 1.9 million in 2005. Almost one-third of all mortgage debt that originated in 2005 was in the form of either subprime or Alt-A loans, three times their share of the market only two years earlier. Over three-quarters of subprime loans had short-term teaser rates that reset to much higher rates after two or three years. Median credit scores for these borrowers were almost 100 points lower than for Alt-A borrowers, who themselves had lower scores than those in the prime market. Over one-third of subprime loans and two-thirds of

---

18. An Alt-A loan is a loan made to a borrower who is close to being eligible for a prime loan but does not quite qualify. For a description of the differences in attributes between subprime borrowers and Alt-A borrowers, see Christopher Mayer et al., The Rise in Mortgage Defaults, 23 J. Econ. Perspectives 27 (2009).

Alt-A loans did not require that borrowers document their income. See Mayer et al., supra, at 27 (2009).

One source of debate is the extent to which federal policy itself created incentives for financial institutions to take on too much risk. As described earlier, a variety of federal policies and statutes promote homeownership among American households, ranging from the favorable treatment of homeownership under the tax code (see pages 538-539) to laws specifically incentivizing banks to lend to low and moderate income home buyers such as the Community Reinvestment Act and the statutorily mandated affordable housing goals governing Fannie Mae and Freddie Mac (see page 658). A number of commentators have suggested that these latter regulations led banks to make imprudent loans to buyers who should never have become home buyers. See, e.g., Peter J. Wallison, Dissent from the Majority Report of the Financial Crisis Inquiry Commission 2-3 (2011). Other studies have refuted these claims by arguing that while Fannie Mae and Freddie Mac certainly purchased their share of poorly underwritten loans, private, unregulated investors did the same as they pooled loans into "private label" MBS. See U.S. Dept. of Housing and Urban Development, Report to Congress on the Root Causes of the Foreclosure Crisis 41-43 (2010).

If the incentives of investors in mortgage credit are somewhat complicated, are the incentives of the borrowers any clearer? Why did so many individuals borrow money and purchase homes that they could not afford? There is no doubt that some buyers sought to leverage low cost debt to make potentially lucrative investments. Some committed fraud by submitting inflated property appraisals and/or inaccurate personal financial disclosures to loan underwriters. Some expected to flip their homes within one or two years before the below-market "teaser" rates adjusted to much higher market rates. Others who wanted to live in their homes for longer periods either assumed that the meteoric rise in housing prices would go on forever or that when the game of musical chairs ended they would safely be able to refinance their loans into more sustainable fixed interest rate loans. And some, of course, were uninformed and became victims. Certainly, the idea that homeownership is an essential part of the American Dream is a powerful American ideology creating a predisposition among many to want to become homeowners. When the individual desire of an unsophisticated person to become a homeowner interacts with strong market pressures by mortgage bankers and financial institutions to originate loans, the results can be combustible.

Commonwealth v. Fremont Investment & Loan

Supreme Judicial Court of Massachusetts, 2008
897 N.E.2d 548

BOTSFORD, J. The Commonwealth, acting through the Attorney General, commenced this consumer protection enforcement action against the defendant Fremont Investment & Loan and its parent company, Fremont General

Corporation (collectively, Fremont), claiming that Fremont, in originating and servicing certain "subprime"[19] mortgage loans between 2004 and 2007 in Massachusetts, acted unfairly and deceptively in violation of G.L. c. 93A, §2. Fremont appeals from a preliminary injunction granted by a judge in the Superior Court in favor of the Attorney General that restricts, but does not remove, Fremont's ability to foreclose on loans with features that the judge described as "presumptively unfair." All of the loans at issue are secured by mortgages on the borrowers' homes.

Based on the record before him, the judge concluded that the Attorney General had established a likelihood of success on the merits of her claim that in originating home mortgage loans with four characteristics that made it almost certain the borrower would not be able to make the necessary loan payments, leading to default and then foreclosure, Fremont had committed an unfair act or practice within the meaning of G.L. c. 93A, §2. We granted the Commonwealth's application for direct appellate review. We affirm the motion judge's grant of the preliminary injunction, as modified.

1. *Background.* Fremont is an industrial bank chartered by the State of California. Between January, 2004, and March, 2007, Fremont originated 14,578 loans to Massachusetts residents secured by mortgages on owner-occupied homes. Of the loans originated during that time period, roughly 3,000 remain active and roughly 2,500 continue to be owned or serviced by Fremont. An estimated fifty to sixty per cent of Fremont's loans in Massachusetts were subprime.[20] Because subprime borrowers present a greater risk to the lender, the interest rate charged for a subprime loan is typically higher than the rate charged for conventional or prime mortgages.[21] After funding the loan, Fremont generally sold it on the secondary market, which largely insulated Fremont from losses arising from borrower default. Fremont General Corporation, Annual Report (Form 10-K) 1, 6 (Mar. 6, 2006).

In originating loans, Fremont did not interact directly with the borrowers; rather, mortgage brokers acting as independent contractors would help a borrower select a mortgage product, and communicate with a Fremont account executive to request a selected product and provide the borrower's loan application and credit report. If approved by Fremont's underwriting department, the loan would proceed to closing and the broker would receive a broker's fee.

---

19. "Subprime" loans are loans made to borrowers who generally would not qualify for traditional loans offered at the generally prevailing rate of interest for conventional mortgages.

20. The judge made this estimate based on the fact that sixty-four per cent of all Fremont's loans were adjustable rate mortgage loans (ARM loans), and 38.4 per cent were "stated income" loans, in which the borrower provided no documentation of his or her income. The judge inferred, based on the limited record available at the preliminary injunction stage, that all of the stated income loans were subprime ARM loans, and a majority of the remaining ARM loans were also subprime.

21. It is not clear that the higher interest rates on Fremont's loans were always appropriate. Federal agencies have warned that the subprime lending market creates incentives to inflate interest rates unnecessarily. Board of Governors of the Federal Reserve System, Federal Deposit Insurance Corporation, Office of the Comptroller of the Currency, Office of Thrift Supervision, Interagency Guidance on Subprime Lending at 5 (Mar. 1, 1999). In 51.4 per cent of Fremont's loans generally, and seventy-three per cent of a sample of delinquent Fremont loans analyzed by the Attorney General, Fremont paid a "yield spread premium" to the broker as compensation for placing the borrower into a higher interest rate bracket than the one for which he or she would otherwise qualify.

Fremont's subprime loan products offered a number of different features to cater to borrowers with low income. A large majority of Fremont's subprime loans were adjustable rate mortgage (ARM) loans, which bore a fixed interest rate for the first two or three years, and then adjusted every six months to a considerably higher variable rate for the remaining period of what was generally a thirty year loan. Thus, borrowers' monthly mortgage payments would start out lower and then increase substantially after the introductory two-year or three-year period. To determine loan qualification, Fremont generally required that borrowers have a debt-to-income ratio of less than or equal to fifty per cent—that is, that the borrowers' monthly debt obligations, including the applied-for mortgage, not exceed one-half their income. However, in calculating the debt-to-income ratio, Fremont considered only the monthly payment required for the introductory rate period of the mortgage loan, not the payment that would ultimately be required at the substantially higher "fully indexed" interest rate.[22] As an additional feature to attract subprime borrowers, who typically had little or no savings, Fremont offered loans with no down payment. Instead of a down payment, Fremont would finance the full value of the property, resulting in a "loan-to-value ratio" approaching one hundred per cent. Most such financing was accomplished through the provision of a first mortgage providing eighty per cent financing and an additional "piggy-back loan" providing twenty per cent.[23]

As of the time the Attorney General initiated this case in 2007, a significant number of Fremont's loans were in default.[24] An analysis by the Attorney General of ninety-eight of those loans indicated that all were ARM loans with a substantial increase in payments required after the first two (or in a few cases, three) years, and that ninety per cent of the ninety-eight had a one hundred per cent loan-to-value ratio.

The judge granted a preliminary injunction in a memorandum of decision dated February 25, 2008. In his decision, the judge found no evidence in the preliminary injunction record that Fremont encouraged or condoned misrepresentation of borrowers' incomes on stated income loans, or that Fremont deceived borrowers by concealing or misrepresenting the terms of its loans. However, the judge determined that the Attorney General was likely to prevail on the claim that Fremont's loans featuring a combination of the following four characteristics qualified as "unfair" under G.L. c. 93A, §2: (1) the loans were ARM loans with an introductory rate period of three years or less; (2) they featured an introductory

22. The "fully indexed" rate refers to the interest rate that represents the LIBOR rate at the time of the loan's inception plus the rate add specified in the loan documents. The judge noted that calculation of the debt-to-income ratio based on the fully indexed rate generally yields a ratio that exceeds fifty per cent.

23. Two other features bear mention, although they are not directly relevant to the preliminary injunction. As previously indicated (see footnote 20, supra), 38.4 per cent of all Fremont's loans were stated income loans without income documentation required. In addition, 12.2 per cent of Fremont's loans offered the borrower lower monthly payments based on a forty-year amortization schedule, with a balloon payment required at the end of thirty years; the usual amortization schedule was based on a thirty-year period.

24. As of January 15, 2008, Fremont had allegedly indicated to the Attorney General that it intended to foreclose on approximately twenty per cent of its loans. We take notice that the industry-wide delinquency rate has increased in the intervening months.

rate for the initial period that was at least three per cent below the fully indexed rate; (3) they were made to borrowers for whom the debt-to-income ratio would have exceeded fifty per cent had Fremont measured the borrower's debt by the monthly payments that would be due at the fully indexed rate rather than under the introductory rate; and (4) the loan-to-value ratio was one hundred per cent, or the loan featured a substantial prepayment penalty (defined by the judge as greater than the "conventional prepayment penalty" defined in G.L. c. 183C, §2) or a prepayment penalty that extended beyond the introductory rate period.

The judge reasoned that Fremont as a lender should have recognized that loans with the first three characteristics just described were "doomed to foreclosure" unless the borrower could refinance the loan at or near the end of the introductory rate period, and obtain in the process a new and low introductory rate.[25] The fourth factor, however, would make it essentially impossible for subprime borrowers to refinance unless housing prices increased, because if housing prices remained steady or declined, a borrower with a mortgage loan having a loan-to-value ratio of one hundred per cent or a substantial prepayment penalty was not likely to have the necessary equity or financial capacity to obtain a new loan. The judge stated that, "[g]iven the fluctuations in the housing market and the inherent uncertainties as to how that market will fluctuate over time . . . it is unfair for a lender to issue a home mortgage loan secured by the borrower's principal dwelling that the lender reasonably expects will fall into default once the introductory period ends unless the fair market value of the home has increased at the close of the introductory period. To issue a home mortgage loan whose success relies on the hope that the fair market value of the home will increase during the introductory period is as unfair as issuing a home mortgage loan whose success depends on the hope that the borrower's income will increase during that same period."

The judge concluded that the balance of harms favored granting the preliminary injunction, and that the public interest would be served by doing so. The injunction he granted requires Fremont to do the following: (1) to give advance notice to the Attorney General of its intent to foreclose on any of its home mortgage loans; and (2) as to loans that possess each of the four characteristics of unfair loans just described and that are secured by the borrower's principal dwelling (referred to in the injunction as "presumptively unfair" loans), to work with the Attorney General to "resolve" their differences regarding foreclosure—presumably through a restructure or workout of the loan. If the loan cannot be worked out, Fremont is required to obtain approval for foreclosure from the court. The judge made clear that the injunction in no way relieved borrowers of their obligation ultimately to prove that a particular loan was unfair and foreclosure should not be permitted, or their obligation to repay the loans they had received.

---

25. The judge's prognosis of doom followed from the fact that the interest payments required when the introductory rate period ended and the fully indexed rate came into play would be significantly greater than the payments called for under the introductory rate (so-called "payment shock"). As a result, the borrower's debt-to-income ratio would necessarily increase, probably and foreseeably beyond the borrower's breaking point.

2. *Standard of review.* We review the grant or denial of a preliminary injunction to determine whether the judge abused his discretion, that is, whether the judge applied proper legal standards and whether there was reasonable support for his evaluation of factual questions.

Fremont's basic contention is that, while the terms of its subprime loans may arguably seem "unfair" within the meaning of G.L. c. 93A, §2, if judged by current standards applicable to the mortgage lending industry, they did not violate any established concept of unfairness at the time they were originated; the judge, in Fremont's view, applied new rules or standards for defining what is "unfair" in a retroactive or ex post facto fashion — a result that is not in accord with the proper interpretation of c. 93A, §2, and also represents "bad policy," because (among other reasons) lenders cannot know what rules govern their conduct, which will reduce their willingness to extend credit, hurting Massachusetts consumers. We do not agree that the judge applied a new standard retroactively.

Fremont highlights the judge's statement that at the time Fremont made the loans in question between 2004 and March of 2007, loans with the four characteristics the judge identified as unfair were not considered by the industry or more generally to be unfair; Fremont argues this acknowledgment by the judge is proof that the judge was creating a new definition or standard of unfairness. The argument lacks merit. First, the judge's statement that Fremont's combination of loan features were not recognized to be unfair does not mean the converse: that the loans were recognized to be fair. More to the point, at the core of the judge's decision is a determination that when Fremont chose to combine in a subprime loan the four characteristics the judge identified, Fremont knew or should have known that they would operate in concert essentially to guarantee that the borrower would be unable to pay and default would follow unless residential real estate values continued to rise indefinitely[26] — an assumption that, in the judge's view, logic and experience had already shown as of January, 2004, to be unreasonable. The judge concluded that the Attorney General was likely to prove that Fremont's actions, in originating loans with terms that in combination would lead predictably to the consequence of the borrowers' default and foreclosure, were within established concepts of unfairness at the time the loans were made, and thus in violation of G.L. c. 93A, §2. The record supports this conclusion.

Fremont correctly points out that as a bank in the business of mortgage lending, it is subject to State and Federal regulation by a variety of agencies. Well before 2004, State and Federal regulatory guidance explicitly warned lending institutions making subprime loans that, even if they were in compliance with banking-specific laws and regulations and were "underwrit[ing] loans on a safe and sound basis, [their] policies could still be considered unfair and deceptive practices" under G.L. c. 93A. Consumer Affairs and Business Regulation Massachusetts Division of Banks, Subprime Lending (Dec. 10, 1997). More particularly, the principle

---

26. It would be necessary for housing values to continue to rise so that the borrower could refinance his or her loan at the end of the introductory rate period, before the (likely) unaffordable indexed rate came into play.

had been clearly stated before 2004 that loans made to borrowers on terms that showed they would be unable to pay and therefore were likely to lead to default, were unsafe and unsound, and probably unfair. Thus, an interagency Federal guidance published January 31, 2001, jointly by the Office of the Comptroller of the Currency (OCC), the Board of Governors of the Federal Reserve System, the FDIC, and the Office of Thrift Supervision, stated: "Loans to borrowers who do not demonstrate the capacity to repay the loan, *as structured*, from sources other than the collateral pledged are generally considered unsafe and unsound" (emphasis supplied). Expanded Guidance for Subprime Lending Programs at 11 (Jan. 31, 2001). On February 21, 2003, one year before the first of Fremont's loans at issue, the OCC warned that certain loans could be unfair to consumers:

> When a loan has been made based on the foreclosure value of the collateral, rather than on a determination that the borrower has the capacity to make the scheduled payments under the terms of the loan, based on the borrower's current and expected income, current obligations, employment status, and other relevant financial resources, the lender is effectively counting on its ability to seize the borrower's equity in the collateral to satisfy the obligation and to recover the typically high fees associated with such credit. Not surprisingly, such credits experience foreclosure rates higher than the norm.
>
> [S]uch disregard of basic principles of loan underwriting lies at the heart of predatory lending. . . .
>
> [OCC Advisory Letter, Guidelines for National Banks to Guard Against Predatory and Abusive Lending Practices, AL 2003-2 at 2 (Feb. 21, 2003).]

The record here suggests that Fremont made no effort to determine whether borrowers could "make the scheduled payments under the terms of the loan." Rather, as the judge determined, loans were made in the understanding that they would have to be refinanced before the end of the introductory period. Fremont suggested in oral argument that the loans were underwritten in the expectation, reasonable at the time, that housing prices would improve during the introductory loan term, and thus could be refinanced before the higher payments began. However, it was unreasonable, and unfair to the borrower, for Fremont to structure its loans on such unsupportable optimism. As a bank and mortgage lender, Fremont had been warned repeatedly before 2004 (in the context of guidance on loan safety and soundness) that it needed to consider the performance of its loans in declining markets. See, e.g., Consumer Affairs and Business Regulation, Massachusetts Division of Banks, Subprime Lending (Dec. 10, 1997) ("[M]ost subprime loans have been originated during robust economic conditions and have not been tested by a downturn in the economy. Management must ensure that the institution has adequate financial and operational strength to address these concerns effectively"). Fremont cannot now claim that it was taken by surprise by the effects of an economic decline, or that it should not be held responsible.

Finally, the conclusion that Fremont's loans featuring the four characteristics at issue violated established concepts of unfairness is supported by the consent agreement that Fremont entered into with the FDIC on March 7, 2007, the date Fremont stopped making loans. The consent agreement contains no admission of wrongdoing by Fremont, and we do not consider it as evidence of liability on Fremont's part. However, we view it as evidence of existing policy and guidance provided to the mortgage lending industry. The fact that the FDIC ordered Fremont to cease and desist from the use of almost precisely the loan features that are included in the judge's list of presumptively unfair characteristics indicates that the FDIC considered that under established mortgage lending standards, the marketing of loans with these features constituted unsafe and unsound banking practice with clearly harmful consequences for borrowers. Such unsafe and unsound conduct on the part of a lender, insofar as it leads directly to injury for consumers, qualifies as "unfair" under G.L. c. 93A, §2. . . .

Because the Attorney General, in the name of the Commonwealth, brings this case to carry out her statutory mandate to enforce the Consumer Protection Act, it is necessary to consider whether the preliminary injunction order promotes the public interest. Commonwealth v. Mass. CRINC, 392 Mass. 79, 88-89, 466 N.E.2d 792 (1984). Fremont argues that it does not, primarily because in Fremont's view, the order imposes new standards on lending practices that were considered permissible and acceptable when the loans were made. The result, Fremont claims, will be an unwillingness on the part of lenders to extend credit to Massachusetts consumers because they will be unwilling to risk doing business in an environment where standards are uncertain and the rules may change after the fact.

Our previous discussion, and rejection, of Fremont's claim that the judge retroactively applied new unfairness standards disposes of Fremont's public interest argument; we do not accept the premise that, in concluding that Fremont is likely to be found to have violated established concepts of unfairness, the judge's order has created an environment of uncertainty that lenders will shun. The injunction order crafted by the judge strikes a balance between the interests of borrowers who face foreclosure and loss of their homes under home loan mortgage terms that are at least presumptively unfair, on the one hand; and the interest of the lender in recovering the value of its loans to borrowers who received the benefit of those loaned funds and continue to have a contractual obligation to repay, on the other. The order does not bar foreclosure as a remedy for the lender, nor does it relieve borrowers of their obligations ultimately to repay the loans. Rather, it requires, where the mortgage loan terms include all four features deemed presumptively unfair, that Fremont explore alternatives to foreclosure in the first instance (a step that Fremont has indicated its desire to take in any event), and then seek approval of the court. If the court does not approve the foreclosure, that decision merely leaves the preliminary injunction in place until the Commonwealth has an opportunity to try to prove that the particular loan at issue actually violated c. 93A—a burden that is never shifted to Fremont. We conclude the order serves the public interest.

NOTES AND QUESTIONS

1. Notice that in *Fremont* the loan applicants did not interact directly with bank employees. Instead, they applied through independent mortgage brokers

who received fees upon the closing of the loans. Once the loan was originated, Fremont would typically sell it in the secondary mortgage market, and eventually it would be bundled into a mortgage-backed security. The process for getting a home was quite different 25 years ago, when applicants approached a savings and loan association directly, the institution made the underwriting decision, and then held any loans made to maturity. How might the change in the structure of the mortgage market over the past quarter century have contributed to the subprime crisis?

2. Why would home purchasers seek loans that, according to the opinion in *Fremont*, were "doomed to foreclosure"? For an interesting perspective on the question, using insights from law and economics and cognitive psychology, see Oren Bar-Gill, The Law, Economics and Psychology of Subprime Mortgage Contracts, 94 Cornell L. Rev. 1073 (2009).

3. A number of factors contributed to the subprime mortgage crisis, including some of the terms that were unique to subprime mortgages — teaser rates that were later to be reset, prepayment penalties that made it difficult to refinance upon reset, and zero or negative amortization. According to one account, these terms may have exacerbated the problem, but the main culprit was the practice of lending to risky borrowers who made very small down payments. See Mayer et al., supra, at 27. A significant literature in economics demonstrates that loans with higher loan-to-value ratios are more likely to default. Can you see why? See Min Qi & Xiaolong Yang, Loss Given Default of High Loan-to-Value Residential Mortgages, 33 J. Banking & Fin. 788 (2009), and sources cited therein.

4. Fremont Investment & Loan filed for Chapter 11 bankruptcy in June 2008. See Tiffany Kary, Fremont Files Bankruptcy After CapitalSource Sale (Bloomberg 2008). As of December 9th, 2013, 515 financial institutions had made it onto the Federal Deposit Insurance Corporation (FDIC) Failed Banks List. See http://www.fdic.gov/bank/individual/failed/banklist.html. Many others, including big names like Citibank, had seen their capital reserves diminish quickly and had applied for and received federal bailout money under the Troubled Asset Relief Program. Fannie Mae and Freddie Mac have been taken over by the federal government, their private investors' equity eliminated. Some major investment banks and insurance companies, such as Bear Stearns, Lehman Brothers, and AIG, have essentially become insolvent and either have shut their doors or gone into what amounts to federal receivership. While the causes of each institutional collapse are varied, subprime mortgages have played a direct or indirect role in many of them. Indeed, the bursting of the real estate bubble and the collapse of the subprime market contributed greatly to the credit crunch that launched the United States into its worst recession since the Great Depression. See Richard A. Posner, A Failure of Capitalism: The Crisis of '08 and the Descent into Depression (2009); Steven L. Schwarcz, Protecting Financial Markets: Lessons from the Subprime Mortgage Meltdown, 93 Minn. L. Rev. 373 (2008).

U.S. Bank Natl. Assn. v. Ibanez

Supreme Judicial Court of Massachusetts, 2010
941 N.E.2d 40

GANTS, J. After foreclosing on two properties and purchasing the properties back at the foreclosure sales, U.S. Bank National Association (U.S. Bank), as trustee for the Structured Asset Securities Corporation Mortgage Pass-Through Certificates, Series 2006-Z; and Wells Fargo Bank, N.A. (Wells Fargo), as trustee for ABFC 2005-OPT 1 Trust, ABFC Asset Backed Certificates, Series 2005-OPT 1 (plaintiffs), filed separate complaints in the Land Court asking a judge to declare that they held clear title to the properties in fee simple. We agree with the judge that the plaintiffs, who were not the original mortgagees, failed to make the required showing that they were the holders of the mortgages at the time of foreclosure. As a result, they did not demonstrate that the foreclosure sales were valid to convey title to the subject properties, and their requests for a declaration of clear title were properly denied.

Procedural history. On July 5, 2007, U.S. Bank, as trustee, foreclosed on the mortgage of Antonio Ibanez, and purchased the Ibanez property at the foreclosure sale. On the same day, Wells Fargo, as trustee, foreclosed on the mortgage of Mark and Tammy LaRace, and purchased the LaRace property at that foreclosure sale.

In September and October of 2008, U.S. Bank and Wells Fargo brought separate actions in the Land Court under G.L. c. 240, §6, which authorizes actions "to quiet or establish the title to land situated in the commonwealth or to remove a cloud from the title thereto." The two complaints sought identical relief: (1) a judgment that the right, title, and interest of the mortgagor (Ibanez or the LaRaces) in the property was extinguished by the foreclosure; (2) a declaration that there was no cloud on title arising from publication of the notice of sale in the Boston Globe; and (3) a declaration that title was vested in the plaintiff trustee in fee simple. U.S. Bank and Wells Fargo each asserted in its complaint that it had become the holder of the respective mortgage through an assignment made *after* the foreclosure sale.

In both cases, the mortgagors—Ibanez and the LaRaces—did not initially answer the complaints, and the plaintiffs moved for entry of default judgment. In their motions for entry of default judgment, the plaintiffs addressed two issues: (1) whether the Boston Globe, in which the required notices of the foreclosure sales were published, is a newspaper of "general circulation" in Springfield, the town where the foreclosed properties lay. See G.L. c. 244, §14 (requiring publication every week for three weeks in newspaper published in town where foreclosed property lies, or of general circulation in that town); and (2) whether the plaintiffs were legally entitled to foreclose on the properties where the assignments of the mortgages to the plaintiffs were neither executed nor recorded in the registry of deeds until after the foreclosure sales. The two cases were heard together by the Land Court, along with a third case that raised the same issues.

On March 26, 2009, judgment was entered against the plaintiffs. The judge ruled that the foreclosure sales were invalid because, in violation of G.L. c. 244, §14, the notices of the foreclosure sales named U.S. Bank (in the Ibanez foreclosure) and Wells Fargo (in the LaRace foreclosure) as the mortgage holders where they had not yet been assigned the mortgages. The judge found, based on each plaintiff's assertions in its complaint, that the plaintiffs acquired the mortgages by assignment only after the foreclosure sales and thus had no interest in the mortgages being foreclosed at the time of the publication of the notices of sale or at the time of the foreclosure sales.

The plaintiffs then moved to vacate the judgments. At a hearing on the motions on April 17, 2009, the plaintiffs conceded that each complaint alleged a postnotice, postforeclosure sale assignment of the mortgage at issue, but they now represented to the judge that documents might exist that could show a prenotice, preforeclosure sale assignment of the mortgages. The judge granted the plaintiffs leave to produce such documents, provided they were produced in the form they existed in at the time the foreclosure sale was noticed and conducted. In response, the plaintiffs submitted hundreds of pages of documents to the judge, which they claimed established that the mortgages had been assigned to them before the foreclosures. Many of these documents related to the creation of the securitized mortgage pools in which the Ibanez and LaRace mortgages were purportedly included.

The judge denied the plaintiffs' motions to vacate judgment on October 14, 2009, concluding that the newly submitted documents did not alter the conclusion that the plaintiffs were not the holders of the respective mortgages at the time of foreclosure. We granted the parties' applications for direct appellate review.

Factual background. We discuss each mortgage separately, describing when appropriate what the plaintiffs allege to have happened and what the documents in the record demonstrate.

The Ibanez mortgage. On December 1, 2005, Antonio Ibanez took out a $103,500 loan for the purchase of property at 20 Crosby Street in Springfield, secured by a mortgage to the lender, Rose Mortgage, Inc. (Rose Mortgage). The mortgage was recorded the following day. Several days later, Rose Mortgage executed an assignment of this mortgage in blank, that is, an assignment that did not specify the name of the assignee. The blank space in the assignment was at some point stamped with the name of Option One Mortgage Corporation (Option One) as the assignee, and that assignment was recorded on June 7, 2006. Before the recording, on January 23, 2006, Option One executed an assignment of the Ibanez mortgage in blank.

According to U.S. Bank, Option One assigned the Ibanez mortgage to Lehman Brothers Bank, FSB, which assigned it to Lehman Brothers Holdings Inc., which then assigned it to the Structured Asset Securities Corporation, which then assigned the mortgage, pooled with approximately 1,220 other mortgage loans, to U.S. Bank, as trustee for the Structured Asset Securities Corporation Mortgage Pass-Through Certificates, Series 2006-Z. With this last assignment, the

Ibanez and other loans were pooled into a trust and converted into mortgage-backed securities that can be bought and sold by investors—a process known as securitization.

For ease of reference, the chain of entities through which the Ibanez mortgage allegedly passed before the foreclosure sale is:

Rose Mortgage, Inc. (originator)
|
Option One Mortgage Corporation (record holder)
|
Lehman Brothers Bank, FSB
|
Lehman Brothers Holdings Inc. (seller)
|
Structured Asset Securities Corporation (depositor)
|
U.S. Bank National Association, as trustee for the Structured Asset Securities Corporation Mortgage Pass-Through Certificates, Series 2006-Z

According to U.S. Bank, the assignment of the Ibanez mortgage to U.S. Bank occurred pursuant to a December 1, 2006, trust agreement, which is not in the record. What is in the record is the private placement memorandum (PPM), dated December 26, 2006, a 273-page, unsigned offer of mortgage-backed securities to potential investors. The PPM describes the mortgage pools and the entities involved, and summarizes the provisions of the trust agreement, including the representation that mortgages "will be" assigned into the trust. According to the PPM, "[e]ach transfer of a Mortgage Loan from the Seller [Lehman Brothers Holdings Inc.] to the Depositor [Structured Asset Securities Corporation] and from the Depositor to the Trustee [U.S. Bank] will be intended to be a sale of that Mortgage Loan and will be reflected as such in the Sale and Assignment Agreement and the Trust Agreement, respectively." The PPM also specifies that "[e]ach Mortgage Loan will be identified in a schedule appearing as an exhibit to the Trust Agreement." However, U.S. Bank did not provide the judge with any mortgage schedule identifying the Ibanez loan as among the mortgages that were assigned in the trust agreement.

On April 17, 2007, U.S. Bank filed a complaint to foreclose on the Ibanez mortgage in the Land Court under the Servicemembers Civil Relief Act (Servicemembers Act), which restricts foreclosures against active duty members of the uniformed services. See 50 U.S.C. Appendix §§501, 511, 533 (2006 & Supp. II 2008). In the complaint, U.S. Bank represented that it was the "owner (or assignee) and holder" of the mortgage given by Ibanez for the property. A judgment issued on behalf of U.S. Bank on June 26, 2007, declaring that the mortgagor was not entitled to protection from foreclosure under the Servicemembers Act. In June, 2007, U.S. Bank also caused to be published in the Boston Globe the notice of the foreclosure sale required by G.L. c. 244, §14. The notice identified U.S. Bank as the "present holder" of the mortgage.

At the foreclosure sale on July 5, 2007, the Ibanez property was purchased by U.S. Bank, as trustee for the securitization trust, for $94,350, a value significantly less than the outstanding debt and the estimated market value of the property. The foreclosure deed (from U.S. Bank, trustee, as the purported holder of the mortgage, to U.S. Bank, trustee, as the purchaser) and the statutory foreclosure affidavit were recorded on May 23, 2008. On September 2, 2008, more than one year after the sale, and more than five months after recording of the sale, American Home Mortgage Servicing, Inc., "as successor-in-interest" to Option One, which was until then the record holder of the Ibanez mortgage, executed a written assignment of that mortgage to U.S. Bank, as trustee for the securitization trust. This assignment was recorded on September 11, 2008.

The LaRace mortgage. On May 19, 2005, Mark and Tammy LaRace gave a mortgage for the property at 6 Brookburn Street in Springfield to Option One as security for a $103,200 loan; the mortgage was recorded that same day. On May 26, 2005, Option One executed an assignment of this mortgage in blank.

According to Wells Fargo, Option One later assigned the LaRace mortgage to Bank of America in a July 28, 2005, flow sale and servicing agreement. Bank of America then assigned it to Asset Backed Funding Corporation (ABFC) in an October 1, 2005, mortgage loan purchase agreement. Finally, ABFC pooled the mortgage with others and assigned it to Wells Fargo, as trustee for the ABFC 2005-OPT 1 Trust, ABFC Asset-Backed Certificates, Series 2005-OPT 1, pursuant to a pooling and servicing agreement (PSA).

For ease of reference, the chain of entities through which the LaRace mortgage allegedly passed before the foreclosure sale is:

Option One Mortgage Corporation (originator and record holder)
|
Bank of America
|
Asset Backed Funding Corporation (depositor)
|
Wells Fargo, as trustee for the ABFC 2005-OPT 1, ABFC Asset-Backed Certificates, Series 2005-OPT 1

Wells Fargo did not provide the judge with a copy of the flow sale and servicing agreement, so there is no document in the record reflecting an assignment of the LaRace mortgage by Option One to Bank of America. The plaintiff did produce an unexecuted copy of the mortgage loan purchase agreement, which was an exhibit to the PSA. The mortgage loan purchase agreement provides that Bank of America, as seller, "does hereby agree to and does hereby sell, assign, set over, and otherwise convey to the Purchaser [ABFC], without recourse, on the Closing Date . . . all of its right, title and interest in and to each Mortgage Loan." The agreement makes reference to a schedule listing the assigned mortgage loans, but this schedule is not in the record, so there was no document before the judge showing that the LaRace mortgage was among the mortgage loans assigned to the ABFC.

Wells Fargo did provide the judge with a copy of the PSA, which is an agreement between the ABFC (as depositor), Option One (as servicer), and Wells Fargo (as trustee), but this copy was downloaded from the Securities and Exchange Commission Web site and was not signed. The PSA provides that the depositor "does hereby transfer, assign, set over and otherwise convey to the Trustee, on behalf of the Trust . . . all the right, title and interest of the Depositor . . . in and to . . . each Mortgage Loan identified on the Mortgage Loan Schedules," and "does hereby deliver" to the trustee the original mortgage note, an original mortgage assignment "in form and substance acceptable for recording," and other documents pertaining to each mortgage.

The copy of the PSA provided to the judge did not contain the loan schedules referenced in the agreement. Instead, Wells Fargo submitted a schedule that it represented identified the loans assigned in the PSA, which did not include property addresses, names of mortgagors, or any number that corresponds to the loan number or servicing number on the LaRace mortgage. Wells Fargo contends that a loan with the LaRace property's zip code and city is the LaRace mortgage loan because the payment history and loan amount matches the LaRace loan.

On April 27, 2007, Wells Fargo filed a complaint under the Servicemembers Act in the Land Court to foreclose on the LaRace mortgage. The complaint represented Wells Fargo as the "owner (or assignee) and holder" of the mortgage given by the LaRaces for the property. A judgment issued on behalf of Wells Fargo on July 3, 2007, indicating that the LaRaces were not beneficiaries of the Servicemembers Act and that foreclosure could proceed in accordance with the terms of the power of sale. In June, 2007, Wells Fargo caused to be published in the Boston Globe the statutory notice of sale, identifying itself as the "present holder" of the mortgage.

At the foreclosure sale on July 5, 2007, Wells Fargo, as trustee, purchased the LaRace property for $120,397.03, a value significantly below its estimated market value. Wells Fargo did not execute a statutory foreclosure affidavit or foreclosure deed until May 7, 2008. That same day, Option One, which was still the record holder of the LaRace mortgage, executed an assignment of the mortgage to Wells Fargo as trustee; the assignment was recorded on May 12, 2008. Although executed ten months after the foreclosure sale, the assignment declared an effective date of April 18, 2007, a date that preceded the publication of the notice of sale and the foreclosure sale.

Discussion. The plaintiffs brought actions under G.L. c. 240, §6, seeking declarations that the defendant mortgagors' titles had been extinguished and that the plaintiffs were the fee simple owners of the foreclosed properties. As such, the plaintiffs bore the burden of establishing their entitlement to the relief sought. Sheriff's Meadow Found., Inc. v. Bay-Courte Edgartown, Inc., 401 Mass. 267, 269, 516 N.E.2d 144 (1987). To meet this burden, they were required "not merely to demonstrate better title . . . than the defendants possess, but . . . to prove sufficient title to succeed in [the] action." Id. See NationsBanc Mtge. Corp. v.

Eisenhauer, 49 Mass. App. Ct. 727, 730, 733 N.E.2d 557 (2000). There is no question that the relief the plaintiffs sought required them to establish the validity of the foreclosure sales on which their claim to clear title rested.

Massachusetts does not require a mortgage holder to obtain judicial authorization to foreclose on a mortgaged property. See G.L. c. 183, §21; G.L. c. 244, §14. With the exception of the limited judicial procedure aimed at certifying that the mortgagor is not a beneficiary of the Servicemembers Act, a mortgage holder can foreclose on a property, as the plaintiffs did here, by exercise of the statutory power of sale, if such a power is granted by the mortgage itself. See Beaton v. Land Court, 367 Mass. 385, 390-391, 393, 326 N.E.2d 302, appeal dismissed, 423 U.S. 806 (1975).

Where a mortgage grants a mortgage holder the power of sale, as did both the Ibanez and LaRace mortgages, it includes by reference the power of sale set out in G.L. c. 183, §21, and further regulated by G.L. c. 244, §§11-17C. Under G.L. c. 183, §21, after a mortgagor defaults in the performance of the underlying note, the mortgage holder may sell the property at a public auction and convey the property to the purchaser in fee simple, "and such sale shall forever bar the mortgagor and all persons claiming under him from all right and interest in the mortgaged premises, whether at law or in equity." Even where there is a dispute as to whether the mortgagor was in default or whether the party claiming to be the mortgage holder is the true mortgage holder, the foreclosure goes forward unless the mortgagor files an action and obtains a court order enjoining the foreclosure. See Beaton v. Land Court, supra at 393, 326 N.E.2d 302.

Recognizing the substantial power that the statutory scheme affords to a mortgage holder to foreclose without immediate judicial oversight, we adhere to the familiar rule that "one who sells under a power [of sale] must follow strictly its terms. If he fails to do so there is no valid execution of the power, and the sale is wholly void." Moore v. Dick, 187 Mass. 207, 211, 72 N.E. 967 (1905). See Roche v. Farnsworth, 106 Mass. 509, 513 (1871) (power of sale contained in mortgage "must be executed in strict compliance with its terms"). See also McGreevey v. Charlestown Five Cents Sav. Bank, 294 Mass. 480, 484, 2 N.E.2d 543 (1936).[27]

One of the terms of the power of sale that must be strictly adhered to is the restriction on who is entitled to foreclose. The "statutory power of sale" can be exercised by "the mortgagee or his executors, administrators, successors or assigns." G.L. c. 183, §21. Under G.L. c. 244, §14, "[t]he mortgagee or person having his estate in the land mortgaged, or a person authorized by the power of sale, or the attorney duly authorized by a writing under seal, or the legal guardian or conservator of such mortgagee or person acting in the name of such mortgagee or person" is empowered to exercise the statutory power of sale. Any effort to

---

27. We recognize that a mortgage holder must not only act in strict compliance with its power of sale but must also "act in good faith and . . . use reasonable diligence to protect the interests of the mortgagor," and this responsibility is "more exacting" where the mortgage holder becomes the buyer at the foreclosure sale, as occurred here. See Williams v. Resolution GGF OY, 417 Mass. 377, 382-383, 630 N.E.2d 581 (1994). . . . Because the issue was not raised by the defendant mortgagors or the judge, we do not consider whether the plaintiffs committed a breach of this obligation.

foreclose by a party lacking "jurisdiction and authority" to carry out a foreclosure under these statutes is void. Chace v. Morse, 189 Mass. 559, 561, 76 N.E. 142 (1905), citing Moore v. Dick, supra. See Davenport v. HSBC Bank USA, 275 Mich. App. 344, 347-348, 739 N.W.2d 383 (2007) (attempt to foreclose by party that had not yet been assigned mortgage results in "structural defect that goes to the very heart of defendant's ability to foreclose by advertisement," and renders foreclosure sale void).

A related statutory requirement that must be strictly adhered to in a foreclosure by power of sale is the notice requirement articulated in G.L. c. 244, §14. That statute provides that "no sale under such power shall be effectual to foreclose a mortgage, unless, previous to such sale," advance notice of the foreclosure sale has been provided to the mortgagor, to other interested parties, and by publication in a newspaper published in the town where the mortgaged land lies or of general circulation in that town. Id. "The manner in which the notice of the proposed sale shall be given is one of the important terms of the power, and a strict compliance with it is essential to the valid exercise of the power." Moore v. Dick, supra at 212, 72 N.E. 967. See Chace v. Morse, supra ("where a certain notice is prescribed, a sale without any notice, or upon a notice lacking the essential requirements of the written power, would be void as a proceeding for foreclosure"). See also McGreevey v. Charlestown Five Cents Sav. Bank, supra. Because only a present holder of the mortgage is authorized to foreclose on the mortgaged property, and because the mortgagor is entitled to know who is foreclosing and selling the property, the failure to identify the holder of the mortgage in the notice of sale may render the notice defective and the foreclosure sale void. . . .

For the plaintiffs to obtain the judicial declaration of clear title that they seek, they had to prove their authority to foreclose under the power of sale and show their compliance with the requirements on which this authority rests. Here, the plaintiffs were not the original mortgagees to whom the power of sale was granted; rather, they claimed the authority to foreclose as the eventual assignees of the original mortgagees. Under the plain language of G.L. c. 183, §21, and G.L. c. 244, §14, the plaintiffs had the authority to exercise the power of sale contained in the Ibanez and LaRace mortgages only if they were the assignees of the mortgages at the time of the notice of sale and the subsequent foreclosure sale. See In re Schwartz, 366 B.R. 265, 269 (Bankr. D. Mass. 2007) ("Acquiring the mortgage after the entry and foreclosure sale does not satisfy the Massachusetts statute"). See also Jeff-Ray Corp. v. Jacobson, 566 So. 2d 885, 886 (Fla. Dist. Ct. App. 1990) (per curiam) (foreclosure action could not be based on assignment of mortgage dated four months after commencement of foreclosure proceeding).

The plaintiffs claim that the securitization documents they submitted establish valid assignments that made them the holders of the Ibanez and LaRace mortgages before the notice of sale and the foreclosure sale. We turn, then, to the documentation submitted by the plaintiffs to determine whether it met the requirements of a valid assignment.

Like a sale of land itself, the assignment of a mortgage is a conveyance of an interest in land that requires a writing signed by the grantor. See G.L. c. 183,

§3; Saint Patrick's Religious, Educ. & Charitable Ass'n v. Hale, 227 Mass. 175, 177, 116 N.E. 407 (1917). In a "title theory state" like Massachusetts, a mortgage is a transfer of legal title in a property to secure a debt. See Faneuil Investors Group, Ltd. Partnership v. Selectmen of Dennis, 458 Mass. 1, 6, 933 N.E.2d 918 (2010). Therefore, when a person borrows money to purchase a home and gives the lender a mortgage, the homeowner-mortgagor retains only equitable title in the home; the legal title is held by the mortgagee. See Vee Jay Realty Trust Co. v. DiCroce, 360 Mass. 751, 753, 277 N.E.2d 690 (1972), quoting Dolliver v. St. Joseph Fire & Marine Ins. Co., 128 Mass. 315, 316 (1880) (although "as to all the world except the mortgagee, a mortgagor is the owner of the mortgaged lands," mortgagee has legal title to property); Maglione v. BancBoston Mtge. Corp., 29 Mass. App. Ct. 88, 90, 557 N.E.2d 756 (1990). Where, as here, mortgage loans are pooled together in a trust and converted into mortgage-backed securities, the underlying promissory notes serve as financial instruments generating a potential income stream for investors, but the mortgages securing these notes are still legal title to someone's home or farm and must be treated as such.

Focusing first on the Ibanez mortgage, U.S. Bank argues that it was assigned the mortgage under the trust agreement described in the PPM, but it did not submit a copy of this trust agreement to the judge. The PPM, however, described the trust agreement as an agreement to be executed in the future, so it only furnished evidence of an intent to assign mortgages to U.S. Bank, not proof of their actual assignment. Even if there were an executed trust agreement with language of present assignment, U.S. Bank did not produce the schedule of loans and mortgages that was an exhibit to that agreement, so it failed to show that the Ibanez mortgage was among the mortgages to be assigned by that agreement. Finally, even if there were an executed trust agreement with the required schedule, U.S. Bank failed to furnish any evidence that the entity assigning the mortgage—Structured Asset Securities Corporation—ever held the mortgage to be assigned. The last assignment of the mortgage on record was from Rose Mortgage to Option One; nothing was submitted to the judge indicating that Option One ever assigned the mortgage to anyone before the foreclosure sale. Thus, based on the documents submitted to the judge, Option One, not U.S. Bank, was the mortgage holder at the time of the foreclosure, and U.S. Bank did not have the authority to foreclose the mortgage.

Turning to the LaRace mortgage, Wells Fargo claims that, before it issued the foreclosure notice, it was assigned the LaRace mortgage under the PSA. The PSA, in contrast with U.S. Bank's PPM, uses the language of a present assignment ("does hereby . . . assign" and "does hereby deliver") rather than an intent to assign in the future. But the mortgage loan schedule Wells Fargo submitted failed to identify with adequate specificity the LaRace mortgage as one of the mortgages assigned in the PSA. Moreover, Wells Fargo provided the judge with no document that reflected that the ABFC (depositor) held the LaRace mortgage that it was purportedly assigning in the PSA. As with the Ibanez loan, the record holder of the LaRace loan was Option One, and nothing was submitted to the judge which demonstrated that the LaRace loan was ever assigned by Option One to another entity before the publication of the notice and the sale.

Where a plaintiff files a complaint asking for a declaration of clear title after a mortgage foreclosure, a judge is entitled to ask for proof that the foreclosing entity was the mortgage holder at the time of the notice of sale and foreclosure, or was one of the parties authorized to foreclose under G.L. c. 183, §21, and G.L. c. 244, §14. . . .

We do not suggest that an assignment must be in recordable form at the time of the notice of sale or the subsequent foreclosure sale, although recording is likely the better practice. Where a pool of mortgages is assigned to a securitized trust, the executed agreement that assigns the pool of mortgages, with a schedule of the pooled mortgage loans that clearly and specifically identifies the mortgage at issue as among those assigned, may suffice to establish the trustee as the mortgage holder. However, there must be proof that the assignment was made by a party that itself held the mortgage. See In re Samuels, 415 B.R. 8, 20 (Bankr. D. Mass. 2009). A foreclosing entity may provide a complete chain of assignments linking it to the record holder of the mortgage, or a single assignment from the record holder of the mortgage. . . . The key in either case is that the foreclosing entity must hold the mortgage at the time of the notice and sale in order accurately to identify itself as the present holder in the notice and in order to have the authority to foreclose under the power of sale (or the foreclosing entity must be one of the parties authorized to foreclose under G.L. c. 183, §21, and G.L. c. 244, §14).

The judge did not err in concluding that the securitization documents submitted by the plaintiffs failed to demonstrate that they were the holders of the Ibanez and LaRace mortgages, respectively, at the time of the publication of the notices and the sales. The judge, therefore, did not err in rendering judgments against the plaintiffs and in denying the plaintiffs' motions to vacate the judgments.

We now turn briefly to three other arguments raised by the plaintiffs on appeal. First, the plaintiffs initially contended that the assignments in blank executed by Option One, identifying the assignor but not the assignee, not only "evidence[ ] and confirm[ ] the assignments that occurred by virtue of the securitization agreements," but "are effective assignments in their own right." But in their reply briefs they conceded that the assignments in blank did not constitute a lawful assignment of the mortgages. Their concession is appropriate. We have long held that a conveyance of real property, such as a mortgage, that does not name the assignee conveys nothing and is void; we do not regard an assignment of land in blank as giving legal title in land to the bearer of the assignment. . . . Second, the plaintiffs contend that, because they held the mortgage note, they had a sufficient financial interest in the mortgage to allow them to foreclose. In Massachusetts, where a note has been assigned but there is no written assignment of the mortgage underlying the note, the assignment of the note does not carry with it the assignment of the mortgage. Barnes v. Boardman, 149 Mass. 106, 114, 21 N.E. 308 (1889). Rather, the holder of the mortgage holds the mortgage in trust for the purchaser of the note, who has an equitable right to obtain an assignment of the mortgage, which may be accomplished by filing an action in court and obtaining an equitable order of assignment. Id. ("In some jurisdictions it is held that the mere transfer of the debt, without any assignment or even mention of the mortgage, carries the mortgage with it, so as to enable the assignee to assert his title in an action at law . . . . This doctrine has not prevailed in Massachusetts, and the tendency of the decisions here has been, that in such cases the mortgagee would hold the legal title in trust for the purchaser of the debt, and that the latter might obtain a conveyance by a bill in equity"). See Young v. Miller, 72 Mass. 152, 6 Gray 152, 154 (1856). In the absence of a valid written assignment of a mortgage or a court order of assignment, the mortgage holder remains unchanged. This common-law principle was later incorporated in the statute enacted in 1912 establishing the statutory power of sale, which grants such a power to "the mortgagee or his executors, administrators, successors or assigns," but not to a party that is the equitable beneficiary of a mortgage held by another. G.L. c. 183, §21, inserted by St.1912, c. 502, §6.

Third, the plaintiffs initially argued that postsale assignments were sufficient to establish their authority to foreclose, and now argue that these assignments are sufficient when taken in conjunction with the evidence of a presale assignment. . . . If the plaintiffs did not have their assignments to the Ibanez and LaRace mortgages at the time of the publication of the notices and the sales, they lacked authority to foreclose under G.L. c. 183, §21, and G.L. c. 244, §14, and their published claims to be the present holders of the mortgages were false. Nor may a postforeclosure assignment be treated as a preforeclosure assignment simply by declaring an "effective date" that precedes the notice of sale and foreclosure, as did Option One's assignment of the LaRace mortgage to Wells Fargo. Because an assignment of a mortgage is a transfer of legal title, it becomes effective with respect to the power of sale only on the transfer; it cannot become effective before the transfer. See In re Schwartz, supra at 269. . . .

In this case, based on the record before the judge, the plaintiffs failed to prove that they obtained valid written assignments of the Ibanez and LaRace mortgages before their foreclosures, so the postforeclosure assignments were not confirmatory of earlier valid assignments.

Finally, we reject the plaintiffs' request that our ruling be prospective in its application. A prospective ruling is only appropriate, in limited circumstances, when we make a significant change in the common law. See Papadopoulos v. Target Corp., 457 Mass. 368, 384, 930 N.E.2d 142 (2010) (noting "normal rule of retroactivity"); Payton v. Abbott Labs, 386 Mass. 540, 565, 437 N.E.2d 171 (1982). We have not done so here. The legal principles and requirements we set forth are well established in our case law and our statutes. All that has changed is the plaintiffs' apparent failure to abide by those principles and requirements in the rush to sell mortgage-backed securities.

Conclusion. For the reasons stated, we agree with the judge that the plaintiffs did not demonstrate that they were the holders of the Ibanez and LaRace mortgages at the time that they foreclosed these properties, and therefore failed to demonstrate that they acquired fee simple title to these properties by purchasing them at the foreclosure sale.

Judgments affirmed.

CORDY, J. (concurring, with whom BOTSFORD, J., joins). I concur fully in the opinion of the court, and write separately only to underscore that what is surprising about these cases is not the statement of principles articulated by the court regarding title law and the law of foreclosure in Massachusetts, but rather the utter carelessness with which the plaintiff banks documented the titles to their assets. There is no dispute that the mortgagors of the properties in question had defaulted on their obligations, and that the mortgaged properties were subject to foreclosure. Before commencing such an action, however, the holder of an assigned mortgage needs to take care to ensure that his legal paperwork is in order. Although there was no apparent actual unfairness here to the mortgagors, that is not the point. Foreclosure is a powerful act with significant consequences, and Massachusetts law has always required that it proceed strictly in accord with the statutes that govern it. As the opinion of the court notes, such strict compliance is necessary because Massachusetts both is a title theory State and allows for extrajudicial foreclosure.

The type of sophisticated transactions leading up to the accumulation of the notes and mortgages in question in these cases and their securitization, and, ultimately the sale of mortgage-backed securities, are not barred nor even burdened by the requirements of Massachusetts law. The plaintiff banks, who brought these cases to clear the titles that they acquired at their own foreclosure sales, have simply failed to prove that the underlying assignments of the mortgages that they allege (and would have) entitled them to foreclose ever existed in any legally cognizable form before they exercised the power of sale that accompanies those assignments. The court's opinion clearly states that such assignments do not need to be in recordable form or recorded before the foreclosure, but they do have to have been effectuated.

What is more complicated, and not addressed in this opinion, because the issue was not before us, is the effect of the conduct of banks such as the plaintiffs here, on a bona fide third-party purchaser who may have relied on the foreclosure title of the bank and the confirmative assignment and affidavit of foreclosure recorded by the bank subsequent to that foreclosure but prior to the purchase by the third party, especially where the party whose property was foreclosed was in fact in violation of the mortgage covenants, had notice of the foreclosure, and took no action to contest it.

NOTES AND QUESTIONS

1. *Securitization and the increasing complexity of real estate finance.* As the *Ibanez* case demonstrates, we have come a long way from the days of *It's a Wonderful Life,* in which the lender held on to mortgage loans from origination to payment. Mortgage loans today are sliced, diced, packaged, and distributed. They are also

repeatedly transferred. Do you think it mattered to the case that Massachusetts was a "title" theory state where the mortgagee is deemed to have legal title to the property? Did the fact that the mortgage foreclosure was by nonjudicial power of sale a factor in the case—implicitly or explicitly? Should it have mattered?

2. *Cutting corners.* As the number of foreclosure filings shot up between 2007 and 2012, many mortgage servicers were accused of abusing the system by either cutting corners or intentionally skirting the requirements of state real property law. *Ibanez* is an example of this carelessness. Among the problems disclosed by one exhaustive federal investigation were instances of "robo-signing" (i.e., the process of lenders and their agents quickly signing affidavits and other foreclosure documents without personally verifying their accuracy), disparities in or absence of necessary documentation such as the note or assignment of the mortgage, improper imposition of fees, and, in some instances, foreclosure actions against properties whose borrowers were not delinquent. See U.S. Federal Reserve System et al., Interagency Review of Foreclosure Policies and Practices 3-4 (2011).

Should mortgagors who can show a failure by their mortgagees to adhere to statutory or common law rules such as pre-foreclosure assignments of their mortgages or appropriate signatures on affidavits be entitled to have their foreclosure actions dismissed? Should it matter whether they were clearly in default under their loans? In many, but not all instances, the failures of mortgage servicers from 2008 through 2012 revolved around their failure to adhere to state legal formalities. The borrowers in the vast majority of cases were delinquent and would ultimately likely lose their properties anyway. In light of this, some members of the financial community suggested that the public outcry and ensuing litigation was a bit overblown. See, e.g., Editorial, The Politics of Foreclosure, Wall St. J., Oct. 9, 2010, at A14; Max Abelson, The Foreclosure Fiasco and Wall Street's Shrug, N.Y. Observer, Oct. 12, 2010. Other commentators took the opposite stance. For example, Professor Dana argues that adherence to formalities does indeed matter since it could result in a homeowner retaining his home. Following the law also demonstrates the law's equal treatment of people who are not wealthy or powerful; it reflects society's emphasis on the importance of the home; and it may prevent the occurrence of another foreclosure crisis by increasing lender precautions. David A. Dana, Why Mortgage "Formalities" Matter, 24 Loy. Consumer L. Rev. 505 (2012); see also Nestor M. Davidson, New Formalism in the Aftermath of the Housing Crisis, 93 B.U. L. Rev. 389 (2013).

There has been quite a bit of litigation challenging flaws in the foreclosure process. In particular, some borrowers have sought to dismiss foreclosure actions on the grounds that the person who signed the affidavit engaged in "robo-signing." Courts have frequently dismissed robo-signing claims either because they lacked factual proof or because the borrower failed to show that the affidavit contained erroneous facts. For instance, in Cerecedes v. U.S. Bankcorp, the plaintiffs alleged that bank employees had robo-signed their foreclosure documents. The court noted its awareness of media reports of robo-signing, but held that the plaintiffs had pled their claim in too conclusory of a fashion. The court also noted that the plaintiffs had not disputed that they were in default. Cerecedes v.

U.S. Bankcorp, 2011 WL 2711071 (C.D. Cal. July 11, 2011). However, in *Glarum v. LaSalle Bank Natl. Assn.*, 83 So. 3d 780 (Fla. App. 2011), the court gave more weight to a robo-signing claim. The court held that the loan servicer's employee's affidavit claiming that the borrowers had defaulted and owed $340,000 was inadmissible hearsay because he had not personally verified the amount due and was not competent to do so. See also *Beals v. Bank of America, N.A.*, 2011 WL 5415174 (D.N.J. Nov. 4, 2011) ("[E]ven though [the borrower] was indisputably in default and the "robo-signing" might involve only the question of who could properly foreclose, the validity and legitimacy of assignment documents are an important part of the foreclosure process."). For more analysis of the problem of robo-signing, see generally Richard E. Gottlieb, et al., The Foreclosure Firestorm: "Robo-Signing" Allegations Have More Bark Than Bite, 67 Bus. Law. 649 (2012).

With respect to the issue in *Ibanez*, courts are split on the precision they require with respect to the timing of assignments. See, e.g., Countrywide Home Loans, Inc. v. Taylor, 843 N.Y.S.2d 495 (Sup. Ct. 2007) (requiring evidence of an assignment prior to the foreclosure complaint filing); US Bank N.A. v. Mallory, 982 A.2d 986 (Pa. Super. Ct. 2009) (recording the assignment is unnecessary for a valid foreclosure); U.S. Bank Natl. Assn. v. Cook, 2009 WL 35286 (N.D. Ill. Jan. 6, 2009) (bank employee's testimony about inclusion of mortgage in Pooling and Servicing Agreement containing assignment language sufficed to prove timely assignment); Tina v. Countrywide Home Loans, Inc., 2008 WL 4790906 (S.D. Cal. Oct. 30, 2008) (nonjudicial foreclosure sale does not require showing the original note prior to the sale). For a discussion of these cases, see David R. Greenberg, Comment, Neglected Formalities in the Mortgage Assignment Process and the Resulting Effects on Residential Foreclosures, 83 Temp. L. Rev. 253 (2010); see also pages 752-753 for a discussion of litigation against mortgagees for using the Mortgage Electronic Registration System (MERS) as their nominee in foreclosure actions.

3. *Foreclosure reform?* As the housing bubble burst, mortgage loan defaults ballooned, millions of homeowners found themselves "underwater," foreclosure filings skyrocketed, and allegations of mortgage foreclosure irregularities such as robo-signing became commonplace, state mortgage foreclosure proceedings came under severe stress. States reacted in a wide variety of ways to these pressures. For example, California, Colorado, Michigan, and Nevada temporarily enacted mortgage foreclosure moratoria to allow borrowers time to catch their breath and pursue mortgage modifications. See Frank S. Alexander et al., Legislative Responses to the Foreclosure Crisis in Nonjudicial Foreclosure States, 31 Rev. Banking & Fin. L. 341, 365 (2011). Some states required lenders and mortgage servicers to contact delinquent borrowers and offer them single points of contact, housing counseling, and mortgage mediation. Minimum notice periods between delinquency and notice of foreclosure and between notice of foreclosure and sale were frequently lengthened. See, e.g., id. at 357-409; Center for Responsible Lending and Consumers Union, Closing the Gaps: What States Should Do to Protect Homeowners from Foreclosure 2-5 (May 2013). Perhaps the most comprehensive state mortgage foreclosure reform initiative is the California Homeowner

Bill of Rights. See California Foreclosure Reduction Act, SB 900, 2011-2012 Leg. Reg. Sess. (Cal. 2012).

As is common in our nation, innovations in regulation began in the state legislatures and spread from there. Foreclosure law reform also has recently emerged from other sources, such as the concerted enforcement action by 49 state attorneys general challenging the mortgage foreclosure practices of five banks. In 2012, these officials, along with federal enforcement officials, entered into a $25 billion settlement with five large banks (Ally, Bank of America, Citibank, J.P. Morgan Chase, and Wells Fargo). See, e.g., Consent Judgment, United States v. Bank of America Corp., Civ. Act. 12-0361 (Apr. 4, 2012). In addition to money to support mortgage foreclosure assistance, the consent decree provides for a variety of consumer safeguards and mandated pre-foreclosure procedures.

In 2013, the newly established Consumer Finance Protection Bureau (CFPB) issued its own set of rules to create uniform mortgage servicing standards throughout the United States. Subject to certain exemptions for smaller servicers, the rules require mortgage servicers to make a good-faith effort to contact borrowers by the thirty-sixth day of delinquency and to inform them about loss mitigation options. By the forty-fifth day, delinquent borrowers must be sent written notice of these options plus the name of a contact person at the servicer. Foreclosures may not be commenced until a homeowner is more than 120 days delinquent, and if the borrower submits a loss mitigation application, a foreclosure action must not be begun until the application is acted upon. A servicer may not pursue foreclosure simultaneous with consideration of a loss mitigation application (i.e., "dual-tracking"). If a foreclosure action is already started when a borrower submits a loss mitigation application, the servicer may not move for judgment or a sale if the application is complete 37 days prior to the sale. If the application is denied, specific reasons must be afforded and the servicer must provide a right of appeal. Should a servicer violate these regulations, homeowners can bring legal action seeking damages, attorneys' fees, and costs. See Mortgage Servicing Rules Under the Real Estate Settlement Procedures Act (Regulation X), 78 Fed. Reg. 10696 (codified at 12 C.F.R. §1024) (Feb. 14, 2013).

The various changes in foreclosure practice instituted by states, the state attorneys general, and the CFPB were all designed to inform borrowers of their rights after delinquency and to give them ample time to seek loan modifications and pursue other mitigation remedies prior to losing their homes. Of course, as with any additional layer of legal protection, the effectiveness of these new rules will depend upon borrowers having access to legal counsel or, at a minimum, housing counselors. Recent federal and state programs have also provided substantial new resources for housing counseling, although the need still far outstrips supply and the results of counseling are sometimes mixed. See J. Michael Collins & Maximilian D. Schmeiser, The Effects of Foreclosure Counseling for Distressed Homeowners, 32 J. Poly. Analysis & Mgmt. 83 (2013); Neil Mayer et al., Has Foreclosure Counseling Helped Troubled Homeowners?, Urban Institute Metropolitan Housing and Communities Center Brief No. 1 (January 2012), available at http://www.urban

.org/UploadedPDF/412492-Has-Foreclosure-Counseling-Helped-Troubled-Homeowners.pdf.

It is very possible that these new protections may also increase the time it takes for lenders to foreclose on delinquent borrowers. Even before many of these procedural reforms were fully phased in, the time it took to foreclose mortgages had escalated sharply in response to the crushing growth in foreclosure filings. For example, according to RealtyTrak, in the fourth quarter of 2012, it took 1,089 days to foreclose a home in New York State, up from less than 300 days in 2007. Similarly, in California, a state that typically uses the more speedy power of nonjudicial sale foreclosure process, time to foreclosure more than doubled to 347 days. See RealtyTrak, 2013 Short Sale Trends (2013), available at http://www.slideshare.net/fullscreen/RealtyTrac/2013-short-sale-trends/1. Additional delay may be beneficial to some borrowers, particularly those who can successfully modify their mortgages and those who benefit from additional periods of time in residency. But are these benefits worth the potential costs? Delay may increase costs to lenders, which could be spread among all borrowers in the form of higher interest rates. In addition, delay could lead to increased disinvestment in homes as owners fail to maintain properties. This disinvestment might ultimately generate negative externalities for neighbors and communities. See Kristopher Gerardi et al., Do Borrower Rights Improve Borrower Outcomes? Evidence from the Foreclosure Process, 73 J. Urb. Econ. 1 (2013); see also page 660 (discussing externalities of mortgage foreclosure).

4. *Avoiding the next crisis.* In addition to enacting requirements that mortgage servicers provide borrowers with procedural protections, the Dodd-Frank Wall Street Reform and Consumer Protection Act, Pub. L. No. 111-203, 124 Stat. 1376 (2010) (codified as amended in scattered sections of the U.S.C.), contains several provisions to rein in risky lending practices. The most important is the requirement that creditors make a reasonable and good-faith determination based on verified and documented information that the consumer has a reasonable ability to repay a loan according to its terms. A lender will be presumed to be in compliance with the law if the loan falls within the category of "qualified mortgages." It is expected that most lenders will seek to make loans that fit within this definition so as to avoid potential liability. The final rules promulgated in 2013 by the CFPB generally exclude loans with negative amortization, interest-only payments, balloon payments, or terms that exceed 30 years. In addition "no-doc" loans generally do not fall within the definition of qualified loans. Also, a loan will not usually be considered "qualified" if the points and fees paid by the consumer exceed 3 percent of the total loan amount (excluding certain "bona fide discount points"). The CFPB also provides for a set of underwriting requirements for qualified loans that includes a rule that monthly payments be calculated based upon the highest payment that will apply in the first five years of the loan and that the total debt-to-income ratio be less than or equal to 43 percent. For higher cost loans that otherwise meet the "qualified mortgage" definition, there is a rebuttable presumption that the loans meet the ability to repay requirements. The rules governing qualifying mortgages are set forth in 78 Fed. Reg. 6408-6620 (Jan. 30, 2013) and 78 Fed. Reg. 35430-35506 (June 12, 2013).

5. *Helping "underwater" borrowers.* As a result of the collapse of housing prices between 2007 and 2011, approximately one out of four homeowners had mortgage balances that exceeded the value of their properties. These "underwater" borrowers were unable to sell their homes because no purchaser would want to buy a house encumbered by a mortgage in excess of its value. Many were unable to refinance their mortgages to take advantage of low market interest rates because they had no equity in their homes. Among the options faced by these underwater borrowers were to (1) wait out the storm and try to keep current on their debt; (2) default and let the mortgagee foreclose; (3) try to get the mortgagee to agree to a "short sale" of the property to a third party in which the lender would write off part of the debt; (4) hand over the deed to the mortgagee in a deed in lieu of foreclosure (see page 659); and (5) negotiate with the mortgagee to modify the terms of the mortgage loan. Beginning in 2009 as part of the Troubled Asset Relief Program (TARP), the federal government created a series of programs to provide lenders with financial incentives to modify mortgages. These programs initially reduced the interest rates and lengthened the amortization terms of mortgages. Ultimately, the programs also provided subsidies to enable mortgagees to forgive principal. When the federal mortgage modification initiatives were originally announced, they were expected to benefit three to four million homeowners. As of March 31, 2013, only 862,279 mortgages were in active permanent modification. See Office of the Special Inspector General for the Troubled Asset Relief Program, Quarterly Report to Congress 63-64 (April 2013). For an analysis of the factors leading to the limited effectiveness of federal loan modification programs, see Sumit Agarwal et al., Policy Intervention in Debt Renegotiation: Evidence from the Home Affordable Modification Program (Fisher College of Bus., Working Paper No. 2012-03-020, 2013), available at http://papers.ssrn.com/sol3/papers.cfm?abstract_id=2138314.

Mortgage modification has proved vexing for a number of reasons. At the beginning of the mortgage meltdown, lenders were ill equipped to respond to borrower requests for modifications and frequently failed to return phone calls or lost paperwork. In addition, since a very large proportion of the loans were sold through the secondary mortgage market and securitized, it often has proven difficult for borrowers to identify the entity with which they should be negotiating. Oftentimes, the servicing agent for the mortgage pool either lacked authority or the appropriate incentives to modify the mortgage. Plus, the transaction costs of loan modifications are substantial. An additional problem cropped up when second mortgage liens existed that would need to be extinguished for the modification to be successful. A number of legal and business scholars proposed solutions to deal with some of these issues. See, e.g., Christopher Mayer et al., A New Proposal for Loan Modifications, 26 Yale J. on Reg. 417 (2009); Eric A. Posner & Luigi Zingales, A Loan Modification Approach to the Housing Crisis, 11 Am. L. & Econ. Rev. 575 (2009).

One of the key policy issues involving mortgage modification is the problem of moral hazard. Ideally, one would like to modify only those mortgages made by borrowers who would default in the absence of the modification. The problem is how to identify those mortgages and avoid the problem of strategic default. See Christopher J. Mayer et al., Mortgage Modification and Strategic Behavior: Evidence from a Legal Settlement with Countrywide (Columbia Law & Econ., Working Paper No. 404, 2012), available at http://ssrn.com/abstract=1836451. An additional and related problem concerns horizontal equity. Is it fair for one household that, in retrospect, has borrowed too much and perhaps bought too expensive a home to benefit from government policy, while another household that put down more equity or purchased a cheaper home receives no assistance? Compare Robert Gavin & Jenifer B. McKim, Bailout Lament: What About Me? Many Who Played by Rules See Unfairness, Boston Globe, Feb. 22, 2009, at A1 (quoting commentators concerned with fairness to people who "play by the rules"), with Tara Siegel Bernard, Help Paying Mortgages Elicits Anger, N.Y. Times, Apr. 3, 2010, at B1 (noting the unfairness of federal policy regarding loan modifications, but concluding that it is still a good idea). What do you think? Should federal and state policy provide financial assistance to rescue underwater borrowers? What are the arguments in favor of assistance? Against it?

The town of Richmond, California has proposed a creative way to deal with the problem of underwater mortgages. It plans to use its power of eminent domain to force mortgagees (largely investors in MBS) to sell them to the city at their current fair market value. The city would then allow homeowners to refinance the mortgages at this reduced value. See Shaila Dewan, A City Invokes Seizure Laws to Save Homes, N.Y. Times, July 30, 2013, at A1. In Chapter 12 (pages 1123-1131) you will learn more about the power of eminent domain and be able to evaluate the constitutionality of Richmond's proposal. For now, if you were advising the mayor and/or city council, would you encourage them to proceed?

6. *The future of housing finance.* The nation has made modest progress as it slowly emerges from the wreckage caused by the deflation of the housing bubble that began in 2007. As this chapter indicates, the federal government through the Dodd-Frank Act as well as the regulations promulgated by the CFPB has sought to limit the sort of risky lending practices that gave rise to the housing bubble in the first place. The CFPB, state legislatures, and state attorneys general have taken steps to fix some of the shortcomings of state mortgage foreclosure and practice. HUD has experimented with new and hopefully better incentives for mortgagees to modify underwater mortgage loans and create liquidity in the sales market. One area that will demand attention in the future is the structure of our housing finance system.

Recall from pages 645-646 that over the past half decade, Fannie Mae and Freddie Mac were instrumental in forging a national mortgage market. In 2010, approximately 46 percent of all home mortgage loans were either held in Fannie Mae or Freddie Mac portfolios or in their MBS pools. This proportion was only 8 percent in 1980. See Dwight Jaffee & John M. Quigley, The Future of the Government-Sponsored Enterprises: The Role for Government in the U.S. Mortgage Market, in Housing and the Financial Crisis 361, 367 (Edward L. Glaeser & Todd Sinai eds. 2013). As the housing bubble inflated, Fannie Mae and Freddie Mac took risks that were imprudent and engaged in transactions that greatly intensified the crisis. As the bubble burst, they were left with enormous liabilities and were ultimately bailed out by the federal government to the tune of $188 million. See id. at 361. At present, the agencies are effectively owned by the taxpayers. For two recent popular accounts of the role of Fannie Mae and Freddie Mac in the mortgage crisis, see James R. Hagerty, The Fateful History of Fannie Mae: New Deal Birth to Mortgage Crisis Fall (2012); Gretchen Morgenson & Joshua Rosner, Reckless Endangerment: How Outsized Ambition, Greed, and Corruption Led to Economic Armageddon (2011).

One of the reasons why Fannie Mae and Freddie Mac were able to take enormous risks investing in subprime mortgages was their status as government sponsored enterprises. In effect, investors failed to monitor Fannie Mae and Freddie Mac sufficiently or price their debt appropriately because they were treated as if they possessed the full faith and credit of the United States (which at least formally they did not). Ultimately, the United States did indeed treat them as "too big to fail."

There is substantial debate about the future of housing finance in the United States and whether we need entities such as Fannie Mae and Freddie Mac. Some commentators have argued that they be abolished and that the availability of single family home purchase mortgage loans be governed solely by the private market. Others believe that Fannie Mae and Freddie Mac should be reconstituted or replaced with some type of federal agency that might provide market-based insurance to promote liquidity in the market and help ensure the continuance of the 30-year, fixed rate, fully amortizing mortgage loan. Others favor a more active agency that supports low and moderate income housing development. Those favoring a government agency agree that it should not have private shareholders like Fannie Mae and Freddie Mac did (can you see why?). Some analysts and interest groups have promoted a housing finance system that obtains capital from covered bonds. What do you think? Should government play a major role in housing finance or should the free market rule? For a discussion of the various options and viewpoints, see U.S. Dept. of Treasury & U.S. Dept. of Housing and Urban Development, Reforming America's Housing Finance Market: A Report to Congress (2011); Jaffee & Quigley, supra; Testimony on the Protect American Taxpayers and Homeowners Act: Hearing on H.R. 2767 Before the H. Committee on Financial Services, 113th Cong. (July 18, 2013) (statement of Peter J. Wallison, Arthur F. Burns Fellow in Financial Policy Studies, American Enterprise Institute).

4. Mortgage Substitutes: The Installment Land Contract

An *installment land sale contract* or a *contract for deed* is an arrangement whereby the purchaser takes possession and the seller contracts to convey title to the purchaser when the purchaser has paid the purchase price in regular installments over a fixed period of time. These payments may be allocated to principal and interest in a fashion similar to amortized mortgage payments, or there may be annual payments of interest and a balloon payment at the end. If the purchaser pays the contract price in full, the seller agrees to deliver a deed conveying legal title to the purchaser.

There is little functional difference between a purchase money mortgage and an installment land sale contract. Both are devices to secure payment of unpaid purchase money. But the installment land sale contract, which provides financing by the *seller*, not by an institutional lender, is widely used in transfers of real estate, particularly low cost housing and vacation lots. The buyer may not have a sufficient down payment to qualify for a loan from an institutional lender, or the buyer may be considered by the institutional lender as a poor credit risk. With an installment land sale contract, no bank loan is necessary; the down payment can be minimal, and the seller may be willing to sell to persons deemed poor credit risks by institutional lenders. Installment land contracts have also been favored by sellers in those states where judicial foreclosure is the only method of foreclosing a mortgage. The reason why sellers use the installment land contract is that it includes a clause providing that the buyer forfeits the land and the payments if the buyer goes into default. Thus sellers hope to avoid expensive and time-consuming judicial foreclosure.

Bean v. Walker

New York Supreme Court, Appellate Division
Fourth Department, 1983
464 N.Y.S.2d 895

DOERR, J. Presented for our resolution is the question of the relative rights between a vendor and a defaulting vendee under a land purchase contract. Special Term, in granting summary judgment in favor of plaintiffs, effectively held that the defaulting vendee has no rights. We cannot agree.

The facts may be briefly stated. In January 1973 plaintiffs agreed to sell and defendants agreed to buy a single-family home in Syracuse for the sum of $15,000.[28] The contract provided that this sum would be paid over a 15-year period at 5% interest, in monthly installments of $118.62. The sellers retained legal title to the property which they agreed to convey upon payment in full according to the terms of the contract. The purchasers were entitled to possession of the property, and all taxes, assessments and water rates, and insurance became the obligation of the purchasers. The contract also provided that in the event purchasers defaulted in making payment and failed to cure the default within 30 days, the sellers could elect to call the remaining balance immediately due or elect to declare the contract terminated and repossess the premises. If the latter alternative was chosen, then a forfeiture clause came into play whereby the seller could retain all the

---

28. The house now has an alleged market value of $44,000.

money paid under the contract as "liquidated" damages and "the same shall be in no event considered a penalty but rather the payment of rent."

Defendants went into possession of the premises in January 1973 and in the ensuing years claim to have made substantial improvements on the property. They made the required payments under the contract until August 1981 when they defaulted following an injury sustained by defendant Carl Walker. During the years while they occupied the premises as contract purchasers defendants paid to plaintiff $12,099.24, of which $7,114.75 was applied to principal. Thus, at the time of their default, defendants had paid almost one-half of the purchase price called for under the agreement. After the required 30-day period to cure the default,[29] plaintiffs commenced this action sounding in ejectment seeking a judgment "that they be adjudged the owner in fee" of the property and granting them possession thereof. The court granted summary judgment to plaintiffs.

If the only substantive law to be applied to this case was that of contracts, the result reached would be correct. However, under the facts presented herein the law with regard to the transfer of real property must also be considered. The reconciliation of what might appear to be conflicting concepts is not insurmountable.

While there are few New York cases which directly address the circumstances herein presented, certain general principles may be observed. "It is well settled that the owner of the real estate from the time of the execution of a valid contract for its sale is to be treated as the owner of the purchase money and the purchaser of the land is to be treated as the equitable owner thereof. The purchase money becomes personal property" (New York C. & H. R.R. Co. v. Cottle, 187 App. Div. 131, 144, 175 N.Y.S. 178 affd. 229 N.Y. 514, 129 N.E. 896). Thus, notwithstanding the words of the contract and implications which may arise therefrom, the law of property declares that, upon the execution of a contract for sale of land, the vendee acquires equitable title. . . . The vendor holds the legal title in trust for the vendee and has an equitable lien for the payment of the purchase price. . . . The vendee in possession, for all practical purposes, is the owner of the property with all the rights of an owner subject only to the terms of the contract. The vendor may enforce his lien by foreclosure or an action at law for the purchase price of the property—the remedies are concurrent (Flickinger v. Glass, 222 N.Y. 404, 118 N.E. 792; Zeiser v. Cohn, 207 N.Y. 407, 101 N.E. 184). . . . The conclusion to be reached, of course, is that upon the execution of a contract an interest in real property comes into existence by operation of law, superseding the terms of the contract. An analogous result occurs in New York if an owner purports to convey title to real property as security for a loan; the conveyance is deemed to create a lien rather than an outright conveyance, even though the deed was recorded (Schulte v. Cleri, 39 A.D.2d 692, 332 N.Y.S.2d 518) and "one who has taken a deed absolute in form as security for an obligation, in order to foreclose the debtor's

---

29. Defendant's offer to bring the payments up-to-date and pay a higher interest rate on the balance due were unavailing.

right to redeem, must institute a foreclosure, and is entitled to have the premises sold in the usual way" (14 Carmody-Wait 2d, §92:2, p. 612).

Cases from other jurisdictions are more instructive. In Skendzel v. Marshall, 261 Ind. 226, 301 N.E.2d 641 (addressing itself to a land sale contract), the court observed that while legal title does not vest in the vendee until the contract terms are satisfied, he does acquire a vested equitable title at the time the contract is consummated. When the parties enter into the contract all incidents of ownership accrue to the vendee who assumes the risk of loss and is the recipient of all appreciation of value. The status of the parties becomes like that of mortgagor-mortgagee. Viewed otherwise would be to elevate form over substance (Skendzel v. Marshall, supra, p. 234, 301 N.E.2d 641). The doctrine that equity deems as done that which ought to be done is an appropriate concept which we should apply to the present case.

Where sale of real property is evidenced by contract only and the purchase price has not been paid and is not to be paid until some future date in accordance with the terms of the agreement, the parties occupy substantially the position of mortgagor and mortgagee at common law. In New York a mortgage merely creates a lien rather than conveying title (Moulton v. Cornish, 138 N.Y. 133, 33 N.E. 842), but this was not always so. At common law the mortgage conveyed title, and it was to protect the buyer from summary ejectment that Courts of Equity evolved the concept of "equitable" title as distinct from "legal" title (Barson v. Mulligan, 191 N.Y. 306, 313-314, 84 N.E. 75; see also, 2 Rasch, Real Property Law and Practice, §1684; 14 Carmody-Wait 2d §92:1). The doctrine of equitable conversion had important consequences. The equitable owner suffered the risk of loss (Sewell v. Underhill, 197 N.Y. 168, 171, 172, 91 N.E. 1120) as does a contract vendee in possession today (see General Obligations Law, §5-1311, subd. 1, par. [b]), but concomitantly, the equitable owner was also entitled to any increase in value; "since a purchaser under a binding contract of sale is in equity regarded as the owner of the property, he is entitled to any benefit or increase in value that may accrue to it" (6 Warren's Weed, New York Real Property, Vendee and Vendor, §6.01). Similarly, upon the parties' death, the vendor's interest is regarded as personal property (i.e., the right to receive money), while the vendee's interest is treated as real property (Barson v. Mulligan, supra, 191 N.Y. at pp. 313-314, 84 N.E. 75).

Because the common-law mortgagor possessed equitable title, the legal owner (the mortgagee) could not recover the premises summarily, but had to first extinguish the equitable owner's equity of redemption. Thus evolved the equitable remedy of mortgage foreclosure, which is now governed by statute (RPAPL, §1301 et seq.). In our view, the vendees herein occupy the same position as the mortgagor at common law; both have an equitable title only, while another person has legal title. We perceive no reason why the instant vendees should be treated any differently than the mortgagor at common law. Thus the contract vendors may not summarily dispossess the vendees of their equitable ownership without first bringing an action to foreclose the vendees' equity of redemption. This view reflects the modern trend in other jurisdictions. See Skendzel v. Marshall, supra (followed in Sebastian v. Floyd, 585 S.W.2d 381 (Ky. 1979); Thomas v. Klein, 99 Idaho 105, 577 P.2d 1153 (1978); Anderson Contracting Co. v. Daugherty, 274 Pa. Super. 13, 417 A.2d 1227 (1979); H & L Land Co. v. Warner, 258 So. 2d 293 (Fla. App. 1972)), and has been recognized in New York (Hudson v. Matter, 219 App. Div. 252, 219 N.Y.S. 555; Gerder Servs. v. Johnson, 109 Misc. 2d 216, 439 N.Y.S.2d 794). . . .

The key to the resolution of the rights of the parties lies in whether the vendee under a land sale contract has acquired an interest in the property of such a nature that it must be extinguished before the vendor may resume possession. We hold that such an interest exists since the vendee acquires equitable title and the vendor merely holds the legal title in trust for the vendee, subject to the vendor's equitable lien for payment of the purchase price in accordance with the terms of the contract. The vendor may not enforce his rights by the simple expedient of an action in ejectment but must instead proceed to foreclose the vendee's equitable title or bring an action at law for the purchase price, neither of which remedies plaintiffs have sought.

The effect of the judgment granted below is that plaintiffs will have their property with improvements made over the years by defendants, along with over $7,000 in principal payments on a purchase price of $15,000, and over $4,000 in interest. The basic inequity of such a result requires no further comment (see Hudson v. Matter, 219 App. Div. 252, 219 N.Y.S. 555; Gerder Servs. v. Johnson, 109 Misc. 2d 216, 439 N.Y.S.2d 794).[30] If a forfeiture would result in the inequitable disposition of property and an exorbitant monetary loss, equity can and should intervene (Thomas v. Klein, 99 Idaho 105, 107, 577 P.2d 1153 (1978); Ellis v. Butterfield, 98 Idaho 644, 648, 570 P.2d 1334 (1977)).

The interest of the parties here can only be determined by a sale of the property after foreclosure proceedings with provisions for disposing of the surplus or for a deficiency judgment. In arguing against this result, plaintiffs stress that in New York a defaulting purchaser may not recover money paid pursuant to an executory contract (Lawrence v. Miller, 86 N.Y. 131). Although we have no quarrel with this general rule of law (see, e.g., Dmochowski v. Rosati, 96 A.D.2d 718, 465 N.Y.S.2d 367, decided herewith), we observe that this rule has generally been applied to cases involving down payments (see Gerder Servs. v. Johnson, supra, 109 Misc. 2d at p.217, 439 N.Y.S.2d 794 and cases cited therein), or to cases wherein the vendee was not in possession (see, e.g., Leonard v. Ickovic, 55 N.Y.S.2d 727, 447 N.Y.S.2d 153, 431 N.E.2d 638 (factually distinguishable because the defaulting vendee was not in possession and was not attempting to defend his equitable title, but rather to recover money paid under a theory of joint venture); Havens v. Patterson, 43 N.Y. 218 (the defaulting party had abandoned possession

30. Some jurisdictions refuse to enforce the forfeiture provision of a land contract if the proportion of the purchase price paid is so substantial that the amount forfeited would be an invalid "penalty" (see, e.g., Hook v. Bomar, 320 F.2d 536 (5th Cir. 1963) (applying Florida law); Rothenberg v. Follman, 172 N.W.2d 845 (Mich. App. 1969); Morris v. Sykes, 624 P.2d 681 (Utah 1981); Johnson v. Carman, 572 P.2d 371 (Utah 1977); Behrendt v. Abraham, 410 P.2d 828 (Cal. 1966); Land Dev., Inc. v. Padgett, 369 P.2d 888 (Alaska 1962)).

eight years earlier, whereupon the vendor retook possession and made substantial improvements)).

By our holding today we do not suggest that forfeiture would be an inappropriate result in all instances involving a breach of a land contract. If the vendee abandons the property and absconds, logic compels that the forfeiture provisions of the contract may be enforced. Similarly, where the vendee has paid a minimal sum on the contract and upon default seeks to retain possession of the property while the vendor is paying taxes, insurance and other upkeep to preserve the property, equity will not intervene to help the vendee (Skendzel v. Marshall, supra, 261 Ind. at pp. 240, 241, 301 N.E.2d 641). Such is not the case before us.

Accordingly, the judgment should be reversed, the motion should be denied and the matter remitted to Supreme Court for further proceedings in accordance with this Opinion.

NOTES

1. Not all states will treat installment sales contracts as financing devices. See, e.g., Russell v. Richards, 702 P.2d 993 (N.M. 1985). In an illuminating examination of installment land contracts, Professor Freyfogle has catalogued the many uncertainties of forfeiture law. Eric T. Freyfogle, Vagueness and the Rule of Law: Reconsidering Installment Land Contract Forfeitures, 1988 Duke L.J. 609. In nearly all states, the seller must give notice of a possible forfeiture, either in a manner prescribed by statute or in a reasonable manner satisfactory to a court. Accepting late payments may waive the seller's right to forfeiture in the future, as it may mislead the purchaser into believing that promptness is not required. Purchasers in default may have the right to specific performance by paying the entire purchase price. The seller's declaration of forfeiture may bar the seller from suing for the remainder of the purchase price. The purchaser, even a willfully defaulting one, may be entitled to restitution of some payments in excess of what is fair to the seller to cover his loss. Some courts require foreclosure by the seller, but with exceptions not easy to apply.

2. History is repeating itself. In the development of mortgage law, the chancellor protected defaulting borrowers when it was necessary to do equity. In time, the chancellor gave all borrowers a right of redemption, regardless of their merits, and the previous ad hockery disappeared. The same, it seems, is now happening with installment land contracts. See Carol M. Rose, Crystals and Mud in Property Law, 40 Stan. L. Rev. 577, 583-585 (1988).

The Restatement (Third) of Property, Mortgages §3.4(b) (1997) provides that a contract for deed creates a mortgage. See Grant S. Nelson, The Contract for Deed as a Mortgage: The Case for the Restatement Approach, 1998 BYU L. Rev. 1111.

3. Are installment sales contracts a potentially useful tool to promote homeownership among low and moderate income households? See Heather K. Way, Informal Homeownership in the United States and the Law, 29 St. Louis U. Pub. L. Rev. 113 (2009).

In this chapter we deal with the system our country has developed to assure purchasers of land that they have good title to the land purchased. At the heart of the system is the public records office, where all instruments affecting land titles (deeds, mortgages, liens, wills, and so forth) are recorded. Before buying, a purchaser should search (or, more accurately, pay a professional to search) the public records office to discover the evidence of title recorded in that office. From the evidence of title in the records office, a professional (often a lawyer) will conclude who has the fee simple title to the land, which may be encumbered with a mortgage or a servitude. Relying on the professional's opinion of title, the purchaser decides whether or not to buy the land.

In a few localities, title registration is available. Under title registration, the state registers title and issues a title certificate to the owner, which is reissued to each new purchaser of the property.

Public records are not always perfect, and purchasers might want further security. So private insurance companies sell title insurance to purchasers for a premium. In many localities, particularly in the Far West and large urban areas, title insurance companies maintain their own private record storage systems, which duplicate the public records and store the information in a computerized system.

With title insurance companies serving as backup to the recording system, security of title in the United States ought to be, and is, very high. This, however, results less from any merits in our land title transfer system than from the ingenuity of professionals in the title industry, who manage to provide security in spite of the recording system's manifest and long-recognized defects.

A. The Recording System

1. Introduction

Public recording of deeds, mortgages, leases, and other instruments affecting land title began in this country in the Plymouth and Massachusetts Bay colonies around 1640. It was not an English custom. Indeed, not until the twentieth century did England have a general public registration system; deeds and other muniments of title were handed from purchaser to purchaser and were usually kept in boxes in the office of the owner's solicitor. Today, in every

American state, statutes provide for land title records to be maintained by the county recorder (or other equivalent public official) in each county. The land title records include copies of documents filed with the recorder and indexes to these copied documents. (The original document presented for recordation is copied by the recorder and returned to the grantee.) Increasingly, jurisdictions are computerizing their land records, although the practice has only begun to affect the law of title.

The recording acts generally do not affect the validity of a deed or other instrument. A deed is valid and good against the grantor upon delivery without recordation. The recording system serves other functions. First, it establishes a system of public recordation of land titles. Anyone—creditor, tax collector, prospective purchaser, or just plain curious—can ascertain who owns land in the county by searching the records. Second, the recording system preserves in a secure place important documents that, in private hands, may be easily lost or misplaced. In most states recorded copies of documents can be admitted directly into evidence in judicial proceedings, without producing or accounting for the original. In other states, the recorded copy can be admitted, but only after showing why the original cannot be produced. In order to increase the reliability of the public records, statutes typically require that a deed be acknowledged before a notary public or other public official before it is entitled to recordation.

Recording statutes often specify what instruments can be recorded, but generally any kind of deed, mortgage, lease, option, or other instrument creating or affecting an interest in land can be recorded. A judgment or decree affecting title to land can also be recorded. Prior to judgment in a lawsuit affecting title to real property, any party may record a *lis pendens* (notice of pending action), which will effectively put subsequent claimants on notice of the claims being litigated. In addition, wills and affidavits of heirship of an intestate are entitled to be recorded. About one-third of the states have statutes permitting recordation of affidavits containing statements of fact relating to title.

Finally, recording acts have the function of protecting purchasers for value and lien creditors against prior unrecorded interests. At common law, as between successive grantees, priority of title was determined by priority in time of conveyance. The theory was that once the grantor conveyed his interest to a grantee, the grantor no longer had an interest to convey to any subsequent grantee. Thus:

> *Example 1.* O mortgages Blackacre to A. O subsequently conveys Blackacre to B who does not know of the mortgage. At common law B takes the land subject to A's mortgage. (In equity, the doctrine of *bona fide purchaser* would protect B against A's mortgage if A's mortgage were purely equitable and not a legal interest. Equity refused to enforce prior hidden equitable interests against bona fide purchasers of the legal title.)

The recording acts in general have adopted and broadened the equitable doctrine of bona fide purchaser. Under the recording acts, *a subsequent bona fide purchaser is protected against prior unrecorded interests.* Thus a purchaser of property will want to search the records to make sure that there are no adverse prior recorded claims, and a purchaser records his deed in order to prevent a subsequent purchaser from a previous owner from prevailing over him. *But remember*: The common law rule of "prior in time, prior in effect," illustrated by *Example 1*, continues to control unless a person can qualify for protection under the applicable recording act.

2. The Indexes

It is impossible for a buyer of land to search out and find all the interests in a particular tract of land without using an index to the thousands, or millions, of documents filed in the recorder's office. There are two types of indexes currently used in the United States: (1) tract index and (2) grantor-grantee index. Both are useful in searching title. Public tract indexes, indexing documents by a parcel identification number assigned to the particular tract, do not exist in most states. The primary obstacle to establishing public tract indexes was the fact that early deeds in eastern states described land by metes and bounds (see page 617). No short formula was available by which a tract of land could be described. This obstacle remains today where land has not been subdivided and conveyed by subdivision tract numbers, or conveyed by reference to a government survey, or, in recent years, has not acquired a parcel identification number in localities where such numbers are available.

The most common method of indexing is the grantor-grantee system. Under this system separate indexes are kept for grantors and grantees. In the *grantor index* all instruments are indexed alphabetically and chronologically under the grantor's surname. In the *grantee index* all instruments are indexed under the grantee's surname. Thus a deed from Able to Baker will be indexed under Able's name in the grantor index and under Baker's name in the grantee index. Usually many volumes compose the grantor index and similarly the grantee index. For example, the recorder's office may have consolidated all of its nineteenth-century grantor index volumes into one volume indexing grantors prior to 1900. For twentieth-century grantors, there may be one volume for each decade: 1900 to 1910, 1910 to 1920, and so forth until 1980. After 1980 there may be one volume for each year and for the most recent year a monthly and daily index. These volumes covering different time spans result from periodic consolidation by the recorder. The more consolidation, the easier it is to search title because there are fewer volumes to check.

There may also be separate grantor and grantee indexes for each type of instrument—one index for deeds, one for mortgages, one for wills, one for liens, and so on. In our description of searching title below, we use the term grantor index to refer comprehensively to all the volumes indexing grantors. Similarly, the term grantee index refers to all volumes indexing grantees.

The reference in the index to a document sets forth its essentials: the grantor, the grantee, description of the land, kind of instrument, date of recording, and volume and page numbers where the instrument can be found set forth in full. The title searcher must, of course, examine the complete instrument; the index is merely a helpful method of locating the instrument among the many volumes in the recorder's office.

How to search title. You will more easily comprehend the issues arising under the recording system if you understand how title is searched in the grantor-grantee indexes. The best way to learn is by doing, and we recommend that you go to the court house in your county and search the title of your parents' house, the apartment where you are living, or some other property you are interested in. The records are public, and employees in the recorder's office in most localities are quite helpful in giving a law student a start. Barring a personal search, you will have to learn from the following description.[1]

Searching title bears some resemblance to what the genealogist does in establishing kindred; first, trace backward for ancestors, and then under each ancestor fill in the names and relationships of his or her descendants. Similarly, in searching title you go backward in time to an acceptable source or "root of title," then search forward from that source. Since you use the grantee index to search backwards and the grantor index to search forward, both indexes must be searched.

Assume that a man named Dubek is selling to your client a tract of land called (as any astrologer might have predicted) Blackacre. Since you want to find out how Dubek received title, you look in the *grantee* index under Dubek's name from the present time backward until you find a deed to Dubek from, let us say, Cotter in 1977. Now you want to know how Cotter received title, so you look, again in the grantee index, under Cotter's name from 1977 backwards in time until you find a deed to Cotter from Barker in 1952. Now you want to know how Barker received title, and so you run Barker's name in the grantee index from 1952 backwards in time to his source of title. By running each grantee's name back through the grantee index you can discover the preceding source of title (the grantor) of each person who purports to own Blackacre.

Suppose you run the grantee index back to 1900, which is as far as you deem necessary, and you find that in 1900 record title was in Oliver. Now you must switch to the *grantor* index and search that index forward in time under the name of each grantor (remember: you have ascertained the names of each grantor by running the grantee index). You start with Oliver in the year 1900. You look under Oliver's name in 1900, 1901, 1902, and so forth, until you find a deed from Oliver to Anderson, executed and recorded in 1915. Having found that Oliver parted with record title to Blackacre in 1915, you stop looking under Oliver's name and start, with the volume for 1915, looking under the name of Anderson to find the first deed out from Anderson. This deed you find is a deed from Anderson to Barker executed in 1934 and recorded in 1939. You then drop Anderson's name in 1939, and run Barker's name in the grantor index from *1934*

---

1. We describe here only the search in the recorder's office, but a title searcher typically must search in other places as well. Transfers by will may be kept in the probate court; claims of *lis pendens*, mechanics' liens, state and federal tax liens, zoning ordinances, building codes, and other pertinent items may be found in other places. See William B. Stoebuck & Dale A. Whitman, The Law of Property 874-877 (3d ed. 2000).

1980 - - - - - GRANTOR INDEX FEB. 2,81 THRU FEB. 20,81 - - - - - SUFFOLK COUNTY REGISTRY OF DEEDS   PAGE 180

MO-DY	GRANTOR	GRANTEE	TOWN	BOOK	PGE	INST	DESCRIPTION
02-05	SECURITY PLANNERS LTD INC EAL	RELEASE		9669	238	REL	U S TAX LIEN A515.35
02-05	SECURITY WAREHOUSE INC EAL	RELEASE		9669	236	REL	U S TAX LIEN B467.535
02-05	SECURITY WAREHOUSE INC EAL	RELEASE		9669	237	REL	U S TAX LIEN B442.251
02-05	SECURITY WAREHOUSE INC EAL	RELEASE		9669	247	REL	U S TAX LIEN
02-05	SEGAL, EDITH EAL	RELEASE		9669	243	REL	U S TAX LIEN
02-05	SEGAL, MARY L. EAL	RELEASE		9669	241	REL	U S TAX LIEN
02-05	SEGAL, MARY L. EAL	RELEASE		9669	242	REL	U S TAX LIEN
02-05	SEGAL, MAX EAL	RELEASE		9669	243	REL	U S TAX LIEN
02-05	SEGAL, MICHAEL G. EAL	RELEASE		9669	242	REL	U S TAX LIEN
02-05	SEGAL, MICHAEL D. EAL	RELEASE		9669	241	REL	U S TAX LIEN
02-04	SEGAL, ROSALYN A. EAL	AMENDMENT		9661	225	AMGT	MASTER CNDNNM DEED 9344,337 PLANS
02-03	SEGALINI, ROLAND JR EAL	J R MCLAUGHLIN TR		9667	240	MTG	UNIT #00-21 OF THE CANTERBURY VILLAGE CNDNNM
02-12	SEGALINI, ROLAND JR TR	M C MAGUIRE EAL	BRI	9676	306	DEED	57 AUSTIN ST LT 45 PL 3500,5366PEING LT 3A PL 1932,383
02-20	SEIDNER, MICHAEL A.	HOUSEHOLD FIN CORP	BRI	9683	284	MTG	SUMMIT AVE&ALLSTON ST LT 3 PL 2306,435
02-11	SEKENSKI, EDWARD A. JR EAL	LEVY & SUSPENDED	CHE	9675	316	LES	WALTHAM DIST CT MADE FEB 11. 1981 BELLINGHAM ST 2 PCS
02-11	SEKENSKI, LINDA C. EAL	LEVY & SUSPENDED	CHE	9675	316	LES	WALTHAM DIST CT MADE FEB 11. 1981 BELLINGHAM ST 2 PCS,
02-05	SELBY AUTO SUPPLY CO INC EAL	RELEASE		9669	240	REL	U S TAX LIEN B443.434
02-05	SELLARD, FRANK EAL	RELEASE		9669	248	REL	U S TAX LIEN
02-09	SELWYN, BARBARA E. EAL	SHAWMUT BK BOSTON N A		9671	113	MTG	19-21 RICKER TERR LT 30 PL 2M3G FND WDLSX #OUT OF CO
02-13	SELYA, ANNE EAL	DISCHARGE		9677	193	DIS	MTG A660.419
02-13	SELYA, DAVID EAL	DISCHARGE		9677	193	DIS	MTG A660.419
02-04	SEMINERIO, SANTINA TR	A DESALVATORE EAL	BRI	9673	170	DEED	MURDOCK&SPARHAWK STS LT 4 PL D APRIL 4,1887
02-03	SENA, LAURA EAL	NOTICE PETN	S B	9665	316	NOT	8 HUMPHREYS ST FCL TAX 2143,090
02-02	SENNET, CAROL EAL	C SENNETT EAL	T P	9665	234	DFED	162 SHFRRIN ST LT 546 PL 4730 LND
02-18	SEPULVEDA, PABLO	J A PROROK JR	ROX	9680	135	DEED	3 ESTRELLA ST
02-06	SERVICENTER LTD EAL	WESTINGHOUSE CR CORP	ROX	9670	338	MTG	BPOOKLINE AVE,FRANCISE BINNEY ST&GFENWOOD RD PL D 1-25-1979
02-06	SERVICENTER LTD EAL	WESTINGHOUSE CR CORP		9671	1	ASST	LFAS&GRENTS ETC SEE INSTR

A page from the Grantor Index, Register of Deeds, Suffolk County, Massachusetts

(the date of execution of the deed) until you find, in 1952, the deed from Barker to Cotter, which was executed and recorded on the same day in 1952. You next run Cotter's name in the grantor index from 1952 until you find the deed from Cotter to Dubek, executed and recorded in 1977. Finally you run Dubek's name in the grantor index from 1977 to the present.

As you can see, you have discovered a chain of title that looks like this:

1900-1915	Oliver owns; conveys to Anderson in 1915
1915-1934	Anderson owns; conveys to Barker in 1934 by deed not recorded until 1939
1934-1952	Barker owns; conveys to Cotter in 1952
1952-1977	Cotter owns; conveys to Dubek in 1977

In running the grantor index under Oliver's name from 1900 to 1915 (to the first deed out, to Anderson) you pick up any mortgages given by Oliver, any attachments or lawsuits filed against Oliver, and any conveyances by Oliver of interests less than a fee simple. Similarly, with respect to each other owner, you pick up all of the claims against the particular owner by running the grantor index under the owner's name forward from the time of the *execution* of the first deed giving title to such owner to the time of *recording* of the first deed out from such owner.

Why must you search under Barker's name from 1934 (the date of execution of the *A* to *B* deed) rather than from 1939 (the date of recording)? The deed from Anderson to Barker passed title to Barker in 1934. Barker thus could convey title to a person after that time. Suppose that Barker mortgaged the property in 1936, which mortgage was recorded. If you ran the grantor index under Barker's name only from 1939 forward, you would not pick up the mortgage. As pointed out above, you also have to run the grantor index under the name of Anderson from 1934 to 1939, because Anderson was the record owner until 1939. If in 1937 Anderson had given a deed to Florence, a bona fide purchaser who recorded, Florence would prevail over Barker's then unrecorded deed. The search sketched above, the minimum required in all jurisdictions without tract indexes, is the standard title search. This search produces a chain of title going back to a source deemed satisfactory. Many jurisdictions require a more extensive search of title, however. The more extensive searches and the problems they raise are examined in the discussion of Chain of Title Problems beginning at page 724.

How far back? How far back in the abysm of time a title searcher must search to find a satisfactory root of title varies both with local custom and with the identity of the client. In some jurisdictions the practice is to go back to a sovereign, in others 60 years, in still others a shorter period. The search is not ordinarily limited to the period of the statute of limitations because the statute may not have begun to run on various types of interests (such as a remainder, an easement, a covenant, or mineral rights). Because a purchaser is liable under CERCLA for costs of cleaning up contaminated land unless the purchaser makes "all appropriate inquiry" into possible contamination and qualifies as a bona fide purchaser (see page 591), purchasers of commercial properties make far more extensive searches to ascertain previous owners and possible polluters of the particular property they are interested in buying.

Agencies of the federal government customarily require a search back to the original source. This perfectionism led to the circulation some years ago of a spurious but delightful story. A New Orleans lawyer had searched title back to 1803 for his client, a federal agency. The agency asked who owned the land prior to that date. The lawyer replied:

> Gentlemen:
>
> I am in receipt of your letter of the fifth of this month inquiring as to the state of the title prior to the year 1803.
>
> Please be advised that in the year 1803 the United States of America acquired the Territory of Louisiana from the Republic of France by purchase. The Republic of France previously acquired title from the Spanish Crown by conquest. Spain acquired title by virtue of the discoveries of one Christopher Columbus, a Genoese sailor who had been duly authorized to embark upon his voyage of discovery by Isabella, Queen of Spain. Before granting such authority, Isabella, a pious and cautious woman, obtained the sanction of His Holiness, the Pope. The Pope is the Vicar on earth of Jesus Christ, the only son and heir apparent of God. God made Louisiana.

Luthi v. Evans

Supreme Court of Kansas, 1978
576 P.2d 1064

PRAGER, J. On February 1, 1971, Grace V. Owens was the owner of interests in a number of oil and gas leases located in Coffey county. On that date Owens, by a written instrument designated "Assignment of Interest in Oil and Gas Leases," assigned to defendant International Tours, Inc. (hereinafter Tours) all of such oil and gas interests. This assignment provided as follows:

Assignment of Interest in Oil and Gas Leases

KNOW ALL MEN BY THESE PRESENTS:

That the undersigned Grace Vannocker Owens, formerly Grace Vannocker, Connie Sue Vannocker, formerly Connie Sue Wilson, Larry R. Vannocker, sometimes known as Larry Vannocker, individually and also doing business as Glacier Petroleum Company and Vannocker Oil Company, hereinafter called Assignors, for and in consideration of $100.00 and other valuable consideration, the receipt whereof is hereby acknowledged, do hereby sell, assign, transfer and set over unto International Tours, Inc., a Delaware Corporation, hereinafter called Assignee, all their right, title, and interest (which includes all overriding royalty interest and working interest) in and to the following Oil and Gas Leases located in Coffey County, Kansas, more particularly specified as follows, to-wit:

[The court omitted the description of the leases assigned, but, to make the case more understandable, we reproduce here the description of one of the leases referred to in the actual instrument:

WILEY (Phillips CP #50098)
    Entire 7/8 Working Interest in Lease
    Dated: June 8, 1936

From: Lillian Wiley
To: E.L. Harrigan and T.F. Harrigan
Recorded: Book 6L pages 137 and 138
Insofar as lease covers NE4 Sec. 14-23-14 (160 a.)

Similar descriptions of six other leases from Rossillon, Scott, Shotwell, Vannocker, McCartney, and Cochran are set forth in the instrument of assignment.]

together with the rights incident thereto and the personal property thereon, appurtenant thereto or used or obtained in connection therewith.

And for the same consideration the Assignors covenant with the Assignee, his heirs, successors or assigns: That the Assignors are the lawful owners of and have good title to the interest above assigned in and to said Lease, estate, rights and property, free and clear from all liens, encumbrances or adverse claims; That said Lease is valid and subsisting Lease on the land above described, and all rentals and royalties due thereunder have been paid and all conditions necessary to keep the same in full force have been duly performed, and that the Assignor will warrant and forever defend the same against all persons whomsoever, lawfully claiming or to claim the same. *Assignors intend to convey, and by this instrument convey, to the Assignee all interest of whatsoever nature in all working interests and overriding royalty interest in all Oil and Gas Leases in Coffey County, Kansas, owned by them whether or not the same are specifically enumerated above with all oil field and oil and gas lease equipment owned by them in said County whether or not located on the leases above described,* or elsewhere in storage in said County, but title is warranted only to the specific interests above specified, and assignors retain their title to all minerals in place and the corresponding royalty (commonly referred to as land owners royalty) attributable thereto. The effective date of this Assignment is February 1, 1971, at 7:00 o'clock A.M.

/s/ *Grace Vannocker Owens*
Connie Sue Vannocker
Larry R. Vannocker

(Acknowledgment by Grace Vannocker Owens before notary public with seal impressed thereon dated Feb. 5, 1971, appears here.) (emphasis supplied.)

This assignment was filed for record in the office of the register of deeds of Coffey county on February 16, 1971.

It is important to note that in the first paragraph of the assignment, seven oil and gas leases were specifically described. Those leases are not involved on this appeal. In addition to the seven leases specifically described in the first paragraph, Owens was also the owner of a working interest in an oil and gas lease known as the Kufahl lease which was located on land in Coffey county. The Kufahl lease was not one of the leases specifically described in the assignment.

The second paragraph of the assignment states that the assignors intended to convey, and by this instrument conveyed to the assignee, "all interest of whatsoever nature in all working interests and overriding royalty interest in all Oil and Gas Leases in Coffey County, Kansas, owned by them whether or not the same are specifically enumerated above. . . ." The interest of Grace V. Owens in the Kufahl lease, being located in Coffey county, would be included under this general description.

On January 30, 1975, the same Grace V. Owens executed and delivered a second assignment of her working interest in the Kufahl lease to the defendant,

J.R. Burris. Prior to the date of that assignment, Burris personally checked the records in the office of the register of deeds and, following the date of the assignment to him, Burris secured an abstract of title to the real estate in question. Neither his personal inspection nor the abstract of title reflected the prior assignment to Tours.

The controversy on this appeal is between Tours and Burris over ownership of what had previously been Owens's interest in the Kufahl lease. It is the position of Tours that the assignment dated February 1, 1971, effectively conveyed from Owens to Tours, Owens's working interest in the Kufahl lease by virtue of the general description contained in paragraph two of that assignment. Tours then contends that the recording of that assignment in the office of the register of deeds of Coffey county gave constructive notice of such conveyance to subsequent purchasers, including Burris. Hence, Tours reasons, it is the owner of Owens's working interest in the Kufahl lease.

Burris admits that the general description and language used in the second paragraph of Owens's assignment to Tours was sufficient to effect a valid transfer of the Owens interest in the Kufahl lease to Tours *as between the parties to that instrument.* Burris contends, however, that the general language contained in the second paragraph of the assignment to Tours, as recorded, which failed to state with specificity the names of the lessor and lessee, the date of the lease, any legal description, and the recording data, was not sufficient to give constructive notice to a subsequent innocent purchaser for value without actual notice of the prior assignment. Burris argues that as a result of those omissions in the assignment to Tours, it was impossible for the register of deeds of Coffey county to identify the real estate involved and to make the proper entries in the numerical index. Accordingly, even though he checked the records at the courthouse, Burris was unaware of the assignment of the Kufahl lease to Tours and he did not learn of the prior conveyance until after he had purchased the rights from Grace V. Owens. The abstract of title also failed to reflect the prior assignment to Tours. Burris maintains that as a result of the omissions and the inadequate description of the interest in real estate to be assigned under the second paragraph of the assignment to Tours, the Tours assignment, as recorded, was not sufficient to give constructive notice to a subsequent innocent purchaser for value. It is upon this point that Burris prevailed before the district court. On appeal, the Court of Appeals held the general description contained in the assignment to Tours to be sufficient, when recorded, to give constructive notice to a subsequent purchaser for value, including Burris.

At the outset, it should be noted that a deed or other instrument in writing which is intended to convey an interest in real estate and which describes the property to be conveyed as "all of the grantor's property in a certain county," is commonly referred to as a "Mother Hubbard" instrument. The language used in the second paragraph of the assignment from Owens to Tours in which the assignor conveyed to the assignee "all interest of whatsoever nature in all working interests . . . in all Oil and Gas Leases in Coffey County, Kansas," is an example of a "Mother Hubbard" clause. The so-called Mother Hubbard clauses or descriptions are seldom used in this state, but in the past have been found to be convenient for death bed transfers and in situations where time is of the essence and specific information concerning the legal description of property to be conveyed is not available. Instruments of conveyance containing a description of the real estate conveyed in the form of a "Mother Hubbard" clause have been upheld in Kansas for many years as between the parties to the instrument. (In re Estate of Crawford, 176 Kan. 537, 271 P.2d 240; Bryant v. Fordyce, 147 Kan. 586, 78 P.2d 32.)

The parties in this case agree, and the Court of Appeals held, that the second paragraph of the assignment from Owens to Tours, providing that the assignors convey to the assignee all interests in all oil and gas leases in Coffey County, Kansas, owned by them, constituted a valid transfer of the Owens interest in the Kufahl lease to Tours *as between the parties to that instrument.* We agree. We also agree with the parties and the Court of Appeals that a single instrument, properly executed, acknowledged, and delivered, may convey separate tracts by specific description and by general description capable of being made specific, where the clear intent of the language used is to do so. We agree that a subsequent purchaser, who has *actual* notice or knowledge of such an instrument, is bound thereby and takes subject to the rights of the assignee or grantor.

This case involves a legal question which is one of first impression in this court. As noted above, the issue presented is whether or not the recording of an instrument of conveyance which uses a "Mother Hubbard" clause to describe the property conveyed, constitutes *constructive notice to a subsequent purchaser.* The determination of this issue requires us to examine the pertinent Kansas statutes covering the conveyance of interests in land and the statutory provisions for recording the same. . . .

The recordation of instruments of conveyance and the effect of recordation is covered in part by K.S.A. 58-2221, 58-2222, and 58-2223. These statutes are directly involved in this case and are as follows:

58-2221. *Recordation of instruments conveying or affecting real estate; duties of register of deeds.* Every instrument in writing that conveys real estate, any estate or interest created by an oil and gas lease, or whereby any real estate, may be affected, proved or acknowledged, and certified in the manner hereinbefore prescribed, may be recorded in the office of register of deeds of the county in which such real estate is situated: *Provided,* It shall be the duty of the register of deeds to file the same for record immediately, and in those counties where a numerical index is maintained in his or her office the register of deeds shall compare such instrument, before copying the same in the record, with the last record of transfer in his or her office of the property described and if the register of deeds finds such instrument contains apparent errors, he or she shall not record the same until he or she shall have notified the grantee where such notice is reasonably possible.

The grantor, lessor, grantee or lessee or any other person conveying or receiving real property or other interest in real property upon recording the instrument in the office of register of deeds shall furnish the register of deeds the full name and last known post-office address of the person to whom the property is conveyed or his or her designee. The register of deeds shall forward such information to the county clerk of the county who shall make any necessary changes in address records for mailing tax statements.

58-2222. *Same; filing imparts notice.* Every such instrument in writing, certified and recorded in the manner hereinbefore prescribed, shall, from the time of filing the same with the register

COFFEY COUNTY KANSAS

GENERAL INDEX

LOCKWOOD CO., INC., ATCHISON 104143-4-89

TIME OF RECEPTION				GRANTOR	GRANTEE
Year	Month	Day	Hour	Part		
1971	Feb.	16	8:50	A.M.	Owens, Grace Vanocker et al	International Tours, Inc.

INSTRUMENT	RECORDED		DESCRIPTION OF PROPERTY
	Vol.	Page	
Assign. of int. by Robt. Vanocker	13 016	1/2-115	*(handwritten legal descriptions)*

Above is the entry in the grantor index of the assignment from Owens to Tours. The land involved is described by reference to the United States Government Survey. Observe that land involved in the Wiley lease, referred to in the case, is described in the index as NE4 (northeast quarter) in 14-23-14 (Section 14, Township 23, Range 14). The other tracts were described by similar references. The Kufahl land did not come within the legal descriptions mentioned in the index.

of deeds for record, impart notice to all persons of the content thereof; and all subsequent purchasers and mortgagees shall be deemed to purchase with notice.

    58-2223. *Same; unrecorded instrument valid only between parties having actual notice.* No such instrument in writing shall be valid, except between the parties thereto, and such as have actual notice thereof, until the same shall be deposited with the register of deeds for record.

    . . . [W]e must also consider the Kansas statutes which govern the custody and the recordation of instruments of conveyance, and the duties of the register of deeds in regard thereto, as contained at K.S.A. 19-1201 through K.S.A. 19-1219. We will discuss only those statutes which we deem pertinent in the present controversy. . . . K.S.A. 19-1205 requires the register of deeds to keep a general index, direct and inverted, in his office. The register is required to record in the general index under the appropriate heading the names of grantors and grantees, the nature of the instrument, the volume and page where recorded, and, where appropriate, *a description of the tract.*

    K.S.A. 19-1207 requires the register to keep a book of plats with an index thereof. K.S.A. 19-1209 provides that the county commissioners of any county may order the register of deeds to furnish a numerical index containing "the name of the instrument, the name of the grantor, the name of the grantee, *a brief description of the property,* and the volume and page in which each instrument indexed is recorded." K.S.A. 19-1210 makes it the duty of the register to make correct entries in the numerical index, of all instruments recorded concerning real estate, under the appropriate headings, and "*in the subdivision devoted to the particular quarter section described in the instrument making the conveyance.*"[2]

    . . . It . . . seems obvious to us that the purpose of the statutes authorizing the recording of instruments of conveyance is to impart to a subsequent purchaser notice of instruments which affect the title to a *specific tract of land* in which the subsequent purchaser is interested at the time. From a reading of all of the statutory provisions together, we have concluded that the legislature intended that recorded instruments of conveyance, to impart constructive notice to a subsequent purchaser or mortgagee, should describe the land conveyed with sufficient specificity so that the specific land conveyed can be identified. . . . A description of the property conveyed should be considered sufficient if it identifies the property or affords the means of identification within the instrument itself or by specific reference to other instruments recorded in the office of the register of deeds. Such a specific description of the property conveyed is required in order to impart constructive notice to a subsequent purchaser.

---

    2. Observe that the Kansas statutes require each county to maintain a grantor-grantee index ("a general index, direct and inverted"). The statutes give the counties the option of establishing, in addition, a tract ("numerical") index by quarter sections of the U.S. government survey (see pages 706-709). An index by quarter sections is better than no tract index at all, but such an index contains references to instruments affecting land in the quarter section other than the land the searcher is interested in.

    Where tract indexes are available, the jurisdictions are split over whether the title searcher must search the tract index as well as the grantor-grantee index and over whether the searcher can rely on the tract index alone and not search the grantor-grantee index. In some states only recordation in the grantor-grantee index gives constructive notice.—EDS.

Again, we wish to emphasize that an instrument which contains a "Mother Hubbard" clause, describing the property conveyed in the general language involved here, is valid, enforceable, and effectively transfers the entire property interest as between the parties to the instrument. Such a transfer is not effective as to subsequent purchasers and mortgagees unless they have *actual* knowledge of the transfer. If, because of emergency, it becomes necessary to use a "Mother Hubbard" clause in an instrument of conveyance, the grantee may take steps to protect his title against subsequent purchasers. He may take possession of the property. Also, as soon as a specific description can be obtained, the grantee may identify the specific property covered by the conveyance by filing an affidavit or other appropriate instrument or document with the register of deeds.

We also wish to make it clear that in situations where an instrument of conveyance containing a sufficient description of the property conveyed is duly recorded but not properly indexed, the fact that it was not properly indexed by the register of deeds will not prevent constructive notice under the provisions of K.S.A. 58-2222. (See Gas Co. v. Harris, 79 Kan. 167, 100 Pac. 72.)

From what we have said above, it follows that the recording of the assignment from Owens to Tours, which did not describe with sufficient specificity the property covered by the conveyance, was not sufficient to impart constructive notice to a subsequent purchaser such as J.R. Burris in the present case. Since Burris had no *actual* knowledge of the prior assignment from Owens to Tours, the later assignment to Burris prevails over the assignment from Owens to Tours.

The judgment of the Court of Appeals is reversed and the judgment of the district court is affirmed.

NOTES AND QUESTIONS

1. Note that the Kansas court states in the third paragraph from the end of its opinion that "the fact that it [a deed] was not properly indexed by the register of deeds will not prevent constructive notice." 4 American Law Property §17.25 (1952) states that:

> [T]he rule appears to be well established that in the absence of statutory provision to that effect, an index is not an essential part of the record. In other words, a purchaser is charged with constructive notice of a record even though there is no official index which will direct him to it.

Is this a sound rule? See Dyer v. Martinez, 54 Cal. Rptr. 3d 907 (Cal. App. 2007) (rejecting the rule on the ground that a title search could not have disclosed the *lis pendens* in the index); Howard Sav. Bank v. Brunson, 582 A.2d 1305 (N.J. Super. Ct. 1990) (rejecting rule); Leeds Bldg. Products, Inc. v. Sears Mortgage Corp., 477 S.E.2d 565 (Ga. 1996) (approving rule); First Citizens National Bank v. Sherwood, 879 A.2d 178, 182 (Pa. 2005) (applying rule). Suppose that a mortgagee records its mortgage, the mortgage is properly indexed in the grantor-grantee index, but it is not recorded in the tract index. Is it "properly recorded" so as to provide constructive notice to subsequent mortgagees? See MidCountry

Bank v. Krueger, 782 N.W.2d 238 (Minn. 2010) (mortgage properly recorded and provides constructive notice).

2. Should the recorder of deeds be liable for negligence if the recorder fails to index a deed properly? In most states the recorder is protected by the doctrine of governmental immunity. See, e.g., Antonis v. Liberati, 821 A.2d 666 (Pa. Commw. Ct. 2003) (recorder immune under doctrine of sovereign immunity).

3. In Luthi v. Evans, Grace Owens assigned her working interest in the Kufahl lease twice. The first assignee, Tours, lost to the second assignee, Burris. Does Tours have any claim against Owens? Under principles of restitution, Tours can have a constructive trust imposed upon Owens to prevent Owens's unjust enrichment. Since Owens sold Tours's oil and gas interest to Burris, Owens must give Tours the amount Owens received from Burris.

Compare Question 3, page 127, where the same principle is incidentally involved. When the finder of a jewel sells the jewel, the finder must give the proceeds of the sale to the true owner.

NOTE: DESCRIPTION BY GOVERNMENT SURVEY

On the formation of the Union it became federal government policy, initiated by the Continental Congress in 1785, to make no disposition of lands in the public domain until the lands were surveyed and a plat of the survey was filed in the General Land Office. This great survey, using a method adapted by Thomas Jefferson[3] from earlier New England surveys, was as remarkable in its own time as Domesday Book had been 700 years earlier. It became the basis of land description in Alabama, Florida, Mississippi, in all states east of the Mississippi

---

3. Thomas Jefferson, principal supporter of the L'Enfant gridiron plan for Washington, D.C., is the intellectual father of the gridiron plan of development in America. Jefferson thought that a rectangular survey was easy to lay out, comprehensible by unsophisticated settlers, and, like geometry, a thing of beauty. In addition, the imposition of a formal rectilinear order on the wilderness served social purposes. It encouraged division of land into small uniform tracts, which could be—and were—given to soldiers who had fought in the Continental army. By act of Congress, section 16 of each township in the survey was granted to each of the states formed out of the territory for the purpose of supporting public schools. All this reflected Jefferson's belief that the future of the country lay with small rural landowners, coming together in townships with the school section at the center, all active in the democratic process. The grid system, as Jefferson conceived it, was a device for the promotion of an agrarian egalitarian society. As it turned out, however, the grid system also was ideally suited to the land speculation that gripped the country in the nineteenth century; nationally surveyed land was easy to describe in deeds and sell from the auctioneer's block.

Jefferson's faithful devotion to the gridiron plan also resulted in the most characteristic design of our urban environment. Unlike European cities, with their winding streets of uneven widths, American cities were, until late in the nineteenth century, built in monotonous conformance to the grid system; almost all were Jeffersonian. The most audacious application of the grid occurred in San Francisco, where streets charge straight up impossibly steep slopes and plunge down the other side, totally oblivious of the topography of the place. This led to the invention of that unique San Francisco carryall, the cable car, to take people up and down the hills.

In defense of Jefferson, in these days when the grid is looked upon by city planners as dull and unimaginative, it should be noted that he suggested a checkerboard plan, with the black squares for development and the white ones for open space. But in the few cities where this idea was followed, the open squares proved too great a temptation as building sites, and in time they were obliterated. An exception is Savannah, Georgia, where open squares still survive, providing breathing room in one of our most architecturally interesting cities. See John W. Reps, The Making of Urban America: A History of City Planning in the United States 294-324 (1965).

River and north of the Ohio River, in all states west of the Mississippi except Texas, and in portions of a few states that were never a part of the public domain because they were embraced in grants by prior governments. This survey did not include the original 13 colonies nor Kentucky, Maine, Tennessee, Vermont, and West Virginia, and land descriptions in those states are not based on the U.S. Government Survey. See 3 American Law of Property §12.100 (1952).

All of the public land in the United States in the areas above described was first surveyed into rectangular tracts by running parallel lines north and south and by crossing them at approximately right angles with other parallel lines so as to form rectangles six miles square. The first north and south line established for any surveyed area was a selected true meridian, which is called a *principal* or *prime meridian*. There are 34 such meridians in the area surveyed. Parallel to the principal meridian, running north and south, are *range lines*. They are six miles apart, and the six-mile strips bounded by the range lines are called *ranges*. For each principal meridian there is a *base line* running east and west on a true parallel of latitude. Parallel to the base line, at six-mile intervals, are *township lines*. The six-mile strips bounded by township lines are called *townships*, as also are the six-mile squares formed by the intersection of range and township lines. These townships are for survey purposes only and do not necessarily coincide with any unit of political subdivision or municipality. Each survey township is numbered and

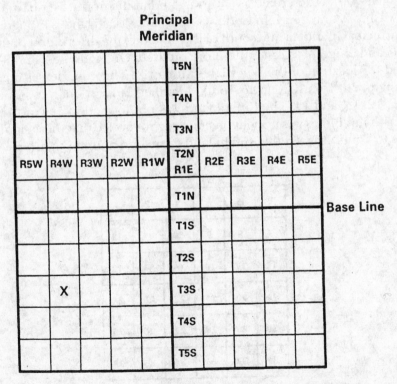

Figure 8-1
Range and Township Lines

located by describing its location north or south of the base line and east or west of the principal meridian. Thus on the chart (Figure 8-1) illustrating a township grid pattern, an X is placed on Township 3 South, Range 4 West of the Principal Meridian. Can you spot Township 4 North, Range 1 West?

Since the curvature of the earth causes all lines running north and south to converge toward the north, correction lines are run at intervals of 24 miles north and south of the base line to avoid an accumulation of errors. As a consequence, not all townships are exactly square, and some quarter sections are slightly larger than others.

Each township was surveyed into 36 tracts called *sections*, each one-mile square and containing, as near as may be, 640 acres. The sections are numbered consecutively, beginning with section 1 in the northeast corner of the township and proceeding west to section 6; thence back to the east in the next tier down numbering 7 through 12; and so on back and forth until section 36 is reached in the southeast corner. The section corners are marked by monuments or stakes, and halfway between these monuments were placed other markers called "quarter-corners." Imaginary lines drawn from these latter markers divide the section into quarter sections of 160 acres each. Quarter sections were not further subdivided by the government survey, but they may be divided further in accordance with rules laid down by the General Land Office.

Observe that in Luthi v. Evans the Wiley lease, which Owens assigned to Tours (pages 699-700), is described as covering land in the northeast quarter of section 14, township 23, range 14. In Coffey County, Kansas, all land is located east of the sixth principal meridian and south of the baseline; the description of township 23 as *south* and range 14 as *east* is therefore omitted. On Figures 8-2 and 8-3, we have marked the location of the Wiley land with an X. The other leases mentioned in the assignment from Owens to Tours described land in quarter sections in sections 1, 12, 13, and 14. The Kufahl land was not located in any of these quarter sections. Thus Burris was not put on constructive notice that the assignment from Owens to Tours affected the Kufahl land located in another quarter section.

6	5	4	3	2	1
7	8	9	10	11	12
18	17	16	15	14ₓ	13
19	20	21	22	23	24
30	29	28	27	26	25
31	32	33	34	35	36

Figure 8-2
Sections in Township 23S, Range 14E

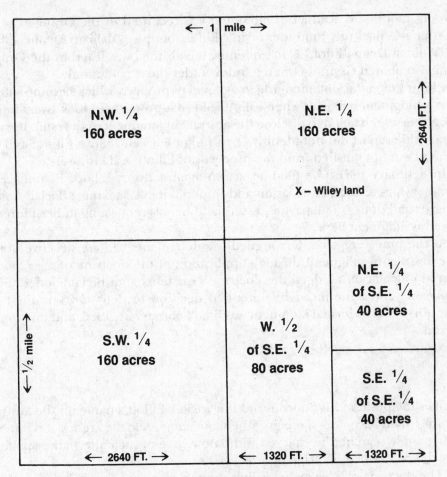

Figure 8-3
Enlargement of Section 14, Township 23S, Range 14E

Orr v. Byers

Court of Appeal of California, Fourth District, 1988
244 Cal. Rptr. 13

SONENSHINE, J. The question presented in this appeal is whether an abstract of judgment containing a misspelled name imparts constructive notice of its contents under the doctrine of *idem sonans*. We conclude it does not and, accordingly, affirm the trial court's ruling.

I.

The facts are not in dispute. In October 1978, James Orr obtained a judgment in excess of $50,000 against William Elliott. The written judgment prepared by Orr's attorney identified Elliott erroneously as "William Duane Elliot." The following month, an abstract of judgment was recorded in the Orange County Recorder's Office, this time identifying Elliott both as "William Duane Elliot" and "William Duane Eliot." Consequently, the abstract was listed in the Orange County Combined Grantor-Grantee Index under those names only.

Elliott thereafter obtained title to a parcel of property which became subject to Orr's judgment lien. But when Elliott sold that property to Rick Byers in July 1979, a title search failed to disclose the abstract of judgment. As a result, the preliminary title report did not identify Orr's judgment lien against Elliott, and the judgment was not satisfied from the proceeds of Elliott's sale to Byers.

In February 1981, Orr filed an action against Byers, Elliott, Pomona First Federal Savings & Loan Association and Imperial Bank[4] seeking a declaration of the rights and duties of all parties. Essentially, he was requesting judicial foreclosure of his judgment lien.

At the June 1985 trial, Orr argued the defendants had constructive notice of the abstract of judgment through application of the doctrine of *idem sonans.* The trial judge acknowledged the doctrine's existence, but he concluded it was inapplicable and announced his intended decision to deny Orr's request for declaratory relief. A formal judgment was filed February 21, 1986, and this appeal followed.[5]

II.

Orr takes the position his attorney did not *misspell* Elliott's name on the abstract but rather, used *alternative spellings* of the same name. And, he argues, it is imperative that a title searcher be charged with knowledge of such alternative spellings under the established doctrine of *idem sonans.*

"The doctrine of *idem sonans* is that though a person's name has been inaccurately written, the identity of such person will be presumed from the similarity of sounds between the correct pronunciation and the pronunciation as written. Therefore, absolute accuracy in spelling names is not required in legal proceedings, and if the pronunciations are practically alike, the rule of *idem sonans* is applicable. (46 Cal. Jur. 3d, Names, §4, p. 110, fns. omitted; see also Napa State Hospital v. Dasso, 153 Cal. 698, 701, 96 P. 355 (1908)). The rule is inapplicable, however, under circumstances "where the written name is material." (Emeric v. Alvarado, 90 Cal. 444, 466, 27 P. 356 (1891)). "[T]o be material, [a variance] must be such as has misled the opposite party to his prejudice." (Black's Law Dict., p. 671 (5th ed. 1979)).

4. As part of the transaction, Byers borrowed $120,000 from Pomona First Federal which held a first trust deed on the property. Byers thereafter obtained a line of credit with Imperial Bank and delivered to Imperial a trust deed encumbering the property. Imperial ultimately acquired the property through foreclosure proceedings.

5. Respondents inform us the appellant in this case is actually the law firm which prepared the erroneous abstract of judgment. Apparently, . . . Orr's malpractice action against that firm was settled prior to trial of this case, with Orr's cause of action against Byers being assigned to the law firm in exchange for payment of a sum equal to the amount of the judgment lien.

Orr insists all that is required to invoke the doctrine is a similarity in pronunciation; thus, the trial court erred in refusing to do so here. We cannot agree. There is no question the names Eliot, Elliot and Elliott are *idem sonans*. But we refuse to extend the doctrine's application in the manner urged.

In virtually all of the cases cited by Orr, the doctrine was applied solely to establish sameness of identity. (See, e.g., Kriste v. International Sav. etc. Bk., 17 Cal. App. 301, 119 P. 666 (1911), Galliano v. Kilfoy, 94 Cal. 86, 29 P. 416 (1892), Hall v. Rice, 64 Cal. 443, 1 P. 891 (1884).) Furthermore, and contrary to Orr's assertion, the rule does not have "widespread application" in the area of real property law. Simply stated, the doctrine of *idem sonans* remains viable for purposes of identification. But it has not, to our knowledge, been applied in this state to give constructive notice to good faith purchasers for value. . . .

Nor are we impressed with the reasoning behind the decision in Green v. Meyers, 98 Mo. App. 438, 72 S.W. 128 (1903), a case Orr urges us to follow. In *Green*, a purchaser of property from an individual named Eleanor G. Sibert was charged with notice of a judgment against Sibert appearing in the judgment abstract as entered against E.G. Seibert. The appellate court concluded: "The names Seibert and Sibert are not only *idem sonans*—they not only sound the same in utterance—but they are, practically, the same name. Therefore, no matter which way it may be spelled by the party, . . . or by the recording officer, it is notice. It is common knowledge that proper names are spelled in a variety of ways, and everybody is presumed to have such knowledge. Thus, 'Reed,' 'Reid,' and 'Read,' are different ways of spelling one name. Manifestly, the record of a judgment against 'Reed' is notice to a subsequent purchaser from the same man signing the deed as 'Reid.' Persons searching the judgment docket for liens ought to know the different forms in which the same name may be spelled, and to make their searches accordingly, unless, indeed, the spelling is so entirely unusual that a person cannot be expected to think of it." (Id., 72 S.W. at p. 129.)

The *Green* court recognized "[s]ome confusion has arisen in the authorities as to whether the rule as to *idem sonans* applies to records. It is said that the law of notice by record is addressed to the eye and not the ear, and that therefore the rule cannot apply to records. It is true that record notice is principally a matter of sight and not sound. Yet it is, above all, a matter for the consideration of the mind, and if the record of a name spelled in one way should directly suggest to the ordinary mind that it is also commonly spelled another way, the searcher should be charged with whatever the record showed in some other spelling under the same capital letter. It is not necessary to decide here whether this would be carried out to the extent of holding that the searcher for information in the record should look under some other capital for another mode of finding the same name, as, for instance, 'Kane' and 'Cain,' 'Phelps' and 'Felps,' etc. But that the rule of *idem sonans* has been applied to records has been too often accepted by the supreme court of this state for us to question it." (Ibid.) . . .

In our view, the case at bar presents a situation where the written name is material. We therefore decline to follow *Green*'s holding which, in essence, dispenses with the formalities of record notice. Moreover, the *Green* opinion entirely ignores the added burden placed on the searcher who is charged with knowledge of the alternative spellings.

In refusing to apply the doctrine here, the trial judge found requiring a title searcher to comb the records for other spellings of the same name would place an undue burden on the transfer of property.[6] The court observed "if you put the burden on those people in addition to what comes up when the name is properly spelled, to track down and satisfy themselves about whatever comes up when the name is improperly spelled in all different ways that it might be improperly spelled, it leads to, I think, an unjustifiable burden." We agree.

Indeed, not every name disclosed by a search corresponds to the individual who is subject to the lien. Thus, if a search uncovered alternative spellings of the same name, the searcher would be required to locate every lien against every individual with a name similar to the one being searched and determine whether that lien impacted the transaction under consideration.

We reject Orr's contention "modern technology has provided a solution to the burden at relative inexpense to the title industry." He advocates use of a system known as Soundex whereby each last name is reduced to a code consisting of a letter and a three digit number. He argues use of that system here would have revealed all three spelling variations.

Testimony at trial disclosed the Soundex system is presently utilized by two title companies in the area, and that the doctrine of *idem sonans* "is one of the reasons why some companies use [that] system." But the same witness also told of a drawback to its use: According to Donald Henley, a developer of software and computer systems for the title insurance industry, "the problem with Soundex is that you may get a lot of extraneous names if it is computer generated. And the task of going through all these names and determining which name affects your search, you know, can be lengthy if it is a popular name in a large county."

We conclude the burden is properly on the judgment creditor to take appropriate action to ensure the judgment lien will be satisfied. The procedure is simple enough. In fact, "[t]he judgment lien is one of the simplest and most effective means by which a judgment creditor may seek to secure payment of the judgment and establish a priority over other judgment creditors." (8 Witkin, Cal. Procedure, Enforcement of Judgment, §62, p.77 (3d ed. 1986), quoting from 16 Cal. Law Rev. Com. Reports, p. 1041.) Indeed, to rule otherwise is to grant the judgment creditor a "free ride."

---

6. Orr asserts he "is not suggesting that a search for each and every possible misspelling of a name be undertaken." Rather, he contends "when a name consists of a double consonant (especially a name which is regularly spelled with either single or double consonants without phonetic dissimilarity, like Elliott), it is reasonable to require and simple for the searcher to look for listings under these variations in spelling."

At oral argument, Orr's attorney displayed a local telephone directory which he brought to illustrate his position the practice of searching for alternative spellings is commonplace today. Indeed, the following notations appear in the November 1987 edition of the Pacific Bell White Pages for Orange County Central & North: (1) directly above the listings for "Eliot," are the words "See Also-Elliot-Elliott," (2) preceding the listings for "Elliot," appear the words "See Also-Eliot-Elliott," and (3) before the name "Elliott," the reader is instructed to "See Also-Eliot-Eliot."

As respondents succinctly state, Orr asks us "to change the law of constructive notice to accommodate [his] error in such a way that future title searches will be required to be performed only by trained individuals with elaborate and expensive equipment at their disposal or else to go uninsured in a world where prudence demands title insurance. Neither result is satisfactory, especially considering that the simple alternative is to require [judgment creditors] simply to spell the names of their judgment debtors properly."

Judgment affirmed. Respondents to receive costs.

NOTES AND PROBLEM

1. For discussion of *idem sonans* and its application to the title searcher, see 4 American Law of Property §17.18 (1952), stating that names like that of the record owner, spelled differently but pronounced alike, give constructive notice so long as they begin with the same letter. See also id. §18.30. Brady v. Mullen, 649 A.2d 47 (N.H. 1994), following Orr v. Byers, rejects the doctrine of *idem sonans* in searching attachment lien indexes. See also Coco v. Ranalletta, 733 N.Y.S.2d 849 (Sup. Ct. 2001), aff'd, 759 N.Y.S.2d 274 (App. Div. 2003); Lively v. Northfield Savings Bank, 940 A.2d 700 (Vt. 2007).

Judgment liens and federal tax liens become liens on all the debtor's land located in the county where the lien is filed. Such liens are filed in the index under the name of the debtor. Do you see why searching a grantor-grantee index and not a tract index is required to find judgment liens and federal tax liens?

2. Elizabeth Taylor owns Whiteacre, and the record title is in her name. Elizabeth marries Eddie Fisher and gives a mortgage on Whiteacre to Carol Burnett, signing the mortgage "Elizabeth Taylor Fisher."[7] This mortgage is indexed under the name of "Fisher." Subsequently Elizabeth divorces Eddie, resumes her maiden name, and sells Whiteacre to Adam Sandler, signing the deed, "Elizabeth Taylor." Sandler has no actual notice of the Burnett mortgage. In a jurisdiction where indexing is a part of the record, does Sandler prevail over Burnett?

Suppose that Elizabeth had signed the mortgage "Elizabeth Taylor-Fisher," and that the mortgage had been indexed under the name of "Taylor-Fisher." Would this indexing give constructive notice to Sandler? See Teschke v. Keller, 650 N.E.2d 1279 (Mass. App. 1995) (holding indexing under hyphenated name insufficient to provide constructive notice of claims against either of the unhyphenated versions of the debtor's name).

Suppose that after the divorce and before the conveyance to Sandler, Taylor's landlord had obtained a judgment against Betty Taylor d/b/a Betty Taylor Jewelry. The name Betty was used in the judgment because the lease was signed that way. The judgment created a lien on all Taylor's property, and the judgment

---

7. If the late real Elizabeth Taylor had been involved, would the title searcher have to look under the names of all her husbands—Hilton, Wilding, Todd, Fisher, Burton, Burton again, Warner, and Fortensky? How would the searcher know the dates of her marriages and the dates of her divorces or husbands' deaths? And suppose she continued to use a husband's name after his death or divorce?

was filed and indexed under the name of "Betty Taylor." The title examiner hired by Sandler does not search under the name "Betty Taylor." Does Taylor's landlord prevail over Sandler? Is the title examiner liable? See J.I. Case Credit v. Barton, 621 F. Supp. 610 (E.D. Ark. 1985) (holding examiner must search under diminutives and noting that documents reciting an erroneous middle initial must also be read); Bank of America v. DE&S Properties, Inc., 2010 WL 5657039 (Pa. Com. Pl. Aug. 9, 2010) (holding lien not discharged when recorded under "Alex" rather "Aleksander"). Compare Frederick Ward Assocs., Inc. v. Venture, Inc., 636 A.2d 496 (Md. Ct. Spec. App. 1994) (holding instrument indexed under nickname or incorrect first name that is "sufficiently dissimilar" to record name of owner is not valid against subsequent bona fide purchaser).

3. *Computerized indexes.* In recent years, in urban counties with many daily real estate transactions, recording clerks have begun to type the indexing information into a computer (and not enter it by hand, as was done in Luthi v. Evans). This enables the title searcher to search the grantor-grantee indexes by computer back to the date computer entries began. When older index books are consolidated, they will be consolidated into the computer (much as library card catalogs have been replaced by computer retrieval systems). In a few localities, the copies of deeds are micrographically stored, and the computer system permits the deed itself to be called up on the screen.

In some localities computerized tract indexes have been established. This requires giving each parcel a parcel identification number (PIN). The tax assessor's number may be used as a PIN, or the PIN may be derived from aerial photography, surveyor's coordinates, or field inspection. Parcel identification numbers are not based on legal descriptions. In 1973, Paul E. Basye, A Uniform Land Parcel Identifier—Its Potential for All Our Land Records, 22 Am. U. L. Rev. 251 (1973), reported that the recorder's office in Suffolk County, Massachusetts (Boston), records approximately 7,000 instruments a month; in Cook County, Illinois (Chicago), about 15,000 documents a month; and in Los Angeles County between 5,000 and 6,000 instruments a day! These data were collected before the surge in condominium sales, which has generated a significant increase in the amount of paper recorded. Obviously, to avoid being overwhelmed by growing amounts of paper, recording offices in urban counties will necessarily turn to computerization. Old records will probably not be computerized in public record offices because of the high cost, and complete computerization will take a generation or two to be phased in. Indeed, a more recent article reports between 8,000 and 10,000 electronic documents are recorded every day. See David E. Ewan & Mark Ladd, Race to the (Virtual) Courthouse: How Standards Drive Electronic Recording of Real Property Documents, Prob. & Prop., Feb. 2008, at 8; see also Brian Henry & Mary Dunn, Understanding Electronic Recording: Current Legislation and Trends, 38 Mich. Real Prop. Rev. 55 (2011).

For an examination of some of the historical and technological aspects of land recordation systems, see Charles Szypszak, Real Estate Records, the Captive Public, and Opportunities for the Public Good, 43 Gonz. L. Rev. 5 (2007).

3. Types of Recording Acts

The earliest type of recording act was what we today call a race statute. Under a race statute, as between successive purchasers of Blackacre, the person who wins the race to record prevails. Whether a subsequent purchaser has actual knowledge of the prior purchaser's claim is irrelevant. Thus:

> *Example 2. O*, owner of Blackacre, conveys Blackacre to *A*, who does not record the deed. *O* subsequently conveys Blackacre to *B* for a valuable consideration. *B* actually knows of the deed to *A*. *B* records the deed from *O* to *B*. Under a race statute, *B* prevails over *A*, and *B* owns Blackacre.

The virtue of a race statute for the title searcher is that it limits inquiry into matters off the record. The question of who knew what (in *Example 2*, whether *B* actually knew of the deed to *A*), which is often difficult to ascertain and harder to prove, is not relevant. Transfer of title is more efficient where off-record inquiries are eliminated. Race statutes applicable to conveyances generally exist today only in Louisiana and North Carolina. A few other states have race statutes applicable to mortgages, but notice or race-notice statutes for deeds. The second type of recording statute is a *notice statute* (see the Florida statute set forth on page 717 below). It developed from judicial decisions interpreting race statutes. Early in the nineteenth century some courts held that if a subsequent purchaser had notice of a prior unrecorded instrument, the purchaser could not prevail over the prior grantee, for such would work a fraud on the prior grantee.[8] In time, legislatures amended the statutes to reflect the judicial interpretation. In *Example 2* above, if a notice statute were applicable, *B* would not prevail over *A* because *B* has notice of *A*'s prior deed.

In addition to protecting only subsequent purchasers without notice, a notice statute differs from a race statute in another respect. A race statute protects a subsequent purchaser only if the subsequent purchaser records first. A notice statute protects a subsequent purchaser against prior unrecorded instruments even though the subsequent purchaser fails to record (read the Florida statute on page 717 carefully and you will see that this is so). Thus:

> *Example 3. O*, owner of Blackacre, conveys Blackacre to *A*, who does not record the deed. *O* subsequently conveys Blackacre to *B* for a valuable consideration. *B* has no knowledge of *A*'s deed. Under a notice statute, *B* prevails over *A* even though *B* does not record the deed from *O* to *B*.

---

8. For sharp criticism of the courts for having defeated the early race statutes by introducing the equitable doctrine of notice, see Francis S. Philbrick, Limits of Record Search and Therefore of Notice (pt. 1), 93 U. Pa. L. Rev. 125 (1944).

You should not underestimate the difficulties of proving that a subsequent purchaser did in fact have actual notice of a prior instrument when the purchaser claims to have had none. In Messersmith v. Smith, page 718, for example, how could you have shown that E.B. Seale did have actual notice?

For the sordid tale of a lawyer who falsely swore that, as a subsequent purchaser, he had no notice, but was undone by his wife in a subsequent divorce action, see Beavers v. Kaiser, 537 N.W.2d 653 (N.D. 1995); Beavers v. Walters, 537 N.W.2d 647 (N.D. 1995).

The virtue of a notice statute is its fairness as between two conflicting claimants, but inasmuch as the question of whether the subsequent purchaser has notice depends on facts not on record, notice statutes are less efficient than race statutes. In *Example 3*, for instance, suppose that, after the conveyance to *B* and before *B* records, *A* records his deed. Thereafter *C* desires to purchase from *B*. *C*, searching title, would find *A*'s deed on record, and *C* then would have to ascertain from facts off the record whether *B* had notice of *A*'s deed. If *B* did not have notice, *B* prevails over *A*, and *C* can buy from *B* and, standing in *B*'s shoes, prevail over *A*.[9]

The third type of recording statute is a *race-notice statute* (see the California statute set forth on page 717). Under a race-notice statute a subsequent purchaser is protected against prior unrecorded instruments only if the subsequent purchaser (1) is without notice of the prior instrument and (2) records before the prior instrument is recorded. The race-notice statute incorporates features of both a notice statute and a race statute. Thus:

> *Example 4. O*, owner of Blackacre, conveys Blackacre to *A*, who does not record the deed. *O* subsequently conveys Blackacre to *B*, who does not know of *A*'s deed. Then *A* records. Then *B* records. *A* prevails over *B* because, even though *B* had no notice of *A*'s deed, *B* did not record before *A* did.

The virtues of a race-notice statute, compared to a race or notice statute, are debatable. It has been suggested that a race-notice statute tends to eliminate lawsuits turning on extrinsic evidence about which deed was delivered first. In *Example 3*, for instance, whether *A* or *B* wins depends upon whether *O* delivered *A*'s deed or *B*'s deed first. Under a race-notice statute, the allegation that *B*'s deed was delivered after *A*'s (or *A*'s after *B*'s) is irrelevant if one of the deeds has been recorded; the first to record wins. It has also been suggested that a race-notice statute is preferable because, by punishing nonrecording, it provides motivation to record, making the public records complete. See B. Taylor Mattis, Recording Acts: Anachronistic Reliance, 25 Real Prop., Prob. & Tr. J. 17, 94-101 (1990) (rejecting these arguments and concluding notice statute is preferable).

About half the states have notice statutes, and half have race-notice statutes. Among the notice jurisdictions are Illinois, Massachusetts, Texas, and Virginia; among the race-notice ones are Georgia, Michigan, New Jersey, and New York. For a listing of states by types of recording acts, see 4 American Law of Property §17.5 (1952 & Supp. 1977).

---

9. Why does *C* prevail over *A* in a notice jurisdiction when *A* records before *B* does? *A*'s recordation puts *C* on notice as to *A*'s deed so *C* cannot claim to be a subsequent purchaser without notice. The answer is: *C* claims protection under the *shelter rule*. A person who takes from a bona fide purchaser protected by the recording act has the same rights as his grantor. This rule is necessary if the recording act is to give *B* the benefit of his bargain by protecting his market.

The shelter rule does not extend to *B*'s grantor, *O*, however. If *O* repurchased Blackacre from *B*, *O* would not prevail over *A*. There is too much risk of undiscoverable collusion between *O* and *B* to permit *B* to transfer the property back to his grantor freed of *A*'s claim. See Sun Valley Land & Minerals, Inc. v. Burt, 853 P.2d 607 (Idaho App. 1993).

Notice statute. Fla. Stat. Ann. §695.01(1) (West 2012):

> No conveyance, transfer or mortgage of real property, or of any interest therein, nor any lease for a term of one year or longer, shall be good and effectual in law or equity against creditors or subsequent purchasers for a valuable consideration and without notice, unless the same be recorded according to the law.

Race-notice statute. Cal. Civ. Code §1214 (West 2013):

> Every conveyance of real property or an estate for years therein, other than a lease for a term not exceeding one year, is void as against any subsequent purchaser or mortgagee of the same property, or any part thereof, in good faith and for a valuable consideration, whose conveyance is first duly recorded, and as against any judgment affecting the title, unless the conveyance shall have been duly recorded prior to the record of notice of action.

For further discussion of race, notice, and race-notice statutes, see Powell on Real Property §82.02[1][c] (Michael A. Wolf gen. ed. 2009).

PROBLEMS AND NOTE

1. *O* conveys Blackacre to *A*, who does not record. *O* subsequently dies, leaving *H* as her heir. *H* then conveys Blackacre to *B*, who records. *B* purchases for a valuable consideration and without notice of the deed from *O* to *A*. Who prevails? In the leading case of Earle v. Fiske, 103 Mass. 491 (1870), it was held that *B* prevails. But how can this be? If *H* did not inherit Blackacre from *O*, how can *H* convey Blackacre to *B*? See Burnett v. Holliday Bros., 305 S.E.2d 238 (S.C. 1983).

2. *O* conveys Whiteacre to *A*, who does not record. *O* subsequently conveys to *B*, who purchases in good faith and for a valuable consideration, but does not record. *A* then records and conveys to *C*. *C* purchases in good faith and for a valuable consideration. *B* records. *C* records. Who prevails under a notice statute? A race-notice statute?

3. *O*, owner of Blackacre, which is worth $50,000, borrows $10,000 from *A* and gives *A* a mortgage on Blackacre. *A* does not record. *O* then borrows $14,000 from *B* and, after telling *B* of the prior mortgage to *A*, gives *B* a mortgage on Blackacre. *B* records. *O* then borrows $5,000 from *C* and gives *C* a mortgage on Blackacre. *C* has no notice of *A*'s mortgage. *C* records.

Subsequently, Blackacre is discovered to be contaminated with hazardous wastes, and its value plummets. *O* defaults. Upon foreclosure sale, Blackacre sells for $20,000. How should this amount be distributed among *A*, *B*, and *C*? Suppose all of the figures in this problem, except for the original worth of $50,000, were $5,000. How should the fund be distributed? The dissenting opinion of Dixon, J., in Hoag v. Sayre, 33 N.J. Eq. 552 (1881), suggesting that the parties should be given their expectations, is the starting point for discussion by most commentators. See 2 Grant Gilmore, Security Interests in Personal Property §§39.1-39.4 (1965); 4 American Law of Property §17.33 (1952).

4. The lawyer or other agent in charge of closing a transaction is liable in negligence to the grantee for failure to record a deed promptly if the grantee

suffers as a result. See Antonis v. Liberati, 821 A.2d 666 (Pa. Commw. Ct. 2003); Meerhoff v. Huntington Mortgage Co., 658 N.E.2d 1109 (Ohio App. 1995). The lawyer may be liable to the buyer even though he is the lawyer for the seller. Some cases have held that lawyers performing title work are liable to reasonably foreseeable persons who detrimentally rely on the lawyer's title work. See Century 21 Deep South Properties, Ltd. v. Corson, 612 So. 2d 359 (Miss. 1993); Petrillo v. Bachenberg, 655 A.2d 1354 (N.J. 1995).

The actual copying by the recorder of a document into the records does not necessarily mean that the document is "recorded" within the terms of the recording act. If it is not authorized, it may not be "recorded" so as to give constructive notice. Almost without exception, statutes require that, in order for an instrument to enter the records, it must be acknowledged before a notary public or other official. In addition, some states require that a transfer tax must be paid before a deed is recorded. If the record does not show that the tax has been paid, a deed actually of record may be deemed not to be legally recorded.

Messersmith v. Smith

Supreme Court of North Dakota, 1953
60 N.W.2d 276

MORRIS, C.J. This is a statutory action to quiet title to three sections of land in Golden Valley County.[10] The records in the office of the register of deeds of that county disclose the following pertinent facts concerning the title: For some time prior to May 7, 1946, the record title owners of this property were Caroline Messersmith and Frederick Messersmith. On that date, Caroline Messersmith executed and delivered to Frederick Messersmith a quitclaim deed to the property which was not recorded until July 9, 1951. Between the date of that deed and the time of its recording the following occurred: On April 23, 1951, Caroline Messersmith, as lessor, executed a lease to Herbert B. Smith, Jr., lessee, which was recorded May 14, 1951. On May 7, 1951, Caroline Messersmith, a single woman, conveyed to Herbert B. Smith, Jr., by mineral deed containing a warranty of title, an undivided one-half interest in and to all oil, gas and other minerals in and under or that may be produced upon the land involved in this case. This deed was recorded May 26, 1951. On May 9, 1951, Herbert B. Smith, Jr., executed a mineral deed conveying to E.B. Seale an undivided one-half interest in all of the

---

10. Golden Valley County (pop. 2,000) is located in the badlands of western North Dakota, on the Montana border. In January 1951 Amerada Petroleum Corporation, drilling a discovery well some 100 miles from Golden Valley, found a "pint of oil," which was widely reported in the press. Drilling continued and on April 4, 1951, the Clarence Iverson Well No. 1 struck oil. Brokers, oil men, and speculators began moving into western North Dakota. Soon it was realized that the Williston oil basin, with vast quantities of oil, had been discovered. Golden Valley County, smack in the middle of the basin, began to run oil fever.—EDS.

**Caroline Messersmith's house in 1997, after Frederick Messersmith
moved out. This was the first house built on a platted street in
Dickinson.**

oil, gas and other minerals in and under or that may be produced upon the land. This deed was also recorded in the office of the Registry of Deeds of Golden Valley County, on May 26, 1951. Seale answered plaintiff's complaint by setting up his deed and claiming a one-half interest in the minerals as a purchaser without notice, actual or constructive, of plaintiff's claim. To this answer the plaintiff replied by way of a general denial and further alleged that the mineral deed by which Seale claims title is void; that it was never acknowledged, not entitled to record and was obtained by fraud, deceit and misrepresentation. The defendant Herbert B. Smith, Jr., defaulted.

For some time prior to the transactions herein noted, Caroline Messersmith and her nephew, Frederick S. Messersmith, were each the owner of an undivided one-half interest in this land, having acquired it by inheritance. The land was unimproved except for being fenced. It was never occupied as a homestead. Section 1 was leased to one tenant and Sections 3 and 11 to another. They used the land for grazing. One party had been a tenant for a number of years, paying $150 a year. The amount paid by the other tenant is not disclosed. The plaintiff lived in Chicago. Caroline Messersmith lived alone in the City of Dickinson where she had resided for many years. She looked after the renting of the land, both before and after she conveyed her interest therein to her nephew. She never told her tenants about the conveyance.

On April 23, 1951, the defendant Smith, accompanied by one King and his prospective wife, went to the Messersmith home and negotiated an oil and gas lease with Miss Messersmith covering the three sections of land involved herein. According to Miss Messersmith, all that was discussed that day concerned royalties. According to the testimony of Mr. Smith and Mr. King, the matter of the mineral deed was discussed.

Two or three days later, Smith and King returned. Again the testimony varies as to the subject of conversation. Miss Messersmith said it was about royalties. Smith and King say it was about a mineral deed for the purchase of her mineral rights. No agreement was reached during this conversation. On May 7, 1951, Smith returned alone and again talked with Miss Messersmith. As a result of this visit, Miss Messersmith executed a mineral deed for an undivided one-half interest in the oil, gas and minerals under the three sections of land. Smith says this deed was acknowledged before a notary public at her house. She says no notary public ever appeared there. She also says that Smith never told her she was signing a mineral deed and that she understood she was signing a "royalty transfer." The consideration paid for this deed was $1,400, which is still retained by Miss Messersmith. After leaving the house Smith discovered a slight error in the deed. The term "his heirs" was used for the term "her heirs." He returned to the home of Miss Messersmith the same day, explained the error to her, tore up the first deed, and prepared another in the same form, except that the error was corrected. According to Smith's testimony, he took the second deed to the same notary public to whom Miss Messersmith had acknowledged the execution of the first deed and the notary called Miss Messersmith for her acknowledgment over the telephone and then placed on the deed the usual notarial acknowledgment, including the notary's signature and seal. The notary, who took many acknowledgments about that time, has no independent recollection of either of these acknowledgments. It is the second deed that was recorded on May 26, 1951, and upon which the defendant, E.B. Seale, relied when he purchased from the defendant, Herbert B. Smith, Jr., the undivided one-half interest in the minerals under the land in question. . . .

The trial court found "that such deeds, or either of them, were not procured through fraud or false representation." The evidence does not warrant this court in disturbing that finding.

The determination that the mineral deed from Caroline Messersmith to Herbert B. Smith, Jr., was not fraudulently obtained by the grantee does not mean that the defendant, who in turn received a deed from Smith, is entitled to prevail as against the plaintiff in this action. At the time Miss Messersmith executed the mineral deed she owned no interest in the land, having previously conveyed her interest therein to the plaintiff. Smith in turn had no actual interest to convey to the defendant Seale. If Seale can assert title to any interest in the property in question, he must do so because the plaintiff's deed was not recorded until July 9, 1951, while the deed from Caroline Messersmith to Smith and the deed from Smith to the defendant Seale were recorded May 26, 1951, thus giving him a record title prior in time to that of the plaintiff. . . . The defendant Seale asserts that priority of record gives him a title superior to that of the plaintiff by virtue of the following statutory provision, Section 47-1941, NDRC 1943:

> Every conveyance of real estate not recorded as provided in section 47-1907 shall be void as against any subsequent purchaser in good faith, and for a valuable consideration, of the same real estate, or any part or portion thereof, whose conveyance, whether in the form of a warranty deed, or deed of bargain and sale, or deed of quitclaim and release, of the form in common use or otherwise, first is recorded, or as against an attachment levied thereon or any judgment lawfully obtained, at the suit of any party, against the person in whose name the title to such land appears of record, prior to the recording of such conveyance. The fact that such first recorded conveyance of such subsequent purchaser for a valuable consideration is in the form, or contains the terms, of a deed of quitclaim and release aforesaid, shall not affect the question of good faith of the subsequent purchaser, or be of itself notice to him of any unrecorded conveyance of the same real estate or any part thereof.

Section 47-1945, NDRC 1943, in part, provides:

> The deposit and recording of an instrument proved and certified according to the provisions of this chapter are constructive notice of the execution of such instrument to all purchasers and encumbrancers subsequent to the recording.

As against the seeming priority of record on the part of Seale's title, the plaintiff contends that the deed from Caroline Messersmith to Smith was never acknowledged and, not having been acknowledged, was not entitled to be recorded, and hence can confer no priority of record upon the grantee or subsequent purchasers from him.

It may be stated as a general rule that the recording of an instrument affecting the title to real estate which does not meet the statutory requirements of the recording laws affords no constructive notice. J.I. Case Co. v. Sax Motor Co., 64 N.D. 757, 256 N.W. 219; First National Bank v. Casselton Realty & Investment Co., 44 N.D. 353, 175 N.W. 720, 29 A.L.R. 911. The applicability of the rule is easily determined where the defect appears on the face of the instrument, but difficulty frequently arises where the defect is latent. Perhaps the most common instance of this nature arises when an instrument is placed of record bearing a certificate of acknowledgment sufficient on its face despite the fact that the statutory procedure for acknowledgment has not been followed. See Annotations 19 A.L.R. 1074; 72 A.L.R. 1039.

The certificate of acknowledgment on the mineral deed to Smith, while it is presumed to state the truth, is not conclusive as to the fact of actual acknowledgment by the grantor.

In Severtson v. Peoples, 28 N.D. 372, 148 N.W. 1054, 1055, this court, in the syllabus, said:

> 4. A certificate of acknowledgment, regular on its face, is presumed to state the truth; and proof to overthrow such certificate must be very strong and convincing, and the burden of overthrowing the same is upon the party attacking the truth of such certificate. 5. To constitute an acknowledgment, the grantor must appear before the officer for the purpose of acknowledging the instrument, and such grantor must, in some manner with a view to giving it authenticity, make an admission to the officer of the fact that he had executed such instrument. 6. Where, in fact, the grantor has never appeared before the officer and acknowledged the execution of the instrument, evidence showing such fact is admissible, even as against an innocent purchaser for value and without notice.

It avails the purchaser nothing to point out that a deed is valid between the parties though not acknowledged by the grantor—see Bumann v. Burleigh County, 73 N.D. 655, 18 N.W.2d 10—for Caroline Messersmith, having previously conveyed to the plaintiff, had no title. The condition of the title is such that Seale must rely wholly upon his position as an innocent purchaser under the recording act.

Before a deed to real property can be recorded its execution must be established in one of the ways prescribed by Section 47-1903, NDRC 1943. No attempt was made to prove the execution of this deed other than "by acknowledgment by the person executing the same." It is the fact of acknowledgment that the statute requires as a condition precedent to recording. Subsequent sections of Chapter 47-19, NDRC 1943, prescribe before whom and how proof of the fact of acknowledgment may be made. A general form of certificate of acknowledgment is set forth in Section 47-1927. The certificate on the mineral deed follows this form and states:

> On this 7th day of May, in the year 1951, before me personally appeared Caroline Messersmith, known to me to be the person described in and who executed the within and foregoing instrument, and acknowledged to me that she executed the same.

But Caroline Messersmith did not appear before the notary and acknowledge that she executed the deed that was recorded. In the absence of the fact of acknowledgment the deed was not entitled to be recorded, regardless of the recital in the certificate. The deed not being entitled to be recorded, the record thereof did not constitute notice of its execution, Section 47-1945, or contents, Section 47-1919. The record appearing in the office of the register of deeds not being notice of the execution or contents of the mineral deed, the purchaser from the grantee therein did not become a "subsequent purchaser in good faith, and for a valuable consideration" within the meaning of Section 47-1941, NDRC 1943.

In this case we have the unusual situation of having two deeds covering the same property from the same grantor, who had no title, to the same grantee. The only difference between the two was a minor defect in the first deed, for which it was destroyed. The evidence is conflicting as to whether or not the first deed was acknowledged. The second deed clearly was not. It is argued that the transaction should be considered as a whole, with the implication that if the first deed was actually acknowledged, the failure to secure an acknowledgment of the second deed would not be fatal to the right to have it recorded and its efficacy as constructive notice. We must again point out that the right which the defendant Seale attempts to assert is dependent exclusively upon compliance with the recording statutes. His claim of title is dependent upon the instrument that was recorded and not the instrument that was destroyed. Assuming that Smith is right in his assertion that the first deed was acknowledged before a notary public, we cannot borrow that unrecorded acknowledgment from the destroyed deed and, in effect, attach it to the unacknowledged deed for purposes of recording and the constructive notice that would ensue. . . .

The judgment appealed from is reversed.

On Petition for Rehearing

MORRIS, C.J. The respondent has petitioned for a rehearing and additional briefs have been filed. From the cases cited and statements of counsel, it appears that there may be a misapprehension concerning the scope of our opinion. We would emphasize the fact that at the time Caroline Messersmith signed and delivered the deed to Herbert B. Smith, Jr., she had no title to convey. Smith therefore obtained no title to convey to E.B. Seale who, as grantee of Smith, claims to be an innocent purchaser. The title had already been conveyed to Frederick Messersmith. The deed to Smith had never been acknowledged and was therefore not entitled to be recorded, although it bore a certificate of acknowledgment in regular form. Seale, whose grantor had no title, seeks through the operation of our recording statutes to divest Frederick Messersmith of the true title and establish a statutory title in himself.

We are here dealing with a prior unrecorded valid and effective conveyance that is challenged by a subsequent purchaser to whom no title was conveyed and who claims that the recording laws vest title in him by virtue of a deed that was not acknowledged in fact and therefore not entitled to be placed of record. This situation differs materially from a case where an attack is made by a subsequent purchaser on a prior recorded deed which actually conveyed title to the grantee but was not entitled to be recorded because of a latent defect. The questions presented by the latter situation we leave to be determined when they arise.

The petition for rehearing is denied.

NOTES AND QUESTIONS

1. In denying the petition for rehearing, the court in *Messersmith* draws a distinction between the following two cases:

> *Example 5.* O conveys to A, who does not record. O subsequently conveys to B, who has no notice of A's deed and gives a valuable consideration. B's deed is entered into the records, but it has a defective acknowledgment. B conveys to C, who has no notice of A's deed, gives a valuable consideration, and records his deed. This is the *Messersmith* case, where it is held that B's deed is not "recorded" and therefore C is not a "subsequent purchaser in good faith . . . whose conveyance . . . first is recorded."[11]
>
> *Example 6.* O conveys to A by a deed with a defective acknowledgment. A records his deed. O subsequently conveys to B, who records. The court in the last paragraph of the *Messersmith* opinion says this case "differs materially" from *Example 5* and leaves open the question whether B would prevail over A.[12] (Of course, if B actually searched the record and found A's deed, B would have actual notice; the issue of constructive notice arises only if B does not have actual notice.)

---

11. Should a race-notice statute protect the subsequent purchaser who first records his own conveyance *only if* all prior conveyances in his chain of title are also recorded? See Bank of New Glarus v. Swartwood, 725 N.W.2d 944 (Wis. App. 2006); B. Taylor Mattis, Recording Acts: Anachronistic Reliance, 25 Real Prop., Prob. & Tr. J. 17, 47-50 (1990).

12. The majority rule in this situation is that when the defect does not appear on the face of the acknowledgment, the deed imparts constructive notice, but if the defect is patent, the deed does not give constructive notice. Leeds Bldg. Prods., Inc. v. Sears Mortgage Corp., 477 S.E.2d 565 (Ga. 1996); Metropolitan Natl. Bank v. United States, 901 F.2d 1297 (5th Cir. 1990).

Does *B* have a more persuasive claim in *Example 6* than *C* does in *Example 5*? Which one can better protect himself against prior claims? See Richard C. Maxwell, The Hidden Defect in Acknowledgment and Title Security, 2 UCLA L. Rev. 83 (1954); John C. Murray, Defective Real Estate Documents: What Are the Consequences? 42 Real Prop., Prob. & Tr. J. 367 (2007).

2. Would Seale have lost in *Messersmith* if North Dakota had a notice statute rather than a race-notice statute?

3. Caroline Messersmith's nephew Frederick, the last descendant of a pioneer family that settled Dickinson, North Dakota, moved back to Dickinson from Chicago and into the family home. Professor Michael J. Davis has sent us a copy of the Dickinson Press, Oct. 22, 1995, which carries a front page story about Frederick, then age 85, unmarried and worth about $2 million. It relates that a guardian had been appointed for Frederick, ailing from senile dementia, and the guardian was trying to set aside Frederick's conflicting wills, earlier probated under North Dakota's unusual procedure permitting probate of a will before death. The guardian claimed undue influence by some of the beneficiaries, including the kindly neighbor to whom Frederick devised the land in Golden Valley County, deeded to Frederick by his aunt Caroline in 1946. Frederick died in 1998, and a legal brouhaha, involving the guardian, cousins, neighbors, charities, and, of course, lawyers, ensued.

4. Six years after the decision in *Messersmith*, the North Dakota legislature amended its recording act to provide that "[n]o action affecting any right, title, interest or lien, to, in or upon real property shall be commenced or maintained . . . in court on the ground that a recorded instrument was not entitled to be recorded." N.D. Century Code §47-19-41 (2012). See In re Nies, 183 B.R. 866 (Bankr. D.N.D. 1995); Robert L. Stroup II, The Unreliable Record Title, 60 N.D. L. Rev. 203, 205 n.9 (1984). Do you think that other states adhering to the rule in *Messersmith* should follow suit?

4.   Chain of Title Problems

The phrase *chain of title* refers generally to the recorded sequence of transactions by which title has passed from a sovereign to the present claimant. It also has a more technical meaning: the period of time for which records must be searched and the documents that must be examined within that time period. In this technical sense, the chain of title includes, and is coextensive with, those instruments that will be picked up by the title search required in the particular jurisdiction. Earlier, at pages 695-699, we described the standard title search required against each owner: from the date of execution of the deed granting title to the owner to the date of recordation of the first deed by such owner conveying title to someone else. Some jurisdictions require a more extended search, and in these jurisdictions the chain of title is defined to include the documents that may be found in the extended search. Thus the meaning of *chain of title* varies from jurisdiction to jurisdiction; it includes the series of recorded documents that, in the particular jurisdiction, give constructive notice to a subsequent purchaser. For discussion of chain of title problems and a listing by states of the extent of search required, see Harry M. Cross, The Record "Chain of Title" Hypocrisy, 57 Colum. L. Rev. 787 (1957). (*Caveat:* Sometimes in legal literature the phrase *chain of title* is used to refer to documents found in a standard title search and not to include documents that might be found in an extended search.)

To help you focus on the precise issue, we preface our treatment of each chain of title problem with a hypothetical example raising the issue. Thus:

> *Example 7.* O conveys to A, who does not record. A conveys to B, who records the A-to-B deed. O conveys to C, a purchaser for value who has no actual knowledge of the deeds from O to A and from A to B. C records. Who prevails, B or C? The issue is: Is the A-to-B deed properly "recorded" so as to give constructive notice to the world?

Board of Education of Minneapolis v. Hughes

Supreme Court of Minnesota, 1912
136 N.W. 1095

BUNN, J. Action to determine adverse claims to a lot in Minneapolis. The complaint alleged that plaintiff owned the lot, and the answer denied this, and alleged title in defendant L.A. Hughes. The trial resulted in a decision in favor of plaintiff, and defendants appealed from an order denying a new trial.

The facts are not in controversy and are as follows: On May 16, 1906, Carrie B. Hoerger, a resident of Faribault, owned the lot in question, which was vacant and subject to unpaid delinquent taxes. Defendant L.A. Hughes offered to pay $25 for this lot. His offer was accepted, and he sent his check for the purchase price of this and two other lots bought at the same time to Ed Hoerger, husband of the owner, together with a deed to be executed and returned. The name of the grantee in the deed was not inserted; the space for the same being left blank. It was executed and acknowledged by Carrie B. Hoerger and her husband on May 17, 1906, and delivered to defendant Hughes by mail. The check was retained and cashed. Hughes filled in the name of the grantee, but not until shortly prior to the date when the deed was recorded, which was December 16, 1910. On April 27, 1909, Duryea & Wilson, real estate dealers, paid Mrs. Hoerger $25 for a quitclaim deed to the lot, which was executed and delivered to them, but which was not recorded until December 21, 1910. On November 19, 1909, Duryea & Wilson executed and delivered to plaintiff a warranty deed to the lot, which deed was filed for record January 27, 1910. It thus appears that the deed to Hughes was recorded before the deed to Duryea & Wilson, though the deed from them to plaintiff was recorded before the deed to defendant.

The questions for our consideration may be thus stated: (1) Did the deed from Hoerger to Hughes ever become operative? (2) If so, is he a subsequent purchaser whose deed was first duly recorded, within the language of the recording act?

1. The decision of the first question involves a consideration of the effect of the delivery of a deed by the grantor to the grantee with the name of the latter omitted from the space provided for it, without express authority to the grantee to insert his own or another name in the blank space. It is settled that a deed that does not name a grantee is a nullity, and wholly inoperative as a conveyance, until the name of the grantee is legally inserted. Allen v. Allen, 48 Minn. 462, 51 N.W. 473; Clark v. Butts, 73 Minn. 361, 76 N.W. 199; Id. 78 Minn. 373, 81 N.W. 11; Casserly v. Morrow, 101 Minn. 16, 111 N.W. 654. It is clear, therefore, and this is conceded, that the deed to defendant Hughes was not operative as a conveyance until his name was inserted as grantee.

Defendant, however, contends that Hughes had implied authority from the grantor to fill the blank with his own name as grantee, and that when he did so the deed became operative. This contention must, we think, be sustained. Whatever the rule may have been in the past, or may be now in some jurisdictions, we are satisfied that at the present day, and in this state, a deed which is a nullity when delivered because the name of the grantee is omitted becomes operative without a new execution or acknowledgment if the grantee, with either express or implied authority from the grantor, inserts his name in the blank space left for the name of the grantee. . . .

Unquestionably the authorities are in conflict; but this court is committed to the rule that in case of the execution and delivery of a sealed instrument, complete in all respects save that the blank for the name of the grantee is not filled, the grantee may insert his name in the blank space, provided he has authority from the grantor to do so, and, further, that this authority may be in parol, and may be implied from circumstances. We consider this the better rule, and also that it should be and is the law that when the grantor receives and retains the consideration, and delivers the deed in the condition described to the purchaser, authority to insert his name as grantee is presumed. Any other rule would be contrary to good sense and to equity. The same result could perhaps be reached by applying the doctrine of estoppel; but we prefer to base our decision on the ground of implied authority. Clearly the facts in the case at bar bring it within the principle announced, and we hold that Hughes, when he received the deed from Mrs. Hoerger, had implied authority to insert his name as grantee, in the absence of evidence showing the want of such authority. The delay in filling up the blank has no bearing on the question of the validity of the instrument when the blank was filled.

It is argued that holding that parol authority to fill the blank is sufficient violates the statute of frauds. This theory is the basis of many of the decisions that conflict with the views above expressed; but we do not think it sound. The cases in this state, and the Wisconsin, Iowa, and other decisions referred to, are abundant authority for the proposition that the authority of the grantee need not be in writing. Our conclusion is, therefore, that the deed to Hughes became operative as a conveyance when he inserted his name as grantee.

2. When the Hughes deed was recorded, there was of record a deed to the lot from Duryea & Wilson to plaintiff, but no record showing that Duryea & Wilson

had any title to convey. The deed to them from the common grantor had not been recorded. We hold that this record of a deed from an apparent stranger to the title was not notice to Hughes of the prior unrecorded conveyance by his grantor. He was a subsequent purchaser in good faith for a valuable consideration, whose conveyance was first duly recorded; that is, Hughes' conveyance dates from the time when he filled the blank space, which was after the deed from his grantor to Duryea & Wilson. He was, therefore, a "subsequent purchaser," and is protected by the recording of his deed before the prior deed was recorded. The statute cannot be construed so as to give priority to a deed recorded before, which shows no conveyance from a record owner. It was necessary, not only that the deed to plaintiff should be recorded before the deed to Hughes, but also that the deed to plaintiff's grantor should be first recorded. Webb, Record of Title, §158; 3 Washburn, Real Property, 292; Losey v. Simpson, 11 N.J. Eq. 246; Burke v. Beveridge, 15 Minn. 160 (205); Schoch v. Birdsall, 48 Minn. 443, 51 N.W. 382.

Our conclusion is that the learned trial court should have held on the evidence that defendant L.A. Hughes was the owner of the lot.

Order reversed, and new trial granted.

QUESTIONS

1. Minnesota at the time of the *Hughes* case was, and at present is, a race-notice jurisdiction. Minn. Stat. Ann. §507.34 (West 2013). Would the result in the case be different in a notice jurisdiction? In a race jurisdiction?[13] Would the result in *Hughes* be different if a tract index were used? See Andy Assocs., Inc. v. Bankers Trust Co., 399 N.E.2d 1160 (N.Y. 1979); Wash. Temple Church of God in Christ, Inc. v. Global Properties and Assocs., Inc., 865 N.Y.S.2d 641 (Sup. Ct. 2008).

2. What are the rights of the Board of Education against Duryea & Wilson and against Carrie B. Hoerger?

3. Suppose that the court had decided that the deed to Hughes became operative on May 17, 1906. What result? See B. Taylor Mattis, Recording Acts: Anachronistic Reliance, 25 Real Prop., Prob. & Tr. J. 17, 50-55 (1990).

The next chain of title problem involves interests in an adjacent or nearby lot owner created by a person who once owned the adjacent lot as well as the tract at hand. Thus:

Example 8. O, owner of Blackacre and Whiteacre, conveys Blackacre to *A* by a deed that also transfers to *A* an easement over Whiteacre. *A* records the deed, and it is described in the index as a deed to Blackacre. *O* subsequently conveys Whiteacre to *B*, a purchaser for value who has no actual knowledge of the easement over Whiteacre conveyed to *A*. *B* records. Is Whiteacre subject

---

13. Although *actual* knowledge of a prior instrument by a subsequent purchaser is irrelevant under a race statute, whether a prior instrument has been first "recorded" (so as to give *constructive notice* of its contents) is important. Thus the problems discussed under Chain of Title Problems, pages 724-733, can arise in a race jurisdiction as well as in notice and race-notice jurisdictions. See Lawing v. Jaynes, 206 S.E.2d 162 (N.C. 1974); Watterson v. Magee, 498 So. 2d 30 (La. App. 1986).

to the easement? The issue is: Does the deed of Blackacre from *O* to *A* give constructive notice to purchasers of Whiteacre?

Guillette v. Daly Dry Wall, Inc.

Supreme Judicial Court of Massachusetts, 1975
325 N.E.2d 572

BRAUCHER, J. A recorded deed of a lot in a subdivision refers to a recorded plan, contains restrictions "imposed solely for the benefit of the other lots shown on said plan," and provides that "the same restrictions are hereby imposed on each of said lots now owned by the seller." A later deed of another lot from the same grantor refers to the same plan but not to the restrictions. The plan does not mention the restrictions, and the later grantee took without knowledge of them. We reject the later grantee's contention that it was not bound by the restrictions because they were not contained in a deed in its chain of title, and affirm a decree enforcing the restrictions.

The plaintiffs, owners of three lots in the subdivision, brought suit in the Superior Court to enjoin the defendant, owner of a lot in the same subdivision, from constructing a multifamily apartment building on its lot. The case was referred to a master, and his report was confirmed. A final decree was entered enjoining the defendant from "constructing any structures designed, intended, or suited for any purpose other than a dwelling for one family and which . . . [do] not conform to the restrictions contained in a deed from Wallace L. Gilmore to Pauline A. Guillette and Kenneth E. Guillette." The defendant appealed, and the case was transferred from the Appeals Court to this court under G.L. c.211A, §10(A). The evidence is not reported.

We summarize the master's findings. Gilmore sold lots in a subdivision called Cedar Hills Section I in Easton to the plaintiffs, the defendant, and others. Two of the plaintiffs, the Walcotts, purchased a lot in August, 1967, by a deed referring to a plan dated in July, 1967. The plaintiff Guillette and her husband, now deceased, purchased a lot in May, 1968, by a deed referring to a plan dated in March, 1968. The 1967 and 1968 plans are the same for all practical purposes; neither mentions restrictions. The plaintiffs Paraskivas purchased a lot in June, 1968, by a deed referring to the 1968 plan. Each of these deeds and five other deeds to lots in the subdivision either set out the restrictions or incorporated them by reference. Only the Guillette deed and one other contained a provision restricting lots retained by the seller.[14] It was the intention of the grantor and the

---

14. Paragraph 8 of the restrictions in the Guillette deed: "The foregoing restrictions are imposed solely for the benefit of the other lots shown on said plan, and may be modified or released at any time by an instrument in writing signed by the seller herein or the legal representative of said seller, and the owner or owners for the time being of each of said lots, said written instructions to be effective immediately upon recording thereof in the proper Registry of Deeds; *and the same restrictions are hereby imposed on each of said lots now owned by the seller*" (emphasis supplied). The italicized language is found only in the Guillette deed and one other. The master found that there had been no release.

plaintiffs to maintain the subdivision as a residential subdivision to include only dwellings for one family.

The master further found that the defendant Daly Dry Wall, Inc. (Daly), purchased its lot from Gilmore in April, 1972, and that the deed to Daly contained no reference to any restrictions but did refer to the 1968 plan. Daly made no inquiry concerning restrictions and did not know of any development pattern. It had a title examination made. It learned of the restrictions in August, 1972. Subsequently it obtained a building permit for thirty-six apartment-type units.

In similar circumstances, where the common grantor has not bound his remaining land by writing, we have held that the statute of frauds prevents enforcement of restrictions against the grantor or a subsequent purchaser of a lot not expressly restricted. G.L. c.183, §3. Houghton v. Rizzo, 361 Mass. 635, 639-642 (1972), and cases cited. Gulf Oil Corp. v. Fall River Housing Authy., 364 Mass. 492, 500-501 (1974). Where, as here, however, the grantor binds his remaining land by writing, reciprocity of restriction between the grantor and grantee can be enforced. See Snow v. Van Dam, 291 Mass. 477, 482 (1935), and cases cited. In such cases a subsequent purchaser from the common grantor acquires title subject to the restrictions in the deed to the earlier purchaser. Beekman v. Schirmer, 239 Mass. 265, 270 (1921). See Am. Law of Property, §9.31 (1952); Tiffany, Real Property, §§858, 861 (3d ed. 1939); Restatement: Property, §539, comment i (1944). Each of the several grantees, if within the scope of the common scheme, is an intended beneficiary of the restrictions and may enforce them against the others. . . .

The sole issue raised by the defendant is whether it is bound by a restriction contained in deeds to its neighbors from a common grantor, when it took without knowledge[15] of the restrictions and under a deed which did not mention them. It has, it says, only the duty to ascertain whether there were any restrictions in former deeds in its chain of title. See Stewart v. Alpert, 262 Mass. 34, 37-38 (1928). But the deed from Gilmore to the Guillettes conveyed not only the described lot but also an interest in the remaining land then owned by Gilmore. That deed was properly recorded under G.L. c.36, §12, and cannot be treated as an unrecorded conveyance under G.L. c.183, §4. As a purchaser of part of the restricted land, the defendant therefore took subject to the restrictions. See Houghton v. Rizzo, 361 Mass. 635, 642 (1972); Am. Law of Property, §17.24 (1952).

The defendant argues that to charge it with notice of any restriction put in a deed by a common grantor is to "put every title examiner to the almost impossible task of searching carefully each and every deed which a grantor deeds out of a common subdivision." But our statutes provide for indexing the names of grantors and grantees, not lot numbers or tracts. G.L. c.36, §§25, 26. Lot numbers or other descriptive information, even though included in an index, do not change what is recorded. Cf. Gillespie v. Rogers, 146 Mass. 610, 612 (1888), and

---

15. General Laws c.183, §4, as appearing in St. 1941, c.85, denies protection to "persons having actual notice of" an unrecorded conveyance.

cases cited. In such a system the purchaser cannot be safe if the title examiner ignores any deed given by a grantor in the chain of title during the time he owned the premises in question. In the present case the defendant's deed referred to a recorded subdivision plan, and the deed to the Guillettes referred to the same plan. A search for such deeds is a task which is not at all impossible. Cf. Roak v. Davis, 194 Mass. 481, 485 (1907).

Decree affirmed with costs of appeal.

NOTE AND QUESTIONS

1. William B. Stoebuck & Dale A. Whitman, The Law of Property 896-897 (3d ed. 2000), says the cases are equally divided between the position of the Massachusetts court and the position that an easement or restrictive covenant on Whiteacre that appears in a prior deed of Blackacre from the common owner of Blackacre and Whiteacre is not in the purchaser's chain of title to Whiteacre. On the other hand, a more recent article suggests that the latter position is now the majority rule. See Herbert Hovenkamp, Post-Sale Restraints and Competitive Harm: The First Sale Doctrine in Perspective, 66 N.Y.U. Ann. Surv. Am. L. 487, 520 (2011) ("Most courts hold that the servitude must be properly recorded in the chain of title of all persons against whom subsequent enforcement is sought."). For cases taking this latter position, see Krueger v. Oberto, 724 N.E.2d 21 (Ill. App. 1999); Witter v. Taggart, 577 N.E.2d 338 (N.Y. 1991); Simone v. Heidelberg, 877 N.E.2d 1288 (N.Y. 2007); Spring Lakes, Ltd. v. O.F.M. Co., 467 N.E.2d 537 (Ohio 1984).

If you were practicing in Illinois, New York, or Ohio, how would you put the subdivider's covenants in the deeds, so as to give notice to all subsequent purchasers?

2. Would the problem in *Example 8* arise if the jurisdiction had a tract index?

Does a title searcher have a duty to examine the records under the name of each owner prior to the date of the deed transferring title to the owner? Consider this hypothetical example:

> *Example 9.* A conveys Blackacre to B by a general warranty deed. B records. A subsequently acquires title to Blackacre from O. A records the deed from O to A. A then conveys Blackacre to C, a purchaser for value who has no actual knowledge of B's deed. C records. Who prevails, B or C? The issue is: Does the A-to-B deed give C constructive notice?

To put some flesh on the bones of *Example 9*, and make it come alive, suppose that Andrew has signed a contract of sale to buy Blackacre from Olympia. Andrew is buying Blackacre to give to his daughter Barbara. Closing the transaction takes longer than expected because there are liens on the property that must be released. On Barbara's birthday, Andrew executes a warranty deed to Blackacre in favor of Barbara, who records the deed. Several months later, after the snags have been removed, Olympia deeds Blackacre to Andrew. Andrew records his deed. Subsequently Andrew runs into financial troubles and sells Blackacre for a substantial amount to Carol, who has no actual knowledge of Andrew's prior deed to Barbara, executed and recorded before Andrew received title. Carol records her deed from Andrew. Who prevails, Barbara or Carol?

In two well-known older cases, the court held that Barbara prevailed. Ayer v. Philadelphia & Boston Face Brick Co., 34 N.E. 177 (Mass. 1893) (opinion by Holmes, J.); Tefft v. Munson, 57 N.Y. 97 (1874). The court reasoned that when Andrew received title from Olympia it passed automatically to Barbara under the doctrine of estoppel by deed (see pages 634-635). Barbara's deed was recorded, and—unlike a wild deed, unconnected to an owner in the chain of title—Barbara's deed could be discovered by a subsequent purchaser by searching the records under Andrew's name prior to the date title came to him from Olympia.

The majority of cases, and especially the more recent cases, are contra, however. See, e.g., Ryczkowski v. Chelsea Title & Guaranty Co., 449 P.2d 261 (Nev. 1969); Sabo v. Horvath, 559 P.2d 1038 (Alaska 1976). These cases emphasize the cost of searching title under the name of every owner for many (how many?) years prior to the date the owner received title, looking for a possible prior deed given by the owner. This cost does not seem justified in view of the fact that Barbara, in our example, could easily make sure that her deed was recorded after the Olympia-to-Andrew deed. And so the majority, promoting efficiency in land transactions, regards Barbara's deed as outside the chain of title. It does not give constructive notice to subsequent purchasers.

If the jurisdiction has a tract index, this chain of title problem does not arise. Barbara's deed will be seen by a title searcher looking at the tract index, and Carol cannot be a subsequent bona fide purchaser without notice. In addition, it is possible that digitization of land records would change the view of courts with respect to the difficulty of finding Barbara's deed. See Emily Bayer-Pacht, Note, The Computerization of Land Records: How Advances in Recording Systems Affect the Rationale Behind Some Existing Chain of Title Doctrine, 32 Cardozo L. Rev. 340, 364-366 (2010).

As a final chain of title problem, we present the matter of a prior deed recorded after a later purchaser with notice has recorded a subsequent deed. Thus:

Example 10. O conveys to A, who does not record. O subsequently conveys to B, who knows of the conveyance to A. B records. A records. Later B conveys to C, a purchaser for value who has no actual knowledge of the deed from O to A. C records. Who prevails, A or C? The issue is: Does the deed from O to A, when recorded, give constructive notice to C?

Let us picture *Example 10* as a real life situation. Oscar conveys Whiteacre to his second wife, Annie. Annie does not record the deed. Subsequently, Oscar decides that he wants Bob, his son by his first wife, to have Whiteacre. Oscar then conveys Whiteacre to Bob, for love and affection but no other consideration. Bob records his deed. Then Annie, belatedly, goes to the courthouse and records her deed. Next Bob conveys Whiteacre, for a substantial sum, to Carol, who does not actually know of the Oscar-to-Annie deed, which has been recorded after the Oscar-to-Bob deed. Carol records her deed. Who prevails, Annie or Carol?[16]

The question is whether a prior deed from an owner *recorded after* a later deed from the same owner gives constructive notice of the prior deed to subsequent purchasers from the grantee of the second deed. If it does, then Carol has constructive notice of Annie's prior deed and cannot prevail. If it does not, then Carol will prevail because the deed is not in the chain of title. (Of course, Bob cannot prevail over Annie because Bob is not a purchaser, only a donee. Carol, however, can prevail if she has no constructive notice.)

The cases are split. Morse v. Curtis, 2 N.E. 929 (Mass. 1885), is a leading case holding in favor of Carol. It held that a purchaser is not bound to examine the record after the date of a recorded conveyance to discover whether the grantor made a prior conveyance recorded later. This makes good sense in terms of reasonably limiting title search. If a prior deed recorded after the first recorded deed gives constructive notice, the title searcher must search under the name of every owner to the present time to see if the owner gave a prior deed recorded after the first recorded deed. For a case following this view, see Hartig v. Stratman, 729 N.E.2d 237 (Ind. App. 2000) (prior deed recorded one minute after subsequent purchaser's deed does not give subsequent purchaser constructive notice).

Woods v. Garnett, 16 So. 390 (Miss. 1894), is a leading case for the opposite view. That case held that a deed recorded late—after another deed from the same owner—gave constructive notice to subsequent purchasers. The costs of title searching under this view are substantially increased, and title searchers may ignore the law. See Francis S. Philbrick, Limits of Record Search and Therefore of Notice (pt. 3), 93 U. Pa. L. Rev. 391, 415 (1945), pointing out that the practice of title examiners in New York is to search only under each name to the day of the recording of the first deed out from that person, even though the law follows the principle of Woods v. Garnett. The problem in *Example 10* does not arise in a jurisdiction with a tract index because *A*'s late-recorded deed will be seen by the title searcher. Would widespread acceptance of computerized land records cut in favor of the rule in Woods v. Garnett? See Bayer-Pacht, supra, at 364-365.

QUESTION AND PROBLEMS

1. Suppose that the jurisdiction follows the view of Morse v. Curtis and has a race-notice statute. In *Example 10*, will *C* prevail?

Professor Philbrick says that in *Example 10*, in a race-notice jurisdiction, *C* must always fail because *C* "can never satisfy the requirement of prior recording." Philbrick, supra, at 391. The American Law of Property agrees. "The anomaly is that the court in notice-race jurisdictions should have injected into their opinions any consideration of notice, either inquiry notice or record notice, when dealing

16. If Bob were a bona fide purchaser and Carol actually knew of the Oscar to Annie deed, Carol would prevail. Do you see why? See footnote 9, page 716, explaining the shelter rule.

with a problem definitely settled by the requirements of their acts relative to securing priority of record." 4 American Law of Property §17.22 (1952). Is this convincing? If *A*'s deed is not "recorded" so as to give constructive notice to *C*, why is not *C*'s deed "first recorded"? Why should the word "recorded" be given one meaning when the problem is whether *A*'s deed is recorded so as to give constructive notice and another when the problem is whether *C* has recorded first? Have the learned authors confused the fact of an instrument being entered on the records with the legal conclusion that it is recorded? See B. Taylor Mattis, Recording Acts: Anachronistic Reliance, 25 Real Prop., Prob. & Tr. J. 17, 44-45 (1990).

2. Assume *O* owns the land before any conveyance is given. Each conveyance is by a warranty deed. Each person is a bona fide purchaser except as otherwise indicated. The jurisdiction has only a grantor-grantee index.

(a) *A* conveys to *B*, who does not record.

O conveys to *A*, who does not record.

B conveys to *C*, who records.

A conveys to *D*, who records. (*D* is shown the deed from *O* to *A*.)

O conveys to *E*, who records.

Who prevails in a notice jurisdiction? In a race-notice jurisdiction?

(b) *O* conveys to *A*, who does not record.

O conveys to *B*, who knows of the deed from *O* to *A* and does not record.

O conveys to *C*, who does not record.

B conveys to *D*, who does not record. (*D* is shown the deed from *O* to *B*.)

A records.

B records.

D records.

Who prevails in a notice jurisdiction? In a race-notice jurisdiction?

If, after *D* records, *A* conveys to *E*, who promptly records, who prevails in a notice jurisdiction? In a race-notice jurisdiction?

3. *O* sells its property to *A* on June 1, 2005. *A* borrows money from *B* and executes a mortgage in *B*'s favor. *A* also borrows funds from *O* and executes a mortgage that states that it is subordinate to the mortgage from *A* to *B*. The mortgage from *A* to *O* is recorded on August 1; the deed from *O* to *A* is recorded on August 15; and the mortgage from *A* to *B* is recorded on August 30. The deed is dated June 1, 2005. *C* buys the property on January 1, 2006. Is *C* bound by the mortgage from *A* to *O*? Is *C* bound by the mortgage from *A* to *B*? See Bank of New York v. Nally, 820 N.E.2d 644 (Ind. 2005).

5.   Persons Protected by the Recording System

The recording statute in each state must be read carefully to see who comes within the protection of the statute. Observe that the Florida statute (page 717) protects, against unrecorded conveyances or mortgages, "creditors or subsequent purchasers[17] for a valuable consideration," and the California statute (page 717) protects "any subsequent purchaser or mortgagee" and "any judgment affecting the title." By judicial construction, the recording statutes have been held, almost universally, not to protect donees and devisees, even in race jurisdictions. As a result, it is sometimes necessary for a court to decide whether a person is a purchaser (and protected) or a donee (and not protected). This in turn may require the court to determine what is a valuable consideration for purposes of obtaining the protection of the recording act.

An examination of the cases leads to the conclusion that there is some disagreement as to how much a grantee must pay to be deemed a purchaser. Most courts require more than a nominal value, such as a "substantial" amount, or an amount "not grossly inadequate." See William B. Stoebuck & Dale A. Whitman, The Law of Property 879 (3d ed. 2000). Why do you suppose that courts require more "consideration" here than is necessary to enforce a contract?

If a deed recites that it is for "$1 and other good and valuable consideration," this raises a presumption that the grantee is a purchaser for a valuable consideration, and places the burden of going forward to establish the falsity of the recital of consideration on the party attacking the deed.

Daniels v. Anderson

Supreme Court of Illinois, 1994
642 N.E.2d 128

[In 1977, William A. Daniels contracted to buy two lots from Stephen Jacula. The contract of sale also gave Daniels a right of first refusal if Jacula ever decided to sell an adjacent parcel (called "the Contiguous Parcel"), for the same price as any prospective buyer offered. The contract of sale was not recorded. When Daniels received a deed from Jacula it did not mention the right of first refusal. The deed was recorded. Some eight years later, in 1985, Nicholas Zografos contracted with Jacula to buy the Contiguous Parcel for $60,000. Daniels was not notified of Zografos's offer. Zografos paid Jacula $10,000 initially and gave Jacula a note for the balance.

Zografos paid $15,000 more in February 1986, and another $15,000 in March 1986. In June 1986, Daniels' wife told Zografos of Daniels' right of first refusal on the parcel. Zografos paid the remaining $20,000 to Jacula in August 1986, when he received a deed that he recorded.

Daniels sued Jacula and Zografos, asking for specific performance of his preemptive option. Zografos defended that he was a subsequent bona fide purchaser without notice of the option. The trial court held that Zografos was not a subsequent bona fide purchaser because he had actual notice of the option when he took title in August 1986. The trial court ordered Zografos to convey

---

17. The term *purchaser* is uniformly held to apply to all parties who have paid consideration for the interest acquired, including a mortgagee or a lessee.

the Contiguous Parcel to Daniels, and ordered Daniels to pay Zografos the full purchase price of $60,000 plus $11,000 in property taxes Zografos had paid on the Contiguous Parcel.

The appellate court affirmed. 252 Ill. App. 3d 289. Zografos appeals to the Supreme Court of Illinois.]

FREEMAN, J. . . . Zografos testified that he did not know of Daniels' right of first refusal until Daniels' wife told him in June 1986. By that time, Zografos had already contracted to buy the Contiguous Parcel and had paid $40,000 of the $60,000 purchase price. The trial court found that Zografos was not a bona fide purchaser based solely on this June 1986 notice.

In the appellate court, Zografos contended that he was a bona fide purchaser of the Contiguous Parcel despite his June 1986 notice of Daniels' interest. Zografos invoked the doctrine of equitable conversion in support of his bona fide purchaser defense. He argued that although he did not take legal title to the Contiguous Parcel until August 1986, he became the equitable owner of the Contiguous Parcel in September 1985, when he entered into the contract. (See Shay v. Penrose, 25 Ill. 2d 447, 449, 185 N.E.2d 218 (1962)). . . . Thus, Zografos reasoned, he became a bona fide purchaser because he took equitable title prior to receiving the June 1986 notice of Daniels' interest. The appellate court concluded that Zografos waived this theory. 252 Ill. App. 3d at 299.

Zografos repeats this theory before this court. We agree with the appellate court that Zografos did not assert this theory in any pleading, memorandum, argument, or post-trial motion in the trial court. Rather, Zografos raised this theory for the first time on appeal. "It has frequently been held that the theory upon which a case is tried in the lower court cannot be changed on review, and that an issue not presented to or considered by the trial court cannot be raised for the first time on review." Kravis v. Smith Marine, Inc., 60 Ill. 2d 141, 147, 324 N.E.2d 417 (1975).

. . . We uphold the appellate court's finding that Zografos has waived application of the doctrine of equitable conversion.

We must next address, absent consideration of the equitable conversion doctrine, the issue of when during the executory stages of a real estate installment contract does the buyer become a bona fide purchaser. Zografos contends that, during this executory period, the buyer can rely solely on the public records and ignore even actual notice of an outstanding, unrecorded interest.

This contention is erroneous. The legal principles are quite established. As we earlier noted, a bona fide purchaser, by definition, takes title to real property without notice of the interests of others. A buyer who, prior to the payment of any consideration receives notice of an outstanding interest, pays the consideration at his or her peril with respect to the holder of the outstanding interest. Such a buyer is not protected as a bona fide purchaser and takes the property bound by the outstanding interest. (Moshier v. Knox College, 32 Ill. 138, 143 (1863)). The law reasons that consummation of the purchase, after notice of the outstanding interest, is a fraud upon the holder of that interest. 8 J. Grimes, Thompson on Real Property §4321, at 416-17 (1963).

Where a buyer receives notice of an outstanding interest subsequent to paying some, but prior to paying the full purchase price, authorities differ on whether the buyer is a bona fide purchaser. As the appellate court noted, some of the authorities state that partial payment of the consideration is insufficient to render the buyer a bona fide purchaser. 252 Ill. App. 3d at 300-02 (and authorities cited therein); 8 J. Grimes, Thompson on Real Property §4322, at 418, 420-21 (1963).

However, a majority of jurisdictions have relaxed this harsh rule. Instead, they apply a pro tanto rule, which protects the buyer to the extent of the payments made prior to notice, but no further. (R. Cunningham, W. Stoebuck, D. Whitman, Property 795 (1984); 8 J. Grimes, Thompson on Real Property §4322, at 418-19 (1963); 5 B. Jones, Tiffany on Real Property §1305 (3d ed. 1939)). This court recognized this pro tanto rule in dicta in Redden v. Miller, 95 Ill. 336, 346 (1880).

Courts have identified at least three methods to apply this pro tanto protection. First, the most common method is to award the land to the holder of the outstanding interest and award the buyer the payments that he or she made. The second method is to award the buyer a fractional interest in the land proportional to the amount paid prior to notice. The third method is to allow the buyer to complete the purchase, but to pay the remaining installments to the holder of the outstanding interest. (R. Cunningham, W. Stoebuck, D. Whitman, Property 795-96 (1984); 8 J. Grimes, Thompson on Real Property §4322, at 418 (1984)). Courts exercise considerable latitude in these cases, taking into account the relative equities of the parties. . . .

In the present case, the trial court ordered Zografos to convey the Contiguous Parcel to Daniels and ordered Daniels to pay Zografos the full purchase price. The trial court also ordered Daniels to reimburse Zografos for the property taxes that Zografos had paid on the property. We agree with the appellate court that the trial court's disposition of this issue, between Daniels and Zografos, satisfied these well-settled principles of equity. (252 Ill. App. 3d at 305.) We cannot say that the trial court abused its discretion. . . .

Affirmed.

Lewis v. Superior Court

Court of Appeal of California, Second District, 1994
37 Cal. Rptr. 2d 63

[In early February 1992, Robert and Josephine Lewis contracted to buy a residence from Shipley for $2.3 million. After the Lewises opened escrow, and just a few days before they acquired title, Fontana Films recorded a *lis pendens* (notice of lawsuit affecting title to the property) against Shipley. The *lis pendens* was recorded on February 24, but not indexed until February 29, the day after the Lewises acquired title. Under the contract of sale, the Lewises paid Shipley $350,000 on February 25. Closing took place on February 28, and the deed from Shipley to the Lewises was recorded on that day. The Lewises gave Shipley their note for $1,950,000, which they paid in March 1992. Within the next year the Lewises spent an additional $1,050,000 in renovating the property. In September 1993, the Lewises were served in Fontana's lawsuit and learned about the *lis pendens*. The Lewises brought suit for summary judgment to remove the *lis pendens* and clear their title. The trial court denied the motion for summary judgment.

The Lewises appealed. The court of appeal held that the *lis pendens* was not properly recorded until it was indexed, which occurred the day after the title passed to the Lewises. The opinion of the court continues.]

WOODS, J. . . . Relying on the case of Davis v. Ward, 109 Cal. 186, 41 P. 1010 (1895), [Fontana] contends that even if the Lewises took title before the indexing of the Fontana lis pendens, they nevertheless were not bona fide purchasers because they did not fully pay for the property until after indexing. [Fontana] appears to be making a make-weight argument that if the court determines that the date of recordation is not the effective date by reason of an absence of indexing until later, then the date for determining the Lewises' status is the date they paid $1,950,000 as the balance of the purchase price on the property. By then, [Fontana] contends, the deed had long since been indexed and the Lewises were chargeable with notice of the lis pendens.

. . . [We] conclude that the *Davis* case payment of value rule does not apply in the instant case for a number of reasons. . . .

In *Davis*, Ward mortgaged some property to Davis' predecessor. Apparently by mutual mistake, the mortgage identified the wrong parcel of land. Ward later sold half of the property to Fleming, who paid cash, and half to Brown, who paid part cash and part notes. (Davis v. Ward, supra, 109 Cal. at pp. 187-191.) Davis sued to have the mortgage reformed and foreclosed. Evidence at trial proved that Fleming and Brown both took without notice of the prior sale because the mortgage was recorded against the wrong property and could not have been discovered by searching the record of the property actually purchased. The evidence also showed, however, that when Brown received notice of Davis' claim—apparently by being sued—he had paid only $200 of the purchase price. (Id., at p. 190.) Fleming and Brown both won nonsuits on the ground that they were bona fide purchasers.

On appeal, the Supreme Court affirmed the nonsuit as to Fleming, the cash purchaser. However, it reversed Brown's nonsuit, holding that he was not a bona fide purchaser because he could not show that "the purchase money had been paid before notice." (109 Cal. at p. 189.) The court relied in part on Jewett v. Palmer, 7 Johnson Ch. 68 (1823 Ch.), where the court explained, "A plea of a purchase for a valuable consideration, without notice, must be with the money actually paid; or else, according to Lord Hardwicke, you are not hurt. The averment must be, not only that the purchaser had not notice at or before the execution of the deeds, but that the purchase money was paid before notice." (Davis v. Ward, supra, at p. 190.)

As we discuss in more detail below, the Supreme Court did not decide what remedy should be applied. It simply reversed a nonsuit, saying nothing about how the trial court should adjust the parties' rights.

(a). The payment of value rule stated in *Davis* cannot be reconciled with modern real property law and practice and should be strictly limited to its facts.

Davis was premised, in part, on Lord Hardwicke's assertion that a purchaser who loses his property is "not hurt" if he has not fully paid for the land. This claim is inconsistent with both equitable considerations and modern market expectations.

Any purchaser without notice who makes a down payment and unequivocally obligates himself to pay the balance has every reason to believe that, if he makes the payments when due, his right to the property will be secure. Such a purchaser may drastically alter his position on the basis of this understanding, such as by selling his prior residence, moving his family and making significant improvements to the property. If his property is taken, his injury remains even if his money is returned. Aside from ignoring this undeniable reality, *Davis* also ignores the ancient principle that real property is unique and its loss cannot be compensated in money. (Glynn v. Marquette, 152 Cal. App. 3d 277, 280, 199 Cal. Rptr. 306 (1984) (specific performance available in land sale contracts because it is assumed real property is unique)). . . . We discern that Lord Hardwicke was simply expostulating an erroneous rule of law.

While this court is bound to follow existing Supreme Court authority, we resist any attempt to apply an outdated theory to modern real property transactions. Since *Davis* was grounded on an archaic and misunderstood principle of real property conveyancing, we confine it to its facts and its narrow purpose. . . .

(b). *Davis* cannot rationally be applied to cases involving only constructive notice.

In *Davis*, Brown received actual notice of the litigation affecting his property; there was no constructive notice, and the court did not opine on what the effect of constructive notice would have been. . . .

One might argue that a buyer in this situation—someone who continues to pay his seller in the face of actual notice of a competing claim—should be at risk of losing his post-notice investment, if only because the assertion of the claim could give rise to a defense to the payment obligation (in other words, the buyer becomes a volunteer). But constructive notice should not have that effect, and nothing in *Davis* requires such a result.

Applying *Davis* to a case of constructive notice penalizes a completely innocent purchaser for simply living up to his payment obligations. This is a purchaser who is "innocent" in every sense of the recording statutes, because he has already acquired title and has already received whatever title information or title insurance he was entitled to under his purchase agreement. If constructive notice before payment threatens him with loss of title, he will have to undertake a title search before each and every payment—360 title searches for a typical 30-year note! Such an obviously absurd result is fundamentally contrary to the whole purpose of the recording statutes, but it would be the unavoidable result of holding that constructive notice is enough to trigger the *Davis* payment of value rule. . . .

(d). Because the court in *Davis* merely reversed Brown's nonsuit and remanded the case, it did not determine the proper remedy. However, the trial court, exercising its equitable powers, could have easily preserved all of the parties' interests in the property except Ward's, in recognition that Ward, as the wrongdoer, should be the one to sacrifice his interest—i.e., his claim against Brown for the balance of his purchase price. The likely and appropriate remedy would have been for Davis to acquire Ward's interest in the property. In other words, Davis would become the payee of Brown's note to Ward, and Brown's position would remain unchanged: he would continue to pay the note, but would make payments to Davis rather than Ward, whose interest would be extinguished. Under this approach, the wrongdoer is penalized, the aggrieved party is compensated and the innocent purchaser's rights are preserved. This result would be possible because, at least as far as the opinion reveals, by the time of trial Brown's note to Ward was still outstanding, so the trial court had something on which to act.

Davis reaches (or at least permits) this correct result, but for the wrong reasons. Davis should have prevailed not because Brown was not a good faith purchaser, but rather because Ward continued to hold an interest that, in equity, belonged to Davis, as the party damaged by Ward's wrongful conduct. . . .

(f). Applying *Davis* would unfairly penalize the Lewises for paying cash for the property, rather than financing the purchase price.

In *Davis*, the court recognized that if Ward had assigned the notes to a bank for value and without notice, "the defense of both Brown and the bank to this action would be complete, for in that event, the notes would have been payment." (Davis v. Ward, supra, 109 Cal. at p. 191.) In other words, the fact that the seller ends up being fully paid transforms the buyer into a good-faith purchaser when otherwise he would not be. This distinction makes no sense; from the buyer's perspective, he is in the same position, and equally obligated to repay a note over time, whether the seller or a bank holds the mortgage.

Here, the Lewises did not merely obligate themselves to pay the purchase price; they paid the price in cash before receiving notice of the litigation. Bringing this case within *Davis'* sweep would lead to a thoroughly anomalous result: the Lewises, cash buyers, would be at risk of losing their property, while another purchaser, who paid only a small down payment and financed the balance, would be considered a bona fide purchaser. No one could comfortably acquiesce in so unfair an outcome.

Disposition

Let a peremptory writ of mandate issue directing the superior court to vacate its order denying petitioners' motion for summary judgment, and thereafter issue a new and different order granting said motion and expunging the lis pendens. Petitioners to recover costs of these proceedings.

Alexander v. Andrews, 64 S.E.2d 487 (W. Va. 1951). Thomas and Mary, husband and wife, owned their home, worth $7,700, as tenants in common. Mary died on April 25, 1946, devising her half interest to their son, Charles, who lived in the house with his parents. On May 8, Thomas conveyed his half interest in the house to his daughter, Sarah, for love and affection. On May 14, Thomas by a second deed conveyed his half interest in the house to Charles, who did not know of the prior deed to Sarah. Charles paid Thomas $1,000 and promised to take care of him for the rest of his life and bury him. Charles promptly recorded his deed. Sarah recorded her deed on July 8. Charles lived in the house with Thomas and took care of him until Thomas died in October 1948.

After the death of Thomas, Sarah claimed a half interest in the house by virtue of her prior deed from Thomas. Charles claimed to be a subsequent purchaser without notice of Sarah's deed. The court held that Charles is a protected subsequent purchaser only to the extent of the $1,000 paid before Sarah recorded her deed. The remainder of his consideration, lifetime care and burial costs, was paid after Sarah recorded her deed, which gave constructive notice to Charles of her prior claim.

NOTES

1. *Creditors.* A number of recording statutes protect "creditors" against unrecorded deeds and mortgages (see the Florida statute on page 717). Courts have interpreted these statutes to protect only creditors who have established a lien, such as by attachment or judgment, and not all creditors. Merely lending money to the record owner does not give priority over unrecorded instruments. In some states, lien creditors are construed to come within broad language extending protection to "all persons except parties to the conveyance."

In many states, a creditor is not protected until the creditor prosecutes a lawsuit to judgment and forecloses a lien or holds an execution sale. The buyer at the sale, who may be the creditor, is protected under the recording act as a subsequent bona fide purchaser for value if the buyer has no notice of the unrecorded claim at the time of sale.

In many states, special statutes give persons who provide labor or materials on a building project a lien on the property from the time such labor or material is provided.

For an examination of which creditors should be protected under the policies of the recording act, see Dan S. Schechter, Judicial Lien Creditors Versus Prior Unrecorded Transferees of Real Property: Rethinking the Goals of the Recording System and Their Consequences, 62 S. Cal. L. Rev. 105 (1988).

2. *Quitclaim deeds.* In a few jurisdictions, a purchaser by quitclaim deed cannot claim the position of a bona fide purchaser without notice. This rests upon the idea that a refusal of the grantor to warrant title should create a strong suspicion that the title is defective. See Diversified, Inc. v. Hall, 23 S.W.3d 403 (Tex. App. 2000); Polhemus v. Cobb, 653 So. 2d 964 (Ala. 1995). It may even be held that a quitclaim deed in the chain of title puts all subsequent purchasers on inquiry notice. They must make further investigation about the deed. See Richardson v. Amresco Residential Mortgage Corp., 592 S.E.2d 65 (Va. 2004); Schwalm v.

Deanhardt, 906 P.2d 167 (Kan. App. 1995). In a large majority of jurisdictions, however, a quitclaim deed is treated the same as a warranty deed for purpose of giving notice. There are many reasons why a grantor may use a quitclaim deed other than a questionable title.

6. Inquiry Notice

There are three kinds of notice a person may have with respect to a prior claim: actual, record, and inquiry. Actual notice arises where one is personally aware of a conflicting interest in real property, often due to another's possession of the property. The latter two are forms of constructive notice—notice that the law deems you to have regardless of your actual knowledge. Record notice consists of notice one has based on properly recorded instruments. Inquiry notice is based on facts that would cause a reasonable person to make inquiry into the possible existence of an interest in real property. See generally Swanson v. Swanson, 769 N.W.2d 614 (N.D. 2011); Gorzeman v. Thompson, 986 P.2d 29 (Or. App. 1999).

Harper v. Paradise

Supreme Court of Georgia, 1974
210 S.E.2d 710

INGRAM, J. This appeal involves title to land. It is from a judgment and directed verdict granted to the appellees and denied to the appellants in the Superior Court of Oglethorpe County.

Appellants claim title as remaindermen under a deed to a life tenant with the remainder interest to the named children of the life tenant. This deed was delivered to the life tenant but was lost or misplaced for a number of years and was not recorded until 35 years later.

On February 1, 1922, Mrs. Susan Harper conveyed by warranty deed a 106.65-acre farm in Oglethorpe County to her daughter-in-law, Maude Harper, for life with remainder in fee simple to Maude Harper's named children. The deed, which recited that it was given for Five Dollars and "natural love and affection," was lost, or misplaced, until 1957 when it was found by Clyde Harper, one of the named remaindermen, in an old trunk belonging to Maude Harper. The deed was recorded in July, 1957.

Susan Harper died sometime during the period 1925-1927 and was survived by her legal heirs, Price Harper, Prudie Harper Jackson, Mildred Chambers and John W. Harper, Maude Harper's husband. In 1928, all of Susan Harper's then living heirs, except John W. Harper, joined in executing an instrument to Maude Harper, recorded March 19, 1928, which contained the following language:

> Deed, Heirs of Mrs. Susan Harper, to Mrs. Maude Harper. Whereas Mrs. Susan Harper did on or about the . . . day of March, 1927 [1922?], make and deliver a deed of gift to the land hereinafter

more fully described to Mrs. Maude Harper the wife of John W. Harper, which said deed was delivered to the said Mrs. Maude Harper and was not recorded; and Whereas said deed has been lost or destroyed and cannot be found; and Whereas the said Mrs. Susan Harper has since died and leaves as her heirs at law the grantors herein; Now therefore for and in consideration of the sum of $1.00, in hand paid, the receipt of which is hereby acknowledged, the undersigned, Mrs. Prudence Harper Jackson, Price Harper and Ben Grant as guardian of Mildred Chambers, do hereby remise, release and forever quit claim to the said Mrs. Maude Harper, her heirs and assigns, all of their right, title, interest, claim or demand that they and each of them have or may have had in and to the [described property]. To have and to hold the said property to the said Mrs. Maude Harper, her heirs and assigns, so that neither the said grantors nor their heirs nor any person or persons claiming under them shall at any time hereafter by any way or means, have, claim or demand any right, title or interest in and to the aforesaid property or its appurtenances or any part thereof. This deed is made and delivered to the said Mrs. Maude Harper to take the place of the deed made and executed and delivered by Mrs. Susan Harper during her lifetime as each of the parties hereto know that the said property was conveyed to the said Mrs. Maude Harper by the said Mrs. Susan Harper during her lifetime and that the said Mrs. Maude Harper was on said property and in possession thereof.

On February 27, 1933, Maude Harper executed a security deed, recorded the same day, which purported to convey the entire fee simple to Ella Thornton to secure a fifty dollar loan. The loan being in default, Ella Thornton foreclosed on the property, receiving a sheriff's deed executed and recorded in 1936. There is an unbroken chain of record title out of Ella Thornton to the appellees, Lincoln and William Paradise, who claim the property as grantees under a warranty deed executed and recorded in 1955. The appellees also assert title by way of peaceful, continuous, open and adverse possession by them and their predecessors in title beginning in 1940.

The appellees trace their title back through Susan Harper, but they do not rely on the 1922 deed from Susan Harper to Maude Harper as a link in their record chain of title. If appellees relied on the 1922 deed, then clearly the only interest they would have obtained would have been Maude Harper's life estate which terminated upon her death in 1972. . . .

Appellees contended that the 1928 instrument executed by three of Susan Harper's then living heirs must be treated under Code §67-2502 as having been executed by the heirs as agents or representatives of Susan Harper, thereby making both the 1922 and 1928 deeds derivative of the same source. That Code section provides:

All innocent persons, firms or corporations acting in good faith and without actual notice, who purchase for value, or obtain contractual liens, from distributees, devisees, legatees, or heirs at law, holding or apparently holding land or personal property by will or inheritance from a deceased person, shall be protected in the purchase of said property or in acquiring such a lien thereon as against unrecorded liens or conveyances created or executed by said deceased person upon or to said property in like manner and to the same extent as if the property had been purchased of or the lien acquired from the deceased person.

Appellees argue that since both deeds must be treated as having emanated from the same source, the 1928 deed has priority under Code §29-401 because it was recorded first. Code §29-401 provides:

> Every deed conveying lands shall be recorded in the office of the clerk of the superior court of the county where the land lies. The record may be made at any time, but such deed loses its priority over a subsequent recorded deed from the same vendor, taken without notice of the existence of the first.

In the present case, . . . after the death of the original grantor, Susan Harper, her heirs could have joined in a deed to an innocent person acting in good faith and without actual notice of the earlier deed. If such a deed had been made, conveying a fee simple interest without making any reference to a prior unrecorded lost or misplaced deed, Code §67-2502 might well apply to place that deed from the heirs within the protection of Code §29-401.

However, the 1928 deed relied upon by appellees was to the same person, Maude Harper, who was the life tenant in the 1922 deed. The 1928 deed recited that it was given in lieu of the earlier lost or misplaced deed from Susan Harper to Maude Harper and that Maude Harper was in possession of the property. Thus Maude Harper is bound to have taken the 1928 deed with knowledge of the 1922 deed. See King v. McDuffie, 144 Ga. 318, 320, 87 S.E. 22. The recitals of the 1928 deed negate any contention that the grantors in that deed were holding or apparently holding the property by will or inheritance from Susan Harper. Indeed, the recitals of the 1928 deed actually serve as a disclaimer by the heirs that they were so holding or apparently holding the land.

Therefore, Code §67-2502 is not applicable under the facts of this case and cannot be used to give the 1928 deed priority over the 1922 deed under the provisions of Code §29-401. The recitals contained in the 1928 deed clearly put any subsequent purchaser on notice of the existence of the earlier misplaced or lost deed, and, in terms of Code §29-401, the 1928 deed, though recorded first, would not be entitled to priority.

We conclude that it was incumbent upon the appellees to ascertain through diligent inquiry the contents of the earlier deed and the interests conveyed therein. See Henson v. Bridges, 218 Ga. 6(2), 126 S.E.2d 226. Cf. Talmadge Bros. & Co. v. Interstate Building & Loan Assn., 105 Ga. 550, 553, 31 S.E. 618, holding that "a deed in the chain of title, discovered by the investigator, is constructive notice of all other deeds which were referred to in the deed discovered," including an unrecorded plat included in the deed discovered. Although the appellees at trial denied having received any information as to the existence of the interests claimed by the appellants, the transcript fails to indicate any effort on the part of the appellees to inquire as to the interests conveyed by the lost or misplaced deed when they purchased the property in 1955. "A thorough review of the record evinces no inquiry whatsoever by the defendants, or attempt to explain why such inquiry would have been futile. Thus it will be presumed that due inquiry would have disclosed the existent facts." Henson v. Bridges, supra, p. 10, of 218 Ga., p. 228 of 126 S.E.2d.

The appellees also contend that they have established prescriptive title by way of peaceful, continuous, open and adverse possession by them and their predecessors in title beginning in 1940. However, the remaindermen named in the 1922 deed had no right of possession until the life tenant's death in 1972. "Prescription does not begin to run in favor of a grantee under a deed from a life tenant, against a remainderman who does not join in the deed, until the falling in of the life-estate by the death of the life tenant." Mathis v. Solomon, 188 Ga. 311, 312, 4 S.E.2d 24, 25.

. . . The trial court erred in granting appellees' motion for directed verdict and in overruling the appellants' motion for directed verdict. Therefore, the judgment of the trial court is reversed with direction that judgment be entered in favor of the appellants.

Judgment reversed with direction.

NOTE

Commercial leases often run on for many pages, and the lessor and lessee may not want the amount of rent payable to be made a public record. Should a recorded memorandum of lease put a subsequent purchaser on inquiry notice of the contents of a lease? Suppose that a shopping center developer leases one space to Howard Johnson for a restaurant; the lease contains a covenant by the lessor that no other restaurant will be permitted in the shopping center. A memorandum of lease is recorded, but the full lease—including the covenant against competition—is not recorded. Subsequently, the developer leases another space in the shopping center to McDonald's restaurant. Is Howard Johnson entitled to an injunction against McDonald's? See Howard D. Johnson Co. v. Parkside Dev. Corp., 348 N.E.2d 656 (Ind. App. 1976) (holding that, even though a memorandum of lease by the common lessor to Howard Johnson is in McDonald's chain of title, the memorandum does not give constructive notice of the full contents of the lease; McDonald's was not put on inquiry notice from Howard Johnson's existing restaurant together with the custom of shopping center developers to use noncompetition covenants); Mister Donut of America, Inc. v. Kemp, 330 N.E.2d 810 (Mass. 1975) (holding memorandum of lease gives constructive notice of contents); Genovese Drug Stores, Inc. v. Connecticut Packing Co., 732 F.2d 286 (2d Cir. 1984) (holding memorandum of lease of adjacent property (such as Howard Johnson's) in shopping center is not in chain of title of subsequent lessee (such as McDonald's)).

Waldorff Insurance and Bonding, Inc. v. Eglin National Bank

District Court of Appeal of Florida, First District, 1984
453 So. 2d 1383

SHIVERS, J. Waldorff Insurance and Bonding, Inc. (Waldorff) appeals the supplemental final judgment of foreclosure entered against it in favor of Eglin National Bank (Bank) on a condominium unit [in the 216-unit Gulf Terrace Condominium in Destin]. Appellant argues that the trial court erred in not finding its interest in the condominium unit superior to the liens of two mortgages held by the Bank. We agree and reverse.

Choctaw Partnership (Choctaw) developed certain properties in Okaloosa County by constructing condominiums. On June 8, 1972, Choctaw executed a promissory note and mortgage on these properties in the amount of $850,000. . . . [This mortgage was promptly recorded.] This note and mortgage was eventually assigned to appellee Bank on January 17, 1975. At that time, the principal balance remaining on this note and mortgage was $41,562.61.

Waldorff entered into a written purchase agreement with Choctaw for condominium unit 111 on April 4, 1973. Choctaw was paid $1,000 at that time as a deposit on Unit 111. The total purchase price of Unit 111 was to be $23,550. In April or May 1973, Waldorff began occupancy of the unit. Furniture worth $5,000 was purchased by Waldorff and placed in the unit. Waldorff continually occupied the unit for about 1½ years thereafter, paying the monthly maintenance fee, the fee for maid service, the fee for garbage pick-up, and paying for repairs to the unit. At the time of the hearing in this case on February 21, 1983, the furniture was still in the unit, the utility bills and monthly maintenance fees were paid by Waldorff, and Waldorff had the keys to the unit and controlled it.

On October 10, 1973, Choctaw executed a note and mortgage for the principal sum of $600,000 in favor of the Bank. Among the properties included in this mortgage was the condominium unit involved in the instant case, Unit 111.

On June 28, 1974, Choctaw executed yet another note and mortgage, this one in favor of the Bank for the principal sum of $95,000. This mortgage secured a number of units, one of which was Unit 111. Choctaw was apparently a client of Waldorff, and in 1974, Choctaw owed Waldorff over $35,000 for insurance premiums. Choctaw agreed to consider the purchase price of Unit 111 paid in full in return for cancellation of the debt owed by Choctaw to Waldorff. Waldorff "wrote off" the debt, and Choctaw executed a quitclaim deed to Unit 111 in favor of Waldorff. The deed was recorded in March 1975.

In 1976, the Bank brought a foreclosure action against Choctaw, Waldorff and others. A final judgment of foreclosure was entered in September 1976, but that judgment did not foreclose Waldorff's interest in Unit 111. Instead, the 1976 final judgment explicitly retained jurisdiction to determine the ownership of Unit 111. A hearing was held on February 21, 1983. The issue at this hearing was whether Waldorff's occupancy, together with the purchase agreement, was sufficient notice so as to make Waldorff's interest in Unit 111 superior to that of the Bank. At this hearing, evidence was taken concerning the agreements between Choctaw and Waldorff and Waldorff's occupancy of Unit 111. There was evidence that condominium units other than 111 were also occupied and that many of these units were occupied by persons who had no legal interest in the units, e.g., persons invited by Choctaw to occupy the units for a time as part of Choctaw's marketing campaign.

The trial court entered a supplemental final judgment of foreclosure which found that Waldorff's occupancy of Unit 111 was "equivocal" because Choctaw allowed at least 8 other condominium units to be furnished and used for

Gulf Terrace Condominium
Destin, Florida

occupancy by various persons. The trial court also found that Waldorff did not pay the consideration promised for Unit 111 because the debt owed by Choctaw to Waldorff was used as a bad debt write-off for federal income tax purposes rather than being credited to Choctaw. The trial court found that "even if defendant could establish some right to Unit 111 by occupancy, defendant failed to pay the agreed consideration for the quitclaim deed and, therefore, the conveyance is void." Based on these findings, the trial court held the Bank's mortgage liens superior to Waldorff's interest.

A contract to convey legal title to real property on payment of the purchase price creates an equitable interest in the purchaser. Lafferty v. Detwiler, 155 Fla. 95, 20 So. 2d 338, 343 (1944); Felt v. Morse, 80 Fla. 154, 85 So. 656 (1920). Beneficial ownership passes to the purchaser while the seller retains mere naked legal title. Arko Enterprises, Inc. v. Wood, 185 So. 2d 734 (Fla. 1st DCA 1966); Tingle v. Hornsby, 111 So. 2d 274 (Fla. 1st DCA 1959). Subsequent successors to the legal title take such title burdened with the equitable interests of which they have either actual or constructive notice. Hoyt v. Evans, 91 Fla. 1053, 109 So. 311 (1926). In the instant case, it appears clear that the April 4, 1973, Agreement to Purchase entered into between Choctaw and Waldorff vested equitable title in Waldorff. Therefore, the interests acquired by the Bank pursuant to the October 1973 and June 1974 mortgages would be subordinate to Waldorff's equitable interest if the Bank had either actual or constructive notice of that interest.

In Blackburn v. Venice Inlet Co., 38 So. 2d 43 (Fla. 1948), the court stated:

It is settled law in Florida that actual possession is constructive notice to all the world, or anyone having knowledge of said possession of whatever right the occupants have in the land. Such possession, when open, visible and exclusive, will put upon inquiry those acquiring any title to or a lien upon the land so occupied to ascertain the nature of the rights the occupants really have in the premises. [38 So. 2d at 46.]

In the instant case, Waldorff was in open, visible and exclusive possession of Unit 111 at the time of the making of the October 1973 and June 1974 mortgages.

The trial court found, however, that Waldorff's possession of Unit 111 was "equivocal" because other units in the condominium project were occupied by persons who had no interest in the units. We do not agree with this analysis. Although many of the condominium units were held by a common grantor, Choctaw, the units were separate parcels intended to be alienated individually. The mortgage executed on June 28, 1974, which secures both the $95,000 note and the $600,000 note of October 10, 1973, described the property mortgaged in terms of individual units, specifically including Unit 111. The status of other units within the condominium project, therefore, is irrelevant to the question of the possession of Unit 111. The issue in the instant case concerned only the rights of the parties involved in Unit 111, not the condominium project as a whole or any other individual units.

Appellee argues, however, that it would have been difficult to ascertain whether any person physically occupying any of the units in the project had a claim of ownership interest in the unit being occupied. Although we agree that it would be more inconvenient for a prospective lender to make several inquiries rather than a single one, we do not find this argument persuasive. We find the ancient, but oft-cited, case of Phelan v. Brady, 119 N.Y. 587, 23 N.E. 1109 (N.Y. 1890), to be instructive in this matter. On May 1, 1886, Mrs. Brady took possession of a tenement building containing 48 apartments occupied by 20 different occupants as tenants from month to month. Her possession was pursuant to a contract for sale secured for her by her attorney. Three of the apartments were occupied by Mrs. Brady and her husband, who kept a liquor store in part of the building. Mrs. Brady began collecting rents immediately upon taking possession of the premises. Mrs. Brady's deed, however, was not recorded until August 26, 1886, subsequent to the recordation of Phelan's mortgage which had been executed by the record owner of the property on July 23, 1886. The court stated:

At the time of the execution and delivery of the mortgage to the plaintiff, the defendant Mrs. Brady was in the actual possession of the premises under a perfectly valid, but unrecorded, deed. Her title must therefore prevail as against the plaintiff. It matters not, so far as Mrs. Brady is concerned, that the plaintiff in good faith advanced his money upon an apparently perfect record title of the defendant John E. Murphy. Nor is it of any consequence, so far as this question is concerned, whether the plaintiff was in fact ignorant of any right or claim of Mrs. Brady to the premises. It is enough that she was in possession under her deed and the contract of purchase, as that fact operated in law as notice to the plaintiff of all her rights. It may be true, as has been argued by plaintiff's counsel, that, when a party takes a conveyance of property situated as this was, occupied by numerous tenants, it would be inconvenient and difficult for him to ascertain the rights or interests that are claimed by all or any of them. But this circumstance cannot change the rule. Actual possession of real estate is sufficient to a person proposing to take a mortgage on the property, and to all the world, of the existence of any right which the person in possession is able to establish. [23 N.E. at 1110-1111.]

Moreover, cases citing Phelan v. Brady have stated that the possession involved there was not equivocal. Swanstrom v. Day, 46 Misc. 311, 93 N.Y.S. 192 (N.Y. Sup. Ct. 1905); Baker v. Thomas, 61 Hun. 17, 15 N.Y.S. 359 (N.Y. Sup. Ct. 1891).

We also agree with appellant that the trial court erred in finding that the conveyance of the property from Choctaw to Waldorff was void due to lack of consideration for the quitclaim deed. Although Waldorff may have erred in attempting to take a "bad debt" tax deduction after cancelling the debt Choctaw owed to Waldorff for insurance premiums, Choctaw was relieved from payment of that debt, and this constituted a valuable consideration flowing to Choctaw. Booth v. Bond, 56 Cal. App. 2d 153, 132 P.2d 520 (Cal. Dist. Ct. App. 1942); see generally Dorman v. Publix-Saenger-Sparks Theatres, 135 Fla. 284, 184 So. 886 (1939); 17 C.J.S. Contracts §§74, 87 (1963).

The parties agree that the 1972 mortgage lien is superior to Waldorff's interest in Unit 111. Appellee, however, stated at oral argument that it did not disagree with the proposition that a proper application of the funds from the 1976 foreclosure sale of the rest of the condominium project should first satisfy the 1972 mortgage. Our decision renders moot appellant's other points on appeal. Accordingly, the supplemental final judgment of foreclosure is reversed and the cause remanded for entry of a judgment consistent with this opinion.

Reversed and remanded.

PROBLEM, NOTE, AND QUESTIONS

1. You are the attorney for a prospective purchaser of a 50-unit apartment house. The present owner has shown the prospective purchaser copies of the leases on file in her office. Can the purchaser rely on these leases? Suppose that the landlord had orally extended tenant A's one-year lease for two more years and has given tenant B a written option to renew for a five-year term, which option does not appear in the landlord's records. Suppose also that tenant C has a five-year lease and has prepaid the rent, though there is nothing in the lease to indicate this. Will the prospective purchaser take subject to the aforementioned rights of tenants A, B, and C? See Gates Rubber Co. v. Ulman, 262 Cal. Rptr. 630 (Cal. App. 1989); Martinique Realty Corp. v. Hall, 166 A.2d 803 (N.J. Super. Ct. 1960). What would you advise the prospective purchaser to do? See 4 American Law of Property §17.12 (1952).

2. *Miller v. Green, 58 N.W.2d 704 (Wis. 1953).* Mary Green leased her farm to Eugene Miller for the year 1950. In November, 1950, after Miller had harvested his crop, Green contracted to sell the farm to Miller for $3,500. Neither the lease nor the contract was recorded. In December, Green had a better offer and sold the farm to W.E. Hines for $3,800. Hines recorded his deed. Hines knew that Miller had leased the land the preceding year but did not know of the contract of sale. The court held that Hines had inquiry notice of Miller's claim because of Miller's acts during November: Miller had (1) hauled 60 loads of manure to the farm and (2) plowed two acres of land. Hines had the obligation to inquire who had done these acts and whether the person had any claim to the land.

3. What types of red flags must be present for a subsequent purchaser to be on notice of a prior interest in a property? In some instances, courts will require quite a bit of reason for concern. For example, in Grose v. Sauvageau, 942 P.2d 398 (Wyo. 1997), Grose purchased property from Ryberg, but never recorded the quitclaim deed because of a variety of deficiencies in the document. After pigs repeatedly escaped from the subject property and injured horses on Sauvageau's farm, and after an unsuccessful City Council reelection campaign that engendered opposition from Grose, Sauvageau apparently sought to exact her revenge by searching title and discovering that there was no deed to show ownership of the property by Grose. Sauvageau then went to the record owner (Ryberg) and purchased the property. The Wyoming Supreme Court held that while Sauvageau "was well aware that the Groses had possession of the property and had made improvements upon it, she diligently searched the records only to discover that the Grose's possession of the property was entirely consistent with the rights of the record owner. Therefore, the Grose's possession of the property did not create a situation which would put Sauvageau on guard as to the possibility of an unrecorded instrument or an alternative claim to the property." 942 P.2d at 403. But see Horse Creek Conservation Dist. v. State ex rel. Wyoming Attorney General, 221 P.3d 306 (Wyo. 2009) (examination of record insufficient if one party has actual notice of unrecorded claim). See also In re Kasparek, 426 B.R. 332 (BAP 10th Cir. 2010); In re Horob Livestock, Inc., 382 B.R. 459 (Bankr. D. Mont. 2007); In re Whiting, 311 B.R. 539 (Bankr. N.D. Cal. 2004).

4. Is the doctrine of inquiry notice sound? Does it make the transfer of land more costly and title less certain? Should the courts abolish inquiry notice and require actual notice?

5. *Negligence and title law.* In a recent article, Professor Sterk describes the development of title doctrine as increasingly importing negligence principles from tort law. With respect to inquiry notice, he observes that "a reasonable purchaser would have asked enough questions to discover the true owner's interest; if this purchaser did not, the purchaser was at fault, and is not protected by the true owner's failure to record." See Stewart E. Sterk, Strict Liability and Negligence in Property Theory, 160 U. Pa. L. Rev. 2129, 2143 (2012). As with tort cases, Sterk argues that importing negligence standards into property law creates incentives for the true owner to take precautions.

7. Marketable Title Acts

Marketable title acts, enacted in a large number of states, have as their purpose limiting title searches to a reasonable period, typically the last 30 or 40 years. The essential idea is quite simple: When one person has a record title to land for a designated period of time, inconsistent claims or interests are extinguished. Some of the acts take the form of a statute of limitations barring a claim not recorded within the designated period. Others declare that the record owner with a clear title going back for the designated period has marketable record title that is free and clear of adverse claims. Thus, except for the interests excepted from the statute, title searches may be safely limited to the number of years specified in the statute. Under a marketable title act, all claimants of interests in land, to be safe, must file a notice of claim every 30 to 40 years after the recording of their instruments of acquisition. See Uniform Marketable Title Act (1990) (30 years); Fla. Stat. Ann. §§712.01 et seq. (West 2013); Mich. Comp. Laws Ann. §§565.101 et seq. (West 2013); N.C. Gen. Stat. §§47B-1 et seq. (2013).

Walter E. Barnett, Marketable Title Acts—Panacea or Pandemonium?
53 Cornell L. Rev. 45, 52-54 (1967)[*]

Marketable title acts are intended to operate in conjunction with, rather than as a substitute for, the recording acts. They seek to extinguish old title defects automatically with the passage of time. The acts provide that if a person has an unbroken chain of title from the present back to his "root of title," then he has the sort of title in favor of which their extinguishment feature will operate. His "root of title" is the most recent transaction in his chain of title that has been of record at least forty years.[18] With certain specified exceptions, claims and interests that depend on matters antedating the root of title are declared null and void. The acts seek to avoid the constitutional problems of an outright extinguishment of property interests by providing, in one of the specified exceptions, that the holders of old interests and claims may preserve them by recording a notice of claim.

The acts do not require a person seeking their benefits to be a bona fide purchaser. In fact, although the acts refer to "the time when marketability is being determined," no "purchase" or other transaction affecting the land need occur to trigger the extinguishment of old defects and interests.

The following example illustrates the intended operation of a marketable title act. Suppose that in 1889 O, the owner of Blackacre, gives X a ninety-nine-year lease, which is recorded that same year. In 1890, O conveys to A, the deed reciting that it is subject to the recorded lease to X. In 1920 A conveys to B, the deed making no mention of the lease. In 1941, B conveys to C, the deed making no mention of the lease. All these deeds were recorded when executed. Under a forty-year marketable title act such as the Model Act, C's title to Blackacre would be free and clear of the ninety-nine-year lease as of 1960, when the 1920 deed from A to B had been of record for forty years. This result assumes that the lessee, X, is not in possession. It is immaterial that the recorded lease gave constructive notice to both B and C, or that both had actual knowledge of its existence. It is likewise immaterial that no transaction affecting the land has taken place between 1941 and the present. The lease is still extinguished in 1960 if X has not filed a notice of claim. C's

18. The 40-year period is most common and is the one used for illustrative purposes throughout this article. . . .

root of title is the 1920 deed from *A* to *B*, and he has an unbroken chain of title for at least forty years since it was recorded. In 1981, *C* or his successor will have a new root of title—the 1941 deed from *B* to *C*—and any claims or interests antedating *its* recording will be extinguished. Thus, title to Blackacre undergoes an automatic "cleansing" whenever forty years elapse from the recording of a transaction that is capable of serving as a root of title. If one asks why the 1890 deed from *O* to *A* did not serve to extinguish the lease in 1930, the answer is that, although the 1890 deed *is* the root of title from 1930 to 1960, its reference to the lease preserves the lease from extinguishment, under one of the act's specified exceptions. If the 1920 deed had made a similar reference to the lease, it would not have been extinguished in 1960. *C* would have had to wait until 1981, when he could show a chain of title from a root at least forty years old, with neither the root nor any subsequent instrument in the chain referring specifically to the lease.

To ensure that his leasehold is preserved from extinction, *X* must file a notice of claim under the act every forty years after the date of his lease. Otherwise, he runs the risk that some recorded transaction will fail to refer to his lease and thus, forty years later, become a root of title that will cut off his rights. Actually, *X* could protect himself in the example given simply by filing one notice of claim in 1960, just before the 1920 deed from *A* to *B* has been of record forty years. But *X* may not know whether or when such transactions have occurred, unless he periodically secures an abstract of title. Regularly filing a notice of claim is his surest protection.

PROBLEM AND NOTES

1. The jurisdiction has a 40-year marketable title act. In 1971, *O*, owner of Blackacre, unimproved land, dies intestate. *O*'s heir, *H*, is unaware that *O* owns Blackacre. In 1972, *F* forges *H*'s name to a deed to Blackacre to *A*. This deed is recorded. In 1974, *A* conveys Blackacre to *B*.

In 2014, *H*'s daughter and sole heir, *C*, discovers the 1972 forgery. *C* brings suit against *B* to establish title to Blackacre. Who prevails? See Marshall v. Hollywood, Inc., 236 So. 2d 114 (Fla. 1970); William B. Stoebuck & Dale A. Whitman, The Law of Property 903 (3d ed. 2000).

2. The marketable title acts except certain interests, which do not have to be re-recorded. These exceptions may include mineral rights, easements, interests of persons in possession, claims of the federal government, or other interests. These exceptions defeat the act's objective of limiting title search because the title examiner much check back beyond the set period of years to be sure no interest excepted exists on record. In recent years, in an effort to preserve views, protect the environment, and reap charitable tax deductions, property owners have granted conservation or historic preservation easements to nonprofit organizations. Since these easements are perpetual, their relationship with marketable title acts sometimes generates interesting questions. For an article that explores some of the issues, see Jennifer Cohoon McStotts, In Perpetuity or for Forty Years, Whichever Is Less: The Effects of Marketable Record Title Acts on Conservation and Preservation Easements, 27 J. Land Resources & Envtl. L. 41 (2007).

3. Some states, without general marketable title statutes, require the periodic re-recordation of certain types of interests in order to preserve them. If not re-recorded, the interests expire. The usual re-recordation period is 30 years. Interests affected by these special re-recordation requirements may include possibilities of reverter and rights of entry (see page 315), easements, covenants, and mineral interests. See Texaco v. Short, 454 U.S. 516 (1982) (upholding a retroactive Indiana statute requiring re-recordation of unused mineral interests every 20 years).

4. One law review article uses an economic framework to model optimal search activities in connection with real estate transactions. See Matthew Baker et al., Optimal Title Search, 31 J. Legal Stud. 139 (2002). Their model, which suggests that it is not efficient to search the entire record of property transactions, provides theoretical support for marketable title acts. The authors also show empirically that state title search requirements can be explained by several relevant economic indicators, including the risk of defects in that state, the cost of title searches, and the frequency of property turnovers.

8.   Recording Systems and the Mortgage Meltdown

The law of title and land recordation rarely finds its way into the headlines of major newspapers. Nevertheless, as mortgage foreclosures swelled during the Great Recession, the weaknesses of our current system for recording mortgages became apparent throughout the nation. As described in Chapter 7, at pages 645-646, over the past quarter century the vast majority of residential loans have been securitized. In contrast to the world before securitization—when a lender held onto the promissory note and mortgage until the loan matured, was prepaid, or was foreclosed upon—securitization entails multiple transfers of beneficial ownership of the debt and the potential for huge recording costs if mortgages would constantly need to be assigned and recorded with each transfer. Ultimately, lenders and the secondary mortgage market agencies came together to create a private solution to this problem—the Mortgage Electronic Registration Systems, Inc. (MERS). A lender participating in the MERS system recorded its mortgage in the relevant local land registry under the name of MERS (as its "nominee"). Subsequent assignments of the mortgage were recorded in the records of MERS, but not in the public land registry. A significant amount of litigation ensued challenging whether MERS had standing to foreclose on the mortgage since it held "legal" but not beneficial title to the mortgage. Although most courts eventually found that MERS did, indeed, have standing, the litigation contributed to the ongoing judicial backlog in mortgage foreclosures. See, e.g., Gomes v. Countrywide Home Loans, 121 Cal. Rptr. 3d 819, 823 (Cal. App. 2011) (MERS had authority to initiate foreclosure); but cf. MERS v. Saunders, 2 A.3d 289, 297 (Me. 2010) (MERS lacked standing to foreclose).

Some commentators have criticized the use of MERS on the ground that it amounts to the "privatization" of the nation's land recording system. See, e.g., Christopher L. Peterson, Two Faces: Demystifying the Mortgage Electronic Registration System's Land Title Theory, 53 Wm. & Mary L. Rev. 111, 125 (2011). Among the complaints are the lack of transparency and accountability inherent in such a change. See id. at 125-133. Indeed, the use of MERS no doubt contributed to the difficulties delinquent borrowers experienced in modifying their mortgages (see the discussion in Chapter 7 at pages 684-685). At its best, mortgage modification is a difficult and laborious process. But because MERS has no authority to act on behalf of the lender and because the "real" owner of the debt is not listed in the public land records, borrowers often have great difficulty determining the right party with which to negotiate. See Donald J. Kochan, Certainty of Title: Perspectives After the Mortgage Foreclosure Crisis on the Essential Role of Effective Recording Systems, 66 Ark. L. Rev. 267, 291 (2013); Gerald Korngold, Legal and Policy Choices in the Aftermath of the Subprime and Mortgage Financing Crisis, 60 S.C. L. Rev. 728, 746 (2009).

One of the reasons for the creation of MERS was the concern among market participants with the cumbersome nature of mortgage recording and high transaction costs, particularly as the volume of mortgage originations exploded in the mid-2000s. This high volume of activity also exposed other flaws in connection with our system for recording interests in land. Sometimes documents are lost or never recorded. In other instances, documents are recorded but fail to comply with legal formalities. See Kochan, supra, at 293-295. Some of these irregularities are related to recording systems, but others are caused by the sheer carelessness of lenders and their agents. For a discussion of efforts to bring more accountability to the system, see the discussion in Chapter 7 at pages 681-683.

The weaknesses in our system of land records exposed by the wave of mortgage foreclosures have generated a wide variety of proposals, ranging from complete digitization to nationalization. See, e.g., Kochan, supra, at 311-314; Tanya Marsh, Foreclosures and the Failure of the American Land Title Recording System, 111 Colum. L. Rev. Sidebar 19, 24-26 (2011).

B. Registration of Title

Myres S. McDougal[19] & John W. Brabner-Smith, Land Title Transfer: A Regression

48 Yale L.J. 1125, 1126-1131 (1939)

It takes no prophet to foresee that fundamental reforms in land utilization are hot upon us. Yet for the achievement of such reforms without payment of

---

19. Myres S. McDougal, Yale's great angry man of property in the 1940s, assailed, with memorable invective, lawyers, judges, legislators, and scholars for failing to reform property doctrines to serve modern needs. McDougal's outrage is summed up in the final line of his evisceration of volume three of the Restatement of Property: "To make a superb inventory of Augean stables is not to cleanse them." Myres S. McDougal, Future Interests Restated: Tradition Versus Clarification and Reform, 55 Harv. L. Rev. 1077, 1115 (1942).

McDougal's casebook, Property, Wealth, Land (1948), written with David Haber, was what the French call a *succès d'estime*—a huge success with the critics but a failure at the box office. Although it found few adoptions, Property, Wealth, Land was filled with imaginative ways of looking at property and trenchant criticism of the received wisdom, and it greatly influenced the way property law is taught.

undue and continued tribute to private monopolies and without fruitless bother and delay—perhaps even if they are to be achieved at all—major changes must be effected in our antiquated, precommerce "system" of land transfer. Cheap, expeditious, and secure methods must be designed, if they are not already available, to replace the present complicated and dilatory methods which, while costly to the individual and burdensome to the public, afford no adequate security of title. Streamlined need cannot long endure horse-and-buggy obstacles to the liquidity of land. It is an ancient query, but its relevance grows: why should not a lot or a farm be as easily acquired and as securely held as a ship or a share of stock or an automobile?

Why *cannot* a lot or a farm be so easily acquired and securely held? The answer can be found in any courthouse. It is in the wild disorder and the incompleteness of the public records. First, the disorder. Suppose a bank had been in business 100 years with 100,000 customers and had repeatedly honored some thirty different kinds of instruments against each account, copying each instrument serially into big books, before returning it to the customer, and keeping only alphabetical indexes—thirty different indexes—to these books. Imagine the expense and delay which might ensue in determining a customer's balance every time he demanded a little money. Preposterous as it may seem, that is a comparison not unfair to our "indigenous" system of land title "recordation" inherited from the Pilgrim Fathers. "The fact is," Professor John R. Rood has written, "that the path of the searcher for a safe title to land . . . is beset by more traps, sirens, harpies, and temptations, than ever plagued the wandering Ulysses, the faithful Pilgrim, or the investor in gilt-edged securities." Such a searcher must go back to a good "root" of title, varying in different states from 40 to 60 or a 100 years or more, and come down to date. As he ploughs through the Joneses, Smiths, and Johnsons and through the deeds, mortgages, judgments, taxes, and mechanics' liens he can never be sure that he isn't missing something fatal to his title. Worse yet, all this laborious retracing of the tortuous path of title is perpetual motion. Every time the land is sold or mortgaged or subdivided—no matter into how small parts—it all has to be done over again; or else private title plants, better ordered than the public records, must be constructed and maintained at great expense. Furthermore, whether our searcher maintains a plant or continually retraces his steps, the accelerating fecundity of the records, added to the disorder, scarcely lessens his labors.

Next, the incompleteness of the records. Here again the perils are legion. In simple truth the notion that we have anywhere in this country (apart from the Torrens statutes) any such thing as "record title" is sheer delusion. There are too many facts affecting the validity of a title which not only do not appear in the records but which often cannot be ascertained by any reasonable search outside the records. Contributors to the literature of land transfer . . . have vied with each other in the number of such facts they could list. Among the most frequently recurring items are: adverse possession and prescriptions; forgeries and other frauds; matters of heirship, marriage, and divorce; copyists' and recorders' errors; infancy, insanity, and other disabilities; authority of corporate officers; invalidity of acknowledgments; identity of persons; invalidity of mortgage foreclosures and of judgments and decrees; want of legal delivery of instruments; violations of the usury laws; unprobated wills, praetermitted heirs, and posthumous children; falsity of affidavits; revocation of powers of attorney by death or insanity; parol partitions and dedications; inchoate mechanics' liens; extent of restrictive covenants; non-recordation of prior government patent; and facts about boundaries. Such are some of the hazards external to the records which may disturb the peace of the faithful searcher for an indefeasible title. Obviously, for even the most scant security he must go much beyond the official sources of information. Often he does not go far enough. Is it any wonder that volumes of reports are filled with cases about "marketability" of titles and that court calendars are crowded with actions to quiet title?

Let us now suppose that some reasonably prudent man—some "rational" seeker for the "good life"—were to set out to reform this mess. What steps would he take? First, he would undoubtedly make provision for getting rid of existing stale claims and threats by a cheap and expeditious procedure for quieting titles or by a short Statute of Limitations or by both. Next, once the account of any particular lot or farm or other convenient unit of land in single ownership had been balanced by such new procedure, he would require a common-sense change in the method of keeping the public books. This change would take the form of a new and improved "tract" index. So far as possible all the facts about the title to any one piece of land, whatever the convenient unit, would be entered on one page, a "register" page. Where the interests making up a "title" are unusually complicated, memorials on the register page could refer an examiner to the field documents creating such interests. For convenience a copy of the register page, called a certificate of title, would be given to the owner. On subsequent voluntary transfers of the land, for double protection against fraud, surrender of this certificate would be required in addition to the vendor's deed. Then a new register page, with all obsolete entries removed, would be opened for the purchaser and a copy handed to him. And so on. Transfers of less than the fee would be memorialized on both the register page and the certificate, and the documents effecting such transfers filed. Involuntary transfers could be made only on order of the court making the transfer.

With the public records at long last in acceptable order, our bold reformer could then proceed to kill caveat emptor, protect the bona fide purchaser, and so create a new security of title. This he would accomplish by making the public records as nearly conclusive, as nearly unimpeachable, as is constitutionally possible. He would need to except only the Federal Government and persons in actual occupation of the premises, making adverse claim, on the date of the initial registration. No other claimants to any piece of land could get their claims honored, against bona fide purchasers for value, who did not have such claims properly entered in the public register. Under such a system, there could scarcely be need of an insurance fund to protect purchasers. Yet occasionally an odd claimant of an interest less than the fee might fail to get his interest properly registered because of oversight or error by a public official. For the protection of such claimants an ample fund could be collected by imposing on the first registrant a small fee (of not more than one-tenth of 1 percent of the value of the land).

Should our estimable reformer now, by chance, turn to any of the voluminous literature on the Torrens system, he would find that his ideas had long been anticipated. Substantially the system he advocates has had an honorable history in Europe of over five hundred years. Its present use spreads wide about the world. It "prevails throughout" Germany (including Austria), Hungary, Australia, Tasmania, Papua, New Zealand, Fiji, the "great majority of the provinces of Canada," and other scattered British colonies and protectorates. It is of "large importance" in England and Ireland. In the United States at least five states—California, Illinois, Massachusetts, Minnesota, and Ohio—have had substantial experience with the system. Statutes have existed in fourteen other states. The system has had the approval of the American Bar Association and of the Commissioners on Uniform State Laws and has even been embodied in a uniform statute. It has had the blessing and active support of a long line of distinguished and disinterested scholars. Predictions have long been current that title registration must inevitably, because of its easily demonstrable superiority, supersede title "recordation" throughout the country. Dissenting voices have usually come from those whose interests were obviously served by the existing chaos.

The system of registering title is widely known as the "Torrens system," named after Sir Richard Torrens who in 1858 introduced registration of title into South Australia, from which it spread to many other parts of the world under his name. Registration of title rests upon these principles: (1) A lawsuit adjudicates title to be in the plaintiff, subject to any mortgage, easement, or other interest the court finds to exist. All other claims are wiped out. This adjudicated state of the title is officially registered on a conclusive certificate of title. (2) When the registered land is transferred, a new certificate is issued by the registrar, after making a substantive review of what has happened to the title since the last certificate was issued. (3) An insurance indemnity fund is established to compensate those who lose interests because of errors of the registrar or operation of the system. As you can see, title registration puts title assurance in the hands of the government whereas the recording system puts title assurance in private hands using the public records.

At one time, statutes in 19 states authorized voluntary registration of title, but about half of these have been repealed. Today only in five states—Hawaii, Illinois (Cook County), Massachusetts, Minnesota (Hennepin and Ramsey Counties), and Ohio (Hamilton County)—is there any substantial amount of land with registered title.

Why has the Torrens system failed to take hold in the United States? First, the initial cost of a lawsuit adjudicating title has been a substantial deterrent to widespread use. Second, although the certificate of title is supposed to be conclusive, exceptions have been provided for certain interests, either by legislatures or courts. Exceptions may include federal tax liens, statutory liens, real property tax liens, short-term leases, possessory claims, and visible easements. A fraudulent registration may make a title registration certificate unreliable. As with the early race recording statutes, courts have been reluctant to protect certificate holders against prior known unrecorded claims, though the object of title registration is to put title in the certificate holder. See Carol M. Rose, Crystals and Mud in Property Law, 40 Stan. L. Rev. 577, 588-589 (1988). Since title registration does not in fact prove conclusive, there is less incentive to go to the expense of registering title. Third, title registration has been opposed by title insurance companies, title abstract companies, and lawyers who have a financial interest in preserving the present system.

Finally, inadequate or inadequately trained personnel in the public records office have, at least in California and Illinois, brought on crises that have resulted in legislative repeal of title registration. In 1989, in Cook County, Illinois, there was a two-year backlog in the issuance of Torrens certificates in the county recorder's office. Some years earlier, an employee had been convicted of taking payments to expedite service to patrons. United States v. Gannon, 684 F.2d 433 (7th Cir. 1981). Upon the recommendation of a blue-ribbon committee appointed by the Cook County recorder, the Illinois legislature in 1991 repealed its Torrens act, prohibiting additional title registrations under it, and closing the registration office in 1997. 765 Ill. Comp. Stat. Ann. 40/1, 40/3 (West 2013).

For a description of the Torrens system and an evaluation of its merits, see John L. McCormack, Torrens and Recording: Land Title Assurance in the Computer Age, 18 Wm. Mitchell L. Rev. 61 (1992) (citing many earlier studies). McCormack concludes that the failure of Torrens in Chicago was "mainly caused by incompetent, unsatisfactory administration. . . . This incompetence is largely due to the fiscal or political constraints which bind many county governments and is really not the fault of the people who administer and work for these governments." Id. at 113 n.220. In his view, "it is clear that Torrens or any other true registration system is more costly and difficult for government to administer than recording. This higher cost is inherent in title registration systems because much of the data consolidation, evaluation and management done by private parties under recording is done by government employees or their agents under registration." Id. at 113.

Thomas J. Miceli & C.F. Sirmans, Torrens vs. Title Insurance: An Economic Analysis of Land Title Systems

Illinois Real Estate Letter (Fall 1997)

To operate efficiently, our real estate markets require a system for establishing and protecting ownership interests. Since Colonial times, the predominant system for achieving this end in the US has been the "recording system," which relies on the maintenance of a public record containing the history of all transactions for all privately owned land. The would-be buyer of a parcel can consult this record to gather *evidence* that the seller has good title and there are no competing claims. However, because there is a possibility that unrecorded claims exist, that there are errors in the public record, or that the opinion of an attorney conducting a *title search* will be found incorrect, the buyer does not obtain *proof* that the seller holds good title. A buyer thus faces some risk of losing his interest if an unknown party later asserts a claim. This risk leads most buyers to purchase private *title insurance*, which provides financial indemnification in the event of a loss. It is also typical for a mortgage lender to require a real estate buyer to purchase title insurance for at least the amount of the mortgage loan. Although the "plants," or "factories," of profit-seeking title insurance companies are generally more efficiently organized and accurate than the public records, the possibility of a successful claim remains.

The Torrens Approach

In 1858, Sir Robert Torrens developed an alternative system for assuring title to land, modeled after a method for recording ownership interests in ships that Torrens had encountered in his work as an Australian customs administrator. The Torrens system ultimately spread to many English-speaking countries, including England, which adopted a version of the system in 1925 as part of sweeping land reform legislation. Since the late 1800s, as many as twenty-one states in the US have enacted Torrens legislation, though the system was used extensively in only a few jurisdictions, including Illinois, primarily in Cook County.[20] (The state repealed its Torrens Act in 1992.)

The Torrens system differs from the traditional recording system in that it establishes a legal procedure whereby the state *guarantees* the owner's title. The process begins with a court proceeding that involves an examination of the history of title to the real estate in question, in an effort to identify potential claimants. The court ultimately issues a certificate to the owner that establishes legal ownership against any claims that remain undeclared or unrecorded at the time of registration. (Any claim that is known or discovered, such as a current mortgage, is recorded on the certificate.) Once the property is registered in the system, subsequent transfers do not require such an extensive procedure; a purchaser need only examine the certificate to verify ownership and learn of any valid claims. Ease of transfer following the registration represents an important benefit of Torrens; under the recording system a full title search must be done in connection with each transfer.

The key difference between the Torrens system and the recording system, therefore, is that under the latter, a good-faith purchaser bears the risk of losing his interest in the land if a claimant later appears, whereas under the former the

---

20. Other states where Torrens was used extensively are Massachusetts and Minnesota. Currently, land can be registered in only a few states; as of 1991 these were Colorado, Georgia, Hawaii, Massachusetts, Minnesota, New York, North Carolina, Ohio, Virginia, and Washington.

owner's certificate defeats any competing claims not declared at the initial proceeding. Undeclared claimants, however, can seek monetary compensation from a public Torrens indemnity fund financed by registration fees. Because a certificate holder possesses a claim that is (with some exceptions) incontestable, he has no need (in theory) to purchase private title insurance, though in practice holders of Torrens certificates often do buy such coverage, for reasons noted below.

Torrens vs. Recording in Practice

The initial experimentation with Torrens in the US was based on several features on which Torrens is purported to offer advantages over the recording system.[21] The principal advantage of land registration is that it clears clouded titles, thereby promoting land's marketability and development. Thus, much of the early motivation for Torrens registration in the US was to promote land development during periods of rapid urbanization. Registration also facilitated redevelopment following idiosyncratic events like the Great Chicago Fire of 1871, in which the public land records were destroyed. In addition to clearing title for development reasons, land registration has been used to clarify boundaries when early property lines have become blurred or historical surveying techniques were found unreliable,[22] and to protect absentee owners against loss of their land to "squatters" under adverse possession statutes.[23] It can be argued, in fact, that registration's prevention of involuntary transfer of title by adverse possession is efficiency-enhancing.

Yet despite its advantages, Torrens has been put to fairly limited use in our country. This lack of success suggests that the system's disadvantages outweigh its advantages in most jurisdictions. The principal disadvantage is the initial cost of registering a parcel, an outlay high enough to deter switching by all but those owners whose land is unmarketable due to title flaws. Potentially offsetting this high up-front cost is a supposed savings in the transaction costs for subsequent transfers of the property; recall that the title history of a registered parcel need not be searched anew with each sale, and that an unrecorded claimant can not seek an interest in the land (he can pursue only compensation from the indemnity fund).

Another *potential* savings under the Torrens system is that property owners would seem not to have to buy private title insurance; the government, in effect, insures their title. In practice, however, researchers Blair Shick and Irving Plotkin

---

21. See Blair Shick and Irving Plotkin, *Torrens in the United States*, Lexington, MA: Lexington Books, 1978.

22. These motivations were especially relevant in Massachusetts and Minnesota.

23. Adverse possession statutes exist in all 50 states, and though the definition of *adverse* can vary across jurisdictions, a typical requirement is that possession be open, continuous, exclusive, and with a claim of right. The usual economic justifications for adverse possession are that it clears title to land and prevents owners from leaving productive land idle. While Torrens does not address the second of these concerns, economists recognize that leaving land idle is not necessarily an inefficient use, in light of the *option* value of future development. See Thomas J. Miceli & C.F. Sirmans, "An Economic Theory of Adverse Possession," *International Review of Law & Economics* 15 (1995): 161-173.

found that in jurisdictions where Torrens and recording coexisted, land owners bought title insurance with about the same frequency under the two systems. The authors further determined that the cost of insuring was the same for registered and unregistered land. Owners of registered land buy private insurance (and lenders often require it) because certification of ownership under Torrens admits several exceptions that continue to pose threats of loss. Examples include tax and mechanics' liens, claims from bankruptcy proceedings, and claims from Native American tribes. In addition, the public indemnity funds, which potentially compensate victims of these losses, can go bankrupt as a result of underfunding.

A final reason for Torrens's failure in the US, unrelated to its merits, has been resistance by parties, especially lawyers and private title insurers, with vested interests in the recording system. Thus history, politics, and the voluntary nature of the system have contributed to the failure of Torrens to thrive in the US, despite a legal expert's view that someone without knowledge of traditional practices would identify registration as the best system. Our successful implementation of land registration would likely require its mandatory imposition, as was done in England with "remarkable success."[24]

Conflicting Results

Attempts to measure supposed transaction cost savings under Torrens in jurisdictions where it has coexisted with the recording system have shown conflicting results. . . .

Transfer & Development Incentives

The principal economic difference between Torrens and recording, as noted above, is how they assign property rights to the land when a claim is asserted. Simply stated, under Torrens the possessor keeps the land and the claimant receives monetary compensation, whereas under the recording system (with title insurance) the claimant gets the land and the possessor is compensated. (For simplicity, we consider only claims of full ownership, though the analysis would be the same for partial claims.) From an economic perspective, the question (aside from transaction costs) is which system is better at promoting *efficient* land use.

Achieving efficiency involves two components: encouraging land's transfer to the highest-valuing user (*exchange* efficiency), and creating incentives for efficient land development (*investment,* or *production,* efficiency). First, consider incentives for efficient transfer. Suppose that the possessor of a parcel values it at $70,000 (the minimum sum he would accept to surrender it voluntarily), but that its market value is only $50,000. The $20,000 difference represents the *subjective*

---

24. See John E. Cribbett, *Principles of the Law of Property*, 2nd, 1975: 316.

value that the possessor assigns to the land, an amount that presumably increases with the length of occupancy, especially for residential users.[25]

Now suppose that someone unknown to the possessor asserts a claim to the land. In the typical case of this nature the claimant has never occupied the land, and therefore has no subjective interest in the property, so we might assume that the claimant values the land at its $50,000 market value. (In any case, the claimant likely values the land less than does the possessor; otherwise he would negotiate its purchase.) An implication is that the claimant would be indifferent between receiving the land and obtaining compensation equal to its market value. In contrast, the possessor, for whom the value is $50,000 plus a subjective amount, would obviously be better off if he were allowed to retain the land rather than being forced to surrender it at its market value.

The example, as outlined so far, might seem to suggest that Torrens is superior to the recording system in terms of maximizing the value of the land, in that Torrens assigns the land to the highest valuer, in this case the possessor. This conclusion is not necessarily true, however. To see why not, consider that if a court awards the land to the claimant, this assignment is not likely to represent the final ownership situation. After all, the displaced possessor (with $50,000 in title insurance proceeds) will pay up to $70,000 to recoup the land, whereas the claimant will accept any amount in excess of $50,000. Thus, unless there are significant transaction costs, the land still ends up in the hands of the highest valuer (the original owner), who repurchases it for a price between $50,000 and $70,000, perhaps $60,000. (The exact price in such a negotiation depends on the bargaining abilities of the parties involved.)

The preceding example shows that title will likely end up with the highest-valuing user regardless of how it is initially assigned, a result suggesting that the title system does *not* affect the final allocation of rights to the land.[26] The initial assignment of rights will likely matter, however, for the distribution of income. Specifically, suppose that financial compensation under both systems is equal to the land's market value. In this situation, the initial possessor would prefer Torrens, under which he retains the land rather than having to repurchase it for a $60,000 figure that exceeds his $50,000 title insurance settlement. The claimant, by contrast, prefers recording, under which he gets title and then sells the land back to the first possessor for $60,000 rather than receiving $50,000 from the Torrens indemnity fund.

The fact that possessors are better off distributionally than successful claimants under Torrens suggests that, *politically*, the Torrens system should be able to replace the recording system, especially since land possessors vastly outnumber would-be claimants. From an *economic* perspective, however, we know that a large

---

25. Oliver Wendell Holmes once observed that "man, like a tree in the cleft of a rock, gradually shapes roots to its surroundings, and when the roots have grown to a certain size, can't be displaced without cutting at its life." We should also recognize, however, that the passage of time can bring about events, such as children's graduation from school or the homeowner's retirement from work, that might *reduce* subjective values.

26. This situation illustrates the *Coase Theorem*; see Ronald Coase, "The Problem of Social Cost," *Journal of Law and Economics* 3 (1960): 1-44. [On the Coase Theorem, recall footnote 32 on page 50.—EDS.]

but apathetic majority (the risk of a claim on any parcel is minuscule) will often fail against an active minority.

The preceding discussion is based on an assumption that transaction costs in connection with a resale would be low. If these costs were high, the Torrens system would be preferable at a societal level, because it assigns the land initially to the highest-valuing user (recall that we expect a current possessor to realize a subjective value that a claimant would lack). In contrast, another costly transaction would be required under the recording system, and if the transaction costs exceeded the difference between the possessor's value and the claimant's ($20,000 in our example), this transfer might not occur at all; the result would be an inefficient assignment of rights.

The title system also affects incentives for land *development* when possessors face the risk of claims. Indeed, recall that an important argument for experiments with Torrens in the US was its initial ability to stimulate land development. The supposed advantage of Torrens in this respect is that developers need not fear the loss of their land, so they can invest as if there were no risk of a claim (just as we might buy more consumer goods if we did not have to fear theft). It is not necessarily true, however, that the recording system provides inferior incentives to invest in land. As long as developers purchase sufficient title insurance to cover the value of the land and improvements, they are able to invest without fear of losing their financial interests in their properties, even though they may lose the land itself, just as we insure expensive consumer goods. (Of course, this conclusion is based on an assumption that a developer is primarily interested in land as an investment, and that he attaches little or no uncompensable subjective value to it.) Both systems therefore have the potential to provide the same level of protection to investors.

[Further work by Miceli and Sirmans studies home sales in Cook County, Illinois, a jurisdiction that for many years simultaneously had a recording system and a Torrens system. See, e.g., Thomas J. Miceli et al., A Question of Title: Property Rights and Asset Values, 41 Regional Sci. & Urban Econ. 499 (2011); Thomas J. Miceli et al., Title Systems and Land Values, 45 J.L. & Econ. 565 (2002). The authors made use of this natural experiment to estimate under which system land values would be higher. According to their results, land values under the Torrens system were greater.

For other appraisals of the Torrens system, see C. Dent Bostick, Land Title Registration: An English Solution to an American Problem, 63 Ind. L.J. 55 (1987); Charles Szypszak, Public Registries and Private Solutions: An Evolving American Real Estate Conveyance Regime, 24 Whittier L. Rev. 663 (2003); William B. Stoebuck & Dale A. Whitman, The Law of Property 923-930 (3d ed. 2000).]

C. Title Insurance

Title insurance developed because of the inadequacies and inefficiencies of the public records in protecting private titles. Title insurance is bought by one premium paid at the time the policy is issued. The premium is based on the amount of insurance purchased, which ordinarily, in a homeowner's policy, is the amount of the purchase price of the property and, in a lender's policy, the amount of the loan. Title insurance has no fixed term and continues for as long as the insured maintains an interest in the property. Title insurance creates liability to the insured only and does not run with the land to subsequent purchasers. A subsequent purchaser must take out a new policy if the purchaser wants title insurance. In a nutshell, title insurance is the opinion of the insurer concerning the validity of title, backed by an agreement to make that opinion good if it should prove to be mistaken and loss results as a consequence.

In most states, title insurance companies are free to use whatever contract forms they choose. However, under pressure by large institutional lenders and by quasi-governmental corporations operating the secondary mortgage market (Federal National Mortgage Association, Federal Home Loan Mortgage Corporation, Government National Mortgage Association)—all of whom need uniform national forms—most title insurance companies today use uniform policy forms based upon forms developed by the American Land Title Association. ALTA has two basic forms of title insurance policies, a mortgagee's policy and an owner's policy. The mortgagee's policy insures the mortgage lender and not the homeowner. The homeowner who desires title insurance must take out a separate owner's policy.

Basically, title insurance guarantees that the insurance company has searched the public records and insures against any defects in the public records, unless such defects are specifically excepted from coverage in the policy. The standard policy excludes losses arising from government regulations affecting the use, occupancy, or enjoyment of land (for example, zoning ordinances, subdivision regulations, and building codes), unless a notice of enforcement or violation is recorded in the public records. The standard policy also excludes claims of persons in possession not shown by the public records, as well as unrecorded easements, implied easements (see page 831), and easements arising by prescription (see pages 842-847). Standard policies also exclude defects that would be revealed by a survey or inspection.

Extended coverage, adding various kinds of protection, can be purchased for an increased premium.

The American Land Title Association's standard mortgage policy insuring the mortgage lender is substantially similar to the owner's policy. It varies principally in that it insures that the mortgage lien is valid, enforceable, and a first and prior lien against all other liens, including mechanics' liens. Almost all institutional lenders require title insurance (at the borrower's expense). Because all secondary-market purchasers of mortgages also require lender's title insurance, there has been an explosive growth of title insurance in the last 30 years.

Walker Rogge, Inc. v. Chelsea Title & Guaranty Co.

Supreme Court of New Jersey, 1989
562 A.2d 208

[Walker Rogge, Inc., acting through its president, John Rogge, purchased a tract of land from Alexander Kosa. Kosa had acquired the property from one Aiello.

Before Rogge signed the contract of sale on December 12, 1979, Kosa showed him a 1975 survey by Price Walker. This survey indicated the tract consisted of 18.33 acres. The Kosa-Rogge contract described the land by reference to the Price Walker survey and indicated that quantity of land to be "19 acres more or less." It called for a price of $363,000, which was to be adjusted on the basis of $16,000 per acre "for deviations from the amount of 19 acres." (Because the tract included a house, the actual sale price was greater than the product of the number of acres times the price per acre.) Signed on December 12, 1979, the contract called for closing on December 31, with time of the essence.

Rogge requested that the title work be handled by Chelsea Title & Guaranty Co., which insures titles, examines titles, and conducts real estate closings. Chelsea had issued two prior title policies on the property. In the deed from Aiello to Kosa the property description, based on a survey done by one Schilling, stated that the property contained 12.486 acres. A copy of this deed was in Chelsea's files.

The deed from Kosa to Rogge described the property in accordance with the 1975 Price Walker survey, but the deed did not indicate the acreage of the tract. Similarly, the title commitment or binder issued by Chelsea before closing, as well as the title insurance policy, described the property by reference to the Price Walker survey, without indicating the total acreage of the property. No one can remember why a description based on the Price Walker survey, rather than the description in the Aiello-to-Kosa deed, was inserted in Chelsea's title commitment, Kosa's deed, and Chelsea's title insurance policy.]

POLLOCK, J. After the closing, Chelsea issued a title policy, which states that

SUBJECT TO THE EXCLUSIONS FROM COVERAGE, THE EXCEPTIONS CONTAINED IN SCHEDULE B AND THE PROVISIONS OF THE CONDITIONS AND STIPULATIONS HEREOF,

Chelsea Title and Guaranty Company, a New Jersey corporation herein called the Company, insures, as of Date of Policy shown in Schedule A [January 10, 1980], against loss or damage, not exceeding the amount of insurance stated in Schedule A [$363,000], and costs, attorneys' fees and expenses which the Company may become obligated to pay hereunder, sustained or incurred by the insured [Walker Rogge] by reason of:

1) Title in the estate or interest described in Schedule A being vested otherwise than as stated herein;
2) Any defect in or lien or encumbrance on such title;
3) Lack of a right of access to and from the land; or
4) Unmarketability of such title.

Repeating the identical exception in Schedule B of the title commitment, that schedule in the title policy states: "This policy does not insure against loss or damage by reason of the following: . . . 3. Encroachments, overlaps, boundary line disputes and other matters which could be disclosed by an accurate survey and inspection of the premises." . . .

Over the six years following the closing, Walker Rogge paid off the purchase money mortgage, but did not obtain a more recent survey. Then in 1985 Rogge sought to acquire lots adjacent to the property in question preparatory to subdividing the entire property. In connection with the subdivision, Rogge hired a new surveyor, Dennis Duffy, who concluded after extensive field work, research, and title searching that the property in question contained not 18.33 acres, as was stated in the 1975 Price Walker survey, but 12.43 acres, a quantity much closer to the recital of 12.486 acres in the Aiello deed. . . .

On learning from Duffy that it had acquired only twelve acres, Walker Rogge instituted the present action. In its complaint, Walker Rogge alleged that the 5.5 acre shortage was an insurable loss under the policy and that Chelsea was liable in negligence in failing to disclose documents in its files revealing that the property contained fewer than eighteen acres. . . . At the conclusion of the trial, the court determined that the policy covered the shortage in acreage. The court found that title to the property was not vested as described in the policy, that the shortage constituted a defect in title, and that the title was unmarketable. Furthermore, the court found the survey exception "so vague as to be meaningless."

Although Chelsea had billed Walker Rogge $75 for a title examination, the court found that Rogge had ordered only a title policy, and not a title search. Damages were computed by deducting the 12.5 acres actually received, as determined by the Duffy survey, from the 18 acres for which Rogge had paid. By multiplying 5.5 acres times the $16,000 per-acre purchase price, the court calculated that damages were $88,000. Costs and prejudgment interest were awarded, but counsel fees were denied.

The Appellate Division affirmed the judgment, but remanded the matter for clarification of the damages. 222 N.J. Super. 363, 536 A.2d 1309. . . .

As we have previously stated, "[a] title insurance policy is a contract of indemnity under which the insurer for a valuable consideration agrees to indemnify the insured in a specified amount against loss through defects of title to, or liens or encumbrances upon realty in which the insured has an interest." Sandler v. New Jersey Realty Title Ins. Co., 36 N.J. 471, 478-79, 178 A.2d 1 (1962). Like other policies of insurance, title policies are liberally construed against the insurer and in favor of the insured. Id. at 479, 178 A.2d 1. Notwithstanding that principle of construction, courts should not write for the insured a better policy of insurance than the one purchased. Last v. West Am. Ins. Co., 139 N.J. Super. 456, 460, 354 A.2d 364 (App. Div. 1976).

Real estate title insurance policies, like other aspects of the transfer of real estate, are unavoidably technical. That technicality counsels a prudent purchaser to consult qualified experts such as lawyers and surveyors. The reason is that the purchase of real estate, even something as commonplace as a single-family residence, is qualitatively different from the purchase of personal property such as furniture, automobiles, and securities. Lawyers, who are familiar with the technicalities and terminology of real estate law, are not only helpful but virtually essential for the protection of the rights of anyone purchasing real property. Every home buyer knows as much. Anyone who buys real estate without the aid of a surveyor runs the risk that he or she may not receive all the land for which he or she paid. In brief, title insurance is no substitute for a survey. . . .

In the absence of a recital of acreage, a title company does not insure the quantity of land. Title companies are in the business of guaranteeing title, not acreage. See Contini v. Western Title Ins. Co., 40 Cal. App. 3d 536, 542-43, 115 Cal. Rptr. 257, 260-61 (1974). To obtain such insurance, an insured should provide the title company with an acceptable survey that recites the quantity of land described or obtain from the company an express guaranty of the quantity of land insured in the policy.

Consistent with that premise, title insurance policies generally provide either that they are subject to such state of facts as an accurate survey would disclose or to the facts shown on an acceptable survey. Thus, one of the reasons that purchasers obtain surveys is to find out how much land they are buying. Another reason for obtaining a survey is to eliminate from the title policy the exception for such state of facts as an accurate survey would disclose. . . .

At the outset, we find that the survey exception is neither vague nor unenforceable. . . . Whatever else the phrase "other matters" might mean in a survey exception, it clearly refers to the dimensions of the lot lines and the size of the lot. The size of a tract simply cannot be ascertained with any certainty from a search of public records alone. The reason is that land exists on the ground, not on paper. When a description refers to a point in the line of another, only a survey can reveal the actual size of a piece of property and the amount of land included in a deed. A shortage in acreage is one of the facts that an accurate survey and inspection would disclose.

. . . The purpose of the survey exception is to exclude coverage when the insured fails to provide the insurer with a survey. 13A M. Lieberman, New Jersey Practice §1701 at 194 (3d ed. 1966). From a search of relevant public records, a title company cannot ascertain the risks that an accurate survey would disclose. It is for this reason that the title company puts that risk on the insured, who can control it either by obtaining a survey or arranging for the elimination of the survey exception. . . . Had plaintiff obtained a survey from Duffy before the Kosa closing, instead of waiting until it wanted to subdivide the property, it could have eliminated the risk of paying for property it did not receive. . . .

We now turn to plaintiff's negligence claim against Chelsea. In support of that claim, plaintiff points to Chelsea's separate charge for "title examination" and to its reliance on Chelsea to conduct a reasonable search. Courts and commentators, like the lower courts in this case, have divided on the question whether a title company should be exposed to liability in tort for negligence in searching records as well as to liability in contract under its policy of insurance.

The basic question is whether the issuance of the title commitment and policy places a duty on a title insurance company to search for and disclose to the insured any reasonably discoverable information that would affect the insured's decision to close the contract to purchase. In this state, the rule has been that a title company's liability is limited to the policy and that the company is not liable in tort for negligence in searching records. Underlying that rule is the premise that the duty of the title company, unlike the duty of a title searcher, does not depend on negligence, but on the agreement between the parties. . . . If, however, the title company agrees to conduct a search and provide the insured with an abstract of title in addition to the title policy, it may expose itself to liability for negligence as a title searcher in addition to its liability under the policy. Trenton Potteries Co. v. Title Guar. & Trust Co., 176 N.Y. 65, 68 N.E. 132, 135 (1903). In that regard, the trial court expressly found that

> it is the conclusion of this court that plaintiff did not engage Chelsea to undertake two separate functions; that is, to prepare a title report, then a policy of title insurance. The title search which was completed by Chelsea was simply an internal procedure for Chelsea's own purposes in deciding whether or not to issue a title policy. Even though plaintiff was billed for the title search, it is the conclusion of this court that the real transaction between the parties was a policy of insurance. This conclusion means that plaintiff's remedy against Chelsea lies in contract, not in negligence. Consequently, the negligence charges against Chelsea are dismissed.

Notwithstanding Chelsea's separate $75 charge for "title examination," the trial court's finding is supported by substantial credible evidence in the record. Rova Farms Resort v. Investors Ins. Co., 65 N.J. 474, 484, 323 A.2d 495 (1974). Chelsea conducted the search in conjunction with its obligation to issue the title commitment and policy. It did not prepare a separate abstract of title for plaintiff, but made the search for its own benefit.

Some out-of-state courts and commentators favor the view that a title company should be liable in tort as well as contract if it negligently fails to discover and disclose information that would be of interest to the insured. The underlying notion is that the insured has the reasonable expectation that the title company will search the title. 9 J. Appleman, Insurance Law and Practice §5212 at 72 (1981); see Note, Title Insurance: The Duty to Search, 71 Yale L.J. 1161, 1171 (1962)....

Other courts have acknowledged in dictum a title company's obligation to make a reasonable search. Those courts have been reluctant, however, to impose on the title companies a duty in tort. For example, in L. Smirlock Realty Corp. v. Title Guar. Co., 52 N.Y.2d 179, 437 N.Y.S.2d 57, 418 N.E.2d 650 (1981), the New York Court of Appeals . . . carefully pointed out that the basis for the imposition of liability on the company was the title policy, and the court was not reaching the question whether the company was liable in negligence. Id. 418 N.E.2d at 652. Similarly, the Illinois Appellate Court in a suit on the policy has stated that an "insurer has a duty to search the records and examine the applicable law before issuing its commitment or policy." McLaughlin v. Attorneys' Title Guar. Fund, 61 Ill. App. 3d 911, 916, 18 Ill. Dec. 891, 895, 378 N.E.2d 355, 359 (Ill. App. Ct. 1978). Although an intermediate court in Washington found a duty to search and disclose that arose by implication from the nature of the policy, Shotwell v. Transamerica Title Ins. Co., 16 Wash. App. 627, 631, 558 P.2d 1359, 1361 (1976), on appeal the Washington Supreme Court expressly reserved the question of the existence of such a duty. 91 Wash. 2d 161, 165-66, 588 P.2d 208, 211 (1978).

At one time the California courts adopted the view that a title company was subject to liability in tort similar to that of a title abstractor. Jarchow v. Transamerica Title Ins., 48 Cal. App. 3d 917, 122 Cal. Rptr. 470 (1975). In 1982, however, the

California Legislature extinguished this cause of action by passing a statute that expressly stated that title commitments are not abstracts of title and that the issuance of a title commitment does not give rise to the same duties as are incurred when a company issues such an abstract. Cal. Insurance Code §12340.11 (West 1988). More recently, the California courts have distinguished title commitments from an abstract of title by stating that a title commitment "generally constitutes no more than a statement of the terms and conditions upon which the insurer is willing to issue its title policy [and] liability for negligence based upon the [title commitment] in addition to liability under the policy does not seem supportable." Lawrence v. Chicago Title Ins. Co., 192 Cal. App. 3d 70, 76, 237 Cal. Rptr. 264, 268 (1987). . . .

Similarly, the Supreme Court of New Mexico has refused to hold a title company liable when it failed to discover a recorded adverse claim. The court held that "[d]efendant clearly had no duty under the policy to search the records, and any search it may have actually undertaken, was undertaken solely for its own protection as indemnitor against losses covered by its policy." Horn v. Lawyers Title Ins. Co., 89 N.M. 709, 711, 557 P.2d 206, 208 (1976).

The Texas Court of Appeals has reached a similar result. As that court recently stated, "[t]he title insurance company is not, as is an abstract company, employed to examine title; rather, the title insurance company is employed to guarantee the status of title and to insure against existing defects. Thus, the relationship between the parties is limited to that of indemnitor and indemnitee." Houston Title Co. v. Ojeda de Toca, 733 S.W.2d 325, 327 (1978). . . .

Although we recognize that an insured expects that a title company will conduct a reasonable title examination, the relationship between the company and the insured is essentially contractual. See Spring Motors Distribs., Inc. v. Ford Motor Co., 98 N.J. 555, 579-80, 489 A.2d 660 (1985). The end result of the relationship between the title company and the insured is the issuance of the policy. . . .

From this perspective, the insured expects that in consideration for payment of the premium, it will receive a policy of insurance. The insurer's expectation is that in exchange for that premium it will insure against certain risks subject to the terms of the policy. If the title company fails to conduct a reasonable title examination or, having conducted such an examination, fails to disclose the results to the insured, then it runs the risk of liability under the policy. In many, if not most, cases conduct that would constitute the failure to make a reasonable title search would also result in a breach of the terms of the policy.

The expectation of the insured that the insurer will conduct a reasonable search does not necessarily mean that the insurer may not limit its liability in the title commitment and policy. If the company may not so limit its liability, then it would be exposed to consequential damages resulting from its negligence. Under general contract principles, however, consequential damages are not recoverable unless they were within the specific contemplation of the parties. Donovan v. Backstadt, 91 N.J. 434, 444-45, 453 A.2d 160 (1982). Another difference is that in an action under the title policy, the insured may establish a cause of action for breach of contract without establishing that the title company breached the standard of care appropriate for a reasonable title search. In an action in tort for the failure to conduct such a search, the insured would be required to establish the appropriate standard of care applicable to title searching.

Both Chelsea and amicus, New Jersey Land Title Association, recognize that negligence principles provide an alternative basis for imposing liability on Chelsea. Notwithstanding the essentially contractual nature of the relationship between a title company and its insured, the company could be subject to a negligence action if the "act complained of was the direct result of duties voluntarily assumed by the insurer in addition to the mere contract to insure title." Brown's Tie and Lumber v. Chicago Title, 115 Idaho 56, 59, 764 P.2d 423, 426 (1988). As support for its negligence claim against Chelsea, Walker Rogge points to various facts. For example, Chelsea had twice insured the property in question and on four other occasions it had opened files on the property. In addition, Chelsea's own back title plant reflected that the tract comprised twelve, not eighteen, acres. One of Chelsea's employees, moreover, supervised the closing, at which time the purchase price was computed on that basis. Because it restricted plaintiff's claim to the policy, the trial court did not determine whether Chelsea knew or should have known of the difference in acreage and of its materiality to the transaction. The court did not, therefore, determine whether Chelsea assumed an independent duty to assure the quantity of acreage, whether it breached that duty, or whether the breach caused any damage to Walker Rogge. Consequently, we are obliged to remand the matter to the trial court for a determination of those issues. In remanding, we do not decide whether Chelsea was obligated to bring the difference in acreage to the attention of its insured under an implied duty of fair dealing. That issue has played no role at the trial or appellate level. We leave to the discretion of the trial court whether the matter should be resolved on the present record or should be supplemented by additional testimony. . . .

The judgment of the Appellate Division is affirmed in part, reversed in part, and, as modified, the matter is remanded to the Law Division.

NOTES AND QUESTIONS

1. On the title insurer's liability for failing to disclose defects in title, see Joyce D. Palomar, Title Insurance Law §12.3 (Supp. 2008) (stating that about half the jurisdictions that have addressed the issue imply a title insurer's duty to conduct a standard title search and disclose all discoverable defects to the title insurance applicant); see also D. Barlow Burke, Jr., Law of Title Insurance §§12.01-12.06 (Supp. 2008). For a recent case disagreeing with the holding in *Walker Rogge*, see MacDonald v. Old Republic Natl. Title Ins. Co., 882 F. Supp. 2d 236 (D. Mass. 2012) (allowing claim for negligence).

In the *Walker Rogge* case, if a lawyer had been hired by Rogge to search title, would the lawyer be liable for not reporting to Rogge the discrepancy in acreage between that described in the Aiello-to-Kosa deed and that called for in the Kosa-Rogge contract? See Fleming v. Nicholson, 724 A.2d 1026 (Vt. 1998).

2. Does a grantee have less or more protection of his title under the standard title insurance policy than under a general warranty deed? See Jerome J. Curtis, Jr., Title Assurance in Sales of California Residential Realty: A Critique of Title Insurance and Title Covenants with Suggested Reforms, 7 Pac. L.J. 1 (1976).

One advantage title insurance has over general warranty deeds is that the title insurance company agrees to defend at its expense all litigation against the insured based upon a defect insured against in the policy. Moreover, eviction is not a prerequisite to a suit on an insurance policy, as it is to a suit for breach of a covenant of general warranty.

3. Suppose that in Brown v. Lober, page 620, where the purchasers received only one-third of the mineral rights, the purchasers had taken out a title insurance policy. Would the title insurance company be liable? Suppose that Paradise, the buyer in Harper v. Paradise, page 741, had purchased a title insurance policy. Would he have been protected against the old deed found in the trunk in the attic?

4. The typical title insurance policy will except from coverage those items that an accurate survey would reveal. A lender or purchaser of real property can obtain protection from the risk created by this exception by having a new survey done and purchasing an "endorsement" from the title company. For example, in Amidano v. Meridian Title Insurance Co., 615 A.2d 654 (N.J. App. Div. 1992), the owner of property obtained an endorsement based upon a survey that limited the exceptions to a set of specifically identified encroachments and easements. The court held that the title insurance company was responsible for damages incurred by the property owner in connection with the existence of an easement that was not included in this list.

Lick Mill Creek Apartments v. Chicago Title Insurance Co.
Court of Appeal of California, Sixth District, 1991
283 Cal. Rptr. 231

AGLIANO, P.J. Plaintiffs Lick Mill Creek Apartments and Prometheus Development Company, Inc., appeal from a judgment of dismissal entered after the trial court sustained, without leave to amend, the demurrer of defendants Chicago Title Insurance Company and First American Title Insurance Company to plaintiffs' first amended complaint. The trial court determined, based on undisputed facts alleged in the complaint, that title insurance policies issued by defendants did not provide coverage for the costs of removing hazardous substances from plaintiffs' property. For the reasons stated below, we conclude the trial court's ruling was correct and affirm the judgment. . . .

The real property which is the subject of this case comprises approximately 30 acres of land near the Guadalupe River in Santa Clara County. Prior to 1979, various corporations operated warehouses and/or chemical processing plants on the property. Incident to this use of the property, the companies maintained underground tanks, pumps, and pipelines for the storage, handling, and disposal of various hazardous substances. These hazardous substances eventually contaminated the soil, subsoil, and groundwater.

In 1979, Kimball Small Investments 103 (KSI) purchased the property. Between 1979 and 1981, the California Department of Health Services ordered KSI to remedy the toxic contamination of the property. KSI, however, did not comply with this order.

In early October 1986, plaintiffs acquired lot 1 of the property from KSI. In connection with this acquisition, plaintiffs purchased title insurance from Chicago Title Insurance Company (Chicago Title). The insurance policy issued was of the type known as an American Land Title Insurance Association (ALTA) policy (policy 1). Prior to issuing this policy, Chicago Title commissioned a survey and inspection of the property by Carroll Resources Engineering & Management (Carroll Resources). Plaintiffs subsequently purchased lots 2 and 3 from KSI and secured two additional ALTA policies (policies 2 and 3) from Chicago Title and First American Title Insurance Company (First American). The entire site was surveyed and inspected. During its survey and inspection, Carroll Resources noted the presence of certain pipes, tanks, pumps, and other improvements on the property. At the time each of the policies was issued, the Department of Health Services, the Regional Water Quality Control Board, and the Santa Clara County Environmental Health Department maintained records disclosing the presence of hazardous substances on the subject property.

Following their purchase of the property, plaintiffs incurred costs for removal and clean-up of the hazardous substances in order "to mitigate plaintiffs' damages and avoid costs of compliance with government mandate." Then, claiming their expenses were a substitute, i.e., a payment made under threat of compulsion of law, for restitution to the State Hazardous Substance Account (Health & Saf. Code, §25300 et seq.) and "response costs" as defined under the Comprehensive Environmental Response, Compensation, and Liability Act (CERCLA) (42 U.S.C. §9601 et seq.), plaintiffs sought indemnity from defendants for the sums expended in their cleanup efforts. Defendants, however, denied coverage.

Discussion . . .

Here the insuring clauses of policies 1, 2, and 3 are identical and provide the following: "Subject to the Exclusions From Coverage, the Exceptions Contained in Schedule B and the Provisions of the Conditions and Stipulations Hereof [The Insurer] Insures, As of Date of Policy Shown in Schedule A, Against Loss or Damage, Not Exceeding the Amount of Insurance Stated in Schedule A, and Costs, Attorneys' Fees and Expenses Which the Company May Become Obligated to Pay Hereunder, Sustained or Incurred by the Insured by Reason of: ¶ (1) Title to the Estate or Interest Described in Schedule A Being Vested Otherwise Than as Stated Therein; ¶ (2) Any Defect in or Lien or Encumbrance on Such Title; ¶ (3) Lack of a Right of Access to and From the Land; or ¶ (4) Unmarketability of Such Title."

Marketability of Title

Plaintiffs first contend the policies in the instant case expressly insured that title to the subject property was marketable and, since the presence of hazardous substances on the property impaired its marketability, defendants were obliged to pay cleanup costs. Plaintiffs' position, however, is dependent upon their view that California courts have adopted a definition of marketable title that encompasses the property's market value. Our review of relevant authority establishes no support for this position. . . .

The case of Hocking v. Title Ins. & Trust Co., 37 Cal. 2d 644, 234 P.2d 625, 40 A.L.R.2d 1238 (1951), . . . illustrates the distinction between marketability of title and marketability of the land. In *Hocking*, the plaintiff purchased unimproved property and received a grant deed, describing it as two lots in a particular block according to a recorded subdivision map. However, because the subdivider had not complied with various local ordinances regarding subdivision of land, the city would not issue building permits until the plaintiff complied with the ordinances. The plaintiff sought damages from the title insurer claiming defective title. The *Hocking* court noted the distinction between the land and its title: "It is defendants' position that plaintiff confuses title with physical condition of the property she purchased and of the adjacent streets, and that 'One can hold perfect title to land that is valueless; one can have marketable title to land while the land itself is unmarketable.' The truth of this proposition would appear elementary. It appears to be the condition of her *land* in respect to improvements related thereto (graded and paved streets), rather than the condition of her *title* to the land, which is different from what she expected to get." (37 Cal. 2d at p. 651; italics in original.) Thus, the court held that the owner's inability to make economic use of the land due to the subdivider's violations of law did not render the title defective or unmarketable within the terms of the title insurance policy. "Although it is unfortunate that plaintiff has been unable to use her lots for the building purposes she contemplated, it is our view that the facts which she pleads do not affect the marketability of her *title* to the land, but merely impair the market *value* of the property. She appears to possess fee simple title to the property for whatever it may be worth; if she has been damaged by false representations in respect to the condition and value of the land her remedy would seem to be against others than the insurers of the title she acquired." (37 Cal. 2d at p. 652, italics in original.) Similarly, here plaintiffs have pled facts relating to marketability of the land rather than marketability of title.

Other jurisdictions have also recognized the distinction. In Chicago Title Ins. Co. v. Kumar, 24 Mass. App. 53, 506 N.E.2d 154, 156 (1987), the defendant had purchased property on which hazardous substances were discovered. The defendant sought payment for cleanup costs from its title insurer. (Ibid.) The insurer sought a declaration as to its obligations under the policy. The defendant owner filed a counterclaim, seeking a declaration that the presence of hazardous substances constituted a defect in title and the state's statutory power to impose a lien to secure payment of cleanup costs rendered his title unmarketable. (Ibid.)

Relying on Hocking v. Title Ins. & Trust Co., supra, 37 Cal. 2d 644, 651, the court found in favor of the insurer, stating "the defendant confuses economic lack of marketability, which relates to physical conditions affecting the use of the property, with title marketability, which relates to defects affecting legally recognized rights and incidents of ownership. . . . The presence of hazardous material may affect the market value of the defendant's land, but, on the present record [since no lien had been recorded], it does not affect the title to the land." (506 N.E.2d at p. 157.)[27] . . .

We find no ambiguity in the insuring clause: defendants are obligated to insure plaintiffs against unmarketability of title on the subject property. Because marketability of title and the market value of the land itself are separate and distinct, plaintiffs cannot claim coverage for the property's physical condition under this clause of the insurance policies.

Encumbrance on Title

The policies in question insure plaintiffs against "any defect in or lien or encumbrance" on title. Although no lien had been recorded or asserted at the time the title insurance policies were issued, plaintiffs contend the presence of hazardous substances on the property constituted an encumbrance on title.

Encumbrances are defined by statute as "taxes, assessments, and all liens upon real property." (Civ. Code, §1114.) Where a property is contaminated with hazardous substances, a subsequent owner of the property may be held fully responsible for the financial costs of cleaning up the contamination. (42 U.S.C. §9607(a); Health & Saf. Code, §§25323.5, 25363.) A lien may also be imposed on the property to cover such cleanup costs. (42 U.S.C. §9607(*l*)). Plaintiffs reason that because any transfer of contaminated land carries with it the responsibility for cleanup costs, liability for such costs constitutes an "encumbrance on title" and is covered. We disagree.

In United States v. Allied Chemical Corp., 587 F. Supp. 1205 (N.D. Cal. 1984), the plaintiff alleged a breach of warranty that property conveyed was free of encumbrance where hazardous substances were present on the property at the time it was conveyed. The court dismissed the plaintiff's cause of action, stating: "Plaintiff argues that the term 'encumbrance' is broad enough to include the presence of hazardous substances. However, the only authorities cited have interpreted 'encumbrance' to include only liens, easements, restrictive covenants and other such interests in or rights to the land held by third persons. (See Evans v. Faught, 231 Cal. App. 2d 698, 706 [1965].) Plaintiff has given no authority establishing its broad argument that any physical condition, including the presence of hazardous substances, is an 'encumbrance' if 'not visible or known' at the time of conveyance. The court declines to interpret 'encumbrance' as broadly as plaintiff urges. The court finds that, under current law, the term 'encumbrance' does not

---

27. Plaintiffs did not purchase an environmental protection endorsement (ALTA form 8.1 policy).

extend to the presence of hazardous substances alleged in this case." (Id. at p. 1206.) . . .

In Chicago Title Ins. Co. v. Kumar, supra, 506 N.E.2d 154, the court also held that the presence of hazardous substances on the land at the time title was conveyed did not constitute an encumbrance. "The mere possibility that the Commonwealth may attach a future lien . . . , as a result of the release of hazardous material (existing but unknown at the time a title insurance policy is issued) when the Commonwealth has neither expended moneys on the property requiring reimbursement nor recorded the necessary statement of claim, is insufficient to create a 'defect in or lien or encumbrance on . . . title.'" (Id. at p. 156.)

In South Shore Bank v. Stewart Title Guar. Co., 688 F. Supp. 803 (D. Mass. 1988), the plaintiff sought a declaration that the title insurance company was liable for the cleanup costs related to hazardous substances on the property where there was no recorded lien at the time the policy was issued. The court held as a matter of law there was no coverage under the policy, stating "[p]laintiff has neither alleged nor offered any facts to show a defect in title. Hence, it has no cause of action against [the title insurer]." (Id. at p. 806.)

In Holmes v. Alabama Title Co., Inc., 507 So. 2d 922 (Ala. 1987), the landowners' parcels contained an abandoned coal mine. Surface fractures began to appear, indicating that methane gas might eventually escape. The landowners brought suit against their title insurers and others. The reviewing court found in favor of the insurers, reasoning: "The purpose of title insurance is not to protect the insured against loss arising from physical damage to property; rather, it is to protect the insured against defects in the title." (Id. at p. 925.) (Accord Title & Trust Co. of Florida v. Barrows, 381 So. 2d 1088, 1090 (Fla. Dist. Ct. App. 1979); Mafetone v. Forest Manor Homes, Inc., 34 A.D.2d 566, 310 N.Y.S.2d 17, 18 (1970); Edwards v. St. Paul Title Ins. Co., 39 Colo. App. 235, 563 P.2d 979, 980 (1977)). . . .

Exclusions in Policies 1 and 3

Plaintiffs contend the governmental regulation and police power exclusions included in policies 1 and 3 are inapplicable.[28] We need not decide this question, since we have found no coverage under the identical insuring clauses of each policy. . . .

As previously discussed, the language of the insuring clauses of all three policies unambiguously provides coverage only for defects relating to title. These clauses make no reference to the physical condition of the land. . . .

---

28. Policies 1 and 3 contain exclusions from coverage as follows: "Any law, ordinance or governmental regulation (including but not limited to building and zoning ordinances) restricting or regulating or prohibiting the occupancy, use or enjoyment of the land, or regulating the character, dimensions or location of any improvement now or hereafter erected on the land, or prohibiting a separation in ownership or a reduction in the dimensions or area of the land, or the effect of any violation of any such law, ordinance or governmental regulation." The police power exclusion states as follows: "Rights of eminent domain or governmental rights of police power unless notice of the exercise of such rights appears in the public records at Date of Policy."

Disposition

The judgment is affirmed.

NOTES

1. In Somerset Savings Bank v. Chicago Title Ins. Co., 649 N.E.2d 1123 (Mass. 1995), the insured bought land which had once been owned by the Boston & Maine Railroad. A Massachusetts statute prohibited building on a former railroad right of way without consent of the State Office of Transportation. The Office of Transportation refused consent to building on the land. The insured sued the insurance company. The court held the company was not liable on the contract because public land use restrictions were not encumbrances on title and did not make title unmarketable, though they might decrease the value of the property. The court also refused to impose any general duty on the insurance company to search for and disclose any information that would affect the insured's decision to purchase. Nonetheless, the court returned the case to the trial court to determine whether the company had assumed a duty to search and disclose by its advertising claim that it knew local laws and practices, which might be fairly interpreted as an assurance that all matters recorded at the local registry affecting a decision to buy would be disclosed.

The court further held that an exculpatory clause against negligence in the policy did not, because unfair and unconscionable, bar a claim based on breach of an assumed duty to search and disclose.

2. In addition to actions based on contract, property owners often seek to recover against title companies based on negligence. Mistakes that might give rise to liability are illustrated by cases like Surace v. Commonwealth Land Title Ins. Co., 879 N.Y.S.2d 542 (App. Div. 2009), where the court held that a title insurer breached its policy and acted negligently by failing to record a mortgage in a timely fashion. But when an insurance commitment contains an error, the company may escape liability for damages that result from investment decisions by the insured. See, e.g., First Midwest Bank, N.A. v. Stewart Title Guaranty Co., 843 N.E.2d 327 (Ill. 2006) (title insurer not liable for negligence in failing to report covenant in title commitment because the insurer is not in the business of supplying information to guide business decisions). One article has suggested that jurisdictions are evenly split on the issue of tort liability for title insurers. See James Bruce Davis, More Than They Bargained For: Are Title Insurance Companies Liable in Tort for Undisclosed Title Defects?, 45 Cath. U. L. Rev. 71 (1995). But see John C. Murray, Attorney Malpractice in Real Estate Transactions: Is Title Insurance the Answer?, 42 Real Prop., Prob. & Tr. J. 221 (2007) (suggesting that tort liability for title insurers is still the minority rule).

3. Plaintiff purchased a home and obtained a policy of title insurance with an exclusion for losses resulting from "[g]overnmental police power, and the existence or violation of any law or government regulation." According to the policy, the exclusion did not apply "to violations or the enforcement of these matters if

notice of the violation or enforcement appears on Public Records at the Policy Date." One week after the plaintiff closed title on the property, it was demolished pursuant to a condemnation order of the city. The property had been listed in the city's condemnation records for one year prior to the purchase. May the plaintiff maintain an action under the policy? Compare Glenn v. First American Title Ins. Co., 2009 WL 1830745 (Mich. App. June 25, 2009) (holding condemnation records were not "records that give notice to matters affecting title under state law"), with New England Fed. Credit Union v. Stewart Title Guarantee Co., 765 A.2d 450 (Vt. 2000) (holding that public records giving constructive notice regarding matters of real property are not limited to municipal land records).

4. In 1947, the Iowa legislature outlawed title insurance. In its place, the state created a system in which "title guaranty certificates" are issued by the state for fees that are significantly cheaper than title insurance premiums. The certificates are based upon title opinions issued by attorneys in the state who participate in the program. Surplus fees—after paying claims and program administrative costs—fund housing programs in the state. For an evaluation of the Iowa program, see Shannon S. Strickler, Note, Iowa's Title Guaranty System: Is It Superior to Other States' Commercial Title Insurance?, 51 Drake L. Rev. 385 (2003).

V

Land Use Controls

In Chapter 1 (see page 46) we introduced the concept of "externalities"; since then, we have considered the relevance of the concept in a number of settings. It takes only a moment's reflection to see that the presence of external costs and benefits becomes especially important to understanding the role of property institutions in controlling conflicting uses of land — the concern of this part. As the examples in Chapter 1's introduction should have suggested, land use activities present the paradigm case of externalities, and much of the law to be studied now can be fruitfully examined as responses to this central fact. But there is more to the subject than just that, and economic considerations should not provide the only perspective. History, a sense of changing times and attitudes, is especially important to understanding many of the major developments in land use. So, too, for politics, especially with regard to zoning and related devices. Finally, some of the nicest (which is to say, perhaps, least tractable) issues presented in the following chapters involve fundamental questions of distributional justice and basic fairness.

The materials that follow are arranged chronologically. They begin, in Chapter 9, with the law of nuisance, the earliest formal legal method of controlling conflicting land uses; then turn in Chapter 10 to the law of servitudes that developed somewhat later; and then survey in Chapter 11 the law of zoning, a creature of the twentieth century. Zoning gives rise to the important problem of regulatory takings of property, examined together with eminent domain in Chapter 12.

All of these methods of land use control are alive and well. Each method has a different institution at its center. The content of nuisance law is set down, essentially but not entirely, by common law courts. Servitudes are defined primarily by private arrangements in light of market forces. Zoning is largely a legislative (and, thus, political) matter, and so too for eminent domain. Withal, however, courts and markets and legislative and administrative bodies always play some part, whatever the method of control.

9

Judicial Land Use Controls: The Law of Nuisance

As a subject of study, the law of nuisance is part torts and part property—torts because nuisance liability arises from negligent or otherwise wrongful activity, and property because the liability is for interference with the use and enjoyment of *land*. Nuisance law is a means by which common law judges resolve conflicting land uses. The guiding principle is an ancient maxim: *Sic utere tuo ut alienum non laedas*, meaning that one should use one's own property in such a way as not to injure the property of another. But what kind of guide is that? Suppose two neighbors are engaged in incompatible land uses, such that if *A* gets his way *B* can't get her way, and vice versa. *Sic utere* gets you nowhere. How, then, is the conflict to be resolved?

That question is what this chapter is about. What you learn will prove instructive in the subsequent chapters as well.

A. An Introduction to the Substantive Law

Morgan v. High Penn Oil Co.

Supreme Court of North Carolina, 1953
77 S.E.2d 682

Civil action to recover temporary damages for a private nuisance, and to abate such nuisance by injunction.

The salient facts appear in the numbered paragraphs which immediately follow. . . .

2. The land of the plaintiffs is a composite tract, which they acquired by two separate purchases antedating 3 August, 1945. It contains a dwelling-house, a restaurant, and accommodations for thirty-two habitable trailers. The dwelling-house existed at the time of the purchases of the plaintiffs, and has been occupied by them as their home since 3 August, 1945. The plaintiffs constructed the restaurant and the trailer accommodations immediately after they established their residence on the premises, and have been renting these improvements since their completion to third persons. They have been supplementing their income from these sources by taking lodgers in their dwelling. . . .

5. The High Penn Oil Company operated [an] oil refinery at virtually all times between 10 October, 1950, and the date of the rendition of the judgement in this action. . . .

9. The oil refinery is approximately 1,000 feet from the dwelling of the plaintiffs.

10. These structures are situated within a radius of one mile of the oil refinery: a church; at least twenty-nine private dwellings; four tourist and trailer camps; a grocery store; two restaurants; a nursery appropriated to the propagation of young trees, shrubs, and plants; three motor vehicle service stations; two motor vehicle repair shops; a railroad track; the terminus of a gasoline pipe line; numerous large storage tanks capable of storing sixty million gallons of gasoline; and the headquarters of at least four motor truck companies engaged in the transportation of petroleum products and other property for hire. Railway tank cars and motor tank trucks are filled with gasoline at the storage tanks for conveyance to various places at virtually all hours of the day and night. . . .

16. The evidence of the plaintiffs tended to show that for some hours on two or three different days during each week of its operation by the High Penn Oil Company, the oil refinery emitted nauseating gases and odors in great quantities; that the nauseating gases and odors invaded the nine acres owned by the plaintiffs and the other lands located within "a mile and three-quarters or two miles" of the oil refinery in such amounts and in such densities as to render persons of ordinary sensitiveness uncomfortable and sick; that the operation of the oil refinery thus substantially impaired the use and enjoyment of the nine acres by the plaintiffs and their renters; and that the defendants failed to put an end to the atmospheric pollution arising out of the operation of the oil refinery after notice and demand from the plaintiffs to abate it. The evidence of the plaintiffs tended to show, moreover, that the oil refinery was the only agency discharging gases or odors in annoying quantities into the air in the Friendship section. . . .

18. [The jury found the refinery to be a nuisance and set damages at $2,500. The trial judge entered a judgment to that effect and further enjoined the defendant from continuing the nuisance. The defendant appealed.]

ERVIN, J.[1] . . . The High Penn Oil Company contends that the evidence is not sufficient to establish either an actionable or an abatable private nuisance. . . .

The law of private nuisance rests on the concept embodied in the ancient legal maxim *Sic utere tuo ut alienum non laedas*, meaning, in essence, that every person should so use his own property as not to injure that of another. . . . As a consequence, a private nuisance exists in a legal sense when one makes an improper use of his own property and in that way injures the land or some incorporeal right of one's neighbor. . . .

---

1. "Ervin, J." refers to Sam J. Ervin, Jr. In 1954, a year after the decision in the *Morgan* case, Sam Ervin was elected to the U.S. Senate; 20 years after that he presided over the Senate Select Committee on Presidential Campaign Activities. "[T]o millions of Americans he was the hero of the unfolding drama of the Watergate affair that led, eventually, to the resignation of President Nixon in 1974." N.Y. Times, Apr. 24, 1985, at B12 (obituary).—EDS.

Much confusion exists in respect to the legal basis of liability in the law of private nuisance because of the deplorable tendency of the courts to call everything a nuisance, and let it go at that. . . . The confusion on this score vanishes in large part, however, when proper heed is paid to the sound propositions that private nuisance is a field of tort liability rather than a single type of tortious conduct; that the feature which gives unity to this field of tort liability is the interest invaded, namely, the interest in the use and enjoyment of land; that any substantial nontrespassory invasion of another's interest in the private use and enjoyment of land by any type of liability forming conduct is a private nuisance; that the invasion which subjects a person to liability for private nuisance may be either intentional or unintentional; that a person is subject to liability for an intentional invasion when his conduct is unreasonable under the circumstances of the particular case; and that a person is subject to liability for an unintentional invasion when his conduct is negligent, reckless or ultrahazardous. See Scope and Introduction Note to Chapter 40, American Law Institute's Restatement of the Law of Torts. . . .

An invasion of another's interest in the use and enjoyment of land is intentional in the law of private nuisance when the person whose conduct is in question as a basis for liability acts for the purpose of causing it, or knows that it is resulting from his conduct, or knows that it is substantially certain to result from his conduct. Restatement of the Law of Torts, section 825. . . . A person who intentionally creates or maintains a private nuisance is liable for the resulting injury to others regardless of the degree of care or skill exercised by him to avoid such injury. . . .

When the evidence is interpreted in the light most favorable to the plaintiffs, it suffices to support a finding that in operating the oil refinery the High Penn Oil Company intentionally and unreasonably caused noxious gases and odors to escape onto the nine acres of the plaintiffs to such a degree as to impair in a substantial manner the plaintiffs' use and enjoyment of their land. This being so, the evidence is ample to establish the existence of an actionable private nuisance, entitling the plaintiffs to recover temporary damages from the High Penn Oil Company. . . .

When the evidence is taken in the light most favorable to the plaintiffs, it also suffices to warrant the additional inferences that the High Penn Oil Company intends to operate the oil refinery in the future in the same manner as in the past; that if it is permitted to carry this intent into effect, the High Penn Oil Company will hereafter cast noxious gases and odors onto the nine acres of the plaintiffs with such recurring frequency and in such annoying density as to inflict irreparable injury upon the plaintiffs in the use and enjoyment of their home and their other adjacent properties; and that the issuance of an appropriate injunction is necessary to protect the plaintiffs against the threatened irreparable injury. This being true, the evidence is ample to establish the existence of an abatable private nuisance, entitling the plaintiffs to such mandatory or prohibitory injunctive relief as may be required to prevent the High Penn Oil Company from continuing the nuisance. . . .

For the reasons given, the evidence is sufficient to withstand the motion of the High Penn Oil Company for a compulsory nonsuit. . . .

NOTES AND QUESTIONS

1. *Unreasonableness.* Issues of "unreasonableness" have come to play an important role in the law of nuisance. Precisely what that role amounts to, however, is obscure. The opinion in *Morgan* states the textbook rules: An interference with use and enjoyment of land, in order to give rise to liability, must be substantial; it must also be *either* intentional and unreasonable *or* the unintentional result of negligent, reckless, or abnormally dangerous activity. See Restatement (Second) of Torts §§821F, 822 (1979).

Regarding the question of unreasonableness, the case of unintentional nuisance seems clear enough. Liability here is based on traditional tort categories—negligence, recklessness, abnormally dangerous activities—all of which "embody in some degree the concept of unreasonableness." Id. §821B comment e, at 90. The intentional nuisance is another matter, and an important one given that most modern-day nuisances are intentional in the sense that the *Morgan* case and the Restatement use that term. Thus, situations giving rise to allegations of nuisance today typically involve interference with use and enjoyment of land—from air and water pollution, noise, odors, vibrations, flooding, excessive light (or inadequate light)—that continues over time and is known by the defendant to result from its activities. Despite the presence of intent in these instances, nuisance liability arises only if the resulting interference is substantial and unreasonable.

What does *unreasonable* mean in this context of an intentional tort? On one view, the term has a function here that is quite different from the role it plays in the law of negligence. Rather than inviting a comparison of whether the social benefits of the defendant's conduct outweigh its expected costs, the relevant inquiry is said to concern the *level* of interference that results from the conduct—particularly, whether the interference crosses some threshold that marks the point of liability. For example, in Jost v. Dairyland Power Coop., 172 N.W.2d 647 (Wis. 1969), the court upheld the exclusion of evidence offered by the defendant to show that the utility of its operations outweighed the gravity of the harm caused to the plaintiffs. Of the defendant's operation, a power plant, the court said, "Whether its economic or social importance dwarfed the claim of a small farmer is of no consequence in this lawsuit." 172 N.W.2d at 653.

The view of the *Jost* case is contrary to the Restatement's position that, to determine unreasonableness in a case of intentional nuisance, the court is to consider whether "the gravity of the harm outweighs the utility of the actor's conduct. . . ." Restatement (Second) of Torts, supra, §826(1); see also id. §827 (factors relevant to gravity of the harm are the extent and character of the harm, the social value of the plaintiff's use, its suitability to the locality in question, and the burden on the plaintiff of avoiding the harm); §828 (factors relevant to utility of the actor's conduct are its social value, its suitability to the locality in question, and the impracticality of the defendant preventing the harm). Which view dominates is not clear, though it can be said that relatively few courts have followed the Restatement explicitly. See Jeff L. Lewin, *Boomer* and the American Law of Nuisance: Past, Present, and Future, 54 Alb. L. Rev. 189, 212-214 (1990).

2. *More on unreasonableness: trespass compared.* Typically, an intentional tort results in liability without regard to the amount of harm or the reasonableness of the activity causing it. Trespass, involving a *physical invasion* of land, is a case in point. While liability for unintentional trespass is virtually identical to that for unintentional nuisance,[2] the two torts differ markedly if the element of intent is present. In such an instance, trespass is treated like the other intentional torts; nuisance, on the other hand, is usually subjected to inquiries about reasonableness and amount of harm. Thus, unless the plaintiff can show a physical invasion by a tangible thing (that is, a trespass), the defendant can escape liability for intentional conduct on grounds of reasonableness or amount of harm that would be irrelevant if there has been a physical invasion by a tangible thing. This seems anomalous. Is there any sense to a system of rules that treats the intentional release of contaminated water onto neighboring land one way (trespass) and the intentional release of polluting gases another way (nuisance)? Some torts scholars have thought not, and at their urging the Restatement added a provision that an intentional invasion is "unreasonable" for purposes of nuisance law if, (1) as before, the gravity of the harm caused outweighs the utility of the actor's conduct; *or* if, (2) alternatively, "the harm caused by the conduct is serious and the financial burden of compensating for this and similar harm to others would not make the continuation of the conduct not feasible." Restatement (Second) of Torts, supra, §826(b); see also id. §829A ("an intentional invasion of another's interest in the use and enjoyment of land is unreasonable if the harm resulting from the invasion is severe and greater than the other should be required to bear without compensation"). Is alternative (2) a restatement of the threshold-level test of liability? Do the remedies available to a plaintiff differ under the two alternatives? See Jeff L. Lewin, Compensated Injunctions and the Evolution of Nuisance Law, 71 Iowa L. Rev. 775, 779-785 (1986). For a case explicitly rejecting alternative (2), see Carpenter v. Double R Cattle Co., Inc., 701 P.2d 222 (Idaho 1985).

Why should an activity that causes serious harm be excused from liability under alternative (2) if the obligation to pay would make continuation of the

---

2. See Restatement (Second) of Torts §165 (1965):

One who recklessly or negligently, or as a result of an abnormally dangerous activity, enters land in the possession of another or causes a thing or third person so to enter is subject to liability to the possessor if, but only if, his presence or the presence of the thing or the third person upon the land causes harm to the land, to the possessor, or to a thing or a third person in whose security the possessor has a legally protected interest.

See also Restatement (Second) of Torts, supra, §821D comment e, at 102 (commenting on the similarity of the two torts). Since a physical invasion—e.g., by polluted water—can also interfere with use and enjoyment of land and thus be a nuisance, the choice of theory with regard to unintentional conduct is usually a matter of indifference, statutes of limitations and variations in the interest protected aside.

activity "not feasible"? Why should it be excused under alternative (1) simply because the utility of the conduct in question outweighs the harm it causes?

Section 826(b) of the Restatement moves intentional nuisance in the doctrinal direction of intentional trespass, though still there are differences. (Do you see them?) At times one finds a court taking the opposite approach, treating an intentional trespass like an intentional nuisance. A case in point is Martin v. Reynolds Metals Co., 342 P.2d 790 (Or. 1959). The plaintiffs in *Martin* were cattle ranchers who alleged that their herds were poisoned by fumes from the defendant's aluminum plant. The trial court found the defendant liable on a *trespass* theory; on appeal the defendant argued that trespass was inappropriate because there had been no physical invasion of the plaintiffs' land. The court rejected the argument, choosing "in this atomic age" to define a trespass "as any intrusion which invades the possessor's protected interest in exclusive possession, whether that intrusion is by visible or invisible pieces of matter or by energy which can be measured only by the mathematical language of the physicist." 342 P.2d at 793-794. But then, having found an intentional trespass, the court went on to apply a balancing test of reasonableness in order to determine liability. Trespass and nuisance were harmonized, but by subjecting both to the utilitarian calculus of intentional nuisance. Compare Wilson v. Interlake Steel Co., 649 P.2d 922 (Cal. 1982), holding that excessive noise alone will not support a trespass action absent some kind of physical invasion or physical damage to property. Intangible intrusions, the court said, must be approached on a nuisance theory.

As anomalous as it may at first seem, might the trespass-nuisance dichotomy in fact be sensible — at least as to the typical trespass (where *A* enters *B*'s land) and the typical nuisance (where pollution, say, from *A*'s operations interferes with neighbors *B, C, D, . . . N*)? Is there a way to generalize the difference between the typical fact settings of the two torts, so as to arrive at better doctrine? See Thomas W. Merrill, Trespass, Nuisance, and the Costs of Determining Property Rights, 14 J. Legal Stud. 13 (1985).

The questions just raised are closely related to issues concerning appropriate remedies in nuisance cases, a matter considered in the next section of this chapter.

3. *Nuisances, nuisances, nuisances: fear and loathing.* Usually, people don't want halfway houses in their neighborhoods, especially facilities for parolees. Apprehension about criminal activity is one worry, declining property values another. Some courts have found such considerations sufficient for nuisance liability, others not. See, e.g., Arkansas Release Guidance Found. v. Needler, 477 S.W.2d 821 (Ark. 1972) (defendant liable because plaintiffs had substantial grounds to feel insecure and property values had gone down); Nickolson v. Connecticut Halfway House, 218 A.2d 383 (Conn. 1966) (apprehension about future criminal activity and mere depreciation of property values do not give rise to nuisance liability); see also Adkins v. Thomas Solvent Co., 487 N.W.2d 715 (Mich. 1992), a suit for nuisance damages brought by property owners in the vicinity of a toxic waste dump. The plaintiffs claimed that the threat of groundwater contamination in the area had pushed down property values. The evidence

established that prices had indeed declined, but also that contamination would not occur. The court held that negative publicity resulting from unfounded fears did not constitute a significant interference with the use and enjoyment of the plaintiffs' land. To similar effect, see Smith v. Kansas Gas Service Co., 163 P.3d 1052 (Kan. 2007), involving natural gas erupting from the defendant's natural gas storage facility. Plaintiffs whose property had not been physically damaged won a jury verdict for almost $8 million to cover alleged losses in the market value of their properties resulting from the stigma of being located in a dangerous area. The Kansas Supreme Court reversed, holding that stigma damages are recognized only where the plaintiff's property has sustained actual physical injury as a result of the defendant's conduct. This appears to be the general rule. (Compare the *Stambovsky* case on page 582 of this book, involving property values adversely affected by public fear of ghosts.)

Light and air. In Amphitheaters, Inc. v. Portland Meadows, 198 P.2d 847 (Or. 1948), the operator of a drive-in theater sued the owner of an amusement park whose bright lights interfered with the use of the drive-in. The court found no nuisance, holding that the conflict arose not from unreasonable conduct by the defendant but from the abnormally sensitive nature of the plaintiff's use. Generally speaking, nuisance law protects ordinary uses, not abnormally sensitive ones. What if, instead of too much light, there is too little, as when a property owner's trees deny sunlight to a neighbor's solar energy panels? Compare Prah v. Maretti, 321 N.W.2d 182 (Wis. 1982) (may be a nuisance if the gravity of the harm to the plaintiff outweighs the utility of the defendant's conduct), with Sher v. Leiderman, 226 Cal. Rptr. 698 (Cal. App. 1986) (criticizing *Prah* as an unjustified departure from established law and holding that blocking light to a neighbor's property does not constitute a nuisance, except in cases where malice is the over-riding motive). Which gets us to . . .

Spite and spam. Courts commonly find nuisance liability in instances where a landowner builds a structure (such as a "spite fence") of no use whatsoever other than to vex a neighbor. And speaking of vexing, consider spam. Commercial unsolicited email is a nuisance, but is it a nuisance? One would think not, given that *nuisance* is conventionally defined as interference with the use and enjoyment of *land*, but the argument to the contrary is convincingly made by Adam Mossoff, Spam — Oy, What a Nuisance!, 19 Berkeley Tech. L.J. 625 (2004). It's hardly clear in any event why there can't be a law of nuisance that concerns interference with the use and enjoyment of personal property, just as there is a law of trespass to chattels (see page 104). The latter has been applied in cases involving spam, but Professor Mossoff regards nuisance as a better and less troublesome approach to the problem. See also Jeremiah Kelman, E-Nuisance: Unsolicited Bulk E-Mail at the Boundaries of Common Law Property Rights, 78 S. Cal. L. Rev. 363 (2004) (a student note for which Mr. Kelman received the 2005 Scribes Award for best law review note in the nation).

Plain old ugly. The issue here is so-called aesthetic nuisance. Most courts hold that unsightliness alone does not a nuisance make (unless, of course, spite is the only motive). Still, a junkyard in a residential area might be a nuisance if unreasonably operated and unduly offensive. See, e.g., Allison v. Smith, 695 P.2d 791 (Colo. App. 1984). In Wernke v. Halas, 600 N.E.2d 117 (Ind. App. 1992), feuding neighbors used ugliness as ammunition, mounting toilet seats in their yards in a manner visible to the lot next door. These, the court said, were not nuisances; "tasteless decoration is merely an aesthetic annoyance. . . ." 600 N.E.2d at 122. But what about the spite motivating the "tasteless decoration"? Then again, we all know a mounted toilet seat is *art*.

NOTE: LATERAL AND SUBJACENT SUPPORT

From the perspective of property, the law of private nuisance is regarded as defining one of a number of so-called rights incident to land ownership; other rights commonly placed in the category are freedom from trespass, water rights, and the right to support. See, e.g., 6A American Law of Property (1954 & Supp. 1977). Trespass was touched upon above (see Note 2, page 783), and we introduced the law of water rights in Chapter 1, Note 2, page 38. The subject here is support, lateral and subjacent.

Lateral support refers to that provided to one piece of land by the parcels of land surrounding it; subjacent support refers to support from underneath as opposed to the sides. The common law right of lateral support imposes a duty on neighboring land to provide the support that the subject parcel would need and receive under *natural* conditions; ordinarily, then, there is no right to support of *structures* on the land. A cause of action for interference with the right to lateral support does not arise until subsidence actually occurs or is threatened, and then it runs against the excavator (who may, of course, be a predecessor of the present possessor). Liability is absolute; negligence need not be shown. If, however, the supported land had been built upon in such a way that subsidence would not have occurred but for the improvements, there is no liability without negligence, at least so long as the excavator gives notice of his plans. Generally speaking, there is also no liability, absent negligence, if subsidence of improved or unimproved land is shown to have been caused by withdrawal of fluids (e.g., groundwater) or their release as a result of excavation.

The right of lateral support can be waived; it can also be expressly expanded, as by grant of a right to additional support. Moreover, a number of jurisdictions have statutes that enlarge or otherwise modify the common law right, in recognition of its unsuitability to modern, dense, high-rise building practices.

Issues of subjacent support arise when one person owns surface rights and another person owns some kind of subsurface rights, such as a mineral interest. The situation is analogous to that of lateral support, and the law pretty much tracks that outlined above.

Could problems of lateral and subjacent support be handled satisfactorily simply through application of nuisance law? Are there any fundamental differences in the bodies of doctrine? Cf. Richard A. Epstein, Nuisance Law: Corrective Justice and Its Utilitarian Constraints, 8 J. Legal Stud. 49, 94-96 (1979).

B.   *Remedies (and More on the Substantive Law)*

Estancias Dallas Corp. v. Schultz

Court of Civil Appeals of Texas, 1973
500 S.W.2d 217

STEPHENSON, J. This is an appeal from an order of the trial court granting a permanent injunction. Trial was by jury and judgment was rendered upon the jury verdict. The parties will be referred to here as they were in the trial court.

Plaintiffs, Thad Schultz and wife, brought this suit asking that defendant, Estancias Dallas Corporation, be permanently enjoined from operating the air conditioning equipment and tower on the property next to plaintiffs' residence. The jury found: that the noise emitted solely from defendant's air conditioning equipment constitutes a nuisance; that the nuisance began May 1, 1969; that it is permanent; that the nuisance has been continuous since it began; that Mrs. Schultz has been damaged $9000 and Thad Schultz $1000, considering material personal discomfort, inconvenience, annoyance and impairment of health as the elements of damages. . . .

Defendant's [point of error is] that the trial court erred in granting the injunction . . . because the trial court failed to balance the equities in its favor.

Even though this matter has arisen many times, we have found little in-depth writing on the subject. The case cited most frequently in this state is Storey v. Central Hide & Rendering Co., 148 Tex. 509, 226 S.W.2d 615 (1950). The rule of law was clearly established in this case that even though a jury finds facts constituting a nuisance, it was held that there should be a balancing of equities in order to determine if an injunction should be granted. The Supreme Court then stated certain guidelines for the trial courts to follow in making such determinations by quoting as follows from 31 Tex. Jur. §35 Nuisances:

> According to the doctrine of "comparative injury" or "balancing of equities" the court will consider the injury which may result to the defendant and the public by granting the injunction as well as the injury to be sustained by the complainant if the writ be denied. If the court finds that the injury to the complainant is slight in comparison to the injury caused the defendant and the public by enjoining the nuisance, relief will ordinarily be refused. It has been pointed out that the cases in which a nuisance is permitted to exist under this doctrine are based on the stern rule of necessity rather than on the right of the author of the nuisance to work a hurt, or injury to his neighbor. The necessity of others may compel the injured party to seek relief by way of an action at law for damages rather than by a suit in equity to abate the nuisance.
>
> "Some one must suffer these inconveniences rather than that the public interest should suffer. . . . These conflicting interests call for a solution of the question by the application of the broad principles of right and justice, leaving the individual to his remedy by compensation and maintaining the public interests intact; this works hardships on the individual, but they are incident to civilization with its physical developments, demanding more and more the means of rapid transportation of persons and property."
>
> On the other hand, an injunction may issue where the injury to the opposing party and the public is slight or disproportionate to the injury suffered by the complainant. [226 S.W.2d at 618-619.] . . .

There is no specific mention in the judgment that the trial court balanced the equities. However, that question was raised by the pleadings, evidence was heard, and there is an implied finding that the trial court balanced the equities in favor of plaintiffs by entering the judgment granting the injunction. We do not find that the trial court abused its discretion in balancing the equities in favor of plaintiffs.

It is significant that the Supreme Court of Texas in the *Storey* case, supra, placed great emphasis upon public interest. Also, in all of the other cases cited above, the appellate courts in their opinions refer to the benefit to the public generally in permitting a nuisance to continue through the balancing of equities. We find little or no testimony in the record before us reflecting benefit to the public generally. There is no evidence that there is a shortage of apartments in the City of Houston and that the public would suffer by having no place to live.

Our record shows that this apartment complex was completed about March or April of 1969 with about 155 rentable apartments in eight buildings. The air conditioning unit complained of here served the entire complex. This unit is located at the back side of defendant's property, about five and one-half feet from plaintiffs' property line, about fifty-five feet from plaintiffs' back door, and about seventy feet from plaintiffs' bedroom. According to much of the testimony, the unit sounds like a jet airplane or helicopter. The plaintiffs testified: That this was a quiet neighborhood before these apartments were constructed. That they can no longer do any entertaining in their backyard because of the noise. That they cannot carry on a normal conversation in their home with all their doors and windows closed. That the noise interferes with their sleep at night. Several of the neighbors gave similar testimony. Plaintiffs testified that the value of their land before was $25,000 and $10,000 after the noise began. One of the neighbors, a real estate broker, placed the value at $25,000 before and $12,500 after. A witness who qualified as an expert metallurgical consultant testified as to the results of tests made at various points as to the sound factors in decibels before and after defendant made changes in an effort to reduce the noise.

A witness testified: That he was the original owner of the apartments. That it cost about $80,000 to construct this air conditioning system and that separate units for the eight buildings would have cost $40,000 more. That it would now cost $150,000 to $200,000 to change to that system. That these apartments could not be rented without air conditioning.

Applying the rules of law set forth above in the quotation from the *Storey* case, supra (226 S.W.2d at 619), the nuisance in this case will not be permitted to exist " 'based on the stern rule of necessity rather than on the right of the author of the nuisance to work a hurt, or injury to his neighbor.' " There is not evidence before us to indicate the " 'necessity of others . . . compel[s] the injured party to seek relief by way of an action at law for damages rather than by a suit in equity to abate the nuisance.' " Furthermore, although plaintiffs had a count in their pleading seeking damages, in response to a motion made by defendant, the court forced plaintiffs to elect at the close of their evidence. Thus, defendant's own trial tactics prevented the development of a full record upon which we could predicate the doctrine of balancing the equities.

Plaintiffs were not required to recover damages for a temporary nuisance, that is, for the time when the nuisance began until the date of the trial, in order to secure a permanent injunction. They were entitled to such injunction based upon the affirmative answers given by the jury as set out above. . . .

Affirmed.

NOTES AND QUESTIONS

1. Allegations of nuisance based on air-conditioning noise are not uncommon, judging by the collection of cases in Annot., 79 A.L.R.3d 320 (1977). As Havelock Ellis put it, "what we call 'Progress' is the exchange of one Nuisance for another Nuisance." Havelock Ellis, Impressions and Comments 5 (1914).

2. Why was a nuisance found in the *Estancias* case? The plaintiffs had suffered past damages—up to the date of trial—of $10,000 ($9,000 damage to Mrs. Schultz, $1,000 to Thad Schultz). As to future damages if the air-conditioning noise were allowed to continue, presumably these were reflected ("capitalized") in the $12,500 to $15,000 reduction in property value suggested by the evidence. The defendant had tried, unsuccessfully, to abate the air-conditioning noise. If a quiet system (separate air-conditioning units for each apartment) had been installed at the time the defendant's apartment building was originally constructed, it would have cost an additional $40,000; to change to such a system later would cost at least $150,000. The apartments could not be rented without air conditioning.

Do these numbers show that the utility of the defendant's conduct outweighed the gravity of the harm to the plaintiffs? Or might it be that the apartment building simply should not have been built in this neighborhood? Suppose the area were zoned for apartments. Should that matter? See John Franklin, Note, Zoning Ordinances and Common-Law Nuisance, 16 Syracuse L. Rev. 860 (1965).

3. Do you find credible the high costs of noise abatement suggested by the defendant's evidence in the *Estancias* case? In any event, why not simply limit the plaintiffs' remedy, and the defendant's liability, to damages? Presumably, the defendant would then, as to the future, abate the noise if that were cheaper than paying damages or pay damages and continue with the present system if that proved the less costly alternative. The conflict between plaintiffs and defendant would be resolved at the least cost, and the plaintiffs—at worst—would be compensated for any hardship caused by the noise. The result, in short, would be efficient (meaning the cost of conflict would be minimized) and fair (meaning the injury would be redressed). Do you agree? But would the plaintiffs then be relegated to a series of lawsuits for damages? See Comment, Equity and the Eco-System: Can Injunctions Clear the Air?, 68 Mich. L. Rev. 1254, 1280 (1970).

4. Given the facts in *Estancias*, might not the injunction affirmed by the court be equally (if not more) effective than damages in accomplishing the ends of fairness and efficiency just discussed? The argument would run as follows: The granting of an injunction to the Schultzes need not represent the final resolution of the conflict between them and the defendant; the parties can bargain over whether

the injunction will be enforced. Put another way, "injunctions are for sale by the plaintiff; the plaintiff expects to demand enforcement of the injunction only if the defendant refuses to pay a good round price for the plaintiff's consent to its dissolution." W. Page Keeton & Clarence Morris, Notes on "Balancing the Equities," 18 Tex. L. Rev. 412, 416 (1940); see also Barton H. Thompson, Jr., Note, Injunction Negotiations: An Economic, Moral, and Legal Analysis, 27 Stan. L. Rev. 1563 (1975) ("the enjoined party may, and often will, attempt to buy off the injunction").

Assume for now that we could count on such post-injunction bargaining by the parties in the *Estancias* case.[3] On that assumption, what, if any, are the advantages of injunctive relief as opposed to an award of damages?

5. Note the discussion in *Estancias* of the doctrine of "balancing the equities." The doctrine, sometimes called comparative hardship or equitable hardship, has an apparent efficiency objective — to avoid the greater harm (or social cost). Why is that objective not served by the nuisance calculus itself, which compares the utility of the conduct to the gravity of the harm it causes? There is some claim that the doctrine is also used to avoid the extortion problem. See, e.g., Barton H. Thompson, Jr., Note, Injunction Negotiations, supra, at 1577-1580. Why was the doctrine not applied in *Estancias*? Should it have been?

"Balancing the equities" figures prominently in the case that follows.

Boomer v. Atlantic Cement Co.

Court of Appeals of New York, 1970
257 N.E.2d 870

BERGAN, J. Defendant operates a large cement plant near Albany. These are actions for injunction and damages by neighboring land owners alleging injury to property from dirt, smoke, and vibration emanating from the plant. A nuisance has been found after trial, temporary damages have been allowed; but an injunction has been denied.

The public concern with air pollution arising from many sources in industry and in transportation is currently accorded ever wider recognition accompanied by a growing sense of responsibility in State and Federal Governments to control it. Cement plants are obvious sources of air pollution in the neighborhoods where they operate.

But there is now before the court private litigation in which individual property owners have sought specific relief from a single plant operation. The threshold question raised by the division of view on this appeal is whether the court

---

3. In fact, no bargaining occurred. Inquiring of counsel, we learned that there was at first some thought that the defendant would simply try to buy the plaintiffs' property (apparently the cheapest alternative, judging from the evidence) — but this didn't happen. Instead, the offensive air-conditioning equipment was moved from the back of the defendant's building to the front. The plaintiffs would probably have resisted negotiations in any event. They had turned down a pre-trial settlement offer of $12,500, and their lawyer thought it unlikely that they would have sold their property after judgment, because they were an elderly couple who had lived in the neighborhood for many years.

should resolve the litigation between the parties now before it as equitably as seems possible; or whether, seeking promotion of the general public welfare, it should channel private litigation into broad public objectives.

A court performs its essential function when it decides the rights of parties before it. Its decision of private controversies may sometimes greatly affect public issues. Large questions of law are often resolved by the manner in which private litigation is decided. But this is normally an incident to the court's main function to settle controversy. It is a rare exercise of judicial power to use a decision in private litigation as a purposeful mechanism to achieve direct public objectives greatly beyond the rights and interests before the court.

Effective control of air pollution is a problem presently far from solution even with the full public and financial powers of government. In large measure adequate technical procedures are yet to be developed and some that appear possible may be economically impracticable.

It seems apparent that the amelioration of air pollution will depend on technical research in great depth; on a carefully balanced consideration of the economic impact of close regulation; and of the actual effect on public health. It is likely to require massive public expenditure and to demand more than any local community can accomplish and to depend on regional and interstate controls.

A court should not try to do this on its own as a by-product of private litigation and it seems manifest that the judicial establishment is neither equipped in the limited nature of any judgment it can pronounce nor prepared to lay down and implement an effective policy for the elimination of air pollution. This is an area beyond the circumference of one private lawsuit. It is a direct responsibility for government and should not thus be undertaken as an incident to solving a dispute between property owners and a single cement plant—one of many—in the Hudson River valley.

The cement making operations of defendant have been found by the court at Special Term to have damaged the nearby properties of plaintiffs in these two actions. That court, as it has been noted, accordingly found defendant maintained a nuisance and this has been affirmed at the Appellate Division. The total damage to plaintiffs' properties is, however, relatively small in comparison with the value of defendant's operation and with the consequences of the injunction which plaintiffs seek.

The ground for the denial of injunction, notwithstanding the finding both that there is a nuisance and that plaintiffs have been damaged substantially, is the large disparity in economic consequences of the nuisance and of the injunction. This theory cannot, however, be sustained without overruling a doctrine which has been consistently reaffirmed in several leading cases in this court and which has never been disavowed here, namely that where a nuisance has been found and where there has been any substantial damage shown by the party complaining an injunction will be granted.

The rule in New York has been that such a nuisance will be enjoined although marked disparity be shown in economic consequence between the effect of the injunction and the effect of the nuisance.

The problem of disparity in economic consequence was sharply in focus in Whalen v. Union Bag & Paper Co., 208 N.Y. 1, 101 N.E. 805. A pulp mill entailing an investment of more than a million dollars polluted a stream in which plaintiff, who owned a farm, was "a lower riparian owner." The economic loss to plaintiff from this pollution was small. This court, reversing the Appellate Division, reinstated the injunction granted by the Special Term against the argument of the mill owner that in view of "the slight advantage to plaintiff and the great loss that will be inflicted on defendant" an injunction should not be granted (p. 2, 101 N.E. p. 805). "Such a balancing of injuries cannot be justified by the circumstances of this case," Judge Werner noted (p. 4, 101 N.E. p. 805). He continued: "Although the damage to the plaintiff may be slight as compared with the defendant's expense of abating the condition, that is not a good reason for refusing an injunction" (p. 5, 101 N.E. p. 806).

Thus the unconditional injunction granted at Special Term was reinstated. The rule laid down in that case, then, is that whenever the damage resulting from a nuisance is found not "unsubstantial," viz., $100 a year, injunction would follow. This states a rule that had been followed in this court with marked consistency. . . .

Although the court at Special Term and the Appellate Division held that injunction should be denied, it was found that plaintiffs had been damaged in various specific amounts up to the time of the trial and damages to the respective plaintiffs were awarded for those amounts. The effect of this was, injunction having been denied, plaintiffs could maintain successive actions at law for damages thereafter as further damage was incurred.

The court at Special Term also found the amount of permanent damage attributable to each plaintiff, for the guidance of the parties in the event both sides stipulated to the payment and acceptance of such permanent damage as a settlement of all the controversies among the parties. The total of permanent damages to all plaintiffs thus found was $185,000. The basis of adjustment has not resulted in any stipulation by the parties.

This result at Special Term and at the Appellate Division is a departure from a rule that has become settled; but to follow the rule literally in these cases would be to close down the plant at once. This court is fully agreed to avoid that immediately drastic remedy; the difference in view is how best to avoid it.[4]

One alternative is to grant the injunction but postpone its effect to a specified future date to give opportunity for technical advances to permit defendant to eliminate the nuisance; another is to grant the injunction conditioned on the payment of permanent damages to plaintiffs which would compensate them for the total economic loss to their property present and future caused by defendant's operations. For reasons which will be developed the court chooses the latter alternative.

---

4. Respondent's investment in the plant is in excess of $45,000,000. There are over 300 people employed there.

If the injunction were to be granted unless within a short period—e.g., 18 months—the nuisance be abated by improved methods, there would be no assurance that any significant technical improvement would occur.

The parties could settle this private litigation at any time if defendant paid enough money and the imminent threat of closing the plant would build up the pressure on defendant. If there were no improved techniques found, there would inevitably be applications to the court at Special Term for extensions of time to perform on showing of good faith efforts to find such techniques.

Moreover, techniques to eliminate dust and other annoying by-products of cement making are unlikely to be developed by any research the defendant can undertake within any short period, but will depend on the total resources of the cement industry nationwide and throughout the world. The problem is universal wherever cement is made.

For obvious reasons the rate of the research is beyond control of defendant. If at the end of 18 months the whole industry has not found a technical solution a court would be hard put to close down this one cement plant if due regard be given to equitable principles.

On the other hand, to grant the injunction unless defendant pays plaintiffs such permanent damages as may be fixed by the court seems to do justice between the contending parties. All of the attributions of economic loss to the properties on which plaintiffs' complaints are based will have been redressed.

The nuisance complained of by these plaintiffs may have other public or private consequences, but these particular parties are the only ones who have sought remedies and the judgment proposed will fully redress them. The limitation of relief granted is a limitation only within the four corners of these actions and does not foreclose public health or other public agencies from seeking proper relief in a proper court.

It seems reasonable to think that the risk of being required to pay permanent damages to injured property owners by cement plant owners would itself be a reasonable effective spur to research for improved techniques to minimize nuisance.

The power of the court to condition on equitable grounds the continuance of an injunction on the payment of permanent damages seems undoubted. . . .

The damage base here suggested is consistent with the general rule in those nuisance cases where damages are allowed. "Where a nuisance is of such a permanent and unabatable character that a single recovery can be had, including the whole damage past and future resulting therefrom, there can be but one recovery" (66 C.J.S. Nuisances §140, p. 947). It has been said that permanent damages are allowed where the loss recoverable would obviously be small as compared with the cost of removal of the nuisance (Kentucky-Ohio Gas Co. v. Bowling, 264 Ky. 470 477, 95 S.W.2d 1). . . .

Thus it seems fair to both sides to grant permanent damages to plaintiffs which will terminate this private litigation. The theory of damage is the "servitude on land" of plaintiffs imposed by defendant's nuisance. (See United States v. Causby, 328 U.S. 256, 261, 262, 267, where the term "servitude" addressed to the land was used by Justice Douglas relating to the effect of airplane noise on property near an airport.)

The judgment, by allowance of permanent damages imposing a servitude on land, which is the basis of the actions, would preclude future recovery by plaintiffs or their grantees.

This should be placed beyond debate by a provision of the judgment that the payment by defendant and the acceptance by plaintiffs of permanent damages found by the court shall be in compensation for servitude on the land. . . .

The orders should be reversed, without costs, and the cases remitted to Supreme Court, Albany County to grant an injunction which shall be vacated upon payment by defendant of such amounts of permanent damage to the respective plaintiffs as shall for this purpose be determined by the court.

JASEN, J. (dissenting). I agree with the majority that a reversal is required here, but I do not subscribe to the newly enunciated doctrine of assessment of permanent damages, in lieu of an injunction, where substantial property rights have been impaired by the creation of a nuisance. . . .

I see grave dangers in overruling our long-established rule of granting an injunction where a nuisance results in substantial continuing damage. In permitting the injunction to become inoperative upon the payment of permanent damages, the majority is, in effect, licensing a continuing wrong. It is the same as saying to the cement company, you may continue to do harm to your neighbors so long as you pay a fee for it. Furthermore, once such permanent damages are assessed and paid, the incentive to alleviate the wrong would be eliminated, thereby continuing air pollution of an area without abatement. . . .

NOTES AND QUESTIONS

1. For illuminating discussion of the background and aftermath of *Boomer*, see Symposium on Nuisance Law: Twenty Years After *Boomer v. Atlantic Cement Co.*, 54 Alb. L. Rev. 169-399 (1990); Daniel A. Farber, Reassessing *Boomer*: Justice, Efficiency, and Nuisance Law, in Property Law and Legal Education 7 (Peter Hay & Michael H. Hoeflich eds. 1988). Farber notes two points in particular: First, the consequences of the nuisance in *Boomer* were much more serious than the opinion of the N.Y. Court of Appeals suggests. The cement company had a quarry a half mile from its plant, and blasting operations at the quarry frightened neighborhood children, cracked the walls, ceilings, and exteriors of homes in the vicinity, and filled the air with fine dust that covered everything. Second, on remand the trial court awarded damages in amounts that came to considerably more than the $185,000 mentioned in the Court of Appeals opinion:

> The trial judge agreed with the plaintiffs that damages would not be limited to the decrease in fair market value. On the other hand, he also rejected the plaintiffs' theory that damages should be awarded under a "contract price theory," that is, for the amount Atlantic would have had to pay to persuade the plaintiffs themselves to agree to lift a permanent injunction. . . . By the time

of the judge's decision, all but one of the cases had settled. In the remaining case, the judge found the decline in market value to be $140,000, and awarded $175,000 in damages.

. . . We know from [subsequent proceedings] that Atlantic's total liability, including the settlements, ultimately came to $710,000, some four times the amount mentioned in the Court of Appeals decision denying permanent injunctive relief. [Id. at 11-12.]

2. *The liability issue.* But why was a nuisance even found in *Boomer*? In a subsequent case, Copart Indus., Inc. v. Consolidated Edison Co., 362 N.E.2d 968 (N.Y. 1977), the N.Y. Court of Appeals confronted a set of facts essentially identical to those in *Boomer*, yet found no nuisance. The court in *Copart* claimed to follow the Restatement. It considered the liability category of abnormally dangerous conditions to be inapplicable and concluded that neither intent nor negligence had been established. *Boomer* was distinguished on the ground that it involved an intentional and unreasonable invasion.

Do you agree with that characterization of the *Boomer* case? Notice the statement in *Boomer* that the trial court based liability simply on the fact that the plaintiffs' property had been damaged. See also the opinion below, 287 N.Y.S.2d 112 (Sup. Ct. 1967). Given that, which of the theories of nuisance liability discussed earlier (see pages 782-783) might *Boomer* reflect? For a suggested answer, and a criticism of *Copart*, see David Silverstone, Comment, Internalizing Externalities: Nuisance Law and Economic Efficiency, 53 N.Y.U. L. Rev. 219 (1978).

Assume that in *Boomer* the costs of pollution abatement would exceed the benefits. Is this a reason to find no liability on the part of the defendant? On the assumption stated, are there reasons (apart from fairness) for holding the defendant liable? See Guido Calabresi & Jon T. Hirschoff, Toward a Test for Strict Liability in Torts, 81 Yale L.J. 1055 (1972).

3. *The remedy issue: injunctions.* Is it not an accurate characterization of *Boomer* to say that the court, in essence, denied injunctive relief and that it did so by "balancing the equities"? What do you think of the method of striking the balance? Consider the following from Mahoney v. Walter, 205 S.E.2d 692, 698 (W. Va. 1974):

> One of the chief problems with this doctrine [of balancing the equities] is that it compares the general loss to the public, such as loss of jobs, while it only considers specific loss to the private land owner, i.e., the specific money damage to his property, notwithstanding he may be damaged in many general ways which cannot be translated into specific damages.

See also Comment, Equity and the Eco-System: Can Injunctions Clear the Air?, 68 Mich. L. Rev. 1254, 1284 n.158 (1970):

> Most cases in which injunctions are sought involve injury to only one or a few persons, but in the air pollution context many are being injured. If the plaintiff were to bring a class action, the weighing of the benefit which would result from granting the injunction would include all the members of the class. Class actions are sometimes difficult to bring, however, and it therefore seems appropriate as a general rule that if a judge can recognize harm to third persons from granting an injunction, he should be able to consider harm to third persons from not granting the injunction.

Is balancing the equities a sensible (or necessary) way to reach a decision about granting or denying injunctive relief; should one look instead at factors other than those suggested by the balancing doctrine (which are what)?

In the discussion after the *Estancias* case we considered in a preliminary way the issue of damages versus injunctive relief (see Note 4 on page 789). But *Estancias* was a case involving just a few parties, whereas in *Boomer* there was a sizable number of plaintiffs, and perhaps a larger number of plaintiffs in the wings. Is this a difference that matters? See the Note on "Externalities" in Chapter 1 (page 46) and consider some findings reported in a series of articles by Hoffman and Spitzer. The first article concluded, on the basis of a set of experiments, that in two-party situations like *Estancias* the parties will likely bargain to efficient outcomes, whereas in many-party situations like *Boomer* post-litigation bargaining difficulties could well arise. Surprisingly, however, the subsequent studies, based on further experiments, suggested that even in situations involving up to 40 parties, post-litigation bargaining can be expected to lead to efficient solutions with no problems of freeriding or holding out whatsoever![5]

But, experiments aside, what happens in the real world? Frankly, it's hard to tell, for there are very few empirical studies, and those that exist look at very small samples. For example, a follow-up of 20 appellate decisions in nuisance cases found that no post-judgment bargaining by the parties took place in any of them, probably because of bad feelings between the parties and distaste for bargaining (more particularly, bargaining that entailed exchanging rights for cash). See Ward Farnsworth, Do Parties in Nuisance Cases Bargain After Judgment? A Glimpse Inside the Cathedral, 66 U. Chi. L. Rev. 373 (1999); see also Ward Farnsworth, The Economics of Enmity, 69 U. Chi. L. Rev. 211 (2002); Peter H. Huang, Reasons within Passions: Emotions and Intentions in Property Rights Bargaining, 79 Or. L. Rev. 435 (2000). A more recent case study, however, cuts in the opposite direction. See Gideon Parchomovsky & Peter Siegelman, Selling Mayberry: Communities and Individuals in Law and Economics, 92 Cal. L. Rev. 75 (2004), investigating American Electric Power Company's buyout of an entire town—Cheshire, Ohio—in 2002. Though AEP never admitted as much, its purchase was probably a means to avoid nuisance litigation over the pollutants it dumped into the community's air. Cheshire is (was) small as towns go, with a population of only 220 (about 90 families), but that's large in terms of negotiation problems. Yet the deal went through with no major hassles, no litigation, no holdouts, just the opposite of what economic theory would suggest. A possible explanation, one of several considered by the authors, is that it is a *community* that was on the table, and an offer to buy out some residents can cause a community

---

5. See Elizabeth Hoffman & Matthew L. Spitzer, The Coase Theorem: Some Experimental Tests, 25 J.L. & Econ. 73 (1982); Elizabeth Hoffman & Matthew L. Spitzer, Experimental Law and Economics: An Introduction, 85 Colum. L. Rev. 991 (1985); Elizabeth Hoffman & Matthew L. Spitzer, Experimental Tests of the Coase Theorem with Large Bargaining Groups, 15 J. Legal Stud. 149 (1986). For comments on the limitations of experimental studies such as these, see Mark Kelman, Comment on Hoffman and Spitzer's *Experimental Law and Economics*, 85 Colum. L. Rev. 1037 (1985); Stewart E. Sterk, Neighbors in American Land Law, 87 Colum. L. Rev. 55, 72-74 (1987).

to unravel: "[A] polluter could offer to buy 60% of the affected properties for an above-market price. If the remaining 40% of the town is not viable on its own, all residents will have an incentive to sell. . . ." Id. at 83. And in the end, "all but two resident and four nonresident property owners agreed to sell." Id. at 91.

4. *The remedy issue: permanent damages.* Notice the nature of the relief awarded in *Boomer.* Does the fact that a court can award permanent damages dispel the concern, mentioned in the discussion after *Estancias,* that denial of injunctive relief relegates plaintiffs to a series of lawsuits? Do permanent damages have any other advantages? Any disadvantages? On the last question, consider the reasons why the damages might fail to give the aggrieved parties "full" compensation. See Farber, supra, at 14-19. Consider also the observation of the dissenting judge in *Boomer,* who argued that an award of permanent damages destroys any incentive on the part of the defendant to abate its pollution in the future—presumably even if new, cost-effective technology is developed. Is there any solution to this problem, other than periodic or temporary damages (which, of course, will give rise to a multiplicity of actions)? Do periodic damages generate incentive problems of their own? See William F. Baxter & Lillian R. Altree, Legal Aspects of Airport Noise, 15 J.L. & Econ. 1 (1972).

Spur Industries, Inc. v. Del E. Webb Development Co.

Supreme Court of Arizona, 1972
494 P.2d 700

CAMERON, J. From a judgment permanently enjoining the defendant, Spur Industries, Inc., from operating a cattle feedlot near the plaintiff Del E. Webb Development Company's Sun City, Spur appeals. Webb cross-appeals. Although numerous issues are raised, we feel that it is necessary to answer only two questions. They are:

1. Where the operation of a business, such as a cattle feedlot is lawful in the first instance, but becomes a nuisance by reason of a nearby residential area, may the feedlot operation be enjoined in an action brought by the developer of the residential area?

2. Assuming that the nuisance may be enjoined, may the developer of a completely new town or urban area in a previously agricultural area be required to indemnify the operator of the feedlot who must move or cease operation because of the presence of the residential area created by the developer?

The facts necessary for a determination of this matter on appeal are as follows. The area in question is located in Maricopa County, Arizona, some 14 or 15 miles west of the urban area of Phoenix, on the Phoenix-Wickenburg Highway, also known as Grand Avenue. About two miles south of Grand Avenue is Olive Avenue which runs east and west. 111th Avenue runs north and south as does the Agua Fria River immediately to the west. See Exhibits A and B [on pages 798-799].

Farming started in this area about 1911. In 1929, with the completion of the Carl Pleasant Dam, gravity flow water became available to the property located

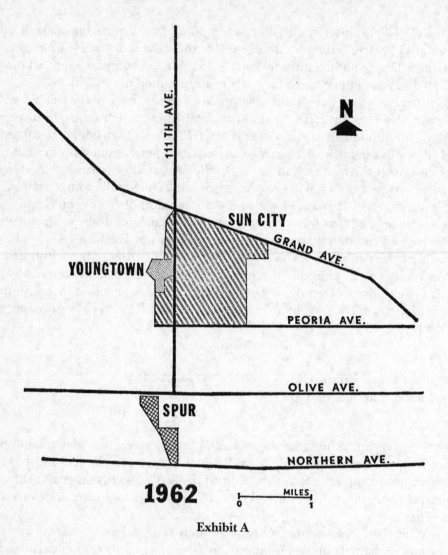

Exhibit A

to the west of the Agua Fria River, though land to the east remained dependent upon well water for irrigation. By 1950, the only urban areas in the vicinity were the agriculturally related communities of Peoria, El Mirage, and Surprise located along Grand Avenue. Along 111th Avenue, approximately one mile south of Grand Avenue and 1½ miles north of Olive Avenue, the community of Youngtown was commenced in 1954. Youngtown is a retirement community appealing primarily to senior citizens.

In 1956, Spur's predecessors in interest, H. Marion Welborn and the Northside Hay Mill and Trading Company, developed feedlots about ½ mile south of Olive Avenue, in an area between the confluence of the usually dry Agua Fria and New Rivers. The area is well suited for cattle feeding and in 1959, there were 25 cattle feeding pens or dairy operations within a 7 mile radius of the location

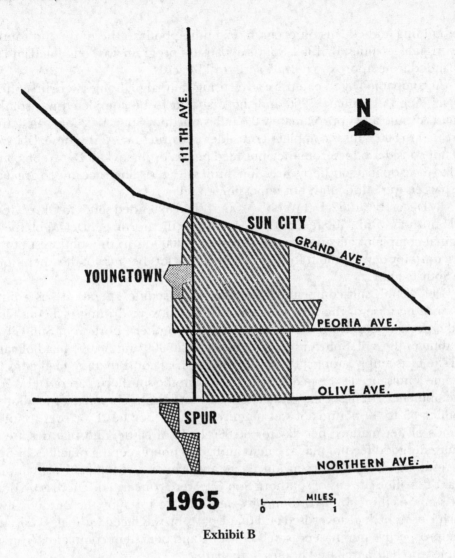

111 TH AVE.

N

SUN CITY

GRAND AVE.

YOUNGTOWN

PEORIA AVE.

OLIVE AVE.

SPUR

NORTHERN AVE.

1965   MILES
                         0   1

Exhibit B

developed by Spur's predecessors. In April and May of 1959, the Northside Hay Mill was feeding between 6,000 and 7,000 head of cattle and Welborn approximately 1,500 head on a combined area of 35 acres.

In May of 1959, Del Webb began to plan the development of an urban area to be known as Sun City. For this purpose, the Marinette and the Santa Fe Ranches, some 20,000 acres of farmland, were purchased for $15,000,000 or $750.00 per acre. This price was considerably less than the price of land located near the urban area of Phoenix, and along with the success of Youngtown was a factor influencing the decision to purchase the property in question.

By September 1959, Del Webb had started construction of a golf course south of Grand Avenue and Spur's predecessors had started to level ground for more feedlot area. In 1960, Spur purchased the property in question and began a rebuilding and expansion program extending both to the north and south of the original facilities. By 1962, Spur's expansion program was completed and had expanded from approximately 35 acres to 114 acres.

Accompanied by an extensive advertising campaign, homes were first offered by Del Webb in January 1960 and the first unit to be completed was south of Grand Avenue and approximately 2½ miles north of Spur. By 2 May 1960, there were 450 to 500 houses completed or under construction. At this time, Del Webb did not consider odors from the Spur feed pens a problem and Del Webb continued to develop in a southerly direction, until sales resistance became so great that the parcels were difficult if not impossible to sell. . . .

By December 1967, Del Webb's property had extended south to Olive Avenue and Spur was within 500 feet of Olive Avenue to the north. . . . Del Webb filed its original complaint alleging that in excess of 1,300 lots in the southwest portion were unfit for development for sale as residential lots because of the operation of the Spur feedlot.

Del Webb's suit complained that the Spur feeding operation was a public nuisance because of the flies and the odor which were drifting or being blown by the prevailing south to north wind over the southern portion of Sun City. At the time of the suit, Spur was feeding between 20,000 and 30,000 head of cattle, and the facts amply support the finding of the trial court that the feed pens had become a nuisance to the people who resided in the southern part of Del Webb's development. The testimony indicated that cattle in a commercial feedlot will produce 35 to 40 pounds of wet manure per day, per head, or over a million pounds of wet manure per day for 30,000 head of cattle, and that despite the admittedly good feedlot management and good housekeeping practices by Spur, the resulting odor and flies produced an annoying if not unhealthy situation as far as the senior citizens of southern Sun City were concerned. There is no doubt that some of the citizens of Sun City were unable to enjoy the outdoor living which Del Webb had advertised and that Del Webb was faced with sales resistance from prospective purchasers as well as strong and persistent complaints from the people who had purchased homes in that area. . . .

It is noted, however, that neither the citizens of Sun City nor Youngtown are represented in this lawsuit and the suit is solely between Del E. Webb Development Company and Spur Industries, Inc.

May Spur Be Enjoined?

The difference between a private nuisance and a public nuisance is generally one of degree. A private nuisance is one affecting a single individual or a definite small number of persons in the enjoyment of private rights not common to the public, while a public nuisance is one affecting the rights enjoyed by citizens as a part of the public. To constitute a public nuisance, the nuisance must affect a considerable number of people or an entire community or neighborhood. . . .

Where the injury is slight, the remedy for minor inconveniences lies in an action for damages rather than in one for an injunction. . . . Moreover, some courts have held, in the "balancing of conveniences" cases, that damages may be the sole remedy. See Boomer v. Atlantic Cement Co., 26 N.Y.2d 219, 309 N.Y.S.2d 312, 257 N.E.2d 870, 40 A.L.R.3d 590 (1970), and annotation comments, 40 A.L.R.3d 601.

Thus, it would appear from the admittedly incomplete record as developed in the trial court, that, at most, residents of Youngtown would be entitled to damages rather than injunctive relief.

We have no difficulty however, in agreeing with the conclusion of the trial court that Spur's operation was an enjoinable public nuisance as far as the people in the southern portion of Del Webb's Sun City were concerned.

§36-601, subsec. A reads as follows:

> §36-601. Public nuisances dangerous to public health
>
> A. The following conditions are specifically declared public nuisances dangerous to the public health:
> 1. Any condition or place in populous areas which constitutes a breeding place for flies, rodents, mosquitoes and other insects which are capable of carrying and transmitting disease-causing organisms to any person or persons.

By this statute, before an otherwise lawful (and necessary) business may be declared a public nuisance, there must be a "populous" area in which people are injured:

> . . . [I]t hardly admits a doubt that, in determining the question as to whether a lawful occupation is so conducted as to constitute a nuisance as a matter of fact, the locality and surroundings are of the first importance. (Citations omitted.) A business which is not per se a public nuisance may become such by being carried on at a place where the health, comfort, or inconvenience of a populous neighborhood is affected. . . . What might amount to a serious nuisance in one locality by reason of the density of the population, or character of the neighborhood affected, may in another place and under different surroundings be deemed proper and unobjectionable. . . . [MacDonald v. Perry, 32 Ariz. 39, 49-50, 255 P. 494, 497 (1927).]

It is clear that as to the citizens of Sun City, the operation of Spur's feedlot was both a public and a private nuisance. They could have successfully maintained an action to abate the nuisance. Del Webb, having shown a special injury in the loss of sales, had standing to bring suit to enjoin the nuisance. . . . The judgment of the trial court permanently enjoining the operation of the feedlot is affirmed.

Must Del Webb Indemnify Spur?

A suit to enjoin a nuisance sounds in equity and the courts have long recognized a special responsibility to the public when acting as a court of equity. . . .

In addition to protecting the public interest, however, courts of equity are concerned with protecting the operator of a lawful, albeit noxious, business from the result of a knowing and willful encroachment by others near his business.

In the so-called coming to the nuisance cases, the courts have held that the residential landowner may not have relief if he knowingly came into a neighborhood reserved for industrial or agricultural endeavors and has been damaged thereby. . . .

Were Webb the only party injured, we would feel justified in holding that the doctrine of "coming to the nuisance" would have been a bar to the relief asked by Webb, and, on the other hand, had Spur located the feedlot near the outskirts of a city and had the city grown toward the feedlot, Spur would have to suffer the cost of abating the nuisance as to those people locating within the growth pattern of the expanding city: "The case affords, perhaps, an example where a business established at a place remote from population is gradually surrounded and becomes part of a populous center, so that a business which formerly was not an interference with the rights of others has become so by the encroachment of the population. . . ." City of Ft. Smith v. Western Hide & Fur Co., 153 Ark. 99, 103, 239 S.W. 724, 726 (1922).

We agree, however, with the Massachusetts court that: "The law of nuisance affords no rigid rule to be applied in all instances. It is elastic. It undertakes to require only that which is fair and reasonable under all the circumstances. In a commonwealth like this, which depends for its material prosperity so largely on the continued growth and enlargement of manufacturing of diverse varieties, 'extreme rights' cannot be enforced. . . ." Stevens v. Rockport Granite Co., 216 Mass. 486, 488, 104 N.E. 371, 373 (1914).

There was no indication in the instant case at the time Spur and its predecessors located in western Maricopa County that a new city would spring up, full-blown, alongside the feeding operation and that the developer of that city would ask the court to order Spur to move because of the new city. Spur is required to move not because of any wrongdoing on the part of Spur, but because of a proper and legitimate regard of the courts for the rights and interests of the public.

Del Webb, on the other hand, is entitled to the relief prayed for (a permanent injunction), not because Webb is blameless, but because of the damage to the people who have been encouraged to purchase homes in Sun City. It does not equitably or legally follow, however, that Webb, being entitled to the injunction, is then free of any liability to Spur if Webb has in fact been the cause of the damage Spur has sustained. It does not seem harsh to require a developer, who has taken advantage of the lesser land values in a rural area as well as the availability of large tracts of land on which to build and develop a new town or city in the area, to indemnify those who are forced to leave as a result.

Having brought people to the nuisance to the foreseeable detriment of Spur, Webb must indemnify Spur for a reasonable amount of the cost of moving or shutting down. It should be noted that this relief to Spur is limited to a case wherein a developer has, with foreseeability, brought into a previously agricultural or industrial area the population which makes necessary the granting of an injunction against a lawful business and for which the business has no adequate relief.

It is therefore the decision of this court that the matter be remanded to the trial court for a hearing upon the damages sustained by the defendant Spur as a reasonable and direct result of the granting of the permanent injunction. Since the result of the appeal may appear novel and both sides have obtained a measure of relief, it is ordered that each side will bear its own costs.

Affirmed in part, reversed in part, and remanded for further proceedings consistent with this opinion.

NOTES AND QUESTIONS

1. *Public nuisance.* A public nuisance, according to the Restatement, "is an unreasonable interference with a right common to the general public." Circumstances said to bear on the issue of unreasonableness are: whether the conduct in question significantly interferes with public health, safety, peace, comfort, or convenience; whether the conduct is proscribed by statute or ordinance (as in *Spur*); whether the conduct is of a continuing nature or has produced a permanent or long-lasting effect. See Restatement (Second) of Torts §821B (1979). Essentially, though, the underlying bases of liability for public nuisance are the same as those for private nuisance—there must be substantial harm caused by intentional and unreasonable conduct or by conduct that is negligent, reckless, or abnormally dangerous. And, as with private nuisance, unreasonableness turns heavily on considerations of gravity and utility. Thus, as one early public nuisance case is said to have put it, "*Le utility del chose excusera le noisomeness del stink.*" Quoted in id. §826 comment a, at 120.

Note, then, that the difference between public and private nuisance lies in the interests protected: public nuisance protects public rights; private nuisance protects rights in the use and enjoyment of land. In *Spur*, the court states (at page 801) that as to the citizens of Sun City the defendant's feedlot was both a public and a private nuisance. This reflects the reasoning of most courts; they take the position that interference with the use and enjoyment of land such as occurred in *Spur* is a private nuisance no matter how many landowners are involved. The interference can also be a public nuisance if it interferes with a general public right, again as in *Spur*.

The distinction between private and public nuisance can be important in several respects. First, since a private nuisance arises from interference with the use and enjoyment of land, *only* owners of interests in land can bring suit. Second, since a public nuisance arises from interference with public rights, any member of the affected public can sue, but usually *only* if the person bringing suit can show "special injury" (or "special damage," or "particular damage")—injury or damage of a kind different from that suffered by other members of the public.

The special injury requirement is a remnant of English history. The original remedies for public nuisances were criminal prosecutions or abatement actions initiated by public officials. No private cause of action was recognized until 1536 and then only if the plaintiff suffered harm over and above that caused to other members of the community. The justifications for the rule are said to be that it is needed to protect the defendant from a multiplicity of actions (could this concern not be handled through class actions or by limiting the plaintiff's remedy to abatement?) and that redress of wrongs to the general public should be left to public officials. Moreover, some commentators make the dubious assertion "that any harm or interference shared by the public at large will normally be, if not entirely theoretical or potential, at least minor, petty and trivial so far as the individual is concerned." Id. §821C comment a, at 95.

The restriction on standing to sue imposed by the special injury rule has often been criticized, especially by environmentalists, and, perhaps in response, the law has been liberalized by statute, judicial decision, and the Restatement. See, e.g., id. §821C (suits for damages may be brought only by persons suffering special injury; abatement actions may be brought by those same persons, by public officials, *and* by any person who "has standing to sue as a representative of the general public, as a citizen in a citizen's action or as a member of a class in a class action"). The Restatement's objective is to leave courts free to proceed with more recent developments expanding citizen access to courts. Motivating concerns are probably that special injury can be difficult to prove (especially if harm is only threatened and has not yet occurred) and that public prosecution can be inhibited by political pressure, inertia, and lack of resources. For a good overview, see John E. Bryson & Angus Macbeth, Public Nuisance, the Restatement (Second) of Torts, and Environmental Law, 2 Ecology L.Q. 241 (1972).

2. *"Coming to the nuisance."* Note the discussion in *Spur* of the "coming to the nuisance" defense. See pages 801-802. Though there are cases to the contrary, the prevailing view is that moving into the vicinity of a nuisance does not completely bar a suit for damages or injunctive relief, but it is a "relevant factor" (much like the factors, suggested earlier in this chapter, that an area is zoned for the activity in question or has come to be commonly used for such an activity). See Restatement (Second) of Torts, supra, §840D. What role does this "relevant factor" play? Does it matter whether the plaintiff knew of the nuisance prior to moving into the area? Whether the defendant could foresee future settlement in the vicinity? Whether the plaintiff bought property before the nuisance came into being, but developed it after? What the plaintiff paid for the property? Is "coming to the nuisance" concerned with fairness or with efficiency?

The answer to the last question is that both concerns have played a role in doctrinal development. As to the first series of questions, all the factors mentioned—perhaps others as well—have a bearing. Working out the role of "coming to the nuisance" in particular cases, then, can be a complicated business from both fairness and efficiency points of view. See, e.g., Robert C. Ellickson, Alternatives to Zoning: Covenants, Nuisance Rules, and Fines as Land Use Controls, 40 U. Chi. L. Rev. 681, 758-761 (1973); Edward H. Rabin, Nuisance Law: Rethinking Fundamental Assumptions, 63 Va. L. Rev. 1299, 1321-1329 (1977).

Recall the principle of first in time that figured so prominently in Chapter 1. Is "coming to the nuisance" yet another application? See Lawrence Berger, An Analysis of the Doctrine That "First in Time Is First in Right," 64 Neb. L. Rev. 349, 378-381 (1985); Donald Wittman, First Come, First Served: An Economic Analysis of "Coming to the Nuisance," 9 J. Legal Stud. 557 (1980).

Did the court in *Spur* end up taking "coming to the nuisance" into account, or not? In any event, is the resolution in *Spur* preferable to a judgment that denies all relief by virtue of the plaintiff's moving into the area or to one that grants it notwithstanding that fact? Compare Pendoley v. Ferreira, 187 N.E.2d 142 (Mass. 1963) (piggery; injunction granted but time provided for defendant to make new arrangements).[6]

3. *Four rules.* A conventional view of long standing held that nuisance claims could be resolved in one of three ways: abate the activity in question by granting the plaintiff injunctive relief (the *Morgan* and *Estancias* cases, pages 779 and 787); let the activity continue if the defendant pays damages (the *Boomer* case, page 790); let the activity continue by denying all relief (the converse of the first alternative). *Spur* adds a new possibility, a fourth rule of decision that is the converse of the second alternative: abate the activity if the plaintiff pays damages.[7]

This "rule four" has an interesting intellectual history: An Arizona court and two Ivy League scholars came up with it at more or less the same time, but through very different approaches. The court in *Spur*, it appears, developed the rule out of the logic of necessity. None of the three traditional approaches yielded a result the court regarded as appropriate. Hence rule four. In the same year, Calabresi and Melamed, working at Harvard, developed the rule as the logical product of a modeling exercise. They reasoned that an entitlement exists (for example, an entitlement to use the air resource) that can be located in either the plaintiff or the defendant (the receptor or the polluter) and that can be protected by an injunction or so-called property rule that permits violation of the entitlement only if one gets the permission of its owner, or—alternatively—by damages, a so-called liability rule that permits violation of the entitlement if one pays a judicially determined sum to its owner. Given that the entitlement can be in either of two parties and that it can be protected by either of two means, there must be four possible outcomes or rules of decision rather than the three traditionally relied on by the courts. Hence rule four again. See Guido Calabresi & A. Douglas Melamed, Property Rules, Liability Rules, and Inalienability: One View of the Cathedral, 85 Harv. L. Rev. 1089 (1972).[8]

---

6. An alternative solution to cases like *Spur* is suggested by "right to farm" statutes designed to protect established agricultural uses from encroachment by urban development. A typical statute provides that no nuisance action may be brought against an "agricultural operation" if the operation has been lawfully ongoing for a year or more prior to the action and if the conditions complained of in the action have existed substantially unchanged since the date the agricultural operation began. John E. Cribbet, Concepts in Transition: The Search for a New Definition of Property, 1986 U. Ill. L. Rev. 1, 19-20, reported that some 35 states had enacted such legislation since 1979. The Iowa Supreme Court subsequently found its state's statute to be unconstitutional. Bormann v. Board of Supervisors, 584 N.W.2d 309 (Iowa 1998).

7. The approach taken in *Spur* could work by degrees. The courts could adopt a doctrine of "comparative nuisance," akin to the contributory or comparative negligence doctrine of standard tort law, and apportion costs between the parties according to degrees of comparative responsibility. Under such an approach, a court might provide injunctive relief but also require a plaintiff whose share of responsibility for the nuisance was (perhaps) 20 percent to pay 20 percent of the defendant's compliance costs. If the suit were for damages, the defendant's liability would be reduced in the same manner. See Jeff L. Lewin, *Boomer* and the American Law of Nuisance: Past, Present, and Future, 54 Alb. L. Rev. 189, 276-291 (1990); Jeff L. Lewin, Comparative Nuisance, 50 U. Pitt. L. Rev. 1009 (1989).

8. A central topic in Calabresi & Melamed is the law of nuisance—and *Spur*, of course, is itself a nuisance case—but the conceptions developed in the article can illuminate any number of legal topics. We first mentioned them, for example, in the context of adverse possession (see the discussion on page 161), and they will be brought into play again when we consider the problem of changed conditions in the law of servitudes (see Note 1 on page 933).

Calabresi and Melamed claim that with the full complement of four rules, one can go a long way toward achieving both efficiency and fairness in any given nuisance dispute (subject, of course, to the inherent limitations of judicial intervention). Their case turns in substantial part on matters we raised in discussing the *Estancias* and *Boomer* cases, having to do with the various advantages and disadvantages of damages and injunctive relief. See, e.g., Louis Kaplow & Steven Shavell, Property Rules Versus Liability Rules, 109 Harv. L. Rev. 713 (1996); James E. Krier & Stewart J. Schwab, Property Rules and Liability Rules: The Cathedral in Another Light, 70 N.Y.U. L. Rev. 440 (1995). Analysis of the pros and cons over the years has resulted in a large literature, much of which is considered and extended in Ian Ayres, Optional Law: The Structure of Legal Entitlements (2005); see also Lee Anne Fennell, Property and Half-Torts, 116 Yale L.J. 1400 (2007); Keith N. Hylton, Property Rules and Liability Rules, Once Again, 2 Rev. L. & Econ. 137 (2006).

Did the court in *Spur* give Del Webb a *choice* either to pay damages to the defendant or to tolerate the presence of its feedlot? Compare the opinion in the *Boomer* case at pages 792-793. Could the parties, after the decision, agree that Spur need not abate? If so, would Del Webb, in conducting negotiations, take into account the situation of the real parties in interest?[9]

On the merits and demerits of the novel approach taken by the court in *Spur*, see Jeff L. Lewin, Compensated Injunctions and the Evolution of Nuisance Law, 71 Iowa L. Rev. 775 (1986); R. E. Hawkins, "In and Of Itself": Some Thoughts on the Assignment of Property Rights in Nuisance Cases, 36 U. Toronto Fac. L. Rev. 209 (1978).

NOTE: NUISANCE LAW AND ENVIRONMENTAL CONTROLS

As much of the material in this chapter suggests, nuisance law has an obvious bearing on environmental problems—pollution, for example, interferes with use and enjoyment of land as well as with public rights and thus seems a natural target for control as a nuisance.

That the law of nuisance has a place in environmental control seems clear, but there are a number of reasons to conclude that its contributions must be

---

9. In fact, the case was settled in another fashion, as the editors learned by inquiring of counsel. Spur moved its feedlot away, and Del Webb paid an undisclosed amount to compensate for the costs of relocation, loss of profits, and related expenses.

Pending at the time of the *Spur* litigation reported in the principal case was a suit by residents of Sun City seeking damages from Spur for maintaining a nuisance. After the main decision in *Spur*, the feedlot company cross-complained against Del Webb, seeking indemnification for any damages for which Spur might be held liable in the residents' suit. The trial court granted a motion by Del Webb to dismiss the cross-complaint, but the Arizona Supreme Court reversed, holding that Spur might indeed be entitled to recover. See Spur Feeding Co. v. Superior Court, 505 P.2d 1377 (Ariz. 1973). The residents' lawsuit was subsequently settled for an undisclosed amount.

The *Spur* case, its background, and its aftermath are detailed by Andrew P. Morriss, Cattle vs. Retirees: Sun City and the Battle of *Spur Industries v. Del E. Webb Development Co.*, in Property Stories 337 (Gerald Korngold & Andrew P. Morriss eds. 2d ed. 2009).

limited ones. Nuisance litigation is an expensive, cumbersome, and somewhat fortuitous means for resolving modern environmental problems, typified as they are by continuing and multiple causes, widespread effects and multiple victims, and scientifically complex issues as to cause, effect, and remedy. Potential plaintiffs, each usually bearing only a small part of the social costs of a large problem, have weak incentives to bring expensive lawsuits that promise limited rewards and difficult problems of proof; judges are poorly equipped to deal in a competent fashion with issues that demand considerable scientific expertise and are probably even less able to devise and oversee an ongoing program of technological controls; arguably, judges also lack the (political) competence to make the large-scale value judgments implicit in far-reaching environmental controls—judgments better left to more politically accountable government branches.

The shortcomings of nuisance litigation as a means of environmental control could, perhaps, be overcome to some degree through such techniques as class actions, provision of attorneys' fees to plaintiffs bringing suit "in the public interest," special environmental courts, and so on. The general conclusion, though, is that nuisance litigation is ill-suited to other than small-scale, incidental, localized, scientifically uncomplicated pollution problems. Indeed, judges themselves at times reveal a marked reluctance to use nuisance suits as the means for an ambitious program of environmental control—see once again the opinion in *Boomer*.

An alternative to judicial resolution of pollution problems is legislative and administrative intervention—the mainstay of environmental control efforts for many years. Air and water pollution were the subjects of royal proclamations in fourteenth-century England and of some parliamentary action not long thereafter; primitive legislative programs to control these same problems existed in the United States at least by the 1800s. By and large, American efforts began at the local level and were followed by state legislation as the dimensions of pollution problems, and knowledge about them, expanded. While there were some early federal pollution control programs, they were generally modest, intended in most instances merely to provide support for state activities. The federal presence was not really felt at all until about 1950; especially since 1970, however, the national government has occupied a dominant position. Today there are federal programs on virtually every aspect of environmental problems (air and water pollution, noise, pesticides, solid waste, and toxic pollutants are examples). State and local programs still operate, but largely within a framework of requirements set at the national level.

To date, virtually all legislative-administrative efforts to control environmental problems—at any level of government—have taken the form of *regulation*. A regulatory program (sometimes called in the trade a program of command and control) typically proceeds by prohibiting certain activities, requiring installation of prescribed technologies, and setting standards limiting emissions from pollution sources. Once established, the measures are backed up by civil and criminal sanctions.

Regulation, then, proceeds by telling pollution sources how much, and sometimes how, to control. *Incentive systems* stand in sharp contrast. Rather than command, they induce. The classic example is the emission or effluent fee—a charge on each unit of air or water pollution, set so as to yield an appropriate level of control in the aggregate (the higher the charge, the less pollution). A variant—marketable or transferable rights—sets a fixed number of pollution rights, distributes them by one means or another, and then permits trading in the rights thereafter (the fewer the rights, the less pollution).

As should be clear, incentive systems are much more decentralized than regulation; pollution sources are left largely to do as they wish, provided that they pay the price of the fee or that they hold the required rights. The advocates of incentive systems have maintained for years that a primary advantage of the decentralized approach is its promise of achieving desired levels of pollution control at lower cost than under regulation. The argument is straightforward: sources with low control costs will control to greater degrees than sources facing higher costs, with the result that the total outlay for a given level of quality will be minimized. (Can you see why?) Advocates also argue that incentive systems encourage more technological innovation than does regulation. But proponents of regulation have arguments of their own. The regulatory approach, for example, is said to be more direct, more certain, and easier to monitor. It avoids the problem of "commodifying" environmental quality (recall the discussion of commodification in connection with the sale of body parts; see pages 103-104). And it is the more acceptable alternative politically.

And so it has been, until relatively recent times. While regulation remains the dominant approach to environmental problems in the United States (and elsewhere), incentive systems—marketable rights in particular—have made substantial inroads that may prove to be of enormous significance. The most notable instance is found in the acid rain provisions of the 1990 amendments to the federal Clean Air Act, which set up a system of pollution allowances that can be banked and traded by sources of sulfur dioxide (primarily power plants). For a quick picture of the program, see Roger W. Findley & Daniel A. Farber, Environmental Law in a Nutshell 160-163 (7th ed. 2008), observing that "[sulfur] dioxide allowances became truly marketable when the Chicago Board of Trade voted to create a private market for them. The federal program seems to have succeeded in reducing the cost of controlling acid rain, aided by some fortuitous economic shifts. A similar market system . . . is likely to be used when Congress adopts climate change legislation." Id. at 163.

No one maintains that command-and-control regulation should be abandoned as a means of environmental policy, though there are those who come close to taking that position. See, e.g., Terry L. Anderson & Donald R. Leal, Free Market Environmentalism (rev. ed. 2001). The point, rather, is that regulation should not be regarded as the exclusive means. And this is an observation that pertains to more than pollution problems. Recall, for instance, the discussion of transferable fishing rights discussed in Chapter 1, at page 53.

10

Private Land Use Controls: The Law of Servitudes

In this chapter we study land use arrangements arising out of private agreements. Usually, but not always, the agreements involve two or more parcels of land, and the purpose of the agreements is to increase the total value of all the parcels involved. And usually, but not always, the effect of the agreements is to burden one parcel of land for the benefit of another parcel. For example, the owner of Tract 1 may have an easement to cross Tract 2 to reach a public road. Burdens and benefits are often reciprocal, as when all lots in a subdivision are restricted to residential use. These agreements create interests in land, binding and benefiting not only the parties to the agreement in question but also their successors. These interests are commonly called, as a class, servitudes.

A. Introduction: Classifying Servitudes

Students, not to mention law professors and practicing lawyers, often find the law of servitudes complex and confusing. Servitude law's complexity stems largely from the fact that the same functional interest may be classified under different doctrinal labels, each with its own set of requirements. Traditional servitude law draws a dichotomy between two major types: easements and covenants.[1] Covenants are further divided into another dichotomy: covenants enforceable at law (called "real covenants") and covenants enforceable in equity ("equitable servitudes"). These labels can be misleading, however, because there is considerable functional overlap among interests bearing different labels. From a strictly functional perspective, all servitudes fall into five types:

1. *A* is given the right to enter upon *B*'s land;
2. *A* is given the right to enter upon *B*'s land and remove something attached to the land;
3. *A* is given the right to enforce a restriction on the use of *B*'s land;
4. *A* is given the right to require *B* to perform some act on *B*'s land; and
5. *A* is given the right to require *B* to pay money for the upkeep of specified facilities.

---

1. There are also two minor types: *profits à prendre*, called "profits" for short, and licenses, both very much like easements in form, but not—as we shall see—always treated in the same fashion.

Doctrinally, *A*'s interest in example 1 is an easement. *A*'s interest in example 2 is a profit. *A*'s interest in example 3 may be treated as an easement (a negative easement, unlike the affirmative easement illustrated by example 1), a real covenant, or an equitable servitude, depending on several factors, including the remedy that *A* seeks in the event the restriction is breached. Finally, *A*'s interest in the last two examples may be treated as a real covenant or an equitable servitude, depending again on the remedy that is sought.

The functional overlap among the different doctrinal categories is the result of history, not policy. In the common law world,[2] easements and covenants evolved more or less in historical succession, one after the other. When easements were hedged in during the Industrial Revolution by judges who regarded them as interfering with marketability (see pages 887-889), landowners sought enforcement in the law courts of promissory agreements (covenants) against successors to the promisor's land. But, as we will later discuss (see page 893), the law courts, ever jealous of fetters on land, threw up roadblocks against these "covenants running with the land." Finally, turning to equity, landowners found a more sympathetic ear. The chancellor began to enforce restrictive covenants, which came to be known as equitable servitudes. The doctrinal complexity of servitude law, then, has the saving grace of making it possible to skin the cat in more than one way. The law of servitudes is a study of how the tides of urbanization and the demands of the market for efficient control of externalities swept around the artificial barriers limiting one form of servitude and forced courts to recognize and develop other forms.

The pressing question today is whether this doctrinal complexity and functional overlap is still necessary. The Restatement (Third) of Property, Servitudes, which the American Law Institute adopted in 2000, has merged the three interests—easements, real covenants, and equitable servitudes—into one, simply called the "servitude," subject to one simplified set of principles for creation, modification, enforcement, and termination. In time the Restatement's approach may come to be the dominant view of the courts, but that time has not yet arrived. As you will see in some of the cases included in this chapter, the previous Restatement, which reflected the traditional approach, continues to be cited by the courts. Hence, it is necessary for students to continue to learn the traditional law of easements and covenants with all of its complexity. For this reason we have organized this chapter on the basis of the traditional dichotomy between easements and covenants. However, as we go through the materials in each doctrinal topic, we will look at the Restatement (Third)'s reforms, pointing out where the Restatement (Third)'s view is now getting the upper hand and where the traditional doctrine still dominates in the courts. We will try to

---

2. Servitudes are not unique to the common law. The civil law, which derives from Roman law, has recognized them longer than the common law. And Roman law's influence was not limited to the civil law. The English law of easements owes much to Roman law and has been characterized as "the most Roman part of English law." Barry Nicholas, An Introduction to Roman Law 148 (1962).

crystallize the differences between old and new and then ask you to think about the competing views.

B. Easements

1. Historical Background, and Some Terminology

In this chapter, we put great emphasis on how and why the law of servitudes developed over time, because this rather disorderly body of law is as much a product of history as of logic.

In the medieval period, manorial and village land was cultivated throughout most of England using a common field system. Arable land was divided into strips, and each tenant would be assigned possession—originally by the lord of the manor or by the village inhabitants in council—of a number of scattered, noncontiguous strips. To be fair, the allocation consisted of a little bit of the good land, a little bit of the bad, and a little bit of the middling. Communal decisions were made as to what crops were to be planted and what strips were to lie fallow in order to restore fertility. Attached to each tenant's holding were certain common rights, for instance, the right to pasture cattle after the crop was cut. Bordering the arable land was wasteland, in which were additional common rights. These rights gave to members of the community *profits à prendre*—rights to take off the land things that were thought of as "part" of the land (for example, timber, minerals, wild game, and fish). Profits were the common wealth.[3]

"This system of agriculture," the English historian Holdsworth wrote,

> came to appear more and more anomalous with the lapse of time. It was impossible to do anything without the consent of a large number of persons who were not likely to agree; and any attempts to carry through improvements were met by the decided opposition of what was in those days the most ignorant and conservative class in the community. We are not surprised, therefore, to hear that it was denounced by all writers on agriculture from the sixteenth to the nineteenth century. . . . [B]ut, though some enclosures took place in the sixteenth and seventeenth centuries, large masses of land remained unenclosed—it was so common in the seventeenth century that it was transplanted by the early colonists to New England. One reason for its long life was no doubt the fact that the attempt to alter the existing common-field system was often combined with the extensive enclosure of common land, which reasonably enough roused much popular feeling. [2 William S. Holdsworth, History of English Law 60 (4th ed. 1927).]

For a number of reasons, the common field system began to break apart during the reign of the Tudors. With the growth in population and prosperity in the sixteenth century, the price of wool—commonly used for clothing—began to rise. Many landowners gave up cultivation and turned to sheep farming, with gradual dispossession of the commoners and the small farmers who lived on the

---

3. For an illustrative map of an open field village, see Robert C. Ellickson, Property in Land, 102 Yale L.J. 1315, 1389 (1993).

produce of the strips. Some enterprising farmers wanted to experiment with new agricultural techniques to produce better and more crops. Others wanted to breed cattle selectively to increase the output of dairy produce, and this required enclosures to control access to the cows. (Selective breeding led eventually to the fine, glossy-coated herds, with extended udders, seen grazing today on the English countryside—beasts very different from the angular medieval cows.) The manorial economy had broken down. The better farmers aimed to meet the demands of the market, not the needs of a great household and the local villagers. As population grew and the price of foodstuffs increased, so did the demand for enclosure of land in separately owned tracts, thereby withdrawing some portion of open fields or wasteland from use in common.

In the sixteenth century, enclosures began with small cultivators rearranging their holdings by bargaining among themselves. The movement picked up speed, ultimately catastrophic to the rural peasantry forced off the lands, when the lords of the manors began leasing the demesne lands of the manors to large farmers, evicting the customary tenants at the end of their leases and breaking up the village community. In the eighteenth century, privately sponsored acts of Parliament authorized specific enclosures when individual bargaining among those concerned failed.

Common fields and shared pastures gave way to fenced fields and consolidated farms amidst considerable outcry and social disorder, for a large share of the peasantry forced off the land drifted into the cities. Nonetheless, the enclosure movement proved irresistible in England as well as throughout Western Europe. By 1820, the transformation to closed fields was nearly complete in England; the only commons left were small patches of green in the middle of villages. And by that date England was well into the Industrial Revolution, which during the 70 years from 1770 to 1840 brought about the rapid growth of towns and completely altered the lives of erstwhile countryfolk.[4]

The primary modern forms of servitudes—easements, real covenants, and equitable servitudes—are largely products of the nineteenth century. In the days of common fields there was little need for defining rights of way; people wandered where they wished through the unfenced countryside, causing little injury. But enclosures pushed the law of *profits à prendre* off center stage[5] and, together with the Industrial Revolution, brought about a need for the development of a new, systematic body of law dealing with easements of way as well as with other servitudes regulating interdependent land uses.[6]

---

4. See 1 William Cunningham, The Growth of English Industry and Commerce 526-533 (5th ed. 1910); 2 id. at 545-561.

5. The most important profits that have survived to modern times are the right to take timber from land and the right to remove sand and gravel and minerals (coal, oil, and gas). Oil, gas, and mineral law has developed into a separate and complex branch of doctrine, with unique rules applicable only to these subsurface interests. Nonmineral profits are generally governed by the same rules as easements. See Restatement (Third) of Property, Servitudes §1.2 (2000).

6. Our treatment of the historical development of servitudes owes a substantial debt to Uriel Reichman, Servitudes in Residential Private Government Systems 92-187 (unpublished J.S.D. thesis, University of Chicago 1975).

The first English textbook on easements, Gale on Easements,[7] was published in 1839, just as the law of easements was quickening. Prior to Gale's book, the law, recognizing only specific types of servitudes that it lumped together with other incorporeal hereditaments having nothing to do with land use,[8] had had no general theory of easements. Besides rights of way, recognized easements included the right to place clothes on lines over neighboring land, the right to nail fruit trees on a neighbor's wall, and the rights to water cattle at a pond and take water for domestic purposes. Observe that each of these easements, granted by a servient owner, gave a neighbor the right to enter or perform an act on the servient land. They are known as affirmative easements, and in the last 150 years they have grown enormously in both the types and extent of use made by the dominant owner over the servient land.

The early law also recognized a few types of negative easements—easements forbidding one landowner from doing something on his land that might harm a neighbor. But the courts were reluctant to create new negative easements, for reasons we will discuss later, at pages 887-889, and strictly fenced them in.

In addition to the distinction between affirmative and negative easement, easements are also classified as *appurtenant* or *in gross*. Both types of easements give easement owners the right to make some specific use (or in the case of a negative easement, restrict some particular use) of land that they do not own. An easement appurtenant gives that right to whomever owns a parcel of land that the easement benefits. An easement in gross gives the right to some person without regard to ownership of land. Stated somewhat differently, an easement appurtenant benefits the easement owner in the use of land belonging to that owner, but an easement in gross benefits the easement owner personally rather than in connection with use of land which that person owns. If it is unclear which type of easement is intended by the parties, the law construes in favor of an easement appurtenant. For example, in a case where the sellers reserved an easement "for the watering of livestock owned by the sellers," the court held that the easement was appurtenant

---

7. Charles J. Gale & Thomas D. Whatley, Law of Easements (1st ed. London 1839). The latest edition is Jonathan Gaunt, Gale on Easements (Hon. Paul Morgan ed. 19th rev. ed. 2012).

8. *Incorporeal hereditaments* is a euphonious collective name for certain intangible rights that, as the term "hereditament" indicates, descended as real property to the primogenitary heir. Although the idea of an incorporeal hereditament originally grew out of feudal ways of thinking (see A.W.B. Simpson, A History of the Land Law 106-107, 121-122 (2d ed. 1986)), the classification proved useful in sorting out those types of medieval rights that ought to descend to the eldest son and those that ought to be treated as personal property and divided among all the children. Incorporeal hereditaments (inherited by the eldest son) included, along with easements and profits, such rights as advowsons (right to appoint the parson of a church), corodies (right to board and lodging, usually in a religious house, assigned to an impoverished relative), peerages, and franchises (rights granted by the crown to hold a fair or market, or to take the chattels of a condemned felon, or to hang convicted thieves). Offices—constable, keeper of a park, falconer, master of the hounds, and such—were also inheritable as incorporeal hereditaments.

There is a modern point to this ancient learning. Some property is inappropriate for common ownership. Single ownership of the right by the eldest son was more efficient (particularly in hanging thieves) than group ownership by all the children. It made sense to give the easements and profits appurtenant to land to the eldest son, who inherited the land. (Compare the law of heirlooms, which gave heirlooms to the heir; see footnote 24 on page 407.) Why might profits in gross have been assigned to the eldest son and not to all the children? See page 864.

to the neighboring tract the sellers owned. Nelson v. Johnson, 679 P.2d 662 (Idaho 1984). See Restatement (Third) of Property, Servitudes §4.5 (2000).

Easements appurtenant require both a *dominant tenement* (or estate) and a *servient tenement.* The easement attaches to and benefits the dominant tenement. Appurtenant easements are usually transferable. The easement transfers along with the dominant tenement to successive owners. However, appurtenant easement can be made personal to the easement owner only and not transferable to others.

Because an easement in gross does not benefit any land, it involves no dominant estate, only a servient estate. Easements in gross may be alienable or inalienable. Easements in gross are sometimes said to be "personal," but they are personal only in the sense that they do not attach to any parcel of land owned by the easement owner, not in the sense that they may not be transferred to another person. The transferability of easements in gross raises special problems, which are treated subsequently in this chapter at pages 857-865.

2.   Creation of Easements

An *easement,* being an interest in land, is within the Statute of Frauds (so too for *profits*). Creation of an easement generally requires a written instrument signed by the party to be bound thereby. However, in addition to the usual exceptions of fraud, part performance, and estoppel, an easement may, under certain circumstances, be created by implication or by prescription.

Willard v. First Church of Christ, Scientist

Supreme Court of California, 1972
498 P.2d 987

PETERS, J. In this case we are called upon to decide whether a grantor may, in deeding real property to one person, effectively reserve an interest in the property to another. We hold that in this case such a reservation vests the interest in the third party.

Plaintiffs Donald E. and Jennie C. Willard filed an action to quiet title to a lot in Pacifica against the First Church of Christ, Scientist (the church). After a trial, judgment was entered quieting the Willards' title. The church has appealed.

Genevieve McGuigan owned two abutting lots in Pacifica known as lots 19 and 20. There was a building on lot 19, and lot 20 was vacant. McGuigan was a member of the church, which was located across the street from her lots, and she permitted it to use lot 20 for parking during services. She sold lot 19 to one Petersen, who used the building as an office. He wanted to resell the lot, so he listed it with Willard, who is a realtor. Willard expressed an interest in purchasing both lots 19 and 20, and he and Petersen signed a deposit receipt for the sale of the two lots. Soon thereafter they entered into an escrow, into which Petersen delivered a deed for both lots in fee simple.

At the time he agreed to sell lot 20 to Willard, Petersen did not own it, so he approached McGuigan with an offer to purchase it. She was willing to sell the lot provided the church could continue to use it for parking. She therefore referred the matter to the church's attorney, who drew up a provision for the deed that stated the conveyance was "subject to an easement for automobile parking during church hours for the benefit of the church on the property at the southwest corner of the intersection of Hilton Way and Francisco Boulevard . . . such easement to run with the land only so long as the property for whose benefit the easement is given is used for church purposes." Once this clause was inserted in the deed, McGuigan sold the property to Petersen, and he recorded the deed.

Willard paid the agreed purchase price into the escrow and received Petersen's deed 10 days later. He then recorded this deed, which did not mention an easement for parking by the church. While Petersen did mention to Willard that the church would want to use lot 20 for parking, it does not appear that he told him of the easement clause contained in the deed he received from McGuigan.

Willard became aware of the easement clause several months after purchasing the property. He then commenced this action to quiet title against the church. At the trial, which was without a jury, McGuigan testified that she had bought lot 20 to provide parking for the church, and would not have sold it unless she was assured the church could thereafter continue to use it for parking. The court found that McGuigan and Petersen intended to convey an easement to the church, but that the clause they employed was ineffective for that purpose because it was invalidated by the common law rule that one cannot "reserve" an interest in property to a stranger to the title.

The rule derives from the common law notions of reservations from a grant and was based on feudal considerations. A reservation allows a grantor's whole interest in the property to pass to the grantee, but revests a newly created interest in the grantor.[9] (4 Tiffany, The Law of Real Property (3d ed. 1939) §972.) While a reservation could theoretically vest an interest in a third party, the early common law courts vigorously rejected this possibility, apparently because they mistrusted and wished to limit conveyance by deed as a substitute for livery by seisin.[10] (See Harris, Reservations in Favor of Strangers to the Title (1953) 6 Okla. L. Rev. 127, 132-133.) Insofar as this mistrust was the foundation of the rule, it is clearly an inapposite feudal shackle today. Consequently, several commentators have attacked the rule as groundless and have called for its abolition. (See, e.g., Harris, supra,

9. The effect of a reservation should be distinguished from an exception, which prevents some part of the grantor's interest from passing to the grantee. The exception cannot vest an interest in the third party, and the excepted interest remains in the grantor. (6 Powell, The Law of Real Property (Rohan ed. 1971) §892.) [This citation to Powell is unhelpful. The useful reference is Powell on Real Property §34.04[5] (Michael A. Wolf gen. ed. 2009).—Eds.]

10. Our late colleague and redoubtable historian Brian Simpson told us the court's history is wrong. Livery of seisin was required to transfer a possessory freehold estate (page 243), whereas easements were created by grant, i.e., a sealed instrument. Professor Simpson believed the rule against creating easements in third parties is traceable to the principle that only parties to a deed can take advantage of it. The same principle underlies the rule that third parties cannot sue on a contract (unless they are in privity of estate with a party). See pages 893-896, 918-919.—Eds.

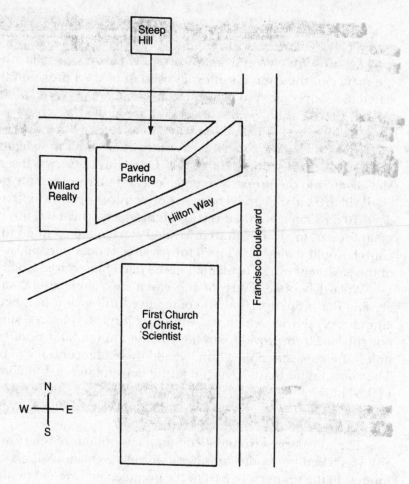

Figure 10-1

6 Okla. L. Rev. at p. 154; Meyers & Williams, Oil and Gas Conveyancing; Grants and Reservations by Owners of Fractional Mineral Interests (1957) 43 Va. L. Rev. 639, 650-651; Comment, Real Property: Easements: Creation by Reservation or Exception (1948) 36 Cal. L. Rev. 470, 476; Annot., Reservation or exception in deed in favor of stranger, 88 A.L.R.2d 1199, 1202; cf. 4 Tiffany, supra, §974, at p. 54; 2 American Law of Property (Casner ed. 1952) §8.29, at p. 254.)

California early adhered to this common law rule. (Eldridge v. See Yup Company (1860) 17 Cal. 44.) In considering our continued adherence to it, we must realize that our courts no longer feel constricted by feudal forms of conveyancing. Rather, our primary objective in construing a conveyance is to try to give effect to the intent of the grantor. . . . In general, therefore, grants are to be interpreted in the same way as other contracts and not according to rigid feudal standards. . . . The common law rule conflicts with the modern approach to construing deeds because it can frustrate the grantor's intent. Moreover, it produces an inequitable result because the original grantee has presumably paid a reduced price for title to the encumbered property. In this case, for example, McGuigan testified that she had discounted the price she charged Petersen by about one-third because of the easement. . . .

In view of the obvious defects of the rule, this court has found methods to avoid it where applying it would frustrate the clear intention of the grantor. In Butler v. Gosling (1900) 130 Cal. 422 [62 P. 596], the court prevented the reserved title to a portion of the property from vesting in the grantee by treating the reservation as an exception to the grant. In Boyer v. Murphy (1927) 202 Cal. 23 [259 P. 38], the court, noting that its primary objective was to give effect to the grantor's intention (id., at pp. 28-29), held that the rule was inapplicable where the third party was the grantor's spouse. (See Fleming v. State Bar (1952) 38 Cal. 2d 341, 345, fn. 2 [239 P.2d 866].) Similarly, the . . . courts of other states[11] have found ways of circumventing the rule.

The highest courts of two states have already eliminated the rule altogether, rather than repealing it piecemeal by evasion. In Townsend v. Cable (Ky. 1964) 378 S.W.2d 806, the Court of Appeals of Kentucky abandoned the rule. It said: "We have no hesitancy in abandoning this archaic and technical rule. It is entirely inconsistent with the basic principle followed in the construction of deeds, which is to determine the intention of grantor as gathered from the four corners of the instrument." (Id., at p. 808.) (See also Blair v. City of Pikeville (Ky. 1964) 384 S.W.2d 65, 66; Combs v. Hounshell (Ky. 1961) 347 S.W.2d 550, 554.) Relying on *Townsend*, the Supreme Court of Oregon, in Garza v. Grayson (1970) 255 Ore. 413 [467 P.2d 960], rejected the rule because it was "derived from a narrow and highly technical interpretation of the meaning of the terms 'reservation' and 'exception' when employed in a deed" (id., at p. 961), and did not sufficiently justify frustrating the grantor's intention in some cases even though it is riddled with exceptions, we follow the lead of Kentucky and Oregon and abandon it entirely.

Willard contends that the old rule should nevertheless be applied in this case to invalidate the church's easement because grantees and title insurers have relied upon it. He has not, however, presented any evidence to support this contention, and it is clear that the facts of this case do not demonstrate reliance on the old rule. There is no evidence that a policy of title insurance

11. (See generally Harris, Reservations in Favor of Strangers to the Title, supra, 6 Okla. L. Rev. 127, 139-150.) Some courts, like the court in Butler v. Gosling, supra, mitigate the harshness of the rule by treating the reservation as an exception that retained the interest in the grantor. (See Lemon v. Lemon (1918) 273 Mo. 484, 201 S.W. 103.) While this approach did prevent the reserved interest from passing to the grantee, it did not achieve the grantor's intention of vesting that interest in the third party. Other courts gave effect to the grantor's intention by estopping those who claimed under a chain of title including the deed containing the reservation from challenging it on the basis of the common law rule. (See Beinlein v. Johns (1898) 102 Ky. 570, 19 Ky. L.R. 1969, 44 S.W. 128; Hodge v. Boothby (1861) 48 Me. 68; Dalton v. Eller (1926) 153 Tenn. 418, 284 S.W. 68.) This approach has the effect of emasculating the common law rule without expressly abandoning it. One court found that a reservation created a trust in favor of the stranger (Burns v. Bastien (1935) 174 Okla. 40, 50 P.2d 377), but this approach seems unduly elaborate to achieve the grantor's intent. Finally, several courts, like the court in Boyer, supra, will disregard the rule entirely when the stranger is the grantor's spouse. (See Saunders v. Saunders (1940) 373 Ill. 302, 26 N.E.2d 126, 129 A.L.R. 306; Du Bois v. Judy (1920) 291 Ill. 340, 126 N.E. 104; Derham v. Hovey (1917) 195 Mich. 243, 161 N.W. 883, 21 A.L.R. 999; Glasgow v. Glasgow (1952) 221 S.C. 322, 70 S.E.2d 432.) Thus, as in California, the rule has been riddled with exceptions in other states.

was issued, and therefore no showing of reliance by a title insurance company. Willard himself could not have relied upon the common law rule to assure him of an absolute fee because he did not even read the deed containing the reservation. This is not a case of an ancient deed where the reservation has not been asserted for many years. The church used lot 20 for parking throughout the period when Willard was purchasing the property and after he acquired title to it, and he may not claim that he was prejudiced by lack of use for an extended period of time.

The determination whether the old common law rule should be applied to grants made prior to our decision involves a balancing of equitable and policy considerations. We must balance the injustice which would result from refusing to give effect to the grantor's intent against the injustice, if any, which might result by failing to give effect to reliance on the old rule and the policy against disturbing settled titles. The record before us does not disclose any reliance upon the old common law rule, and there is no problem of an ancient title. Although in other cases the balancing of the competing interests may warrant application of the common law rule to presently existing deeds, in the instant case the balance falls in favor of the grantor's intent, and the old common law rule may not be applied to defeat her intent.

Willard also contends that the church has received no interest in this case because the clause stated only that the grant was "subject to" the church's easement, and not that the easement was either excepted or reserved. In construing this provision, however, we must look to the clause as a whole which states that the easement "is given." Even if we assume that there is some ambiguity or conflict in the clause, the trial court found on substantial evidence that the parties to the deed intended to convey the easement to the church.

The judgment is reversed.

NOTES AND QUESTIONS

1. *Modern authority.* Restatement (Third) of Property, Servitudes §2.6(2) (2000), provides that an easement can be created in favor of a third party, but contrary authority in a number of states is cited in the Reporter's Note. Cases reaffirming the common law rule that a grantor cannot reserve an easement in favor of a third party include Tripp v. Huff, 606 A.2d 792 (Me. 1992); Estate of Thomson v. Wade, 509 N.E.2d 309 (N.Y. 1987); Beachside Bungalow Preservation Assn. of Far Rockaway, Inc. v. Oceanview Associates, LLC, 753 N.Y.S.2d 133 (App. Div. 2003); see also John E. Lansche, Jr., Note, Ancient, Antiquated & Archaic: South Carolina Fails to Embrace the Rule That a Grantor May Reserve an Easement in Favor of a Third Party, 52 S.C. L. Rev. 269 (2000).

2. *Drafting to avoid the common law rule.* How would you draft documents so as to carry out Genevieve McGuigan's intent and not violate the common law rule that an easement cannot be reserved in favor of a third party? If the church had lost, would the church's attorney who drew up the deed be liable for malpractice?

See Jesse Dukeminier, Cleansing the Stables of Property: A River Found at Last, 65 Iowa L. Rev. 151, 174 (1979).

3. *Reservations and exceptions.* In *Willard,* the court held that an easement can be reserved in favor of a third party but stated in footnote 9 that an easement cannot be excepted in favor of a third party. What is the difference between an exception and a reservation? How did the court determine that Genevieve McGuigan had reserved rather than excepted an easement? (The deed said "subject to an easement.")

A *reservation* is a provision in a deed creating some *new* servitude which did not exist before as an independent interest. For example, *O* conveys Blackacre to *A* reserving a 20-foot-wide easement of way along the south boundary of Blackacre. The easement did not exist as an independent interest prior to the conveyance by *O.* An *exception* is a provision in a deed that excludes from the grant some *preexisting* servitude on the land. For example, after the above conveyance, *A* conveys Blackacre to *B,* except for the easement previously reserved by *O.*

When the grantor attempted to reserve an easement at early common law, there were difficulties. A new right, such as some feudal obligation or the payment of rent, could be reserved if it was to issue out of the land granted, but the English courts held that an easement could not be reserved because it did not issue out of the land granted. English courts ultimately found a way around this obstacle by inventing the *regrant theory.* They held that an easement "reserved" by the grantor was not a reservation at all (which would be void), but a *regrant* of an easement by the grantee to the grantor. Thus a deed from *O* to *A* and her heirs, reserving an easement in *O,* was treated as if it were two deeds. The deed grants *A* a fee simple; then *A* is treated as granting an easement back to *O.*

The regrant theory may have been a brilliant way around the crabbed interpretation of what could be reserved in a grant, but it brought a new difficulty of its own. Because a reserved easement theoretically involved a regrant by the grantee, the Statute of Frauds required the deed to be signed by the grantee as well as by the grantor. In this country, where deeds are usually signed only by the grantor, this could have caused trouble. But American courts deftly held that the grantee had, by accepting the deed, made it her own and adopted the seal and signature of the grantor! Thus was a legal fiction invented to overcome a faulty premise.

Now that you understand the difference between a reservation and an exception, does the court's statement in footnote 9 that an exception cannot vest an easement in a third party make sense?

4. *Appurtenant or in gross?* Is the church's easement in the *Willard* case *appurtenant* or *in gross?* If the Christian Science Church sold the church on Hilton Way and Francisco Boulevard to a Methodist Church, and erected a new church a block away to the west on Hilton Way, would the easement belong to the Methodist Church or to the Christian Science Church, or would the easement be extinguished?

An easement can have a duration comparable to any of the possessory estates. An easement can be in fee simple (perpetual duration), or for life, or for a term of years. How would you describe the duration of the easement in *Willard?*

NOTE: LICENSES

An easement must be distinguished from a license. A *license* is oral or written permission given by the occupant of land allowing the licensee to do some act that otherwise would be a trespass. Licenses are very common: the plumber fixing a drain, the guest coming to dinner, the purchaser of a theater ticket all have licenses. This privilege to use the land resembles an easement, but a license is revocable whereas an easement is not.

There are two distinct exceptions to the rule that a license is revocable. First, a license coupled with an interest cannot be revoked. A license coupled with an interest is one that is incidental to ownership of a chattel on the licensor's land. For example, *O* grants to *A* the right to take timber from Blackacre, owned by *O*. *A* has an interest (a *profit à prendre*) and an irrevocable license to enter the land and take the timber. The irrevocability of a license coupled with an interest bears some resemblance to the doctrine of easements by necessity. (See pages 839-842.) The second exception is a license that becomes irrevocable under the rules of estoppel. A license that cannot be revoked is treated as an easement in Restatement (Third) of Property, Servitudes §2(4) (2000).

Holbrook v. Taylor

Supreme Court of Kentucky, 1976
532 S.W.2d 763

STERNBERG, J. This is an action to establish a right to the use of a roadway, which is 10 to 12 feet wide and about 250 feet long, over the unenclosed, hilly woodlands of another. The claimed right to the use of the roadway is twofold: by prescription and by estoppel. Both issues are heatedly contested. The evidence is in conflict as to the nature and type of use that had been made of the roadway. The lower court determined that a right to the use of the roadway by prescription had not been established, but that it had been established by estoppel. The landowners, feeling themselves aggrieved, appeal. We will consider the two issues separately.

In Grinestaff v. Grinestaff, Ky., 318 S.W.2d 881 (1958), we said that an easement may be created by express written grant, by implication, by prescription, or by estoppel. It has long been the law of this commonwealth that

> (an) easement, such as a right of way, is created when the owner of a tenement to which the right is claimed to be appurtenant, or those under whom he claims title, have openly, peaceably, continuously, and under a claim of right adverse to the owner of the soil, and with his knowledge and acquiescence, used a way over the lands of another for as much as 15 years.

Flener v. Lawrence, 187 Ky. 384, 220 S.W. 1041 (1920); Rominger v. City Realty Company, Ky., 324 S.W.2d 806 (1959).

In 1942 appellants purchased the subject property. In 1944 they gave permission for a haul road to be cut for the purpose of moving coal from a newly opened mine. The roadway was so used until 1949, when the mine closed. During that time the appellants were paid a royalty for the use of the road. In 1957 appellants built a tenant house on their property and the roadway was used by them and their tenant. The tenant house burned in 1961 and was not replaced. In 1964 the appellees bought their three-acre building site, which adjoins appellants, and the following year built their residence thereon. At all times prior to 1965, the use of the haul road was by permission of appellants. There is no evidence of any probative value which would indicate that the use of the haul road during that period of time was either adverse, continuous, or uninterrupted. The trial court was fully justified, therefore, in finding that the right to the use of this easement was not established by prescription.

As to the issue of estoppel, we have long recognized that a right to the use of a roadway over the lands of another may be established by estoppel. In Lashley Telephone Co. v. Durbin, 190 Ky. 792, 228 S.W. 423 (1921), we said:

> Though many courts hold that a licensee is conclusively presumed as a matter of law to know that a license is revocable at the pleasure of the licensor, and if he expend money in connection with his entry upon the land of the latter, he does so at his peril, . . . yet it is the established rule in this state that where a license is not a bare, naked right of entry, but includes the right to erect structures and acquire an interest in the land in the nature of an easement by the construction of improvements thereon, the licensor may not revoke the license and restore his premises to their former condition after the licensee has exercised the privilege given by the license and erected the improvements at considerable expense. . . .

In Gibbs v. Anderson, 288 Ky. 488, 156 S.W.2d 876 (1941), Gibbs claimed the right, by estoppel, to the use of a roadway over the lands of Anderson. The lower court denied the claim. We reversed. Anderson's immediate predecessor in title admitted that he had discussed the passway with Gibbs before it was constructed and had agreed that it might be built through his land. He stood by and saw Gibbs expend considerable money in this construction. We applied the rule announced in Lashley Telephone Co. v. Durbin, supra, and reversed with directions that a judgment be entered granting Gibbs the right to the use of the passway.

In McCoy v. Hoffman, Ky., 295 S.W.2d 560 (1956), the facts are that Hoffman had acquired the verbal consent of the landowner to build a passway over the lands of the owner to the state highway. Subsequently, the owner of the servient estate sold the property to McCoy, who at the time of the purchase was fully aware of the existence of the roadway and the use to which it was being put. McCoy challenged Hoffman's right to use the road. The lower court found that a right had been gained by prescription. In this court's consideration of the case, we affirmed, not on the theory of prescriptive right but on the basis that the owner of the servient estate was estopped. After announcing the rule for establishing a right by prescription, we went on to say:

> . . . On the other hand, the right of revocation of the license is subject to the qualification that where the licensee has exercised the privilege given him and erected improvements or made substantial expenditures on the faith or strength of the license, it becomes irrevocable and continues for so long a time as the nature of the license calls for. In effect, under this condition the license becomes in reality a grant through estoppel. . . .

In Akers v. Moore, Ky., 309 S.W.2d 758 (1958), this court again considered the right to the use of a passway by estoppel. Akers and others had used the Moore branch as a public way of ingress and egress from their property. They sued Moore and others who owned property along the branch seeking to have the court recognize their right to the use of the roadway and to order the removal of obstructions which had been placed in the roadway. The trial court found that Akers and others had acquired a prescriptive right to the use of the portion of the road lying on the left side of the creek bed, but had not acquired the right to the use of so much of the road as lay on the right side of the creek bed. Consequently, an appeal and a cross-appeal were filed. Considering the right to use of the strip of land between the right side of the creek bed and the highway, this court found that the evidence portrayed it very rough and apparently never improved, that it ran alongside the house in which one of the protestors lived, and that by acquiescence or by express consent of at least one of the protestors the right side of the roadway was opened up so as to change the roadway from its close proximity to the Moore residence. The relocated portion of the highway had only been used as a passway for about six years before the suit was filed. The trial court found that this section of the road had not been established as a public way by estoppel. We reversed. In doing so, we stated:

> We consider the fact that the appellees, Artie Moore, et al., had stood by and acquiesced in (if in fact they had not affirmatively consented to) the change being made and permitted the appellants to spend money in fixing it up to make it passable and use it for six years without objecting. Of course, the element of time was not sufficient for the acquisition of the right of way by adverse possession. But the law recognizes that one may acquire a license to use a passway or roadway where, with the knowledge of the licensor, he has in the exercise of the privilege spent money in improving the way or for other purposes connected with its use on the faith or strength of the license. Under such conditions the license becomes irrevocable and continues for so long a time as its nature calls for. This, in effect, becomes a grant through estoppel. Gibbs v. Anderson, 288 Ky. 488, 156 S.W.2d 876; McCoy v. Hoffman, Ky., 295 S.W.2d 560. It would be unconscionable to permit the owners of this strip of land of trivial value to revoke the license by obstructing and preventing its use.

In the present case the roadway had been used since 1944 by permission of the owners of the servient estate. The evidence is conflicting as to whether the use of the road subsequent to 1965 was by permission or by claim of right. Appellees contend that it had been used by them and others without the permission of appellants; on the other hand, it is contended by appellants that the use of the roadway at all times was by their permission. The evidence discloses that during the period of preparation for the construction of appellees' home and during the time the house was being built, appellees were permitted to use the roadway as ingress and egress for workmen, for hauling machinery and material to the building site, for construction of the dwelling, and for making improvements generally to the premises. Further, the evidence reflects that after construction of the residence, which cost $25,000, was completed, appellees continued to regularly use the roadway as they had been doing. Appellant J.S. Holbrook testified that in order for appellees to get up to their house he gave them permission to use and repair the roadway. They widened it, put in a culvert and graveled part of it with "red dog," also known as cinders, at a cost of approximately $100. There is no other location over which a roadway could reasonably be built to provide an outlet for appellees.

No dispute had arisen between the parties at any time over the use of the roadway until the fall of 1970. Appellant J.S. Holbrook contends that he wanted to secure a writing from the appellees in order to relieve him from any responsibility for any damage that might happen to anyone on the subject road. On the other hand, Mrs. Holbrook testified that the writing was desired to avoid any claim which may be made by appellees of a right to the use of the roadway. Appellees testified that the writing was an effort to force them to purchase a small strip of land over which the roadway traversed, for the sum of $500. The dispute was not resolved and appellants erected a steel cable across the roadway to prevent its use and also constructed "no-trespassing" signs. Shortly thereafter, the suit was filed to require the removal of the obstruction and to declare the right of appellees to the use of the roadway without interference.

The use of the roadway by appellees to get to their home from the public highway, the use of the roadway to take in heavy equipment and material and supplies for construction of the residence, the general improvement of the premises, the maintenance of the roadway, and the construction by appellees of a $25,000 residence, all with the actual consent of appellants or at least with their tacit approval, clearly demonstrates the rule laid down in Lashley Telephone Co. v. Durbin, supra, that the license to use the subject roadway may not be revoked.

The evidence justifies the finding of the lower court that the right to the use of the roadway had been established by estoppel.

The judgment is affirmed.

Shepard v. Purvine, 248 P.2d 352, 361-362 (Or. 1952). "These people were close friends and neighbors, and they were not dealing at arm's length. One's word was considered as good as his bond. Under the circumstances, for plaintiffs to have insisted upon a deed would have been embarrassing; in effect it would have been expressing a doubt as to their friend's integrity. We do not believe the evidence warrants a conclusion that plaintiffs were negligent in not insisting upon a formal transfer of the rights accorded. An oral license promptly acted upon in the manner plaintiffs acted is just as valid, binding, and irrevocable as a deeded right of way."

Henry v. Dalton, 151 A.2d 362, 366 (R.I. 1959). "We are of the opinion that in reason and justice the better rule is expressed in the case of Crosdale v. Lanigan, 129 N.Y. 604, 29 N.E. 824. There the plaintiff was required to remove a wall built on the property of the defendant pursuant to a license. The court stated the rule at page 610 of 129 N.Y., at page 825 of 29 N.E. as follows: '. . . a parol license to do an act on the land of the licensor, while it justifies anything done by the licensee before revocation, is, nevertheless, revocable at the option of the licensor, and this, although the intention was to confer a continuing right and money had been expended by the licensee upon the faith of the license. This is plainly the rule of the statute. It is also, we believe, the rule required by public policy. It prevents the burdening of lands with restrictions founded upon oral agreements, easily misunderstood. It gives security and certainty to titles, which are most important to be preserved against defects and qualifications not founded upon solemn instruments. The jurisdiction of courts to enforce oral contracts for the sale of land is clearly defined and well understood, and is indisputable; but to change what commenced in a license into an irrevocable right, on the ground of equitable estoppel, is another and quite different matter. It is far better, we think, that the law requiring interests in land to be evidenced by deed, should be observed, than to leave it to the chancellor to construe an executed license as a grant, depending upon what, in his view, may be equity in the special case. . . .'

"Counsel for the complainants urge that the statute of frauds was conceived and is designed to protect against fraud and should not be used to assist in the perpetration of fraud. We are in accord with this contention, but are not convinced that in the circumstances of the instant case the respondent's revocation of the complainants' license is fraudulent within any acceptable definition of that term. The right which complainants seek to establish in the land of the respondent is essentially an easement and should be the subject of a grant, expressed in the solemnity of a written instrument. It is no hardship for one in the position of these complainants either to secure an easement in perpetuity in the manner provided by the statute, or, such being refused, to weigh the advantages inuring to them as against the uncertainty implicit in the making of expenditures on the basis of a revocable license."

NOTES AND QUESTIONS

1. *The Restatement (Third)'s view on easements by estoppel.* Restatement (Third) of Property, Servitudes §2.10 (2000), provides that a servitude may be created by estoppel. Comment e says, "Normally the change in position that triggers application of the rule stated in this subsection is an investment in improvements either to the servient estate or to other land of the investor." See also id. illustration 5. See generally Stewart E. Sterk, Estoppel in Property Law, 77 Neb. L. Rev. 756, 769-784 (1998).

2. *Scope and terms of easement by estoppel.* Suppose that Taylor's house burns down. Can Taylor build a new house using the right of way across Holbrook's land? Restatement (Third) of Property, supra, §4.1 comment g, provides: "The expectations that create the servitude will also define its scope and terms. The relevant expectations are those that reasonable people in the position of the landowner and the person who relied on the grant of permission or representation would have had under the circumstances."

3. *Duration of easement by estoppel.* For how long does a license made irrevocable by estoppel last? As long as necessary to prevent unjust enrichment by the

licensor? That appeared to be the position of the first Restatement. (The license remains irrevocable "to the extent reasonably necessary to realize upon [the] expenditures." Restatement of Property §519(4) (1944).) Restatement (Third) of Property, however, abandons that position in favor of the view that "the irrevocable license is treated the same as any other easement," unless the parties intended or reasonably expected that it would remain irrevocable only so long as reasonably necessary to recover expenditures. Restatement (Third) of Property, Servitudes ch. 4 Introductory Note, at 496 (2000).

4. *Damages or injunction?* Where the facts justify an application of estoppel, should the court give the servient landowner damages rather than denying all relief? Remember that the court has the choice of giving the servient owner an injunction, damages, or nothing. If it is considered unfair for the landowner to revoke permission to cross, is it fair for the appellees to gain the benefit without paying anything for it? Would an award of damages be an efficient solution? See Stewart E. Sterk, Neighbors in American Land Law, 87 Colum. L. Rev. 55, 77-78 (1987).

Van Sandt v. Royster

Supreme Court of Kansas, 1938
83 P.2d 698

ALLEN, J. The action was brought to enjoin defendants from using and maintaining an underground lateral sewer drain through and across plaintiff's land. The case was tried by the court, judgment was rendered in favor of defendants, and plaintiff appeals.

In the city of Chanute, Highland avenue, running north and south, intersects Tenth street running east and west. In the early part of 1904 Laura A.J. Bailey was the owner of a plot of ground lying east of Highland avenue and south of Tenth street. Running east from Highland avenue and facing north on Tenth street the lots are numbered respectively, 19, 20, and 4. In 1904 the residence of Mrs. Bailey was on lot 4 on the east part of her land.[12]

In the latter part of 1903 or the early part of 1904, the city of Chanute constructed a public sewer in Highland avenue, west of lot 19. About the same time a private lateral drain was constructed from the Bailey residence on lot 4 running in a westerly direction through and across lots 20 and 19 to the public sewer.

On January 15, 1904, Laura A.J. Bailey conveyed lot 19 to John J. Jones, by general warranty deed with the usual covenants against encumbrances, and containing no exceptions or reservations. Jones erected a dwelling on the north part of the lot. In 1920 Jones conveyed the north 156 feet of lot 19 to Carl D. Reynolds;

---

12. The residence on lot 4, locally known as "Gray's Mansion," was originally built in 1880 by Laura Bailey's husband, Mahlon Bailey, a surgeon who later became a prominent banker in Chanute. There are six red brick chimneys located at various points on the house. Reportedly, many townspeople bemoan the addition of these chimneys because they block the view of the ornate cupola. We are grateful to Professor Greg Vetter and his wife, Dr. Christy Vetter (a native of Chanute), for providing us with this information. — EDS.

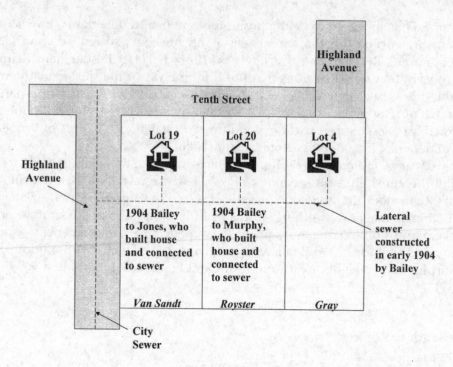

Figure 10-2

in 1924 Reynolds conveyed to the plaintiff, who has owned and occupied the premises since that time.

In 1904 Laura A.J. Bailey conveyed lot 20 to one Murphy, who built a house thereon, and by mesne conveyances the title passed to the defendant, Louise H. Royster. The deed to Murphy was a general warranty deed without exceptions or reservations. The defendant Gray has succeeded to the title to lot 4 upon which the old Bailey home stood at the time Laura A.J. Bailey sold lots 19 and 20.

In March, 1936, plaintiff discovered his basement flooded with sewage and filth to a depth of six or eight inches, and upon investigation he found for the first time that there existed on and across his property a sewer drain extending in an easterly direction across the property of Royster to the property of Gray. The refusal of defendants to cease draining and discharging their sewage across plaintiff's land resulted in this lawsuit. . . .[13]

The drain pipe in the lateral sewer was several feet under the surface of the ground. There was nothing visible on the ground in the rear of the houses to indicate the existence of the drain or the connection of the drain with the houses.

---

13. Professor Vetter reports that several residents of Chanute have told him stories about Mss. Van Sandt and Royster dumping buckets of sewage on each other's front porch. The court mentioned only the Van Sandt sewage problem, but it is possible that both houses experienced clogging and that the court was either misinformed or simply did not report the full facts.—EDS.

**A view of houses on lots 19, 20, and 4 (right to left) from the intersection
of Highland Avenue and Tenth Street**

Lot 4 (locally known as "Gray's Mansion")

As a conclusion of law the court found that "an appurtenant easement existed in the said lateral sewer as to all three of the properties involved in the controversy here." Plaintiff's prayer for relief was denied and it was decreed that plaintiff be restrained from interfering in any way with the lateral drain or sewer.

Plaintiff contends that the evidence fails to show that an easement was ever created in his land, and, assuming there was an easement created as alleged, that he took the premises free from the burden of the easement for the reason that he was a bona fide purchaser, without notice, actual or constructive.

Defendants contend: (1) That an easement was created by implied reservation on the severance of the servient from the dominant estate of the deed from Mrs. Bailey to Jones; (2) there is a valid easement by prescription.

In finding No. 11, the court found that the lateral sewer "was an appurtenance to the properties belonging to plaintiff and Louise Royster, and the same is necessary to the reasonable use and enjoyment of the said properties of the parties."

As an easement is an interest which a person has in land in the possession of another, it necessarily follows that an owner cannot have an easement in his own land. (Johnston v. City of Kingman, 141 Kan. 131, 39 P.2d 924; Ferguson v. Ferguson, 106 Kan. 823, 189 Pac. 925.) However, an owner may make use of one part of his land for the benefit of another part, and this is very frequently spoken of as a quasi easement.

> When one thus utilizes part of his land for the benefit of another part, it is frequently said that a quasi easement exists, the part of the land which is benefited being referred to as the "quasi dominant tenement" and the part which is utilized for the benefit of the other part being referred to as the "quasi servient tenement." The so-called quasi easement is evidently not a legal relation in any sense, but the expression is a convenient one to describe the particular mode in which the owner utilizes one part of the land for the benefit of the other. . . .
>
> If the owner of land, one part of which is subject to a quasi easement in favor of another part, conveys the quasi dominant tenement, an easement corresponding to such quasi easement is ordinarily regarded as thereby vested in the grantee of the land, provided, it is said, the quasi easement is of an apparent, continuous and necessary character. [2 Tiffany on Real Property, 2d ed., 1272, 1273.]

Following the famous case of Pyer v. Carter, 1 Hurl & N. 916, some of the English cases and many early American cases held that upon the transfer of the quasi-servient tenement there was an implied reservation of an easement in favor of the conveyor. Under the doctrine of Pyer v. Carter, no distinction was made between an implied reservation and an implied grant.

The case, however, was overthrown in England by Suffield v. Brown, 4 De G.J. & S. 185, and Wheeldon v. Burrows, L. R. 12 Ch. D. 31. In the former case the court said:

> It seems to me more reasonable and just to hold that if the grantor intends to reserve any right over the property granted, it is his duty to reserve it expressly in the grant, rather than to limit and cut down the operation of a plain grant (which is not pretended to be otherwise than in conformity with the contract between the parties), by the fiction of an implied reservation. If this

plain rule be adhered to, men will know what they have to trust, and will place confidence in the language of their contracts and assurances. . . . But I cannot agree that the grantor can derogate from his own absolute grant so as to claim rights over the thing granted, even if they were at the time of the grant continuous and apparent easements enjoyed by an adjoining tenement which remains the property of him the grantor. [Pp. 190, 194.]

Many American courts of high standing assert that the rule regarding implied grants and implied reservations is reciprocal and that the rule applies with equal force and in like circumstances to both grants and reservations. (Washburn on Easements, 4th ed. 75; Miller v. Skaggs, 79 W. Va. 645, 91 S.E. 536, Ann. Cas. 1918 D. 929.)

On the other hand, perhaps a majority of the cases hold that in order to establish an easement by implied reservation in favor of the grantor the easement must be one of strict necessity, even when there was an existing drain or sewer at the time of the severance.

Thus in Howley v. Chaffee et al., 88 Vt. 468, 474, 93 Atl. 120, L.R.A. 1915 D. 1010, the court said:

> With the character and extent of implied grants, we now have nothing to do. We are here only concerned with determining the circumstances which will give rise to an implied reservation. On this precise question the authorities are in conflict. Courts of high standing assert that the rule regarding implied grants and implied reservations of "visible servitudes" is reciprocal, and that it applies with equal force and in like circumstances to both grants and reservations. But upon a careful consideration of the whole subject, studied in the light of the many cases in which it is discussed, we are convinced that there is a clear distinction between implied grants and implied reservations, and that this distinction is well founded in principle and well supported by authority. It is apparent that no question of public policy is here involved, as we have seen is the case where a way of necessity is involved. To say that a grantor reserves to himself something out of the property granted, wholly by implication, not only offends the rule that one shall not derogate from his own grant, but conflicts with the grantor's language in the conveyance, which, by the rule, is to be taken against him, and is wholly inconsistent with the theory on which our registry laws are based. If such an illogical result is to follow an absolute grant, it must be by virtue of some legal rule of compelling force. The correct rule is, we think, that where, as here, one grants a parcel of land by metes and bounds, by a deed containing full covenants of warranty and without any express reservation, there can be no reservation by implication, unless the easement claimed is one of strict necessity, within the meaning of that term as explained in Dee v. King, 73 Vt. 375.

See, also, Brown v. Fuller, 165 Mich. 162, 130 N.W. 621, 33 L.R.A., n.s., 459, Ann. Cas. 1912 C 853. The cases are collected in 58 A.L.R. 837.

We are inclined to the view that the circumstance that the claimant of the easement is the grantor instead of the grantee, is but one of many factors to be considered in determining whether an easement will arise by implication. An easement created by implication arises as an inference of the intentions of the parties to a conveyance of land. The inference is drawn from the circumstances under which the conveyance was made rather than from the language of the conveyance. The easement may arise in favor of the conveyor or the conveyee. In the Restatement of Property, Tentative Draft No. 8, section 28, the factors determining the implication of an easement are stated:

Sec. 28. Factors Determining Implication of Easements or Profits. In determining whether the circumstances under which a conveyance of land is made imply an easement or a profit, the following factors are important: *(a)* whether the claimant is the conveyor or the conveyee, *(b)* the terms of the conveyance, *(c)* the consideration given for it, *(d)* whether the claim is made against a simultaneous conveyee, *(e)* the extent of necessity of the easement or the profit to the claimant, *(f)* whether reciprocal benefits result to the conveyor and the conveyee, *(g)* the manner in which the land was used prior to its conveyance, and *(h)* the extent to which the manner of prior use was or might have been known to the parties.

Comment j, under the same section, reads:

The extent to which the manner of prior use was or might have been known to the parties. The effect of the prior use as a circumstance in implying, upon a severance of possession by conveyance, an easement or a profit results from an inference as to the intention of the parties. To draw such an inference, the prior use must have been known to the parties at the time of the conveyance, or, at least, have been within the possibility of their knowledge at the time. Each party to a conveyance is bound not merely to what he intended, but also to what he might reasonably have foreseen the other party to the conveyance expected. Parties to a conveyance may, therefore, be assumed to intend the continuance of uses known to them which are in a considerable degree necessary to the continued usefulness of the land. Also they will be assumed to know and to contemplate the continuance of reasonably necessary uses which have so altered the premises as to make them apparent upon reasonably prudent investigation. The degree of necessity required to imply an easement in favor of the conveyor is greater than that required in the case of the conveyee (see comment b). Yet, even in the case of the conveyor, the implication from necessity will be aided by a previous use made apparent by the physical adaptation of the premises to it.

Illustrations:

9. *A* is the owner of two adjacent tracts of land, Blackacre and Whiteacre. Blackacre has on it a dwelling house. Whiteacre is unimproved. Drainage from the house to a public sewer is across Whiteacre. This fact is unknown to *A*, who purchased the two tracts with the house already built. By reasonable effort, *A* might discover the manner of drainage and the location of the drain. *A* sells Blackacre to *B*, who has been informed as to the manner of drainage and the location of the drain and assumes that *A* is aware of it. There is created by implication an easement of drainage in favor of *B* across Whiteacre.

10. Same facts as in illustration 9, except that both *A* and *B* are unaware of the manner of drainage and the location of the drain. However, each had reasonable opportunity to learn of such facts. A holding that there is created by implication an easement of drainage in favor of *B* across Whiteacre is proper.

At the time John J. Jones purchased lot 19 he was aware of the lateral sewer, and knew that it was installed for the benefit of the lots owned by Mrs. Bailey, the common owner. The easement was necessary to the comfortable enjoyment of the grantor's property. If land may be used without an easement, but cannot be used without disproportionate effort and expense, an easement may still be implied in favor of either the grantor or grantee on the basis of necessity alone. This is the situation as found by the trial court.

Neither can it be claimed that plaintiff purchased without notice. At the time plaintiff purchased the property he and his wife made a careful and thorough inspection of the property. They knew the house was equipped with modern plumbing and that the plumbing had to drain into a sewer. Under the facts as found by the court, we think the purchaser was charged with notice of the lateral sewer. It was an apparent easement as that term is used in the books. (Wiesel v. Smira, 49 R.I. 246, 142 Atl. 148, 58 A.L.R. 818; 19 C.J. 868.)

The author of the annotation on Easements by Implication in 58 A.L.R. 832, states the rule as follows:

> While there is some conflict of authority as to whether existing drains, pipes, and sewers may be properly characterized as apparent, within the rule as to apparent or visible easements, the majority of the cases which have considered the question have taken the view that appearance and visibility are not synonymous, and that the fact that the pipe, sewer, or drain may be hidden underground does not negative its character as an apparent condition; at least, where the appliances connected with and leading to it are obvious.

As we are clear that an easement by implication was created under the facts as found by the trial court, it is unnecessary to discuss the question of prescription.

The judgment is affirmed.

NOTES AND QUESTIONS

1. *The theory and requirements of easements implied from a prior existing use.* The easement in *Van Sandt* is an easement from a prior existing use. (The prior existing use is sometimes called a "quasi-easement.") The easement is implied to protect the probable expectations of the grantor and grantee that the existing use will continue after the transfer. The inference that the parties intended to create an easement is not conclusive, however. It may be negated by contrary evidence. See Zotos v. Armstrong, 828 N.E.2d 551 (Mass. App. 2005). Three requirements are usually stated to imply an easement from a prior existing use: (1) severance of title to land initially undivided; (2) an apparent, existing, and continuing use of one parcel at the time of severance; and (3) reasonable necessity for the use at the time of severance. The court in *Van Sandt* referred to these requirements, albeit indirectly. Which of them was in question?

An interesting example of an easement implied from a prior use is the implied right of relatives of a deceased person to cross private property for the purposes of accessing the cemetery where the decedent is buried. This "graveyard right" is basically an implied easement in gross and is recognized by statute in some states and by case law in many others. See Alfred L. Brophy, Grave Matters: The Ancient Rights of the Graveyard, 2006 BYU L. Rev. 1469.

2. *The Restatement (Third)'s approach.* The first Restatement of Property collapsed the common law's traditional distinction between easements implied from a prior existing use and easements recognized on the basis of necessity (which we will take up in the next case, Othen v. Rosier). Following most of the case law, the Restatement (Third) returns to the common law distinction and states the above three requirements for servitudes implied from a prior existing use. Restatement (Third) of Property, Servitudes §2.12 (2000). Regarding the third requirement

(reasonable necessity), it lists several factors that "tend to establish that the parties had reasonable grounds to expect that the conveyance would not terminate the right to continue the prior use. . . ." Among these factors is that continuance is "reasonably necessary to enjoyment of the parcel. . . ." Id. §2.12(2).

3. *What is "reasonable necessity"?* Reasonable necessity is not absolute necessity. As the Restatement (Third) explains, "Reasonable necessity usually means that alternative access . . . cannot be obtained without a substantial expenditure of money or labor. It may also be measured by the amount of waste involved in duplicating facilities or the cost of reestablishing an entitlement to make the prior use." Restatement (Third) of Property, supra, §2.12 comment e. Thus, in Russakoff v. Scruggs, 400 S.E.2d 529 (Va. 1991), the court found that residents' use of a man-made lake located within their residential development was reasonably necessary for recreational purposes.

4. *Implied reservation versus implied grant.* Several jurisdictions, including New York and Texas, follow an old rule that distinguishes between an easement implied in favor of the grantor—an implied reservation—and one implied in favor of a grantee—an implied grant. According to this rule, although an implied grant requires only reasonable necessity, an implied reservation requires strict necessity. A few states still adhere to the old rule. See Houston Bellaire, Ltd. v. TCP LB Portfolio I, L.P., 981 S.W.2d 916 (Tex. Civ. App. 1998). However, the Restatement (Third), along with the weight of authority today, rejects the old rule and states that only reasonable necessity is required for an implied servitude, regardless of whether the servitude is implied in favor of the grantor or the grantee. Restatement (Third) of Property, supra, §2.12 Reporter's Note, at 167.

5. *What is an "apparent" use? The notice problem.* The use involved in *Van Sandt* concerned an underground sewer pipe. In what sense was that use "apparent"? Courts once limited the term to easily visible uses on the surface, but most courts today have broadened the term to include any use that is discoverable through reasonable inspection. In *Van Sandt*, the court concluded that the use was apparent because Van Sandt knew that his house was equipped with modern plumbing and that the plumbing had to drain into a sewer. Is this convincing? See Joel Eichengrun, The Problem of Hidden Easements and the Subsequent Purchaser Without Notice, 40 Okla. L. Rev. 3 (1987). Restatement (Third) takes a somewhat different approach. Rather than adopting an expansive definition of "apparent," it treats underground utilities as a special case. If a court implies an easement on the basis of an existing use, and the easement is hidden (such as a pipeline), should the easement be valid against a subsequent purchaser of the servient land who has no notice of the easement? See id. §2.12(4) (implying easement where "the prior use was for underground utilities serving either parcel").

6. *Expanding the scope of an implied easement.* Can an easement implied from one use be expanded to include a different use, one that did not exist at the time of severance? Changes that occur as the result of technological changes and normal development present little difficulty. Restatement (Third) of Property, supra, §4.10 comment c. So, an easement of way that originated a hundred years ago by means of horse-drawn carriage today permits access by automobile. But suppose

that at the time of severance between lots 1 (the servient tract) and 2 (the dominant tract) the use of lot 2 by *A*, its owner, was confined to agriculture. Could *A* later use her easement for residential purposes? Restatement (Third), in line with its position that the method of a servitude's creation may affect the scope of its use, takes the position that "[t]he purpose of an easement created by . . . prior use under §2.12 is generally defined specifically so that only the use that created the easement and closely related ancillary uses are included within the purpose." Restatement (Third) of Property, supra, §4.10 comment d.

7. *Termination of an easement by merger of tenements.* If the dominant tenement and the servient tenement come into the same ownership, the easement is extinguished altogether. It will not be revived by a severance of the united title into the former dominant and servient tenements. When the united title is subsequently redivided, a new easement by implication can arise if the circumstances at that time indicate a new easement was intended. See Shah v. Smith, 908 N.E.2d 983 (Ohio App. 2009).

Othen v. Rosier

Supreme Court of Texas, 1950
226 S.W.2d 622

BREWSTER, J. Petitioner, Albert Othen, brought this suit to enforce a roadway easement on lands of respondents, Estella Rosier et al., claiming the easement both of necessity and by prescription.

The land of both parties is a part of the Tone Survey of 2493 acres, all of which was formerly owned by one Hill. [The Rosiers own tracts of 100 acres and 16.31 acres, over which Othen claims an easement. Along the west side of the Rosiers' 100 acres runs Belt Line Road, a public highway running north and south. Othen owns tracts of 60 acres and 53 acres, lying to the east of, and contiguous to, the Rosiers' land (see Figure 10-3).

The chronological order of the conveyances of these tracts is as follows. First, Hill conveyed the 100-acre tract on August 26, 1896; by mesne conveyances this tract came into the hands of the Rosiers in 1924. Second, Hill conveyed the 60-acre tract in 1897, and by mesne conveyances Othen acquired it in 1904. These two conveyances left Hill owning the 53-acre tract and the 16.31-acre tract (and possibly other land). On the same day, January 26, 1899, Hill conveyed the 53-acre tract and the 16.31-acre tract to separate purchasers, who conveyed the 53 acres to Othen in 1913 and the 16.31 acres to the Rosiers in 1924.]

. . . The Tone Survey touches three roads: the Belt Line Road, which runs along its west side; the Duncanville Road, which borders it on the south; and the Fish Creek Road, which is its north boundary. But Othen's 113 acres is not contiguous to any of them; so he must cross somebody else's land to get out to a highway. That he had accomplished before the happening which precipitated this litigation by going through a gate in the west line of his 60 acres and in the east line of Rosiers' 16.31 acres, a short but unproved distance south of

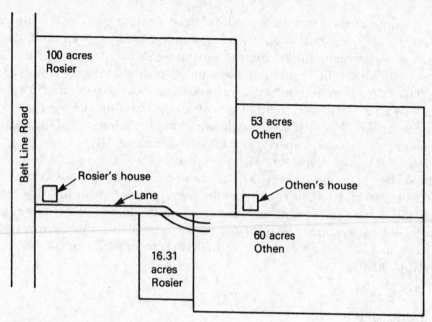

100 acres conveyed by Hill in 1896.
60 acres conveyed by Hill in 1897.
53 acres and 16.31 acres conveyed by Hill in 1899.

Figure 10-3

the south line of Rosiers' 100 acres; thence west-northwesterly across the 16.31 acres into a fenced lane which runs along the south side of Rosiers' 100 acres; thence through this lane to a gate, which opens into the Belt Line Road. Near this gate and in the southwest corner of the 100 acres was the Rosiers' dwelling house, orchard, stock lots and barns. The Rosiers travel and use the lane above described for such purposes as go with the operation of a farm, as well as for their stock to travel to and from the 16.31 acres, which they use as a pasture and from which they get fire wood. On the 16.31 acres is a tenant house, which has been occupied some of the 18 or 20 years previous to the trial by tenants of the Rosiers; and they have made the same use of the lane as Othen has made. The south fence of this lane was built about 1895. Its north fence and the outside gate were constructed about 1906. Before Othen bought his 60 acres in 1904 he had lived on it for two years as a tenant and had moved away for about a year; and he has continuously used the disputed roadway to get to and from the highway from and to his home.

It seems undisputed that the Rosiers made whatever repairs were necessary to keep the land usable. And, so far as the record shows, nobody else recognized any obligation or claimed any right so to keep it. The surface waters flowing into the lane had cut out a large ditch which threatened to encroach across the roadway and render it impassable unless a bridge should be built across it, and these waters threatened erosion damage to Rosiers' cultivated land. To remedy that situation the Rosiers caused a levee 300 feet long to be constructed as close as possible to the south fence of the lane, with something like half of it in the lane and the other half curving southeasterly into the 16.31 acres. This levee impounded the waters draining southward off Rosiers' 100 acres and made the lane so muddy that for weeks at a time it was impassable except by horseback, thereby, Othen alleged, depriving him of ingress and egress to and from his farm. So he filed this suit praying a temporary writ of injunction enjoining the Rosiers from further maintaining this levee and a "mandatory writ of injunction commanding and enjoining and restraining the said defendant from further interfering with" his "use of such easement and roadway" and for damages.

The trial court found that Othen had an easement of necessity and adjudged it to him "upon, over and across" land of the Rosiers beginning at the northeast corner of the 16.31 acres and extending westward "along the said 16.31 acre tract and having a width of approximately 40 feet" to a point in its north boundary immediately east of the northwest corner of the 16.31 acres, thence across that boundary line and westward along the south boundary line of Rosiers' 100 acres to its southwest corner and into the Belt Line Road. The judgment further ordered the Rosiers "to take such action as is necessary to put said easement and roadway, so described, in as usable a condition as same was prior to the erection of said levee."

The Court of Civil Appeals . . . concluded that Othen has no easement either of necessity or by prescription and rendered judgment for the Rosiers, Chief Justice Bond dissenting. 221 S.W.2d 594. That conclusion is attacked here in two points of error.

In support of his claim to an easement of necessity, Othen quotes from 15 Tex. Jur., Sec. 16. p. 785, as follows:

> Furthermore, the grantor impliedly reserves for himself a right of way where he sells land surrounded by other land of which he is owner, and to which he can have access or egress only through the granted premises, and the servient estate is charged with the burden in the hands of any vendee holding under the conveyance.

That statement is in line with the recent holding by this court in Bains v. Parker, 143 Texas 57, 182 S.W.2d 397: "Where a vendor retains a tract of land which is surrounded partly by the tract conveyed and partly by the lands of a stranger, there is an implied reservation of a right of way by necessity over the land conveyed where grantor has no other way out." In 28 C.J.S., Easements, §§34 and 35, pp. 694 et seq., it is made clear that before an easement can be held to be created by implied reservation it must be shown: (1) that there was a unity of ownership of the alleged dominant and servient estates; (2) that the roadway is a necessity, not a mere convenience; and (3) *that the necessity existed at the time of severance of the two estates.* And see 17 Am. Jur., Easements, §§43 and 49, pp. 953 and 963.

Under the foregoing authorities, Othen's claim to an implied reservation of an easement in a roadway means that when Hill, the original owner, sold the

116.31 acres to the Rosiers[14] it was then necessary, not merely convenient, for him to travel over it from the 113 acres now owned by Othen in order to get to and from the Belt Line Road. In determining that question we shall ignore the Duncanville Road to the South, which was established in 1910, as well as the Fish Creek Road to the north, although the record is silent as to when the latter came into existence.

As already stated, the entire Tone Survey of 2493 acres was owned by one Hill, in whom was unity of ownership of the lands now owned by the parties to this suit. On August 26, 1896, he sold the 100 acres in question to Rosiers' predecessors in title, retaining the south 60 acres now owned by Othen, which he conveyed on February 20, 1897. In the deed of date August 26, 1896, did he impliedly reserve the roadway easement from the 60 acres, which he retained over and across the 16.31 acres which he did not convey until January 26, 1899, thence on and along the south side of the 100 acres to the Belt Line Road? Obviously, no such easement arose as to the 16.31 acres over which the trial court decreed Othen a roadway, because Hill did not part with his title to it until two years and five months after he sold the 100 acres and about two years after he sold the 60 acres which Othen now owns; one cannot be said to have an easement in lands, the fee simple title to which is in himself. Alley v. Carleton, 29 Texas 74, 94 Am. Dec. 260. Under the record before us we cannot hold that petitioner has shown any implied easement as to the 100 acres by reason of the deed of August 26, 1896, because the record nowhere shows that the roadway along the south line of the 100 acres was a necessity on the date of that deed, rather than a mere convenience. The burden to prove that was on Othen. Bains v. Parker, supra. There was testimony that it was the only outlet to a public road since about 1900 and for the "last 40 years"; *but there was none as to the situation on August 26, 1896.* One Posey did testify that the owner of the "Othen land" (necessarily the 60 acres) in 1897 "came out up across the south side of the place to the road there," but he did not testify that it was then the only roadway out. On that proposition his testimony was: "Q. Now, then, *is* there any other outlet from Mr. Othen's place to a highway, outside of the road—to a public road? A. Well, I don't know of any." (Italics ours.) The record does not show just how much of the Tone Survey Hill owned when he conveyed the 100 acres on August 26, 1896, but it does appear from a stipulation of the parties that he owned as much as 1350 acres of it until January 26, 1899; and Othen's 53 acres and Rosiers' 16.31 acres were a part of that tract. So, for all the record shows, Hill may easily have been able to cross the 53 acres and around north of the 100 acres on to the Belt Line Road, or he may as easily have been able to go from the 16.31 acres southwesterly to that road across land which he still owned. Certainly Othen should have excluded any such possibility by proof if he would raise an implied reservation in derogation of the warranties in Hill's deed of date August 26, 1896. Rights claimed in derogation of the warranties are implied with

---

14. The court misspoke here. As the court itself makes clear later in the opinion, Hill did not convey either the 100 acres or the 16.31 acres directly to the Rosiers but to intermediate purchasers who then conveyed their respective parcels to the Rosiers in 1924. — EDS.

great caution, hence they should be made clearly to appear. Sellers v. Texas Cent. Ry. Co., 81 Texas 458, 17 S.W. 32, 13 L.R.A. 657; Scarborough v. Anderson Bros. Const. Co. (Civ. App.), 90 S.W.2d 305 (er. dism.).

What we have said determines Othen's claim to a way of necessity; such an easement necessarily can arise only from an implied grant or implied reservation. This results from [the] rule that the mere fact that the claimant's land is completely surrounded by the land of another does not, of itself, give the former a way of necessity over the land of the latter, where there is no privity of ownership. . . .

> It is dependent upon an implied grant or reservation, and cannot exist unless it is affirmatively shown that there was formerly unity of ownership of the alleged dominant and servient estates, for no one can have a way of necessity over the land of a stranger. Necessity alone, without reference to any relations between the respective owners of the land, is not sufficient to create such a right. [Ward v. Bledsoe (Civ. App.), 105 S.W.2d 1116.]

Petitioner's other point complains of the holding of the Court of Civil Appeals that, as a matter of law, he has no easement by prescription.

An important essential in the acquisition of a prescriptive right is an adverse use of the easement.

> Generally, the hostile and adverse character of the user necessary to establish an easement by prescription is the same as that which is necessary to establish title by adverse possession. If the enjoyment is consistent with the right of the owner of the tenement, it confers no right in opposition to such ownership.

17 Am. Jur., Easements, Sec. 63, p. 974, citing cases from 22 jurisdictions, among which are Weber v. Chaney (Civ. App.), 5 S.W.2d 213 (er. ref.), and Callan v. Walters (Civ. App.), 190 S.W. 829. Therefore, the same authority declares in Sec. 67, at page 978,

> The rule is well settled that use by express or implied permission or license, no matter how long continued, cannot ripen into an easement by prescription, since user as of right, as distinguished from permissive user, is lacking,

citing, among other cases, Klein v. Gehrung, 25 Texas Supp. 232, 78 Am. Dec. 565.

In Klein v. Gehrung, it is said: "The foundation of prescriptive title is the presumed grant of the party whose rights are adversely affected; but where it appears that the enjoyment has existed by the consent or license of such party, no presumption of grant can be made."

In Weber v. Chaney, supra, the Webers sued to require Chaney to reopen a road through his farm to public use. Before Chaney closed it such of the public as had occasion to do so used the road as if it had been an established highway. Chaney, his family, tenants and employees likewise used it. Although Chaney never made any objection to the public using the road, he at all times maintained three closed gates across it and the public usually closed them after passing through.

It was held that this use by the public was a permissive use which, in the absence of any adverse claim of right against Chaney, could never ripen into a prescriptive right against him so as to constitute the road a public highway.

Callan v. Walters, supra, holds that where both the owner and the claimant were using a common stairway, each to get into his own building, the claimant's use was not adverse because not exclusive. "The use of a way over the land of another when the owner is also using the same is not such adverse possession as will serve as notice of a claim of right, for the reason that the same is not inconsistent with a license from the owner."

In Sassman v. Collins, 53 Texas Civ. App. 71, 115 S.W. 337 (er. ref.), Collins sued to enforce a roadway across Sassman's land, alleging that he had an easement therein both of necessity and by prescription. Collins and others did use the roadway to get to a public road but Sassman and his predecessors in title likewise used it for the same purpose. The court held that under those circumstances the use of the roadway by the claimant and others is presumed to be with the consent of the owner and not adverse. . . .

It is undisputed that the road along the Rosiers' 100 acres has been fenced on both sides since about 1906; that the gate opening from the lane into the Belt Line Road was erected at the same time and has been kept closed by the Rosiers and Othen as well as by all parties using the lane as an outlet to the road; that the Rosiers and their tenants have used the lane for general farm purposes as well as to haul wood from the 16.31 acres and to permit their livestock to get to and from the pasture. Under those facts, we conclude that Othen's use of the roadway was merely permissive, hence constituted only a license, which could not and did not ripen into a prescriptive right.

But Othen insists that he had prescriptive title of 10 years to the easement before the lane was fenced and the gate opening into the Belt Line Road was erected in 1906, because "at least since 1895 and probably since 1893 said roadway has been established and claimed by petitioner and others." Othen testified that about 1900 he moved onto the 113 acres in question as a tenant and lived there two years, moved away for about 11 months, then "bought it and moved back." It is obvious that he did not use the roadway in any way for any period of 10 years prior to 1906. The testimony as to its use by Othen's predecessors is, in our opinion, too vague and uncertain to amount to any evidence of prescriptive right to the roadway decreed by the trial court. For example, when Othen was asked to "tell the court what the condition of that passageway was there," he answered: "Well, in that day and time it was just prairie and there were some hog wallows which would hold water. You would just pick your place round about; if there was a hog wallow, go around it and come on in. But that was the general direction through there." Another witness, asked whether in 1901 there was a road "by the side of the present Rosier property," replied: "It was on the present Rosier property, and at that time went up through the edge of the field." When asked by Othen's counsel, "Do you know anything about where this road used to run?", Mrs. Rosier said: "Well, it didn't run up exactly next to the Belt Line like it is running now." It cannot be said that this showed only a slight divergence in the directions taken by the roadway before 1904, therefore Othen did not discharge his burden of showing that his predecessors' adverse possession was in the same place and within the definite lines claimed by him and fixed by the trial court. . . .

Moreover, since Hill did not part with his title to Othen's alleged dominant estate until 1897 (as to the 60 acres) and until 1899 (as to the 53 acres) and did not part with his title to 16.31 acres of the Rosiers' alleged servient estate until 1899, Othen could not under any circumstances have perfected prescriptive title to a roadway easement on the 16.31 acres prior to 1906.

> Since a person cannot claim adversely to himself, the courts uniformly maintain that the prescriptive period does not begin to run while the dominant and servient tracts are under the same ownership. [17 Am. Jur., Easements, Sec. 69, p. 980.]

It follows that the judgment of the Court of Civil Appeals is affirmed.

A NOTE ON *OTHEN*

Professor Dan Schechter has provided us with the following information about Albert Othen, based on a telephone conversation he had with Othen's grandson: Albert ("Bert") Othen was "wiry and tough, about 5'5" and 135 lbs." He farmed cotton as his cash crop but also raised corn, hogs and milo (an animal feed crop). Of his two parcels, the south parcel, i.e., the 60-acre parcel, was the "expensive" land, bought at $10 per acre. The 53-acre parcel was purchased at $7 per acre.

Professor Schechter further reports:

> There was a rumor in the neighborhood that there was some bad blood between the families, something [connected] with rivalry about an old beau, and the Rosiers eventually closed off the lane. The Othens filed suit. After they lost, the neighbor to the south felt that the Othens had been treated unfairly and gave them a right of way to Camp Wisdom Road, a much longer and more difficult way out. . . . Almost 40 years after the trouble first started, [Othen's daughter] bumped into Juanita Rosier at a cotton gin. They fell into each other's arms, made up, and talked over old times. . . . The land is mostly housing now. The city made the [Othen] family tear down the old home place in 1988, because it was a fire hazard. That was very sad for the whole family, but it just couldn't be helped.

NOTES, QUESTIONS, AND PROBLEM: EASEMENTS BY NECESSITY

1. *Basis of easement by necessity.* Is an easement by necessity implied because of public policy or because it effectuates the intent of the parties? In the early English cases, it was said that one who grants a thing must be understood to have granted that without which the granted thing cannot exist. By the seventeenth century, an easement by necessity came to be supported by a public policy that

no land be made inaccessible. In the nineteenth century, when courts sought to ground rights in the contract between the parties, the easement by necessity was said to carry out the presumed intent of the parties. In most cases, it does not matter which justification is given, but if the parties expressly provide that no way of necessity exists, the court must decide whether such a provision is valid. Compare Mersac, Inc. v. National Hills Condominium Assn., Inc., 480 S.E.2d 16 (Ga. 1997) (holding retained land locked when developer inadvertently failed to retain an easement of access; doctrine of implied reservation of easement by grantor not recognized).

2. *How much necessity?* There is some conflict in the cases over the degree of necessity required for an easement by necessity. The traditional and still dominant view, reflected by Othen v. Rosier, requires strict necessity. See, e.g., Schwab v. Timmons, 589 N.W.2d 1 (Wis. 1999) (refusing to recognize an easement by necessity when allegedly "landlocked" parcel had access to a public road on foot, down a steep cliff; the fact that the cost of building a road over the cliff would be $700,000 was deemed irrelevant). A few jurisdictions go so far as to hold that a surface way of necessity will not be implied if the tract has access by navigable water. In a minority of jurisdictions, however, only reasonable necessity is required. Courts in these jurisdictions have granted an easement by necessity where access to the land exists but is claimed to be inadequate, difficult, or costly. See, e.g., Weaver v. Cummins, 751 N.E. 2d 628 (Ill. App. 2001). The Restatement (Third) endorses the minority view. See Restatement (Third) of Property, Servitudes §2.15 (2000). Comment d states, "If property cannot otherwise be used without disproportionate effort or expense, the rights are necessary within the meaning of this section." Which view seems more sensible to you?

On easements by necessity, see Stewart E. Sterk, Neighbors in American Land Law, 87 Colum. L. Rev. 55 (1987) (attempting to ground easements by necessity, implication, and estoppel in a social obligation of neighbors to cooperate); John Martinez, No More Free Easements: Judicial Takings for Private Necessity, 40 Real

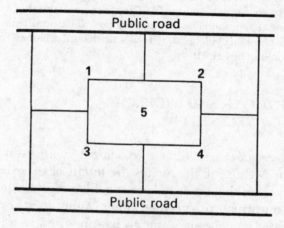

Figure 10-4

Est. L.J. 425 (2012) (arguing that finding an easement by necessity requires compensation because it is a judicial taking under the Fifth Amendment; for more on judicial takings, see pages 1222-1238).

3. *A* owns five adjoining tracts of forest land, numbered 1 through 5. All five lots had previously been owned by *O* as a single tract; *A* purchased each lot from *O* in a separate transaction, lot 1 first, lot 2 second, lot 3 third, lot 4 fourth, and finally lot 5. Lots 1 and 2 are bounded by a public road on the north. Lots 3 and 4 are bounded by a public road on the south. Lot 5 has no access to a public road except through one of the other four lots. See figure 10-4.

A dies intestate. Her five children, *B*, *C*, *D*, *E*, and *F*, are her heirs. In the decree of distribution settling *A*'s estate, the court assigns lot 1 to *B*, lot 2 to *C*, lot 3 to *D*, lot 4 to *E*, and lot 5 to *F.* Nothing is said in the decree about lot 5 having an easement of way. Sometime later *F* sues the owners of lots 1 through 4, claiming an easement by necessity. What result? See 2 American Law of Property §8.91 (1952). Cf. Horner v. Heersche, 447 P.2d 811 (Kan. 1968); McQuinn v. Tantalo, 339 N.Y.S.2d 541 (App. Div. 1973).

4. *Duration of an easement by necessity.* An easement by necessity endures only so long as it is necessary. If the dominant owner secures another way out from the landlocked parcel, the easement by necessity ceases. Thus if *A*, owner of a landlocked parcel with an easement by necessity over *B*'s land, acquires an easement over *C*'s land enabling *A* to reach a public road, the easement by necessity disappears.

In Van Sandt v. Royster, page 825, suppose that the city constructs a public sewer in Tenth Street, and that the owner of lot 4 can connect with it. Does the owner of lot 4 lose the implied sewer easement over lots 19 and 20?

5. *Private condemnation actions.* In some states, statutes or constitutional provisions give an owner of landlocked land the right to condemn an easement across neighboring land upon showing the requisite necessity. The condemnation is a judicial proceeding, and the landowner must pay damages to the owner of the land where the easement is sought. Under these statutes, it does not matter how the landlocking occurred; prior common ownership of the dominant and servient estates is not required. See, e.g., Minn. Stat. §164.08 (2012); N.D. Cent. Code §24-07-06 (2012).

Under provisions of this sort, should it matter if a grantor voluntarily landlocked himself? In Ruvalcaba v. Kwang Ho Baek, 282 P.3d 1083 (Wash. 2012), the court said that it does. In that case, the grantor landlocked himself when he conveyed the access portion of an initially unsevered parcel of land, retaining for himself the landlocked portion. The grantor brought a private condemnation action under a provision in the state constitution and a state statute giving landowners power to condemn private rights of way when reasonably necessary. They brought the claim 35 years after their parcel became landlocked. Eschewing a bright-line rule that would automatically bar landlocked plaintiffs from condemning a private right of way any time a landowner voluntarily landlocks his own property, the court held the combination of the grantor's voluntary action together with the facts that he waited 35 years before bringing the action and that his claim was based on financial impracticability, rather than access as such, made it impossible for a finder of fact to find that reasonable necessity existed on these facts.

Why should the servient owner of a common law easement by necessity receive no compensation whereas the servient owner of a privately condemned easement by necessity receives compensation from the benefitted owner?

In Leo Sheep Co. v. United States, 440 U.S. 668 (1979), the Court held that the United States had no easement by necessity to reach landlocked government lands because it has the power of eminent domain.

NOTES, QUESTIONS, AND PROBLEM: EASEMENTS BY PRESCRIPTION

1. As mentioned in Chapter 2 (see footnote 15 on page 152), easements may be acquired by prescription, which in many ways is similar to adverse possession but in some ways distinctly different. Adverse possession involves a statute of limitations running on the right to bring an action to recover *possession* of land; the statute operates to extinguish the remedy of the previous owner, leaving the adverse possessor in indefeasible possession. The result is that the adverse possessor has a new title based on his possession. A statute of limitations upon the recovery of possession does not cover actions concerning easements, which involve *use* and not possession of land. Yet the reasons underlying the protection of long-continued adverse possession apply also to long-continued use. In as much as legislatures enacted no legislation to protect ancient easements, courts developed the doctrine of prescription. Prescription rests upon the idea, taken from Roman law, that rights can be acquired simply by the passage of time.

The earliest type of prescriptive easement was the easement based upon a use from time immemorial. In 1275, to settle old claims to earlier possession, Parliament enacted a statute prohibiting challenges to rights of possession enjoyed since the accession to the throne of Richard I (the Lionheart) in 1189. This legislation applied only to writs of right to recover seisin, but the courts thereafter by analogy held that any continuous use in the nature of an easement or profit from 1189 was unchallengeable. The year 1189 was fixed as the time beyond which legal memory could not go, and the claimant of an easement by prescription would allege use since "the memory of man runneth not to the contrary." As the year 1189 receded into history, it became more and more difficult to prove that the claimant and his predecessors had enjoyed the use since 1189. In time, "as parliament failed to intervene to amend the law, the judges set their ingenuity to work, by fictions and presumptions, to atone for the supineness of the legislature, and to amend, so far as in them lay, the law." Bryant v. Foot, (1867) L.R. 2 Q.B. 161, 181. They first set down the rule that if a use had existed so long as any living person could remember, it was presumed to have existed from the year 1189. Later, by analogy to a statute of limitations enacted in 1623 providing a 20-year limitation on suits in ejectment, the judges held that, if a use had continued for 20 years, it presumptively had existed since 1189. However, these presumptions did not provide an effective system of prescription because they were only presumptions and could be overcome by evidence showing that some time since 1189 (perhaps 25 years before the lawsuit) the use could not or did not exist. And so, "endowed with a great power of imagination for the purpose of supporting ancient uses" (Neaverson v. Peterborough R.D.C., [1902] 1 Ch. 557, 573), the judges invented the *fiction of the lost grant*. If a use was shown to have existed for 20 years, it was presumed that a grant of an easement had been made and that the grant had been lost. The presumption of grant could not be rebutted by evidence that no grant had in fact been made. Thus was the 20 years' adverse use clothed with a rightful beginning and the necessity of proof of use from 1189 obviated.

In this country, it would have been impossible to require a continuous use since 1189, and American courts rejected the theory that prescriptive easements rest upon use from time immemorial. They developed the law of prescription, applying by analogy the statutes of limitation relating to the recovery of possession. Courts set the same period for prescriptive easements as the statutes fixed for recovery of possession, and generally required the same manner of use as is required for adverse possession: open and notorious, continuous, adverse, and under claim of right. The fiction of the lost grant—an ingenious invention to overcome the onerous burden of proving use from time immemorial, never required in the United States—should not have crossed the Atlantic. Once prescriptive easements were put on the same basis as adverse possession (the running of the statute of limitations upon a cause of action), the lost grant theory should have been seen as irrelevant.[15] But, in slavish adherence to the verbal formulation of eighteenth-century English law, and unmindful of its historical justification, some American courts adopted the fiction of the lost grant, although the majority rejected it.

The lost grant theory draws a confusing distinction between acquiescence and permission. Under lost grant theory, the owner of land is presumed to consent or acquiesce in the use; after all, the owner (or his predecessor) is thought to have granted the easement. On the other hand, if the use is made with the permission of the owner, the use is not adverse. To secure a prescriptive easement under lost grant theory, the claimant must show that the use was not permissive and also that the owner acquiesced (did not object). Language that the owner must acquiesce in the easement sometimes appears, like a pentimento, in opinions in jurisdictions that have erased the lost grant theory.

---

15. To illustrate, a prescriptive easement for parking vehicles obtained against a tenant is not valid against the landlord because actions in ejectment and trespass (the usual methods of preventing a prescriptive easement) are available only to the owner of a possessory interest (the tenant). Dieterich Intl. v. J.S. & J. Servs., 5 Cal. Rptr. 2d 388 (Cal. App. 1992). (Compare adverse possession, Problem 3, page 176.) Under a lost grant theory, the landlord would be barred simply by the passage of time if the landlord were capable of making a grant. See Jerome J. Curtis, Jr., Reviving the Lost Grant, 23 Real Prop., Prob. & Tr. J. 535 (1988).

Consider the fiction of the lost grant in relation to the following problem: To reach her land more easily, in 1982 *A* makes a road across *O*'s land. In 1994, *O* writes *A* a letter saying: "You are hereby notified that the portion of my land which you made into a road is my private property. No person has the right to cross this land, and you are liable to me in damages. I hereby forbid you to pass over any portion of my land, especially that portion which you unlawfully made into a road." *A* ignores *O*'s letter and continues to use the road for the prescriptive period of 20 years. In 2002 does *A* have a prescriptive easement? See Dartnell v. Bidwell, 98 A. 743 (Me. 1916) (holding that a letter interrupts prescription because it rebuts any claim of acquiescence or grant); cf. Dowley v. Morency, 737 A.2d 1061 (Me. 1999) (discussing meaning of acquiescence). Would a letter to a possessor stop adverse possession from running?

In a jurisdiction not following the fiction of the lost grant, to prevent a prescriptive easement from being acquired, the owner must effectively interrupt or stop the adverse use. Suppose, under the preceding facts, that in 1994 *O* had erected a fence across the road, and that *A* tore down the fence and continued to use the road. Does *A* acquire a prescriptive easement in 2002? See Restatement (Third) of Property, Servitudes §2.17 comment j illustration 35 (2000). Some states have statutes that allow landowners to interrupt an adverse use by simply giving written notice to persons using the owner's land of the owner's intent to dispute any claim arising from such use. See, e.g., Conn. Gen. Stat. §47-38 (2012); Iowa Code Ann. §§564.4-564.7 (1992); R.I. Gen. Laws §34-7-6 (2012).

On prescriptive as well as implied easements, see Michael V. Hernandez, Restating Implied, Prescriptive, and Statutory Easements, 40 Real Prop., Prob. & Trust J. 75 (2005).

2. *Compensation for prescriptive easements?* Where *A* acquires a prescriptive easement over *O*'s land, should *A* have to pay *O* damages? This question arose in Warsaw v. Chicago Metallic Ceilings, Inc., 676 P.2d 584 (Cal. 1984). Although six of the seven judges agreed that any change in the no-compensation rule must come from the legislature, the judges divided on the soundness of the no-compensation rule. Four members of the court thought the rule sound because (1) prescription protected a long use or possession against largely unmeritorious claims of an "alleged owner," (2) the rule reduced litigation, and (3) land use historically has been favored over disuse. Three members of the court thought that allowing persons to acquire prescriptive rights without compensation had no justification. See Thomas W. Merrill, Property Rules, Liability Rules, and Adverse Possession, 79 Nw. U. L. Rev. 1122 (1984); Noel Elfant, Comment, Compensation for the Involuntary Transfer of Property Between Private Parties: Application of a Liability Rule to the Law of Adverse Possession, 79 Nw. U. L. Rev. 758 (1984), both mentioned in the discussion on page 161.

Compare the law of nuisance, for example, Note 3 on pages 795-797, and the law of mistaken improver, Note 4 on page 169, both of which give a court power to grant damages or an injunction.

3. *Exclusivity of use.* In Othen v. Rosier, the court presumed that the use of the road by Othen was permissive rather than adverse because it was not exclusive.

Why should this be presumed? In order to gain title by adverse possession, a person must show exclusive possession for the required period. There is good reason for this requirement when one is claiming exclusive ownership of the land ousting the legal owner. But why should it apply so as to bar a claim to a nonexclusive prescriptive easement to be used by the servient owner as well? It appears that most courts require exclusive use for prescription, but define it differently from the adverse possession requirement. "[E]xclusivity for a prescriptive easement is not as strictly construed as for adverse possession. The use need not be exclusive in the sense that it must be used by one person only. Rather, the right must not depend upon a similar right in others. . . ." Nordin v. Kuno, 287 N.W.2d 923, 926 (Minn. 1980). But see Catholic Bishop of Chicago v. Chicago Title & Trust Co., 954 N.E.2d 797, 801-803 (Ill. App. 2011) (treating exclusivity as synonymous in the prescriptive easement and adverse possession contexts). Thus, in most states, the user can acquire a prescriptive easement even though the easement is also used by the servient owner. See Jon W. Bruce & James W. Ely, Jr., The Law of Easements and Licenses in Land ¶ 5.07 (rev. ed. 2001); Dena Cohen, Note, Exclusiveness in the Law of Prescription, 8 Cardozo L. Rev. 611 (1987).

4. Adjacent to Conrad Hilton's home is a golf club. Every day several golf balls are driven onto Hilton's property, and the players come onto his property to retrieve them. If this continues, will the golf club acquire a prescriptive easement over Hilton's property? See MacDonald Properties, Inc. v. Bel-Air Country Club, 140 Cal. Rptr. 367 (Cal. App. 1977). If so, what should Hilton do to prevent a prescriptive easement from arising?

In Malouf v. Dallas Athletic Country Club, 837 S.W.2d 674 (Tex. Civ. App. 1992), the court held that a golf club was not liable in trespass to adjoining homeowners for damages resulting from errant golf balls. The court said that an action in trespass required an intent to commit trespass (compare Note 2 on pages 783-784) and the golfers did not intend to send their balls on the neighbors' land. The "hooks" and "slices" were an unintended consequence of play. Can the golf club acquire a prescriptive easement without a trespass? What are the neighbors to do to prevent their windows from being broken?

5. *Public prescriptive easements.* In most states a public prescriptive easement can be obtained by long continuous use by the public under a claim of right. The landowner must be put on notice, by the kind and extent of use, that an adverse right is being claimed by the general public, not by individuals.[16] Where a public road is being claimed, the same requirements generally apply as are applied to a private prescriptive easement. Note, however, that public prescriptive easements may be difficult to prove. Courts often place greater burdens on claimants to a public prescriptive easement than they do on persons asserting private prescriptive easements. Claimants must prove that the nature and extent of the use is sufficient to establish notice to the landowner that the public in general, rather than simply a group of individuals, is claiming a use right. Moreover, the

---

16. In Rockefeller Center, in New York City, a private street called Rockefeller Plaza is situated between the GE Building and the sunken skating rink. In order to preserve Rockefeller Center's right of ownership of the street, each year the street is closed to all traffic, even pedestrian, for one day—a Sunday in July is usually chosen as interfering least with tenants and visitors. Lawyers for Rockefeller Center believe that this formality is necessary to prevent the public from acquiring a permanent right of way in the street.

exclusivity requirement may block creation of a public prescriptive easement. Courts are divided on the applicability of exclusivity to public prescriptive easements. Compare, e.g., Heller v. Gremaux, 53 P.3d 1259 (Mont. 2002) (exclusivity not required), with Selletin v. Terkildsen, 343 N.W.2d 894 (Neb. 1984) (exclusivity required). Where exclusivity is required, it is difficult to establish in cases of public prescriptive easements because exclusivity is usually defined as use that is separate or distinct from that of the public. Finally, some states do not recognize public prescriptive easements at all, on the ground that an "unorganized public" cannot establish rights for the public as a whole. See Miller v. Grossman Shoes, Inc., 404 A.2d 302 (Conn. 1982); Forest Hills Garden Corp. v. Baroth, 555 N.Y.S.2d 1000 (Sup. Ct. 1990).

Some courts use the theory of implied dedication, rather than prescription, for public easements. Dedications may be express or implied. Express dedications are essentially grants and usually involve gratuitous transfers of land to a government body or the public at large. Subdivision maps, for example, commonly contain dedications of roads to the public. The theory of implied dedication owes something to the lost grant fiction, for it seeks a substitute for a grant in an implied dedication. It may be used where the landowner evidences an intent to dedicate, and the state accepts by maintaining the land used by the public. Or implied dedication theory may be used as a substitute for prescription. For discussion of the obligations a public prescriptive easement imposes on governmental authorities, see Stewart E. Sterk, Publicly Held Servitudes in the New Restatement, 27 Conn. L. Rev. 157 (1994).

Beach access. In states bordering the sea, the availability of coastal beaches for public use is a matter of considerable importance. In most states, the state holds, in public trust, the beach from the water to the mean high-tide line (the foreshore or wet sand area). The dry sand portion of the beach between the mean high-tide line and the vegetation line is subject to private ownership. Public access requires both a way of access from inland to the coast and a lateral easement up and down the beach. The prescriptive easement doctrine has not been notably successful in providing public access, largely because most courts presume that public use of beaches is with the permission of the owner, and the burden of proving adverse use cannot be met. See City of Daytona Beach v. Tona-Rama, Inc., 294 So. 2d 73 (Fla. 1974). In a few states, suits for prescriptive easements for beach access have been successful. See Concerned Citizens of Brunswick County Taxpayers Assn. v. Holden Beach Enterprises, 404 S.E.2d 677 (N.C. 1991) (holding pathway to beach could shift over prescriptive period so long as there was substantial identity of use; barricades placed by owner did not destroy the public's continuity of use because they were ineffective in stopping the public); see also Joseph J. Kalo, The Changing Face of the Shoreline: Public and Private Rights to the Natural and Nourished Dry Sand Beaches of North Carolina, 78 N.C. L. Rev. 1869 (2000). In California, on the other hand, public prescriptive easements have been abolished by statute except on land within 1,000 yards from the ocean. Even on such land the landowner can prevent a public prescriptive easement either by posting annually a sign ("Right to pass by permission of the owner, revocable at any time") or recording a similar notice in the public records. The landowner's act granting permission defeats any claim of public adverse use. Cal. Civ. Code §1009 (2012).[17]

Because beach access is usually presumed to be with the permission of the owner and because each individual beach access case must be litigated separately under the prescriptive easement doctrine, courts in some jurisdictions have turned to other doctrines with greater potential for opening the beaches. In Florida, Oregon, and Texas, courts have roused, from a sleep of some centuries, the medieval doctrine of customary rights—uses that existed for so long that "the memory of man runneth not to the contrary"—and have held that long usage of beaches by the public is protected as a customary right. *City of Daytona Beach*, 294 So. 2d 73; Stevens v. City of Cannon Beach, 854 P.2d 449 (Or. 1993); Matcha v. Mattox, 711 S.W.2d 95 (Tex. Civ. App. 1986). Similarly, the Hawaiian court has rooted in the history of the Hawaiian Islands the public's right to use the beaches up to the vegetation line or line of debris. Public Access Shoreline Hawaii v. Hawai'i County Planning Commn., 903 P.2d 1246 (Haw. 1995). See Alfred L. Brophy, Aloha Jurisprudence: Equity Rules in Property, 85 Or. L. Rev. 771 (2006); Jon W. Bruce & James W. Ely, Jr., The Law of Easements and Licenses in Land ¶¶ 5.26, 6.2, 6.3 (rev. ed. 2009) (citing a wealth of articles and comments on beach access).

Another method of recognizing a public interest in beaches is the public trust doctrine, discussed in the following case.

Matthews v. Bay Head Improvement Association

Supreme Court of New Jersey, 1984
471 A.2d 355, cert. denied, 469 U.S. 821 (1984)

SCHREIBER, J. The public trust doctrine acknowledges that the ownership, dominion and sovereignty over land flowed by tidal waters, which extend to the mean high water mark, is vested in the State in trust for the people. The public's right to use the tidal lands and water encompasses navigation, fishing and recreational uses, including bathing, swimming and other shore activities. Borough of Neptune City v. Borough of Avon-by-the-Sea, 61 N.J. 296, 309, 294 A.2d 47 (1972). In *Avon* we held that the public trust applied to the municipally-owned dry sand beach immediately landward of the high water mark. The major issue in this case is whether, ancillary to the public's right to enjoy the tidal lands, the

---

17. In Texas, public access to beaches, permitted under various common law theories, has adapted to shoreline movements under a doctrine known as "rolling easements." Recently, however, the Texas Supreme Court held that beach access easements do not "roll" when the shift in the shoreline's shape are sudden. See Severance v. Patterson, 370 S.W.3d 705 (Tex. 2012). The court based its decision on the doctrine of avulsion, which we saw earlier in footnote 8 on page 617, drawing a distinction between shoreline movement due to erosion (to which rolling easements continue to apply) and those caused by avulsion (to which rolling easements do not apply). See Celeste Pagano, Where's the Beach? Coastal Access in the Age of Rising Tides, 42 Sw. L. Rev. 1 (2012).

public has a right to gain access through and to use the dry sand area not owned by a municipality but by a quasi-public body.

The Borough of Point Pleasant instituted this suit against the Borough of Bay Head and the Bay Head Improvement Association (Association), generally asserting that the defendants prevented Point Pleasant inhabitants from gaining access to the Atlantic Ocean and the beachfront in Bay Head. The proceeding was dismissed as to the Borough of Bay Head because it did not own or control the beach. Subsequently, . . . Stanley Van Ness, as Public Advocate, joined as plaintiff-intervenor. When the Borough of Point Pleasant ceased pursuing the litigation, the Public Advocate became the primary moving party. The Public Advocate asserted that the defendants had denied the general public its right of access during the summer bathing season to public trust lands along the beaches in Bay Head and its right to use private property fronting on the ocean incidental to the public's right under the public trust doctrine. The complaint was amended on several occasions, eliminating the Borough of Point Pleasant as plaintiff and adding more than 100 individuals, who were owners or had interests in properties located on the oceanfront in Bay Head, as defendants. . . .

Facts

The Borough of Bay Head (Bay Head) borders the Atlantic Ocean. Adjacent to it on the north is the Borough of Point Pleasant Beach, on the south the Borough of Mantoloking, and on the west Barnegat Bay. Bay Head consists of a fairly narrow strip of land, 6,667 feet long (about 1 1/4 miles). A beach runs along its entire length adjacent to the Atlantic Ocean. There are 76 separate parcels of land that border the beach. All except six are owned by private individuals. Title to those six is vested in the Association.

The Association was founded in 1910 and incorporated as a nonprofit corporation in 1932. . . . Its constitution delineates the Association's object to promote the best interests of the Borough and "in so doing to own property, operate bathing beaches, hire life guards, beach cleaners and policemen. . . ."

Nine streets in the Borough, which are perpendicular to the beach, end at the dry sand. The Association owns the land commencing at the end of seven of these streets for the width of each street and extending through the upper dry sand to the mean high water line, the beginning of the wet sand area or foreshore. In addition, the Association owns the fee in six shore front properties, three of which are contiguous and have a frontage aggregating 310 feet. Many owners of beachfront property executed and delivered to the Association leases of the upper dry sand area. These leases are revocable by either party to the lease on thirty days' notice. Some owners have not executed such leases and have not permitted the Association to use their beaches. . . .

The Association controls and supervises its beach property between the third week in June and Labor Day. It engages about 40 employees who serve as lifeguards, beach police and beach cleaners. Lifeguards, stationed at five operating

A long-forgotten, 4,134-foot-long seawall, dating to 1882, buried beneath the sand in Bay Head, N.J., helped weather Hurricane Sandy's record surges and large waves, according to scientists.

beaches, indicate by use of flags whether the ocean condition is dangerous (red), requires caution (yellow), or is satisfactory (green). In addition to observing and, if need be, assisting those in the water, when called upon lifeguards render first aid. Beach cleaners are engaged to rake and keep the beach clean of debris. Beach police are stationed at the entrances to the beaches where the public streets lead into the beach to ensure that only Association members or their guests enter. Some beach police patrol the beaches to enforce its membership rules.

Membership is generally limited to residents of Bay Head. Class A members are property owners. Class B are non-owners. . . . Upon application residents are routinely accepted. . . .

Except for fishermen, who are permitted to walk through the upper dry sand area to the foreshore, only the membership may use the beach between 10:00 A.M. and 5:30 P.M. during the summer season. The public is permitted to use the Association's beach from 5:30 P.M. to 10:00 A.M. during the summer and, with no hourly restrictions, between Labor Day and mid-June.

No attempt has ever been made to stop anyone from occupying the terrain east of the high water mark. During certain parts of the day, when the tide is low, the foreshore could consist of about 50 feet of sand not being flowed by the water. The public could gain access to the foreshore by coming from the Borough of Point Pleasant Beach on the north or from the Borough of Mantoloking on the south. . . .

The Public Trust

In Borough of Neptune City v. Borough of Avon-by-the-Sea, 61 N.J. 296, 303, 294 A.2d 47 (1972), Justice Hall alluded to the ancient principle "that land covered by tidal waters belonged to the sovereign, but for the common use of all the people." The genesis of this principle is found in Roman jurisprudence, which held that "[b]y the law of nature" "the air, running water, the sea, and consequently the shores of the sea," were "common to mankind." Justinian, Institutes 2.1.1 (T. Sandars trans. 1st Am. ed. 1876). No one was forbidden access to the sea, and everyone could use the seashore "to dry his nets there, and haul them from the sea. . . ." Id., 2.1.5. The seashore was not private property, but "subject to the same law as the sea itself, and the sand or ground beneath it." Id. This underlying concept was applied in New Jersey in Arnold v. Mundy, 6 N.J.L. 1 (Sup. Ct.[18] 1821).

[I]n *Arnold* . . . Chief Justice Kirkpatrick, in an extensive opinion, . . . concluded that all navigable rivers in which the tide ebbs and flows and the coasts of the sea, including the water and land under the water, are "common to all the citizens, and that each [citizen] has a right to use them according to his necessities, subject only to the laws which regulate that use. . . ." Id. at 93. Regulation included erecting docks, harbors and wharves, and improving fishery and oyster beds. This common property . . . [belonged] to the Crown of England, and upon the Revolution these royal rights became vested in the people of New Jersey. Later in Illinois Central R.R. v. Illinois, 146 U.S. 387, 453 (1892), the Supreme Court, in referring to the common property, stated that "[t]he State can no more abdicate its trust over property in which the whole people are interested . . . than it can abdicate its police powers. . . ."

In *Avon*, Justice Hall reaffirmed the public's right to use the waterfront as announced in Arnold v. Mundy. He observed that the public has a right to use the land below the mean average high water mark where the tide ebbs and flows. These uses have historically included navigation and fishing. In *Avon* the public's rights were extended "to recreational uses, including bathing, swimming and other shore activities." 61 N.J. at 309, 294 A.2d 47. . . . Extension of the public trust doctrine to include bathing, swimming and other shore activities is consonant with and furthers the general welfare. The public's right to enjoy these privileges must be respected.

In order to exercise these rights guaranteed by the public trust doctrine, the public must have access to municipally-owned dry sand areas as well as the foreshore. The extension of the public trust doctrine to include municipally-owned dry sand areas was necessitated by our conclusion that enjoyment of rights in the foreshore is inseparable from use of dry sand beaches. See Lusardi v. Curtis Point Property Owners Ass'n, 86 N.J. 217, 228, 430 A.2d 881 (1981). In *Avon* we struck down a municipal ordinance that required nonresidents to pay a higher fee than

---

18. Although the court refers to the court that decided *Arnold* as the Supreme Court, this is not historically accurate. Prior to 1947, the court of last resort in New Jersey was known as the Court of Errors and Appeals, not the Supreme Court. It was abolished and replaced by the New Jersey Supreme Court in 1947. Thanks to Craig Oren for bringing this matter to our attention. — EDS.

residents for the use of the beach. We held that where a municipal beach is dedicated to public use, the public trust doctrine "dictates that the beach and the ocean waters must be open to all on equal terms and without preference and that any contrary state or municipal action is impermissible." 61 N.J. at 309, 294 A.2d 47. The Court was not relying on the legal theory of dedication, although dedication alone would have entitled the public to the full enjoyment of the dry sand. Instead the Court depended on the public trust doctrine, impliedly holding that full enjoyment of the foreshore necessitated some use of the upper sand, so that the latter came under the umbrella of the public trust.

In Van Ness v. Borough of Deal, 78 N.J. 174, 393 A.2d 571 (1978), we stated that the public's right to use municipally-owned beaches was not dependent upon the municipality's dedication of its beaches to use by the general public. The Borough of Deal had dedicated a portion of such beach for use by its residents only. We found such limited dedication "immaterial" given the public trust doctrine's requirement that the public be afforded the right to enjoy all dry sand beaches owned by a municipality. 78 N.J. at 179-80, 393 A.2d 571.

Public Rights in Privately-Owned Dry Sand Beaches

In *Avon* and *Deal* our finding of public rights in dry sand areas was specifically and appropriately limited to those beaches owned by a municipality. We now address the extent of the public's interest in privately-owned dry sand beaches. This interest may take one of two forms. First, the public may have a right to cross privately owned dry sand beaches in order to gain access to the foreshore. Second, this interest may be of the sort enjoyed by the public in municipal beaches under *Avon* and *Deal*, namely, the right to sunbathe and generally enjoy recreational activities. . . .

Exercise of the public's right to swim and bathe below the mean high water mark may depend upon a right to pass across the upland beach. Without some means of access the public right to use the foreshore would be meaningless. To say that the public trust doctrine entitles the public to swim in the ocean and to use the foreshore in connection therewith without assuring the public of a feasible access route would seriously impinge on, if not effectively eliminate, the rights of the public trust doctrine. This does not mean the public has an unrestricted right to cross at will over any and all property bordering on the common property. The public interest is satisfied so long as there is reasonable access to the sea. . . .

The bather's right in the upland sands is not limited to passage. Reasonable enjoyment of the foreshore and the sea cannot be realized unless some enjoyment of the dry sand area is also allowed.[19] The complete pleasure of swimming

---

19. Some historical support for this proposition may be found in an analogous situation where fishermen, in exercising the right of public fishery in tidal waters, were permitted to draw nets on the beach above the ordinary high water mark in the act of fishing. S. Moore & H. Moore, The History and Law of Fisheries 96 (1903).

must be accompanied by intermittent periods of rest and relaxation beyond the water's edge. See State ex rel. Thornton v. Hay, 254 Or. 584, 599-602, 462 P.2d 671, 678-79 (1969) (Denecke, J., concurring). The unavailability of the physical situs for such rest and relaxation would seriously curtail and in many situations eliminate the right to the recreational use of the ocean. This was a principal reason why in *Avon* and *Deal* we held that municipally-owned dry sand beaches "must be open to all on equal terms. . . ." *Avon*, 61 N.J. at 308, 294 A.2d 47. We see no reason why rights under the public trust doctrine to use of the upland dry sand area should be limited to municipally-owned property. It is true that the private owner's interest in the upland dry sand area is not identical to that of a municipality. Nonetheless, where use of dry sand is essential or reasonably necessary for enjoyment of the ocean, the doctrine warrants the public's use of the upland dry sand area subject to an accommodation of the interests of the owner.

We perceive no need to attempt to apply notions of prescription, City of Daytona Beach v. Tona-Rama, Inc., 294 So. 2d 73 (Fla. 1974), dedication, Gion v. City of Santa Cruz, 2 Cal. 3d 29, 465 P.2d 50, 84 Cal. Rptr. 162 (1970), or custom, State ex rel. Thornton v. Hay, 254 Or. 584, 462 P.2d 671 (1969), as an alternative to application of the public trust doctrine. Archaic judicial responses are not an answer to a modern social problem. Rather, we perceive the public trust doctrine not to be "fixed or static," but one to "be molded and extended to meet changing conditions and needs of the public it was created to benefit." *Avon*, 61 N.J. at 309, 294 A.2d 47.

Precisely what privately-owned upland sand area will be available and required to satisfy the public's rights under the public trust doctrine will depend on the circumstances. Location of the dry sand area in relation to the foreshore, extent and availability of publicly-owned upland sand area, nature and extent of the public demand, and usage of the upland sand land by the owner are all factors to be weighed and considered in fixing the contours of the usage of the upper sand.

Today, recognizing the increasing demand for our State's beaches and the dynamic nature of the public trust doctrine, we find that the public must be given both access to and use of privately-owned dry sand areas as reasonably necessary. While the public's rights in private beaches are not co-extensive with the rights enjoyed in municipal beaches, private landowners may not in all instances prevent the public from exercising its rights under the public trust doctrine. The public must be afforded reasonable access to the foreshore as well as a suitable area for recreation on the dry sand.

The Beaches of Bay Head

The Bay Head Improvement Association, which services the needs of all residents of the Borough for swimming and bathing in the public trust property, owns the street-wide strip of dry sand area at the foot of seven public streets that extends to the mean high water line. It also owns the fee in six other upland sand properties connected or adjacent to the tracts it owns at the end of two streets. In addition, it holds leases to approximately 42 tracts of upland sand area. The question that we must address is whether the dry sand area that the Association owns or leases should be open to the public to satisfy the public's rights under the public trust doctrine. Our analysis turns upon whether the Association may restrict its membership to Bay Head residents and thereby preclude public use of the dry sand area. . . .

The Association's activities paralleled those of a municipality in its operation of the beachfront. . . . When viewed in its totality—its purposes, relationship with the municipality, communal characteristic, activities, and virtual monopoly over the Bay Head beachfront—the quasi-public nature of the Association is apparent. The Association makes available to the Bay Head public access to the common tidal property for swimming and bathing and to the upland dry sand area for use incidental thereto, preserving the residents' interests in a fashion similar to *Avon*. . . .

Accordingly, membership in the Association must be open to the public at large. In this manner the public will be assured access to the common beach property during the hours of 10:00 A.M. to 5:30 P.M. between mid-June and September, where they may exercise their right to swim and bathe and to use the Association's dry sand area incidental to those activities. . . .

The Public Advocate has urged that all the privately-owned beachfront property likewise must be opened to the public. Nothing has been developed on this record to justify that conclusion. We have decided that the Association's membership and thereby its beach must be open to the public. That area might reasonably satisfy the public need at this time. We are aware that the Association possessed, as of the initiation of this litigation, about 42 upland sand lots under leases revocable on 30 days' notice. If any of these leases have been or are to be terminated, or if the Association were to sell all or part of its property, it may necessitate further adjudication of the public's claims in favor of the public trust on part or all of these or other privately-owned upland dry sand lands depending upon the circumstances. . . .

. . . It is not necessary for us to determine under what circumstances and to what extent there will be a need to use the dry sand of private owners who either now or in the future may have no leases with the Association. Resolution of the competing interests, private ownership and the public trust, may in some cases be simple, but in many it may be most complex. In any event, resolution would depend upon the specific facts in controversy. . . .

We realize that considerable uncertainty will continue to surround the question of the public's right to cross private land and to use a portion of the dry sand as discussed above. Where the parties are unable to agree as to the application of the principles enunciated herein, the claim of the private owner shall be honored until the contrary is established. . . .

The judgment of the Appellate Division is reversed in part and affirmed in part. Judgment is entered for the plaintiff against the Association. Judgment of dismissal against the individual property owners is affirmed without prejudice.

NOTES AND QUESTIONS

1. *Post*-Matthews *developments regarding beach access in New Jersey.* Subsequent to its decision in *Matthews,* the New Jersey Supreme Court expanded the *Matthews* doctrine. In Raleigh Avenue Beach Assn. v. Atlantis Beach Club, 879 A.2d 112 (N.J. 2005), the court held that the public's right to reasonable access to beaches extends to the dry-sand portion of beaches owned by strictly private entities as well as quasi-public entities such as the Bay Head Improvement Association. In *Raleigh Avenue,* the beach owner, Atlantis Beach Club, was strictly private, performing no city-like functions and having no symbiotic relationship with the municipality. The beach on the Atlantis property was the only beach in the township, and it was open to the public free of charge until 1996, when the beach club was established. The court stated that "*Matthews* established the framework for application of the public trust doctrine to private-owned upland sand beaches." 879 A.2d at 121. Is this a satisfactory explanation of the extension of *Matthews* to *Raleigh Avenue?* For an argument that such a right is justified on the basis of promoting human flourishing through improved public health and enhanced sociability, see Gregory S. Alexander, The Social-Obligation Norm in American Property Law, 94 Cornell L. Rev. 745, 801-810 (2009); see also Robert Thompson, Beach Access, Trespass, and the Social Enactment of Property, 17 Roger Williams U. L. Rev. 351 (2012).

For discussions of *Matthews* and *Raleigh Avenue,* see Timothy M. Mulvaney & Brian Weeks, "Waterlocked": Public Access to New Jersey's Coastline, 34 Ecology L.Q. 579 (2007); Marc R. Poirer, Modified Private Property: New Jersey's Public Trust Doctrine, Private Development and Exclusion, and Shared Public Uses of Natural Resources, 15 S.E. Envtl. L.J. 71 (2006). Subsequent to the *Raleigh Avenue* decision the New Jersey Department of Environmental Protection promulgated "Public Access Rules" implementing the decision. See N.J. Admin. Code tit. 7, §7:7E-8.11 (2012). The rules were significantly revised in 2012 to allow the state to work out separate arrangements for beach access with each waterfront community. See http://www.state.nj.us/dep/cmp/access.

2. *Origins of the public trust doctrine.* Though its roots lie in Roman law, the modern version of the public trust doctrine is conventionally traced to the 1892 U.S. Supreme Court decision in Illinois Central Railroad Co. v. Illinois, 146 U.S. 387 (1892). In that case, the Illinois legislature in 1886 granted to the railroad in fee simple submerged lands comprising virtually the entire Chicago lakefront. Four years later, regretting the grant, the legislature revoked it. The Supreme Court upheld the revocation, explaining that the legislature did not have the power to convey the entire city lakefront free of trust, thus barring all future legislatures from protecting the public interest. See Joseph D. Kearney & Thomas W. Merrill, The Origins of the Public Trust Doctrine: What Really Happened in *Illinois Central,* 71 U. Chi. L. Rev. 799 (2004). The seminal article that revived interest in the public trust doctrine is Joseph L. Sax, The Public Trust Doctrine in Natural Resource Law: Effective Judicial Intervention, 68 Mich. L. Rev. 471 (1970); see also Carol M. Rose, Joseph Sax and the Idea of the Public Trust, 25 Ecology L.Q. 351 (1998).

For discussions of how the public trust doctrine is applied in the various states, see Michael C. Blumm & Erika Doot, Oregon's Public Trust Doctrine: Public Rights in Waters, Wildlife, and Beaches, 42 Envtl. L. 375 (2012); Alexandra B. Klass, Modern Public Trust Principles: Recognizing Rights and Integrating Standards, 82 Notre Dame L. Rev. 699 (2006); Carol Necole Brown, Drinking from a Deep Well: The Public Trust Doctrine and Western Water Law, 34 Fla. St. U. L. Rev. 1 (2006); Jack H. Archer et al., The Public Trust Doctrine and the Management of America's Coasts (1994); Matthew Thor Kirsch, Note, Upholding the Public Trust in State Constitutions, 46 Duke L.J. 1169 (1997); see also Haochen Sun, Toward a New Social-Political Theory of the Public Trust Doctrine, 35 Vt. L. Rev. 563 (2011).

3. *Scope of the public trust.* The public trust doctrine extends to all land covered by the ebb and flow of the tide and, in addition, all inland lakes and rivers that are navigable. Phillips Petroleum Co. v. Mississippi, 484 U.S. 469 (1988). In Michigan, the public trust doctrine protects the public right of access to privately owned beaches along the Great Lakes. In Glass v. Goeckel, 703 N.W.2d 58 (Mich. 2005), the court held that public access along the shore is permitted between the current edge of the lake and the "ordinary high water mark." Any prior state grants of private property rights inconsistent with this public easement, the court said, are invalid. See Kenneth K. Kilbert, The Public Trust Doctrine and the Great Lakes Shores, 58 Clev. St. L. Rev. 1 (2010).

4. *Conflicting views on the public trust doctrine.* The public trust doctrine has been the topic of considerable controversy among both scholars and public policy activists. Property rights advocates have attacked it as a threat to private property, inconsistent with the rule of law, and inefficient. See, e.g., Jedidiah Brewer & Gary D. Libecap, Property Rights and the Public Trust Doctrine in Environmental Protection and Natural Resource Conservation, 53 Austl. J. Agric. & Resource Econ. 1 (2009); James L. Huffman, Background Principles and the Rule of Law, 35 Ecology L.Q. 1 (2008); Randy T. Simmons, Property and the Public Trust Doctrine, in 39 Prop. & Envtl. Res. Center Poly. Series 1 (2007). Proponents have argued that it functions as a background principle that permits property law to accommodate changing conditions and that it serves a socializing function by bringing people into dealings with others. See, e.g., Michael C. Blumm, The Public Trust Doctrine and Private Property: The Accommodation Principle, 27 Pace Envtl. L. Rev. 649 (2010); Carol M. Rose, The Comedy of the Commons: Customs, Commerce, and Inherently Public Property, 53 U. Chi. L. Rev. 711, 781 (1986).

5. *Legislative repudiation of the public trust doctrine.* Is the public trust doctrine subject to legislative revision or even repudiation? At least one state has enacted a statute making the doctrine inapplicable to water rights and to state public land decision making. See Idaho Code §58-1201 (2012). Whether the state's legislature has this power depends on the legal source of the public trust doctrine—federal versus state law, constitutional versus common law—and on whether the doctrine is a rule of construction or a fixed qualification on legal title. In Illinois, the doctrine is considered a fixed qualification on title and, hence, is not subject to legislative change. See Lake Michigan Federation v. U.S. Army Corp of Engineers, 742

F. Supp. 441 (N.D. Ill. 1990). For an examination of these issues and an assessment of one state's legislative partial repudiation of the public trust doctrine,
see Michael C. Blumm, Harrison C. Dunning & Scott W. Reed, Renouncing the
Public Trust Doctrine: An Assessment of the Validity of Idaho House Bill 794, 24
Ecology L.Q. 461 (1997).

6. *A right to roam?* Should a public right to roam over privately owned wilderness
land be recognized? Such a right now exists in Scotland as a result of Land Reform
(Scotland) Act 2003. Under the act, "any person" is entitled to walk on any land
in Scotland, including privately owned land, except for certain narrowly defined
categories, such as a building or other structure, the "curtilage" (i.e., fenced-in
grounds immediately surrounding a building) of a building that is not a house,
and school grounds. See John A. Lovett, Progressive Property in Action: The Land
Reform (Scotland) Act 2003, 89 Neb. L. Rev. 739 (2011). A more qualified right
exists in England and Wales under the Countryside and Rights of Way Act 2000,
ch. 37 (Eng.). The statute classifies private land that contains mountains, moors,
heaths, or downland as "open country" and requires owners of such land to permit
members of the public to roam freely across it. This statutory right to roam is subject to several qualifications. Access is permitted only by foot, and there are extensive requirements of reasonable behavior. The right does not include commercial
activity or camping, swimming in non-tidal areas, fishing, hunting, or other activities that threaten wildlife. The right does not apply to cultivated areas, land covered
by buildings, land used as parks or gardens, or golf courses. The stated purposes of
creating the right were to "'improv[e] public health and reduc[e] social divisions'"
and to establish a degree of "'social equity.'" Kevin Gray & Susan Gray, Elements
of Land Law 1372 (5th ed. 2009) (quoting Access to the Open Countryside in
England and Wales: A Consultation Paper). See Heidi Gorovitz Robertson, Public
Access to Private Land for Walking: Environmental and Individual Responsibility as
Rationale for Limiting the Right to Exclude, 23 Geo. Intl. Envtl. L. Rev. 211 (2011);
Jerry L. Anderson, Britain's Right to Roam: Redefining the Landowner's Bundle of
Sticks, 19 Geo. Intl. Envtl. L. Rev. 375 (2007).

In this country, Professor Eric Freyfogle has argued that for much of America's
history the full right to exclude was the exception for private open land rather
than the norm. In many parts of the country, the public had a legal right to roam
on privately owned countryside so long as it did not invade fenced-in areas or
interfere with owners' uses. This public right declined as a pro-development ethic
developed in the latter half of the nineteenth century, Freyfogle contends. See
Eric T. Freyfogle, On Private Property 29-60 (2007).

3.   Assignability of Easements

The benefits and burdens of appurtenant easements pass automatically to assignees of the land to which they are appurtenant, if the parties so intend and the burdened party has notice of the easement. Where the benefit is in gross, however,
the benefit may not be assignable.

Miller v. Lutheran Conference & Camp Association

Supreme Court of Pennsylvania, 1938
200 A. 646

STERN, J. This litigation is concerned with interesting and somewhat novel legal questions regarding rights of boating, bathing and fishing in an artificial lake.

Frank C. Miller, his brother Rufus W. Miller, and others, who owned lands on Tunkhannock Creek in Tobyhanna Township, Monroe County, organized a corporation known as the Pocono Spring Water Ice Company, to which, in September, 1895, they made a lease for a term of ninety-nine years of so much of their lands as would be covered by the backing up of the water as a result of the construction of a 14-foot dam which they proposed to erect across the creek. The company was to have "the exclusive use of the water and its privileges." It was chartered for the purpose of "erecting a dam . . . , for pleasure, boating, skating, fishing and the cutting, storing and selling of ice." The dam was built, forming "Lake Naomi," somewhat more than a mile long and about one-third of a mile wide.

By deed dated March 20, 1899, the Pocono Spring Water Ice Company granted to "Frank C. Miller, his heirs and assigns forever, the exclusive right to fish and boat in all the waters of the said corporation at Naomi Pines, Pa." On February 17, 1900, Frank C. Miller (his wife Katherine D. Miller not joining) granted to Rufus W. Miller, his heirs and assigns forever, "all the one-fourth interest in and to the fishing, boating, and bathing rights and privileges at, in, upon and about Lake Naomi . . . ; which said rights and privileges were granted and conveyed to me by the Pocono Spring Water Ice Company by their indenture of the 20th day of March, A.D. 1899." On the same day, Frank C. Miller and Rufus W. Miller executed an agreement of business partnership, the purpose of which was the erection and operation of boat and bath houses on Naomi Lake and the purchase and maintenance of boats for use on the lake, the houses and boats to be rented for hire and the net proceeds to be divided between the parties in proportion to their respective interests in the bathing, boating and fishing privileges, namely, three-fourths to Frank C. Miller and one-fourth to Rufus W. Miller, the capital to be contributed and the losses to be borne in the same proportion. In pursuance of this agreement the brothers erected and maintained boats and bath houses at different points on the lake, purchased and rented out boats, and conducted the business generally, from the spring of 1900 until the death of Rufus W. Miller on October 11, 1925, exercising their control and use of the privileges in an exclusive, uninterrupted and open manner and without challenge on the part of anyone.[20]

___

20. In the early 1900s, Rufus Miller, a prominent Philadelphia minister in the Reformed Church, established Pocono Pines Assembly on the shore of Lake Naomi (named for Ruth's mother-in-law in the Bible). The Assembly was a religious camp providing vacations each summer for members of the Reformed Church and other like-minded Protestants in eastern Pennsylvania. The Assembly vacationers used the lake for many years with the permission of the Miller brothers. After Rufus died in 1925, the Assembly, in financial distress, sold its lakefront property to the Lutheran Conference and Camp Association, which renamed the property Lutherland and planned to bring to the lake each summer between 1,300 and 2,000 Lutherans from New York,

Discord began with the death of Rufus W. Miller, which terminated the partnership. Thereafter Frank C. Miller, and the executors and heirs of Rufus W. Miller, went their respective ways, each granting licenses without reference to the other. Under date of July 13, 1929, the executors of the Rufus W. Miller estate granted a license for the year 1929 to defendant, Lutheran Conference and Camp Association, which was the owner of a tract of ground abutting on the lake for a distance of about 100 feet, purporting to grant to defendant, its members, guests and campers, permission to boat, bathe and fish in the lake, a certain percentage of the receipts therefrom to be paid to the estate. Thereupon Frank C. Miller and his wife Katherine D. Miller, filed the present bill in equity, complaining that defendant was placing diving floats on the lake and "encouraging and instigating visitors and boarders" to bathe in the lake, and was threatening to hire out boats and canoes and in general to license its guests and others to boat, bathe and fish in the lake. The bill prayed for an injunction to prevent defendant from trespassing on the lands covered by the waters of the lake, from erecting or maintaining any structures or other encroachments thereon, and from granting any bathing licenses. The court issued the injunction.

It is the contention of plaintiffs that, while the privileges of boating and fishing were granted in the deed from the Pocono Spring Water Ice Company to Frank C. Miller, no *bathing* rights were conveyed by that instrument. In 1903 all the property of the company was sold by the sheriff under a writ of fieri facias on the mortgage bond which the company had executed in 1898. As a result of that sale the Pocono Spring Water Ice Company was entirely extinguished, and the title to its rights and property came into the ownership of the Pocono Pines Ice Company, a corporation chartered for "the supply of ice to the public." In 1928 the title to the property of the Pocono Pines Ice Company became vested in Katherine D. Miller. Plaintiffs therefore maintain that the bathing rights, never having passed to Frank C. Miller, descended in ownership from the Pocono Spring Water Ice Company through the Pocono Pines Ice Company to plaintiff Katherine D. Miller, and that Frank C. Miller could not, and did not, give Rufus W. Miller any title to them. They further contend that even if such bathing rights ever did vest in Frank C. Miller, all of the boating, bathing and fishing privileges were easements in gross which were inalienable and indivisible, and when Frank C. Miller undertook to convey a one-fourth interest in them to Rufus W. Miller he not only failed to transfer a legal title to the rights but, in attempting to do so, extinguished the rights altogether as against Katherine D. Miller, who was the successor in title of the Pocono Spring Water Ice Company. It is defendant's contention, on the other hand, that the deed of 1899 from the Pocono Spring Water Ice Company to Frank C. Miller should be construed as transferring the bathing

---

New Jersey, and Pennsylvania. Frank and Katherine objected to the use of the lake by the Lutherans. The sale had been arranged by Rufus's children to carry on his religious work, and the lawsuit resulted in an irreparable split in the Miller families. See Emma Miller Waygood, Changing Times in the Poconos (1972) (memoir of the Assembly, Lutherland, and the Rufus Miller family by his daughter); Irene Miller Gross, Naomi, A Family Affair (1972) (memoir by Frank's daughter, not mentioning Rufus's family). — Eds.

Lake Naomi, 1918

as well as the boating and fishing privileges, but that if Frank C. Miller did not obtain them by grant he and Rufus W. Miller acquired them by prescription, and that all of these rights were alienable and divisible. . . .

Coming to the merits of the controversy, it is initially to be observed that no boating, bathing or fishing rights can be, or are, claimed by defendant as a riparian owner. Ordinarily, title to land bordering on a navigable stream extends to low water mark subject to the rights of the public to navigation and fishery between high and low water, and in the case of land abutting on creeks and non-navigable rivers to the middle of the stream, but in the case of a non-navigable lake or pond where the land under the water is owned by others, no riparian rights attach to the property bordering on the water, and an attempt to exercise any such rights by invading the water is as much a trespass as if an unauthorized entry were made up the dry land of another: Baylor v. Decker, 133 Pa. 168; Smoulter v. Boyd, 209 Pa. 146, 152; Gibbs v. Sweet, 20 Pa. Superior Ct. 275, 283; Fuller v. Cole, 33 Pa. Superior Ct. 563; Cryer v. Sawkill Pines Camp, Inc., 88 Pa. Superior Ct. 71.

It is impossible to construe the deed of 1899 from the Pocono Spring Water Ice Company to Frank C. Miller as conveying to the latter any privileges of bathing. It is clear and unambiguous. It gives to Frank C. Miller the exclusive right to *fish and boat. Expressio unius est exclusio alterius.* No *bathing* rights are mentioned. This omission may have been the result of oversight or it may have been deliberate, but in either event the legal consequence is the same. . . .

But, while Frank C. Miller acquired by grant merely boating and fishing privileges, the facts are amply sufficient to establish title to the bathing rights by prescription. True, these rights, not having been granted in connection with, or to be attached to, the ownership of any land, were not easements appurtenant but in gross. There is, however, no inexorable principle of law which forbids an adverse enjoyment of an easement in gross from ripening into a title thereto by prescription. In Tinicum Fishing Co. v. Carter, 61 Pa. 21, it was questioned whether a fishing right could be created by prescription, although there is an intimation (p. 40) that some easements in gross might so arise if there be evidence sufficient to establish them. Certainly the casual use of a lake during a few months each year for boating and fishing could not develop into a title to such privileges by prescription. But here the exercise of the bathing right was not carried on sporadically by Frank C. Miller and his assignee Rufus W. Miller for their personal enjoyment but systematically for commercial purposes in the pursuit of which they conducted an extensive and profitable business enterprise. The circumstances thus presented must be viewed from a realistic standpoint. Naomi Lake is situated in the Pocono Mountains district, has become a summer resort for campers and boarders, and, except for the ice it furnishes, its bathing and boating facilities are the factors which give it its prime importance and value. They were exploited from the time the lake was created, and are recited as among the purposes for which the Pocono Spring Water Ice Company was chartered. From the early part of 1900 down to at least the filing of the present bill in 1929, Frank C. Miller and Rufus W. Miller openly carried on their business of constructing and operating bath houses and licensing individuals and camp associations to use the lake for bathing. This was known to the stockholders of the Pocono Spring Water Ice Company and necessarily also to Katherine D. Miller, the wife of Frank C. Miller; no objection of any kind was made, and Frank C. Miller and Rufus W. Miller were encouraged to expend large sums of money in pursuance of the right of which they considered and asserted themselves to be the owners. Under such circumstances it would be highly unjust to hold that a title by prescription to the bathing rights did not vest in Frank C. Miller and Rufus W. Miller which is just as valid, as far as Katherine D. Miller is concerned, as that to the boating and fishing rights which Frank C. Miller obtained by express grant.

We are thus brought to a consideration of the next question, which is whether the boating, bathing and fishing privileges were assignable by Frank C. Miller to Rufus W. Miller. What is the nature of such rights? In England it has been said that easements in gross do not exist at all, although rights of that kind have been there recognized.[21] In this country such privileges have sometimes been spoken of as licenses, or as contractual in their nature, rather than as easements in gross. These are differences of terminology rather than of substance. We may assume, therefore, that these privileges are easements in gross, and we see no reason to consider them otherwise. It has uniformly been held that a profit in gross—for example, a right of mining or fishing—may be made assignable: Funk v. Haldeman, 53 Pa. 229; Tinicum Fishing Co. v. Carter, 61 Pa. 21, 39; see cases cited 19 C.J. 870, note 25. In regard to easements in gross generally, there has been much controversy in the courts and by textbook writers and law students as to whether they have the attribute of assignability. There are dicta in Pennsylvania that they are nonassignable: Tinicum Fishing Co. v. Carter, supra, 38, 39; Lindenmuth v. Safe Harbor

---

21. See Michael F. Sturley, Easements in Gross, 96 L.Q. Rev. 557 (1980). Profits in gross, on the other hand, can exist in England.—EDS.

Water Power Corporation, 309 Pa. 58, 63, 64; Commonwealth v. Zimmerman, 56 Pa. Superior Ct. 311, 315, 316. But there is forcible expression and even definite authority to the contrary: Tide Water Pipe Co. v. Bell, 280 Pa. 104, 112, 113; Dalton Street Railway Co. v. Scranton, 326 Pa. 6, 12. Learned articles upon the subject are to be found in 32 Yale Law Journal 813; 38 Yale Law Journal 139; 22 Michigan Law Review 521; 40 Dickinson Law Review 46. There does not seem to be any reason why the law should prohibit the assignment of an easement in gross if the parties to its creation evidence their intention to make it assignable. Here, as in Tide Water Pipe Company v. Bell, supra, the rights of fishing and boating were conveyed to the grantee—in this case Frank C. Miller—"his heirs and assigns," thus showing that the grantor, the Pocono Spring Water Ice Company, intended to attach the attribute of assignability to the privileges granted. Moreover, as a practical matter, there is an obvious difference in this respect between easements for personal enjoyment and those designed for commercial exploitation; while there may be little justification for permitting assignments in the former case, there is every reason for upholding them in the latter.

The question of assignability of the easements in gross in the present case is not as important as that of their divisibility. It is argued by plaintiffs that even if held to be assignable such easements are not divisible, because this might involve an excessive user or "surcharge of the easement" subjecting the servient tenement to a greater burden than originally contemplated. The law does not take that extreme position. It does require, however, that, if there be a division, the easements must be used or exercised as an entirety. This rule had its earliest expression in Mountjoy's Case, which is reported in Co. Litt. 164b, 165a. It was there said, in regard to the grant of a right to dig for ore, that the grantee, Lord Mountjoy, "must assign his whole interest to one, two, or more; but then, if there be two or more, they could make no division of it, but work together with one stock." In Caldwell v. Fulton, 31 Pa. 475, 477, 478, and in Funk v. Haldeman, 53 Pa. 229, that case was followed, and it was held that the right of a grantee to mine coal or to prospect for oil might be assigned, but if to more than one they must hold, enjoy and convey the right as an entirety, and not divide it in severalty. There are cases in other jurisdictions which also approve the doctrine of Mountjoy's Case, and hold that a mining right in gross is essentially integral and not susceptible of apportionment; an assignment of it is valid, but it cannot be aliened in such a way that it may be utilized by grantor and grantee, or by several grantees, separately; there must be a joint user, nor can one of the tenants alone convey a share in the common right: Grubb v. Baird, Federal Case No. 5849 (Circuit Court, Eastern District of Pennsylvania); Harlow v. Lake Superior Iron Co., 36 Mich. 105, 121; Stanton v. T. L. Herbert & Sons, 141 Tenn. 440, 211 S.W. 353.

These authorities furnish an illuminating guide to the solution of the problem of divisibility of profits or easements in gross. They indicate that much depends upon the nature of the right and the terms of its creation, that "surcharge of the easement" is prevented if assignees exercise the right as "one stock," and that a proper method of enjoyment of the easement by two or more owners of it may usually be worked out in any given instance without insuperable difficulty.

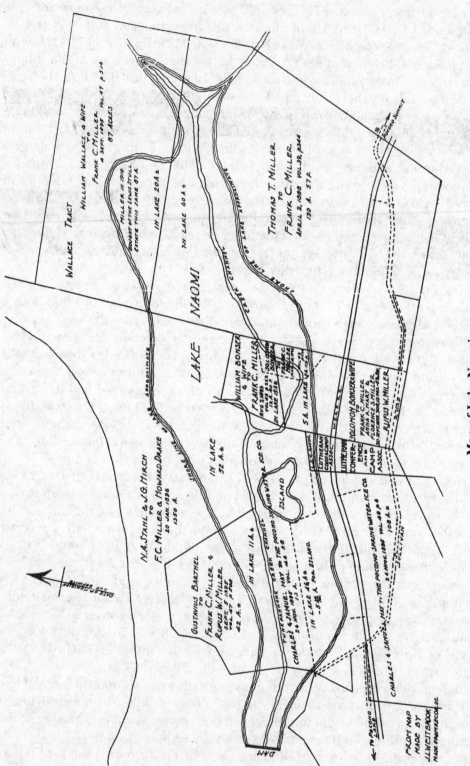

Map of Lake Naomi

In the present case it seems reasonably clear that in the conveyance of February 17, 1900, it was not the intention of Frank C. Miller to grant, and of Rufus W. Miller to receive, a separate right to subdivide and sublicense the boating, fishing and bathing privileges on and in Lake Naomi, but only that they should together use such rights for commercial purposes, Rufus W. Miller to be entitled to one-fourth and Frank C. Miller to three-fourths of the proceeds resulting from their combined exploitation of the privileges. They were to hold the rights, in the quaint phraseology of Mountjoy's Case, as "one stock." Nor do the technical rules that would be applicable to a tenancy in common of a corporeal hereditament apply to the control of these easements in gross. Defendant contends that, as a tenant in common of the privileges, Rufus W. Miller individually was entitled to their use, benefit and possession and to exercise rights of ownership in regard thereto, including the right to license third persons to use them, subject only to the limitation that he must not thereby interfere with the similar rights of his co-tenant. But the very nature of these easements prevents their being so exercised, inasmuch as it is necessary, because of the legal limitations upon their divisibility, that they should be utilized in common, and not by two owners severally, and, as stated, this was evidently the intention of the brothers.

Summarizing our conclusions, we are of opinion (1) that Frank C. Miller acquired title to the boating and fishing privileges by grant and he and Rufus W. Miller to the bathing rights by prescription; (2) that he made a valid assignment of a one-fourth interest in them to Rufus W. Miller; but (3) that they cannot be commercially used and licenses thereunder granted without the common consent and joinder of the present owners, who with regard to them must act as "one stock." It follows that the executors of the estate of Rufus W. Miller did not have the right, in and by themselves, to grant a license to defendant.

The decree is affirmed; costs to be paid by defendant.

NOTES, QUESTIONS, AND PROBLEM

1. *Transferability of easements in gross.* Where an easement is appurtenant, the burden on the servient tenement is limited by the needs of the dominant tenement. An easement in gross has no such limitation; therefore, American courts have attempted to prevent the burden on the servient tenement from increasing beyond what was intended by the original parties.

Some early cases held that an easement in gross was not transferable. Such a rule proved inconvenient when railroad or utility companies, holding easements in gross, attempted to transfer them. So the law changed. The first Restatement of Property §489 (1944) provided that an easement in gross can be assigned if of a commercial character (used primarily for economic benefit rather than personal satisfaction). Restatement (Third) of Property, Servitudes §§4.6(1)(c), 5.8 (2000), provides that all easements in gross are assignable regardless of their commercial character. Most modern cases permit any easement in gross to be assignable if the parties so intended. See O'Donovan v. McIntosh, 728 A.2d 681 (Me. 1999).

About the only easements in gross that are not assignable under modern cases are recreational easements (easements for hunting, fishing, boating, and camping). Restricting their assignability appears to rest on the courts' conclusion that they are intended to be personal and on the fear of burdening the servient land beyond the original contemplation of the parties. See Alan David Hegi, Note, The Easement in Gross Revisited: Transferability and Divisibility Since 1945, 39 Vand. L. Rev. 109 (1986).

Once courts decided that the benefit of an easement in gross is assignable, the question became whether the benefit holder could divide the benefit with another person. The general view is that an easement in gross is divisible when the creating instrument so indicates or when the easement is exclusive. The term "exclusive" in this context means that the easement owner has the sole right to engage in the activity that the easement permits.

2. *Divisibility of easements in gross.* In *Miller*, the question was how to deal with the concern that division of the easement might create an excessive burden on the servient estate. Rather than declaring the easement nonassignable and nondivisible, the court applied the "one stock" rule of the law of profits. This means Frank and Rufus's executor must use the lake as one person; either one can veto the other's use. Is it sound to apply this rule to easements?

Courts today have largely abandoned this approach. Restatement (Third) of Property, supra, §5.9, provides that easements in gross may be divided unless contrary to the intent of the parties creating the easement or unless the division unreasonably increases the burden on the servient estate. Accord Orange County v. Citgo Pipeline Co., 934 S.W.2d 472 (Tex. Civ. App. 1996). On this view, the benefit of an easement in gross may be divided and utilized independently by its holders, assuming that this is not contrary to the intent of the original parties and that division would not place an unreasonable burden on the servient estate. However, the Restatement points out that division of benefits in gross are more likely than subdivision of appurtenant benefits to run counter to the servient owner's expectations because division permits independent use of the easement in gross by each of the transferees. Restatement (Third) of Property, supra, §5.9 comment b. Under the Restatement's approach, the exclusivity or non-exclusivity of the easement is still relevant. "Division of an exclusive easement is less likely to be contrary to the intent of the parties than division of a non-exclusive easement." Id.

3. *Lake Naomi today.* Professor Barlow Burke of American University visited Lake Naomi in 1994 and reports that the rights to boat, bathe, and fish in Lake Naomi are now held by the Lake Naomi Club, a private club with 1,400 members that maintains the beaches and the dam. The Lutheran Conference & Camp Association became insolvent, and its land was sold to developers who have erected houses for the well-to-do, with tennis courts and swimming pools and beaches. Indeed, the whole area has been developed with housing, sometimes second homes for (mostly) Philadelphians.

4. *A*, owner of Blackacre, conveys an easement over Blackacre to *B* for the benefit of Whiteacre, which *B* once owned but sold to *C* several months earlier.

B then conveys the easement to *C*. Who, if anyone, has an easement across Blackacre? See Yaali, Ltd. v. Barnes & Noble, Inc., 506 S.E.2d 116 (Ga. 1998). How, if at all, does this case differ from Willard v. First Church of Christ, Scientist, which we saw on pages 814-818? Is the result sensible?

4. Scope of Easements

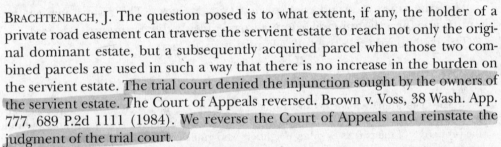

Brown v. Voss

Supreme Court of Washington, 1986
715 P.2d 514

BRACHTENBACH, J. The question posed is to what extent, if any, the holder of a private road easement can traverse the servient estate to reach not only the original dominant estate, but a subsequently acquired parcel when those two combined parcels are used in such a way that there is no increase in the burden on the servient estate. The trial court denied the injunction sought by the owners of the servient estate. The Court of Appeals reversed. Brown v. Voss, 38 Wash. App. 777, 689 P.2d 1111 (1984). We reverse the Court of Appeals and reinstate the judgment of the trial court.

[Figure 10-5] depicts the involved parcels.

In 1952 the predecessors in title of parcel A granted to the predecessor owners of parcel B a private road easement across parcel A for "ingress to and egress from" parcel B. Defendants acquired parcel A in 1973. Plaintiffs bought parcel B on April 1, 1977 and parcel C on July 31, 1977, but from two different owners. Apparently the previous owners of parcel C were not parties to the easement grant.

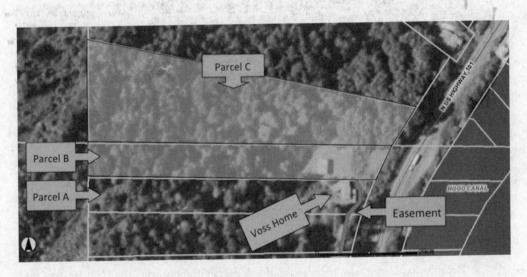

Figure 10-5

When plaintiffs acquired parcel B a single family dwelling was situated thereon. They intended to remove that residence and replace it with a single family dwelling which would straddle the boundary line common to parcels B and C.

Plaintiffs began clearing both parcels B and C and moving fill materials in November 1977. Defendants first sought to bar plaintiffs' use of the easement in April 1979 by which time plaintiffs had spent more than $11,000 in developing their property for building.

Defendants placed logs, a concrete sump and a chain link fence within the easement. Plaintiffs sued for removal of the obstructions, an injunction against defendants' interference with their use of the easement and damages. Defendants counterclaimed for damages and an injunction against plaintiffs using the easement other than for parcel B.

The trial court awarded each party $1 in damages. The award against the plaintiffs was for a slight inadvertent trespass outside the easement.

The trial court made the following findings of fact:

VI

The plaintiffs have made no unreasonable use of the easement in the development of their property. There have been no complaints of unreasonable use of the roadway to the south of the properties of the parties by other neighbors who grant[ed] easements to the parties to this action to cross their properties to gain access to the property of the plaintiffs. Other than the trespass there is no evidence of any damage to the defendants as a result of the use of the easement by the plaintiffs. There has been no increase in volume of travel on the easement to reach a single family dwelling whether built on tract B or on tracts B and C. There is no evidence of any increase in the burden on the subservient estate from the use of the easement by the plaintiffs for access to parcel C.

VIII

If an injunction were granted to bar plaintiffs' access to tract C across the easement to a single family residence, Parcel C would become landlocked; plaintiffs would not be able to make use of their property; they would not be able to build their single family residence in a manner to properly enjoy the view of the Hood Canal and the surrounding area as originally anticipated at the time of their purchase and even if the single family residence were constructed on parcel B, if the injunction were granted, plaintiffs would not be able to use the balance of their property in parcel C as a yard or for any other use of their property in conjunction with their home. Conversely, there is and will be no appreciable hardship or damage to the defendants if the injunction is denied.

IX

If an injunction were to be granted to bar the plaintiffs' access to tract C, the framing and enforcing of such an order would be impractical. Any violation of the order would result in the parties back in court at great cost but with little or no damages being involved.

X

Plaintiffs have acted reasonably in the development of their property. Their trespass over a "little" corner of the defendants' property was inadvertent, and de minimis. The fact that the defendants' counter claim seeking an injunction to bar plaintiffs' access to parcel C was filed as leverage against the original plaintiffs' claim for an interruption of their easement rights, may be considered in determining whether equitable relief by way of an injunction should be granted.

Relying upon these findings of fact, the court denied defendants' request for an injunction and granted the plaintiffs the right to use the easement for access to parcels B & C "as long as plaintiffs' properties (B and C) are developed and used solely for the purpose of a single family residence." Clerk's Papers, at 10.

The Court of Appeals reversed, holding [that an injunction must issue]. . . .

The easement in this case was created by express grant. Accordingly, the extent of the right acquired is to be determined from the terms of the grant properly construed to give effect to the intention of the parties. See Zobrist v. Culp, 95 Wash. 2d 556, 561, 627 P.2d 1308 (1981); Seattle v. Nazarenus, 60 Wash. 2d 657, 665, 374 P.2d 1014 (1962). By the express terms of the 1952 grant, the predecessor owners of parcel B acquired a private road easement across parcel A and the right to use the easement for ingress to and egress from parcel B. Both plaintiffs and defendants agree that the 1952 grant created an easement appurtenant to parcel B as the dominant estate. Thus, plaintiffs, as owners of the dominant estate, acquired rights in the use of the easement for ingress to and egress from parcel B.

However, plaintiffs have no such easement rights in connection with their ownership of parcel C, which was not a part of the original dominant estate under the terms of the 1952 grant. As a general rule, an easement appurtenant to one parcel of land may not be extended by the owner of the dominant estate to other parcels owned by him, whether adjoining or distinct tracts, to which the easement is not appurtenant. E.g., Heritage Standard Bank & Trust Co. v. Trustees of Schs., 84 Ill. App. 3d 653, 40 Ill. Dec. 104, 405 N.E.2d 1196 (1980); Kanefsky v. Dratch Constr. Co., 376 Pa. 188, 101 A.2d 923 (1954); S.S. Kresge Co. of Mich. v. Winkleman Realty Co., 260 Wis. 372, 50 N.W.2d 920 (1952); 28 C.J.S. Easements §92, at 772-73 (1941).

Plaintiffs, nonetheless, contend that extension of the use of the easement for the benefit of nondominant property does not constitute a misuse of the easement, where as here, there is no evidence of an increase in the burden on the servient estate. We do not agree. If an easement is appurtenant to a particular parcel of land, any extension thereof to other parcels is a misuse of the easement. Wetmore v. Ladies of Loretto, Wheaton, 73 Ill. App. 2d 454, 220 N.E.2d 491 (1966); see also, e.g., Robertson v. Robertson, 214 Va. 76, 197 S.E.2d 183 (1973); Penn Bowling Rec. Ctr., Inc. v. Hot Shoppes, Inc., 179 F.2d 64 (D.C. Cir. 1949). As noted by one court in a factually similar case, "[I]n this context this classic rule of property law is directed to the rights of the respective parties rather than the actual burden on the servitude." National Lead Co. v. Kanawha Block Co., 228 F. Supp. 357, 364 (S.D. W. Va. 1968), aff'd, 409 F.2d 1309 (4th Cir. 1969). Under the express language of the 1952 grant, plaintiffs only have rights in the use of the easement for the benefit of parcel B. Although, as plaintiffs contend, their planned use of the easement to gain access to a single family residence located partially on parcel B and partially on parcel C is perhaps no more than technical misuse of the easement, we conclude that it is misuse nonetheless.

However, it does not follow from this conclusion alone that defendants are entitled to injunctive relief. Since the awards of $1 in damages were not appealed, only the denial of an injunction to defendants is in issue. Some fundamental principles applicable to a request for an injunction must be considered. (1) The proceeding is equitable and addressed to the sound discretion of the trial court. (2) The trial court is vested with a broad discretionary power to shape and fashion injunctive relief to fit the *particular facts, circumstances, and equities of the case before it.* Appellate courts give great weight to the trial court's exercise of that discretion. (3) One of the essential criteria for injunctive relief is actual and substantial injury sustained by the person seeking the injunction.

The trial court found as facts, upon substantial evidence, that plaintiffs have acted reasonably in the development of their property, that there is and was no damage to the defendants from plaintiffs' use of the easement, that there was no increase in the volume of travel on the easement, that there was no increase in the burden on the servient estate, that defendants sat by for more than a year while plaintiffs expended more than $11,000 on their project, and that defendants' counterclaim was an effort to gain "leverage" against plaintiffs' claim. In addition, the court found from the evidence that plaintiffs would suffer considerable hardship if the injunction were granted whereas no appreciable hardship or damages would flow to defendants from its denial. Finally, the court limited plaintiffs' use of the combined parcels solely to the same purpose for which the original parcel was used—i.e., for a single family residence.

Neither this court nor the Court of Appeals may substitute its effort to make findings of fact for those supported findings of the trial court. . . . Therefore, the only valid issue is whether, under these established facts, as a matter of law, the trial court abused its discretion in denying defendants' request for injunctive relief. Based upon the equities of the case, as found by the trial court, we are persuaded that the trial court acted within its discretion. The Court of Appeals is reversed and the trial court is affirmed.

DORE, J. (dissenting). The majority correctly finds that an extension of this easement to nondominant property is a misuse of the easement. The majority, nonetheless, holds that the owners of the servient estate are not entitled to injunctive relief. I dissent.

The comments and illustrations found in the Restatement of Property §478 (1944) address the precise issue before this court. Comment e provides in pertinent part that "if one who has an easement of way over Whiteacre appurtenant to Blackacre uses the way with the purpose of going to Greenacre, the use is improper even though he eventually goes to Blackacre rather than to Greenacre." Illustration 6 provides:

> 6. By prescription, *A* has acquired, as the owner and possessor of Blackacre, an easement of way over an alley leading from Blackacre to the street. He buys Whiteacre, an adjacent lot,

to which the way is not appurtenant, and builds a public garage one-fourth of which is located on Blackacre and three-fourths of which is located on Whiteacre. *A* wishes to use the alley as a means of ingress and egress to and from the garage. He has no privilege to use the alley to go to that part of the garage which is built on Whiteacre, and he may not use the alley until that part of the garage built on Blackacre is so separated from the part built on Whiteacre that uses for the benefit of Blackacre are distinguishable from those which benefit Whiteacre.

The majority grants the privilege to extend the agreement to nondominant property on the basis that the trial court found no appreciable hardship or damage to the servient owners. However, as conceded by the majority, any extension of the use of an easement to benefit a nondominant estate constitutes a misuse of the easement. Misuse of an easement is a trespass. Raven Red Ash Coal Co. v. Ball, 184 Va. 534, 39 S.E.2d 231 (1946); Selvia v. Reitmeyer, 156 Ind. App. 203, 295 N.E.2d 869 (1973). The Browns' use of the easement to benefit parcel C, especially if they build their home as planned, would involve a continuing trespass for which damages would be difficult to measure. Injunctive relief is the appropriate remedy under these circumstances. *Selvia*, at 212, 295 N.E.2d 869; Gregory v. Sanders, 635 P.2d 795, 801 (Wyo. 1981). In Penn Bowling Rec. Ctr., Inc. v. Hot Shoppes, Inc., 179 F.2d 64, 66 (D.C. Cir. 1949) the court states:

> It is contended by appellant that since the area of the dominant and nondominant land served by the easement is less than the original area of the dominant tenement, the use made by appellant of the right of way to serve the building located on the lesser area is not materially increased or excessive. It is true that where the nature and extent of the use of an easement is, by its terms, unrestricted, the use of the dominant tenement may be increased or enlarged. . . . But the owner of the dominant tenement may not subject the servient tenement to use or servitude in connection with other premises to which the easement is not appurtenant. See Williams v. James, Eng. Law. Rep. (1867), 2 C.P. 577. And when an easement is being used in such a manner, an injunction will be issued to prevent such use. Cleve et al. v. Nairin, 204 Ky. 342, 264 S.W. 741 [(1924)]; Diocese of Trenton v. Toman et al., 74 N.J. Eq. 702, 70 A. 606 [(1908)]; Shock v. Holt Lumber Co. et al., 107 W. Va. 259, 148 S.E. 73 [(1929)]. Appellant, therefore, may not use the easement to serve both the dominant and nondominant property, even though the area thereof is less than the original area of the dominant tenement.

See also Kanefsky v. Dratch Constr. Co., 376 Pa. 188, 101 A.2d 923 (1954). Thus, the fact that an extension of the easement to nondominant property would not increase the burden on the servient estate does not warrant a denial of injunctive relief.

The Browns are responsible for the hardship of creating a landlocked parcel. They knew or should have known from the public records that the easement was not appurtenant to parcel C. See Seattle v. Nazarenus, 60 Wash. 2d 657, 670, 374 P.2d 1014 (1962). In encroachment cases this factor is significant. As stated by the court in Bach v. Sarich, 74 Wash. 2d 575, 582, 445 P.2d 648 (1968): "The benefit of the doctrine of balancing the equities, or relative hardship, is reserved for the innocent defendant who proceeds without knowledge or warning that his structure encroaches upon another's property or property rights."

In addition, an injunction would not interfere with the Browns' right to use the easement as expressly granted, i.e., for access to parcel B. An injunction would merely require the Browns to acquire access to parcel C if they want to build a home that straddles parcels B and C. One possibility would be to condemn a private way of necessity over their existing easement in an action under RCW 8.24.010. See Brown v. McAnally, 97 Wash. 2d 360, 644 P.2d 1153 (1982).

I would affirm the Court of Appeals decision as a correct application of the law of easements. If the Browns desire access to their landlocked parcel they have the benefit of the statutory procedure for condemnation of a private way of necessity.

NOTES, QUESTIONS, AND PROBLEMS

1. *Digging into* Brown v. Voss. This Note is based on Professor Elizabeth Samuels's illuminating exploration of the litigation in Brown v. Voss in Stories Out of School: Teaching the Case of *Brown v. Voss*, 16 Cardozo L. Rev. 1445 (1995). The whole article is well worth reading. Professor Samuels analyzes, among other things, the strategies of the lawyers and how well the lawyers' narratives in court matched their clients' stories as well as whether, under economic theory, damages or an injunction is more appropriate in this case.

All of the tracts involved were on a wooded hillside overlooking Hood Canal. As Figure 10-5 indicates, all three parcels fronted on, and had access to, State Road 101, which parallels Hood Canal. The map used by the trial court did not make this clear. Parcel B is a long, narrow lot consisting of 1.4 acres. Parcel C is 5.05 acres, three and a half times larger. Brown testified at the trial that the exact location of the house had not been determined, and Professor Samuels, inspecting the property after the lawsuit, discovered that the Browns had prepared a large, flat area high up on Parcel C, which she thought "a perfect site for a large house."

The Browns bought their two parcels directly from the sellers without consulting a real estate broker or a lawyer. They started using the easement in November 1977 to clear their parcels and bring in fill. They did not tell the Vosses what they were going to build on their property or where they were going to build. They did not seek permission to use the easement to benefit Parcel C, because they assumed they could use the easement to service their entire tract. Throughout the dispute the Browns did not attempt to bargain with the Vosses because they thought the Vosses had no right about which it was necessary to bargain. They believed it was none of the Vosses' business what they were going to build on their tract.

Smarting from not knowing what was going on as the trucks were going in and out, and not being consulted about where the new road would go on the Browns' land, Voss got his dander up. A retired military man whose last position was as an air traffic controller at a military airport, Voss began raising objections. He disputed the location of the easement and complained that Brown and his contractors were trespassing, both through their driving off of the easement and by backing up and turning vehicles on a triangular piece of the Vosses' land where the easement joined Parcel B. Voss erected a chain link fence along the east side of the easement, which Brown believed encroached on the easement.

Brown was in no mood to negotiate. In his own words, Brown was "an extremely adamant person" about his rights who would not be "intimidated by property threats." He hired a surveyor and invited Voss to join him in walking the property line between their tracts as well as the location of the easement, but he told Voss he was only to listen and not to talk with either him or the surveyor. Voss was highly offended by this. He thought Brown downright unneighborly. The quarreling continued for several months until the parties came to blows. Brown said Voss assaulted him, and Voss said Brown, who was 15 years younger, knocked him down. Voss unsuccessfully sought to have Brown prosecuted for assault, and the Browns' lawyer sent Voss a letter threatening legal action against him. A few months later the Browns filed their lawsuit to enjoin the Vosses from interfering with their easement. In the lawsuit, the Browns complained that the Vosses had intentionally placed logs and a concrete sump on the easement "preventing its full use."

After the lawsuit was filed, the Vosses hired a lawyer, who advised them to counterclaim for an injunction preventing the Browns from using the easement to reach Parcel C. The original dispute over location and misuse of the easement now turned into a legal issue of use of the easement by nondominant land. To the Browns, this counterclaim came as a bolt out of the blue—something Voss had never complained of before. The Browns' position in reply was that Parcels B and C had merged into one tract with one owner, that the parcel lines had disappeared, and that they had a right to use the easement to service their entire tract. They thought the traditional rule against use by nondominant land made no sense because, if they located their house straddling the former parcel lines, they would be permitted to enter one part of their house and not another.[22] Moreover, the Browns had bought the two lots with the idea of building a large new home, a home which might be too large to erect on Parcel B alone, and they testified they would not have bought these lots had they known of this limitation on the easement. They felt terribly wronged by this new claim by the Vosses, which they viewed as spiteful and entirely unreasonable. And in the trial their lawyer presented their position exactly this way.

---

22. Under the traditional rule granting an injunction against use of an easement by a nondominant tenement, this is exactly the result. In Penn Bowling Recreation Center, Inc. v. Hot Shoppes, Inc., 179 F.2d 64 (D.C. Cir. 1949), cited by the court and by the dissent, the dominant owner bought a lot next door and erected a building on both the dominant and nondominant land housing a bowling alley on the dominant land and a luncheonette on the nondominant land. The court enjoined the use of the easement for the luncheonette and held that any use by the dominant tenement could be prohibited until the building was so altered that the easement could not be used by the nondominant part (luncheonette).

See also Schadewald v. Brulé, 570 N.W.2d 788 (Mich. App. 1997), refusing to follow Brown v. Voss ("it is not the rule in Michigan"). The court granted an injunction for extending use of an easement to a two-car garage built on nondominant land.

The Restatement (Third) of Property, supra, §4.11, endorses the conventional rule from which the court in Brown v. Voss departed.

The Vosses' lawyer believed the case turned solely on the rule that an easement cannot be extended to nondominant land. As a result, at the trial he did not let the Vosses tell their story—how they had tried to be good neighbors and how uncooperative the Browns had been. He viewed this as irrelevant. The Vosses' lawyer also made what was perhaps a crucial error: he did not offer into evidence a correct map of the properties, which would show that Parcel C had direct access to Route 101 and was not landlocked.

The trial and appeals dragged on for seven years. Finally, the Washington Supreme Court ruled that although the legal rule that an easement cannot be used for nondominant land is enforceable—in this case, only by an award of damages of $1—the trial court did not abuse its discretion in denying the Vosses injunctive relief. The Vosses' lawyer wrote them that they had won the case. Subsequently, when a bill for the Browns' legal costs arrived, they were rather surprised, but they paid it without complaint. By this time, the Browns were out of the picture.

The Browns were not able to build their dream house. They had bought Parcel B on an installment land contract and, after failing to make payments to the seller while the lawsuit was proceeding, the seller declared a forfeiture. The Browns lost Parcel C in a tax sale resulting from their failure to pay taxes on the property for three years. Dogged by financial reverses, the Browns pulled up stakes and moved to Alaska before the Washington Supreme Court handed down its decision. The owner of Parcel B, who had sold it to the Browns, now sold it to the Vosses, thereby merging Parcels A and B into common ownership, terminating the bitterly contested easement.

When Professor Samuels contacted Mr. Brown by telephone in Alaska, "[f]ifteen years after the lawsuit began, he continued to express frustration and anger with Mr. Voss, whom he called 'one of the scum-baggiest persons I've ever met' [and whose wife he called a 'bozo']. When he learned near the end of our conversation that Mr. Voss now owns Parcel B, he commented—after long moments of silence—that Mr. Voss did not deserve to have the property and that 'it's unfortunate we didn't bury him right there.'" Id. at 1487.

For more on Brown v. Voss, see Pamela McClaran, Note, Extending the Benefit of an Easement: A Closer Look at a Classic Rule—*Brown v. Voss*, 62 Wash. L. Rev. 295 (1987). For more on which is the better remedy, an injunction or damages, see Note 3 on pages 795-797, the discussion in Note 3 on pages 805-806, and the thoroughgoing analysis in John A. Lovett, A Bend in the Road: Easement Relocation and Pliability in the New Restatement (Third) of Property: Servitudes, 38 Conn. L. Rev. 1 (2005).

2. *Objections to* Brown v. Voss. Brown v. Voss, which departs from the traditional rule that an easement may not be used in connection with a nondominant estate and that any such use is subject to an injunction, has been the subject of a fair amount of commentary, both pro and con. Professor Lee Strang endorses the *Brown* view so long as no unreasonable burden on the servient estate results and so long as the benefits to the dominant estate outweigh the burdens of the servient estate. See Lee Strang, Damages as the Appropriate Remedy for "Abuse" of

an Easement: Moving Toward Consistency, Efficiency, and Fairness in Property Law, 15 Geo. Mason L. Rev. 933 (2008). Professor Stewart Sterk also supports the *Brown* approach but for different, broader reasons. Sterk argues that in cases where the use exceeds the scope of an easement, liability rules are more efficient than property rules because of high search costs. The owner of the dominant estate is unlikely to be aware of the traditional legal rule and resolving uncertainty about the scope of her rights involves costs that are high relative to the harm done to the servient estate. See Stewart E. Sterk, Property Rules, Liability Rules, and Uncertainty About Property Rights, 106 Mich. L. Rev. 1285, 1323-1327 (2008). There are several potential objections to the *Brown* approach. One concern is that by giving the power of private eminent domain to the dominant estate owner, the *Brown* rule eliminates any need for the parties to negotiate to a consensual solution. Parties do not always negotiate even under the traditional rule (they did not in *Brown* itself, as Professor Samuels's article indicates), but that rule at least creates an incentive for them to do so. Second, with respect to *Brown* itself, it is doubtful that lot C, the nondominant estate, would have been landlocked had the court granted an injunction to Voss. As Professor Samuels indicates, lot C had access to State Road 101. Moreover, it is difficult to believe that Voss would have sold an extension of the easement to include lot C for only one dollar, the amount of damages that the court awarded.

3. *Subdivision of dominant tenements.* Suppose that the owner of the dominant tenement wants to subdivide her land into 100 subdivision tracts. Will each tract have the right to use the easement over the servient tenement? Restatement (Third) of Property, Servitudes §4.10 (2000), says:

> [T]he holder of an easement or profit . . . is entitled to use the servient estate in a manner that is reasonably necessary for the convenient enjoyment of the servitude. The manner, frequency, and intensity of the use may change over time to take advantage of developments in technology and *to accommodate normal development of the dominant estate* or enterprise benefited by the servitude. Unless authorized by the terms of the servitude, the holder is not entitled to cause unreasonable damage to the servient estate or interfere unreasonably with its enjoyment. (Emphasis added.)

The comment to this section points out that what is normal development for an area changes over time and what may be considered abnormal at any one time may become normal at a later time. See also John W. Weaver, Easements Are Nuisances, 25 Real Prop., Prob. & Tr. J. 103 (1990) (proposing that the easement owner be able to expand the easement upon payment of compensation to the servient owner, i.e., apply the nuisance rule of Boomer v. Atlantic Cement Co., page 790). Note also that under the Restatement provision quoted above the use of an easement may change over time to take advantage of new technological developments, unless language in the granting instrument provides otherwise. See, e.g., Center v. Bluebonnet, 264 S.W.3d 381 (Tex. App. 2008). See generally John V. Orth, Reappraisals in the Law of Property 57-62 (2010).

4. *Private condemnation as a solution?* As the dissenting opinion in *Brown* pointed out (see page 870), Washington State has a statute permitting private

condemnation actions. See Rev. Code Wash. §8.24.010 (2012). Under this statute, if the Browns' lot was in fact landlocked, they could condemn a right of way across Voss's land.

5. *Scope of easements of way.* A private easement of way does not usually permit the easement owner to install on the easement aboveground or underground utilities, such as electrical lines and sewer pipes. Most courts hold such uses are not reasonably foreseeable by the parties. Kuras v. Kope, 533 A.2d 1202 (Conn. 1987). See Restatement (Third) of Property, supra, §4.10. Such courts view the purpose of the easement of way as entrance and exit of people and vehicles. If an easement of way were viewed as providing general access to the dominant estate, should utilities be permitted?

6. *Changes in location.* Suppose *O* grants *A* an easement of way over Blackacre, which *O* owns, to reach adjacent land owned by *A*. The easement location is fixed by mutual agreement. Subsequently *O* proposes to change the location of the easement, at *O*'s expense, in order to facilitate development of *O*'s land. *A* objects. What result?

The established rule is that the location of an easement, once fixed by the parties, cannot be changed by the servient owner without permission of the dominant owner. See Davis v. Bruk, 411 A.2d 660 (Me. 1980) (advancing reasons why servient owner cannot unilaterally change location of easement). Restatement (Third) of Property, supra, §4.8, changes this rule. It grants the servient owner the right to make "reasonable changes in the location or dimensions of an easement . . . to permit normal use and development of the servient estate, but only if the changes do not (a) significantly lessen the utility of the easement, (b) increase the burdens on the owner of the easement in its use and enjoyment, or (c) frustrate the purpose for which the easement was created." Id. §4.8(3). This is a default rule; it does not apply if the parties have provided otherwise. The rule is followed in several modern decisions. See St. James Village, Inc. v. Cunningham, 210 P.3d 190 (Nev. 2009) (adopting Restatement position); M.P.M. Builders v. Dwyer, 809 N.E.2d 1053 (Mass. 2004) (same); Lewis v. Young, 705 N.E.2d 649 (N.Y. 1998); Umphres v. Mayer Enterprises, Inc., 889 S.W.2d 86 (Mo. App. 1994) (granting dominant owner damages when servient owner relocated easement but refusing an injunction requiring servient owner to restore original easement); Soderberg v. Weisel, 687 A.2d 839 (Pa. Super. Ct. 1997) (relocating prescriptive easement). But see Herren v. Pettengill, 528 S.E.2d 735 (Ga. 2000). Compare Susan French, Relocating Easements: Restatement (Third) §4.8(3), 38 Real Prop., Prob. & Tr. J. 1 (2003) (explaining and justifying new Restatement rule), with John Orth, Relocating Easements: A Response to Professor French, 38 Real Prop., Prob. & Tr. J. 643 (2004) (criticizing new Restatement rule).

7. *Scope of prescriptive easements.* A prescriptive easement is not as broad in scope as an easement created by grant, by implication, or by necessity. Although the uses of a prescriptive easement are not confined to the actual uses made during the prescriptive period, the uses made of a prescriptive easement must be consistent with the general kind of use by which the easement was created and with what the servient owner might reasonably expect to lose by failing to interrupt

the adverse use. For example, a prescriptive easement acquired by pedestrian traffic or by herding livestock with men and horses across land has been held not usable by motor vehicles. "Anyone who does not think there is a significant difference between horses and motorcycles may wish to ponder why it is that carriages in Central Park are pulled by horses, not Hondas." Connolly v. McDermott, 208 Cal. Rptr. 796, 799 (Cal. App. 1984).

8. *A solution for landlocked owners?* Go back to Othen v. Rosier (page 833). Does *Brown v. Voss* show a way out of the problem of the landlocked owner's dilemma in that case? Using the terminology discussed in the last chapter, at pages 805-806, we can note that the court in *Brown* protected the servient tenement with a liability rule (damages) rather than a property rule (injunction). Could not the same approach have been used in *Othen*?

5. Termination of Easements

Preseault v. United States

United States Court of Appeals, Federal Circuit, 1996
100 F.3d 1525

[Under the Transportation Act of 1920, in order to abandon a line, a railroad must receive permission of the Interstate Commerce Commission (ICC). In 1983, Congress enacted the Rails-to-Trails Act, 16 U.S.C. §1247(d) (1994). The Rails-to-Trails Act has two purposes: (1) preserving discontinued railroad corridors for future railroad use and (2) permitting public recreational use of discontinued railroad rights of way. The act gives the ICC[23] authority to authorize *abandonment* of the line *or* to permit *discontinuance* of rail service and transfer of the railroad right of way to a public or private group willing to maintain the right of way as a public trail. In this case, the railroad shut down service in 1970 and in 1975 removed the railroad tracks, but it never applied to the ICC for an abandonment order. In 1985 the railroad entered into an agreement with the state of Vermont and the city of Burlington that the latter would maintain the former railroad strip as a public trail. In 1986, the ICC approved the trails agreement and authorized the railroad to discontinue service. The owners of the underlying fee simple over which the tracks formerly ran — the Preseaults — sued, claiming the Rails-to-Trails Act was unconstitutional. In Preseault v. Interstate Commerce Commission, 494 U.S. 1 (1990), the United States Supreme Court held that the act was constitutional as an appropriate exercise of congressional power to regulate interstate commerce but further held that the Preseaults may have a remedy under the Fifth Amendment for a taking of their property as defined by state law.

23. The ICC Termination Act of 1995, 109 Stat. 803, abolished the ICC and transferred its responsibilities to the newly created Surface Transportation Board, with a saving clause for suits initiated before 1996.

Determining what interest petitioners would have enjoyed under Vermont law, in the absence of the ICC's recent actions, will establish whether petitioners possess the predicate property interest that must underlie any takings claim. . . .

The scope of the Commission's authority to regulate abandonments, thereby delimiting the ambit of federal power, is an issue quite distinct from whether the Commission's exercise of power over matters within its jurisdiction effected a taking of petitioner's property. . . . The Commission's actions may delay property owners' enjoyment of their reversionary interests, but that delay burdens and defeats the property interest rather than suspends or defers the vesting of those property rights. . . . Any other conclusion would convert the ICC's power to pre-empt conflicting state regulation of interstate commerce into the power to pre-empt the rights guaranteed by state property law, a result incompatible with the Fifth Amendment. [449 U.S. at 20, 22 (O'Connor, J., concurring).]

The Preseaults now bring suit claiming that the federal government, acting through the ICC, took their property when it authorized the conversion of the former railroad right of way to public trail use. They rely upon the traditional rule of takings law that permanent physical occupation of property by the government or the public is a taking of the owners' property. (See Loretto v. Teleprompter Manhattan CATV Corp., 458 U.S. 419 (1982), reproduced at page 1132.)]

PLAGER, J. In this Takings case, the United States denies liability under the Fifth Amendment of the Constitution[24] for actions it took pursuant to the Federal legislation known as the Rails-to-Trails Act. The original parties to the case were the property owners, J. Paul and Patricia Preseault, plaintiffs, and the United States (the "Government"), defendant. The State of Vermont (the "State"), claiming an interest in the properties involved, intervened and, under the joinder rules of the Court of Federal Claims, entered its appearance as a co-defendant. The Court of Federal Claims, on summary judgment after hearings and argument, concluded that the law was on the Government's side, and rendered judgment against the complaining property owners. Preseault v. United States, 27 Fed. Cl. 69 (1992). The property owners appeal. . . .

A. Introduction and Summary

In brief, the issue in this case is whether the conversion, under the authority of the Rails-to-Trails Act and by order of the Interstate Commerce Commission, of a long unused railroad right-of-way to a public recreational hiking and biking trail constituted a taking of the property of the owners of the underlying fee simple estate. . . .

B. Factual Background

The Preseaults own a fee simple interest in a tract of land near the shore of Lake Champlain in Burlington, Vermont, on which they have a home. This tract of

---

24. U.S. Const. amend. V ("nor shall private property be taken for public use, without just compensation").

land is made up of several previously separate properties, the identities of which date back to before the turn of the century. The dispute centers on three parcels within this tract, areas over which the original railroad right-of-way ran. The areas are designated by the trial court as parcels A, B, and C. Two of those parcels, A and B, derive from the old Barker Estate property. The third parcel, C, is part of what was the larger Manwell property.

The Rutland-Canadian Railroad Company, a corporation organized under the laws of Vermont, acquired in 1899 the rights-of-way at issue on parcels A, B, and C, over which it laid its rails and operated its railroad. . . .

Meanwhile, ownership of the properties over which the rights-of-way ran passed through the hands of successors in interest, eventually arriving in the hands of the Preseaults. A map of the Preseault tract, showing the various parcels and the areas subject to the railroad's rights-of-way, is reproduced [on the next page].

C. The Property Interests

In Preseault [v. Interstate Commerce Commission, 494 U.S. 1], Justice Brennan writing for the Supreme Court noted the importance of determining the nature of the interests created by these turn-of-the-century transfers:

> The alternative chosen by Congress [the Rails-to-Trails program] is less costly than a program of direct federal trail acquisition because, under any view of takings law, only some rail-to-trail conversions will amount to takings. Some rights-of-way are held in fee simple. Others are held as easements that do not even as a matter of state law revert upon interim use as nature trails.

Id. at 16. . . .

Clearly, if the Railroad obtained fee simple title to the land over which it was to operate, and that title inures, as it would, to its successors, the Preseaults today would have no right or interest in those parcels and could have no claim related to those parcels for a taking. If, on the other hand, the Railroad acquired only easements for use, easements imposed on the property owners' underlying fee simple estates, and if those easements were limited to uses that did not include public recreational hiking and biking trails ("nature trails" as Justice Brennan referred to them), or if the easements prior to their conversion to trails had been extinguished by operation of law leaving the property owner with unfettered fee simples, the argument of the Preseaults becomes viable.

The determinative issues in the case, then, are three: (1) who owned the strips of land involved, specifically did the Railroad by the 1899 transfers acquire only easements, or did it obtain fee simple estates; (2) if the Railroad acquired only easements, were the terms of the easements limited to use for railroad purposes, or did they include future use as public recreational trails; and (3) even if the grants of the Railroad's easements were broad enough to encompass recreational trails, had these easements terminated prior to the alleged taking so that the property owners at that time held fee simples unencumbered by the easements. . . .

The question of what estates in property were created by these turn-of-the-century transfers to the Railroad requires a close examination of the conveying instruments, read in light of the common law and statutes of Vermont then in effect. . . . With regard to the two parcels, A and B, derived from the Barker Estate, [the Railroad, exercising a power of eminent domain given it by the state, acquired its interest by a Commissioner's Award. It surveyed and located the land it wanted for its tracks, and, since the land owners and the Railroad could not agree on the damages to be paid, three disinterested commissioners were appointed who fixed the damages and executed a document called a Commissioner's Award. The document made no reference to an easement or a fee simple.] In her opinion, the trial judge concluded that . . . "the portion of the right-of-way consisting of the parcel of land condemned from the Barker Estate and taken by commissioner's award is indisputably an easement under the law of the State of Vermont." [Preseault v. United States, 24 Cl. Ct. 818 at 827 (1992).]

As a result of our independent examination of the question we conclude that there is little real dispute about this. . . . With few exceptions the Vermont cases are consistent in holding that, practically without regard to the documentation and manner of acquisition, when a railroad for its purposes acquires an estate in land for laying track and operating railroad equipment thereon, the estate acquired is no more than that needed for the purpose, and that typically means an easement, not a fee simple estate. . . .

Determining the provenance of the third parcel, C, derived from the Manwell tract, tests the above stated proposition even further. The operative instrument is a warranty deed, dated August 2, 1899, from Frederick and Mary Manwell to the Railroad. The deed contains the usual habendum clause found in a warranty deed, and purports to convey the described strip of land to the grantee railroad "to have and to hold the above granted and bargained premises . . . unto it the said grantee, its successors and assigns forever, to its and their own proper use, benefit and behoof forever." The deed further warrants that the grantors have "a good, indefeasible estate, in fee simple, and have good right to bargain and sell the same in manner and form as above written. . . ." In short, the deed appears to be the standard form used to convey a fee simple title from a grantor to a grantee.

But did it? . . .

At trial, the Preseaults argued that, although the Manwell deed purports to grant a fee simple, the deed was given following survey and location of the right-of-way and therefore it should be construed as conveying only an easement in accordance with Vermont railroad law. . . .

In Hill v. Western Vermont Railroad, 32 Vt. 68 (1859), . . . [t]he court observed that railroads acquire needed land either by order of a designated public body (through the exercise of eminent domain) or by consent of the landowner, although even in the latter case "the proceeding is, in some sense, compulsory." Id. at 75. Thus,

in either mode of appropriating land for the purposes of the company, there is this implied limitation upon the power, that the company will take only so much land or estate therein as is necessary for their public purposes. It does not seem to us to make much difference in regard to either they quantity or the estate whether the price is fixed by the commissioners or by the parties.

Id. at 76. . . .

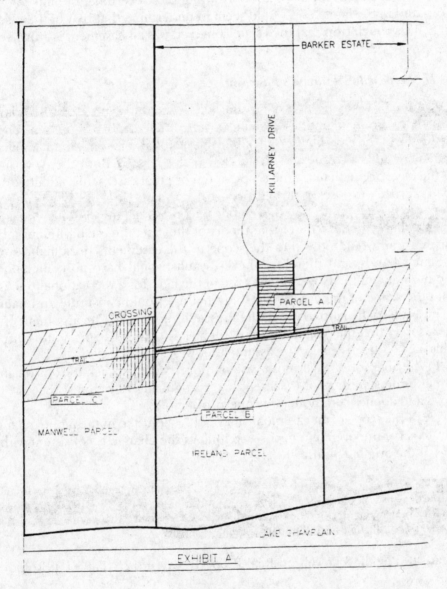

Figure 10-6
Map from Court's opinion

Thus it is that a railroad that proceeds to acquire a right-of-way for its road acquires only that estate, typically an easement, necessary for its limited purposes, and that the act of survey and location is the operative determinant, and not the particular form of transfer, if any. Here, the evidence is that the Railroad had obtained a survey and location of its right-of-way, after which the Manwell deed was executed confirming and memorializing the Railroad's action. On balance it would seem that, consistent with the view expressed in *Hill*, the proceeding retained its eminent domain flavor, and the railroad acquired only that which it needed, an easement for its roadway. Nothing the Government points to or that we can find in the later cases would seem to undermine that view of the case; the trial court's conclusion that the estate conveyed was an easement is affirmed. . . .

D. The Scope of the Railroad's Easement

We turn then to the question of whether the easements granted to the Railroad, to which the Preseaults' title was subject, are sufficiently broad in their scope so that the use of the easements for a public recreational trail is not a violation of the Preseaults' rights as owners of the underlying fee estate. Both the Government and the State argue that . . . the scope of the original easements, admittedly limited to railroad purposes, is properly construed today to include other public purposes as well, and that these other public purposes include a public recreational hiking and biking trail. Under that theory of the case, the establishment in 1986 of such a trail would be within the scope of the easements presumably now in the State's hands, and therefore the Preseaults would have no complaint. On the other hand, if the Government's use of the land for a recreational trail is not within the scope of the easements, then that use would constitute an unauthorized invasion of the land to which the Preseaults hold title. The argument on this issue assumes that the easements were still in existence in 1986, and for purposes of this part of the discussion we assume they were. . . .

In the absence of a Vermont case on point, we must seek the answer in traditional understandings of easement law, recognizing as we must that Vermont follows and applies common law property principles.

. . . [T]he scope of an easement [may be] . . . adjusted in the face of changing times to serve the original purpose, so long as the change is consistent with the terms of the original grant:

> It is often said that the parties are to be presumed to have contemplated such a scope for the created easement as would reasonably serve the purposes of the grant. . . . This presumption often allows an expansion of use of the easement, but does not permit a change in use not reasonably foreseeable at the time of establishment of the easement.

Richard R. Powell, 3 Powell on Real Property ¶ 34.12[2] (Patrick J. Rohan ed., 1996). . . .

When the easements here were granted to the Preseaults' predecessors in title at the turn of the century, specifically for transportation of goods and persons via railroad, could it be said that the parties contemplated that a century later the easements would be used for recreational hiking and biking trails, or that it was necessary to so construe them in order to give the grantee railroad that for which it bargained? We think not. Although a public recreational trail could be described as a roadway for the transportation of persons, the nature of the usage is clearly different. In the one case, the grantee is a commercial enterprise using the easement in its business, the transport of goods and people for compensation. In the other, the easement belongs to the public, and is open for use for recreational purposes, which happens to involve people engaged in exercise or recreation on foot or on bicycles. It is difficult to imagine that either party to the original transfers had anything remotely in mind that would resemble a public recreational trail.

Furthermore, there are differences in the degree and nature of the burden imposed on the servient estate. It is one thing to have occasional railroad trains crossing one's land. Noisy though they may be, they are limited in location, in number, and in frequency of occurrence. Particularly is this so on a relatively remote spur. When used for public recreational purposes, however, in a region that is environmentally attractive, the burden imposed by the use of the easement is at the whim of many individuals, and, as the record attests, has been impossible to contain in numbers or to keep strictly within the parameters of the easement. . . .

Most state courts that have been faced with the question of whether conversion to a nature trail falls within the scope of an original railroad easement have held that it does not. . . .

Given that the easements in this case are limited by their terms and as a matter of law to railroad purposes, we are unable to join the dissent's effort to read into Vermont law a breadth of scope for the easements that is well outside the parameters of traditional common law understanding. . . .

E. Abandonment

Even assuming for sake of argument that the . . . original conveyances [may be read so as to permit trail use,] . . . there remains yet a further obstacle to the Government's successful defense. The Preseaults contend that under Vermont law the original easements were abandoned, and thus extinguished, in 1975. If that is so, the State could not, over ten years later in 1986, have re-established the easement even for the narrow purposes provided in the original conveyances without payment of the just compensation required by the Constitution. . . .

Typically the grant under which such rights-of-way are created does not specify a termination date. The usual way in which such an easement ends is by abandonment, which causes the easement to be extinguished by operation of law. See generally Restatement of Property §504. Upon an act of abandonment, the then owner of the fee estate, the "burdened" estate, is relieved of the burden of the easement. In most jurisdictions, including Vermont, this happens automatically when abandonment of the easement occurs. . . .

Vermont law recognizes the well-established proposition that easements, like other property interests, are not extinguished by simple non-use. As was said in Nelson v. Bacon, 113 Vt. 161, 32 A.2d 140, 146 (1943), "one who acquires title to an easement in this manner [by deed in that case] has the same right of property therein as an owner of the fee and it is not necessary that he should make use of his right in order to maintain his title." Thus in cases involving a passageway through an adjoining building (*Nelson*), or a shared driveway (Sabins v. McAllister, 116 Vt. 302, 76 A.2d 106 (1950), overruled in part on other grounds by Lague v. Royea, 152 Vt. 499, 568 A.2d 357 (1989)), the claimed easement was not extinguished merely because the owner had not made use of it regularly.

Something more is needed. The Vermont Supreme Court in *Nelson* summarized the rule in this way: "In order to establish an abandonment there must be in addition to nonuser, acts by the owner of the dominant tenement conclusively and unequivocally manifesting *either* a present intent to relinquish the easement or a purpose inconsistent with its future existence." *Nelson*, 32 A.2d at 146 (emphasis added); see also *Lague*, 152 Vt. at 503, 568 A.2d at 359; Barrett v. Kunz, 158 Vt. 15, 604 A.2d 1278 (1992). The record here establishes that these easements, along with the other assets of the railroad, came into the hands of the State of Vermont in the 1960s. The State then leased them to an entity called the Vermont Railway, which operated trains over them. In 1970, the Vermont Railway ceased active transport operations on the line which included the right-of-way over the parcels at issue, and used the line only to store railroad cars. In 1975 the Railroad removed all of the railroad equipment, including switches and tracks, from the portion of the right-of-way running over the three parcels of land now owned by the Preseaults. In light of these facts, the trial court concluded that under Vermont law this amounted to an abandonment of the easements, and adjudged that the easements were extinguished as a matter of law in 1975. . . .

The Government and the State argue that there are facts inconsistent with that determination, but we are not persuaded that any of them significantly undercut the trial court's conclusion. For example, when the Vermont Railway removed its tracks in 1975, it did not remove the two bridges or any of the culverts on the line, all of which remained "substantially intact." That is not surprising. The Railroad was under no obligation to restore the former easement to its original condition. Tearing out existing structures would simply add to its costs, whereas the rails that were taken up could be used for repairs of defective rails elsewhere on the line. It is further argued that, since the rail line continues to operate to a point approximately one and one-third miles south of the Preseaults' property, it is possible to restore the line to full operation. The fact that restoration of the northern portion of the line would be technically feasible tells us little. The question is not what is technically possible to do in the future, but what was done in the past.

Almost immediately after the tracks were removed, members of the public began crossing over the easement. Perhaps illustrating the difficulty in getting government paperwork to catch up with reality, or perhaps indicating that revenue collectors do not give up easily, the State of Vermont and Vermont Railway, as they had done before the removal of the tracks, continued to collect fees under various license and crossing agreements from persons wishing to establish fixed crossings. In January 1976, the Preseaults executed a crossing agreement with the Vermont Railway which gave the Preseaults permission to cross the right-of-way. In March 1976, the Preseaults entered into a license agreement with the State and the Vermont Railway to locate a driveway and underground utility service across the railroad right-of-way. As late as 1991, 985 Associates (through Paul Preseault) paid a $10 license fee to "Vermont Railroad" (sic), presumably pursuant to one of the 1976 agreements. The Preseaults paid "under protest." Much of this activity suggests that, initially at least, the adjacent property owners decided it was cheaper to pay a nominal license fee to the State than to litigate the question of whether the State had the right to extract the fee. In view of all the contrary evidence of physical abandonment, we find this behavior by the State's revenue collectors unconvincing as persuasive evidence of a purpose or intent not to abandon the use of the right-of-way for actual railroad purposes.

One uncontrovertible piece of evidence in favor of abandonment is that, in the years following the shutting down of the line in 1970 and the 1975 removal of the tracks, no move has been made by the State or by the Railroad to reinstitute service over the line, or to undertake replacement of the removed tracks and other infrastructure necessary to return the line to service. . . . Other events occurring after 1975 are also of little probative value.[25]

The trial judge in this case . . . concluded that as a fact the Railroad had effected in 1975 an abandonment of the easement running over parcels A, B, and C. . . . We affirm the determination of the trial court that abandonment of the easements took place in 1975. That determination provides an alternative ground for concluding that a governmental taking occurred.

F.   The Taking

. . . The ICC in a January 1986 Order authorized Vermont Railway ex post facto to discontinue service and approved the agreement between the state and the city of Burlington for trail use by the former right of way. . . .

In due course an eight foot wide paved strip was established on the former right-of-way over parcels A, B, and C. The path is some 60 feet from the Preseaults' front door. On each side of the Preseaults' driveway, where it crosses the easement, two concrete posts and one metal post were installed to block automobile traffic. The city also erected two stop signs on the path and built a water main under and along the path. The Preseaults have been unable to build on the land under the easement or to construct a driveway connecting their land through parcels A and B to the nearest public street.

The path is used regularly by members of the public for walking, skating, and bicycle riding. On warm weekends up to two hundred people an hour go through the Preseaults' property. People using the path often trespass on the Preseaults'

---

25. Since the 1950s, Rutland Railway and later the Vermont Railway have licensed the Burlington Electric Light Department, a municipal utility, to install and maintain electrical transmission and distribution lines within the right-of-way. The City of Burlington installed a water line on the property under an agreement with the Vermont Railway. The Government says this occurred in 1974, but the Preseaults say it was in 1976.

front yard. On one occasion Mr. Preseault was nearly run over by a cyclist as he walked across the path.

Thus, if the Preseaults have interests under state property law that have traditionally been recognized and protected from governmental expropriation, and if, over their objection, the Government chooses to occupy or otherwise acquire those interests, the Fifth Amendment compels compensation. The record establishes two bases on which the Preseaults are entitled to recover. One, if the easements were in existence in 1986 when, pursuant to ICC Order, the City of Burlington established the public recreational trail, its establishment could not be justified under the terms and within the scope of the existing easements for railroad purposes. The taking of possession of the lands owned by the Preseaults for use as a public trail was in effect a taking of a new easement for that new use, for which the landowners are entitled to compensation.

Two, as an alternative basis, in 1986 when the ICC issued its Order authorizing the City to establish a public recreational biking and pedestrian trail on parcels A, B, and C, there was as a matter of state law no railroad easement in existence on those parcels, nor had there been for more than ten years. The easement had been abandoned in 1975, and the properties were held by the Preseaults in fee simple, unencumbered by any former property rights of the Railroad. When the City, pursuant to federal authorization, took possession of parcels A, B, and C and opened them to public use, that was a physical taking of the right of exclusive possession that belonged to the Preseaults as an incident of their ownership of the land.

The Government argues that, since it was the City that actually established the trail, the United States should not be considered the responsible actor. If a taking occurred, says the Government, it was the City and the State who did it. . . .

In the case before us there was a . . . physical entry upon the private lands of the Preseaults, acting under the Federal Government's authority pursuant to the ICC's Order.

. . . [W]hen the Federal Government puts into play a series of events which result in a taking of private property, the fact that the Government acts through a state agent does not absolve it from the responsibility, and the consequences, of its actions.

Summary and Conclusion

. . .

Whether, at the time a railroad applies to abandon its use of an easement limited to railroad purposes, a taking occurs under an ICC order to "railbank" the easement for possible future railroad use, and allowing in the interim for use of the easement for trail purposes, is a question not now before us. We offer no opinion at this time on that question. We conclude that the occupation of the Preseaults' property by the City of Burlington under the authority of the Federal

Government constituted a taking of their property for which the Constitution requires that just compensation be paid. The judgment of the Court of Federal Claims, holding the Government not liable, is reversed. The matter is remanded to that court for further proceedings consistent with this opinion.

[Three of the nine judges sitting en banc in this case dissented. In their view, the Railroad had not abandoned the easement because, even though the tracks were removed, there was no clear and unequivocal signal of intent to abandon. Lack of intent to abandon is confirmed by the crossing and license agreements entered into by the Railroad. On the scope of the easement, the dissenters thought a railroad easement can be used as a public trail that merely shifts the use from one public use to another and imposes no greater burden on the servient tenement.

Upon remand, a U.S. Court of Federal Claims judge awarded the Preseaults $234,000 plus interest from the time the government opened the nature trail. The Burlington (Vt.) Free Press, May 26, 2001, at 2B.]

NOTES AND PROBLEM

1. *The Rails-to-Trails Act.* For more on the Rails-to-Trails Act, see Chevy Chase Land Co. v. United States, 733 A.2d 1055 (Md. 1999) (holding conversion to trail usage was within the easement's scope); S. Mike Gentine, Riding the Trails to Bad Law: The Inevitably Unjust Results of the National Trails System and Current Takings Jurisprudence, 47 Real Prop., Tr. & Est. L.J. 173 (2012); Danaya C. Wright & Jeffrey M. Hester, Pipes, Wires, and Bicycles: Rails-to-Trails, Utility Licenses, and the Shifting Scope of Railroad Easements from the Nineteenth to the Twenty-First Centuries, 27 Ecology L.Q. 351 (2000); Emily Drumm, Note, Addressing the Flaws of the Rails-to-Trails Act, 8 Kan. J.L. & Pub. Poly. 158 (1999).

2. *A fee simple or an easement?* Whether a deed of a strip of land gives the grantee a fee simple or an easement has been often litigated, particularly when the strip is to be used as a right of way. If the strip is referred to as a "right of way," the court usually finds an easement is granted. But there are cases finding an intention to create a fee simple in other words of the deed or in the form of deed. In Brown v. State, 924 P.2d 908 (Wash. 1996), the court found a fee simple was granted because a statutory warranty deed for a fee simple (see page 615) was used. (But compare the *Preseault* case.) And in City of Manhattan Beach v. Superior Court, 914 P.2d 160 (Cal. 1996), in which the grantor in 1888 quitclaimed a "right-of-way for a steam railroad," the court, four to three, found a fee simple was granted on the basis of extrinsic evidence of the grantor's conduct subsequent to the conveyance. In the latter case, after ceasing operations, the railroad sold the parcel to the city for a park and jogging path. The litigation was instigated by two "heir-hunters," who had found and, in exchange for a fractional interest, notified some 80 persons that they were heirs of the original grantors and had an interest in the abandoned railroad right of way. The majority and the dissenting opinions cite numerous cases from many jurisdictions, going both ways on particular facts.

3. *Methods of terminating easements.* Easements can be terminated in a number of ways. The easement owner may agree to *release* the easement. Because easements are interests in property, subject to the Statute of Frauds, normally a release requires a writing. If the duration of an easement is limited in some way, it ends through *expiration* at the end of the stated period. Similarly, an easement created to end upon the occurrence of some event (sometimes called a defeasible easement) expires automatically if and when the stated event occurs. Easements by necessity end when the necessity that gave rise to it ends. See Note 4 on page 841. An easement ends by *merger* if the easement owner later becomes the owner of the servient estate. See Note 7 on page 833. An easement may end through *estoppel* if the servient owner reasonably relies upon a statement or representation by the easement owner. As *Preseault* indicates, an easement may terminate by *abandonment.* Normally, mere non-use by the easement owner does not constitute abandonment, but in several states a prescriptive easement ends by abandonment upon non-use for the statutory period of time. See Zadnichek v. Fidler, 894 So. 2d 702 (Ala. App. 2004) (holding non-use alone does not constitute abandonment of a right-of-way easement but suggesting that the benefitted owner's act of obtaining alternative means of access to the benefitted parcel could constitute evidence of intent to abandon). An easement may terminate by *condemnation* if the government exercises its eminent domain power to take title to a fee interest in the servient estate for a purpose that is inconsistent with continued existence of the easement. Finally, an easement may be terminated by *prescription.* If the servient owner wrongfully and physically prevents the easement from being used for the prescriptive period, the easement is terminated. Spiegel v. Ferraro, 541 N.E.2d 15 (N.Y. 1989); Faulconer v. Williams, 964 P.2d 246 (Or. 1998); Restatement (Third) of Property, Servitudes §7.7 (2000).

As we will see later in this chapter (see pages 927-936), under the law of covenants and equitable servitudes it has long been the case that courts may modify or even terminate real covenants and equitable servitudes on the basis of changed conditions. The traditional law of easements, however, does not recognize a changed conditions doctrine. Traditional easements doctrine has dealt with obsolete easements on the basis of what is in effect a frustration of purpose doctrine. See Restatement (Third) of Property, Servitudes §7.10 Reporter's Note (2000). However, as part of its effort to unify the law of easements, covenants, and equitable servitudes, the Restatement (Third) of Property provides that the changed conditions doctrine applies to all types of servitudes. See Restatement (Third) of Property, Servitudes §7.10(1) (2000). Under that provision a court may modify or, if modification is not feasible or is ineffective, terminate a servitude if a post-creation change of circumstances has made it practically impossible to accomplish the purpose for which the servitude was created.

4. The owner of Blackacre, on which is an easement in favor of Whiteacre, fails to pay property taxes. The county forecloses on Blackacre for failure to pay taxes and sells Blackacre to a new owner. Does the foreclosure terminate the easement? See Hearn v. Autumn Woods Office Park Prop. Owners Assn., 757 So. 2d 155 (Miss. 1999); Restatement (Third) of Property, supra, §7.9.

6. Negative Easements

A negative easement is the right of the dominant owner to stop the servient owner from doing something on the servient land. Prior to Queen Victoria's reign, English courts had recognized four types of negative easements: the right to stop your neighbor from (1) blocking your windows, (2) interfering with air flowing to your land in a defined channel, (3) removing the support of your building (usually by excavating or removing a supporting wall), and (4) interfering with the flow of water in an artificial stream.[26] If the judges had let the list of negative easements expand naturally with the changes taking place in urban development, the excessive complexity characterizing the law of servitudes may never have developed. But the expansion of the English law of easements was curbed in the first half of the nineteenth century.

Judges, for several reasons, were not disposed to permit the creation of new types of easements, negative easements in particular. First, England was without an effective system of public records of land titles until 1925, and the purchaser of land was bound by its servitudes regardless of notice, actual or constructive. The purchaser could protect himself by viewing the land, but negative easements were not so easy to discover as affirmative easements, such as an easement of way. To expand the list of negative easements would increase the risk to the purchaser that the land was subject to undiscoverable rights. Thus, to keep land titles unencumbered, judges did not favor negative easements.

Second, the traditional negative easements could arise by prescription in England; for example, a person whose windows had not been blocked by a neighbor for 20 years received a prescriptive easement for light over the neighbor's land.[27] If new types of negative easements could arise by prescription, the servient owner's rights to change the land use would be unduly restricted. A neighbor, sensing some harm from a change on the neighboring land, might claim, "You cannot do act X on your land because it has never been done before. I have a prescriptive right to prevent it." Judicial recognition of such claims would hopelessly cloud the conditions under which development could take place.

The final objection to negative easements was conceptual. From the time of the Year Books (see footnote 16 on page 31), English judges had a hard time deciding whether negative obligations should be analyzed as easements or as covenants. An easement could be created only by grant. From this it was deduced

26. All landowners have the duty, imposed by law, of supporting adjoining *land* (see page 786) and of not interfering unreasonably with the flow of water in adjacent *natural* streams (see pages 38-39). Landowners can bargain among themselves for additional rights and duties respecting support of buildings and not interfering with artificial streams. These bargains, creating recognized negative easements, are enforceable against successor owners.

27. This doctrine, known as the *doctrine of ancient lights*, has never been accepted in the United States. American courts have held that negative easements cannot be acquired by prescription. Analogizing to statutes of limitations, which set time periods on causes of action, the courts have reasoned that prescription does not apply unless the servient owner has a cause of action against the user. Since a landowner has no cause of action against a neighbor for erecting a building with windows overlooking his land, the neighbor can acquire no prescriptive right to unobstructed light and air. Hence the doctrine of ancient lights has been rejected in this country.

that a right in land could not be an easement unless it could be pictured as an intelligible object of a grant. English judges found it difficult to picture, in their minds, a negative right being granted from *A* to *B*. Judges could imagine an affirmative easement (for example, a right of way) being granted from *A* to *B*, because *B* was given the right to do an affirmative act on *A*'s land. On the other hand, a negative easement resembled an obligation of *A*. If *A* purported to grant to *B* the right not to have a piggery on *A*'s land, *B*'s rights depended on the behavior of *A*. A negative right thus seemed more naturally to be acquired by a covenant, that is, by a promise by *A* that *A* would not establish a piggery on *A*'s land.

For these reasons the English law courts in the nineteenth century called a halt to the creation of negative easements other than the four traditional kinds. They refused to recognize any new negative servitudes as easements.

Two of the conditions that influenced, and perhaps justified, the English law of servitudes did not exist in the United States in the nineteenth century, when the English law crossed the Atlantic. In all American states a recording system existed to protect subsequent purchasers against unrecorded claims; during the post-Civil War industrialization period, reliance on record searches became universally common in this country. An effective recording system is of the greatest importance because it provides information about existing servitudes at small cost and protects against hidden claims—which English judges rightly feared. Subsequent purchasers were further protected in this country by rejection of the English idea that negative easements could be created by prescription. American courts held that prescription does not apply until the rights of the "servient owner" are interfered with and a cause of action against the "dominant owner" arises.

The third objection to negative easements—that they cannot be conceptualized as the subject of a grant—could also have been overcome. This is merely a peculiar and entirely unnecessary way of looking at the matter. Any negative restriction can be cast in terms of either a promise or a grant. *A* promises *B* that *A* will not put a piggery on *A*'s land, or *A* grants to *B* the right not to have a piggery on *A*'s land. *B* has a right; *A* has a duty not to establish a pig farm. Whether rights are created in the form of a grant or in the form of a promise, the resulting legal relationship (right in *B*, duty in *A*) is the important thing. Unless there is some overriding policy reason, a right created by promise should be treated the same way as a right created by grant.

American courts thus might have rejected the artificial English barriers to the creation of servitudes. They might have fashioned a law that enforced all servitudes of whatever type against subsequent purchasers with notice, in more or less the same manner as they enforce other interests in land against subsequent purchasers with notice. In short, they might have relied upon the market system to ensure that the bargains creating these servitudes were advantageous to affected parties and hence economically efficient. And courts might have relied on the recording system to protect subsequent purchasers and to find parties from whom releases could be obtained, thus clearing servitudes from the land. And courts might have concentrated their talents on removing obsolete servitudes when the market did not function to remove them. But alas, they did not.

In the main, American courts accepted the English restrictions on creating new types of easements. Nonetheless, although the list of four negative easements is seemingly closed in England, it is not necessarily closed in the United States. Now and then a new type of negative easement is recognized. In Petersen v. Friedman, 328 P.2d 264 (Cal. App. 1958), the court enforced an express easement of unobstructed view of the San Francisco Bay over a neighbor's house, compelling the neighbor to remove obstructing television aerials. In England, the right to an unspoiled view cannot exist as an easement. A solar easement, preventing a person from blocking a neighbor's solar collector, has also been recognized in this country. See Troy A. Rule, Shadows on the Cathedral: Solar Access Laws in a Different Light, 2010 U. Ill. L. Rev. 851; Sara C. Bronin, Solar Rights, 89 B.U. L. Rev. 1217 (2009).

Although the English law courts closed the books on negative easements 150 years ago, chancery soon thereafter began to enforce negative covenants between the parties as equitable servitudes (see page 898). Equitable servitudes became the equivalent of negative easements, but subject to a different set of rules developed in chancery. The American courts followed suit. Today there is little pressure on the courts to expand the traditional list of negative easements because negative restrictions on land can be, and usually are, treated as equitable servitudes. American courts frequently refer to equitable servitudes as negative easements, acknowledging both the similarity of these interests and equity's circumvention of the law.

Restatement (Third) of Property, supra, §1.2 comment h, treats negative easements as restrictive covenants.

7. Conservation and Other Novel Easements

The most noteworthy new negative easement is the conservation easement, developed in the last 40 years to preserve scenic and historic areas and open space. An owner of land can give a public body or a private charitable organization (such as a land trust) a conservation easement, preventing the servient owner from building on the land except as specified in the grant. The value of the conservation easement (which is usually the development value of the land) is deductible as a charitable gift on income tax returns. Because of doubts about the validity and transferability of negative easements in gross at common law, statutes have been enacted in almost all states authorizing conservation easements. The catalyst for this wave of statutes was the Uniform Conservation Easement Act (UCEA), first promulgated in 1981. The stated purpose of the UCEA is to enable "durable restrictions and affirmative obligations to be attached to real property to protect natural resources" and to ensure that these restrictions "are immune from certain common law impediments which might otherwise be raised." UCEA, Prefatory Note at 164. The UCEA was the model for Restatement (Third) of Property, Servitudes §1.6 (2000), which defines the term "conservation servitudes." Conservation easements have been generally effective in protecting undeveloped land against various threats to its wild character, including adverse possession. See Alexandra B. Klass, Adverse Possession and Conservation: Expanding Traditional Notions of Use and Possession, 77 U. Colo. L. Rev. 283 (2006).

The growth of conservation easements in recent decades has been remarkable. The Land Trust Alliance's 2005 National Land Trust Census reported that the acres protected by conservation easements increased by 148 percent between 2000 and 2005, from approximately 2.5 million acres to approximately 6.2 million acres. See http://www.landtrustalliance.org/about-us/land-trust-census/executive-summary.

Conservation easements owe their growing popularity to a variety of factors. Not the least of these, of course, is the environmental concern of some owners that subsequent owners may succumb to pressure for residential or commercial development. Another concern of owners is that the family farm may be sold when they die. A third major incentive is the significant tax deduction available for donations of conservation easements to local government units or charitable land trusts.[28] Indeed, the real boom in conservation easements began when Congress amended the Internal Revenue Code in 1976 to allow tax deductions for donations of such interests.

Conservation easements are perpetual in duration, are transferable, and can be in gross. See Restatement (Third) of Property, Servitudes §1.6 comments & Statutory Note, and §4.3(4) (2000). These features, especially perpetual duration, have led some commentators to express concern about conservation easements and the specter of dead-hand control. See Julia D. Mahoney, Perpetual Restrictions on Land and the Problem of the Future, 88 Va. L. Rev. 739, 744 (2002) (arguing that conservation easements "impose significant potential costs on future generations by deliberately making non-development decisions hard to change"); Nancy A. McLaughlin, Conservation Easements: Perpetuity and Beyond, 34 Ecology L.Q. 673 (2007); Jessica Owley, Changing Property in a Changing World: A Call for the End of Perpetual Conservation Easements, 30 Stan. Envtl. L. Rev. 121 (2011); Gerald Korngold, Solving the Contentious Issues of Conservation Easements: Promoting for the Future and Engaging in the Public Land Use Process, 2007 Utah L. Rev. 1039; Julia D. Mahoney, The Illusion of Perpetuity and the Preservation of Privately Owned Lands, 44 Nat. Resources J. 573 (2004); Barton H. Thompson Jr., The Trouble with Time: Influencing the Conservation Choices of Future Generations, 44 Nat. Resources J. 601 (2004); see also Nancy A. McLaughlin, Rethinking the Perpetual Nature of Conservation Easements, 29 Harv. Envtl. L. Rev. 421 (2005) (proposing application of the charitable trust law doctrine of *cy pres* to allow modification of conservation easements); Abraham Bell & Gideon Parchomovsky, Of Property and Antiproperty, 102 Mich. L. Rev.

---

28. Land trusts are nonprofit organizations that work to conserve land by accepting donations of land and conservation easements and purchasing land to maintain natural habitats or provide public recreation. They are community-based and rely on community members for support. For an argument that land trusts are an effective vehicle for developing a sense of community, see James J. Kelly, Jr., Land Trusts That Conserve Communities, 59 DePaul L. Rev. 69 (2009).

1 (2003) (proposing an "antiproperty easement" as an alternative to conventional conservation easements); Christopher S. Elmendorf, Securing Ecological Investments on Other People's Land: A Transaction-Costs Perspective, 44 Nat. Resources J. 529 (2004) (proposing a "liability-rule conservation easement"). For discussion of the problems with perpetual restrictions on property, comparing conservation easements with other restrictive property arrangements that involve no temporal limitations, see Sarah Harding, Perpetual Property, 61 Fla. L. Rev. 285 (2009); Susan French, Perpetual Trusts, Conservation Servitudes, and the Problem of the Future, 27 Cardozo L. Rev. 2523 (2006).

Critics have also objected to the substantial tax deductions given as incentives to donate conservation easements. See Daniel I. Halperin, Incentives for Conservation Easements: The Charitable Deduction or a Better Way?, 74 Law & Contemp. Probs. 29 (2011) (recommending a cap on tax credits for conservation easements and evaluation of the public value of a conservation easement by the Bureau of Land Management). Donors often overvalue such easements and have taken deductions that exceed the benefit to the public. See Timothy Lindstrom, Income Tax Aspects of Conservation Easements, 5 Wyo. L. Rev. 1, 17-18 (2005). Despite efforts by some state legislatures to stiffen requirements for conservation purposes, so-called sham easements (conservation easements of questionable public value) continue to be reported. One investigation, for example, found that generous tax deductions were being claimed in exclusive subdivisions for land located between high priced houses. Deductions were also claimed for conservation easements of land located along fairways at golf courses. See http:// www.rockymountainnews.com/news/2008/feb/09/abuses-taint-land-deals. For a detailed and comprehensive study of charitable deductions for conservations, see Nancy A. McLaughlin, Internal Revenue Code Section 170(h): National Perpetuity Standards for Federally Subsidized Conservation Easements—Part I: The Standards, 45 Real Prop., Tr. & Est. L.J. 473 (2010); Part II: Comparison to State Law, 46 Real Prop., Tr. & Est. L.J. 1 (2011). See generally Symposium, Conservation Easements: New Perspectives in an Evolving World, 74 Law & Contemp. Probs. 1 (2011). For a comparative look at conservation easements, see Gerald Korngold, Globalizing Conservation Easements: Private Law Approaches for International Environmental Protection, 28 Wis. Intl. L.J. 585 (2011).

More recently, the Uniform Environmental Covenants Act of 2003 has been promulgated. The purpose of the act is to help remediation and development of so-called brownfields (parcels previously contaminated by industrial use). The act facilitates use of environmental covenants, which are agreements between parties responsible for environmental clean-up projects. Environmental covenants impose activity and use restrictions on contaminated land and permit the contaminated land to be developed within the limits imposed by these restrictions. The servitudes that the agreements create primarily take the form of covenants rather than easements, although elements of both may be combined. The act is designed to eliminate potential obstacles to enforcement of environmental covenants under common law doctrines such as the horizontal privity and touch and concern requirements and other traditional rules that we will study in the next part of this chapter. The act has been adopted in several states.

Variations on the conservation easement idea have appeared in recent years. Some homeowners have entered into preservation easement agreements with private historic preservation associations. These agreements assure that architecturally significant homes cannot be torn down or substantially altered even after they are acquired by new owners. See, e.g., Abby Goodnough, Amid Historic Homes, New England Moves to Preserve a Modern Heritage, N.Y. Times, Dec. 4, 2011, at 20. A twist on the preservation easement is the "facade preservation easement," which is a device for preventing the facade of a house that is registered on the national Register of Historic Places from being altered. Federal tax law permits the house owner who donates such an easement to a nonprofit preservation group to take an income tax deduction for the value of the easement. Yet another innovative negative easement is the primary residence easement. This device is a reaction to the growing popularity of vacation homes whose owners leave the property vacant for most of the year—"drive-by neighbors," as they have been called. Under a plan in use in Charleston, S.C., the owners of historic homes donate to the Historic Charleston Foundation an easement that restricts the owner, present or future, from using it as a vacation home. The foundation is authorized to take action against any owner who fails to comply with the restriction. Primary residence easements are not authorized by any specific legislation. Are they enforceable at common law?

C.   Covenants Running with the Land

1.   Historical Background

a.   Covenants Enforceable at Law: Real Covenants

Thwarted by the law courts' refusal to recognize new types of negative easements, landowners turned—in the early nineteenth century—to the law of contracts. They sought judicial recognition of a contract right respecting land use enforceable not only against the promisor landowner, but against his successors in title as well.

Why were landowners so interested in imposing restrictions on the use of land? Suppose that O owns a large tract of land on which he wants to put several different uses—a factory, a residence, and a market. If O wishes to maximize the value of all parts of his tract, he will locate these uses so as to minimize the harms they might impose on each other, taking into consideration the interrelationships among the various activities. Because a factory produces smoke and a grocery produces traffic, O may place them at some distance from each other and from the residence; he may even provide a green belt of trees to serve as a buffer zone.

Similarly, bargains between neighboring property owners can operate to allocate resources efficiently by arranging land uses so as to minimize conflicts. For example, if A (owner of a residence on Whiteacre) and B (owner of a vacant lot, Blackacre) agree that a factory should not be built on Blackacre, presumably the agreement between *A* and *B* maximizes their well-being (and society's too, if there are no third-party effects that *A* and *B* have neglected to take into account). If *A* pays *B* $1,000 for *B*'s promise, the gain to *A* from not having a factory for a neighbor is likely to be greater than $1,000, and the loss to *B* of the opportunity of putting a factory on his land is likely to be less than $1,000; otherwise, we can presume that *A* and *B* would not have reached their bargain. Both *A* and *B*, then, are better off. So too if *A*, rather than giving *B* $1,000, agrees instead by a reciprocal promise not to use Whiteacre for a factory. Here the value of both Whiteacre and Blackacre for residential use is presumably greater than the value of the opportunities for industrial use that have been forgone.

Thus bargains among neighbors of the sort just discussed can serve to minimize the harmful impacts ("external costs") that arise from conflicting resource uses. Such bargains, though, are less likely to be struck if only the original promisor is bound and only the original promisee benefitted. The promisee wants assurances that he and his successors in interest will be protected against the original promisor and his successors in interest. What is needed, then, is some sort of *property right* that is enforceable by and against subsequent purchasers of Whiteacre and Blackacre. A mere contract right—the right of the original promisee to sue the original promisor alone—will seldom be sufficient to enable the market to allocate conflicting land uses efficiently. Do you see why? The answer relates to the discussion of transaction costs at pages 48-49. See also James E. Krier, Book Review, 122 U. Pa. L. Rev. 1664, 1678-1680 (1974).

In the early nineteenth century, contract rights and duties were not generally assignable. Promises were not enforceable against a person who was not a party to the contract.[29] As Lord Haldane observed in Dunlop Pneumatic Tyre Co. v. Selfridge & Co., [1915] App. Cas. 847, 853, "[I]n the law of England certain principles are fundamental. One is that only a person who is a party to a contract can sue on it." The law had, however, developed one exception to the rule of non-assignability. *Where there is privity of estate*, the judges held, the contract is enforceable by and against assignees, at least as to certain promises. It had long been established that privity of estate existed between a landlord and a tenant and that most covenants in leases would run with the land. They would be enforceable by and against a successor landlord or a successor tenant (see page 470). But it was unclear, at the beginning of the nineteenth century, whether privity of estate might exist in other circumstances.

Landowners in England tried to persuade the law courts to expand the required relationship of privity of estate to include contracts between neighbors so that the contracts would be enforceable against successor landowners. These attempts ultimately failed. The courts concluded that privity of estate, required for the burden of a covenant to run at law to successors, was satisfied only by a

---

29. Likewise, deeds were not enforceable by persons not parties to the deed. See footnote 10, page 815.

landlord-tenant relationship. Keppell v. Bailey, 39 Eng. Rep. 1042 (Ch. 1834). To this day, the burden of a covenant between landowners will not run at law in England. Thus a promise by A, owner of Blackacre, to B, owner of Whiteacre, not to permit a piggery on Blackacre is not enforceable at law against the successor owner.

Unlike the English courts, American courts did not define privity of estate to include only a landlord-tenant relationship. They permitted, under varying circumstances, covenants to run in favor of and against successor owners. They developed the American *real covenant*, a promise respecting the use of land that runs with the land *at law*. The cases on real covenants are in some disarray and are often obscure and disputed, but you will be able to understand the issues and the confusion if you pay close attention to the following analytic model.

Suppose that B, owner of Blackacre, has promised A, owner of Whiteacre, that Blackacre shall not be used for industrial purposes. B sells Blackacre to C, and A sells Whiteacre to D. C constructs a factory on Blackacre. D sues C for damages. Will the covenant run to C and D? Let us begin with the diagram shown on the next page.

If A, before any assignment, sues B, A is suing on the contract. There is privity of contract between A and B, and the law of contracts governs. No question arises whether a covenant runs. The question whether a covenant runs arises only when a person who is not a party to the covenant is suing or being sued.

Note that there are two ends of the covenant, the benefit end originally held by A and the burden end originally held by B.[30] The burdened parcel is the servient tenement. If A conveys Whiteacre to D, and B still owns Blackacre and constructs the factory, and D sues B, D must allege that the *benefit* runs to D. The burden remains with B, the original promisor. If B conveys Blackacre to C, who constructs the factory, and A, still owning Whiteacre, sues C, A must allege that the *burden* runs to C. If, as in the diagram above, both Whiteacre and Blackacre are conveyed to D and C respectively, and D sues C, D must allege that *both the burden and the benefit run*. It is important to keep in mind whether the running of the benefit or the running of the burden is involved in the case because the test for running of the burden is traditionally more onerous than the test for running of the benefit.

Observe that in the diagram we have two types of privity of estate that we shall discuss: (1) *horizontal privity*, meaning privity of estate between the original covenanting parties; and (2) *vertical privity*, meaning privity of estate between one of the covenanting parties and a successor in interest. These are called horizontal and vertical privity because, probably, countless law professors have put the above diagram on the blackboard to analyze the issues; as a result the terms have become part of the legal language. First, let us explore the meaning of *horizontal privity*.

---

30. The benefited parcel is, in analogous terms used in speaking of easements, the dominant tenement. The burdened parcel is the servient tenement.

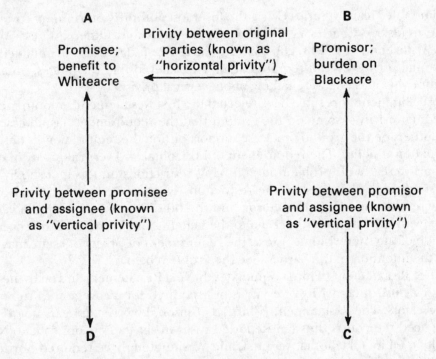

Figure 10-7

In this country, as noted above, courts did not hold privity of estate to be satisfied only in landlord-tenant relationships. Analogizing to the fact that the landlord transferred an estate to the tenant, courts defined horizontal privity of estate between landowners to be a successive (grantor-grantee) relationship.[31] Thus, if in our diagram *B*'s promise had been in a deed conveying Blackacre from *A* to *B*, *A* and *B* would be in privity of estate. Giving privity this meaning allows enforcement of the covenant against successors when the covenant is created in conjunction with the transfer of some other interest in land, for example, a deed conveying a fee simple, but not otherwise.[32]

The first Restatement of Property declared that horizontal privity of estate is required for the *burden* of a covenant to run at law. Restatement of Property §534 (1944). The Restatement went on to say, in accordance with most authority, that horizontal privity is not required for the *benefit* to run. Id. §548. The policy of the Restatement was to put various obstacles in the way of the burden running at law, but to permit the benefit to run freely. The Restatement's requirement of horizontal privity for the burden to run was sharply denounced by Judge (and

31. This is the meaning of privity of estate when the question is whether a successor adverse possessor can tack on the period of a prior adverse possessor (see pages 175-176), and when the question is whether covenants for title run with the land (see page 633).

32. Massachusetts took the unique position that horizontal privity requires that both parties must have a mutual interest in the same land, apart from the covenant. Morse v. Aldrich, 56 Mass. (19 Pick.) 449 (1837).

onetime Yale Dean) Charles Clark, the foremost authority on running covenants at the time. See Charles E. Clark, Real Covenants and Other Interests Which "Run With Land" 137-143, 206-262 (2d ed. 1947). Judge Clark maintained that horizontal privity was not required at all. He believed that the judges, in talking about privity of estate, were talking about vertical privity.

All commentators since have rejected the first Restatement's requirement of horizontal privity—some on the ground that the requirement has no case support, others on the ground that, case support or not, the requirement is unsound as a matter of policy. The requirement of horizontal and vertical privity of estate ordinarily creates no problem in enforcing restrictions on lots in a subdivision. The subdivider who imposes the restrictions in a deed is in horizontal privity of estate with the original promisor, and the other lot owners, being in vertical privity with the subdivider, succeed to the benefits and burdens of the covenant. Outside of the subdivision context, the requirement of privity of estate may frustrate the intention of the parties. See the Problem below.

The Restatement (Third) repudiates the first Restatement and takes the position that horizontal privity of estate is not required for a covenant to run at law to successors. The Restatement (Third)'s position, however, appears not to have influenced the courts thus far. Reported cases in six states, Connecticut, North Carolina, Ohio, Oklahoma, Virginia, and Washington, have required horizontal privity for enforcement of restrictive covenants, and no post-2000 (the year of the Restatement's adoption) cases have been found to the contrary. See Michael Lewyn, The Puzzling Persistence of Horizontal Privity, 27 Prob. & Prop. 32, 33 (2013). A real covenant can be a *negative* promise (a promise not to do an act) or an *affirmative* promise (a promise to do an act). A covenant is not enforceable against an assignee who has no notice of it.

PROBLEM

A and *B*, neighboring landowners, decide that they will mutually restrict their lots to single family residential use. They sign an agreement wherein each promises on behalf of herself, and her heirs and assigns, that her lot will be used for single family residential purposes only. This agreement is recorded in the county courthouse under the name of each signer. *B* sells her lot to *C*. *C* builds an apartment house on his lot. *A* sues *C* for damages. What result? Suppose that *A* rather than *C* had built the apartment house. Is *C* entitled to damages against *A*? See William B. Stoebuck, Running Covenants: An Analytical Primer, 52 Wash. L. Rev. 861, 877-881 (1977).

If the agreement between *A* and *B* was drafted by a lawyer and the court requires horizontal privity of estate, presumably the lawyer is liable to *A* for malpractice. The lawyer could put the parties in privity of estate by, first, directing *A* and *B* to convey their lots to *X* (a straw, perhaps the lawyer's secretary); and, second, directing *X* to convey *A*'s lot back to *A* by a deed containing a promise by the grantee *A* for the benefit of *B*'s lot, and then directing *X* to convey *B*'s lot back to *B* by a deed containing a promise by the grantee *B* for the benefit of *A*'s lot.

Vertical privity. Traditional doctrine requires vertical privity for both the burden and the benefit of a real covenant to run. Just what does vertical privity mean? Conventionally, it is said that under the law of real covenants the burden and the benefit run with *estates* in land, not with the land itself. With respect to the vertical privity requirement, this is understood to mean that a covenant is enforceable at law by and against remote parties only if those parties have succeeded to the original parties' estates in the land in question. *[handwritten: Vertical privity]*

But there is a qualification to this point. The vertical privity requirement applicable to the running of burdens is different from—and more demanding than—the requirement applicable to the running of benefits. On the *burden* side, the covenant is enforceable only against someone who has succeeded to the same estate as that of the original promisor. See Restatement of Property §535 (1944). If the promisor had a fee simple, the party against whom enforcement is sought must have succeeded to that fee simple estate. Hence, the burden of a real covenant does not run to, that is, is not enforceable at law against, an adverse possessor because an adverse possessor does not succeed to the original owner's estate but takes a new title by operation of law. *[handwritten: Same as estate as original promisor] [handwritten: N/A to adverse possessor b/c of new title]*

A more relaxed standard is used for the running of the benefit, however. The promise is enforceable by a person who succeeds to the original promisee's estate or to a lesser interest carved out of that estate. See Restatement of Property §547 (1944). *[handwritten: Benefit running]*

To illustrate these rules, consider the following hypotheticals:

O, owner of a 2 acre parcel, divides that parcel and conveys 1 acre to *A*, keeping the other acre herself. The deed, properly recorded, includes mutual covenants by *A*, on behalf of herself, her heirs and assigns, and *O*, her heirs and assigns, that the conveyed and the retained parcel will be used for residential purposes only.

(a) *B* takes *A*'s parcel by adverse possession. *B* later opens a restaurant on the premises. *O* brings an action against *B* for damages for breach of the covenant made by *A*. *O* will lose. The burden does not run against *B* because *B*, as an adverse possessor, is not in vertical privity with *A*, the original promisor.[33]

(b) *O* leases her parcel to *C* for five years. *A* opens a nursery school on her parcel. *C* brings an action against *A* for damages for breaching the covenant. The question is, does the benefit of the covenant run at law in favor of *C*, a lessee of the original promisee? Under the traditional law, the answer is yes. As *O*'s lessee, *C* succeeded to an estate carved out of *O*'s original estate and is therefore in vertical privity with *O*.

---

33. Adverse possession does not begin to run against either a real covenant or an equitable servitude until the promise is breached.

The Restatement (Third) of Property, Servitudes, fundamentally changes these rules, as we discuss in the next section (see pages 819-820).

b.   Covenants Enforceable in Equity: Equitable Servitudes

Although in England the law courts, bound by the learning of the past, failed to respond positively to market demands for negative servitudes prohibiting some objectionable use enforceable against successor owners, the chancellor, by design or by result, came to the aid of the market in the famous case of Tulk v. Moxhay.

Tulk v. Moxhay

Court of Chancery, England, 1848
2 Phillips 774, 41 Eng. Rep. 1143

In the year 1808 the Plaintiff, being then the owner in fee of the vacant piece of ground in Leicester Square, as well as of several of the houses forming the Square, sold the piece of ground by the description of "Leicester Square garden or pleasure ground, with the equestrian statue then standing in the centre thereof, and the iron railing and stone work round the same," to one Elms in fee: and the deed of conveyance contained a covenant by Elms, for himself, his heirs, and assigns, with the Plaintiff, his heirs, executors, and administrators,

> that Elms, his heirs, and assigns should, and would from time to time, and at all times thereafter at his and their own costs and charges, keep and maintain the said piece of ground and square garden, and the iron railing round the same in its then form, and in sufficient and proper repair as a square garden and pleasure ground, in an open state, uncovered with any buildings, in neat and ornamental order; and that it should be lawful for the inhabitants of Leicester Square, tenants of the Plaintiff, on payment of a reasonable rent for the same, to have keys at their own expense and the privilege of admission therewith at any time or times into the said square garden and pleasure ground.

The piece of land so conveyed passed by divers mesne conveyances into the hands of the Defendant, whose purchase deed contained no similar covenant with his vendor: but he admitted that he had purchased with notice of the covenant in the deed of 1808.

The Defendant having manifested an intention to alter the character of the square garden, and asserted a right, if he thought fit, to build upon it, the Plaintiff, who still remained owner of several houses in the square, filed this bill for an injunction; and an injunction was granted by the Master of the Rolls to restrain the Defendant from converting or using the piece of ground and square garden, and the iron railing round the same, to or for any other purpose than as a . . . square garden and pleasure ground in an open state, and uncovered with buildings. . . .

THE LORD CHANCELLOR [Cottenham]. . . . That this Court has jurisdiction to enforce a contract between the owner of land and his neighbour purchasing a part of it, that the latter shall either use or abstain from using the land purchased in a particular way, is what I never knew disputed. Here there is no question about the contract: the owner of certain houses in the square sells the land adjoining, with a covenant from the purchaser not to use it for any other purpose than as a square garden. And it is now contended, not that the vendee could violate the contract, but that he might sell the piece of land, and that the purchaser from him may violate it without this Court having any power to interfere. If that were so, it would be impossible for an owner of land to sell part of it without incurring the risk of rendering what he retains worthless. It is said that, the covenant being one which does not run with the land, this court cannot enforce it; but the question is, not whether the covenant runs with the land, but whether a party shall be permitted to use the land in a manner inconsistent with the contract entered into by his vendor, and with notice of which he purchased. Of course, the price would be affected by the covenant, and nothing could be more inequitable than the original purchaser should be able to sell the property the next day for a greater price, in consideration of the assignee being allowed to escape from the liability which he had himself undertaken.

Leicester Square today

Leicester Square, 1852

It is said that "an injunction is for sale," meaning the person who holds it may sell it to the enjoined party if the price is right. And this is what happened after the decision in Tulk v. Moxhay.

At the time of Tulk v. Moxhay, Leicester Square was changing from a residential to a commercial area, and the central garden had become an unkempt receptacle for rubbish. In 1851 James Wyld, a geographer, purchased the garden from Moxhay's widow. With the consent of the Tulk family, who received an option to purchase an undivided half of the garden at the end of 10 years, Wyld erected in the garden a building to house a 60-foot high plaster scale model of the earth. This building, called "Wyld's Monster Globe" in the etching above, dwarfed the surrounding houses. After 10 years this was pulled down, and John A. Tulk, grandson of the plaintiff in Tulk v. Moxhay, exercised the option to purchase. John A. Tulk hoped to convert the garden to building land, as Moxhay had tried to do formerly. After much public outcry, the garden was acquired by the government for a public park in 1874. Leicester Square today is the center of London's cinema district. For more on the history of Leicester Square, see 1 Zechariah Chafee & Sidney P. Simpson, Cases on Equity 704 (1934).

That the question does not depend upon whether the covenant runs with the land is evident from this, that if there was a mere agreement and no covenant, this Court would enforce it against a party purchasing with notice of it; for if an equity is attached to the property by the owner, no one purchasing with notice of that equity can stand in a different situation from the party from whom he purchased. . . .

I think the cases cited before the Vice-Chancellor and this decision of the Master of the Rolls perfectly right, and, therefore, that this motion must be refused, with costs.

NOTES, QUESTIONS, AND PROBLEMS

1. *The background of* Tulk v. Moxhay. The fascinating story behind Tulk v. Moxhay and the history of Leicester Square is told in James Charles Smith, *Tulk v. Moxhay*: The Fight to Develop Leicester Square, in Property Stories 171 (Gerald Korngold & Andrew P. Morriss eds. 2d ed. 2009). Professor Smith reports that the origin of the central restriction involved in the case was not the 1808 deed from Tulk to Elms but a certificate of partition executed earlier in 1789. The land of which the garden was a part was partitioned to pay the original owner's mortgagees. The court imposed the restrictions to protect land that the mortgagees acquired near the garden. Professor Smith speculates that had Moxhay's lawyers considered this fact they might have challenged Tulk's standing. Tulk owned none of the benefitted land and hence was not an intended beneficiary of the judicial restriction. Id. at 178 n.24.

2. *The covenants in* Tulk. Examine each of the covenants made by Elms. How would you classify the rights and duties intended by the deed of conveyance? Is the covenant sued on really an easement of view in promissory form?

The chancellor reasoned that it would be inequitable for Elms, who bought the land at a price reflecting the burdens, to be able to charge his purchaser the price of unburdened land. He therefore enforced the negative covenant. Does this reasoning suggest that the other covenants should also be enforceable against the defendant? Although in a few cases after Tulk v. Moxhay the court suggested it was prepared to enforce affirmative covenants, in 1881 it was settled in England that only negative covenants are enforceable as equitable servitudes. Haywood v. Brunswick Permanent Benefit Bldg. Socy., (1881) 8 Q.B.D. 403. An equitable servitude was viewed as an interest in property analogous to a negative easement. In the United States, as we shall see, affirmative obligations have been enforced as equitable servitudes.

3. *The traditional requirements for equitable servitudes.* An equitable servitude, enforceable by an injunction as in Tulk v. Moxhay, is a covenant respecting the use of land enforceable against successor owners or possessors in equity regardless of its enforceability at law. Equity requires that (1) the parties intend the promise to run, (2) that a subsequent purchaser have actual or constructive notice of the covenant,[34] and (3) that the covenant touch and concern the land (of which more later). Horizontal privity of estate is of no importance in equity. Nor is vertical privity required for the *burden* to run. All subsequent owners and possessors

---

34. Covenants run in equity against successors who give no consideration (donees, heirs, will beneficiaries), whether or not they have notice. A fundamental principle of the recording system is that only subsequent purchasers, and not donees, are protected against prior interests of which they have no notice. See page 734.

are bound by the servitude, just as they are bound by an easement. 2 American Law of Property §9.31 (1952). The *benefit* runs to all assignees. It may also run to adverse possessors, but this question has not been litigated. Id. §9.27. In some jurisdictions, however, a covenant made for the benefit of a third-party beneficiary cannot be enforced by the beneficiary unless he can show that he acquired title to his land from the original covenantee, either before or after the covenant was made. In these jurisdictions, privity of estate may be required in equity for enforcement of the benefit by the third-party beneficiaries. See the discussion on pages 918-919.

4. *Injunction or damages (or a different remedy)?* The traditional difference between real covenants and equitable servitudes relates to the remedy sought. The usual remedy for breach of a real covenant is damages in a suit at law. The usual remedy for breach of an equitable servitude is an injunction. Damages and injunctions are not the only remedies that plaintiffs may seek, however. As we will see in the *Neponsit* case, which follows shortly (see pages 909), the plaintiff may seek enforcement of a lien, which is an equitable proceeding. Another possible remedy sometimes sought is a declaratory judgment. Under state law, the equitable or legal nature of a declaratory judgment proceeding varies from jurisdiction to jurisdiction. In jurisdictions where the proceeding is legal in nature, the rules governing real covenants apply. See, e.g., Cunningham v. City of Greensboro, 711 S.E.2d 477 (N.C. App. 2011).

Refer back to the Problem on page 896. If injunctive relief had been sought there, what result?

If an injunction is granted, the plaintiff can, if the plaintiff wishes, "sell the injunction" to the defendant, as happened in Tulk v. Moxhay. By fixing the selling price of the injunction, the plaintiff can make his own determination of the amount of damages, whereas if the plaintiff sues for damages the jury determines the amount of damages.

Today, in most states, law and equity have merged, and a court in an equitable action for an injunction can give damages instead. See Boomer v. Atlantic Cement Co., page 790 (denying injunction but granting damages); Spur Industries v. Del E. Webb Development Co., page 797 (granting injunction but requiring plaintiff to pay damages); cf. Sonoma Development, Inc. v. Miller, 515 S.E.2d 577 (Va. 1999) (in suit for injunction, court, without explanation, treated covenant as a real covenant, held horizontal privity existed, and granted injunction). So does it matter anymore whether a covenant is characterized as a real covenant or an equitable servitude? As we have already discussed (see page 810), the Restatement (Third) says no. Under its approach, the same rules apply to all covenants running with the land, and a court may enforce the covenant by "any appropriate remedy or combination of remedies, which may include declaratory judgment, compensatory damages, punitive damages, nominal damages, injunctions, restitution, and imposition of liens." Id. §8.3. However, as we have also seen, a number of courts continue to distinguish between the requirements for real covenants and equitable servitudes, so to that extent at least the distinction between law and equity still matters.

5. *The property theory of equitable servitudes.* Although an equitable servitude started out as a promise enforced in equity, in the course of time it turned into an interest in land. Unlike a real covenant, which attaches to an estate in land, an equitable servitude " 'sinks its tentacles into the soil,' burdening the land itself and not the estate." Powell on Real Property §60.01[4] (Michael A. Wolf gen. ed. 2009). What this means is that equitable servitudes have no privity requirement.[35] In this respect they are like easements.

One important consequence of the property theory is that, after the original promisor has conveyed the burdened land, the promisor cannot be sued on the covenant, either in law or in equity. The original promisor has lost control of the land when she assigns her entire interest, and it would be unfair to penalize her for the conduct of some future owner. Concomitantly, the original promisee may not enforce restrictions after he has conveyed the benefited land. See Haldeman v. Teicholz, 611 N.Y.S.2d 669 (App. Div. 1994); Restatement (Third) of Property, Servitudes §4.4 (2000).

2. Creation of Covenants

A real covenant must be created by a written instrument signed by the covenantor. It is an interest in land within the meaning of the Statute of Frauds. If the deed creating a real covenant is signed by the grantor only, and it contains a promise by the grantee, the promise is enforceable against the grantee. The grantee is bound by the act of accepting such a deed. A real covenant cannot arise by estoppel, implication, or prescription, as can an easement.

Similarly, an equitable servitude is an interest in land. But unlike a real covenant, it may be implied in equity under certain limited circumstances. An equitable servitude, which arises out of a promise, cannot be obtained by prescription.

Sanborn v. McLean

Supreme Court of Michigan, 1925
206 N.W. 496

WIEST, J. Defendant Christina McLean owns the west 35 feet of lot 86 of Green Lawn subdivision, at the northeast corner of Collingwood avenue and Second boulevard, in the city of Detroit, upon which there is a dwelling house, occupied by herself and her husband, defendant John A. McLean. The house fronts Collingwood avenue. At the rear of the lot is an alley. Mrs. McLean derived title from her husband and, in the course of the opinion, we will speak of both as defendants. Mr. and Mrs. McLean started to erect a gasoline filling station at

35. Having said that, we need to add a qualification. See the discussion regarding vertical privity on the benefit side in Note 5, on pages 918-920.

the rear end of their lot, and they and their contractor, William S. Weir, were enjoined by decree from doing so and bring the issues before us by appeal. Mr. Weir will not be further mentioned in the opinion.

Collingwood avenue is a high-grade residence street between Woodward avenue and Hamilton boulevard, with single, double, and apartment houses, and plaintiffs who are owners of land adjoining, and in the vicinity of defendants' land, and who trace title, as do defendants, to the proprietors of the subdivision, claim that the proposed gasoline station will be a nuisance per se, is in violation of the general plan fixed for use of all lots on the street for residence purposes only, as evidenced by restrictions upon 53 of the 91 lots fronting on Collingwood avenue, and that defendants' lot is subject to a reciprocal negative easement barring a use so detrimental to the enjoyment and value of its neighbors. Defendants insist that no restrictions appear in their chain of title and they purchased without notice of any reciprocal negative easement, and deny that a gasoline station is a nuisance per se. We find no occasion to pass upon the question of nuisance, as the case can be decided under the rule of reciprocal negative easement.

This subdivision was planned strictly for residence purposes, except lots fronting Woodward avenue and Hamilton boulevard. The 91 lots on Collingwood avenue were platted in 1891, designed for and each one sold solely for residence purposes, and residences have been erected upon all of the lots. Is defendants' lot subject to a reciprocal negative easement? If the owner of two or more lots, so situated as to bear the relation, sells one with restrictions of benefit to the land retained, the servitude becomes mutual, and, during the period of restraint, the owner of the lot or lots retained can do nothing forbidden to the owner of the lot sold. For want of a better descriptive term this is styled a reciprocal negative easement. It runs with the land sold by virtue of express fastening and abides with the land retained until loosened by expiration of its period of service or by events working its destruction. It is not personal to owners but operative upon use of the land by any owner having actual or constructive notice thereof. It is an easement passing its benefits and carrying its obligations to all purchasers of land subject to its affirmative or negative mandates. It originates for mutual benefit and exists with vigor sufficient to work its ends. It must start with a common owner. Reciprocal negative easements are never retroactive; the very nature of their origin forbids. They arise, if at all, out of a benefit accorded land retained, by restrictions upon neighboring land sold by a common owner. Such a scheme of restrictions must start with a common owner; it cannot arise and fasten upon one lot by reason of other lot owners conforming to a general plan. If a reciprocal negative easement attached to defendants' lot it was fastened thereto while in the hands of the common owner of it and neighboring lots by way of sale of other lots with restrictions beneficial at that time to it. This leads to inquiry as to what lots, if any, were sold with restrictions by the common owner before the sale of defendants' lot. While the proofs cover another avenue we need consider sales only on Collingwood.

December 28, 1892, Robert J. and Joseph R. McLaughlin, who were then evidently owners of the lots on Collingwood avenue, deeded lots 37 to 41 and 58 to 62, inclusive, with the following restrictions:

No residence shall be erected upon said premises, which shall cost less than $2,500 and nothing but residences shall be erected upon said premises. Said residences shall front on Helene (now Collingwood) avenue and be placed no nearer than 20 feet from the front street line.

July 24, 1893, the McLaughlins conveyed lots 17 to 21 and 78 to 82, both inclusive, and lot 98 with the same restrictions. Such restrictions were imposed for the benefit of the lands held by the grantors to carry out the scheme of a residential district, and a restrictive negative easement attached to the lots retained, and title to lot 86 was then in the McLaughlins. Defendants' title, through mesne conveyances, runs back to a deed by the McLaughlins dated September 7, 1893, without restrictions mentioned therein. Subsequent deeds to other lots were executed by the McLaughlins, some with restrictions and some without. Previous to September 7, 1893, a reciprocal negative easement had attached to lot 86 by acts of the owners, as before mentioned, and such easement is still attached and may now be enforced by plaintiffs, provided defendants, at the time of their purchase, had knowledge, actual or constructive, thereof. The plaintiffs run back with their title, as do defendants, to a common owner. This common owner, as before stated, by restrictions upon lots sold, had burdened all the lots retained with reciprocal restrictions. Defendants' lot and plaintiff Sanborn's lot, next thereto, were held by such common owner, burdened with a reciprocal negative easement and, when later sold to separate parties, remained burdened therewith and right to demand observance thereof passed to each purchaser with notice of the easement. The restrictions were upon defendants' lot while it was in the hands of the common owners, and abstract of title to defendants' lot showed

Corner House Lot 86 of Green Lawn Subdivision
Collingwood Avenue at Second Boulevard Detroit 1987

the common owners and the record showed deeds of lots in the plat restricted to perfect and carry out the general plan and resulting in a reciprocal negative easement upon defendants' lot and all lots within its scope, and defendants and their predecessors in title were bound by constructive notice under our recording acts. The original plan was repeatedly declared in subsequent sales of lots by restrictions in the deeds, and while some lots sold were not so restricted the purchasers thereof, in every instance, observed the general plan and purpose of the restrictions in building residences. For upward of 30 years the united efforts of all persons interested have carried out the common purpose of making and keeping all the lots strictly for residences, and defendants are the first to depart therefrom.

When Mr. McLean purchased on contract in 1910 or 1911, there was a partly built dwelling on lot 86, which he completed and now occupies. He had an abstract of title which he examined and claims he was told by the grantor that the lot was unrestricted. Considering the character of use made of all the lots open to a view of Mr. McLean when he purchased, we think he was put thereby to inquiry, beyond asking his grantor whether there were restrictions. He had an abstract showing the subdivision and that lot 86 had 97 companions; he could not avoid noticing the strictly uniform residence character given the lots by the expensive dwellings thereon, and the least inquiry would have quickly developed the fact that lot 86 was subjected to a reciprocal negative easement, and he could finish his house and, like the others, enjoy the benefits of the easement. We do not say Mr. McLean should have asked his neighbors about restrictions, but we do say that with the notice he had from a view of the premises on the street, clearly indicating the residences were built and the lots occupied in strict accordance with a general plan, he was put to inquiry, and had he inquired he would have found of record the reason for such general conformation, and the benefits thereof serving the owners of lot 86 and the obligations running with such service and available to adjacent lot owners to prevent a departure from the general plan by an owner of lot 86.

While no case appears to be on all fours with the one at bar the principles we have stated, and the conclusions announced, are supported by Allen v. City of Detroit, 167 Mich. 464 (36 L.R.A. [N.S.] 890); McQuade v. Wilcox, 215 Mich. 302 (16 A.L.R. 997); French v. White Star Refining Co., 229 Mich. 474; Silberman v. Uhrlaub, 116 N.Y. App. Div. 869 (102 N.Y. Supp. 299); Boyden v. Roberts, 131 Wis. 659 (111 N.W. 701); Howland v. Andrus, 80 N.J. Eq. 276 (83 Atl. 982).

We notice the decree in the circuit directed that the work done on the building be torn down. If the portion of the building constructed can be utilized for any purpose within the restrictions it need not be destroyed.[36]

With this modification the decree in the circuit is affirmed, with costs to plaintiffs.

---

36. In Webb v. Smith, 568 N.W.2d 378 (Mich. App. 1997), the court ordered a very expensive home, erected in violation of subdivision restrictions, torn down.

NOTES AND QUESTIONS

1. *Notice.* In McQuade v. Wilcox, 183 N.W. 771 (Mich. 1921), Mary Wilcox, the owner of a large tract of land, divided it into lots for residential subdivision. By each deed, save the deed to lot 2, Wilcox restricted the lot sold to a single family residential dwelling, and *by the same instrument restricted her remaining lots to the same use.* After she had sold almost all the other lots in the subdivision, and after expensive residences had been built on them, Wilcox sold lot 2, a four-acre lot on which was her home, to a purchaser who wanted to convert it into a restaurant. Wilcox's deed conveying lot 2 contained no restrictions, and the purchaser had no actual notice of the restrictions on lot 2 appearing in the earlier deeds to the other lots. The court held, as did Guillette v. Daly Dry Wall, Inc., page 728, that the recording of the deeds to the other lots, which contained a restriction on lot 2, gave constructive notice to the purchaser of lot 2 that lot 2 was restricted. Therefore the purchaser of lot 2 was bound by the restrictions.

Inasmuch as prior deeds by the McLaughlins to other lots in Green Lawn subdivision gave constructive notice of their contents to the purchaser of lot 86, why did the court talk of "inquiry notice" in Sanborn v. McLean? Is it because the defendants McLean would not have found any written restriction on lot 86 had they searched the title to other lots in Green Lawn subdivision and would not have constructive notice of any such restriction?

2. *What is a "scheme" or general plan?* On what constitutes a scheme or general plan, from which restrictions will be implied in equity, see Restatement (Third) of Property, Servitudes §2.14 (2000). The plan usually imposes uniform restrictions on all lots. But uniformity is not required. The plan may be that some lots are intended to be restricted in certain ways, while others are restricted in other ways or not at all. In Evans v. Pollock, 796 S.W.2d 465 (Tex. 1990), it was held that the evidence indicated that the restrictions prohibiting commercial use and permitting only one dwelling per lot were intended to apply to lakefront lots but not to hilltop lots. The court stressed that the provision permitting restrictions to be waived or modified with consent of owners of three-fourths of the lakefront lots was a strong indication these restrictions were intended to apply only to the lakefront lots.

3. *Majority and contrary views.* A majority of courts imply negative restrictions from a general plan, as was done in Sanborn v. McLean. But a few jurisdictions take the Statute of Frauds more seriously. In California, an equitable servitude must be created by a written instrument identifying the burdened lot; it will not be implied from the existence of restrictions on other lots in a subdivision. Riley v. Bear Creek Planning Comm., 551 P.2d 1213 (Cal. 1976). If a recorded subdivision map contains restrictions on the property, which are said to be covenants running with the land, such written restrictions are enforceable by and against subsequent purchasers of lots in the subdivision. Citizens for Covenant Compliance v. Anderson, 906 P.2d 1314 (Cal. 1995).

In Massachusetts, covenants will not be implied from a general plan, but if the covenants on the burdened lot are in writing a general plan may be used to show that the neighbors in the subdivision were intended as beneficiaries and may enforce the covenants. Snow v. Van Dam, 197 N.E. 224 (Mass. 1935).

4. *The Virginia approach.* In Virginia, the courts have limited equitable servitudes, including those that were expressly created, to general plan covenants on all lots in a subdivision. See Barner v. Chappell, 585 S.E.2d 590 (Va. 2003); Sonoma Development, Inc. v. Miller, 515 S.E.2d 577 (Va. 1999). A covenant that was not created incident to a general plan may be recognized as a real covenant *if* it meets the requirements for real covenants. In Virginia, those requirements still include horizontal privity. However, if a non-general-plan covenant meets all of the requirements of real covenant at law, the court will enforce it by injunction. The effect of these decisions appears to be that in Virginia, there is no real difference between a real covenant and an equitable servitude except that non-general-plan covenants will not be enforced as equitable servitudes, i.e., enforced by an injunction, unless horizontal privity exists.

5. *Who has the benefit—prior purchasers? subsequent purchasers?* Suppose in a residential subdivision *O*, the developer conveyed lot 1 in 2011 to *X*, lot 2 in 2012 to *Y*, and lot 3 in 2012 to *Z*. In each deed, *O* inserted an express covenant by the buyer that the lot is restricted to single family residential use and that this covenant is for the benefit of "*O*, his heirs and assigns." The deed makes no reference, however, to restrictions on purchasers of other lots in the subdivision. In 2013, *X* begins construction of a convenience store on lot 1. Are *Y* and *Z* entitled to sue him for an injunction? The answer is yes. *Y* and *Z*, as subsequent purchasers from *O*, are successors to the benefit of *X*'s covenant to him.

More difficult is the reverse situation, where a prior purchaser seeks to enforce a covenant against a subsequent purchaser from a common grantor. In the above example, suppose that *Z* is the one who breaches the covenant, and *X* sues to enforce it against *Z*. *X*, as a prior purchaser from *O*, apparently is a stranger to the agreement made between *O* and *Z*. There are two theories by which a prior purchaser in a subdivision can enforce an agreement subsequently made by his grantor and a subsequent purchaser, with the intention to benefit the land previously sold. The first is the theory adopted by the court in Sanborn v. McLean, the *implied reciprocal servitude* theory. According to this theory, when a common grantor later sells a parcel from his remaining land, the prior purchaser is enforcing a reciprocal servitude that is implied from a common plan of development.

This theory is unavailable in two situations: first, in one of the minority of jurisdictions interpreting the Statute of Frauds as barring implied servitudes (see Note 3, above), and second, where the developer had no common plan. In these situations, an alternative theory may be available—*the third-party beneficiary* theory. Applying that theory (which we encountered in Chapter 6 in discussing subleases and assignments, see pages 471-472) to the earlier example, the express restriction in the deed to *Z* was for the benefit of all of the residents of the development, and equity is merely permitting *X* to enforce it as a third-party beneficiary. In most of the cases decided in recent decades, courts have followed this theory where there is evidence (e.g., language in the deed or a common plan) that the parties intended the prior purchaser to have the benefit of the covenant. See, e.g., Zamiarski v. Koziak, 239 N.Y.S.2d 221 (App. Div. 1963). Some courts have imposed limitations on the theory's application, however. For example, as we will see later in this chapter (see pages 918-919), when it comes to enforcing promises respecting land use, some courts have hemmed it in with a requirement that the third-party beneficiary be in privity of estate with the original promise. This limitation does not cause any difficulty when subdivision restrictions are sued on by neighbors in the subdivision, because they receive their titles from the developer or other original promise, but it does prevent enforcement by someone to whom the original promise has never conveyed land. See Brown v. Heirs of Fuller, 347 A.2d 127 127 (Me. 1975). Restatement (Third) of Property, Servitudes §2.6(2) adopts the third-party beneficiary theory.

3.   Validity and Enforcement of Covenants

Tulk v. Moxhay relaxed the requirements for the enforcement of covenants in equity, but it did not eliminate all of the common law's requirements. As mentioned briefly in Note 3 on page 901, equity imposes three requirements: (1) *intent* that the benefit and/or the burden of the covenant run to successors of the original parties; (2) *notice* on the part of purchasers of the original promisor; and (3) that the covenant *touch and concern* land. In addition, vertical privity may be required in some jurisdictions for the benefit (but not the burden) of a covenant to run in equity. In this section we take up these requirements. Historically, courts have used them as the means to examine whether there are certain types of obligations that parties should not be able to attach to land and what, if any, limits should exist on who can enforce a covenant. As we will see, the Restatement (Third) of Property, Servitudes, generally focuses on these questions directly rather than under the guise of one or more of the traditional doctrinal requirements.

The next case, *Neponsit*, raises the vertical privity and touch and concern requirements. It does so in the context of an early example of a residential phenomenon that has become extraordinarily popular today, the homeowners association, or common interest community, as it is also known. We examine common interest communities in more detail later, beginning at page 937.

Neponsit Property Owners' Association, Inc. v. Emigrant Industrial Savings Bank[37]

Court of Appeals of New York, 1938
15 N.E.2d 793

LEHMAN, J. The plaintiff, as assignee of Neponsit Realty Company, has brought this action to foreclose a lien upon land which the defendant owns. The lien, it is

---

37. Professor Craig Oren calls to our attention that the Emigrant Industrial Savings Bank was an outgrowth of the Irish Emigrant Society, an institution to aid Irish immigrants to America during the great potato famine (1845 to 1850). The bank was founded in 1850 to counter discrimination against the Irish by established banks. It required its new depositors and borrowers to give the date and place of birth and names of parents and siblings. The bank, renamed Emigrant Savings Bank in 1967, transferred its records to the New York City Public Library, where they are a treasure trove for genealogists. — EDS.

alleged, arises from a covenant, condition or charge contained in a deed of conveyance of the land from Neponsit Realty Company to a predecessor in title of
the defendant.[38] The defendant purchased the land at a judicial sale. The referee's deed to the defendant and every deed in the defendant's chain of title since
the conveyance of the land by Neponsit Realty Company purports to convey the
property subject to the covenant, condition or charge contained in the original
deed. . . .

It appears that in January, 1911, Neponsit Realty Company, as owner of a
tract of land in Queens county, caused to be filed in the office of the clerk of the
county a map of the land. The tract was developed for a strictly residential community, and Neponsit Realty Company conveyed lots in the tract to purchasers,
describing such lots by reference to the filed map and to roads and streets shown
thereon. In 1917, Neponsit Realty Company conveyed the land now owned by
the defendant to Robert Oldner Deyer and his wife by deed which contained the
covenant upon which the plaintiff's cause of action is based.

That covenant provides:

And the party of the second part for the party of the second part and the heirs, successors and
assigns of the party of the second part further covenants that the property conveyed by this
deed shall be subject to an annual charge in such an amount as will be fixed by the party of the
first part, its successors and assigns, not, however exceeding in any year the sum of four ($4.00)

---

38. An action to enforce a lien to secure a promise to pay money cannot succeed if the debt is not owed.
After the original covenantors, Robert Deyer and his wife, conveyed the land, they are no longer liable on the
debt because they have no interest in the land (see page 903). Only if the debt is owed by the assignee defendant
bank can the lien be enforced. — Eds.

Dollars per lot 20 x 100 feet. The assigns of the party of the first part may include a Property Owners' Association which may hereafter be organized for the purposes referred to in this paragraph, and in case such association is organized the sums in this paragraph provided for shall be payable to such association. The party of the second part for the party of the second part and the heirs, successors and assigns of the party of the second part covenants that they will pay this charge to the party of the first part, its successors and assigns on the first day of May in each and every year, and further covenants that said charge shall on said date in each year become a lien on the land and shall continue to be such lien until fully paid. Such charge shall be payable to the party of the first part or its successors or assigns, and shall be devoted to the maintenance of the roads, paths, parks, beach, sewers and such other public purposes as shall from time to time be determined by the party of the first part, its successors or assigns. And the party of the second part by the acceptance of this deed hereby expressly vests in the party of the first part, its successors and assigns, the right and power to bring all actions against the owner of the premises hereby conveyed or any part thereof for the collection of such charge and to enforce the aforesaid lien therefor.

     These covenants shall run with the land and shall be construed as real covenants running with the land until January 31st, 1940, when they shall cease and determine.

Every subsequent deed of conveyance of the property in the defendant's chain of title, including the deed from the referee to the defendant, contained, as we have said, a provision that they were made subject to covenants and restrictions of former deeds of record.

There can be no doubt that the Neponsit Realty Company intended that the covenant should run with the land and should be enforceable by a property owners association against every owner of property in the residential tract which the realty company was then developing. The language of the covenant admits of no other construction. Regardless of the intention of the parties, a covenant will run with the land and will be enforceable against a subsequent purchaser of the land at the suit of one who claims the benefit of the covenant, only if the covenant complies with certain legal requirements. These requirements rest upon ancient rules and precedents. The age-old essentials of a real covenant, aside from the form of the covenant, may be summarily formulated as follows: (1) it must appear that grantor and grantee intended that the covenant should run with the land; (2) it must appear that the covenant is one "touching" or "concerning" the land with which it runs; (3) it must appear that there is "privity of estate" between the promisee or party claiming the benefit of the covenant and the right to enforce it, and the promisor or party who rests under the burden of the covenant. (Clark on Covenants and Interests Running with Land, p. 74.) Although the deeds of Neponsit Realty Company conveying lots in the tract it developed "contained a provision to the effect that the covenants ran with the land, such provision in the absence of the other legal requirements is insufficient to accomplish such a purpose." (Morgan Lake Co. v. N.Y., N.H. & H.R.R. Co., 262 N.Y. 234, 238.) In his opinion in that case, Judge Crane posed but found it unnecessary to decide many of the questions which the court must consider in this case.

The covenant in this case is intended to create a charge or obligation to pay a fixed sum of money to be "devoted to the maintenance of the roads, paths, parks, beach, sewers and such other public purposes as shall from time to time be determined by the party of the first part [the grantor], its successors or assigns." It is an affirmative covenant to pay money for use in connection with, but not upon, the land which it is said is subject to the burden of the covenant. Does such a covenant "touch" or "concern" the land? These terms are not part of a statutory definition, a limitation placed by the State upon the power of the courts to enforce covenants *intended* to run with the land by the parties who entered into the covenants. Rather they are words used by courts in England in old cases to describe a limitation which the courts themselves created or to formulate a test which the courts have devised and which the courts voluntarily apply. (Cf. Spencer's Case, Coke, vol. 3, part 5, p. 16; Mayor of Congleton v. Pattison, 10 East, 316.) In truth the test so formulated is too vague to be of much assistance and judges and academic scholars alike have struggled, not with entire success, to formulate a test at once more satisfactory and more accurate. "It has been found impossible to state any absolute tests to determine what covenants touch and concern land and what do not. The question is one for the court to determine in the exercise of its best judgment upon the facts of each case." (Clark, op. cit. p. 76.)

Even though that be true, a determination by a court in one case upon particular facts will often serve to point the way to correct decision in other cases upon analogous facts. Such guideposts may not be disregarded. It has been often said that a covenant to pay a sum of money is a personal affirmative covenant which usually does not concern or touch the land. Such statements are based upon English decisions which hold in effect that only covenants, which compel the covenanter to submit to some *restriction on the use* of his property, touch or concern the land, and that the burden of a covenant which requires the covenanter to do an affirmative act, even on his own land, for the benefit of the owner of a "dominant" estate, does not run with his land. (Miller v. Clary, 210 N.Y. 127.) In that case the court pointed out that in many jurisdictions of this country the narrow English rule has been criticized and a more liberal and flexible rule has been substituted. In this State the courts have not gone so far. We have not abandoned the historic distinction drawn by the English courts. So this court has recently said:

> Subject to a few exceptions not important at this time, there is now in this State a settled rule of law that a covenant to do an affirmative act, as distinguished from a covenant merely negative in effect, does not run with the land so as to charge the burden of performance on a subsequent grantee [citing cases]. This is so though the burden of such a covenant is laid upon the very parcel which is the subject-matter of conveyance. [Guaranty Trust Co. v. N.Y. & Queens County Ry. Co., 253 N.Y. 190, 204, opinion by Cardozo, Ch. J.]

Both in that case and in the case of Miller v. Clary (supra) the court pointed out that there were some exceptions or limitations in the application of the general rule. Some promises to pay money have been enforced, as covenants running with the land, against subsequent holders of the land who took with notice of the covenant. (Cf. Greenfarb v. R.S.K. Realty Corp., 256 N.Y. 130; Morgan Lake Co. v. N.Y., N.H. & H.R.R. Co., supra.) It may be difficult to classify these exceptions or to formulate a test of whether a particular covenant to pay money or to perform some other act falls within the general rule that ordinarily an affirmative covenant is a personal and not a real covenant, or falls outside the limitations placed upon the general rule. At least it must "touch" or "concern" the land in a substantial degree, and though it may be inexpedient and perhaps impossible to formulate a rigid test or definition which will be entirely satisfactory or which can be applied mechanically in all cases, we should at least be able to state the problem and find a reasonable method of approach to it. It has been suggested that a covenant which runs with the land must affect the legal relations—the advantages and the burdens—of the parties to the covenant, as owners of particular parcels of land and not merely as members of the community in general, such as taxpayers or owners of other land. (Clark, op. cit. p. 76. Cf. Professor Bigelow's article on The Contents of Covenants in Leases, 12 Mich. L. Rev. 639; 30 Law Quarterly Review 319.) That method of approach has the merit of realism. The test is based on the effect of the covenant rather than on technical distinctions. Does the covenant impose, on the one hand, a burden upon an interest in land, which on the other hand increases the value of a different interest in the same or related land?[39] Even though we accept that approach and test, it still remains true that whether a particular covenant is sufficiently connected with the use of land to run with the land, must be in many cases a question of degree. A promise to pay for something to be done in connection with the promisor's land does not differ essentially from a promise by the promisor to do the thing himself, and both promises constitute, in a substantial sense, a restriction upon the owner's right to use the land, and a burden upon the legal interest of the owner. On the other hand, a covenant to perform or pay for the performance of an affirmative act disconnected with the use of the land cannot ordinarily touch or concern the land in any substantial degree. Thus, unless we exalt technical form over substance, the distinction between covenants which run with land and covenants which are personal, must depend upon the effect of the covenant on the legal rights which otherwise would flow from ownership of land and which are connected with the land. The problem then is: Does the covenant in purpose and effect *substantially* alter these rights?

Looking at the problem presented in this case . . . and stressing the intent and substantial effect of the covenant rather than its form, it seems clear that the covenant may properly be said to touch and concern the land of the defendant and its burden should run with the land. True, it calls for payment of a sum of money to be expended for "public purposes" upon land other than the land conveyed by Neponsit Realty Company to [defendant's] predecessor in title. By that conveyance the grantee, however, obtained not only title to particular lots,

---

39. A fuller statement of Professor Bigelow's test for touch and concern, alluded to by the court, runs as follows: "[I]f the covenantor's legal interest in land is rendered less valuable by the covenant's performance, then the burden of the covenant satisfies the requirement that the covenant touch and concern land. If, on the other hand, the covenantee's legal interest in land is rendered more valuable by the covenant's performance, then the benefit of the covenant satisfies the requirement that the covenant touch and concern land." Powell on Real Property §60.04[3][a] (Michael A. Wolf gen. ed. 2009). This test may have the virtue of realism, as Judge Lehman suggests, but does it escape the vice of circularity?—Eds.

but an easement or right of common enjoyment with other property owners in roads, beaches, public parks or spaces and improvements in the same tract. For full enjoyment in common by the defendant and other property owners of these easements or rights, the roads and public places must be maintained. In order that the burden of maintaining public improvements should rest upon the land benefited by the improvements, the grantor exacted from the grantee of the land with its appurtenant easement or right of enjoyment a covenant that the burden of paying the cost should be inseparably attached to the land which enjoys the benefit. It is plain that any distinction or definition which would exclude such a covenant from the classification of covenants which "touch" or "concern" the land would be based on form and not on substance.

Another difficulty remains. Though between the grantor and the grantee there was privity of estate, the covenant provides that its benefit shall run to the assigns of the grantor who "may include a Property Owners' Association which may hereafter be organized for the purposes referred to in this paragraph." The plaintiff has been organized to receive the sums payable by the property owners and to expend them for the benefit of such owners. Various definitions have been formulated of "privity of estate" in connection with covenants that run with the land, but none of such definitions seems to cover the relationship between the plaintiff and the defendant in this case. The plaintiff has not succeeded to the ownership of any property of the grantor. It does not appear that it ever had title to the streets or public places upon which charges which are payable to it must be expended. It does not appear that it owns any other property in the residential tract to which any easement or right of enjoyment in such property is appurtenant. It is created solely to act as the assignee of the benefit of the covenant, and it has no interest of its own in the enforcement of the covenant.

The arguments that under such circumstances the plaintiff has no right of action to enforce a covenant running with the land are all based upon a distinction between the corporate property owners association and the property owners for whose benefit the association has been formed. If that distinction may be ignored, then the basis of the arguments is destroyed. How far privity of estate in technical form is necessary to enforce in equity a restrictive covenant upon the use of land, presents an interesting question. Enforcement of such covenants rests upon equitable principles (Tulk v. Moxhay, 2 Phillips, 774; Trustees of Columbia College v. Lynch, 70 N.Y. 440; Korn v. Campbell, 192 N.Y. 490), and at times, at least, the violation "of the restrictive covenant may be restrained at the suit of one who owns property, or for whose benefit the restriction was established, irrespective of whether there were privity either of estate or of contract between the parties, or whether an action at law were maintainable." (Cheseboro v. Moers, 233 N.Y. 75, 80.) The covenant in this case does not fall exactly within any classification of "restrictive" covenants, which have been enforced in this State (Cf. Korn v. Campbell, 192 N.Y. 490), and no right to enforce even a restrictive covenant has been sustained in this State where the plaintiff did not own property which would benefit by such enforcement so that some of the elements of an equitable servitude are present. In some jurisdictions

Houses in Neponsit, 1980

it has been held that no action may be maintained without such elements. (But cf. Van Sant v. Rose, 260 Ill. 401.) We do not attempt to decide now how far the rule of Trustees of Columbia College v. Lynch (supra) will be carried, or to formulate a definite rule as to when, or even whether, covenants in a deed will be enforced, upon equitable principles, against subsequent purchasers with notice, at the suit of a party without privity of contract or estate. (Cf. Equitable Rights and Liabilities of Strangers to a Contract, by Harlan F. Stone, 18 Columbia Law Review 291.) There is no need to resort to such a rule if the courts may look behind the corporate form of the plaintiff.

The corporate plaintiff has been formed as a convenient instrument by which the property owners may advance their common interests. We do not ignore the corporate form when we recognize that the Neponsit Property Owners' Association, Inc., is acting as the agent or representative of the Neponsit property owners. As we have said in another case: when Neponsit Property Owners' Association, Inc., "was formed, the property owners were expected to, and have looked to that organization as the medium through which enjoyment of their common right might be preserved equally for all." (Matter of City of New York [Public Beach], 269 N.Y. 64, 75.) Under the conditions thus presented we said: "it may be difficult, or even impossible, to classify into recognized categories the nature of the interest of the membership corporation and its members in the land. The corporate entity cannot be disregarded, nor can the separate interests of the members of the corporation" (p. 73). Only blind adherence to an ancient formula devised to meet entirely different conditions could constrain the court to hold that a corporation formed as a medium for the enjoyment of common rights of property owners owns no property which would benefit by enforcement of common rights and has no cause of action in equity to enforce the covenant upon which such common rights depend. Every reason which in other circumstances may justify the ancient formula may be urged in support of the conclusion that the formula should not be applied in this case. In substance if not in form the covenant is a restrictive covenant which touches and concerns the defendant's land, and in substance, if not in form, there is privity of estate between the plaintiff and the defendant. . . .

The order [denying a motion by defendant for judgment on the pleadings] should be affirmed.

NOTES AND QUESTIONS

1. *Background of* Neponsit. One of the mysteries about *Neponsit* is the motives of the two parties. Why did the case get litigated all the way to the highest court in New York when the amount in question ($340 plus interest) was minimal and the obligation was due to terminate in a few years? Professor Stewart Sterk has offered some possible explanations. First, he suggests, Emigrant Bank, which had filed a weak brief, may have wanted to establish a precedent that assessment covenants were enforceable.

During the Depression, Emigrant and other banks had foreclosed on various residential properties, some of them in areas subject to assessment covenants. Those properties could have
been more valuable for resale purposes if potential purchasers could be assured that common
areas would be maintained. Hence, it might have been in Emigrant's interest to establish that
assessment covenants would be enforceable. From that perspective, *Neponsit* would have been an
attractive test case [because of the minimal amount and the near termination date]. [Stewart E.
Sterk, Neponsit Property Owners' Association v. Emigrant Industrial Savings Bank, in Property
Stories 379, 397 (Gerald Korngold & Andrew P. Morriss eds. 2d ed. 2009).]

Another possible explanation, according to Professor Sterk, is that the litigation
was a grudge suit between the Association and disgruntled members.

2. *Equitable servitude or real covenant?* The court in *Neponsit* applied the "age-
old" requirements for real covenants. Enforcement of a lien, however, is an equitable proceeding, so why did the court apply the real covenant requirements?
Although the court did not discuss the matter, the most likely answer is that
because enforcement of the lien resulted in money damages the court assumed
real covenant law applied even though the proceeding was in equity.

3. *The significance of* Neponsit. *Neponsit* is the first major decision on the validity of a very important type of covenant, the assessment covenant in common
interest communities. Although today such covenants are generally enforceable, at the time of *Neponsit* their validity and enforceability in circumstances like
Neponsit were very much in doubt.

Homeowner association enforcement of assessment covenants posed two
issues at the time of the case: (1) whether a homeowner association, which owned
no land, had standing to enforce the covenant, and (2) whether covenants to pay
money were enforceable against successors of the original promisor. The court
framed these issues in terms of the requirements of *vertical privity* and *touch and
concern*, respectively. We will take up the latter issue first because in some ways it
is the easier of the two.

4. *Touch and concern: affirmative covenants.* One problem in *Neponsit* was the
fact that the covenant in question—a covenant to pay money—was affirmative
rather than restrictive in character. The court analyzed the covenant's enforceability through the lens of the touch and concern requirement, which aims to
identify those covenants whose content relates to land use or enjoyment in such
a way that it is appropriately enforceable by and against successors. As the court
in *Neponsit* noted, courts and commentators have had difficulty formulating a
precise test by which to make this determination. *Neponsit*'s test, adopted from an
influential law review article, is just one more flawed attempt (flawed for the reason we suggest in the footnote on page 913). About the best we can do is to offer
some generalizations and point out some gray areas.

Covenants *restricting* the use of land have almost always been held to touch
and concern land. These negative covenants directly affect the uses to which the
land can be put and substantially affect its value. On the other hand, as *Neponsit*
indicates, courts have been wary of enforcing affirmative covenants against successors. There are several reasons for this caution. Courts are reluctant to issue
orders to perform a series of acts requiring continuing judicial supervision.

Moreover, some courts have traditionally viewed affirmative covenants as clogs on titles. As to covenants to pay money specifically, courts have been concerned that such an obligation may impose a large personal liability on a successor. Today simple covenants to pay dues to homeowner associations are nearly always enforced. Somewhat less certain are more complex monetary obligations to homeowner associations (or common interest communities, as they are also called). Compare Streams Sports Club, Ltd. v. Richmond, 457 N.E.2d 1226 (Ill. 1983) (covenant requiring condominium owners to become dues-paying members of an adjacent sports club that the developer owned (and later sold to Streams Sports) touched and concerned the land), with Midsouth Golf, LLC v. Fairfield Harbourside Condominium Assn., Inc., 652 S.E.2d 378 (N.C. App. 2007) (condominium association's recreational amenity fees covenant did not touch and concern the owners' properties).

The touch and concern requirement has been the subject of much debate. Compare Richard A. Epstein, Notice and Freedom of Contract in the Law of Servitudes, 55 S. Cal. L. Rev. 1353, 1360-1364 (1982) ("denies the original parties their contractual freedom by subordinating their desires to the interests of future third parties"; produces high transaction costs when the servitude is created, because of unpredictability), with Jeffrey E. Stake, Toward an Economic Understanding of Touch and Concern, 1988 Duke L.J. 925, 971-974 (arguing that the test permits courts to allocate efficiently the burden between the promisor and his successor and the benefit between the promisee and his successor); Stewart E. Sterk, Freedom from Freedom of Contract: The Enduring Value of Servitude Restrictions, 70 Iowa L. Rev. 615, 661 (1985) (advocating retention of the touch and concern test as a "check against externalities, inadequate foresight, and intergenerational imposition").

Restatement (Third) eliminates the touch and concern requirement, replacing it with a default rule that a covenant is valid. A covenant is invalid at its inception if it is "illegal or unconstitutional or [against] public policy." Restatement (Third) of Property, Servitudes, §3.1 (2000). Grounds for finding a violation of public policy include, but are not limited to, spiteful or capricious servitudes; servitudes burdening a "fundamental constitutional right" or imposing an unreasonable restraint on alienation (defined in §§3.4, 3.5). The Restatement's goal is to encourage courts to articulate more specifically why they find a particular covenant objectionable at its inception. To date, no court has clearly adopted the Restatement (Third)'s approach. For pros and cons on the Restatement, see Susan F. French, The Touch and Concern Doctrine and the Restatement (Third) of Servitudes, 77 Neb. L. Rev. 653 (1998); A. Dan Tarlock, Touch and Concern Is Dead, Long Live the Doctrine, 77 Neb. L. Rev. 804 (1998); Note, Touch and Concern, the Restatement (Third) of Property: Servitudes, and a Proposal, 122 Harv. L. Rev. 938 (2009).

5. *Vertical privity on the benefit side.* Vertical privity has never been required for the burden of an equitable servitude to run. On the benefit side at the time of *Neponsit*, it was unclear whether homeowner associations, which commonly own

no land, had standing to enforce development covenants. *Neponsit* is the leading case supporting standing for homeowner associations. How did the court resolve the questions whether vertical privity is required for the benefit to run and, if it is, how that requirement was met in the case?

Most jurisdictions today do not require vertical privity for the enforcement of covenants, in law or equity. A plaintiff may enforce the covenant regardless of whether he or she has succeeded to land from the original promisee. See, e.g., Runyon v. Paley, 416 S.E.2d 177 (N.C. 1992); Allemong v. Frendzel, 363 S.E.2d 487 (W. Va. 1987); Restatement (Third) of Property, Servitudes §2.6(2) (2000). The matter is still in doubt in a few jurisdictions, however. Compare, e.g., Malley v. Hanna, 480 N.E.2d 1068 (N.Y. 1985), with Nature Conservancy v. Congel, 689 N.Y.S.2d 317 (App. Div. 1999). The New York Court of Appeals reaffirmed the vertical privity requirement, citing *Neponsit,* in 328 Owners Corp. v. 330 West 86 Oaks Corp., 865 N.E.2d 1228 (N.Y. 2007).

Today it is well settled that homeowner associations do have standing to enforce development covenants, both in law and equity, if they have been given enforcement power. Restatement (Third) of Property, Servitudes §6.8 (2000) provides that a homeowner association has standing to enforce development covenants unless the declaration of covenants denies it. The basis for standing is the homeowner association's status as a third-party beneficiary.

Section 5.2 discards the vertical privity requirement for both the burden and the benefit. Rather, as to both real covenants and equitable servitudes it distinguishes between negative (or restrictive) promises and affirmative ones. It treats *negative* promises the same as easements, meaning that all owners and possessors of burdened land are bound by negative covenants regardless of the extent of their interest or the manner in which they obtained their interest. Likewise, all owners and possessors of benefitted land are entitled to enforce the covenant.

The Restatement views *affirmative* covenants differently. Some background helps to understand the Restatement (Third)'s approach. Recall that under the first Restatement only a relaxed form of vertical privity was required for the benefit of covenants to run, either in law or equity, but that a strict form of vertical privity was required for the burden to run at law. Privity was not required for the benefit to run in equity. As we have discussed, affirmative covenants traditionally were not enforceable in equity or were enforceable only by a lien imposed on the property itself rather than a judgment against the defendant personally. Hence, the effect of the vertical privity doctrine under the traditional rules was to shield lessees and life tenants of burdened land from liability on affirmative covenants. At the same time, they could enjoy the benefits of the same covenants. As to adverse possessors, the vertical privity requirement shielded the adverse possessor from liability on affirmative covenants but barred enjoyment of the benefits. Restatement (Third) of Property, Servitudes §5.2 comment b (2000).

In allocating the benefits and burdens of affirmative covenants, the Restatement (Third) focuses on who can better perform the covenant and what the parties' probable expectations are. According to the Restatement, these policies weigh differently for lessees, life tenants, and adverse possessors and between benefits and burdens. The following is a quick summary of the Restatement's rules:

Lessees—

Benefits: The benefits of covenants to repair, maintain, or render services to the property run to lessees. So also do benefits that the lessee may enjoy without diminishing the benefit's value to the lessor and without materially increasing the burden of performance on the person obligated to perform the covenant.

Burdens: The only affirmative covenants that bind lessees are those that can more reasonably be performed by a person in possession than by the holder of the reversion. Id. §5.3.

Life tenants—

Benefits and burdens: Both the benefits and burdens of affirmative covenants run to *legal* (i.e., non-trust) life tenants.[40] Id. §5.4. However, the life tenant's liability for performance of an affirmative covenant is limited to the value of the life estate.

Adverse possessors—

Burdens: Adverse possessors who have not yet gained title are liable on the affirmative covenants burdening the property.

Benefits: The benefits of affirmative covenants run to adverse possessors who have not yet gained title to the property only under limited circumstances. Id. §5.2. Those circumstances are that the covenant was to repair, maintain, or render services to the property, or that the benefit is one that can be enjoyed by the person in possession without diminishing the benefit's value to the owner of the property and without materially increasing the burden of performance on the party obligated to perform the covenant. Id. §5.5. All the appurtenant benefits and burdens of servitudes burdening the land when adverse possession began run to adverse possessors who have acquired title. Id. §5.2.

6. *Benefits in gross and enforcement of servitudes.* An old doctrine, closely related to vertical privity on the benefit side, to which the court in *Neponsit* alluded, is the rule that if the benefit is in gross — that is, not benefitting a dominant estate — the burden will not run. The jurisdictions are divided over the vitality of this rule. See Powell on Real Property §60.04[3][a] (Michael A. Wolf gen. ed. 2009). As a corollary of this rule a person must own land that benefits from a covenant as a prerequisite to standing to enforce the covenant. In other words, holders of benefits in gross are denied enforcement rights. See, e.g., Shaff v. Leyland, 914 A.2d 1240 (N.H. 2006); McLeod v. Baptiste, 433 S.E.2d 834 (S.C. 1993).

The traditional rule originates from English servitude law, which developed equitable servitudes by analogizing them to negative easements. Since English

---

40. Section 5.4 does not apply to life beneficiaries under a trust. In such situations, the trustee holds legal title to the property and ordinarily is available to perform duties under affirmative burdens and to make appropriate allocations of burdens and benefits among the beneficiaries. Id. §5.4 comment a.

law did not recognize easements in gross, it followed that a dominant estate was required for an equitable servitude. This analogy does not apply in American law, which does recognize easements in gross. Are there nevertheless sound policy reasons supporting the rule that the burden won't run if the benefit is in gross? Are the information and transaction costs of transferring the benefit to the servient owner in order to extinguish the burden, greater when the benefit is in gross than when it is appurtenant?

Refer back to *Neponsit*. Was the benefit of the assessment covenant in that case appurtenant or in gross?

Restatement (Third) of Property, Servitudes §2.6 comment d (2000), provides that benefits in gross are freely permitted and the burden will run when the benefit is in gross. See Eastling v. BP Products North America, Inc., 578 F.3d 831 (8th Cir. 2009) (adopting the Restatement's position). However, in keeping with its general philosophy of removing artificial objections to running covenants and dealing with covenants that create problems over time, the Restatement provides a special termination rule for servitudes in gross: "If it has become impossible or impracticable to locate the beneficiaries of a servitude held in gross, a court may modify or terminate the servitude with the consent of those beneficiaries who can be located, subject to suitable provisions for protection of the interests of those who have not been located." Id. §7.13. The Restatement rejects the traditional requirement of land ownership as a prerequisite for enforcement of covenants. It provides that a person who holds the benefit of a covenant may enforce it so long as that person establishes a "legitimate interest" in enforcement. Id. §8.1.

NOTE: DEFEASIBLE FEES AS LAND USE CONTROL DEVICES

Defeasible fees (determinable fee, fee simple subject to condition subsequent, and fee simple subject to executory limitation, see pages 244-247, 289-292) may be employed to control land use. A defeasible fee differs from a servitude in that the remedy for its breach is forfeiture, whereas the remedy for breach of a servitude is damages, injunction, or enforcement of a lien.

Defeasible fees were popular land use control devices in the late nineteenth and early twentieth centuries before the modern development of equitable servitudes. But they are infrequently used today to control land use except in gifts for charitable purposes. A purchaser of land will likely object to a condition with a forfeiture remedy, both because it makes the purchaser's capital investment risky and because it may make the land unmortgageable and therefore unimprovable.

A defeasible fee can be used to create a right of enforcement in a third party or in a person who owns no land. In view of this, does it make sense to deny enforcement of a covenant by a third-party beneficiary (see pages 918-919) or by a person owning no land?

4.   Discriminatory Covenants

Shelley v. Kraemer

Supreme Court of the United States, 1948
334 U.S. 1

VINSON, C.J. These cases present for our consideration questions relating to the validity of court enforcement of private agreements, generally described as restrictive covenants, which have as their purpose the exclusion of persons of designated race or color from the ownership or occupancy of real property. Basic constitutional issues of obvious importance have been raised. On February 16, 1911, thirty out of a total of thirty-nine owners of property fronting both sides of Labadie Avenue . . . in the city of St. Louis, signed an agreement, which was subsequently recorded, providing in part:

> . . . the said property is hereby restricted to the use and occupancy for the term of Fifty (50) years from this date, so that . . . hereafter no part of said property or any portion thereof shall be, for said term of Fifty-years, occupied by any person not of the Caucasian race, it being intended hereby to restrict the use of said property for said period of time against the occupancy as owners or tenants of any portion of said property for resident or other purpose by people of the Negro or Mongolian Race. . . .

On August 11, 1945, pursuant to a contract of sale, petitioners Shelley, who are Negroes, for valuable consideration received from one Fitzgerald a warranty deed to the parcel in question. The trial court found that petitioners had no actual knowledge of the restrictive agreement at the time of the purchase.

On October 9, 1945, respondents, as owners of other property subject to the terms of the restrictive covenant, brought suit . . . praying that petitioners Shelley be restrained from taking possession of the property and that judgment be entered divesting title out of petitioners Shelley and revesting title in the immediate grantor or in such other person as the court should direct. . . .

Petitioners have placed primary reliance on their contentions, first raised in the state courts, that judicial enforcement of the restrictive agreements in these cases has violated rights guaranteed to petitioners by the Fourteenth Amendment of the Federal Constitution and Acts of Congress passed pursuant to that Amendment. . . . Specifically, petitioners urge that they have been denied the equal protection of the laws. . . .

I.

It cannot be doubted that among the civil rights intended to be protected from discriminatory state action by the Fourteenth Amendment are the rights to acquire, enjoy, own and dispose of property. Equality in the enjoyment of property rights was regarded by the framers of that Amendment as an essential pre-condition to the realization of other basic civil rights and liberties which the Amendment was intended to guarantee. . . .

It is likewise clear that restrictions on the right of occupancy of the sort sought to be created by the private agreements in these cases could not be squared with the requirements of the Fourteenth Amendment if imposed by state statute or local ordinance. We do not understand respondents to urge the contrary. . . .

But the present cases . . . do not involve action by state legislatures or city councils. Here the particular patterns of discrimination and the areas in which the restrictions are to operate, are determined, in the first instance, by the terms of agreements among private individuals. Participation of the State consists in the enforcement of the restrictions so defined. The crucial issue with which we are here confronted is whether this distinction removes these cases from the operation of the prohibitory provisions of the Fourteenth Amendment. Since the decision of this Court in the Civil Rights Cases, 109 U.S. 3 [(1883)], the principle has become firmly embedded in our constitutional law that the action inhibited by the first section of the Fourteenth Amendment is only such action as may fairly be said to be that of the States. That Amendment erects no shield against merely private conduct, however discriminatory or wrongful.

We conclude . . . that the restrictive agreements standing alone cannot be regarded as violative of any rights guaranteed to petitioners by the Fourteenth Amendment. So long as the purposes of those agreements are effectuated by voluntary adherence to their terms, it would appear clear that there has been no action by the State and the provisions of the Amendment have not been violated.

But here there was more. These are cases in which the purposes of the agreements were secured only by judicial enforcement by state courts of the restrictive terms of the agreements. . . .

II.

That the action of state courts and judicial officers in their official capacities is to be regarded as action of the State within the meaning of the Fourteenth Amendment, is a proposition which has long been established by decisions of this Court. . . .

The action of state courts in imposing penalties or depriving parties of other substantive rights without providing adequate notice and opportunity to defend, has, of course, long been regarded as a denial of the due process of law guaranteed by the Fourteenth Amendment. . . .

But the examples of state judicial action which have been held by this Court to violate the Amendment's commands are not restricted to situations in which the judicial proceedings were found in some manner to be procedurally unfair. It has been recognized that the action of state courts in enforcing a substantive common-law rule formulated by those courts, may result in the denial of rights guaranteed by the Fourteenth Amendment, even though the judicial proceedings in such cases may have been in complete accord with the most rigorous conceptions of procedural due process.

The short of the matter is that from the time of the adoption of the Fourteenth Amendment until the present, it has been the consistent ruling of this Court that the action of the States to which the Amendment has reference, includes action of state courts and state judicial officials. Although, in construing the terms of the Fourteenth Amendment, differences have from time to time been expressed as to whether particular types of state action may be said to offend the Amendment's prohibitory provisions, it has never been suggested that state court action is immunized from the operation of those provisions simply because the act is that of the judicial branch of the state government. . . .

III.

We have no doubt that there has been state action in these cases in the full and complete sense of the phrase. The undisputed facts disclose that petitioners were willing purchasers of properties upon which they desired to establish homes. The owners of the properties were willing sellers; and contracts of sale were accordingly consummated. It is clear that but for the active intervention of the state courts, supported by the full panoply of state power, petitioners would have been free to occupy the properties in question without restraint.

. . . The judicial action in each case bears the clear and unmistakable imprimatur of the State. . . . And when the effect of that action is to deny rights subject to the protection of the Fourteenth Amendment, it is the obligation of this Court to enforce the constitutional commands.

We hold that in granting judicial enforcement of the restrictive agreements in these cases, the States have denied petitioners the equal protection of the laws and that, therefore, the action of the state courts cannot stand. We have noted that freedom from discrimination by the States in the enjoyment of property rights was among the basic objectives sought to be effectuated by the framers of the Fourteenth Amendment. That such discrimination has occurred in these cases is clear. Because of the race or color of these petitioners they have been denied rights of ownership or occupancy enjoyed as a matter of course by other citizens of different race or color. . . .

The historical context in which the Fourteenth Amendment became a part of the Constitution should not be forgotten. Whatever else the framers sought to achieve, it is clear that the matter of primary concern was the establishment of equality in the enjoyment of basic civil and political rights and the preservation of those rights from discriminatory action on the part of the States based on considerations of race or color. Seventy-five years ago this Court announced that the provisions of the Amendment are to be construed with this fundamental purpose in mind.

Upon full consideration, we have concluded that in these cases the States have acted to deny petitioners the equal protection of the laws guaranteed by the Fourteenth Amendment. Having so decided, we find it unnecessary to consider whether petitioners have also been deprived of property without due process of law or denied privileges and immunities of citizens of the United States.

For the reasons stated, the judgment of the Supreme Court of Missouri and the judgment of the Supreme Court of Michigan must be reversed.

Reversed.

NOTES AND QUESTIONS

1. *Money damages.* In Barrows v. Jackson, 346 U.S. 249 (1953), the Supreme Court held that a court cannot give money damages against a seller who breaches a covenant not to convey to a nonwhite. Such action is state action.

2. *Non-constitutional grounds for* Shelley*'s result.* Were there any available non-constitutional bases for declaring the racially restrictive covenant in *Shelley* not only unenforceable but invalid? Did the covenant meet all of the common law requirements for covenants running with the land? See Carol Rose, Property Stories: *Shelley v. Kraemer,* in Property Stories 189, 200-204 (Gerald Korngold & Andrew P. Morriss eds. 2d ed. 2009).

3. *Post-*Shelley *use of racially restrictive covenants.* In an important book, Professors Richard Brooks and Carol Rose have established that with respect to covenants *Shelley* changed very little. After the decision, racially restrictive covenants continued to have an important role in perpetuating residential racial segregation in urban areas. They served as important signals of neighborhood racial preferences to real estate brokers and lenders. It was not until 1968, when the federal Fair Housing Act was first enacted, that the communicative function of racially restrictive covenants was seriously addressed. Richard R.W. Brooks & Carol M. Rose, Saving the Neighborhood: Racially Restrictive Covenants, Law, and Social Norms (2013). Also on the signaling function of restrictive covenants, see Valerie Jaffee, Note, Private Law or Social Norms? The Use of Restrictive Covenants in Beaver Hills, 116 Yale L.J. 1302 (2007). See generally Jeannine Bell, Beyond White Flight: Move-In Violence and the Persistence of Racial Segregation in American Housing (2013).

4. *The Fair Housing Act.* A covenant with a racially discriminatory effect may violate the federal Fair Housing Act, enacted as Title VIII of the Civil Rights Act of 1968, 42 U.S.C.A. §§3601-3631. The act makes it unlawful to refuse to sell or rent or otherwise make unavailable a dwelling to any person because of race, color, religion, sex, national origin, familial status, or handicap. See pages 453-454. Still, there may be ways around the prohibition. See Lior Jacob Strahilevitz, Information and Exclusion 55-71 (2011) (discussing "exclusionary amenities" and "exclusionary vibes" that circumvent anti-discrimination protection).

Since the enactment of the Fair Housing Act and the revival the same year of §1982 of the Civil Rights Act of 1866, page 455, the federal courts have channeled all litigation alleging housing discrimination to these two acts, avoiding constitutional holdings. But the constitutional prohibition of discriminatory state action is very much alive when the claim does not come within the purview of the legislation. See Shelley Ross Saxer, Shelley v. Kramer's Fiftieth Anniversary: "A Time for Keeping; A Time for Throwing Away"?, 47 U. Kan. L. Rev. 61 (1998). For an examination of the enforceability of a private covenant created in Georgia forbidding sale of land to Yankees (defined as a person who was born, or has lived for more than one year, north of the Mason-Dixon line), see Alfred L. Brophy & Shubha Ghosh, Whistling Dixie: The Invalidity and Unconstitutionality of Covenants Against Yankees, 10 Vill. Envtl. L.J. 57 (1999).

A deed containing a restrictive covenant against a particular race or religion or ethnic group violates §3604(c) of the Fair Housing Act, which prohibits the printing or publishing of any statement indicating a racial, religious, or ethnic preference with respect to the buyer of a dwelling. See page 454. In Mayers v. Ridley, 465 F.2d 630 (D.C. Cir. 1972), the court permanently enjoined the District of Columbia recorder of deeds from recording deeds containing racial covenants.

When a person buys a house, a title abstractor (usually a lawyer or an abstract company) furnishes the buyer a title abstract reporting all covenants on record. If there is a racial covenant on the property, imposed in the 1940s, does a title report of such a covenant violate §3604(c) of the Fair Housing Act?

5. *Restrictive covenants against group homes.* Covenants restricting property to "residential use only" or "single family residence" have been the subject of considerable litigation. Suppose that a private, not-for-profit corporation that assists mentally impaired persons purchases a house in a residential subdivision all lots of which are restricted by covenant to "single family" residences. The corporation plans to use the house as a group home for eight unrelated mentally impaired residents. The homeowner association charged with enforcing all restrictive covenants sues to enjoin such use on the ground that it would violate the restriction.

Two separate issues may be raised. The first is one of interpretation: Does the use of the house as a group home fall within the meaning of the phrase "single family residence"? On this question, the cases are mixed. Most courts have found that the intended use is permissible either on the theory that the restriction was intended to regulate an architectural style rather than the relationship among the structure's inhabitants, see, e.g., Blevins v. Barry-Lawrence County Assn. for Retarded Citizens, 707 S.W.2d 407 (Mo. 1986), or that "single family" was intended to be interpreted to include groups of otherwise unrelated persons who function as a family. See, e.g., Berger v. State, 364 A.2d 993 (N.J. 1976). But see Shaver v. Hunter, 626 S.W.2d 574, 578 (Tex. App. 1981) ("single family dwelling" limited to occupancy by persons related by blood, marriage, or adoption). See Restatement (Third) of Property, Servitudes §4.1 comment i, Reporter's Note (2000). Where a covenant merely speaks of "residential use only," many courts have held that this includes group homes on the ground that the restriction was intended to exclude commercial use and group homes are not a commercial use. See, e.g., Knudtson v. Trainor, 345 N.W.2d 4 (Neb. 1984). But see Hagemann v. Worth, 782 P.2d 1072 (Wash. App. 1989) (group home found to be a commercial use).

The second issue that may arise in these cases is whether such a restrictive term violates the federal Fair Housing Act or some other anti-discrimination statute. In Hill v. Community of Damien of Molokai, 911 P.2d 861 (N.M. 1996), the court, after first concluding that a group home for persons with AIDS fell within the meaning of a "single family residence" covenant, held that the covenant violated §3604(f)(1) of the FHA by discriminating on the basis of handicap. The court held that the covenant would impose no undue hardship on the neighbors and that the neighbors could reasonably accommodate the group home.

For the impact of the Fair Housing Act on zoning ordinances excluding group homes, see City of Edmonds v. Oxford House, page 1072.

5. Termination of Covenants

Covenants, like easements, can be terminated on a number of grounds. They may be discharged by: (1) *merger* on the basis of unity of ownership of the benefit and burden by the same person; (2) a formal *release*, which is normally written and recorded; (3) *acquiescence*, which arises when the plaintiff has failed to enforce the servitude against other breaches and then seeks to enforce the servitude against the defendant; (4) *abandonment*, which resembles acquiescence except that it makes the servitude unenforceable as to the entire parcel rather than only as to the plaintiff immediately involved; (5) the equitable doctrine of *unclean hands*, according to which the court will refuse to enjoin a violation of a servitude that the plaintiff previously violated; (6) the equitable doctrine of *laches*, which involves an unreasonable delay by the plaintiff to enforce a servitude against the defendant causing prejudice to the defendant (laches does not extinguish the servitude but only bars enforcement); and (7) *estoppel*, if the defendant has relied upon the plaintiff's conduct making it inequitable to allow the plaintiff to enforce the servitude. See Powell on Real Property §60.10[1] (Michael A. Wolf gen. ed. 2009). Servitudes may also be terminated through the exercise of the government's eminent domain power (discussed later on page 936) and on the basis of *prescription*.

Notice that all of the foregoing grounds for termination have to do with changes *inside* the area restricted by covenants. Another ground, *changed conditions*, concerns changes outside the restricted area. Consider the following.

Western Land Co. v. Truskolaski

Supreme Court of Nevada, 1972
495 P.2d 624

BATJER, J. The respondents, homeowners in the Southland Heights subdivision in southwest Reno, Nevada, brought an action in the district court to enjoin the appellant from constructing a shopping center on a 3.5-acre parcel of land located within the subdivision at the northeast corner of Plumas and West Plumb Lane. In 1941 the appellant subdivided this 40-acre development, and at that time it subjected the lots to certain restrictive covenants which specifically restricted the entire 40 acres of the subdivision to single family dwellings and further prohibited any stores, butcher shops, grocery or mercantile business of any kind. The district court held these restrictive covenants to be enforceable, and enjoined the appellant from constructing a supermarket or using the 3.5 acres in any manner other than that permitted by the covenants. The appellant contends that the district court erred in enforcing these covenants because the subdivision had so radically changed in recent years as to nullify their purpose. We agree with the holding of the district court that the restrictive covenants remain of substantial value to the homeowners in the subdivision, and that the changes that have occurred since 1941 are not so great as to make it inequitable or oppressive to restrict the property to single family residential use.

In 1941 the Southland Heights subdivision was outside of the Reno city limits. The property surrounding the subdivision was primarily used for residential and agricultural purposes, with very little commercial development of any type in the immediate area. At that time Plumb Lane extended only as far east as Arlington Avenue.

By the time the respondents sought equitable relief in an effort to enforce the restrictive covenants, the area had markedly changed. In 1941 the city of

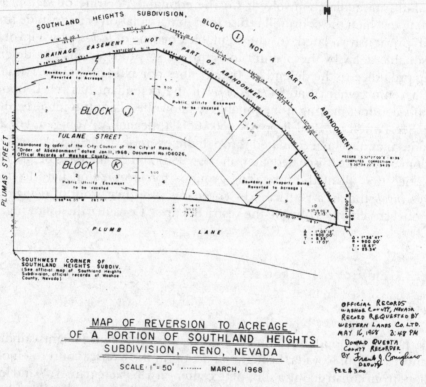

MAP OF REVERSION TO ACREAGE
OF A PORTION OF SOUTHLAND HEIGHTS
SUBDIVISION, RENO, NEVADA

SCALE: 1" = 50' .... MARCH, 1968

On May 16, 1968, Western Land Company filed with the county recorder this map abandoning the Southland Heights subdivision map as applied to the acreage litigated in Western Land Co. v. Truskolaski. Earlier that spring the city council of Reno had approved the abandonment and reversion of Tulane Street and also had approved the abandonment of the subdivision map applied to this acreage. The utility companies also had consented to the abandonment of the public utility easements. This abandonment procedure was undertaken pursuant to Nev. Stat. §278.490 (1991), which permits the abandonment of a subdivision map by the owner of the subdivided land. After the decision in Western Land Co. v. Truskolaski, what is the status of this acreage? Does the original subdivision map apply? Can it be re-subdivided in a different manner for residential use?

Reno had a population of slightly more than 20,000; that figure had jumped to approximately 95,100 by 1969. One of the significant changes, as the appellant aptly illustrates, is the increase in traffic in the surrounding area. Plumb Lane had been extended to Virginia Street, and in 1961 the city of Reno condemned 1.04 acres of land on the edge of the subdivision to allow for the widening of Plumb Lane into a four-lane arterial boulevard. A city planner, testifying for the appellant, stated that Plumb Lane was designed to be and now is the major east-west artery through the southern portion of the city. A person who owns property across Plumas from the subdivision testified that the corner of Plumb Lane and Plumas is "terribly noisy from 5:00 P.M. until midnight." One of the findings of the trial court was that traffic on Plumb Lane had greatly increased in recent years.

Another significant change that had occurred since 1941 was the increase in commercial development in the vicinity of the subdivision. On the east side of Lakeside Drive, across from the subdivision property, is a restaurant and the Lakeside Plaza Shopping Center. A supermarket, hardware store, drug store, flower shop, beauty shop and a dress shop are located in this shopping center. Still further east of the subdivision, on Virginia Street, is the Continental Lodge, and across Virginia Street is the Park Lane Shopping Center.

Even though traffic has increased and commercial development has occurred in the vicinity of the subdivision, the owners of land within Southland Heights testified to the desirability of the subdivision for residential purposes. The traffic density within the subdivision is low, resulting in a safe environment for the children who live and play in the area. Homes in Southland Heights are well cared for and attractively landscaped.

The trial court found that substantial changes in traffic patterns and commercial activity had occurred since 1941 in the vicinity of the subdivision. Although it was shown that commercial activity outside of the subdivision had increased considerably since 1941, the appellant failed to show that the area in question is now unsuitable for residential purposes.

Even though nearby avenues may become heavily traveled thoroughfares, restrictive covenants are still enforceable if the single family residential character of the neighborhood has not been been adversely affected, and the purpose of the restrictions has not been thwarted. Burden v. Lobdell, 93 Ill. App. 2d 476, 235 N.E.2d 660 (1968); Gonzales v. Gackle Drilling Company, 67 N.M. 130, 353 P.2d 353 (1960); Continental Oil Co. v. Fennemore, 38 Ariz. 277, 299 P. 132 (1931). Although commercialization has increased in the vicinity of the subdivision, such activity has not rendered the restrictive covenants unenforceable because they are still of real and substantial value to those homeowners living within the subdivision. West Alameda Heights H. Assn. v. Board of Co. Comrs., 169 Colo. 491, 458 P.2d 253 (1969); Burden v. Lobdell, supra; Hogue v. Dreeszen, 161 Neb. 268, 73 N.W.2d 159 (1955).

The appellant asks this court to reverse the judgment of the district court and declare as a matter of law that the objects and purposes for which the restrictive covenants were originally imposed have been thwarted, and that it is now inequitable to enforce such restrictions against the entity that originally created them. This we will not do. The record will not permit us to find as a matter of law that there has been such a change in the subdivision or for that matter in the area to relieve the appellant's property of the burden placed upon it by the covenants. There is sufficient evidence to sustain the findings of the trial court that the objects and purposes of the restrictions have not been thwarted, and that they remain of substantial value to the homeowners in the subdivision.

The case of Hirsch v. Hancock, 173 Cal. App. 2d 745, 343 P.2d 959 (1959) as well as the other authorities relied upon by the appellant [Key v. McCabe, 54 Cal. 2d 736, 356 P.2d 169, 8 Cal. Rptr. 425 (1960); Strong v. Hancock, 201 Cal. 530, 258 P. 60 (1927); Downs v. Kroeger, 200 Cal. 743, 254 P. 1101 (1927)], are inapposite for in those cases the trial court found many changes within as well as outside the subdivision and concluded from the evidence that the properties were entirely unsuitable and undesirable for residential use and that they had no suitable economic use except for business or commercial purposes, and the appellate courts in reviewing those cases held that the evidence supported the findings and sustained the judgments of the trial courts.

On the other hand, in the case of West Alameda Heights H. Assn. v. Board of Co. Comrs., supra, upon facts similar to those found in this case, the trial court decided that the changed conditions in the neighborhood were such as to render the restrictive covenants void and unenforceable. The appellate court reversed and held that the trial court misconceived and misapplied the rule as to change of conditions and said, 169 Colo. at 498, 458 P.2d at 256: "As long as the original purpose of the covenants can still be accomplished and substantial benefit will inure to the restricted area by their enforcement, the covenants stand even though the subject property has a greater value if used for other purposes."

There is substantial evidence in the record to support the trial court's findings of fact and conclusions of law that the covenants were of real and substantial value to the residents of the subdivision. Where the evidence is conflicting and the credibility of the witnesses is in issue, the judgment will not be disturbed on appeal if the evidence is substantially in support of the judgment of the lower court. Here the appellant has not carried its burden of showing that the subdivision is not now suitable for residential purposes because of changed conditions.

In another attempt to show that the restrictive covenants have outlived their usefulness, the appellant points to actions of the Reno city council. On August 1, 1968, the council adopted a Resolution of Intent to reclassify this 3.5-acre parcel from R-1 [residential] to C-1(b) [commercial]. The council never did change the zoning, but the appellant contends that since the council did indicate its willingness to rezone, it was of the opinion that the property was more suitable for commercial than residential use. This argument of the appellant is not persuasive. A zoning ordinance cannot override privately-placed restrictions, and a trial court cannot be compelled to invalidate restrictive covenants merely because of a zoning change. Rice v. Heggy, 158 Cal. App. 2d 89, 322 P.2d 53 (1958).[41] Another of the appellant's

---

41. Zoning regulations do not modify or terminate a covenant unless they make compliance with the servitude illegal. Since residential as well as commercial uses are usually permitted in a district zoned commercial (but commercial uses forbidden in a residential district), the residential covenant is still enforceable in a commercial district. The general rule is that where zoning and restrictive covenants conflict, the more restrictive prevails. Restatement (Third) of Property, Servitudes §3.1 comment c (2000); Teachers Ins. & Annuity Assn. v. Furlohi, 83 Cal. Rptr. 2d 455 (Cal. App. 1999).—Eds.

arguments regarding changed conditions involves the value of the property for residential as compared to commercial purposes. A professional planning consultant, testifying for the appellant, stated that the land in question is no longer suitable for use as a single family residential area. From this testimony the appellant concludes that the highest and best use for the land is non-residential. Even if this property is more valuable for commercial than residential purposes, this fact does not entitle the appellant to be relieved of the restrictions it created, since substantial benefit inures to the restricted area by their enforcement. West Alameda Heights H. Assn. v. Board of Co. Comrs., supra; Cawthon v. Anderson, 211 Ga. 77, 84 S.E.2d 66 (1954).

In addition to the alleged changed circumstances, the appellant contends that the restrictive covenants are no longer enforceable because they have been abandoned or waived due to violations by homeowners in the area. Paragraph 3 of the restrictive agreement provides that no residential structure shall be placed on a lot comprising less than 6,000 square feet. Both lot 24 and lot 25 of block E contain less than 6,000 square feet and each has a house located on it. This could hardly be deemed a violation of the restrictions imposed by the appellant inasmuch as it was the appellant that subdivided the land and caused these lots to be smaller than 6,000 feet.

Paragraph 7 of the agreement provides that a committee shall approve any structure which is moved onto the subdivision, or if there is no committee, that the structure shall conform to and be in harmony with existing structures. The appellant did show that two houses were moved on to lots within the subdivision, but the appellant failed to show whether a committee existed and if so approved or disapproved, or whether the houses failed to conform or were out of harmony with the existing structures. Finally, in an effort to prove abandonment and waiver, the appellant showed that one house within the subdivision was used as a painting contractor's office for several years in the late 1940s, and that more recently the same house had been used as a nursery for a baby sitting business. However, the same witnesses testified that at the time of the hearing this house was being used as a single family residence.

Even if the alleged occurrences and irregularities could be construed to be violations of the restrictive covenants they were too distant and sporadic to constitute general consent by the property owners in the subdivision and they were not sufficient to constitute an abandonment or waiver. In order for community violations to constitute an abandonment, they must be so general as to frustrate the original purpose of the agreement. Thodos v. Shirk, 79 N.W.2d 733 (Iowa 1956).

Affirmed.

Rick v. West

New York Supreme Court, Westchester County, 1962
228 N.Y.S.2d 195

[Chester Rick owned 62 acres of vacant land, which he subdivided in 1946. A declaration of covenants, restricting the land to single family dwellings, was filed in the courthouse. In 1956, Rick sold to Catherine West a half-acre lot, upon which she built a house. In 1957, the land was zoned for residential use. Subsequently, Rick contracted for the sale of 45 acres to an industrialist, the sale being conditioned upon rezoning of the tract to industrial use. The town board rezoned the 45 acres, but West would not release the covenant in her favor and the sale fell through. In 1959, unable to sell more than a few lots, Rick conveyed the remaining acreage to the plaintiffs. In 1961, the plaintiffs contracted to sell 15 acres from the tract to Peekskill Hospital, but again West refused to consent to release of the covenant. The plaintiffs sued, claiming the covenant was no longer enforceable because of a change of conditions. The court held for the defendant, stating that there was no evidence of any substantial change in the general neighborhood and no change at all within the plaintiffs' tract.]

HOYT, J. The parcel in question would doubtless by its topography and proximity to fast-growing suburban areas make a desirable location for the hospital. The hospital authorities would like to acquire it, and the plaintiffs would like to sell it, and it may be asked why should defendant owning a most respectable, but modest, home be permitted to prevent the sale, or in any event why should the covenants be not determined nonenforceable and the defendant relegated to pecuniary damages.

Plaintiffs' predecessor owned the tract free and clear of all restrictions. He could do with the parcel as he saw best. He elected to promote a residential development and in the furtherance of his plan, and as an inducement to purchasers he imposed the residential restrictions. The defendant relied upon them and has a right to continue to rely thereon. It is not a question of balancing equities or equating the advantages of a hospital on this site with the effect it would have on defendant's property. Nor does the fact that defendant is the only one of the few purchasers from plaintiffs' predecessor in title who has refused to release the covenants make defendant's insistence upon the enforcement of the covenants less deserving of the court's protection and safeguarding of her rights.

The opinion of Judge Cardozo in Evangelical Lutheran Church of the Ascension, of Snyder, N.Y. v. Sahlem (254 N.Y. 161, 166, 168) is quoted at length since the questions therein presented are so similar to those in the case at bar.

> By the settled doctrine of equity, restrictive covenants in respect of land will be enforced by preventive remedies while the violation is still in prospect, unless the attitude of the complaining owner in standing on his covenant is unconscionable or oppressive. Relief is not withheld because the money damage is unsubstantial or even none at all. . . .
>
>   Here, in the case at hand, no process of balancing the equities can make the plaintiff's the greater when compared with the defendant's, or even place the two in equipoise. The defendant, the owner, has done nothing but insist upon adherence to a covenant which is now as valid and binding as at the hour of its making. His neighbors are willing to modify the restriction and forgo a portion of their rights. He refuses to go with them. Rightly or wrongly he believes that the comfort of his dwelling will be imperilled by the change, and so he chooses to abide by the covenant as framed. The choice is for him only. . . . He will be protected in his refusal by all the power of the law.

For the reasons stated in the above-quoted portion of Judge Cardozo's opinion, and since section 346 of the Real Property Law provides no basis for awarding pecuniary damages when the restriction is not outmoded and when it affords real benefit to the person seeking its enforcement, no consideration can or should be given to any award of pecuniary damages to the defendant in lieu of the enforcement of the restrictions. . . .

Restatement (Third) of Property, Servitudes (2000)

§7.10 Modification and Termination of Servitudes Because of Changed Conditions

(1) When a change has taken place since the creation of a servitude that makes it impossible as a practical matter to accomplish the purpose for which the servitude was created, a court may modify the servitude to permit the purpose to be accomplished. If modification is not practicable, or would not be effective, a court may terminate the servitude. Compensation for resulting harm to the beneficiaries may be awarded as a condition of modifying or terminating a servitude.

(2) If the purpose of the servitude can be accomplished, but because of changed conditions the servient estate is no longer suitable for uses permitted by the servitude, a court may modify the servitude to permit other uses under conditions designed to preserve the benefits of the original servitude.

(3) The rules stated in §7.11 govern modification or termination of conservation servitudes held by public bodies and conservation organizations, which are not subject to this section.

NOTES AND QUESTIONS

1. *Scope of the changed conditions doctrine.* Western Land Co. v. Truskolaski and Rick v. West are typical cases refusing to terminate covenants. The changed conditions doctrine is a stringent one. In most cases when conditions change, the court continues to enforce the covenant by injunctive relief. But ought that to be the case?

Generally, a court can enforce a restrictive covenant by an injunction or by an award of damages for breach. Which remedy is preferable, as a matter of fairness and efficiency, when conditions radically change? Should it matter whether multiple parties have the benefit of the covenant (as in *Western Land*) or only one party (as in Rick v. West)? For matters bearing on the answer, see Note 3 on pages 795-797. See also Glen O. Robinson, Explaining Contingent Rights: The Puzzle of "Obsolete" Covenants, 91 Colum. L. Rev. 546, 548-560, 570-576 (1991) (a revealing search into theoretical justifications for the changed conditions doctrine); Carol M. Rose, Servitudes, Security, and Assent: Some Comments on Professors French and Reichman, 55 S. Cal. L. Rev. 1403, 1410-1415 (1982); Timothy C. Shephard, Comment, Termination of Servitudes: Expanding the Remedies for "Changed Conditions," 31 UCLA L. Rev. 226 (1983).

Can you imagine situations when restrictive covenants should *not* be enforced unless the parties who seek enforcement pay compensation to the parties who maintain that changed conditions have rendered the restrictions unenforceable? Is such a remedy of "reverse damages" even conceivable? (It is. See the discussion in Note 3 on page 805.)

For an argument that the changed conditions doctrine unduly interferes with property rights and that courts should specifically enforce covenants in spite of changed conditions, see Richard A. Epstein, Notice and Freedom of Contract in the Law of Servitudes, 55 S. Cal. L. Rev. 1353, 1364-1368 (1982). For a reply, see Stewart E. Sterk, Freedom from Freedom of Contract: The Enduring Value of Servitude Restrictions, 70 Iowa L. Rev. 615, 652-654 (1985).

2. *Current New York statute.* Rick v. West has been superseded by N.Y. RPAPL §951, which provides:

§1951. *Extinguishment of non-substantial restrictions on the use of land*

1. No restriction on the use of land created at any time by covenant, promise or negative easement, or created on or after September 1, 1958, by a special limitation or condition subsequent governed by section 1953, shall be enforced by injunction or judgment compelling a conveyance of the land burdened by the restriction or an interest therein, nor shall such restriction be declared or determined to be enforceable, if, at the time the enforceability of the restriction is brought in question, it appears that the restriction is of no actual and substantial benefit to the persons seeking its enforcement or seeking a declaration or determination of its enforceability, either because the purpose of the restriction has already been accomplished or, by reason of changed conditions or other cause, its purpose is not capable of accomplishment, or for any other reason.

2. When relief against such a restriction is sought in an action to quiet title or to obtain a declaration with respect to enforceability of the restriction or to determine an adverse claim arising from the restriction, or is sought by way of defense or counterclaim in an action to enforce the restriction or to obtain a declaration with respect to its enforceability, if the court shall find that the restriction is of no actual and substantial benefit to the persons seeking its enforcement or seeking a declaration or determination of its enforceability, either because the purpose of the restriction has already been accomplished or, by reason of changed conditions or other cause, its purpose is not capable of accomplishment, or for any other reason, it may adjudge that the restriction is not enforceable by injunction or as provided in subdivision 2 of section 1953 and that it shall be completely extinguished upon payment, to the person or persons who would otherwise be entitled to enforce it in the event of a breach at the time of the action, of such damages, if any, as such person or persons will sustain from the extinguishment of the restriction.

Had this statute been in effect at the time of *Rick* would the result have been the same? Does this statute substitute a liability rule for a property rule? See In re East Fifth Street Housing Preservation Development Fund Corp., 79 B.R. 568 (Bankr. S.D.N.Y. 1987) (relief under §1951 denied where benefit of restrictive covenant outweighs financial burden of enforcement on owner). Is this a good idea?

For fascinating stories of holdouts in New York City, see Andrew Alpern & Seymour Durst, Holdouts! (1984). The book discusses numerous instances where skyscrapers were built over and around business establishments—especially bars—owned by stubborn proprietors. Examples: Hurley's at 49th Street and Sixth Avenue, which stood up to the Rockefellers, and P.J. Clarke's midtown on Third Avenue. Also compare London, which has many interesting variations in cityscape resulting from holdouts, with Paris, where holdouts were not permitted against the grand redevelopment plans of Baron Haussmann.

Virginia Lee Burton's colorfully illustrated children's book, The Little House (1942), traces the quiet life of a rural cottage that imagines what life in

"Talk about argument, cajolery, threats!"

a city would be like, only to find itself years later in the middle of urban slums. Development ultimately prevails, and the little house is finally moved to greener pastures. (Maybe she should have sued for an injunction!)

3. *Changed conditions doctrine for easements.* Note that §7.10 of the Restatement, set forth on page 933, applies to easements as well as to equitable servitudes and real covenants. Traditionally, the changed conditions doctrine applied only to covenants. Obsolete easements were terminated on the theory that the easement no longer serves its intended purpose. Restatement (Third) of Property, §7.10, Reporter's Note. Because the concept is the same under either formulation, the Restatement combines the two under the label "changed conditions." In more recent cases, the Restatement's approach has been followed, see, e.g., Boissy v. Chevion, 33 A.3d 1109 (N.H. 2011), and rejected, see AKG Real Estate, LLC v. Kosterman, 717 N.W.2d 835 (Wis. 2006).

4. *Postscript for* Western Land Co. v. Truskolaski. After their victory in *Western Land,* the neighbors agreed to the developer's use of the 3.5 acre parcel for commercial uses generating low traffic. Professor Owen L. Anderson writes:

> I have visited the corner of Plumb and Plumas in Reno on two occasions for the very purpose of determining what happened. The 3.5 acres in question have been in commercial use for at least 10 years, perhaps longer. The area consists of small offices, realtors, insurance, floral, etc. with offstreet parking immediately outside of each office. It is a bit like a strip mall, but there are no high-traffic retail stores. Also, there are groupings of offices that are separated from each other by small private access roads and parking. The balance of the subdivision appears to be residential. [Letter dated April 16, 1999.]

5. *Duration of covenants.* In general, the duration of covenants is a matter of the intention of the parties. For servitudes other than conservation easements (which are perpetual—see page 890) and easements by necessity (see Note 4 on page 841), the duration is indeterminate. See Restatement (Third) of Property, Servitudes §4.3 (2000). There is no general public policy against perpetual covenants. However, in Citibrook II, L.L.C. v. Morgan's Foods of Missouri, Inc., 239 S.W.3d 631 (Mo. App. 2007), the court held that a covenant restricting "forever" the use of the land for the exclusive purpose of building and operating a Kentucky Fried Chicken store was invalid because it was unreasonable in duration. The court might have reached the same result on the narrower ground that this covenant constituted an unreasonable restraint of alienation by limiting the ownership of the property to a very small pool of persons, but that was not the court's basis for its decision.

6. *Termination by condemnation.* If the government condemns an existing easement or condemns the servient land so as to destroy an existing easement, the government must pay compensation to the easement owner. If the government uses land in violation of a restrictive covenant, the large majority of cases hold that the government must pay damages to the landowners having the benefit. Similarly, if the government condemns land on which there is an affirmative covenant to pay money, the government must pay the beneficiary of the covenant for loss of the benefit.

6.   Common Interest Communities

Earlier, in the *Neponsit* case, page 909, we introduced a common interest community. Since *Neponsit*, homeowners associations in common interest communities have grown greatly in number and spread to all corners of the United States. The Community Associations Institute estimates that as of 2011, there were 314,200 common interest communities (CICs) in the United States, housing over 62 million people. Cmty. Assns. Inst., Data on U.S. Community Associations, at http://www.caionline.org/info/research/Pages/default.aspx. The majority of common interest communities are homeowner associations; a smaller percentage are condominiums; and a much smaller percentage are cooperatives.

One reason for the boom in CICs in the United States is that local governments use public powers to tilt the market for new housing construction in favor of CICs rather than other forms of housing. Their incentive for doing so is that this permits them to shift many local costs, such as parks, streets, etc., to developers as the price for permission to develop. See Steven Siegel, The Public Role in Establishing Private Residential Communities: Towards a New Formulation of Local Government Land Use Policies That Eliminates the Legal Requirements to Privatize New Communities in the United States, 38 Urb. Law. 859 (2010); Hannah Wiseman, Public Communities, Private Rules, 98 Geo. L.J. 697 (2010).

Almost every state has adopted a statutory scheme for organizing a common interest community. Some of these are modeled after the Uniform Common Interest Ownership Act (1982, amended 2008). These statutes require a declaration of rules governing the community, which must be disclosed to purchasers. In most common interest communities, a homeowners association, in which all homeowners are automatically members, enforces the servitudes set forth in the declaration establishing the common interest community. The association, governed by a board elected by its members, may adopt new regulations reasonably necessary to manage the common property, administer the servitude regime, protect community members from unreasonable interference in the enjoyment of their individual property, and carry out other functions set forth in the declaration establishing the common interest community.

"The distinctive feature of a common-interest community," declares the Restatement (Third) of Property, Servitudes §6.2 comment a (2000), "is the obligation that binds the owners of individual lots or units to contribute to the support of common property, or other facilities, or to support the activities of an association, whether or not the owner uses the common property or facilities, or agrees to join the association." Although the rules about servitudes covered earlier in this chapter are generally applicable to common interest communities, the homeowners association in addition has power to raise funds reasonably necessary to carry out its functions. In most such communities, the power to levy assessments is enforceable by fines and a lien on the individual property (as it was in *Neponsit*).

Condominiums. The condominium form of shared ownership, known for centuries in Europe, was virtually unheard of in the United States until the 1960s, when it rather suddenly became very popular. Scholars have attributed this to various causes: the rising cost of single family homes; the availability of shared amenities (swimming pools, tennis courts, clubhouses, playgrounds) at lower cost; the tax subsidy to owner-occupied housing (deductibility of mortgage interest and real property taxes and failure to include the imputed rental value of owner-occupied housing in taxable personal income); the increasing affluence of apartment dwellers permitting a greater proportion to invest in equity ownership (as seen among two-earner childless couples and the elderly); the belief that real estate is an inflation-proof investment; the availability of FHA mortgage insurance on condominiums, eliminating risk to lenders; the fear of rent control by investors in rental housing. See Henry B. Hansmann, Condominium and Cooperative Housing: Transactional Efficiency, Tax Subsidies, and Tenure Choice, 20 J. Legal Stud. 25 (1991).

The basic idea of a condominium is simple. Each unit (or interior space) in a condominium is owned *separately in fee simple* by an individual owner. The exterior walls, the land beneath, the hallways, and other common areas are owned by the unit owners as *tenants in common*. Because each unit is owned separately, each owner obtains mortgage financing by a separate mortgage on the owner's individual unit. Real estate taxes are assessed or allocated to each unit separately. The failure of one unit owner to pay mortgage interest or taxes does not jeopardize the other unit owners.

The condominium form of ownership can be adapted to residential or commercial use, and can apply to units in high rise buildings or to lateral developments such as townhouses and detached dwellings. The declaration of condominium, filed before the first sale is made, will provide for an association of unit owners to make and enforce rules, to manage the common areas, and to set maintenance charges levied against unit owners. Each purchaser, by accepting a deed, becomes an association member and must abide by its bylaws. All 50 states have some form of condominium statute governing this type of shared ownership.

Each condominium unit owner is liable for a monthly charge to maintain common facilities and insure against casualty and liability. The condominium documents fix the fraction of each unit owner's pro rata burden of common expenses. This fraction also may govern the unit owner's voice in management and may be used by the tax assessor in apportioning the project's total value among the separate units. The association may also have the right to make improvements and assess the unit owners their fractional share. Enforcement of condominium obligations may be covered by the state condominium statute or the condominium declaration.

Cooperatives. New York City is probably the only housing market in the country with a substantial number of cooperative apartments (over 400,000). In a housing cooperative, the title to the land and building is held by a corporation; the residents own all the shares of stock in the corporation and control it through an elected board of directors. Each resident also has a long-term renewable lease of an apartment unit. Hence, residents are both owners of the cooperative corporation (by virtue of stock ownership) and tenants of the corporation.

The cooperative property is usually subject to one blanket mortgage securing the money lender for the money borrowed to buy the land and erect the building. If one cooperator fails to pay his share of the mortgage interest or taxes, the other cooperators must make it up or the entire property may be foreclosed upon. Thus, in a cooperative more than a condominium, the investment of one person depends upon the financial stability of others.

As a result, members of a cooperative have a strong incentive to screen applicants to ensure that they can carry their share of the collective mortgage. Financial screening also provides an opportunity for social screening. New York courts have held that cooperative boards can deny entry to anyone for any reason and without giving any reason, provided the board does not violate federal and state civil rights laws. Weisner v. 791 Park Ave. Corp., 160 N.E.2d 720 (N.Y. 1959). Because cooperatives can screen prospective members, and because of long experience with the cooperative form of housing, they continue to flourish in New York City despite the growth of condominiums in the rest of the country. (In a condominium in New York, the boards typically can prevent entry only by exercising a preemptive option; they rarely screen applicants by social criteria.)

The conventional wisdom is that compared with cooperatives, the condominium is the relatively more efficient and desirable housing form. Why, then, do cooperatives persist in New York City, where over 80 percent of common interest buildings are cooperatives? One reason is the greater exclusivity that cooperatives offer. Tenants in exclusive cooperatives in Manhattan place a premium on having neighbors of high status or well-seasoned money in conservative surroundings. As a result of their screening procedures, numerous prominent persons have been excluded from cooperative apartments. Notables rejected by cooperatives include Barbra Streisand, Madonna, ex-President Richard Nixon, and Sean Lennon, son of John, turned down at his mother's building. In 1999, the Grammy Award-winning singer Mariah Carey was rejected by the cooperative board after trying to buy a $7.5 million, 16-room apartment owned by Barbra Streisand at the exclusive Ardsley building on Central Park West. No reason was given, and under New York state law none is required. One Manhattan real estate broker thinks she knows why Carey was rejected. "She is young, she's female, she's newly divorced," the broker reportedly stated. All this creates "a concern that the [building's] more well-heeled elderly women might have of their husbands riding the elevator with her." See House Rules Mightier than Movie Moguls, People Magazine, May 31st, 1999. Real estate brokers have become matchmakers, steering buyers to buildings where they are likely to be accepted.

The taste for exclusivity explains only part of the market for cooperatives in New York City. Dean Michael Schill and two co-authors have argued that the major factors explaining the persistence of cooperatives in New York City are the high transaction costs in switching from cooperative to condominium ownership and the problem of collective action involved in getting cooperative shareholders to agree to dissolve the corporation. The collective action problem is exacerbated by the fact that New York state law requires agreement of two-thirds of shares for dissolution. Moreover, some cooperative corporation bylaws require as high as 80 percent. See Michael H. Schill, Ioan Voicu & Jonathan Miller, The Condominium versus Cooperative Puzzle: An Empirical Analysis of Housing in New York City, 36 J. Legal Stud. 275 (2007).

If the applicant can prove racial or ethnic discrimination, the cooperative will have to admit the applicant or pay damages. In Broome v. Biondi, 17 F. Supp. 2d 211 (S.D.N.Y. 1997), an African-American attorney with the law firm of Skadden Arps and his Caucasian wife, also an attorney, won a $640,000 judgment against a cooperative for racial discrimination in turning down their application for an apartment. See Sabrina Malpeli, Comment, Cracking Down on Cooperative Board Decisions That Reject Applicants Based on Race: Broome v. Biondi, 73 St. John's L. Rev. 313 (1999).

In common interest communities, any requirement of horizontal or vertical privity is met because the original purchasers are all in privity with the developer and subsequent purchasers are in privity with the original purchasers. Any requirement that a covenant touch and concern the land is usually satisfied. Negative covenants restricting use are almost always held to touch and concern, as are affirmative covenants to pay dues to a homeowners association (see page 918). But, because the rules of a common interest community and the powers of the homeowners association can adversely affect the interests of individual members, courts have been called upon to determine whether individual members shall be protected from imposition by those who control the association. The emerging issue is by what standards the common interest communities' rules and regulations should be judged.

 ## Nahrstedt v. Lakeside Village Condominium Association, Inc.

Supreme Court of California, 1994
878 P.2d 1275

KENNARD, J. A homeowner in a 530-unit condominium complex sued to prevent the homeowners association from enforcing a restriction against keeping cats, dogs, and other animals in the condominium development. The owner asserted that the restriction, which was contained in the project's declaration[42] recorded by the condominium project's developer, was "unreasonable" as applied to her because she kept her three cats indoors and because her cats were "noiseless" and "created no nuisance." Agreeing with the premise underlying the owner's complaint, the Court of Appeal concluded that the homeowners association could enforce the restriction only upon proof that plaintiff's cats would be likely to interfere with the right of other homeowners "to the peaceful and quiet enjoyment of their property."

Those of us who have cats or dogs can attest to their wonderful companionship and affection. Not surprisingly, studies have confirmed this effect. . . . But the issue before us is not whether in the abstract pets can have a beneficial effect

---

42. The declaration is the operative document for a common interest development, setting forth, among other things, the restrictions on the use or enjoyment of any portion of the development. (Civ. Code, §§1351, 1353.) In some states, the declaration is also referred to as the "master deed."

on humans. Rather, the narrow issue here is whether a pet restriction that is contained in the recorded declaration of a condominium complex is enforceable against the challenge of a homeowner. As we shall explain, the Legislature, in Civil Code section 1354, has required that courts enforce the covenants, conditions and restrictions contained in the recorded declaration of a common interest development "unless unreasonable."

Because a stable and predictable living environment is crucial to the success of condominiums and other common interest residential developments, and because recorded use restrictions are a primary means of ensuring this stability and predictability, the Legislature in section 1354 has afforded such restrictions a presumption of validity and has required of challengers that they demonstrate the restriction's "unreasonableness" by the deferential standard applicable to equitable servitudes. Under this standard established by the Legislature, enforcement of a restriction does not depend upon the conduct of a particular condominium owner. Rather, the restriction must be uniformly enforced in the condominium development to which it was intended to apply unless the plaintiff owner can show that the burdens it imposes on affected properties so substantially outweigh the benefits of the restriction that it should not be enforced against any owner. Here, the Court of Appeal did not apply this standard in deciding that plaintiff had stated a claim for declaratory relief. Accordingly, we reverse the judgment of the Court of Appeal and remand for further proceedings consistent with the views expressed in this opinion.

I.

Lakeside Village is a large condominium development in Culver City, Los Angeles County. It consists of 530 units spread throughout 12 separate 3-story buildings. The residents share common lobbies and hallways, in addition to laundry and trash facilities.

The Lakeside Village project is subject to certain covenants, conditions and restrictions (hereafter CC&R's) that were included in the developer's declaration recorded with the Los Angeles County Recorder on April 17, 1978, at the inception of the development project. Ownership of a unit includes membership in the project's homeowners association, the Lakeside Village Condominium Association (hereafter Association), the body that enforces the project's CC&R's, including the pet restriction, which provides in relevant part: "No animals (which shall mean dogs and cats), livestock, reptiles or poultry shall be kept in any unit."[43] In January 1988, plaintiff Natore Nahrstedt purchased a Lakeside Village condominium and moved in with her three cats. When the Association learned of the cats' presence, it demanded their removal and assessed fines against Nahrstedt for each successive month that she remained in violation of the condominium project's pet restriction.

---

43. The CC&R's permit residents to keep "domestic fish and birds."

Nahrstedt then brought this lawsuit against the Association, its officers, and two of its employees, asking the trial court to invalidate the assessments, to enjoin future assessments, . . . and to declare the pet restriction "unreasonable" as applied to indoor cats (such as hers) that are not allowed free run of the project's common areas. Nahrstedt also alleged she did not know of the pet restriction when she bought her condominium. . . .

The Association demurred to the complaint. . . . The trial court sustained the demurrer as to each cause of action and dismissed Nahrstedt's complaint. Nahrstedt appealed.

A divided Court of Appeal reversed the trial court's judgment of dismissal. In the majority's view, the complaint stated a claim for declaratory relief based on its allegations that Nahrstedt's three cats are kept inside her condominium unit and do not bother her neighbors. According to the majority, whether a condominium use restriction is "unreasonable," as that term is used in section 1354, hinges on the facts of a particular homeowner's case. Thus, the majority reasoned, Nahrstedt would be entitled to declaratory relief if application of the pet restriction in her case would not be reasonable. . . .

On the Association's petition, we granted review to decide when a condominium owner can prevent enforcement of a use restriction that the project's developer has included in the recorded declaration of CC&R's. . . .

II.

Today, condominiums, cooperatives, and planned-unit developments with homeowners associations have become a widely accepted form of real property ownership. These ownership arrangements are known as "common interest" developments.

Lakeside Village Condominiums
Culver City

. . . [S]ubordination of individual property rights to the collective judgment of the owners association together with restrictions on the use of real property comprise the chief attributes of owning property in a common interest development. As the Florida District Court of Appeal observed in Hidden Harbour Estates, Inc. v. Norman (Fla. Dist. Ct. App. 1975) 309 So. 2d 180, a decision frequently cited in condominium cases: "[I]nherent in the condominium concept is the principle that to promote the health, happiness, and peace of mind of the majority of the unit owners since they are living in such close proximity and using facilities in common, each unit owner must give up a certain degree of freedom of choice which he [or she] might otherwise enjoy in separate, privately owned property. Condominium unit owners comprise a little democratic sub-society of necessity more restrictive as it pertains to use of condominium property than may be existent outside the condominium organization."

One significant factor in the continued popularity of the common interest form of property ownership is the ability of homeowners to enforce restrictive CC&R's against other owners (including future purchasers) of project units. (Natelson, Law of Property Owners Associations 1989 §1.3.2.1, p. 19. . . .) Generally, however, such enforcement is possible only if the restriction that is sought to be enforced meets the requirements of equitable servitudes or of covenants running with the land. . . .

When restrictions limiting the use of property within a common interest development satisfy the requirements of covenants running with the land or of equitable servitudes, what standard or test governs their enforceability? In California, as we explained at the outset, our Legislature has made common interest development use restrictions contained in a project's recorded declaration "enforceable . . . unless unreasonable." (Civil Code, §1354, subd. (a).)

In states lacking such legislative guidance, some courts have adopted a standard under which a common interest development's recorded use restrictions will be enforced so long as they are "reasonable." (See Riley v. Stoves (1974) 22 Ariz. App. 223, 228, 526 P.2d 747, 752 [asking whether the challenged restriction provided "a reasonable means to accomplish the private objective"].) . . . Others would limit the "reasonableness" standard only to those restrictions adopted by majority vote of the homeowners or enacted under the rulemaking power of an association's governing board, and would not apply this test to restrictions included in a planned development project's recorded declaration or master deed. Because such restrictions are presumptively valid, these authorities would enforce them regardless of reasonableness. The first court to articulate this view was the Florida Fourth District Court of Appeal.

In Hidden Harbour Estates v. Basso (Fla. Dist. Ct. App. 1981) 393 So. 2d 637, the Florida court distinguished two categories of use restrictions: use restrictions set forth in the declaration or master deed of the condominium project itself, and rules promulgated by the governing board of the condominium owners association or the board's interpretation of a rule. The latter category of use restrictions, the court said, should be subject to a "reasonableness" test, so as to "somewhat fetter the discretion of the board of directors." Such a standard, the court explained, best assures that governing boards will "enact rules and make decisions that are reasonably related to the promotion of the health, happiness and peace of mind" of the project owners, considered collectively.

By contrast, restrictions contained in the declaration or master deed of the condominium complex, the Florida court concluded, should not be evaluated under a "reasonableness" standard. Rather, such use restrictions are "clothed with a very strong presumption of validity" and should be upheld even if they exhibit some degree of unreasonableness. Nonenforcement would be proper only if such restrictions were arbitrary or in violation of public policy or some fundamental constitutional right. The Florida court's decision was cited with approval by a Massachusetts appellate court in Noble v. Murphy (1993) 34 Mass. App. Ct. 452, 612 N.E.2d 266.

In *Noble*, managers of a condominium development sought to enforce against the owners of one unit a pet restriction contained in the project's master deed. The Massachusetts court upheld the validity of the restriction. The court stated that "[a] condominium use restriction appearing in originating documents which predate the purchase of individual units" was entitled to greater judicial deference than restrictions "promulgated after units have been individually acquired." The court reasoned that "properly-enacted and evenly-enforced use restrictions contained in a master deed or original bylaws of a condominium" should be insulated against attack "except on constitutional or public policy grounds." This standard, the court explained, best "serves the interest of the majority of owners [within a project] who may be presumed to have chosen not to alter or rescind such restrictions," and it spares overcrowded courts "the burden and expense of highly particularized and lengthy litigation."

Indeed, giving deference to use restrictions contained in a condominium project's originating documents protects the general expectations of condominium owners "that restrictions in place at the time they purchase their units will be enforceable." (Note, Judicial Review of Condominium Rulemaking (1981) 94 Harv. L. Rev. 647, 653; Ellickson, Cities and Homeowners' Associations (1982) 130 U. Pa. L. Rev. 1519, 1526-1527 [stating that association members "unanimously consent to the provisions in the association's original documents" and courts therefore should not scrutinize such documents for "reasonableness"].) This in turn encourages the development of shared ownership housing—generally a less costly alternative to single dwelling ownership—by attracting buyers who prefer a stable, planned environment. It also protects buyers who have paid a premium for condominium units in reliance on a particular restrictive scheme.

III.

. . . Thus, when enforcing equitable servitudes, courts are generally disinclined to question the wisdom of agreed-to restrictions. . . . This rule does not apply, however, when the restriction does not comport with public policy. Equity will not enforce any restrictive covenant that violates public policy. (See Shelley v.

Kraemer (1948) 334 U.S. 1, 68 S. Ct. 836, 92 L. Ed. 1161 [racial restriction unenforceable]; §53, subd. (b) [voiding property use restrictions based on "sex, race, color, religion, ancestry, national origin, or disability"].) Nor will courts enforce as equitable servitudes those restrictions that are arbitrary, that is, bearing no rational relationship to the protection, preservation, operation or purpose of the affected land. (See Laguna Royale Owners Assn. v. Darger (1981) 119 Cal. App. 3d 670, 684, 174 Cal. Rptr. 136.)

These limitations on the equitable enforcement of restrictive servitudes that are either arbitrary or violate fundamental public policy are specific applications of the general rule that courts will not enforce a restrictive covenant when "the harm caused by the restriction is so disproportionate to the benefit produced" by its enforcement that the restriction "ought not to be enforced." (Rest., Property, §539, com. f, pp. 3229-3230.) When a use restriction bears no relationship to the land it burdens, or violates a fundamental policy inuring to the public at large, the resulting harm will always be disproportionate to any benefit. . . .

With these principles of equitable servitude law to guide us, we now turn to Civil Code section 1354. As mentioned earlier, under subdivision (a) of section 1354 the use restrictions for a common interest development that are set forth in the recorded declaration are "enforceable equitable servitudes, unless unreasonable." In other words, such restrictions should be enforced unless they are wholly arbitrary, violate a fundamental public policy, or impose a burden on the use of affected land that far outweighs any benefit.

This interpretation of section 1354 is consistent with the views of legal commentators as well as judicial decisions in other jurisdictions that have applied a presumption of validity to the recorded land use restrictions of a common interest development. (Noble v. Murphy, supra, 612 N.E.2d 266, 270; Hidden Harbour Estates v. Basso, supra, 393 So. 2d 637, 639-640; Note, Judicial Review of Condominium Rulemaking, supra, 94 Harv. L. Rev. 647, 653.) As these authorities point out, and as we discussed previously, recorded CC&R's are the primary means of achieving the stability and predictability so essential to the success of a shared ownership housing development. . . .

When courts accord a presumption of validity to all such recorded use restrictions and measure them against deferential standards of equitable servitude law, it discourages lawsuits by owners of individual units seeking personal exemptions from the restrictions. This also promotes stability and predictability in two ways. It provides substantial assurance to prospective condominium purchasers that they may rely with confidence on the promises embodied in the project's recorded CC&R's. And it protects all owners in the planned development from unanticipated increases in association fees to fund the defense of legal challenges to recorded restrictions.

How courts enforce recorded use restrictions affects not only those who have made their homes in planned developments, but also the owners associations charged with the fiduciary obligation to enforce those restrictions. (See Posey v. Leavitt (1991) 229 Cal. App. 3d 1236, 1247, 280 Cal. Rptr. 568; Advising Cal. Condominium and Homeowner Associations (Cont. Ed. Bar 1991) §6.11, pp. 259-261.) When courts treat recorded use restrictions as presumptively valid, and place on the challenger the burden of proving the restriction "unreasonable" under the deferential standards applicable to equitable servitudes, associations can proceed to enforce reasonable restrictive covenants without fear that their actions will embroil them in costly and prolonged legal proceedings. Of course, when an association determines that a unit owner has violated a use restriction, the association must do so in good faith, not in an arbitrary or capricious manner, and its enforcement procedures must be fair and applied uniformly. . . .

There is an additional beneficiary of legal rules that are protective of recorded use restrictions: the judicial system. Fewer lawsuits challenging such restrictions will be brought, and those that are filed may be disposed of more expeditiously, if the rules courts use in evaluating such restrictions are clear, simple, and not subject to exceptions based on the peculiar circumstances or hardships of individual residents in condominiums and other shared-ownership developments.

Contrary to the dissent's accusations that the majority's decision "fray[s]" the "social fabric," we are of the view that our social fabric is best preserved if courts uphold and enforce solemn written instruments that embody the expectations of the parties rather than treat them as "worthless paper" as the dissent would. Our social fabric is founded on the stability of expectation and obligation that arises from the consistent enforcement of the terms of deeds, contracts, wills, statutes, and other writings. To allow one person to escape obligations under a written instrument upsets the expectations of all the other parties governed by that instrument (here, the owners of the other 529 units) that the instrument will be uniformly and predictably enforced. . . .

Refusing to enforce the CC&R's contained in a recorded declaration, or enforcing them only after protracted litigation that would require justification of their application on a case-by-case basis, would impose great strain on the social fabric of the common interest development. It would frustrate owners who had purchased their units in reliance on the CC&R's. It would put the owners and the homeowners association in the difficult and divisive position of deciding whether particular CC&R's should be applied to a particular owner. Here, for example, deciding whether a particular animal is "confined to an owner's unit and create[s] no noise, odor, or nuisance" is a fact-intensive determination that can only be made by examining in detail the behavior of the particular animal and the behavior of the particular owner. Homeowners associations are ill-equipped to make such investigations, and any decision they might make in a particular case could be divisive or subject to claims of partiality.

Enforcing the CC&R's contained in a recorded declaration only after protracted case-by-case litigation would impose substantial litigation costs on the owners through their homeowners association, which would have to defend not only against owners contesting the application of the CC&R's to them, but also against owners contesting any case-by-case exceptions the homeowners association might make. In short, it is difficult to imagine what could more disrupt the harmony of a common interest development than the course proposed by the dissent.

IV.

Here, the Court of Appeal failed to consider the rules governing equitable servitudes in holding that Nahrstedt's complaint challenging the Lakeside Village restriction against the keeping of cats in condominium units stated a cause of action for declaratory relief. Instead, the court concluded that factual allegations by Nahrstedt that her cats are kept inside her condominium unit and do not bother her neighbors were sufficient to have the trial court decide whether enforcement of the restriction against Nahrstedt would be reasonable. For this conclusion, the court relied on two Court of Appeal decisions, Bernardo Villas Management Corp. v. Black (1987) 190 Cal. App. 3d 153, 235 Cal. Rptr. 509 and Portola Hills Community Assn. v. James (1992) 4 Cal. App. 4th 289, 5 Cal. Rptr. 2d 580, both of which had invalidated recorded restrictions covered by section 1354.

In *Bernardo Villas*, the manager of a condominium project sued two condominium residents to enforce a restriction that prohibited them from keeping any "truck, camper, trailer, boat . . . or other form of recreational vehicle" in the carports. In holding that the restriction was unreasonable as applied to the clean new pickup truck with camper shell that the defendants used for personal transportation, the Court of Appeal observed that parking the truck in the development's carport would "not interfere with other owners' use or enjoyment of their property."

Thereafter, a different division of the same district Court of Appeal used a similar analysis in *Portola Hills*. There, the court refused to enforce a planned community's landscape restriction banning satellite dishes against a homeowner who had installed a satellite dish in his backyard. After expressing the view that "[a] homeowner is allowed to prove a particular restriction is unreasonable as applied to his property," the court observed that the defendant's satellite dish was not visible to other project residents or the public, leading the court to conclude that the ban promoted no legitimate goal of the homeowners association.

At issue in both Bernardo Villas Management Corp. v. Black, supra, 190 Cal. App. 3d 153, 235 Cal. Rptr. 509, and Portola Hills Community Assn. v. James, supra, 4 Cal. App. 4th 289, 5 Cal. Rptr. 2d 580, were recorded use restrictions contained in a common interest development's declaration that had been recorded with the county recorder. Accordingly, the use restrictions involved in these two cases were covered by section 1354, rendering them presumptively reasonable and enforceable under the rules governing equitable servitudes. . . . In determining whether a restriction is "unreasonable" under section 1354, and thus not enforceable, the focus is on the restriction's effect on the project as a whole, not on the individual homeowner. Although purporting to evaluate the use restrictions in accord with section 1354, both *Bernardo Villas* and *Portola Hills* failed to apply the deferential standards of equitable servitude law just mentioned. Accordingly, to the extent they differ from the views expressed in this opinion, we disapprove *Bernardo Villas*[44] and *Portola Hills*.

V.

Under the holding we adopt today, the reasonableness or unreasonableness of a condominium use restriction that the Legislature has made subject to section 1354 is to be determined not by reference to facts that are specific to the objecting homeowner, but by reference to the common interest development as a whole. As we have explained, when, as here, a restriction is contained in the declaration of the common interest development and is recorded with the county recorder, the restriction is presumed to be reasonable and will be enforced uniformly against all residents of the common interest development unless the restriction is arbitrary, imposes burdens on the use of lands it affects that substantially outweigh the restriction's benefits to the development's residents, or violates a fundamental public policy. . . .

We conclude, as a matter of law, that the recorded pet restriction of the Lakeside Village condominium development prohibiting cats or dogs but allowing some other pets is not arbitrary, but is rationally related to health, sanitation and noise concerns legitimately held by residents of a high-density condominium project such as Lakeside Village, which includes 530 units in 12 separate 3-story buildings.

Nahrstedt's complaint alleges no facts that could possibly support a finding that the burden of the restriction on the affected property is so disproportionate to its benefit that the restriction is unreasonable and should not be enforced.

. . . [W]e discern no fundamental public policy that would favor the keeping of pets in a condominium project. There is no federal or state constitutional provision or any California statute that confers a general right to keep household pets in condominiums or other common interest developments.

. . . For many owners, the pet restriction may have been an important inducement to purchase into the development. Because the homeowners collectively have the power to repeal the pet restriction, its continued existence reflects their desire to retain it.

. . . We reverse the judgment of the Court of Appeal, and remand for further proceedings consistent with the views expressed in this opinion.

ARABIAN, J., dissenting. "There are two means of refuge from the misery of life: music and cats."[45]

___

44. Suppose that the pick-up truck is necessary in the owner's line of work. Is it reasonable to deprive him of his means of livelihood? Does this restriction have the effect of excluding workers in the building trades? — EDS.

45. Albert Schweitzer.

Natore Nahrstedt with Boo-Boo

I respectfully dissent. While technical merit may commend the majority's analysis, its application to the facts presented reflects a narrow, indeed chary, view of the law that eschews the human spirit in favor of arbitrary efficiency. In my view, the resolution of this case well illustrates the conventional wisdom, and fundamental truth, of the Spanish proverb, "It is better to be a mouse in a cat's mouth than a man in a lawyer's hands."

I find the provision known as the "pet restriction" contained in the covenants, conditions, and restrictions (CC&R's) governing the Lakeside Village project patently arbitrary and unreasonable within the meaning of Civil Code section 1354. Beyond dispute, human beings have long enjoyed an abiding and cherished association with their household animals. Given the substantial benefits derived from pet ownership, the undue burden on the use of property imposed on condominium owners who can maintain pets within the confines of their units without creating a nuisance or disturbing the quiet enjoyment of others substantially outweighs whatever meager utility the restriction may serve in the abstract. It certainly does not promote "health, happiness [or] peace of mind" commensurate with its tariff on the quality of life for those who value the companionship of animals. Worse, it contributes to the fraying of our social fabric. . . .

From the statement of the facts through the conclusion, the majority's analysis . . . simply takes refuge behind the "presumption of validity" now accorded all CC&R's irrespective of subject matter. They never objectively scrutinize defendants' blandishments of protecting "health and happiness" or realistically assess the substantial impact on affected unit owners and their use of their property. . . .

Here, such inquiry should start with an evaluation of the interest that will suffer upon enforcement of the pet restriction. In determining the "burden on the use of land," due recognition must be given to the fact that this particular "use" transcends the impersonal and mundane matters typically regulated by condominium CC&R's, such as whether someone can place a doormat in the hallway or hang a towel on the patio rail or have food in the pool area, and reaches the very quality of life of hundreds of owners and residents. Nonetheless, the majority accept uncritically the proffered justification of preserving "health and happiness" and essentially consider only one criterion to determine enforceability: was the restriction recorded in the original declaration? If so, it is "presumptively valid," unless in violation of public policy.

Given the application of the law to the facts alleged and by an inversion of relative interests, it is difficult to hypothesize any CC&R's that would not pass muster. Such sanctity has not been afforded any writing save the commandments delivered to Moses on Mount Sinai, and they were set in stone, not upon worthless paper.

Moreover, unlike most conduct controlled by CC&R's, the activity at issue here is strictly confined to the owner's interior space; it does not in any manner invade other units or the common areas. Owning a home of one's own has always epitomized the American dream. More than simply embodying the notion of having "one's castle," it represents the sense of freedom and self-determination emblematic of our national character. Granted, those who live in multi-unit developments cannot exercise this freedom to the same extent possible on a large estate. But owning pets that do not disturb the quiet enjoyment of others does not reasonably come within this compromise. Nevertheless, with no demonstrated or discernible benefit, the majority arbitrarily sacrifice the dream to the tyranny of the "commonality."

. . . [T]he majority's . . . view, shorn of grace and guiding philosophy, is devoid of the humanity that must temper the interpretation and application of all laws, for in a civilized society that is the source of their authority. As judicial architects of the rules of life, we better serve when we construct halls of harmony rather than walls of wrath.

I would affirm the judgment of the Court of Appeal.

California Civil Code §1360.5 (West 2012, enacted 2000)

§1360.5 Responsibility for pets

(a) No governing documents shall prohibit the owner of a separate interest within a common interest development from keeping at least one pet within the common interest development, subject to reasonable rules and regulations of the association. This section may not be construed to affect any other rights provided by law to an owner of a separate interest to keep a pet within the development.

(b) For purposes of this section, "pet" means any domesticated bird, cat, dog, aquatic animal kept within an aquarium, or other animal as agreed to between the association and the homeowner.

(c) If the association implements a rule or regulation restricting the number of pets an owner may keep, the new rule or regulation shall not apply to prohibit an owner from continuing to keep any pet that the owner currently keeps in his or her separate interest if the pet otherwise conforms with the previous rules or regulations relating to pets.

NOTES AND QUESTIONS

1. *The aftermath of* Nahrstedt. After losing the lawsuit, Natore Nahrstedt moved out of Lakeside Village, with her three cats, Boo-Boo, Dockers, and Tulip. Her legal bill was around $50,000.

2. *The economic impact of pet restrictions.* A recent study found that pet restrictions have significant effects on condominium prices. Specifically, sales of condominiums with no or limited pet restrictions sold for 11.6 percent more than comparable condominiums with no pets allowed. See Zhenguo Lin et al., Pet Policy and Housing Prices: Evidence from the Condominium Market, 47 J. Real Est. Fin. Econ. 109 (2013).

3. *Housing discrimination?* Many people are allergic to cats or dogs, which bring on asthma and other temporarily disabling reactions. Under Cal. Civ. Code §1360.5, have these persons been deprived of a choice to live in a pet-free condominium? Does this deny them equal protection of the laws? Does the statute violate the Fair Housing Act by discriminating against the handicapped? See pages 458-459; Robert G. Schwemm, Housing Discrimination: Law and Litigation §11D:2 (2002).

4. *The Restatement (Third)'s approach.* Recall that Restatement (Third) of Property, Servitudes §3.1 (2000) (see page 918) establishes a presumption that a servitude is valid unless it is illegal, unconstitutional, or violates public policy. Among the identified bases for violating public policy are "unreasonably burden[ing] a fundamental constitutional right" and "impos[ing] an unreasonable restraint of alienation under §3.4 or §3.5." The two cited provisions distinguish between direct and indirect restraints on alienation. Direct restraints (which we discussed in Chapter 3 on pages 232-233) include prohibitions on transfers without the consent of the association, rights of first refusal, and requirements that transfers be made only to persons meeting certain eligibility requirements. Under §3.4, such restraints are invalid if they are *unreasonable*. The Restatement says of the reasonableness standard: "Determining reasonableness . . . requires balancing the utility of the purpose served by the restraint against the harm that is likely to flow from its enforcement." Id. §3.4 comment c.

Indirect restraints (those most commonly imposed in common interest communities) include restrictions on use and restrictions that might limit the sales value of the property but do not directly interfere with free functioning of the market in land (e.g., restrictions on pets, paint color, signs). The test for the validity of such indirect restraints is more lenient than that applicable to direct restraints. Under §3.5, an otherwise valid indirect restraint is invalid only if it

Doonesbury © G.B. Trudeau.
Reprinted with permission of Universal Uclick. All rights reserved.

"*lacks rational justification.*" (Emphasis added.) The Restatement indicates that under this standard "there is no need to weigh the benefits of the restriction against its burdens." Id. §3.5 Reporter's Note.

The Restatement, like the *Nahrstedt* court, draws a distinction between regulations included in the deeds or declaration of the common interest development and the regulations subsequently adopted by property owners associations for community governance. A reasonableness standard is applied to the latter, including the exercise of powers to approve architectural plans. Id.

See also id. §6.13, for further discussion of what board actions are reasonable in a common interest community.

5. *The standard applicable to subsequent HOA actions.* The court in *Nahrstedt* referred, with apparent approval, to Hidden Harbour Estates v. Basso, where a Florida court stated that use restrictions subsequently imposed by action of the condominium association board are subject to a more stringent standard than the deferential standard applied to restrictions included in the original declaration. Subsequently, the California Supreme Court held that the deferential *Nahrstedt* standard applies to use restrictions included in recorded amendments to declarations. Villa de las Palmas Homeowners Assn. v. Terifaj, 90 P.3d 1223 (Cal. 2004). The court distinguished between restrictions in a recorded amended declaration and an unrecorded restriction promulgated by the board, as to which the deferential standard presumably does not apply. The court based its decision on what it considered the unambiguous language of Cal. Civ. Code §1354(a) (West 2007), the same provision involved in *Nahrstedt.*

In Evergreen Highlands Assn. v. West, 73 P.3d 1 (Colo. 2003), the court held that an association had the power to amend the declaration by adding a new provision imposing mandatory assessments. The declaration stated that the owners of 75 percent or more of the development's lots may "change or modify" any one or more of "said restrictions." The court construed this language to permit a new mandatory assessment provision. Without discussing what standard applied to test the validity of new provisions, the court summarily stated that the assessment provision was reasonable.

6. *Litigation fees.* Litigation between homeowners associations and their members is extensive. Who pays the legal fees? In Noble v. Murphy, 612 N.E.2d 266 (Mass. App. 1993), another violation-of-pet-restriction case cited in *Nahrstedt,* the court assessed against the losing defendants (the pet owners) the association's attorneys' fees of $15,000. A condominium bylaw provided that the association could recoup the cost and expense of eliminating bylaw violations from the offending unit owner. In Mountain View Condominium Assn. v. Bomersbach, 734 A.2d 468 (Pa. Comm. 1999), the court held the condominium association could collect $46,500 in attorneys' fees in a 10-year-long dispute with a unit owner over a $500 lien.

But the money for legal fees can also flow in the other direction. In Riss v. Angel, 934 P.2d 669 (Wash. 1997), the court held that the homeowners association was liable for over $200,000 in legal fees incurred by a unit owner in fighting what the court thought was an unreasonable action by the board. Being a member of a common interest community can be dangerous to your pocketbook if one of the unit owners is litigious.

PROBLEMS

In a common interest community, the developer imposes the following restrictions. Which, if any, are invalid under the Restatement (Third) of Property §3.1? Under the *Nahrstedt* version of the reasonableness requirement?

1. "No flag of any kind, including the American flag, may be displayed." See 4 U.S.C. §5 Note (Pub. L. No. 109-243, 120 Stat. 572 (July 24, 2006)); Cal. Govt. Code §434.5 (2012); Ky. Rev. Stat. Ann §2.042 (2012).

2. "No sign except house location number may be displayed, nor may Christmas lights be displayed outside of a house." See Osborne v. Power, 890 S.W.2d 570 (Ark. 1994); cf. City of Ladue v. Gilleo, 512 U.S. 43 (1994), reproduced at page 1031; Brian Jason Fleming, Note, Regulation of Political Signs in Private Homeowner Associations: A New Approach, 59 Vand. L. Rev. 571 (2006).

3. "No solar energy device shall be installed on the roof of any house." See Mass. Ann. Laws ch. 184, §23(c) (2012); Fla. Stat. Ann. §163.04 (2012).

4. "No house shall be used to provide day care for nonresidents of the house." See Woodvale Condominium Trust v. Scheff, 540 N.E.2d 206 (Mass. App. 1989); Cal. Health & Safety Code §1597.40(c) (West 2012).

5. "No religious services or activities of any kind are allowed in the development's auditorium or any other common areas." When a number of association members met in the auditorium on Saturday morning for religious services, the association's board of directors sought to enjoin them from violating the restriction. Would it make a difference if a local state statute prohibited condominium associations from "unreasonably restrict[ing] any unit owner's right to peaceably assemble . . ."? Fla. Stat. Ann. §718.123 (2012). See Neuman v. Grandview at Emerald Hills, Inc., 861 So. 2d 494 (Fla. App. 2003).

6. "Outdoor clotheslines and clothes drying are not permitted." See Anne Marie Chaker, To Hang, or Not to Hang, Ann Arbor News, Oct. 20, 2007 at E1.

7. "No signs, billboards, or advertising without the prior approval of the architectural control committee." When a resident places on her door a Christmas wreath that features a peace symbol, the architecture control committee orders her to remove it.

8. "No smoking of cigarettes, cigars, or any other tobacco product, marijuana or illegal substance anywhere within the boundaries of the complex. This prohibition shall include the outside common area, enclosed common area, exclusive use common area and units within the complex."

 Craziest CIC rules? An article in The Week, an on-line magazine, listed the top "insane" homeowner association rules. They include the following restrictions:

Too many roses. A Rancho Santa Fe, California CIC levied monthly fines against Jeffrey DeMarco for exceeding the prescribed number of rose bushes per acre. DeMarco not only lost in court but had to pay the CIC's $70,000 legal bill. When he could not pay it, he lost his home.

No dogs on the lobby floor. Pamela McMahan, a geriatric resident of a Long Beach, California condominium who walks with a cane, was fined $25 each time she failed to carry her dog across the lobby. The condominium rules provide that pets' feet must never touch the floor of the lobby. The property manager explained that the rule was aimed against dogs jumping up on people or defecating in the lobby. After piling up so many fines, Ms. McMahan was forced to move.

No brown lawns. Sixty-six-year old Joseph Prudente ended up in jail for failing to properly maintain his lawn. A large increase in his monthly mortgage payment put him in financial straits, but his Bayonet Point, Florida CIC took him to court nevertheless. A group of neighbors took pity on him, gathering a collection that paid for new sod, flowers, and a working sprinkler system, and sprung him from jail.

No inconsistent shingles. Distraught when a plane crashed into his home, killing his wife and baby, Joe Woodard rebuilt the home using shingles that did not match those of his neighbors. His CIC successfully enjoined to stop him from using the nonconforming shingles. Mr. Woodard explained to a local reporter that he had wanted to avoid painful memories by slightly changing the look of his house.

40 West 67th Street Corp. v. Pullman

New York Court of Appeals, 2003
790 N.E.2d 1174

ROSENBLATT, J. In Levandusky v. One Fifth Ave Corp. [553 N.E.2d 1317 (N.Y. 1990)], we held that the business judgment rule is the proper standard of judicial review when evaluating decisions made by residential cooperative corporations.

In the case before us, defendant is a shareholder-tenant in the plaintiff cooperative building. The relationship between defendant and the cooperative, including the conditions under which a shareholder's tenancy may be terminated, is
governed by the shareholder's lease agreement. The cooperative terminated
defendant's tenancy in accordance with a provision in the lease that authorized it
to do so based on a tenant's "objectionable" conduct.

Defendant has challenged the cooperative's action and asserts, in essence,
that his tenancy may not be terminated by the court based on a review of the
facts under the standard articulated in *Levandusky*. He argues that termination
may rest only upon a court's independent evaluation of the reasonableness of
the cooperative's action. We disagree. In reviewing the cooperative's actions, the
business judgment standard governs a cooperative's decision to terminate a tenancy in accordance with the terms of the parties' agreement.

I.

Plaintiff cooperative owns the building located at 40 West 67th Street in
Manhattan, which contains 38 apartments. In 1998, defendant bought into the
cooperative and acquired 80 shares of stock appurtenant to his proprietary lease
for Apartment 7B.

Soon after moving in, defendant engaged in a course of behavior that, in the
view of the cooperative, began as demanding, grew increasingly disruptive and
ultimately became intolerable. After several points of friction between defendant
and the cooperative,[46] defendant started complaining about his elderly upstairs
neighbors, a retired college professor and his wife who had occupied apartment
8B for over two decades. In a stream of vituperative letters to the cooperative—16
letters in the month of October 1999 alone—he accused the couple of playing
their television set and stereo at high volumes late into the night, and alleged that
they were running a loud and illegal bookbinding business in their apartment.
Defendant further charged that the couple stored toxic chemicals in their apartment for use in their "dangerous and illegal" business. Upon investigation, the
cooperative's Board determined that the couple did not possess a television set
or stereo and that there was no evidence of a bookbinding business or any other
commercial enterprise in their apartment.

Hostilities escalated, resulting in a physical altercation between defendant
and the retired professor.[47] Following the altercation, defendant distributed flyers to the cooperative residents in which he referred to the professor, by name,
as a potential "psychopath in our midst" and accused him of cutting defendant's

---

46. Initially, defendant sought changes in the building services, such as the installation of video surveil-
lance, 24-hour door service and replacement of the lobby mailboxes. After investigation, the Board deemed
these proposed changes inadvisable or infeasible.

47. Defendant brought charges against the professor which resulted in the professor's arrest. Eventually,
the charges were adjourned in contemplation of dismissal.

telephone lines. In another flyer, defendant described the professor's wife and the wife of the Board president as having "close intimate personal relations." Defendant also claimed that the previous occupants of his apartment revealed that the upstairs couple have "historically made excessive noise." The former occupants, however, submitted an affidavit that denied making any complaints about noise from the upstairs apartment and proclaimed that defendant's assertions to the contrary were "completely false."

Furthermore, defendant made alterations to his apartment without Board approval, had construction work performed on the weekend in violation of house rules, and would not respond to Board requests to correct these conditions or to allow a mutual inspection of his apartment and the upstairs apartment belonging to the elderly couple. Finally, defendant commenced four lawsuits against the upstairs couple, the president of the cooperative and the cooperative management, and tried to commence three more.

In reaction to defendant's behavior, the cooperative called a special meeting pursuant to Article III, section (1)(f) of the lease agreement, which provides for termination of the tenancy if the cooperative by a two-thirds vote determines that "because of objectionable conduct on the part of the Lessee . . . the tenancy of the Lessee is undesirable. . . ." The cooperative informed the shareholders that the purpose of the meeting was to determine whether defendant "engaged in repeated actions inimical to cooperative living and objectionable to the Corporation and its stockholders that make his continued tenancy undesirable. . . ."

Timely notice of the meeting was sent to all shareholders in the cooperative, including defendant. At the ensuing meeting, held in June 2000, owners of more than 75% of the outstanding shares in the cooperative were present. Defendant chose not attend. By a vote of 2,048 shares to zero, the shareholders in attendance passed a resolution declaring defendant's conduct "objectionable" and directing the Board to terminate his proprietary lease and cancel his shares. The resolution contained the findings upon which the shareholders concluded that defendant's behavior was inimical to cooperative living. Pursuant to the resolution, the Board sent defendant a Notice of Termination requiring him to vacate his apartment by August 31, 2000. Ignoring the notice, defendant remained in the apartment, prompting the cooperative to bring this suit for possession and ejectment, a declaratory judgment cancelling defendant's stock, and a money judgment for use and occupancy, along with attorneys' fees and costs.

Supreme Court . . . declined to apply the business judgment rule to sustain the shareholders' vote and the Board's issuance of the Notice of Termination. Instead, the court invoked RPAPL 711(1) and held that to terminate a tenancy, a cooperative must prove its claim of objectionable conduct by competent evidence to the satisfaction of the court.

Disagreeing with Supreme Court, a divided Appellate Division . . . held that *Levandusky* prohibited judicial scrutiny of actions of cooperative boards "taken in good faith and in the exercise of honest judgment in the lawful and legitimate furtherance of corporate purposes." . . . We agree with the Appellate Division majority that the business judgment rule applies and therefore affirm.

II. *The* Levandusky *Business Judgment Rule*

The heart of this dispute is the parties' disagreement over the proper standard of review to be applied when a cooperative exercises its agreed-upon right to terminate a tenancy based on a shareholder-tenant's objectionable conduct. In the agreement establishing the rights and duties of the parties, the cooperative reserved to itself the authority to determine whether a member's conduct was objectionable and to terminate the tenancy on that basis. The cooperative argues that its decision to do so should be reviewed in accordance with *Levandusky*'s business judgment rule. Defendant contends that the business judgment rule has no application under these circumstances and that RPAPL 711 requires a court to make its own evaluation of the Board's conduct based on a judicial standard of reasonableness.

Levandusky established a standard of review analogous to the corporate business judgment rule for a shareholder-tenant challenge to a decision of a residential cooperative corporation. The business judgment rule is a common law doctrine by which courts exercise restraint and defer to good faith decisions made by boards of directors in business settings. . . . The rule has been long recognized in New York. . . . In *Levandusky*, the cooperative board issued a stop work order for a shareholder-tenant's renovations that violated the proprietary lease. The shareholder-tenant brought a CPLR article 78 proceeding to set aside the stop work order. The Court upheld the Board's action, and concluded that the business judgment rule "best balances the individual and collective interests at stake" in the residential cooperative setting (*Levandusky*, [553 N.E.2d at 1321]).

In the context of cooperative dwellings, the business judgment rule provides that a court should defer to a cooperative board's determination "[s]o long as the board acts for the purposes of the cooperative, within the scope of its authority and in good faith" (id. at [1322]). In adopting this rule, we recognized that a cooperative board's broad powers could lead to abuse through arbitrary or malicious decisionmaking, unlawful discrimination or the like. However, we also aimed to avoid impairing "the purposes for which the residential community and its governing structures were formed: protection of the interest of the entire community of residents in an environment managed by the board for the common benefit" (id. at [1321]). The Court concluded that the business judgment rule best balances these competing interests and also noted that the limited judicial review afforded by the rule protects the cooperative's decisions against "undue court involvement and judicial second-guessing" (id. at [1322]).

Although we applied the business judgment rule in *Levandusky*, we did not attempt to fix its boundaries, recognizing that this corporate concept may not necessarily comport with every situation encountered by a cooperative and its shareholder-tenants. Defendant argues that when it comes to terminations the business judgment rule conflicts with RPAPL 711(1) and is therefore inoperative.[48] We see no such conflict. In the realm of cooperative governance and in the lease provision before us, the cooperative's determination as to the tenant's objectionable behavior stands as competent evidence necessary to sustain the cooperative's determination. If that were not so, the contract provision for termination of the lease—to which defendant agreed—would be meaningless.

We reject the cooperative's argument that RPAPL 711(1) is irrelevant to these proceedings, but conclude that the business judgment rule may be applied consistently with the statute. Procedurally, the business judgment standard will be applied across the cases, but the manner in which it presents itself varies with the form of the lawsuit. . . .

[T]he procedural vehicle driving this case is RPAPL 711(1), which requires "competent evidence" to show that a tenant is objectionable. Thus, in this context, the competent evidence that is the basis for the shareholder vote will be reviewed under the business judgment rule, which means courts will normally defer to that vote and the shareholders' stated findings as competent evidence that the tenant is indeed objectionable under the statute. As we stated in *Levandusky*, a single standard of review for cooperatives is preferable, and "we see no purpose in allowing the form of the action to dictate the substance of the standard by which the legitimacy of corporate action is to be measured" (id. at [1323]).

In addition, RPAPL 711 was derived from former Civil Practice Act §1410(6), which was enacted in 1920 (L 1920, ch 133). Before that, a landlord could evict a tenant based on the landlord's sole and unfettered determination that the tenant was objectionable. By enacting former CPA 1410(6), the legislature imposed on the landlord the burden of proving that the tenant was objectionable. While RPAPL 711(1) applies to the termination before us, we are satisfied that the relationships among shareholders in cooperatives are sufficiently distinct from traditional landlord-tenant relationships that the statute's "competent evidence" standard is satisfied by the application of the business judgment rule.

Despite this deferential standard, there are instances when courts should undertake review of board decisions. In order to trigger further judicial scrutiny, an aggrieved shareholder-tenant must make a showing that the Board acted (1) outside the scope of its authority, (2) in a way that did not legitimately further the corporate purpose or (3) in bad faith. We next consider the lack of these elements.

---

48. RPAPL 711(1), in pertinent part, states: ". . . A proceeding seeking to recover possession of real property by reason of the termination of the term fixed in the lease pursuant to a provision contained therein giving the landlord the right to terminate the time fixed for occupancy under such agreement if he deem the tenant objectionable, shall not be maintainable unless the landlord shall by competent evidence establish to the satisfaction of the court that the tenant is objectionable."

III.

[The court found that the Board acted within the scope of its authority in terminating the tenancy; that its purpose was to further the overall welfare of the cooperative; and that there was no indication that the Board acted in bad faith or arbitrarily or that it engaged in malice, favoritism, or discrimination. The court concluded:]

The very concept of cooperative living entails a voluntary, shared control over rules, maintenance and the composition of the community. Indeed, as we observed in *Levandusky*, a shareholder-tenant voluntarily agrees to submit to the authority of a cooperative board, and consequently the board "may significantly restrict the bundle of rights a property owner normally enjoys" (id. at [1320]). When dealing, however, with termination, courts must exercise a heightened vigilance in examining whether the Board's action meets the *Levandusky* test.

We have considered defendant's remaining contentions, and find them without merit. Accordingly, the order of the Appellate Division should be affirmed, with costs.

Order affirmed, with costs.

NOTES AND QUESTIONS

1. *The business judgment rule applied to homeowner associations.* The New York Appellate Division has subsequently applied the business judgment rule to the decisions of homeowner association boards. See Forest Close Assn., Inc. v. Richards, 845 N.Y.S.2d 418 (App. Div. 2007); Captain's Walk Homeowners Assn. v. Penney, 794 N.Y.S.2d 82 (App. Div. 2005).

In Lamden v. La Jolla Shores Clubdominium Homeowners Assn., 980 P.2d 940 (Cal. 1999), the court applied the business judgment rule to sustain the decision of a homeowner association board. When a condominium became infested with termites, the association's board decided to use spot treatment rather than to fumigate the entire building. When more termite infestation became apparent in one unit five years later, the unit owner brought an action against the board for damages allegedly resulting from the board's decision not to fumigate the whole building. Ruling for the board, the court stated that in making financial decisions all that was required of the board was that it exercise its discretion in good faith, after reasonable investigation, and in the best interests of the association and its members. The court distinguished *Nahrstedt* on the ground that the no-pets rule was an equitable servitude, governed by California Civil Code §1354, whereas the board's action in *Lamden* involved no equitable servitude, only a financial decision.

At least one other court has applied the business judgment rule to homeowner associations. See Riverside Park Condominium Unit Owners Assn. v. Lucas, 691 N.W.2d 862 (N.D. 2005) (applied to amendment of no-pet rule).

2. *Which standard?* At least three different standards of judicial review are now in use by courts. At the most deferential end of the spectrum is the business judgment rule, illustrated in *Pullman*. Somewhat less deferential is the *Nahrstedt*

version of the reasonableness standard (restrictions enforced unless they are wholly arbitrary, violate a fundamental public policy, or impose a burden on the affected land that far outweighs the benefit). The third, and most intrusive, standard of review is, as mentioned in *Nahrstedt*, the one applied by the Florida courts to restrictions adopted by the association's board, as opposed to those included in the original declaration of covenants. The Florida courts confusingly call their standard a "reasonableness" test (no strong presumption of validity; balancing utility of restriction's purpose versus harms resulting from its enforcement). Should one of these three standards apply to all original covenants in all common interest communities (and if so, which one), or should different standards apply to different types of decisions by association boards? By different types of common interest communities?

The debate over standards to govern judicial review of common interest community rules has given rise to a large and growing literature. Commentaries favoring some form of deference include Robert C. Ellickson, Cities and Homeowners Associations, 130 U. Pa. L. Rev. 1519 (1982); Richard A. Epstein, Covenants and Constitutions, 73 Cornell L. Rev. 906 (1988); Clayton P. Gillette, Courts, Covenants, and Communities, 61 U. Chi. L. Rev. 1375 (1994); Robert G. Natelson, Consent, Coercion and "Reasonableness" in Private Law: The Special Case of the Property Owners Association, 51 Ohio St. L.J. 41 (1990); Laura T. Rahe, Note, The Right to Exclude: Preserving the Autonomy of the Homeowners' Association, 34 Urb. Law. 521 (2002); Patrick A. Randolph, Jr., Changing the Rules: Should Courts Limit the Power of Common Interest Communities to Alter Unit Owners' Privileges in the Face of Vested Expectations?, 38 Santa Clara L. Rev. 1081 (1998); and Stewart E. Sterk, Minority Protection in Residential Private Governments, 77 B.U. L. Rev. 273 (1997). Authors calling for closer judicial scrutiny include Gregory S. Alexander, Dilemmas of Group Autonomy: Residential Associations and Community, 75 Cornell L. Rev. 1 (1989); Paula A. Franzese & Steven Siegel, Trust and Community: The Common Interest Community as Metaphor and Paradox, 72 Mo. L. Rev. 1111 (2007); and Paula A. Franzese, Common Interest Communities: Standards of Review and Review of Standards, 3 Wash. U. J.L. & Poly. 663 (2000); see also Gerald Korngold, Resolving the Flaws of Residential Servitudes and Owners Associations: For Reformation Not Termination, 1990 Wis. L. Rev. 513; James L. Winokur, Reforming Servitude Regimes: Toward Associational Federalism and Community, 1990 Wis. L. Rev. 537; James L. Winokur, The Mixed Blessings of Promissory Servitudes: Toward Optimizing Economic Utility, Individual Liberty, and Personal Identity, 1989 Wis. L. Rev. 1.

3. *Trouble in paradise?* There is also disagreement about the level of satisfaction among residents of common interest communities. Compare, e.g., Paula A. Franzese, Does It Take a Village? Privatization, Patterns of Restrictiveness and the Demise of Community, 47 Vill. L. Rev. 553, 572 (2002) ("With increasing frequency, common interest community residents are balking at the restrictions that accompany association living."), with Wayne Hyatt, Reinvention Redux: Continuing the Evolution of Master-Planned Communities, 38 Real Prop., Prob. & Tr. J. 45 (2003) (disputing Franzese's evaluation). Professor Lee Anne Fennell

observes, "While this form of ownership is plainly thriving, significant numbers of these communities have become hotbeds of litigation and acrimony." Lee Anne Fennell, Contracting Communities, 2004 U. Ill. L. Rev. 829, 831. Professor Fennell's article suggests several reasons why common interest communities sometimes fail to satisfy the preferences of their residents, and she offers some solutions. See also Lee Anne Fennell, Revealing Options, 118 Harv. L. Rev. 1399, 1444-1471 (2005) (proposing "entitlements subject to self-made options" as a device for improving consumer satisfaction in CICs); see also Lee Anne Fennell, The Unbounded Home: Property Values Beyond Property Lines (2009).

4. *The impact of the mortgage crisis on CICs.* The homeowner mortgage default crisis (discussed previously beginning at page 659) affected CICs as well as homes that are not part of residential developments. For CICs, the damage that has resulted from the crisis has been collateral as well as direct. In CICs, non-defaulting unit owners must absorb unpaid assessments themselves until title can be transferred to a new owner. This forces non-defaulting neighbors to shoulder the cost for defaulted units. Typically, this situation does not present an issue if a new owner can be placed in the unit. However, the weakened housing market has increased the difficulty in finding new owners to take title to the property. Furthermore, lenders have begun to strategically drag out foreclosure proceedings to prevent the lender from taking title and responsibility for the payments. As a result, other unit owners and not the lender must cover the payments. For a full discussion of the problem, see Andrea J. Boyack, Community Collateral Damage: A Question of Priorities, 43 Loy. U. Chi. L.J. 53 (2011).

Mulligan v. Panther Valley Property Owners Assn., 766 A.2d 1186 (N.J. App. 2001). Panther Valley is a gated residential community in Allamuchy Township, Warren County, N.J., consisting of more than 2,000 houses, including single family homes, townhouses, and condominium units, and organized as a common interest community. The members of the Panther Valley Property Owners Association voted to amend the community's declaration of covenants and the association bylaws by declaring that no individual registered as a Tier 3 sex offender under Megan's Law[49] could reside in Panther Valley. A Tier 3 sex offender is a person who is deemed to have the highest risk of repeating the crime. One member of the association, Elinor Mulligan, challenged this amendment on the ground that it violated public policy. The court decided to apply a reasonableness test rather than New York's business judgment test because the changes were made by a vote of the members rather than by the board of directors. The court found that the record was insufficient to decide the question, but since it was the plaintiff's burden to establish such a record, the association was entitled to judgment. The court said:

---

49. For more on Megan's Law, and whether a seller who has received notice that a sex offender lives nearby must disclose this to the buyer, see page 590. For a discussion of sex-offender covenants and statutes like Megan's Law, see Asmara M. Tekle, Safe: Restrictive Covenants and the Next Wave of Sex Offender Legislation, 62 SMU L. Rev. 1817 (2009).

"Although not contained within the record before us, we are aware that other similar common interest communities within the State have passed similar restrictions upon residency by Tier 3 registrants. 156 N.J.L.J. 361 (May 3, 1999). We do not know from the record how many common interest communities exist within the State and we do not know from the record how many of those communities have seen fit to adopt comparable restrictions and whether they have determined to include a broader group than Tier 3 registrants. We are thus unable to determine whether the result of such provisions is to make a large segment of the housing market unavailable to one category of individual and indeed perhaps to approach 'the ogre of vigilantism and harassment,' the potential dangers of which the Supreme Court recognized even while upholding the constitutionality of Megan's Law. Doe v. Poritz, 142 N.J. 1, 110, 662 A.2d 367 (1995).

"The record is deficient in another regard as well for it is entirely unclear if the Association performs quasi-municipal functions, such that its actions perhaps should be viewed as analogous to governmental actions in some regards. As to this issue, see, e.g., David J. Kennedy, Note, Residential Associations as State Actors: Regulating the Impact of Gated Communities on Nonmembers, 105 Yale L.J. 761 (1995); John B. Owens, Westec Story: Gated Communities and the Fourth Amendment, 34 Am. Crim. L. Rev. 1127 (1997). We do know . . . that the Association has turned over to the township the responsibility for traffic enforcement, for instance, and is precluded from acting independently in that sphere.[50] The record does not disclose whether certain services are provided by the township and others by the Association. . . .

"We recognize, of course, that Tier 3 registrants (and indeed convicted criminals) are not a protected group within the terms of New Jersey's Law Against Discrimination. N.J.S.A. 10:5-3. Nor have we been pointed to any authority deeming them handicapped. . . . It does not necessarily follow, however, that large segments of the State could entirely close their doors to such individuals, confining them to a narrow corridor and thus perhaps exposing those within that remaining corridor to a greater risk of harm than they might otherwise have had to confront."

Gated communities. Some common interest communities provide what are usually deemed municipal services. These include policing, garbage disposal,

---

50. In 1976, the Panther Valley Association asked the township and county to assume jurisdiction to enforce the traffic laws over its private roads. This request was granted. In 1995, the association, apparently dissatisfied with county enforcement, amended its rules to provide that "[d]riving in excess of the posted speed limits is prohibited." After the 1995 amendment, the association issued 126 speeding citations. One of these citations by the association's manager, using a K-15 radar unit to monitor speed, was sent to Elinor Mulligan informing her of a speeding violation and of an impending fine. Mulligan filed a complaint with the Warren County prosecutor, alleging that the association, by granting jurisdiction to the township and county, had surrendered the authority to impose independent fines upon its members who committed traffic violations within its borders. In State v. Panther Valley Property Owners Assn., 704 A.2d 1010 (N.J. App. 1998), the court agreed with Mulligan. — EDS.

street cleaning, enforcing traffic regulations against non-homeowners (levying fines on the offender or the owner of the unit to which the car is speeding), or penalizing persons who park in a fire zone (which is not a violation of a private covenant but a violation of state law). Do these actions by the association run the risk of being deemed state actions and thus subject to constitutional and statutory restrictions on municipalities? The New Jersey court in *Mulligan* suggests they might be, but the New Jersey Supreme Court later put this notion to rest. In Committee for a Better Twin Rivers v. Twin Rivers Homeowners' Assn., 929 A.2d 1060 (N.J. 2007), the court addressed the free speech rights of members of common interest communities. The case involved a challenge to an association's rules restricting the number and location of any external signs posted by residents and members' access to the association's monthly newsletter. Rejecting the claim that common interest communities had become quasi-governmental entities, the court said that board decisions were not subject to state action review but rather to a rule of reasonableness. It emphasized that the development's primary use was private and that the association had not invited the public to use its property. The development was, the court said, "a private, residential community whose residents have contractually agreed to abide by the common rules and regulations of the Association. The mutual benefit and reciprocal nature of those rules and regulations, and their enforcement, is essential to the fundamental nature of the communal living agreement that residents enjoy." 929 A.2d at 1073. The court held that the restrictions were valid under the circumstances. In an important part of its opinion, however, the court stated that in some circumstances constitutional protections under New Jersey's state constitution *may* apply when CICs unreasonably restrict residents' free speech rights because under New Jersey law state action is not a prerequisite for its constitutional rights to free speech and assembly to attach. The court provided no concrete guidance regarding the circumstances under which constitutional protection might attach. The court also noted that CIC residents are protected by common law principles that render as void restrictive covenants that violate public policy. For a discussion of the case, see Paula A. Franzese & Steven Siegel, The *Twin Rivers* Case: Of Homeowners Associations, Free Speech Rights and Privatized Mini-Governments, 5 Rutgers J.L. & Poly. 4 (2008).

Some commentators have argued that common interest communities should be classed as "state actors," subjecting their actions to constitutional regulation. See Lisa J. Chadderdon, No Political Speech Allowed: Common Interest Developments, Homeowners Associations, and Restrictions on Free Speech, 21 J. Land Use & Envtl. L. 233 (2006); David Kennedy, Note, Residential Associations as State Actors: Regulating the Impact of Gated Communities on Nonmembers, 105 Yale L.J. 761 (1995).

For commentary on gated communities in general, see, e.g., Setha Low, Behind the Gates: Life, Security, and the Pursuit of Happiness in Fortress America (2003); Edward J. Blakely & Mary Gail Snyder, Fortress America: Gated Communities in the United States (1997); David L. Callies et al., *Ramapo* Looking Forward: Gated Communities, Covenants, and Concerns, 35 Urb.

Law. 177 (2003); Paula A. Franzese, Privatization and Its Discontents: Common Interest Communities and the Rise of Government for the "Nice," 37 Urb. Law. 335 (2005). For an argument that courts explicitly recognize the novelty and importance of the geography of gated communities and that they are mindful of the potentially harmful social effects of these geographical features, see Ron Levi, Gated Communities in Law's Gaze: Material Forms and the Production of a Social Body in Legal Adjudication, 34 Law & Soc. Inq. 635 (2009) (discussing *Mulligan* as an example).

Timothy Egan, The Serene Fortress: Many Seek Security in Private Communities

N.Y. Times, Sept. 3, 1995, §1, at 1

There are no pesky doorbellers, be they politicians or Girl Scouts, allowed inside this community of high ceilings sprouting under the fir trees east of Seattle. A random encounter is the last thing people here want.

There is a new park, every blade of grass in shape—but for members only. Four private guards man the entrance gates 24 hours a day, keeping the 500 residents of Bear Creek in a nearly crime-free bubble. And should a dog try to stray outside its yard, the pet would be instantly zapped by an electronic monitor.

The streets are private. The sewers are private. There is gun control. Residents tax themselves heavily, dictate house colors and shrubbery heights for their neighbors, and have built in the kinds of natural buffers and environmental protections that are the envy of nearby middle-class communities that remain open to the public.

Bear Creek is doing for itself virtually everything that local government used to do. But in place of municipal rules are a set of regulations so restrictive that many could be found unconstitutional should a city government enact them.

More than ever, a walled-in private town like Bear Creek is exactly what the American homeowner wants—even here in the Pacific Northwest, a largely white, low-crime corner of the country with barely a hundred-year history of city-building.

The fastest-growing residential communities in the nation are private and usually gated, governed by a thicket of covenants, codes and restrictions. By some estimates, nearly four million Americans live in these closed-off, gated communities. About 28 million live in an area governed by a private community association, including condominiums and cooperatives, and that number is expected to double in the next decade, said the Community Associations Institute of Alexandria, Va.

And the very things that Republicans in Congress are trying to do away with for the nation as a whole—environmental protection, gun control, heavy regulation—are most pronounced in these predominantly Republican private enclaves.

Americans have long had gated communities, usually peopled by the very rich and built around a lake or golf course. For retirees, Sun Belt states like

Florida and Arizona have been a lure. What is different now is that a big portion of middle-class families, in nonretirement, largely white areas of the country, have chosen to wall themselves off, opting for private government, schools and police.

One of the biggest consequences of this trend, urban experts and even many residents of the new tracts say, is that the nation will surely become more balkanized. Critics worry that as homeowners withdraw into private domains, the larger sense of community spirit will disappear.

"The worst scenario for America with this trend would be to have a nation of gated communities where each group chooses to live among people just like themselves and ignores everyone else," said Milenko Matanovic, director of the Pomegranate Center, a nonprofit group from Issaquah, Wash., that works to build community links among new suburbs. . . .

In Bear Creek, most homes range in cost from $300,000 to $600,000, and there are at least a half-dozen private committees governing everything from house colors (usually nothing stronger than beige or gray)[51] to whether basketball hoops can be attached to the garage (they are prohibited). . . .

---

51. A very expensive gated community in Rancho Santa Fe, California goes further. The board of directors has the authority to determine what vehicle color is acceptable. — EDS.

Private communities are popular in many areas of the nation. In Southern California, real estate agents say a third of all new developments built in the last five years have been gated and are regulated by private governments. The suburbs outside Dallas, Phoenix, Washington, D.C., and major cities in Florida are also big strongholds of private communities. Last year, Minnesota's first gated community, Bearpath, was built near Eden Prairie. . . .

Gerald Frug, a professor of local government at the Harvard Law School, said the new private communities, while harkening back to another era, were unlike anything America has ever seen.

"The village was open to the public," he said. "The village did not have these kinds of restrictions. The village had poor people, retarded people. Somebody could hand you a leaflet. These private communities are totally devoid of random encounters. So you develop this instinct that everyone is just like me, and then you become less likely to support schools, parks or roads for everyone else."

See Sheryll D. Cashin, Privatized Communities and the "Secession of the Successful": Democracy and Fairness Beyond the Gate, 28 Fordham Urb. L.J. 1675 (2001).

11

Legislative Land Use Controls: The Law of Zoning

There is no doubt whatever about the influence of architecture
and structure upon human character and action. We make our buildings
and afterwards they make us. —

Winston Churchill

A. Introduction

1. Historical Background

From the end of the Civil War to the beginning of the twentieth century, city
life in the United States changed more dramatically than at any time since the
founding of the Republic. "Industrialism, the main creative force of the 19th
Century," Lewis Mumford observed in his great work, The City in History (1961),
"produced the most degraded human environment the world had yet seen."
Id. at 433. The extraordinary changes it brought—congestion, overcrowding,
noise, tenement housing, moral turpitude, factories belching smoke from soft
coal, and foul odors—were beyond the corrective powers of the doctrines on
nuisance and servitudes considered in Chapters 9 and 10. Courts, not wishing
to hinder the development that was making America rich, were reluctant to
declare anything a nuisance except a use highly objectionable in a particular
context. Any number of insults could be visited by one neighbor upon others, yet not be legal nuisances. As the Boston social reformer Elmer Severance
Forbes reported, not entirely managing to conceal his Brahmin caste:

> A citizen built a beautiful house with an area of 5,000 square feet of land . . . and presently
> found himself confronted by a garage. A gentleman expended $17,000 on his place . . . and
> by and by a fellow citizen built a row of seven one-story shacks on the opposite side of the
> street. A third citizen, whose property cost him $50,000, awakened one morning to discover
> a Chinese laundry in the basement adjoining his own, and . . . by the master stroke of fate
> and an unscrupulous neighbor [the value of his property plunged] to $13,000. [Elmer S.
> Forbes, Rural and Suburban Housing, in Proceedings of the Second National Conference
> on Housing (1912).]

Nuisance law had other limitations. It did not prevent nuisances from arising,
but merely gave damages or an injunction after the fact in an expensive lawsuit by one neighbor against another. And, from the developer's point of view,

nuisance law added the risk that capital sunk in land development might later be declared a nuisance.

Restrictive covenants also were incapable of dealing effectively with relations among neighbors in urban areas. They were useful only in new subdivisions and other developments of large acreage occurring under a single owner, who imposed the covenants. At the turn of the century most development was lot-by-lot. With the exception of some experimental new towns, large housing developments, such as Levittown and its progeny, did not appear until after World War II. Hence early in the twentieth century, environmentalists or social reformers or city planners (whatever they might be called) turned to zoning, which was in theory designed to *prevent* harmful neighborhood effects.

The ideological roots of zoning are traceable to Ebenezer Howard, an Englishman who in 1898 published a little book entitled Tomorrow: A Peaceful Path to Real Reform (known since its revised edition in 1902 by the title Garden Cities of Tomorrow). Appalled by the chaos of London, which sprawled across the horizon as the most populous metropolis in the world, Howard proposed resettling people in Garden Cities, new towns in the country limited to 30,000 people and surrounded by agricultural greenbelts. Uses of land would be separated — houses here, commerce there (in a glass-covered market), public buildings in the center, and industry somewhere else — so one use would not harm another. Howard venerated the home as crucial to the transmission of culture and the formation of character in children, so he sheltered it from the impersonal and sometimes hostile external world.

It is not surprising that Howard's Garden City ideal found fertile ground in the United States. From the beginning — with William Penn's creation of Philadelphia as "a green country town," incorporating ample gardens or orchards around each house, and Thomas Jefferson's "dominant image of an undefiled green republic, a quiet land of forests, villages, and farms"[1] — a strong current projecting pastoral life as the ideal has run through American culture. Our most influential writers — Emerson, Thoreau, Melville, Hawthorne — celebrated life in the country, and the reigning architectural genius, Frank Lloyd Wright, regarded the overcrowded city as an artificial form of living that should be dismantled. Still, American city planners and reformers were not much interested in building the Garden City ideal. They were, however, much interested in its underlying principles, which they turned into the foundation for modern city planning: (1) separation of uses, (2) protection of the single family home, (3) low rise development, and (4) medium density population.

While Howard provided these ideological principles of zoning, other visionaries made important contributions to the public acceptance of city planning. The architect Daniel Burnham staged the Chicago World's Columbian Exposition in 1893, which through its enormous success captured the imagination of the public and fired up the City Beautiful movement, a nationwide effort to beautify cities with great civic

---

1. Leo Marx, The Machine in the Garden: Technology and the Pastoral Ideal in America 6 (1964). See also Morton White & Lucia White, The Intellectual Versus the City (2d ed. 2000).

World's Columbian Exposition, Chicago, 1893

monuments and public works. In 1901, the United States Congress was moved to produce, with Burnham's guidance, a new master plan for Washington, restoring and revitalizing L'Enfant's 1791 plan for the city. Other cities—Cleveland, Kansas City, Denver—followed with visionary city plans. The magnificent American railroad stations—Washington's Union Station, New York's Pennsylvania Station (modeled after the Roman Baths of Caracalla, and now demolished), Grand Central Terminal, and Kansas City's cavernous Union Station—are products of the City Beautiful movement. So is San Francisco's sumptuous city hall, reminiscent of St. Peter's in Rome.

Within 20 years, however, the City Beautiful movement ran out of steam, a decline encouraged by another architect, Swiss-born LeCorbusier. LeCorbusier observed that the low density development envisioned in Garden Cities, joined together in successive rings of suburbia, consumed an enormous amount of land. So he proposed a vertical rather than a horizontal Garden City, residential towers built in green parks (1,200 persons to the acre, twice as many as on the Upper East Side of Manhattan, and only 15 percent of the ground covered) and connected by elevated highways to blocks of office towers also set in green parks. Each residential superblock would include all the amenities of a healthy family life: playgrounds, schools, pools, neighborhood grocery, and sunbathing on roof gardens. This was the Radiant City, practical for high densities but sharing the same essential anti-urban stance of the Garden City. LeCorbusier's ideas had an immense impact on public housing built in tower blocks, on urban renewal projects in the 1950s and 1960s, and, in some areas of the country, like Chicago's North Michigan Avenue, on housing for the rich.

For good reading on the history of city planning and development in twen-tieth-century America, see Stanley Buder, Visionaries and Planners: The Garden City Movement and the Modern Community (1990); Walter L. Creese, The Search for Enrichment: The Garden City Before and After (1992); Kenneth T. Jackson, Crabgrass Frontier: The Suburbanization of the United States (1985); Jane Jacobs, The Death and Life of Great American Cities (1961) (a scathing denunciation of Garden City and Radiant City by a lover of city life); John W. Reps, The Making of Urban America: A History of City Planning in the United States (1965); Vincent Scully, American Architecture and Urbanism (1969); see also M. Christine Boyer, Dreaming the Rational City: The Myth of American City Planning (1983).

Although Howard, Burnham, and LeCorbusier had different views about urbanity—Howard rejected it, Burnham welcomed it, and LeCorbusier did a little of both—they shared a common certitude that rational planning was actually possible and an optimistic belief that planning bodies could control the shortsighted and uncoordinated decisions of individual landowners, which had resulted in ugly and chaotic cities. Their ideas—the Garden City, City Beautiful, the Radiant City—generated a large and continuing interest in improvement of the city in the United States. In 1909, Los Angeles enacted an ordinance restricting industry to specified districts, away from residential areas. In 1916, New York City enacted the first comprehensive zoning program, which assigned several classes of land uses to different zones and restricted the height and bulk of buildings.

Important interests had a stake in controlling the course of this sort of development. In New York City, for instance, residents were upset that their properties were being cut off from light and air by sprouting skyscrapers, while Fifth Avenue retailers worried that the mingling of immigrant workers with wealthy patrons would be bad for business. In all towns, homeowners sought some kind of insurance that their major asset would not be devalued by neighboring industrial and apartment uses.[2] Citizens, business people, and social reformers decided that zoning was essential to healthy housing with light and air, to economic interests, and to environmental planning. For accounts of the early adoption of zoning in the United States, see Stanislaw J. Makielski, The Politics of Zoning (1966); Seymour I. Toll, Zoned American (1969); see also Martha A. Lees, Preserving Property Values? Preserving Proper Homes? Preserving Privilege? The Pre-*Euclid* Debate over Zoning for Exclusively Private Residential Areas, 1916-1926, 56 U. Pitt. L. Rev. 367 (1994).

Zoning spread rapidly in the years after 1916, especially following the appearance of a model zoning statute in 1922, the Standard State Zoning Enabling Act. By 1925, 368 municipalities had zoning ordinances. With the spread of zoning came constitutional attacks—assertions that the new controls amounted to takings of property without compensation or worked deprivations of property without due process of law. By the mid-1920s, a few state courts had struck down zoning as unconstitutional, but others had upheld it. Everyone, especially city planners and realtors, wanted an answer from the United States Supreme Court.

---

2. See William A. Fischel, An Economic History of Zoning and a Cure for Its Exclusionary Effects, 41 Urb. Stud. 317 (2004); William A. Fischel, The Homevoter Hypothesis (2001).

Real estate dealers and realty boards selected as a test case the zoning ordinance of tiny Euclid, Ohio (pop. 3,300 in 1920), a suburb of Cleveland (pop. 800,000). They thought it a favorable case for a broad holding of unconstitutionality for several reasons. First, it took three-quarters of the value out of part of the plaintiff's land. Second, the court might see little Euclid as interfering with the natural and desirable expansion of Cleveland. And third, the ordinance had six use districts, three height districts, and four area districts, which appeared difficult to justify as nuisance prevention.

In 1924, a federal district court found the Euclid ordinance unconstitutional:

> The plain truth is that the true object of the ordinance in question is to place all the property in an undeveloped area of 16 square miles in a straitjacket. The purpose to be accomplished is really to regulate the mode of living of persons who may hereafter inhabit it. In the last analysis, the result to be accomplished is to classify the population and segregate them according to their income or situation in life. The true reason why some persons live in a mansion and others in a shack, why some live in a single family dwelling and others in a double-family dwelling, why some live in a two-family dwelling and others in an apartment, or why some live in a well-kept apartment and others in a tenement, is primarily economic. It is a matter of income and wealth, plus the labor and difficulty of procuring adequate domestic service. Aside from contributing to these results and furthering such class tendencies, the ordinance has also an esthetic purpose; that is to say, to make this village develop into a city along lines now conceived by the village council to be attractive and beautiful. . . . Whether these purposes and objects would justify the taking of plaintiff's property as and for a public use need not be considered. It is sufficient to say that, in our opinion, and as applied to plaintiff's property, it may not be done without compensation under the guise of exercising the police power. [Ambler Realty Co. v. Village of Euclid, 297 F. 307, 316 (N.D. Ohio 1924).]

The judge knew his decision was an important one. "This case," he said, "is obviously destined to go higher." 297 F. at 308.

Village of Euclid v. Ambler Realty Co.

Supreme Court of the United States, 1926
272 U.S. 365

JUSTICE SUTHERLAND delivered the opinion of the Court.

The Village of Euclid is an Ohio municipal corporation. It adjoins and practically is a suburb of the City of Cleveland. Its estimated population is between 5,000 and 10,000, and its area from twelve to fourteen square miles, the greater part of which is farm lands or unimproved acreage. It lies, roughly, in the form of a parallelogram measuring approximately three and one-half miles each way. East and west it is traversed by three principal highways: Euclid Avenue, through the southerly border, St. Clair Avenue, through the central portion, and Lake Shore Boulevard, through the northerly border in close proximity to the shore of Lake Erie. The Nickel Plate railroad lies from 1,500 to 1,800 feet north of Euclid Avenue, and the Lake Shore railroad 1,600 feet farther to the north. The three highways and the two railroads are substantially parallel.

Appellee is the owner of a tract of land containing 68 acres, situated in the westerly end of the village, abutting on Euclid Avenue to the south and the Nickel Plate railroad to the north. Adjoining this tract, both on the east and on the west, there have been laid out restricted residential plats upon which residences have been erected.

On November 13, 1922, an ordinance was adopted by the Village Council, establishing a comprehensive zoning plan for regulating and restricting the location of trades, industries, apartment houses, two-family houses, etc., the lot area to be built upon, the size and height of buildings, etc.

The entire area of the village is divided by the ordinance into six classes of use districts, denominated U-1 to U-6, inclusive; three classes of height districts, denominated H-1 to H-3, inclusive; and four classes of area districts, denominated A-1 to A-4, inclusive. The use districts are classified in respect of the buildings which may be erected within their respective limits, as follows: U-1 is restricted to single family dwellings, public parks, water towers and reservoirs, suburban and interurban electric railway passenger stations and rights of way, and farming, noncommercial greenhouse nurseries and truck gardening; U-2 is extended to include two-family dwellings; U-3 is further extended to include apartment houses, hotels, churches, schools, public libraries, museums, private clubs, community center buildings, hospitals, sanitariums, public playgrounds and recreation buildings, and a city hall and courthouse; U-4 is further extended to include banks, offices, studios, telephone exchanges, fire and police stations, restaurants, theatres and moving picture shows, retail stores and shops, sales offices, sample rooms, wholesale stores for hardware, drugs and groceries, stations for gasoline and oil (not exceeding 1,000 gallons storage) and for ice delivery, skating rinks and dance halls, electric substations, job and newspaper printing, public garages for motor vehicles, stables and wagon sheds (not exceeding five horses, wagons or motor trucks) and distributing stations for central store and commercial enterprises; U-5 is further extended to include billboards and advertising signs (if permitted), warehouses, ice and ice cream manufacturing and cold storage plants, bottling works, milk bottling and central distribution stations, laundries, carpet cleaning, dry cleaning and dyeing establishments, blacksmith, horseshoeing, wagon and motor vehicle repair shops, freight stations, street car barns, stables and wagon sheds (for more than five horses, wagons or motor trucks), and wholesale produce markets and salesrooms; U-6 is further extended to include plants for sewage disposal and for producing gas, garbage and refuse incineration, scrap iron, junk, scrap paper and rag storage, aviation fields, cemeteries, penal and correctional institutions, insane and feeble minded institutions, storage of oil and gasoline (not to exceed 25,000 gallons), and manufacturing and industrial operations of any kind other than, and any public utility not included in, a class U-1, U-2, U-3, U-4 or U-5 use. There is a seventh class of uses which is prohibited altogether.

Class U-1 is the only district in which buildings are restricted to those enumerated. In the other classes the uses are cumulative; that is to say, uses in class U-2 include those enumerated in the preceding class, U-1; class U-3 includes uses enumerated in the preceding classes, U-2 and U-1; and so on. In addition to the enumerated uses, the ordinance provides for accessory uses, that is, for uses customarily incident to the principal use, such as private garages. Many regulations are provided in respect of such accessory uses.

The height districts are classified as follows: In class H-1, buildings are limited to a height of two and one-half stories or thirty-five feet; in class H-2, to four stories or fifty feet; in class H-3, to eighty feet. To all of these, certain exceptions are made, as in the case of church spires, water tanks, etc.

The classification of area districts is: In A-1 districts, dwellings or apartment houses to accommodate more than one family must have at least 5,000 square feet for interior lots and at least 4,000 square feet for corner lots; in A-2 districts, the area must be at least 2,500 square feet for interior lots, and 2,000 square feet for corner lots; in A-3 districts, the limits are 1,250 and 1,000 square feet, respectively; in A-4 districts, the limits are 900 and 700 square feet, respectively. The ordinance contains, in great variety and detail, provisions in respect of width of lots, front, side and rear yards, and other matters, including restrictions and regulations as to the use of bill boards, sign boards and advertising signs. . . .

Appellee's tract of land comes under U-2, U-3, and U-6. The first strip of 620 feet immediately north of Euclid Avenue falls in class U-2, the next 130 feet to the north, in U-3, and the remainder in U-6. The uses of the first 620 feet, therefore, do not include apartment houses, hotels, churches, schools, or other public and semi-public buildings, or other uses enumerated in respect to U-3 to U-6, inclusive. The uses of the next 130 feet include all of these, but exclude industries, theatres, banks, shops, and the various other uses set forth in respect of U-4 to U-6, inclusive.

Annexed to the ordinance, and made a part of it, is a zone map, showing the location and limits of the various use, height and area districts, from which it appears that the three classes overlap one another; that is to say, for example, both U-5 and U-6 use districts are in A-4 area districts, but the former is in H-2 and the latter in H-3 height districts. . . .

The lands lying between the two railroads for the entire length of the village area and extending some distance on either side to the north and south, having an average width of about 1,600 feet, are left open, with slight exceptions, for industrial and all other uses. This includes the larger part of appellee's tract. . . .

The enforcement of the ordinance is entrusted to the inspector of buildings, under rules and regulations of the board of zoning appeals. Meetings of the board are public, and minutes of its proceedings are kept. It is authorized to adopt rules and regulations to carry into effect provisions of the ordinance. Decisions of the inspector of buildings may be appealed to the board by any person claiming to be adversely affected by any such decision. The board is given power in specific cases of practical difficulty or unnecessary hardship to interpret the ordinance in harmony with its general purpose and intent, so that the public health, safety and general welfare may be secure and substantial justice done. Penalties are prescribed for violations, and it is provided that the various provisions are to be regarded as independent and the holding of any provision to be unconstitutional, void or ineffective shall not affect any of the others.

The ordinance is assailed on the grounds that it is in derogation of §1 of the Fourteenth Amendment to the Federal Constitution in that it deprives appellee of liberty and property without due process of law and denies it the equal protection of the law, and that it offends against certain provisions of the Constitution of the State of Ohio. The prayer of the bill is for an injunction restraining the enforcement of the ordinance and all attempts to impose or maintain as to appellee's property any of the restrictions, limitations or conditions. The court below held the ordinance to be unconstitutional and void, and enjoined its enforcement. 297 Fed. 307.

Before proceeding to a consideration of the case, it is necessary to determine the scope of the inquiry. The bill alleges that the tract of land in question is vacant and has been held for years for the purpose of selling and developing it for industrial uses, for which it is especially adapted, being immediately in the path of progressive industrial development; that for such uses it has a market value of about $10,000 per acre, but if the use be limited to residential purpose the market value is not in excess of $2,500 per acre; that the first 200 feet of the parcel back from Euclid Avenue, if unrestricted in respect of use, has a value of $150 per front foot, but if limited to residential uses, and ordinary mercantile business be excluded therefrom, its value is not in excess of $50 per front foot.

It is specifically averred that the ordinance attempts to restrict and control the lawful uses of appellee's land so as to confiscate and destroy a great part of its value; that it is being enforced in accordance with its terms; that prospective buyers of land for industrial, commercial and residential uses in the metropolitan district of Cleveland are deterred from buying any part of this land because of the existence of the ordinance and the necessity thereby entailed of conducting burdensome and expensive litigation in order to vindicate the right to use the land for lawful and legitimate purposes; that the ordinance constitutes a cloud upon the land, reduces and destroys its value, and has the effect of diverting the normal industrial, commercial and residential development thereof to other and less favorable locations.

The record goes no farther than to show, as the lower court found, that the normal, and reasonably to be expected, use and development of that part of appellee's land adjoining Euclid Avenue is for general trade and commercial purposes, particularly retail stores and like establishments, and that the normal, and reasonably to be expected, use and development of the residue of the land is for industrial and trade purposes. Whatever injury is inflicted by the mere existence and threatened enforcement of the ordinance is due to restrictions in respect of these and similar uses; to which perhaps should be added—if not included in the foregoing—restrictions in respect of apartment houses. Specifically, there is nothing in the record to suggest that any damage results from the presence in the ordinance of those restrictions relating to churches, schools, libraries and other public and semipublic buildings. It is neither alleged nor proved that there is, or may be, a demand for any part of appellee's land for any of the last named uses; and we cannot assume the existence of facts which would justify an injunction upon this record in respect of this class of restrictions. For present purposes the provisions of the ordinance in respect of these uses may, therefore, be put aside as unnecessary to be considered. It is also unnecessary to consider the effect of the restrictions in respect of U-1 districts, since none of appellee's land falls within that class.

We proceed, then, to a consideration of those provisions of the ordinance to which the case as it is made relates, first disposing of a preliminary matter.

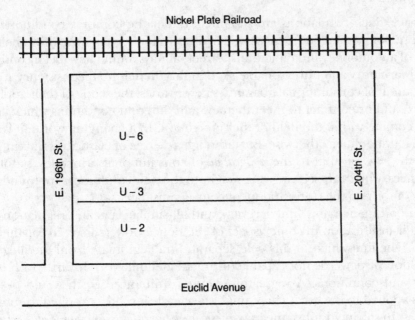

Figure 11-1
Ambler Realty Property

A motion was made in the court below to dismiss the bill on the ground that, because complainant [appellee] had made no effort to obtain a building permit or apply to the zoning board of appeals for relief as it might have done under the terms of the ordinance, the suit was premature. The motion was properly overruled. The effect of the allegations of the bill is that the ordinance of its own force operates greatly to reduce the value of appellee's lands and destroy their marketability for industrial, commercial and residential uses; and the attack is directed, not against any specific provision or provisions, but against the ordinance as an entirety. Assuming the premises, the existence and maintenance of the ordinance, in effect, constitutes a present invasion of appellee's property rights and a threat to continue it. Under these circumstances, the equitable jurisdiction is clear. . . .

It is not necessary to set forth the provisions of the Ohio Constitution which are thought to be infringed. The question is the same under both Constitutions, namely, as stated by appellee: Is the ordinance invalid in that it violates the constitutional protection "to the right of property in the appellee by attempted regulations under the guise of the police power, which are unreasonable and confiscatory"?

Building zone laws are of modern origin. They began in this country about twenty-five years ago. Until recent years, urban life was comparatively simple; but with the great increase and concentration of population, problems have developed, and constantly are developing, which require, and will continue to require, additional restrictions in respect of the use and occupation of private lands in urban communities. Regulations, the wisdom, necessity and validity of which, as applied to existing conditions, are so apparent that they are now uniformly sustained, a century ago, or even half a century ago, probably would have been rejected as arbitrary and oppressive. Such regulations are sustained, under the complex conditions of our day, for reasons analogous to those which justify traffic regulations, which, before the advent of automobiles and rapid transit street railways, would have been condemned as fatally arbitrary and unreasonable. And in this there is no inconsistency, for while the meaning of constitutional guaranties never varies, the scope of their application must expand or contract to meet the new and different conditions which are constantly coming within the field of their operation. In a changing world, it is impossible that it should be otherwise. But although a degree of elasticity is thus imparted, not to the *meaning*, but to the *application* of constitutional principles, statutes and ordinances, which, after giving due weight to the new conditions, are found clearly not to conform to the Constitution, of course, must fall.

The ordinance now under review, and all similar laws and regulations, must find their justification in some aspect of the police power, asserted for the public welfare. The line which in this field separates the legitimate from the illegitimate assumption of power is not capable of precise delimitation. It varies with circumstances and conditions. A regulatory zoning ordinance, which would be clearly valid as applied to the great cities, might be clearly invalid as applied to rural communities. In solving doubts, the maxim *sic utere tuo ut alienum non laedas*, which lies at the foundation of so much of the common law of nuisances, ordinarily will furnish a fairly helpful clew. And the law of nuisances, likewise, may be consulted, not for the purpose of controlling, but for the helpful aid of its analogies in the process of ascertaining the scope of, the power. Thus the question whether the power exists to forbid the erection of a building of a particular kind or for a particular use, like the question whether a particular thing is a nuisance, is to be determined, not by an abstract consideration of the building or of the thing considered apart, but by considering it in connection with the circumstances and the locality. . . . A nuisance may be merely a right thing in the wrong place — like a pig in the parlor instead of the barnyard. If the validity of the legislative classification for zoning purposes be fairly debatable, the legislative judgment must be allowed to control. . . .

There is no serious difference of opinion in respect of the validity of laws and regulations fixing the height of buildings within reasonable limits, the character of materials and methods of construction, and the adjoining area which must be left open, in order to minimize the danger of fire or collapse, the evils of overcrowding, and the like, and excluding from residential sections offensive trades, industries and structures likely to create nuisances. . . .

Here, however, the exclusion is in general terms of all industrial establishments, and it may thereby happen that not only offensive or dangerous industries will be excluded, but those which are neither offensive nor dangerous will share the same fate. But this is no more than happens in respect of many practice-forbidding laws which this Court has upheld although drawn in general terms so as to include individual cases that may turn out to be innocuous in themselves. . . . The inclusion of a reasonable margin to insure effective enforcement, will not put upon a law, otherwise valid, the stamp of invalidity. Such laws may also find their justification in the fact that, in some fields, the bad fades into the good by such insensible degrees that the two are not capable of being readily distinguished and separated in terms of legislation. In the light of these considerations, we are not prepared to say that the end in view was not sufficient to justify the general rule of the ordinance, although some industries of an innocent character might fall within the proscribed class. It can not be said that the ordinance in this respect "passes the bounds of reason and assumes the character of a merely arbitrary fiat." Purity Extract Co. v. Lynch, 226 U.S. 192, 204. Moreover, the restrictive provisions of the ordinance in this particular may be sustained upon the principles applicable to the broader exclusion from residential districts of all business and trade structures, presently to be discussed.

It is said that the Village of Euclid is a mere suburb of the City of Cleveland; that the industrial development of that city has now reached and in some degree extended into the village and, in the obvious course of things, will soon absorb the entire area for industrial enterprises; that the effect of the ordinance is to divert this natural development elsewhere with the consequent loss of increased values to the owners of the lands within the village borders. But the village, though physically a suburb of Cleveland, is politically a separate municipality, with powers of its own and authority to govern itself as it sees fit within the limits of the organic law of its creation and the State and Federal Constitutions. Its governing authorities, presumably representing a majority of its inhabitants and voicing their will, have determined, not that industrial development shall cease at its boundaries, but that the course of such development shall proceed within definitely fixed lines. If it be a proper exercise of the police power to relegate industrial establishments to localities separated from residential sections, it is not easy to find a sufficient reason for denying the power because the effect of its exercise is to divert an industrial flow from the course which it would follow, to the injury of the residential public if left alone, to another course where such injury will be obviated. It is not meant by this, however, to exclude the possibility of cases where the general public interest would so far outweigh the interest of the municipality that the municipality would not be allowed to stand in the way.

We find no difficulty in sustaining restrictions of the kind thus far reviewed. The serious question in the case arises over the provisions of the ordinance excluding from residential districts, apartment houses, business houses, retail stores and shops, and other like establishments. This question involves the validity of what is really the crux of the more recent zoning legislation, namely, the creation and maintenance of residential districts, from which business and trade of every sort, including hotels and apartment houses, are excluded. Upon that question this Court has not thus far spoken. The decisions of the state courts are numerous and conflicting; but those which broadly sustain the power greatly outnumber those which deny altogether or narrowly limit it; and it is very apparent that there is a constantly increasing tendency in the direction of the broader view. . . .

The matter of zoning has received much attention at the hands of commissions and experts, and the results of their investigations have been set forth in comprehensive reports. These reports, which bear every evidence of painstaking consideration, concur in the view that the segregation of residential, business, and industrial buildings will make it easier to provide fire apparatus suitable for the character and intensity of the development in each section; that it will increase the safety and security of home life; greatly tend to prevent street accidents, especially to children, by reducing the traffic and resulting confusion in residential sections; decrease noise and other conditions which produce or intensify nervous disorders; preserve a more favorable environment in which to rear children, etc. With particular reference to apartment houses, it is pointed out that the development of detached house sections is greatly retarded by the coming of apartment houses, which has sometimes resulted in destroying the entire section for private house purposes; that in such sections very often the apartment house is a mere parasite, constructed in order to take advantage of the open spaces and attractive surroundings created by the residential character of the district. Moreover, the coming of one apartment house is followed by others, interfering by their height and bulk with the free circulation of air and monopolizing the rays of the sun which otherwise would fall upon the smaller homes, and bringing, as their necessary accompaniments, the disturbing noises incident to increased traffic and business, and the occupation, by means of moving and parked automobiles, of larger portions of the streets, thus detracting from their safety and depriving children of the privilege of quiet and open spaces for play, enjoyed by those in more favored localities—until, finally, the residential character of the neighborhood and its desirability as a place of detached residences are utterly destroyed. Under these circumstances, apartment houses, which in a different environment would be not only entirely unobjectionable but highly desirable, come very near to being nuisances.

If these reasons, thus summarized, do not demonstrate the wisdom or sound policy in all respects of those restrictions which we have indicated as pertinent to the inquiry, at least, the reasons are sufficiently cogent to preclude us from saying, as it must be said before the ordinance can be declared unconstitutional, that such provisions are clearly arbitrary and unreasonable, having no substantial relation to the public health, safety, morals, or general welfare. . . .

It is true that when, if ever, the provisions set forth in the ordinance in tedious and minute detail, come to be concretely applied to particular premises, including those of the appellee, or to particular conditions, or to be considered in connection with specific complaints, some of them, or even many of them, may be found to be clearly arbitrary and unreasonable. But where the equitable remedy of injunction is sought, as it is here, not upon the ground of a present infringement or denial of a specific right, or of a particular injury in process of actual execution, but upon the broad ground that the mere existence and threatened enforcement of the ordinance, by materially and adversely affecting values and curtailing the opportunities of the market, constitute a present and irreparable injury, the court will not scrutinize its provisions, sentence by sentence, to ascertain by a process of piecemeal dissection whether there may be, here and there, provisions of a minor character, or relating to matters of administration, or not shown to contribute to the injury complained of, which, if attacked separately, might not withstand the test of constitutionality. In respect of such provisions, of which specific complaint is not made, it cannot be said that the land owner has suffered or is threatened with an injury which entitles him to challenge their constitutionality. . . .

The relief sought here is . . . an injunction against the enforcement of any of the restrictions, limitations or conditions of the ordinance. And the gravamen of the complaint is that a portion of the land of the appellee cannot be sold for certain enumerated uses because of the general and broad restraints of the ordinance. What would be the effect of a restraint imposed by one or more of the innumerable provisions of the ordinance, considered apart, upon the value or marketability of the lands is neither disclosed by the bill nor by the evidence, and we are afforded no basis, apart from mere speculation, upon which to rest a conclusion that it or they would have any appreciable effect upon those matters. Under these circumstances, therefore, it is enough for us to determine, as we do, that the ordinance in its general scope and dominant features, so far as its provisions are here involved, is a valid exercise of authority, leaving other provisions to be dealt with as cases arise directly involving them.

And this is in accordance with the traditional policy of this Court. In the realm of constitutional law, especially, this Court has perceived the embarrassment which is likely to result from an attempt to formulate rules or decide questions beyond the necessities of the immediate issue. It has preferred to follow the method of a gradual approach to the general by a systematically guarded application and extension of constitutional principles to particular cases as they arise, rather than by out of hand attempts to establish general rules to which future cases must be fitted. This process applies with peculiar force to the solution of questions arising under the due process clause of the Constitution as applied to the exercise of the flexible powers of police, with which we are here concerned.

Decree reversed.

Mr. Justice Van Devanter, Mr. Justice McReynolds, and Mr. Justice Butler, dissent.

NOTES AND QUESTIONS

1. The zoning scheme of the Euclid ordinance is known today as Euclidean zoning. Districts are graded from "highest" (single family residences) to "lowest" (worst kind of industry). Under Euclidean zoning, the uses permitted in each district are cumulative; higher uses are permitted in areas zoned for lower uses but not vice versa. Thus one can put a single family house in an apartment district, and both uses in a commercial district, but not a commercial use in a residential district nor an apartment house in a single family district. In an attempt to preserve large tracts for future industrial use, improving the fiscal base, some cities have turned to noncumulative zoning, prohibiting houses and commerce in industrial zones (often called industrial parks).

The terms "higher" and "lower" uses do not refer to economic value. *A*, whose lot is zoned residential, has a higher use than *B*, whose lot is zoned commercial, but *A*'s lot ordinarily has a lower value. Commercially zoned property usually sells at a higher price than residentially zoned property.

On *Euclid*, see Michael Allan Wolf, The Zoning of America (2008); Symposium on the Seventy-Fifth Anniversary of *Euclid v. Ambler*, 51 Case W. Res. L. Rev. 593 (2001); Richard H. Chused, *Euclid*'s Historical Imagery, 51 Case W. Res. L. Rev.

597 (2001), noting that *Euclid* actually served to enable many of the very problems that enlightened land use planning is supposed to overcome. In particular
(and as the trial court in the case sensed), Euclidean zoning can be seen as "overt
licensing of segregation by class." Id. at 615. More on this theme at the end of this
chapter. See page 1104.

2. Justice George Sutherland, the author of the majority opinion in the *Euclid*
case, was a noted conservative. In the 1930s, he joined with Justices Van Devanter,
McReynolds, and Butler (the so-called Four Horsemen, tenacious agents of
destruction), who, managing to pick up a fifth vote, struck down important New
Deal legislation as depriving citizens of liberty or property without (substantive)
due process of law. "Substantive due process" refers to fundamental rights and
liberties, as found by the Court but not enumerated in the Bill of Rights. It is
grounded in a notion of "natural rights." From the end of the nineteenth century to President Franklin Roosevelt's second term, substantive due process was
the weapon the Court most frequently used to strike down social legislation it
deemed unwise, such as minimum wage and maximum hours of work legislation. Although it fell into disuse in protecting economic liberty when Roosevelt
appointed new justices to replace the Four Horsemen, substantive due process
has not been abandoned by the Court. Indeed, in the last quarter of the twentieth century there was a reassertion of substantive due process to support personal
rather than economic liberties. See, e.g., Moore v. City of East Cleveland, 431 U.S.
494 (1977), reproduced at page 1069.

Why would Justice Sutherland and his conservative allies on the Court endorse
a seemingly radical reform like zoning? Perhaps because, as already suggested, they
recognized that zoning could protect the value of land owned by the propertied
class—not to mention the values of the class itself—by, among other things, excluding people regarded as undesirable neighbors. If this is the point, it took a while to
dawn on the justices. According to Alfred McCormack, A Law Clerk's Recollections,
46 Colum. L. Rev. 710, 712 (1946), after oral argument in *Euclid* a majority of the
Court was ready to hold that the zoning ordinance was unconstitutional.

It was in this context that Alfred Bettman, leader of the National Conference on City
Planning, emerged as a crucial strategic and theoretical player. He did not directly participate
in either the trial or the first hearing before the Supreme Court. In one of history's most bizarre
twists of fate, Bettman drafted a brief to file for use when the Supreme Court first heard the
case, but missed the deadline by waiting until after the oral argument before seeking to file.
[A]bout two-and-one-half weeks after the *Euclid* oral argument, (from which Justice Sutherland
was absent), Bettman wrote to his old friend and fellow Cincinnatian, Chief Justice William
Howard Taft, noting how important the case was and asking if he could belatedly file an amicus
brief. Taft wrote back to Bettman later that month telling him that his request had been brought
up in conference and granted. Shortly thereafter, the Court ordered that the case be reargued
the following term. . . .

[In his approach to the case,] Bettman declined to use . . . broad and unlimited arguments,
preferring instead to contend that specific claims of unfairness could be dealt with individually
without barring zoning altogether. He argued that legislative authority extended to the prevention of nuisances, and that creating single use zones was an appropriate method for avoiding
future conflicts in land uses. . . .

> [By contrasting the wholesome neighborhood of single family homes with the hectic congestion of areas filled with apartment buildings,] Bettman could call forth a host of phrases well suited to convince the conservative instincts of Supreme Court Justices that zoning was a positive good. The moral strength of upper class children was at risk, Bettman warned. Keeping the kids away from a "disorderly, noisy, slovenly, blighted and slum-like district" was the only protection. [Chused, supra, at 610-613.]

See also Nadav Shoked, The Reinvention of Ownership: The Embrace of Residential Zoning and the Modern Populist Reading of Property, 28 Yale. J. on Reg. 91 (2011) (comparing different "readings" of the *Euclid* decision); Emily Talen, Zoning and Diversity in Historical Perspective, 11 J. Plan. Hist. 330 (2012) (discussing what framers of zoning thought about diversity).

3. The Court in *Euclid* concerned itself solely with whether the police power could be exercised to zone property without depriving the plaintiff of (substantive) due process of law. Another argument might have been made that the severe reduction in value of the plaintiff's land by the zoning ordinance effected a "taking" of plaintiff's property, which cannot be done under the Fifth Amendment without compensating the plaintiff. If the government had taken title to the plaintiff's land, the government would have had to pay for it. Should it also have to pay if it leaves title in the plaintiff but destroys much of the land's economic value? The argument that government regulation of land can constitute a compensable taking if it "goes too far" was accepted by the Court in Pennsylvania Coal Co. v. Mahon, 260 U.S. 393 (1922), reproduced at page 1153. We explore the issue of regulatory takings in the next chapter. Suffice it to say for now that zoning ordinances are routinely upheld in the face of takings allegations, especially if they are controlling nuisance-like conditions or so long as they leave the property owner with some reasonable use.

4. Notice that the plaintiff in *Euclid* did not challenge any specific provisions of the ordinance in question but rather attacked the zoning law in its entirety. The Supreme Court in turn held zoning *in general* to be constitutional but added that concrete applications of specific provisions could prove to be arbitrary and unreasonable; such problems would be dealt with as they arose. Two years later, in Nectow v. City of Cambridge, 277 U.S. 183 (1928), the Court followed through on this warning by deciding that the zoning ordinance, as applied to the plaintiff's land, was arbitrary and unreasonable. After *Nectow*, the Supreme Court went out of the zoning business for nearly half a century, leaving the policing of zoning laws to state courts. In recent years, however, the Court has become active in the area once again. We shall have occasion to consider some of its opinions in the balance of this chapter and in the next.

5. "Today, zoning is virtually universal in the metropolitan areas of the United States. . . . Of cities with over 250,000 population only Houston, Texas, has not enacted a zoning ordinance." Robert C. Ellickson, Alternatives to Zoning: Covenants, Nuisance Rules, and Fines as Land Use Controls, 40 U. Chi. L. Rev. 681, 692 (1973). And Houston is an exception in only the strictest sense; "extensive government regulation belies the city's free market reputation in land use management. . . . [G]overnment policies have altered land use decisions for decades,

and recent interventions continue the trend toward greater regulation." Teddy M. Kapur, Land Use Regulation in Houston Contradicts the City's Free Market Reputation, 34 Envtl. L. Rep. 10045 (2004). Moreover, Houston has in recent years turned increasingly to nuisance law to regulate undesirable land uses. See, e.g., Bradley Olson, Nuisance Laws Stoke Regulatory Arsenal, Hous. Chron., Apr. 10, 2009; Houston Using Nuisance Laws on Business, Hous. Chron., Apr. 11, 2009. A study by two economists at the Federal Reserve Bank of Dallas suggests that the absence of zoning laws has kept land values in Houston stable, reducing volatility in housing prices. See Amber C. McCullagh & Robert W. Gilmer, Neither Boom Nor Bust: How Houston's Housing Market Differs from Nation's, Federal Reserve Bank of Dallas, Houston Branch (Jan. 2008).

As the discussion of *Euclid* suggests, and as the material on exclusionary zoning (see pages 1080-1105) shows, zoning can affect the spatial location of households of varying socioeconomic groups differentially. Would the same dynamic occur in other cities without zoning, as in Houston? According to one commentator, planning tools other than zoning were used by elites in Houston in order to reach their objectives. See John Mixon, Four Land Use Vignettes from Unzoned(?) Houston, 24 Notre Dame J.L. Ethics & Pub. Poly. 159 (2010). One empirical study compared three neighborhoods in Houston and concluded that homogenous neighborhoods composed of relatively high income and well-educated residents could use deed restrictions as planning and exclusionary devices more effectively than low and moderate income neighborhoods. See Zhu Qian, Shaping Urban Form Without Zoning: Investigating Three Neighborhoods in Houston, 26 Planning, Practice & Research 21, 40 (2011). Another compared levels of land use and social segregation in Houston and Dallas and found no significant differences. This led the author to conclude that private deed covenants regulating land use (utilized in Houston) can achieve comparable results in terms of segregation as can zoning (utilized in Dallas). See Christopher Berry, Land Use Regulation and Residential Segregation: Does Zoning Matter?, 3 Am. L. & Econ. Rev. 251, 271 (2001). For an analysis of the role of private land use covenants in fostering racial and economic segregation, see Richard R.W. Brooks & Carol M. Rose, Saving the Neighborhood: Racially Restrictive Covenants, Law, and Social Norms 166-232 (2013).

2.   The Structure of Authority Underlying Zoning

a.   Enabling Legislation

Zoning is an exercise of the police power—essentially, the power of government to protect health, safety, welfare, and morals. Generally speaking, the police power is held to reside in the state, but in the case of zoning all states have adopted enabling acts that delegate zoning authority to local governments.

The Standard State Zoning Enabling Act, mentioned earlier at page 970, was adopted at one time or another in all 50 states and is still in effect (with modifications) in many of them. A few states—most notably California, New Jersey, and Pennsylvania—have in recent years enacted tailor-made statutes that depart significantly from the Standard Act; even these, however, reflect its continuing influence.

The Standard Act empowers municipalities to "regulate and restrict the height, number of stories, and size of buildings and other structures, the percentage of lot that may be occupied, the size of yards, courts, and other open spaces, the density of population, and the location and use of buildings, structures, and land for trade, industry, residence, or other purposes." It permits division of municipalities into districts (zones) of appropriate number, shape, and area, and provides that regulations may vary from district to district. The regulations must be "made in accordance with a comprehensive plan and designed to lessen congestion in the streets; to secure safety from fire, panic, and other dangers; to promote health and the general welfare; to provide adequate light and air; to prevent the overcrowding of land; to avoid undue concentration of population; to facilitate the adequate provision of transportation, water, sewerage, schools, parks, and other public requirements. Such regulations shall be made with reasonable consideration, among other things, to the character of the district and its peculiar suitability for particular uses, and with a view to conserving the value of buildings and encouraging the most appropriate use of land throughout [the] municipality."

Under the Standard Act, to enact a zoning ordinance a city must create a planning (or zoning) commission and a board of adjustment (sometimes called a board of zoning appeals). The commission and the board are composed of citizens appointed by the mayor. The commission, advised by planning experts, has the function of recommending a comprehensive plan and a zoning ordinance to the city council. The zoning ordinance must be enacted by the city council. Thus expert planners, citizen commissioners, and politicians are all involved in enacting a zoning ordinance.

If the ordinance needs amending later, the commission recommends the amendment to the city council, which must adopt the amendment for it to become legally effective.

The board of adjustment plays a different role. It was originally conceived as a device to ensure that broad zoning regulations do not operate inequitably on particular parcels of land. It may grant a variance when the zoning restrictions cause the owner practical difficulty or unnecessary hardship. It also may grant a special exception when specific requirements set forth in the zoning ordinance are met. More on this later.

b.   The Comprehensive Plan

The Standard Act says that zoning regulations shall be "in accordance with a comprehensive plan." A comprehensive plan is a statement of the local government's objectives and standards for development. Usually made up of maps, charts, and descriptive text, it shows—at least in a general way—the boundaries of height, area, bulk, and use zones, and the locations of streets, bridges, parks, public buildings, and the like. The plan is based on surveys and studies of the city's present situation and future needs, the idea being to anticipate change and promote harmonious development. To require some sort of master plan and regulations "in accordance" with it, as enabling legislation typically does, reflects the view that zoning itself is but a means of giving effect to a larger planning enterprise that has led to formulation of the comprehensive plan. See Charles M. Haar, "In Accordance with a Comprehensive Plan," 68 Harv. L. Rev. 1154, 1155 (1955).

But only about half of the states require comprehensive plans, and sometimes only in the weakest of terms. As to those with plan requirements, judicial attitudes vary greatly. Some hold, absent very specific language in the enabling legislation, that the plan need not be written down in a document separate from the zoning ordinance itself; some consider that the statement of purpose in the zoning ordinance's preamble is evidence of an underlying plan to which the ordinance conforms; some have found the scheme of regulations in the ordinance to be "the plan." Even when a written plan exists, zoning regulations inconsistent with it are not necessarily invalid, so long as they are considered reasonable and in the public interest. There is some evidence that this relaxed judicial attitude is changing, however. "The definite trend appears to be toward finding the plan as a sort of impermanent constitution, flexible in its interpretation, but more than a guide to growth that may be rejected in some circumstance." Edward J. Sullivan, The Role of the Comprehensive Plan, 31 Urb. Law. 915, 924 (1999); see also Edward J. Sullivan, Ramapo Plus Thirty: The Changing Role of the Plan in Land Use Regulation, 35 Urb. Law. 75 (2003); Edward J. Sullivan, Comprehensive Planning Law, 36 Urb. Law. 541 (2004); Edward J. Sullivan, Recent Developments in Comprehensive Planning Law, 42 Urb. Law. 665 (2010); American Law of Zoning §6:6 (Patricia Salkin ed. 5th ed. 2008). For an annotation of cases illustrating contemporary judicial attitudes toward comprehensive plans, see 83 Am. Jur. 2d Zoning & Planning 22 (2d ed. 2008). See, e.g., Urrutia v. Blaine County, 2 P.3d 738, 742-743 (Idaho 2000) ("a comprehensive plan does not operate as legally controlling zoning law, but rather serves to guide and advise the governmental agencies responsible for making zoning decisions"); Citizens for Mount Vernon v. City of Mount Vernon, 947 P.2d 1208, 1214-1215 (Wash. 1997) ("[C]omprehensive plans generally are not used to make specific land use decisions. Instead . . . a comprehensive plan is a 'guide' or 'blueprint' to be used when making land use decisions. . . . [C]onflicts surrounding the appropriate use are resolved in favor of the more specific regulations, usually zoning regulations.").

Why have judges been so easygoing about comprehensive plan requirements? Part of the answer probably lies in judicial (and general public) skepticism about the planning enterprise, which once seemed to proceed on the assumption that an area could be mapped, once and for all, with few changes necessary thereafter. But eventually planning professionals came to recognize what judges had perhaps already figured out: the future is too unpredictable to allow for comprehensive long-term planning; a better approach is to focus on the short-term and mid-term and to be flexible.

Not only do planners have limited capacity to anticipate the future; local authorities have limited capacity to control (as opposed to react to) what it holds. For example, after World War II, the federal government greatly expanded a program of insuring mortgages on single family homes. With risks thus reduced, banks opened their coffers to home buyers, creating a huge demand for single family residences (which builders sometimes sold on a down payment of only $100!). The federal government reinforced the desirability of the single family house by making mortgage interest and real estate taxes deductible on the income tax. Large scale developers entered the housing market and also built huge shopping malls with acres of free parking, dooming downtown shops.[3] Federally financed urban renewal destroyed residential neighborhoods populated by racial minorities and working-class whites. Public housing was sited in segregated neighborhoods, creating ghettos. The federal interstate highway program, begun in the 1950s, made formerly unthinkable commutes seem reasonable; it opened rural areas to development and, together with the jet airplane, devastated the railroads. Federal defense spending favored suburban locations over urban ones. Prosperity turned one car per family into two and then into three, requiring more roads and more parking. National franchises of fast foods, motel beds, and discount goods demanded spaces along a highway strip, bedizened with neon. Protected by social security and pensions, retired workers moved to Florida, Arizona, and elsewhere in the sunbelt, which was made livable year-round by technological advances in air-conditioning. Minorities and the poor moved into, or were left in, the center cities, as uneasy whites moved to the suburbs, where they got increased space for the same housing dollar. Waves of immigration also reshaped metropolitan areas—central cities and suburbs alike. Most recently, low income families have joined the exodus to the suburbs.

In the face of this tidal wave of personal mobility and suburbanization, the appropriate allocation of land proved much more complicated and unforeseeable than could be writ in stone by a local planning commission in a comprehensive plan. By the late 1960s, zoning had become a much more reactive enterprise, responding piece by piece to changing conditions, unanticipated demands, and specific proposals.

---

3. Witold Rybczynski's book, City Life (1995), reports at 207 that from 1970 to 1990 a new shopping center opened every seven hours in the United States. Rybczynski, the Meyerson Professor of Urbanism at the University of Pennsylvania, attributes the success of enclosed shopping malls to the fact that they are strictly policed, regularly cleaned, and properly maintained.

I think that what attracts people to malls is that they are perceived as public spaces where rules of personal conduct are enforced. In other words, they are more like public streets used to be before police indifference and overzealous protectors of individual rights effectively ensured that *any* behavior, no matter how antisocial, is tolerated. This is what malls offer: a reasonable (in most eyes) level of public order; the right not to be subjected to outlandish conduct, not to be assaulted and intimidated by boorish adolescents, noisy drunks, and aggressive panhandlers. It does not seem much to ask. [Id. at 210.]

Enclosed shopping malls are popular abroad too. They flourish in the developing countries in Southeast Asia and even in Paris, where giant *hypermarchés* have opened on the *périphériques* around the city.

For a rich and illuminating essay about the powerful impact of government (at all levels) on the suburbanization of America, see Jerry Frug, The Geography of Community, 48 Stan. L. Rev. 1047 (1996). Frug argues that the move to suburbs separated people by income and race and thereby destroyed the heterogeneity of cities.

3. The Economics of Zoning

A voluminous literature considers the motivations for zoning and land use regulations and the impact of regulation on the price of land and housing. The usual justification for zoning is that it solves the problem of externalities in environments where bargaining (servitudes) or judicial determination (nuisance law) are not sufficient. See, e.g., Robert C. Ellickson et al., Land Use Controls 40-44 (4th ed. 2013); Keith R. Ihlanfeldt, Does Comprehensive Land-Use Planning Improve Cities?, 85 Land Econ. 74 (2013). But there are also other motivations for zoning, and hardly any of them are consistent with the externality rationale. See William A. Fischel, The Economics of Zoning Laws (1985). In addition to the class- and race-based motives hinted at by the district court judge in *Euclid*, and made more explicit in the *Mount Laurel* saga (considered beginning at page 1080), some communities seek to use zoning as a way to raise property values by creating scarcity, although the multiplicity of jurisdictions in any particular housing market can make it difficult for localities to be successful at such "monopoly zoning." See John M. Quigley & Larry A. Rosenthal, The Effects of Land Use Regulation on the Price of Housing: What Do We Know? What Can We Learn?, 8 Cityscape: A Journal of Policy Development and Research 69, 82-83 (2005).

Zoning is just one of many ways governments control the use of land. Others include regulations over the subdivision of properties, environmental review and mitigation requirements, and a variety of fees charged to developers (such as the exactions and impact fees to be considered in Chapter 12). Often these charges are justified on the same ground as zoning, namely that they internalize the externalities of development. See Michael H. Schill, Regulations and Housing Development: What We Know, 8 Cityscape: A Journal of Policy Development and Research 5 (2005).

Much of the empirical literature suggests that land use regulation increases the price of land and often the price of housing. See Jeffrey Zabel & Maurice Dallton, The Impact of Minimum Lot Size Regulations on House Prices in Eastern Massachusetts, 41 Regional Sci. & Urb. Econ. 571, 583 (2011); Edward Glaeser & Bryce A. Ward, The Causes and Consequences of Land Use Regulation: Evidence from Greater Boston, 65 J. Urb. Econ. 265 (2009); Vicki Been, Impact Fees and Housing Affordability, 8 Cityscape: A Journal of Policy Development and Research 139 (2005); John M. Quigley & Steven Raphael, Is Housing Unaffordable? Why Isn't It More Affordable?, 18 J. Econ. Perspectives 191 (2004). Higher land prices are consistent with both the externality justification for zoning and the monopoly zoning rationale. If zoning minimizes negative externalities or provides positive amenities, it will make property more desirable and therefore increase prices. Similarly, prices will also increase if zoning is used to create scarcity. (What are the implications of these ordinances for economic efficiency?)

It can be tricky to determine whether the price of any particular property will increase as a result of land use regulation. Take, for example, a parcel of property owned by landowner L. Absent regulation, its value would be equal to its highest and best use — say single family homes on quarter-acre lots. Suppose the municipality then enacts an ordinance requiring that homes be on one-acre lots. Will the result be higher prices (and lower profits) for developers who subsequently buy from L, higher prices for home buyers who purchase from developers, or reduced profits for L, or some mix? Or take the case of a builder who buys a piece of vacant land from a landowner, planning to subdivide it and build a dozen houses. Then the local government enacts an impact fee or requires the developer to provide expensive amenities such as roads or parks on its property in return for permission to build. Who bears the cost of these fees? Will they result in more or less housing being built? See Been, supra.

The short of it is that zoning and land use regulation do much to shape the pattern of life in our communities. In this chapter, we will examine a variety of impacts on the natural environment, see pages 1053-1061, on access to adult materials and entertainment, see pages 1041-1042, and on socioeconomic and racial integration, see pages 1080-1105. Recent empirical research also suggests linkages between zoning and the incidence of mortgage foreclosures, school quality, and crime (perhaps you can imagine what some of the cause and effect relationships might be). See, e.g., Arnab Chakraborty, Dustin Allred & Robert H. Boyer, Zoning Restrictiveness and Housing Foreclosures: Exploring a New Link to the Subprime Mortgage Crisis, 23 Housing Poly. Debate 431 (2013); Jonathan Rothwell, Housing Costs, Zoning, and Access to High-Scoring Schools (Brookings Institution Metropolitan Policy Program, April 2012); James M. Anderson et al., Reducing Crime by Shaping the Built Environment with Zoning: An Empirical Study of Los Angeles, 161 U. Pa. L. Rev. 699 (2013).

B.   The Nonconforming Use

PA Northwestern Distributors, Inc. v. Zoning Hearing Board

Supreme Court of Pennsylvania, 1991
584 A.2d 1372

LARSEN, J. This appeal presents an issue of first impression to this Court, i.e., whether a zoning ordinance which requires the amortization and discontinuance of a lawful preexisting nonconforming use is confiscatory and violative of the constitution as a taking of property without just compensation.

On May 4, 1985, after obtaining the necessary permits and certificates to conduct its business on leased premises, appellant, PA Northwestern Distributors, Inc., opened an adult book store in Moon Township, Pennsylvania. Four days later, the Moon Township Board of Supervisors published a public notice of its intention to amend the Moon Township Zoning Ordinance to regulate "adult commercial enterprises." On May 23, 1985, following a public hearing on the matter, the Moon Township Board of Supervisors adopted Ordinance No. 243, effective on May 28, 1985, which ordinance imposes extensive restrictions on the location and operation of "adult commercial enterprises." Section 805 of the ordinance provides as follows:

> *Amortization.* Any commercial enterprise which would constitute a pre-existing use and which would be in conflict with the requirements set forth in this amendment to the Moon Township Zoning Ordinance has 90 days from the date that the ordinance becomes effective to come into compliance with this ordinance. This 90-day grace period is designed to be a period of amortization for those pre-existing businesses which cannot meet the standards set forth in this amendment to the Moon Township Zoning Ordinance.

Appellant's adult book store, by definition, is an adult commercial enterprise under the ordinance, and it does not and cannot meet the place restrictions set forth in the ordinance in that it is not located within an area designated for adult commercial enterprises.[4] The Zoning Officer of Moon Township notified appellant that it was out of compliance with the ordinance. Appellant filed an appeal to the Zoning Hearing Board of the Township of Moon, appellee herein. The appeal was limited to challenging the validity of the amortization provision set forth in the ordinance.

Following a hearing, the Zoning Hearing Board upheld the validity of the amortization provision as applied, and appellant filed an appeal to the Court of Common Pleas of Allegheny County. No further evidence was taken, and appellant's appeal was dismissed. On appeal, Commonwealth Court affirmed, 124 Pa. Commw. 228, 555 A.2d 1368, basing its decision on Sullivan v. Zoning Board of Adjustment, 83 Pa. Commw. 228, 478 A.2d 912 (1984). We granted appellant's petition for allowance of appeal, and we now reverse. . . .

In the case of *Sullivan,* supra, the Commonwealth Court determined that provisions for the amortization of nonconforming uses are constitutional exercises of the police power so long as they are reasonable. It was the opinion of the Commonwealth Court in that case, that the "distinction between an ordinance restricting future uses and one requiring the termination of present uses within a reasonable period of time is merely one of degree. . . ." 83 Pa. Commw.

---

4. Section 803 of the ordinance requires that no adult commercial enterprise can operate within 500 feet of a pre-existing school, hospital, nursing home, group care facility, park, church, establishment selling alcoholic beverages, or another adult commercial enterprise. Section 804 requires that no adult commercial enterprise can operate within 1,000 feet of an area zoned residential. Appellant's adult book store is located closer to a school, a church and a residential district than permitted under these place restrictions.

at 244, 478 A.2d at 920. To determine whether the amortization provisions are reasonable, the Commonwealth Court stated:

> Each case in this class must be determined on its own facts; and the answer to the question of whether the provision is reasonable must be decided by observing its impact upon the property under consideration. The true issue is that of whether, considering the nature of the present use, the length of the period for amortization, the present characteristics of and the foreseeable future prospects for development of the vicinage and other relevant facts and circumstances, the beneficial effects upon the community that would result from the discontinuance of the use can be seen to more than offset the losses to the affected landowner. [83 Pa. Commw. at 247, 478 A.2d at 920.]

Following this standard, the Zoning Hearing Board herein heard evidence regarding the impact upon the property in question with respect to the nature of the present use, the period for amortization, the characteristics of the vicinage, etc., and determined that the amortization provision was reasonable as applied. In this regard the Zoning Hearing Board stated that the "real and substantial benefits to the Township of elimination of the nonconforming use from this location . . . more than offset the losses to the affected landowner." Opinion of the Board at 13 (May 20, 1987).

If the Commonwealth Court opinion in *Sullivan*, supra, had been a correct statement of the law in this Commonwealth, we would be constrained to find that appellee herein had not committed an error of law or an abuse of discretion. For the following reasons, however, we find that *Sullivan* is not a correct statement of the law regarding amortization provisions in this Commonwealth.

In this Commonwealth, all property is held in subordination to the right of its reasonable regulation by the government, which regulation is clearly necessary to preserve the health, safety, morals, or general welfare of the people. Moreover, "a presumption of validity attaches to a zoning ordinance which imposes the burden to prove its invalidity upon the one who challenges it." National Land and Investment Co. v. Easttown Township Board of Adjustment, 419 Pa. 504, 522, 215 A.2d 597, 607 (1965). This Court has noted, however, that the presumption of a zoning ordinance's validity must be tempered by the Court's appreciation of the fact that zoning involves governmental restrictions upon a property owner's *constitutionally guaranteed* right to use his or her property, unfettered by governmental restrictions, except where the use violates any law, the use creates a nuisance, or the owner violates any covenant, restriction or easement.[5]

Many other jurisdictions have upheld the validity of amortization provisions in zoning ordinances, finding that it is appropriate to balance the property interests of the individual with the health, safety, morals or general welfare of the

---

5. At the hearing before the Zoning Hearing Board herein, no evidence was presented to show that appellant's adult book store had violated any law, created a nuisance in the community, or violated any covenant, restriction or easement. In fact, evidence presented at the hearing tended to show that appellant was operating its adult book store well within the parameters of the law in that prosecutions against appellant's employees for violations of the obscenity law, 18 Pa. C.S.A. §5903, had resulted in acquittals. Hearing Transcript at 45-46 (Nov. 13, 1986).

community at large, and that, where reasonable, amortization provisions succeed in effectuating orderly land use planning and development in a way that the natural attrition of nonconforming uses cannot. See cases collected at Annotation, Validity of Provisions for Amortization of Nonconforming Uses, 22 A.L.R.3d (1968 & Supp. 1990).

Although this Court has never before considered the validity of an amortization provision in a zoning ordinance, it has long been the law of this Commonwealth that municipalities lack the power to compel a change in the nature of an existing lawful use of property. . . . In addition, municipalities may not prevent the owner of nonconforming property from making those necessary additions to an existing structure as are needed to provide for its natural expansion, so long as such additions would not be detrimental to the public welfare, safety, and health.

A lawful nonconforming use establishes in the property owner a vested property right which cannot be abrogated or destroyed, unless it is a nuisance, it is abandoned, or it is extinguished by eminent domain. . . .

The effect of the amortization provision herein is to deprive appellant of the lawful use of its property in that the ordinance forces appellant to cease using its property as an adult book store within 90 days. Appellee argues that appellant is free to relocate to one of the few sites in the Township of Moon that complies with the place restrictions of the ordinance, or to change its use to sell some other commodity, in an attempt to convince this Court that the ordinance has not effectuated a "taking" of appellant's property without just compensation. The Pennsylvania Constitution, Pa. Const. art. I, §1, however, protects the right of a property owner to use his or her property in any lawful way that he or she so chooses. If government desires to interfere with the owner's use, where the use is lawful and is not a nuisance nor is it abandoned, it must compensate the owner for the resulting loss. A gradual phasing out of nonconforming uses which occurs when an ordinance only restricts future uses differs in significant measure from an amortization provision which restricts future uses *and* extinguishes a lawful nonconforming use on a timetable which is not of the property owner's choosing.

The language of the Missouri Supreme Court in Hoffman v. Kinealy, 389 S.W.2d 745, 753 (Mo. 1965), is apropos to the issue of this case:

> [I]t would be a strange and novel doctrine indeed which would approve a municipality taking private property for public use without compensation if the property was not too valuable and the taking was not too soon, and prompts us to repeat the caveat of Mr. Justice Holmes in Pennsylvania Coal Co. v. Mahon, 260 U.S. 393, 416, 43 S. Ct. 158, 160, 67 L. Ed. 322, 326, 28 A.L.R. 1321, that "[we] are in danger of forgetting that a strong public desire to improve the public condition is not enough to warrant achieving the desire by a shorter cut than the constitutional way of paying for the change." . . .

Thus, we hold that the amortization and discontinuance of a lawful pre-existing nonconforming use is per se confiscatory and violative of the Pennsylvania Constitution, Pa. Const. art. I, §1. There are important policy considerations which support this determination. If municipalities were free to amortize nonconforming uses out of existence, future economic development could be seriously compromised. . . .

It is clear that if we were to permit the amortization of nonconforming uses in this Commonwealth, *any* use could be amortized out of existence without just compensation. Although such a zoning option seems reasonable when the use involves some activity that may be distasteful to some members of the public, *no* use would be exempt from the reach of amortization, and *any* property owner could lose the use of his or her property without compensation. Even a home-owner could find one day that his or her "castle" had become a nonconforming use and would be required to vacate the premises within some arbitrary period of time, *without just compensation.* Such a result is repugnant to a basic protection accorded in this Commonwealth to vested property interests.

Accordingly, we find that the amortization provision, Section 805, of Ordinance No. 243 of the Township of Moon is unconstitutional on its face, and we reverse the order of the Commonwealth Court, which affirmed the order of the Court of Common Pleas of Allegheny County dismissing appellant's appeal from the decision of the Zoning Hearing Board of the Township of Moon.

NIX, C.J., concurring. While I agree with the result reached by the majority, that Section 805 of Ordinance No. 243 is invalid in this case, I must disagree with the finding that any provision for the amortization of nonconforming uses would be per se confiscatory and unconstitutional. I would uphold the Commonwealth Court's decision relying on Sullivan v. Zoning Board of Adjustment, 83 Pa. Commw. 228, 478 A.2d 912 (1984), and hold that a reasonable amortization provision is valid if it reflects the consideration of certain factors. The instant provision, however, falls short of the reasonableness requirements and therefore must be struck down.

The weight of authority supports the conclusion that a reasonable amortization provision would not be unconstitutional. See generally 22 A.L.R.3d 1134 (1968). It has been stated that a blanket rule against amortization provisions should be rejected because such a rule has a debilitating effect on effective zoning, unnecessarily restricts a state's police power, and prevents the operation of a reasonable and flexible method of eliminating nonconforming uses in the public interest. Lachapelle v. Goffstown, 107 N.H. 485, 225 A.2d 624 (1967). The New Hampshire court found acceptable amortization provisions which were reasonable as to time and directed toward some reasonable aspect of land use regulation under properly delegated police power. Id. Other cases have considered several factors in determining the reasonableness of these provisions. Those factors weigh any circumstance bearing upon a balancing of public gain against private loss, including the length of the amortization period in relation to the nature of the nonconforming use; length of time in relation to the investment; and the degree of offensiveness of the nonconforming use in view of the character of the surrounding neighborhood. . . . *[reasonable factors]*

I believe that a per se prohibition against amortization provisions is too restrictive. A community should have a right to change its character without being locked into pre-existing definitions of what is offensive. As this Court has also noted, "nonconforming uses, inconsistent with a basic purpose of zoning, represent conditions which should be reduced to conformity as speedily as is compatible with the law and the Constitution." Hanna v. Board of Adjustment of Borough of Forest Hills, 408 Pa. 306, 312-13, 183 A.2d 539, 543 (1962). I believe that amortization provisions are an effective method of reconciling interests of the community with those of property owners. Where the provisions are reasonable in consideration of the elements herein discussed, they provide adequate notice to the property owner so that no deprivation of property or use thereof is suffered, yet they simultaneously afford a township the opportunity to alter the character of its neighborhoods when the alteration takes the form of a reasonable land use regulation.

In this case, however, the amortization provision is not a reasonable one because it fails to provide adequate time for elimination of the nonconforming use. The period allowed for the dissolution of appellant's business is ninety days. Certainly ninety days is an insufficient period of time to allow a merchant to close a business. Any contractual obligations appellant has incurred in anticipation of operating the business probably cannot be terminated within such a short period of time without severe hardship on appellant's part. Three months also would not permit appellant to obtain an alternative means of income. Moreover, forcing appellant to liquidate his enterprise within ninety days could prevent him from obtaining a reasonable return on his investment. I therefore agree that the instant provision is confiscatory.[6]

PROBLEMS, NOTES, AND QUESTIONS

1. Should nonconforming uses be protected? Consider this problem. *A* and *B* each have $50,000 to invest. *A* purchases a vacant lot for $50,000. Ten years later the city passes a zoning ordinance zoning *A*'s land for single family dwellings. The value of *A*'s land is reduced to $12,500 by this action. As we shall see in Chapter 12, it is likely that *A* has no grounds to sue the city for this loss of value.

B purchases a vacant lot next to *A*'s lot for $10,000 and builds and equips a store on the premises for $40,000, for a total investment of $50,000. The store earns *B* a 10 percent net profit each year after paying all business expenses including *B*'s salary. After 10 years the city passes a zoning ordinance zoning *B*'s land for single family dwellings. The value of *B*'s land, like *A*'s land, is reduced by three-fourths. If this ordinance requires *B* to discontinue his nonconforming use immediately, the courts almost surely would declare it unconstitutional as a taking of *B*'s property. Why should this be so? Is *B* harmed more than *A*? If the ordinance were retroactive, would you prefer to be in *A*'s shoes or *B*'s? See generally

---

6. Zoning measures designed to control the location of adult bookstores and the like can give rise to First Amendment concerns. We address these later. See pages 1041-1042. —Eds.

Christopher Serkin, Existing Uses and the Limits of Land Use Regulations, 84 N.Y.U. L. Rev. 1222 (2009).

2. *Changes.* The right to maintain a nonconforming use runs with land; hence it survives a change of *ownership.* (But see the discussion of Village of Valatie v. Smith in Note 3 below.) As to change of *use,* some jurisdictions provide that nonconforming uses may expand, especially to meet natural changes such as increased demand. Moreover, some allow one nonconforming use to be changed to another nonconforming use, but usually only if the change reduces (or at least does not increase) the impact of the use on the zone in question. Suppose the owner of a nonconforming apartment building redoes it in a way that leaves the general structure intact but results in a few more apartments inside. Is that sort of change permitted? See Rudolf Steiner Fellowship Foundation v. De Luccia, 685 N.E.2d 192 (N.Y. 1997) (suggesting that the answer would be no); In re Paxinosa Ave., 80 A.2d 789 (Pa. 1951) (suggesting the answer would be yes.)

Destruction of a nonconforming use (by act of God or otherwise) usually terminates it, and so too for *abandonment,* which requires intent to abandon the nonconforming use. Some ordinances go further and, to eliminate litigation over intent, prohibit the continuation of a nonconforming use if it is "discontinued" for a period of time, say two years. If operations cease for the given period, the nonconforming use may be held discontinued, even though the owner intends to resume the nonconforming use. Consider this problem: Because of family feuding, a fire, and declining business, Lundy's, a famous and popular Brooklyn seafood restaurant, closed its doors in 1979. The restaurant windows were boarded up and the equipment and furniture stayed locked inside the vacant restaurant. In 1995, 16 years later, Lundy's reopened under a new owner. If Lundy's restaurant had been a nonconforming use, would this closure constitute an abandonment of the nonconforming use? Does "mothballing" forfeit the protected status?

In Toys "R" Us v. Silva, 676 N.E.2d 862 (N.Y. 1996), the owner of a nonconforming warehouse in a residential district contracted to sell the premises to a real estate developer. The owner emptied the warehouse. The zoning ordinance provided that either abandonment with intent or discontinuance of the nonconforming use for two years forfeited the nonconforming status. The sale fell through. In an effort to preserve its nonconforming use status, the owner transferred a small amount of goods back into the warehouse after 19 months and assigned a property manager there. The court held, however, that the nonconforming use was lost because it was "substantially" discontinued for two years; complete discontinuance was not necessary for loss of the privilege. See also Ka-Hur Enterprises v. Zoning Board of Appeals of Provincetown, 676 N.E.2d 838 (Mass. 1997).

Compare Stokes v. Board of Permit Appeals, 61 Cal. Rptr. 2d 181 (Cal. App. 1997), holding that the owners of a gay bathhouse in San Francisco, which closed at the beginning of the AIDS epidemic and remained vacant for seven years, had intentionally abandoned the nonconforming use status when they filed an application to convert the bathhouse to a shelter for the homeless, although this offer was refused by the city. In addition, nonconforming use status was lost by discontinuance; see also Duffy v. Milder, 896 A.2d 27 (R.I. 2006) (request for zoning change manifested intention to abandon use).

3. *Amortization.* Would a longer period have mattered in the *PA Northwestern* case? Should it have? The court in the *Sullivan* case (quoted on page 988) reasoned that "the distinction between an ordinance restricting future uses and one requiring the termination of present uses within a reasonable period of time is merely one of degree." Is this correct? Does protection of the landowner's investment-backed expectations in continuing the existing use raise claims of fairness not present where new uses are prohibited? The same general issue is involved in whether persons should be "grandfathered" from legislation and whether overruling of cases by courts should be retroactive or only prospective.

Courts in the two dozen or so jurisdictions approving the amortization technique claim to require a reasonable period for the particular nonconforming use in question. In practice, however, there appears to be considerable deference to rough-and-ready lines. For any given use, one can find cases upholding, and other cases invalidating, periods ranging from 1 to 30 or more years. See, e.g., American Law of Zoning §12:74 (Patricia E. Salkin ed. 5th ed. 2008). This kind of (apparent) sloppiness threatens to make amortization especially vulnerable to challenge. See Craig A. Peterson & Claire McCarthy, Amortization of Legal Land Use Nonconformities as Regulatory Takings: An Uncertain Future, 35 Wash. U. J. Urb. & Contemp. L. 37 (1989); Osborne M. Reynolds, Jr., The Reasonableness of Amortization Periods for Nonconforming Uses—Balancing the Private Interest and the Public Welfare, 34 Wash. U. J. Urb. & Contemp. L. 99 (1988); see also Joseph Michaels, Amortization and the Constitutional Methodology for Terminating Nonconforming Uses, 41 Urb. Law. 807 (2009); Julie R. Shank, A Taking Without Just Compensation? The Constitutionality of Amortization Provisions for Nonconforming Uses, 109 W. Va. L. Rev. 225 (2006).

Factors usually listed as relevant to an assessment of the reasonableness of a particular amortization period are the nature of the use in question, the amount invested in it, the number of improvements, the public detriment caused by the use, the character of the surrounding neighborhood, and the amount of time needed to "amortize" the investment. Would you add to the list? May an amortization period be based on the depreciation regulations of the Internal Revenue Service, and a nonconforming use forced out when it is fully amortized for tax purposes? See National Advertising Co. v. County of Monterey, 464 P.2d 33 (Cal.), cert. denied, 398 U.S. 946 (1970) (yes). Must the amortization period permit the owner of improvements sufficient time to depreciate his property entirely? See Art Neon Co. v. City and County of Denver, 488 F.2d 118 (10th Cir. 1973), cert. denied, 417 U.S. 932 (1974) (use may be terminated prior to full depreciation); Modjeska Sign Studios, Inc. v. Berle, 373 N.E.2d 255 (N.Y. 1977) (same); Outdoor Graphics, Inc. v. City of Burlington, Iowa, 103 F.3d 690, 695 n.7 (8th Cir. 1996) ("reasonable time"); Suffolk Asphalt Supply Inc. v. Board of Trustees of Village of Westhampton Beach, 872 N.Y.S.2d 516 (App. Div. 2009) (five years).

Refer back to Note 2 on page 993. In Village of Valatie v. Smith, 632 N.E.2d 1264 (N.Y. 1994), the court noted that, in the absence of amortization legislation, the right to continue a nonconforming use runs with the land; with amortization, however, the right ends at the termination of the applicable period, whether or not the property has been sold. The twist was that the amortization provision at issue in the case was triggered *upon sale* of the property, thus wiping out the run-with-the-land feature. The court found this to be reasonable.

4. *Vested rights.* Related to the law of nonconforming uses is the more general doctrine of vested rights. In the case of nonconforming uses, a pre-existing operation is protected; plans to engage in some particular use are insufficient. In the case of vested rights doctrine, a proposed use might be protected if sufficient commitments have been made — plans drawn, permits obtained, the site prepared, construction begun — in reliance on existing zoning requirements that are subsequently changed in a way that invalidates the proposed use. Vested rights doctrine varies in practice from jurisdiction to jurisdiction (some of which have statutes or ordinances on the question), but the critical variables include how far the developer has gone in obtaining governmental approvals, how much money has been invested in good faith, and on what the money has been spent. See generally American Law of Zoning, supra, §§12:20-12:34.

Another theory, estoppel, is sometimes applied when developers rely reasonably and to their detriment on the issuance of a permit and proceed to make substantial expenditures. But the developer cannot rely on a permit unless he proceeds in good faith, making all the inquiries as to the permit's validity as are expected of a reasonable person. Parkview Assocs. v. City of New York, 519 N.E.2d 1372 (N.Y. 1988), is illustrative. In this case the Department of Building erroneously interpreted a zoning map and issued a permit to Parkview Associates for a 31-story apartment building at 108 E. 96th St. Some eight months later, alerted by watchful neighbors who saw the building rise far above the 19 stories permitted in the district, the Department revoked the building permit. The New York Court of Appeals rejected Parkview's claim "that its reliance on the permit caused substantial and irreparable harm requiring that the City be estopped from revoking the permit."

> Insofar as estoppel is not available to preclude a municipality from enforcing the provisions of its zoning laws and the mistaken or erroneous issuance of a permit does not estop a municipality from correcting errors, even where there are harsh results, the City should not be estopped here from revoking that portion of the building permit which violated the long-standing zoning limits. . . . Even if there was municipal error in one map and in the mistaken administrative issuance of the original permit, those factors would be completely outweighed in this case by the doctrine that reasonable diligence would have readily uncovered for a good-faith inquirer the existence of the unequivocal limitations . . . in the original metes and bounds description of the enabling legislation, and that this boundary has never been changed by the Board of Estimate. The policy reasons which foreclose estoppel against a governmental entity in all but the rarest cases thus have irrefutable cogency in this case. [519 N.E.2d at 1375.]

Parkview was required to remove the top 12 stories of its building. Two Congressmen from New York proposed using these stories for low income housing, but the City was not interested. It cost Parkview $1 million to remove the top 12 stories. See Alan S. Oser, As Building Slows, So Does Demolition, N.Y. Times, Apr. 18, 1993, §10, at 1.

Suppose that Parkview could not have readily discovered that the building permit had been issued in error. Would it have to remove the 12 top stories or would the neighbors have to live with the too-tall building? The cases go both ways, but neither way seems very satisfactory. An alternative approach would allow the City to enforce the regulations but require it to compensate Parkview $1 million to cover its loss. Such an approach has been rejected by most courts on the ground it would expose local authorities to virtually unlimited liability. Compare Taylor v. Stevens County, 759 P.2d 447 (Wash. 1988), with Village of Camden v. National Fire Ins. Co., 589 N.Y.S.2d 293 (Sup. Ct. 1992), aff'd, 603 N.Y.S.2d 781 (App. Div. 1993).

On whether estoppel differs in any significant way from vested rights doctrine, see Richard B. Cunningham & David H. Kremer, Vested Rights, Estoppel, and the Land Development Process, 29 Hastings L.J. 625 (1978).

In the *Parkview* case, the developer applied for a variance after the building permit was revoked (see the next section on variances). The variance was denied. The property owner's reliance on an erroneously issued building permit does not constitute a hardship entitling the owner to a variance. See Bloom v. Zoning Board of Appeals, 658 A.2d 559 (Conn. 1995).

C. Achieving Flexibility in Zoning

By segregating various classes of uses in tightly drawn districts, Euclidean zoning can work inequitable hardships and promote inefficient patterns of land use. We saw, for instance, how certain zoning restrictions can slow new construction, reduce the supply of new homes, and thereby increase the cost of housing, as discussed at pages 986-987. Zoning laws can also inhibit socially and aesthetically desirable diversity. See Jane Jacobs, The Death and Life of Great American Cities 152-177, 222-269 passim (1961). On a number of grounds, then, there is a need to provide flexibility in zoning. The approach to nonconforming uses, considered in the last section, could be regarded as one way of doing so; this section surveys a number of others. They range from modest techniques to modify traditional zoning regulations, to distinctly non-Euclidean approaches, to public control of land use.

As you study the materials that follow, note the differing requirements of each of the flexibility devices and the differing methods (and decision makers) they employ. Keep especially in mind that the power to regulate "flexibly" can be the power to favor, or disfavor, for illegitimate reasons.

1. Variances and Special Exceptions

Recall that the Standard State Zoning Enabling Act authorizes appointment of a board of adjustment. The board may, "in appropriate cases and subject to appropriate conditions and safeguards, make special exceptions to the terms of the ordinance in harmony with its general purpose and intent . . . ," and may authorize "in specific cases such variance from the terms of the ordinance as will not be contrary to the public interest, where, owing to special conditions, a literal enforcement of the provisions of the ordinance will result in unnecessary hardship, and so that the spirit of the ordinance shall be observed and substantial justice done." The act thus authorizes two rather different means of promoting flexibility: the variance and the special exception (or, as the latter is commonly called, special-use permit or conditional-use permit).

a.   Variances

Commons v. Westwood Zoning Board of Adjustment, 410 A.2d 1138 (N.J. 1980). As is typical, New Jersey's enabling statute delegates to boards of adjustment the power to grant a variance, provided two conditions are met. First, the variance must be necessary to avoid imposing *undue hardship* on the owner of the land in question. (Undue hardship "involves the underlying notion that no effective use can be made of the property in the event the variance is denied.") To show hardship, the owner must first have made reasonable efforts to comply with the zoning ordinance—say by trying, in the case of an undersized lot, to sell it to, or buy additional land from, a neighbor, in either case at a fair price. And the owner's hardship must not have been self-inflicted, such as by earlier disposing of part of his land with the result that what was left fell short of area requirements. Second, "the grant of the variance must not substantially impinge upon the public good and the intent and purpose of the zoning plan and ordinance." This requires paying attention to "the manner in and extent to which the variance will impact upon the character of the area."

Weingarten wanted to build a one-family residence on the only undeveloped lot in a residential neighborhood. Because his lot did not meet the existing zoning ordinance's minimum lot size requirements (it had a frontage of 30 feet and a total area of 5,190 square feet, whereas the zoning ordinance required a frontage of 75 feet and total area of 7,500 square feet), Weingarten sought a variance, proposing to build a narrow but deep four-bedroom home. Neighbors opposed this plan, and the board of adjustment denied the variance, finding "that the applicant failed to demonstrate any evidence to establish hardship" and "that the granting of the variance would substantially impair the intent and purpose of the Zone Plan and Zoning Ordinance of the Borough of Westwood."

On appeal by Weingarten, the court held that the record did not support the board of adjustment's conclusions. The board could not base its decision on the size of the house, because the planned construction did not violate any of the traditional zoning purposes of light, air, and open space reflected in the ordinance. And while minimum lot size requirements, "conserving the value of the surrounding properties," and "aesthetic considerations" were all appropriate "desiderata of zoning," the board did not rest its decision on evidence about such matters, but instead simply drew conclusions that were unsupported by the facts.

"Until the 1947 amendment to the zoning ordinance the plaintiffs or their predecessors in title could have constructed a one-family house on the lot. Ownership commenced in 1927 when the Borough of Westwood had no zoning ordinance. Furthermore an attempt, albeit unsuccessful, had been made to acquire an additional ten-foot strip from Mr. Butler, owner of the property bordering to the south. A 40-foot frontage would have at least brought the property into conformity with one home in the neighborhood and within close proximity of the size of the lots of two other houses. In addition there had been discussion concerning the possible sale of the property to a neighbor, there being a substantial divergence in the offering and asking prices. Lastly, one could reasonably conclude that, if a variance were not granted, the land would be zoned into inutility. In view of all the above, it cannot be said that there was not any evidence to establish hardship.

"Passing to the [questions of impact on the public good and on the general zoning plan], the board of adjustment made only the conclusive statement that the variance would substantially impair the intent and purpose of the zone plan and ordinance. The manner in which the variance would cause that effect is not explained. The board found that the lot was the only 30-foot parcel in the block, that the applicant builder had never constructed a house on a 30-foot lot, and that the proposed house would be 19 feet in width. How these facts relate to the zone plan is not made clear. The proposed use, side yards and setback meet the requirements of the ordinance. The proposed sales price of the home would be within the range of the value of the houses in the neighborhood. The total acreage of the land, exceeding 5,000 square feet, is comparable to 17 other properties in the neighborhood."

The court remanded for further proceedings, noting not only that the board should address the problems noted by the court, but also that the applicant—who had the burden of proof—should submit plans for the proposed house.

NOTES AND QUESTIONS

1. In granting a variance, zoning boards may impose reasonable conditions related to the use of the property that minimize the adverse impact of the use on neighbors. Such conditions may relate, for example, to fences, landscaping, outdoor lighting and noises, and enclosure of buildings. On the other hand, zoning boards may not condition a variance upon use of the property by the original applicants only, as this has no relation to ameliorating the effects of the proposed land use and is unrelated to the legitimate purposes of zoning. A variance thus must "run with the land." St. Onge v. Donovan, 522 N.E.2d 1019 (N.Y. 1988).

2. *Personal hardship.* Suppose that the owner wants to add a porch onto the back of his house for use by an invalid child. The home itself already violates side-yard requirements, and the porch would simply extend the line of the existing violation. High shrubbery protects the privacy of neighboring lots and there is

no evidence that the porch will affect their value. Adding the porch elsewhere is not feasible. Should a variance be granted on grounds of practical difficulties or unnecessary hardship? See Aronson v. Board of Appeals of Stoneham, 211 N.E.2d 228 (Mass. 1965) (no: existing violations cannot be made a basis for further violations, and "hardship" does not include personal infirmity). Cf. Crossley v. Town of Pelham, 578 A.2d 319 (N.H. 1990) (opinion by Souter, J., recently retired from the U.S. Supreme Court, holding irrelevant hardships that are the product of personal circumstances). That personal hardships are irrelevant seems to be the prevailing view, but in a couple of rare instances courts have upheld grants of area variances for increased access by persons with disabilities. See Mastandrea v. North, 760 A.2d 677 (Md. 2000) (upholding a variance for a brick and concrete pathway within a waterfront "critical area" so a wheelchair-bound woman could access a creek); Welch v. Law, 504 N.Y.S.2d 790 (App. Div. 1986) (upholding a variance for a 10-inch setback in order to accommodate a catwalk that would allow an ailing elderly woman to more easily access her home).

3. *Self-imposed hardship.* Suppose that property is purchased by someone who knows or should know that the land cannot be developed in accordance with zoning restrictions unless a variance is granted. Does this foreclose the buyer from being granted a variance, on the ground that the hardship is self-imposed? Although courts go off in various directions on the question, the most sensible view is this: If the seller could have qualified for a variance, then the buyer should stand in the same position, there being no point in making one rather than the other seek the relief. Decisions to this effect include H.A. Steen Indus. v. Zoning Hearing Bd. of Bensalem Township, 410 A.2d 386 (Pa. Commw. Ct. 1980), and Conley v. Town of Brookhaven Zoning Bd. of Appeals, 353 N.E.2d 594 (N.Y. 1976). Contrast the situation where the buyer purchases a lot that was undersized precisely because the original developer of the neighborhood had laid out that parcel to be used as a common area and not for development. Here the hardship is self-imposed. See Swift v. Zoning Bd. of East Hempfield, 382 A.2d 150 (Pa. Commw. Ct. 1978).

Other examples of self-imposed hardship are straightforward. See, e.g., Korean Buddhist Dae Won Sa Temple of Hawaii v. Sullivan, 953 P.2d 1315 (Haw. 1998) (affirming denial of a variance to a Buddhist temple that had bought property and begun construction of a roof that exceeded zoning height restrictions prior to seeking a variance, although the buyer knew a variance was required); Dudlik v. Upper Moreland Township Zoning Hearing Bd., 840 A.2d 1048 (Pa. Commw. Ct. 2004) (affirming denial of a variance for a lot that did not meet minimum lot size requirements for single family dwellings because the applicant had sold adjacent lots that would have been compliant).

4. *Area versus use.* The *Commons* case involved a so-called area (or dimensional) variance, having to do with setback requirements and the like, as opposed to a use variance relaxing restrictions on permissible uses in a particular area (e.g., allowing a commercial use in a residential zone). The burden of proof is said to be greater for a use variance than for an area variance. See, e.g., Hertzberg v. Zoning Bd. of Adjustment of Pittsburgh, 721 A.2d 43 (Pa. 1998).

Why might this be? Does an area variance necessarily have less impact on the neighborhood than a use variance? And as between area and use, is it always clear which is which? In *Hertzberg*, for example, the appellant was seeking an area variance for a "lodging house" of about 3,400 square feet to be operated in a commercial zone permitting lodging houses, but only if they were at least 5,000 square feet. The zone did not permit group care and institutional facilities. The lodging house was to be used "to provide up to twenty resident women suffering from emotional disabilities with basic needs, counseling and life skills training in an environment which is continuously supervised and includes twenty-four hour crisis intervention services." The court treated the case as one involving an area or dimensional variance. A dissenting justice saw it as a "disguised use variance." 721 A.2d at 53.

A twist on the method of *Hertzberg*—which eased the burden of proof as to the standard of unnecessary hardship in instances involving area variances—is to change the standard itself, whether by legislation or judicial interpretation. New York, for instance, amended its statute governing area variances in 1992, and in 1995 the New York Court of Appeals affirmed that the statute did not require an applicant for an area variance to prove "practical difficulties." Instead, the zoning board must engage in balancing test, weighing the benefit to the applicant against the detriment to the health, safety, and welfare of the neighborhood or community if the variance is granted. Sasso v. Osgood, 657 N.E.2d 254 (N.Y. 1995). Applicants for use variances, on the other hand, must show that the land can't earn a reasonable return without the requested variance; that the alleged hardship is unique and doesn't apply to a substantial portion of the neighborhood; that the requested variance won't alter the essential characteristics of the neighborhood; and that the alleged hardship was not self-created. 657 N.E.2d at 254.

5. *Grant versus denial.* In one respect at least, the decision in *Commons* is uncommon: According to conventional wisdom, issuance of variances is reversed far more often than denial. This is not to say that variance administration is policed as closely as it should be. "The criteria for obtaining a variance are rigorous. If the courts really superintended their issuance, more than ninety percent of the variances granted would probably be found invalid. . . . Illegal issuance is a widespread phenomenon nationwide." Donald G. Hagman & Julian C. Juergensmeyer, Urban Planning and Land Development Control Law 173 (2d ed. 1986). One commentator suggests that the conventional wisdom is that the "variance is widely abused." David W. Owens, The Zoning Variance: Reappraisal and Recommendations for Reform of a Much-Maligned Tool, 29 Colum. J. Envtl. L. 279, 280 (2004). Why do you think this is so? See Jesse Dukeminier & Clyde L. Stapleton, The Zoning Board of Adjustment: A Case Study in Misrule, 50 Ky. L.J. 273 (1962); Ronald M. Shapiro, The Zoning Variance Power—Constructive in Theory, Destructive in Practice, 29 Md. L. Rev. 3 (1969) ("[T]he board of appeals variance procedure, conceived as the 'safety valve' of the zoning ordinance, has ruptured into a steady leak."). On zoning boards generally, see Jerry L. Anderson et al., A Study of American Zoning Board Composition and Public Attitudes Toward Zoning Issues, 40 Urb. Law. 689 (2008).

A study of three Denver metropolitan area municipalities (Denver, Englewood, and Wheat Ridge) found that variances were approved between 67 and 71 percent of the time. According to the study's author, denial of variances was generally consistent with pertinent law. On the other hand, "decision-makers—to a sizable degree—do *not* render decisions consistent with their jurisdiction's governing legal standard, at least when those decisions result in the granting of a variance." See Randall W. Sampson, Theory and Practice in the Granting of Dimensional Land Use Variances: Is the Legal Standard Conscientiously Applied, Consciously Ignored, or Something in Between?, 39 Urb. Law. 877, 903-905 (2007).

6. *Zoning bored.* See Lacy Street Hospitality Service v. City of Los Angeles, 22 Cal. Rptr. 3d 805 (Cal. App. 2004) (unpublished). Appellant sought a variance, which was granted. Neighbors protested to the zoning board, which recommended to the Los Angeles City Council that it reverse the grant. Appellant appeared before the city council and managed to videotape the entire proceeding. The city council reversed the grant, and the appellant took the case to court. After losing before the trial court, appellant sought review by the Court of Appeal, which took a look at the videotape. The tape showed that most of the council members were not paying attention at the hearing, or if they were they were doing other things as well—talking with aides, eating, reviewing paperwork. One council member started a cell phone conversation just as appellant's presentation began; two other members started a conversation of their own; one member started working the room, talking to colleagues. When appellant finished, the opposition spoke but also got little if any attention.

The city argued that the hearing was fair because both sides were treated the same way, but, as a concurring opinion in the appellate court's decision noted, all the parties "had the right to be equally heard, not equally ignored." The court concluded that "the council cannot be said to have made a reasoned decision based upon hearing all the evidence and argument, which is the essence of sound decision making and to which [appellant] was entitled as a matter of due process." A rehearing was ordered, and Lacy Street eventually received its variance.

b. Special Exceptions

Cope v. Inhabitants of the Town of Brunswick, 464 A.2d 223 (Me. 1983). Developers sought to build an apartment complex in a "suburban residential" use area of Brunswick, Maine. To do so, they needed to qualify for an exception. The zoning ordinance in Brunswick, Maine delegated to the local zoning board the authority to grant the exception if: (1) the other requirements of the ordinance were met, (2) the use "will not adversely affect the health, safety, or general welfare of the public," (3) the use "will not tend to defeat the purpose of this ordinance . . . or of the comprehensive plan for the development of the Town of Brunswick," and (4) the use "will not tend to devaluate or alter the essential characteristic of the surrounding property." The board denied the developers' application for an exception because the requested use did not meet the requirements of (2) and

(4): it would "endanger the safety of the public" and "drastically change the basic characteristic of the existing neighborhood from one of a small quiet not very heavily traveled area to one more dense and heavily traveled." The court said:

"The issue before us arises from the fact that local zoning boards, like municipalities, have no inherent authority to regulate the use of private property. Instead, the power of a town, and therefore that of the local zoning board of appeals, is conferred upon the town by the State. This power may not be delegated from the legislature to the municipality or from the municipality to a local administrative body without a sufficiently detailed statement of policy to [provide a guide to property owners and a limitation on arbitrary decisions by zoning authorities].

"The present case calls into question the constitutionality of two of the standards contained in section 1107 of the ordinance. Under the ordinance, the Board is directed to base its decision upon a determination of whether the proposed use would 'adversely affect the health, safety or general welfare of the public,' and whether the use would 'alter the essential characteristics of the surrounding property.' Upon the authority of prior decisions of this Court, we hold that the ordinance improperly delegates legislative authority to the Board and is therefore void. . . .

"The legislative body may specify conditions under which certain uses may exist and may delegate to the Board discretion in determining whether or not the conditions have been met. The legislative body cannot, however, delegate to the Board a discretion which is not limited by legislative standards. It cannot give the Board discretionary authority to approve or disapprove applications for permits as the Board thinks best serves the public interest without establishing standards to limit and guide the Board. . . .

"Defendants seek to avoid the implications of the foregoing decisions by relying upon the later decision of Barnard v. Zoning Board of Appeals of the Town of Yarmouth, 313 A.2d 741 (Me. 1974). The ordinance at issue in that case provided that the Board of Appeals had authority to grant variances, 'where necessary to avoid undue hardship, provided there is no substantial departure from the intent of the ordinances.' Although acknowledging that the standard was broadly stated, we concluded that it was nonetheless sufficient to guide the Board in granting or denying *variances*.

"Contrary to defendants' assertion, *Barnard* does not represent a departure from our earlier decisions. The standard provided by the ordinance in *Barnard* was sufficient because it related to the granting of a variance and described only the negative findings which were required to be made before the prohibited use could be allowed by variance. In determining absence of a 'substantial departure from the intent of the ordinances,' it would be the other provisions of the ordinance which would provide substantive guidance for the decision. Moreover, *Barnard* does not have application in judging the sufficiency of standards to permit use by exception as opposed to use by variance. A use by exception, such as the apartment complex proposed in this case, differs substantially from a use by variance [in that a variance permits an owner to use land in a manner otherwise prohibited by the zoning ordinance, whereas a special exception allows an owner to put property to a use that the ordinance expressly permits]. An exception is a conditional use under a zoning ordinance and results from a legislative determination that such use will not ordinarily be detrimental or injurious to the neighborhood within the zone. Whether the use will generally comply with the health, safety and welfare of the public and the essential character of the area is a legislative question. The delegation is improper if the Board is permitted to decide that same legislative question anew, without specific guidelines which permit the Board to determine what unique or distinctive characteristics of a particular apartment building will render it detrimental or injurious to the neighborhood.

"We therefore conclude that the relevant portions of subsections (2) and (4) of section 1107 of the Brunswick zoning ordinance upon which the Board relied in denying the permit to plaintiffs are facially unconstitutional. Those standards refer only to the same general considerations which the legislative body was required to address and resolve in enacting the ordinance. . . .

"Stated simply, by enacting the ordinance, the voters of Brunswick determined that an apartment building was generally suitable for location in a suburban residential zone. The ordinance did not provide the Board with any basis for determining that a particular location was unsuitable because of the existence of certain characteristics which rendered the general legislative determination inapplicable. Since the Board found that plaintiffs were in compliance with all requirements of the ordinance except for those which we now find to be invalid, a permit for the exception should issue."

NOTES AND QUESTIONS

1. *Variances and special exceptions compared.* See Daniel R. Mandelker, Delegation of Power and Function in Zoning Administration, 1963 Wash. U. L.Q. 60, 62-63 (emphasis added):

> Confusion about the role of exceptions and variances is endemic to zoning, reflecting the confusion over underlying purposes, and shows little sign of being resolved. The variance is an administratively-authorized departure from the terms of the zoning ordinance, granted in cases of unique and individual hardship, in which a strict application of the terms of the ordinance would be unconstitutional. The grant of a variance is meant to avoid an unfavorable holding on unconstitutionality.
>
> By way of contrast, an exception is a use *permitted by the ordinance* in a district in which it is not necessarily incompatible, but where it might cause harm if not watched. Exceptions are authorized under conditions which will insure their compatibility with surrounding uses. Typically, a use which is the subject of a special exception demands a large amount of land, may be public or semipublic in character and might often be noxious or offensive. Not all of these characteristics will apply to every excepted use, however. Hospitals in residential districts are one example, because of the extensive area they occupy, and because of the potential traffic and other problems which may affect a residential neighborhood. A filling station in a light commercial district is another example because of its potentially noxious effects.

2. The theory of special exceptions is clear enough; practice under the theory varies. One approach, illustrated by the *Cope* case, reflects an effort by zoners

to use special exceptions as an essentially discretionary device: Listed uses will be granted an exception only if very general criteria—no adverse effects on health, welfare, and safety, for example—are found to be met. The approach gives zoners considerable leverage over applicants and also, obviously, invites abuse. Hence the reaction of the court in *Cope*, shared by a number of jurisdictions. See, e.g., Kosalka v. Town of Georgetown, 752 A.2d 183 (Me. 2000) (vacating municipality's denial of a conditional use permit to construct a campground on grounds that the local regulation—which required all use permit developments to "conserve natural beauty"—was an unconstitutional delegation of legislative authority). But some states do tolerate the sorts of standards at issue in *Cope*. See, e.g., Coronet Homes, Inc. v. McKenzie, 439 P.2d 219 (Nev. 1968).

An alternative approach to special exceptions reduces discretion by listing detailed criteria regarding such things as design, location, hours of operation, standards of performance, and the like in the ordinance; if the proposed use meets the criteria, an exception must be granted. See, e.g., Laughter v. Bd. of County Commrs. for Sweetwater County, 110 P.3d 875 (Wyo. 2005), which upheld the constitutionality of a zoning ordinance with the following standard: "[T]o insure that the Conditionally Permitted Use does not unreasonably impose adverse impacts on the health, safety, and general welfare of the County or on adjacent or nearby properties or residents, the County may impose certain special conditions including but not limited to the following: duration of use . . . hours of operation . . . parking requirements. . . ." Since the detailed-criteria approach to special exceptions helps control abuse, why not use it as the chief means of providing more flexibility in Euclidean zoning, and extend it even to cases typically handled through variances?

2. Zoning Amendments and the Spot Zoning Problem

State v. City of Rochester, 268 N.W.2d 885 (Minn. 1978). The case involves zoning amendments, another way to provide flexibility. A single tract of land in Rochester, Minnesota bordered single family homes, multiple-family dwellings, and a vacant lot zoned for "institutional" use and owned by the Mayo Clinic. High-rise condominiums and the Mayo Clinic Complex were one block away and visible from the tract, and the central business district was three blocks away. The tract was zoned for low density residential use (multiple-family dwellings), but the owner wanted to build a 49-unit "luxury condominium," so he applied to have the property rezoned for high density residential use. The Rochester city council approved his application and passed an ordinance rezoning the property. It provided no written reasons or findings supporting the rezoning, but minutes from council meetings showed "that the council members believed the proposed condominium was needed to serve the city's expanded housing requirements. Council members stated that the Gooding property would be an ideal site since it was located within three blocks of the central business district and since high density residential uses already across two streets from the property would be compatible with the proposed condominium and made development of the subject property for any other use unlikely."

Owners of the neighboring homes appealed the city council decision. They sought closer judicial scrutiny of the rezoning by arguing that it was an administrative or quasi-judicial act. The court rejected the opportunity to apply a higher level of review, saying:

"[W]e have consistently held that when a municipality adopts or amends a zoning ordinance, it acts in a legislative capacity under its delegated police powers. As a legislative act, a zoning or rezoning classification must be upheld unless opponents prove that the classification is unsupported by any rational basis related to promoting the public health, safety, morals, or general welfare, or that the classification amounts to a taking without compensation. . . . Our narrow scope of review reflects a policy decision that a legislative body can best determine which zoning classifications best serve the public welfare."

This left the plaintiffs with the job of convincing the court that the rezoning had no reasonable relation to promoting public health, safety, morals, or general welfare—a very tough sell. Given the proximity of the tract of land to commonly used services (city bus lines, public community centers, a child care center, a city library, the central business district and major shopping area) and the fact that the tract was surrounded by medium and high density residential uses, the court concluded that "[t]here was a rational basis for concluding that a six-story condominium would be compatible with existing uses in the neighborhood of the subject property." Plaintiffs' arguments that the new condominium would disrupt the neighboring single family community's stability and character by increasing noise and traffic, and would make the homes lose some of their value, fell short. "All of these factors may make the reasonableness of the zoning change fairly debatable, but under our standard of review, that is not enough to justify the court's interfering with the council's legislative judgment in passing the ordinance."

NOTES AND QUESTIONS

1. *Spot zoning.* The plaintiffs in *City of Rochester* claimed that the zoning amendment was invalid "spot zoning," defined by the court as "zoning changes, typically limited to small plots of land, which establish a use classification inconsistent with surrounding uses and create an island of nonconforming use within a larger zoned district, and which dramatically reduce the value for uses specified in the zoning ordinance of either the rezoned plot or abutting property." 268 N.W.2d at 891. Here's another way to think about spot zoning:

> To the popular mind, spot zoning means the improper permission to use an "island" of land for a more intensive use than permitted on adjacent properties. The popular definition needs several qualifications. Some courts use the term spot zoning to describe a certain set of facts so that the term is neutral with respect to validity or invalidity. Other courts use the term spot zoning to describe a set of facts where the zoning as applied is invalid. . . .

Spot zoning is invalid where some or all of the following factors are present:

1. a small parcel or land is singled out for special and privileged treatment;
2. the singling out is not in the public interest but only for the benefit of the landowner;
3. the action is not in accord with a comprehensive plan.

The list is not meant to suggest that the three tests are mutually exclusive. If spot zoning is invalid, usually all three elements are present, or said another way, the three statements may be merely nuances of one another. [Donald G. Hagman & Julian C. Juergensmeyer, Urban Planning and Land Development Control Law 136-137 (2d ed. 1986).]

Spot zoning usually arises from legislative zoning amendments, although administrative variances and special exceptions are sometimes invalidated by reference to the same concept. See American Law of Zoning §§6:12, 13:3, 14:4 (Patricia E. Salkin ed. 5th ed. 2008). And although spot zoning usually involves preferential treatment of certain landowners, the phrase may be used in connection with restrictions that single out particular parcels to the *detriment* of their owners—a kind of "reverse" spot zoning. See, e.g., In re Realen Valley Forge Greenes Associates, 838 A.2d 718 (Pa. 2003) (agricultural zoning of an island of land "in the heart of one of the most highly developed areas in the region . . . constitute[d] unlawful reverse spot zoning beyond the municipality's proper powers").

The cast of characters in the *City of Rochester* case is fairly typical of spot zoning cases. On one side are the homeowners who want to keep anything but single family residences out of their neighborhood; their aim is to protect their property values, and never mind that the larger public interest might suggest a need for higher density housing projects, a day care center, a retail shopping center, or whatever. On the other side are real estate developers who hope to buy land, build a project, and make some money. The concern with spot zoning is that the very "spot" resulting from a zoning amendment suggests that one or another of groups like these might have brought undue pressure to bear on the political process, whether by way of bribes or more subtle influences—this against a background belief that local land use control processes are corrupt to the core. See, e.g., Robert C. Ellickson et al., Land Use Controls 335-336 (4th ed. 2013).

2. *Judicial review.* So how should the courts respond? Technically speaking, they should respond just like the court in *City of Rochester*, or like the United States Supreme Court in Euclid v. Ambler, discussed earlier. The legislative body's judgment stands absent a showing that it simply has no rational basis; if reasonable minds can differ, the courts defer. On this standard (or nonstandard), virtually no zoning amendment could ever be successfully challenged.

In response to concerns that rezonings are granted too frequently and for the wrong reasons . . . courts and state legislatures gradually have developed doctrines to strengthen judicial review of rezonings. Those doctrines fall into four categories. First, under the change-or-mistake doctrine, a handful of courts adopt a presumption in favor of the zoning status quo, requiring local governments to justify any departure as a response to a change in conditions or a mistake in the original zoning designation. Second, under doctrines limiting contract or conditional zoning, courts limit local governments' power to commit themselves to future zoning changes benefiting specific landowners unless those commitments are authorized by a state statutory procedure that insures a minimum level of participation and uniformity across land use bargains. Third, some jurisdictions require that rezonings be consistent with a written comprehensive plan, thereby recruiting planning expertise to limit political bargaining. Finally, some jurisdictions enlist substantive and procedural norms of administrative law to police land use deals by classifying small-scale rezonings as quasijudicial decisions subject to the same sort of administrative review as decisions by local administrative agencies. . . . [Ellickson et al., supra, at 331-332.]

In this light, the majority opinion in *City of Rochester* was deferential to a fault. The "size of the tract of land involved" was of no interest to the court, and departures from the comprehensive plan concerned it little more. Indeed, the court seemed to deny that spot zoning was even an issue, primarily because adjacent land was already zoned for high density residential use. Should that have mattered?

3. *Legislative or quasi-judicial?* The excerpt from Ellickson et al. mentions a category of cases that approach review of suspicious zoning amendments by treating them as quasi-judicial rather than legislative and subjecting them to decidedly undeferential review. The leading case is Fasano v. Board of County Commissioners, favored by the dissenting judge but rejected by the majority in *City of Rochester.* The court in *Fasano* abandoned its earlier approach to zoning amendments (which required the zoners to show a mistake in the original comprehensive plan, or a change in circumstances since — see again the excerpt from Ellickson et al.) in favor of one that focuses on the particulars of the rezoning in question. The more the rezoning seems to reflect an adjudicative decision about the use of a specific piece of property, as opposed to a general legislative policy decision affecting a large area, the more will be the burden on the zoners to show the need for the change and how it will be served by reclassifying the parcel in question.

Fasano was a bit of a rage for a while, until the academic literature began to pick it apart. See, e.g., Carol M. Rose, New Models for Local Land Use Decisions, 79 Nw. U. L. Rev. 1155, 1157-1164 (1984-1985). Professor Rose agrees that it is problematic to view small-scale land use decisions as legislative products likely to enjoy the protections of the political process. But viewing the decisions as adjudicative is also troublesome. There are the familiar problems of standards and the need for flexibility, and also a number of procedural difficulties. Local governmental authorities are always involved in the zoning process at some point, and they do — and should — make contact with their constituents in the community. They also take positions on land use issues when they campaign. But can they then, by prevailing standards of appropriate *judicial* conduct, subsequently make legitimate adjudicative decisions (and if they can't, who can)? And what about the nitty-gritty? If there are hearings, must witnesses be sworn? Subject to cross-examination? On these latter points, the courts of at least one state, Kentucky, have answered in the negative. See id. at 1164 n.47.

The Oregon Supreme Court subsequently retreated from the position it had adopted in *Fasano.* See Neuberger v. City of Portland, 603 P.2d 771 (Or. 1979), characterized as "overruling" *Fasano,* "at least in part," because of "extensive legislative and administrative activity in the land use area since *Fasano* was decided—seeming to imply that the time has come for Oregon courts to defer more to other branches of government in the area of land use law." Norvell v. Portland Metro. Area Local Govt. Boundary Commn., 604 P.2d 896, 899 (Or. App. 1979). That view has come to be pretty widely shared. Several of the state courts that at first subscribed to the *Fasano* doctrine later rejected it, and "such momentum as the doctrine had has petered out." William B. Stoebuck & Dale A. Whitman, The Law of Property 620 (3d ed. 2000).

4. *Plebiscites: another twist on legislative versus quasi-judicial.* A plebiscite is a direct vote by citizens on some public question, commonly taking one of two forms. In the case of a referendum, the local governing body approves an ordinance and then refers it to the electorate for a final decision. An initiative goes right from a qualifying petition, initiated by citizens, to the ballot. See American Law of Zoning §§11:1-11:17 (Patricia E. Salkin ed. 5th ed. 2008). Both methods are reserved for legislative functions; thus neither can be used for small-scale rezoning in states adopting the *Fasano* point of view that small-scale rezoning is quasi-judicial in nature. As to other states, the courts divide, some permitting and some prohibiting plebiscites for zoning or rezoning decisions. At least one state, in a novel approach to the matter, has held that small-scale rezoning is legislative and thus appropriate for a referendum or initiative, but quasi-judicial when the issue is the applicable standard of review. See Margolis v. District Court, 638 P.2d 297 (Colo. 1981).

What is the concern with small-scale rezoning by popular procedures? Ronald H. Rosenberg, Referendum Zoning: Legal Doctrine and Practice, 53 U. Cin. L. Rev. 381 (1984), reports on a study of one Ohio county. Typically, Rosenberg found, the issues at stake were poorly presented to the public, giving at best only a superficial understanding. Voter turnout was generally very low, and the procedures used meant that in some instances a small handful of neighbors had effective veto power. Hence small-scale rezonings can be "conspicuously undemocratic," and large rezonings are too complex to be decided on a yes-or-no basis. Moreover, in both cases the popular procedures tend to discourage full and open discussion in a public forum—such as before the legislative body—and to devalue expert input. See id. at 431-433. For similar sentiments, see Marcilynn A. Burke, The Emperor's New Clothes: Exposing the Failures of Regulating Land Use Through the Ballot Box, 84 Notre Dame L. Rev. 1453 (2009); David L. Callies, Nancy C. Neuffer & Carlito P. Caliboso, Ballot Box Zoning: Initiative, Referendum and the Law, 39 Wash. U. J. Urb. & Contemp. L. 53 (1991).

NOTE: OTHER MEANS FOR ACHIEVING
FLEXIBILITY IN ZONING

Contract and conditional rezoning. Zoning amendments are sometimes enacted subject to an understanding, explicit or otherwise, that the property owner seeking the change will abide by certain conditions. Conditional rezoning is typically used to describe a situation where the property owner agrees unilaterally to use the land in the specified manner, whereas contract rezoning refers to a bilateral agreement between the owner and the zoning authority, perhaps with the owner covenanting to restrict the use of the property in exchange for the authority's promise to rezone. But there is much confusion about the foregoing terminology and considerable disagreement about the validity of each of the methods described. Each method enhances flexibility by providing a means to control the consequences of rezoning, but both raise concerns about spot zoning and departures from the comprehensive plan. In addition to this, contract rezoning might be seen to involve unlawful delegations of legislative authority. Contract rezoning was once widely considered illegal, but many courts gradually came to accept conditional rezoning. For historical analysis of contract zoning, see Daniel P. Selmi, The Contract Transformation in Land Use Regulation, 63 Stan. L. Rev. 591 (2011). Some states now recognize the legitimacy of each, by statute or case law. But there is a difference between endorsing method on the one hand and particular applications on the other. The conditions imposed on the property owner must pass muster as reasonable, or having a rational basis, and be free of the taint of undue influence. If the conditions involve so-called exactions—requiring the property owner to provide (or pay a fee to provide) public improvements like streets, recreational facilities, and so forth—then special tests developed in several decisions by the United States Supreme Court come into play. We take these up in the next chapter (see pages 1238-1250).

In recent years, community groups have become increasingly active in demanding that developers of real estate make contributions to benefit the neighborhoods in which their developments are located. In return for these agreements the groups agree to support or at least not to oppose the developers when they seek public funding, zoning changes, or other discretionary approvals. The benefits sought by communities might include such things as money for child care, institutional support, job set-asides, and affordable housing. Although developers negotiate directly with community groups, sometimes local governments incorporate the community benefits agreement into the overall project development agreement so that the government might enforce its provisions. For examples of community benefit agreements, see Scott Cummings, Mobilization Lawyering: Community Economic Development in the Figueroa Corridor, in Cause Lawyers and Social Movements (A. Sarat et al. eds. 2006); Julian Gross, Community Benefits Agreements: Making Development Projects Accountable (2005).

Are community benefits agreements an example of reasonable bargaining with developers, or extortion, or something in between? For a discussion of some of the issues, legal and otherwise, see Patricia Salkin, Community Benefits Agreements: Opportunities and Traps for Developers, Municipalities, and Community Organizations, 59 American Planning Association, Planning and Environmental Law 3 (2007); Patricia Salkin & Amy Lavine, Understanding Community Benefits Agreements, Practical Real Estate Lawyer 19 (July 2009); Matthew Schuerman, Mr. Bollinger's Battle, New York Observer, Feb. 18, 2007.

Floating zones. The floating zone represents a relatively new method—post-dating the standard techniques of variances, special exceptions, and rezoning—by which to deal with the rigidities of typical Euclidean zoning. A floating zone achieves flexibility by, in essence, defining a zone but reserving the decision about its location for the future. Two steps are usually involved: First, the local government creates (but does not pin down) a use district by an ordinance that specifies standards and criteria to govern the uses permitted in the zone. Second, and later in time, the zone is brought to earth, attached to a particular area through a zoning amendment.

Floating zones are used regularly enough, although only a handful of states has approved them explicitly. A smaller handful has found the approach invalid, usually on grounds that the floating zone does not conform with a comprehensive plan, or amounts to spot zoning, or entails an improper delegation of legislative power.

Cluster zones and PUDs. Cluster zoning is a flexibility device whereby a developer is permitted to construct dwellings in a pattern not in literal compliance with the area restrictions of a zoning ordinance. Residences in a cluster zone are typically relieved from observing the usual frontage or setback regulations and side- or rear-yard requirements. Overall population density is generally no greater in a cluster zone than in other residential areas, however, because open spaces are preserved as an element of the cluster. A central idea of the concept is to provide some of the amenities of a rural environment in an otherwise urban setting.

PUDs are similar to cluster zones. While the terms are often used interchangeably, planned unit developments generally contemplate a mix of residential, commercial, and sometimes even industrial uses. Cluster zones, then, involve area variations; PUDs involve area and use variations.

Both cluster zones and PUDs can be accomplished in a number of ways: through special exceptions issued by a board of adjustment; through subdivision controls administered by a planning board; through floating zones created, ultimately, by the local legislative body. The floating zone is the most common approach, and cluster zones and PUDs have been challenged with all the arguments leveled at floating zones. Generally speaking, though, the courts have been tolerant, so long as adequate standards are specified in the ordinance in question.

D. Expanding the Aims (and Exercising the Muscle) of Zoning

The best laid schemes o' mice an' men
Gang aft a-gley,
An' lea'e us nought but grief an' pain
For promised joy!—

Robert Burns,
To a Mouse (1785)

Recall the early objectives of zoning, at least as stated by the Supreme Court in Euclid v. Ambler, the first case in this chapter. The central idea seemed to be little more than the control of nuisances, though in a comprehensive fashion. Thus the height, spacing, and location of buildings were controlled, justifiably, as means to provide light and air, to help avoid and control the dangers of fire, to prevent overcrowding, and to exclude offensive industries from areas where people lived. Ends and means alike appeared to be innocuous and relatively unintrusive.

But the picture painted by the Court in *Euclid* was somewhat misleading. Recall, for example, that the Euclid ordinance excluded apartment buildings from areas zoned for single family and two-family dwellings, a result the trial court characterized as economic segregation but that the Supreme Court managed to justify in the same terms as it did the more benign aspects of Euclidean zoning. The facts and holding in the case, then, could be read as a generous endorsement of social engineering in the name of public health, safety, and welfare.

It is beside the point whether zoning authorities actually read the case this way; the point is that they came to act as though they did. Over the years after *Euclid*, the aims of zoning gradually expanded, no doubt for a host of reasons—population growth, increased pressures on the public fisc, the rise of activist government generally, racial prejudice, an expanding environmental consciousness, and so on. Zoning authorities began taking initiatives that the Court in *Euclid* would never have imagined (and others that the Court could have foreseen but chose to ignore).

There are any number of ways to organize a study of the new initiatives and judicial reaction to them. We shall concentrate on the rise of aesthetics as a factor in zoning, on efforts to control household composition, and on efforts to control the nature and size of local populations.

1.   Aesthetic Regulation

State ex rel. Stoyanoff v. Berkeley

Supreme Court of Missouri, 1970
458 S.W.2d 305

PRITCHARD, COMMISSIONER. Upon summary judgment the trial court issued a peremptory writ of mandamus to compel appellant to issue a residential building permit to respondents. The trial court's judgment is that the below-mentioned ordinances are violative of Section 10, Article I of the Constitution of Missouri, 1945, V.A.M.S., in that restrictions placed by the ordinances on the use of property deprive the owners of their property without due process of law. Relators' petition pleads that they applied to appellant Building Commissioner for a building permit to allow them to construct a single family residence in the City of Ladue, and that plans and specifications were submitted for the proposed residence, which was unusual in design, "but complied with all existing building and zoning regulations and ordinances of the City of Ladue, Missouri."

It is further pleaded that relators were refused a building permit for the construction of their proposed residence upon the ground that the permit was not approved by the Architectural Board of the City of Ladue. Ordinance 131, as amended by Ordinance 281 of that city, purports to set up an Architectural Board to approve plans and specifications for buildings and structures erected within the city and in a preamble to

> conform to certain minimum architectural standards of appearance and conformity with surrounding structures, and that unsightly, grotesque and unsuitable structures, detrimental to the stability of value and the welfare of surrounding property, structures and residents, and to the general welfare and happiness of the community, be avoided, and that appropriate standards of beauty and conformity be fostered and encouraged.

It is asserted in the petition that the ordinances are invalid, illegal and void, "are unconstitutional in that they are vague and provide no standard nor uniform rule by which to guide the architectural board," that the city acted in excess of statutory powers (§89.020, RS Mo 1959, V.A.M.S.) in enacting the ordinances, which "attempt to allow respondent to impose aesthetic standards for buildings in the City of Ladue, and are in excess of the powers granted the City of Ladue by said statute."

Relators filed a motion for summary judgment and affidavits were filed in opposition thereto. Richard D. Shelton, Mayor of the City of Ladue, deposed that the facts in appellant's answer were true and correct, as here pertinent: that the City of Ladue constitutes one of the finer suburban residential areas of Metropolitan St. Louis, the homes therein are considerably more expensive than in cities of comparable size, being homes on lots from three fourths of an acre to three or more acres each; that a zoning ordinance was enacted by the city regulating the height, number of stories, size of buildings, percentage of lot occupancy, yard sizes, and the location and use of buildings and land for trade, industry, residence and other purposes; that the zoning regulations were made in accordance with a comprehensive plan "designed to promote the health and general welfare of the residents of the City of Ladue," which in furtherance of said objectives duly enacted said Ordinances numbered 131 and 281. Appellant also asserted in his answer that these ordinances were a reasonable exercise of the city's governmental, legislative and police powers, as determined by its legislative body, and as stated in the above-quoted preamble to the ordinances. It is then pleaded that relators' description of their proposed residence as "'unusual in design' is the understatement of the year. It is in fact a monstrosity of grotesque design, which would seriously impair the value of property in the neighborhood."

The affidavit of Harold C. Simon, a developer of residential subdivisions in St. Louis County, is that he is familiar with relators' lot upon which they seek to build a house, and with the surrounding houses in the neighborhood; that the houses therein existent are virtually all two-story houses of conventional architectural design, such as Colonial, French Provincial or English; and that the house which relators propose to construct is of ultramodern design which would clash with and not be in conformity with any other house in the entire neighborhood.

It is Mr. Simon's opinion that the design and appearance of relators' proposed residence would have a substantial adverse effect upon the market values of other residential property in the neighborhood, such average market value ranging from $60,000 to $85,000 each.

As a part of the affidavit of Russell H. Riley, consultant for the city planning and engineering firm of Harland Bartholomew & Associates, photographic exhibits of homes surrounding relators' lot were attached. . . . [The surrounding houses consisted of a conventional frame residence, several of a Colonial style, and one of a Tudor style.] In substance Mr. Riley went on to say that the City of Ladue is one of the finer residential suburbs in the St. Louis area. . . . The homes are considerably more expensive than average homes found in a city of comparable size. The ordinance which has been adopted by the City of Ladue is typical of those which have been adopted by a number of suburban cities in St. Louis County and in similar cities throughout the United States, the need therefor being based upon the protection of existing property values by preventing the construction of houses that are in complete conflict with the general type of houses in a given area. The intrusion into this neighborhood of relators' unusual, grotesque and nonconforming structure would have a substantial adverse effect on market values of other homes in the immediate area. According to Mr. Riley the standards of Ordinance 131, as amended by Ordinance 281, are usually and customarily applied in city planning work and are:

> (1) whether the proposed house meets the customary architectural requirements in appearance and design for a house of the particular type which is proposed (whether it be Colonial, Tudor English, French Provincial, or Modern), (2) whether the proposed house is in general conformity with the style and design of surrounding structures, and (3) whether the proposed house lends itself to the proper architectural development of the City; and that in applying said standards the Architectural Board and its Chairman are to determine whether the proposed house will have an adverse effect on the stability of values in the surrounding area.

Photographic exhibits of relators' proposed residence were also attached to Mr. Riley's affidavit. They show the residence to be of a pyramid shape, with a flat top, and with triangular shaped windows or doors at one or more corners. . . .

[R]elators' position is that "the creation by the City of Ladue of an architectural board for the purpose of promoting and maintaining 'general conformity with the style and design of surrounding structures' is totally unauthorized by our Enabling Statute." (§§89.020, 89.040, RS Mo 1959, V.A.M.S.) It is further contended by relators that Ordinances 131 and 281 are invalid and unconstitutional as being an unreasonable and arbitrary exercise of the police power (as based entirely on aesthetic values); and that the same are invalid as an unlawful delegation of legislative powers (to the Architectural Board).

Section 89.020 provides . . . [for regulation of lot size; height, size, spacing, and use of buildings; and population density—all for the purpose of promoting health, safety, and welfare.] Section 89.040 provides . . . [that regulations be made in accordance with a comprehensive plan and designed "to promote health *and the general welfare. . . . Such regulations shall be made with reasonable consideration,*

Houses in Ladue on the same street as the proposed Stoyanoff house

among other things, to the character of the district and its peculiar suitability for particular uses, and with a view to conserving the values of buildings and encouraging the most appropriate use of land throughout such municipality." (Italics added by the court.)]

Relators say that "Neither Sections 89.020 or 89.040 nor any other provision of Chapter 89 mentions or gives a city the authority to regulate architectural design and appearance. There exists no provision providing for an architectural board and no entity even remotely resembling such a board is mentioned under the enabling legislation." Relators conclude that the City of Ladue lacked any power to adopt Ordinance 131 as amended by Ordinance 281 "and its intrusion into this area is wholly unwarranted and without sanction in the law." As to this aspect of the appeal realtors rely upon the 1961 decision of State ex rel. Magidson v. Henze, Mo. App., 342 S.W.2d 261. That case had the identical question presented. An Architectural Control Commission was set up by an ordinance of the City of University City. In its report to the Building Commissioner, the Architectural Control Commission disapproved the Magidson application for permits to build four houses. It was commented that the proposed houses did not provide for the minimum number of square feet, and "In considering the existing character of this neighborhood, the Commission is of the opinion that houses of the character proposed in these plans are not in harmony with and will not contribute to nor protect the general welfare of this neighborhood" (loc. cit. 264). The court held that §89.020, RS Mo 1949, V.A.M.S., does not grant to the city the right to impose upon the landowner aesthetic standards for the buildings he chooses to erect.

As is clear from the affidavits and attached exhibits, the City of Ladue is an area composed principally of residences of the general types of Colonial, French Provincial and English Tudor. The city has a comprehensive plan of zoning to maintain the general character of buildings therein. The *Magidson* case, supra, did not consider the effect of §89.040, supra, and the italicized portion relating to the character of the district, its suitability for particular uses, and the conservation of the values of buildings therein. These considerations, sanctioned by statute, are directly related to the general welfare of the community. . . . In Marrs v. City of Oxford (D.C.D. Kan.) 24 F.2d 541, 548, it was said, "The stabilizing of property values, and giving some assurance to the public that, if property is purchased in a residential district, its value as such will be preserved, is probably the most cogent reason back of zoning ordinances." The preamble to Ordinance 131, quoted above in part, demonstrates that its purpose is to conform to the dictates of §89.040, with reference to preserving values of property by zoning procedure and restrictions on the use of property. This is an illustration of what was referred to in Deimeke v. State Highway Commission, Mo., 444 S.W.2d 480, 484, as a growing number of cases recognizing a change in the scope of the term "general welfare." In the *Deimeke* case on the same page it is said, "Property use which offends sensibilities and debases property values affects not only the adjoining property owners in that vicinity but the general public as well because when such property values are destroyed or seriously impaired, the tax base of the community is affected and the public suffers economically as a result."

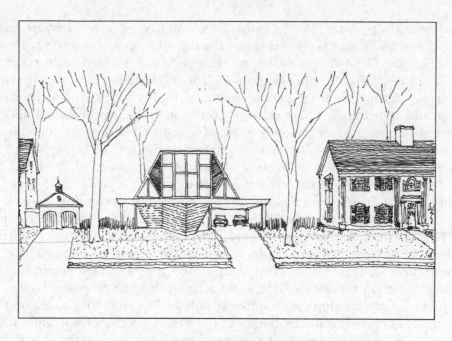

**A 2001 rendering by architect Stephen Harby showing what the
Stoyanoff house might have looked like**

arguments of both parties

Relators say further that Ordinances 131 and 281 are invalid and unconstitutional as being an unreasonable and arbitrary exercise of the police power. It is argued that a mere reading of these ordinances shows that they are based entirely on aesthetic factors in that the stated purpose of the Architectural Board is to maintain "conformity with surrounding structures" and to assure that structures "conform to certain minimum architectural standards of appearance." The argument ignores the further provisos in the ordinance: . . . and that unsightly, grotesque and unsuitable structures, *detrimental to the stability of value and the welfare of surrounding property, structures, and residents,* and *to the general welfare and happiness of the community,* be avoided, and that appropriate standards of beauty and conformity be fostered and encouraged. (Italics added.) Relators' proposed residence does not descend to the "patently offensive character of vehicle graveyards in close proximity to such highways" referred to in the *Deimeke* case, supra (444 S.W.2d 484). Nevertheless, the aesthetic factor to be taken into account by the Architectural Board is not to be considered alone. Along with that inherent factor is the effect that the proposed residence would have upon the property values in the area. In this time of burgeoning urban areas, congested with people and structures, it is certainly in keeping with the ultimate ideal of general welfare that the Architectural Board, in its function, preserve and protect existing areas in which structures of a general conformity of architecture have been erected. The area under consideration is clearly, from the record, a fashionable one. In State ex rel. Civello v. City of New Orleans, 154 La. 271, 97 So. 440, 444, the court said, "If by the term 'aesthetic considerations' is meant a regard merely for outward appearances, for good taste in the matter of the beauty of the neighborhood itself, we do not observe any substantial reason for saying that such a consideration is not a matter of general welfare. The beauty of a fashionable residence neighborhood in a city is for the comfort and happiness of the residents, and it sustains in a general way the value of property in the neighborhood." . . .

The denial by appellant of a building permit for relators' highly modernistic residence in this area where traditional Colonial, French Provincial and English Tudor styles of architecture are erected does not appear to be arbitrary and unreasonable when the basic purpose to be served is that of the general welfare of persons in the entire community.

In addition to the above-stated purpose in the preamble to Ordinance 131, it establishes an Architectural Board of three members, all of whom must be architects. Meetings of the Board are to be open to the public, and every application for a building permit, except those not affecting the outward appearance of a building, shall be submitted to the Board along with plans, elevations, detail drawings and specifications, before being approved by the Building Commissioner. The Chairman of the Board shall examine the application to determine if it conforms to proper architectural standards in appearance and design and will be in general conformity with the style and design of surrounding structures and conducive to the proper architectural development of the city. If he so finds, he approves and returns the application to the Building Commissioner. If he does not find conformity, or has doubt, a full meeting of the Board is called, with notice of the time and place thereof given to the applicant. The Board shall disapprove the application if it determines the proposed structure will constitute an unsightly, grotesque or unsuitable structure in appearance, detrimental to the welfare of surrounding property or residents. If it cannot make that decision, the application shall be returned to the Building Commissioner either with or without suggestions or recommendations, and if that is done without disapproval, the Building Commissioner may issue the permit. If the Board's disapproval is given and the applicant refuses to comply with recommendations, the Building Commissioner shall refuse the permit. Thereafter provisions are made for an appeal to the Council of the city for review of the decision of the Architectural Board. Ordinance 281 amends Ordinance 131 only with respect to the application initially being submitted to and considered by all members of the Architectural Board.

Relators claim that the above provisions of the ordinance amount to an unconstitutional delegation of power by the city to the Architectural Board. It is argued that the Board cannot be given the power to determine what is unsightly and grotesque and that the standards, "whether the proposed structure will conform to proper architectural standards in appearance and design, and will be in general conformity with the style and design of surrounding structures and conducive to the proper architectural development of the City . . ." and "the Board shall disapprove the application if it determines that the proposed structure will constitute an unsightly, grotesque or unsuitable structure in appearance, detrimental to the welfare of surrounding property or residents . . . ," are inadequate. . . . Ordinances 131 and 281 are sufficient in their general standards calling for a factual determination of the suitability of any proposed structure with reference to the character of the surrounding neighborhood and to the determination of any adverse effect on the general welfare and preservation of property values of the community. Like holdings were made involving Architectural Board ordinances in State ex rel. Saveland Park Holding Corp. v. Wieland, 269 Wis. 262, 69 N.W.2d 217, and Reid v. Architectural Board of Review of the City of Cleveland Heights, 119 Ohio App. 67, 192 N.E.2d 74.

The judgment is reversed.

NOTES

1. Courts, developing the law of nuisance, rarely declared an ugly site a nuisance. Obnoxious smells, deafening noises, yes, but unsightliness, no. There were no common standards to determine beauty; as the old saw puts it, beauty is in the eye of the beholder.

As we have seen, courts early viewed zoning under the police power as a form of nuisance control. Naturally, then, by an analogy to nuisance, they held that the police power can be exercised to further public health, safety, and general welfare, but not for purely aesthetic purposes. When billboards proliferated along highways in the first part of the twentieth century, and cities passed ordinances against them, courts first held these ordinances invalid, but, later, as public outrage against blaring billboards grew, courts held they could be regulated as menaces to public health and safety. After all, they might be blown down and fall on someone, they blocked sunlight and air, and the ground behind them might be used for dumping wastes (or doing other bad things). As the Missouri Supreme Court put it in the watershed case, "The sign boards . . . endanger the public health, promote immorality, constitute hiding places and retreats for criminals and all classes of miscreants." St. Louis Gunning Advertising Co. v. City of St. Louis, 137 S.W. 929, 942 (Mo. 1911). This disingenuous reasoning, of course, masked the real objection: billboards are ugly.

Not until the 1950s did courts begin to accept the legitimacy of zoning based exclusively on aesthetic considerations. In Berman v. Parker, 348 U.S. 26 (1954), an urban renewal case involving the use of the federal police power in the District of Columbia, the Supreme Court approved an expanded conception of the "public welfare." The values it represents, said the Court, "are spiritual as well as physical, aesthetic as well as monetary. It is within the power of the legislature to determine that the community should be beautiful as well as healthy, spacious as well as clean, well-balanced as well as carefully patrolled." 348 U.S. at 33. Perhaps a majority of jurisdictions today follow *Berman* and accept aesthetics as a legitimate police power goal in itself. But a good number still waffle on the issue, and a few are opposed to aesthetic regulation. For head counts, see Samuel Bufford, Beyond the Eye of the Beholder: A New Majority of Jurisdictions Authorize Aesthetic Regulation, 48 UMKC L. Rev. 127 (1980); James P. Karp, The Evolving Meaning of Aesthetics in Land-Use Regulation, 15 Colum. J. Envtl. L.

307, 313 n.35 (1990) (31 states have "either held or indicated strongly in dicta that aesthetics can stand alone" as justification for exercise of the police power); Kenneth Pearlman et al., Beyond the Eye of the Beholder Once Again: A New Review of Aesthetic Regulation, 38 Urb. Law. 1119 (2006). As a result of this judicial change of view, architectural review boards have proliferated in many states.

Aesthetic considerations are an important factor in historic zoning and historic preservation legislation, and in these contexts the courts have felt less inhibition in admitting the legitimacy of aesthetic objectives. See Penn Central Transp. Co. v. City of New York, reproduced at page 1162.

There is an extensive bibliography on the matters discussed here. Readings of particular interest include Raymond R. Coletta, The Case for Aesthetic Nuisance: Rethinking Traditional Judicial Attitudes, 48 Ohio St. L.J. 141 (1987); John J. Costonis, Law and Aesthetics: A Critique and a Reformulation of the Dilemmas, 80 Mich. L. Rev. 355 (1982); James C. Smith, Law, Beauty, and Human Stability: A Rose Is a Rose Is a Rose, 78 Cal. L. Rev. 787 (1990) (reviewing John J. Costonis, Icons and Aliens: Law, Aesthetics, and Environmental Change (1989)); Stephen F. Williams, Subjectivity, Expression, and Privacy: Problems of Aesthetic Regulation, 62 Minn. L. Rev. 1 (1977) (noting the "merit in the intuitive judicial anxiety about purely aesthetic purposes," id. at 58).

2. Notice that the court in *Stoyanoff* did not rest its decision on the legitimacy of aesthetics as a zoning objective, relying instead largely on protection of property values. (To the same effect are the *Saveland Park* and *Reid* cases cited by the court. *Reid* in particular is remarkably similar to *Stoyanoff*.)

> What appears to be an aesthetically aimed regulation is often upheld because it "protects property values," and therefore need not depend for its validity on its curbing a "merely aesthetic" nuisance. It should be clearly understood that this is escapist reasoning that evades the real issues.
>
> The effect on market value, after all, is derivative or symptomatic—not primary or of the essence. If the activities curbed by the regulation would otherwise make the surrounding property less valuable, it must be because those activities would radiate some kind of undesirable impact.
>
> If that impact is received and felt through visual sensibility, then the "economic" interest in question simply masks what has been referred to above as an "aesthetic" interest. In other words, without the aesthetic nuisance, there would be no market devaluation.
>
> The decline in market value, therefore, ought to be regarded as a kind of socially computerized, objective evidence that the regulated activity is by a social consensus deemed intrinsically ugly, negatively suggestive, or destructive of prior existing beauty. [Frank Michelman, Toward a Practical Standard for Aesthetic Regulation, 15 Prac. Law. 36, 36-37 (1969).]

3. And then there is the case of Sandra Cisneros, author of The House on Mango Street (1984), a novel drawn from her own experience. Her purple house located in the King William historical district of San Antonio did not conform to the Historic and Design Review Commission's mandate that houses may only be the color they were when originally constructed, a color available at the time of original construction, or a color of another house in the district. Cisneros left a legal pad outside her home on which many neighbors and passers-by indicated

their approval of her home. Ultimately, the Board withdrew its objections, but the house is no longer purple. Today it is bright red with a green door. See Sara Rimer, Novelist's Purple Palette Is Not to Everyone's Taste, N.Y. Times, July 13, 1998, at A14.

In the same vein, perhaps as a child you read (or had read to you) The Big Orange Splot, by D. Manus Pinkwater (1977). Eric Felleman, Michigan Law 2013, says of the book: "This deep and engrossing story revolves around a man whose house is identical to all the others on his street until a bucket of orange paint is dropped on it. Resisting pressure from his neighbors to restore the house to its original state, he instead turns it into a wacky piece of self-expression, and one-by-one convinces his neighbors to follow suit." Mr. Felleman adds that his feelings today about aesthetic zoning stem from reading the book more than 20 years ago.

4. *Locavores.* Aesthetic grounds (among others) figure in the recent and ongoing spate of controversies about whether and how zoning authorizes should regulate home farming in residential neighborhoods. For an overview, see Sarah B. Schindler, Of Backyard Chickens and Front Yard Gardens: The Conflict Between Local Governments and Locavores, 87 Tul. L. Rev. 231 (2012).

Anderson v. City of Issaquah
Court of Appeals of Washington, 1993
851 P.2d 744

KENNEDY, J. Appellants M. Bruce Anderson, Gary D. LaChance, and M. Bruce Anderson, Inc. (hereinafter referred to as "Anderson"), challenge the denial of their application for a land use certification, arguing, inter alia, that the building design requirements contained in Issaquah Municipal Code (IMC) 16.16.060 are unconstitutionally vague. The superior court rejected this constitutional challenge. We reverse and direct that Anderson's land use certification be issued.

Facts

Anderson owns property located at 145 N.W. Gilman Boulevard in the City of Issaquah (City). In 1988, Anderson applied to the City for a land use certification to develop the property. The property is zoned for general commercial use. Anderson desired to build a 6800-square-foot commercial building for several retail tenants.

After obtaining architectural plans, Anderson submitted the project to various City departments for the necessary approvals. The process went smoothly until the approval of the Issaquah Development Commission (Development Commission) was sought. This commission was created to administer and enforce the City's land use regulations. It has the authority to approve or deny applications for land use certification.

Section 16.16.060 of the IMC enumerates various building design objectives which the Development Commission is required to administer and enforce. Insofar as is relevant to this appeal, the Development Commission is to be guided by the following criteria:

> IMC 16.16.060(B). Relationship of Building and Site to Adjoining Area.
>
> 1. Buildings and structures shall be made compatible with adjacent buildings of conflicting architectural styles by such means as screens and site breaks, or other suitable methods and materials.
> 2. Harmony in texture, lines, and masses shall be encouraged. . . .
>
> IMC 16.16.060(D). Building Design.
>
> 1. Evaluation of a project shall be based on quality of its design and relationship to the natural setting of the valley and surrounding mountains.
> 2. Building components, such as windows, doors, eaves and parapets, shall have appropriate proportions and relationship to each other, expressing themselves as a part of the overall design.
> 3. Colors shall be harmonious, with bright or brilliant colors used only for minimal accent.
> 4. Design attention shall be given to screening from public view all mechanical equipment, including refuse enclosures, electrical transformer pads and vaults, communication equipment, and other utility hardware on roofs, grounds or buildings.
> 5. Exterior lighting shall be part of the architectural concept. Fixtures, standards and all exposed accessories shall be harmonious with the building design.
> 6. Monotony of design in single or multiple building projects shall be avoided. Efforts should be made to create an interesting project by use of complimentary details, functional orientation of buildings, parking and access provisions and relating the development to the site. In multiple building projects, variable siting of individual buildings, heights of buildings, or other methods shall be used to prevent a monotonous design.[7]

As initially designed, Anderson's proposed structure was to be faced with off-white stucco and was to have a blue metal roof. It was designed in a "modern" style with an unbroken "warehouse" appearance in the rear, and large retail style windows in the front. The City moved a Victorian era residence, the "Alexander House," onto the neighboring property to serve as a visitors' center. Across the street from the Anderson site is a gasoline station that looks like a gasoline station. Located nearby and within view from the proposed building site are two more gasoline stations, the First Mutual Bank Building built in the "Issaquah territorial style," an Elk's hall which is described in the record by the Mayor of Issaquah as a "box building," an auto repair shop, and a veterinary clinic with a cyclone fenced dog run. The area is described in the record as "a natural transition

---

7. The Issaquah Municipal Code aims to avoid "monotonous" design, whereas in some cities architectural regulations promote homogeneity. See Kenneth Regan, Note, You Can't Build That Here: The Constitutionality of Aesthetic Zoning and Architectural Review, 58 Fordham L. Rev. 1013, 1019 (1990). Is one of these more troublesome than the other from a free-expression point of view? See Samuel C. Poole III & Ilene Katz Kobert, Architectural Appearance Review Regulations and the First Amendment: The Constitutionally Infirm "Excessive Difference" Test, 12 Zoning & Plan. L. Rep. 89, 93-95 (1989).—Eds.

area between old downtown Issaquah and the new village style construction of Gilman [Boulevard]."

The Development Commission reviewed Anderson's application for the first time at a public hearing on December 21, 1988. Commissioner Nash commented that "the facade did not fit with the concept of the surrounding area." Commissioner McGinnis agreed. Commissioner Nash expressed concern about the building color and stated that he did not think the building was compatible with the image of Issaquah. Commissioner Larson said that he would like to see more depth to the building facade. Commissioner Nash said there should be some interest created along the blank back wall. Commissioner Garrison suggested that the rear facade needed to be redesigned.

At the conclusion of the meeting, the Development Commission voted to continue the hearing to give Anderson an opportunity to modify the building design.

On January 18, 1989, Anderson came back before the Development Commission with modified plans which included changing the roofing from metal to tile, changing the color of the structure from off-white to "Cape Cod" gray with "Tahoe" blue trim, and adding brick to the front facade. During the ensuing discussion among the commissioners, Commissioner Larson stated that the revisions to the front facade had not satisfied his concerns from the last meeting. In response to Anderson's request for more specific design guidelines, Commissioner McGinnis stated that the Development Commission had "been giving direction; it is the applicant's responsibility to take the direction/suggestions and incorporate them into a revised plan that reflects the changes." Commissioner Larson then suggested that "the facade can be broken up with sculptures, benches, fountains, etc." Commissioner Nash suggested that Anderson "drive up and down Gilman and look at both good and bad examples of what has been done with flat facades."

As the discussion continued, Commissioner Larson stated that Anderson "should present a [plan] that achieves what the Commission is trying to achieve through its comments/suggestions at these meetings" and stated that "architectural screens, fountains, paving of brick, wood or other similar method[s] of screening in lieu of vegetative landscaping are examples of design suggestions that can be used to break up the front facade." Commissioner Davis objected to the front facade, stating that he could not see putting an expanse of glass facing Gilman Boulevard. "The building is not compatible with Gilman." Commissioner O'Shea agreed. Commissioner Nash stated that "the application needs major changes to be acceptable." Commissioner O'Shea agreed. Commissioner Nash stated that "this facade does not create the same feeling as the building/environment around this site."

Commissioner Nash continued, stating that he "personally like[d] the introduction of brick and the use of tiles rather than metal on the roof." Commissioner Larson stated that he would like to see a review of the blue to be used: "Tahoe blue may be too dark." Commissioner Steinwachs agreed. Commissioner Larson noted that "the front of the building could be modulated [to] have other design techniques employed to make the front facade more interesting."

With this, the Development Commission voted to continue the discussion to a future hearing.

On February 15, 1989, Anderson came back before the Development Commission. In the meantime, Anderson's architects had added a 5-foot over-hang and a 7-foot accent overhang to the plans for the front of the building. More brick had been added to the front of the building. Wood trim and accent colors had been added to the back of the building and trees were added to the landscaping to further break up the rear facade.

Anderson explained the plans still called for large, floor to ceiling windows as this was to be a retail premises: "[A] glass front is necessary to rent the space. . . ." Commissioner Steinwachs stated that he had driven Gilman Boulevard and taken notes. The following verbatim statements by Steinwachs was placed into the minutes:

"My General Observation From Driving Up and Down Gilman Boulevard."

I see certain design elements and techniques used in various combinations in various locations to achieve a visual effect that is sensitive to the unique character of our Signature Street. I see heavy use of brick, wood, and tile. I see minimal use of stucco. I see colors that are mostly earth-tones, avoiding extreme contrasts. I see various methods used to provide modulation in both horizontal and vertical lines, such as gables, bay windows, recesses in front faces, porches, rails, many vertical columns, and breaks in roof lines. I see long, sloping, conspicuous roofs with large overhangs. I see windows with panels above and below windows. I see no windows that extend down to floor level. This is the impression I have of Gilman Boulevard as it relates to building design.

Commissioner Nash agreed stating, "There is a certain feeling you get when you drive along Gilman Boulevard, and this building does not give this same feeling." Commissioner Steinwachs wondered if the applicant had any option but to start "from scratch." Anderson responded that he would be willing to change from stucco to wood facing but that, after working on the project for 9 months and experiencing total frustration, he was not willing to make additional design changes.

At that point, the Development Commission denied Anderson's application, giving four reasons:

1. After four [sic] lengthy review meetings of the Development Commission, the applicant has not been sufficiently responsive to concerns expressed by the Commission to warrant approval or an additional continuance of the review.

2. The primary concerns expressed relate to the building architecture as it relates to Gilman Boulevard in general, and the immediate neighborhood in particular.

3. The Development Commission is charged with protecting, preserving and enhancing the aesthetic values that have established the desirable quality and unique character of Issaquah.

4. We see certain design elements and techniques used in various combinations in various locations to achieve a visual effect that is sensitive to the unique character of our Signature Street. On Gilman Boulevard we see heavy use of brick, wood and tile. We see minimal use of stucco. We see various methods used to provide both horizontal and vertical modulation, including gables, breaks in rooflines, bay windows, recesses and protrusions in front face. We see long, sloping, conspicuous roofs with large overhangs. We see no windows that extend to ground level.

We see brick and wood panels at intervals between windows. We see earthtone colors avoiding extreme contrast.

Anderson, who by this time had an estimated $250,000 into the project, timely appealed the adverse ruling to the Issaquah City Council (City Council). After a lengthy hearing and much debate, the City Council decided to affirm the Development Commission's decision by a vote of 4 to 3.

The City Council considered formal written findings and conclusions on April 3, 1989. The City Council verbally adopted its action on that date but required that certain changes be made to the proposed findings and conclusions. Those changes were made and the final findings and conclusions were signed on April 5, 1989. . . .

Thirteen days later, on April 18, 1989, Anderson filed a complaint in King County Superior Court. . . .

Following trial, the court dismissed Anderson's complaint, rejecting the same claims now raised in this appeal.

Discussion

Constitutionality of IMC 16.16.060 (Building Design Provisions).

Rule

[A] statute which either forbids or requires the doing of an act in terms so vague that men [and women] of common intelligence must necessarily guess at its meaning and differ as to its application, violates the first essential of due process of law.

Connally v. General Constr. Co., 269 U.S. 385, 391 (1926). . . .

In the area of land use, a court looks not only at the face of the ordinance but also at its application to the person who has sought to comply with the ordinance and/or who is alleged to have failed to comply. Burien Bark Supply v. King Cy., 106 Wash. 2d 868, 871, 725 P.2d 994 (1986); Grant Cy. v. Bohne, 89 Wash. 2d 953, 955, 577 P.2d 138 (1978). The purpose of the void for vagueness doctrine is to limit arbitrary and discretionary enforcements of the law. Burien Bark Supply, 106 Wash. 2d at 871.

Looking first at the face of the building design sections of IMC 16.16.060, we note that an ordinary citizen reading these sections would learn only that a given building project should bear a good relationship with the Issaquah Valley and surrounding mountains; its windows, doors, eaves and parapets should be of "appropriate proportions," its colors should be "harmonious" and seldom "bright" or "brilliant"; its mechanical equipment should be screened from public view; its exterior lighting should be "harmonious" with the building design and "monotony should be avoided." The project should also be "interesting." IMC 16.16.060(D)(1)-(6). If the building is not "compatible" with adjacent buildings, it should be "made compatible" by the use of screens and site breaks "or other suitable methods and materials." "Harmony in texture, lines, and masses [is] encouraged." The landscaping should provide an "attractive . . . transition" to adjoining properties. IMC 16.16.060(B) (1)-(3).

As is stated in the brief of amici curiae,[8] we conclude that these code sections "do not give effective or meaningful guidance" to applicants, to design professionals, or to the public officials of Issaquah who are responsible for enforcing the code. Although it is clear from the code sections here at issue that mechanical equipment must be screened from public view and that, probably, earth tones or pastels located within the cool and muted ranges of the color wheel are going to be preferred, there is nothing in the code from which an applicant can determine whether his or her project is going to be seen by the Development Commission as "interesting" versus "monotonous" and as "harmonious" with the valley and the mountains. Neither is it clear from the code just what else, besides the valley and the mountains, a particular project is supposed to be harmonious with, although "[h]armony in texture, lines, and masses" is certainly encouraged. IMC 16.16.060(B)(2).

In attempting to interpret and apply this code, the commissioners charged with that task were left with only their own individual, subjective "feelings" about the "image of Issaquah" and as to whether this project was "compatible" or "interesting." The commissioners stated that the City was "making a statement" on its "signature street" and invited Anderson to take a drive up and down Gilman Boulevard and "look at good and bad examples of what has been done with flat facades." One commissioner drove up and down Gilman, taking notes, in a no doubt sincere effort to define that which is left undefined in the code.[9]

The point we make here is that neither Anderson nor the commissioners may constitutionally be required or allowed to guess at the meaning of the code's building design requirements by driving up and down Gilman Boulevard looking at "good and bad" examples of what has been done with other buildings, recently or in the past. We hold that the code sections here at issue are unconstitutionally vague on their face. The words employed are not technical words which are commonly understood within the professional building design industry. Neither do these words have a settled common law meaning.

As they were applied to Anderson, it is also clear the code sections at issue fail to pass constitutional muster. Because the commissioners themselves had no objective guidelines to follow, they necessarily had to resort to their own subjective "feelings." The "statement" Issaquah is apparently trying to make on its "signature street" is not written in the code. In order to be enforceable, that "statement" must be written down in the code, in understandable terms. See, e.g., Morristown Road Assocs. v. Mayor & Common Council & Planning Bd., 163 N.J. Super. 58, 394 A.2d 157 (1978). The unacceptable alternative is what happened

8. The amici curiae are the Seattle Chapter of the American Institute of Architects, the Washington Council of the American Institute of Architects, and the Washington Chapter of the American Society of Landscape Architects.

9. Although Commissioner Steinwachs stated that he saw heavy use of brick, wood and tile, minimal use of stucco, many gables, bay windows, and long, sloping vertical roofs, it is clear from the record that also to be seen on Gilman Boulevard are a number of approved and completed projects that do not bear these characteristics. Examples include a Shuck's Auto Supply store at 607 N.W. Gilman Boulevard; a strip mall known as Town and County Square at 1135 Gilman Boulevard; a Mobil gasoline station located at 55 N.W. Gilman Boulevard and a Skipper's Restaurant located at the southeast corner of Front Street and Gilman Boulevard.

here. The commissioners enforced not a building design code but their own arbitrary concept of the provisions of an unwritten "statement" to be made on Gilman Boulevard. The commissioners' individual concepts were as vague and undefined as those written in the code. This is the very epitome of discretionary, arbitrary enforcement of the law.

Although the City argues that its code is not unconstitutionally vague, it primarily relies upon the procedural safeguards contained in the code. Because aesthetic considerations are subjective in concept, the City argues that they cannot be reduced to a formula or a number. The vagueness test does not require a statute to meet impossible standards of specificity. Chicago, M., St. P. & P.R.R. v. Washington State Human Rights Commn., 87 Wash. 2d at 802, 805, 527 P.2d 307 (1976).

As well illustrated by the appendices to the brief of amici curiae, aesthetic considerations are not impossible to define in a code or ordinance.[10] Moreover, the procedural safeguards contained in the Issaquah Municipal Code (providing for appeal to the city council and to the courts) do not cure the constitutional defects here apparent.

Certainly, the IMC grants Anderson the right to appeal the adverse decision of the Development Commission. But just as IMC 16.16.060 provides no standards by which an applicant or the Development Commission or the City Council can determine whether a given building design passes muster under the code, it provides no ascertainable criteria by which a court can review a decision at issue, regardless of whether the court applies the arbitrary and capricious standard as the City argues is appropriate or the clearly erroneous standard as Anderson argues is appropriate. Under either standard of review, the appellate process is to no avail where the statute at issue contains no ascertainable standards and where, as here, the Development Commission was not empowered to adopt clearly ascertainable standards of its own. The procedural safeguards provided here do not save the ordinance.

Anderson has argued strenuously in this appeal that a municipality has no power to deny a proposed development for aesthetic reasons alone. Anderson argues this issue is "settled" by Washington case law. See Polygon Corp. v. Seattle, 90 Wash. 2d 59, 70, 578 P.2d 1309 (1978); Duckworth v. Bonney Lake, 91 Wash. 2d 19, 30, 586 P.2d 860 (1978); and Victoria Tower Partnership v. Seattle, 59 Wash. App. 592, 603, 800 P.2d 380 (1990) (holding a city can consider aesthetic impacts only "along with other adverse impacts"), review denied, 116 Wash. 2d 1012, 807 P.2d 884 (1991). Relying on these same cases, the City argues that, although Anderson's land use certification admittedly was denied solely on the basis of aesthetics, IMC 16.16 is valid because aesthetic concerns are only one of the bases contained in the code for the exercise of police power relating to land use. The amici point out that the modern view is that aesthetics alone will justify

10. Appendix A to the brief of amici curiae is a portion of the design objectives plan for entry way corridors for Bozeman, Montana. Appendix B is a portion of the development code for San Bernardino, California. Both codes contain extensive written criteria illustrated by schematic drawings and photographs. The illustrations clarify a number of concepts which otherwise might be difficult to describe with the requisite degree of clarity.

a regulation, provided that there are adequate standards and they are appropriately applied. See 1 A. & D. Rathkopf, Zoning and Planning §14.02[4] (1986).

We believe the issue of whether a community can exert control over design issues based solely on accepted community aesthetic values is far from "settled" in Washington case law. The possibility certainly has not been foreclosed by our Supreme Court. See *Polygon*, 90 Wash. 2d at 70, 578 P.2d 1309 ("While this court has not held that aesthetic factors alone will support an exercise of the police power, such considerations taken together with other factors can support such action."); see also *Duckworth*, 91 Wash. 2d at 30, 586 P.2d 860 ("While we have indicated that aesthetic considerations alone may not support invocation of the police powers. . . .").

Clearly, however, aesthetic standards are an appropriate component of land use governance. Whenever a community adopts such standards they can and must be drafted to give clear guidance to all parties concerned. Applicants must have an understandable statement of what is expected from new construction. Design professionals need to know in advance what standards will be acceptable in a given community. It is unreasonable to expect applicants to pay for repetitive revisions of plans in an effort to comply with the unarticulated, unpublished "statements" a given community may wish to make on or off its "signature street." It is equally unreasonable, and a deprivation of due process, to expect or allow a design review board such as the Issaquah Development Commission to create standards on an ad hoc basis, during the design review process.

Conclusion

It is not disputed that Anderson's project meets all of the City's land use requirements except for those unwritten and therefore unenforceable requirements relating to building design which the Development Commission unsuccessfully tried to articulate during the course of several hearings. We order that Anderson's land use certification be issued, provided however, that those changes which Anderson agreed to through the hearing before the City Council may validly be imposed.

NOTES AND QUESTIONS

1. The view of the Washington Court of Appeals closely parallels that of some eminent architects. (Note that the court refers favorably to the amicus brief filed by the American Institute of Architects.) Consider the views of the architects whose criticism of modern architecture brought on the postmodernist architectural movement.

The courts have ruled that beauty is an urban amenity to be sought through the police powers, review boards, and other regulatory measures; but they have omitted to set the standards by which beauty may be defined or the processes through which it may be equitably judged to be present. Local authorities have reacted by appointing "experts" (usually local architects) who use their own discretion in assigning beauty or lack of it to the works of others. The limits set on capriciousness, authoritarianism, or venality in such a system are those internal to the individual review board members. This is rule by man rather than rule by law.

In proceedings based solely on taste, the supplicant architect is left perplexed, and often thousands of dollars are lost as he makes frustrating attempts, scheming rather than designing, to anticipate or to follow the dicta of "experts" whose tastes and philosophies differ from his own or are so capricious as to be incomprehensible to him.

Aesthetically too, the aim is not achieved. Any artist could have told the lawmakers that you cannot legislate beauty and that attempts to do so by the use of experts will result not only in gross injustice but in an ugly deadness in the environment.

Beauty escapes in the pursuit of safety, which promotes a simplistic sameness over a varied vitality. [Robert Venturi, Denise Scott Brown & Steven Izenour, Learning from Las Vegas 189 (1972).][11]

Philadelphia architect Robert Venturi is one of contemporary architecture's most influential thinkers. In his book, Complexity and Contradiction in Architecture (1966), Venturi, tired of the spare aesthetics of glass boxes, parodied the famous dictum of Mies van der Rohe, "less is more," with his own mot, "less is a bore." The postmodern architectural movement was thus born. In 1991 Venturi received the Pritzker Prize, architecture's equivalent of the Nobel.

Venturi and his wife and partner Denise Scott Brown have been tireless critics of design review boards. In a conference in Austin, Texas in 1984, Scott Brown fired another shot:

Design review, from our personal experiences as people at the cutting edge of art—it kills us. I believe that Frank Lloyd Wright would not have had a single building built, nor Le Corbusier, if there had been design review and fine arts boards in cities where they would have had to present their work.

Where there are design review boards, what is accepted is the going and the slightly old-fashioned and the mediocre. Where you have design review, you have the avoidance of risk. You will get nothing bad, but you will get little that's new. [The Land, The City, and the Human Spirit 128 (Larry P. Fuller ed. 1985).]

Scott Brown wrote in 1999 that her "criticisms of the design process have become more not less relevant with time." Denise Scott Brown, With the Best Intentions, Harvard Design Magazine, Winter/Spring 1999, at 37, 39.

What do you suppose Scott Brown would think of Portland, Oregon's adoption of a "design dictate" that outlaws "snout houses"? "[T]he offending structure has been clearly defined in the city code: the garage cannot dominate the front of the house or protrude; the main entrance has to be close to the street and clearly identifiable. . . ." The house, as a supporter of the design requirement put it, has to pass the "trick or treat test." A builder of snout houses complained that "the city of Portland, they've become socialists." He's thinking of moving to Las Vegas. " 'They

---

11. Venturi and Scott Brown, who taught in the Yale architecture school, took their seminar students to Las Vegas to study it. This project appalled the architectural elite, but the resulting book shows there were some fascinating lessons to learn.

**In Portland, snout houses—garage dominating the front of the house
and main entrance inconspicuous—are illegal.**

**This house does not violate Portland's zoning ordinance because the
garage does not dominate the street side of the house.**

have almost no restrictions down there,' he said, with uncontained glee." Timothy Egan, In Portland, Houses Are Friendly. Or Else, N.Y. Times, Apr. 20, 2000, at B1.

For another case like *Anderson,* holding as unconstitutionally vague an architectural regulation prohibiting buildings that are "inappropriate to, or incompatible with, the character of the surrounding neighborhood and cause substantial depreciation in property values," see Waterfront Estates Development, Inc. v. City of Palos Hills, 597 N.E.2d 641 (Ill. App. 1992); see also Hanna v. City of Chicago, 907 N.E.2d 390, 396 (Ill. App. 2009) (words "value," "important," "significant," and "unique" in landmarks ordinance are "vague, ambiguous and overly broad").

2. *Compare private restrictive covenants.* If the *Anderson* case had involved a dispute between the property owner Anderson and an architectural control committee established by private covenants, Anderson very likely would have lost. Private architectural restrictions are governed by a different standard than public restrictions. Cases have held that specific standards are not necessary when architectural approval is required by a private covenant. The architectural committee only has to act reasonably and in good faith. See Gleneagle Civic Assn. v. Hardin, 205 P.3d 462 (Colo. App. 2009); Hammons v. Table Mountain Ranches Owners Assn., 72 P.3d 1153 (Wyo. 2003).

Should architectural boards established by private covenant be subject to less demanding standards than a city board? Does it matter if the architectural covenants are administered by a board within a private gated community that maintains its streets, has a private security force, and provides garbage service for its residents? For criticism of the failure of courts to require specific architectural standards to guide decisions of boards established by covenants, see Note, Validity Rules Concerning Public Zoning and Private Covenants: A Comparison and Critique, 39 S. Cal. L. Rev. 409 (1966); Comment, An Evaluation of the Applicability of Zoning Principles to the Law of Private Land Use Restrictions, 21 UCLA L. Rev. 1655 (1974).

As you study the rest of this chapter, consider whether a zoning restriction that is held to violate the Constitution may validly be imposed as a private covenant.

3. *First Amendment concerns.* No court has ever held that architectural expression is protected by the First Amendment, but it is a common view of commentators that design regulation, because it implicates expressive values, should at least be subject to close scrutiny. See Sheldon H. Nahmod, Artistic Expression and Aesthetic Theory: The Beautiful, the Sublime, and the First Amendment, 1987 Wis. L. Rev. 221; Stephen F. Williams, Subjectivity, Expression, and Privacy: Problems of Aesthetic Regulation, 62 Minn. L. Rev. 1 (1977); Shawn G. Rice, Comment, Zoning Law: Architectural Appearance Ordinances and the First Amendment, 76 Marq. L. Rev. 439 (1993); Kenneth Regan, Note, You Can't Build That Here: The Constitutionality of Aesthetic Zoning and Architectural Review, 58 Fordham L. Rev. 1013 (1990); see also Darrel C. Menthe, Aesthetic Regulation and the Development of First Amendment Jurisprudence, 19 B.U. Pub. Int. L.J. 225 (2010).

For an unusually insightful and comprehensive discussion of this matter, see John Nivala, Constitutional Architecture: The First Amendment and the Single

Family House, 33 San Diego L. Rev. 291 (1996). Using the philosophy of architect Robert Venturi, Professor Nivala argues that "the exterior design of a private single family house speaks on behalf of the inhabitants, expressing who they are and how they choose to live." Id. at 292. He would apply to house architecture the same standard applied in Schad v. Borough of Mount Ephraim, 452 U.S. 61 (1981), to non-obscene live nude dancing: "[W]hen a zoning law infringes upon a protected liberty, it must be narrowly drawn and must further a sufficiently substantial government interest." 452 U.S. at 68.

Compare Hurley v. Irish-American Gay, Lesbian & Bisexual Group of Boston, 515 U.S. 557, 567 (1995), holding that a parade was a constitutionally protected form of free speech:

> The protected expression that inheres in a parade is not limited to its banners and songs, however, for the Constitution looks beyond written or spoken words as mediums of expression. Noting that "symbolism is a primitive but effective way of communicating ideas," . . . our cases have recognized that the First Amendment shields such acts as saluting a flag (and refusing to do so), . . . wearing an armband to protest a war, . . . displaying a red flag, . . . and even "marching, walking or parading" in uniforms displaying the swastika. . . . As some of these examples show, a narrow, succinctly articulable message is not a condition of constitutional protection, which if confined to expressions conveying a "particularized message," . . . would never reach the unquestionably shielded painting of Jackson Pollock, music of Arnold Schönberg, or Jabberwocky verse of Lewis Carroll.

City of Ladue v. Gilleo

Supreme Court of the United States, 1994
512 U.S. 43

JUSTICE STEVENS delivered the opinion of the Court.

An ordinance of the City of Ladue prohibits homeowners from displaying any signs on their property except "residence identification" signs, "for sale" signs, and signs warning of safety hazards. The ordinance permits commercial establishments, churches, and nonprofit organizations to erect certain signs that are not allowed at residences. The question presented is whether the ordinance violates a Ladue resident's right to free speech.[12]

I.

Respondent Margaret P. Gilleo owns one of the 57 single family homes in the Willow Hill subdivision of Ladue.[13] On December 8, 1990, she placed on her front lawn a 24- by 36-inch sign printed with the words "Say No to War in the

---

12. The First Amendment provides: "Congress shall make no law . . . abridging the freedom of speech, or of the press. . . ." The Fourteenth Amendment makes this limitation applicable to the States, see Gitlow v. New York, 268 U.S. 652 (1925), and to their political subdivisions, see Lovell v. Griffin, 303 U.S. 444 (1938).

13. Ladue is a suburb of St. Louis, Missouri. It has a population of almost 9,000, and an area of about 8.5 square miles, of which only 3% is zoned for commercial or industrial use.

Persian Gulf, Call Congress Now." After that sign disappeared, Gilleo put up another but it was knocked to the ground. When Gilleo reported these incidents to the police, they advised her that such signs were prohibited in Ladue. The City Council denied her petition for a variance.[14] Gilleo then filed this action under 42 U.S.C. §1983 against the City, the Mayor, and members of the City Council, alleging that Ladue's sign ordinance violated her First Amendment right of free speech.

The District Court issued a preliminary injunction against enforcement of the ordinance. 774 F. Supp. 1559 (E.D. Mo. 1991). Gilleo then placed an 8.5-by 11-inch sign in the second story window of her home stating, "For Peace in the Gulf." The Ladue City Council responded to the injunction by repealing its ordinance and enacting a replacement.[15] Like its predecessor, the new ordinance contains a general prohibition of "signs" and defines that term broadly.[16] The ordinance prohibits all signs except those that fall within one of ten exemptions. Thus, "residential identification signs" no larger than one square foot are allowed, as are signs advertising "that the property is for sale, lease or exchange" and identifying the owner or agent. Also exempted are signs "for churches, religious institutions, and schools," "[c]ommercial signs in commercially or industrial zoned districts," and on-site signs advertising "gasoline filling stations." Unlike its predecessor, the new ordinance contains a lengthy "Declaration of Findings, Policies, Interests, and Purposes," part of which recites that the

> proliferation of an unlimited number of signs in private, residential, commercial, industrial, and public areas of the City of Ladue would create ugliness, visual blight and clutter, tarnish the natural beauty of the landscape as well as the residential and commercial architecture, impair property values, substantially impinge upon the privacy and special ambience of the community, and may cause safety and traffic hazards to motorists, pedestrians, and children[.] Id. at 36a.

Gilleo amended her complaint to challenge the new ordinance, which explicitly prohibits window signs like hers. The District Court held the ordinance unconstitutional, and the Court of Appeals affirmed. 986 F.2d 1180 (C.A. 8 1993). Relying on the plurality opinion in Metromedia, Inc. v. San Diego, 453

---

14. The ordinance then in effect gave the Council the authority to "permit a variation in the strict application of the provisions and requirements of this chapter . . . where the public interest will be best served by permitting such variation."

15. The new ordinance eliminates the provision allowing for variances and contains a grandfather clause exempting signs already lawfully in place.

16. Section 35-2 of the ordinance declares that "No sign shall be erected [or] maintained" in the City except in conformity with the ordinance; §35-3 authorizes the City to remove nonconforming signs. Section 35-1 defines "sign" as:

> A name, word, letter, writing, identification, description, or illustration which is erected, placed upon, affixed to, painted or represented upon a building or structure, or any part thereof, or any manner upon a parcel of land or lot, and which publicizes an object, product, place, activity, opinion, person, institution, organization or place of business, or which is used to advertise or promote the interests of any person. The word "sign" shall also include "banners," "pennants," "insignia," "bulletin boards," "ground signs," "billboards," "poster billboards," "illuminated signs," "projecting signs," "temporary signs," "marquees," "roof signs," "yard signs," "electric signs," "wall signs," and "window signs," wherever placed out of doors in view of the general public or wherever placed indoors as a window sign. Id. at 39a.

U.S. 490 (1981), the Court of Appeals held the ordinance invalid as a "content based" regulation because the City treated commercial speech more favorably than noncommercial speech and favored some kinds of noncommercial speech over others. Acknowledging that "Ladue's interests in enacting its ordinance are substantial," the Court of Appeals nevertheless concluded that those interests were "not sufficiently 'compelling' to support a content-based restriction."

We granted the City of Ladue's petition for certiorari and now affirm.

II.

While signs are a form of expression protected by the Free Speech Clause, they pose distinctive problems that are subject to municipalities' police powers. Unlike oral speech, signs take up space and may obstruct views, distract motorists, displace alternative uses for land, and pose other problems that legitimately call for regulation. It is common ground that governments may regulate the physical characteristics of signs—just as they can, within reasonable bounds and absent censorial purpose, regulate audible expression in its capacity as noise. See, e.g., Ward v. Rock Against Racism, 491 U.S. 781 (1989); Kovacs v. Cooper, 336 U.S. 77 (1949). However, because regulation of a medium inevitably affects communication itself, it is not surprising that we have had occasion to review the constitutionality of municipal ordinances prohibiting the display of certain outdoor signs.

In Linmark Associates, Inc. v. Willingboro, 431 U.S. 85 (1977), we addressed an ordinance that sought to maintain stable, integrated neighborhoods by prohibiting homeowners from placing "For Sale" or "Sold" signs on their property. Although we recognized the importance of Willingboro's objective, we held that the First Amendment prevented the township from "achieving its goal by restricting the free flow of truthful information." In some respects Linmark is the mirror image of this case. For instead of prohibiting "For Sale" signs without banning any other signs, Ladue has exempted such signs from an otherwise virtually complete ban. Moreover, whereas in Linmark we noted that the ordinance was not concerned with the promotion of aesthetic values unrelated to the content of the prohibited speech, here Ladue relies squarely on that content-neutral justification for its ordinance.

In Metromedia, we reviewed an ordinance imposing substantial prohibitions on outdoor advertising displays within the City of San Diego in the interest of traffic safety and aesthetics. The ordinance generally banned all except those advertising "on-site" activities.[17] The Court concluded that the City's interest in traffic safety and its aesthetic interest in preventing "visual clutter" could justify a prohibition of off-site commercial billboards even though similar on-site signs were allowed. Nevertheless, the Court's judgment in Metromedia, supported by two

---

17. The San Diego ordinance defined "on-site signs" as "those designating the name of the owner or occupant of the premises upon which such signs are placed, or identifying such premises; or signs advertising goods manufactured or produced or services rendered on the premises upon which such signs are placed." Metromedia Inc. v. San Diego, 453 U.S. 490, 494 (1981).

different lines of reasoning, invalidated the San Diego ordinance in its entirety. According to Justice White's plurality opinion, the ordinance impermissibly discriminated on the basis of content by permitting on-site commercial speech while broadly prohibiting noncommercial messages. On the other hand, Justice Brennan, joined by Justice Blackmun, concluded "that the practical effect of the San Diego ordinance [was] to eliminate the billboard as an effective medium of communication" for noncommercial messages, and that the city had failed to make the strong showing needed to justify such "content-neutral prohibitions of particular media of communication." 453 U.S., at 525-527. The three dissenters also viewed San Diego's ordinance as tantamount to a blanket prohibition of billboards, but would have upheld it because they did not perceive "even a hint of bias or censorship in the city's actions" nor "any reason to believe that the overall communications market in San Diego is inadequate." Id. at 552-553 (Stevens, J., dissenting in part); see also id. at 563, 566 (Burger, C.J., dissenting); id. at 569-570 (Rehnquist, J., dissenting).

In City Council of Los Angeles v. Taxpayers for Vincent, 466 U.S. 789 (1984), we upheld a Los Angeles ordinance that prohibited the posting of signs on public property. Noting the conclusion shared by seven Justices in *Metromedia* that San Diego's "interest in avoiding visual clutter" was sufficient to justify a prohibition of commercial billboards, in *Vincent* we upheld the Los Angeles ordinance, which was justified on the same grounds. We rejected the argument that the validity of the City's aesthetic interest had been compromised by failing to extend the ban to private property, reasoning that the "private citizen's interest in controlling the use of his own property justifies the disparate treatment." Id. at 811. . . .

These decisions identify two analytically distinct grounds for challenging the constitutionality of a municipal ordinance regulating the display of signs. One is that the measure in effect restricts too little speech because its exemptions discriminate on the basis of the signs' messages. See *Metromedia*, 453 U.S., at 512-517 (opinion of White, J.). Alternatively, such provisions are subject to attack on the ground that they simply prohibit too much protected speech. See id. at 525-534 (Brennan, J., concurring in judgment). The City of Ladue contends, first, that the Court of Appeals' reliance on the former rationale was misplaced because the City's regulatory purposes are content-neutral, and, second, that those purposes justify the comprehensiveness of the sign prohibition. A comment on the former contention will help explain why we ultimately base our decision on a rejection of the latter.

III.

While surprising at first glance, the notion that a regulation of speech may be impermissibly underinclusive is firmly grounded in basic First Amendment principles. Thus, an exemption from an otherwise permissible regulation of speech may represent a governmental "attempt to give one side of a debatable public question an advantage in expressing its views to the people." First Nat. Bank of

What is a "sign"?

A question for semiotics mavens: Does the illustration above depict a "sign"? To what does an ordinance regulating "signs" apply? To a giant model of an iguana perched on the roof of a bar in Manhattan? To a sculpture, 30 feet high, made of brushed aluminum cylinders? To colossal toothbrushes and teeth placed outside a dentist's office? See Russ VerSteeg, Iguanas, Toads and Toothbrushes: Land-Use Regulation of Art as Signage, 25 Ga. L. Rev. 437 (1991) (citing and discussing cases in point).

Boston v. Belloti, 435 U.S. 765, 785-786 (1978). Alternatively, through the combined operation of a general speech restriction and its exemptions, the government might seek to select the "permissible subjects for public debate" and thereby to "control . . . the search for political truth." Consolidated Edison Co. of N.Y. v. Public Service Commn. of N.Y., 447 U.S. 530, 538 (1980).

The City argues that its sign ordinance implicates neither of these concerns, and that the Court of Appeals therefore erred in demanding a "compelling" justification for the exemptions. The mix of prohibitions and exemptions in the ordinance, Ladue maintains, reflects legitimate differences among the side effects of various kinds of signs. These differences are only adventitiously connected with content, and supply a sufficient justification, unrelated to the City's approval or disapproval of specific messages, for carving out the specified categories from the general ban. Thus, according to the Declaration of Findings, Policies, Interests, and Purposes supporting the ordinance, the permitted signs, unlike the prohibited signs, are unlikely to contribute to the dangers of "unlimited proliferation" associated with categories of signs that are not inherently limited in number. Because only a few residents will need to display "for sale" or "for rent" signs at any given time, permitting one such sign per marketed house does not threaten visual clutter. Because the City has only a few businesses, churches, and schools, the same rationale explains the exemption for on-site commercial and organizational signs. Moreover, some of the exempted categories (e.g., danger signs) respond to unique public needs to permit certain kinds of speech.

Even if we assume the validity of these arguments, the exemptions in Ladue's ordinance nevertheless shed light on the separate question of whether the ordinance prohibits too much speech.

Exemptions from an otherwise legitimate regulation of a medium of speech may be noteworthy for a reason quite apart from the risks of viewpoint and content discrimination: they may diminish the credibility of the government's rationale for restricting speech in the first place. In this case, at the very least, the exemptions from Ladue's ordinance demonstrate that Ladue has concluded that the interest in allowing certain messages to be conveyed by means of residential signs outweighs the City's aesthetic interest in eliminating outdoor signs. Ladue has not imposed a flat ban on signs because it has determined that at least some of them are too vital to be banned.

Under the Court of Appeals' content discrimination rationale, the City might theoretically remove the defects in its ordinance by simply repealing all of the exemptions. If, however, the ordinance is also vulnerable because it prohibits too much speech, that solution would not save it. Moreover, if the prohibitions in Ladue's ordinance are impermissible, resting our decision on its exemptions would afford scant relief for respondent Gilleo. She is primarily concerned not with the scope of the exemptions available in other locations, such as commercial areas and on church property. She asserts a constitutional right to display an antiwar sign at her own home. Therefore, we first ask whether Ladue may properly prohibit Gilleo from displaying her sign, and then, only if necessary, consider the separate question whether it was improper for the City simultaneously to permit certain other signs. In examining the propriety of Ladue's near-total prohibition of residential signs, we will assume, arguendo, the validity of the City's submission that the various exemptions are free of impermissible content or viewpoint discrimination.

IV.

In *Linmark* we held that the City's interest in maintaining a stable, racially integrated neighborhood was not sufficient to support a prohibition of residential "For Sale" signs. We recognized that even such a narrow sign prohibition would have a deleterious effect on residents' ability to convey important information because alternatives were "far from satisfactory." 431 U.S., at 93. Ladue's sign ordinance is supported principally by the City's interest in minimizing the visual clutter associated with signs, an interest that is concededly valid but certainly no more compelling than the interests at stake in *Linmark*. Moreover, whereas the ordinance in *Linmark* applied only to a form of commercial speech, Ladue's ordinance covers even such absolutely pivotal speech as a sign protesting an imminent governmental decision to go to war.

The impact on free communication of Ladue's broad sign prohibition, moreover, is manifestly greater than in *Linmark*. Gilleo and other residents of Ladue are forbidden to display virtually any "sign" on their property. The ordinance defines that term sweepingly. A prohibition is not always invalid merely because it applies to a sizeable category of speech; the sign ban we upheld in *Vincent*, for example, was quite broad. But in *Vincent* we specifically noted that the category of speech in question—signs placed on public property—was not a "uniquely valuable or important mode of communication," and that there was no evidence that "appellees' ability to communicate effectively is threatened by ever-increasing restrictions on expression." 466 U.S., at 812.

Here, in contrast, Ladue has almost completely foreclosed a venerable means of communication that is both unique and important. It has totally foreclosed that medium to political, religious, or personal messages. Signs that react to a local happening or express a view on a controversial issue both reflect and animate change in the life of a community. Often placed on lawns or in windows, residential signs play an important part in political campaigns, during which they are displayed to signal the resident's support for particular candidates, parties, or causes. They may not afford the same opportunities for conveying complex ideas as do other media, but residential signs have long been an important and distinct medium of expression.

Our prior decisions have voiced particular concern with laws that foreclose an entire medium of expression. Thus, we have held invalid ordinances that completely banned the distribution of pamphlets within the municipality, Lovell v. Griffin, 303 U.S. 444 (1938); handbills on the public streets, Jamison v. Texas, 318 U.S. 413 (1943); the door-to-door distribution of literature, Martin v. Struthers, 319 U.S. 141 (1943); Schneider v. State, 308 U.S. 147 (1939), and live entertainment, Schad v. Mount Ephraim, 452 U.S. 61 (1981). Although prohibitions foreclosing entire media may be completely free of content or viewpoint discrimination, the danger they pose to the freedom of speech is readily apparent—by eliminating a common means of speaking, such measures can suppress too much speech.

Ladue contends, however, that its ordinance is a mere regulation of the "time, place, or manner" of speech because residents remain free to convey their desired messages by other means, such as hand-held signs, "letters, handbills, flyers, telephone calls, newspaper advertisements, bumper stickers, speeches, and neighborhood or community meetings." However, even regulations that do not foreclose an entire medium of expression, but merely shift the time, place, or manner of its use, must "leave open ample alternative channels for communication." Clark v. Community for Creative Non-Violence, 468 U.S. 288, 293 (1984). In this case, we are not persuaded that adequate substitutes exist for the important medium of speech that Ladue has closed off. *adequate substitutes*

Displaying a sign from one's own residence often carries a message quite distinct from placing the same sign someplace else, or conveying the same text or picture by other means. Precisely because of their location, such signs provide information about the identity of the "speaker." As an early and eminent student of rhetoric observed, the identity of the speaker is an important component of many attempts to persuade.[18] A sign advocating "Peace in the Gulf" in the front lawn of a retired general or decorated war veteran may provoke a different reaction than the same sign in a 10-year-old child's bedroom window or the same message on a bumper sticker of a passing automobile. An espousal of socialism may carry different implications when displayed on the grounds of a stately mansion than when pasted on a factory wall or an ambulatory sandwich board.

Residential signs are an unusually cheap and convenient form of communication. Especially for persons of modest means or limited mobility, a yard or window sign may have no practical substitute. Even for the affluent, the added costs in money or time of taking out a newspaper advertisement, handing out leaflets on the street, or standing in front of one's house with a handheld sign may make the difference between participating and not participating in some public debate. Furthermore, a person who puts up a sign at her residence often intends to reach neighbors, an audience that could not be reached nearly as well by other means.

A special respect for individual liberty in the home has long been part of our culture and our law; that principle has special resonance when the government seeks to constrain a person's ability to speak there. Most Americans would be understandably dismayed, given that tradition, to learn that it was illegal to display from their window an 8- by 11-inch sign expressing their political views. Whereas the government's need to mediate among various competing uses, including expressive ones, for public streets and facilities is constant and unavoidable, its need to regulate temperate speech from the home is surely much less pressing.

Our decision that Ladue's ban on almost all residential signs violates the First Amendment by no means leaves the City powerless to address the ills that may be associated with residential signs. It bears mentioning that individual residents themselves have strong incentives to keep their own property values up and to prevent "visual clutter" in their own yards and neighborhoods—incentives markedly different from those of persons who erect signs on others' land, in others' neighborhoods, or on public property. Residents' self-interest diminishes the danger of the "unlimited" proliferation of residential signs that concerns the City of Ladue. We are confident that more temperate measures could in large part satisfy Ladue's stated regulatory needs without harm to the First Amendment rights of its citizens. As currently framed, however, the ordinance abridges those rights.

Accordingly, the judgment of the Court of Appeals is Affirmed.

18. See Aristotle 2, Rhetoric, Book 1, ch. 2, in 8 Great Books of the Western World, Encyclopedia Brittanica 595 (M. Adler ed., 2d ed. 1990) ("We believe good men more fully and more readily than others: this is true generally whatever the question is, and absolutely true where exact certainty is impossible and opinions are divided").

NOTES, PROBLEMS, AND QUESTIONS

1. City of Ladue v. Gilleo is analyzed in Stephanie L. Bunting, Note, Unsightly Politics: Aesthetics, Sign Ordinances, and Homeowners' Speech in *City of Ladue v. Gilleo*, 20 Harv. Envtl. L. Rev. 473 (1996); see also David Burnett, Note, Judging the Aesthetics of Billboards, 23 J.L. & Pol. 171 (2007); R. Douglas Bond, Note, Making Sense of Billboard Law, 88 Mich. L. Rev. 2482 (1990).

2. *Signs.* Suppose that a property owner lawfully operates within her home a travel business specializing in cruise ship vacations. She posts a seven and one-half foot anchor in her yard. The city cites this as a violation of its ordinance prohibiting signs advertising home businesses. What result? See Houghtaling v. Medina Bd. of Zoning Appeals, 731 N.E.2d 733 (Ohio App. 1999) (whether or not the anchor is a sign, it is not a sign that advertises the cruise business). May signs advertising lawful home businesses be banned in any event? See, e.g., City of Rochester Hills v. Schultz, 592 N.W.2d 69 (Mich. 1999). On zoning and home businesses generally, see Nicole S. Garnett, On Castles and Commerce: Zoning Law and the Home-Business Dilemma, 42 Wm. & Mary L. Rev. 1191 (2001).

Sometimes the mere characterization of an object as a sign can get a municipality in trouble. For example, in Neighborhood Enterprises, Inc. v. City of St. Louis, 644 F.3d 728 (8th Cir. 2011), a civic organization concerned with eminent domain abuses commissioned a "sign/mural" consisting of the words "End Eminent Domain Abuse" inside a red circle and slash to be painted on a building. The city characterized the "object" as a sign and denied the permit. The civic organization characterized it as a mural and therefore not subject to the regulations. The appellate court held that the zoning code's definition of "sign" was content-based since one must look to the content of the expression to determine whether it was subject to regulation in the first place. 644 F.3d at 736. The court applied strict scrutiny and invalidated the regulation as violative of the First Amendment. 644 F.3d at 738.

3. *Art of one sort or another.* Suppose a property owner places in the front yard a sculpture made of "found art"—junk and other castoff items picked up by a sculptor and arranged in a fashion pleasing to the sculptor and the property owner. The neighbors think it's ugly. May the city require its removal? See Galina Krasilovsky, Note, A Sculpture Is Worth a Thousand Words: The First Amendment Rights of Homeowners Publicly Displaying Art on Private Property, 20 Colum.-VLA J.L. & Arts 521 (1996).

Suppose an ardent feminist places in her front yard a bronze sculpture of a consummately self-assured female nude by Gaston Lachaise (see the following illustration).[19] Can she keep it there? Suppose that she paints the sculpture in life-

---

19. Gaston Lachaise, an art student age 20, met the shapely, majestic Isabel Nagle while walking along the Seine in Paris. An unhappily married Boston Brahmin, and 10 years older than Lachaise, Isabel set him on fire. Lachaise pursued her to Boston where, obsessed with Isabel's physical proportions, he began working furiously on sculptures with her as the model. He wrote her: "You are the Goddess I am searching to express in all things." After 10 years of a passionate love affair, Isabel finally consented to divorce her husband and marry Lachaise. She was the inspiration for all Lachaise's sculptures depicting the female form. Lachaise knew what he liked.

Standing Woman
by Gaston Lachaise (1932)

like colors resembling the nude body, right down to the pubic hair, as the Greeks originally painted their marble statues. Can she keep it there?

Peggy Guggenheim, who famously enjoyed many lovers, placed on the front terrace of her palazzo on the Grand Canal in Venice a bronze sculpture by Marino Marini of a young man astride a horse, with head thrown back, arms outstretched, and flaunting an erect phallus as an expression of ecstasy. The phallus was detachable and was unscrewed whenever nuns came to call. (The palazzo is now owned by the Guggenheim Museum of New York; the sculpture is still on the Venetian terrace.)

And then there's Al Goldstein, publisher of *Screw* magazine, who "placed the statue of a huge hand—with its middle finger extended—in the backyard patio of his $1 million home overlooking the Intracoastal Waterway in Pompano Beach." See Steve d'Oliveira, Publisher Wants to Give Boat Parades a Hand, South Florida Sun-Sentinel, Nov. 11, 1998, at 3B.

4. *Adult entertainment.* Government controls based on the *content* of communication are said to be subject to closer judicial scrutiny than controls that simply regulate the time, place, and manner of communication without regard to content. Yet several Supreme Court decisions regarding zoning controls on adult entertainment call the assertion into question. In recent decades the Court has approved two distinct approaches to control—in each instance against strong dissents that the zoning measures were obviously not content-neutral because they imposed selective limitations on movie theater location based exclusively on the content of the films shown. Young v. American Mini Theatres, Inc., 427 U.S. 50 (1976), upheld a Detroit ordinance that *dispersed* adult theaters by requiring that they not locate within 500 feet of a residential area nor within 1,000 feet of any two other regulated uses (adult bookstores, cabarets, and so forth). City of Renton v. Playtime Theatres, Inc., 475 U.S. 41 (1986), upheld the ordinance of a Seattle suburb that effectively *concentrated* adult theaters in about 5 percent of the city's total land area. The Court explained in *Renton* that both measures *seemed* to be content based, but in fact were time, place, and manner restrictions aimed not at content but at the secondary effects of adult theaters on the quality of urban life—a substantial interest. The Court found that neither ordinance unreasonably limited alternative avenues of communication. It contrasted Schad v. Borough of Mount Ephraim, 452 U.S. 61 (1981), invalidating an ordinance that banned live entertainment (including nude dancers) throughout the Borough of Mount Ephraim. The borough had failed to justify the "substantial restriction" there.[20] The Renton and Detroit ordinances survived because they were "narrowly tailored" to affect only entertainment demonstrated to have the unwanted secondary effects.

Subsequent to the *Mini Theatres* case, many municipalities enacted pornography zoning laws modeled on the Detroit dispersion technique. *Renton* now endorses the opposite approach as well. See generally Kimberly K. Smith, Comment, Zoning Adult Entertainment: A Reassessment of *Renton*, 79 Cal. L. Rev. 119 (1991); see also City of Los Angeles v. Alameda Books, Inc., 475 U.S. 425 (2002) (upholding Los Angeles ordinance controlling concentration of adult entertainment businesses in a given area, including congregation of multiple adult entertainment businesses in a single building), discussed in Mindi M. Jelsema, Note, Zoning Adult Businesses after *Los Angeles v. Alameda Books*, 47 St. Louis U. L.J. 1117 (2003).

---

20. Compare Barnes v. Glen Theatre, 501 U.S. 560 (1991), upholding an Indiana public indecency law proscribing public nudity across the board and thus requiring female dancers who would otherwise be nude to wear pasties and a G-string. "It is without cavil that the public indecency statute is 'narrowly tailored'; Indiana's requirement that the dancers wear at least pasties and a G-string is modest, and the bare minimum necessary to achieve the state's purpose." 501 U.S. at 572. See also City of Erie v. Pap's A.M., 529 U.S. 277 (2000), upholding a similar ordinance.

The Court of Appeals had held the Indiana statute unconstitutional, relying in part on *Schad*. See Miller v. Civil City of South Bend, 904 F.2d 1081 (7th Cir. 1990). For students interested in the general subject—public censorship of erotica—Judge Posner's concurring opinion in *Miller* is must reading. See 904 F.2d at 1089-1104.

Voyeur Dorm operates a web-casting business out of a residential home in Tampa, Florida. Five or six women live there, and paying customers can view all of their activities, 24 hours a day, seven days a week, on the Internet. Zoning officials concluded that Voyeur Dorm was a business offering adult services and thus could not operate in a residential zone, a position upheld by the trial court, but reversed on appeal. See Voyeur Dorm, L.C. v. City of Tampa, 265 F.3d 1232 (11th Cir. 2001) (ordinance does not apply to an adult entertainment business at a location not itself open to the public; the adult entertainment actually occurred in "virtual space").

5. *Art imitates death.* Thanks and a tip of the hat to Professor Michael Doran, who steered us to *The Death of Justina,* a short story by the late John Cheever. (See Cheever, Collected Stories and Other Writings 514 (2009).) In brief: Moses lives with his family in a suburb named Proxmire Manor. His wife calls him at work with the news that her elderly cousin Justina, who had been visiting, is sitting dead on the living-room sofa. Moses goes home to help with arrangements. He calls the family doctor to get a death certificate, which the doctor says he can't provide because Moses's house is in Zone B, limited to residential housing, two-acre lots, and—thanks to a provision rushed through some years before—no funeral homes, no burials, and no death ("you can't bury anything there and you can't die there"). Rejecting the doctor's advice to drive Justina's body to another zone and claim that Justina died there, in the car, Moses seeks a zoning "exception" from the mayor. That action would require a majority vote by the village council, all the members of which are out of town for a good while. The mayor says he cannot act on his own. Justina's death "happened in the wrong zone and if I make an exception for you I'll have to make an exception for everyone and this kind of morbidity, when it gets out of hand, can be very depressing. People don't like to live in a neighborhood where this sort of thing goes on all the time."

After threats from Moses, the mayor relents, making Moses promise to keep the whole business a secret. Justina is buried the next afternoon.

A lawyer would note that Moses was seeking not an exception, but a variance. Recall the discussion in Note 1, page 1003.

2. Protection of Religious Establishments and Uses

Suppose that a zoning ordinance excludes churches from residential areas. Is the ordinance unconstitutional as a significant burden on the free exercise of religion? Is it subject, at least, to close judicial scrutiny to discern whether a compelling governmental interest justifies the exclusion? Or suppose that historic preservation regulations limit the freedom of a religious group to alter its place of worship. Constitutional? See Shelley Ross Saxer, When Religion Becomes a Nuisance: Balancing Land Use and Religious Freedom When Activities of Religious Institutions Bring Outsiders into the Neighborhood, 84 Ky. L.J. 507 (1995); Mark W. Cordes, Where to Pray? Religious Zoning and the First Amendment, 35 U. Kan. L. Rev. 697 (1987); Laurie Reynolds, Zoning the Church: The Police Power

Versus the First Amendment, 64 B.U. L. Rev. 767 (1985). Or suppose that an historic preservation ordinance limits the freedom of a religious group to alter its
place of worship. Constitutional? See Richard F. Babcock & David A. Theriaque,
Landmarks Preservation Ordinances: Are the Religion Clauses Violated by Their
Application to Religious Properties?, 7 J. Land Use & Envtl. L. 165 (1992).

In an effort to expand protection of religious institutions, Congress enacted
the Religious Freedom Restoration Act of 1993. The legislation (RFRA) required
courts to apply strict scrutiny to any government rule or law that substantially burdened a person's exercise of religion, regardless of whether the law was intended
to do so. RFRA was declared unconstitutional in City of Boerne v. Flores, 521
U.S. 507 (1997), as exceeding congressional enforcement powers under the
Fourteenth Amendment. Congress responded with the Religious Land Use and
Institutionalized Persons Act of 2000, 42 U.S.C. §§2000CC-1 through 2000CC-5,
designed to avoid the objections raised in *Flores*. The new legislation (RLUIPA)
prohibits land use regulations that impose substantial burdens on religious exercise unless the government demonstrates that the regulation is in furtherance
of a compelling governmental interest and is the least restrictive means of furthering that interest; further provisions prohibit regulations that treat religious
institutions unequally relative to nonreligious institutions, otherwise discriminate
against them, or totally exclude them from a jurisdiction. The legislative development of RLUIPA is thoroughly described in Kevin M. Powers, The Sword and the
Shield: RLUIPA and the New Battle Ground of Religious Freedom, 22 Buff. Pub.
Int. L.J. 145 (2003-2004).

Guru Nanak Sikh Society of Yuba City v. County of Sutter

United States Court of Appeals, Ninth Circuit, 2006
456 F.3d 978

BEA, CIRCUIT JUDGE: We must decide whether a local government's denial of a
religious group's application for a conditional use permit to construct a temple
on a parcel of land zoned "agricultural" constituted a "substantial burden" under
the Religious Land Use and Institutionalized Persons Act of 2000 (RLUIPA), 42
U.S.C. §§2000cc, et seq. . . .

I. Facts and Background

A. Denial of Guru Nanak's First CUP Application

Guru Nanak is a non-profit organization dedicated to fostering the teachings
and practices of the Sikh religion. In 2001, Guru Nanak attempted to obtain a
conditional use permit (CUP) for the construction of a Sikh temple—a *gurud-
wara*—on its 1.89-acre property on Grove Road in Yuba City ("the Grove Road
property"). . . . The Grove Road property was in an area designated for low density residential use (R-1), intended mainly for large lot single family residences;

churches and temples are only conditionally permitted in R-1 districts, through issuance of a CUP.

The Sutter County Planning Division, part of the County Community Services Department, issued a report recommending that the Planning Commission grant a CUP for the Grove Road property. The report stated that while the permit presented potential conflicts with established residences in the area, the conflicts could be minimized by specifically recommended conditions that would be consistent with the General Plan of Sutter County. However, at a public meeting, the Planning Commission voted unanimously to deny the CUP. The denial was based on citizens' voiced fears that the resulting noise and traffic would interfere with the existing neighborhood. Following the Commission's denial, Guru Nanak began searching for a different parcel of property for the proposed temple.

B.   Denial of Guru Nanak's Second CUP Application

In 2002, Guru Nanak acquired the property at issue in this case, a 28.79-acre parcel located on George Washington Boulevard in an unincorporated area of the County, to build a temple there. The site is zoned "AG" (general agricultural district) in the Sutter County Zoning Code. As in R-1 districts, churches and temples are only conditionally permitted in AG districts, through issuance of a CUP. . . .

Guru Nanak filed an application for a CUP to build a temple limited to approximately 2,850 square feet on the proposed site. The proposed use of the property was for a Sikh temple, assembly hall, worship services, and weddings. . . . Various county and state departments reviewed Guru Nanak's application and added a variety of conditions regarding the environmental impact of the proposed use including a twenty-five foot "no development" buffer along the north side of the property, a requirement that ceremonies remain indoors, and required landscaping. . . .

The Planning Commission held a public meeting to consider Guru Nanak's permit application. A member of Guru Nanak testified that while its previous application was for a 1.9-acre lot in a residential area, the subject application pertained to a 28.8-acre lot that did not border anyone's front or back yard. He also stated that Guru Nanak would accept all the Planning Division's proposed conditions on the land's use. Various potential neighbors spoke against the proposed temple, complaining mainly that the temple would increase traffic and noise, interfere with the agricultural use of their land, and lower property values. The Commission approved the application 4-3, subject to the conditions required by the Planning Division and stipulated to by Guru Nanak, with the commissioners echoing the reasoning voiced by both sides.

Several neighbors filed timely appeals to the Sutter County Board of Supervisors. . . .

The four-member Board of Supervisors unanimously reversed the Planning Commission's approval and denied Guru Nanak's application. Supervisor Kroon flatly rejected the project based on the "right to farm": the property had been agricultural and should remain so. He argued that long-time farmers should not be affected by someone who wishes to change the use of the property. Supervisor Nelson stated that he was concerned that Guru Nanak's proposed use "was too far away from the city" and would not promote orderly growth. He commented that such development is detrimental to the surrounding agricultural uses and that Guru Nanak should locate its church nearer to his and other existing churches. Supervisors Munger and Silva agreed that the proposed temple site's separation from existing infrastructure, termed "leapfrog development," was a poor idea and denied the application on that ground. . . .

II. Analysis

. . . We decide that the County made an individualized assessment of Guru Nanak's CUP, thereby making RLUIPA applicable, and that the County's denial of Guru Nanak's CUP application constituted a substantial burden, as that phrase is defined by RLUIPA. . . .

A. Statutory Claim Under RLUIPA

RLUIPA is Congress's latest effort to protect the free exercise of religion guaranteed by the First Amendment from governmental regulation. In Employment Division, Department of Human Resources of Oregon v. Smith, 494 U.S. 872, 878-82(1990), the Supreme Court decided that the Free Exercise Clause of the First Amendment "does not inhibit enforcement of otherwise valid laws of general application that incidentally burden religious conduct." Cutter v. Wilkinson, 544 U.S. 709 (2005).

In 1993, Congress enacted the Religious Freedom and Restoration Act of (RFRA) in response to the Supreme Court's decision in Smith. RFRA "prohibit[ed] '[g]overnment' from 'substantially burden[ing]' a person's exercise of religion even if the burden results from a rule of general applicability unless the government [could] demonstrate the burden '(1) [was] in furtherance of a compelling governmental interest; and (2) [was] the least restrictive means of furthering that compelling governmental interest.'" City of Boerne v. Flores, 521 U.S. 507, 515-16 (1997) (second and third alterations in original) (quoting 42 U.S.C. §2000bb-1). In City of Boerne, though, the Supreme Court invalidated RFRA, deciding that it was an unconstitutional exercise of congressional power pursuant to Section Five of the Fourteenth Amendment because of a "lack of proportionality or congruence between the means adopted and the legitimate end to be achieved." Id. at 533.

Congress enacted RLUIPA in response to the constitutional flaws with RFRA identified by City of Boerne. "RLUIPA 'replaces the void provisions of RFRA[,]' and prohibits the government from imposing 'substantial burdens' on 'religious exercise' unless there exists a compelling governmental interest and the burden is the least restrictive means of satisfying the governmental interest." San Jose Christian [College v. City of Morgan Hill], 360 F.3d [1024,] 1033-34 [(9th Cir. 2004)] (quoting Wyatt v. Terhune, 315 F.3d 1108, 1112 (9th Cir. 2003) (citation omitted). To avoid RFRA's fate, Congress wrote that RLUIPA would apply only to regulations regarding land use and prison conditions.

RLUIPA applies only if one of three conditions obtain: (1) If the state "program or activity receives Federal financial assistance," 42 U.S.C. §2000cc(2)(A), implicating congressional authority pursuant to the Spending Clause; (2) if the substantial burden imposed by local law "affects . . . [or] would affect, commerce with foreign nations, among the several States, or with Indian tribes," id. §2000cc(2)(B), implicating congressional power pursuant to the Commerce Clause; (3) or, as Guru Nanak argues here, if "the substantial burden is imposed in the *implementation of a land use regulation* or system of land use regulations, under which a government makes, or has in place formal or informal procedures or practices that permit the government to make, *individualized assessments* of the proposed uses for the property involved," 42 U.S.C. §2000cc(2)(C) (emphasis added).

1.   Individualized Land Use Assessments

Before we apply the terms of RLUIPA, of course, we first must determine if RLUIPA even applies, by examining whether the actions of the County are "individualized assessments of the proposed uses for the property involved." Id. The County argues that its denial of Guru Nanak's second CUP application falls outside the legislative scope of RLUIPA because its use permit process is a neutral law of general applicability. However, the plain meaning of §2000cc(2)(C), quoted above, belies this contention. RLUIPA applies when the government may take into account the particular details of an applicant's proposed use of land when deciding to permit or deny that use.

The Sutter County Zoning Code does not permit churches as a matter of right in any of the six types of zoned areas available for church construction. Rather, an entity intending to build a church must first apply for a CUP and be approved by the County. The Zoning Code states, "The County realizes that certain uses . . . may have the potential to negatively impact adjoining properties and uses. Such uses therefore require a more comprehensive review and approval procedure in order to evaluate and mitigate any potentially detrimental impacts." §1500-8210. The Zoning Code also outlines how the Sutter County Planning Commission, which has original jurisdiction over such use applications, should determine whether to approve or reject an application:

> The Planning Commission may approve or conditionally approve a use permit if it finds that the establishment, maintenance, or operation of the use or building applied for will or will not, *under the circumstances of the particular case*, be detrimental to the health, safety, and general welfare of persons residing or working in the neighborhood of such proposed use, or be detrimental or injurious to property and improvement in the neighborhood or to the general welfare of the County. Additionally, the Commission shall find that the use or activity approved by the use permit is consistent with the General Plan [of Sutter County].

§§1500-8216 (emphasis added).

The County Board of Supervisors reviews the Planning Commission's conditional use decisions "de novo and all applications, papers, maps, exhibits and staff recommendations made or presented to the Planning Commission may be considered." Id. §1500-312(f). The Sutter County Zoning Code directs the Planning Commission and the Board of Supervisors to "implement [its] system of land use regulations [by making] individualized assessments of the proposed uses of the land involved." 42 U.S.C. §2000cc.

By its own terms, it appears that RLUIPA does not apply directly to land use regulations, such as the Zoning Code here, which typically are written in general and neutral terms. However, when the Zoning Code is applied to grant or deny a certain use to a particular parcel of land, that application is an "implementation" under 42 U.S.C. §2000cc(2)(C). . . . RLUIPA therefore governs the actions of the County in this case.

2. *Substantial Burden Under RLUIPA*

We next turn to the issue whether the County's denial of Guru Nanak's CUP application substantially burdened its religious exercise within the meaning of RLUIPA.

The statute states, in relevant part:

(a) Substantial burdens

(1) General rule

No government shall impose or implement a land use regulation in a manner that imposes a *substantial burden on the religious exercise* of a person, including a religious assembly or institution, unless the government demonstrates that imposition of the burden on that person, assembly, or institution —
 (A) is in furtherance of a compelling governmental interest; and
 (B) is the least restrictive means of furthering that compelling governmental interest.
42 U.S.C. §2000cc (emphasis added).

Guru Nanak bears the burden to prove the County's denial of its application imposed a substantial burden on its religious exercise. Id. §2000cc-2(b). . . .

[I]nterpreting RLUIPA, this court has held: "[F]or a land use regulation to impose a 'substantial burden,' it must be 'oppressive' to a 'significantly great' extent. That is, a 'substantial burden' on 'religious exercise' must impose a significantly great restriction or onus upon such exercise." *San Jose Christian*, 360 F.3d at 1034 (quoting Merriam-Webster's Collegiate Dictionary 1170 (10th ed. 2002)). Applying *San Jose Christian*'s definition of a substantial burden to the particular facts here, we find the district court correctly granted summary judgment for Guru Nanak. Most important to us the history behind Guru Nanak's two CUP application processes, and the reasons given for ultimately denying these applications, to a significantly great extent lessened the possibility that future CUP applications would be successful. See Saints Constantine & Helen Greek Orthodox Church, Inc. v. City of New Berlin, 396 F.3d 895, 899-900 (7th Cir. 2005) ("*Saint Constantine*") (finding that, to prove a substantial burden under RLUIPA, a religious group need not "show that there was no other parcel of land on which it could build its church"). We need not and do not decide that failing to provide a religious institution with a land use entitlement for a new facility for worship necessarily constitutes a substantial burden pursuant to RLUIPA. At the same time, we do decide the County imposed a substantial burden here based on two considerations: (1) that the County's broad reasons given for its tandem denials could easily apply to all future applications by Guru Nanak; and (2) that Guru Nanak readily agreed to every mitigation measure suggested by the Planning Division, but the County, without explanation, found such cooperation insufficient.

The Zoning Code permits churches in six types of districts. Churches must apply for a CUP within any or all of the six available districts. Each of the district classifications available to churches is intended to provide an area for a distinct form of development. The CUP application process is intended to ensure that a religious group's proposed property use conforms with the type of development that the particular district contemplates.

Guru Nanak initially applied for a CUP to construct a Sikh temple on a 1.89-acre property in an R-1 (One Family Residence) District. The Sutter County Community Services Department had recommended approval of the proposed use because mitigation measures, agreed to by Guru Nanak, would have minimized conflicts with surrounding land. Nevertheless, the County Planning Commission unanimously rejected the application, citing neighbors' complaints regarding increased noise and traffic. . . .

[Next], Guru Nanak proposed a smaller temple, with the same seventy-five person capacity, on a much larger parcel of agricultural land. The agricultural parcel left much more space between the temple and adjacent properties; that space mitigated the temple's noise and traffic impact on surrounding persons. Both the Community Services Department and the Planning Commission approved this second application because the parcel's size, along with additional setback and use conditions, adequately addressed the noise, traffic, and other complaints related to the temple's possible impact on surrounding agricultural uses.

The County Board of Supervisors' denial of Guru Nanak's second application frustrated Guru Nanak's attempt to comply both with the reasons given for the County's first denial and the Planning Division's various requirements for Guru Nanak to locate a temple on land zoned "agricultural." The Board's primary reason for denying Guru Nanak's second application was that the temple would contribute to "leapfrog development." Although the Zoning Code conditionally permits churches and other non-agricultural activities within agricultural districts, the County could use its concern with leapfrog development effectively to deny churches access to all such land; a great majority of agriculturally zoned land near Yuba City is separated from existing urban development. Moreover, many other churches already exist on agriculturally zoned land, including another Sikh temple located on Bogue Road less than a mile away from the proposed temple. The Bogue Road Sikh temple's parcel of land, like Guru Nanak's land, is surrounded by other agricultural parcels of land, to the extent such parcels are within Yuba City's sphere of influence. Hence, the County inconsistently applied its concern with leapfrog development to Guru Nanak. At the very least, such inconsistent decision-making establishes that any future CUP applications for a temple on land zoned "agricultural" would be fraught with uncertainty. . . .

In denying the second CUP application, the Board of Supervisors disregarded, without explanation, the Planning Division's finding that Guru Nanak's acceptance of various mitigation conditions would make the proposed temple have a less-than-significant impact on surrounding land uses. We "cannot view [the denial of the second CUP application] 'in isolation'; [rather, it] 'must be viewed in the context of [Guru Nanak's permit process] history.'" See Westchester Day Sch. v. Vill. of Mamaroneck, 417 F. Supp. 2d 477, 548 (S.D.N.Y. 2006) (quoting Living Water Church of God v. Charter Twp. of Meridian, 384 F. Supp. 2d 1123, 1134 (W.D. Mich. 2005)). . . . Guru Nanak agreed to every mitigation condition the Planning Division found necessary to recommend the land entitlements. Regarding the second application in particular, Guru Nanak agreed to a host of conditions proposed specifically to allay the County's concerns with leapfrog development—including a one-hundred foot setback to allow for pesticide spraying, and that all its religious ceremonies be held indoors and limited to seventy-five people. Nevertheless, in denying the second application, the Board of Supervisors neither related why any of such mitigation conditions were inadequate nor suggested additional conditions that would render satisfactory Guru Nanak's application. . . .

The net effect of the County's two denials—including their underlying rationales and disregard for Guru Nanak's accepted mitigation conditions—is to shrink the large amount of land theoretically available to Guru Nanak under the Zoning Code to several scattered parcels that the County may or may not ultimately approve.[21] Because the County's actions have to a significantly great extent lessened the prospect of Guru Nanak being able to construct a temple in the future, the County has imposed a substantial burden on Guru Nanak's religious exercise. . . .

3. Compelling Interests

The County effectively concedes that it has no compelling interest, much less that the restrictions are narrowly tailored to accomplish such interest. The County presents no such argument in its briefs. Because the County "shall bear the burden of persuasion," 42 U.S.C. §2000cc-2(b), to prove narrowly tailored,

---

21. In denying Guru Nanak's second application, the Board of Supervisors assured Guru Nanak that it would support a future application "if it was in the right location . . . closer towards Yuba City . . . further to the north of this site along with several other churches." The Board of Supervisors also advised that it would informally cooperate with Guru Nanak to locate a suitable site. Admittedly, the availability of other suitable property weighs against a finding of a substantial burden. See San Jose Christian, 360 F.3d at 1035. However, RLUIPA does not contemplate that local governments can use broad and discretionary land use rationales as leverage to select the precise parcel of land where a religious group can worship. See Saint Constantine, 396 F.3d at 900 (noting that RLUIPA's substantial burden test aims to protect religious groups from "subtle forms of discrimination when, as in the case of the grant or denial of zoning variances, a state delegates essentially standardless discretion to nonprofessionals operating without procedural safeguards"). Moreover, given that Guru Nanak had repeatedly followed the guidance of governmental bodies about how to obtain a land entitlement to no avail, we cannot credit the Board's offer to cooperate as assuring Guru Nanak's future success.

compelling interests, we hold that the district court properly invalidated the County's denial of Guru Nanak's CUP application. . . .

III. CEQA Analysis and Injunctive Relief

. . . The County claims that the district court's injunction violated the California Environmental Quality Act (CEQA), Cal. Pub. Res. Code §21000, et seq., when it ordered the County immediately to approve Guru Nanak's CUP application. The district court did not abuse its discretion, however, because the County has already fully reviewed the environmental impact of the application without stating any deficiency. If residents had not appealed the Planning Commission's decision, the Commission's review of the Planning Division's detailed environmental impact report on Guru Nanak's application would have been final. In fact, the Planning Division attached thirty-three detailed conditions to its approval of Guru Nanak's application—all dealing with the environmental impact of the proposed temple. Neither a Commission member nor a Board member ever disagreed with the Planning Division's conclusion that Guru Nanak's application, subject to several mitigation measures, complied with CEQA. . . .

IV. Conclusion

We AFFIRM the district court's order granting summary judgment for Guru Nanak and enjoining the County immediately to approve and grant Guru Nanak's CUP application.

NOTES AND QUESTIONS

1. As the Ninth Circuit observed in *Guru Nanak*, RLUIPA is the latest attempt by Congress to shore up protection of the free exercise of religion guaranteed by the First Amendment. RLUIPA attempts to cure the infirmities of RFRA that led the Supreme Court to hold that RFRA was unconstitutional. To date, the Supreme Court has ruled on the constitutionality of the institutionalized persons' provision of the RLUIPA, but not on the land use provision. See Cutter v. Wilkinson, 544 U.S. 709, 713, 716 n.3 (2005) (holding that the institutionalized persons' provision does not violate the Establishment Clause of the First Amendment, and expressing no view on the validity of the land use provision).

Despite the lack of a decision from the Supreme Court, all of the Circuit Courts that have heard cases involving RLUIPA's land use provision have determined that it is a constitutional exercise of congressional power under the First, Tenth, and Fourteenth Amendments. See, e.g., Westchester Day School v. Village of Mamaroneck, 504 F.3d 338, 353-356 (2d Cir. 2007); Guru Nanak Sikh Society of Yuba City v. County of Sutter, 456 F.3d 978, 992-995 (9th Cir. 2006); and Midrash Sephardi, Inc. v. Town of Surfside, 366 F.3d 1214, 1219 (11th Cir. 2004).

2. As with *Guru Nanak*, most of the cases involving RLUIPA's land use provision consider whether the plaintiff's religious exercise was substantially burdened by the defendant. To resolve the matter, courts have to wrestle with two distinct questions: Did the government's regulation burden the "exercise of religion"? If so, was the burden a "substantial" one? Religious exercise is defined as "any exercise of religion, whether or not compelled by, or central to, a system of religious belief." 42 U.S.C. §2000cc-5(7)(A). In *Guru Nanak*, the question of religious exercise was not at issue. The religious group was seeking to build a temple for religious observance. But not all cases are so easy. For example, take the case of a religious group whose members believed in helping the poor. Would the denial of a conditional use permit to allow the use of church land for a homeless shelter or affordable housing constitute an element of religious exercise? See, e.g., Greater Bible Way v. City of Jackson, 733 N.W.2d 734 (Mich. 2007) (affordable housing); Westgate Tabernacle, Inc. v. Palm Beach County, 14 So. 3d 1027 (Fla. App. 2009) (homeless shelter). See generally Shelley Ross Saxer, Faith in Action: Religious Accessory Uses and Land Use Regulation, 2008 Utah L. Rev. 593.

3. *"Substantial burden."* RLUIPA does not explicitly define "substantial burden." In a RLUIPA case preceding *Guru Nanak*, the Ninth Circuit defined substantial burden as anything that is significantly oppressive. San Jose Christian Coll. v. City of Morgan Hill, 360 F.3d 1024, 1034 (9th Cir. 2004). It has also held that a city's interest in preserving its tax base is not sufficiently compelling to defeat a substantial burden claim, opening possibilities for further RLUIPA claims. See Intl. Church of Foursquare Gospel v. City of San Leandro, 673 F.3d 1059 (9th Cir. 2011). Most of the other Circuit Courts that have heard RLUIPA cases have interpreted the meaning of substantial burden in a manner similar to the Ninth Circuit. See, e.g., Westchester Day School v. Village of Mamaroneck, 504 F.3d 338, 349 (2d Cir. 2007) (finding that there must be a substantial connection between the coerced or impeded conduct and the religious exercise of the institution for the conduct to constitute a substantial burden on that religious exercise); Saints Constantine & Helen Greek Orthodox Church, Inc. v. City of New Berlin, 396 F.3d 895, 901 (7th Cir. 2005) (finding that a burden does not have to be insurmountable to be substantial with respect to the RLUIPA); Lovelace v. Lee, 472 F.3d 174, 187 (4th Cir. 2006) (determining that a substantial burden exists when the plaintiff is substantially pressured by the government to modify her behavior in violation of her religious beliefs). But see Midrash Sephardi, Inc. v. Town of Surfside, 366 F.3d 1214, 1227 (11th Cir. 2004) (adopting a stricter definition of substantial burden than the Seventh Circuit in determining that a substantial burden only exists if the plaintiff has been effectively coerced into changing her religious behavior).

For a description of each federal circuit's version of the substantial burden test, see Adam J. Macleod, Resurrecting the Bogeyman: The Curious Forms of the Substantial Burden Test in RLUIPA, 40 Real Est. L.J. 115 (2011).

4. *"Equal terms."* While the substantial burden claim is the most common land use claim raised under RLUIPA, it is not the only claim available. Another

land use claim often raised under RLUIPA comes from the equal terms provision, which states that religious assemblies and institutions cannot be treated differently than non-religious assemblies and institutions. 42 U.S.C. §2000cc(b)(1). Thus, if a religious institution is forced to get a conditional use permit to hold religious assemblies in an area where non-religious groups can hold similar assemblies without having to get a conditional use permit, the religious institution might have a valid RLUIPA claim under the equal terms provision. One of the advantages of the equal terms claim is that a plaintiff does not have to prove that it was substantially burdened. See, e.g., Digrugilliers v. Consolidated City of Indianapolis, 506 F.3d 613, 616 (7th Cir. 2007).

RLUIPA's equal terms clause may seem straightforward, but courts have taken several approaches in applying it. The Eleventh Circuit subjects any ordinance that differentiates between religious and secular assemblies to strict scrutiny. See *Midrash Sephardi, Inc.*, 366 F.3d at 1214. The Third, Seventh, and Ninth Circuits, however, hold that a violation of the equal terms clause occurs only if a religious institution is treated less well than a similarly situated non-religious entity. See Lighthouse Inst. for Evangelism, Inc. v. City of Long Branch, 510 F.3d 253 (3d Cir. 2007); River of Life Kingdom Ministries v. Village of Hazel Crest, Ill., 611 F.3d 367 (7th Cir. 2010) (en banc); Centro Familiar Cristiano Buenas Nuevas v. City of Yuma, 651 F.3d 1163, 1172 (9th Cir. 2011). But there are differences in approach among these three circuits too. The Third Circuit requires the similarly situated non-religious entity to be similarly situated with respect to the "regulatory purpose" (see *Lighthouse*), whereas the Seventh and Ninth Circuits require that it be similarly situated with respect to "accepted zoning criteria" (see *River of Life* and *Centro Familiar*). A recent Fifth Circuit decision seems to have combined the two approaches. See Opulent Life Church v. City of Holly Springs, 697 F.3d 279, 292-293 (5th Cir. 2012).

Recall that the equal terms clause of RLUIPA operates independently of the substantial burden clause. What are the advantages of allowing religious assemblies to pursue RLUIPA actions under this provision, without having to show a substantial burden? For a summary of each circuit's approach to RLUIPA equal terms claims, see Peter T. Reed, Note, What Are Equal Terms Anyway?, 87 Notre Dame L. Rev. 1313 (2012).

5. If a religious assembly wins a RLUIPA claim, what remedies are available? The statute does not provide specific guidance, stating simply that plaintiffs may "obtain appropriate relief against a government." 42 U.S.C.A. §2000cc-2. But what is "appropriate relief"? In a case interpreting the provisions of RLUIPA that apply to institutionalized persons (such as prisoners), the Supreme Court recently held that plaintiffs are not entitled to money damages, but did not extend its holding to the statute's land use provisions. See Sossamon v. Texas, 131 S. Ct. 1651 (2011). The Ninth Circuit, meanwhile, has explicitly distinguished *Sossamon*'s holding for land use plaintiffs, and left the door open for money damages against municipalities. See *Centro Familiar Cristiano Buenas Nuevas*, 651 F.3d at 1163, 1168; see also Daniel P. Dalton, The Religious Land Use and Institutionalized Persons Act—Recent Developments, 43 Urb. Law. 853, 875 (2011).

6. RLUIPA was enacted in part to alleviate the perceived problem of discrimination against churches in land use. For example, according to the Joint Statement of Senators Edward Kennedy and Orrin Hatch in support of the bill, "churches in general, and new, small, or unfamiliar churches in particular, are frequently discriminated against on the face of zoning codes and also in the highly individualized and discretionary processes of land use regulation." See 146 Cong. Rec. S7774 (July 27, 2000); Patricia E. Salkin & Amy Lavine, The Genesis of RLUIPA and Federalism: Evaluating the Creation of a Federal Statutory Right and Its Impact on Local Government, 40 Urb. Law. 195 (2008). Yet in the wake of RLUIPA's passage, there has been strenuous debate among commentators over whether there is actually widespread discrimination by municipalities against religious uses. Why might such discrimination exist? Why are existing First Amendment protections not sufficient? See Bram Alden, Comment, Reconsidering RLUIPA: Do Religious Land Use Protections Really Benefit Religious Land Users?, 57 UCLA L. Rev. 1779 (2010); Mark Chaves & William Tsitsos, Are Congregations Constrained by Government? Empirical Results from the National Congregations Study, 42 J. Church & St. 335, 342 (2000); Stephen Clowney, Comment, An Empirical Look at Churches in the Zoning Process, 116 Yale L.J. 859 (2007); Daniel P. Lennington, Thou Shalt Not Zone: The Overbroad Applications and Troubling Implications of RLUIPA's Land Use Provisions, 29 Seattle U. L. Rev. 805 (2006). For community perceptions about the need for RLUIPA in areas affected by litigation under the law, see Peter Applebome, A Court Decision Elbows a Village in Favor of Religious Rights, N.Y. Times, Oct. 21, 2007, at A24.

3. Environmental Protection

Zoning and land use regulation are increasingly intertwined with issues of environmental protection. Indeed, one of the principal justifications for zoning from the time of *Euclid* until today is that regulation will keep incompatible land uses from generating externalities. In 1969, Congress passed the National Environmental Policy Act (NEPA), which requires federal agencies to submit reports on the potential environmental impacts of their actions. 42 U.S.C. §4332(C). Since the passage of NEPA, about half the states have enacted their own environmental policy acts, sometimes known as State Environmental Policy Acts, or SEPAs, which similarly require state and local government agencies to complete environmental impact statements or reports before taking or allowing actions that will affect the environment.

Environmental impact reports can have wide ranging effects on zoning. In states that have enacted SEPAs, before a rezoning or conditional use permit can be granted, an environmental impact report must be filed and the agency in charge must determine whether the project should be approved and, if so, what needs to be done to ensure that the impact on the environment will be within acceptable limits. In *Guru Nanak*, considered in the last section, the plaintiff had to satisfy the detailed requirements of the environmental impact report prepared by the Planning Division in order to get a conditional use permit to build its temple, and

managed to do so. But it is easy to envision situations where a long list of requirements would pose a serious obstacle for permit applicants, forcing them to change
locations, take legal action, or abandon the proposed action entirely.

Fisher v. Giuliani

Supreme Court of New York, Appellate Division, First Department, 2001
720 N.Y.S.2d 50

FRIEDMAN, J. This appeal involves a challenge to recent zoning amendments affecting the Manhattan Theater District. Specifically, petitioners allege that the City
was required to prepare an Environmental Impact Statement before implementing the changes to the New York City Zoning Resolution (ZR). For the reasons
that follow, we conclude that, insofar as the amendments created a mechanism
permitting the transfer, as-of-right, of a theater's development rights and implemented design controls, no Environmental Impact Statement was required.
However, because the City failed to analyze the potential environmental impact
of the amendments providing for special permits and discretionary authoriza-
tions, such amendments should be severed and annulled.

For more than 30 years, New York City has recognized the importance of the
Manhattan Theater District—a district that, by some estimates, generates $2 bil-
lion in economic activity annually and employs, in the aggregate, 250,000 people.
A crucial lynchpin in the success of the district is, of course, Broadway theaters.

. . . [I]n 1982, the City amended the Zoning Resolution in response to the
destruction of several theaters. These amendments created a new "Theater
Subdistrict" that restricted the demolition of designated theaters and attempted
to make them more viable by permitting the transfer of development rights to
nearby parcels. . . .

Unlike the earlier provisions of the Zoning Resolution, the 1998 amendments authorize the transfer of development rights from designated theaters
to receiving sites anywhere within the Theater Subdistrict. Under the proposed
amendments, the transfer is limited to a 20% increase in the base Floor-to-Area
ratio (FAR) of the receiving site, inclusive of, or in combination with, all other as-
of-right zoning incentives.[22] The transfer must be accompanied by the execution
of a covenant ensuring the continued operational soundness of the transferring
theater and its continued use as a legitimate theater, as well as a contribution to
a Theater Subdistrict Fund that, among other things, will be used to monitor
transferring theaters. . . .

In addition to the as-of-right transfer mechanism, an additional discretionary mechanism was also established in the Theater Subdistrict. Thus, at certain
sites in the district, including sites on Eighth Avenue, a developer may obtain an

---

22. Floor-to-Area ratio refers to the relationship between the amount of usable floor area that may be
constructed in a building and the area of the lot on which the building stands.

additional 20% of the base FAR via special permit or discretionary authorization (see, ZR §§81-744[b] & [c])....

Before submitting the proposed amendments for public review, the CPC [City Planning Commission], through the Environmental Assessment and Review Division of the Department of City Planning (DCP), conducted an environmental assessment as required by the State Environmental Quality Review Act (SEQRA) and our local regulations, the City Environmental Quality Review (CEQR). Under the statutory scheme, an Environmental Assessment Statement is prepared that sets forth the environmental analysis. If it is determined that the proposed action may have a significant effect on the environment (62 RCNY §5-05[b]), the agency (here CPC) must then issue a positive declaration and an Environmental Impact Statement must be prepared before the proposed zoning may be adopted (43 RCNY §6-07[b]). If, on the other hand, it is determined that the action will have no significant impact, the agency issues a negative declaration and no environmental impact statement need be prepared (43 RCNY §6-07[b][1]).

To assess the potential environmental impact of the proposed zoning changes, the DCP examined the reasonable worst case scenario that could result under the as-of-right amendments and compared it with the development that would otherwise have occurred without the amendments.... The DCP then considered the potential demand for additional development in the study area within the foreseeable future, that is, over the next ten years.

To make these future projections, DCP examined development trends in the larger midtown area during the 10-year period between 1983 through 1993.... Assuming that there would be a similar demand over the next 10 years, the DCP found that the existing zoning capacity could accommodate, more than twice over, the projected demand.

With regard to development under the proposed zoning, the DCP determined that the amendments did modestly increase the density of particular sites via the transfer of development rights from theaters.... However, this would not affect overall market conditions and would not induce development beyond what was already likely to occur.... Viewed otherwise, the higher density of specific sites would accommodate the projected demand for space—it would not change the overall demand.

Next, the DCP analyzed the potential impact that any development might have on traffic, transit, and air quality.... [T]he DCP concluded that any potential development would give rise to less than 50 peak-hour vehicle trips at any given intersection in the area. According to the CEQR Technical Manual, this was below the threshold requiring further analysis because it would not have a significant effect upon traffic and transit. Further analysis also determined that any additional traffic would have no significant impact on air quality.

As to the socioeconomic conditions of the area, the DCP analyzed whether the proposed amendments would lead to the displacement of area residents or businesses. Because the amendments would not induce development different in kind or magnitude from that which was already expected to take place, the

DCP concluded that the change in zoning would not result in any significant displacement.

The findings and conclusions reached by the DCP resulted in a negative declaration, which was supported by an Environmental Assessment Statement that included a 75-page single-spaced report. Thereafter, the Environmental Assessment Statement and negative declaration were filed with a revised Land Use Review Application on January 8, 1998, and, in accordance with public review requirements (see, New York City Charter §§197-c & 201), referred for review to Community Boards Four and Five, the Manhattan Borough Board, and the Manhattan Borough President. After public hearings at which approximately 80 people testified both for and against the proposal, and consideration of written submissions, the CPC adopted the proposed amendments on June 3, 1998.

The matter was then referred to the New York City Council pursuant to City Charter §§197-d and 200(a)(2). By resolutions dated August 6, 1998, the Council, after a further round of public hearings involving the testimony of approximately 100 people, found that no significant environmental impact would result from the proposed action and approved the amendments and map change (subject to certain modifications). This litigation ensued.

Petitioners, among whom are residents of the neighboring Special Clinton District, commenced this CPLR article 78 proceeding, seeking to challenge the adequacy of the environmental review and consequent negative declaration. According to petitioners, the underlying analysis supporting the negative declaration was deficient and preparation of an Environmental Impact Statement was warranted. . . .

Supreme Court, without reaching this latter argument, annulled the Theater Subdistrict Amendments and the Zoning Map Change and directed the DCP to prepare an Environmental Impact Statement. In so doing, the court concluded that the amendments would stimulate development, relying, in large part, upon a newspaper article about the current state of the midtown real estate market. . . .

Stripped to its essentials, the purported flaws identified by petitioners are threefold: first that the DCP (which, as noted, prepared the environmental assessment) underestimated the projected market demand for development in the Theater Subdistrict; second, that the DCP erroneously determined that the amendments would not stimulate development beyond that which would already have occurred; and, third, that the DCP improperly limited its analysis to 10 years into the future and failed to consider that every single square inch of buildable space, might, in fact, be developed. None of these claims has merit.

In analyzing a SEQRA determination, a court is required to sustain an agency's negative declaration unless the court concludes that it "was affected by an error of law or was arbitrary and capricious or an abuse of discretion." Under this standard, it is not the role of the court to weigh the desirability of the proposed action, choose among alternatives, resolve disagreements among experts, or substitute its judgment for that of the agency. Rather, the limited issue for the court's review is whether the agency identified "the relevant areas of environmental concern," took a "hard look" at them, and made a "reasoned elaboration of the basis for its determination."

Viewed against this analytical backdrop, we first address petitioners' claim that the DCP underestimated future demand in the Theater Subdistrict. This charge flows from petitioners' belief that historical development trends in the Theater Subdistrict are no longer meaningful. . . . This argument, however, ignores the forecasting method used by the DCP.

In developing its projections, the DCP examined the larger midtown area, not just the Theater Subdistrict. Thus, in applying the historic trends of the midtown area to the much smaller Theater Subdistrict, it is uncontroverted that the DCP projected future growth in excess of historic levels. Hence, this conservative forecasting method necessarily took into account relatively recent changes in the Theater Subdistrict.

With regard to the claim that the as-of-right amendments will stimulate development, it is true that certain soft sites might enjoy greater profitability (because taller buildings may be permitted). It is also true that theaters will have a wider geographic area in which to sell their development rights. But these observations, without more, do not undermine the rationality of the DCP's determination that market demand and consequent development will remain relatively constant.

As the CPC convincingly notes, potential zoning capacity will not induce development beyond that which would otherwise have occurred unless the demand for additional space exceeds current zoning capacity. Since current zoning capacity already far exceeds demand, the CPC's central conclusion is rational. . . .

Contrary to petitioners' claim, the CPC also properly considered the long-term impact of the proposed as-of-right amendments. At its core, petitioners' argument is that the CPC was required to look beyond 10 years from the enactment of the zoning amendments and assume that every single square foot of buildable area will eventually be developed, regardless of the likelihood that it will occur. This argument is without merit since the DCP was only obligated to examine environmental consequences into the foreseeable future, not to examine theoretical possibilities that were steeped in nothing more than unsupported speculation. To adopt a ten-year time frame was hardly an irrational examination of the long-term foreseeable future. . . .

What the foregoing reveals is that the DCP's detailed analysis, as reflected in the Environmental Assessment Statement, was entirely rational insofar as the as-of-right amendments were concerned. Hence, an Environmental Impact Statement was not required. This, however, does not conclude the matter.

As previously noted, in addition to the as-of-right transfer mechanism established by the zoning amendments, a discretionary mechanism was also established in the Theater Subdistrict. The DCP was of the view that no environmental review of these amendments was required because when an owner applied for a special permit, an assessment would be made at that time. Hence, the DCP believed that it could defer its analysis. This was error.

It is well settled that "SEQRA's goal [is] to incorporate environmental considerations into the decisionmaking process at the earliest opportunity" (Matter of Neville v. Koch, 79 N.Y.2d 416, 426, 583 N.Y.S.2d 802, 593 N.E.2d 256). Thus, the mere fact that environmental review may be required at the time an applicant seeks a special permit does not, by itself, obviate the CPC's obligation to consider possible environmental impact at the time it enacts the zoning changes, at least on a conceptual basis.

In reaching this conclusion, we do not suggest that the grant of additional FAR beyond that permitted as-of-right would have a significant environmental impact. It may very well be that a grant of additional FAR will have no impact. But, whatever the case may be, the DCP was obligated to consider the matter *now*, not just in the future. In view of this, we turn to the remedy for this isolated error. . . .

In sum, because the DCP failed to analyze the potential environmental impact that could arise from discretionary grants of FAR, these provisions of the Zoning Resolution are severed and annulled. However, the remaining aspects of the Zoning Resolution, which include the as-of-right and design control provisions, were enacted after the DCP took a hard look at the relevant environmental concerns and made a reasoned elaboration for its determination that no impact would result. There is, therefore, no basis for annulling these provisions of the Zoning Resolution.

NOTES AND QUESTIONS

1. *Standard of review.* As noted by the court in *Fisher*, the standard of review for overturning administrative rulings is a finding that the actions were "arbitrary and capricious." This means that even if there was substantial objection in the community regarding the plan (as there was in the case), or some disagreement as to its likely environmental impact, the court will not overturn a negative declaration unless the board acted irrationally or abused its discretion. Ultimately, the court in *Fisher* upheld the negative declaration but remanded to the City Planning Commission to determine the environmental impact of the discretionary permits. Does it make sense to mandate an environmental impact assessment for a project of unknown scope? What sorts of information would likely be revealed, and what of value would it add to the decision process?

2. *The Theater District after Fisher.* The city's plan for saving the Theater District was not widely embraced outside of the theater community. Organizations like the American Institute of Architects and the Municipal Art Society strongly opposed the plan, fearing that it would undermine zoning protections. Others were concerned about gentrification and questioned the environmental assessment's determination that there would be no displacement as a result of the plan. The litigation spurred by these concerns delayed much-needed revenue,

causing many theaters and organizations to scramble when they did not receive the $100 million windfall they were expecting from the $10 per square foot fee tacked on to the sale of the air development rights. While Fisher v. Giuliani permitted the initiative to move forward, no developers or theater-owners attempted to capitalize on the arrangement until more than five years after the court's decision. When two deals for over $20 million were set in motion in 2006, the theater owners encountered a snag in realizing the benefits of the arrangement: The city had failed to set up the fund to collect the required additional money for the theater community. The fund, now administered by the Theater Subdistrict Council, wasn't formally created until 2007. More than 10 years after the adoption of the zoning changes requiring the fund's creation, and several completed deals later, the fund now contains over $5 million and is used for grants to support theater productions and audience development. For more details on the theater subdistrict, see Michael Kruse, Constructing the Special Theater Subdistrict: Culture, Politics, and Economics in the Creation of Transferable Development Rights, 40 Urb. Law. 95 (2008).

3. *Transferable development rights.* Transferable development rights, or TDRs, are a land-use planning tool often used to allow historic or landmarked buildings to sell their air-space rights to nearby or contiguous buildings. TDRs also played an important role in Penn Central Transportation Company v. City of New York, 438 U.S. 104 (1978) (considered beginning at page 1162). That case involved the designation of New York's Grand Central Terminal as a historic landmark. The designation blocked vertical development above the station, a blow softened by permitting Grand Central's owner, Penn Central, to transfer its air rights to eight lots located near the terminal. For more discussion of the role of TDRs in land use planning, see Note 3 on page 1177.

4. *"Little NEPAs."* SEPAs, often referred to as "Little NEPAs," differ widely in scope and impact, with some states adopting narrow thresholds and rarely mandating the preparation of an EIS, and others requiring almost any project with an administrative action to do an impact assessment. States might limit the application of their environmental review statute to projects funded by public monies—see, e.g., Md. Code Ann. Nat. Res. §1-301(c) (LexisNexis 2012)—or, as in California, and in New York's SEQRA mentioned in *Fisher*, take a more inclusive approach that requires an impact statement for any project involving a governmental action (such as the issuance of a permit, the conveyance of publicly owned land, or a rezoning). When litigation results under a SEPA, it typically centers on one of two issues: (1) If an EIS was not prepared, was the agency's finding of no significant environmental impact (called a "negative declaration") proper? (2) If an EIS was prepared, did it adequately address all the environmental concerns, including, in some states, proposed methods of mitigating adverse impacts?

Some commentators have been critical of the ultimate impact of state and local environmental review laws, particularly measures that require expensive and time-consuming impact statements for all projects at the local level. Professor

Stewart Sterk argues that SEPAs offer little in terms of increased environmental protection, and are often used by interest groups to promote agendas that have nothing to do with environmental protection. See Stewart E. Sterk, Environmental Review in the Land Use Process: New York's Experience with SEQRA, 13 Cardozo L. Rev. 2041 (1992).

5. *What is the "environment"?* While some states restrict their notion of environmental analysis to the impact on the natural surroundings, others have adopted a broader approach. For example, New York's environmental review statute, SEQRA, defines "environment" comprehensively to include "existing patterns of population concentration, distribution, or growth, and existing community or neighborhood character." N.Y. Envtl. Conserv. Law §8-0105.6 (McKinney Supp. 2013). In Chinese Staff and Workers Assn. v. City of New York, 502 N.E.2d 176 (N.Y. 1986), the court vacated a special permit after the issuance of a conditional negative declaration because the threshold review failed to consider whether a luxury building would alter the Chinatown community or result in displacement of low income residents and businesses. The court said "the impact that a project may have on population patterns or existing community character, with or without a separate impact on the physical environment, is a relevant concern in an environmental analysis since the statute includes these concerns as elements of the environment." 502 N.E.2d at 180. Recall the discussion of the impact of zoning changes on socioeconomic conditions in *Fisher*. See also Land Master Montg I, LLC v. Town of Montgomery, 821 N.Y.S.2d 432 (Sup. Ct. 2006) (holding that SEQRA compliance required examination of affordable housing availability after the proposed elimination of zoning for multi-family units).

6. *Global warming, climate change, and environmental review.* Global warming and climate change have come to play a large role in national discussions of environmental policy. Now there is a growing debate about the extent to which municipalities and developers must account for greenhouse gas emissions in order to comply with state NEPAs. A relatively recent case, Center for Biological Diversity v. Natl. Highway Traffic Safety Admin., 538 F.3d 1172 (9th Cir. 2008), held that NEPA does indeed require such analysis. But see North Carolina Alliance for Transp. Reform v. U.S. Dept. of Transp., 713 F. Supp. 2d 491, 519 (M.D.N.C. 2010) (holding that NEPA does not require consideration of the potential contribution of a highway project to global climate change).

On the state level, some states have required state NEPAs to take into account the impact of projects on global warming and to consider approaches to mitigation. California has been the leader thus far, enacting aggressive legislation that aims to reduce greenhouse gases to 1990 levels by 2020. See Global Warming Solutions Act, Cal. Health & Safety Code §§38500 et seq. (West Supp. 2013). After considerable litigation about whether California's Environmental Quality Act (CEQA) requires analysis of development impact on greenhouse gas emissions, the state enacted SB 97, which required the state office of planning and research to "prepare, develop, and transmit to the Resources Agency guidelines for the feasible mitigation of greenhouse gas emissions or the effects of greenhouse gas emissions, as required by CEQA, including, but not limited to, effects associated with transportation or energy consumption." Cal. Pub. Res. Code §21083.05 (West Supp. 2013). These regulations are set forth in 13 Cal. Admin. Code §§15000 et seq. (2013).

A requirement that cities, states, and the federal government assess the contribution of development-related greenhouse gases to global warming does not necessarily solve the problem of how to estimate such an impact. For a discussion of some of the difficulties involved, see Neal McAliley, NEPA and Assessment of Greenhouse Gas Emissions, 41 Envtl. L. Rep. 10197 (2011).

7. *Smart growth.* "Smart growth" refers to measures to reduce sprawl and associated negative environmental impacts, now common in many states. California, for example, has legislation creating incentives to reduce car travel by increasing housing density around regional transportation hubs. Oregon legislation mandates the creation of "urban growth boundaries" that set outer limits of expansion around all of the state's 241 cities. The result has been increasing population density, but not enough yet to forestall considerable sprawl in areas like Portland, often cited as a model city for smart growth. The passage of Measure 37 in 2004—requiring state or local governments either to waive growth regulation or compensate land owners for losses resulting from it—has raised questions about the future of land use planning in Oregon. See Edward J. Sullivan & Carrie A. Richter, A Taste of Ashes—The *MacPherson* Decision and the Future of Oregon's Planning Program, 58 Plan. & Envtl. Law 3 (2006). Voters ultimately passed Measure 49 in 2007, which severely limited waivers under Measure 37 and is seen as a compromise bill.

For an extensive look (over 1,400 pages) at different legislative models for smart growth, see American Planning Association, Growing Smart Legislative Guidebook: Model Statutes for Planning and the Management of Change (Stuart Meck ed. 2002).

8. *Environmental regulation and the cost of development.* Many of the measures lumped together under the smart-growth rubric are likely to increase the cost of housing and other forms of development. Measures that push development into urban cores result in higher prices for land (urban land is more expensive than land at the outskirts), labor, transportation, and materials. Environmental review requirements can increase development costs by adding delay, uncertainty, and legal expenses to the process. None of this means, of course, that the benefits of environmental improvement are not worth the costs. For discussions of the cost implications of environmental regulation, see Anthony Downs, Growth Management and Affordable Housing: Do They Conflict? (Anthony Downs ed. 2004); Charles Connerly, Smart Growth: Opportunity or Threat to Affordable Housing?, in Gerrit-Jan Knaap et al., The Role of States and Nation-States in Smart Growth Planning 103 (2007); Katherine A. Kiel, Environmental Regulations and the Housing Market: A Review of the Literature, 8 Cityscape: A Journal of Policy Development and Research 187 (2005).

4. Controls on Household Composition

Village of Belle Terre v. Boraas

Supreme Court of the United States, 1974
416 U.S. 1

JUSTICE DOUGLAS delivered the opinion of the Court.

Belle Terre is a village on Long Island's north shore of about 220 homes inhabited by 700 people. Its total land area is less than one square mile. It has restricted land use to one-family dwellings excluding lodging houses, boarding houses, fraternity houses, or multiple-dwelling houses. The word "family" as used in the ordinance means,

> [o]ne or more persons related by blood, adoption, or marriage, living and cooking together as a single housekeeping unit, exclusive of household servants. A number of persons but not exceeding two (2) living and cooking together as a single housekeeping unit though not related by blood, adoption, or marriage shall be deemed to constitute a family.

Appellees the Dickmans are owners of a house in the village and leased it in December 1971 for a term of 18 months to Michael Truman. Later Bruce Boraas became a colessee. Then Anne Parish moved into the house along with three others. These six are students at nearby State University at Stony Brook and none is related to the other by blood, adoption, or marriage. When the village served the Dickmans with an "Order to Remedy Violations" of the ordinance, the owners plus three tenants thereupon brought this action under 42 U.S.C. §1983 for an injunction and a judgment declaring the ordinance unconstitutional. The District Court held the ordinance constitutional, 367 F. Supp. 136, and the Court of Appeals reversed, one judge dissenting, 476 F.2d 806. The case is here by appeal, 28 U.S.C. §1254(2); and we noted probable jurisdiction, 414 U.S. 907.

This case brings to this Court a different phase of local zoning regulations from those we have previously reviewed. Euclid v. Ambler Realty Co., 272 U.S. 365, involved a zoning ordinance classifying land use in a given area into six categories. . . .

The main thrust of the case in the mind of the Court was in the exclusion of industries and apartments, and as respects that it commented on the desire to keep residential areas free of "disturbing noises"; "increased traffic"; the hazard of "moving and parked automobiles"; the "depriving children of the privilege of quiet and open spaces for play, enjoyed by those in more favored localities." Id. at 394. The ordinance was sanctioned because the validity of the legislative classification was "fairly debatable" and therefore could not be said to be wholly arbitrary. Id. at 388.

Our decision in Berman v. Parker, 348 U.S. 26, sustained a land use project in the District of Columbia against a landowner's claim that the taking violated the Due Process Clause and the Just Compensation Clause of the Fifth Amendment. The essence of the argument against the law was, while taking property for ridding an area of slums was permissible, taking it "merely to develop a better balanced, more attractive community" was not, id., at 31. We refused to limit the concept of public welfare that may be enhanced by zoning regulations. We said:

> Miserable and disreputable housing conditions may do more than spread disease and crime and immorality. They may also suffocate the spirit by reducing the people who live there to the status of cattle. They may indeed make living an almost insufferable burden. They may also be an ugly sore, a blight on the community which robs it of charm, which makes it a place from which men turn. The misery of housing may despoil a community as an open sewer may ruin a river.
>
> We do not sit to determine whether a particular housing project is or is not desirable. The concept of the public welfare is broad and inclusive. . . . The values it represents are spiritual as well as physical, aesthetic as well as monetary. It is within the power of the legislature to determine that the community should be beautiful as well as healthy, spacious as well as clean, well-balanced as well as carefully patrolled. [Id. at 32-33.]

If the ordinance segregated one area only for one race, it would immediately be suspect under the reasoning of Buchanan v. Warley, 245 U.S. 60, where the Court invalidated a city ordinance barring a black from acquiring real property in a white residential area by reason of an 1866 Act of Congress, 14 Stat. 27, now 42 U.S.C. §1982, and an 1870 Act, §17, 16 Stat. 144, now 42 U.S.C. §1981, both enforcing the Fourteenth Amendment. 245 U.S., at 78-82. See Jones v. Mayer Co., 392 U.S. 409.

In Seattle Trust Co. v. Roberge, 278 U.S. 116, Seattle had a zoning ordinance that permitted a "'philanthropic home for children or for old people'" in a particular district "'when the written consent shall have been obtained of the owners of two-thirds of the property within four hundred (400) feet of the proposed building.'" Id. at 118. The Court held that provision of the ordinance unconstitutional, saying that the existing owners could "withhold consent for selfish reasons or arbitrarily and may subject the trustee [owner] to their will or caprice." Id. at 122. Unlike the billboard cases (e.g., Cusack Co. v. City of Chicago, 242 U.S. 526), the Court concluded that the Seattle ordinance was invalid since the proposed home for the aged poor was not shown by its maintenance and construction "to work any injury, inconvenience or annoyance to the community, the district or any person." 278 U.S., at 122.

The present ordinance is challenged on several grounds: that it interferes with a person's right to travel; that it interferes with the right to migrate to and settle within a State; that it bars people who are uncongenial to the present residents; that it expresses the social preferences of the residents for groups that will be congenial to them; that social homogeneity is not a legitimate interest of government; that the restriction of those whom the neighbors do not like trenches on the newcomers' rights of privacy; that it is of no rightful concern to villagers whether the residents are married or unmarried; that the ordinance is antithetical to the Nation's experience, ideology, and self-perception as an open, egalitarian, and integrated society.

We find none of these reasons in the record before us. It is not aimed at transients. Cf. Shapiro v. Thompson, 394 U.S. 618. It involves no procedural disparity inflicted on some but not on others such as was presented by Griffin v. Illinois,

351 U.S. 12. It involves no "fundamental" right guaranteed by the Constitution, such as voting, Harper v. Virginia Board, 383 U.S. 663; the right of association, NAACP v. Alabama, 357 U.S. 449; the right of access to the courts, NAACP v. Button, 371 U.S. 415; or any rights of privacy, cf. Griswold v. Connecticut, 381 U.S. 479; Eisenstadt v. Baird, 405 U.S. 438, 453-454. We deal with economic and social legislation where legislatures have historically drawn lines which we respect against the charge of violation of the Equal Protection Clause if the law be " 'reasonable, not arbitrary' " (quoting Royster Guano Co. v. Virginia, 253 U.S. 412, 415) and bears "a rational relationship to a [permissible] state objective." Reed v. Reed, 404 U.S. 71, 76.

It is said, however, that if two unmarried people can constitute a "family," there is no reason why three or four may not. But every line drawn by a legislature leaves some out that might well have been included. That exercise of discretion, however, is a legislative, not a judicial, function.

It is said that the Belle Terre ordinance reeks with an animosity to unmarried couples who live together. There is no evidence to support it; and the provision of the ordinance bringing within the definition of a "family" two unmarried people belies the charge.

The ordinance places no ban on other forms of association, for a "family" may, so far as the ordinance is concerned, entertain whomever it likes.

The regimes of boarding houses, fraternity houses, and the like present urban problems. More people occupy a given space; more cars rather continuously pass by; more cars are parked; noise travels with crowds.

A quiet place where yards are wide, people few, and motor vehicles restricted are legitimate guidelines in a land use project addressed to family needs. This goal is a permissible one within Berman v. Parker, supra. The police power is not confined to elimination of filth, stench, and unhealthy places. It is ample to lay out zones where family values, youth values, and the blessings of quiet seclusion and clean air make the area a sanctuary for people. . . .[23]

Reversed.

JUSTICE MARSHALL, dissenting.

This case draws into question the constitutionality of a zoning ordinance of the incorporated village of Belle Terre, New York, which prohibits groups of more than two unrelated persons, as distinguished from groups consisting of any number of persons related by blood, adoption, or marriage, from occupying a

---

23. With Justice Douglas's pastoral paradise, compare Lewis Mumford's vision of suburbia as:

> a multitude of uniform, unidentifiable houses, lined up inflexibly, at uniform distances, on uniform roads, in a treeless communal waste, inhabited by people of the same class, the same income, the same age group, witnessing the same television performances, eating the same tasteless, prefabricated foods, from the same freezers, conforming in every outward and inward respect to a common mold.

> . . . The end product is an encapsulated life, spent more and more either in a motor car or within the cabin of darkness before a television set. . . . Here indeed we find "The Lonely Crowd." [Lewis Mumford, The City in History 486, 512 (1961).]—EDS.

residence within the confines of the township. Lessor-appellees, the two owners of a Belle Terre residence, and three unrelated student tenants challenged the ordinance on the ground that it establishes a classification between households of related and unrelated individuals, which deprives them of equal protection of the laws. In my view, the disputed classification burdens the students' fundamental rights of association and privacy guaranteed by the First and Fourteenth Amendments. Because the application of strict equal protection scrutiny is therefore required, I am at odds with my Brethren's conclusion that the ordinance may be sustained on a showing that it bears a rational relationship to the accomplishment of legitimate governmental objectives.

I am in full agreement with the majority that zoning is a complex and important function of the State. It may indeed be the most essential function performed by local government, for it is one of the primary means by which we protect that sometimes difficult to define concept of quality of life. I therefore continue to adhere to the principle of Euclid v. Ambler Realty Co., 272 U.S. 365 (1926), that deference should be given to governmental judgments concerning proper land-use allocation. That deference is a principle which has served this Court well and which is necessary for the continued development of effective zoning and land-use control mechanisms. Had the owners alone brought this suit alleging that the restrictive ordinance deprived them of their property or was an irrational legislative classification, I would agree that the ordinance would have to be sustained. Our role is not and should not be to sit as a zoning board of appeals.

I would also agree with the majority that local zoning authorities may properly act in furtherance of the objectives asserted to be served by the ordinance at issue here: restricting uncontrolled growth, solving traffic problems, keeping rental costs at a reasonable level, and making the community attractive to families. The police power which provides the justification for zoning is not narrowly confined. See Berman v. Parker, 348 U.S. 26 (1954). And, it is appropriate that we afford zoning authorities considerable latitude in choosing the means by which to implement such purposes. But deference does not mean abdication. This Court has an obligation to ensure that zoning ordinances, even when adopted in furtherance of such legitimate aims, do not infringe upon fundamental constitutional rights.

When separate but equal was still accepted constitutional dogma, this Court struck down a racially restrictive zoning ordinance. Buchanan v. Warley, 245 U.S. 60 (1917). I am sure the Court would not be hesitant to invalidate that ordinance today. The lower federal courts have considered procedural aspects of zoning, and acted to insure that land-use controls are not used as means of confining minorities and the poor to the ghettos of our central cities. These are limited but necessary intrusions on the discretion of zoning authorities. By the same token, I think it clear that the First Amendment provides some limitation on zoning laws. It is inconceivable to me that we would allow the exercise of the zoning power to burden First Amendment freedoms, as by ordinances that restrict occupancy to individuals adhering to particular religious, political, or scientific beliefs. Zoning officials properly concern themselves with the uses of land—with, for example, the number and kind of dwellings to be constructed in a certain neighborhood or the number of persons who can reside in those dwellings. But zoning authorities cannot validly consider who those persons are, what they believe, or how they choose to live, whether they are Negro or white, Catholic or Jew, Republican or Democrat, married or unmarried.

My disagreement with the Court today is based upon my view that the ordinance in this case unnecessarily burdens appellees' First Amendment freedom of association and their constitutionally guaranteed right to privacy. Our decisions establish that the First and Fourteenth Amendments protect the freedom to choose one's associates. NAACP v. Button, 371 U.S. 415, 430 (1963). Constitutional protection is extended, not only to modes of association that are political in the usual sense, but also to those that pertain to the social and economic benefit of the members. Id. at 430-431; Brotherhood of Railroad Trainmen v. Virginia Bar, 377 U.S. 1 (1964). See United Transportation Union v. State Bar of Michigan, 401 U.S. 576 (1971); Mine Workers v. Illinois State Bar Assn., 389 U.S. 217 (1967). The selection of one's living companions involves similar choices as to the emotional, social, or economic benefits to be derived from alternative living arrangements.

The freedom of association is often inextricably entwined with the constitutionally guaranteed right of privacy. The right to "establish a home" is an essential part of the liberty guaranteed by the Fourteenth Amendment. Meyer v. Nebraska, 262 U.S. 390, 399 (1923); Griswold v. Connecticut, 381 U.S. 479, 495 (1965) (Goldberg, J., concurring). And the Constitution secures to an individual a freedom "to satisfy his intellectual and emotional needs in the privacy of his own home." Stanley v. Georgia, 394 U.S. 557, 565 (1969); see Paris Adult Theatre I v. Slaton, 413 U.S. 49, 66-67 (1973). Constitutionally protected privacy is, in Mr. Justice Brandeis' words, "as against the Government, the right to be let alone . . . the right most valued by civilized man." Olmstead v. United States, 277 U.S. 438, 478 (1928) (dissenting opinion). The choice of household companions — of whether a person's "intellectual and emotional needs" are best met by living with family, friends, professional associates, or others — involves deeply personal considerations as to the kind and quality of intimate relationships within the home. That decision surely falls within the ambit of the right to privacy protected by the Constitution. See Roe v. Wade, 410 U.S. 113, 153 (1973); Eisenstadt v. Baird, 405 U.S. 438, 453 (1972); Stanley v. Georgia, supra, at 564-565; Griswold v. Connecticut, supra, at 483, 486; Olmstead v. United States, supra, at 478 (Brandeis, J., dissenting); Moreno v. Department of Agriculture, 345 F. Supp. 310, 315 (DC 1972), aff'd, 413 U.S. 528 (1973).

The instant ordinance discriminates on the basis of just such a personal lifestyle choice as to household companions. It permits any number of persons related by blood or marriage, be it two or twenty, to live in a single household, but it limits to two the number of unrelated persons bound by profession, love, friendship, religious or political affiliation, or mere economics who can occupy a single home. Belle Terre imposes upon those who deviate from the community norm in their choice of living companions significantly greater restrictions than are applied to residential groups who are related by blood or marriage, and compose the established order within the community. The village has, in effect, acted to fence out those individuals whose choice of lifestyle differs from that of its current residents.

This is not a case where the Court is being asked to nullify a township's sincere efforts to maintain its residential character by preventing the operation of rooming houses, fraternity houses, or other commercial or high density residential uses. Unquestionably, a town is free to restrict such uses. Moreover, as a general proposition, I see no constitutional infirmity in a town's limiting the density of use in residential areas by zoning regulations which do not discriminate on the basis of constitutionally suspect criteria. This ordinance, however, limits the density of occupancy of only those homes occupied by unrelated persons. It thus reaches beyond control of the use of land or the density of population, and undertakes to regulate the way people choose to associate with each other within the privacy of their own homes.

It is no answer to say, as does the majority, that associational interests are not infringed because Belle Terre residents may entertain whomever they choose. Only last Term Mr. Justice Douglas indicated in concurrence that he saw the right of association protected by the First Amendment as involving far more than the right to entertain visitors. He found that right infringed by a restriction on food stamp assistance, penalizing households of "unrelated persons." As Mr. Justice Douglas there said, freedom of association encompasses the "right to invite the stranger into one's home" not only for "entertainment" but to join the household as well. Department of Agriculture v. Moreno, 413 U.S. 528, 538-545 (1973) (concurring opinion). I am still persuaded that the choice of those who will form one's household implicates constitutionally protected rights.

Because I believe that this zoning ordinance creates a classification which impinges upon fundamental personal rights, it can withstand constitutional scrutiny only upon a clear showing that the burden imposed is necessary to protect a compelling and substantial governmental interest, Shapiro v. Thompson, 394 U.S. 618, 634 (1969). And, once it be determined that a burden has been placed upon a constitutional right, the onus of demonstrating that no less intrusive means will adequately protect the compelling state interest and that the challenged statute is sufficiently narrowly drawn, is upon the party seeking to justify the burden. See Memorial Hospital v. Maricopa County, 415 U.S. 250 (1974); Speiser v. Randall, 357 U.S. 513, 525-526 (1958).

A variety of justifications have been proffered in support of the village's ordinance. It is claimed that the ordinance controls population density, prevents noise, traffic and parking problems, and preserves the rent structure of the community and its attractiveness to families. As I noted earlier, these are all legitimate and substantial interests of government. But I think it clear that the means chosen to accomplish these purposes are both overinclusive and underinclusive, and that the asserted goals could be as effectively achieved by means of an ordinance that did not discriminate on the basis of constitutionally protected choices of lifestyle. The ordinance imposes no restriction whatsoever on the number of persons who may live in a house, as long as they are related by marital or sanguinary bonds—presumably no matter how distant their relationship. Nor does the ordinance restrict the number of income earners who may contribute to rent in such a household, or the number of automobiles that may be maintained by its occupants. In that sense the ordinance is underinclusive. On the other hand, the statute restricts the number of unrelated persons who may live in a home to no more than two. It would therefore prevent three unrelated people from occupying a dwelling even if among them they had but one income and no vehicles. While an extended family of a dozen or more might live in a small bungalow, three elderly and retired persons could not occupy the large manor house next door. Thus the statute is also grossly overinclusive to accomplish its intended purposes.

There are some 220 residences in Belle Terre occupied by about 700 persons. The density is therefore just above three per household. The village is justifiably concerned with density of population and the related problems of noise, traffic, and the like. It could deal with those problems by limiting each household to a specified number of adults, two or three perhaps, without limitation on the number of dependent children.[24] The burden of such an ordinance would fall equally upon all segments of the community. It would surely be better tailored to the goals asserted by the village than the ordinance before us today, for it would more realistically restrict population density and growth and their attendant environmental costs. Various other statutory mechanisms also suggest themselves as solutions to Belle Terre's problems—rent control, limits on the number of vehicles per household, and so forth, but, of course, such schemes are matters of legislative judgment and not for this Court. Appellants also refer to the necessity of maintaining the family character of the village. There is not a shred of evidence in the record indicating that if Belle Terre permitted a limited number of unrelated persons to live together, the residential, familial character of the community would be fundamentally affected.

By limiting unrelated households to two persons while placing no limitation on households of related individuals, the village has embarked upon its commendable course in a constitutionally faulty vessel. Cf. Marshall v. United States, 414 U.S. 417, 430 (1974) (dissenting opinion). I would find the challenged ordinance unconstitutional. But I would not ask the village to abandon its goal of providing quiet streets, little traffic, and a pleasant and reasonably priced environment in which families might raise their children. Rather, I would commend the village to continue to pursue those purposes but by means of more carefully drawn and even-handed legislation.

I respectfully dissent.

---

24. By providing an exception for dependent children, the village would avoid any doubts that might otherwise be posed by the constitutional protection afforded the choice of whether to bear a child. See Molino v. Mayor & Council of Glassboro, 116 N.J. Super. 195, 281 A.2d 401 (1971); cf. Cleveland Board of Education v. LaFleur, 414 U.S. 632 (1974).

NOTES

1. In Moore v. City of East Cleveland, 431 U.S. 494 (1977), the Supreme Court limited the holding in *Belle Terre*. *Moore* invalidated a single family zoning ordinance that defined "family" to include no more than one set of grandchildren. Mrs. Moore was convicted of violating the ordinance and sentenced to jail because she had living with her a son and two grandsons who were not brothers. The plurality opinion distinguished *Belle Terre* on the ground that Belle Terre's ordinance applied only to unrelated individuals:

> But one overriding factor sets this case apart from *Belle Terre*. The ordinance there affected only *unrelated* individuals. It expressly allowed all who were related by "blood, adoption, or marriage" to live together, and in sustaining the ordinance we were careful to note that it promoted "family needs" and "family values." . . .
>
> East Cleveland, in contrast, has chosen to regulate the occupancy of its housing by slicing deeply into the family itself. This is no mere incidental result of the ordinance. On its face it selects certain categories of relatives who may live together and declares that others may not. In particular, it makes a crime of a grandmother's choice to live with her grandson in circumstances like those presented here.
>
> When a city undertakes such intrusive regulation of the family, neither *Belle Terre* nor *Euclid* governs; the usual judicial deference to the legislature is inappropriate. "This Court has long recognized that freedom of personal choice in matters of marriage and family life is one of the liberties protected by the Due Process Clause of the Fourteenth Amendment." . . . Of course, the family is not beyond regulation. . . . But when the government intrudes on choices concerning family living arrangements, this Court must examine carefully the importance of the governmental interests advanced and the extent to which they are served by the challenged regulation. . . .
>
> When thus examined, this ordinance cannot survive. The city seeks to justify it as a means of preventing overcrowding, minimizing traffic and parking congestion, and avoiding an undue financial burden on East Cleveland's school system. Although these are legitimate goals, the ordinance before us serves them marginally, at best. For example, the ordinance permits any family consisting only of husband, wife, and unmarried children to live together, even if the family contains a half dozen licensed drivers, each with his or her own car. At the same time it forbids an adult brother and sister to share a household, even if both faithfully use public transportation. The ordinance would permit a grandmother to live with a single dependent son and children, even if his school-age children number a dozen, yet it forces Mrs. Moore to find another dwelling for her grandson John, simply because of the presence of his uncle and cousin in the same household. We need not labor the point. [The ordinance] has but a tenuous relation to alleviation of the conditions mentioned by the city. . . .
>
> Substantive due process has at times been a treacherous field for this Court. There *are* risks when the judicial branch gives enhanced protection to certain substantive liberties without the guidance of the more specific provisions of the Bill of Rights. As the history of the *Lochner* era demonstrates, there is reason for concern lest the only limits to such judicial intervention become the predilections of those who happen at the time to be Members of this Court. That history counsels caution and restraint. But it does not counsel abandonment, nor does it require what the city urges here: cutting off any protection of family rights at the first convenient, if arbitrary boundary — the boundary of the nuclear family.
>
> Appropriate limits on substantive due process come not from drawing arbitrary lines but rather from careful "respect for the teachings of history [and] solid recognition of the basic values that underlie our society." . . . Our decisions establish that the Constitution protects the sanctity of the family precisely because the institution of the family is deeply rooted in this Nation's

history and tradition. It is through the family that we inculcate and pass down many of our most cherished values, moral and cultural.

Ours is by no means a tradition limited to respect for the bonds uniting the members of the nuclear family. The tradition of uncles, aunts, cousins, and especially grandparents sharing a household along with parents and children has roots equally venerable and equally deserving of constitutional recognition. Over the years millions of our citizens have grown up in just such an environment, and most, surely, have profited from it. Even if conditions of modern society have brought about a decline in extended family households, they have not erased the accumulated wisdom of civilization, gained over the centuries and honored throughout our history, that supports a larger conception of the family. Out of choice, necessity, or a sense of family responsibility, it has been common for close relatives to draw together and participate in the duties and the satisfactions of a common home. [431 U.S. at 498-505. Chief Justice Burger and Justices Stewart, White, and Rehnquist dissented.]

2. On issues of household composition, some state courts have taken a less deferential position than that of the Supreme Court in *Belle Terre*; they have found one basis or another—including the state's own constitution—to narrow the territory left open by the Court. A prominent example is McMinn v. Town of Oyster Bay, 488 N.E.2d 1240 (N.Y. 1985). The ordinance in *McMinn* restricted single family housing to any number of people related by blood, marriage, or adoption, or to two people not so related but both over the age of 62. The court invalidated the ordinance because it infringed on the due process protections of the New York constitution. The objectives of the ordinance—to preserve the character of single family neighborhoods, control density, reduce traffic and noise—were acceptable, but the means were not. Occupancy restrictions based on biological or legal relationships, the court said, had no reasonable tie to the city's objectives. The ordinance was overinclusive (prohibiting occupancy by a young unmarried couple) and underinclusive (permitting a dozen distantly related people to live together). The court was mindful of *Belle Terre* and *Moore*, but said neither case set out the definition of "family" minimally necessary under the federal Constitution. In any event, the definition in the ordinance was incompatible with the state constitution and earlier state cases prohibiting definitions of "family" that excluded households that were families in all but the biological sense.[25]

Cases to similar effect are City of Santa Barbara v. Adamson, 610 P.2d 436 (Cal. 1980) (ordinance allowing no more than five unrelated persons to live together was an invasion of privacy unjustified by any compelling governmental interest; less restrictive alternatives were available; *Moore* was read by the court as undermining *Belle Terre*, and California's right of privacy is broader than the federal right in any event); Charter Township of Delta v. Dinolfo, 351 N.W.2d 831 (Mich. 1984) (the ordinance was underinclusive and overinclusive; less restrictive alternatives were available; *Belle Terre* was not accepted as a guide to the state constitution); see also College Area Renters & Landlords Assn. v. City of San Diego, 50 Cal. Rptr. 2d 515 (Cal. App. 1996) (holding unconstitutional an ordinance that limited the number of renters who may occupy a residence while permit-

---

25. On the meaning of "family," recall the discussion of restrictive covenants limiting neighborhoods to "single family dwellings" (Note 5 on page 926).

ting an unlimited number of occupants in owner-occupied residences); Kirsch v. Prince George's County, 626 A.2d 372 (Md. 1993) (invalidating on equal protection grounds a "mini-dorm" ordinance that imposed stricter requirements on housing for unrelated student tenants than on housing for an equal number of unrelated non-student tenants).

Compare City of Ladue v. Horn, 720 S.W.2d 745 (Mo. App. 1986) (Ladue again!), upholding an ordinance—as applied to an unmarried couple living together with three children from earlier marriages—that defined "family" as two or more persons related by blood, marriage, or adoption. The court relied on *Belle Terre* and deferred to the legislative definition set forth in the ordinance. The ordinance was rationally related to public health, safety, and welfare; needed to pass only that "relaxed test" of judicial review; and was thus constitutional notwithstanding the availability of less restrictive alternatives. The state constitution and earlier state cases endorsed "traditional notions of family. . . . There is no doubt that there is a governmental interest in marriage and in preserving the integrity of the biological or legal family. There is no concomitant governmental interest in keeping together a group of unrelated persons, no matter how closely they simulate a family." 720 S.W.2d at 751-752. see also McMaster v. Columbia Bd. of Zoning Appeals, 719 S.E.2d 660, 664 (S.C. 2011) (upholding ordinance limiting to three the maximum number of unrelated persons living together).

Ladue probably represents a rapidly fading view. Some of the states following the more open-minded position sketched above have proceeded on other than constitutional grounds. For example, in Borough of Glassboro v. Vallorosi, 568 A.2d 888 (N.J. 1990), the Supreme Court of New Jersey held that a group of ten unrelated college students living together were a "family" within the definition of a local ordinance that limited houses and duplexes in residential zones to "one or more persons occupying a dwelling unit as a single non-profit housekeeping unit, who are living together as a stable and permanent living unit, being a traditional family unit or the functional equivalency [sic] thereof." (The stated purpose of the ordinance was to confine college students to dormitories and to districts zoned for apartments, in order to preserve "family living style" and neighborhood character.)

The court noted that its earlier decisions had declined to follow *Belle Terre*; restrictions based upon legal or biological relationships were not to be tolerated. On the other hand, localities were allowed to restrict uses in certain residential zones to single housekeeping units, as the Glassboro ordinance did.

> But the standard for determining whether a use qualifies as a single housekeeping unit must be functional, and hence capable of being met by either related or unrelated persons.
>
> . . . The uncontradicted testimony [here] reflects a plan by ten sophomore college students to live together for three years under conditions that correspond substantially to the ordinance's requirement of a "stable and permanent living unit." . . . The students ate together, shared household chores, and paid expenses from a common fund. [568 A.2d at 894 (1990).]

See generally Katia Brener, *Belle Terre* and Single-Family Home Ordinances: Judicial Perceptions of Local Government and the Presumption of Validity, 74

N.Y.U. L. Rev. 447 (1999). For further discussion of the definition of "family," see Adam Lubow, Note, ". . . Not related by blood, marriage, or adoption": A History of the Definition of "Family" in Zoning Law, 16 J. Affordable Housing & Cmty. Dev. L. 144 (2007).

City of Edmonds v. Oxford House, Inc.

Supreme Court of the United States, 1995
514 U.S. 725

JUSTICE GINSBURG delivered the opinion of the Court.

The Fair Housing Act (FHA or Act) prohibits discrimination in housing against, inter alios, persons with handicaps.[26] Section 3607(b)(1) of the Act entirely exempts from the FHA's compass "any reasonable local, State, or Federal restrictions regarding the maximum number of occupants permitted to occupy a dwelling." 42 U.S.C. §3607(b)(1). This case presents the question whether a provision in petitioner City of Edmonds' zoning code qualifies for §3607(b)(1)'s complete exemption from FHA scrutiny. The provision, governing areas zoned for single family dwelling units, defines "family" as "persons [without regard to number] related by genetics, adoption, or marriage, or a group of five or fewer [unrelated] persons." Edmonds Community Development Code (ECDC) §21.30.010 (1991).

The defining provision at issue describes who may compose a family unit; it does not prescribe "the maximum number of occupants" a dwelling unit may house. We hold that §3607(b)(1) does not exempt prescriptions of the family-defining kind, i.e., provisions designed to foster the family character of a neighborhood. Instead, §3607(b)(1)'s absolute exemption removes from the FHA's scope only total occupancy limits, i.e., numerical ceilings that serve to prevent overcrowding in living quarters.

I.

In the summer of 1990, respondent Oxford House opened a group home in the City of Edmonds, Washington for 10 to 12 adults recovering from alcoholism and drug addiction. The group home, called Oxford House-Edmonds, is located in a neighborhood zoned for single family residences. Upon learning that Oxford House had leased and was operating a home in Edmonds, the City issued criminal citations to the owner and a resident of the house. The citations charged violation of the zoning code rule that defines who may live in single

---

26. The FHA, as originally enacted in 1968, prohibited discrimination based on race, color, religion, or national origin. See 82 Stat. 83. Proscription of discrimination based on sex was added in 1974. See Housing and Community Development Act of 1974, §808(b), 88 Stat. 729. In 1988, Congress extended coverage to persons with handicaps and also prohibited "familial status" discrimination, i.e., discrimination against parents or other custodial persons domiciled with children under the age of 18. 42 U.S.C. §3602(k).

family dwelling units. The occupants of such units must compose a "family," and family, under the City's defining rule, "means an individual or two or more persons related by genetics, adoption, or marriage, or a group of five or fewer persons who are not related by genetics, adoption, or marriage." Edmonds Community Development Code (ECDC) §21.30.010. Oxford House-Edmonds houses more than five unrelated persons, and therefore does not conform to the code.

Oxford House asserted reliance on the Fair Housing Act, 102 Stat. 1619, 42 U.S.C. §3601 et seq., which declares it unlawful "to discriminate in the sale or rental, or to otherwise make unavailable or deny, a dwelling to any buyer or renter because of a handicap of . . . that buyer or renter." §3604(f)(1)(A). The parties have stipulated, for purposes of this litigation, that the residents of Oxford House-Edmonds "are recovering alcoholics and drug addicts and are handicapped persons within the meaning" of the Act.

Discrimination covered by the FHA includes "a refusal to make reasonable accommodations in rules, policies, practices, or services, when such accommodations may be necessary to afford [handicapped] persons equal opportunity to use and enjoy a dwelling." §3604(f)(3)(B). Oxford House asked Edmonds to make a "reasonable accommodation" by allowing it to remain in the single family dwelling it had leased. Group homes for recovering substance abusers, Oxford urged, need 8 to 12 residents to be financially and therapeutically viable. Edmonds declined to permit Oxford House to stay in a single family residential zone, but passed an ordinance listing group homes as permitted uses in multifamily and general commercial zones.

Edmonds sued Oxford House in the United States District Court for the Western District of Washington seeking a declaration that the FHA does not constrain the City's zoning code family definition rule. Oxford House counterclaimed under the FHA, charging the City with failure to make a "reasonable accommodation" permitting maintenance of the group home in a single family zone. The United States filed a separate action on the same FHA-"reasonable accommodation" ground, and the two cases were consolidated. Edmonds suspended its criminal enforcement actions pending resolution of the federal litigation.

On cross-motions for summary judgment, the District Court held that ECDC §21.30.010, defining "family," is exempt from the FHA under §3607(b)(1) as a "reasonable . . . restrictio[n] regarding the maximum number of occupants permitted to occupy a dwelling." The United States Court of Appeals for the Ninth Circuit reversed; holding §3607(b)(1)'s absolute exemption inapplicable, the Court of Appeals remanded the cases for further consideration of the claims asserted by Oxford House and the United States. Edmonds v. Washington State Building Code Council, 18 F.3d 802 (1994).

The Ninth Circuit's decision conflicts with an Eleventh Circuit decision declaring exempt under §3607(b)(1) a family definition provision similar to the Edmonds prescription. See Elliott v. Athens, 960 F.2d 975 (1992). We granted certiorari to resolve the conflict, and we now affirm the Ninth Circuit's judgment.

II.

The sole question before the Court is whether Edmonds' family composition rule qualifies as a "restrictio[n] regarding the maximum number of occupants permitted to occupy a dwelling" within the meaning of the FHA's absolute exemption. 42 U.S.C. §3607(b)(1).[27] In answering this question, we are mindful of the Act's stated policy "to provide, within constitutional limitations, for fair housing throughout the United States." §3601. We also note precedent recognizing the FHA's "broad and inclusive" compass, and therefore according a "generous construction" to the Act's complaint-filing provision. Trafficante v. Metropolitan Life Ins. Co., 409 U.S. 205, 209, 212 (1972). Accordingly, we regard this case as an instance in which an exception to "a general statement of policy" is sensibly read "narrowly in order to preserve the primary operation of the [policy]." Commissioner v. Clark, 489 U.S. 726, 739 (1989).

A.

Congress enacted §3607(b)(1) against the backdrop of an evident distinction between municipal land use restrictions and maximum occupancy restrictions.

Land use restrictions designate "districts in which only compatible uses are allowed and incompatible uses are excluded." D. Mandelker, Land Use Law §4.16,

Oxford House, Edmonds, Washington

27. Like the District Court and the Ninth Circuit, we do not decide whether Edmonds' zoning code provision defining "family," as the City would apply it against Oxford House, violates the FHA's prohibitions against discrimination set out in 42 U.S.C. §§3604(f)(1)(A) and (f)(3)(B). [For these prohibitions, see page 454, where §3604 is set forth.—Eds.]

pp. 113-114 (3d ed. 1993) (hereinafter Mandelker). These restrictions typically categorize uses as single family residential, multiple-family residential, commercial, or industrial. See, e.g., 1 E. Ziegler, Jr., Rathkopf's The Law of Zoning and Planning §8.01, pp. 8-2 to 8-3 (4th ed. 1995); Mandelker §1.03, p. 4; 1 E. Yokley, Zoning Law and Practice §7-2, p. 252 (4th ed. 1978).

Land use restrictions aim to prevent problems caused by the "pig in the parlor instead of the barnyard." Village of Euclid v. Ambler Realty Co., 272 U.S. 365, 388 (1926). In particular, reserving land for single family residences preserves the character of neighborhoods, securing "zones where family values, youth values, and the blessings of quiet seclusion and clean air make the area a sanctuary for people." Village of Belle Terre v. Boraas, 416 U.S. 1, 9 (1974); see also Moore v. City of East Cleveland, 431 U.S. 494 (1977). To limit land use to single family residences, a municipality must define the term "family"; thus family composition rules are an essential component of single family residential use restrictions.

Maximum occupancy restrictions, in contradistinction, cap the number of occupants per dwelling, typically in relation to available floor space or the number and type of rooms. See, e.g., Uniform Housing Code §503(b) (1988); BOCA National Property Maintenance Code §§PM-405.3, PM-405.5 (1993) (hereinafter BOCA Code); Standard Housing Code §§306.1, 306.2 (1991); APHA-CDC Recommended Minimum Housing Standards §9.02, p. 37 (1986) (hereinafter APHA-CDC Standards). These restrictions ordinarily apply uniformly to all residents of all dwelling units. Their purpose is to protect health and safety by preventing dwelling overcrowding. See, e.g., BOCA Code §§PM-101.3, PM-405.3, PM-405.5 and commentary; Abbott, Housing Policy, Housing Codes and Tenant Remedies, 56 B.U. L. Rev. 1, 41-45 (1976). . . .

Section 3607(b)(1)'s language—"restrictions regarding the maximum number of occupants permitted to occupy a dwelling"—surely encompasses maximum occupancy restrictions. But the formulation does not fit family composition rules typically tied to land use restrictions. In sum, rules that cap the total number of occupants in order to prevent overcrowding of a dwelling "plainly and unmistakably," see A.H. Phillips, Inc. v. Walling, 324 U.S. 490, 493 (1945), fall within §3607(b)(1)'s absolute exemption from the FHA's governance; rules designed to preserve the family character of a neighborhood, fastening on the composition of households rather than on the total number of occupants living quarters can contain, do not.

B.

Turning specifically to the City's Community Development Code, we note that the provisions Edmonds invoked against Oxford House, ECDC §§16.20.010 and 21.30.010, are classic examples of a use restriction and complementing family composition rule. These provisions do not cap the number of people who may live in a dwelling. In plain terms, they direct that dwellings be used only to house families. Captioned "USES," ECDC §16.20.010 provides that the sole "Permitted Primary Use" in a single family residential zone is "single family dwelling units."

Edmonds itself recognizes that this provision simply "defines those uses permitted in a single family residential zone."

A separate provision caps the number of occupants a dwelling may house, based on floor area:

> Floor Area. Every dwelling unit shall have at least one room which shall have not less than 120 square feet of floor area. Other habitable rooms, except kitchens, shall have an area of not less than 70 square feet. Where more than two persons occupy a room used for sleeping purposes, the required floor area shall be increased at the rate of 50 square feet for each occupant in excess of two. ECDC §19.10.000 (adopting Uniform Housing Code §503(b) (1988)).

This space and occupancy standard is a prototypical maximum occupancy restriction.

Edmonds nevertheless argues that its family composition rule, ECDC §21.30.010, falls within §3607(b)(1), the FHA exemption for maximum occupancy restrictions, because the rule caps at five the number of unrelated persons allowed to occupy a single family dwelling. But Edmonds' family composition rule surely does not answer the question: "What is the maximum number of occupants permitted to occupy a house?" So long as they are related "by genetics, adoption, or marriage," any number of people can live in a house. Ten siblings, their parents and grandparents, for example, could dwell in a house in Edmonds' single family residential zone without offending Edmonds' family composition rule.

Family living, not living space per occupant, is what ECDC §21.30.010 describes. Defining family primarily by biological and legal relationships, the provision also accommodates another group association: five or fewer unrelated people are allowed to live together as though they were family. This accommodation is the peg on which Edmonds rests its plea for §3607(b)(1) exemption. Had the City defined a family solely by biological and legal links, §3607(b)(1) would not have been the ground on which Edmonds staked its case. It is curious reasoning indeed that converts a family values preserver into a maximum occupancy restriction once a town adds to a related persons prescription "and also two unrelated persons."

Edmonds additionally contends that subjecting single family zoning to FHA scrutiny will "overturn Euclidian zoning" and "destroy the effectiveness and purpose of single family zoning." This contention both ignores the limited scope of the issue before us and exaggerates the force of the FHA's antidiscrimination provisions. We address only whether Edmonds' family composition rule qualifies for §3607(b)(1) exemption. Moreover, the FHA antidiscrimination provisions, when applicable, require only "reasonable" accommodations to afford persons with handicaps "equal opportunity to use and enjoy" housing. §§3604(f)(1)(A) and (f)(3)(B).

The parties have presented, and we have decided, only a threshold question: Edmonds' zoning code provision describing who may compose a "family" is not a maximum occupancy restriction exempt from the FHA under §3607(b)(1). It remains for the lower courts to decide whether Edmonds' actions against

Oxford House violate the FHA's prohibitions against discrimination set out in §§3604(f)(1)(A) and (f)(3)(B). For the reasons stated, the judgment of the United States Court of Appeals for the Ninth Circuit is

Affirmed.

[The dissenting opinion of Justice Thomas, joined by Justices Scalia and Kennedy, is omitted.]

NOTES AND PROBLEM

1. See generally Michael J. Davis & Karen L. Gaus, Protecting Group Homes for the Non-Handicapped: Zoning in the Post-*Edmonds* Era, 46 U. Kan. L. Rev. 777 (1998).

2. In Oxford House v. City of St. Louis, 77 F.3d 249 (8th Cir. 1996), the court had before it a St. Louis zoning ordinance defining a single family dwelling to include three unrelated non-handicapped persons residing together and defining group homes with eight or fewer unrelated handicapped residents. Two Oxford Houses within the city had more than eight recovering addicts in each house. The city cited the Oxford Houses for zoning violation. Rather than applying for a variance excepting them from the eight-person rule, Oxford Houses brought a lawsuit against the city, contending that enforcing the eight-person limit against them violated the Fair Housing Act. The court held that the eight-person rule for handicapped persons had a rational basis and was valid. It further held that Oxford Houses' failure to apply for a variance, which would give the city a chance to accommodate them through established procedures, was fatal to their reasonable accommodation claim under the Fair Housing Act. To hold otherwise, the court thought, would force federal courts to act as zoning boards by deciding fact-intensive accommodation issues in the first instance. But see Community House, Inc. v. City of Boise, 490 F.3d 1041 (9th Cir. 2007) (applying more searching scrutiny to ordinances that discriminate against certain groups protected under the Fair Housing Act).

See also Albert v. Zoning Hearing Board of North Abington Township, 854 A.2d 401 (Pa. 2004), holding that a retreat house for recovering alcoholics did not qualify as a single family detached dwelling, and could thus be excluded from an area zoned for such a use, because the average stay for residents of the retreat would be only two to six months. The high rate of turnover, in the court's view, was inconsistent with the idea of a family household. The Fair Housing Act did not figure in the decision, so the question remains whether a court hearing a challenge on that ground would reach the same conclusion.

3. *Reasonable accommodation?* As you may remember from Chapter 6 (see pages 454-458), discrimination on the basis of handicap under the Fair Housing Act occurs when a municipality or landlord (among others) refuses "to make reasonable accommodations in rules, policies, practices, or services, when such accommodations may be necessary to afford such person equal opportunity to use and enjoy a dwelling." 42 U.S.C. §3604(f)(3)(B) (2013). When must a city alter its zoning ordinance to permit group homes? In Schwarz v. City of Treasure Island,

544 F.2d 1201 (11th Cir. 2008), a small town on the Gulf Coast of Florida enacted an ordinance to limit the number of times a single family or two-family dwelling could change occupancy during a twelve-month period as a way to minimize the disruption and noise caused by tourists. The city brought suit against an operator of group homes for former substance abusers for violating this ordinance. The Eleventh Circuit, citing language in *Belle Terre* about the special nature of "single family neighborhoods," found that there was no obligation on the part of the city to accommodate the group home in a neighborhood zoning for single family homes only, but remanded the case with respect to whether the ordinance was valid in neighborhoods zoned to permit multifamily apartments. According to the court, the city might be required to make the accommodation with respect to these neighborhoods if it was "necessary" to provide the residents with the full therapeutic benefits they required from the housing. 544 F.3d at 1227-1228.

4. Suppose that Chris Kohl lists his house for sale with a broker. After eight months, Chris has not sold the house. Chris contacts Oxford House to see if it is interested in leasing the property for a group home. It is. When the neighbors learn of this, they begin a campaign to prevent the property from becoming a group home. They prepare and send to all neighbors a mailing that includes a newspaper article about a resident of a group home raping a nine-year-old girl, a sheet stating that the neighborhood will no longer be safe and property values will plummet if a group home is situated in the neighborhood, and form letters to send to Chris to express concern about the group home. The neighbors call a town meeting at which 100 people show up.

Several neighbors chip in and offer Chris his asking price, and he sells the home to them. Oxford House then sues Chris and the neighbors for damages under the federal Fair Housing Act §3604(f)(1), page 454, for interfering with its right to equal access to housing by making the house unavailable. Are they liable? Michigan Protection and Advocacy Service, Inc. v. Babin, 18 F.3d 337 (6th Cir. 1994).

Suppose that instead of the neighbors buying the home, Chris sells it to Oxford House. The neighbors then bring a lawsuit in state court asking for an injunction preventing operation of a group home on the grounds that its intended occupants fail to satisfy the local zoning ordinance's definition of a family. Eventually, the neighbors drop the case. Oxford House then sues the neighbors in federal court for damages, including delay in securing housing and legal fees, arguing that the state court lawsuit was an act of discrimination in violation of the FHA. What result? See David Franklin, Comment, Civil Rights v. Civil Liberties? The Legality of State Court Lawsuits under the Fair Housing Act, 63 U. Chi. L. Rev. 1607 (1996).

5. "Group homes" is a generic term for any number of small, decentralized treatment facilities housing foster children, the mentally ill, the developmentally disabled, juvenile offenders, ex-drug addicts, alcoholics, and so on. Such people were once congregated in large public institutions, but group homes have become very common in recent years because they are less expensive than centralized facilities and are thought to provide more humane and effective treatment.

Neighbors, of course, dislike group homes—the NIMBY (Not In My Back Yard) phenomenon.[28] A circular mailed out by a Michigan group listed some of the reasons neighbors give for not wanting a group home on their street. The reasons were portrayed like this:

Our road is too wide / Our road is too narrow
It's too dangerous in the country / It's too dangerous in the city
The residents might hurt my kids / My kids might hurt the residents
Our street ends in a cul-de-sac / Our street is a thru street

Other sorts of reasons were: we don't have sidewalks; there's water (someone else said quicksand) nearby; we let our dogs run free; the retarded stay up and scream all night; dust in our neighborhood would be a health hazard to the residents of the home. See Peter Margulies, Building Communities of Virtue: Political Theory, Land Use Policy, and the "Not in My Backyard" Syndrome, 43 Syracuse L. Rev. 945 (1992).

For a comprehensive analysis of the theories for determining fairness in siting "locally undesirable land uses" (LULUs), see Vicki Been, Locally Undesirable Land Uses in Minority Neighborhoods: Disproportionate Siting or Market Dynamics?, 103 Yale L.J. 1383 (1994); Vicki Been, What's Fairness Got to Do With It? Environmental Justice and the Siting of Locally Undesirable Land Uses, 78 Cornell L. Rev. 1001 (1993); Lynn E. Blais, Environmental Racism Reconsidered, 75 N.C. L. Rev. 75 (1996). LULUs have been disproportionately sited in neighborhoods populated by the poor and by people of color. These neighborhoods are now fighting back, using environmental protection and land use laws. For more on this, see Jon C. Dubin, From Junkyards to Gentrification: Explicating a Right to Protective Zoning in Low-Income Communities of Color, 77 Minn. L. Rev. 739 (1993).

---

28. See Peter W. Salsich, Jr., Group Homes, Shelters and Congregate Housing: Deinstitutionalization Policies and the NIMBY Syndrome, 21 Real Prop., Prob. & Tr. J. 413 (1986).

NIMBY is only one—but probably the best known—of the LULU acronyms (a LULU is a Locally Undesirable Land Use). Others include:

BANANA (Build Absolutely Nothing Anywhere Near Anyone)
GUMBY (Gotta Use Many Back Yards)
LASBY (Look At Several Back Yards)
NIABY (Not In Anyone's Back Yard)
NIMBL (Not In My Bottom Line)
NIMTOO (Not In My Term Of Office)
NIRPBY (Never In Rich People's Back Yards)
NIYBY (Not In Your Back Yard)
NOPE (Nowhere On Planet Earth)
YIMBY (Yes In Many Back Yards)

NIMBY et al. has a broad reach, at least on the East Coast. Neighbors are reported to have objected to putting a dog run in a park, building a baseball field, building a middle school or a church or housing for the elderly or a planetarium or a nature trail, putting up a swing set in the yard, replacing wood window frames with aluminum ones, pruning a hedge (this dispute resulted in a double homicide), etc. See David M. Herszenhorn, Today, "Not in My Backyard" Can Cover Almost Anything, N.Y. Times, Apr. 16, 2000, at 29; Kathryn Shattuck, Beware the Cry of "Niyby": Not in *Your* Backyard!, N.Y. Times, May 11, 2000, at B1.

5.   Exclusionary Zoning

All zoning is exclusionary by definition: Its central purpose is to minimize or eliminate unwanted effects—externalities—in a given district, whether the effects be caused by typical nuisances (*Euclid*'s pig in a parlor), by apartments or commercial uses in a high-class single family residential zone, or by group homes. Commonly, however, zoning measures like these aim not to ban uses (nuisances aside), but rather to relegate them to what the zoners regard as their proper place in the community. Contrast another kind of exclusionary zoning, the kind to which that phrase particularly refers today: measures whose purpose or effect is essentially to close an entire community to unwanted groups—typically people of low income who might put a heavy burden on the public fisc yet at the same time contribute little to it, resulting in increased property taxes and reduced land values throughout the community. The attitude here is, "Let them go elsewhere, to some other city."

Southern Burlington County NAACP
v. Township of Mount Laurel
Supreme Court of New Jersey, 1975
336 A.2d 713, appeal dismissed and cert. denied, 423 U.S. 808 (1975)

HALL, J. This case attacks the system of land use regulation by defendant Township of Mount Laurel on the ground that low and moderate income families are thereby unlawfully excluded from the municipality. . . .

The implications of the issue presented are indeed broad and far-reaching, extending much beyond these particular plaintiffs and the boundaries of this particular municipality. . . .

Plaintiffs represent the minority group poor (black and Hispanic)[29] seeking such quarters. But they are not the only category of persons barred from so many municipalities by reason of restrictive land use regulations. We have reference to young and elderly couples, single persons and large, growing families not in the poverty class, but who still cannot afford the only kinds of housing realistically permitted in most places—relatively high-priced, single family detached dwellings on sizeable lots and, in some municipalities, expensive apartments. We will, therefore, consider the case from the wider viewpoint that the effect of Mount Laurel's land use regulation has been to prevent various categories of persons

---

29. Plaintiffs fall into four categories: (1) present residents of the township residing in dilapidated or substandard housing; (2) former residents who were forced to move elsewhere because of the absence of suitable housing; (3) nonresidents living in central city substandard housing in the region who desire to secure decent housing and accompanying advantages within their means elsewhere; (4) three organizations representing the housing and other interests of racial minorities. The township originally challenged plaintiffs' standing to bring this action. The trial court properly held (119 N.J. Super. at 166, 290 A.2d 465) that the resident plaintiffs had adequate standing to ground the entire action and found it unnecessary to pass on that of the other plaintiffs. The issue has not been raised on appeal. . . .

from living in the township because of the limited extent of their income and resources. In this connection, we accept the presentation of the municipality's counsel at oral argument that the regulatory scheme was not adopted with any desire or intent to exclude prospective residents on the obviously illegal bases of race, origin or believed social incompatibility. . . .

I.

The Facts

Mount Laurel is a flat, sprawling township, 22 square miles, or about 14,000 acres, in area, on the west central edge of Burlington County. . . .

In 1950, the township had a population of 2,817, only about 600 more people than it had in 1940. It was then, as it had been for decades, primarily a rural agricultural area with no sizeable settlements or commercial or industrial enterprises. The populace generally lived in individual houses scattered along country roads. There were several pockets of poverty, with deteriorating or dilapidated housing (apparently 300 or so units of which remain today in equally poor condition). After 1950, as in so many other municipalities similarly situated, residential development and some commerce and industry began to come in. By 1960 the population had almost doubled to 5,249 and by 1970 had more than doubled again to 11,221. These new residents were, of course, "outsiders" from the nearby central cities and older suburbs or from more distant places drawn here by reason of employment in the region. The township is now definitely a part of the outer ring of the South Jersey metropolitan area, which area we define as those portions of Camden, Burlington and Gloucester Counties within a semicircle having a radius of 20 miles or so from the heart of Camden city. And 65% of the township is still vacant land or in agricultural use.

The growth of the township has been spurred by the construction or improvement of main highways through or near it. . . . This highway network gives the township a most strategic location from the standpoint of transport of goods and people by truck and private car. There is no other means of transportation.

The location and nature of development have been, as usual, controlled by the local zoning enactments. The general ordinance presently in force, which was declared invalid by the trial court, was adopted in 1964. We understand that earlier enactments provided, however, basically the same scheme but were less restrictive as to residential development. The growth pattern dictated by the ordinance is typical.

Under the present ordinance, 29.2% of all the land in the township, or 4,121 acres, is zoned for industry. This amounts to 2,800 more acres than were so zoned by the 1954 ordinance. . . .

Only industry meeting specified performance standards is permitted. The effect is to limit the use substantially to light manufacturing, research, distribution of goods, offices and the like. Some nonindustrial uses, such as agriculture, farm dwellings, motels, a harness racetrack, and certain retail sales and service establishments, are permitted in this zone. At the time of trial no more than 100 acres . . . were actually occupied by industrial uses. They had been constructed in recent years, mostly in several industrial parks, and involved tax ratables of about 16 million dollars. The rest of the land so zoned has remained undeveloped. If it were fully utilized, the testimony was that about 43,500 industrial jobs would be created, but it appeared clear that, as happens in the case of so many munici-palities, much more land has been so zoned than the reasonable potential for industrial movement or expansion warrants. At the same time, however, the land cannot be used for residential development under the general ordinance.

The amount of land zoned for retail business use under the general ordi-nance is relatively small — 169 acres, or 1.2% of the total. . . .

While the greater part of the land so zoned appears to be in use, there is no major shopping center or concentrated retail commercial area — "downtown" — in the township.

The balance of the land area, almost 10,000 acres, has been developed until recently in the conventional form of major subdivisions. The general ordinance provides for four residential zones, designated R-1, R-1D, R-2 and R-3. All permit only single family, detached dwellings, one house per lot — the usual form of grid development. Attached townhouses, apartments (except on farms for agri-cultural workers) and mobile homes are not allowed anywhere in the township under the general ordinance. This dwelling development, resulting in the previ-ously mentioned quadrupling of the population, has been largely confined to the R-1 and R-2 districts in two sections — the northeasterly and southwesterly corners adjacent to the turnpike and other major highways. The result has been quite intensive development of these sections, but at a low density. The dwellings are substantial; the average value in 1971 was $32,500 and is undoubtedly much higher today.

The general ordinance requirements, while not as restrictive as those in many similar municipalities, nonetheless realistically allow only homes within the financial reach of persons of at least middle income. The R-1 zone requires a min-imum lot area of 9,375 square feet, a minimum lot width of 75 feet at the build-ing line, and a minimum dwelling floor area of 1,100 square feet if a one-story building and 1,300 square feet if one and one-half stories or higher. Originally this zone comprised about 2,500 acres. Most of the subdivisions have been con-structed within it so that only a few hundred acres remain (the testimony was at variance as to the exact amount). The R-2 zone, comprising a single district of 141 acres in the northeasterly corner, has been completely developed. While it only required a minimum floor area of 900 square feet for a one-story dwelling, the minimum lot size was 11,000 square feet; otherwise the requisites were the same as in the R-1 zone.

The general ordinance places the remainder of the township, outside of the industrial and commercial zones and the R-1D district (to be mentioned shortly), in the R-3 zone. This zone comprises over 7,000 acres — slightly more than half of the total municipal area — practically all of which is located in the central part of the township extending southeasterly to the apex of the triangle. The testimony was that about 4,600 acres of it then remained available for housing development. Ordinance requirements are substantially higher, however, in that the minimum lot size is increased to about one-half acre (20,000 square feet). (We understand that sewer and water utilities have not generally been installed, but, of course, they can be.) Lot width at the building line must be 100 feet. Minimum dwelling floor area is as in the R-1 zone. Presently this section is primarily in agricultural use; it contains as well most of the municipality's substandard housing.

The R-1D district was created by ordinance amendment in 1968. The area is composed of a piece of what was formerly R-3 land in the western part of that zone. The district is a so-called "cluster" zone. See generally 2 Williams, American Planning Law: Land Use and the Police Power, §§47.01-47.05 (1974). . . . Here [the] concept is implemented by reduction of the minimum lot area from 20,000 square feet required in the R-3 zone to 10,000 square feet (12,000 square feet for corner lots) but with the proviso that one-family houses—the single permitted dwelling use—"shall not be erected in excess of an allowable development density of 2.25 dwelling units per gross acre." The minimum lot width at the building line must be 80 feet and the minimum dwelling floor area is the same as in the R-3 zone. The amendment further provides that the developer must set aside and dedicate to the municipality a minimum of 15% and a maximum of 25% of the total acreage for such public uses as may be required by the Planning Board, including "but not limited to school sites, parks, playgrounds, recreation areas, public buildings, public utilities." Some dwelling development has taken place in this district, the exact extent of which is not disclosed by the record. It is apparent that the dwellings are comparable in character and value to those in the other residential zones. The testimony was that 486 acres remained available in the district.

A variation from conventional development has recently occurred in some parts of Mount Laurel, as in a number of other similar municipalities, by use of the land use regulation device known as "planned unit development" (PUD). This scheme differs from the traditional in that the type, density and placement of land uses and buildings, instead of being detailed and confined to specified districts by local legislation in advance, is determined by contract, or "deal," as to each development between the developer and the municipal administrative authority, under broad guidelines laid down by state enabling legislation and an implementing local ordinance. The stress is on regulation of density and permitted mixture of uses within the same area, including various kinds of living accommodations with or without commercial and industrial enterprises. The idea may be basically thought of as the creation of "new towns" in virgin territory, full-blown or in miniature, although most frequently the concept has been limited in practice, as in Mount Laurel, to residential developments of various sizes having some variety of housing and perhaps some retail establishments to serve the inhabitants.

New Jersey passed such enabling legislation in 1967, which closely follows a model act found in 114 U. Pa. L. Rev. 140 (1965), and Mount Laurel adopted the implementing enactment as a supplement to its general zoning ordinance in

December of that year. While the ordinance was repealed early in 1971, the township governing body in the interim had approved four PUD projects, which were specifically saved from extinction by the repealer.[30]

These projects, three in the southwesterly sector and one in the northeasterly sector, are very substantial and involve at least 10,000 sale and rental housing units of various types to be erected over a period of years. Their bounds were created by agreement rather than legislative specification on the zoning map, invading industrial, R-1, R-1D, R-3 and even flood plain zones. If completed as planned, they will in themselves ultimately quadruple the 1970 township population, but still leave a good part of the township undeveloped. (The record does not indicate how far development in each of the projects has progressed.) While multi-family housing in the form of rental garden, medium rise and high rise apartments and attached townhouses is for the first time provided for, as well as single family detached dwellings for sale, it is not designed to accommodate and is beyond the financial reach of low and moderate income families, especially those with young children. The aim is quite the contrary; as with the single family homes in the older conventional subdivisions, only persons of medium and upper income are sought as residents.

A few details will furnish sufficient documentation. Each of the resolutions of tentative approval of the projects contains a similar fact finding to the effect that the development will attract a highly educated and trained population base to support the nearby industrial parks in the township as well as the business and commercial facilities. The approvals also sharply limit the number of apartments having more than one bedroom. Further, they require that the developer must provide in its leases that no school-age children shall be permitted to occupy any one-bedroom apartment and that no more than two such children shall reside in any two-bedroom unit. The developer is also required, prior to the issuance of the first building permit, to record a covenant, running with all land on which multi-family housing is to be constructed, providing that in the event more than .3 school children per multi-family unit shall attend the township school system in any one year, the developer will pay the cost of tuition and other school expenses of all such excess numbers of children. In addition, low density, required amenities, such as central air conditioning, and specified developer contributions help to push rents and sales prices to high levels. These contributions include fire apparatus, ambulances, fire houses, and very large sums of money for educational facilities, a cultural center and the township library.[31]

---

30. . . . This court has never passed upon the PUD enabling legislation, any local implementing ordinance or any municipal approval of a PUD project. The basic legal questions, . . . which include among others the matter of what requirements a municipal authority may, in effect, impose upon a developer as a condition of approval, are serious and not all easy of solution. We refer to the Mount Laurel PUD projects as part of the picture of land use regulation in the township and its effect. It may be noted that, at a hearing on the PUD ordinance, the then township attorney stated that ". . . providing for apartments in a PUD ordinance in effect would seem to overcome any court objection that the Township was not properly zoning in denying apartments." [On cluster zoning and PUDs, see page 1010.—EDS.]

31. The current township attorney, at oral argument, conceded, without specification, that many of these various conditions which had been required of developers were illegal.

Still another restrictive land use regulation was adopted by the township through a supplement to the general zoning ordinance enacted in September 1972 creating a new zone, R-4, Planned Adult Retirement Community (PARC). The supplementary enactment designated a sizeable area as the zone—perhaps 200 acres—carved out of the R-1D and R-3 districts in the southwesterly sector. The enactment recited a critical shortage of adequate housing in the township suitable "for the needs and desires of senior citizens and certain other adults over the age of 52." The permission was essentially for single ownership development of the zone for multi-family housing (townhouses and apartments), thereafter to be either rented or sold as cooperatives or condominiums. The extensive development requirements detailed in the ordinance make it apparent that the scheme was not designed for, and would be beyond the means of, low and moderate income retirees. The highly restricted nature of the zone is found in the requirement that all permanent residents must be at least 52 years of age (except a spouse, immediate family member other than a child, live-in domestic, companion or nurse). Children are limited to a maximum of one, over age 18, residing with a parent and there may be no more than three permanent residents in any one dwelling unit.[32]

All this affirmative action for the benefit of certain segments of the population is in sharp contrast to the lack of action, and indeed hostility, with respect to affording any opportunity for decent housing for the township's own poor living in substandard accommodations, found largely in the section known as Springville (R-3 zone). The 1969 Master Plan Report recognized it and recommended positive action. The continuous official reaction has been rather a negative policy of waiting for dilapidated premises to be vacated and then forbidding further occupancy. An earlier non-governmental effort to improve conditions had been effectively thwarted. In 1968 a private non-profit association sought to build subsidized, multi-family housing in the Springville section with funds to be granted by a higher level governmental agency. Advance municipal approval of the project was required. The Township Committee responded with a purportedly approving resolution, which found a need for "moderate" income housing in the area, but went on to specify that such housing must be constructed subject to all zoning, planning, building and other applicable ordinances and codes. This meant single family detached dwellings on 20,000 square foot lots. (Fear was also expressed that such housing would attract low income families from outside the township.) Needless to say, such requirements killed realistic housing for this group of low and moderate income families.

The record thoroughly substantiates the findings of the trial court that over the years Mount Laurel "has acted affirmatively to control development and to attract a selective type of growth" and that "through its zoning ordinances has exhibited economic discrimination in that the poor have been deprived of

---

32. This court has not yet passed on the validity of any land use regulation which restricts residence on the basis of occupant age.

adequate housing and the opportunity to secure the construction of subsidized housing, and has used federal, state, county and local finances and resources solely for the betterment of middle and upper income persons."

There cannot be the slightest doubt that the reason for this course of conduct has been to keep down local taxes on *property* (Mount Laurel is not a high tax municipality) and that the policy was carried out without regard for non-fiscal considerations with respect to *people*, either within or without its boundaries. This conclusion is demonstrated not only by what was done and what happened, as we have related, but also by innumerable direct statements of municipal officials at public meetings over the years which are found in the exhibits. . . .

This policy of land use regulation for a fiscal end derives from New Jersey's tax structure, which has imposed on local real estate most of the cost of municipal and county government and of the primary and secondary education of the municipality's children. The latter expense is much the largest, so, basically, the fewer the school children, the lower the tax rate. Sizeable industrial and commercial ratables are eagerly sought and homes and the lots on which they are situate are required to be large enough, through minimum lot sizes and minimum floor areas, to have substantial value in order to produce greater tax revenues to meet school costs. Large families who cannot afford to buy large houses and must live in cheaper rental accommodations are definitely not wanted, so we find drastic bedroom restrictions for, or complete prohibition of, multi-family or other feasible housing for those of lesser income.

This pattern of land use regulation has been adopted for the same purpose in developing municipality after developing municipality. Almost every one acts solely in its own selfish and parochial interest and in effect builds a wall around itself to keep out those people or entities not adding favorably to the tax base, despite the location of the municipality or the demand for varied kinds of housing. There has been no effective intermunicipal or area planning or land use regulation. All of this is amply demonstrated by the evidence in this case as to Camden, Burlington and Gloucester counties. . . .

One incongruous result is the picture of developing municipalities rendering it impossible for lower paid employees of industries they have eagerly sought and welcomed with open arms (and, in Mount Laurel's case, even some of its own lower paid municipal employees) to live in the community where they work.

The other end of the spectrum should also be mentioned because it shows the source of some of the demand for cheaper housing than the developing municipalities have permitted. Core cities were originally the location of most commerce and industry. Many of those facilities furnished employment for the unskilled and semi-skilled. These employees lived relatively near their work, so sections of cities always have housed the majority of people of low and moderate income, generally in old and deteriorating housing. Despite the municipally confined tax structure, commercial and industrial ratables generally used to supply enough revenue to provide and maintain municipal services equal or superior to those furnished in most suburban and rural areas.

The situation has become exactly the opposite since the end of World War II. Much industry and retail business, and even the professions, have left the cities. Camden is a typical example. The testimonial and documentary evidence in this case as to what has happened to that city is depressing indeed. For various reasons, it lost thousands of jobs between 1950 and 1970, including more than half of its manufacturing jobs (a reduction from 43,267 to 20,671, while all jobs in the entire area labor market increased from 94,507 to 197,037). A large segment of retail business faded away with the erection of large suburban shopping centers. The economically better situated city residents helped fill up the miles of sprawling new housing developments, not fully served by public transit. In a society which came to depend more and more on expensive individual motor vehicle transportation for all purposes, low income employees very frequently could not afford to reach outlying places of suitable employment and they certainly could not afford the permissible housing near such locations. These people have great difficulty in obtaining work and have been forced to remain in housing which is overcrowded, and has become more and more substandard and less and less tax productive. There has been a consequent critical erosion of the city tax base and inability to provide the amount and quality of those governmental services — education, health, police, fire, housing and the like — so necessary to the very existence of safe and decent city life. This category of city dwellers desperately needs much better housing and living conditions than is available to them now, both in a rehabilitated city and in outlying municipalities. They make up, along with the other classes of persons earlier mentioned who also cannot afford the only generally permitted housing in the developing municipalities, the acknowledged great demand for low and moderate income housing.

II.

The Legal Issue

The legal question before us, as earlier indicated, is whether a developing municipality like Mount Laurel may validly, by a system of land use regulation, make it physically and economically impossible to provide low and moderate income housing in the municipality for the various categories of persons who need and want it and thereby, as Mount Laurel has, exclude such people from living within its confines because of the limited extent of their income and resources. Necessarily implicated are the broader questions of the right of such municipalities to limit the kinds of available housing and of any obligation to make possible a variety and choice of types of living accommodations.

We conclude that every such municipality must, by its land use regulations, presumptively make realistically possible an appropriate variety and choice of housing. More specifically, presumptively it cannot foreclose the opportunity of the classes of people mentioned for low and moderate income housing and in its regulations must affirmatively afford that opportunity, at least to the extent of the municipality's fair share of the present and prospective regional need therefor.

These obligations must be met unless the particular municipality can sustain the heavy burden of demonstrating peculiar circumstances which dictate that it should not be required so to do.[33]

We reach this conclusion under state law and so do not find it necessary to consider federal constitutional grounds urged by plaintiffs. We begin with some fundamental principles as applied to the scene before us.

Land use regulation is encompassed within the state's police power. . . .

It is elementary theory that all police power enactments, no matter at what level of government, must conform to the basic state constitutional requirements of substantive due process and equal protection of the laws. . . .

It is required that, affirmatively, a zoning regulation, like any police power enactment, must promote public health, safety, morals or the general welfare. (The last term seems broad enough to encompass the others.) Conversely, a zoning enactment which is contrary to the general welfare is invalid. . . .

Indeed these considerations are specifically set forth in the zoning enabling act as among the various purposes of zoning for which regulations must be designed. N.J.S.A. 40:55-32. Their inclusion therein really adds little; the same requirement would exist even if they were omitted. If a zoning regulation violates the enabling act in this respect, it is also theoretically invalid under the state constitution. We say "theoretically" because, as a matter of policy, we do not treat the validity of most land use ordinance provisions as involving matters of constitutional dimension; that classification is confined to major questions of fundamental import. . . .

We consider the basic importance of housing and local regulations restricting its availability to substantial segments of the population to fall within the latter category.

The demarcation between the valid and the invalid in the field of land use regulation is difficult to determine, not always clear and subject to change. This was recognized almost fifty years ago in the basic case of Village of Euclid v. Ambler Realty Co., 272 U.S. 365 (1926). . . .

This court has also said as much and has plainly warned, even in cases decided some years ago sanctioning a broad measure of restrictive municipal decisions, of the inevitability of change in judicial approach and view as mandated by change in the world around us. . . .

The warning implicates the matter of *whose* general welfare must be served or not violated in the field of land use regulation. Frequently the decisions in this state . . . have spoken only in terms of the interest of the enacting municipality, so that it has been thought, at least in some quarters, that such was the only welfare requiring consideration. It is, of course, true that many cases have dealt only with regulations having little, if any, outside impact where the local decision is ordinarily entitled to prevail. However, it is fundamental and not to be forgotten that the

---

33. While, as the trial court found, Mount Laurel's actions were deliberate, we are of the view that the identical conclusion follows even when municipal conduct is not shown to be intentional, but the effect is substantially the same as if it were.

zoning power is a police power of the state and the local authority is acting only as a delegate of that power and is restricted in the same manner as is the state. So, when regulation does have a substantial external impact, the welfare of the state's citizens beyond the borders of the particular municipality cannot be disregarded and must be recognized and served. . . .

This brings us to the relation of housing to the concept of general welfare just discussed and the result in terms of land use regulation which that relationship mandates. There cannot be the slightest doubt that shelter, along with food, are the most basic human needs. . . .

It is plain beyond dispute that proper provision for adequate housing of all categories of people is certainly an absolute essential in promotion of the general welfare required in all local land use regulation. Further the universal and constant need for such housing is so important and of such broad public interest that the general welfare which developing municipalities like Mount Laurel must consider extends beyond their boundaries and cannot be parochially confined to the claimed good of the particular municipality. It has to follow that, broadly speaking, the presumptive obligation arises for each such municipality affirmatively to plan and provide, by its land use regulations, the reasonable opportunity for an appropriate variety and choice of housing, including, of course, low and moderate cost housing, to meet the needs, desires and resources of all categories of people who may desire to live within its boundaries. Negatively, it may not adopt regulations or policies which thwart or preclude that opportunity.

It is also entirely clear, as we pointed out earlier, that most developing municipalities, including Mount Laurel, have not met their affirmative or negative obligations, primarily for local fiscal reasons. . . .

In sum, we are satisfied beyond any doubt that, by reason of the basic importance of appropriate housing and the long-standing pressing need for it, especially in the low and moderate cost category, and of the exclusionary zoning practices of so many municipalities, conditions have changed, and . . . judicial attitudes must be altered . . . to require, as we have just said, a broader view of the general welfare and the presumptive obligation on the part of developing municipalities at least to afford the opportunity by land use regulations for appropriate housing for all.

We have spoken of this obligation of such municipalities as "presumptive." The term has two aspects, procedural and substantive. Procedurally, we think the basic importance of appropriate housing for all dictates that, when it is shown that a developing municipality in its land use regulations has not made realistically possible a variety and choice of housing, including adequate provision to afford the opportunity for low and moderate income housing or has expressly prescribed requirements or restrictions which preclude or substantially hinder it, a facial showing of violation of substantive due process or equal protection under the state constitution has been made out and the burden, and it is a heavy one, shifts to the municipality to establish a valid basis for its action or non-action. . . .

The substantive aspect of "presumptive" relates to the specifics, on the one hand, of what municipal land use regulation provisions, or the absence thereof, will evidence invalidity and shift the burden of proof and, on the other hand, of what bases and considerations will carry the municipality's burden and sustain what it has done or failed to do. Both kinds of specifics may well vary between municipalities according to peculiar circumstances.

We turn to application of these principles in appraisal of Mount Laurel's zoning ordinance, useful as well, we think, as guidelines for future application in other municipalities.

The township's general zoning ordinance (including the cluster zone provision) permits, as we have said, only one type of housing—single family detached dwellings. This means that all other types—multi-family including garden apartments and other kinds housing more than one family, town (row) houses, mobile home parks—are prohibited.[34] Concededly, low and moderate income housing has been intentionally excluded. While a large percentage of the population living outside of cities prefers a one-family house on its own sizeable lot, a substantial proportion do not for various reasons. Moreover, single family dwellings are the most expensive type of quarters and a great number of families cannot afford them. Certainly they are not pecuniarily feasible for low and moderate income families, most young people and many elderly and retired persons, except for some of moderate income by the use of low cost construction on small lots.

As previously indicated, Mount Laurel has allowed some multi-family housing by agreement in planned unit developments, but only for the relatively affluent and of no benefit to low and moderate income families. And even here, the contractual agreements between municipality and developer sharply limit the number of apartments having more than one bedroom.[35] While the township's PUD ordinance has been repealed, we mention the subject of bedroom restriction because, assuming the overall validity of the PUD technique, . . . the measure could be reenacted and the subject is of importance generally. The design of such limitations is obviously to restrict the number of families in the municipality having school age children and thereby keep down local education costs. Such restrictions are so clearly contrary to the general welfare as not to require further discussion. Cf. Molino v. Mayor and Council of Borough of Glassboro, 116 N.J. Super. 195, 281 A.2d 401 (Law Div. 1971).

Mount Laurel's zoning ordinance is also so restrictive in its minimum lot area, lot frontage and building size requirements, earlier detailed, as to preclude single family housing for even moderate income families. Required lot area of at least 9,375 square feet in one remaining regular residential zone and 20,000 square feet (almost half an acre) in the other, with required frontage of 75 and 100 feet,

---

34. Zoning ordinance restriction of housing to single family dwellings is very common in New Jersey. Excluding six large, clearly rural townships, the percentage of remaining land zoned for multi-family use is only just over 1% of the net residential land supply in 16 of New Jersey's 21 counties. . . . Pennsylvania has held it unconstitutional for a developing municipality to fail to provide for apartments anywhere within it. Appeal of Girsh, 437 Pa. 237, 263 A.2d 395 (1970).

35. Apartment bedroom restrictions are also common in municipalities of the state which do allow multi-family housing. About 60% of the area zoned to permit multi-family dwellings is restricted to efficiency or one-bedroom apartments; another 20% permits two-bedroom units and only the remaining 20% allows units of three bedrooms or larger. . . .

respectively, cannot be called small lots and amounts to low density zoning, very definitely increasing the cost of purchasing and improving land and so affecting the cost of housing.[36] As to building size, the township's general requirements of a minimum dwelling floor area of 1,100 square feet for all one-story houses and 1,300 square feet for all of one and one-half stories or higher is without regard to required minimum lot size or frontage or the number of occupants. . . . Again it is evident these requirements increase the size and so the cost of housing. The conclusion is irresistible that Mount Laurel permits only such middle and upper income housing as it believes will have sufficient taxable value to come close to paying its own governmental way.

Akin to large lot, single family zoning restricting the population is the zoning of very large amounts of land for industrial and related uses. Mount Laurel has set aside almost 30% of its area, over 4,100 acres, for that purpose; the only residential use allowed is for farm dwellings. In almost a decade only about 100 acres have been developed industrially. Despite the township's strategic location for motor transportation purposes, as intimated earlier, it seems plain that the likelihood of anywhere near the whole of the zoned area being used for the intended purpose in the foreseeable future is remote indeed and that an unreasonable amount of land has thereby been removed from possible residential development, again seemingly for local fiscal reasons.

Without further elaboration at this point, our opinion is that Mount Laurel's zoning ordinance is presumptively contrary to the general welfare and outside the intended scope of the zoning power in the particulars mentioned. A facial showing of invalidity is thus established, shifting to the municipality the burden of establishing valid superseding reasons for its action and non-action. We now examine the reasons it advances.

The township's principal reason in support of its zoning plan and ordinance housing provisions, advanced especially strongly at oral argument, is the fiscal one previously adverted to, i.e., that by reason of New Jersey's tax structure which substantially finances municipal governmental and educational costs from taxes on local real property, every municipality may, by the exercise of the zoning power, allow only such uses and to such extent as will be beneficial to the local tax rate. In other words, the position is that any municipality may zone extensively to seek and encourage the "good" tax ratables of industry and commerce and limit the permissible types of housing to those having the fewest school children or to those providing sufficient value to attain or approach paying their own way taxwise.

We have previously held that a developing municipality may properly zone for and seek industrial ratables to create a better economic balance for the community vis-à-vis educational and governmental costs engendered by residential development, provided that such was ". . . done reasonably as part of and in furtherance of a legitimate comprehensive plan for the zoning of the entire

36. These restrictions are typical throughout the state. . . .

municipality." Gruber v. Mayor and Township Committee of Raritan Township, 39 N.J. 1, 9-11, 186 A.2d 489, 493 (1962). We adhere to that view today. But we were not there concerned with, and did not pass upon, the validity of municipal exclusion by zoning of types of housing and kinds of people for the same local financial end. We have no hesitancy in now saying, and do so emphatically, that, considering the basic importance of the opportunity for appropriate housing for all classes of our citizenry, no municipality may exclude or limit categories of housing for that reason or purpose. While we fully recognize the increasingly heavy burden of local taxes for municipal governmental and school costs on homeowners, relief from the consequences of this tax system will have to be furnished by other branches of government. It cannot legitimately be accomplished by restricting types of housing through the zoning process in developing municipalities.

The propriety of zoning ordinance limitations on housing for ecological or environmental reasons seems also to be suggested by Mount Laurel in support of the one-half acre minimum lot size in that very considerable portion of the township still available for residential development. It is said that the area is without sewer or water utilities and that the soil is such that this plot size is required for safe individual lot sewage disposal and water supply. The short answer is that, this being flat land and readily amenable to such utility installations, the township could require them as improvements by developers or install them under the special assessment or other appropriate statutory procedure. The present environmental situation of the area is, therefore, no sufficient excuse in itself for limiting housing therein to single family dwellings on large lots. Cf. National Land and Investment Co. v. Kohn, 419 Pa. 504, 215 A.2d 597 (1965). This is not to say that land use regulations should not take due account of ecological or environmental factors or problems. Quite the contrary. Their importance, at last being recognized, should always be considered. Generally only a relatively small portion of a developing municipality will be involved, for, to have a valid effect, the danger and impact must be substantial and very real (the construction of every building or the improvement of every plot has some environmental impact) — not simply a makeweight to support exclusionary housing measures or preclude growth — and the regulation adopted must be only that reasonably necessary for public protection of a vital interest. Otherwise difficult additional problems relating to a "taking" of a property owner's land may arise.

By way of summary, what we have said comes down to this. As a developing municipality, Mount Laurel must, by its land use regulations, make realistically possible the opportunity for an appropriate variety and choice of housing for all categories of people who may desire to live there, of course including those of low and moderate income. It must permit multi-family housing, without bedroom or similar restrictions, as well as small dwellings on very small lots, low cost housing of other types and, in general, high density zoning, without artificial and unjustifiable minimum requirements as to lot size, building size and the like, to meet the full panoply of these needs. Certainly when a municipality zones for industry and commerce for local tax benefit purposes, it without question must zone to permit adequate housing within the means of the employees involved in such uses. (If planned unit developments are authorized, one would assume that each must include a reasonable amount of low and moderate income housing in its residential "mix," unless opportunity for such housing has already been realistically provided for elsewhere in the municipality.) The amount of land removed from residential use by allocation to industrial and commercial purposes must be reasonably related to the present and future potential for such purposes. In other words, such municipalities must zone primarily for the living welfare of people and not for the benefit of the local tax rate.

We have earlier stated that a developing municipality's obligation to afford the opportunity for decent and adequate low and moderate income housing extends at least to ". . . the municipality's fair share of the present and prospective regional need therefor." Some comment on that conclusion is in order at this point. Frequently it might be sounder to have more of such housing, like some specialized land uses, in one municipality in a region than in another, because of greater availability of suitable land, location of employment, accessibility of public transportation or some other significant reason. But, under present New Jersey legislation, zoning must be on an individual municipal basis, rather than regionally. So long as that situation persists under the present tax structure, or in the absence of some kind of binding agreement among all the municipalities of a region, we feel that every municipality therein must bear its fair share of the regional burden. (In this respect our holding is broader than that of the trial court, which was limited to Mount Laurel-related low and moderate income housing needs.)

The composition of the applicable "region" will necessarily vary from situation to situation and probably no hard and fast rule will serve to furnish the answer in every case. Confinement to or within a certain county appears not to be realistic, but restriction within the boundaries of the state seems practical and advisable. (This is not to say that a developing municipality can ignore a demand for housing within its boundaries on the part of people who commute to work in another state.) Here we have already defined the region at present as "those portions of Camden, Burlington and Gloucester Counties within a semicircle having a radius of 20 miles or so from the heart of Camden City." The concept of "fair share" is coming into more general use and, through the expertise of the municipal planning adviser, the county planning boards and the state planning agency, a reasonable figure for Mount Laurel can be determined, which can then be translated to the allocation of sufficient land therefor on the zoning map. . . .

There is no reason why developing municipalities like Mount Laurel, required by this opinion to afford the opportunity for all types of housing to meet the needs of various categories of people, may not become and remain attractive, viable communities providing good living and adequate services for all their residents in the kind of atmosphere which a democracy and free institutions demand. They can have industrial sections, commercial sections and sections for every kind of housing from low cost and multi-family to lots of more than an acre with very expensive homes. Proper planning and governmental cooperation can prevent over-intensive and too sudden development, insure against future suburban sprawl and slums and assure the preservation of open space and local beauty. We do not intend that developing municipalities shall be overwhelmed by voracious land speculators and developers if they use the powers which they have intelligently and in the broad public interest. Under our holdings today, they can be better communities for all than they previously have been.

III.

The Remedy

[T]he trial court invalidated the zoning ordinance in toto and ordered the township to make certain studies and investigations and to present to the court a plan of affirmative public action designed "to enable and encourage the satisfaction of the indicated needs" for township related low and moderate income housing. Jurisdiction was retained for judicial consideration and approval of such a plan and for the entry of a final order requiring its implementation.

We are of the view that the trial court's judgment should be modified in certain respects. We see no reason why the entire zoning ordinance should be nullified. Therefore we declare it to be invalid only to the extent and in the particulars set forth in this opinion. The township is granted 90 days from the date hereof, or such additional time as the trial court may find it reasonable and necessary to allow, to adopt amendments to correct the deficiencies herein specified. It is the local function and responsibility, in the first instance at least, rather than the court's, to decide on the details of the same within the guidelines we have laid down. If plaintiffs desire to attack such amendments, they may do so by supplemental complaint filed in this cause within 30 days of the final adoption of the amendments.

We are not at all sure what the trial judge had in mind as ultimate action with reference to the approval of a plan for affirmative public action concerning the satisfaction of indicated housing needs and the entry of a final order requiring implementation thereof. Courts do not build housing nor do municipalities. That function is performed by private builders, various kinds of associations, or, for public housing, by special agencies created for that purpose at various levels of government. The municipal function is initially to provide the opportunity through appropriate land use regulations and we have spelled out what Mount Laurel must do in that regard. It is not appropriate at this time, particularly in view of the advanced view of zoning law as applied to housing laid down by this opinion, to deal with the matter of the further extent of judicial power in the field or to exercise any such power. . . . The municipality should first have full opportunity to itself act without judicial supervision. We trust it will do so in the spirit we have suggested, both by appropriate zoning ordinance amendments and whatever additional action encouraging the fulfillment of its fair share of the regional need for low and moderate income housing may be indicated as necessary and advisable. (We have in mind that there is at least a moral obligation in a municipality to establish a local housing agency pursuant to state law to provide housing for its resident poor now living in dilapidated, unhealthy quarters.) The portion of the trial court's judgment ordering the preparation and submission of the aforesaid study, report and plan to it for further action is therefore vacated as at least premature. Should Mount Laurel not perform as we expect, further judicial action may be sought by supplemental pleading in this cause.

The judgment of the Law Division is modified as set forth herein.

NOTES AND QUESTIONS

1. *The general picture.* Exclusionary zoning is not a thing just of the 1970s and '80s. For the last 50 years at least, suburban communities have resorted to various measures in an effort to restrict or bar particular uses—such as apartments, small houses on small lots, mobile homes—and to limit or foreclose entry by particular people, especially the poor and racial minorities.[37]

Simple prejudice has much to do with exclusionary efforts, but—as the court in *Mount Laurel* indicates—fiscal concerns are also a powerful motivation. Ideally, *all* communities want low property taxes. Citizens obviously would rather spend their money in other ways, and they like the fact that low property taxes buoy up property values. Public officials want contented citizens who will keep them in office.

The straightforward way to achieve relatively low taxes is to have a handsome tax base (valuable property, especially nonresidential property), well-to-do residents, and low demand for such public services as water and sewer, schools, police and fire departments, public assistance programs, and so on. Translated into policy, this means measures to ensure a community of substantial and desirable industrial uses and expensive homes located in a low density manner (say on large lots). With such a policy in place, residents will necessarily tend to have high incomes; the typical family will have few children. Most of the workers in the local industries will be unable to live in the community or in other suburbs nearby (the other suburbs will be using exclusionary measures to pursue their own fiscal aims). They will reside in the central city.

2. *Exclusionary zoning techniques.* Putting aside blatant efforts to exclude racial minorities and the poor,[38] and focusing on residential uses, there are a number of

---

37. Local governments were not alone in encouraging the use of zoning techniques that tended to exclude residents with low and moderate incomes. See Andrew H. Whittemore, How the Federal Government Zoned America: The Federal Housing Administration and Zoning, 39 J. Urb. Hist. 620 (2013) (describing the FHA's impact on suburban development).

38. A recent study suggests that low density zoning increases residential segregation by reducing the quantity of affordable housing available in the low density areas. See Jonathan Rothwell & Douglas S. Massey, The Effect of Density Zoning on Racial Segregation in U.S. Urban Areas, 44 Urb. Aff. Rev. 779-801 (2009). Of course, racially discriminatory zoning practices violate the Fair Housing Act. See Town of Huntington v. Huntington Branch, NAACP, 488 U.S. 15 (1988) (per curiam), aff'g 844 F.2d 926 (2d Cir. 1988). The ordinance at issue in *Huntington* prohibited apartments everywhere but in the town's urban renewal area, located in the central city and occupied mostly by minority residents. The town had denied a developer's request that the ordinance be amended to allow construction of subsidized multifamily housing in a white neighborhood. On the Fair Housing Act generally, see pages 453-459.

techniques a community might use to exclude people whose characteristics (low income, high service demand) would interfere with the ideal fiscal picture: controls on minimum housing cost, minimum housing size, and minimum lot size. Related techniques include prohibitions on mobile homes and on multi-family housing. For a summary of the literature on how zoning can increase housing costs, look back to pages 986-987.

The few early efforts to set *minimum housing-cost* requirements were invalidated by the courts, which saw no rational relationship between cost and advancing public health and safety. *Minimum floor-area* requirements, often set without regard to the number of residents in a dwelling (and therefore lacking any apparent health and safety rationale), met with a more mixed judicial reaction. Minimum floor-area requirements were superseded in many communities by housing codes, which were required by the federal government in the Housing Act of 1954 in order to qualify for urban renewal money. Housing codes establish minimum standards for all housing within the municipality; they cover required facilities (number of bathrooms, windows in bedrooms, electrical outlets, etc.) and occupancy limitations. They are similar to building codes, but apply only to housing. In addition, minimum square footage requirements imposed by private developers on a subdivision by way of covenants render publicly imposed lower minimums superfluous.[39]

Minimum lot-size requirements are upheld when found justified by the conditions of the community in question, but their exclusionary effects can provoke judicial skepticism. See, e.g., County Commrs. of Queen Anne County v. Miles, 228 A.2d 450 (Md. 1967) (upholding a five-acre minimum in part of the county with smaller lot sizes in other areas; low density was held to help with municipal concerns about sanitation, traffic problems, and protection of historic areas); Ketchel v. Bainbridge Township, 587 N.E.2d 779 (Ohio 1990) (upholding a three-acre minimum intended to conserve underground water supplies); Appeal of Kit-Mar Builders, Inc., 268 A.2d 765 (Pa. 1970) (striking down two- and three-acre minimums as exclusionary, in the face of arguments that they were designed to deal with sewage treatment and traffic and to help preserve the area's character); C&M Developers, Inc. v. Bedminster Township Zoning Hearing Board, 820 A.2d 143 (Pa. 2002) (striking down an agricultural land preservation measure that set minimum lot sizes).

Minimum setback requirements have been upheld because they increase light and air, reduce the danger from fire, and advance aesthetic concerns. Minimum setback requirements have a cumulative effect on the production of low cost

---

39. Times change; efforts to keep out little houses have transformed into efforts to keep out big ones! "In recent years, oversized homes—labeled 'McMansions' by some—have spread from spacious gated enclaves to close-in suburbs, where they often dwarf their neighbors. Now, town officials, urban planners, and irate neighbors in suburbs across the country are scrambling to find ways to rewrite zoning codes to restrict the size of new houses and additions to existing homes." Lisa W. Foderaro, In Suburbs, They're Cracking Down on the Joneses, N.Y. Times, Mar. 19, 2001, at A1. In his poem "Slum Lords," John Updike says "The Superrich make lousy neighbors—/they buy a house and tear it down/and build another, twice as big, and leave."

housing similar to that of minimum lot sizes. These requirements have been almost universally upheld.

Barring mobile or manufactured homes from residential areas, or perhaps from the entire community, is another method of excluding low cost housing. Such ordinances were almost always upheld in the early cases. And even today, when manufactured homes must meet federal safety standards (and thus often rival or surpass "stick built" housing in size and quality), prejudice against manufactured homes (originally called "trailers") persists.[40] In some recent cases, particularly in the South, courts appear to be standing up to this prejudice. See, e.g., Five C's Inc. v. County of Pasquotank, 672 S.E.2d 737 (N.C. App. 2009) (county may not zone out mobile homes older than 10 years to increase tax base); Cannon v. Coweta County, 389 S.E.2d 329 (Ga. 1990) (holding, four to three, that protection of the neighbors' property values was not a sufficient justification for complete prohibition of manufactured homes in all residential areas; ordinance unconstitutional).

In the decades since *Mount Laurel*, municipalities have enacted new energy conservation regulations, environmental regulations, and growth controls—all of which increase the price of housing. The price may also be affected by the time required to receive permits from the various regulators involved and to battle the neighbor defenders of the status quo. See George Lefcoe, The Neighborhood Defenders, 23 UCLA L. Rev. 823 (1976). See also pages 986-987.

3. *The* Mount Laurel *case.* Notice that *Mount Laurel* is based on state, not federal, constitutional law. Justice Hall was aware that several decisions of the U.S. Supreme Court made federal constitutional law an uneasy basis for exclusionary zoning claims. In Lindsey v. Normet, 405 U.S. 56 (1972), the Supreme Court held that housing is not a fundamental right, and in San Antonio Indep. Sch. Dist. v. Rodriguez, 411 U.S. 1 (1973), the Court held that wealth is not necessarily a suspect classification for purposes of the Equal Protection Clause of the U.S. Constitution. In Village of Belle Terre v. Boraas, 416 U.S. 1 (1974), page 1062, the Supreme Court rejected a challenge to a village's restricting all land use in the village to one-family dwellings, excluding boarding houses, lodging houses, and multiple dwellings. The court found that the prohibition of boarding houses and other multifamily dwellings was reasonable and within the public welfare because such dwellings bring more people, more traffic, and more noise, intruding on "the blessings of quiet seclusion and clean air [which] make the area a sanctuary for people." In 1975, the same year that *Mount Laurel* was decided, the Supreme Court in Warth v. Seldin, 422 U.S. 490 (1975), held that nonresidents lacked standing in federal court to challenge municipal regulations unless they alleged specific concrete facts (such as denial of a building permit for a particular low income housing project) showing they were harmed. And in Arlington Heights v. Metropolitan Hous. Dev. Corp., 429 U.S. 252 (1977), the Court held that plaintiffs must prove discriminatory *intent* if they charge that environmental regulations impact minorities adversely and violate the Equal Protection Clause.

On state courts turning to state constitutions to reach beyond Supreme Court interpretations of the federal Constitution, recall the discussion in Note 2 on page

1070. See also W. John Moore, In Whose Court, 23 Natl. J. 2396 (1991) ("state courts have sometimes simply ignored Supreme Court rulings, relying on the language of their states' constitutions to carve exceptions to high court dogma").

4. *After* Mount Laurel. It appears that the idea behind *Mount Laurel* was essentially one of deregulation: Remove obstacles that local governments had put in the way of less costly housing and let the market respond. Newly constructed housing, even of modest residences, might be beyond the reach of low income people, but the increased supply would let used housing trickle down to them at affordable prices.

Things did not work out quite that way. Communities read the *Mount Laurel* opinion closely. They saw, for example, that it applied only to "developing" communities. A number of communities claimed that they were not "developing." Others pleaded that their local ecology was too sensitive to fall fully under *Mount Laurel*'s dictates. Still others fudged, changing their ordinances in such a way as to create the appearance, but not the reality, of compliance. And a host of questions developed about how a "fair share" within a "region" was to be determined.

The township of Mount Laurel itself was grudging—indeed, less than honest—in complying with the court's mandate. It rezoned for low cost housing three small, widely scattered areas (less than .25 percent of its land) suffering from high noise levels and proximity to industrial uses. This new ordinance was struck down as a complete failure to meet the township's constitutional obligations in Southern Burlington County NAACP v. Township of Mount Laurel, 456 A.2d 390 (N.J. 1983)—popularly known as *Mount Laurel II*.

Mount Laurel II gave the court a chance to address some of the issues left open in *Mount Laurel I*. In the eight years between the cases, the court had learned, it said, that without a strong judicial hand there would not be more housing but only paper, process, and litigation. It also learned, or so it seems, that its original idea of deregulation and an unconstrained market was wrong; rather the need was for measures that *required* the production of low and moderate income housing. So *Mount Laurel II* held, among other rulings, as follows:

Essentially, *every* municipality—not just developing ones—must provide a realistic opportunity for decent housing for its poor, except where (as in many urban areas) the poor represent a disproportionately large percentage of the population as compared to the rest of the region. Good faith attempts on the part of municipalities would be insufficient; each community must provide its fair share, expressed in terms of number of units needed immediately and in the future. It would not be enough for municipalities to remove barriers to low cost construction; they were to undertake affirmative measures and to assist developers in obtaining state and federal aid. Affirmative measures might include inclusionary zoning devices—such as altering density limits in exchange for a developer's commitment to construct certain amounts of low and moderate income housing. (See Note 9 on page 1104.) Zones for mobile homes were to be created if necessary to meet the fair-share obligation. All future *Mount Laurel* litigation would be assigned to a group of three judges, appointed by the chief justice, a measure intended in part to ease the difficulties of calculating fair shares. Finally, the opinion confirmed a "builder's remedy" under which the trial court could allow a developer to go forth with a low income project even though the municipality had not granted a permit if the court found that the municipality had not fulfilled its *Mount Laurel* obligations.

"It is difficult to convey adequately the intensity of the public reaction to the *Mount Laurel* process since 1983," Professor John Payne reported. Where *Mount Laurel I* could be ignored because it was ineffective, *Mount Laurel II* worked, and it stirred up a fire storm. John M. Payne, Rethinking Fair Share: The Judicial Enforcement of Affordable Housing Policies, 16 Real Est. L.J. 20, 22 (1987). Governor Thomas Kean attacked *Mount Laurel II* as an undesirable intrusion on the home rule principle. Two years later, the New Jersey legislature, responding to the ongoing problem of exclusionary zoning and the controversy provoked by the builder's remedy, enacted a Fair Housing Act. N.J. Stat. Ann. §§52:27D-301 to 329 (2001). The statute put a moratorium on the builder's remedy. It also established an administrative agency, the Council on Affordable Housing (COAH), to determine fair-share obligations for each municipality subject to a *Mount Laurel* obligation. Municipalities that filed satisfactory plans to meet their obligations would receive a "substantive certification" from COAH, protecting them from builder's remedies for a period of 10 years. Uncertified municipalities were subject to suit under *Mount Laurel II*. COAH certification decisions could be appealed, but courts were to treat them with deference. New Jersey's Fair Housing Act was upheld by the New Jersey Supreme Court in Hills Dev. Co. v. Bernards Township, 510 A.2d 621 (N.J. 1986) (known as *Mount Laurel III*).

A particularly interesting feature of the Fair Housing Act provided for regional contribution agreements whereby any suburb might, with Council approval, compensate cities for agreeing to absorb up to half of the suburb's fair-share obligation. The legislation itself states that the purpose of the transfer option is to make use of the existing housing stock; suburban contributions would make it possible to rehabilitate substandard housing, presumably in the central cities. Regional contribution agreements proved to be quite popular—over 10,000 units were built or renovated after 1986. See State of New Jersey, Department of Community Affairs, COAH: Reports and Quick Facts (2009), http://www.state.nj.us/dca/affiliates/coah/reports/. In 2008, the New Jersey Legislature amended the Fair Housing Act to eliminate the regional contribution option.

What are the arguments—pro and con—for regional contribution agreements? See Editorial: RCAs, RIP, 193 New Jersey Law Journal 814 (2008); Charles M. Haar, Suburbs Under Siege: Race, Space, and Audacious Judges 113-116 (1996); Michael H. Schill, Deconcentrating the Inner City Poor, 67 Chi.-Kent L. Rev. 795 (1991).

After *Mount Laurel II*, New Jersey state courts, the state legislature, and COAH used a formulaic approach to determine the fair share of affordable housing for which a community would be responsible. In 2004, COAH adopted a new methodology that included the concept of "growth share"; it required municipalities to plan for and facilitate the construction of a number of units that was proportionate to their actual rather than merely projected growth. The growth-share methodology has been controversial. Can you imagine why? See John M. Payne, The Paradox of Progress: Three Decades of the Mount Laurel Doctrine, 5 J. Plan. Hist. 126 (2006). For an interesting theoretical approach to regional contribution agreements, see Lee Anne Fennell, Properties of Concentration, 73 U. Chi. L. Rev. 1227, 1267-1270 (2006).

In 2007, the New Jersey Superior Court struck down the "third round rules" of growth share based upon their use of available data. See In re Adoption of N.J.A.C. 5:94 and 5:95 by the New Jersey Council on Affordable Housing, 914 A.2d 348 (N.J. Super. Ct. 2007). The COAH responded by amending its third round rules in 2008. These revised rules met the same fate, however. In September 2013, the New Jersey Supreme Court invalidated the most recent version of the third round rules. The court held that the growth share methodology is contrary to *Mount Laurel* and to the Fair Housing Act. See In re Adoption of N.J.A.C. 5:96 and 5:97 by the New Jersey Council on Affordable Housing, 74 A.3d 893 (N.J. 2013).

The *Mount Laurel* saga produced another simmering dispute that was decided in July 2013. Earlier, in June 2011, after a disagreement with the New Jersey legislature, Governor Chris Christie had issued a reorganization plan that abolished COAH and transferred all of its functions, powers, duties, and personnel to the state's Department of Community Affairs. This plan was challenged by housing advocates, and in In re Plan for Abolition of the Council on Affordable Hous., No. A-127-11/A-14-12 (2013), the court ruled that the governor had exceeded his authority. For a discussion of the history leading up to this controversy involving the state's response to the *Mount Laurel* rulings, see Alan Mallach, The Mount Laurel Doctrine and the Uncertainties of Social Policy in a Time of Retrenchment, 63 Rutgers L. Rev. 849, 856-859 (2011).

Since the New Jersey Supreme Court dipped its toe (plunged into the deep end?) into exclusionary zoning, over 36,000 units of housing have been built or renovated pursuant to the *Mount Laurel* doctrine. See COAH: Reports and Quick Facts, supra. Some have argued that while the quantity of units built or rehabilitated is small compared to overall need (which is in the 600,000 to 700,000 range through 2014), "[s]omething is surely better than nothing." See Payne, The Paradox of Progress, supra, at 134. Empirical studies of who is living in *Mount Laurel* housing suggest that they are not necessarily the people anticipated by Justice Hall in *Mount Laurel I.* See Naomi Bailin Wish & Stephen Eisdorfer, The Impact of Mount Laurel Initiatives: An Analysis of the Characteristics of Applicants and Occupants, 27 Seton Hall L. Rev. 1268 (1997).

5. *The social science and demographic underpinnings of* Mount Laurel. As the first two *Mount Laurel* decisions emphasize, the battle against exclusionary suburban zoning was undergirded by two sets of considerations: (1) the demographic changes in central cities since World War II, and (2) the belief that households with low incomes (disproportionately minority households) would benefit from living in socioeconomically and racially integrated communities with better schools and lower crime rates. With respect to the first consideration, at the time of *Mount Laurel,* inner cities had lost tremendous shares of their middle and upper income populations to the suburbs, leaving behind an increasingly impoverished, racially

segregated, and fiscally strapped central city. See generally Kenneth T. Jackson, Crabgrass Frontier: The Suburbanization of the United States (1985). Suburbs were seen as overwhelmingly white and affluent, unreachable by the inner-city poor without the addition of new low cost housing and vigorous enforcement of anti-discrimination laws. See Anthony Downs, Opening Up the Suburbs: An Urban Strategy for America (1973). Since the original *Mount Laurel* decision, this view of the suburbs as monolithically white and affluent has broken down. Indeed, according to one recent study, in 2010, while the poverty rate remained significantly higher in cities than in suburbs (21 percent compared to 11 percent), the number of poor people living in suburbs exceeded the number in cities and the rate of poverty growth in suburbs was more than twice the rate of increase in cities. Elizabeth Kneebone & Alan Berube, Confronting Suburban Poverty in America 16-20 (2013).

With respect to the second consideration, social scientists and legal advocates supported opening up the suburbs, believing that moving low and moderate income families to suburban neighborhoods would improve their social mobility by increasing educational opportunities, geographic access to employment, and exposure to peers who were imbued with middle class values. See generally William Julius Wilson, The Truly Disadvantaged (1987); Schill, supra, at 795. A significant amount of empirical data sheds light on the wisdom of these assumptions. For example, the results of the recent Moving to Opportunity Program suggest that low income families who moved from high poverty inner city neighborhoods to the suburbs of five cities experienced better health and feelings of subjective well-being compared to a control group, but had no statistically significant differences with respect to school failure or employment outcomes. Jens Ludwig et al., Long-Term Neighborhood Effects on Low-Income Families: Evidence from Moving to Opportunity, 103 Am. Econ. Rev. 226, 231 (2013).

The affordable housing project that started the controversy in Mount Laurel was not approved until 1997 and opened in 2002. See David L. Kirp, Here Comes the Neighborhood, N.Y. Times, Oct. 19, 2013, at SR3. Social scientists used its opening as a natural experiment, comparing those applicants who had been assigned units in the complex to those who had not. Although the applicants were similar at the time they sought units in Mount Laurel, a decade later Mt. Laurel residents experienced dramatically lower rates of neighborhood disorder, higher rates of employment, higher wages, lower reliance on welfare payments, and their children spent more hours studying and reading, though significant increases in their children's academic performance were not observed. See Rebecca Casciano & Douglas S. Massey, Neighborhood Disorder and Individual Economic Self-Sufficiency: New Evidence from a Quasi-Experimental Study, 41 Soc. Sci. Res. 802, 813 (2012); Rebecca Casciano & Douglas S. Massey, School Context and Educational Outcomes: Results from a Quasi-Experimental Study, 48 Urb. Aff. Rev. 180, 197 (2012). This research is summarized in Douglas S. Massey et al., Climbing Mount Laurel: The Struggle for Affordable Housing and Social Mobility in an American Suburb (2013). The downside appeared negligible: "Even in the Mount Laurel neighborhoods closest to the affordable housing, property values were unaffected. To most residents, the fact that poor families now live in Mount Laurel has proved entirely irrelevant. Today, many well-to-do Mount Laurel residents don't even know that affordable housing exists there." Kirp, supra, at SR3.

Do the rather dramatic growth in poverty in the suburbs over the past 25 years and the impact on low and moderate income households of moving to the suburbs affect your view about the continuing relevance and wisdom of the original decision and subsequent remedial efforts?

6. *Exclusionary zoning in other states.* Exclusionary zoning can be practiced anywhere, and not all state courts have responded in the aggressive fashion of the New Jersey Supreme Court in *Mount Laurel.* Some, quite to the contrary, continue to honor the convention that zoning ordinances (exclusionary ordinances included) are presumed to be constitutional. The rational basis test of judicial review is applied and many measures survive. Others adopt a middle ground by maintaining the presumption of validity but judging the rationality of the measure in question with reference to regional as opposed to purely local interests. Still others are true to the spirit, but not necessarily the letter, of *Mount Laurel.*

In Pennsylvania, for example, municipalities have been required to provide zones for all types of housing, at least within reason, and developers have standing to sue those that don't comply. Unlike the New Jersey system, no subsidies are provided, so builders pursue their remedy only if they believe there is a market for the sorts of housing they propose to build.

New York has taken a more passive approach. Berenson v. Town of New Castle, 341 N.E.2d 236 (N.Y. 1975), held that municipal zoning ordinances would be annulled if they did not include districts for multiple housing when community and regional needs required such housing. *Berenson* did not mandate affirmative relief. See generally Charles M. Haar, Suburbs Under Siege: Race, Space and Audacious Judges (1996).

In an attempt to provide a clear route through the bureaucratic jungle for builders of low cost housing, Massachusetts has enacted a statute allowing public agencies, nonprofit corporations, and limited dividend corporations to apply to the local zoning board of appeals for a comprehensive permit for low income housing, bypassing separate permits needed under housing and building codes or subdivision requirements. If the applicant is denied the permit, the applicant may appeal to a state housing appeals committee. The committee may reverse the denial if it is not consistent with local needs for low and moderate income housing. See Mass. Gen. Laws ch. 40B, §§20-23 (2012). The legislation is appraised in Paul K. Stockman, Note, Anti-Snob Zoning in Massachusetts: Assessing One Attempt at Opening the Suburbs to Affordable Housing, 78 Va. L. Rev. 535 (1992); see also Christopher Baker, Note, Housing in Crisis—A Call to Reform Massachusetts's Affordable Housing Law, 32 B.C. Envtl. Aff. L. Rev. 156 (2005). For an overview of efforts to reconcile the aims of environmental and affordable housing policies in Massachusetts, see Karla L. Chaffee, Note, Massachusetts's Chapter 40R: A Model for Incentive-Based Land Use Planning and Affordable Housing Development, 10 Vt. J. Envtl. L. 181 (2008).

Connecticut has similar legislation, which permits expedited judicial appeals by any developer of an "affordable housing project." Conn. Gen. Stat. §8-30g

(2013). See West Hartford Interfaith Coalition v. Town of West Hartford, 636 A.2d 1342 (Conn. 1994) (upholding trial court reversal of municipality's refusal to rezone so as to permit construction of 10 units of affordable housing). For an evaluation of anti-snob laws in Massachusetts, Connecticut, and Rhode Island, see Spencer M. Cowan, Anti-Snob Land Use Laws, Suburban Exclusion, and Housing Opportunity, 28 J. Urb. Aff. 295 (2006).

In Oregon a state Land Conservation and Development Commission has authority to require a municipality to plan for higher residential densities and permit multiple-unit dwellings when it finds the municipality lags in meeting the housing needs of the region. See Terry D. Morgan, Exclusionary Zoning: Remedies Under Oregon's Land Use Planning Program, 14 Envtl. L. 779 (1984).

7. *Exclusionary zoning and the Tiebout Hypothesis.* Are restrictions on exclusionary zoning definitely a good thing? Consider the following from Robert C. Ellickson & Vicki L. Been, Land Use Controls 771 (3d ed. 2005).

> A number of urban economists have suggested that specialization among suburbs is efficiency-enhancing. The leading article is by Professor Charles Tiebout, A Pure Theory of Local Expenditures, 64 J. Pol. Econ. 416 (1956). The Tiebout Hypothesis (developed with the aid of several simplifying assumptions) is that consumers benefit from being able to "vote with their feet" among municipalities offering varying packages of public goods and taxing policies. Families with children might settle in jurisdictions with excellent schools, for example, while elderly individuals worried about public safety might pick locations with excellent police services. According to Tiebout, the specialization of municipalities and the competition among them will enhance the efficiency of metropolitan organization because people will congregate with others of similar tastes and therefore be more likely to get the public goods they most prefer.
>
> The Tiebout Hypothesis may be contrasted with what might be called a "Waring Blender model," which would call for all land uses and all types of households to be represented in each neighborhood in proportion to their representation in the entire metropolitan area. . . . Note that the Waring Blender model produces great diversity *within* neighborhoods, but no diversity *between* neighborhoods, and thus may limit the variety of residential choices available to households.

An efficient Tiebout outcome requires that everybody living in a locality pay the same amount of taxes (called head taxes) for public goods provided by the local government. (Can you see why?) Local governments in the United States do not rely much on head taxes, but zoning regulations, by effectively setting minimum values on property in the area, can help ensure that residents pay taxes in proportion to the services or public goods they receive. For this reason, exclusionary zoning practices can have efficiency-enhancing properties. Unfortunately, however, they can also have very undesirable effects. First, they distribute wealth away from people with low incomes. Second, they generate spillovers (negative externalities) among communities, and these can result in *in*efficiencies that more than outweigh the efficiency gains of specialization. Such as what? For discussion and a review of the literature, see Schill, supra, at 811-821; Michael H. Schill, The Federal Role in Reducing Regulatory Barriers to Affordable Housing in the Suburbs, 7 J.L. & Pol. 703, 716-722 (1992) (also discussing the case for increased *federal* oversight of suburban exclusionary practices).

8. *Zoning's history and zoning's exclusionary effects.* At the beginning of this chapter, we looked at some of the grand ideas behind the rise of zoning in the United States, but noted also, in connection with our discussion of Euclid v. Ambler, that the picture was in fact not all that pretty. At worst, zoning was a means to achieve segregation by class, income, and race; short of that, it was an effective way to protect the property values of homeowners. An economic history of zoning adds detail to the story. In this connection, consider William A. Fischel, An Economic History of Zoning and a Cure for Its Exclusionary Effects, 41 Urb. Stud. 317 (2004). Professor Fischel is an economist and an expert on land use issues and land use law—an expertise gained not just through research and writing, but by ground-level experience and service with local zoning authorities. He tells a story we can only outline here, and partially at that. His article is brief and well worth reading in full.

Fischel's purpose is to explain how homeowners came to dominate the zoning game—on which see his book, The Homevoter Hypothesis (2001)—and with what consequences. Homeowners, he notes, are usually interested and politically active in their immediate community, in considerable part because for many of them their home is their chief asset. Hence we can see immediately why virtually every suburban zoning measure puts single family residences first and foremost.

We can also see, Fischel believes, why zoning began when it did (the second decade of the last century) and became, as it did, increasingly exclusionary. First, the appearance of electric powered streetcars in the late nineteenth century let urban workers live in exclusively residential areas and commute to (rather than live near) their jobs in the city. Then automobiles and trucks came into regular use, such that homeowners could move away from streetcar lines to suburban areas, and light industry could move away from downtown transportation hubs. Buses also appeared, so apartment dwellers (and their apartments) could move out and away from trolley lines. The problem, at least from the standpoint of single family homeowners, was that businesses and apartment buildings could invade their serene territory. This was a problem that local zoning could address with such exclusionary devices as dedicating most or all of a locality to single family residences, or zoning for large lots, and so on. Tendencies in these respects became more intense with the appearance of interstate highways, civil rights laws, and the environmental movement—which played into the story in ways Fischel sets forth. A little reflection should let you anticipate his arguments.

9. *Inclusionary zoning.* Inclusionary zoning consists of any number of devices designed to require or encourage developers to supply low and moderate income housing. Examples: (1) A requirement—conditioning a building permit on the builder's agreement to provide a certain number of units for lease at below-market rents. The courts have divided on the legality of such measures. (2) An incentive—lifting density limits in exchange for the builder's agreement to build more low income units. See Jennifer M. Morgan, Comment, Zoning for All: Using Inclusionary Zoning Techniques to Promote Affordable Housing, 44 Emory L.J. 359 (1995); Timothy J. Choppin, Note, Breaking the Exclusionary Land Use

Regulation Barrier: Policies to Promote Affordable Housing in the Suburbs, 82 Geo. L.J. 2039 (1994).

Can you see how inclusionary zoning might backfire, becoming exclusionary in effect? See Robert C. Ellickson, The Irony of "Inclusionary" Zoning, 54 S. Cal. L. Rev. 1167 (1981); see also James L. Mitchell, Will Empowering Developers to Challenge Exclusionary Zoning Increase Suburban Housing Choice?, 23 J. Poly. Analysis & Mgmt. 119 (2004), a comparative empirical study of the New Jersey and Pennsylvania approaches to exclusionary zoning. The study found that significantly more inexpensive housing was produced in Pennsylvania than in New Jersey in the years 1970-1990, notwithstanding the judicial mandate in New Jersey to construct less-expensive housing, and the provision of incentives to encourage developers to build it. A possible reason for this striking result is that the New Jersey approach diminished local control and raised questions of equity regarding the subsidies, which in turn provoked strong local opposition.

More recent empirical studies suggest that the impact of inclusionary zoning ordinances has been limited both in volume of new housing and impacts on housing prices. See, e.g., Gerrit-Jan Knaap, Housing Market Impacts of Inclusionary Zoning (National Center for Smart Growth Research and Education 2008) (finding that inclusionary zoning in California has no significant impact on housing permits but that prices for below-median value homes decrease by 0.8 percent and prices for above-median value homes increase by 5 percent); Jenny Schuetz et al., Silver Bullet or Trojan Horse? The Effects of Inclusionary Zoning on Local Housing Markets in the United States, 48 Urb. Stud. 297 (2011) (finding that inclusionary zoning in Boston raises prices and lowers production, but the effects are small).

12

Eminent Domain and the Problem
of Regulatory Takings

Unsatisfied with private arrangements (servitudes) and nuisance law as the means of land use control, the government might and often does embark on more activist courses—leaving property in the hands of its owners but regulating its use, or taking property from its owners and reallocating it to governmentally preferred uses.[1] The first approach, *regulating*, is illustrated by the method of zoning, studied in the last chapter. The second approach, *taking*, is the method of eminent domain to be considered here.

That the government has the power of eminent domain is, as we shall see, a point long beyond dispute. There are constraints, however. The Fifth Amendment enjoins: "nor shall private property be taken for public use, without just compensation."[2] As it happens, this language limits not only the government's right literally to take property through the power of eminent domain, but its freedom to regulate property as well. In regulating through zoning or other means, the government might at times be said to have expropriated what it claimed only to control; so too in carrying out the myriad other activities that attend the modern state. Some of the most intractable issues in the jurisprudence of property concern the matter of under what circumstances such governmental activities should be regarded as takings.

A. The Power of Eminent Domain: Sources and Rationales

Eminent domain is the power of government to force transfers of property from owners to itself.[3] Notice that the Fifth Amendment does not grant the taking power, but only confirms it—"a tacit recognition of a pre-existing power. . . ." United States v. Carmack, 329 U.S. 230, 241-242 (1946). The origins of eminent domain can be traced back to ancient Rome, where property could be taken for public projects (the evidence suggests that owners received compensation). English sovereigns enjoyed similar powers; indeed, they had no obligation to

---

1. Reallocation might be part of a grand scheme (for example, an urban renewal program intended to upgrade a slum area) or might instead involve a narrow, self-serving transfer (say the government wants a piece of land for a post office).

2. Virtually all state constitutions have similar language; in any event, the Fifth Amendment applies to the states through the Due Process Clause of the Fourteenth Amendment.

3. Or to other entities commonly invested with the power of eminent domain, such as public utilities and public schools, or, at times, to other private parties.

pay compensation (save in limited instances regarding seizure of provisions for the use of the royal household—a prerogative later abolished). By the time of the American Revolution, the power of the British government to take private property for public uses was well established. While never required to do so, the British Parliament has commonly paid compensation in the course of appropriating land for public purposes.

Early American practice regarding eminent domain was heavily influenced by the precedent of English experience. The power of government to take private property was recognized, though compensation was hardly universal in colonial times. Gradually, however, statutes came to provide for compensation, and some judges required it even in the absence of legislation. Constitutional provisions began to appear in the late 1700s, and by the end of the first half of the nineteenth century a trend in this direction had developed. Such provisions eventually became the norm; by the time the United States Constitution was held to require compensation by the states, they were already providing it on their own—through constitutional or judge-made law.

Various rationales for the taking power have been offered over the years. Early civil law scholars like Grotius and Pufendorf (to whom you were introduced in Chapter 1—see page 12) argued essentially that sovereign states had original and absolute ownership of property, prior to possession by citizens; individual possession derived from grants from the state and was held subject to an implied reservation that the state might resume its ownership. Another rationale is that eminent domain is the natural consequence of royal prerogatives that inhered in the concept of feudalism; on this view, the taking power is a remnant of feudal tenures. Finally, it has been argued, especially by natural law theorists, that eminent domain is an inherent attribute of sovereignty, necessary to the very existence of government.

Each of these notions has been reflected to some degree in American law, the last being the most common rationale today. Notice that none of the rationales really explains the obligation to compensate, as opposed to the power to take. In fact, there is very little historical evidence on the motivations behind the requirement of just compensation. Various accounts attribute it to a moral imperative of the natural law view of eminent domain; to English practice; to the views of Blackstone, at one time as influential in America as in England, in favor of "full indemnification"; and to a shift from traditional republican ideology to a liberalism that carried with it distrust of legislatures and a concern for individual rights. Related to the last point is speculation that James Madison, in drafting the Fifth Amendment, inserted the compensation requirement to guard the propertied classes from egalitarian redistributions of wealth.

NOTES AND QUESTIONS

1. *The power to take.* Richard Posner sketches a functional justification for the taking power, a justification that stresses efficiency. See Richard A. Posner, Economic Analysis of Law 70-71 (8th ed. 2011):

A good economic argument for eminent domain, although one with greater application to railroads and other right-of-way companies than to the government, is that it is an antimonopoly device. Once the railroad or pipeline has begun to build its line, the cost of abandoning it for an alternative route becomes very high. Knowing this, people owning land in the path of the advancing line will be tempted to hold out for a very high price—a price in excess of the opportunity cost of the land. (This is a problem of bilateral monopoly. . . .) Transaction costs will be high, land-acquisition costs high, and for both reasons the right-of-way company will have to raise the price of its services. The higher price will induce some consumers to shift to substitute services. Right-of-way companies will therefore have a smaller output; as a result they will need, and buy, less land than they would have bought at prices equal to the opportunity costs of the land. Higher land prices will also give the companies an incentive to substitute other inputs for some of the land they would have bought. As a result of all this, land that would have been more valuable to a right-of-way company than to its present owners will remain in its existing, less valuable uses, and this is inefficient. . . .

This analysis shows that the distinction between conflicting claims to a resource and conflicting or incompatible uses of resources is not fundamental. What is fundamental is the distinction between settings of low transaction costs and of high transaction costs. In the former, the law should require the parties to transact in the market, which it can do by making the present owner's property right absolute (or nearly so), so that anyone who thinks the property is worth more has to negotiate with the owner. But in settings of high transaction costs, people must be allowed to use the courts to shift resources to a more valuable use; the market is by definition unable to perform this function in those settings. This distinction is only imperfectly reflected in the law. While some government takings of land do occur in high-transaction-cost settings—taking land for a highway or for an airport or military base that requires the assembly of a large number of contiguous parcels—many others do not (public schools, post offices, government office buildings).

Do Posner's observations suggest that private developers facing land assembly problems be given the power of eminent domain? Or, on the other hand, should the government be denied the power, leaving it to cope with assembly problems just as private developers must? (Private developers use buying agents, option agreements, and straw transactions in their efforts—apparently often successful—to deal with the problem of holdouts.) For an overview of the key legal and economic considerations, see Daniel B. Kelly, Acquiring Land Through Eminent Domain: Justifications, Limitations, and Alternatives, in Research Handbook on the Economics of Property Law 345 (Kenneth Ayotte & Henry E. Smith eds. 2011).

2. *The duty to compensate.* Posner also suggests an economic rationale for the compensation obligation: "without it government would have an incentive to substitute land for cheaper inputs that were, however, more expensive to the government." Posner, supra, at 73. But there might be more to it than that. See William A. Fischel & Perry Shapiro, Takings, Insurance, and Michelman: Comments on Economic Interpretations of "Just Compensation" Law, 17 J. Legal Stud. 269 (1988):

In a world lacking any compensation requirement, the obvious fear is that private investors will be inhibited by the thought that government will snatch away or unthinkingly destroy the fruits of their venture. The fears of what will happen at the end of the process work themselves into the calculation of property owners at the beginning of that process, so that too little capital will be invested in productive enterprises. The compensation requirement thus serves the dual purpose of offering a substantial measure of protection to private entitlements, while disciplining the power of the state, which would otherwise overexpand unless made to pay for the resources that it consumes. [Id. at 269-270.]

Professors Fischel and Shapiro go on to discuss (which is not to say endorse) challenges to this "conventional economic wisdom," in particular the argument that compensation for takings can be *in*efficient in that it encourages landowners to overinvest in capital on their land without regard to its value for efficient government projects (an analogy would be unconditional payments for losses from hurricane damage; owners of shoreland would build on their property without thinking about predictable weather losses). The problem, it has been suggested, might best be handled by a private insurance market. The premium paid by insured property owners would force them to consider costs presently ignored. Id. at 270-271. For an overview of the debate, see Michael H. Schill, Intergovernmental Takings and Just Compensation: A Question of Federalism, 137 U. Pa. L. Rev. 829, 851-856 (1989).

An alternative view of the duty to compensate is framed in terms of fairness. The question to be answered is this: "[I]s it fair to effectuate this social measure without granting this claim to compensation for private loss thereby inflicted?" Frank Michelman, Property, Utility, and Fairness: Comments on the Ethical Foundations of "Just Compensation" Law, 80 Harv. L. Rev. 1165, 1172 (1967). Michelman's is a classic but difficult treatment, built on careful attention to principles of efficiency and fairness and on their interplay. Can you think of other grounds for requiring compensation? What about the argument that it protects against exploitation of relatively powerless groups and individuals? For discussion, see Daniel A. Farber, Economic Analysis and Just Compensation, 12 Intl. Rev. L. & Econ. 125 (1992); Daniel A. Farber, Public Choice and Just Compensation, 9 Const. Commentary 279 (1992); William A. Fischel, The Rest of Michelman 1967, in Research Handbook on the Economics of Property Law 372 (Kenneth Ayotte & Henry E. Smith eds. 2011); William A. Fischel & Perry Shapiro, A Constitutional Choice Model of Compensation for Takings, 9 Intl. Rev. L. & Econ. 115 (1989); Saul Levmore, Just Compensation and Just Politics, 22 Conn. L. Rev. 285 (1990); Saul Levmore, Takings, Torts, and Special Interests, 77 Va. L. Rev. 1333 (1991).

Regarding efficiency and fairness justifications for the duty to compensate in takings law, does it matter that *the government* is the party to be held liable? See Daryl J. Levinson, Making Government Pay: Markets, Politics, and the Allocation of Constitutional Costs, 67 U. Chi. L. Rev. 345 (2000) (arguing that because government actors respond to political incentives, not market incentives, the duty to compensate might work perversely, promoting inefficiency and injustice alike).

B.   The Public-Use Puzzle (and a Note on Just Compensation)

The Fifth Amendment's mention of "public use" is read to mean that property may be taken *only* for such uses; the government may not condemn for "private" purposes, however willing it might be to pay compensation for the forced transfer. Quite obviously, then, the reach of the eminent domain power hinges directly on the breadth or narrowness of meaning attached to "public use."

Kelo v. City of New London

Supreme Court of the United States, 2005
545 U.S. 469

JUSTICE STEVENS delivered the opinion of the Court.

In 2000, the city of New London approved a development plan that, in the words of the Supreme Court of Connecticut, was "projected to create in excess of 1,000 jobs, to increase tax and other revenues, and to revitalize an economically distressed city, including its downtown and waterfront areas." In assembling the land needed for this project, the city's development agent has purchased property from willing sellers and proposes to use the power of eminent domain to acquire the remainder of the property from unwilling owners in exchange for just compensation. The question presented is whether the city's proposed disposition of this property qualifies as a "public use" within the meaning of the Takings Clause of the Fifth Amendment to the Constitution.

The city of New London (hereinafter City) sits at the junction of the Thames River and the Long Island Sound in southeastern Connecticut. Decades of economic decline led a state agency in 1990 to designate the City a "distressed municipality." In 1996, the Federal Government closed the Naval Undersea Warfare Center, which had been located in the Fort Trumbull area of the City and had employed over 1,500 people. In 1998, the City's unemployment rate was nearly double that of the State, and its population of just under 24,000 residents was at its lowest since 1920.

These conditions prompted state and local officials to target New London, and particularly its Fort Trumbull area, for economic revitalization. To this end, respondent New London Development Corporation (NLDC), a private nonprofit entity established some years earlier to assist the City in planning economic development, was reactivated. In January 1998, the State authorized a $5.35 million bond issue to support the NLDC's planning activities and a $10 million bond issue toward the creation of a Fort Trumbull State Park. In February, the pharmaceutical company Pfizer Inc. announced that it would build a $300 million research facility on a site immediately adjacent to Fort Trumbull; local planners hoped that Pfizer would draw new business to the area, thereby serving as a catalyst to the area's rejuvenation. After receiving initial approval from the city council, the NLDC continued its planning activities and held a series of neighborhood meetings to educate the public about the process. In May, the city council authorized the NLDC to formally submit its plans to the relevant state agencies for review. Upon obtaining state-level approval, the NLDC finalized an integrated development plan focused on 90 acres of the Fort Trumbull area.

The Fort Trumbull area is situated on a peninsula that juts into the Thames River. The area comprises approximately 115 privately owned properties, as well as the 32 acres of land formerly occupied by the naval facility (Trumbull State Park now occupies 18 of those 32 acres). The development plan encompasses seven parcels. Parcel 1 is designated for a waterfront conference hotel at the center of a "small urban village" that will include restaurants and shopping. This parcel will also have marinas for both recreational and commercial uses. A pedestrian "riverwalk" will originate here and continue down the coast, connecting the waterfront areas of the development. Parcel 2 will be the site of approximately 80 new residences organized into an urban neighborhood and linked by public walkway to the remainder of the development, including the state park. This parcel also includes space reserved for a new U.S. Coast Guard Museum. Parcel 3, which is located immediately north of the Pfizer facility, will contain at least 90,000 square feet of research and development office space. Parcel 4A is a 2.4-acre site that will be used either to support the adjacent state park, by providing parking or retail services for visitors, or to support the nearby marina. Parcel 4B will include a renovated marina, as well as the final stretch of the riverwalk. Parcels 5, 6, and 7 will provide land for office and retail space, parking, and water-dependent commercial uses.

The NLDC intended the development plan to capitalize on the arrival of the Pfizer facility and the new commerce it was expected to attract. In addition to creating jobs, generating tax revenue, and helping to "build momentum for the revitalization of downtown New London," the plan was also designed to make the City more attractive and to create leisure and recreational opportunities on the waterfront and in the park.

The city council approved the plan in January 2000, and designated the NLDC as its development agent in charge of implementation. The city council also authorized the NLDC to purchase property or to acquire property by exercising eminent domain in the City's name. The NLDC successfully negotiated the purchase of most of the real estate in the 90-acre area, but its negotiations with petitioners failed. As a consequence, in November 2000, the NLDC initiated the condemnation proceedings that gave rise to this case.

Petitioner Susette Kelo has lived in the Fort Trumbull area since 1997. She has made extensive improvements to her house, which she prizes for its water view. Petitioner Wilhelmina Dery was born in her Fort Trumbull house in 1918 and has lived there her entire life. Her husband Charles (also a petitioner) has lived in the house since they married some 60 years ago. In all, the nine petitioners own 15 properties in Fort Trumbull—4 in parcel 3 of the development plan and 11 in parcel 4A. Ten of the parcels are occupied by the owner or a family member; the other five are held as investment properties. There is no allegation that any of these properties is blighted or otherwise in poor condition; rather, they were condemned only because they happen to be located in the development area.

In December 2000, petitioners brought this action in the New London Superior Court. They claimed, among other things, that the taking of their

Susette Kelo's house

properties would violate the "public use" restriction in the Fifth Amendment. After a 7-day bench trial, the Superior Court granted a permanent restraining order prohibiting the taking of the properties located in parcel 4A (park or marina support). It, however, denied petitioners relief as to the properties located in parcel 3 (office space).

After the Superior Court ruled, both sides took appeals to the Supreme Court of Connecticut. That court held, over a dissent, that all of the City's proposed takings were valid. It began by upholding the lower court's determination that the takings were authorized by the State's municipal development statute. That statute expresses a legislative determination that the taking of land, even developed land, as part of an economic development project is a "public use" and in the "public interest." Next, relying on cases such as Hawaii Housing Authority v. Midkiff, 467 U.S. 229 (1984), and Berman v. Parker, 348 U.S. 26 (1954), the court held that such economic development qualified as a valid public use under both the Federal and State Constitutions.

Finally, adhering to its precedents, the court went on to determine, first, whether the takings of the particular properties at issue were "reasonably necessary" to achieving the City's intended public use, and, second, whether the takings were for "reasonably foreseeable needs." The court upheld the trial court's factual findings as to parcel 3, but reversed the trial court as to parcel 4A, agreeing with the City that the intended use of this land was sufficiently definite and had been given "reasonable attention" during the planning process.

The three dissenting justices would have imposed a "heightened" standard of judicial review for takings justified by economic development. Although they agreed that the plan was intended to serve a valid public use, they would have found all the takings unconstitutional because the City had failed to adduce "clear and convincing evidence" that the economic benefits of the plan would in fact come to pass.

We granted certiorari to determine whether a city's decision to take property for the purpose of economic development satisfies the "public use" requirement of the Fifth Amendment.

Two polar propositions are perfectly clear. On the one hand, it has long been accepted that the sovereign may not take the property of A for the sole purpose of transferring it to another private party B, even though A is paid just compensation. On the other hand, it is equally clear that a State may transfer property from one private party to another if future "use by the public" is the purpose of the taking; the condemnation of land for a railroad with common-carrier duties is a familiar example. Neither of these propositions, however, determines the disposition of this case.

As for the first proposition, the City would no doubt be forbidden from taking petitioners' land for the purpose of conferring a private benefit on a particular private party. See *Midkiff*, 467 U.S. at 245 ("A purely private taking could not withstand the scrutiny of the public use requirement; it would serve no legitimate purpose of government and would thus be void"). Nor would the City be allowed to take property under the mere pretext of a public purpose, when its actual purpose was to bestow a private benefit. The takings before us, however, would be executed pursuant to a "carefully considered" development plan. The trial judge and all the members of the Supreme Court of Connecticut agreed that there was no evidence of an illegitimate purpose in this case. Therefore, as was true of the statute challenged in *Midkiff*, 467 U.S. at 245, the City's development plan was not adopted "to benefit a particular class of identifiable individuals."

On the other hand, this is not a case in which the City is planning to open the condemned land—at least not in its entirety—to use by the general public. Nor will the private lessees of the land in any sense be required to operate like common carriers, making their services available to all comers. But although such a projected use would be sufficient to satisfy the public use requirement, this "Court long ago rejected any literal requirement that condemned property be put into use for the general public." Id. at 244. Indeed, while many state courts in the mid-19th century endorsed "use by the public" as the proper definition of public use, that narrow view steadily eroded over time. Not only was the "use by the public" test difficult to administer (e.g., what proportion of the public need have access to the property? at what price?), but it proved to be impractical given the diverse and always evolving needs of society. Accordingly, when this Court began applying the Fifth Amendment to the States at the close of the 19th century, it embraced the broader and more natural interpretation of public use as "public purpose." . . . We have repeatedly and consistently rejected that narrow test ever since.

The disposition of this case therefore turns on the question whether the City's development plan serves a "public purpose." Without exception, our cases have defined that concept broadly, reflecting our longstanding policy of deference to legislative judgments in this field.

In Berman v. Parker, 348 U.S. 26 (1954), this Court upheld a redevelopment plan targeting a blighted area of Washington, D.C., in which most of the housing for the area's 5,000 inhabitants was beyond repair. Under the plan, the area would be condemned and part of it utilized for the construction of streets, schools, and other public facilities. The remainder of the land would be leased or sold to private parties for the purpose of redevelopment, including the construction of low-cost housing.

The owner of a department store located in the area challenged the condemnation, pointing out that his store was not itself blighted and arguing that the creation of a "better balanced, more attractive community" was not a valid public use. Writing for a unanimous Court, Justice Douglas refused to evaluate this claim in isolation, deferring instead to the legislative and agency judgment that the area "must be planned as a whole" for the plan to be successful. The Court explained that "community redevelopment programs need not, by force of the Constitution, be on a piecemeal basis—lot by lot, building by building." The public use underlying the taking was unequivocally affirmed:

> We do not sit to determine whether a particular housing project is or is not desirable. The concept of the public welfare is broad and inclusive. . . . The values it represents are spiritual as well as physical, aesthetic as well as monetary. It is within the power of the legislature to determine that the community should be beautiful as well as healthy, spacious as well as clean, well-balanced as well as carefully patrolled. In the present case, the Congress and its authorized agencies have made determinations that take into account a wide variety of values. It is not for us to reappraise them. If those who govern the District of Columbia decide that the Nation's Capital should be beautiful as well as sanitary, there is nothing in the Fifth Amendment that stands in the way.

In Hawaii Housing Authority v. Midkiff, 467 U.S. 229 (1984), the Court considered a Hawaii statute whereby fee title was taken from lessors and transferred to lessees (for just compensation) in order to reduce the concentration of land ownership. We unanimously upheld the statute and rejected the Ninth Circuit's view that it was a naked attempt on the part of the state of Hawaii to take the property of A and transfer it to B solely for B's private use and benefit. Reaffirming Berman's deferential approach to legislative judgments in this field, we concluded that the State's purpose of eliminating the "social and economic evils of a land oligopoly" qualified as a valid public use. Our opinion also rejected the contention that the mere fact that the State immediately transferred the properties to private individuals upon condemnation somehow diminished the public character of the taking. "[I]t is only the taking's purpose, and not its mechanics," we explained, that matters in determining public use. . . .

Viewed as a whole, our jurisprudence has recognized that the needs of society have varied between different parts of the Nation, just as they have evolved over time in response to changed circumstances. Our earliest cases in particular embodied a strong theme of federalism, emphasizing the "great respect" that we owe to state legislatures and state courts in discerning local public needs. . . . For more than a century, our public use jurisprudence has wisely eschewed rigid formulas and intrusive scrutiny in favor of affording legislatures broad latitude in determining what public needs justify the use of the takings power.

Those who govern the City were not confronted with the need to remove blight in the Fort Trumbull area, but their determination that the area was sufficiently distressed to justify a program of economic rejuvenation is entitled to our deference. The City has carefully formulated an economic development plan that it believes will provide appreciable benefits to the community, including—but by no means limited to—new jobs and increased tax revenue. As with other exercises in urban planning and development, the City is endeavoring to coordinate a variety of commercial, residential, and recreational uses of land, with the hope that they will form a whole greater than the sum of its parts. To effectuate this plan, the City has invoked a state statute that specifically authorizes the use of eminent domain to promote economic development. Given the comprehensive character of the plan, the thorough deliberation that preceded its adoption, and the limited scope of our review, it is appropriate for us, as it was in *Berman*, to resolve the challenges of the individual owners, not on a piecemeal basis, but rather in light of the entire plan. Because that plan unquestionably serves a public purpose, the takings challenged here satisfy the public use requirement of the Fifth Amendment.

To avoid this result, petitioners urge us to adopt a new bright-line rule that economic development does not qualify as a public use. Putting aside the unpersuasive suggestion that the City's plan will provide only purely economic benefits, neither precedent nor logic supports petitioners' proposal. Promoting economic development is a traditional and long accepted function of government. There is, moreover, no principled way of distinguishing economic development from the other public purposes that we have recognized. In our cases upholding takings that facilitated agriculture and mining, for example, we emphasized the importance of those industries to the welfare of the States in question; in *Berman*, we endorsed the purpose of transforming a blighted area into a "well-balanced" community through redevelopment; in *Midkiff*, we upheld the interest in breaking up a land oligopoly that "created artificial deterrents to the normal functioning of the State's residential land market." . . . It would be incongruous to hold that the City's interest in the economic benefits to be derived from the development of the Fort Trumbull area has less of a public character than any of those other interests. Clearly, there is no basis for exempting economic development from our traditionally broad understanding of public purpose.

Petitioners contend that using eminent domain for economic development impermissibly blurs the boundary between public and private takings. Again, our cases foreclose this objection. Quite simply, the government's pursuit of a public purpose will often benefit individual private parties. . . .

It is further argued that without a bright-line rule nothing would stop a city from transferring citizen A's property to citizen B for the sole reason that citizen B will put the property to a more productive use and thus pay more taxes. Such a one-to-one transfer of property, executed outside the confines of an integrated development plan, is not presented in this case. While such an unusual exercise of government power would certainly raise a suspicion that a private purpose was afoot, the hypothetical cases posited by petitioners can be confronted if and when they arise. They do not warrant the crafting of an artificial restriction on the concept of public use. . . .

Just as we decline to second-guess the City's considered judgments about the efficacy of its development plan, we also decline to second-guess the City's determinations as to what lands it needs to acquire in order to effectuate the project. "It is not for the courts to oversee the choice of the boundary line nor to sit in review on the size of a particular project area. Once the question of the public purpose has been decided, the amount and character of land to be taken for the project and the need for a particular tract to complete the integrated plan rests in the discretion of the legislative branch." *Berman*, 348 U.S. at 35-36.

In affirming the City's authority to take petitioners' properties, we do not minimize the hardship that condemnations may entail, notwithstanding the payment of just compensation. We emphasize that nothing in our opinion precludes any State from placing further restrictions on its exercise of the takings power. Indeed, many States already impose "public use" requirements that are stricter than the federal baseline. Some of these requirements have been established as a matter of state constitutional law,[4] while others are expressed in state eminent domain statutes that carefully limit the grounds upon which takings may be exercised.[5] As the submissions of the parties and their amici make clear, the necessity and wisdom of using eminent domain to promote economic development are certainly matters of legitimate public debate. This Court's authority, however, extends only to determining whether the City's proposed condemnations are for a "public use" within the meaning of the Fifth Amendment to the Federal Constitution. Because over a century of our case law interpreting that provision dictates an affirmative answer to that question, we may not grant petitioners the relief that they seek.

The judgment of the Supreme Court of Connecticut is affirmed.

[Justice Kennedy concurred in the judgment, but added that even with a deferential standard of review, a taking should not survive the public use test if there is a clear showing that its purpose is "to favor a particular private party, with only incidental or pretextual public benefits. . . ." That a taking for economic development is not presumptively invalid, as petitioners had urged, "does not foreclose

---

4. See, e.g., County of Wayne v. Hathcock, 471 Mich. 445, 684 N.W.2d 765 (2004).
5. Under California law, for instance, a city may only take land for economic development purposes in blighted areas. Cal. Health & Safety Code Ann. §§33030-33037 (West 1997). See, e.g., Redevelopment Agency of Chula Vista v. Rados Bros., 95 Cal. App. 4th 309 (2002).

the possibility that a more stringent standard of review . . . might be appropriate for a more narrowly drawn category of takings."]

JUSTICE O'CONNOR, with whom THE CHIEF JUSTICE, JUSTICE SCALIA, and JUSTICE THOMAS join, dissenting.

. . . Under the banner of economic development, all private property is now vulnerable to being taken and transferred to another private owner, so long as it might be upgraded—i.e., given to an owner who will use it in a way that the legislature deems more beneficial to the public—in the process. To reason, as the Court does, that the incidental public benefits resulting from the subsequent ordinary use of private property render economic development takings "for public use" is to wash out any distinction between private and public use of property—and thereby effectively to delete the words "for public use" from the Takings Clause of the Fifth Amendment. Accordingly I respectfully dissent.

. . . Petitioners own properties in two of the plan's seven parcels—Parcel 3 and Parcel 4A. Under the plan, Parcel 3 is slated for the construction of research and office space as a market develops for such space. It will also retain the existing Italian Dramatic Club (a private cultural organization) though the homes of three plaintiffs in that parcel are to be demolished.[6] Parcel 4A is slated, mysteriously, for "park support." At oral argument, counsel for respondents conceded the vagueness of this proposed use, and offered that the parcel might eventually be used for parking.

To save their homes, petitioners sued New London and the NLDC, to whom New London has delegated eminent domain power. . . . Petitioners are not holdouts; they do not seek increased compensation, and none is opposed to new development in the area. Theirs is an objection in principle: They claim that the NLDC's proposed use for their confiscated property is not a "public" one for purposes of the Fifth Amendment. While the government may take their homes to build a road or a railroad or to eliminate a property use that harms the public, say petitioners, it cannot take their property for the private use of other owners simply because the new owners may make more productive use of the property.

. . . Where is the line between "public" and "private" property use? We give considerable deference to legislatures' determinations about what governmental activities will advantage the public. But were the political branches the sole arbiters of the public-private distinction, the Public Use Clause would amount to little more than hortatory fluff. An external, judicial check on how the public use requirement is interpreted, however limited, is necessary if this constraint on government power is to retain any meaning. . . .

Our cases have generally identified three categories of takings that comply with the public use requirement, though it is in the nature of things that the boundaries between these categories are not always firm. Two are relatively straightforward and uncontroversial. First, the sovereign may transfer private property to

---

6. The Italian Dramatic Club was founded in 1922 and is apparently a favorite watering hole for New London's government officials and other parts of the city's establishment.—EDS.

public ownership—such as for a road, a hospital, or a military base. . . . Second, the sovereign may transfer private property to private parties, often common carriers, who make the property available for the public's use—such as with a railroad, a public utility, or a stadium. . . . But "public ownership" and "use-by-the-public" are sometimes too constricting and impractical ways to define the scope of the Public Use Clause. Thus we have allowed that, in certain circumstances and to meet certain exigencies, takings that serve a public purpose also satisfy the Constitution even if the property is destined for subsequent private use. See, e.g., Berman v. Parker, 348 U.S. 26 (1954); Hawaii Housing Authority v. Midkiff, 467 U.S. 229 (1984).

This case returns us for the first time in over 20 years to the hard question of when a purportedly "public purpose" taking meets the public use requirement. It presents an issue of first impression: Are economic development takings constitutional? I would hold that they are not. We are guided by two precedents about the taking of real property by eminent domain. In *Berman*, we upheld takings within a blighted neighborhood of Washington, D.C. The neighborhood had so deteriorated that, for example, 64.3% of its dwellings were beyond repair. 348 U.S. at 30. It had become burdened with "overcrowding of dwellings," "lack of adequate streets and alleys," and "lack of light and air." Id. at 34. Congress had determined that the neighborhood had become "injurious to the public health, safety, morals, and welfare" and that it was necessary to "eliminat[e] all such injurious conditions by employing all means necessary and appropriate for the purpose," including eminent domain. Id. at 28. Mr. Berman's department store was not itself blighted. Having approved of Congress' decision to eliminate the harm to the public emanating from the blighted neighborhood, however, we did not second-guess its decision to treat the neighborhood as a whole rather than lot-by-lot. Id. at 34-35. . . .

In *Midkiff*, we upheld a land condemnation scheme in Hawaii whereby title in real property was taken from lessors and transferred to lessees. At that time, the State and Federal Governments owned nearly 49% of the State's land, and another 47% was in the hands of only 72 private landowners. Concentration of land ownership was so dramatic that on the State's most urbanized island, Oahu, 22 landowners owned 72.5% of the fee simple titles. [467 U.S.] at 232. The Hawaii Legislature had concluded that the oligopoly in land ownership was "skewing the State's residential fee simple market, inflating land prices, and injuring the public tranquility and welfare," and therefore enacted a condemnation scheme for redistributing title. Id.

In those decisions, we emphasized the importance of deferring to legislative judgments about public purpose. Because courts are ill equipped to evaluate the efficacy of proposed legislative initiatives, we rejected as unworkable the idea of courts' "deciding on what is and is not a governmental function and . . . invalidating legislation on the basis of their view on that question at the moment of decision, a practice which has proved impracticable in other fields." . . .

Yet for all the emphasis on deference, *Berman* and *Midkiff* hewed to a bedrock principle without which our public use jurisprudence would collapse: "A

purely private taking could not withstand the scrutiny of the public use requirement; it would serve no legitimate purpose of government and would thus be
void." *Midkiff*, 467 U.S. at 245. . . .

The Court's holdings in *Berman* and *Midkiff* were true to the principle underlying the Public Use Clause. In both those cases, the extraordinary, precondemna-
tion use of the targeted property inflicted affirmative harm on society—in *Berman*
through blight resulting from extreme poverty and in *Midkiff* through oligopoly
resulting from extreme wealth. And in both cases, the relevant legislative body
had found that eliminating the existing property use was necessary to remedy the
harm. . . . Thus a public purpose was realized when the harmful use was eliminated. Because each taking directly achieved a public benefit, it did not matter
that the property was turned over to private use. Here, in contrast, New London
does not claim that Susette Kelo's and Wilhelmina Dery's well-maintained homes
are the source of any social harm. Indeed, it could not so claim without adopting
the absurd argument that any single-family home that might be razed to make
way for an apartment building, or any church that might be replaced with a retail
store, or any small business that might be more lucrative if it were instead part of
a national franchise, is inherently harmful to society and thus within the government's power to condemn.

In moving away from our decisions sanctioning the condemnation of harmful property use, the Court today significantly expands the meaning of public use.
It holds that the sovereign may take private property currently put to ordinary
private use, and give it over for new, ordinary private use, so long as the new use is
predicted to generate some secondary benefit for the public—such as increased
tax revenue, more jobs, maybe even esthetic pleasure. . . .

There is a sense in which this troubling result follows from errant language
in *Berman* and *Midkiff*. In discussing whether takings within a blighted neighborhood were for a public use, *Berman* began by observing: "We deal, in other
words, with what traditionally has been known as the police power." 348 U.S.
at 32. From there it declared that "[o]nce the object is within the authority of
Congress, the right to realize it through the exercise of eminent domain is clear."
Id. at 33. Following up, we said in *Midkiff* that "[t]he 'public use' requirement is
coterminous with the scope of a sovereign's police powers." 467 U.S. at 240. This
language was unnecessary to the specific holdings of those decisions.[7] *Berman* and
Midkiff simply did not put such language to the constitutional test, because the
takings in those cases were within the police power but also for "public use" for
the reasons I have described. The case before us now demonstrates why, when
deciding if a taking's purpose is constitutional, the police power and "public use"
cannot always be equated.

. . . The trouble with economic development takings is that private benefit
and incidental public benefit are, by definition, merged and mutually reinforcing.

---

7. As Justice O'Connor was the author of the Court's unanimous opinion in *Midkiff*, this must have been
an awkward paragraph to write.—EDS.

In this case, for example, any boon for Pfizer or the plan's developer is difficult to disaggregate from the promised public gains in taxes and jobs.

. . . The logic of today's decision is that eminent domain may only be used to upgrade—not downgrade—property. At best this makes the Public Use Clause redundant with the Due Process Clause, which already prohibits irrational government action. See *Lingle*, 544 U.S. 528. . . . [W]ho among us can say she already makes the most productive or attractive possible use of her property? The specter of condemnation hangs over all property. Nothing is to prevent the State from replacing any Motel 6 with a Ritz-Carlton, any home with a shopping mall, or any farm with a factory. . . .

Finally, in a coda, the Court suggests that property owners should turn to the States, who may or may not choose to impose appropriate limits on economic development takings. This is an abdication of our responsibility. States play many important functions in our system of dual sovereignty, but compensating for our refusal to enforce properly the Federal Constitution (and a provision meant to curtail state action, no less) is not among them. . . .

JUSTICE THOMAS, dissenting.

. . . [T]he Court replaces the Public Use Clause with a "[P]ublic [P]urpose" Clause, (or perhaps the "Diverse and Always Evolving Needs of Society" Clause), a restriction that is satisfied, the Court instructs, so long as the purpose is "legitimate" and the means "not irrational." This deferential shift in phraseology enables the Court to hold, against all common sense, that a costly urban-renewal project whose stated purpose is a vague promise of new jobs and increased tax revenue, but which is also suspiciously agreeable to the Pfizer Corporation, is for a "public use."

I cannot agree. If such "economic development" takings are for a "public use," any taking is, and the Court has erased the Public Use Clause from our Constitution, as Justice O'Connor powerfully argues in dissent. . . . Today's decision is simply the latest in a string of our cases construing the Public Use Clause to be a virtual nullity, without the slightest nod to its original meaning. In my view, the Public Use Clause, originally understood, is a meaningful limit on the government's eminent domain power. Our cases have strayed from the Clause's original meaning, and I would reconsider them.

. . . The most natural reading of the [Takings] Clause is that it allows the government to take property only if the government owns, or the public has a legal right to use, the property, as opposed to taking it for any public purpose or necessity whatsoever. At the time of the founding, dictionaries primarily defined the noun "use" as "[t]he act of employing any thing to any purpose." 2 S. Johnson, A Dictionary of the English Language 2194 (4th ed. 1773). . . . The term "public use," then, means that either the government or its citizens as a whole must actually "employ" the taken property.

. . . Tellingly, the phrase "public use" contrasts with the very different phrase "general Welfare" used elsewhere in the Constitution. . . . The Framers would have used some such broader term if they had meant the Public Use Clause to have a similarly sweeping scope. . . .

Early American eminent domain practice largely bears out this understanding of the Public Use Clause. . . . States employed the eminent domain power to provide quintessentially public goods, such as public roads, toll roads, ferries, canals, railroads, and public parks. . . .

To be sure, some early state legislatures tested the limits of their state-law eminent domain power. Some States enacted statutes allowing the taking of property for the purpose of building private roads. . . . These statutes were mixed; some required the private landowner to keep the road open to the public, and others did not. . . . Later in the 19th century, moreover, the Mill Acts were employed to grant rights to private manufacturing plants, in addition to grist mills that had common-carrier duties. See, e.g., M. Horwitz, The Transformation of American Law 1780-1860, pp. 51-52 (1977).

[T]he earliest Mill Acts were applied to entities with duties to remain open to the public, and their later extension is not deeply probative of whether that subsequent practice is consistent with the original meaning of the Public Use Clause. . . . At the time of the founding, "[b]usiness corporations were only beginning to upset the old corporate model, in which the raison d'être of chartered associations was their service to the public," Horwitz, supra, at 49-50, so it was natural to those who framed the first Public Use Clauses to think of mills as inherently public entities. The disagreement among state courts, and state legislatures' attempts to circumvent public use limits on their eminent domain power, cannot obscure that the Public Use Clause is most naturally read to authorize takings for public use only if the government or the public actually uses the taken property.

. . . For all these reasons, I would revisit our Public Use Clause cases and consider returning to the original meaning of the Public Use Clause: that the government may take property only if it actually uses or gives the public a legal right to use the property. . . .

. . . Allowing the government to take property solely for public purposes is bad enough, but extending the concept of public purpose to encompass any economically beneficial goal guarantees that these losses will fall disproportionately on poor communities. Those communities are not only systematically less likely to put their lands to the highest and best social use, but are also the least politically powerful. If ever there were justification for intrusive judicial review of constitutional provisions that protect "discrete and insular minorities," United States v. Carolene Products Co., 304 U.S. 144, 152 n.4 (1938), surely that principle would apply with great force to the powerless groups and individuals the Public Use Clause protects. The deferential standard this Court has adopted for the Public Use Clause is therefore deeply perverse. It encourages "those citizens with disproportionate influence and power in the political process, including large corporations and development firms," to victimize the weak. . . .

Those incentives have made the legacy of this Court's "public purpose" test an unhappy one. In the 1950's, no doubt emboldened in part by the expansive understanding of "public use" this Court adopted in *Berman*, cities "rushed to draw plans" for downtown development. B. Frieden & L. Sagalyn, Downtown, Inc.: How America Rebuilds Cities 17 (1989). "Of all the families displaced by urban renewal from 1949 through 1963, 63 percent of those whose race was known were nonwhite, and of these families, 56 percent of nonwhites and 38 percent of whites had incomes low enough to qualify for public housing, which, however, was seldom available to them." Id. at 28. Public works projects in the 1950's and 1960's destroyed predominantly minority communities in St. Paul, Minnesota, and Baltimore, Maryland. Id. at 28-29. In 1981, urban planners in Detroit, Michigan, uprooted the largely "lower-income and elderly" Poletown neighborhood for the benefit of the General Motors Corporation. J. Wylie, Poletown: Community Betrayed 58 (1989). Urban renewal projects have long been associated with the displacement of blacks; "[i]n cities across the country, urban renewal came to be known as 'Negro removal.'" Pritchett, The "Public Menace" of Blight: Urban Renewal and the Private Uses of Eminent Domain, 21 Yale L. & Pol'y Rev. 1, 47 (2003). Over 97 percent of the individuals forcibly removed from their homes by the "slum-clearance" project upheld by this Court in *Berman* were black. 348 U.S. at 30. Regrettably, the predictable consequence of the Court's decision will be to exacerbate these effects. . . .

NOTES AND QUESTIONS

1. *Public use in general.* See Lawrence Berger, The Public Use Requirement in Eminent Domain, 57 Or. L. Rev. 203, 205, 209 (1978):

> The precise meaning of the "public use" requirement has varied over time and according to the type of taking involved. The conventional statement of the historical case development holds that there are two basic opposing views of the meaning of "public use": (1) that the term means advantage or benefit to the public (the so-called broad view); and (2) that it means actual use or right to use of the condemned property by the public (the so-called narrow view). The conventional wisdom goes on to say that right after the Revolution the broad view dominated the courts; that later the narrow view came into fashion; and that later still and to date, the broad—and according to many—the enlightened view has returned to favor. Actually, the history is somewhat more complicated. . . .
>
> While the narrow view of public use held considerable sway, especially in the latter half of the nineteenth century, it never completely took over the field. The two doctrines competed, leaving the commentators in hopeless confusion as to what the "true rule" (for in those days they believed in such things) was. And no wonder the difficulty, for each view as applied to particular cases obviously led to at least what were then regarded as unacceptable results. Thus the narrow use by the public rule would have allowed condemnation for the purpose of erecting a privately owned theater or hotel, something which no one then (or perhaps even now) would seriously advocate. And the broad public advantage test would have allowed a toy manufacturer who provided substantial employment in the vicinity to condemn land for the construction of a plant, likewise then unthinkable.
>
> Thus by the beginning of the twentieth century, doctrine was in a shambles and predictability of result at a minimum. . . .

Doctrine remains in a shambles, even today, especially in cases, like *Kelo*, where the government aims to take property from one group of private owners and transfer it, by sale or lease, to other private owners.

2. *Public use—ends*. What *should* the public-use test be? The question can be approached in two ways. One way, suggested in the excerpt from Berger set out above, focuses on the contemplated ends of an act of condemnation. If the ends are sufficiently "public" in one sense or another, the test is passed. Notice that if the relevant sense of "public" is the broad test of "public benefit" to which Professor Berger refers, then really there is no test at all. Essentially, the public-benefit test permits an act of condemnation so long as the objective it serves is in the public interest, as an exercise of the police power must be. Yet this suggests that what the government is doing by way of eminent domain it could just as well do by way of the police power. Indeed, as Justice O'Connor notes in *Kelo*, the *Midkiff* Court said that the public-use requirement of the Takings Clause is "coterminous with the scope of the sovereign's police powers." Page 1120.

> This pronouncement has dismayed commentators because the outer limit of the police power has traditionally marked the line between *noncompensable* regulation and compensable takings of property. . . . Legitimately exercised, the police power requires no compensation. Thus, if public use is truly coterminous with the police power, a state could freely choose between compensation and noncompensation any time its actions served a "public use." [Thomas W. Merrill, The Economics of Public Use, 72 Cornell L. Rev. 61, 70 (1986).]

See also Richard A. Epstein, Takings: Private Property and the Power of Eminent Domain 170 (1985) (a public-benefit test makes the public-use requirement wholly empty). But is this view of Professors Merrill and Epstein correct? It seems not. To see why, simply

> [s]uppose that public use is truly "coterminous with the police power," as Merrill puts it. The Fifth Amendment's taking provision would then be read to say *nor shall private property be taken pursuant to the police power, without just compensation*. Obviously, compensation would still be required so long as there is a *taking*—that is, condemnation through eminent domain. So treating public use as coterminous with the police power doesn't do away with takings doctrine; rather, it seems to have done away with serious judicial scrutiny of the public-use question. [James E. Krier & Christopher Serkin, Public Ruses, 2004 Mich. St. L. Rev. 859, 862-863.]

In any event, treating public use in terms of ends in either of the senses mentioned by Professor Berger—advantage to the public or use by the public—can result in a very sweeping taking power, as the *Kelo* dissents emphasize.

3. *Public use—means*. Another way to approach the question of public use is in terms of means rather than ends. The idea here is to ask whether the power of eminent domain is really necessary to accomplish whatever aim the government has in mind (recall the discussion of justifications for the taking power in Note 1 on pages 1108-1109). Justice Woodbury suggested such a view long ago, in his concurring opinion in West River Bridge Co. v. Dix, 47 U.S. 507, 545-546 (1848), arguing that takings should be permitted only for pressing needs the attainment of which would be unduly difficult without the *means* of eminent domain.

The case for a means-based test was spelled out many years later in Professor Merrill's article on The Economics of Public Use, supra. Something akin to Merrill's and Woodruff's position was adopted subsequently by the Michigan Supreme Court in County of Wayne v. Hathcock, 684 N.W.2d 765 (Mich. 2004).

The case involved a government plan to stimulate an ailing economy by condemning unblighted land adjacent to Detroit Metropolitan Airport and transferring it to private parties for the purpose of developing a business and technology park with a conference center, hotel, and recreational facility. The court, relying heavily on a dissenting opinion in a notorious earlier case,[8] held that transfer of condemned land to private parties is appropriate as a public use only where "public necessity of the extreme sort" requires eminent domain to assemble land on behalf of enterprises generating public benefits (for example, rights of way, railroads, and highways—this is a means and ends test); or where the condemned property "remains subject to public oversight after transfer" (for example, the property is transferred to a regulated public utility—an ends test); or where the property is taken not in the interests of private parties to whom it is transferred, but rather "because of 'facts of independent public significance'" (for example, to clear blighted land—another ends test). The court ruled that the airport project met none of the criteria. 684 N.W.2d at 783, quoting *Poletown*. On *Hathcock*, see Symposium, The Death of *Poletown*: The Future of Eminent Domain and Urban Development After *County of Wayne v. Hathcock*, 2004 Mich. St. L. Rev. 837.

For more on means tests, see, e.g., Nicole Stelle Garnett, The Public-Use Question as a Takings Problem, 71 Geo. Wash. L. Rev. 934 (2003); Daniel B. Kelly, The "Public Use" Requirement in Eminent Domain: A Rationale Based on Secret Purchases and Private Influence, 92 Cornell L. Rev. 1 (2006).

4. *Public use—the* Kelo *case and the level of scrutiny.* The Court in *Kelo* employed an ends test, but applied it in a very deferential manner, "affording legislatures broad latitude in determining what public needs justify the use of the takings power" (see page 1116). Most state courts take the same approach, but some review the government's justifications for a proposed project with close scrutiny, requiring a showing that the project's aims cannot be achieved by some means less intrusive than eminent domain. See, e.g., Sw. Ill. Dev. Auth. v. Natl. City Envtl., L.L.C., 768 N.E.2d 1 (Ill. 2002).

Putting together all that's been sketched above, we can see that reviewing courts might take any number of approaches to the public-use question. A court might look at ends or means or both; it might look closely, or in a more deferential frame of mind. Is one way of going at the matter better than all the others? Are any of the alternatives satisfactory? More on this when we get to the Notes on "Just Compensation" that appear below.[9]

5. *After* Kelo. Reactions to *Kelo* were fast and furious. Within a month of the decision, state legislatures "moved to protect homes and businesses from the expanded reach of eminent domain." Timothy Egan, Ruling Sets Off Tug of War over Private Property, N.Y. Times, July 30, 2005, at A1. As of 2013, at least 43 states had enacted post-*Kelo* restrictions (sometimes through a referendum

---

8. Poletown Neighborhood Council v. City of Detroit, 304 N.W.2d 455 (Mich. 1981). *Poletown*, subsequently overruled by *Hathcock*, upheld as a public use Detroit's plan to condemn an unblighted residential neighborhood, clear the land, and convey it to General Motors as a site for construction of an assembly plant.

9. Related to the issue of public use is the propriety of a delegation of eminent domain power from the government to private corporations and individuals engaged in "public services" (e.g., common carriers, public utilities). That such delegation is generally permitted is well settled.

process), and other measures, including federal ones, have been put in place or are under consideration. For comprehensive treatments, see Ilya Somin, The Limits of Backlash: Assessing the Political Response to *Kelo*, 93 Minn. L. Rev. 2100 (2009); Marc Mihaly & Turner Smith, *Kelo*'s Trail: A Survey of State and Federal Legislative and Judicial Activity Five Years Later, 38 Ecology L.Q. 703 (2011).

Some observers see all of this activity as a vindication of the *Kelo* Court's approach (recall that the Court noted in its opinion, see page 1117, that state courts and legislatures are free to impose stricter public use requirements than the Court itself saw fit to do). Judge Richard Posner, for example, sees the pronounced adverse reaction to the *Kelo* decision as "evidence of its pragmatic soundness" in shifting the public use debate to democratically accountable entities. See Richard A. Posner, Foreword: A Political Court, 119 Harv. L. Rev. 31, 98 (2005).

Professor Somin disagrees with Posner's assessment. In his view, most of the new measures are likely to prove ineffective.[10] He argues that political ignorance

10. He thinks that effective measures are those that categorically prohibit takings for economic development, or at least forbid them to some significant degree. All in all, 36 state legislatures adopted post-*Kelo* measures, and in 7 additional states measures resulted from legislative- or citizen-initiated referenda. In Somin's terms, more than 60 percent of the measures enacted or initiated by legislatures are ineffective, whereas about 80 percent of the measures enacted by citizen-initiated referenda are effective. See Somin, supra, at 2115 (Table 3). A different sort of proposed reform would make structural changes in the eminent domain process in order to make takings for economic development more responsive to citizen interests. See Michael Heller & Rick Hills, Land Assembly Districts, 121 Harv. L. Rev. 1465 (2008); Amnon Lehavi & Amir N. Licht, Eminent Domain, Inc., 107 Colum. L. Rev. 1704 (2007).

lets legislators get away with cosmetic laws, so there is still a strong case for the vigorous sort of judicial review that the *Kelo* majority refused to provide. Ideally, of course, property rights advocates would prefer even more, namely a flat-out judicial ban on takings for purposes of economic development. For discussion, see Ilya Somin, Controlling the Grasping Hand: Economic Development Takings After *Kelo*, 15 Sup. Ct. Econ. Rev. 183 (2007).

For a fascinating account of the events surrounding *Kelo*, and discussion of key legal and policy issues, written by an award-winning investigative journalist, see Jeff Benedict, The Little Pink House: A True Story of Defiance and Courage (2009). For a review by a veteran land use scholar, see George Lefcoe, Jeff Benedict's *Little Pink House*: The Back Story of the *Kelo* Case, 42 Conn. L. Rev. 925 (2010).

Pfizer closed its New London facility in late 2010. And thanks in part to Hurricane Irene in 2011, the area planned for development in New London became a dump for storm debris.

6. *Eminent domain, federalism, and originalism.* Scholars have long taken for granted the proposition that the federal government may exercise eminent domain anywhere in the United States. After all, the Supreme Court so held in Kohl v. United States, 91 U.S. 367 (1875). An eye-opening article by Will Baude argues that *Kohl* was a wrong turn, one very much at odds with the original understanding of the eminent domain power and early American practice. Baude argues that at the time of the founding and for a long while thereafter, the common practice was for states to condemn private property and then to transfer this property to the national government so federal improvements could be built. This practice prevailed precisely because so many lawyers and legislators at the time felt that the federal government lacked the constitutional authority to condemn land outside the District of Columbia and territories. See William Baude, Rethinking the Federal Eminent Domain Power, 122 Yale L.J. 1738 (2013).

7. *RLUIPA after* Kelo. Recall the discussion of the Religious Land Use and Institutionalized Persons Act in Chapter 11 (beginning at page 1043), which limits the zoning authority of local governments with respect to lands owned by religious congregations. One way a locality might try to get around the constraints of RLUIPA would be by taking the property of churches under the power of eminent domain, rather than regulating the property under the police power. Given *Kelo*'s expansive view of the takings power, should such a move be permitted? For discussion, see St. John's United Church of Christ v. City of Chicago, 502 F.3d 616, 639-642 (7th Cir. 2007) (holding RLUIPA inapplicable to exercises of eminent domain); Christopher Serkin & Nelson Tebbe, Condemning Religion: RLUIPA and the Politics of Eminent Domain, 85 Notre Dame L. Rev. 1 (2009).

NOTES: "JUST COMPENSATION"

1. Why is "public use" a matter of concern to property owners, given that they are entitled to "just compensation" if their property is taken? The answer lies in

part in the measure of what they receive. See, e.g., Coniston Corp. v. Village of Hoffman Estates, 844 F.2d 461, 464 (7th Cir. 1988) (Posner, J.):

"[J]ust compensation" has been held to be satisfied by payment of market value.... Compensation in the constitutional sense is therefore not full compensation, for market value is not the value that every owner of property attaches to his property but merely the value that the marginal owner attaches to *his* property. Many owners are "intramarginal" meaning that because of relocation costs, sentimental attachments, or the special suitability of the property for their particular (perhaps idiosyncratic) needs, they value their property at more than its market value (i.e., it is not "for sale"). Such owners are hurt when the government takes their property and gives them just its market value in return. The taking in effect confiscates the additional (call it "personal") value that they obtain from the property, but this limited confiscation is permitted provided the taking is for a public use.

Earlier we briefly considered the reasons for the just-compensation requirement (see Note 2 on page 1109). One reason, as the word *just* suggests, must surely be justice or fairness. "The constitutional requirement of just compensation derives as much content from the basic equitable principles of fairness . . . as it does from technical concepts of property law." United States v. Fuller, 409 U.S. 488, 490 (1973).[11] Given Judge Posner's remarks in the *Hoffman Estates* case, is fair market value fair? (Fair to whom? In United States v. Commodities Trading Corp., 339 U.S. 121, 123 (1950), the Court said the question is this: "What compensation is 'just' both to an owner whose property is taken and to the public that must pay the bill?")

What about efficiency? Does not the market-value measure of just compensation promote or at least tolerate transfers of property from higher- to lower-valued uses?[12] Concerns from the standpoint of fairness and efficiency alike could be remedied, at least in part, by including in just compensation the "personal value" mentioned by Judge Posner, but the Supreme Court has rejected the idea:

Because of serious practical difficulties in assessing the worth an individual places on particular property at a given time, we have recognized the need for a relatively objective working rule. . . . The Court therefore has employed the concept of fair market value to determine the condemnee's loss. Under this standard, the owner is entitled to receive "what a willing buyer

---

11. The compensation practices of a number of countries are considered in Gregory S. Alexander, The Global Debate over Constitutional Property: Lessons for American Takings Jurisprudence (2006); Andre van der Walt, Constitutional Property Clauses (2006); and Compensation for Expropriation: A Comparative Study (Gavin M. Erasmus ed. 1990).

12. Government authorities are required to negotiate with property owners before beginning eminent domain proceedings, and the vast majority of cases are resolved without litigation. Negotiations can work in favor of property owners, because if they fail the government faces the costs of litigation (but then, so too do the property owners), or because the government is trying to minimize political fallout. An empirical analysis of condemnation awards in New York revealed that courts there usually awarded damages closer to the amounts proposed by condemnors than condemnees but that both the condemnors' and condmenees' assessments were above the fair market values of the properties. As a result, owners usually receive a premium above fair market valuations. See Yun-chien Chang, An Empirical Study of Court-Adjudicated Takings Compensation in New York City: 1990-2003, 8 J. Empirical L. Stud. 384 (2011). Moreover, there is usually provision for relocation assistance to the owners of condemned property. See generally Nicole Stelle Garnett, The Neglected Political Economy of Eminent Domain, 105 Mich. L. Rev. 101 (2006).

would pay in cash to a willing seller" at the time of the taking. [United States v. 564.54 Acres of Land, 441 U.S. 506, 511 (1979), quoting United States v. Miller, 317 U.S. 369, 374 (1943).]

What are these "practical difficulties," and how might the legal system deal with them? See Thomas W. Merrill, The Economics of Public Use, 72 Cornell L. Rev. 61, 82-85, 90-92 (1986). Professor Ellickson has suggested a system of bonuses to compensate for losses of personal value. To limit the administrative costs of such a system, the bonuses could be defined in legislative schedules.[13]

2. *Just compensation and the question of public use.* Recall Note 2 on page 1124, where we considered the various approaches used by reviewing courts as they go about deciding whether the public use requirement has been met in a particular case. Notice that all of the alternatives—whether focused on means or on ends, whether deferential or skeptical—proceed in a yes-or-no fashion: A proposed taking either satisfies the public-use test and may thus go forward upon payment of just compensation as fixed by the court, or a proposed taking flunks the test and the government may go forward only by purchasing the property through voluntary transactions with owners, who set the price for themselves. In short, the public-use requirement is enforced by a property rule, to use the terminology introduced in footnote 18 on page 161.

A difficulty with this approach is that it invites high error costs. Probably the reason courts tend to defer to legislative judgments about public use is that judges want to avoid killing worthwhile government projects that employ eminent domain to overcome holdouts. Unfortunately, judicial deference invites error in the opposite direction, which is to say approving programs notwithstanding questionable benefits and inadequate compensation.

Given this, perhaps it makes sense to abandon the present approach to public use and simply presume—except in extraordinary cases that obviously involve no public benefit at all—to use liability rules instead of property rules to control government abuse of eminent domain. Under this approach, compensation at

---

13. See Robert C. Ellickson, Alternatives to Zoning: Covenants, Nuisance Rules, and Fines as Land Use Controls, 40 U. Chi. L. Rev. 681, 736-737 (1973). Or perhaps homeowners should receive an amount exceeding the fair market value of their property, with those who have lived in their homes the longest times receiving the largest premiums. See Yun-chien Chang, Economic Value or Fair Market Value: What Form of Takings Compensation Is Efficient?, 20 Sup. Ct. Econ. Rev. 35, 86-87 (2012). Saul Levmore suggested in a classic law and economics article that the law should induce property owners to reveal their true valuations by requiring them to state the land's worth for the purposes of assessing property taxes and then giving the state the option to buy the land at the stated price. See Saul Levmore, Self-Assessed Valuation Systems for Tort and Other Law, 68 Va. L. Rev. 771, 789-790 (1982); see also Priya S. Gupta, The Peculiar Circumstances of Eminent Domain in India, 49 Osgoode Hall L.J. 445, 471 (2012) ("because of the extensive black market for real estate in India, the parties to a transaction often declare a sale price that is half or less than half of the actual price paid, in an effort to avoid taxes. Because the government determines market value based on the listed prices of nearby properties, this leads to massive undervaluation" in eminent domain cases). Compare the approach taken in Canada, where allowances over and above market value have been made to compensate for the compulsory nature of the taking; moreover, if a condemnee can prove that her use of a tract of land generates "special advantages" not captured in fair market value, she is entitled to compensation for these (sentimental value is not compensable). See generally Eric C. Todd, The Law of Expropriation and Compensation in Canada (2d ed. 1992). Also compare England, where condemnees used to be awarded fair market value plus 10 percent to soften the blow of compulsory taking. The approach has been abandoned, but people displaced from dwellings are entitled to home loss payments ascertained by an arbitrary formula. See Keith Davies, Law of Compulsory Purchase and Compensation 136, 219 (4th ed. 1984).

fair market value would be used, as at present, in the case of takings for classic public uses (parks, rights of way, and so on), but as the uses in question move away from the classic model in the direction of private to private transfers, compensation awards would increase as a function of increasing judicial skepticism about the public benefits of the government action in question. Courts, of course, might still make errors in judgment, but error costs will be lower than with the present all-or-nothing approach; mistakes might, in particular cases, result in the government having to pay somewhat more than would be the case otherwise, but still the project could go forth. Moreover, governments would have incentives to provide more accurate information about the benefits of proposed programs, rather than (as too often at present) accentuating the positive and eliminating the negative—because doing otherwise might increase compensation awards. See James E. Krier & Christopher Serkin, Public Ruses, 2004 Mich. St. L. Rev. 859. But see Lee Anne Fennell, Taking Eminent Domain Apart, 2004 Mich. St. L. Rev. 957. Professor Fennell points out that the shortfall in just compensation for takings arises not only from the fact that awards based on fair market value ignore a property owner's subjective value (what Judge Posner calls the owner's "personal value," see page 1128), but two additional components of value as well. One of these is the chance of reaping a surplus, over and above subjective value, from trade in a voluntary sale. For example, a number of pieces of property might have, in the aggregate, a value higher than the sum of values of the individual pieces if they were never assembled and used for a large-scale project; this can be called the assembly or aggregation surplus. The second component arises from the nature of forced sales, which compromise the autonomy of owners; they might rightly feel they bear a loss even if they receive payment for subjective value and a portion of any assembly (or other) surplus. These three components together make up what Professor Fennell calls the "uncompensated increment" that results from conventional awards based on fair market value alone. Notice, then, that the approach suggested by Professors Krier and Serkin takes no account of the last of Fennell's three components, the loss of autonomy. Arguably, it could not do so. The problem is one of incommensurability; autonomy, by definition, is lost in the process of forced sales, however much one is compensated. Hence the true calling of the public use requirement might be "to screen out takings for which monetary compensation is not 'just.'" Id. at 1002. But which are those? Keep that question in mind as you puzzle through the next section of this chapter.

3. *Matters of detail.* The law of just compensation is busy and complex. See Christopher Serkin, The Meaning of Value: Assessing Just Compensation for Regulatory Takings, 99 Nw. U. L. Rev. 677 (2005). Consider just a few thorny issues:

Suppose that the government condemns part of a tract of land and that the government's use of that land will reduce (increase) the value of the rest of the tract remaining in the condemnee's hands. How is just compensation computed? See Julius L. Sackman, Nichols on Eminent Domain §8A.02 (3d ed. 2005). Is compensation due if the government's use does not reduce the value of the condemnee's remaining land, but does reduce the rate at which it appreciates? See State v. Doyle, 735 P.2d 733 (Alaska 1987).

May a city downzone property, restricting its permissible uses, so as to be liable in a subsequent condemnation action only for fair market value in light of the restrictive zoning? See Riggs v. Township of Long Beach, 538 A.2d 808 (N.J. 1988). Suppose that there has been no downzoning, but that future zoning changes, reasonably likely to occur, will increase the value of condemned property. How might this bear on the measure of just compensation? See Developments in the Law—Zoning, 91 Harv. L. Rev. 1427, 1498-1499 (1978).

Sometimes the federal government condemns property owned by a state or city. Until 1984, the courts in such cases usually measured compensation in terms of "substitute facilities" doctrine: The state or city was entitled not merely to market value but to the cost of obtaining or constructing the equivalent of what had been taken. In United States v. 50 Acres of Land, 469 U.S. 24 (1984), the Court held that the substitute-facilities measure is not required when the market value of the condemned property is ascertainable, even if the condemnee has a duty to replace the condemned facility, and the cost of the substitute will exceed compensation measured in market-value terms. The idea is to treat public condemnees like private ones. Is that a *good* idea? See Michael H. Schill, Intergovernmental Takings and Just Compensation: A Question of Federalism, 137 U. Pa. L. Rev. 829 (1989).

Recall Richmond, California's inventive plan, first introduced in Chapter 7 (page 685), to condemn underwater mortgages using the eminent domain power and then to permit homeowners who would otherwise be unable to refinance their mortgages to do so. The mortgage lenders quickly filed a lawsuit, alleging that Richmond's threatened seizure of their loans was unlawful. See Robert Rogers, Banks Sue Richmond to Halt Plan to Seize Mortgages, Contra Costa Times, Aug. 8, 2013. The city claims that 47 percent of mortgages in the city remain underwater, and when a home on the street goes into foreclosure, the value of nearby properties also tends to drop (which might in turn cause those respective mortgages to sink underwater). How should the value of the mortgage loans be calculated? If the city's plan itself increases property values in Richmond by reducing foreclosures, should this effect figure into the just compensation Richmond owes the lenders?

C. Physical Occupations and Regulatory Takings

At the outset of this chapter we alluded to governmental actions that, though not intended to take property, might nonetheless be held by the courts to have done so; these cases, we said, present some of the most difficult issues in the law of property. The materials that follow should justify the assertion. Before getting to them, however, it is useful to have in mind a far simpler matter—the general method of straightforward condemnation under the power of eminent domain.

If the government wishes to condemn private property for public use, it must comply with procedures designed to assure owners due process of law. As mentioned earlier (in footnote 12 on page 1128), the government is usually required to begin by attempting negotiated purchases. Failing acquisition by that means, the condemning authority will file a petition in court, followed by notice to all persons with interests in the property in question.[14] Thereafter, a trial is held, at which the government must establish its authority to condemn (which means, in some jurisdictions, that the government must show that a taking is "necessary"). The court can give the government permission to enter and inspect the subject property; it may require the government to make a deposit as security for the eventual condemnation, in an amount based on the compensation estimated to be awarded at the end of the proceedings. Jurisdictions differ on the availability of a jury trial in condemnation actions (none is required under the United States Constitution). If there is a jury trial, it is typically the jury that determines just compensation; issues of public use and necessity are decided by the court. At the conclusion of a successful condemnation action (or within a prescribed time thereafter), the government must pay the compensation awarded plus interest, if any, accrued from the time of the taking. Generally, condemnees may not recover attorneys' fees or other litigation expenses. Dissatisfied condemnees may, of course, appeal.

In a straightforward condemnation action, then, there is no question that the government is taking property (though there might well be questions about whether the taking is for a public use and about the measure of compensation). The cases that follow are different: Now the central issue is *whether* a taking has occurred in consequence of some government activity. The four sections below examine the chief rules of decision that the courts (especially the United States Supreme Court) have fashioned to resolve this issue of regulatory takings. We also consider the question of remedies in the event a regulatory taking is found to have occurred.

1.   Two Categorical Rules

Loretto v. Teleprompter Manhattan CATV Corp.

Supreme Court of the United States, 1982
458 U.S. 419

JUSTICE MARSHALL delivered the opinion of the Court.

This case presents the question whether a minor but permanent physical occupation of an owner's property authorized by government constitutes a "taking" of property for which just compensation is due under the Fifth and Fourteenth Amendments of the Constitution. New York law provides that a landlord must permit a cable television company to install its cable facilities upon his property. N.Y. Exec. Law §828(1) (McKinney Supp. 1981-1982). In this case, the cable installation occupied portions of appellant's roof and the side of her

---

14. Many states, and the federal government, have so-called quick-take statutes that let the government take title and possession prior to final judgment. For a quick overview, see Nicole Stelle Garnett, The Public-Use Question as a Takings Problem, 71 Geo. Wash. L. Rev. 934, 970-974 (2003).

building. The New York Court of Appeals ruled that this appropriation does not amount to a taking. 423 N.E.2d 320 (N.Y. 1981). Because we conclude that such a physical occupation of property is a taking, we reverse.

Appellant Jean Loretto purchased a five-story apartment building located at 303 West 105th Street, New York City, in 1971. The previous owner had granted appellees Teleprompter Corporation and Teleprompter Manhattan CATV (collectively Teleprompter) permission to install a cable on the building and the exclusive privilege of furnishing cable television (CATV) services to the tenants. The New York Court of Appeals described the installation as follows:

> On June 1, 1970 Teleprompter installed a cable slightly less than one-half inch in diameter and of approximately 30 feet in length along the length of the building about 18 inches above the roof top, and directional taps, approximately 4 inches by 4 inches by 4 inches, on the front and rear of the roof. By June 8, 1970 the cable had been extended another 4 to 6 feet and cable had been run from the directional taps to the adjoining building at 305 West 105th Street. [Id. at 324.]

Teleprompter also installed two large silver boxes along the roof cables. The cables are attached by screws or nails penetrating the masonry at approximately two-foot intervals, and other equipment is installed by bolts.

Initially, Teleprompter's roof cables did not service appellant's building. They were part of what could be described as a cable "highway" circumnavigating the city block, with service cables periodically dropped over the front or back of a building in which a tenant desired service. Crucial to such a network is the use of so-called "crossovers"—cable lines extending from one building to another in order to reach a new group of tenants. Two years after appellant purchased the building, Teleprompter connected a "noncrossover" line—i.e., one that provided CATV service to appellant's own tenants—by dropping a line to the first floor down the front of appellant's building.

Prior to 1973, Teleprompter routinely obtained authorization for its installations from property owners along the cable's route, compensating the owners at the standard rate of 5% of the gross revenues that Teleprompter realized from the particular property. To facilitate tenant access to CATV, the State of New York enacted §828 of the Executive Law, effective January 1, 1973. Section 828 provides that a landlord may not "interfere with the installation of cable television facilities upon his property or premises," and may not demand payment from any tenant for permitting CATV, or demand payment from any CATV company "in excess of any amount which the [State Commission on Cable Television] shall, by regulation, determine to be reasonable." The landlord may, however, require the CATV company or the tenant to bear the cost of installation and to indemnify for any damage caused by the installation. Pursuant to §828(1)(b), the State Commission has ruled that a onetime $1 payment is the normal fee to which a landlord is entitled. . . . The Commission ruled that this nominal fee, which the Commission concluded was equivalent to what the landlord would receive if the property were condemned pursuant to New York's Transportation Corporations Law, satisfied constitutional requirements "in the absence of a special showing of greater damages attributable to the taking."

Appellant did not discover the existence of the cable until after she had purchased the building. She brought a class action against Teleprompter in 1976 on behalf of all owners of real property in the State on which Teleprompter has placed CATV components, alleging that Teleprompter's installation was a trespass and, insofar as it relied on §828, a taking without just compensation. She requested damages and injunctive relief. Appellee the City of New York, which has granted Teleprompter an exclusive franchise to provide CATV within certain areas of Manhattan, intervened. The Supreme Court, Special Term, granted summary judgment to Teleprompter and the city, upholding the constitutionality of §828 in both crossover and noncrossover situations. The Appellate Division affirmed without opinion. On appeal, the Court of Appeals, over dissent, upheld the statute. 423 N.E.2d 320 (N.Y. 1981). The court concluded that the law requires the landlord to allow both crossover and noncrossover installations but permits him to request payment from the CATV company under §828(1)(b), at a level determined by the State Cable Commission, only for noncrossovers. The court then ruled that the law serves a legitimate police power purpose — eliminating landlord fees and conditions that inhibit the development of CATV, which has important educational and community benefits. Rejecting the argument that a physical occupation authorized by government is necessarily a taking, the court stated that the regulation does not have an excessive economic impact upon appellant when measured against her aggregate property rights, and that it does not interfere with any reasonable investment-backed expectations. Accordingly, the court held that §828 does not work a taking of appellant's property. Chief Judge Cooke dissented, reasoning that the physical appropriation of a portion of appellant's property is a taking without regard to the balancing analysis courts ordinarily employ in evaluating whether a regulation is a taking.

In light of its holding, the Court of Appeals had no occasion to determine whether the $1 fee ordinarily awarded for a noncrossover installation was adequate compensation for the taking. Judge Gabrielli, concurring, agreed with the dissent that the law works a taking but concluded that the $1 presumptive award, together with the procedures permitting a landlord to demonstrate a greater entitlement, affords just compensation. . . .

The Court of Appeals determined that §828 serves the legitimate public purpose of "rapid development of and maximum penetration by a means of communication which has important educational and community aspects," 423 N.E.2d, at 329, and thus is within the State's police power. We have no reason to question that determination. It is a separate question, however, whether an otherwise valid regulation so frustrates property rights that compensation must be paid. We conclude that a permanent physical occupation authorized by government is a taking without regard to the public interests that it may serve. Our constitutional history confirms the rule, recent cases do not question it, and the purposes of the Takings Clause compel its retention.

In Penn Central Transportation Co. v. New York City, [438 U.S. 104 (1978) (reproduced at page 1162)], the Court surveyed some of the general principles governing the Takings Clause. The Court noted that no "set formula" existed to determine, in all cases, whether compensation is constitutionally due for a government restriction of property. Ordinarily, the Court must engage in "essentially ad hoc, factual inquiries." Id. at 124. But the inquiry is not standardless. The economic impact of the regulation, especially the degree of interference with investment-backed expectations, is of particular significance.

> So, too, is the character of the government action. A "taking" may more readily be found when the interference with property can be characterized as a physical invasion by government, than when interference arises from some public program adjusting the benefits and burdens of economic life to promote the common good. [Id.]

As *Penn Central* affirms, the Court has often upheld substantial regulation of an owner's use of his own property where deemed necessary to promote the public interest. At the same time, we have long considered a physical intrusion by government to be a property restriction of an unusually serious character for purposes of the Takings Clause. Our cases further establish that when the physical intrusion reaches the extreme form of a permanent physical occupation, a taking has occurred. In such a case, "the character of the government action" not only is an important factor in resolving whether the action works a taking but also is determinative.

When faced with a constitutional challenge to a permanent physical occupation of real property, this Court has invariably found a taking. As early as 1872, in Pumpelly v. Green Bay Co., 80 U.S. 166, this Court held that the defendant's construction, pursuant to state authority, of a dam which permanently flooded plaintiff's property constituted a taking. A unanimous Court stated, without qualification, that "where real estate is actually invaded by superinduced additions of water, earth, sand, or other material, or by having any artificial structure placed on it, so as to effectually destroy or impair its usefulness, it is a taking, within the meaning of the Constitution." Id. at 181. Seven years later, the Court reemphasized the importance of a physical occupation by distinguishing a regulation that merely restricted the use of private property. In Northern Transportation Co. v. Chicago, 99 U.S. 635 (1879), the Court held that the city's construction of a temporary dam in a river to permit construction of a tunnel was not a taking, even though the plaintiffs were thereby denied access to their premises, because the obstruction only impaired the use of plaintiffs' property. The Court distinguished earlier cases in which permanent flooding of private property was regarded as a taking, e.g., *Pumpelly*, supra, as involving "a physical invasion of the real estate of the private owner, and a practical ouster of his possession." In this case, by contrast, "[n]o entry was made upon the plaintiffs' lot." 99 U.S. at 642.

Since these early cases, this Court has consistently distinguished between flooding cases involving a permanent physical occupation, on the one hand, and cases involving a more temporary invasion, or government action outside the owner's property that causes consequential damages within, on the other. A taking has always been found only in the former situation. . . .

More recent cases confirm the distinction between a permanent physical occupation, a physical invasion short of an occupation, and a regulation that merely restricts the use of property. In United States v. Causby, 328 U.S. 256 (1946), the Court ruled that frequent flights immediately above a landowner's property constituted a taking, comparing such overflights to the quintessential form of a taking:

> If, by reason of the frequency and altitude of the flights, respondents could not use this land for any purpose, their loss would be complete. It would be as complete as if the United States had entered upon the surface of the land and taken exclusive possession of it. [Id. at 261.]

Although this Court's most recent cases have not addressed the precise issue before us, they have emphasized that physical *invasion* cases are special and have not repudiated the rule that any permanent physical *occupation* is a taking. The cases state or imply that a physical invasion is subject to a balancing process, but they do not suggest that a permanent physical occupation would ever be exempt from the Takings Clause. . . .

In Kaiser Aetna v. United States, 444 U.S. 164 (1979), the Court held that the Government's imposition of a navigational servitude requiring public access to a pond was a taking where the landowner had reasonably relied on Government consent in connecting the pond to navigable water. The Court emphasized that the servitude took the landowner's right to exclude, "one of the most essential sticks in the bundle of rights that are commonly characterized as property." Id. at 176. The Court explained:

> This is not a case in which the Government is exercising its regulatory power in a manner that will cause an insubstantial devaluation of petitioner's private property; rather, the imposition of the navigational servitude in this context will result in an *actual physical invasion* of the privately owned marina. . . . And even if the Government physically invades only an easement in property, it must nonetheless pay compensation. See United States v. Causby, 328 U.S. 256, 265 (1946). [Id. at 180 (emphasis added).]

Although the easement of passage, not being a permanent occupation of land, was not considered a taking per se, *Kaiser Aetna* reemphasizes that a physical invasion is a government intrusion of an unusually serious character.[15]

Another recent case underscores the constitutional distinction between a permanent occupation and a temporary physical invasion. In PruneYard Shopping Center v. Robins, 447 U.S. 74 (1980), the Court upheld a state constitutional requirement that shopping center owners permit individuals to exercise free speech and petition rights on their property, to which they had already invited

---

15. See also Andrus v. Allard, 444 U.S. 51 (1979). That case held that the prohibition of the sale of eagle feathers was not a taking as applied to traders of bird artifacts. "The regulations challenged here do not compel the surrender of the artifacts, and there is no physical invasion or restraint upon them. . . . In this case, it is crucial that appellees retain the rights to possess and transport their property, and to donate or devise the protected birds. . . . [L]oss of future profits — unaccompanied by any physical property restriction — provides a slender reed upon which to rest a takings claim." Id. at 65-66.

the general public. The Court emphasized that the State Constitution does not prevent the owner from restricting expressive activities by imposing reasonable time, place, and manner restrictions to minimize interference with the owner's commercial functions. Since the invasion was temporary and limited in nature, and since the owner had not exhibited an interest in excluding all persons from his property, "the fact that [the solicitors] may have 'physically invaded' [the owners'] property cannot be viewed as determinative." Id. at 84.

In short, when the "character of the governmental action," *Penn Central*, 438 U.S. at 124, is a permanent physical occupation of property, our cases uniformly have found a taking to the extent of the occupation, without regard to whether the action achieves an important public benefit or has only minimal economic impact on the owner.

The historical rule that a permanent physical occupation of another's property is a taking has more than tradition to commend it. Such an appropriation is perhaps the most serious form of invasion of an owner's property interests. . . .

Property rights in a physical thing have been described as the rights "to possess, use and dispose of it." United States v. General Motors Corp., 323 U.S. 373, 378 (1945). To the extent that the government permanently occupies physical property, it effectively destroys *each* of these rights. First, the owner has no right to possess the occupied space himself, and also has no power to exclude the occupier from possession and use of the space. The power to exclude has traditionally been considered one of the most treasured strands in an owner's bundle of property rights.[16] See *Kaiser Aetna*, 444 U.S. at 179-180; see also Restatement of Property §7 (1936). Second, the permanent physical occupation of property forever denies the owner any power to control the use of the property; he not only cannot exclude others, but can make no nonpossessory use of the property. Although deprivation of the right to use and obtain a profit from property is not, in every case, independently sufficient to establish a taking, see Andrus v. Allard, supra, at 66, it is clearly relevant. Finally, even though the owner may retain the bare legal right to dispose of the occupied space by transfer or sale, the permanent occupation of that space by a stranger will ordinarily empty the right of any value, since the purchaser will also be unable to make any use of the property.

Moreover, an owner suffers a special kind of injury when a *stranger* directly invades and occupies the owner's property. . . . [P]roperty law has long protected an owner's expectation that he will be relatively undisturbed at least in the possession of his property. To require, as well, that the owner permit another to exercise complete dominion literally adds insult to injury. See Michelman, Property, Utility,

---

16. The permanence and absolute exclusivity of a physical occupation distinguish it from temporary limitations on the right to exclude. Not every physical invasion is a taking. As PruneYard Shopping Center v. Robins, 447 U.S. 74 (1980), Kaiser Aetna v. United States, 444 U.S. 164 (1979), and the intermittent flooding cases reveal, such temporary limitations are subject to a more complex balancing process to determine whether they are a taking. The rationale is evident: they do not absolutely dispossess the owner of his rights to use, and exclude others from, his property.

The dissent objects that the distinction between a permanent physical occupation and a temporary invasion will not always be clear. This objection is overstated, and in any event is irrelevant to the critical point that a permanent physical occupation is unquestionably a taking. . . .

Loretto's Apartment House
303 West 105th Street, New York City
Note the cable television line, a little to left of center, dropping down the front
of the building to the first floor.

and Fairness: Comments on the Ethical Foundations of "Just Compensation" Law, 80 Harv. L. Rev. 1165, 1228, and n.110 (1967). Furthermore, such an occupation is qualitatively more severe than a regulation of the *use* of property, even a regulation that imposes affirmative duties on the owner, since the owner may have no control over the timing, extent, or nature of the invasion. See [footnote 19 on page 1140].

The traditional rule also avoids otherwise difficult line-drawing problems. Few would disagree that if the State required landlords to permit third parties to install swimming pools on the landlords' rooftops for the convenience of the tenants, the requirement would be a taking. If the cable installation here occupied as much space, again, few would disagree that the occupation would be a taking. But constitutional protection for the rights of private property cannot be made to depend on the size of the area permanently occupied. Indeed, it is possible that in the future, additional cable installations that more significantly restrict a landlord's use of the roof of his building will be made. Section 828 requires a landlord to permit such multiple installations.

Finally, whether a permanent physical occupation has occurred presents relatively few problems of proof. The placement of a fixed structure on land or real property is an obvious fact that will rarely be subject to dispute. Once the fact of occupation is shown, of course, a court should consider the *extent* of the occupation as one relevant factor in determining the compensation due. For that reason, moreover, there is less need to consider the extent of the occupation in determining whether there is a taking in the first instance.

Teleprompter's cable installation on appellant's building constitutes a taking under the traditional test. The installation involved a direct physical attachment of plates, boxes, wires, bolts, and screws to the building, completely occupying space immediately above and upon the roof and along the building's exterior wall.[17]

In light of our analysis we find no constitutional difference between a crossover and a noncrossover installation. The portions of the installation necessary for both crossovers and noncrossovers permanently appropriate appellant's property. Accordingly, each type of installation is a taking.

Appellees raise a series of objections to application of the traditional rule here. Teleprompter notes that the law applies only to buildings used as rental property, and draws the conclusion that the law is simply a permissible regulation of the use of real property. We fail to see, however, why a physical occupation of one type of property but not another type is any less a physical occupation.

---

17. It is constitutionally irrelevant whether appellant (or her predecessor in title) had previously occupied this space, since a "landowner owns at least as much of the space above the ground as he can occupy or use in connection with the land." United States v. Causby, supra, at 264.

The dissent asserts that a taking of about one-eighth of a cubic foot of space is not of constitutional significance. The assertion appears to be factually incorrect, since it ignores the two large silver boxes that appellant identified as part of the installation. Although the record does not reveal their size, appellant states that they are approximately 18" × 12" × 6", and appellees do not dispute this statement. The displaced volume, then, is in excess of 1 1/2 cubic feet. In any event, these facts are not critical; whether the installation is a taking does not depend on whether the volume of space it occupies is bigger than a breadbox.

Insofar as Teleprompter means to suggest that this is not a permanent physical invasion, we must differ. So long as the property remains residential and a CATV company wishes to retain the installation, the landlord must permit it.[18]

Teleprompter also asserts the related argument that the State has effectively granted a tenant the property right to have a CATV installation placed on the roof of his building, as an appurtenance to the tenant's leasehold. The short answer is that §828(1)(a) does not purport to give the *tenant* any enforceable property rights with respect to CATV installation, and the lower courts did not rest their decisions on this ground. Of course, Teleprompter, not appellant's tenants, actually owns the installation. Moreover, the government does not have unlimited power to redefine property rights. See Webb's Fabulous Pharmacies, Inc. v. Beckwith, 449 U.S. 155, 164 (1980) ("a State, by ipse dixit, may not transform private property into public property without compensation").

Finally, we do not agree with appellees that application of the physical occupation rule will have dire consequences for the government's power to adjust landlord-tenant relationships. This Court has consistently affirmed that States have broad power to regulate housing conditions in general and the landlord-tenant relationship in particular without paying compensation for all economic injuries that such regulation entails. See, e.g., Heart of Atlanta Motel, Inc. v. United States, 379 U.S. 241 (1964) (discrimination in places of public accommodation); Queenside Hills Realty Co. v. Saxl, 328 U.S. 80 (1946) (fire regulation); Bowles v. Willingham, 321 U.S. 503 (1944) (rent control); Home Building & Loan Assn. v. Blaisdell, 290 U.S. 398 (1934) (mortgage moratorium); Edgar A. Levy Leasing Co. v. Siegel, 258 U.S. 242 (1922) (emergency housing law); Block v. Hirsh, 256 U.S. 135 (1921) (rent control). In none of these cases, however, did the government authorize the permanent occupation of the landlord's property by a third party. Consequently, our holding today in no way alters the analysis governing the State's power to require landlords to comply with building codes and provide utility connections, mailboxes, smoke detectors, fire extinguishers, and the like in the common area of a building. So long as these regulations do not require the landlord to suffer the physical occupation of a portion of his building by a third party, they will be analyzed under the multifactor inquiry generally applicable to nonpossessory governmental activity. See Penn Central Transportation Co. v. New York City, 438 U.S. 104 (1978).[19]

---

18. It is true that the landlord could avoid the requirements of §828 by ceasing to rent the building to tenants. But a landlord's ability to rent his property may not be conditioned on his forfeiting the right to compensation for a physical occupation. . . .

19. If §828 required landlords to provide cable installation if a tenant so desires, the statute might present a different question from the question before us, since the landlord would own the installation. Ownership would give the landlord rights to the placement, manner, use, and possibly the disposition of the installation. The fact of ownership is, contrary to the dissent, not simply "incidental"; it would give a landlord (rather than a CATV company) full authority over the installation except only as government specifically limited that authority. The landlord would decide how to comply with applicable government regulations concerning CATV and therefore could minimize the physical, esthetic, and other effects of the installation. Moreover, if the landlord

Our holding today is very narrow. We affirm the traditional rule that a permanent physical occupation of property is a taking. In such a case, the property owner entertains a historically rooted expectation of compensation, and the character of the invasion is qualitatively more intrusive than perhaps any other category of property regulation. We do not, however, question the equally substantial authority upholding a State's broad power to impose appropriate restrictions upon an owner's *use* of his property.

Furthermore, our conclusion that §828 works a taking of a portion of appellant's property does not presuppose that the fee which many landlords had obtained by Teleprompter prior to the law's enactment is a proper measure of the value of the property taken. The issue of the amount of compensation that is due, on which we express no opinion, is a matter for the state courts to consider on remand. . . .

JUSTICE BLACKMUN, with whom JUSTICE BRENNAN and JUSTICE WHITE join, dissenting. . . .

In a curiously anachronistic decision, the Court today acknowledges its historical disavowal of set formulae in almost the same breath as it constructs a rigid per se takings rule: "a permanent physical occupation authorized by government is a taking without regard to the public interests that it may serve." To sustain its rule against our recent precedents, the Court erects a strained and untenable distinction between "temporary physical invasions," whose constitutionality concededly "is subject to a balancing process," and "permanent physical occupations," which are "taking[s] without regard to other factors that a court might ordinarily examine."

In my view, the Court's approach "reduces the constitutional issue to a formalistic quibble" over whether property has been "permanently occupied" or "temporarily invaded." Sax, Takings and the Police Power, 74 Yale L.J. 36, 37 (1964). The Court's application of its formula to the facts of this case vividly illustrates that its approach is potentially dangerous as well as misguided. Despite its concession that "States have broad power to regulate . . . the landlord-tenant relationship . . . without paying compensation for all economic injuries that such regulation entails," the Court uses its rule to undercut a carefully considered legislative judgment concerning landlord-tenant relationships. I therefore respectfully dissent. . . .

The Court's recent Takings Clause decisions teach that *nonphysical* government intrusions on private property, such as zoning ordinances and other land-use restrictions, have become the rule rather than the exception. Modern government regulation exudes intangible "externalities" that may diminish the value of private property far more than minor physical touchings. . . .

---

wished to repair, demolish, or construct in the area of the building where the installation is located, he need not incur the burden of obtaining the CATV company's cooperation in moving the cable.

In this case, by contrast, appellant suffered injury that might have been obviated if she had owned the cable and could exercise control over its installation. The drilling and stapling that accompanied installation apparently caused physical damage to appellant's building. Appellant, who resides in the building, further testified that the cable installation is "ugly."

Precisely because the extent to which the government may injure private interests now depends so little on whether or not it has authorized a "physical contact," the Court has avoided per se takings rules resting on outmoded distinctions between physical and nonphysical intrusions. As one commentator has observed, a takings rule based on such a distinction is inherently suspect because "its capacity to distinguish, even crudely, between significant and insignificant losses is too puny to be taken seriously." Michelman, Property, Utility, and Fairness: Comments on the Ethical Foundations of "Just Compensation" Law, 80 Harv. L. Rev. 1165, 1227 (1967).

Surprisingly, the Court draws an even finer distinction today—between "temporary physical invasions" and "permanent physical occupations." When the government authorizes the latter type of intrusion, the Court would find "a taking without regard to the public interests" the regulation may serve. Yet an examination of each of the three words in the Court's "permanent physical occupation" formula illustrates that the newly created distinction is even less substantial than the distinction between physical and nonphysical intrusions that the Court already has rejected.

First, what does the Court mean by "permanent"? Since all "temporary limitations on the right to exclude" remain "subject to a more complex balancing process to determine whether they are a taking," the Court presumably describes a government intrusion that lasts forever. But as the Court itself concedes, §828 does not require appellant to permit the cable installation forever, but only "[s]o long as the property remains residential and a CATV company wishes to retain the installation." This is far from "permanent."

. . . If §828 authorizes a "permanent" occupation, and thus works a taking "without regard to the public interests that it may serve," then all other New York statutes that require a landlord to make physical attachments to his rental property also must constitute takings, even if they serve indisputably valid public interests in tenant protection and safety.[20]

The Court denies that its theory invalidates these statutes, because they "do not require the landlord to suffer the physical occupation of a portion of his building by a third party." But surely this factor cannot be determinative, since the Court simultaneously recognizes that temporary invasions by third parties are not subject to a per se rule. Nor can the qualitative difference arise from the incidental fact that, under §828, Teleprompter, rather than appellant or her tenants, owns the cable installation. If anything, §828 leaves appellant better off than do other housing statutes, since it ensures that her property will not be damaged esthetically or physically, without burdening her with the cost of buying or maintaining the cable.

---

20. See, e.g., N.Y. Mult. Dwell. Law §35 (McKinney 1974) (requiring entrance doors and lights); §36 (windows and skylights for public halls and stairs); §50-a (Supp. 1982) (locks and intercommunication systems); §50-c (lobby attendants); §51-a (peepholes); §51-b (elevator mirrors); §53 (fire escapes); §57 (bells and mail receptacles); §67(3) (fire sprinklers). See also Queenside Hills Realty Co. v. Saxl, 328 U.S. 80 (1946) (upholding constitutionality of New York fire sprinkler provision). . . .

In any event, under the Court's test, the "third party" problem would remain even if appellant herself owned the cable. So long as Teleprompter continuously passed its electronic signal through the cable, a litigant could argue that the second element of the Court's formula—a "physical touching" by a stranger—was satisfied and that §828 therefore worked a taking. Literally read, the Court's test opens the door to endless metaphysical struggles over whether or not an individual's property has been "physically" touched. . . .

Third, the Court's talismanic distinction between a continuous "occupation" and a transient "invasion" finds no basis in either economic logic or Takings Clause precedent. In the landlord-tenant context, the Court has upheld against takings challenges rent control statutes permitting "temporary" physical invasions of considerable economic magnitude. . . .

In sum, history teaches that takings claims are properly evaluated under a multifactor balancing test. By directing that all "permanent physical occupations" automatically are compensable, "without regard to whether the action achieves an important public benefit or has only minimal economic impact on the owner," the Court does not further equity so much as it encourages litigants to manipulate their factual allegations to gain the benefit of its per se rule. I do not relish the prospect of distinguishing the inevitable flow of certiorari petitions attempting to shoehorn insubstantial takings claims into today's "set formula." . . .

For constitutional purposes, the relevant question cannot be solely *whether* the State has interfered in some minimal way with an owner's use of space on her building. Any intelligible takings inquiry must also ask whether the *extent* of the State's interference is so severe as to constitute a compensable taking in light of the owner's alternative uses for the property. Appellant freely admitted that she would have had no other use for the cable-occupied space, were Teleprompter's equipment not on her building.

The Court's third and final argument is that §828 has deprived appellant of her "power to exclude the occupier from possession and use of the space" occupied by the cable. This argument has two flaws. First, it unjustifiably assumes that appellant's tenants have no countervailing property interest in permitting Teleprompter to use that space.[21] Second, it suggests that the New York legislature may not exercise its police power to affect appellant's common-law right to exclude Teleprompter even from one-eighth cubic foot of roof space. . . .

This Court now reaches back in time for a per se rule that disrupts that legislative determination.[22] I would affirm the judgment and uphold the reasoning of the New York Court of Appeals.

---

21. It is far from clear that, under New York law, appellant's tenants would lack all property interests in the few square inches on the exterior of the building to which Teleprompter's cable and hardware attach. Under modern landlord-tenant law, a residential tenancy is not merely a possessory interest in specified space, but also a contract for the provision of a package of services and facilities necessary and appurtenant to that space. . . .

22. Happily, the Court leaves open the question whether §828 provides landlords like appellant sufficient compensation for their actual losses. . . . If, after the remand following today's decision, this minor physical invasion is declared to be a taking deserving little or no compensation, the net result will have been a large expenditure of judicial resources on a constitutional claim of little moment.

NOTES, QUESTIONS, AND A PROBLEM

1. On remand in *Loretto*, the New York Court of Appeals sustained the validity of the statutory provisions empowering the Commission on Cable Television to set compensation for the takings in question at $1. Loretto v. Teleprompter Manhattan CATV Corp., 446 N.E.2d 428 (N.Y. 1983). The Commission concluded that $1 was sufficient compensation because the presence of cable TV usually increases a building's value.

2. *"Per se" (or "categorical") rules.* As Justice Blackmun observes in his dissenting opinion (at page 1143), the majority in *Loretto* decided the case in terms of a per se or categorical rule: A permanent physical occupation authorized by the government is a taking, period. As we shall see—and as Justice Marshall suggests at page 1135, where he notes that there is no "set formula" and mentions "ad hoc, factual inquiries"—not all takings cases are decided in terms of such categorical rules, but some are, and cases involving physical occupation are not the only instance. More on this as we go along, but do start thinking about the virtues and vices of categorical takings rules as compared to an ad hoc approach. See generally Frank Michelman, Takings, 1987, 88 Colum. L. Rev. 1600 (1988); Susan Rose-Ackerman, Against Ad Hocery: A Comment on Michelman, 88 Colum. L. Rev. 1697 (1988); Frank Michelman, A Reply to Susan Rose-Ackerman, 88 Colum. L. Rev. 1712 (1988).

3. *Permanent physical occupation.* The particular categorical rule of *Loretto* is described as "anachronistic" and "aberrational" in John J. Costonis, Presumptive and Per Se Takings: A Decisional Model for the Taking Issue, 58 N.Y.U. L. Rev. 465, 529 (1985). Notwithstanding, the fact remains that *Loretto* represents little more than the U.S. Supreme Court's endorsement of a rule of long standing. If government action is pictured as having worked a permanent physical occupation, it appears that there is always a taking, no matter how inconsequential or trivial the invasion. See, e.g., Frank Michelman, Property, Utility, and Fairness: Comments on the Ethical Foundations of "Just Compensation" Law, 80 Harv. L. Rev. 1165, 1184-1185 (1967).

4. *Temporary physical occupation.* If *Loretto* added anything new, it is the distinction between permanent occupations, as to which the finding of a taking necessarily follows, and the temporary occupations that the Court says call for a balancing process. The distinction had been hinted at, but left uncrystallized, in the *Kaiser Aetna* and *PruneYard* cases discussed by the Court in its opinion. (See pages 1136-1137.) The permanent-versus-temporary distinction came into play in a more recent decision by the Court, Arkansas Game & Fish Commission v. United States, 133 S. Ct. 511 (2012). That case involved government-induced flooding of a temporary nature, and the decision below had held that the government was categorically exempt from takings liability for just that reason. Not so, said the Court, remanding for consideration in light of a variety of factors, including not just the duration of the flooding but also its foreseeability and the character of the land in question.

Why should permanent occupations be treated one way and temporary invasions another way, especially when, as in *Loretto*, the permanent occupation may have, at most, trivial effects on any interest of the property owner? The majority in *Loretto* claims that its per se rule for permanent occupations avoids "difficult line-drawing problems." Do you agree?

5. *The right to exclude again.* We introduced the right to exclude in Chapter 1, at pages 104-110. *Loretto*, taking its lead from *Kaiser Aetna* and other cases, describes the power to exclude as "one of the most treasured strands in an owner's bundle of property rights." (See page 1137; see also page 1136, quoting *Kaiser Aetna*.) If the right to exclude is entitled to such solicitude, why isn't something like rent control a taking by physical occupation? See the Court's discussion on page 1140. The constitutionality of a rent control ordinance was considered by the Court in Yee v. City of Escondido, 503 U.S. 519 (1992). Here is a passage of interest from *Yee*:

> Petitioners' final line of argument rests on a footnote in *Loretto*, in which we rejected the contention that "the landlord could avoid the requirements of [the statute forcing her to permit cable to be permanently placed on her property] by ceasing to rent the building to tenants." We found this possibility insufficient to defeat a physical taking claim, because "a landlord's ability to rent his property may not be conditioned on his forfeiting the right to compensation for a physical occupation." *Loretto* [footnote 18 on page 1140]. Petitioners argue that if they have to leave the mobile home park business in order to avoid the strictures of the Escondido ordinance, their ability to rent their property has in fact been conditioned on such a forfeiture. This argument fails at its base, however, because there has simply been no compelled physical occupation giving rise to a right to compensation that petitioners could have forfeited. Had the city required such an occupation, of course, petitioners would have a right to compensation, and the city might then lack the power to condition petitioners' ability to run mobile home parks on their waiver of this right. . . . But because the ordinance does not effect a physical taking in the first place, this footnote in *Loretto* does not help petitioners.
>
> With respect to physical takings, then, this case is not far removed from FCC v. Florida Power Corp., 480 U.S. 245 (1987), in which . . . [w]e rejected the respondent's claim that "it is a taking under *Loretto* for a tenant invited to lease at a rent of $7.15 to remain at the regulated rent of $1.79." . . . We explained that "it is the invitation, not the rent, that makes the difference. The line which separates [this case] from *Loretto* is the unambiguous distinction between a . . . lessee and an interloper with a government license." [503 U.S. at 531-532.]

6. *Taking personal property.* During his presidency, Richard Nixon accumulated a mass of papers, tape recordings, and other materials covering official, political, and personal matters. After his resignation in 1974, and before he could have all of this material shipped to California, Congress enacted legislation that abrogated various arrangements Nixon had made with respect to the material and authorized the Administrator of General Services to retain possession and control of them. Nixon challenged the legislation with no success. He then brought an action for just compensation under the Fifth Amendment's Takings Clause. Is there a per se taking under *Loretto*? See Nixon v. United States, 978 F.2d 1269 (D.C. Cir. 1992). More on this later. See Note 2 on page 1195.

Hadacheck v. Sebastian

Supreme Court of the United States, 1915
239 U.S. 394

JUSTICE MCKENNA delivered the opinion of the Court.

Habeas corpus prosecuted in the Supreme Court of the State of California for the discharge of plaintiff in error from the custody of defendant in error, Chief of Police of the City of Los Angeles.

Plaintiff in error, to whom we shall refer as petitioner, was convicted of a misdemeanor for the violation of an ordinance of the City of Los Angeles which makes it unlawful for any person to establish or operate a brick yard or brick kiln, or any establishment, factory or place for the manufacture or burning of brick within described limits in the city. . . .

The petition sets forth . . . that petitioner is the owner of a tract of land within the limits described in the ordinance upon which tract of land there is a very valuable bed of clay, of great value for the manufacture of brick of a fine quality, worth to him not less than $100,000 per acre or about $800,000 for the entire tract for brick-making purposes, and not exceeding $60,000 for residential purposes or for any purpose other than the manufacture of brick. That he has made excavations of considerable depth and covering a very large area of the property and that on account thereof the land cannot be utilized for residential purposes or any purpose other than that for which it is now used. That he purchased the land because of such bed of clay and for the purpose of manufacturing brick; that it was at the time of purchase outside of the limits of the city and distant from dwellings and other habitations and that he did not expect or believe, nor did other owners of the property in the vicinity expect or believe, that the territory would be annexed to the city. That he has erected expensive machinery for the manufacture of bricks of fine quality which have been and are being used for building purposes in and about the city.

That if the ordinance be declared valid he will be compelled to entirely abandon his business and will be deprived of the use of his property.

That the manufacture of brick must necessarily be carried on where suitable clay is found and the clay cannot be transported to some other location, and, besides, the clay upon his property is particularly fine and clay of as good quality cannot be found in any other place within the city where the same can be utilized for the manufacture of brick. That within the prohibited district there is one other brick yard besides that of plaintiff in error.

That there is no reason for the prohibition of the business; that its maintenance cannot be and is not in the nature of a nuisance . . . and cannot be dangerous or detrimental to health or the morals or safety or peace or welfare or convenience of the people of the district or city.

That . . . no noises arise therefrom, and no noxious odors, and that by the use of certain means (which are described) provided and the situation of the brick yard an extremely small amount of smoke is emitted from any kiln and what is emitted is so dissipated that it is not a nuisance nor in any manner detrimental to health or comfort. That during the seven years which the brick yard has been conducted no complaint has been made of it, and no attempt has ever been made to regulate it.

That the city embraces 107.62 square miles in area and 75% of it is devoted to residential purposes; that the district described in the ordinance includes only about three square miles, is sparsely settled and contains large tracts of unsubdivided and unoccupied land; and that the boundaries of the district were determined for the sole and specific purpose of prohibiting and suppressing the business of petitioner and that of the other brick yard.

That there are and were at the time of the adoption of the ordinance in other districts of the city thickly built up with residences brick yards maintained more detrimental to the inhabitants of the city. That a petition was filed, signed by several hundred persons, representing such brick yards to be a nuisance and no ordinance or regulation was passed in regard to such petition and the brick yards are operated without hindrance or molestation. That other brick yards are permitted to be maintained without prohibition or regulation.

That no ordinance or regulation of any kind has been passed at any time regulating or attempting to regulate brick yards or inquiry made whether they could be maintained without being a nuisance or detrimental to health.

That the ordinance does not state a public offense and is in violation of the constitution of the State and the Fourteenth Amendment to the Constitution of the United States.

That the business of petitioner is a lawful one, none of the materials used in it are combustible, the machinery is of the most approved pattern and its conduct will not create a nuisance.

There is an allegation that the ordinance if enforced fosters and will foster a monopoly and protects and will protect other persons engaged in the manufacture of brick in the city, and discriminates and will discriminate against petitioner in favor of such other persons who are his competitors, and will prevent him from entering into competition with them.

The petition, after almost every paragraph, charges a deprivation of property, the taking of property without compensation, and that the ordinance is in consequence invalid.

We have given this outline of the petition as it presents petitioner's contentions, with the circumstances (which we deem most material) that give color and emphasis to them.

But there are substantial traverses made by the return to the writ, among others, a denial of the charge that the ordinance was arbitrarily directed against the business of petitioner, and it is alleged that there is another district in which brick yards are prohibited.

There was a denial of the allegations that the brick yard was conducted or could be conducted sanitarily or was not offensive to health. And there were affidavits supporting the denials. In these it was alleged that the fumes, gases, smoke, soot, steam and dust arising from petitioner's brick-making plant have from time to time caused sickness and serious discomfort to those living in the vicinity.

There was no specific denial of the value of the property or that it contained deposits of clay or that the latter could not be removed and manufactured into brick elsewhere. There was, however, a general denial that the enforcement of the ordinance would "entirely deprive petitioner of his property and the use thereof."

How the Supreme Court dealt with the allegations, denials and affidavits we can gather from its opinion. The court said, through Mr. Justice Sloss, 165 California, p. 416:

> The district to which the prohibition was applied contains about three square miles. The petitioner is the owner of a tract of land, containing eight acres, more or less, within the district described in the ordinance. He acquired his land in 1902, before the territory to which the ordinance was directed had been annexed to the city of Los Angeles. His land contains valuable deposits of clay suitable for the manufacture of brick, and he has, during the entire period of his ownership, used the land for brickmaking, and has erected thereon kilns, machinery and buildings necessary for such manufacture. The land, as he alleges, is far more valuable for brickmaking than for any other purpose.

The court considered the business one which could be regulated and that regulation was not precluded by the fact "that the value of investments made in the business prior to any legislative action will be greatly diminished," and that no complaint could be based upon the fact that petitioner had been carrying on the trade in that locality for a long period.

And, considering the allegations of the petition, the denials of the return and the evidence of the affidavits, the court said that the latter tended to show that the district created had become primarily a residential section and that the occupants of the neighboring dwellings are seriously incommoded by the operations of petitioner; and that such evidence, "when taken in connection with the presumptions in favor of the propriety of the legislative determination, overcame the contention that the prohibition of the ordinance was a mere arbitrary invasion of private right, not supported by any tenable belief that the continuance of the business was so detrimental to the interests of others as to require suppression."

The court, on the evidence, rejected the contention that the ordinance was not in good faith enacted as a police measure and that it was intended to discriminate against petitioner or that it was actuated by any motive of injuring him as an individual.

The charge of discrimination between localities was not sustained. . . . "The facts before us," the court finally said, "would certainly not justify the conclusion that the ordinance here in question was designed, in either its adoption or its enforcement, to be anything but what it purported to be, viz., a legitimate regulation, operating alike upon all who came within its terms."

We think the conclusion of the court is justified by the evidence and makes it unnecessary to review the many cases cited by petitioner in which it is decided that the police power of a state cannot be arbitrarily exercised. The principle is familiar, but in any given case it must plainly appear to apply. It is to be remembered that we are dealing with one of the most essential powers of government, one that is the least limitable. It may, indeed, seem harsh in its exercise, usually is on some individual, but the imperative necessity for its existence precludes any limitation upon it when not exerted arbitrarily. A vested interest cannot be asserted against it because of conditions once obtaining. Chicago & Alton R.R. v. Tranbarger, 238 U.S. 67, 78. To so hold would preclude development and fix a city forever in its primitive conditions. There must be progress, and if in its march private interests are in the way they must yield to the good of the community. The logical result of petitioner's contention would seem to be that a city could not be formed or enlarged against the resistance of an occupant of the ground and that if it grows at all it can only grow as the environment of the occupations that are usually banished to the purlieus.

The police power and to what extent it may be exerted we have recently illustrated in Reinman v. Little Rock, 237 U.S. 171. The circumstances of the case were very much like those of the case at bar and give reply to the contentions of petitioner, especially that which asserts that a necessary and lawful occupation that is not a nuisance *per se* cannot be made so by legislative declaration. There was a like investment in property, encouraged by the then conditions; a like reduction of value and deprivation of property was asserted against the validity of the ordinance there considered; a like assertion of an arbitrary exercise of the power of prohibition. Against all of these contentions, and causing the rejection of them all, was adduced the police power. There was a prohibition of a business, lawful in itself, there as here. It was a livery stable there; a brick yard here. They differ in particulars, but they are alike in that which cause and justify prohibition in defined localities — that is, the effect upon the health and comfort of the community.

The ordinance passed upon prohibited the conduct of the business within a certain defined area in Little Rock, Arkansas. This Court said of it: granting that the business was not a nuisance *per se*, it was clearly within the police power of the State to regulate it, "and to that end to declare that in particular circumstances and in particular localities a livery stable shall be deemed a nuisance in fact and in law." And the only limitation upon the power was stated to be that the power could not be exerted arbitrarily or with unjust discrimination. There was a citation of cases. We think the present case is within the ruling thus declared.

There is a distinction between Reinman v. Little Rock and the case at bar. There a particular business was prohibited which was not affixed to or dependent upon its locality; it could be conducted elsewhere. Here, it is contended, the latter condition does not exist, and it is alleged that the manufacture of brick must necessarily be carried on where suitable clay is found and that the clay on petitioner's property cannot be transported to some other locality. This is not urged as a physical impossibility but only, counsel say, that such transportation and the transportation of the bricks to places where they could be used in construction work would be prohibitive "from a financial standpoint." But upon the evidence the Supreme Court considered the case, as we understand its opinion, from the standpoint of the offensive effects of the operation of a brick yard and not from the deprivation of the deposits of clay, and distinguished Ex parte Kelso, 147

California 609, wherein the court declared invalid an ordinance absolutely prohibiting the maintenance or operation of a rock or stone quarry within a certain portion of the city and county of San Francisco. The court there said that the effect of the ordinance was "to absolutely deprive the owners of real property within such limits of a valuable right incident to their ownership,—viz., the right to extract therefrom such rock and stone as they might find it to their advantage to dispose of." The court expressed the view that the removal could be regulated but that "an absolute prohibition of such removal under the circumstances," could not be upheld.

In the present case there is no prohibition of the removal of the brick clay; only a prohibition within the designated locality of its manufacture into bricks. And to this feature of the ordinance our opinion is addressed. Whether other questions would arise if the ordinance were broader, and opinion on such questions, we reserve. . . .

In his petition and argument something is made of the ordinance as fostering a monopoly and suppressing his competition with other brickmakers. The charge and argument are too illusive. It is part of the charge that the ordinance was directed against him. The charge, we have seen, was rejected by the Supreme Court, and we find nothing to justify it. . . .

Judgment affirmed.

NOTES AND QUESTIONS

1. J.M. Guinn, Historical and Biographical Record of Southern California 1201 (1902), contains the following entry for the petitioner Hadacheck:

> J.C. HADACHECK. One of the important and substantial industries to which Los Angeles may lay claim is the [Hadacheck] brick yards at Pico Heights. . . . J.C. Hadacheck . . . is one of the most experienced brick men in Southern California, and had a large amount of experience before casting his fortunes with the city of which he is at present an honored citizen. He was born near Tama City, Tama County, Iowa, in 1869, and . . . was reared on his father's farm. At a comparatively early age he felt the limitations by which he was surrounded, and when seventeen years old, in 1886, started out to make his own living. As a preliminary he went to Salt Lake City and learned the brick business, and eventually had a brick yard of his own, where he manufactured adobe brick with considerable success. . . . In 1893 he settled permanently in Los Angeles, and engaged in the brick business . . . on Pico Heights, where [he is] doing an extensive business and catering to a constantly increasing trade. The yards are run to their utmost capacity, and the making of reliable brick assures a continuance of the present enviable prosperity. Instead of using coal, the machinery is worked by oil.
>
> Mr. Hadacheck is widely known in business and social circles in Los Angeles, where his genial and kindly personality, tact and sympathy have won for him a host of friends and the approval of the business world.

But not sufficient approval to keep him in business when his brickyard stood in the way of housing developers!

2. *The nuisance or "public bad" test of takings.* The *Hadacheck* case can be read to suggest that if the government action in question is depicted as a nuisance-control

measure, then there is no taking notwithstanding the loss worked by the regulation. The underlying notion is that the government is curbing a public bad rather than expropriating a public good. See Ernst Freund, The Police Power §511 (1904):

> If we differentiate eminent domain and police power as distinct powers of government, the difference lies neither in the form nor in the purpose of taking, but in the relation which the property affected bears to the danger or evil which is to be provided against.
>
> Under the police power, rights of property are impaired not because they become useful or necessary to the public, or because some public advantage can be gained by disregarding them, but because their free exercise is believed to be detrimental to public interests; it may be said that the state takes property by eminent domain because it is useful to the public, and under the police power because it is harmful, or as Justice Bradley put it, because "the property itself is the cause of the public detriment."
>
> From this results the difference between the power of eminent domain and the police power, that the former recognizes a right to compensation, while the latter on principle does not.

Though not completely without defenders, the nuisance or public-bad test has been rather roundly criticized as a basis for deciding when a regulation amounts to a taking. See, e.g., Glynn S. Lunney, Jr., Responsibility, Causation, and the Harm-Benefit Line in Takings Jurisprudence, 6 Fordham Envtl. L.J. 433 (1995). Professor Frank Michelman suggested the central problem some years ago:

> The idea is that compensation is required when the public helps itself to good at private expense, but not when the public simply requires one of its members to stop making a nuisance of himself.
>
> For illustration of this approach, let us compare a regulation forbidding continued operation of a brick works which has been annoying residential neighbors with one forbidding an owner of rare meadowland to develop it so as to deprive the public of the benefits of drainage and wildlife conservation. According to the theories we are now to consider, a person affected by the second regulation would have the stronger claim to compensation. But even as to him, the matter is not free of ambiguity. To see this clearly, we can take as a third example a regulation forbidding the erection of billboards along the highway. Shall we construe this regulation as one which prevents the "harms" of roadside blight and distraction, or as one securing the "benefits" of safety and amenity? Shall we say that it prevents the highway abutter from inflicting injury on passing motorists, or that it enhances the value of the public's highway facility? This third example serves to expose one basic difficulty with the method of classifying regulations as compensable or not according to whether they prevent harms or extract benefits. Such a method will not work unless we can establish a benchmark of "neutral" conduct which enables us to say where refusal to confer benefits (not reversible without compensation) slips over into readiness to inflict harms (reversible without compensation). [Frank Michelman, Property, Utility, and Fairness: Comments on the Ethical Foundations of "Just Compensation" Law, 80 Harv. L. Rev. 1165, 1196-1197 (1967).]

A wonderful example of the "basic difficulty" identified by Michelman is Just v. Marinette County, 201 N.W.2d 761 (Wis. 1972), finding that an ordinance regulating wetlands development did not work a taking. As the court saw the case, the issue was whether the ordinance was designed to control a public harm or create a public benefit. Held: The purpose and effect were to control a public harm, not to extract a benefit. The ordinance simply limited land uses that were not "natural and indigenous" (the neutral benchmark). The court contrasted cases finding a taking when an ordinance prohibited bathing, swimming, and boating (is boating a "natural use"?), and when an ordinance limited building height (are high buildings a "natural use"?). See, to the same effect as *Just*, Graham v. Estuary Properties, Inc., 39 So. 2d 1374 (Fla. 1981); Sibson v. State, 336 A.2d 239 (N.H. 1972), overruled in part by Burrows v. Keene, 432 A.2d 15 (N.H. 1981). Contra, State v. Johnson, 265 A.2d 711 (Me. 1970). State courts have divided on the question whether wetlands regulation works a taking. See generally Annot., 19 A.L.R.4th 756 (1983).

3. *Hadacheck* is very similar on its facts to the *Spur* case, page 797. In *Spur*, the feedlot in question was held to be a nuisance, but the court concluded that, as a matter of fairness, the costs of moving or shutting down the feedlot operation should be borne by others. Why did considerations of fairness not compel the same result in *Hadacheck*? Is it not one thing to say that the government can control nuisances and quite another to say that compensation is never required in the course of doing so? See Lawrence Berger, A Policy Analysis of the Taking Problem, 49 N.Y.U. L. Rev. 165, 175 (1974):

> This [nuisance] approach assumes that if the harm [from the nuisance] is great enough, no compensation should be necessary. But why should that be? A result of no compensation will seem fair only when the regulated owner could reasonably have foreseen at the time he purchased or improved the property that the regulation would be imposed; in that event, the price he paid would reflect that expectation. He would have such expectation when, for example, there is a continuing and long standing consensus about the moral obloquy of the activity such as to warn the prospective actor that what he is about to do is against the law. On the other hand, he would be much less likely to foresee future regulation of a brickyard originally constructed in an undeveloped area.

In light of the foregoing, consider three other cases and ask yourself whether compensation should have been awarded in any of them *on grounds of fairness*.

Miller v. Schoene, 276 U.S. 272 (1928). Red cedar rust is a fungus that has no effect on cedars or anything else—except it can kill apple trees. A state regulation requires that the owners of infected red cedars must cut them down to protect apple orchards.

Empire Kosher Poultry, Inc. v. Hallowell, 816 F.2d 907 (3d Cir. 1987). Avian influenza does not endanger human health, but it does kill chickens. A poultry quarantine is set up to protect the chicken industry.

Department of Agric. & Consumer Servs. v. Mid-Florida Growers, Inc., 521 So. 2d 101 (Fla. 1988). The state destroys healthy orange trees to prevent the spread of citrus canker and protect the citrus industry.

4. *A second categorical rule.* Recall the categorical (or per se) rule of *Loretto*: if government action is seen to work a permanent physical occupation, then a taking *always* follows (nuisance controls aside). The *Hadacheck* line of cases stands for another categorical rule, one that cuts in the opposite direction and holds

that nuisance control regulations are *never* takings. But "nuisance" has a special meaning here, as you will come to understand when we consider the *Lucas* case on page 1179.

2. Rules Based on Measuring and Balancing

Pennsylvania Coal Co. v. Mahon

Supreme Court of the United States, 1922
260 U.S. 393

JUSTICE HOLMES delivered the opinion of the Court.

This is a bill in equity brought by the defendants in error to prevent the Pennsylvania Coal Company from mining under their property in such way as to remove the supports and cause a subsidence of the surface and of their house. The bill sets out a deed executed by the Coal Company in 1878, under which the plaintiffs claim. The deed conveys the surface, but in express terms reserves the right to remove all the coal under the same, and the grantee takes the premises with the risk, and waives all claim for damages that may arise from mining out the coal. But the plaintiffs say that whatever may have been the Coal Company's rights, they were taken away by an Act of Pennsylvania, approved May 27, 1921, P.L. 1198, commonly known there as the Kohler Act. The Court of Common Pleas found that if not restrained the defendant would cause the damage to prevent which the bill was brought, but denied an injunction, holding that the statute if applied to this case would be unconstitutional. On appeal the Supreme Court of the State agreed that the defendant had contract and property rights protected by the Constitution of the United States, but held that the statute was a legitimate exercise of the police power and directed a decree for the plaintiffs. A writ of error was granted bringing the case to this Court.

The statute forbids the mining of anthracite coal in such way as to cause the subsidence of, among other things, any structure used as a human habitation, with certain exceptions, including among them land where the surface is owned by the owner of the underlying coal and is distant more than one hundred and fifty feet from any improved property belonging to any other person. As applied to this case the statute is admitted to destroy previously existing rights of property and contract. The question is whether the police power can be stretched so far.

Government hardly could go on if to some extent values incident to property could not be diminished without paying for every such change in the general law. As long recognized, some values are enjoyed under an implied limitation and must yield to the police power. But obviously the implied limitation must have its limits, or the contract and due process clauses are gone. One fact for consideration in determining such limits is the extent of the diminution. When it reaches a certain magnitude, in most if not in all cases there must be an exercise of eminent domain and compensation to sustain the act. So the question depends upon the particular facts. The greatest weight is given to the judgment of the legislature, but it always is open to interested parties to contend that the legislature has gone beyond its constitutional power.

This is the case of a single private house. No doubt there is a public interest even in this, as there is in every purchase and sale and in all that happens within the commonwealth. Some existing rights may be modified even in such a case. Rideout v. Knox, 148 Mass. 368. But usually in ordinary private affairs the public interest does not warrant much of this kind of interference. A source of damage to such a house is not a public nuisance even if similar damage is inflicted on others in different places. The damage is not common or public. The extent of the public interest is shown by the statute to be limited, since the statute ordinarily does not apply to land when the surface is owned by the owner of the coal. Furthermore, it is not justified as a protection of personal safety. That could be provided for by notice. Indeed the very foundation of this bill is that the defendant gave timely notice of its intent to mine under the house. On the other hand the extent of the taking is great. It purports to abolish what is recognized in Pennsylvania as an estate in land—a very valuable estate—and what is declared by the court below to be a contract hitherto binding the plaintiffs. If we were called upon to deal with the plaintiffs' position alone, we should think it clear that the statute does not disclose a public interest sufficient to warrant so extensive a destruction of the defendant's constitutionally protected rights.

But the case has been treated as one in which the general validity of the act should be discussed. The Attorney General of the State, the City of Scranton, and the representatives of other extensive interests were allowed to take part in the argument below and have submitted their contentions here. It seems, therefore, to be our duty to go farther in the statement of our opinion, in order that it may be known at once, and that further suits should not be brought in vain.

It is our opinion that the act cannot be sustained as an exercise of the police power, so far as it affects the mining of coal under streets or cities in places where the right to mine such coal has been reserved. As said in a Pennsylvania case, "For practical purposes, the right to coal consists in the right to mine it." Commonwealth v. Clearview Coal Co., 256 Pa. St. 328, 331. What makes the right to mine coal valuable is that it can be exercised with profit. To make it commercially impracticable to mine certain coal has very nearly the same effect for constitutional purposes as appropriating or destroying it. This we think that we are warranted in assuming that the statute does.

It is true that in Plymouth Coal Co. v. Pennsylvania, 232 U.S. 531, it was held competent for the legislature to require a pillar of coal to be left along the line of adjoining property, that, with the pillar on the other side of the line, would be a barrier sufficient for the safety of the employees of either mine in case the other should be abandoned and allowed to fill with water. But that was a requirement for the safety of employees invited into the mine, and secured an average reciprocity of advantage that has been recognized as a justification of various laws.

The rights of the public in a street purchased or laid out by eminent domain are those that it has paid for. If in any case its representatives have been so short

Justice Oliver Wendell Holmes

sighted as to acquire only surface rights without the right of support, we see no more authority for supplying the latter without compensation than there was for taking the right of way in the first place and refusing to pay for it because the public wanted it very much. The protection of private property in the Fifth Amendment presupposes that it is wanted for public use, but provides that it shall not be taken for such use without compensation. A similar assumption is made in the decisions upon the Fourteenth Amendment. Hairston v. Danville & Western Ry. Co., 208 U.S. 598, 605. When the seemingly absolute protection is found to be qualified by the police power, the natural tendency of human nature is to extend the qualification more and more until at last private property disappears. But that cannot be accomplished in this way under the Constitution of the United States.

The general rule at least is, that while property may be regulated to a certain extent, if regulation goes too far it will be recognized as a taking. It may be doubted how far exceptional cases, like the blowing up of a house to stop a conflagration, go—and if they go beyond the general rule, whether they do not stand as much upon tradition as upon principle. Bowditch v. Boston, 101 U.S. 16. In general it is not plain that a man's misfortunes or necessities will justify his shifting the damages to his neighbor's shoulders. Space v. Lynn & Boston R.R. Co., 172 Mass. 488, 489. We are in danger of forgetting that a strong public desire to improve the public condition is not enough to warrant achieving the desire by a shorter cut than the constitutional way of paying for the change. As we already have said, this is a question of degree—and therefore cannot be disposed of by general propositions. But we regard this as going beyond any of the cases decided by this Court. . . . We assume, of course, that the statute was passed upon the conviction that an exigency existed that would warrant it, and we assume that an exigency exists that would warrant the exercise of eminent domain. But the question at bottom is upon whom the loss of the changes desired should fall. So far as private persons or communities have seen fit to take the risk of acquiring only surface rights, we cannot see that the fact that their risk has become a danger warrants the giving to them greater rights than they bought.

Decree reversed.

JUSTICE BRANDEIS, dissenting.

The Kohler Act prohibits, under certain conditions, the mining of anthracite coal within the limits of a city in such a manner or to such an extent "as to cause the . . . subsidence of any dwelling or other structure used as a human habitation, or any factory, store, or other industrial or mercantile establishment in which human labor is employed." Coal in place is land; and the right of the owner to use his land is not absolute. He may not so use it as to create a public nuisance; and uses, once harmless, may, owing to changed conditions, seriously threaten the public welfare. Whenever they do, the legislature has power to prohibit such uses without paying compensation; and the power to prohibit extends alike to the manner, the character and the purpose of the use. Are we justified in declaring that the Legislature of Pennsylvania has, in restricting the right to mine anthracite, exercised this power so arbitrarily as to violate the Fourteenth Amendment?

Every restriction upon the use of property imposed in the exercise of the police power deprives the owner of some right theretofore enjoyed, and is, in that sense, an abridgement by the State of rights in property without making compensation. But restriction imposed to protect the public health, safety or morals from dangers threatened is not a taking. The restriction here in question is merely the prohibition of a noxious use. The property so restricted remains in the possession of its owner. The State does not appropriate it or make any use of it. The State merely prevents the owner from making a use which interferes with paramount rights of the public. Whenever the use prohibited ceases to be noxious—as it may because of further change in local or social conditions—the restriction will have to be removed and the owner will again be free to enjoy his property as heretofore.

The restriction upon the use of this property can not, of course, be lawfully imposed, unless its purpose is to protect the public. But the purpose of a restriction does not cease to be public, because incidentally some private persons may thereby receive gratuitously valuable special benefits. Thus, owners of low buildings may obtain, through statutory restrictions upon the height of neighboring structures, benefits equivalent to an easement of light and air. Furthermore, a restriction, though imposed for a public purpose, will not be lawful, unless the restriction is an appropriate means to the public end. But to keep coal in place is surely an appropriate means of preventing subsidence of the surface; and ordinarily it is the only available means. Restriction upon use does not become inappropriate as a means, merely because it deprives the owner of the only use to which the property can then be profitably put. The liquor and the oleomargarine cases settled that. Mugler v. Kansas, 123 U.S. 623; Powell v. Pennsylvania, 127 U.S. 678. Nor is a restriction imposed through exercise of the police power inappropriate as a means, merely because the same end might be effected through exercise of the power of eminent domain, or otherwise at public expense. Every restriction upon the height of buildings might be secured through acquiring by eminent domain the right of each owner to build above the limiting height; but it is settled that the State need not resort to that power. If by mining anthracite coal the owner would necessarily unloose poisonous gasses, I suppose no one would doubt the power of the State to prevent the mining, without buying his coal fields. And why may not the State, likewise, without paying compensation, prohibit one from digging so deep or excavating so near the surface, as to expose the community to like dangers? In the latter case, as in the former, carrying on the business would be a public nuisance.

It is said that one fact for consideration in determining whether the limits of the police power have been exceeded is the extent of the resulting diminution in value; and that here the restriction destroys existing rights of property and contract. But values are relative. If we are to consider the value of the coal kept in place by the restriction, we should compare it with the value of all other parts of the land. That is, with the value not of the coal alone, but with the value of the whole property. The rights of an owner as against the public are not increased by dividing the interests in his property into surface and subsoil. The sum of the

Justice Louis Dembitz Brandeis

rights in the parts can not be greater than the rights in the whole. The estate of an owner in land is grandiloquently described as extending *ab orco usque ad coelum*. But I suppose no one would contend that by selling his interest above one hundred feet from the surface he could prevent the State from limiting, by the police power, the height of structures in a city. And why should a sale of underground rights bar the State's power? For aught that appears the value of the coal kept in place by the restriction may be negligible as compared with the value of the whole property, or even as compared with that part of it which is represented by the coal remaining in place and which may be extracted despite the statute. Ordinarily a police regulation, general in operation, will not be held void as to a particular property, although proof is offered that owing to conditions peculiar to it the restriction could not reasonably be applied. But even if the particular facts are to govern, the statute should, in my opinion, be upheld in this case. For the defendant has failed to adduce any evidence from which it appears that to restrict its mining operations was an unreasonable exercise of the police power. Where the surface and the coal belong to the same person, self-interest would ordinarily prevent mining to such an extent as to cause a subsidence. It was, doubtless, for this reason that the legislature, estimating the degrees of danger, deemed statutory restriction unnecessary for the public safety under such conditions.

It is said that this is a case of a single dwelling house; that the restriction upon mining abolishes a valuable estate hitherto secured by a contract with the plaintiffs; and that the restriction upon mining cannot be justified as a protection of personal safety, since that could be provided for by notice. The propriety of deferring a good deal to tribunals on the spot has been repeatedly recognized. . . . May we say that notice would afford adequate protection of the public safety where the legislature and the highest court of the State, with greater knowledge of local conditions, have declared, in effect, that it would not? If public safety is imperiled, surely neither grant, nor contract, can prevail against the exercise of the police power. . . .

This case involves only mining which causes subsidence of a dwelling house. But the Kohler Act contains provisions in addition to that quoted above; and as to these, also, an opinion is expressed. These provisions deal with mining under cities to such an extent as to cause subsidence of—

(a) Any public building or any structure customarily used by the public as a place of resort, assemblage, or amusement, including, but not being limited to, churches, schools, hospitals, theatres, hotels, and railroad stations.

(b) Any street, road, bridge or other public passageway, dedicated to public use or habitually used by the public.

(c) Any track, roadbed, right of way, pipe, conduit, wire, or other facility, used in the service of the public by any municipal corporation or public service company. . . . A prohibition of mining which causes subsidence of such structures and facilities is obviously enacted for a public purpose and it seems, likewise, clear that mere notice of intention to mine would not in this connection secure the public safety. Yet it is said that these provisions of the act cannot be sustained as an exercise of the police power where the right to mine such coal has been reserved.

The conclusion seems to rest upon the assumption that in order to justify such exercise of the police power there must be "an average reciprocity of advantage" as between the owner of the property restricted and the rest of the community; and that here such reciprocity is absent. Reciprocity of advantage is an important consideration, and may even be an essential, where the State's power is exercised for the purpose of conferring benefits upon the property of a neighborhood, as in drainage projects, Wurts v. Hoagland, 114 U.S. 606; or upon adjoining owners, as by party wall provisions, Jackman v. Rosenbaum Co., [260 U.S.] 22. But where the police power is exercised, not to confer benefits upon property owners, but to protect the public from detriment and danger, there is, in my opinion, no room for considering reciprocity of advantage. There was no reciprocal advantage to the owner prohibited from using his oil tanks in 248 U.S. 498; his brickyard, in 239 U.S. 394; his livery stable, in 237 U.S. 171; his billiard hall, in 225 U.S. 623; his oleomargarine factory, in 127 U.S. 678; his brewery, in 123 U.S. 623; unless it be the advantage of living and doing business in a civilized community. That reciprocal advantage is given by the act to the coal operators.

NOTES AND QUESTIONS

1. *Some background.* For discussion of the contemporary significance of *Pennsylvania Coal,* see William M. Treanor, Jam for Justice Holmes: Reassessing the Significance of *Mahon,* 86 Geo. L.J. 813 (1998), followed in the same issue by responses by Professors Richard A. Epstein and Robert Brauneis and a reply by Professor Treanor. See also Robert Brauneis, "The Foundation of Our 'Regulatory Takings' Jurisprudence": The Myth and Meaning of Justice Holmes's Opinion in *Pennsylvania Coal Co. v. Mahon,* 106 Yale L.J. 613 (1996). Historical accounts of the case can be found in Joseph F. DiMento, Mining the Archives of *Pennsylvania Coal:* Heaps of Constitutional Mischief, 11 J. Legal Hist. 396 (1990); Lawrence M. Friedman, A Search for Seizure: *Pennsylvania Coal Co. v. Mahon* in Context, 4 Law & Hist. Rev. 1 (1986); E.F. Roberts, Mining with Mr. Justice Holmes, 39 Vand. L. Rev. 287 (1986); Carol M. Rose, *Mahon* Reconstructed: Why the Takings Issue Is Still a Muddle, 57 S. Cal. L. Rev. 561 (1984). Especially rewarding is the story told in William A. Fischel, Regulatory Takings: Law, Economics, and Politics (1995). Fischel, an economist and land use scholar, visited the site of the case (Scranton), dug through local newspapers and other original sources, and interviewed knowledgeable parties. Here is what he found:

> Pennsylvania Coal and other coal mining companies in the Scranton area had the practice of repairing or paying compensation for surface subsidence brought about by their mining activities. They developed the practice well before the Kohler Act at issue in *Pennsylvania Coal* forbade mining in a way that would cause subsidence, and they adhered to the practice even after the Court's decision in *Pennsylvania Coal* invalidated the Kohler Act as a taking. [James E. Krier, Takings from Freund to Fischel, 84 Geo. L.J. 1895, 1897 (1996) (book review).]

So Holmes's famous (but enigmatic) opinion actually had little if any impact on mining operations.

2. *Takings tests.* We have thus far considered two categorical tests or per se rules of decision for takings cases: Permanent physical occupations are always takings; nuisance-control measures are never takings (but remember Note 4 on page 1152). *Pennsylvania Coal* is the classic statement of a different sort of test—not a hard and fast rule, but rather a standard—softer around its edges, concerned with differences of degree rather than differences in kind, inquiring whether, on balance, matters have gone "too far." The test says, in essence, that when governmental regulation of a use that is not a nuisance works too great a burden on property owners, compensation must be paid if the regulation is to remain in effect. Notice, though, that the regulation itself might provide implicit compensation by way of what Justice Holmes called, on page 1154, "an average reciprocity of advantage." The idea, of course, is that the apparent losers under a government program might not be losers at all (or not, at least, big losers) because they are simultaneously benefitted by the very action that burdens them. Watch for this idea as it plays into later cases. See generally Richard A. Epstein, Takings: Private Property and the Power of Eminent Domain 195-197 (1985).

3. *Diminution in value.* The rule of decision in *Pennsylvania Coal* is usually referred to as the diminution-in-value test. What is its point? Is it concerned with efficiency, with justice, or with both?[23]

Notice Justice Brandeis's response to the majority opinion of Justice Holmes. His first argument is straightforward. The Kohler Act was merely controlling a nuisance, hence no compensation was required. His second argument attacks the diminution-in-value test head-on: diminution relative to what?

The question is an important one. Contemporary takings cases most commonly arise from governmental regulatory activities that involve neither permanent physical occupations nor any pretense of nuisance controls, so the diminution-in-value test has a dominant role to play.[24] The problem is the extraordinary ambiguity of the test. How much of a loss of value is too much?

---

23. Some observers see a balancing test in *Pennsylvania Coal.* The idea here is that one should compare the public benefits of governmental activity against the private harms it works on claimants. If claimants would lose a lot more than the public would gain, a taking should be found, otherwise not. The test fares pretty well in efficiency terms, but begs the question of fairness. As to each point, do you see why? In any event, were there in Holmes's view any public benefits in the Kohler Act? That question is addressed in the *Keystone* case, to which we shall turn momentarily. See also Rose, supra, at 571-581.

24. And mistakenly so in the view of John F. Hart, Land Use Law in the Early Republic and the Original Meaning of the Takings Clause, 94 Nw. U. L. Rev. 1099 (2000), arguing that the Takings Clause was intended to apply to actual appropriations, not to hardships imposed by regulation. Although Hart's view reflects the universal view of legal scholars who have examined the Takings Clause's original meaning, Michael Rappaport has argued that by the time the Fourteenth Amendment incorporated the Takings Clause against the states, regulatory takings liability might have been contemplated. See Michael B. Rappaport, Originalism and Regulatory Takings: Why the Fifth Amendment May Not Protect Against Regulatory Takings But the Fourteenth Amendment May, 45 San Diego L. Rev. 729 (2008). This conjecture raises a host of fascinating questions: Can the Takings Clause really have separate original public meanings as applied to the state and federal governments? What is the import for Rappaport's argument of Will Baude's recent revelation that the Takings Clause apparently did not confer upon the federal government the authority to condemn land in the states? (Recall Note 6 on page 1127.) If Baude and Hart are both right then was the Fifth Amendment's Takings Clause merely a minor provision that governed the federal eminent domain power in the District of Columbia and the territories? Finally, can Justice Thomas justify his basing the meaning of "public use" in the Takings Clause exclusively on those words' original public meaning while ignoring the original public meaning of the word "taken" in the same clause? See Justice Thomas's *Kelo* dissent on page 1121.

Is loss to be measured in absolute terms, or rather in relative ones? If the latter, relative to what?

4. *Conceptual severance.* Consider how Holmes and Brandeis differed in their approach to the last question in particular. Pennsylvania law recognizes three separate estates in mining property: in the surface, in the minerals, and in support of the surface. Holmes saw the Kohler Act as purporting to "abolish" the third estate entirely. See page 1154. Brandeis, on the other hand, reasoned that the "rights of an owner as against the public are not increased by dividing the interests in his property"; the Kohler Act did not take all of a smaller thing (the third estate) but only a part "of the whole property." See page 1157.

Which view is correct? The question—referred to in the literature as the issue of *conceptual severance*[25]—is seemingly crucial but also, thus far, seemingly unresolved. It figured in Keystone Bituminous Coal Association v. DeBenedictis, 480 U.S. 470 (1987), a case that might rightly be called *Pennsylvania Coal* redux. The case arose out of a 1966 Pennsylvania statute designed, as was the Kohler Act involved in *Pennsylvania Coal*, to control subsidence from coal mining. Under the legislation, coal companies had to keep up to 50 percent of their coal in place, and repair subsidence damage even if surface owners had waived their rights. The Court held that the statute did not work a taking, despite its similarities to the Kohler Act, because its purpose was not just to balance private economic interests, but rather to protect the public interest in health, environmental quality, and fiscal integrity. In any event, the Court held, the coal companies had not shown a sufficient diminution in value, a point related to the matter of conceptual severance. The millions of tons of coal that had to remain in place under the Pennsylvania statute were not a separate segment of property, but only a few percent of the total coal owned by the companies. Never mind that Pennsylvania law recognized the "support estate" as a separate interest; "our takings jurisprudence forecloses reliance on such legalistic distinctions within a bundle of property rights." 480 U.S. at 500.

Chief Justice Rehnquist, joined by Justices Powell, O'Connor, and Scalia, dissented. In their view, the majority in *Keystone* had wrongly discounted *Pennsylvania Coal*, "the foundation of our 'regulatory takings' jurisprudence." 480 U.S. at 508.

Conceptual severance figures in the next case as well.

Penn Central Transportation Company v. City of New York

Supreme Court of the United States, 1978
438 U.S. 104

JUSTICE BRENNAN delivered the opinion of the Court.

The question presented is whether a city may, as part of a comprehensive program to preserve historic landmarks and historic districts, place restrictions

---

25. The terminology owes to Margaret Jane Radin, The Liberal Conception of Property: Cross Currents in the Jurisprudence of Takings, 88 Colum. L. Rev. 1667, 1676 (1988). Sometimes people refer to the issue as the "denominator problem." Can you see why?

on the development of individual historic landmarks—in addition to those imposed by applicable zoning ordinances—without effecting a "taking" requiring the payment of "just compensation." Specifically, we must decide whether the application of New York City's Landmarks Preservation Law to the parcel of land occupied by Grand Central Terminal has "taken" its owners' property in violation of the Fifth and Fourteenth Amendments.

Over the past 50 years, all 50 States and over 500 municipalities have enacted laws to encourage or require the preservation of buildings and areas with historic or aesthetic importance. These nationwide legislative efforts have been precipitated by two concerns. The first is recognition that, in recent years, large numbers of historic structures, landmarks, and areas have been destroyed without adequate consideration of either the values represented therein or the possibility of preserving the destroyed properties for use in economically productive ways. The second is a widely shared belief that structures with special historic, cultural, or architectural significance enhance the quality of life for all. Not only do these buildings and their workmanship represent the lessons of the past and embody precious features of our heritage, they serve as examples of quality for today. . . .

New York City, responding to similar concerns and acting pursuant to a New York State enabling Act, adopted its Landmarks Preservation Law in 1965. See N.Y.C. Admin. Code, ch. 8-A, §205-1.0 et seq. (1976). The city acted from the conviction that "the standing of [New York City] as a world-wide tourist center and world capital of business, culture and government" would be threatened if legislation were not enacted to protect historic landmarks and neighborhoods from precipitate decisions to destroy or fundamentally alter their character. . . .

The New York City law is typical of many urban landmark laws in that its primary method of achieving its goals is not by acquisitions of historic properties, but rather by involving public entities in land-use decisions affecting these properties and providing services, standards, controls, and incentives that will encourage preservation by private owners and users. While the law does place special restrictions on landmark properties as a necessary feature to the attainment of its larger objectives, the major theme of the law is to ensure the owners of any such properties both a "reasonable return" on their investments and maximum latitude to use their parcels for purposes not inconsistent with the preservation goals. . . .

Final designation as a landmark results in restrictions upon the property owner's options concerning use of the landmark site. First, the law imposes a duty upon the owner to keep the exterior features of the building "in good repair" to assure that the law's objectives not be defeated by the landmark's falling into a state of irremediable disrepair. Second, the Commission must approve in advance any proposal to alter the exterior architectural features of the landmark or to construct any exterior improvement on the landmark site, thus ensuring that decisions concerning construction on the landmark site are made with due consideration of both the public interest in the maintenance of the structure and the landowner's interest in use of the property.

In the event an owner wishes to alter a landmark site, three separate procedures are available through which administrative approval may be obtained. First, the owner may apply to the Commission for a "certificate of no effect on protected architectural features": that is, for an order approving the improvement or alteration on the ground that it will not change or affect any architectural feature of the landmark and will be in harmony therewith. Denial of the certificate is subject to judicial review.

Second, the owner may apply to the Commission for a certificate of "appropriateness." Such certificates will be granted if the Commission concludes—focusing upon aesthetic, historical, and architectural values—that the proposed construction on the landmark site would not unduly hinder the protection, enhancement, perpetuation, and use of the landmark. Again, denial of the certificate is subject to judicial review. Moreover, the owner who is denied either a certificate of no exterior effect or a certificate of appropriateness may submit an alternative or modified plan for approval. The final procedure—seeking a certificate of appropriateness on the ground of "insufficient return"—provides special mechanisms, which vary depending on whether or not the landmark enjoys a tax exemption, to ensure that designation does not cause economic hardship.

Although the designation of a landmark and landmark site restricts the owner's control over the parcel, designation also enhances the economic position of the landmark owner in one significant respect. Under New York City's zoning laws, owners of real property who have not developed their property to the full extent permitted by the applicable zoning laws are allowed to transfer development rights to . . . other parcels. Subject to a restriction that the floor area of the transferee lot may not be increased by more than 20% above its authorized level, the ordinance permitted transfers from a landmark parcel to [contiguous or nearby] lots. In addition, the 1969 amendment permits, in highly commercialized areas like midtown Manhattan, the transfer of all unused development rights to a single parcel.

This case involves the application of New York City's Landmarks Preservation Law to Grand Central Terminal (Terminal). The Terminal, which is owned by the Penn Central Transportation Co. and its affiliates (Penn Central), is one of New York City's most famous buildings. Opened in 1913, it is regarded not only as providing an ingenious engineering solution to the problems presented by urban railroad stations, but also as a magnificent example of the French beaux-arts style.

The Terminal is located in midtown Manhattan. Its south facade faces 42d Street and that street's intersection with Park Avenue. At street level, the Terminal is bounded on the west by Vanderbilt Avenue, on the east by the Commodore Hotel, and on the north by the Pan-American Building. Although a 20-story office tower, to have been located above the Terminal, was part of the original design, the planned tower was never constructed. The Terminal itself is an eight-story structure which Penn Central uses as a railroad station and in which it rents space not needed for railroad purposes to a variety of commercial interests. The Terminal is one of a number of properties owned by appellant Penn Central in this area of midtown Manhattan. The others include the Barclay, Biltmore, Commodore, Roosevelt, and Waldorf-Astoria Hotels, the Pan-American Building and other office buildings along Park Avenue, and the Yale Club. At least eight of these are eligible to be recipients of development rights afforded the Terminal by virtue of landmark designation.

On August 2, 1967, following a public hearing, the Commission designated the Terminal a "landmark" and designated the "city tax block" it occupies a "landmark site." The Board of Estimate confirmed this action on September 21, 1967. Although appellant Penn Central had opposed the designation before the Commission, it did not seek judicial review of the final designation decision.

On January 22, 1968, appellant Penn Central, to increase its income, entered into a renewable 50-year lease and sublease agreement with appellant UGP Properties, Inc. (UGP), a wholly owned subsidiary of Union General Properties, Ltd., a United Kingdom corporation. Under the terms of the agreement, UGP was to construct a multistory office building above the Terminal. UGP promised to pay Penn Central $1 million annually during construction and at least $3 million annually thereafter. The rentals would be offset in part by a loss of some $700,000 to $1 million in net rentals presently received from concessionaires displaced by the new building.

Appellants UGP and Penn Central then applied to the Commission for permission to construct an office building atop the Terminal. Two separate plans, both designed by architect Marcel Breuer and both apparently satisfying the terms of the applicable zoning ordinance, were submitted to the Commission for approval. The first, Breuer I, provided for the construction of a 55-story office building, to be cantilevered above the existing facade and to rest on the roof of the Terminal. The second, Breuer II Revised, called for tearing down a portion of the Terminal that included the 42d Street facade, stripping off some of the remaining features of the Terminal's facade, and constructing a 53-story office building. The Commission denied a certificate of no exterior effect on September 20, 1968. Appellants then applied for a certificate of "appropriateness" as to both proposals. After four days of hearings at which over 80 witnesses testified, the Commission denied this application as to both proposals.

The Commission's reasons for rejecting certificates respecting Breuer II Revised are summarized in the following statement: "To protect a Landmark, one does not tear it down. To perpetuate its architectural features, one does not strip them off." Breuer I, which would have preserved the existing vertical facades of the present structure, received more sympathetic consideration. The Commission first focused on the effect that the proposed tower would have on one desirable feature created by the present structure and its surroundings: the dramatic view of the Terminal from Park Avenue South. Although appellants had contended that the Pan-American Building had already destroyed the silhouette of the south facade and that one additional tower could do no further damage and might even provide a better background for the facade, the Commission disagreed, stating that it found the majestic approach from the south to be still unique in the city and that a 55-story tower atop the Terminal would be far more detrimental

Breuer I

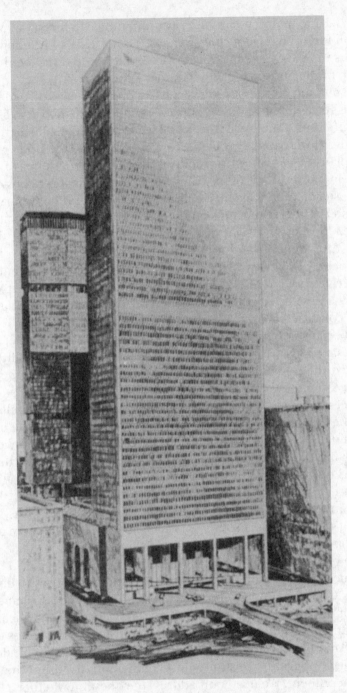

Breuer II

to its south facade than the Pan-American Building 375 feet away. Moreover, the Commission found that from closer vantage points the Pan-Am Building and the other towers were largely cut off from view, which would not be the case of the mass on top of the Terminal planned under Breuer I. . . .

Appellants did not seek judicial review of the denial of either certificate. Because the Terminal site enjoyed a tax exemption, remained suitable for its present and future uses, and was not the subject of a contract of sale, there were no further administrative remedies available to appellants as to the Breuer I and Breuer II Revised plans. . . . Further, appellants did not avail themselves of the opportunity to develop and submit other plans for the Commission's consideration and approval. Instead, appellants filed suit in New York Supreme Court, Trial Term, claiming, inter alia, that the application of the Landmarks Preservation Law had "taken" their property without just compensation in violation of the Fifth and Fourteenth Amendments and arbitrarily deprived them of their property without due process of law in violation of the Fourteenth Amendment. Appellants sought a declaratory judgment, injunctive relief barring the city from using the Landmarks Law to impede the construction of any structure that might otherwise lawfully be constructed on the Terminal site, and damages for the "temporary taking" that occurred between August 2, 1967, the designation date, and the date when the restrictions arising from the Landmarks Law would be lifted. The trial court granted the injunctive and declaratory relief, but severed the question of damages for a "temporary taking."

Appellees appealed, and the New York Supreme Court, Appellate Division, reversed. The Appellate Division held that the restrictions on the development of the Terminal site were necessary to promote the legitimate public purpose of protecting landmarks and therefore that appellants could sustain their constitutional claims only by proof that the regulation deprived them of all reasonable beneficial use of the property. The Appellate Division held that the evidence appellants introduced at trial — "Statements of Revenues and Costs," purporting to show a net operating loss for the years 1969 and 1971, which were prepared for the instant litigation — had not satisfied their burden. . . .

The New York Court of Appeals affirmed. . . .

The issues presented by appellants are (1) whether the restrictions imposed by New York City's law upon appellants' exploitation of the Terminal site effect a "taking" of appellants' property for a public use within the meaning of the Fifth Amendment, which of course is made applicable to the States through the Fourteenth Amendment, . . . and, (2), if so, whether the transferable development rights afforded appellants constitute "just compensation" within the meaning of the Fifth Amendment. We need only address the question whether a "taking" has occurred.

Before considering appellants' specific contentions, it will be useful to review the factors that have shaped the jurisprudence of the Fifth Amendment injunction "nor shall private property be taken for public use, without just compensation." The question of what constitutes a "taking" for purposes of the Fifth Amendment has proved to be a problem of considerable difficulty. While this

Court has recognized that the "Fifth Amendment's guarantee . . . [is] designed to bar Government from forcing some people alone to bear public burdens which, in all fairness and justice, should be borne by the public as a whole," Armstrong v. United States, 364 U.S. 40, 49 (1960), this Court, quite simply, has been unable to develop any "set formula" for determining when "justice and fairness" require that economic injuries caused by public action be compensated by the government, rather than remain disproportionately concentrated on a few persons. See Goldblatt v. Hempstead, 369 U.S. 590, 594 (1962). . . . In engaging in these essentially ad hoc, factual inquiries, the Court's decisions have identified several factors that have particular significance. The economic impact of the regulation on the claimant and, particularly, the extent to which the regulation has interfered with distinct investment-backed expectations are, of course, relevant considerations. So, too, is the character of the governmental action. A "taking" may more readily be found when the interference with property can be characterized as a physical invasion by government, see, e.g., United States v. Causby, 328 U.S. 256 (1946), than when interference arises from some public program adjusting the benefits and burdens of economic life to promote the common good.

"Government hardly could go on if to some extent values incident to property could not be diminished without paying for every such change in the general law," Pennsylvania Coal Co. v. Mahon, 260 U.S. 393, 413 (1922), and this Court has accordingly recognized, in a wide variety of contexts, that government may execute laws or programs that adversely affect recognized economic values. Exercises of the taxing power are one obvious example. A second are the decisions in which this Court has dismissed "taking" challenges on the ground that, while the challenged government action caused economic harm, it did not interfere with interests that were sufficiently bound up with the reasonable expectations of the claimant to constitute "property" for Fifth Amendment purposes. See, e.g., United States v. Willow River Power Co., 324 U.S. 499 (1945) (interest in high-water level of river for runoff for tailwaters to maintain power head is not property); United States v. Chandler-Dunbar Water Power Co., 229 U.S. 53 (1913) (no property interest can exist in navigable waters).

More importantly for the present case, in instances in which a state tribunal reasonably concluded that "the health, safety, morals, or general welfare" would be promoted by prohibiting particular contemplated uses of land, this Court has upheld land-use regulations that destroyed or adversely affected recognized real property interests. See Nectow v. Cambridge, 277 U.S. 183, 188 (1928). Zoning laws are, of course, the classic example, see Euclid v. Ambler Realty Co., 272 U.S. 365 (1926) (prohibition of industrial use). . . .

Zoning laws generally do not affect existing uses of real property, but "taking" challenges have also been held to be without merit in a wide variety of situations when the challenged governmental actions prohibited a beneficial use to which individual parcels had previously been devoted and thus caused substantial individualized harm.

. . . [Thus,] Hadacheck v. Sebastian, 239 U.S. 394 (1915), upheld a law prohibiting the claimant from continuing his otherwise lawful business of operating a brickyard in a particular physical community on the ground that the legislature had reasonably concluded that the presence of the brickyard was inconsistent with neighboring uses. . . .

Pennsylvania Coal Co. v. Mahon, 260 U.S. 393 (1922), is the leading case for the proposition that a state statute that substantially furthers important public policies may so frustrate distinct investment-backed expectations as to amount to a "taking." . . .

Finally, government actions that may be characterized as acquisitions of resources to permit or facilitate uniquely public functions have often been held to constitute "takings." United States v. Causby, 328 U.S. 256 (1946), is illustrative. In holding that direct overflights above the claimant's land, that destroyed the present use of the land as a chicken farm, constituted a "taking," *Causby* emphasized that Government had not "merely destroyed property [but was] using a part of it for the flight of its planes." Id. at 262-263, n.7. . . .

In contending that the New York City law has "taken" their property in violation of the Fifth and Fourteenth Amendments, appellants make a series of arguments, which, while tailored to the facts of this case, essentially urge that any substantial restriction imposed pursuant to a landmark law must be accompanied by just compensation if it is to be constitutional. Before considering these, we emphasize what is not in dispute. Because this Court has recognized, in a number of settings, that States and cities may enact land-use restrictions or controls to enhance the quality of life by preserving the character and desirable aesthetic features of a city, appellants do not contest that New York City's objective of preserving structures and areas with special historic, architectural, or cultural significance is an entirely permissible governmental goal. They also do not dispute that the restrictions imposed on its parcel are appropriate means of securing the purposes of the New York City law. Finally, appellants do not challenge any of the specific factual premises of the decision below. They accept for present purposes both that the parcel of land occupied by Grand Central Terminal must, in its present state, be regarded as capable of earning a reasonable return, and that the transferable development rights afforded appellants by virtue of the Terminal's designation as a landmark are valuable, even if not as valuable as the rights to construct above the Terminal. In appellants' view none of these factors derogate from their claim that New York City's law has effected a "taking."

They first observe that the airspace above the Terminal is a valuable property interest, citing United States v. Causby, supra. They urge that the Landmarks Law has deprived them of any gainful use of their "air rights" above the Terminal and that, irrespective of the value of the remainder of their parcel, the city has "taken" their right to this superadjacent airspace, thus entitling them to "just compensation" measured by the fair market value of these air rights.

Apart from our own disagreement with appellants' characterization of the effect of the New York City law, . . . the submission that appellants may establish a "taking" simply by showing that they have been denied the ability to exploit a property interest that they heretofore had believed was available for development is quite simply untenable. . . . "Taking" jurisprudence does not divide a single parcel into discrete segments and attempt to determine whether rights in a particular segment have been entirely abrogated. In deciding whether a particular governmental action has effected a taking, this Court focuses rather both on the character of the action and on the nature and extent of the interference with rights in the parcel as a whole—here, the city tax block designated as the "landmark site."

Secondly, appellants, focusing on the character and impact of the New York City law, argue that it effects a "taking" because its operation has significantly diminished the value of the Terminal site. Appellants concede that the decisions sustaining other land-use regulations, which, like the New York City law, are reasonably related to the promotion of the general welfare, uniformly reject the proposition that diminution in property value, standing alone, can establish a "taking," see Euclid v. Ambler Realty Co., 272 U.S. 365 (1926) (75% diminution in value caused by zoning law); Hadacheck v. Sebastian, 239 U.S. 394 (1915) (87 1/2% diminution in value), and that the "taking" issue in these contexts is resolved by focusing on the uses the regulations permit. Appellants, moreover, also do not dispute that a showing of diminution in property value would not establish a taking if the restriction had been imposed as a result of historic-district legislation, see generally Maher v. New Orleans, 516 F.2d 1051 (CA5 1975), but appellants argue that New York City's regulation of individual landmarks is fundamentally different from zoning or from historic-district legislation because the controls imposed by New York City's law apply only to individuals who own selected properties.

Stated baldly, appellants' position appears to be that the only means of ensuring that selected owners are not singled out to endure financial hardship for no reason is to hold that any restriction imposed on individual landmarks pursuant to the New York City scheme is a "taking" requiring the payment of "just compensation." Agreement with this argument would, of course, invalidate not just New York City's law, but all comparable landmark legislation in the Nation. We find no merit in it.

It is true, as appellants emphasize, that both historic-district legislation and zoning laws regulate all properties within given physical communities whereas landmark laws apply only to selected parcels. But, contrary to appellants' suggestions, landmark laws are not like discriminatory, or "reverse spot," zoning: that is, a land-use decision which arbitrarily singles out a particular parcel for different, less favorable treatment than the neighboring ones. In contrast to discriminatory zoning, which is the antithesis of land-use control as part of some comprehensive plan, the New York City law embodies a comprehensive plan to preserve structures of historic or aesthetic interest wherever they might be found in the city, and as noted, over 400 landmarks and 31 historic districts have been designated pursuant to this plan. . . .

Next, appellants observe that New York City's law differs from zoning laws and historic-district ordinances in that the Landmarks Law does not impose identical or similar restrictions on all structures located in particular physical communities. It follows, they argue, that New York City's law is inherently incapable of producing the fair and equitable distribution of benefits and burdens of governmental action which is characteristic of zoning laws and historic-district legislation and which they maintain is a constitutional requirement if "just compensation" is not to be afforded. It is, of course, true that the Landmarks Law has a more severe impact on some landowners than on others, but that in itself does not mean that the law effects a "taking." Legislation designed to promote the general welfare commonly burdens some more than others. The owners of the brickyard in *Hadacheck*, of the cedar trees in Miller v. Schoene, and of the gravel and sand mine in Goldblatt v. Hempstead, were uniquely burdened by the legislation sustained in those cases. Similarly, zoning laws often affect some property owners more severely than others but have not been held to be invalid on that account. For example, the property owner in *Euclid* who wished to use its property for industrial purposes was affected far more severely by the ordinance than its neighbors who wished to use their land for residences.

In any event, appellants' repeated suggestions that they are solely burdened and unbenefited is factually inaccurate. This contention overlooks the fact that the New York City law applies to vast numbers of structures in the city in addition to the Terminal—all the structures contained in the 31 historic districts and over 400 individual landmarks, many of which are close to the Terminal. . . .

Appellants' final broad-based attack would have us treat the law as an instance, like that in United States v. Causby, in which government, acting in an enterprise capacity, has appropriated part of their property for some strictly governmental purpose. Apart from the fact that *Causby* was a case of invasion of airspace that destroyed the use of the farm beneath and this New York City law has in nowise impaired the present use of the Terminal, the Landmarks Law neither exploits appellants' parcel for city purposes nor facilitates nor arises from any entrepreneurial operations of the city. The situation is not remotely like that in *Causby* where the airspace above the property was in the flight pattern for military aircraft. The Landmarks Law's effect is simply to prohibit appellants or anyone else from occupying portions of the airspace above the Terminal, while permitting appellants to use the remainder of the parcel in a gainful fashion. . . .

Rejection of appellants' broad arguments is not, however, the end of our inquiry, for all we thus far have established is that the New York City law is not rendered invalid by its failure to provide "just compensation" whenever a landmark owner is restricted in the exploitation of property interests, such as air rights, to a greater extent than provided for under applicable zoning laws. We now must consider whether the interference with appellants' property is of such a magnitude that "there must be an exercise of eminent domain and compensation to sustain [it]." Pennsylvania Coal Co. v. Mahon, 260 U.S. at 413. That inquiry may be narrowed to the question of the severity of the impact of the law on appellants' parcel, and its resolution in turn requires a careful assessment of the impact of the regulation on the Terminal site.

. . . [T]he New York City law does not interfere in any way with the present uses of the Terminal. Its designation as a landmark not only permits but contemplates that appellants may continue to use the property precisely as it has been used for the past 65 years: as a railroad terminal containing office space and concessions. So the law does not interfere with what must be regarded as Penn Central's primary expectation concerning the use of the parcel. More importantly, on this record, we must regard the New York City law as permitting Penn Central not only to profit from the Terminal but also to obtain a "reasonable return" on its investment.

Appellants, moreover, exaggerate the effect of the law on their ability to make use of the air rights above the Terminal in two respects. First, it simply cannot be maintained, on this record, that appellants have been prohibited from occupying *any* portion of the airspace above the Terminal. While the Commission's actions in denying applications to construct an office building in excess of 50 stories above the Terminal may indicate that it will refuse to issue a certificate of appropriateness for any comparably sized structure, nothing the Commission has said or done suggests an intention to prohibit *any* construction above the Terminal. The Commission's report emphasized that whether any construction would be allowed depended upon whether the proposed addition "would harmonize in scale, material and character with [the Terminal]." Since appellants have not sought approval for the construction of a smaller structure, we do not know that appellants will be denied any use of any portion of the airspace above the Terminal.

Second, to the extent appellants have been denied the right to build above the Terminal, it is not literally accurate to say that they have been denied *all* use of even those pre-existing air rights. Their ability to use these rights has not been abrogated; they are made transferable to at least eight parcels in the vicinity of the Terminal, one or two of which have been found suitable for the construction of new office buildings. Although appellants and others have argued that New York City's transferable development-rights program is far from ideal, the New York courts here supportably found that, at least in the case of the Terminal, the rights afforded are valuable. While these rights may well not have constituted "just compensation" if a "taking" had occurred, the rights nevertheless undoubtedly mitigate whatever financial burdens the law has imposed on appellants and, for that reason, are to be taken into account in considering the impact of regulation.

On this record, we conclude that the application of New York City's Landmarks Law has not effected a "taking" of appellants' property. The restrictions imposed are substantially related to the promotion of the general welfare and not only permit reasonable beneficial use of the landmark site but also afford appellants opportunities further to enhance not only the Terminal site proper but also other properties.

Affirmed.

JUSTICE REHNQUIST, with whom THE CHIEF JUSTICE and JUSTICE STEVENS join, dissenting. . . .

The Fifth Amendment provides in part: "nor shall private property be taken for public use, without just compensation." In a very literal sense, the actions of appellees violated this constitutional prohibition. Before the city of New York declared Grand Central Terminal to be a landmark, Penn Central could have used its "air rights" over the Terminal to build a multistory office building, at an apparent value of several million dollars per year. Today, the Terminal cannot be modified in *any* form, including the erection of additional stories, without the permission of the Landmark Preservation Commission, a permission which appellants, despite good-faith attempts, have so far been unable to obtain. Because the Taking Clause of the Fifth Amendment has not always been read literally, however, the constitutionality of appellees' actions requires a closer scrutiny of this Court's interpretation of the three key words in the Taking Clause — "property," "taken," and "just compensation."

Appellees do not dispute that valuable property rights have been destroyed. And the Court has frequently emphasized that the term "property" as used in the Taking Clause includes the entire "group of rights inhering in the citizen's [ownership]." United States v. General Motors Corp., 323 U.S. 373 (1945). The term is not used in the vulgar and untechnical sense of the physical thing with respect to which the citizen exercises rights recognized by law. [Instead, it] . . . denote[s] the *group of rights* inhering in the citizen's relation to the physical thing, *as the right to possess, use and dispose of it.* . . . The constitutional provision is addressed to *every sort of interest* the citizen may possess. Id. at 377-378 (emphasis added). While neighboring landowners are free to use their land and "air rights" in any way consistent with the broad boundaries of New York zoning, Penn Central, absent the permission of appellees, must forever maintain its property in its present state. The property has been thus subjected to a nonconsensual servitude not borne by any neighboring or similar properties.

Appellees have thus destroyed—in a literal sense, "taken"—substantial property rights of Penn Central. While the term "taken" might have been narrowly interpreted to include only physical seizures of property rights, "the construction of the phrase has not been so narrow. The courts have held that the deprivation of the former owner rather than the accretion of a right or interest to the sovereign constitutes the taking." Id. at 378. Because "not every destruction or injury to property by governmental action has been held to be a 'taking' in the constitutional sense," Armstrong v. United States, 364 U.S. at 48, however, this does not end our inquiry. But an examination of the two exceptions where the destruction of property does *not* constitute a taking demonstrates that a compensable taking has occurred here.

As early as 1887, the Court recognized that the government can prevent a property owner from using his property to injure others without having to compensate the owner for the value of the forbidden use. . . . Thus, there is no "taking" where a city prohibits the operation of a brickyard within a residential area, see Hadacheck v. Sebastian, 239 U.S. 394 (1915), or forbids excavation for sand and gravel below the water line, see Goldblatt v. Hempstead, 369 U.S. 590 (1962). Nor is it relevant, where the government is merely prohibiting a noxious use of property, that the government would seem to be singling out a particular property owner.

The nuisance exception to the taking guarantee is not coterminous with the police power itself. The question is whether the forbidden use is dangerous to the safety, health, or welfare of others. . . .

Appellees are not prohibiting a nuisance. The record is clear that the proposed addition to the Grand Central Terminal would be in full compliance with zoning, height limitations, and other health and safety requirements. Instead, appellees are seeking to preserve what they believe to be an outstanding example of beaux-arts architecture. Penn Central is prevented from further developing its property basically because *too good* a job was done in designing and building it. The city of New York, because of its unadorned admiration for the design, has decided that the owners of the building must preserve it unchanged for the benefit of sightseeing New Yorkers and tourists.

Unlike land-use regulations, appellees' actions do not merely *prohibit* Penn Central from using its property in a narrow set of noxious ways. Instead, appellees have placed an *affirmative* duty on Penn Central to maintain the Terminal in its present state and in "good repair." Appellants are not free to use their property as they see fit within broad outer boundaries but must strictly adhere to their past use except where appellees conclude that alternative uses would not detract from the landmark. While Penn Central may continue to use the Terminal as it is presently designed, appellees otherwise "exercise complete dominion and control over the surface of the land," United States v. Causby, 328 U.S. 256, 262 (1946), and must compensate the owner for his loss. Id. . . . Even where the government prohibits a noninjurious use, the Court has ruled that a taking does not take place if the prohibition applies over a broad cross section of land and thereby "secure[s] an average reciprocity of advantage." Pennsylvania Coal Co. v. Mahon, 260 U.S. at 415. It is for this reason that zoning does not constitute a "taking." While zoning at times reduces *individual* property values, the burden is shared relatively evenly and it is reasonable to conclude that on the whole an individual who is harmed by one aspect of the zoning will be benefited by another.

Here, however, a multimillion dollar loss has been imposed on appellants; it is uniquely felt and is not offset by any benefits flowing from the preservation of some 400 other "landmarks" in New York City. Appellees have imposed a substantial cost on less than one one-tenth of one percent of the buildings in New York City for the general benefit of all its people. It is exactly this imposition of general costs on a few individuals at which the "taking" protection is directed. . . .

As Mr. Justice Holmes pointed out in Pennsylvania Coal Co. v. Mahon, "the question at bottom" in an eminent domain case "is upon whom the loss of the changes desired should fall." 260 U.S. at 416. The benefits that appellees believe will flow from preservation of the Grand Central Terminal will accrue to all the citizens of New York City. There is no reason to believe that appellants will enjoy a substantially greater share of these benefits. If the cost of preserving Grand Central Terminal were spread evenly across the entire population of the city of New York, the burden per person would be in cents per year—a minor cost appellees would surely concede for the benefit accrued. Instead, however, appellees would impose the entire cost of several million dollars per year on Penn

Central. But it is precisely this sort of discrimination that the Fifth Amendment prohibits. . . .

Appellees, apparently recognizing that the constraints imposed on a landmark site constitute a taking for Fifth Amendment purposes, do not leave the property owner empty-handed. As the Court notes, the property owner may theoretically "transfer" his previous right to develop the landmark property to adjacent properties if they are under his control. Appellees have coined this system "Transfer Development Rights," or TDR's.

Of all the terms used in the Taking Clause, "just compensation" has the strictest meaning. The Fifth Amendment does not allow simply an approximate compensation but requires "a full and perfect equivalent for the property taken." Monongahela Navigation Co. v. United States, 148 U.S. 312, 326 (1893). . . .

Appellees contend that, even if they have "taken" appellants' property, TDR's constitute "just compensation." Appellants, of course, argue that TDR's are highly imperfect compensation. Because the lower courts held that there was no "taking," they did not have to reach the question of whether or not just compensation has already been awarded. . . . [I]n other cases the Court of Appeals has noted that TDR's have an "uncertain and contingent market value" and do "not adequately preserve" the value lost when a building is declared to be a landmark. French Investing Co. v. City of New York, 350 N.E.2d 381, 383 (N.Y. 1976). On the other hand, there is evidence in the record that Penn Central has been offered substantial amounts for its TDR's. Because the record on appeal is relatively slim, I would remand to the Court of Appeals for a determination of whether TDR's constitute a "full and perfect equivalent for the property taken."

NOTES AND QUESTIONS

1. Recall Note 4 on page 1162. *Keystone* and *Penn Central* clearly reject conceptual severance, do they not? What about the rule regarding nuisance controls discussed in Notes 2 and 4 on pages 1150, 1152?

2. "*Distinct investment-backed expectations.*" The majority opinion in *Penn Central* added something new to the conventional collection of takings tests, but just what is less than clear. The "distinct investment-backed expectations" formulation is drawn from Professor Michelman's influential article on takings, particularly the portion dealing with diminution in value. See Frank Michelman, Property, Utility, and Fairness: Comments on the Ethical Foundations of "Just Compensation" Law, 80 Harv. L. Rev. 1165, 1229-1234 (1967). Is the test in *Penn Central* different from the diminution-in-value test? Michelman saw the latter as calling for compensation when a claimant is deprived of "distinctly perceived, sharply crystallized, investment-backed expectations." Id. at 1223. His discussion suggests that *Pennsylvania Coal* (page 1153) is a case in point, for in *Pennsylvania Coal* the claimant had a distinct interest—the support estate—that was wiped out by the Kohler Act. But what then of the distinct interest of Penn Central in the air rights above Grand Central Terminal? See Mary B. Spector, Note, Vertical and

Horizontal Aspects of Takings Jurisprudence: Is Airspace Property?, 7 Cardozo L. Rev. 489, 510-516 (1986).

Over the years since *Penn Central*, courts and commentators alike have been puzzled by the meaning of the phrase "distinct investment-backed expectations" (DIBE). "Some courts have given up. They effectively read investment-backed expectations out of taking law by holding expectations are frustrated only when a land-use regulation denies all economically viable use of land." Daniel R. Mandelker, Investment-Backed Expectations in Taking Law, 27 Urb. Law. 215, 245 (1995). Other courts have found DIBE only in instances when regulations interfere with investments that have already been made, as opposed to regulations limiting possible future investment activities. See, e.g., Gregory S. Alexander, Ten Years of Takings, 46 J. Legal Ed. 586, 589-590 (1996) (citing cases). We will revisit the issue in a case called *Palazzolo* later in this chapter (see pages 1199-1207).

On DIBE generally, see David A. Dana & Thomas W. Merrill, Property: Takings 156-164 (2002) (a highly recommended and refreshingly slim volume).

3. *TDRs.* Transferable development rights (TDRs) like those involved in *Penn Central* represent an important and controversial approach to land use planning. The concept, still evolving, has many variants and has spawned an enormous literature. Here we can do little more than introduce the subject and suggest a few issues.

Essentially, the TDR approach severs development rights from other rights in land and treats them as a separate item. The right to develop is restricted at particular sites or in so-called conservation areas, but owners of the restricted land are given TDRs that can be used for development, beyond that which would otherwise be permitted, on receiving lots or in so-called transfer areas. Depending on the method used, recipients of TDRs may sell their rights or use them on land they own (in a transfer area, for example). The idea, of course, is to ease the burdens of land use restrictions by providing some form of compensation.

TDRs have already been put to a variety of uses: to preserve historic sites, as in *Penn Central*; to preserve farmland and open space; to create incentives for low income housing; to regulate land use generally. Whatever its purpose, the approach gives rise to a number of issues. Where should development be restricted, and where permitted? How many rights should there be, and how should they be allocated? How is their marketability to be assured? The central question for our purposes concerns the bearing of TDRs on the takings issue.

Notice that the Court in *Penn Central* left unresolved the question whether TDRs can provide the "just compensation" required if a taking has occurred. See page 1173. It appears to be the Court's view, however, that TDRs can ease the burden of a regulation such that it will not amount to a taking. Can you make sense of that line of thinking? If a given regulation without TDRs would be a taking but the same regulation with TDRs would not be a taking, isn't that just a roundabout way of saying that the TDRs do in fact amount to "just compensation," even though the value of the TDRs may fall short of the fair market value ordinarily required in cases of condemnation? If so, the takings issue and the just-compensation requirement can be made, more or less, to disappear. See in

Figure 12-1
Development Rights Transfer

The landmark building (A) utilizes only a fraction of the development rights of the site, the remainder of which (B) are transferred to various other sites within a transfer district and appear as additional bulk on top of neighboring buildings (dark areas).

Source: John Costonis, Space Adrift (1974), © 1974 (University of Illinois).

this connection Justice Scalia's opinion in Suitum v. Tahoe Regional Planning Agency, 520 U.S. 725, 747-748 (1997):

> Just as a cash payment from the government would not relate to whether the regulation "goes too far" . . . but rather to whether there has been adequate compensation for the taking; and just as a chit or coupon from the government, redeemable by and hence marketable to third parties, would relate not to the question of taking but to the question of compensation; so also the marketable TDR, a peculiar type of chit which enables a third party not to get cash from the government but to use his land in ways the government would not otherwise permit, relates not to taking but to compensation. . . .
>
> Putting TDRs on the taking rather than the just-compensation side of the equation . . . is a clever, albeit transparent, device that seeks to take advantage of a peculiarity of our Takings-Clause jurisprudence: Whereas once there *is* a taking, the Constitution requires just (i.e. full) compensation, . . . a regulatory taking generally does not *occur* so long as the land retains substantial (albeit not its full) value. . . . If money that the government-regulator gives to the landowner can be counted on the question of whether there *is* a taking . . . rather than on the question of whether the compensation for the taking is adequate, the government can get away with paying much less.

Do TDRs let government purchase property on the cheap with "funny money" it mints by unduly restricting development in transfer areas so as to make the

TDRs (which would permit more intense development) valuable in those areas? Doesn't this just move the takings issue around, rather than make it go away? See Richard A. Epstein, Takings: Private Property and the Power of Eminent Domain 188-190 (1985); Note, The Unconstitutionality of Transferable Development Rights, 84 Yale L.J. 1101 (1975).

As TDRs have become increasingly familiar in New York City, they have been put to increasingly sophisticated and varied uses. See Vicki Been & John Infranca, Transferable Development Rights Programs: "Post-Zoning"?, 78 Brook. L. Rev. 435 (2013).

3.   A Third Categorical Rule

Think back to the diminution-in-value test of *Pennsylvania Coal* (stated on page 1156): "if regulation goes too far it will be recognized as a taking." If, then, a regulation wipes out all value, won't this always be going "too far"? But what if the regulation claims to control a nuisance (recall *Hadacheck*, page 1146)? Or what if the property owner had no "investment-backed expectations" (*Penn Central*, on page 1162)? The following materials address these questions.

Lucas v. South Carolina Coastal Council

Supreme Court of the United States, 1992
505 U.S. 1003

JUSTICE SCALIA delivered the opinion of the Court.

[South Carolina began managing its coastal zone in 1977, when it enacted a Coastal Zone Management Act (the federal government had enacted similar legislation in 1972). The 1977 law required owners of coastal land in "critical areas" (including beaches and immediately adjacent sand dunes) to obtain a permit from the South Carolina Coastal Council prior to committing the land to a use other than the use the critical area was devoted to on September 28, 1977.

In 1986, petitioner Lucas paid $975,000 for two residential lots on an island off the coast of South Carolina. He intended to build single-family houses on the lots and, because no parts of the parcels were critical areas under the 1977 legislation, he did not need to get a permit. His plans to build, however, were halted by new legislation, the Beachfront Management Act, enacted by the state in 1988. The act had the direct effect of barring Lucas from building any permanent habitable structures on his two lots. A state trial court found that the act made Lucas's property "valueless."

Lucas filed suit in state court, claiming a taking. The trial court agreed, but the South Carolina Supreme Court reversed, holding that when a land use regulation is designed "to prevent serious public harm," no compensation is due regardless of the regulation's effect on the property's value. 404 S.E.2d 895, 898 (S.C. 1991).

The United States Supreme Court granted certiorari.]

Prior to Justice Holmes' exposition in Pennsylvania Coal Co. v. Mahon, 260 U.S. 393 (1922), it was generally thought that the Takings Clause reached only a "direct appropriation" of property, Legal Tender Cases, 12 Wall. 457, 551 (1871), or the functional equivalent of a "practical ouster of [the owner's] possession." Transportation Co. v. Chicago, 99 U.S. 635, 642 (1879). . . . Justice Holmes recognized in *Mahon*, however, that if the protection against physical appropriations of private property was to be meaningfully enforced, the government's power to redefine the range of interests included in the ownership of property was necessarily constrained by constitutional limits. . . . These considerations gave birth in that case to the oft-cited maxim that, "while property may be regulated to a certain extent, if regulation goes too far it will be recognized as a taking."

Nevertheless, our decision in *Mahon* offered little insight into when, and under what circumstances, a given regulation would be seen as going "too far" for purposes of the Fifth Amendment. In 70-odd years of succeeding "regulatory takings" jurisprudence, we have generally eschewed any "set formula" for determining how far is too far, preferring to "engag[e] in . . . essentially ad hoc, factual inquiries," Penn Central Transportation Co. v. New York City, 438 U.S. 104, 124 (1978). . . . See Epstein, Takings: Descent and Resurrection, 1987 Sup. Ct. Rev. 1, 4. We have, however, described at least two discrete categories of regulatory action as compensable without case-specific inquiry into the public interest advanced in support of the restraint. The first encompasses regulations that compel the property owner to suffer a physical "invasion" of his property. In general (at least with regard to permanent invasions), no matter how minute the intrusion, and no matter how weighty the public purpose behind it, we have required compensation [citing *Loretto*, reproduced at page 1132].

The second situation in which we have found categorical treatment appropriate is where regulation denies all economically beneficial or productive use of land. . . . As we have said on numerous occasions, the Fifth Amendment is violated when land-use regulation "does not substantially advance legitimate state interests *or denies an owner economically viable use of his land*." [Agins v. City of Tiburon, 447 U.S. 255, 260 (1980).][26]

---

26. Regrettably, the rhetorical force of our "deprivation of all economically feasible use" rule is greater than its precision, since the rule does not make clear the "property interest" against which the loss of value is to be measured. When, for example, a regulation requires a developer to leave 90% of a rural tract in its natural state, it is unclear whether we would analyze the situation as one in which the owner has been deprived of all economically beneficial use of the burdened portion of the tract, or as one in which the owner has suffered a mere diminution in value of the tract as a whole. (For an extreme—and, we think, unsupportable—view of the relevant calculus, see Penn Central Transportation Co. v. New York City, 920, 366 N.E.2d 1271, 1276-1277 (N.Y. 1977), aff'd, 438 U.S. 104 (1978), where the state court examined the diminution in a particular parcel's value produced by a municipal ordinance in light of total value of the taking claimant's other holdings in the vicinity.) Unsurprisingly, this uncertainty regarding the composition of the denominator in our "deprivation" fraction has produced inconsistent pronouncements by the Court. Compare Pennsylvania Coal Co. v. Mahon, 260 U.S. 393, 414 (1922) (law restricting subsurface extraction of coal held to effect a taking), with Keystone Bituminous Coal Assn. v. DeBenedictis, 480 U.S. 470, 497-502 (1987) (nearly identical law held not to effect a taking); see also id. at 515-520 (Rehnquist, C.J., dissenting); Rose, *Mahon* Reconstructed: Why the Takings Issue is Still a Muddle, 57 S. Cal. L. Rev. 561, 566-569 (1984). The answer to this difficult question may lie in how the owner's reasonable expectations have been shaped by the State's law of property—i.e., whether and to what degree the

We have never set forth the justification for this rule. Perhaps it is simply, as Justice Brennan suggested, that total deprivation of beneficial use is, from the landowner's point of view, the equivalent of a physical appropriation. See San Diego Gas & Electric Co. v. San Diego, 450 U.S. at 652 (Brennan, J., dissenting). "[F]or what is the land but the profits thereof[?]" 1 E. Coke, Institutes ch. 1, §1 (1st Am. ed. 1812). Surely, at least, in the extraordinary circumstance when *no* productive or economically beneficial use of land is permitted, it is less realistic to indulge our usual assumption that the legislature is simply "adjusting the benefits and burdens of economic life," *Penn Central Transportation Co.*, 438 U.S. at 124, in a manner that secures an "average reciprocity of advantage" to everyone concerned. Pennsylvania Coal Co. v. Mahon, 260 U.S. at 415. And the *functional* basis for permitting the government, by regulation, to affect property values without compensation—that "Government hardly could go on if to some extent values incident to property could not be diminished without paying for every such change in the general law," id. at 413—does not apply to the relatively rare situations where the government has deprived a landowner of all economically beneficial uses.

On the other side of the balance, affirmatively supporting a compensation requirement, is the fact that regulations that leave the owner of land without economically beneficial or productive options for its use—typically, as here, by requiring land to be left substantially in its natural state—carry with them a heightened risk that private property is being pressed into some form of public service under the guise of mitigating serious public harm. . . . "From the government's point of view, the benefits flowing to the public from preservation of open space through regulation may be equally great as from creating a wildlife refuge through formal condemnation or increasing electricity production through a dam project that floods private property." *San Diego Gas & Elec. Co.*, 450 U.S. at 652 (Brennan, J., dissenting). The many statutes on the books, both state and federal, that provide for the use of eminent domain to impose servitudes on private scenic lands preventing developmental uses, or to acquire such lands altogether, suggest the practical equivalence in this setting of negative regulation and appropriation. . . .

We think, in short, that there are good reasons for our frequently expressed belief that when the owner of real property has been called upon to sacrifice *all* economically beneficial uses in the name of the common good, that is, to leave his property economically idle, he has suffered a taking.[27]

State's law has accorded legal recognition and protection to the particular interest in land with respect to which the takings claimant alleges a diminution in (or elimination of) value. In any event, we avoid this difficulty in the present case, since the "interest in land" that Lucas has pleaded (a fee simple interest) is an estate with a rich tradition of protection at common law, and since the South Carolina Court of Common Pleas found that the Beachfront Management Act left each of Lucas's beachfront lots without economic value.

27. Justice Stevens criticizes the "deprivation of all economically beneficial use" rule as "wholly arbitrary," in that "[the] landowner whose property is diminished in value 95% recovers nothing," while the landowner who suffers a complete elimination of value "recovers the land's full value." This analysis errs in its assumption that the landowner whose deprivation is one step short of complete is not entitled to compensation. Such an owner might not be able to claim the benefit of our categorical formulation, but, as we have acknowledged time

The trial court found Lucas's two beachfront lots to have been rendered valueless by respondent's enforcement of the coastal-zone construction ban. Under Lucas's theory of the case, which rested upon our "no economically viable use" statements, that finding entitled him to compensation. Lucas believed it unnecessary to take issue with either the purposes behind the Beachfront Management Act, or the means chosen by the South Carolina Legislature to effectuate those purposes. The South Carolina Supreme Court, however, thought otherwise. In its view, the Beachfront Management Act was no ordinary enactment, but involved an exercise of South Carolina's "police powers" to mitigate the harm to the public interest that petitioner's use of his land might occasion. 404 S.E.2d, at 899. By neglecting to dispute the findings enumerated in the Act or otherwise to challenge the legislature's purposes, petitioner concede[d] that the beach/dune area of South Carolina's shores is an extremely valuable public resource; that the erection of new construction, *inter alia*, contributes to the erosion and destruction of this public resource; and that discouraging new construction in close proximity to the beach/dune area is necessary to prevent a great public harm. Id. at 898. In the court's view, these concessions brought petitioner's challenge within a long line of this Court's cases sustaining against Due Process and Takings Clause challenges the State's use of its "police powers" to enjoin a property owner from activities akin to public nuisances. See Mugler v. Kansas, 123 U.S. 623 (1887) (law prohibiting manufacture of alcoholic beverages); Hadacheck v. Sebastian, 239 U.S. 394 (1915) (law barring operation of brick mill in residential area); Miller v. Schoene, 276 U.S. 272 (1928) (order to destroy diseased cedar trees to prevent infection of nearby orchards); Goldblatt v. Hempstead, 369 U.S. 590 (1962) (law effectively preventing continued operation of quarry in residential area).

It is correct that many of our prior opinions have suggested that "harmful or noxious uses" of property may be proscribed by government regulation without the requirement of compensation. For a number of reasons, however, we think the South Carolina Supreme Court was too quick to conclude that that principle decides the present case. The "harmful or noxious uses" principle was the Court's early attempt to describe in theoretical terms why government may, consistent with the Takings Clause, affect property values by regulation without incurring an obligation to compensate—a reality we nowadays acknowledge explicitly with

---

and again, "[t]he economic impact of the regulation on the claimant and . . . the extent to which the regulation has interfered with distinct investment-backed expectations" are keenly relevant to takings analysis generally. Penn Central Transportation Co. v. New York City, 438 U.S. 104 (1978). It is true that in at least some cases the landowner with 95% loss will get nothing, while the landowner with total loss will recover in full. But that occasional result is no more strange than the gross disparity between the landowner whose premises are taken for a highway (who recovers in full) and the landowner whose property is reduced to 5% of its former value by the highway (who recovers nothing). Takings law is full of these "all-or-nothing" situations.

Justice Stevens similarly misinterprets our focus on "developmental" uses of property (the uses proscribed by the Beachfront Management Act) as betraying an "assumption that the only uses of property cognizable under the Constitution are developmental uses." We make no such assumption. . . . [T]here are plainly a number of noneconomic interests in land whose impairment will invite exceedingly close scrutiny under the Takings Clause. See, e.g., Loretto v. Teleprompter Manhattan CATV Corp., 458 U.S. 419, 436 (1982) (interest in excluding strangers from one's land).

David Lucas's lots, Isle of Palms, South Carolina
The lots are in the gated community of Wild Dunes.

respect to the full scope of the State's police power. . . . "Harmful or noxious use" analysis was, in other words, simply the progenitor of our more contemporary statements that "land-use regulation does not effect a taking if it substantially advance[s] legitimate state interests. . . ." Nollan [v. California Coastal Commn., 483 U.S. 825, 834 (1987)]. . . .

The transition from our early focus on control of "noxious" uses to our contemporary understanding of the broad realm within which government may regulate without compensation was an easy one, since the distinction between "harm-preventing" and "benefit-conferring" regulation is often in the eye of the beholder. It is quite possible, for example, to describe in *either* fashion the ecological, economic, and aesthetic concerns that inspired the South Carolina legislature in the present case. One could say that imposing a servitude on Lucas's land is necessary in order to prevent his use of it from "harming" South Carolina's ecological resources; or, instead, in order to achieve the "benefits" of an ecological preserve. . . . Whether one or the other of the competing characterizations will come to one's lips in a particular case depends primarily upon one's evaluation of the worth of competing uses of real estate. . . . A given restraint will be seen as mitigating "harm" to the adjacent parcels or securing a "benefit" for them, depending upon the observer's evaluation of the relative importance of the use that the restraint favors. . . . Whether Lucas's construction of single-family residences on his parcels should be described as bringing "harm" to South Carolina's adjacent ecological resources thus depends principally upon whether the describer believes that the State's use interest in nurturing those resources is so important that *any* competing adjacent use must yield.[28]

When it is understood that "prevention of harmful use" was merely our early formulation of the police power justification necessary to sustain (without compensation) *any* regulatory diminution in value; and that the distinction between regulation that "prevents harmful use" and that which "confers benefits" is difficult, if not impossible, to discern on an objective, value-free basis; it becomes self-evident that noxious-use logic cannot serve as a touchstone to distinguish regulatory "takings"—which require compensation—from regulatory deprivations that do not require compensation. *A fortiori* the legislature's recitation of a noxious-use justification cannot be the basis for departing from our categorical rule that total regulatory takings must be compensated. If it were, departure would virtually always be allowed. The South Carolina Supreme Court's approach would essentially nullify *Mahon*'s affirmation of limits to the noncompensable exercise of the police power. Our cases provide no support for this: None of them that employed the logic of "harmful use" prevention to sustain a regulation involved an allegation that the regulation wholly eliminated the value of the claimant's land. . . .

Where the State seeks to sustain regulation that deprives land of all economically beneficial use, we think it may resist compensation only if the logically antecedent inquiry into the nature of the owner's estate shows that the proscribed use interests were not part of his title to begin with. This accords, we think, with our "takings" jurisprudence, which has traditionally been guided by the understandings of our citizens regarding the content of, and the State's power over, the "bundle of rights" that they acquire when they obtain title to property. It seems to us that the property owner necessarily expects the uses of his property to be restricted, from time to time, by various measures newly enacted by the State in legitimate exercise of its police powers. . . . And in the case of personal property, by reason of the State's traditionally high degree of control over commercial dealings, he ought to be aware of the possibility that new regulation might even render his property economically worthless (at least if the property's only economically productive use is sale or manufacture for sale), see Andrus v. Allard, 444 U.S. 51, 66-67 (1979) (prohibition on sale of eagle feathers). In the case of land, however, we think the notion pressed by the Council that title is somehow held subject to the "implied limitation" that the State may subsequently eliminate all economically valuable use is inconsistent with the historical compact recorded in the Takings Clause that has become part of our constitutional culture.

Where "permanent physical occupation" of land is concerned, we have refused to allow the government to decree it anew (without compensation), no matter

---

28. In Justice Blackmun's view, even with respect to regulations that deprive an owner of all developmental or economically beneficial land uses, the test for required compensation is whether the legislature has recited a harm-preventing justification for its action. Since such a justification can be formulated in practically every case, this amounts to a test of whether the legislature has a stupid staff. We think the Takings Clause requires courts to do more than insist upon artful harm-preventing characterizations.

how weighty the asserted "public interests" involved, Loretto v. Teleprompter Manhattan CATV Corp., 458 U.S. at 426—though we assuredly *would* permit the government to assert a permanent easement that was a pre-existing limitation upon the landowner's title. . . . We believe similar treatment must be accorded confiscatory regulations, i.e., regulations that prohibit all economically beneficial use of land: Any limitation so severe cannot be newly legislated or decreed (without compensation), but must inhere in the title itself, in the restrictions that background principles of the State's law of property and nuisance already place upon land ownership. A law or decree with such an effect must, in other words, do no more than duplicate the result that could have been achieved in the courts—by adjacent landowners (or other uniquely affected persons) under the State's law of private nuisance, or by the State under its complementary power to abate nuisances that affect the public generally, or otherwise.[29]

On this analysis, the owner of a lake bed, for example, would not be entitled to compensation when he is denied the requisite permit to engage in a landfilling operation that would have the effect of flooding others' land. Nor the corporate owner of a nuclear generating plant, when it is directed to remove all improvements from its land upon discovery that the plant sits astride an earthquake fault. Such regulatory action may well have the effect of eliminating the land's only economically productive use, but it does not proscribe a productive use that was previously permissible under relevant property and nuisance principles. The use of these properties for what are now expressly prohibited purposes was *always* unlawful, and (subject to other constitutional limitations) it was open to the State at any point to make the implication of those background principles of nuisance and property law explicit. . . . In light of our traditional resort to "existing rules or understandings that stem from an independent source such as state law" to define the range of interests that qualify for protection as "property" under the Fifth (and Fourteenth) amendments, . . . this recognition that the Takings Clause does not require compensation when an owner is barred from putting land to a use that is proscribed by those "existing rules or understandings" is surely unexceptional. When, however, a regulation that declares "off-limits" all economically productive or beneficial uses of land goes beyond what the relevant background principles would dictate, compensation must be paid to sustain it.[30] The "total taking" inquiry we require today will ordinarily entail (as the application of state nuisance law ordinarily entails) analysis of, among other things, the degree of harm to public lands and resources, or adjacent private property, posed by the claimant's proposed activities, see, e.g., Restatement (Second) of Torts §§826, 827, the social value of the claimant's activities and their suitability to the locality

---

29. The principal "otherwise" that we have in mind is litigation absolving the State (or private parties) of liability for the destruction of "real and personal property, in cases of actual necessity, to prevent the spreading of a fire" or to forestall other grave threats to the lives and property of others. Bowditch v. Boston, 101 U.S. 16, 18-19 (1880). . . .

30. Of course, the State may elect to rescind its regulation and thereby avoid having to pay compensation for a permanent deprivation. See First English Evangelical Lutheran Church [of Glendale v. County of Los Angeles, 482 U.S. 304, 321 (1987), to be considered later. See page 1219].

in question, see, e.g., id., §§828(a) and (b), 831, and the relative ease with which the alleged harm can be avoided through measures taken by the claimant and the government (or adjacent private landowners) alike, see, e.g., id., §§827(e), 828(c), 830. The fact that a particular use has long been engaged in by similarly situated owners ordinarily imports a lack of any common-law prohibition (though changed circumstances or new knowledge may make what was previously permissible no longer so, see Restatement (Second) of Torts, supra, §827, comment g). So also does the fact that other landowners, similarly situated, are permitted to continue the use denied to the claimant.

It seems unlikely that common-law principles would have prevented the erection of any habitable or productive improvements on petitioner's land. . . . The question, however, is one of state law to be dealt with on remand. We emphasize that to win its case South Carolina must do more than proffer the legislature's declaration that the uses Lucas desires are inconsistent with the public interest, or the conclusory assertion that they violate a common-law maxim such as *sic utere tuo ut alienum non laedas*. As we have said, a State, by *ipse dixit*, may not transform private property into public property without compensation. . . ." Webb's Fabulous Pharmacies, Inc. v. Beckwith, 449 U.S. 155, 164 (1980). Instead, as it would be required to do if it sought to restrain Lucas in a common-law action for public nuisance, South Carolina must identify background principles of nuisance and property law that prohibit the uses he now intends in the circumstances in which the property is presently found. Only on this showing can the State fairly claim that, in proscribing all such beneficial uses, the Beachfront Management Act is taking nothing.

The judgment is reversed and the cause remanded for proceedings not inconsistent with this opinion.

[Justice Kennedy concurred in the judgment, mentioning several points: (1) The majority opinion established a framework for remand but did not decide the ultimate question of whether a temporary taking had actually occurred. (2) The finding that Lucas's property had no value was "curious." "I share the reservations of some of my colleagues about a finding that a beach front lot loses all value because of a development restriction." (3) "The finding of no value must be considered under the Takings Clause by reference to the owner's reasonable, investment-backed expectations. . . . There is an inherent tendency towards circularity in this synthesis, of course; for if the owner's reasonable expectations are shaped by what courts allow as a proper exercise of governmental authority, property tends to become what courts say it is. Some circularity must be tolerated in these matters, however, as it is in other spheres. . . . The definition, moreover, is not circular in its entirety. The expectations protected by the Constitution are based on objective rules and customs that can be understood as reasonable by all parties involved." (4) "In my view, reasonable expectations must be understood in light of the whole of our legal tradition. The common law of nuisance is too narrow a confine for the exercise of regulatory power in a complex and interdependent society."

Justice Souter filed a separate statement saying he would dismiss the writ of certiorari as having been improvidently granted. "The petition for review was granted on the assumption that the state by regulation had deprived the owner of his entire economic interest in the subject-property. Such was the state trial court's conclusion, which the state supreme court did not review. It is apparent now that in light of our prior cases . . . the trial court's conclusion is highly questionable. . . . [T]he Court is certainly right to refuse to take up the issue, which is not fairly included within the question presented. . . . This alone is enough to show that there is little utility in attempting to deal with this case on the merits."

In addition to the foregoing, there were two dissenting opinions, which follow.]

JUSTICE BLACKMUN, dissenting.

Today the Court launches a missile to kill a mouse.

. . . Relying on an unreviewed (and implausible) state trial court finding that this restriction left Lucas' property valueless, this Court granted review to determine whether compensation must be paid in cases where the State prohibits all economic use of real estate. According to the Court, such an occasion never has arisen in any of our prior cases, and the Court imagines that it will arise "relatively rarely" or only in "extraordinary circumstances." Almost certainly it did not happen in this case.

Nonetheless, the Court presses on to decide the issue, and as it does, it ignores its jurisdictional limits, remakes its traditional rules of review, and creates simultaneously a new categorical rule and an exception (neither of which is rooted in our prior case law, common law, or common sense). I protest not only the Court's decision, but each step taken to reach it. More fundamentally, I question the Court's wisdom in issuing sweeping new rules to decide such a narrow case. . . .

My fear is that the Court's new policies will spread beyond the narrow confines of the present case. For that reason, I, like the Court, will give far greater attention to this case than its narrow scope suggests—not because I can intercept the Court's missile, or save the targeted mouse, but because I hope perhaps to limit the collateral damage. . . .

If the state legislature is correct that the prohibition on building in front of the setback line prevents serious harm, then, under this Court's prior cases, the Act is constitutional. . . . The Court consistently has upheld regulations imposed to arrest a significant threat to the common welfare, whatever their economic effect on the owner. . . .

Petitioner never challenged the legislature's findings that a building ban was necessary to protect property and life. Nor did he contend that the threatened harm was not sufficiently serious to make building a house in a particular location a "harmful" use, that the legislature had not made sufficient findings, or that the legislature was motivated by anything other than a desire to minimize damage to coastal areas. . . .

Nothing in the record undermines the General Assembly's assessment that prohibitions on building in front of the setback line are necessary to protect people and property from storms, high tides, and beach erosion. Because that legislative determination cannot be disregarded in the absence of such evidence, . . . and because its determination of harm to life and property from building is sufficient to prohibit that use under this Court's cases, the South Carolina Supreme Court correctly found no taking.

. . . The Court creates its new takings jurisprudence based on the trial court's finding that the property had lost all economic value. This finding is almost certainly erroneous. Petitioner still can enjoy other attributes of ownership, such as the right to exclude others, "one of the most essential sticks in the bundle of rights that are commonly characterized as property." Kaiser Aetna v. United States, 444 U.S. 164, 176 (1979). Petitioner can picnic, swim, camp in a tent, or live on the property in a movable trailer. State courts frequently have recognized that land has economic value where the only residual economic uses are recreation or camping. . . . Petitioner also retains the right to alienate the land, which would have value for neighbors and for those prepared to enjoy proximity to the ocean without a house. . . .

Clearly, the Court was eager to decide this case. . . .

The Court does not reject the South Carolina Supreme Court's decision simply on the basis of its disbelief and distrust of the legislature's findings. It also takes the opportunity to create a new scheme for regulations that eliminate all economic value. From now on, there is a categorical rule finding these regulations to be a taking unless the use they prohibit is a background common-law nuisance or property principle. . . .

This Court repeatedly has recognized the ability of government, in certain circumstances, to regulate property without compensation no matter how adverse the financial effect on the owner may be. More than a century ago, the Court explicitly upheld the right of States to prohibit uses of property injurious to public health, safety, or welfare without paying compensation: "A prohibition simply upon the use of property for purposes that are declared, by valid legislation, to be injurious to the health, morals, or safety of the community, cannot, in any just sense, be deemed a taking or an appropriation of property." Mugler v. Kansas, 123 U.S. at 668-669 (1887). On this basis, the Court upheld an ordinance effectively prohibiting operation of a previously lawful brewery, although the "establishments will become of no value as property." . . .

The Court recognizes that "our prior opinions have suggested that 'harmful or noxious uses' of property may be proscribed by government regulation without the requirement of compensation," but seeks to reconcile them with its categorical rule by claiming that the Court never has upheld a regulation when the owner alleged the loss of all economic value. Even if the Court's factual premise were correct, its understanding of the Court's cases is distorted. In none of the cases did the Court suggest that the right of a State to prohibit certain activities without paying compensation turned on the availability of some residual valuable use. Instead, the cases depended on whether the government interest was sufficient to prohibit the activity, given the significant private cost.

These cases rest on the principle that the State has full power to prohibit an owner's use of property if it is harmful to the public. "[S]ince no individual has a right to use his property so as to create a nuisance or otherwise harm others, the State has not 'taken' anything when it asserts its power to enjoin the nuisance-like activity." *Keystone Bituminous Coal*, 480 U.S. at 491, n. 20. It would make no sense under this theory to suggest that an owner has a constitutionally protected right to harm others, if only he makes the proper showing of economic loss. . . .

Ultimately even the Court cannot embrace the full implications of its *per se* rule: It eventually agrees that there cannot be a categorical rule for a taking based on economic value that wholly disregards the public need asserted. Instead, the Court decides that it will permit a State to regulate all economic value only if the State prohibits uses that would not be permitted under "background principles of nuisance and property law."[31] Until today, the Court explicitly had rejected the contention that the government's power to act without paying compensation turns on whether the prohibited activity is a common-law nuisance. The brewery closed in *Mugler* itself was not a common-law nuisance, and the Court specifically stated that it was the role of the legislature to determine what measures would be appropriate for the protection of public health and safety. See 123 U.S. at 661. In upholding the state action in *Miller*, the Court found it unnecessary to "weigh with nicety the question whether the infected cedars constitute a nuisance according to common law; or whether they may be so declared by statute." 276 U.S. at 280. Instead the Court has relied in the past, as the South Carolina court has done here, on legislative judgments of what constitutes a harm.

The Court rejects the notion that the State always can prohibit uses it deems a harm to the public without granting compensation because "the distinction between 'harm-preventing' and 'benefit-conferring' regulation is often in the eye of the beholder." Since the characterization will depend "primarily upon one's evaluation of the worth of competing uses of real estate," the Court decides a legislative judgment of this kind no longer can provide the desired "objective, value-free basis" for upholding a regulation. The Court, however, fails to explain how its proposed common-law alternative escapes the same trap.

The threshold inquiry for imposition of the Court's new rule, "deprivation of all economically valuable use," itself cannot be determined objectively. As the Court admits, whether the owner has been deprived of all economic value of his property will depend on how "property" is defined. The "composition of the denominator in our 'deprivation' fraction," [see footnote 26 at page 1180] is the dispositive inquiry. Yet there is no "objective" way to define what that denominator should be. "We have long understood that any land-use regulation can be characterized as the 'total' deprivation of an aptly defined entitlement. . . .

---

31. Although it refers to state nuisance and property law, the Court apparently does not mean just any state nuisance and property law. Public nuisance was first a common law creation, see Newark, The Boundaries of Nuisance, 65 L.Q. Rev. 480, 482 (1949) (attributing development of nuisance to 1535), but by the 1800s in both the United States and England, legislatures had the power to define what is a public nuisance, and particular uses often have been selectively targeted. See Prosser, Private Action for Public Nuisance, 52 Va. L. Rev. 997, 999-1000 (1966); J. Stephen, A General View of the Criminal Law of England 105-107 (2d ed. 1890). The Court's references to "common-law" background principles, however, indicate that legislative determinations do not constitute "state nuisance and property law" for the Court.

Alternatively, the same regulation can always be characterized as a mere 'partial' withdrawal from full, unencumbered ownership of the landholding affected by the regulation. . . ." Michelman, Takings, 1987, 88 Colum. L. Rev. 1600, 1614 (1988). . . .

Even more perplexing, however, is the Court's reliance on common-law principles of nuisance in its quest for a value-free takings jurisprudence. In determining what is a nuisance at common law, state courts make exactly the decision that the Court finds so troubling when made by the South Carolina General Assembly today: They determine whether the use is harmful. Common-law public and private nuisance law is simply a determination whether a particular use causes harm. See Prosser, Private Action for Public Nuisance, 52 Va. L. Rev. 997 (1966) ("*Nuisance* is a French word which means nothing more than harm"). There is nothing magical in the reasoning of judges long dead. They determined a harm in the same way as state judges and legislatures do today. If judges in the 18th and 19th centuries can distinguish a harm from a benefit, why not judges in the 20th century, and if judges can, why not legislators? There simply is no reason to believe that new interpretations of the hoary common-law nuisance doctrine will be particularly "objective" or "value free."[32] Once one abandons the level of generality of *sic utere tuo ut alienum non laedas*, one searches in vain, I think, for anything resembling a principle in the common law of nuisance.

Finally, the Court justifies its new rule that the legislature may not deprive a property owner of the only economically valuable use of his land, even if the legislature finds it to be a harmful use, because such action is not part of the " 'long recognized' " "understandings of our citizens." These "understandings" permit such regulation only if the use is a nuisance under the common law. Any other course is "inconsistent with the historical compact recorded in the Takings Clause." It is not clear from the Court's opinion where our "historical compact" or "citizens' understanding" comes from, but it does not appear to be history.

The principle that the State should compensate individuals for property taken for public use was not widely established in America at the time of the Revolution.

> The colonists . . . inherited . . . a concept of property which permitted extensive regulation of the use of that property for the public benefit—regulation that could even go so far as to deny all productive use of the property to the owner if, as Coke himself stated, the regulation "extends to the public benefit . . . for this is for the public, and every one hath benefit by it." [F. Bosselman, D. Callies & J. Banta, The Taking Issue 80-81 (1973), quoting The Case of the King's Prerogative in Saltpetre, 12 Co. Rep. 12-13 (1606).]

See also Treanor, The Origins and Original Significance of the Just Compensation Clause of the Fifth Amendment, 94 Yale L.J. 694, 697, n. 9 (1985).

---

32. "There is perhaps no more impenetrable jungle in the entire law than that which surrounds the word 'nuisance.' It has meant all things to all people, and has been applied indiscriminately to everything from an alarming advertisement to a cockroach baked in a pie." W. Keeton, D. Dobbs, R. Keeton & D. Owen, Prosser and Keeton on The Law of Torts 616 (5th ed. 1984) (footnotes omitted). . . .

Even into the 19th century, state governments often felt free to take property for roads and other public projects without paying compensation to the owners. See M. Horwitz, The Transformation of American Law, 1780-1860, pp. 63-64 (1977) (hereinafter Horwitz); Treanor, 94 Yale L.J., at 695. As one court declared in 1802, citizens "were bound to contribute as much of [land], as by the laws of the country, were deemed necessary for the public convenience." M'Clenachan v. Curwin, 3 Yeates 362, 373 (Pa. 1802). There was an obvious movement toward establishing the just compensation principle during the 19th century, but "there continued to be a strong current in American legal thought that regarded compensation simply as a 'bounty given . . . by the State' out of 'kindness' and not out of justice." Horwitz 65, quoting Commonwealth v. Fisher, 1 Pen. & W. 462, 465 (Pa. 1830). Although, prior to the adoption of the Bill of Rights, America was replete with land-use regulations describing which activities were considered noxious and forbidden, see Bender, The Takings Clause: Principles or Politics?, 34 Buffalo L. Rev. 735, 751 (1985); L. Friedman, A History of American Law 66-68 (1973), the Fifth Amendment's Takings Clause originally did not extend to regulations of property, whatever the effect. Most state courts agreed with this narrow interpretation of a taking. "Until the end of the nineteenth century . . . jurists held that the constitution protected possession only, and not value." Siegel, Understanding the Nineteenth Century Contract Clause: The Role of the Property-Privilege Distinction and "Takings" Clause Jurisprudence, 60 S. Cal. L. Rev. 1, 76 (1986). . . . Even when courts began to consider that regulation in some situations could constitute a taking, they continued to uphold bans on particular uses without paying compensation, notwithstanding the economic impact, under the rationale that no one can obtain a vested right to injure or endanger the public. . . .

In addition, state courts historically have been less likely to find that a government action constitutes a taking when the affected land is undeveloped. . . .

Nor does history indicate any common-law limit on the State's power to regulate harmful uses even to the point of destroying all economic value. Nothing in the discussions in Congress concerning the Takings Clause indicates that the Clause was limited by the common-law nuisance doctrine. Common-law courts themselves rejected such an understanding. They regularly recognized that it is "for the legislature to interpose, and by positive enactment to prohibit a use of property which would be injurious to the public." [Commonwealth v. Tewksbury, 11 Metc., at 57 (Mass. 1846).] Chief Justice Shaw explained in upholding a regulation prohibiting construction of wharves, the existence of a taking did not depend on "whether a certain erection in tide water is a nuisance at common law or not." [Commonwealth v. Alger, 7 Cush., at 104 (Mass. 1851).] . . .

In short, I find no clear and accepted "historical compact" or "understanding of our citizens" justifying the Court's new takings doctrine. Instead, the Court seems to treat history as a grab bag of principles, to be adopted where they support the Court's theory, and ignored where they do not. If the Court decided that the early common law provides the background principles for interpreting the Takings Clause, then regulation, as opposed to physical confiscation, would not be compensable. If the Court decided that the law of a later period provides the background principles, then regulation might be compensable, but the Court would have to confront the fact that legislatures regularly determined which uses were prohibited, independent of the common law, and independent of whether the uses were lawful when the owner purchased. What makes the Court's analysis unworkable is its attempt to package the law of two incompatible eras and peddle it as historical fact. . . .

I dissent.

JUSTICE STEVENS, dissenting. . . .

In my opinion, the Court is doubly in error. The categorical rule the Court establishes is an unsound and unwise addition to the law and the Court's formulation of the exception to that rule is too rigid and too narrow.

. . . Although in dicta we have sometimes recited that a law "effects a taking if [it] . . . denies an owner economically viable use of his land," Agins v. City of Tiburon, 447 U.S. 255, 260, (1980), our *rulings* have rejected such an absolute position. We have frequently—and recently—held that, in some circumstances, a law that renders property valueless may nonetheless not constitute a taking. See, e.g., First English Evangelical Lutheran Church of Glendale v. County of Los Angeles, 482 U.S. 304, 313 (1987); Goldblatt v. Hempstead, 369 U.S. 590, 596 (1962). . . .

In addition to lacking support in past decisions, the Court's new rule is wholly arbitrary. A landowner whose property is diminished in value 95% recovers nothing, while an owner whose property is diminished 100% recovers the land's full value. . . .

Moreover, because of the elastic nature of property rights, the Court's new rule will also prove unsound in practice. In response to the rule, courts may define "property" broadly and only rarely find regulations to effect total takings. This is the approach the Court itself adopts in its revisionist reading of venerable precedents. We are told that—notwithstanding the Court's findings to the contrary in each case—the brewery in *Mugler*, the brickyard in *Hadacheck*, and the gravel pit in *Goldblatt* all could be put to "other uses" and that, therefore, those cases did not involve total regulatory takings.[33]

On the other hand, developers and investors may market specialized estates to take advantage of the Court's new rule. The smaller the estate, the more likely that a regulatory change will effect a total taking. Thus, an investor may, for example, purchase the right to build a multifamily home on a specific lot, with the

---

33. Of course, the same could easily be said in this case: Lucas may put his land to "other uses"—fishing or camping, for example—or may sell his land to his neighbors as a buffer. In either event, his land is far from "valueless."

This highlights a fundamental weakness in the Court's analysis: its failure to explain why only the impairment of "economically beneficial or productive use" (emphasis added) of property is relevant in takings analysis. I should think that a regulation arbitrarily prohibiting an owner from continuing to use her property for bird watching or sunbathing might constitute a taking under some circumstances; and, conversely, that such uses are of value to the owner. Yet the Court offers no basis for its assumption that the only uses of property cognizable under the Constitution are developmental uses.

result that a zoning regulation that allows only single-family homes would render the investor's property interest "valueless." In short, the categorical rule will likely have one of two effects: Either courts will alter the definition of the "denominator" in the takings "fraction," rendering the Court's categorical rule meaningless, or investors will manipulate the relevant property interests, giving the Court's rule sweeping effect. To my mind, neither of these results is desirable or appropriate, and both are distortions of our takings jurisprudence.

Finally, the Court's justification for its new categorical rule is remarkably thin. The Court mentions in passing three arguments in support of its rule; none is convincing. First, the Court suggests that "total deprivation of feasible use is, from the landowner's point of view, the equivalent of a physical appropriation." This argument proves too much. From the "landowner's point of view," a regulation that diminishes a lot's value by 50% is as well "the equivalent" of the condemnation of half of the lot. Yet, it is well established that a 50% diminution in value does not by itself constitute a taking. See Euclid v. Ambler Realty Co., 272 U.S. 365, 384 (1926) (75% diminution in value). Thus, the landowner's perception of the regulation cannot justify the Court's new rule.

Second, the Court emphasizes that because total takings are "relatively rare" its new rule will not adversely affect the government's ability to "go on." This argument proves too little. Certainly it is true that defining a small class of regulations that are per se takings will not greatly hinder important governmental functions—but this is true of *any* small class of regulations. The Court's suggestion only begs the question of why regulations of *this* particular class should always be found to effect takings.

Finally, the Court suggests that "regulations that leave the owner . . . without economically beneficial . . . use . . . carry with them a heightened risk that private property is being pressed into some form of public service." As discussed more fully below, I agree that the risks of such singling out are of central concern in takings law. However, such risks do not justify a per se rule for total regulatory takings. There is no necessary correlation between "singling out" and total takings: a regulation may single out a property owner without depriving him of all of his property, see, e.g., Nollan v. California Coastal Commn., 483 U.S. 825, 837 (1987); and it may deprive him of all of his property without singling him out, see, e.g., Mugler v. Kansas, 123 U.S. 623 (1887); Hadacheck v. Sebastian, 239 U.S. 394 (1915). What matters in such cases is not the degree of diminution of value, but rather the specificity of the expropriating act. For this reason, the Court's third justification for its new rule also fails. . . .

Like many bright-line rules, the categorical rule established in this case is only "categorical" for a page or two in the U.S. Reports. No sooner does the Court state that "total regulatory takings must be compensated," than it quickly establishes an exception to that rule.

The exception provides that a regulation that renders property valueless is not a taking if it prohibits uses of property that were not "previously permissible under relevant property and nuisance principles." The Court thus rejects the basic holding in Mugler v. Kansas, 123 U.S. 623 (1887). . . .

Under our reasoning in *Mugler*, a State's decision to prohibit or to regulate certain uses of property is not a compensable taking just because the particular uses were previously lawful. Under the Court's opinion today, however, if a State should decide to prohibit the manufacture of asbestos, cigarettes, or concealable firearms, for example, it must be prepared to pay for the adverse economic consequences of its decision. . . .

The Court's holding today effectively freezes the State's common law, denying the legislature much of its traditional power to revise the law governing the rights and uses of property. . . .

Arresting the development of the common law is not only a departure from our prior decisions; it is also profoundly unwise. The human condition is one of constant learning and evolution—both moral and practical. Legislatures implement that new learning; in doing so they must often revise the definition of property and the rights of property owners. . . .

Of course, some legislative redefinitions of property will effect a taking and must be compensated—but it certainly cannot be the case that every movement away from common law does so. There is no reason, and less sense, in such an absolute rule. We live in a world in which changes in the economy and the environment occur with increasing frequency and importance. . . . The rule that should govern a decision in a case of this kind should focus on the future, not the past. . . .[34]

The Court's categorical approach rule will, I fear, greatly hamper the efforts of local officials and planners who must deal with increasingly complex problems in land-use and environmental regulation. As this case—in which the claims of an *individual* property owner exceed $1 million—well demonstrates, these officials face both substantial uncertainty because of the ad hoc nature of takings law and unacceptable penalties if they guess incorrectly about that law.

Viewed more broadly, the Court's new rule and exception conflict with the very character of our takings jurisprudence. We have frequently and consistently recognized that the definition of a taking cannot be reduced to a "set formula" and that determining whether a regulation is a taking is "essentially [an] ad hoc, factual inquir[y]." . . .

The presumption that a permanent physical occupation, no matter how slight, effects a taking is wholly consistent with this principle. A physical taking entails a certain amount of "singling out." Consistent with this principle, physical occupations by third parties are more likely to effect takings than other physical occupations. . . .

---

34. Even measured in terms of efficiency, the Court's rule is unsound. The Court today effectively establishes a form of insurance against certain changes in land-use regulations. Like other forms of insurance, the Court's rule creates a "moral hazard" and inefficiencies: In the face of uncertainty about changes in the law, developers will overinvest, safe in the knowledge that if the law changes adversely, they will be entitled to compensation. See generally Farber, Economic Analysis and Just Compensation, 12 Intl. Rev. of Law & Econ. 125 (1992).

In analyzing takings claims, courts have long recognized the difference between a regulation that targets one or two parcels of land and a regulation that enforces a statewide policy. . . .

In considering Lucas' claim, the generality of the Beachfront Management Act is significant. The Act does not target particular landowners, but rather regulates the use of the coastline of the entire State. Indeed, South Carolina's Act is best understood as part of a national effort to protect the coastline, one initiated by the federal Coastal Zone Management Act of 1972. Pursuant to the federal Act, every coastal State has implemented coastline regulations. Moreover, the Act did not single out owners of undeveloped land. The Act also prohibited owners of developed land from rebuilding if their structures were destroyed. . . . In short, the South Carolina Act imposed substantial burdens on owners of developed and undeveloped land alike. This generality indicates that the Act is not an effort to expropriate owners of undeveloped land.

Accordingly, I respectfully dissent.

NOTES AND QUESTIONS

1. *Conceptual severance again.* Begin by returning to a subject already mentioned on several occasions in this chapter (see pages 1162, 1176). Where did conceptual severance stand after the Court's opinion in *Lucas*? For discussion, see Marc R. Lisker, Regulatory Takings and the Denominator Problem, 27 Rutgers L.J. 663 (1996). Generally speaking, state courts appear to reject conceptual severance; they consider the impact of a land use regulation on the value of a property owner's entire parcel, as opposed to its impact on just the regulated part. On the other hand, the Court of Appeals for the Federal Circuit (discussed in Note 4 on page 1221) arguably tends in just the opposite direction. See Lost Tree Village Corp. v. United States, 707 F.3d 1286 (Fed. Cir. 2013).

2. *Real property versus personal property.* Recall the reference to former President Nixon's presidential papers in Note 6 on page 1145. Notice that in his opinion for the Court in *Lucas* (see page 1184), Justice Scalia draws a distinction between real and personal property when it comes to regulatory takings, stating that the "historical compact" applies only to the former, not the latter. For a challenge to that view, see Eduardo M. Peñalver, Is Land Special?, 32 Ecology L.Q. 227 (2004).

3. *Which background principles?* Notice that the majority's articulation of the "background principles" framework cites the Restatement (Second) of Torts, which directs courts to determine whether a particular land use is a nuisance by weighing both the costs and benefits associated with that use. See page 1184. The Second Restatement was promulgated in 1977, though its provisions on nuisance largely mirrored those articulated in the Restatement of Property, which was published in the 1930s. See Louise A. Halper, Untangling the Nuisance Knot, 26 B.C. Envtl. Aff. L. Rev. 89, 120-128 (1998). Historically, the common law of private nuisance in the United States and England focused on whether the defendant's land use had substantially interfered with the plaintiff's property rights. If so, the

use was a nuisance, regardless of any offsetting benefits. See the *Morgan* case in Chapter 9 (at page 779) and Justice Blackmun's dissent at 1190. The idea that courts hearing nuisance claims should consider whether the medicine was worse than the disease was first articulated by an American court in 1868, and gradually gained broader acceptance over the decades that followed. See George P. Smith II, Nuisance Law: The Morphogenesis of an Historical Revisionist Theory of Contemporary Economic Jurisprudence, 74 Neb. L. Rev. 658, 688-692 (1995); Morton J. Horwitz, The Transformation of American Law 1870-1960: The Crisis of Legal Orthodoxy 27-29 (1992). Indeed, the Restatement's nuisance provisions were still very controversial in the 1970s, and contemporary leading tort treatises differed with the Restatement over the relevance of benefits produced by the defendant's use. See Halper, supra, at 127-130. If the basic concept of what counts as a nuisance was changing radically in the nineteenth and twentieth centuries, how is a court to determine what the relevant background principles are?

Why does the existence of background principles alter the takings analysis, and what are the results of making this inquiry central to takings doctrine? See Timothy M. Mulvaney, Foreground Principles, 20 Geo. Mason L. Rev. 837 (2013).

4. *More on categorical rules.* We saw earlier (see Note 2 on page 1144) that certain government actions are treated, categorically, as always amounting to takings (namely actions that work permanent physical occupations—the *Loretto* rule, and those that effectively wipe out all economic value—the *Lucas* rule). But there are also certain government actions that are treated, categorically, as *never* amounting to takings. One, introduced in connection with *Hadacheck* (see Note 4 on page 1152), has to do with control of nuisances, meaning, after *Lucas*, common law nuisances. Another, referred to in footnote 29 on page 1185, is the so-called conflagration rule excluding takings liability for damages caused by fire control measures. Two others are the forfeiture rule, which allows the government to seize property used in the commission of crimes, and the navigation servitude, which excludes government liability for property damage caused by federal regulation of navigable waters. See generally David A. Dana & Thomas W. Merrill, Property: Takings 110-120 (2002).

5. *Of missiles and mice.* Consider the opening words of Justice Blackmun's dissenting opinion in *Lucas*: "Today, the court launches a missile to kill a mouse." The missile has two components—the Court's new categorical rule (land use regulations that prohibit all economic uses of property are takings . . .) and the exception to it (. . . unless the prohibited uses are common law nuisances). But the target is just a mouse, because rarely if at all will regulatory programs wipe out value altogether. And supposing they do, was it not already clear, from the decision in *Pennsylvania Coal*, that there would be liability for a taking? State courts had acted accordingly for many years. So is *Lucas* insignificant?

Opinions on that question were sharply divided right after the Court's decision. Environmentalists in particular feared that the case would have a chilling effect on constructive regulation. But many other observers found much ado about nothing. See, e.g., Ronald H. Rosenberg, The Non-Impact of the United States Supreme Court Regulatory Takings Cases on the State Courts: Does the

Supreme Court Really Matter?, 6 Fordham Envtl. L.J. 523, 545-548 (1995), reporting that a review of state court opinions in the two-and-one-half year period following *Lucas* found 80 cases mentioning the case. Only 57 of those considered it in any detail, and "only three can be said to have relied on *Lucas* in finding a regulatory taking." Id. at 545. For a good selection of law review commentary on *Lucas*, see Symposium, 45 Stan. L. Rev. 1369 (1993).

6. *The aftermath of* Lucas. On remand from the decision in *Lucas*, the South Carolina Supreme Court concluded that there was no common law basis for holding that Mr. Lucas's intended use of his land was not a part of the bundle of rights inhering in his title. The trial court was thus instructed to make findings of damages—for the period beginning with the enactment of the 1988 Beachfront Management Act and running to the date of the court's order—to compensate Mr. Lucas for a temporary taking. Lucas v. South Carolina Coastal Council, 424 S.E.2d 484 (S.C. 1992). The case ended in a negotiated settlement. The state purchased Lucas's two lots for $850,000 and paid him another $725,000 in interest, attorneys' fees, and costs. Strapped for the money (a total of $1,575,000), the state resold the lots to a construction company!

For Mr. Lucas's own account of his trials and tribulations, see David Lucas, Lucas vs. the Green Machine (1995), which mentions in its concluding pages the effort on various fronts to enact so-called takings legislation, which has enjoyed success mostly at the state level. For a fascinating account of the *Lucas* case's richer context, see Vicki Been, Lucas v. The Green Machine: Using the Takings Clause to Promote More Efficient Regulation?, in Property Stories 299 (Gerald Korngold & Andrew P. Morriss eds. 2d ed. 2009).

A considerable number of states have enacted "takings assessment" statutes that require agencies to determine whether regulatory activity might constitute a taking of private property. Several states have gone further, enacting "compensation" statutes that provide for payment when government action has a significant impact on value—say by reducing it more than 25 percent, or burdening land use "inordinately." Enthusiasts see a "rebellion" in such measures; critics see the "taxpayers' worst nightmare," "an extension of the worst parts of the Reagan Revolution." See Land Rights: The 1990s' Property Rights Rebellion (Bruce Yandle ed. 1995); Margaret Kriz, Taking Issue, Natl. J., June 1, 1996, at 1200, 1204. A 2008 report by the Georgetown Environmental Law & Policy Institute examines the compensation laws of Florida, Oregon, and several other states, and concludes that the legislation was counterproductive, rolling back existing land use rules, inhibiting new controls, and serving the interests of developers and timber companies. See John Echeverria & Thekla Hansen-Young, The Track Record on Takings Legislation: Lessons from Democracy's Laboratories (Georgetown Environmental Law & Policy Institute Papers & Reports 2008).

7. *Courts versus legislatures.* Notice how *Lucas* altered the nuisance exception discussed earlier in this chapter (see Notes 2 and 4 on pages 1150, 1152):

The practical effect of this . . . is to transfer authority from legislatures to courts. Essentially, it implies that legislative judgments of harm are not legitimate, but judge-made judgments are. This transfer is a concern because serious environmental harms, such as the ozone hole or degradation of the Chesapeake Bay, often arise from many small, seemingly safe uses of property that only together cause great harm. Environmental protection began with judge-made law, but shifted to legislative statutes long ago precisely because courts have difficulty recognizing and regulating such diffuse sources of harm. [Timothy D. Searchinger, Private Property Rights and Environmental Harm, EDF Letter (A Report to Members of the Environmental Defense Fund), Oct. 1992, at 4.]

See also the report of an interview with John A. Humbach, a professor of law at Pace University, in News Notes—High Court Takings Analysis Likelyto Burden Regulators, Envt. Rep. (BNA) Decisions No. 22 (July 10, 1992) (unpaginated):

> Humbach said that what troubled him about the ruling was that the Supreme Court reassigned from the legislative branch to the courts final authority for determining what land uses are injurious. This is bad, he said, because the courts are not responsive to a voting constituency and are not so well suited to respond to change. In addition, the courts are institutionally isolated from the "tug and pull of the political process," he said.

The thrust of both sets of remarks, in part, is that legislative bodies can be trusted as much as, if not more than, the courts. The justices in the majority in *Lucas* seem to disagree.[35] Or do they? Might it depend on which courts are involved? Keep these questions in mind until we get to Justice Scalia's opinion in the *Stop the Beach* case (the report of which begins at page 1222).

8. Pennsylvania Coal, Penn Central, *and* Lucas. Suppose that a government regulation, enacted to control some land use that is troublesome but decidedly not a common law nuisance, has the eventual effect of reducing—substantially, but not to zero—the market value of land owned by *O*. May *O* assert a takings claim based on the diminution-in-value test of *Pennsylvania Coal* (page 1153)? Suppose that *O* purchased the property from its erstwhile owner after the government regulation was enacted. In the words of *Penn Central* (see Note 2 on page 1176), does this mean that *O* has no "distinct investment-backed expectation," and thus no takings claim? Suppose that *O* purchased the land after the regulation was enacted and that the regulation does wipe out the value of *O*'s land. Does the fact of post-enactment purchase mean, in the words of *Lucas* (at page 1184), "that the proscribed use interests were not part of his title to begin with"?[36]

On all of these questions, consider the following case.

---

35. See John F. Hart, Colonial Land Use Law and Its Significance for Modern Takings Doctrine, 109 Harv. L. Rev. 1252, 1297-1298 (1996):

> The Supreme Court has suggested that only land use regulation comporting with judicially constructed nuisance doctrine is entitled to deference, and that expansion of the nuisance concept "cannot be newly legislated or decreed" by modern legislatures. This insistence . . . rests on the historical premise that American nuisance law traditionally was defined by judicial common law and not by statute or ordinance.
>
> This premise is wrong. Throughout the colonial period, lawmakers regularly used statutes and ordinances to define nuisances.

36. Some post-*Lucas* state court decisions so held. For discussion, see Gregory M. Stein, Who Gets the Taking Claim? Changes in Land Use Law, Pre-Enactment Owners, and Post-Enactment Buyers, 61 Ohio St. L.J. 89 (2000); see also Lynn E. Blais, Takings, Statutes, and the Common Law: Considering Inherent Limitations on Title, 70 S. Cal. L. Rev. 1 (1996).

Palazzolo v. Rhode Island

Supreme Court of the United States, 2001
533 U.S. 606

JUSTICE KENNEDY delivered the opinion of the Court.

Petitioner Anthony Palazzolo owns a waterfront parcel of land in the town of
Westerly, Rhode Island. Almost all of the property is designated as coastal wetlands
under Rhode Island law. After petitioner's development proposals were rejected
by respondent Rhode Island Coastal Resources Management Council (Council),
he sued in state court, asserting the Council's application of its wetlands regulations took the property without compensation in violation of the Takings Clause
of the Fifth Amendment, binding upon the State through the Due Process Clause
of the Fourteenth Amendment. Petitioner sought review in this Court, contending the Supreme Court of Rhode Island erred in rejecting his takings claim. . . .

I.

. . . In 1959 petitioner, a lifelong Westerly resident, decided to invest in three
undeveloped, adjoining parcels along this eastern stretch of Atlantic Avenue. To
the north, the property faces, and borders upon, Winnapaug Pond; the south of
the property faces Atlantic Avenue and the beachfront homes abutting it on the
other side, and beyond that the dunes and the beach. To purchase and hold the
property, petitioner and associates formed Shore Gardens, Inc. (SGI). After SGI
purchased the property petitioner bought out his associates and became the sole
shareholder. In the first decade of SGI's ownership of the property the corporation submitted a plat to the town subdividing the property into 80 lots; and it
engaged in various transactions that left it with 74 lots, which together encompassed about 20 acres. During the same period SGI also made initial attempts to
develop the property and submitted intermittent applications to state agencies to
fill substantial portions of the parcel. Most of the property was then, as it is now,
salt marsh subject to tidal flooding. The wet ground and permeable soil would
require considerable fill—as much as six feet in some places—before significant
structures could be built. SGI's proposal, submitted in 1962 to the Rhode Island
Division of Harbors and Rivers (DHR), sought to dredge from Winnapaug Pond
and fill the entire property. The application was denied for lack of essential information. A second, similar proposal followed a year later. A third application, submitted in 1966 while the second application was pending, proposed more limited
filling of the land for use as a private beach club. These latter two applications
were referred to the Rhode Island Department of Natural Resources, which indicated initial assent. The agency later withdrew approval, however, citing adverse
environmental impacts. SGI did not contest the ruling.

No further attempts to develop the property were made for over a decade.
Two intervening events, however, become important to the issues presented.
First, in 1971, Rhode Island enacted legislation creating the Council, an agency
charged with the duty of protecting the State's coastal properties. Regulations

promulgated by the Council designated salt marshes like those on SGI's property as protected "coastal wetlands," on which development is limited to a great extent. Second, in 1978 SGI's corporate charter was revoked for failure to pay corporate income taxes; and title to the property passed, by operation of state law, to petitioner as the corporation's sole shareholder.

In 1983 petitioner, now the owner, renewed the efforts to develop the property. An application to the Council, resembling the 1962 submission, requested permission to construct a wooden bulkhead along the shore of Winnapaug Pond and to fill the entire marsh land area. The Council rejected the application, noting it was "vague and inadequate for a project of this size and nature." The agency also found that "the proposed activities will have significant impacts upon the waters and wetlands of Winnapaug Pond," and concluded that "the proposed alteration . . . will conflict with the Coastal Resources Management Plan presently in effect." Petitioner did not appeal the agency's determination.

Petitioner went back to the drawing board, this time hiring counsel and preparing a more specific and limited proposal for use of the property. . . .

The application fared no better with the Council than previous ones. . . . This time petitioner appealed the decision to the Rhode Island courts, challenging the Council's conclusion as contrary to principles of state administrative law. The Council's decision was affirmed.

Petitioner filed an inverse condemnation action in Rhode Island Superior Court, asserting that the State's wetlands regulations, as applied by the Council to his parcel, had taken the property without compensation in violation of the Fifth and Fourteenth Amendments. The suit alleged the Council's action deprived him of "all economically beneficial use" of his property, resulting in a total taking requiring compensation under Lucas v. South Carolina Coastal Council, 505 U.S. 1003 (1992). He sought damages in the amount of $3,150,000, a figure derived from an appraiser's estimate as to the value of a 74-lot residential subdivision. The State countered with a host of defenses. After a bench trial, a justice of the Superior Court ruled against petitioner, accepting some of the State's theories.

The Rhode Island Supreme Court affirmed. 746 A.2d 707 (2000). Like the Superior Court, the State Supreme Court recited multiple grounds for rejecting petitioner's suit. [Two of these were] that petitioner had no right to challenge regulations predating 1978, when he succeeded to legal ownership of the property from SGI, and that the claim of deprivation of all economically beneficial use was contradicted by undisputed evidence that he had $200,000 in development value remaining on an upland parcel of the property. In addition to holding petitioner could not assert a takings claim based on the denial of all economic use the court concluded he could not recover under the more general test of Penn Central Transp. Co. v. City New York, 438 U.S. 104 (1978). On this claim, too, the date of acquisition of the parcel was found determinative, and the court held he could have had "no reasonable investment-backed expectations that were affected by this regulation" because it predated his ownership.

We disagree with the Supreme Court of Rhode Island as to the first of these conclusions; and, we hold, the court was correct to conclude that the owner is not deprived of all economic use of his property because the value of upland portions is substantial. We remand for further consideration of the claim under the principles set forth in *Penn Central.*

II.

. . . In Pennsylvania Coal Co. v. Mahon, 260 U.S. 393 (1922), the Court recognized that there will be instances when government actions do not encroach upon or occupy property yet still affect and limit its use to such an extent that a taking occurs. In Justice Holmes' well-known, if less than self-defining, formulation, "while property may be regulated to a certain extent, if a regulation goes too far it will be recognized as a taking."

Since *Mahon,* we have given some, but not too specific, guidance to courts confronted with deciding whether a particular government action goes too far and effects a regulatory taking. First, we have observed, with certain qualifications, that a regulation which "denies all economically beneficial or productive use of land" will require compensation under the Takings Clause. *Lucas,* 505 U.S. at 1015. Where a regulation places limitations on land that fall short of eliminating all economically beneficial use, a taking nonetheless may have occurred, depending on a complex of factors including the regulation's economic effect on the landowner, the extent to which the regulation interferes with reasonable investment-backed expectations, and the character of the government action. *Penn Central,* supra, at 124. . . .

Petitioner seeks compensation under these principles. . . .

A. [Omitted.]

B.

. . . When the Council promulgated its wetlands regulations, the disputed parcel was owned not by petitioner but by the corporation of which he was sole shareholder. When title was transferred to petitioner by operation of law, the wetlands regulations were in force. The state court held the postregulation acquisition of title was fatal to the claim for deprivation of all economic use, and to the *Penn Central* claim. While the first holding was couched in terms of background principles of state property law, see *Lucas,* 505 U.S. at 1015, and the second in terms of petitioner's reasonable investment-backed expectations, see *Penn Central,* 438 U.S. at 124, the two holdings together amount to a single, sweeping, rule: A purchaser or a successive title holder like petitioner is deemed to have notice of an earlier-enacted restriction and is barred from claiming that it effects a taking.

The theory underlying the argument that post-enactment purchasers cannot challenge a regulation under the Takings Clause seems to run on these lines: Property rights are created by the State. So, the argument goes, by prospective legislation the State can shape and define property rights and reasonable investment-backed expectations, and subsequent owners cannot claim any injury from lost value. After all, they purchased or took title with notice of the limitation.

The State may not put so potent a Hobbesian stick into the Lockean bundle. The right to improve property, of course, is subject to the reasonable exercise of state authority, including the enforcement of valid zoning and land-use restrictions. The Takings Clause, however, in certain circumstances allows a landowner to assert that a particular exercise of the State's regulatory power is so unreasonable or onerous as to compel compensation. Just as a prospective enactment, such as a new zoning ordinance, can limit the value of land without effecting a taking because it can be understood as reasonable by all concerned, other enactments are unreasonable and do not become less so through passage of time or title. Were we to accept the State's rule, the postenactment transfer of title would absolve the State of its obligation to defend any action restricting land use, no matter how extreme or unreasonable. A State would be allowed, in effect, to put an expiration date on the Takings Clause. This ought not to be the rule. Future generations, too, have a right to challenge unreasonable limitations on the use and value of land.

Nor does the justification of notice take into account the effect on owners at the time of enactment, who are prejudiced as well. Should an owner attempt to challenge a new regulation, but not survive the process of ripening his or her claim (which, as this case demonstrates, will often take years), under the proposed rule the right to compensation may not be asserted by an heir or successor, and so may not be asserted at all. The State's rule would work a critical alteration to the nature of property, as the newly regulated landowner is stripped of the ability to transfer the interest which was possessed prior to the regulation. The State may not by this means secure a windfall for itself. . . . The proposed rule is, furthermore, capricious in effect. The young owner contrasted with the older owner, the owner with the resources to hold contrasted with the owner with the need to sell, would be in different positions. The Takings Clause is not so quixotic. A blanket rule that purchasers with notice have no compensation right when a claim becomes ripe is too blunt an instrument to accord with the duty to compensate for what is taken. . . .

In *Lucas* the Court observed that a landowner's ability to recover for a government deprivation of all economically beneficial use of property is not absolute but instead is confined by limitations on the use of land which "inhere in the title itself." This is so, the Court reasoned, because the landowner is constrained by those "restrictions that background principles of the State's law of property and nuisance already place upon land ownership." It is asserted here that *Lucas* stands for the proposition that any new regulation, once enacted, becomes a background principle of property law which cannot be challenged by those who acquire title after the enactment.

We have no occasion to consider the precise circumstances when a legislative enactment can be deemed a background principle of state law or whether those circumstances are present here. It suffices to say that a regulation that otherwise would be unconstitutional absent compensation is not transformed into a background principle of the State's law by mere virtue of the passage of title. This relative standard would be incompatible with our description of the concept in *Lucas*, which is explained in terms of those common, shared understandings of permissible limitations derived from a State's legal tradition. A regulation or common-law rule cannot be a background principle for some owners but not for others. The determination whether an existing, general law can limit all economic use of property must turn on objective factors, such as the nature of the land use proscribed. See *Lucas*, supra, at 1030 ("The 'total taking' inquiry we require today will ordinarily entail . . . analysis of, among other things, the degree of harm to public lands and resources, or adjacent private property, posed by the claimant's proposed activities"). A law does not become a background principle for subsequent owners by enactment itself. . . .

For reasons we discuss next, the state court will not find it necessary to explore these matters on remand in connection with the claim that all economic use was deprived; it must address, however, the merits of petitioner's claim under *Penn Central*. That claim is not barred by the mere fact that title was acquired after the effective date of the state-imposed restriction.

III.

As . . . the date of transfer of title does not bar petitioner's takings claim, we have before us the alternative ground relied upon by the Rhode Island Supreme Court in ruling upon the merits of the takings claims. It held that all economically beneficial use was not deprived because the uplands portion of the property can still be improved. On this point, we agree with the court's decision. Petitioner accepts the Council's contention and the state trial court's finding that his parcel retains $200,000 in development value under the State's wetlands regulations. He asserts, nonetheless, that he has suffered a total taking and contends the Council cannot sidestep the holding in *Lucas* "by the simple expedient of leaving a landowner a few crumbs of value."

Assuming a taking is otherwise established, a State may not evade the duty to compensate on the premise that the landowner is left with a token interest. This is not the situation of the landowner in this case, however. A regulation permitting a landowner to build a substantial residence on an 18-acre parcel does not leave the property "economically idle." *Lucas*, supra, at 1019.

In his brief submitted to us petitioner attempts to revive this part of his claim by reframing it. He argues, for the first time, that the upland parcel is distinct from the wetlands portions, so he should be permitted to assert a deprivation limited to the latter. This contention asks us to examine the difficult, persisting question of what is the proper denominator in the takings fraction. See Michelman, Property, Utility, and Fairness: Comments on the Ethical Foundations of "Just Compensation Law," 80 Harv. L. Rev. 1165, 1192 (1967). Some of our cases indicate that the extent of deprivation effected by a regulatory action is measured against the value of the parcel as a whole, see, e.g., Keystone Bituminous Coal Assn. v. DeBenedictis, 480 U.S. 470, 497 (1987); but we have at times expressed discomfort with the logic of this rule, see *Lucas*, supra, at 1016-1017, a sentiment echoed by some commentators, see, *e.g.*, Epstein, Takings: Descent and

Resurrection, 1987 Sup. Ct. Rev. 1, 16-17; Fee, Unearthing the Denominator in Regulatory Takings Claims, 61 U. Chi. L. Rev. 1535 (1994). Whatever the merits of these criticisms, we will not explore the point here. Petitioner did not press the argument in the state courts, and the issue was not presented in the petition for certiorari. The case comes to us on the premise that petitioner's entire parcel serves as the basis for his takings claim, and, so framed, the total deprivation argument fails.

For the reasons we have discussed, the State Supreme Court erred in ruling that acquisition of title after the effective date of the regulations barred the takings claims. The court did not err in finding that petitioner failed to establish a deprivation of all economic value, for it is undisputed that the parcel retains significant worth for construction of a residence. The claims under the *Penn Central* analysis were not examined, and for this purpose the case should be remanded. . . .

JUSTICE O'CONNOR, concurring.

I join the opinion of the Court but with my understanding of how the issues discussed in Part II-B of the opinion must be considered on remand.

Part II-B of the Court's opinion addresses the circumstance, present in this case, where a takings claimant has acquired title to the regulated property after the enactment of the regulation at issue. As the Court holds, the Rhode Island Supreme Court erred in effectively adopting the sweeping rule that the preacquisition enactment of the use restriction ipso facto defeats any takings claim based on that use restriction. Accordingly, the Court holds that petitioner's claim under Penn Central Transp. Co. v. City of New York, 438 U.S. 104 (1978), "is not barred by the mere fact that title was acquired after the effective date of the state-imposed restriction."

The more difficult question is what role the temporal relationship between regulatory enactment and title acquisition plays in a proper *Penn Central* analysis. Today's holding does not mean that the timing of the regulation's enactment relative to the acquisition of title is immaterial to the *Penn Central* analysis. Indeed, it would be just as much error to expunge this consideration from the takings inquiry as it would be to accord it exclusive significance. Our polestar instead remains the principles set forth in *Penn Central* itself and our other cases that govern partial regulatory takings. Under these cases, interference with investment-backed expectations is one of a number of factors that a court must examine. Further, the regulatory regime in place at the time the claimant acquires the property at issue helps to shape the reasonableness of those expectations.

The Fifth Amendment forbids the taking of private property for public use without just compensation. We have recognized that this constitutional guarantee is "designed to bar Government from forcing some people alone to bear public burdens which, in all fairness and justice, should be borne by the public as a whole." The concepts of "fairness and justice" that underlie the Takings Clause, of course, are less than fully determinate. Accordingly, we have eschewed "any 'set formula' for determining when 'justice and fairness' require that economic injuries caused by public action be compensated by the government, rather than remain disproportionately concentrated on a few persons." The outcome instead "depends largely 'upon the particular circumstances [in that] case.'" *Penn Central*, supra, at 124. . . .

The Rhode Island Supreme Court concluded that, because the wetlands regulations predated petitioner's acquisition of the property at issue, petitioner lacked reasonable investment-backed expectations and hence lacked a viable takings claim. The court erred in elevating what it believed to be "[petitioner's] lack of reasonable investment-backed expectations" to "dispositive" status. Investment-backed expectations, though important, are not talismanic under *Penn Central*. Evaluation of the degree of interference with investment-backed expectations instead is one factor that points toward the answer to the question whether the application of a particular regulation to particular property "goes too far." Pennsylvania Coal Co. v. Mahon, 260 U.S. 393, 415 (1922).

Further, the state of regulatory affairs at the time of acquisition is not the only factor that may determine the extent of investment-backed expectations. For example, the nature and extent of permitted development under the regulatory regime vis-à-vis the development sought by the claimant may also shape legitimate expectations without vesting any kind of development right in the property owner. We also have never held that a takings claim is defeated simply on account of the lack of a personal financial investment by a postenactment acquirer of property, such as a donee, heir, or devisee. . . . Courts instead must attend to those circumstances which are probative of what fairness requires in a given case.

. . . As I understand it, our decision today does not remove the regulatory backdrop against which an owner takes title to property from the purview of the *Penn Central* inquiry. It simply restores balance to that inquiry. Courts properly consider the effect of existing regulations under the rubric of investment-backed expectations in determining whether a compensable taking has occurred. As before, the salience of these facts cannot be reduced to any "set formula." The temptation to adopt what amount to per se rules in either direction must be resisted. The Takings Clause requires careful examination and weighing of all the relevant circumstances in this context. The court below therefore must consider on remand the array of relevant factors under *Penn Central* before deciding whether any compensation is due.

[Justice Scalia concurred, but wrote "separately to make clear that my understanding of how the issue discussed in Part II-B of the Court's opinion must be considered on remand is not Justice O'Connor's." In his view, "the fact that a restriction existed at the time the purchaser took title (other than a restriction forming part of the 'background principles of the State's law of property and nuisance') should have no bearing upon the determination of whether the restriction is so substantial as to constitute a taking."

Justice Stevens concurred in part and dissented in part. "In cases . . . in which landowners have notice of a regulation when they purchase a piece of property but the regulatory event constituting the taking does not occur until after they take title to the property," he would treat the owners' notice as relevant but not necessarily dispositive as to whether the regulation goes "too far."

Justice Ginsburg, joined by Justices Souter and Breyer, dissented. She agreed with Justice O'Connor that "transfer of title can impair a takings claim." Justice Breyer added that he would agree with Justice O'Connor "that the simple fact that a piece of property has changed hands (for example, by inheritance) does not always and *automatically* bar a takings claim." In short, "postregulatory acquisition of the property (through automatic operation of the law) by itself should not prove dispositive."]

NOTES AND QUESTION

1. Palazzolo *on remand*. The decision in *Palazzolo* remanded the case to the Rhode Island Supreme Court, which in turn remanded to the trial court with directions to examine the takings claim according to the principles of *Penn Central*. See Palazzolo v. State of Rhode Island, 785 A.2d 561 (R.I. 2001). In July 2005, Justice Gale of the Rhode Island Superior Court held that the wetlands regulation involved in the case did not amount to a taking under a *Penn Central* analysis.

2. Palazzolo *and* Lucas. Prior to the decision in *Palazzolo,* most state courts addressing the issue held that limitations imposed by state environmental and land use legislation amounted to what *Lucas* called background principles that limited the rights of land owners who purchased their property after the limitations were enacted. In *Palazzolo*, the Court precluded this categorical approach—a point expanded upon by Justice O'Connor—but also acknowledged that some statutes might nevertheless qualify as background principles, and lower courts have since relied on this statement to soften the impact of *Lucas.* See John D. Echeverria, A Preliminary Assessment of *Palazzolo v. Rhode Island,* 31 ELR 11112 (News and Analysis, 2001). Moreover, they have developed a dozen or more other categorical defenses to *Lucas* claims, based on background principles. See, e.g., James L. Huffman, Background Principles and the Rule of Law: Fifteen Years After *Lucas,* 35 Ecology L.Q. 1 (2008); Michael C. Blumm & J.B. Ruhl, Background Principles, Takings, and Libertarian Property: A Reply to Professor Huffman, 37 Ecology L.Q. 805 (2010); Michael C. Blumm & Lucus Ritchie, *Lucas*'s Unlikely Legacy: The Rise of Background Principles as Categorical Takings Defenses, 29 Harv. Envtl. L. Rev. 321 (2005).

3. *The fourth dimension.* Suppose a local planning agency imposes a moratorium on development while studying the impact of growth on the area and preparing a comprehensive land use plan. During the period of the moratorium, undeveloped land loses its value entirely. Does this result in a per se taking under *Lucas?* An earlier decision by the United States Supreme Court suggested, but did not hold, that the answer is yes. See First English Evangelical Lutheran Church of Glendale v. County of Los Angeles, 482 U.S. 304 (1987). Justice Stevens dissented in that case, for reasons that will become clear. In the case that follows, he writes the majority opinion, affirming a court of appeals decision that, it appears, was heavily influenced by the reasoning of that dissent. As you will see, Stevens's

opinion raises once again the issue of conceptual severance that we have considered at several points already in this chapter. See, e.g., Note 4 on page 1162,
Note 1 on page 1176, and Note 1 on 1195. In those earlier instances, the issue
involved the standard three dimensions of space; now, it involves the fourth
dimension — time.

Tahoe-Sierra Preservation Council, Inc. v. Tahoe Regional Planning Agency

United States Supreme Court, 2002
535 U.S. 302

JUSTICE STEVENS delivered the opinion of the Court.

The question presented is whether a moratorium on development imposed
during the process of devising a comprehensive land-use plan constitutes a per
se taking of property requiring compensation under the Takings Clause of the
United States Constitution. This case actually involves two moratoria ordered
by respondent Tahoe Regional Planning Agency (TRPA) to maintain the status
quo while studying the impact of development on Lake Tahoe and designing a
strategy for environmentally sound growth. The first, Ordinance was effective
from August 24, 1981, until August 26, 1983, whereas the second more restrictive Resolution was in effect from August 27, 1983, until April 25, 1984. As a
result of these two directives, virtually all development on a substantial portion
of the property subject to TRPA's jurisdiction was prohibited for a period of 32
months. . . .

The relevant facts are undisputed. . . . All agree that Lake Tahoe is "uniquely
beautiful," that President Clinton was right to call it a "'national treasure that
must be protected and preserved,'" and that Mark Twain aptly described the clarity of its waters as "'not merely transparent, but dazzlingly, brilliantly so.'" Lake
Tahoe's exceptional clarity is attributed to the absence of algae that obscures the
waters of most other lakes. . . . Unfortunately, the lake's pristine state has deteriorated rapidly over the past 40 years. . . . The lake's unsurpassed beauty, it seems, is
the wellspring of its undoing. The upsurge of development in the area has caused
"increased nutrient loading of the lake largely because of the increase in impervious coverage of land in the Basin resulting from that development." "Impervious
coverage — such as asphalt, concrete, buildings, and even packed dirt — prevents
precipitation from being absorbed by the soil. . . . Those areas in the Basin that
have steeper slopes produce more runoff; therefore, they are usually considered
high hazard" lands. Moreover, certain areas near streams or wetlands known as
"Stream Environment Zones" (SEZs) are especially vulnerable to the impact of
development because, in their natural state, they act as filters for much of the
debris that runoff carries. Because "[t]he most obvious response to this problem
. . . is to restrict development around the lake — especially in SEZ lands, as well as
in areas already naturally prone to runoff," conservation efforts have focused on
controlling growth in these high hazard areas.

In the 1960's, when the problems associated with the burgeoning development began to receive significant attention, jurisdiction over the Basin, which occupies 501 square miles, was shared by the States of California and Nevada, five counties, several municipalities, and the Forest Service of the Federal Government. In 1968, the legislatures of the two States adopted the Tahoe Regional Planning Compact, which Congress approved in 1969. The compact set goals for the protection and preservation of the lake and created TRPA as the agency assigned "to coordinate and regulate development in the Basin and to conserve its natural resources."

Pursuant to the compact, in 1972 TRPA adopted a Land Use Ordinance. . . . Unfortunately, the 1972 ordinance allowed numerous exceptions and did not significantly limit the construction of new residential housing. California became so dissatisfied with TRPA that it withdrew its financial support and unilaterally imposed stricter regulations on the part of the Basin located in California. Eventually the two States, with the approval of Congress and the President, adopted an extensive amendment to the compact that became effective on December 19, 1980.

The 1980 Tahoe Regional Planning Compact . . . contained a finding by the Legislatures of California and Nevada "that in order to make effective the regional plan as revised by [TRPA], it is necessary to halt temporarily works of development in the region which might otherwise absorb the entire capability of the region for further development or direct it out of harmony with the ultimate plan." Accordingly, for the period prior to the adoption of the final plan ("or until May 1, 1983, whichever is earlier"), the Compact itself prohibited the development of new subdivisions, condominiums, and apartment buildings, and also prohibited each city and county in the Basin from granting any more permits in 1981, 1982, or 1983 than had been granted in 1978.

During this period TRPA was also working on the development of a regional water quality plan to comply with the Clean Water Act, 33 U.S.C. §1288. Despite the fact that TRPA performed these obligations in "good faith and to the best of its ability," after a few months it concluded that it could not meet the deadlines in the Compact. On June 25, 1981, it therefore enacted Ordinance 81-5 imposing the first of the two moratoria on development that petitioners challenge in this proceeding. The ordinance provided that it would become effective on August 24, 1981, and remain in effect pending the adoption of the permanent plan required by the Compact. . . . It is undisputed . . . that Ordinance 81-5 prohibited the construction of any new residences on SEZ lands in either State and on class 1, 2, and 3 lands in California.

[There were other delays thereafter.] TRPA therefore adopted Resolution 83-21, "which completely suspended all project reviews and approvals, including the acceptance of new proposals," and which remained in effect until a new regional plan was adopted on April 26, 1984. Thus, Resolution 83-21 imposed an 8-month moratorium prohibiting all construction on high hazard lands in either State. In combination, Ordinance 81-5 and Resolution 83-21 effectively prohibited all construction on sensitive lands in California and on all SEZ lands in the entire Basin for 32 months, and on sensitive lands in Nevada (other than SEZ lands) for eight months. It is these two moratoria that are at issue in this case.

On the same day that the 1984 plan was adopted, the State of California filed an action seeking to enjoin its implementation on the ground that it failed to establish land-use controls sufficiently stringent to protect the Basin. Id. at 1236. The District Court entered an injunction that was upheld by the Court of Appeals and remained in effect until a completely revised plan was adopted in 1987. Both the 1984 injunction and the 1987 plan contained provisions that prohibited new construction on sensitive lands in the Basin. As the case comes to us, however, we have no occasion to consider the validity of those provisions.

Approximately two months after the adoption of the 1984 Plan, petitioners filed parallel actions against TRPA and other defendants in federal courts in Nevada and California that were ultimately consolidated for trial in the District of Nevada. The petitioners include the Tahoe Sierra Preservation Council, a nonprofit membership corporation representing about 2,000 owners of both improved and unimproved parcels of real estate in the Lake Tahoe Basin, and a class of some 400 individual owners of vacant lots located either on SEZ lands or in other parts of districts 1, 2, or 3. Those individuals purchased their properties prior to the effective date of the 1980 Compact, primarily for the purpose of constructing "at a time of their choosing" a single-family home "to serve as a permanent, retirement or vacation residence." When they made those purchases, they did so with the understanding that such construction was authorized provided that "they complied with all reasonable requirements for building."

Petitioners' complaints gave rise to protracted litigation that has produced four opinions by the Court of Appeals for the Ninth Circuit and several published District Court opinions. . . . [W]e limit our discussion to the lower courts' disposition of the claims based on the 2-year moratorium (Ordinance 81-5) and the ensuing 8-month moratorium (Resolution 83-21).

The District Court . . . noted that all of the claims in this case "are of the 'regulatory takings' variety." Citing our decision in Agins v. City of Tiburon, 447 U.S. 255 (1980), it then stated that a "regulation will constitute a taking when either: (1) it does not substantially advance a legitimate state interest;[37] or (2) it denies the owner economically viable use of her land." The District Court rejected the first alternative based on its finding that "further development on high hazard lands such as [petitioners'] would lead to significant additional damage to the lake." With respect to the second alternative, the court first considered whether the analysis adopted in Penn Central Transp. Co. v. New York City, 438 U.S. 104 (1978), would lead to the conclusion that TRPA had effected a "partial taking," and then whether those actions had effected a "total taking."

---

37. The Court recanted this statement from *Agins* three years after its decision in the Tahoe case. See Lingle v. Chevron U.S.A., Inc., 544 U.S. 528, 540, 545-547 (2005), declaring that the "substantially advances" formula prescribes a due process inquiry, not a takings test, and thus has no place in the Court's takings jurisprudence, a conclusion that did not require the Court "to disturb any of our prior holdings." The Court made an exception for its rules on exactions, a subject we take up beginning on page 1238. On the significance of *Lingle*, see, e.g., D. Benjamin Barros, At Last, Some Clarity: The Potential Long-Term Impact of *Lingle v. Chevron* and the Separation of Takings and Substantive Due Process, 69 Alb. L. Rev. 343 (2005).—EDS.

Emphasizing the temporary nature of the regulations, the testimony that the "average holding time of a lot in the Tahoe area between lot purchase and home construction is twenty-five years," and the failure of petitioners to offer specific evidence of harm, the District Court concluded that "consideration of the Penn Central factors clearly leads to the conclusion that there was no taking." In the absence of evidence regarding any of the individual plaintiffs, the court evaluated the "average" purchasers' intent and found that such purchasers "did not have reasonable, investment-backed expectations that they would be able to build single-family homes on their land within the six-year period involved in this lawsuit."[38]

The District Court had more difficulty with the "total taking" issue. Although it was satisfied that petitioners' property did retain some value during the moratoria, it found that they had been temporarily deprived of "all economically viable use of their land." The court concluded that those actions therefore constituted "categorical" takings under our decision in Lucas v. South Carolina Coastal Council, 505 U.S. 1003 (1992). It rejected TRPA's response that Ordinance 81-5 and Resolution 83-21 were "reasonable temporary planning moratoria" that should be excluded from *Lucas*' categorical approach. The court thought it "fairly clear" that such interim actions would not have been viewed as takings prior to our decisions in *Lucas* and First English Evangelical Lutheran Church of Glendale v. County of Los Angeles, 482 U.S. 304 (1987), because "[z]oning boards, cities, counties and other agencies used them all the time to maintain the status quo pending study and governmental decision making." After expressing uncertainty as to whether those cases required a holding that moratoria on development automatically effect takings, the court concluded that TRPA's actions did so, partly because neither the ordinance nor the resolution, even though intended to be temporary from the beginning, contained an express termination date. Accordingly, it ordered TRPA to pay damages to most petitioners for the 32-month period from August 24, 1981, to April 25, 1984, and to those owning class 1, 2, or 3 property in Nevada for the 8-month period from August 27, 1983, to April 25, 1984.

Both parties appealed. TRPA successfully challenged the District Court's takings determination, and petitioners unsuccessfully challenged the dismissal of their claims based on the 1984 and 1987 plans. Petitioners did not, however, challenge the District Court's findings or conclusions concerning its application of *Penn Central.* With respect to the two moratoria, the Ninth Circuit noted that petitioners had expressly disavowed an argument "that the regulations constitute a taking under the ad hoc balancing approach described in *Penn Central*" and that they did not "dispute that the restrictions imposed on their properties are appropriate

---

38. The court stated that petitioners "had plenty of time to build before the restrictions went into effect—and almost everyone in the Tahoe Basin knew in the late 1970s that a crackdown on development was in the works." In addition, the court found "the fact that no evidence was introduced regarding the specific diminution in value of any of the plaintiffs' individual properties clearly weighs against a finding that there was a partial taking of the plaintiffs' property."

means of securing the purpose set forth in the Compact." Accordingly, the only question before the court was "whether the rule set forth in *Lucas* applies—that is, whether a categorical taking occurred because Ordinance 81-5 and Resolution 83-21 denied the plaintiffs' 'all economically beneficial or productive use of land.'" Moreover, because petitioners brought only a facial challenge, the narrow inquiry before the Court of Appeals was whether the mere enactment of the regulations constituted a taking.

Contrary to the District Court, the Court of Appeals held that because the regulations had only a temporary impact on petitioners' fee interest in the properties, no categorical taking had occurred. It reasoned:

> Property interests may have many different dimensions. For example, the dimensions of a property interest may include a physical dimension (which describes the size and shape of the property in question), a functional dimension (which describes the extent to which an owner may use or dispose of the property in question), and a temporal dimension (which describes the duration of the property interest). At base, the plaintiffs' argument is that we should conceptually sever each plaintiff's fee interest into discrete segments in at least one of these dimensions—the temporal one—and treat each of those segments as separate and distinct property interests for purposes of takings analysis. Under this theory, they argue that there was a categorical taking of one of those temporal segments.

Putting to one side "cases of physical invasion or occupation," the court read our cases involving regulatory taking claims to focus on the impact of a regulation on the parcel as a whole. In its view a "planning regulation that prevents the development of a parcel for a temporary period of time is conceptually no different than a land-use restriction that permanently denies all use on a discrete portion of property, or that permanently restricts a type of use across all of the parcel." In each situation, a regulation that affects only a portion of the parcel—whether limited by time, use, or space—does not deprive the owner of all economically beneficial use.

The Court of Appeals distinguished *Lucas* as applying to the "relatively rare" case in which a regulation denies all productive use of an entire parcel, whereas the moratoria involve only a "temporal slice" of the fee interest and a form of regulation that is widespread and well established. It also rejected petitioners' argument that our decision in *First English* was controlling. According to the Court of Appeals, *First English* concerned the question whether compensation is an appropriate remedy for a temporary taking and not whether or when such a taking has occurred. Faced squarely with the question whether a taking had occurred, the court held that *Penn Central* was the appropriate framework for analysis. Petitioners, however, had failed to challenge the District Court's conclusion that they could not make out a taking claim under the *Penn Central* factors.

. . . Because of the importance of the case, we granted certiorari limited to the question stated at the beginning of this opinion. We now affirm.

. . . Petitioners assert that our opinions in *First English* and *Lucas* have already endorsed their view, and that it is a logical application of the principle that the Takings Clause was "designed to bar Government from forcing some people alone to bear burdens which, in all fairness and justice, should be borne by the public as a whole." Armstrong v. United States, 364 U.S. 40, 49 (1960).

We shall first explain why our cases do not support their proposed categorical rule—indeed, fairly read, they implicitly reject it. Next, we shall explain why the *Armstrong* principle requires rejection of that rule as well as the less extreme position advanced by petitioners at oral argument. In our view the answer to the abstract question whether a temporary moratorium effects a taking is neither "yes, always" nor "no, never"; the answer depends upon the particular circumstances of the case. . . .

The text of the Fifth Amendment itself provides a basis for drawing a distinction between physical takings and regulatory takings. Its plain language requires the payment of compensation whenever the government acquires private property for a public purpose, whether the acquisition is the result of a condemnation proceeding or a physical appropriation. But the Constitution contains no comparable reference to regulations that prohibit a property owner from making certain uses of her private property. Our jurisprudence involving condemnations and physical takings is as old as the Republic and, for the most part, involves the straightforward application of per se rules. Our regulatory takings jurisprudence, in contrast, is of more recent vintage and is characterized by "essentially ad hoc, factual inquiries," *Penn Central*, 438 U.S. at 124. . . .

This longstanding distinction between acquisitions of property for public use, on the one hand, and regulations prohibiting private uses, on the other, makes it inappropriate to treat cases involving physical takings as controlling precedents for the evaluation of a claim that there has been a "regulatory taking," and vice versa. . . . Land-use regulations are ubiquitous and most of them impact property values in some tangential way—often in completely unanticipated ways. Treating them all as per se takings would transform government regulation into a luxury few governments could afford. By contrast, physical appropriations are relatively rare, easily identified, and usually represent a greater affront to individual property rights. . . .

Perhaps recognizing this fundamental distinction, petitioners wisely do not place all their emphasis on analogies to physical takings cases. Instead, they rely principally on our decision in Lucas v. South Carolina Coastal Council, 505 U.S. 1003 (1992)—a regulatory takings case that, nevertheless, applied a categorical rule. . . .

[O]ur decision in *Lucas* is not dispositive of the question presented. . . . The categorical rule that we applied in *Lucas* states that compensation is required when a regulation deprives an owner of "all economically beneficial uses" of his land. Under that rule, a statute that "wholly eliminated the value" of Lucas' fee simple title clearly qualified as a taking. But our holding was limited to "the extraordinary circumstance when no productive or economically beneficial use of land is permitted." The emphasis on the word "no" in the text of the opinion was, in effect, reiterated in a footnote explaining that the categorical rule would not apply if the diminution in value were 95% instead of 100%. Anything less than a "complete elimination of value," or a "total loss," the Court acknowledged, would require the kind of analysis applied in *Penn Central*.

Certainly, our holding that the permanent "obliteration of the value" of a fee simple estate constitutes a categorical taking does not answer the question whether a regulation prohibiting any economic use of land for a 32-month period has the same legal effect. Petitioners seek to bring this case under the rule announced in *Lucas* by arguing that we can effectively sever a 32-month segment from the remainder of each landowner's fee simple estate, and then ask whether that segment has been taken in its entirety by the moratoria. Of course, defining the property interest taken in terms of the very regulation being challenged is circular. With property so divided, every delay would become a total ban; the moratorium and the normal permit process alike would constitute categorical takings. Petitioners' "conceptual severance" argument is unavailing because it ignores *Penn Central*'s admonition that in regulatory takings cases we must focus on "the parcel as a whole." . . . Thus, the District Court erred when it disaggregated petitioners' property into temporal segments corresponding to the regulations at issue and then analyzed whether petitioners were deprived of all economically viable use during each period. . . .

An interest in real property is defined by the metes and bounds that describe its geographic dimensions and the term of years that describes the temporal aspect of the owner's interest. See Restatement of Property §§7-9 (1936). Both dimensions must be considered if the interest is to be viewed in its entirety. Hence, a permanent deprivation of the owner's use of the entire area is a taking of "the parcel as a whole," whereas a temporary restriction that merely causes a diminution in value is not. Logically, a fee simple estate cannot be rendered valueless by a temporary prohibition on economic use, because the property will recover value as soon as the prohibition is lifted. . . .

Considerations of "fairness and justice" [as mentioned in *Armstrong*, supra] arguably could support the conclusion that TRPA's moratoria were takings of petitioners' property based on any of seven different theories. First, even though we have not previously done so, we might now announce a categorical rule that, in the interest of fairness and justice, compensation is required whenever government temporarily deprives an owner of all economically viable use of her property. Second, we could craft a narrower rule that would cover all temporary land-use restrictions except those "normal delays in obtaining building permits, changes in zoning ordinances, variances, and the like" which were put to one side in our opinion in *First English*. Third, we could adopt a rule like the one suggested by an amicus supporting petitioners that would "allow a short fixed period for deliberations to take place without compensation—say maximum one year—after which the just compensation requirements" would "kick in." Fourth, with the benefit of hindsight, we might characterize the successive actions of TRPA as a "series of rolling moratoria" that were the functional equivalent of a permanent taking. Fifth, were it not for the findings of the District Court that TRPA acted diligently and in good faith, we might have concluded that the agency was stalling in order to avoid promulgating the environmental threshold carrying capacities and regional plan mandated by the 1980 Compact. Sixth, apart from the District Court's finding that TRPA's actions represented a proportional response to a serious risk of harm to the lake, petitioners might have argued that the moratoria did not substantially advance a legitimate state interest. Finally, if petitioners had challenged the application of the moratoria to their individual parcels, instead of making a facial challenge, some of them might have prevailed under a *Penn Central* analysis.

As the case comes to us, however, none of the last four theories is available. The "rolling moratoria" theory was presented in the petition for certiorari, but our order granting review did not encompass that issue. . . . And, as we have already noted, recovery on either a bad faith theory or a theory that the state interests were insubstantial is foreclosed by the District Court's unchallenged findings of fact. Recovery under a *Penn Central* analysis is also foreclosed both because petitioners expressly disavowed that theory, and because they did not appeal from the District Court's conclusion that the evidence would not support it. Nonetheless, each of the three per se theories is fairly encompassed within the question that we decided to answer.

With respect to these theories, the ultimate constitutional question is whether the concepts of "fairness and justice" that underlie the Takings Clause will be better served by one of these categorical rules or by a *Penn Central* inquiry into all of the relevant circumstances in particular cases. From that perspective, the extreme categorical rule that any deprivation of all economic use, no matter how brief, constitutes a compensable taking surely cannot be sustained. Petitioners' broad submission would apply to numerous "normal delays in obtaining building permits, changes in zoning ordinances, variances, and the like," as well as to orders temporarily prohibiting access to crime scenes, businesses that violate health codes, fire-damaged buildings, or other areas that we cannot now foresee. Such a rule would undoubtedly require changes in numerous practices that have long been considered permissible exercises of the police power.

More importantly, for reasons set out at some length by Justice O'Connor in her concurring opinion in Palazzolo v. Rhode Island, 533 U.S. at 636 (2001), we are persuaded that the better approach to claims that a regulation has effected a temporary taking "requires careful examination and weighing of all the relevant circumstances." . . . In rejecting petitioners' per se rule, we do not hold that the temporary nature of a land-use restriction precludes finding that it effects a taking; we simply recognize that it should not be given exclusive significance one way or the other. . . .

Accordingly, the judgment of the Court of Appeals is affirmed.

CHIEF JUSTICE REHNQUIST, with whom JUSTICES SCALIA and THOMAS join, dissenting.

For over half a decade petitioners were prohibited from building homes, or any other structures, on their land. Because the Takings Clause requires the government to pay compensation when it deprives owners of all economically viable use of their land, see Lucas v. South Carolina Coastal Council, 505 U.S. 1003 (1992), and because a ban on all development lasting almost six years does not resemble any traditional land-use planning device, I dissent.

. . . Respondent is surely responsible for its own regulations, and it is also responsible for the Compact as it is the governmental agency charged with administering the Compact. It follows that respondent was the "moving force" behind petitioners' inability to develop its land from April 1984 through the enactment of the 1987 plan. Without the environmental thresholds established by the Compact and Resolution 82-11, the 1984 Plan would have gone into effect and petitioners would have been able to build single-family residences. And it was certainly foreseeable that development projects exceeding the environmental thresholds would be prohibited; indeed, that was the very purpose of enacting the thresholds.

Because respondent caused petitioners' inability to use their land from 1981 through 1987, that is the appropriate period of time from which to consider their takings claim.

I now turn to determining whether a ban on all economic development lasting almost six years is a taking. *Lucas* reaffirmed our "frequently expressed" view that "when the owner of real property has been called upon to sacrifice all economically beneficial uses in the name of the common good, that is, to leave his property economically idle, he has suffered a taking." 505 U.S., at 1019. . . . The District Court in this case held that the ordinances and resolutions in effect between August 24, 1981, and April 25, 1984, "did in fact deny the plaintiffs all economically viable use of their land." 34 F. Supp. 2d 1226, 1245 (D. Nev. 1999). The Court of Appeals did not overturn this finding. And the 1984 injunction, issued because the environmental thresholds issued by respondent did not permit the development of single-family residences, forced petitioners to leave their land economically idle for at least another three years. The Court does not dispute that petitioners were forced to leave their land economically idle during this period. But the Court refuses to apply *Lucas* on the ground that the deprivation was "temporary."

Neither the Takings Clause nor our case law supports such a distinction. For one thing, a distinction between "temporary" and "permanent" prohibitions is tenuous. The "temporary" prohibition in this case that the Court finds is not a taking lasted almost six years. The "permanent" prohibition that the Court held to be a taking in *Lucas* lasted less than two years. See 505 U.S. at 1011-1012. The "permanent" prohibition in *Lucas* lasted less than two years because the law, as it often does, changed. The South Carolina Legislature in 1990 decided to amend the 1988 Beachfront Management Act to allow the issuance of "special permits for the construction or reconstruction of habitable structures seaward of the baseline." Id. at 1011-1012. Land-use regulations are not irrevocable. And the government can even abandon condemned land. See United States v. Dow, 357 U.S. 17, 26 (1958). Under the Court's decision today, the takings question turns entirely on the initial label given a regulation, a label that is often without much meaning. There is every incentive for government to simply label any prohibition on development "temporary," or to fix a set number of years. As in this case, this initial designation does not preclude the government from repeatedly extending the "temporary" prohibition into a long-term ban on all development. The Court now holds that such a designation by the government is conclusive even though in fact the moratorium greatly exceeds the time initially specified. . . .

Our opinion in First English Evangelical Lutheran Church of Glendale v. County of Los Angeles, 482 U.S. 304 (1987), rejects any distinction between temporary and permanent takings when a landowner is deprived of all economically beneficial use of his land. *First English* stated that "temporary takings which, as here, deny a landowner all use of his property, are not different in kind from permanent takings, for which the Constitution clearly requires compensation." Id. at 318. . . .

More fundamentally, even if a practical distinction between temporary and permanent deprivations were plausible, to treat the two differently in terms of takings law would be at odds with the justification for the *Lucas* rule. The *Lucas* rule is derived from the fact that a "total deprivation of use is, from the landowner's point of view, the equivalent of a physical appropriation." 505 U.S., at 1017. The regulation in *Lucas* was the "practical equivalence" of a long-term physical appropriation, i.e., a condemnation, so the Fifth Amendment required compensation. The "practical equivalence," from the landowner's point of view, of a "temporary" ban on all economic use is a forced leasehold. . . .

. . . From petitioners' standpoint, what happened in this case is no different than if the government had taken a 6-year lease of their property. The Court ignores this "practical equivalence" between respondent's deprivation and the deprivation resulting from a leasehold. . . .

. . . In addition to the "practical equivalence" from the landowner's perspective of such a regulation and a physical appropriation, we have held that a regulation denying all productive use of land does not implicate the traditional justification for differentiating between regulations and physical appropriations. . . .

The Court also reads *Lucas* as being fundamentally concerned with value, rather than with the denial of "all economically beneficial or productive use of land," 505 U.S., at 1015. But *Lucas* repeatedly discusses its holding as applying where "no productive or economically beneficial use of land is permitted." Id. at 1017. . . . Moreover, the Court's position that value is the sine qua non of the *Lucas* rule proves too much. Surely, the land at issue in *Lucas* retained some market value based on the contingency, which soon came to fruition, that the development ban would be amended.

. . . Because the rationale for the *Lucas* rule applies just as strongly in this case, the "temporary" denial of all viable use of land for six years is a taking.

The Court worries that applying *Lucas* here compels finding that an array of traditional, short-term, land-use planning devices are takings. But since the beginning of our regulatory takings jurisprudence, we have recognized that property rights "are enjoyed under an implied limitation." *Mahon*, supra, at 413. Thus, in *Lucas*, after holding that the regulation prohibiting all economically beneficial use of the coastal land came within our categorical takings rule, we nonetheless inquired into whether such a result "inhere[d] in the title itself, in the restrictions that background principles of the State's law of property and nuisance already place upon land ownership." 505 U.S., at 1029. . . .

When a regulation merely delays a final land use decision, we have recognized that there are other background principles of state property law that prevent the delay from being deemed a taking. We thus noted in *First English* that our discussion of temporary takings did not apply "in the case of normal delays in obtaining building permits, changes in zoning ordinances, variances, and the like." 482 U.S. at 321. . . . Zoning regulations existed as far back as colonial Boston, see Treanor, The Original Understanding of the Takings Clause and the Political Process, 95 Colum. L. Rev. 782, 789 (1995), and New York City enacted the first comprehensive zoning ordinance in 1916. Thus, the short-term delays attendant to zoning and permit regimes are a longstanding feature of state property law and part of a landowner's reasonable investment-backed expectations.

But a moratorium prohibiting all economic use for a period of six years is not one of the longstanding, implied limitations of state property law. . . . Typical moratoria thus prohibit only certain categories of development, such as fast-food restaurants, see Schafer v. New Orleans, 743 F.2d 1086 (C.A.5 1984), or adult businesses, see Renton v. Playtime Theatres, Inc., 475 U.S. 41 (1986), or all commercial development, see Arnold Bernhard & Co. v. Planning & Zoning Comm'n, 479 A.2d 801 (Conn. 1984). Such moratoria do not implicate *Lucas* because they do not deprive landowners of all economically beneficial use of their land. As for moratoria that prohibit all development, these do not have the lineage of permit and zoning requirements and thus it is less certain that property is acquired under the "implied limitation" of a moratorium prohibiting all development. . . .

But this case does not require us to decide as a categorical matter whether moratoria prohibiting all economic use are an implied limitation of state property law, because the duration of this "moratorium" far exceeds that of ordinary moratoria. . . .

Lake Tahoe is a national treasure and I do not doubt that respondent's efforts at preventing further degradation of the lake were made in good faith in furtherance of the public interest. But, as is the case with most governmental action that furthers the public interest, the Constitution requires that the costs and burdens be borne by the public at large, not by a few targeted citizens. . . .

NOTES AND QUESTIONS

1. On the *Tahoe* case, see Laura S. Underkuffler, *Tahoe*'s Requiem: The Death of the Scalian View of Property and Justice, 21 Const. Com. 727 (2006); Steven J. Eagle, Planning Moratoria and Regulatory Takings: The Supreme Court's Fairness Mandate Benefits Landowners, 31 Fla. St. U. L. Rev. 429 (2004).

2. *Temporal conceptual severance. Tahoe* holds that for purposes of a takings analysis, severing a property interest in terms of time is no more appropriate than severing it in terms of space. So if there isn't necessarily (in fact, almost surely isn't) a taking when government regulation wipes out, perhaps permanently, half of the value of a piece of property (or all the value of half of the piece of property), then, the logic of the opinion goes, why should the situation be any

different when government regulation wipes out all the value of the property for half of . . . of what?

3. *Actual severance?* Suppose a tenant obtains a five-year lease to a commercial property, and pays the entire rent to the landlord up front. One day after the tenant takes possession, the government announces that it will need to occupy the premises for the next five years, stating a valid public use. Under *Tahoe*, is this a per se taking of the tenant's entire leasehold interest, such that *Lucas* applies, or a possible taking depending on the outcome of the *Penn Central* balancing test? See Nicholas Spear, Comment, Taking Leases, 80 U. Chi. L. Rev. 2005 (2013).

4. *The triumph of* Penn Central *?* By rejecting temporal conceptual severance, *Tahoe* clarified that the *Lucas* rule was inapplicable to a broad swath of regulatory activities. (Permanent wipeouts of all a parcel's economic value rarely result from government regulation, but temporary wipeouts occur frequently.) Does *Tahoe* signal more broadly that the majority of the Court is interested in having the law of takings be governed by multi-factor, context-sensitive standards, like the *Penn Central* test, rather than bright-line rules of the sort embraced in *Lucas* and *Loretto*? In Arkansas Game & Fish Commn. v. United States, 133 S. Ct. 511 (2012), a unanimous Supreme Court reversed a lower court ruling, which held that as a per se matter the government could not be liable under the Takings Clause for causing the temporary flooding of private property. The Court instructed lower courts to apply the standard *Penn Central* inquiry instead of a flooding-specific bright-line rule that had been suggested in a Supreme Court precedent from the 1920s. 133 S. Ct. at 519-522.

NOTES: MATTERS OF REMEDY

1. *Logic and conventional wisdom.* What should be the remedy for physical occupations and regulatory takings? Logic would suggest a straightforward answer: The remedy should be compensation. After all, if the government takes property—condemns it—under the power of eminent domain, the obligation to pay just compensation follows. Should it not follow as well where the government takes property by other means? The suit for compensation would usually proceed by way of a so-called inverse condemnation action. As its name suggests, inverse condemnation is simply the opposite of a government eminent domain proceeding: The claimant rather than the government institutes the suit, alleging that a taking has occurred and seeking recompense for it. A forced purchase, rather than a forced sale, is the claimant's objective.

Though one would logically expect compensation through inverse condemnation to be commonplace, for many years it was not. To be sure, the remedy was routinely granted as to takings by physical occupation (including in that category loss of access, destruction of property, or an actual transfer of title, possession, or control to the government), but it was typically denied as to regulatory takings. Instead, the courts awarded declaratory or injunctive relief invalidating the regulation or its application. If the government wished to proceed thereafter, it either had to bring an eminent domain proceeding or amend the regulation to avoid the taking problem. If the government chose the latter alternative, losses sustained by the claimant during the period the regulation was in effect went uncompensated.

Thus was the conventional wisdom, but it was changed by First English Evangelical Lutheran Church of Glendale v. County of Los Angeles, 482 U.S. 304 (1987), cited and discussed by the Court in *Tahoe* (see in particular pages 1211-1213). *First English* held that *if* a government regulation results in a taking, then the government must pay just compensation from the time the regulation first worked the taking until the time the government rescinds the regulation or changes it in such a way that no taking occurs. Hence an undue delay—normal delays brought on by the development permitting process and the like are put to the side—results in liability for a temporary taking. *Tahoe* leaves this rule untouched.

2. *The pros and cons of the compensation remedy.* Most states (not all)[39] took the view that to charge the government with the duty to compensate for regulatory takings would inhibit community planning and chill exercises of the police power. Regulators would become too cautious. Judicial imposition of a compensation requirement, moreover, would usurp the legislature's power to make decisions about public expenditures. Scholarly commentary added to the list of concerns, the following being the chief points: if compensation is required, there arises the problem of determining just what interest the government has "purchased"; when the overly harsh regulation is later repealed, the claimant in the inverse condemnation suit will have received an undeserved windfall (an observation that obviously assumes compensation awards are based on permanent losses); cases involving physical invasion or property destruction are off the point because they, unlike regulatory takings, are more likely to involve irreparable losses.

The majority opinion in *First English* stressed the other side of the story. Regulatory action can destroy use and enjoyment of property just as effectively as physical occupation or destruction, and in the latter cases compensation has always been required. Logic, then, requires that overzealous regulation also be compensable, especially because invalidation of itself fails to compensate for losses that were wrongfully imposed. The government should have the duty to pay compensation for losses accruing from the time a regulation effected a taking until the time the regulation is rescinded or amended. (Alternatively, the government could condemn the property or, presumably, leave the regulation in place and be liable for an award based on the permanent, not temporary, loss of value.) Policy considerations could not work to limit the express guarantees of the Fifth Amendment. In any event, the concerns were unpersuasive. The threat

---

39. At least eight states had already held, prior to *First English*, that their own constitutions required compensation for regulatory takings, and seven of these required compensation for temporary takings. See Gene R. Rankin, The First Bite at the Apple: State Supreme Court Takings Jurisprudence Antedating *First English*, 22 Urb. Law. 417, 429 (1990).

of governmental financial liability for unconstitutional exercises of the police power would help produce more rational land use controls, ones that more carefully weighed costs against benefits. It would also encourage state and local officials to err on the constitutional side of police power regulation.

Do other arguments, pro or con, occur to you? Where do you come out in the debate?[40]

3. *Procedural matters.* Consider a few statements from *First English* and some problems to which they give rise:

(a) "[T]he Just Compensation Clause of the Fifth Amendment requires that the government pay the landowner for the value of the use of the land during this period" of a regulatory taking. But what precisely is the measure of damages?

There are various possibilities, such as fair rental value, option price, interest on lost profits, before-and-after valuation, and benefit to the government. In Wheeler v. City of Pleasant Grove, 896 F.2d 1347 (11th Cir. 1990), the court calculated damages based on "the market rate [of] return computed over the period of the temporary taking on the difference between the property's fair market value without the regulatory restriction and its fair market value with the restriction."

(b) "Though, as a matter of law, an illegitimate taking might not occur until the government refuses to pay, the interference that effects a taking might begin much earlier, and compensation is measured from that time." Does the cause of action for a regulatory taking accrue on the date the offending regulation is enacted, or when the government refuses to pay, or on some other date? In any event, may a suit for compensation be barred by a statute of limitations running from that date? See Scott v. City of Sioux City, 432 N.W.2d 144 (Iowa 1988); Millison v. Wilzack, 551 A.2d 899 (Md. App. 1989). See generally Gregory M. Stein, Pinpointing the Beginning and Ending of a Temporary Regulatory Taking, 70 Wash. L. Rev. 953 (1995).

(c) "[In] *Williamson County Regional Planning Commn.* . . . we noted that 'no constitutional violation occurs until just compensation has been denied.'" What this means, among other things, is that inverse condemnation suits seeking compensation for regulatory takings are generally to be pursued in the first instance in state courts. Constitutional challenges in the federal courts are usually not ripe

40. It is possible, of course, that takings liability has effects on government decision making that vary with the level of government involved. On one view, takings liability doesn't deter governments at all, because taxpayers, not government officials, are the ones paying the awards. See Daryl J. Levinson, Making Government Pay: Markets, Politics, and the Allocation of Constitutional Costs, 67 U. Chi. L. Rev. 345 (2000). Professor Serkin argues that this might be true of large units of government (big cities, states, the federal government) but not of small local governments dependent on property taxes for most of their revenues. Small governments tend to be unduly risk averse because a big judgment could wipe out their assets. Perhaps, then, their takings liability should be reduced to account for this. See Christopher Serkin, Big Differences for Small Governments: Local Governments and the Takings Clause, 81 N.Y.U. L. Rev. 1624 (2006); see also Christopher Serkin, Local Property Law: Adjusting the Scale of Property Protection, 107 Colum. L. Rev. 883 (2007) (proposing variations in the limits placed on local government regulation of land use).

until a state denies compensation, because states are free to take property for legitimate governmental purposes, provided only that they pay.[41]

Here is a related matter: suppose a *federal* regulation, otherwise legitimate, so burdens some claimant as to work a taking. Is the regulation to be invalidated as unconstitutional? The answer is no, if compensation is available under the Tucker Act, 28 U.S.C. §1491. See, e.g., Preseault v. ICC, 494 U.S. 1 (1990).

4. *The Tucker Act and the Court of Federal Claims.* The Tucker Act provides jurisdiction in the U.S. Court of Federal Claims for damage claims against the federal government founded on the Constitution, a regulation, or an express or implied contract. If a regulation works a taking, then the claim for compensation is founded on the Constitution and within the court's jurisdiction (unless Congress has provided otherwise).

The Court of Federal Claims came about as part of a reorganization and renaming of the former Court of Claims, established in 1855 to provide a forum for monetary claims against the federal government. Appeals from the court's decisions go to the Federal Circuit, also established as part of the reorganization. Cases like *Preseault,* supra, effectively move a large number of takings cases against the federal government into the Court of Federal Claims.

5. *Intellectual property.* What if the federal government infringes someone's intellectual property? These claims are also adjudicated in the Court of Federal Claims, as per 28 U.S.C. §1498. See Zoltek Corp. v. United States, 672 F.3d 1309 (Fed. Cir. 2012) (en banc).

---

41. Two points. First, the rule in *Williamson* can end up keeping a takings claimant with a federal claim from getting access to a federal court. See San Remo Hotel, L.P. v. City & County of San Francisco, California, 545 U.S. 323 (2005) (requirement that aggrieved property owners first seek compensation in state courts does not foreclose state courts from simultaneously hearing arguments for compensation under state constitutions and United States Constitution, and federal claims actually decided by state courts preclude claimants from retrying claims in federal court); Stewart E. Sterk, The Demise of Federal Takings Litigation, 48 Wm. & Mary L. Rev. 251 (2006); David A. Dana & Thomas W. Merrill, Property: Takings 258-265 (2002). Second, notice our statement in the text: "states are free to take property for legitimate governmental purposes, provided only that they pay." Suppose the governmental purpose is illegitimate—the alleged taking would not be for a public use, say, or the legislative objective is unconstitutional. Invalidation of the measure in question can follow as a matter of course, but is relief in damages available? See Wheeler v. City of Pleasant Grove, 833 F.2d 267, 270 n.3 (11th Cir. 1987), discussing 42 U.S.C.A. §1983, which provides for civil rights suits seeking damages for deprivation of constitutional rights under color of state law:

> Technically, the fifth amendment's just compensation clause is not applicable where there has been no "public use." Such may be the case where . . . the land use regulation that effected the taking was not enacted in furtherance of the public health, safety, morals, or general welfare. The affected landowner may nevertheless have a damage cause of action under section 1983 since the taking may violate his fourteenth amendment rights to due process.

See also Matthew C. Zinn, Ultra Vires Takings, 97 Mich. L. Rev. 245 (1998). On §1983 as an alternative to inverse condemnation actions, see Kenneth B. Bley, Use of the Civil Rights Acts to Recover Damages in Land Use Cases, SF64 ALI-ABA 435 (2001). It bears mention that §1983 suits for damages might well carry a right to jury trial, something not necessarily available under state law. See City of Monterey v. Del Monte Dunes, 526 U.S. 687 (1999).

4.   Judicial Takings

We have considered how legislatures and administrative agencies at various levels of government might violate the Takings Clause. Notice that the Takings Clause is written in the passive voice ("nor shall private property be taken . . ."). Can a court "take" property? Consider the following case.

Stop the Beach Renourishment, Inc. v. Florida Department of Environmental Protection

United States Supreme Court, 2010
560 U.S. 702

JUSTICE SCALIA announced the judgment of the Court and delivered the opinion of the Court with respect to Parts I, IV, and V, and an opinion with respect to Parts II and III, in which THE CHIEF JUSTICE, JUSTICE THOMAS, and JUSTICE ALITO join.

We consider a claim that the decision of a State's court of last resort took property without just compensation in violation of the Takings Clause of the Fifth Amendment, as applied against the States through the Fourteenth. . . .

I.

Generally speaking, state law defines property interests, Phillips v. Washington Legal Foundation, 524 U.S. 156, 164 (1998), including property rights in navigable waters and the lands underneath them, see United States v. Cress, 243 U.S. 316, 319-320 (1917). . . . In Florida, the State owns in trust for the public the land permanently submerged beneath navigable waters and the foreshore (the land between the low-tide line and the mean high-water line). Fla. Const., Art. X, §11; Broward v. Mabry, 50 So. 826, 829-830 (Fla. 1909). Thus, the mean high-water line (the average reach of high tide over the preceding 19 years) is the ordinary boundary between private beachfront, or littoral property, and state-owned land. See Miller v. Bay-To-Gulf, Inc., 193 So. 425, 427-428 (Fla. 1940) (per curiam); Fla. Stat. §§177.27(14)-(15), 177.28(1) (2007).

Littoral owners have, in addition to the rights of the public, certain "special rights" with regard to the water and the foreshore, *Broward*, 50 So. at 830, rights which Florida considers to be property, generally akin to easements. . . . These include the right of access to the water, the right to use the water for certain purposes, the right to an unobstructed view of the water, and the right to receive accretions and relictions to the littoral property. . . . This is generally in accord with well-established common law, although the precise property rights vary among jurisdictions. . . .

At the center of this case is the right to accretions and relictions. Accretions are additions of alluvion (sand, sediment, or other deposits) to waterfront land; relictions are lands once covered by water that become dry when the water recedes. . . . In order for an addition to dry land to qualify as an accretion, it must have occurred gradually and imperceptibly—that is, so slowly that one could not see the change occurring, though over time the difference became apparent. . . . When, on the other hand, there is a "sudden or perceptible loss of or addition to land by the action of the water or a sudden change in the bed of a lake or the course of a stream," the change is called an avulsion.

In Florida, as at common law, the littoral owner automatically takes title to dry land added to his property by accretion; but formerly submerged land that has become dry land by avulsion continues to belong to the owner of the seabed (usually the State). . . . Thus, regardless of whether an avulsive event exposes land previously submerged or submerges land previously exposed, the boundary between littoral property and sovereign land does not change; it remains (ordinarily) what was the mean high-water line before the event. See Bryant v. Peppe, 238 So. 2d 836, 838-839 (Fla. 1970); J. Gould, Law of Waters §158, p. 290 (1883). It follows from this that, when a new strip of land has been added to the shore by avulsion, the littoral owner has no right to subsequent accretions. Those accretions no longer add to his property, since the property abutting the water belongs not to him but to the State. . . .

In 1961, Florida's Legislature passed the Beach and Shore Preservation Act, 1961 Fla. Laws ch. 61-246, as amended, Fla. Stat. §§61.011-161.45 (2007). The Act establishes procedures for "beach restoration and nourishment projects," §161.088, designed to deposit sand on eroded beaches (restoration) and to maintain the deposited sand (nourishment). §§161.021(3), (4). A local government may apply to the Department of Environmental Protection for the funds and the necessary permits to restore a beach, see §§161.101(1), 161.041(1). When the project involves placing fill on the State's submerged lands, authorization is required from the Board of Trustees of the Internal Improvement Trust Fund, see §253.77(1), which holds title to those lands, §253.12(1).

Once a beach restoration "is determined to be undertaken," the Board sets what is called "an erosion control line." §§161.161(3)-(5). It must be set by reference to the existing mean high-water line, though in theory it can be located seaward or landward of that. See §161.161(5). Much of the project work occurs seaward of the erosion-control line, as sand is dumped on what was once submerged land. The fixed erosion-control line replaces the fluctuating mean high-water line as the boundary between privately owned littoral property and state property. §161.191(1). Once the erosion-control line is recorded, the common law ceases to increase upland property by accretion (or decrease it by erosion). §161.191(2). Thus, when accretion to the shore moves the mean high-water line seaward, the property of beachfront landowners is not extended to that line (as the prior law provided), but remains bounded by the permanent erosion-control line. Those landowners "continue to be entitled," however, "to all common-law riparian rights" other than the right to accretions. §161.201. . . . Finally, by regulation, if the use of submerged land would "unreasonably infringe on riparian rights," the project cannot proceed unless the local governments show that they own or have a property interest in the upland property adjacent to the project site. Fla. Admin. Code Rule 18-21.004(3)(b) (2009).

In 2003, the city of Destin and Walton County applied for the necessary permits to restore 6.9 miles of beach within their jurisdictions that had been eroded by several hurricanes. The project envisioned depositing along that shore sand dredged from further out. See Walton Cty. v. Stop the Beach Renourishment, Inc., 998 So. 2d 1102, 1106 (Fla. 2008). It would add about 75 feet of dry sand seaward of the mean high-water line (to be denominated the erosion-control line). The Department issued a notice of intent to award the permits, and the Board approved the erosion-control line.

The petitioner here, Stop the Beach Renourishment, Inc., is a nonprofit corporation formed by people who own beachfront property bordering the project area (we shall refer to them as the Members). It brought an administrative challenge to the proposed project, which was unsuccessful; the Department approved the permits. Petitioner then challenged that action in state court under the Florida Administrative Procedure Act, Fla. Stat. §120.68 (2007). The District Court of Appeal for the First District concluded that, contrary to the Act's preservation of "all common-law riparian rights," the order had eliminated two of the Members' littoral rights: (1) the right to receive accretions to their property; and (2) the right to have the contact of their property with the water remain intact. . . . This, it believed, would be an unconstitutional taking, which would "unreasonably infringe on riparian rights," and therefore require the showing under Fla. Admin. Code Rule 18-21.004(3)(b) that the local governments owned or had a property interest in the upland property. . . .

The Florida Supreme Court . . . faulted the Court of Appeal for not considering the doctrine of avulsion, which it concluded permitted the State to reclaim the restored beach on behalf of the public. . . . It described the right to accretions as a future contingent interest, not a vested property right, and held that there is no littoral right to contact with the water independent of the littoral right of access, which the Act does not infringe. . . . Petitioner sought rehearing on the ground that the Florida Supreme Court's decision itself effected a taking of the Members' littoral rights contrary to the Fifth and Fourteenth Amendments to the Federal Constitution. The request for rehearing was denied. We granted certiorari.

II.

Before coming to the parties' arguments in the present case, we discuss some general principles of our takings jurisprudence. The Takings Clause—"nor shall private property be taken for public use, without just compensation," U.S. Const., Amdt. 5—applies as fully to the taking of a landowner's riparian rights as it does to the taking of an estate in land.[42] See Yates v. Milwaukee, 10 Wall. 497, 504 (1871). Moreover, though the classic taking is a transfer of property to the State or to another private party by eminent domain, the Takings Clause applies to other

---

42. We thus need not resolve whether the right of accretion is an easement, as petitioner claims, or, as Florida claims, a contingent future interest.

state actions that achieve the same thing. Thus, when the government uses its own property in such a way that it destroys private property, it has taken that property. . . . Similarly, our doctrine of regulatory takings "aims to identify regulatory actions that are functionally equivalent to the classic taking." . . . Finally (and here we approach the situation before us), States effect a taking if they recharacterize as public property what was previously private property. . . .

The Takings Clause (unlike, for instance, the Ex Post Facto Clauses, see Art. I, §9, cl. 3; §10, cl. 1) is not addressed to the action of a specific branch or branches. It is concerned simply with the act, and not with the governmental actor ("nor shall private property be taken"). There is no textual justification for saying that the existence or the scope of a State's power to expropriate private property without just compensation varies according to the branch of government effecting the expropriation. Nor does common sense recommend such a principle. It would be absurd to allow a State to do by judicial decree what the Takings Clause forbids it to do by legislative fiat. . . .

Our precedents provide no support for the proposition that takings effected by the judicial branch are entitled to special treatment, and in fact suggest the contrary. PruneYard Shopping Center v. Robins, 447 U.S. 74, 100 (1980), involved a decision of the California Supreme Court overruling one of its prior decisions which had held that the California Constitution's guarantees of freedom of speech and of the press, and of the right to petition the government, did not require the owner of private property to accord those rights on his premises. The appellants, owners of a shopping center, contended that their private property rights could not "be denied by invocation of a state constitutional provision or by judicial reconstruction of a State's laws of private property," id. at 79. We held that there had been no taking, citing cases involving legislative and executive takings, and applying standard Takings Clause analysis. See id. at 82-84. . . .

Webb's Fabulous Pharmacies is even closer in point. There the purchaser of an insolvent corporation had interpleaded the corporation's creditors, placing the purchase price in an interest-bearing account in the registry of the Circuit Court of Seminole County, to be distributed in satisfaction of claims approved by a receiver. The Florida Supreme Court construed an applicable statute to mean that the interest on the account belonged to the county, because the account was "considered 'public money,'" Beckwith v. Webb's Fabulous Pharmacies, 374 So. 2d 951, 952-953 (Fla. 1979) (per curiam). We held this to be a taking. We noted that "[t]he usual and general rule is that any interest on an interpleaded and deposited fund follows the principal and is to be allocated to those who are ultimately to be the owners of that principal," 449 U.S. at 162. "Neither the Florida Legislature by statute, nor the Florida courts by judicial decree," we said, "may accomplish the result the county seeks simply by recharacterizing the principal as 'public money.'" Id. at 164.

In sum, the Takings Clause bars the State from taking private property without paying for it, no matter which branch is the instrument of the taking. To be sure, the manner of state action may matter: Condemnation by eminent domain, for example, is always a taking, while a legislative, executive, or judicial restriction of property use may or may not be, depending on its nature and extent. But the particular state actor is irrelevant. If a legislature or a court declares that what was once an established right of private property no longer exists, it has taken that property, no less than if the State had physically appropriated it or destroyed its value by regulation. "[A] State, by ipse dixit, may not transform private property into public property without compensation." Id. . . .

Justice Kennedy concludes that the Florida Supreme Court's action here does not meet the standard for a judicial taking, while purporting not to determine what is the standard for a judicial taking, or indeed whether such a thing as a judicial taking even exists. That approach is invalid for the reasons we have discussed.

Justice Kennedy says that we need not take what he considers the bold and risky step of holding that the Takings Clause applies to judicial action, because the Due Process Clause "would likely prevent a State from doing by judicial decree what the Takings Clause forbids it to do by legislative fiat." He invokes the Due Process Clause "in both its substantive and procedural aspects," not specifying which of his arguments relates to which.

The first respect in which Justice Kennedy thinks the Due Process Clause can do the job seems to sound in Procedural Due Process. Because, he says, "[c]ourts, unlike the executive or legislature, are not designed to make policy decisions" about expropriation, "[t]he Court would be on strong footing in ruling that a judicial decision that eliminates or substantially changes established property rights" violates the Due Process Clause. Let us be clear what is being proposed here. This Court has held that the separation-of-powers principles that the Constitution imposes upon the Federal Government do not apply against the States. See Dreyer v. Illinois, 187 U.S. 71, 83-84 (1902). But in order to avoid the bold and risky step of saying that the Takings Clause applies to all government takings, Justice Kennedy would have us use Procedural Due Process to impose judicially crafted separation-of-powers limitations upon the States: courts cannot be used to perform the governmental function of expropriation. The asserted reasons for the due-process limitation are that the legislative and executive branches "are accountable in their political capacity" for takings, and "[c]ourts . . . are not designed to make policy decisions" about takings. These reasons may have a lot to do with sound separation-of-powers principles that ought to govern a democratic society, but they have nothing whatever to do with the protection of individual rights that is the object of the Due Process Clause.

Of course even taking those reasons at face value, it is strange to proclaim a democracy deficit and lack of special competence for the judicial taking of an individual property right, when this Court has had no trouble deciding matters of much greater moment, contrary to congressional desire or the legislated desires of most of the States, with no special competence except the authority we possess to enforce the Constitution. In any case, our opinion does not trust judges with the relatively small power Justice Kennedy now objects to. It is we who propose setting aside judicial decisions that take private property; it is he who insists that judges cannot be so limited. Under his regime, the citizen whose property has been judicially redefined to belong to the State would presumably be given the

Orwellian explanation: "The court did not take your property. Because it is neither politically accountable nor competent to make such a decision, it cannot
take property."

   Justice Kennedy's injection of separation-of-powers principles into the Due
Process Clause would also have the ironic effect of preventing the assignment of
the expropriation function to the branch of government whose procedures are,
by far, the most protective of individual rights. So perhaps even this first respect
in which Justice Kennedy would have the Due Process Clause do the work of
the Takings Clause pertains to Substantive, rather than Procedural, Due Process.
His other arguments undoubtedly pertain to that, as evidenced by his assertion
that "[i]t is . . . natural to read the Due Process Clause as limiting the power of
courts to eliminate or change established property rights," his endorsement of
the proposition that the Due Process Clause imposes "limits on government's
ability to diminish property values by regulation," and his contention that "the
Due Process Clause would likely prevent a State from doing by judicial decree
what the Takings Clause forbids it to do by legislative fiat."

   The first problem with using Substantive Due Process to do the work of
the Takings Clause is that we have held it cannot be done. "Where a particular Amendment 'provides an explicit textual source of constitutional protection'
against a particular sort of government behavior, 'that Amendment, not the more
generalized notion of "substantive due process," must be the guide for analyzing
these claims.'" Albright v. Oliver, 510 U.S. 266, 273 (1994) (four-Justice plurality
opinion). . . . The second problem is that we have held for many years (logically
or not) that the "liberties" protected by Substantive Due Process do not include
economic liberties. See, e.g., Lincoln Fed. Labor Union v. Northwestern Iron &
Metal Co., 335 U.S. 525, 536 (1949). Justice Kennedy's language ("If a judicial
decision . . . eliminates an established property right, the judgment could be set
aside as a deprivation of property without due process of law.") propels us back
to what is referred to (usually deprecatingly) as "the *Lochner* era." See Lochner
v. New York, 198 U.S. 45, 56-58 (1905). That is a step of much greater novelty,
and much more unpredictable effect, than merely applying the Takings Clause
to judicial action. And the third and last problem with using Substantive Due
Process is that either (1) it will not do all that the Takings Clause does, or (2) if
it does all that the Takings Clause does, it will encounter the same supposed difficulties that Justice Kennedy finds troublesome.

   We do not grasp the relevance of Justice Kennedy's speculation that the
Framers did not envision the Takings Clause would apply to judicial action. They
doubtless did not, since the Constitution was adopted in an era when courts had
no power to "change" the common law. See 1 Blackstone 69-70 (1765); Rogers v.
Tennessee, 532 U.S. 451, 472-478 (2001) (Scalia, J., dissenting). Where the text
they adopted is clear, however ("nor shall private property be taken for public
use"), what counts is not what they envisioned but what they wrote. Of course
even after courts, in the 19th century, did assume the power to change the common law, it is not true that the new "common-law tradition . . . allows for incremental modifications to property law," so that "owners may reasonably expect or

anticipate courts to make certain changes in property law." In the only sense in which this could be relevant to what we are discussing, that is an astounding statement. We are talking here about judicial elimination of established private property rights. If that is indeed a "common-law tradition," Justice Kennedy ought to be able to provide a more solid example for it than the only one he cites, a state-court change (from "noxious" to "harmful") of the test for determining whether a neighbor's vegetation is a tortious nuisance. Fancher v. Fagella, 650 S.E.2d 519, 522 (Va. 2007). But perhaps he does not really mean that it is a common-law tradition to eliminate property rights, since he immediately follows his statement that "owners may reasonably expect or anticipate courts to make certain changes in property law" with the contradictory statement that "courts cannot abandon settled principles." If no "settled principl[e]" has been abandoned, it is hard to see how property law could have been "change[d]," rather than merely clarified.

Justice Kennedy has added "two additional practical considerations that the Court would need to address before recognizing judicial takings." One of them is simple and simply answered: the assertion that "it is unclear what remedy a reviewing court could enter after finding a judicial taking." Justice Kennedy worries that we may only be able to mandate compensation. That remedy is even rare for a legislative or executive taking, and we see no reason why it would be the exclusive remedy for a judicial taking. If we were to hold that the Florida Supreme Court had effected an uncompensated taking in the present case, we would simply reverse the Florida Supreme Court's judgment that the Beach and Shore Preservation Act can be applied to the property in question. Justice Kennedy's other point—that we will have to decide when the claim of a judicial taking must be asserted—hardly presents an awe-inspiring prospect. These, and all the other "difficulties," "difficult questions," and "practical considerations," that Justice Kennedy worries may perhaps stand in the way of recognizing a judicial taking, are either nonexistent or insignificant.

Finally, we cannot avoid comment upon Justice Kennedy's donning of the mantle of judicial restraint—his assertion that it is we, and not he, who would empower the courts and encourage their expropriation of private property. He warns that if judges know that their action is covered by the Takings Clause, they will issue "sweeping new rule[s] to adjust the rights of property owners," comfortable in the knowledge that their innovations will be preserved upon payment by the State. That is quite impossible. As we have said, if we were to hold that the Florida Supreme Court had effected an uncompensated taking in this case, we would not validate the taking by ordering Florida to pay compensation. We would simply reverse the Florida Supreme Court's judgment that the Beach and Shore Preservation Act can be applied to the Members' property. The power to effect a compensated taking would then reside, where it has always resided, not in the Florida Supreme Court but in the Florida Legislature—which could either provide compensation or acquiesce in the invalidity of the offending features of the Act. Cf. Davis v. Michigan Dept. of Treasury, 489 U.S. 803, 817-818 (1989). The only realistic incentive that subjection to the Takings Clause might provide to any court would be the incentive to get reversed, which in our experience few judges value.

Justice Kennedy, however, while dismissive of the Takings Clause, places no other constraints on judicial action. He puts forward some extremely vague applications of Substantive Due Process, and does not even say that they (whatever they are) will for sure apply. . . .

Moreover, and more importantly, Justice Kennedy places no constraints whatever upon this Court. Not only does his concurrence only think about applying Substantive Due Process; but because Substantive Due Process is such a wonderfully malleable concept, see, e.g., Lawrence v. Texas, 539 U.S. 558, 562 (2003) (referring to "liberty of the person both in its spatial and in its more transcendent dimensions"), even a firm commitment to apply it would be a firm commitment to nothing in particular. . . .

III.

Respondents put forward a number of arguments which contradict, to a greater or lesser degree, the principle discussed above, that the existence of a taking does not depend upon the branch of government that effects it. . . .

[R]espondents argue that federal courts lack the knowledge of state law required to decide whether a judicial decision that purports merely to clarify property rights has instead taken them. But federal courts must often decide what state property rights exist in nontakings contexts, see, e.g., Board of Regents of State Colleges v. Roth, 408 U.S. 564, 577-578 (1972) (Due Process Clause). And indeed they must decide it to resolve claims that legislative or executive action has effected a taking. For example, a regulation that deprives a property owner of all economically beneficial use of his property is not a taking if the restriction "inhere[s] in the title itself, in the restrictions that background principles of the State's law of property and nuisance already place upon land ownership." *Lucas,* 505 U.S. at 1029. A constitutional provision that forbids the uncompensated taking of property is quite simply insusceptible of enforcement by federal courts unless they have the power to decide what property rights exist under state law.

Respondents also warn us against depriving common-law judging of needed flexibility. That argument has little appeal when directed against the enforcement of a constitutional guarantee adopted in an era when, as we said supra, courts had no power to "change" the common law. But in any case, courts have no peculiar need of flexibility. It is no more essential that judges be free to overrule prior cases that establish property entitlements than that state legislators be free to revise pre-existing statutes that confer property entitlements, or agency-heads pre-existing regulations that do so. And insofar as courts merely clarify and elaborate property entitlements that were previously unclear, they cannot be said to have taken an established property right. . . .

For its part, petitioner proposes an unpredictability test. Quoting Justice Stewart's concurrence in Hughes v. Washington, 389 U.S. 290, 296 (1967), petitioner argues that a judicial taking consists of a decision that "constitutes a sudden change in state law, unpredictable in terms of relevant precedents." See Brief for Petitioner 17, 34-50. The focus of petitioner's test is misdirected. What counts is not whether there is precedent for the allegedly confiscatory decision, but whether the property right allegedly taken was established. A "predictability of change" test would cover both too much and too little. Too much, because a judicial property decision need not be predictable, so long as it does not declare that what had been private property under established law no longer is. A decision that clarifies property entitlements (or the lack thereof) that were previously unclear might be difficult to predict, but it does not eliminate established property rights. And the predictability test covers too little, because a judicial elimination of established private-property rights that is foreshadowed by dicta or even by holdings years in advance is nonetheless a taking. . . .

IV.

We come at last to petitioner's takings attack on the decision below. . . . Petitioner argues that the Florida Supreme Court took two of the property rights of the Members by declaring that those rights did not exist: the right to accretions, and the right to have littoral property touch the water (which petitioner distinguishes from the mere right of access to the water). Under petitioner's theory, because no prior Florida decision had said that the State's filling of submerged tidal lands could have the effect of depriving a littoral owner of contact with the water and denying him future accretions, the Florida Supreme Court's judgment in the present case abolished those two easements to which littoral property owners had been entitled. This puts the burden on the wrong party. There is no taking unless petitioner can show that, before the Florida Supreme Court's decision, littoral-property owners had rights to future accretions and contact with the water superior to the State's right to fill in its submerged land. Though some may think the question close, in our view the showing cannot be made.

Two core principles of Florida property law intersect in this case. First, the State as owner of the submerged land adjacent to littoral property has the right to fill that land, so long as it does not interfere with the rights of the public and the rights of littoral landowners. See Hayes v. Bowman, 91 So. 2d 795, 799-800 (Fla. 1957) (right to fill conveyed by State to private party); State ex rel. Buford v. Tampa, 102 So. 336, 341 (1924) (same). Second, as we described supra, if an avulsion exposes land seaward of littoral property that had previously been submerged, that land belongs to the State even if it interrupts the littoral owner's contact with the water. See *Bryant*, 238 So. 2d, at 837, 838-839. The issue here is whether there is an exception to this rule when the State is the cause of the avulsion. Prior law suggests there is not. In Martin v. Busch, 112 So. 274 (Fla. 1927), the Florida Supreme Court held that when the State drained water from a lakebed belonging to the State, causing land that was formerly below the mean high-water line to become dry land, that land continued to belong to the State. Id. at 287; see also *Bryant*, supra, at 838-839 (analogizing the situation in *Martin* to an avulsion). "The riparian rights doctrine of accretion and reliction," the Florida Supreme Court later explained, "does not apply to such lands." *Bryant*, supra, at 839 (quoting *Martin*, supra, at 578, 112 So., at 288 (Brown, J., concurring)).

This is not surprising, as there can be no accretions to land that no longer abuts the water.

Thus, Florida law as it stood before the decision below allowed the State to fill in its own seabed, and the resulting sudden exposure of previously submerged land was treated like an avulsion for purposes of ownership. The right to accretions was therefore subordinate to the State's right to fill. . . .

The Florida Supreme Court decision before us is consistent with these background principles of state property law. Cf. *Lucas*, 505 U.S. at 1028-1029. It did not abolish the Members' right to future accretions, but merely held that the right was not implicated by the beach-restoration project, because the doctrine of avulsion applied. See 998 So. 2d, at 1117, 1120-1121. The Florida Supreme Court's opinion describes beach restoration as the reclamation by the State of the public's land, just as *Martin* had described the lake drainage in that case. Although the opinion does not cite *Martin* and is not always clear on this point, it suffices that its characterization of the littoral right to accretion is consistent with *Martin* and the other relevant principles of Florida law we have discussed. . . .

The result under Florida law may seem counter-intuitive. After all, the Members' property has been deprived of its character (and value) as oceanfront property by the State's artificial creation of an avulsion. Perhaps state-created avulsions ought to be treated differently from other avulsions insofar as the property right to accretion is concerned. But nothing in prior Florida law makes such a distinction, and *Martin* suggests, if it does not indeed hold, the contrary. Even if there might be different interpretations of *Martin* and other Florida property-law cases that would prevent this arguably odd result, we are not free to adopt them. The Takings Clause only protects property rights as they are established under state law, not as they might have been established or ought to have been established. We cannot say that the Florida Supreme Court's decision eliminated a right of accretion established under Florida law. . . .

V.

Because the Florida Supreme Court's decision did not contravene the established property rights of petitioner's Members, Florida has not violated the Fifth and Fourteenth Amendments. The judgment of the Florida Supreme Court is therefore affirmed.

It is so ordered.

Justice Stevens took no part in the decision of this case.

JUSTICE KENNEDY, with whom JUSTICE SOTOMAYOR joins, concurring in part and concurring in the judgment.

The Court's analysis of the principles that control ownership of the land in question, and of the rights of petitioner's members as adjacent owners, is correct in my view, leading to my joining Parts I, IV, and V of the Court's opinion. As Justice Breyer observes, however, this case does not require the Court to determine whether, or when, a judicial decision determining the rights of property owners can violate the Takings Clause of the Fifth Amendment of the United States Constitution. This separate opinion notes certain difficulties that should be considered before accepting the theory that a judicial decision that eliminates an "established property right," constitutes a violation of the Takings Clause. . . .

If a judicial decision, as opposed to an act of the executive or the legislature, eliminates an established property right, the judgment could be set aside as a deprivation of property without due process of law. The Due Process Clause, in both its substantive and procedural aspects, is a central limitation upon the exercise of judicial power. And this Court has long recognized that property regulations can be invalidated under the Due Process Clause. . . . It is thus natural to read the Due Process Clause as limiting the power of courts to eliminate or change established property rights.

The Takings Clause also protects property rights, and it "operates as a conditional limitation, permitting the government to do what it wants so long as it pays the charge." Eastern Enterprises v. Apfel, 524 U.S. 498, 545 (1998) (Kennedy, J., concurring in judgment and dissenting in part). Unlike the Due Process Clause, therefore, the Takings Clause implicitly recognizes a governmental power while placing limits upon that power. Thus, if the Court were to hold that a judicial taking exists, it would presuppose that a judicial decision eliminating established property rights is "otherwise constitutional" so long as the State compensates the aggrieved property owners. Id. There is no clear authority for this proposition.

When courts act without direction from the executive or legislature, they may not have the power to eliminate established property rights by judicial decision. "Given that the constitutionality" of a judicial decision altering property rights "appears to turn on the legitimacy" of whether the court's judgment eliminates or changes established property rights "rather than on the availability of compensation, . . . the more appropriate constitutional analysis arises under general due process principles rather than under the Takings Clause." Id. Courts, unlike the executive or legislature, are not designed to make policy decisions about "the need for, and likely effectiveness of, regulatory actions." *Lingle*, [544 U.S.] at 545. State courts generally operate under a common-law tradition that allows for incremental modifications to property law, but "this tradition cannot justify a carte blanch judicial authority to change property definitions wholly free of constitutional limitations." Walston, The Constitution and Property: Due Process, Regulatory Takings, and Judicial Takings, 2001 Utah L. Rev. 379, 435.

The Court would be on strong footing in ruling that a judicial decision that eliminates or substantially changes established property rights, which are a legitimate expectation of the owner, is "arbitrary or irrational" under the Due Process Clause. . . . Thus, without a judicial takings doctrine, the Due Process Clause would likely prevent a State from doing "by judicial decree what the Takings Clause forbids it to do by legislative fiat." The objection that a due process claim might involve close questions concerning whether a judicial decree extends beyond what owners might have expected is not a sound argument; for the same close questions would arise with respect to whether a judicial decision is a taking. . . .

To announce that courts too can effect a taking when they decide cases involving property rights, would raise certain difficult questions. Since this case does not require those questions to be addressed, in my respectful view, the Court should not reach beyond the necessities of the case to announce a sweeping rule that court decisions can be takings, as that phrase is used in the Takings Clause. The evident reason for recognizing a judicial takings doctrine would be to constrain the power of the judicial branch. Of course, the judiciary must respect private ownership. But were this Court to say that judicial decisions become takings when they overreach, this might give more power to courts, not less.

Consider the instance of litigation between two property owners to determine which one bears the liability and costs when a tree that stands on one property extends its roots in a way that damages adjacent property. See, e.g., Fancher v. Fagella, 650 S.E.2d 519 (Va. 2007). If a court deems that, in light of increasing urbanization, the former rule for allocation of these costs should be changed, thus shifting the rights of the owners, it may well increase the value of one property and decrease the value of the other. This might be the type of incremental modification under state common law that does not violate due process, as owners may reasonably expect or anticipate courts to make certain changes in property law. The usual due process constraint is that courts cannot abandon settled principles. . . .

But if the state court were deemed to be exercising the power to take property, that constraint would be removed. Because the State would be bound to pay owners for takings caused by a judicial decision, it is conceivable that some judges might decide that enacting a sweeping new rule to adjust the rights of property owners in the context of changing social needs is a good idea. Knowing that the resulting ruling would be a taking, the courts could go ahead with their project, free from constraints that would otherwise confine their power. The resulting judgment as between the property owners likely could not be set aside by some later enactment. . . . And if the litigation were a class action to decide, for instance, whether there are public rights of access that diminish the rights of private ownership, a State might find itself obligated to pay a substantial judgment for the judicial ruling. Even if the legislature were to subsequently rescind the judicial decision by statute, the State would still have to pay just compensation for the temporary taking that occurred from the time of the judicial decision to the time of the statutory fix. See *First English*, 482 U.S. at 321.

The idea, then, that a judicial takings doctrine would constrain judges might just well have the opposite effect. It would give judges new power and new assurance that changes in property rights that are beneficial, or thought to be so, are fair and proper because just compensation will be paid. The judiciary historically has not had the right or responsibility to say what property should or should not be taken.

Indeed, it is unclear whether the Takings Clause was understood, as a historical matter, to apply to judicial decisions. The Framers most likely viewed this Clause as applying only to physical appropriation pursuant to the power of eminent domain. See Lucas v. South Carolina Coastal Council, 505 U.S. 1003, 1028 n.15 (1992). And it appears these physical appropriations were traditionally made by legislatures. See 3 J. Story, Commentaries on the Constitution of the United States §1784, p. 661 (1833). Courts, on the other hand, lacked the power of eminent domain. See 1 W. Blackstone, Commentaries 135 (W. Lewis ed. 1897). The Court's Takings Clause jurisprudence has expanded beyond the Framers' understanding, as it now applies to certain regulations that are not physical appropriations. See *Lucas*, supra, at 1014 (citing *Mahon*, 260 U.S. at 393). But the Court should consider with care the decision to extend the Takings Clause in a manner that might be inconsistent with historical practice.

There are two additional practical considerations that the Court would need to address before recognizing judicial takings. First, it may be unclear in certain situations how a party should properly raise a judicial takings claim. "[I]t is important to separate out two judicial actions — the decision to change current property rules in a way that would constitute a taking, and the decision to require compensation." Thompson, Judicial Takings, 76 Va. L. Rev. 1449, 1515 (1990). In some contexts, these issues could arise separately. For instance, assume that a state-court opinion explicitly holds that it is changing state property law, or that it asserts that is not changing the law but there is no "fair or substantial basis" for this statement. (Most of these cases may arise in the latter posture, like inverse condemnation claims where the State says it is not taking property and pays no compensation.) Call this Case A. The only issue in Case A was determining the substance of state property law. It is doubtful that parties would raise a judicial takings claim on appeal, or in a petition for a writ of certiorari, in Case A, as the issue would not have been litigated below. Rather, the party may file a separate lawsuit — Case B — arguing that a taking occurred in light of the change in property law made by Case A. After all, until the state court in Case A changes the law, the party will not know if his or her property rights will have been eliminated. So res judicata probably would not bar the party from litigating the takings issue in Case B.

Second, it is unclear what remedy a reviewing court could enter after finding a judicial taking. It appears under our precedents that a party who suffers a taking is only entitled to damages, not equitable relief: The Court has said that "[e]quitable relief is not available to enjoin an alleged taking of private property for a public use . . . when a suit for compensation can be brought against the sovereign subsequent to the taking," Ruckelshaus v. Monsanto Co., 467 U.S. 986, 1016 (1984), and the Court subsequently held that the Takings Clause requires the availability of a suit for compensation against the States, *First English*, supra, at 321-322. It makes perfect sense that the remedy for a Takings Clause violation is only damages, as the Clause "does not proscribe the taking of property; it proscribes taking without just compensation." . . .

It is thus questionable whether reviewing courts could invalidate judicial decisions deemed to be judicial takings; they may only be able to order just compensation. In the posture discussed above where Case A changes the law and Case B addresses whether that change is a taking, it is not clear how the Court, in Case B, could invalidate the holding of Case A. If a single case were to properly address both a state court's change in the law and whether the change was a taking, the Court might be able to give the state court a choice on how to proceed if there were a judicial taking. The Court might be able to remand and let the state court determine whether it wants to insist on changing its property law and paying just compensation or to rescind its holding that changed the law. . . . But that decision would rest with the state court, not this Court; so the state court could still force the State to pay just compensation. And even if the state court decided to rescind its decision that changed the law, a temporary taking would have occurred in the interim. See id.

These difficult issues are some of the reasons why the Court should not reach beyond the necessities of the case to recognize a judicial takings doctrine. It is not wise, from an institutional standpoint, to reach out and decide questions that have not been discussed at much length by courts and commentators. . . . If and when future cases show that the usual principles, including constitutional principles that constrain the judiciary like due process, are somehow inadequate to protect property owners, then the question whether a judicial decision can effect a taking would be properly presented. In the meantime, it seems appropriate to recognize that the substantial power to decide whose property to take and when to take it should be conceived of as a power vested in the political branches and subject to political control.

JUSTICE BREYER, with whom JUSTICE GINSBURG joins, concurring in part and concurring in the judgment.

I agree that no unconstitutional taking of property occurred in this case, and I therefore join Parts I, IV, and V of today's opinion. I cannot join Parts II and III, however, for in those Parts the plurality unnecessarily addresses questions of constitutional law that are better left for another day. . . .

NOTES AND QUESTIONS

1. *What if?* No opinion commanded a five-justice majority in *Stop the Beach*. As a result, it is unclear whether lawsuits alleging that a judicial decision violates the Takings Clause are viable. Compare Northern Natural Gas Co. v. ONEOK Field Servs. Co., 296 P.3d 1106, 1127 (Kan. 2013) (referring to Justice Scalia's opinion as "a plurality opinion with no precedential value"), with Investors Savings Bank v. Keybank Natl. Assn., 38 A.3d 638, 643-644 (N.J. Super. Ct. 2012) (interpreting *Stop the Beach* as holding "that a taking may occur if a judicial decision articulates a new rule that alters a clearly established right of private property"). The 4-2-2 split in *Stop the Beach* resulted from the recusal of Justice Stevens, who faced calls from journalists to remove himself from the case because his wife owns a beachfront condominium in Fort Lauderdale, Florida. A 2013 law review article by Justice Stevens explains that he recused himself despite his doubts about how the litigation might conceivably affect the condominium's value. See John Paul Stevens, The Ninth Vote in the "Stop the Beach" Case, 88 Chi.-Kent L. Rev. 553, 556 (2013).

The same article also reveals how Stevens would have voted had he decided not to recuse. Justice Stevens would have urged his colleagues to dismiss the case as one in which certiorari had "been improvidently granted because there was no justification for using it as a vehicle for discussing the subject of judicial takings." Id. In Justice Stevens's view, Justice Scalia's "advisory" opinion was wrong for three primary reasons. First, any taking in the case was a legislative or administrative agency taking, not a judicial taking. Second, the Due Process Clause already gives the federal courts authority to deem state judicial decisions concerning property rights unconstitutional. Third, the plurality should have exercised restraint rather than (1) deciding a constitutional question that did not need to be decided in light of the Court's unanimity on the question of Florida law, and (2) articulating a constitutional rule of greater breadth than was required to resolve the case. Id. at 557-564. Justice Stevens thus expressed sympathy for the positions taken by Justices Kennedy and Breyer. Of course, with Justice Kagan having replaced Justice Stevens on the Court, the precise sentiments of the new "ninth vote" regarding judicial takings are presently unknown.

2. *Why this case?* As Justice Stevens's article indicates, it is at the very least odd that the Supreme Court devoted its first sustained attention to judicial takings in a case where all the justices agreed that the state court decision in question was consistent with longstanding precedents. So why did the Court grant certiorari in *Stop the Beach*? As Justice Scalia's opinion noted, the controlling Florida precedent, Martin v. Busch, was not cited by the Florida Supreme Court in its *Stop the Beach* opinion. That omission was not the fault of Florida's lawyers, who insisted in the lower courts that *Martin* controlled. Perhaps chastened after seeing their principal precedent ignored by the Florida Supreme Court and by Stop the Beach Renourishment Inc.'s certiorari petition, the state's lawyers also neglected to mention the case in their brief opposing certiorari. But after the Supreme Court agreed to consider the case, Florida brought *Martin* to the justices' attention and the Solicitor General (Elena Kagan) argued forcefully that in light of *Martin* the Florida Supreme Court had not deviated from existing Florida law. Given this sequence of events, it seems plausible that the justices and their clerks did not know of Martin v. Busch's existence when they agreed to hear the case. See Eduardo M. Peñalver & Lior Jacob Strahilevitz, Judicial Takings or Due Process?, 97 Cornell L. Rev. 305, 344-345 (2012).

3. *Should the courts be liable for changing the contours of property entitlements?* As the opinions in *Stop the Beach* indicated, the question of judicial takings has been percolating for many years, both in judicial opinions and in an influential law review article. See Hughes v. Washington, 389 U.S. 290, 296 (1967) (Stewart, J., concurring); Barton H. Thompson, Jr., Judicial Takings, 76 Va. L. Rev. 1449 (1990). Suppose that a litigant's property value was substantially reduced by a decades-old state court decision that altered existing property law. The litigant files a judicial takings suit a week after *Stop the Beach* is decided. What result? See Smith v. United States, 709 F.3d 1114, 1116-1117 (Fed. Cir. 2013) (*Stop the Beach* did not create a new judicial takings cause of action, but merely applied existing

precedents regarding judicial takings claims); Willits v. Peabody Coal Co., 400 S.W.3d 442, 451 (Mo. App. 2013) (same).

4. *Other judicial takings?* Recall the *Keystone* decision discussed in Note 4 on page 1162. In it, the Supreme Court held that a contemporary law nearly identical to the one that had been held a taking in *Pennsylvania Coal* was not a taking. So was *Keystone* itself a judicial taking then? If so, what is the remedy for a judicial taking by the Supreme Court?

5. *Judging judicial takings.* A voluminous literature has examined the Court's *Stop the Beach* decision, with much of it expressing misgivings about the plurality's approach. See, e.g., D. Benjamin Barros, The Complexities of Judicial Takings, 45 U. Rich. L. Rev. 903 (2011); Mary Doyle & Stephen J. Schnably, Going Rogue: *Stop the Beach Renourishment* as an Object of Morbid Fascination, 64 Hastings L.J. 83 (2012); John D. Echeverria, *Stop the Beach Renourishment*: Why the Judiciary Is Different, 35 Vt. L. Rev. 475 (2010); Stephanie Stern, Protecting Property Through Politics: State Legislative Checks and Judicial Takings, 97 Minn. L. Rev. 2176 (2013).

Frederic Bloom and Christopher Serkin provide an ambitious partial defense of judicial takings liability, arguing that such liability can be conceptualized as a form of "transition relief," whereby parties disadvantaged by judicial changes to legal rules are made whole. On this account, judicial takings help soften "the harshest effects of desirable legal change." Frederic Bloom & Christopher Serkin, Suing Courts, 79 U. Chi. L. Rev. 553, 556 (2012).

6. *Judicial takings and due process: neither, one, or both?* An important source of disagreement between Justices Scalia and Kennedy is the question of what constitutional provision should police judicial abrogations of existing entitlements: the Takings Clause or the Due Process Clause? This question is the focus of Peñalver & Strahilevitz, supra. Peñalver and Strahilevitz argue that intentionality—a factor largely ignored by all the opinions in *Stop the Beach*—helps sort between those grievances best addressed by the Takings Clause and those implicating the Due Process Clause. When the state intentionally seizes property to further a legitimate public end, the Takings Clause usually applies. When the state either lacks intent to seize private property or seizes the property in furtherance of an illegitimate state interest, the Due Process Clause typically governs. 97 Cornell L. Rev. at 312. The importance of governmental intent as a factor in the takings inquiry was reiterated by the Supreme Court in a case decided a few years after *Stop the Beach.* Arkansas Game & Fish Commn. v. United States, 133 S. Ct. 511, 522 (2012).

7. *Moral hazard?* Suppose a property owner's existing entitlement to Blackacre is being challenged by a neighbor. The owner elects not to hire the best lawyer that money can buy, and the neighbor prevails in the trial court, with the result that the court declares the neighbor to be Blackacre's new owner. The original owner then sues the state, alleging a judicial taking. If he prevails, then the state now owes him Blackacre's fair market value. Might this possibility of a judicial takings recovery cause the original owner to underinvest in legal representation at trial? And could systematic underinvestment in counsel destabilize property doctrine? See Peñalver & Strahilevitz, supra, at 335-354. In circumstances like

these, is it appropriate to impose a cost on the government (via takings liability) without permitting the government to recoup these costs from the neighbor who convinced the state courts to transfer Blackacre to her? For an illuminating discussion of related topics, see Abraham Bell & Gideon Parchomovsky, Givings, 111 Yale L.J. 547 (2001).

8. *Avulsions, accretions, and relictions.* Although students often assume that land is fixed and stable, the plurality opinion nicely illustrates the ways in which the boundaries of waterfront land may change and the challenges that these changes pose for property doctrine. We can expect these topics to take on further significance in the coming decades thanks to climate change. For further explorations of these interesting topics, see J. Peter Byrne, The Cathedral Engulfed: Sea-Level Rise, Property Rights, and Time, 73 La. L. Rev. 69 (2012); Joseph D. Kearney & Thomas W. Merrill, Contested Shore: Property Rights in Reclaimed Land and the Battle for Streeterville, 107 Nw. U. L. Rev. 1057 (2013). For a contemporary account of the hurdles faced by affluent beachfront communities confronting beach erosion, see William D. Cohan & Vanessa Grigoriadis, From Coast to Toast, Vanity Fair (August 2013).

9. *Avulsions and easements.* Consider the following scenario: a public easement exists permitting beach access across private property. A hurricane alters the beach's boundaries and buries the public easement under water. Does the easement migrate to a nearby parcel so as to preserve public access? See Severance v. Patterson, 370 S.W.3d 705, 708 (Tex. 2012) ("[P]ublic easements may gradually change size and shape as the respective Gulf-front properties they burden imperceptibly change, but they do not 'roll' onto previously unencumbered private beachfront parcels or onto new portions of previously encumbered private beachfront parcels when avulsive events cause dramatic changes in the coastline."). For a critique of *Severance* as out of step with both prior Texas precedents and the approach taken by other jurisdictions, see Celeste Pagano, Where's the Beach? Coastal Access in the Age of Rising Tides, 42 Sw. L. Rev. 1 (2012).

5. The Problem of Exactions

As we saw in the last chapter (at pages 986, 1009), exactions are local government measures that require developers to provide goods and services or pay money (called impact fees) as a condition to getting project approval. For a good account, see William A. Fischel, Regulatory Takings: Law, Economics, and Politics 341-351 (1995). Professor Fischel says that exactions were once small potatoes. Developers were willing to pay for sidewalks, sewer connections, and so forth in exchange for building permits, because these public goods yielded private benefits to the developers' projects. When communities wanted improvements that benefited everybody in the area generally—improvements not so directly linked to satisfying service demands created by new development itself—they relied on property taxes and government grants to provide the wherewithal.

This situation changed, and eventually exactions became a common substitute means of funding public improvements. Fischel attributes the transformation to the dramatic expansion of land use regulation that began about 1970. Exactions are toothless without overlying regulations that limit development in the first place; for local communities, enacting regulations is like printing money, because the legal restrictions can be relaxed in exchange for goods, services, and fees. The politics of the strategy are pretty obvious, and finally exactions became so common and troublesome that the Supreme Court intervened, as traced in the three cases that follow. The first two cases deal with exaction of good and services, the third with exaction of fees.

Nollan v. California Coastal Commission

Supreme Court of the United States, 1987
483 U.S. 825

JUSTICE SCALIA delivered the opinion of the Court. . . .

The Nollans own a beachfront lot in Ventura County, California. A quarter-mile north of their property is Faria County Park, an oceanside public park with a public beach and recreation area. Another public beach area, known locally as "the Cove," lies 1,800 feet south of their lot. A concrete seawall approximately eight feet high separates the beach portion of the Nollans' property from the rest of the lot. The historic mean high tide line determines the lot's oceanside boundary.

The Nollans originally leased their property with an option to buy. The building on the lot was a small bungalow, totaling 504 square feet, which for a time they rented to summer vacationers. After years of rental use, however, the building had fallen into disrepair, and could no longer be rented out.

The Nollans' option to purchase was conditioned on their promise to demolish the bungalow and replace it. In order to do so, under Cal. Pub. Res. Code Ann. §§30106, 30212, and 30600 (West 1986), they were required to obtain a coastal development permit from the California Coastal Commission. On February 25, 1982, they submitted a permit application to the Commission in which they proposed to demolish the existing structure and replace it with a three-bedroom house in keeping with the rest of the neighborhood.

The Nollans were informed that their application had been placed on the administrative calendar, and that the Commission staff had recommended that the permit be granted subject to the condition that they allow the public an easement to pass across a portion of their property bounded by the mean high tide line on one side, and their seawall on the other side. This would make it easier for the public to get to Faria County Park and the Cove. The Nollans protested imposition of the condition, but the Commission overruled their objections and granted the permit subject to their recordation of a deed restriction granting the easement. . . .

[In June 1982, the Nollans filed a petition asking the Ventura County Superior Court to invalidate the access condition, arguing that it could not be imposed absent evidence that their proposed development would have an impact on public access to the beach. The court agreed and remanded to the Commission for a hearing on that issue. The Commission subsequently held a hearing and reaffirmed the condition. The Nollans again petitioned the superior court, arguing that imposition of the condition was a taking. When the court ruled in their favor on other grounds, the Commission took the case to the court of appeal, which reversed, holding among other things that imposition of the access condition was not a taking. The Nollans then appealed to the Supreme Court, raising only the takings question.]

Had California simply required the Nollans to make an easement across their beachfront available to the public on a permanent basis in order to increase public access to the beach, rather than conditioning their permit to rebuild their house on their agreeing to do so, we have no doubt there would have been a taking. To say that the appropriation of a public easement across a landowner's premises does not constitute the taking of a property interest but rather (as Justice Brennan contends) "a mere restriction on its use," is to use words in a manner that deprives them of all their ordinary meaning. Indeed, one of the principal uses of the eminent domain power is to assure that the government be able to require conveyance of just such interests, so long as it pays for them. . . . Perhaps because the point is so obvious, we have never been confronted with a controversy that required us to rule upon it, but our cases' analysis of the effect of other governmental action leads to the same conclusion. . . .

Given, then, that requiring uncompensated conveyance of the easement outright would violate the Fourteenth Amendment, the question becomes whether requiring it to be conveyed as a condition for issuing a land-use permit alters the outcome. We have long recognized that land-use regulation does not effect a taking if it "substantially advance[s] legitimate state interests" and does not "den[y] an owner economically viable use of his land," Agins v. Tiburon, 447 U.S. 255, 260 (1980). See also Penn Central Transportation Co. v. New York City, 438 U.S. 104, 127 (1978) ("[A] use restriction may constitute a 'taking' if not reasonably necessary to the effectuation of a substantial government purpose"). Our cases have not elaborated on the standards for determining what constitutes a "legitimate state interest" or what type of connection between the regulation and the state interest satisfies the requirement that the former "substantially advance" the latter. They have made clear, however, that a broad range of governmental purposes and regulations satisfies these requirements. See Agins v. Tiburon, supra, at 260-262 (scenic zoning); Penn Central Transportation Co. v. New York City, supra (landmark preservation); Euclid v. Ambler Realty Co., 272 U.S. 365 (1926) (residential zoning); Laitos & Westfall, Government Interference with Private Interests in Public Resources, 11 Harv. Envtl. L. Rev. 1, 66 (1987). The Commission argues that among these permissible purposes are protecting the public's ability to see the beach, assisting the public in overcoming the "psychological barrier" to using the beach created by a developed shorefront, and preventing congestion on the public beaches. We assume, without deciding, that this is so—in which case the Commission unquestionably would be able to deny

**The beach in front of the Nollans' house (wintertime);
in summer the beach is wider.**

The Nollans' house as built, first on the left

the Nollans their permit outright if their new house (alone, or by reason of the cumulative impact produced in conjunction with other construction) would substantially impede these purposes, unless the denial would interfere so drastically with the Nollans' use of their property as to constitute a taking. See *Penn Central.* The Commission argues that a permit condition that serves the same legitimate police-power purpose as a refusal to issue the permit should not be found to be a taking if the refusal to issue the permit would not constitute a taking. We agree. Thus, if the Commission attached to the permit some condition that would have protected the public's ability to see the beach notwithstanding construction of the new house—for example, a height limitation, a width restriction, or a ban on fences—so long as the Commission could have exercised its police power (as we have assumed it could) to forbid construction of the house altogether, imposition of the condition would also be constitutional. Moreover (and here we come closer to the facts of the present case), the condition would be constitutional even if it consisted of the requirement that the Nollans provide a viewing spot on their property for passersby with whose sighting of the ocean their new house would interfere. Although such a requirement, constituting a permanent grant of continuous access to the property, would have to be considered a taking if it were not attached to a development permit, the Commission's assumed power to forbid construction of the house in order to protect the public's view of the beach must surely include the power to condition construction upon some concession by the owner, even a concession of property rights, that serves the same end. If a prohibition designed to accomplish that purpose would be a legitimate exercise of the police power rather than a taking, it would be strange to conclude that providing the owner an alternative to that prohibition which accomplishes the same purpose is not.

The evident constitutional propriety disappears, however, if the condition substituted for the prohibition utterly fails to further the end advanced as the justification for the prohibition. . . . [H]ere, the lack of nexus between the condition and the original purpose of the building restriction converts that purpose to something other than what it was. The purpose then becomes, quite simply, the obtaining of an easement to serve some valid governmental purpose, but without payment of compensation. Whatever may be the outer limits of "legitimate state interests" in the takings and land-use context, this is not one of them. In short, unless the permit condition serves the same governmental purpose as the development ban, the building restriction is not a valid regulation of land use but "an out-and-out plan of extortion." J.E.D. Associates, Inc. v. Atkinson, 432 A.2d 12, 14-15 (N.H. 1981). . . . The Commission claims that it concedes as much, and that we may sustain the condition at issue here by finding that it is reasonably related to the public need or burden that the Nollans' new house creates or to which it contributes. We can accept, for purposes of discussion, the Commission's proposed test as to how close a "fit" between the condition and the burden is required, because we find that this case does not meet even the most untailored standards. The Commission's principal contention to the contrary essentially turns on a play on the word "access." The Nollans' new house, the Commission found, will interfere with "visual access" to the beach. That in turn (along with other shorefront development) will interfere with the desire of people who drive past the Nollans' house to use the beach, thus creating a "psychological barrier" to "access." The Nollans' new house will also, by a process not altogether clear from the Commission's opinion but presumably potent enough to more than offset the effects of the psychological barrier, increase the use of the public beaches, thus creating the need for more "access." These burdens on "access" would be alleviated by a requirement that the Nollans provide "lateral access" to the beach.

Rewriting the argument to eliminate the play on words makes clear that there is nothing to it. It is quite impossible to understand how a requirement that people already on the public beaches be able to walk across the Nollans' property reduces any obstacles to viewing the beach created by the new house. It is also impossible to understand how it lowers any "psychological barrier" to using the public beaches, or how it helps to remedy any additional congestion on them caused by construction of the Nollans' new house. We therefore find that the Commission's imposition of the permit condition cannot be treated as an exercise of its land-use power for any of these purposes. Our conclusion on this point is consistent with the approach taken by every other court that has considered the question, with the exception of the California state courts. . . .

. . . We view the Fifth Amendment's Property Clause to be more than a pleading requirement, and compliance with it to be more than an exercise in cleverness and imagination. As indicated earlier, our cases describe the condition for abridgment of property rights through the police power as a "*substantial* advanc[ing]" of a legitimate state interest. We are inclined to be particularly careful about the adjective where the actual conveyance of property is made a condition to the lifting of a land-use restriction, since in that context there is heightened risk that the purpose is avoidance of the compensation requirement, rather than the stated police-power objective.

We are left, then, with the Commission's justification for the access requirement unrelated to land-use regulation:

> Finally, the Commission notes that there are several existing provisions of pass and repass lateral access benefits already given by past Faria Beach Tract applicants as a result of prior coastal permit decisions. The access required as a condition of this permit is part of a comprehensive program to provide continuous public access along Faria Beach as the lots undergo development or redevelopment.

That is simply an expression of the Commission's belief that the public interest will be served by a continuous strip of publicly accessible beach along the coast. The Commission may well be right that it is a good idea, but that does not establish that the Nollans (and other coastal residents) alone can be compelled to contribute to its realization. Rather, California is free to advance its "comprehensive program," if it wishes, by using its power of eminent domain for this "public purpose," see U.S. Const., Amdt. 5; but if it wants an easement across the Nollans' property, it must pay for it.

Reversed.

[A dissenting opinion by Justice Brennan, joined by Justices Marshall, Blackmun, and Stevens, is omitted.]

Dolan v. City of Tigard
Supreme Court of the United States, 1994
512 U.S. 374

CHIEF JUSTICE REHNQUIST delivered the opinion of the Court.

Petitioner challenges the decision of the Oregon Supreme Court which held that the city of Tigard could condition the approval of her building permit on the dedication of a portion of her property for flood control and traffic improvements. We granted certiorari to resolve a question left open by our decision in Nollan v. California Coastal Commn., 483 U.S. 825 (1987), of what is the required degree of connection between the exactions imposed by the city and the projected impacts of the proposed development.

[Pursuant to a comprehensive land use management program adopted by Oregon in 1973, the city of Tigard, population 30,000, developed a Community Development Code (CDC) that (1) required property owners in the area zoned as Central Business District to comply with a 15 percent open space and landscaping requirement that limited total site coverage, including structures and paved parking, to 85 percent of the parcel; (2) required that new development dedicate land for pedestrian and bicycle pathways; and (3) required, in accord with a Master Drainage Plan, various improvements to the Fanno Creek Basin. Petitioner Florence Dolan owned a plumbing and electric supply store located on Main Street in the Central Business District of the city. The store occupied about 9,700 square feet on the eastern side of a 1.67-acre parcel, which included a gravel parking lot. Fanno Creek flows through the southwestern corner of the lot and along its western boundary, and its year-round flow of the creek rendered the area within the creek's 100-year floodplain virtually unusable for commercial development. The city's comprehensive plan included the Fanno Creek floodplain as part of the city's greenway system.]

Petitioner applied to the city for a permit to redevelop the site. Her proposed plans called for nearly doubling the size of the store to 17,600 square feet, and paving a 39-space parking lot. . . . [T]he Commission required that petitioner dedicate the portion of her property lying within the 100-year floodplain for improvement of a storm drainage system along Fanno Creek and that she dedicate an additional 15-foot strip of land adjacent to the floodplain as a pedestrian/bicycle pathway. The dedication required by that condition encompasses approximately 7,000 square feet, or roughly 10% of the property. In accordance with city practice, petitioner could rely on the dedicated property to meet the 15% open space and landscaping requirement mandated by the city's zoning scheme. The city would bear the cost of maintaining a landscaped buffer between the dedicated area and the new store. . . .

The Commission made a series of findings concerning the relationship between the dedicated conditions and the projected impacts of petitioner's project. [The Commission found that Dolan's customers would utilize the pedestrian/bicycle pathway, and that the path's availability would reduce traffic demand on nearby streets. It also found that paving large portions of the parcel would increase stormwater flow into an already strained creek and drainage basin. Petitioner's appeal to the Land Use Board of Appeals was unsuccessful, as was a subsequent appeal to the Oregon Court of Appeals, which] rejected petitioner's contention that in Nollan v. California Coastal Commn., 483 U.S. 825 (1987), we had abandoned the "reasonable relationship" test in favor of a stricter "essential nexus" test. The Oregon Supreme Court affirmed. The court also disagreed with petitioner's contention that the *Nollan* Court abandoned the "reasonably related" test. Instead, the court read *Nollan* to mean that an "exaction is reasonably related to an impact if the exaction serves the same purpose that a denial of the permit would serve." The court decided that both the pedestrian/ bicycle pathway condition and the storm drainage dedication had an essential nexus to the development of the proposed site. . . .

. . . Without question, had the city simply required petitioner to dedicate a strip of land along Fanno Creek for public use, rather than conditioning the grant of her permit to redevelop her property on such a dedication, a taking would have occurred. *Nollan*, supra, at 831. Such public access would deprive petitioner of the right to exclude others, "one of the most essential sticks in the bundle of rights that are commonly characterized as property." Kaiser Aetna v. United States, 444 U.S. 164, 176 (1979).

On the other side of the ledger, the authority of state and local governments to engage in land use planning has been sustained against constitutional challenge as long ago as our decision in Euclid v. Ambler Realty Co., 272 U.S. 365 (1926). "Government hardly could go on if to some extent values incident to property could not be diminished without paying for every such change in the general law." Pennsylvania Coal Co. v. Mahon, 260 U.S. 393, 413 (1922). A land use regulation does not effect a taking if it substantially advance[s] legitimate state interests and does not den[y] an owner economically viable use of his land. Agins v. Tiburon, 447 U.S. 255, 260 (1980). . . . Petitioner contends that the city has forced her to choose between the building permit and her right under the Fifth Amendment to just compensation for the public easements. Petitioner does not quarrel with the city's authority to exact some forms of dedication as a condition for the grant of a building permit, but challenges the showing made by the city to justify these exactions. She argues that the city has identified no special benefits conferred on her, and has not identified any special quantifiable burdens created by her new store that would justify the particular dedications required from her which are not required from the public at large.

In evaluating petitioner's claim, we must first determine whether the essential nexus exists between the legitimate state interest and the permit condition exacted by the city. *Nollan*, 483 U.S. at 837. If we find that a nexus exists, we must then decide the required degree of connection between the exactions and the projected impact of the proposed development. We were not required to reach this question in *Nollan*, because we concluded that the connection did not meet even the loosest standard. Id. at 838. Here, however, we must decide this question.

We addressed the essential nexus question in *Nollan*. . . . How enhancing the public's ability to traverse to and along the shorefront [in that case] served the same governmental purpose of visual access to the ocean from the roadway was beyond our ability to countenance. The absence of a nexus left the Coastal Commission in the position of simply trying to obtain an easement through gimmickry, which converted a valid regulation of land use into an out-and-out plan of extortion. . . .

No such gimmicks are associated with the permit conditions imposed by the city in this case. Undoubtedly, the prevention of flooding along Fanno Creek and the reduction of traffic congestion in the Central Business District qualify as the type of legitimate public purposes we have upheld. It seems equally obvious that a nexus exists between preventing flooding along Fanno Creek and limiting development within the creek's 100-year floodplain. Petitioner proposes to double the size of her retail store and to pave her now-gravel parking lot, thereby expanding the impervious surface on the property and increasing the amount of stormwater run-off into Fanno Creek.

The same may be said for the city's attempt to reduce traffic congestion by providing for alternative means of transportation. . . . The second part of our analysis requires us to determine whether the degree of the exactions demanded by the city's permit conditions bear the required relationship to the projected impact of petitioner's proposed development. . . . The city required that petitioner dedicate to the city as Greenway all portions of the site that fall within the existing 100-year floodplain [of Fanno Creek] . . . and all property 15 feet above [the floodplain] boundary." In addition, the city demanded that the retail store be designed so as not to intrude into the greenway area. The city relies on the Commission's rather tentative findings that increased stormwater flow from petitioner's property can only add to the public need to manage the [floodplain] for drainage purposes to support its conclusion that the requirement of dedication of the floodplain area on the site is related to the applicant's plan to intensify development on the site.

The city made the following specific findings relevant to the pedestrian/ bicycle pathway:

> In addition, the proposed expanded use of this site is anticipated to generate additional vehicular traffic thereby increasing congestion on nearby collector and arterial streets. Creation of a convenient, safe pedestrian/bicycle pathway system as an alternative means of transportation could offset some of the traffic demand on these nearby streets and lessen the increase in traffic congestion.

The question for us is whether these findings are constitutionally sufficient to justify the conditions imposed by the city on petitioner's building permit. . . . [The Court observed that state courts had developed a number of tests regarding the necessary connection between a required dedication and the proposed development, some of them tolerating just a loose connection, others demanding a very strict connection, and still others "a reasonable relationship" between the required dedication and the impact of the proposed development.]

. . . We think a term such as "rough proportionality" best encapsulates what we hold to be the requirement of the Fifth Amendment. No precise mathematical calculation is required, but the city must make some sort of individualized determination that the required dedication is related both in nature and extent to the impact of the proposed development.

. . . We turn now to analysis of whether the findings relied upon by the city here, first with respect to the floodplain easement, and second with respect to the pedestrian/bicycle path, satisfied these requirements.

It is axiomatic that increasing the amount of impervious surface will increase the quantity and rate of storm-water flow from petitioner's property. Therefore, keeping the floodplain open and free from development would likely confine the pressures on Fanno Creek created by petitioner's development. In fact, because petitioner's property lies within the Central Business District, the Community Development Code already required that petitioner leave 15% of it as open space and the undeveloped floodplain would have nearly satisfied that requirement. But the city demanded more—it not only wanted petitioner not to build in the floodplain, but it also wanted petitioner's property along Fanno Creek for its Greenway system. The city has never said why a public greenway, as opposed to a private one, was required in the interest of flood control.

The difference to petitioner, of course, is the loss of her ability to exclude others. As we have noted, this right to exclude others is "one of the most essential sticks in the bundle of rights that are commonly characterized as property." *Kaiser Aetna*, 444 U.S. at 176. It is difficult to see why recreational visitors trampling along petitioner's floodplain easement are sufficiently related to the city's legitimate interest in reducing flooding problems along Fanno Creek, and the city has not attempted to make any individualized determination to support this part of its request.

The city contends that the recreational easement along the Greenway is only ancillary to the city's chief purpose in controlling flood hazards. It further asserts that unlike the residential property at issue in *Nollan*, petitioner's property is commercial in character and therefore, her right to exclude others is compromised. . . . The city maintains that "[t]here is nothing to suggest that preventing [petitioner] from prohibiting [the easements] will unreasonably impair the value of [her] property as a [retail store]." PruneYard Shopping Center v. Robins, 447 U.S. 74, 83 (1980).

Admittedly, petitioner wants to build a bigger store to attract members of the public to her property. She also wants, however, to be able to control the time and manner in which they enter. The . . . city wants to impose a permanent recreational easement upon petitioner's property that borders Fanno Creek. Petitioner would lose all rights to regulate the time in which the public entered onto the Greenway, regardless of any interference it might pose with her retail store. Her right to exclude would not be regulated, it would be eviscerated.

If petitioner's proposed development had somehow encroached on existing greenway space in the city, it would have been reasonable to require petitioner to provide some alternative greenway space for the public either on her property or elsewhere. . . . But that is not the case here. We conclude that the findings upon which the city relies do not show the required reasonable relationship between the floodplain easement and the petitioner's proposed new building.

With respect to the pedestrian/bicycle pathway, we have no doubt that the city was correct in finding that the larger retail sales facility proposed by petitioner will increase traffic on the streets of the Central Business District. The city estimates that the proposed development would generate roughly 435 additional trips per day. Dedications for streets, sidewalks, and other public ways are generally reasonable exactions to avoid excessive congestion from a proposed property use. But on the record before us, the city has not met its burden of demonstrating that the additional number of vehicle and bicycle trips generated by the petitioner's development reasonably relate to the city's requirement for a dedication of the pedestrian/bicycle pathway easement. The city simply found that the creation of the pathway "could offset some of the traffic demand . . . and lessen the increase in traffic congestion."

As Justice Peterson of the Supreme Court of Oregon explained in his dissenting opinion, however, [t]he findings of fact that the bicycle pathway system *could* offset some of the traffic demand is a far cry from a finding that the bicycle pathway system *will*, or is *likely to*, offset some of the traffic demand. No precise mathematical calculation is required, but the city must make some effort to quantify its findings in support of the dedication for the pedestrian/bicycle pathway beyond the conclusory statement that it could offset some of the traffic demand generated.

Cities have long engaged in the commendable task of land use planning, made necessary by increasing urbanization particularly in metropolitan areas such as Portland. The city's goals of reducing flooding hazards and traffic congestion, and providing for public greenways, are laudable, but there are outer limits to how this may be done. A strong public desire to improve the public condition [will not] warrant achieving the desire by a shorter cut than the constitutional way of paying for the change. *Pennsylvania Coal*, 260 U.S. at 416.

The judgment of the Supreme Court of Oregon is reversed, and the case is remanded for further proceedings consistent with this opinion.

[The dissenting opinion by Justice Stevens, joined by Justices Blackmun and Ginsburg, is omitted.]

NOTES AND QUESTIONS

1. *The* Nollan *and* Dolan *cases.* In *Nollan*, the Court held that there must be some logical connection—some "nexus"—between an exaction and the regulation excepted in exchange for it. Under this rule, says Fischel, "a community could give an exception to a leash law to dog owners who contributed to a clean-up

fund, but it could not give an exception to dog owners who promised to paint their houses white." William A. Fischel, Regulatory Takings: Law, Economics, and Politics 58 (1995). Then, in *Dolan*, the Court went further and held that even when a nexus exists, there must also be some "rough proportionality" between the thing exacted and the development permitted in exchange.

Fischel argues that the *Dolan* rule should have replaced the *Nollan* rule, rather than just supplement it, because *Nollan* forecloses desirable deals between developers and local communities, and also because it encourages counterproductive lawsuits. (You will see this theme developed by Justice Kagan in the Supreme Court's most recent exactions case, to which we will turn momentarily.)

2. Is *Dolan* limited to exactions, or does it instead apply to any sort of land use regulation challenged as a taking? See City of Monterey v. Del Monte Dunes, 526 U.S. 687, 702-703 (1999), where

> the Court expressly disavowed any expansion of *Dolan*'s rough proportionality test beyond the exactions context. This limitation is understandable; wholesale application of *Dolan* to regulatory takings jurisprudence would abruptly dismantle nearly seventy-five years of zoning law. Yet *Dolan*'s proportionality rule, thus limited, represents a logical anomaly. Land use bargains are constrained by proportionality requirements, while land use decisions made by local governments are not.
>
> The result is a conceptual disconnect. . . . The current state of land use jurisprudence, which couples relatively open-ended regulatory power with tight restrictions on regulatory bargains, represents the worst of both worlds. It leaves landowners exposed to excessive land use regulation while constricting their ability to bargain for regulatory adjustments. Without meaningful constraints on the underlying land use regulations, limits on land use bargains cannot provide landowners with protection against overregulation. Instead, these bargaining limits add insult to injury by preventing mutually beneficial land use deals and generating vast inefficiencies that harm landowners and communities. [Lee Anne Fennell, Hard Bargains and Real Steals: Land Use Exactions Revisited, 86 Iowa L. Rev. 1, 4-5 (2000).]

For criticism of the Supreme Court's bifurcated approach to takings problems—with heightened scrutiny applied to exactions, but deference to most other regulatory acts facing takings challenges—see Mark Fenster, Takings Formalism and Regulatory Formulas: Exactions and the Consequences of Clarity, 96 Cal. L. Rev. 609 (2004).

3. *Do* Nollan *and* Dolan *really matter?* Any number of commentators have suggested that nexus/rough proportionality review significantly limits the ability of localities to impose conditions on development. See David A. Dana, Land Use Regulation in an Age of Heightened Scrutiny, 75 N.C. L. Rev. 1243, 1286-1287 (1997) (canvassing the literature). Professor Dana himself is not so sure. He develops a game-theoretic model "challenging the predictions that nexus/rough proportionality review will lead regulators to reduce significantly their development conditions demands." Id. at 1288.

A number of states have managed to avoid application of the *Nollan-Dolan* exaction rules to local land use regulators by finding that the condition involved in a particular case is actually not an "exaction." See, e.g., Smith v. Town of Mendon, 822 N.E.2d 1214 (N.Y. 2004). In some states, however, the courts fess up. See, e.g., Flower Mound, Texas v. Stafford, 135 S.W.3d 620 (Tex. 2004).

4. *Impact fees.* Recall that the introduction to this section on exactions pointed out that what was exacted might be goods and services on the one hand, or money on the other, in the form of impact fees. Do *Nollan* and *Dolan* apply to them? Some state courts said they did, and others said they did not. Now the Supreme Court has spoken, in the case that follows.

Koontz v. St. Johns River Water Management District

Supreme Court of the United States, 2013
133 S. Ct. 2586

JUSTICE ALITO delivered the opinion of the Court.

Our decisions in Nollan v. California Coastal Comm'n, 483 U.S. 825 (1987), and Dolan v. City of Tigard, 512 U.S. 374 (1994), provide important protection against the misuse of the power of land-use regulation. In those cases, we held that a unit of government may not condition the approval of a land-use permit on the owner's relinquishment of a portion of his property unless there is a "nexus" and "rough proportionality" between the government's demand and the effects of the proposed land use. In this case, the St. Johns River Water Management District (District) believes that it circumvented *Nollan* and *Dolan* because of the way in which it structured its handling of a permit application submitted by Coy Koontz, Sr. The District did not approve his application on the condition that he surrender an interest in his land. Instead, the District, after suggesting that he could obtain approval by signing over such an interest, denied his application because he refused to yield. The Florida Supreme Court blessed this maneuver and thus effectively interred those important decisions. Because we conclude that *Nollan* and *Dolan* cannot be evaded in this way, the Florida Supreme Court's decision must be reversed.

I.

In 1972, petitioner purchased an undeveloped 14.9-acre tract of land on the south side of Florida State Road 50, a divided four-lane highway east of Orlando. The property is located less than 1,000 feet from that road's intersection with Florida State Road 408, a tolled expressway that is one of Orlando's major thoroughfares.

A drainage ditch runs along the property's western edge, and high-voltage power lines bisect it into northern and southern sections. The combined effect of the ditch, a 100-foot wide area kept clear for the power lines, the highways, and other construction on nearby parcels is to isolate the northern section of petitioner's property from any other undeveloped land. Although largely classified as wetlands by the State, the northern section drains well; the most significant standing water forms in ruts in an unpaved road used to access the power lines. The natural topography of the property's southern section is somewhat more diverse, with a small creek, forested uplands, and wetlands that sometimes have water as much as a foot deep. A wildlife survey found evidence of animals that often frequent developed areas: raccoons, rabbits, several species of bird, and a turtle. The record also indicates that the land may be a suitable habitat for opossums.

The same year that petitioner purchased his property, Florida enacted the Water Resources Act, which divided the State into five water management districts and authorized each district to regulate "construction that connects to, draws water from, drains water into, or is placed in or across the waters in the state." . . . Under the Act, a landowner wishing to undertake such construction must obtain from the relevant district a Management and Storage of Surface Water (MSSW) permit, which may impose "such reasonable conditions" on the permit as are "necessary to assure" that construction will "not be harmful to the water resources of the district." . . .

In 1984, in an effort to protect the State's rapidly diminishing wetlands, the Florida Legislature passed the Warren S. Henderson Wetlands Protection Act, which made it illegal for anyone to "dredge or fill in, on, or over surface waters" without a Wetlands Resource Management (WRM) permit. . . . Under the Henderson Act, permit applicants are required to provide "reasonable assurance" that proposed construction on wetlands is "not contrary to the public interest," as defined by an enumerated list of criteria. See Fla. Stat. §373.414(1). Consistent with the Henderson Act, the St. Johns River Water Management District, the district with jurisdiction over petitioner's land, requires that permit applicants wishing to build on wetlands offset the resulting environmental damage by creating, enhancing, or preserving wetlands elsewhere.

Petitioner decided to develop the 3.7-acre northern section of his property, and in 1994 he applied to the District for MSSW and WRM permits. Under his proposal, petitioner would have raised the elevation of the northernmost section of his land to make it suitable for a building, graded the land from the southern edge of the building site down to the elevation of the high-voltage electrical lines, and installed a dry-bed pond for retaining and gradually releasing stormwater runoff from the building and its parking lot. To mitigate the environmental effects of his proposal, petitioner offered to foreclose any possible future development of the approximately 11-acre southern section of his land by deeding to the District a conservation easement on that portion of his property.

The District considered the 11-acre conservation easement to be inadequate, and it informed petitioner that it would approve construction only if he agreed to one of two concessions. First, the District proposed that petitioner reduce the size of his development to 1 acre and deed to the District a conservation easement on the remaining 13.9 acres. To reduce the development area, the District suggested that petitioner could eliminate the dry-bed pond from his proposal and instead install a more costly subsurface stormwater management system beneath the building site. The District also suggested that petitioner install retaining walls rather than gradually sloping the land from the building site down to the elevation of the rest of his property to the south.

In the alternative, the District told petitioner that he could proceed with the development as proposed, building on 3.7 acres and deeding a conservation easement to the government on the remainder of the property, if he also agreed to hire contractors to make improvements to District-owned land several miles away. Specifically, petitioner could pay to replace culverts on one parcel or fill in ditches on another. Either of those projects would have enhanced approximately 50 acres of District-owned wetlands. When the District asks permit applicants to fund offsite mitigation work, its policy is never to require any particular offsite project, and it did not do so here. Instead, the District said that it "would also favorably consider" alternatives to its suggested offsite mitigation projects if petitioner proposed something "equivalent."

Believing the District's demands for mitigation to be excessive in light of the environmental effects that his building proposal would have caused, petitioner filed suit in state court. Among other claims, he argued that he was entitled to relief under Fla. Stat. §373.617(2), which allows owners to recover "monetary damages" if a state agency's action is "an unreasonable exercise of the state's police power constituting a taking without just compensation."

. . . After considering testimony from several experts who examined petitioner's property, the trial court found that the property's northern section had already been "seriously degraded" by extensive construction on the surrounding parcels. In light of this finding and petitioner's offer to dedicate nearly three-quarters of his land to the District, the trial court concluded that any further mitigation in the form of payment for offsite improvements to District property lacked both a nexus and rough proportionality to the environmental impact of the proposed construction. It accordingly held the District's actions unlawful under our decisions in *Nollan* and *Dolan*.

The [Florida] Supreme Court reversed, 77 So. 3d 1220 (Fla. 2011). A majority of that court distinguished *Nollan* and *Dolan* on two grounds. First, the majority thought it significant that in this case, unlike *Nollan* or *Dolan*, the District did not approve petitioner's application on the condition that he accede to the District's demands; instead, the District denied his application because he refused to make concessions. . . . Second, the majority drew a distinction between a demand for an interest in real property (what happened in *Nollan* and *Dolan*) and a demand for money. . . .

Recognizing that the majority opinion rested on a question of federal constitutional law on which the lower courts are divided, we granted the petition for a writ of certiorari, and now reverse.

II.

We have said in a variety of contexts that "the government may not deny a benefit to a person because he exercises a constitutional right." Regan v. Taxation With Representation of Wash., 461 U.S. 540, 545 (1983). . . . In Perry v. Sindermann, 408 U.S. 593 (1972), for example, we held that a public college would violate a professor's freedom of speech if it declined to renew his contract because he was an outspoken critic of the college's administration. And in Memorial Hospital v. Maricopa County, 415 U.S. 250 (1974), we concluded that a county impermissibly burdened the right to travel by extending healthcare benefits only to those indigent sick who had been residents of the county for at least one year. Those cases reflect an overarching principle, known as the unconstitutional conditions doctrine, that vindicates the Constitution's enumerated rights by preventing the government from coercing people into giving them up.

Nollan and *Dolan* "involve a special application" of this doctrine that protects the Fifth Amendment right to just compensation for property the government takes when owners apply for land-use permits. . . . Our decisions in those cases reflect two realities of the permitting process. The first is that land-use permit applicants are especially vulnerable to the type of coercion that the unconstitutional conditions doctrine prohibits because the government often has broad discretion to deny a permit that is worth far more than property it would like to take. By conditioning a building permit on the owner's deeding over a public right-of-way, for example, the government can pressure an owner into voluntarily giving up property for which the Fifth Amendment would otherwise require just compensation. . . .

A second reality of the permitting process is that many proposed land uses threaten to impose costs on the public that dedications of property can offset. Where a building proposal would substantially increase traffic congestion, for example, officials might condition permit approval on the owner's agreement to deed over the land needed to widen a public road. Respondent argues that a similar rationale justifies the exaction at issue here: petitioner's proposed construction project, it submits, would destroy wetlands on his property, and in order to compensate for this loss, respondent demands that he enhance wetlands elsewhere. Insisting that landowners internalize the negative externalities of their conduct is a hallmark of responsible land-use policy, and we have long sustained such regulations against constitutional attack. See Village of Euclid v. Ambler Realty Co., 272 U.S. 365 (1926).

Nollan and *Dolan* accommodate both realities by allowing the government to condition approval of a permit on the dedication of property to the public so long as there is a "nexus" and "rough proportionality" between the property that the government demands and the social costs of the applicant's proposal. . . . Our precedents thus enable permitting authorities to insist that applicants bear the full costs of their proposals while still forbidding the government from engaging in "out-and-out . . . extortion" that would thwart the Fifth Amendment right to just compensation. . . . Under *Nollan* and *Dolan* the government may choose whether and how a permit applicant is required to mitigate the impacts of a proposed development, but it may not leverage its legitimate interest in mitigation to pursue governmental ends that lack an essential nexus and rough proportionality to those impacts.

The principles that undergird our decisions in *Nollan* and *Dolan* do not change depending on whether the government approves a permit on the condition that the applicant turn over property or denies a permit because the applicant refuses to do so. . . .

A contrary rule would be especially untenable in this case because it would enable the government to evade the limitations of *Nollan* and *Dolan* simply by phrasing its demands for property as conditions precedent to permit approval. Under the Florida Supreme Court's approach, a government order stating that a permit is "approved if" the owner turns over property would be subject to *Nollan* and *Dolan*, but an identical order that uses the words "denied until" would not. Our unconstitutional conditions cases have long refused to attach significance to the distinction between conditions precedent and conditions subsequent. . . . To do so here would effectively render *Nollan* and *Dolan* a dead letter.

The Florida Supreme Court puzzled over how the government's demand for property can violate the Takings Clause even though "no property of any kind was ever taken," 77 So. 3d at 1225, but the unconstitutional conditions doctrine provides a ready answer. Extortionate demands for property in the land-use permitting context run afoul of the Takings Clause not because they take property but because they impermissibly burden the right not to have property taken without just compensation. As in other unconstitutional conditions cases in which someone refuses to cede a constitutional right in the face of coercive pressure, the impermissible denial of a governmental benefit is a constitutionally cognizable injury.

Nor does it make a difference, as respondent suggests, that the government might have been able to deny petitioner's application outright without giving him the option of securing a permit by agreeing to spend money to improve public lands. See Penn Central Transp. Co. v. New York City, 438 U.S. 104 (1978). Virtually all of our unconstitutional conditions cases involve a gratuitous governmental benefit of some kind. . . . Yet we have repeatedly rejected the argument that if the government need not confer a benefit at all, it can withhold the benefit because someone refuses to give up constitutional rights. . . . Even if respondent would have been entirely within its rights in denying the permit for some other reason, that greater authority does not imply a lesser power to condition permit approval on petitioner's forfeiture of his constitutional rights. See *Nollan*, 483 U.S. at 836-837 (explaining that "[t]he evident constitutional propriety" of prohibiting a land use "disappears . . . if the condition substituted for the prohibition utterly fails to further the end advanced as the justification for the prohibition").

That is not to say, however, that there is no relevant difference between a consummated taking and the denial of a permit based on an unconstitutionally extortionate demand. Where the permit is denied and the condition is never imposed, nothing has been taken. While the unconstitutional conditions doctrine recognizes that this burdens a constitutional right, the Fifth Amendment mandates a particular remedy—just compensation—only for takings. In cases where there is an excessive demand but no taking, whether money damages are available is not a question of federal constitutional law but of the cause of action—whether state or federal—on which the landowner relies. Because petitioner brought his claim pursuant to a state law cause of action, the Court has no occasion to discuss what remedies might be available for a *Nollan/Dolan* unconstitutional conditions violation either here or in other cases.

[R]espondent argues that we need not decide whether its demand for off-site improvements satisfied *Nollan* and *Dolan* because it gave petitioner another avenue for obtaining permit approval. Specifically, respondent said that it would have approved a revised permit application that reduced the footprint of petitioner's proposed construction site from 3.7 acres to 1 acre and placed a conservation easement on the remaining 13.9 acres of petitioner's land. Respondent argues that regardless of whether its demands for offsite mitigation satisfied *Nollan* and *Dolan*, we must separately consider each of petitioner's options, one of which did not require any of the offsite work the trial court found objectionable.

Respondent's argument is flawed because the option to which it points—developing only 1 acre of the site and granting a conservation easement on the rest—involves the same issue as the option to build on 3.7 acres and perform offsite mitigation. We agree with respondent that, so long as a permitting authority offers the landowner at least one alternative that would satisfy *Nollan* and *Dolan*, the landowner has not been subjected to an unconstitutional condition. But respondent's suggestion that we should treat its offer to let petitioner build on 1 acre as an alternative to offsite mitigation misapprehends the governmental benefit that petitioner was denied. Petitioner sought to develop 3.7 acres, but respondent in effect told petitioner that it would not allow him to build on 2.7 of those acres unless he agreed to spend money improving public lands. Petitioner claims that he was wrongfully denied a permit to build on those 2.7 acres. For that reason, respondent's offer to approve a less ambitious building project does not obviate the need to determine whether the demand for offsite mitigation satisfied *Nollan* and *Dolan*.

III.

We turn to the Florida Supreme Court's alternative holding that petitioner's claim fails because respondent asked him to spend money rather than give up an easement on his land. A predicate for any unconstitutional conditions claim is that the government could not have constitutionally ordered the person asserting the claim to do what it attempted to pressure that person into doing. . . . For that reason, we began our analysis in both *Nollan* and *Dolan* by observing that if the government had directly seized the easements it sought to obtain through the permitting process, it would have committed a per se taking. See *Dolan*, 512 U.S. at 384; *Nollan*, 483 U.S. at 831. The Florida Supreme Court held that petitioner's claim fails at this first step because the subject of the exaction at issue here was money rather than a more tangible interest in real property. 77 So. 3d, at 1230. Respondent and the dissent take the same position, citing the concurring and dissenting opinions in Eastern Enterprises v. Apfel, 524 U.S. 498 (1998), for the proposition that an obligation to spend money can never provide the basis for a takings claim.

[I]f we accepted this argument it would be very easy for land-use permitting officials to evade the limitations of *Nollan* and *Dolan*. Because the government need only provide a permit applicant with one alternative that satisfies the nexus and rough proportionality standards, a permitting authority wishing to exact an easement could simply give the owner a choice of either surrendering an easement or making a payment equal to the easement's value. Such so-called "in lieu of" fees are utterly commonplace, Rosenberg, The Changing Culture of American Land Use Regulation: Paying for Growth with Impact Fees, 59 S.M.U. L. Rev. 177, 202-203 (2006), and they are functionally equivalent to other types of land use exactions. For that reason and those that follow, we reject respondent's argument and hold that so-called "monetary exactions" must satisfy the nexus and rough proportionality requirements of *Nollan* and *Dolan*.

In *Eastern Enterprises*, the United States retroactively imposed on a former mining company an obligation to pay for the medical benefits of retired miners and their families. A four-Justice plurality concluded that the statute's imposition of retroactive financial liability was so arbitrary that it violated the Takings Clause. 524 U.S. at 529-537. Although Justice Kennedy concurred in the result on due process grounds, he joined four other Justices in dissent in arguing that the Takings Clause does not apply to government-imposed financial obligations that "d[o] not operate upon or alter an identified property interest." Id. at 540 (opinion concurring in judgment and dissenting in part); see id. at 554-556 (Breyer, J., dissenting) ("The 'private property' upon which the [Takings] Clause traditionally has focused is a specific interest in physical or intellectual property."). Relying on the concurrence and dissent in *Eastern Enterprises*, respondent argues that a requirement that petitioner spend money improving public lands could not give rise to a taking.

Respondent's argument rests on a mistaken premise. Unlike the financial obligation in *Eastern Enterprises*, the demand for money at issue here did "operate upon . . . an identified property interest" by directing the owner of a particular piece of property to make a monetary payment. Id. at 540 (opinion of Kennedy, J.). In this case, unlike *Eastern Enterprises*, the monetary obligation burdened petitioner's ownership of a specific parcel of land. In that sense, this case bears resemblance to our cases holding that the government must pay just compensation when it takes a lien—a right to receive money that is secured by a particular piece of property. . . . The fulcrum this case turns on is the direct link between the government's demand and a specific parcel of real property. Because of that direct link, this case implicates the central concern of *Nollan* and *Dolan*: the risk that the government may use its substantial power and discretion in land-use permitting to pursue governmental ends that lack an essential nexus and rough proportionality to the effects of the proposed new use of the specific property at issue, thereby diminishing without justification the value of the property.

In this case, moreover, petitioner does not ask us to hold that the government can commit a regulatory taking by directing someone to spend money. As a result, we need not apply *Penn Central*'s "essentially ad hoc, factual inquir[y]," 438 U.S. at 124, at all, much less extend that "already difficult and uncertain rule" to the "vast category of cases" in which someone believes that a regulation is too costly. *Eastern Enterprises*, 524 U.S. at 542 (opinion of Kennedy, J.). Instead, petitioner's claim rests on the more limited proposition that when the government commands the relinquishment of funds linked to a specific, identifiable property interest such as a bank account or parcel of real property, a "per se [takings] approach" is the proper mode of analysis under the Court's precedent. Brown v. Legal Foundation of Wash., 538 U.S. 216, 235 (2003). . . .

Respondent and the dissent argue that if monetary exactions are made subject to scrutiny under *Nollan* and *Dolan,* then there will be no principled way of distinguishing impermissible land-use exactions from property taxes. We think they exaggerate both the extent to which that problem is unique to the land-use permitting context and the practical difficulty of distinguishing between the power to tax and the power to take by eminent domain.

It is beyond dispute that "[t]axes and user fees . . . are not 'takings.'" Id. at 243 n.2 (Scalia, J., dissenting). We said as much in County of Mobile v. Kimball, 102 U.S. 691, 703 (1881), and our cases have been clear on that point ever since. . . . This case therefore does not affect the ability of governments to impose property taxes, user fees, and similar laws and regulations that may impose financial burdens on property owners.

At the same time, we have repeatedly found takings where the government, by confiscating financial obligations, achieved a result that could have been obtained by imposing a tax. Most recently, in *Brown,* we were unanimous in concluding that a State Supreme Court's seizure of the interest on client funds held in escrow was a taking despite the unquestionable constitutional propriety of a tax that would have raised exactly the same revenue. Our holding in *Brown* followed from Phillips v. Washington Legal Foundation, 524 U.S. 156 (1998), and Webb's Fabulous Pharmacies, Inc. v. Beckwith, 449 U.S. 155 (1980), two earlier cases in which we treated confiscations of money as takings despite their functional similarity to a tax. Perhaps most closely analogous to the present case, we have repeatedly held that the government takes property when it seizes liens, and in so ruling we have never considered whether the government could have achieved an economically equivalent result through taxation. . . .

Two facts emerge from those cases. The first is that the need to distinguish taxes from takings is not a creature of our holding today that monetary exactions are subject to scrutiny under *Nollan* and *Dolan.* Rather, the problem is inherent in this Court's long-settled view that property the government could constitutionally demand through its taxing power can also be taken by eminent domain.

Second, our cases show that teasing out the difference between taxes and takings is more difficult in theory than in practice. *Brown* is illustrative. Similar to respondent in this case, the respondents in *Brown* argued that extending the protections of the Takings Clause to a bank account would open a Pandora's Box of constitutional challenges to taxes. . . . But also like respondent here, the *Brown* respondents never claimed that they were exercising their power to levy taxes when they took the petitioners' property. Any such argument would have been implausible under state law; in Washington, taxes are levied by the legislature, not the courts. . . .

The same dynamic is at work in this case because Florida law greatly circumscribes respondent's power to tax. See Fla. Stat. Ann. §373.503 (authorizing respondent to impose ad valorem tax on properties within its jurisdiction); §373.109 (authorizing respondent to charge permit application fees but providing that such fees "shall not exceed the cost . . . for processing, monitoring, and inspecting for compliance with the permit"). If respondent had argued that its demand for money was a tax, it would have effectively conceded that its denial of petitioner's permit was improper under Florida law. Far from making that concession, respondent has maintained throughout this litigation that it considered petitioner's money to be a substitute for his deeding to the public a conservation easement on a larger parcel of undeveloped land.

This case does not require us to say more. We need not decide at precisely what point a land-use permitting charge denominated by the government as a "tax" becomes "so arbitrary . . . that it was not the exertion of taxation but a confiscation of property." Brushaber v. Union Pacific R. Co., 240 U.S. 1, 24-25 (1916). For present purposes, it suffices to say that despite having long recognized that "the power of taxation should not be confused with the power of eminent domain," Houck v. Little River Drainage Dist., 239 U.S. 254, 264 (1915), we have had little trouble distinguishing between the two.

Finally, we disagree with the dissent's forecast that our decision will work a revolution in land use law by depriving local governments of the ability to charge reasonable permitting fees. Numerous courts—including courts in many of our Nation's most populous States—have confronted constitutional challenges to monetary exactions over the last two decades and applied the standard from *Nollan* and *Dolan* or something like it. . . . Yet the "significant practical harm" the dissent predicts has not come to pass. . . .

The . . . dissent's argument that land use permit applicants need no further protection when the government demands money is really an argument for over-ruling *Nollan* and *Dolan*. After all, the Due Process Clause protected the Nollans from an unfair allocation of public burdens, and they too could have argued that the government's demand for property amounted to a taking under the *Penn Central* framework. See *Nollan*, 483 U.S. at 838. We have repeatedly rejected the dissent's contention that other constitutional doctrines leave no room for the nexus and rough proportionality requirements of *Nollan* and *Dolan*. Mindful of the special vulnerability of land use permit applicants to extortionate demands for money, we do so again today. . . .

We hold that the government's demand for property from a land-use permit applicant must satisfy the requirements of *Nollan* and *Dolan* even when the government denies the permit and even when its demand is for money. The Court expresses no view on the merits of petitioner's claim that respondent's actions here failed to comply with the principles set forth in this opinion and those two cases. The Florida Supreme Court's judgment is reversed, and this case is remanded for further proceedings not inconsistent with this opinion.

It is so ordered.

JUSTICE KAGAN, with whom JUSTICE GINSBURG, JUSTICE BREYER, and JUSTICE SOTOMAYOR join, dissenting.

In the paradigmatic case triggering review under Nollan v. California Coastal Comm'n, 483 U.S. 825 (1987), and Dolan v. City of Tigard, 512 U.S. 374 (1994), the government approves a building permit on the condition that the land-owner relinquish an interest in real property, like an easement. The significant legal questions that the Court resolves today are whether *Nollan* and *Dolan* also apply when that case is varied in two ways. First, what if the government does not approve the permit, but instead demands that the condition be fulfilled before it will do so? Second, what if the condition entails not transferring real property, but simply paying money? This case also raises other, more fact-specific issues I will address: whether the government here imposed any condition at all, and whether petitioner Coy Koontz suffered any compensable injury.

I think the Court gets the first question it addresses right. The *Nollan-Dolan* standard applies not only when the government approves a development permit conditioned on the owner's conveyance of a property interest (i.e., imposes a condition subsequent), but also when the government denies a permit until the owner meets the condition (i.e., imposes a condition precedent). That means an owner may challenge the denial of a permit on the ground that the govern-ment's condition lacks the "nexus" and "rough proportionality" to the develop-ment's social costs that *Nollan* and *Dolan* require. Still, the condition-subsequent and condition-precedent situations differ in an important way. When the govern-ment grants a permit subject to the relinquishment of real property, and that condition does not satisfy *Nollan* and *Dolan*, then the government has taken the property and must pay just compensation under the Fifth Amendment. But when the government denies a permit because an owner has refused to accede to that same demand, nothing has actually been taken. The owner is entitled to have the improper condition removed; and he may be entitled to a monetary remedy created by state law for imposing such a condition; but he cannot be entitled to constitutional compensation for a taking of property. So far, we all agree.

Our core disagreement concerns the second question the Court addresses. The majority extends *Nollan* and *Dolan* to cases in which the government condi-tions a permit not on the transfer of real property, but instead on the payment or expenditure of money. That runs roughshod over Eastern Enterprises v. Apfel, 524 U.S. 498 (1998), which held that the government may impose ordinary finan-cial obligations without triggering the Takings Clause's protections. The bound-aries of the majority's new rule are uncertain. But it threatens to subject a vast array of land-use regulations, applied daily in States and localities throughout the country, to heightened constitutional scrutiny. I would not embark on so unwise an adventure, and would affirm the Florida Supreme Court's decision.

I also would affirm for two independent reasons establishing that Koontz cannot get the money damages he seeks. First, respondent St. Johns River Water Management District never demanded anything (including money) in exchange for a permit; the *Nollan-Dolan* standard therefore does not come into play (even assuming that test applies to demands for money). Second, no taking occurred in this case because Koontz never acceded to a demand (even had there been one), and so no property changed hands; as just noted, Koontz therefore cannot claim just compensation under the Fifth Amendment. The majority does not take issue with my first conclusion, and affirmatively agrees with my second. But the majority thinks Koontz might still be entitled to money damages, and remands to the Florida Supreme Court on that question. I do not see how, and expect that court will so rule.

Claims that government regulations violate the Takings Clause by unduly restricting the use of property are generally "governed by the standards set forth in Penn Central Transp. Co. v. New York City, 438 U.S. 104 (1978)." Lingle v. Chevron U.S.A. Inc., 544 U.S. 528, 538 (2005). Under *Penn Central*, courts examine a regulation's "character" and "economic impact," asking whether the action goes beyond "adjusting the benefits and burdens of economic life to promote the common good" and whether it "interfere[s] with distinct investment-backed expectations." *Penn Central*, 438 U.S. at 124. . . .

Our decisions in *Nollan* and *Dolan* are different: They provide an independent layer of protection in "the special context of land-use exactions." *Lingle*, 544 U.S. at 538. In that situation, the "government demands that a landowner dedicate an easement" or surrender a piece of real property "as a condition of obtaining a development permit." Id. at 546. If the government appropriated such a property interest outside the permitting process, its action would constitute a taking, necessitating just compensation. Id. at 547. *Nollan* and *Dolan* prevent the government from exploiting the landowner's permit application to evade the constitutional obligation to pay for the property. They do so, as the majority explains, by subjecting the government's demand to heightened scrutiny: The government may condition a land-use permit on the relinquishment of real property only if it shows a "nexus" and "rough proportionality" between the demand made and "the impact of the proposed development." . . . *Nollan* and *Dolan* thus serve not to address excessive regulatory burdens on land use (the function of *Penn Central*), but instead to stop the government from imposing an "unconstitutional condition." . . .

Accordingly, the *Nollan-Dolan* test applies only when the property the government demands during the permitting process is the kind it otherwise would have to pay for—or, put differently, when the appropriation of that property, outside the permitting process, would constitute a taking. . . . [T]he majority acknowledges this basic point about *Nollan* and *Dolan*: It too notes that those cases rest on the premise that "if the government had directly seized the easements it sought to obtain through the permitting process, it would have committed a per se taking." . . . Only if that is true could the government's demand for the property force a landowner to relinquish his constitutional right to just compensation.

Here, Koontz claims that the District demanded that he spend money to improve public wetlands, not that he hand over a real property interest. I assume for now that the District made that demand (although I think it did not. . . .). The key question then is: Independent of the permitting process, does requiring a person to pay money to the government, or spend money on its behalf, constitute a taking requiring just compensation? Only if the answer is yes does the *Nollan-Dolan* test apply.

But we have already answered that question no. Eastern Enterprises v. Apfel, 524 U.S. 498, as the Court describes, involved a federal statute requiring a former mining company to pay a large sum of money for the health benefits of retired employees. Five Members of the Court determined that the law did not effect a taking, distinguishing between the appropriation of a specific property interest and the imposition of an order to pay money. Justice Kennedy acknowledged in his controlling opinion that the statute "impose[d] a staggering financial burden" (which influenced his conclusion that it violated due process). Id. at 540 (opinion concurring in judgment and dissenting in part). Still, Justice Kennedy explained, the law did not effect a taking because it did not "operate upon or alter" a "specific and identified propert[y] or property right[ ]." Id. at 540-541. Instead, "[t]he law simply imposes an obligation to perform an act, the payment of benefits. The statute is indifferent as to how the regulated entity elects to comply or the property it uses to do so." Id. at 540. Justice Breyer, writing for four more Justices, agreed. He stated that the Takings Clause applies only when the government appropriates a "specific interest in physical or intellectual property" or "a specific, separately identifiable fund of money"; by contrast, the Clause has no bearing when the government imposes "an ordinary liability to pay money." Id. at 554-555 (dissenting opinion).

Thus, a requirement that a person pay money to repair public wetlands is not a taking. Such an order does not affect a "specific and identified propert[y] or property right[ ];" it simply "imposes an obligation to perform an act" (the improvement of wetlands) that costs money. Id. at 540-541 (opinion of Kennedy, J.). To be sure, when a person spends money on the government's behalf, or pays money directly to the government, it "will reduce [his] net worth"—but that "can be said of any law which has an adverse economic effect" on someone. Id. at 543. Because the government is merely imposing a "general liability" to pay money . . . and therefore is "indifferent as to how the regulated entity elects to comply or the property it uses to do so," . . . the order to repair wetlands, viewed independent of the permitting process, does not constitute a taking. And that means the order does not trigger the *Nollan-Dolan* test, because it does not force Koontz to relinquish a constitutional right.

The majority tries to distinguish *Apfel* by asserting that the District's demand here was "closely analogous" (and "bears resemblance") to the seizure of a lien on property or an income stream from a parcel of land. . . .

But . . . [w]hen the government dissolves a lien, or appropriates a determinate income stream from a piece of property—or, for that matter, seizes a particular "bank account or [the] accrued interest" on it—the government indeed takes a "specific" and "identified property interest." *Apfel*, 524 U.S. at 540-541 (opinion of Kennedy, J.). But nothing like that occurred here. The District did not demand any particular lien, or bank account, or income stream from property. It just ordered Koontz to spend or pay money (again, assuming it ordered anything at all). Koontz's liability would have been the same whether his property produced income or not—e.g., even if all he wanted to build was a family home. . . .

The majority thus falls back on the sole way the District's alleged demand related to a property interest: The demand arose out of the permitting process for Koontz's land. . . . But under the analytic framework that *Nollan* and *Dolan* established, that connection alone is insufficient to trigger heightened scrutiny. As I have described, the heightened standard of *Nollan* and *Dolan* is not a free-standing protection for land-use permit applicants; rather, it is "a special application of the doctrine of unconstitutional conditions, which provides that the government may not require a person to give up a constitutional right—here the right to receive just compensation when property is taken"—in exchange for a land-use permit. *Lingle*, 544 U.S. at 547. As such, *Nollan* and *Dolan* apply only if the demand at issue would have violated the Constitution independent of that proposed exchange. Or put otherwise, those cases apply only if the demand would have constituted a taking when executed outside the permitting process. And here, under *Apfel*, it would not.

The majority's approach, on top of its analytic flaws, threatens significant practical harm. By applying *Nollan* and *Dolan* to permit conditions requiring monetary payments—with no express limitation except as to taxes—the majority extends the Takings Clause, with its notoriously "difficult" and "perplexing" standards, into the very heart of local land-use regulation and service delivery. 524 U.S. at 541. Cities and towns across the nation impose many kinds of permitting fees every day. Some enable a government to mitigate a new development's impact on the community, like increased traffic or pollution—or destruction of wetlands. . . . Others cover the direct costs of providing services like sewage or water to the development. . . . Still others are meant to limit the number of landowners who engage in a certain activity, as fees for liquor licenses do. . . . All now must meet *Nollan* and *Dolan*'s nexus and proportionality tests. The Federal Constitution thus will decide whether one town is overcharging for sewage, or another is setting the price to sell liquor too high. And the flexibility of state and local governments to take the most routine actions to enhance their communities will diminish accordingly.

That problem becomes still worse because the majority's distinction between monetary "exactions" and taxes is so hard to apply. The majority acknowledges, as it must, that taxes are not takings. . . . But once the majority decides that a simple demand to pay money—the sort of thing often viewed as a tax—can count as an impermissible "exaction," how is anyone to tell the two apart? The question, as Justice Breyer's opinion in *Apfel* noted, "bristles with conceptual difficulties." 524 U.S. at 556. And practical ones, too: How to separate orders to pay money from . . . well, orders to pay money, so that a locality knows what it can (and cannot) do. . . .

Perhaps the Court means in the future to curb the intrusion into local affairs that its holding will accomplish; the Court claims, after all, that its opinion is intended to have only limited impact on localities' land-use authority. The majority might, for example, approve the rule, adopted in several States, that *Nollan* and *Dolan* apply only to permitting fees that are imposed ad hoc, and not to fees that are generally applicable. See, e.g., Ehrlich v. Culver City, 911 P.2d 429 (Cal. 1996). . . . Maybe today's majority accepts that distinction; or . . . maybe not. At the least, the majority's refusal "to say more" about the scope of its new rule now casts a cloud on every decision by every local government to require a person seeking a permit to pay or spend money.

At bottom, the majority's analysis seems to grow out of a yen for a prophylactic rule: Unless *Nollan* and *Dolan* apply to monetary demands, the majority worries, "land-use permitting officials" could easily "evade the limitations" on exaction of real property interests that those decisions impose. But that is a prophylaxis in search of a problem. No one has presented evidence that in the many States declining to apply heightened scrutiny to permitting fees, local officials routinely short-circuit *Nollan* and *Dolan* to extort the surrender of real property interests having no relation to a development's costs. . . . And if officials were to impose a fee as a contrivance to take an easement (or other real property right), then a court could indeed apply *Nollan* and *Dolan*. See, e.g., Norwood v. Baker, 172 U.S. 269 (1898) (preventing circumvention of the Takings Clause by prohibiting the government from imposing a special assessment for the full value of a property in advance of condemning it). That situation does not call for a rule extending, as the majority's does, to all monetary exactions. Finally, a court can use the *Penn Central* framework, the Due Process Clause, and (in many places) state law to protect against monetary demands, whether or not imposed to evade *Nollan* and *Dolan*, that simply "go[ ] too far." *Mahon*. . . .

I also would affirm the judgment below for two independent reasons, even assuming that a demand for money can trigger *Nollan* and *Dolan*. First, the District never demanded that Koontz give up anything (including money) as a condition for granting him a permit. And second, because (as everyone agrees) no actual taking occurred, Koontz cannot claim just compensation even had the District made a demand. The majority nonetheless remands this case on the theory that Koontz might still be entitled to money damages. I cannot see how, and so would spare the Florida courts.

Nollan and *Dolan* apply only when the government makes a "demand[ ]" that a landowner turn over property in exchange for a permit. *Lingle*, 544 U.S. at 546. I understand the majority to agree with that proposition: After all, the entire unconstitutional conditions doctrine, as the majority notes, rests on the fear that the government may use its control over benefits (like permits) to "coerc[e]" a person into giving up a constitutional right. A *Nollan-Dolan* claim therefore depends on a showing of government coercion, not relevant in an ordinary challenge to a permit denial. . . . Before applying *Nollan* and *Dolan*, a court must find that the permit denial occurred because the government made a demand of the landowner, which he rebuffed.

And unless *Nollan* and *Dolan* are to wreck land-use permitting throughout the country—to the detriment of both communities and property owners—that demand must be unequivocal. If a local government risked a lawsuit every time it made a suggestion to an applicant about how to meet permitting criteria, it would cease to do so; indeed, the government might desist altogether from communicating with applicants. That hazard is to some extent baked into *Nollan* and *Dolan*; observers have wondered whether those decisions have inclined some local governments to deny permit applications outright, rather than negotiate agreements that could work to both sides' advantage. See W. Fischel, Regulatory Takings 346 (1995). But that danger would rise exponentially if something less than a clear condition—if each idea or proposal offered in the back-and-forth of reconciling diverse interests—triggered *Nollan-Dolan* scrutiny. At that point, no local government official with a decent lawyer would have a conversation with a developer. Hence the need to reserve *Nollan* and *Dolan*, as we always have, for reviewing only what an official demands, not all he says in negotiations.

With that as backdrop, consider how this case arose. To arrest the loss of the State's rapidly diminishing wetlands, Florida law prevents landowners from filling or draining any such property without two permits. . . . Koontz's property qualifies as a wetland, and he therefore needed the permits to embark on development. His applications, however, failed the District's preliminary review: The District found that they did not preserve wetlands or protect fish and wildlife to the extent Florida law required. . . . At that point, the District could simply have denied the applications; had it done so, the *Penn Central* test—not *Nollan* and *Dolan*—would have governed any takings claim Koontz might have brought. . . .

Rather than reject the applications, however, the District suggested to Koontz ways he could modify them to meet legal requirements. The District proposed reducing the development's size or modifying its design to lessen the impact on wetlands. . . . Alternatively, the District raised several options for "off-site mitigation" that Koontz could undertake in a nearby nature preserve, thus compensating for the loss of wetlands his project would cause. . . . The District never made any particular demand respecting an off-site project (or anything else); as Koontz testified at trial, that possibility was presented only in broad strokes, "[n]ot in any great detail." . . . And the District made clear that it welcomed additional proposals from Koontz to mitigate his project's damage to wetlands. . . . Even at the final hearing on his applications, the District asked Koontz if he would "be willing to go back with the staff over the next month and renegotiate this thing and try to come up with" a solution. . . . But Koontz refused, saying (through his lawyer) that the proposal he submitted was "as good as it can get." . . .

In short, the District never made a demand or set a condition—not to cede an identifiable property interest, not to undertake a particular mitigation project, not even to write a check to the government. Instead, the District suggested to Koontz several non-exclusive ways to make his applications conform to state law. The District's only hard-and-fast requirement was that Koontz do something—anything—to satisfy the relevant permitting criteria. Koontz's failure to obtain the permits therefore did not result from his refusal to accede to an allegedly extortionate demand or condition; rather, it arose from the legal deficiencies of his applications, combined with his unwillingness to correct them by any means. *Nollan* and *Dolan* were never meant to address such a run-of-the-mill denial of a land-use permit. As applications of the unconstitutional conditions doctrine, those decisions require a condition; and here, there was none. . . .

. . . The majority's errors here are consequential. The majority turns a broad array of local land-use regulations into federal constitutional questions. It deprives state and local governments of the flexibility they need to enhance their communities—to ensure environmentally sound and economically productive development. It places courts smack in the middle of the most everyday local government activity. As those consequences play out across the country, I believe the Court will rue today's decision. I respectfully dissent.

NOTES AND QUESTIONS

1. *Property taxes.* For discussions of the distinction between property taxes (not subject to the Takings Clause) and user fees, a distinction that the *Koontz* majority regards as "more difficult in theory than in practice," see David A. Dana & Thomas W. Merrill, Property: Takings 225-226 (2002); Richard A. Epstein, Takings: Private Property and the Power of Eminent Domain 99-100, 283-289 (1985); Eduardo M. Peñalver, Regulatory Taxings, 105 Colum. L. Rev. 2182 (2004); and Ilya Somin, Two Steps Forward for the "Poor Relation" of Constitutional Law: Reflections on *Koontz, Arkansas Game and Fish Commission,* and the Future of the Takings Clause, 2012-2013 Cato Sup. Ct. Rev. (forthcoming).

2. *Effect on negotiations?* Will the consequences of *Koontz* be less negotiation between governments and landowners? Recall Anderson v. City of Issaquah at page 1020. Might *Koontz* cause governments to follow Issaquah's lead in the way that it deals with would-be developers? If the government simply denies a permit unconditionally, the landowner will be forced to invoke *Penn Central,* which rarely ends well for plaintiffs. But as soon as the government responds with "yes if" then per se takings theories under *Nollan* and *Dolan* are in play, though even then the landowner may still find the remedies available to be unsatisfying. For a thoughtful analysis of the connection between the doctrinal issue in *Koontz* and the realities of land use negotiations and administrative review, see Mark Fenster, Failed Exactions, 36 Vt. L. Rev. 623, 643-646 (2012).

3. *Off-site versus on-site.* After *Koontz,* does it matter whether a landowner is asked by local government officials to perform remediation on his parcel or on a different site? Is there any reason why that distinction should make a difference for the purposes of the Takings Clause?

4. *Limiting principles.* What *isn't* an exaction after *Koontz?* Has the Supreme Court cast overboard some of the most promising boundary principles for differentiating unconstitutional exactions and permissible land use planning? For an examination, see Lee Anne Fennell & Eduardo M. Peñalver, *Exactions Creep,* 2014 Sup. Ct. Rev. (forthcoming), available at http://papers.ssrn.com/sol3/papers.cfm?abstract_id=2345028.

5. *Further reading.* Students interested in takings can explore a rich but dauntingly large academic literature. In addition to the sources already cited throughout this chapter, some illuminating classic works are Bruce A. Ackerman, Private

Property and the Constitution (1977); Michael A. Heller & James E. Krier, Deterrence and Distribution in the Law of Takings, 112 Harv. L. Rev. 997 (1999); Jed Rubenfeld, Usings, 102 Yale L.J. 1077 (1993); and Joseph L. Sax, Takings, Private Property and Public Rights, 91 Yale L.J. 149 (1971). For a recent and ambitious exploration of the treatment of property in the Constitution's Takings and Due Process Clauses, see James Y. Stern, Property's Constitution, 101 Cal. L. Rev. 277 (2013).

Appendix A

ANSWERS TO REVIEW PROBLEMS
CHAPTER 3, PAGE 272

Regarding all of the Problems, we assume O started out with a fee simple absolute.

1. After the conveyance, A has a fee simple subject to condition subsequent, and O has a right of entry in fee simple absolute. There are no other interests.

2. Assuming that building residences is a breach of the condition (which it almost certainly is), A has breached the condition subsequent, but the fee does not automatically terminate. It terminates only if and when the right of entry is properly exercised. Who has the right of entry? In most states the right of entry is devisable by will, but, as the *Mahrenholz* case (page 226) indicates, there are a few states in which it is not. If the right of entry is devisable under local law, then B has it. If it is not devisable under local law, then O's heirs (whoever they are) have it because a right of entry is descendible in all states. In either case, though, no one has taken steps to exercise the right, so A's fee is still in effect.

3. After the conveyance, A has a fee simple determinable, and O has a possibility of reverter in fee simple absolute. A possibility of reverter does not have to be expressly stated to be created because it arises by operation of law.

4. Assuming that building a factory on Blackacre is a violation of the limitation, which it clearly is, A has violated the limitation with the result that the fee automatically terminates, without any action taken by O or anyone else. Title to Blackacre depends on succession to O's possibility of reverter. If possibilities of reverter may be devised under local law (as most states permit), then B owns Blackacre in fee simple absolute. Otherwise, O's heirs (whoever they are) hold the fee simple absolute as tenants in common.

5. After the conveyance, the Finger Lakes Land Trust has a fee simple subject to executory limitation, and Land Conservancy has an executory interest in fee simple absolute. It will become possessory if and when Greenacre is ever developed. In this respect, a fee simple subject to executory limitation operates the same way as a fee simple determinable. (Note that the executory interest is valid under the common law Rule Against Perpetuity because both interests were conveyed to charities.)

6. After the conveyance, A has a fee simple absolute. A's promise creates a covenant, one which binds not only A but everyone who succeeds to ownership in Greenacre. The covenant does *not* make the fee subject to either a condition or a limitation. We will study covenants that "run with the land," as they are called, in Chapter 10.

7. The essential difference between a covenant, on the one hand, and a condition or limitation, on the other, concerns the effect of breach. As we have seen, in the case of both a condition and a limitation the effect of a breach or violation of the restriction is forfeiture of the fee simple, either automatically or upon the exercise of a right of entry. With a covenant, however, no forfeiture follows a breach. Rather, the person who holds the benefit of the covenant may either enjoin the breach or seek damages.

8. After the conveyance, A has a fee simple subject to executory limitation, and B has an executory interest. Note that A's fee simple is defeasible only during A's lifetime, i.e., in the event that A ever drinks alcohol or alcoholic beverages. Hence, B's executory interest is valid under the common law Rule Against Perpetuities (A is the validating life). The state of title after the given events death depends on the alienability of executory interests. As we will see in Chapter 4, executory interests are generally alienable. So, B's conveyance to C is valid, giving C the same executory interest that B had. When A subsequently drinks whiskey, that act causes the fee simple to terminate, and C's executory interest now vests in possession as a fee simple absolute. C need not take any action for this to occur.

Appendix B

ANSWERS TO REVIEW PROBLEMS
CHAPTER 4, PAGE 292

Regarding all of the Problems, we assume O started out with a fee simple absolute.

1. After the conveyance, A has a life estate; B has a vested remainder for life; and there is a contingent remainder in fee simple absolute in C's unascertained heirs. There is also a reversion in fee simple in O. Reversions, like possibilities of reverter, arise by operation of law and need not be expressly stated.

B's remainder is vested because we do not treat the expiration of A's preceding life estate as a condition precedent. In theory we could do so. The fact that we do not illustrates the common law's preference for early vesting. (One of the reasons for this preference was to reduce the incidence of invalid future interests under the Rule Against Perpetuities.) Another (more technical) way to classify the vested remainder for life is as a remainder vested subject to limitational defeasance. The limitation is B's death.

2. After the conveyance, A has a springing executory interest in fee simple absolute. O has a fee simple subject to an executory limitation (or subject to an executory interest, if you will). Immediately and automatically upon A's first wedding anniversary, if it ever occurs, A's executory interest will divest O's fee simple and become possessory in a fee simple absolute.

3. After the conveyance, A has a term of years followed by a contingent remainder in fee simple in which X and Y have an interest. There is also a reversion in fee simple in O. The remainder is contingent because it is subject to an unfulfilled condition precedent (attaining age 21).

4. X's attaining age 21 vests the contingent remainder in him or her, so that X now has a vested remainder in fee simple subject to partial divestment (also called subject to open) by Y and also subject to open because A is alive and may have more children some or all of whom may reach age 21. There is no reversion (the vesting of X's remainder simultaneously divests O's reversion). Y now has a shifting executory interest in fee simple which will vest if Y reaches age 21.

5. X's vested remainder is transmissible at death because it is not subject to any condition that X survive to the time of possession. So, it passes to X's successors in interest, i.e., X's devisees under any valid will or X's heirs. Those persons take *exactly the same* interest that X had. Y still has a shifting executory interest in fee simple. There is no reversion.

6. After the conveyance, *A* has a life estate; *X* has a vested remainder in fee simple subject to open; and there is a shifting executory interest in fee simple in *A*'s unborn children. There is no reversion.

7. The birth of *Y* vests the remainder in him or her and simultaneously partially divests *X*'s remainder (reducing *X*'s share from 100 percent to 50 percent). Both *X*'s and *Y*'s remainders are subject to open (partial divestment) so long as *A* is still alive and capable of having more children. Once *A* dies, however, the class of *A*'s children closes and *X*'s and *Y*'s interests become indefeasibly vested in fee simple absolute. With *A*'s life estate terminated, *X* and *Y* take possession and own the property in fee simple absolute as tenants in common (each has an undivided interest—a concept that we will study in Chapter 5).

8. After the conveyance, *A* has a life estate; *B* has a remainder in fee simple that is vested subject to complete divestment; *C* has a shifting executory interest in fee simple absolute. There is no reversion.

9. After the conveyance, *A* has a life estate; *B* has a vested remainder in fee simple determinable; *O* has a possibility of reverter in fee simple absolute.

10. After the conveyance, *A* has a springing executory interest in fee simple absolute. *O* has a fee simple subject to executory limitation (or, if you will, an executory interest). If and when *A* graduates from college, *A*'s executory interest will vest in possession, divesting *O*'s fee simple.

Table of Cases

Italics indicate principal cases.

Author Index

Subject Index